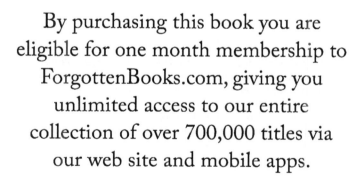

ISBN 978-0-331-04858-2
PIBN 10296054

RHEINPROVINZ
und NASSAU
Maßstab 1:1000000

Eisenbahnen mit Schnellzugverkehr
"   ohne   "
Klein- und Strassenbahnen
Erzbischofs- und Bischofssitze
Generalkommandos, Schlösser, Burgruinen,
Kur- und Badeorte
Hauptorte der Provinzen, Regierungsbezirke
und Kreise. Kreise, die nicht nach ihren Haupt-
orten benannt werden, in dieser Schrift: Unt-
Taunus
Höhenangaben in Metern

THE RHINE

INCLUDING

THE BLACK FOREST & THE VOSGES

HANDBOOK FOR TRAVELLERS

BY

KARL BAEDEKER

WITH 69 MAPS AND 59 PLANS

SEVENTEENTH REVISED EDITION

LEIPZIG: KARL BAEDEKER, PUBLISHER

LONDON: T. FISHER UNWIN, 1 ADELPHI TERRACE, W.C.

NEW YORK: CHARLES SCRIBNER'S SONS, 153 FIFTH AVENUE

1911

'Go, little book, God send thee good passage,
And specially let this be thy prayere
Unto them all that thee will read or hear,
Where thou art wrong, after their help to call,
Thee to correct in any part or all.'

PREFACE.

The German original of the Handbook to the Rhine, first published in 1828, was the pionier of the long series of the Baedeker guidebooks now issued in three languages. The 'Rheinreise von Mainz bis Köln', by *Prof. J. A. Klein*, was soon taken over by *Karl Baedeker* (1801-59), who himself revised it, issuing a second edition in 1836. The first English edition was published in 1861.

The chief object of the Handbook, which is now issued for the 17th time and corresponds with the thirty-first German edition, is to supply the traveller with such information as will render him as nearly as possible independent of hotel-keepers, commissionnaires, and guides, and thus enable him the more thoroughly to enjoy and appreciate the objects of interest he meets with on his tour.

The Handbook is based almost entirely upon the personal observation of the Editor, and the country described has been repeatedly explored by him with a view to procure the latest possible information; but, as changes are constantly taking place, he will highly appreciate any communications with which travellers may kindly favour him, if the result of their own experience. Those already received from numerous correspondents, which he gratefully acknowledges, have in many cases proved most serviceable.

The contents of the Handbook are divided into SIX SECTIONS, each of which may be separately removed from the volume by cutting the gauze backing visible on opening the book at the requisite pages. Linen covers for these sections may be obtained through any bookseller.

The MAPS and PLANS, on which special care has been bestowed, will, it is hoped, render material service to the traveller in planning his tour.

TIME TABLES. Information regarding trains, steamboats, and diligences is most trustworthy when obtained from local sources. The best German publications of the kind are the '*Reichs-Kursbuch*' (2 *M*; published at Berlin), '*Hendschel's Telegraph*' (2 *M*, smaller edition 1 *M*; these two issued eight times a year), and '*Storm's Kursbuch für's Reich*' (80 pf.).

DISTANCES by road are given approximately in English miles; but in the case of mountain-excursions they are expressed by the time in which they can be accomplished by average walkers. A kilomètre approximately equals $5/8$ English mile; 8 kil. = 5 M. HEIGHTS are given in English feet (1 Engl. ft. = 0,3048 mètre), and the POPULATIONS in accordance with the most recent census.

HOTELS. The Editor has endeavoured to enumerate, not only the first-class hotels, but others also of more modest pretensions, which may be safely selected by the 'voyageur en garçon', with little sacrifice of comfort and great saving of expenditure. Although changes frequently take place, and prices generally have an upward tendency, the average charges as stated in the Handbook from the personal experience of the Editor, from data furnished by numerous correspondents, and from information supplied by hotel-keepers themselves, will enable the traveller to form a fair estimate of his probable expenditure. It is advisable to ascertain the charge for rooms in advance. The asterisks indicate those hotels which the Editor has reason to believe to be provided with the comforts and conveniences expected in up-to-date establishments, and also to be well managed and with a reasonable scale of charges. Houses of a more modest character, when good of their class, are described as 'good' or 'very fair'.

To hotel-proprietors, tradesmen, and others the Editor begs to intimate that a character for fair dealing and courtesy towards travellers is the sole passport to his commendation, and that advertisements of every kind are strictly excluded from his Handbooks. Hotel-keepers are also warned against persons representing themselves as agents for Baedeker's Handbooks.

Abbreviations.

R. = room, route	omn. = omnibus	pf. = pfennig
B. = breakfast	N.= north, northern, etc.	fr. = franc
L. = luncheon	S. = south, etc.	c. = centime
D. = dinner	E. = east, etc.	hr. = hour
S. = supper	W. = west, etc.	min. = minute
déj.= déjeuner (luncheon)	r. = right	ca. = circa, about
rfmts. = refreshments	l. = left	Pl. = plan
pens. = pension (i.e.	M. = English mile	p. = page
board and lodging)	ft. = Engl. foot	m. = mètre
carr. = carriage	ℳ = mark	comp. = compare

The letter d with a date, after the name of a person, indicates the year of his death. The number of feet given after the name of a place indicates its height above the sea-level. The number of miles placed before the principal places on railway-routes and highroads generally indicates their distance from the starting-point of the route or sub-route.

Asterisks are used as marks of commendation.

CONTENTS.

III. West Part of Rhenish Prussia and Lorraine.

IV. The Rhine from Coblenz to Mayence. Frankfort. Taunus.

V. Grand-Duchies of Hesse (right bank of the Rhine) and Baden.

VI. Rhenish Hesse. Bavarian Palatinate. Alsace.

Maps.

Plans.

INTRODUCTION.

I. Season and Plan of Tour.

The climate of W. Germany is influenced by the comparative proximity of the North Sea, which renders the temperature remarkably mild. While the annual mean temperature in E. Germany is only about 42-48° Fahr., in the valley of the Rhine it rises to over 51°. Thus, owing to the early springs and the long warm autumns, a tour in the Rhenish provinces is still enjoyable at a season when the Alps and the mountainous districts of Central Germany are beginning to feel the frosts of the coming winter.

The following survey will serve to give an idea of the time requisite for a visit to the chief points of interest in the Rhenish provinces.

II. Language.

A slight acquaintance with German is very desirable for those who desire to explore the more remote parts of the Rhenish Provinces. Tourists who do not deviate from the beaten track will generally find English or French spoken at the principal hotels and the usual resorts of strangers; but if they are entirely ignorant of German they must be prepared occasionally to submit to the extortions practised by porters, cab-drivers, and others of a like class, which even the data furnished by the Handbook will not always enable them to avoid.

English travellers often impose considerable trouble by ordering things almost unknown in German usage; and if ignorance of the language be added to want of conformity to the customs, misunderstandings and disputes are apt to ensue. The reader is therefore recommended to acquire if possible such a moderate proficiency in the language as to render him intelligible to the servants, and to endeavour to adapt his requirements to the habits of the country.

III. Money. Travelling Expenses.

Money. The German mark ($\mathcal{M}$), which is nearly equivalent to the English shilling, is divided into 100 pfennigs. Banknotes of 20, 50, 100, and 1000 $\mathcal{M}$ are issued by the German Imperial Bank ('*Deutsche Reichsbank*'), and others of 100 and 500 $\mathcal{M}$, with a limited circulation, by four other chartered banks. There are also treasury-bills ('Reichskassen-Scheine') of 5 $\mathcal{M}$ and 10 $\mathcal{M}$. The current gold coins are pieces of 10 $\mathcal{M}$ und 20 $\mathcal{M}$, the intrinsic value of which is somewhat lower than that of the English half-sovereign and sovereign (1l. being worth about 20 $\mathcal{M}$ 43 pf.). The paper currency is of the same value as the precious metals. The silver coins are pieces of 5, 3 (the old 'thaler' or dollar), 2, 1, and $1/_2$ mark (50 pf.). In nickel there are coins of 25, 20, 10, and 5 pfennigs, and in copper there are pieces of 2 and 1 pfennig.

English sovereigns and banknotes may be exchanged at all the principal towns in Germany, and napoleons are also favourably received (20 fr. $=$ 16s. $=$ 16 $\mathcal{M}$ 20 pf., and often a little more). Those who travel with large sums should carry them in the form of letters of credit or in circular notes of 5l. or 10l., rather than in banknotes or gold, as the value of the former, if lost or stolen, is recoverable. The cheques issued by the chief American express companies and by the American Bankers Association may also be recommended.

Travelling Expenses. The expense of a tour in the Rhenish Provinces depends of course on a great variety of circumstances; but it may be stated generally that travelling in Germany, and even on the Rhine, is less expensive, and in some respects more comfortable, than in most other countries in Europe. The pedestrian of moderate requirements, who has attained tolerable proficiency in the language and avoids the beaten track as much as possible, will have no difficulty in limiting his expenditure to 10-12 ℳ per day; but those who prefer driving to walking, frequent the most expensive hotels, and require the services of guides and commissionnaires, must be prepared to expend at least 25-30 ℳ daily.

IV. Passports. Custom House.

PASSPORTS are now unnecessary in Germany, except for students who wish to matriculate at a German university, but they are frequently useful in proving the identity of the traveller, in procuring admission to collections, and in obtaining delivery of registered letters. Cyclists and motorists (comp. p. xvii) should always carry passports.

Passports may be obtained in London direct from the Passport Department of the *Foreign Office*, Whitehall (fee 2s.), or through any of the usual tourist-agents. — In the United States applications for passports should be made to the *Bureau of Citizenship*, State Department, Washington, D. C.

CUSTOM HOUSE formalities are now almost everywhere lenient. As a rule, however, articles purchased during the journey, which are not destined for personal use, should be declared at the frontier.

V. Routes from London to the Rhine.

Cologne, as the focus of the Rhenish districts, is taken as the goal of the under-noted routes; but it will be easy to make the requisite allowances if some other point be the tourist's destination. — *Luggage* may be registered through to destination (booking-fee 4-6d. per package), but is examined at the frontier (see below). *Bicycles* are registered as ordinary luggage for an extra fee of 5s. — Second-class passengers may travel in the saloon of the steamers for a small extra fee (from 2s. upwards). — Uniformed *Interpreters* attend the Continental trains at the chief points of departure and arrival. — German (Central Europe) time is 1 hr., and Dutch railway-time (Amsterdam time) 20 min. ahead of Greenwich time. — For fuller details as to hours of trains, sleeping carriages, station-omnibuses, etc., see the time-tables of the *South Eastern & Chatham* and the *Great Eastern Railways, Cook's Continental Time Tables,* or *Bradshaw's Continental Railway Guide.*

a. Viâ Ostend.

Duration of direct journey 13-15 hrs. Through-fares, 1st class 2l. 15s. 3d., 2nd class 1l. 18s. 2d.; return-fares 4l. 18s. 11d., 3l. 8s. 7d. Extra-fare on 'train de luxe' (9 a.m.) 10s. 6d; sleeping-car from Ostend on the afternoon train (2.20 p.m.), 1st. cl. 10s. 2d., 2nd. cl. 8s. 6d. extra. Return-tickets valid for 60 days.

SOUTH EASTERN & CHATHAM RAILWAY from *Charing Cross, Victoria,* or *Cannon Street* to (78 M.) *Dover Pier* in about 2 hrs. — STEAMER from Dover to (69 M.) *Ostend* in 3¼-4 hrs. — RAILWAY to (217 M.) *Cologne* viâ *Brussels* in 7-8 hrs. (comp. p. 1).

Luggage is examined at *Herbestal* (p. 2). Passengers by the morning service may, on notice given to the conductor of the train at Ostend, Bruges, or Ghent, obtain dinner-baskets at Malines (4½ fr., wine included).

b. Viâ Flushing.

Duration of journey about 14½ hrs. Through-fares 2*l.* 14*s.* 5*d.*, 1*l.* 16*s.* 10*d.*; return (available for 60 days) 4*l.* 8*s.* 6*d.*, 3*l.* 0*s.* 10*d.*

RAILWAY from *Victoria, Holborn,* or *St. Paul's* to (50 M.) *Queenboro Pier* in 1¼-1½ hr. — STEAMER from Queenboro to (120 M.) *Flushing* in 7¼-7¾ hrs. — RAILWAY from Flushing to *Cologne* viâ *Venlo*, 185 M. in 6-7 hrs., viâ *Wesel* and *Oberhausen*, 208 M. in 5¾-7 hrs.

Luggage examined at *Kaldenkirchen* (p. 17) or *Goch* (p. 20). Table d'hôte on the day-steamer 4*s.* Restaurant-cars attached to the chief trains from Flushing.

c. Viâ Hoek van Holland.

Duration of journey 14 hrs. Fares 2*l.* 14*s.* 5*d.*, 1*l.* 16*s.* 10*d.*; return (60 days) 4*l.* 8*s.* 6*d.*, 3*l.* 0*s.* 10*d.*

GREAT EASTERN RAILWAY from *Liverpool Street* to (70½ M.) *Harwich* in 1½ hr. — STEAMER from Harwich to (108 M.) *Hoek van Holland* in 7 hrs. — RAILWAY from Hoek van Holland to (181 M.) *Cologne*, see p. 17. — Restaurant-car attached to the boat-train from Hoek van Holland.

d. Viâ Calais.

Duration of journey 13½-14½ hrs. Fares 3*l.* 5*s.* 8*d.*, 2*l.* 5*s.* 3*d.*; return (60 days) 5*l.* 16*s.* 10*d.*, 4*l.* 2*s.*; extra-fare on 'train de luxe' (9 a.m.) 13*s.* 4*d.*

RAILWAY from *Charing Cross, Victoria,* or *Cannon Street* to (78 M.) *Dover Pier* in 2 hrs. — STEAMER from Dover to (25 M.) *Calais* in 1⅓ hr. — RAILWAY from Calais to *Brussels* and (259 M.) *Cologne* in 9 hrs.

Luggage examined at *Herbestal* (p. 2). Restaurant or dining cars attached to the chief trains.

VI. Railways.

RAILWAYS. Railway-travelling is cheaper in Germany than in most other parts of Europe, and the carriages are generally clean and comfortable. Those of the second class, with spring-seats, are sometimes as good as the first in England. Smoking is permitted in all the carriages, except those 'Für Nicht-Raucher' and the coupés for ladies; in first-class compartments, however, all the inmates must agree. The average fares for the different classes by ordinary trains ('*Personen-Züge*'; often without first-class carriages) and the so-called '*Eil-Züge*' (fast trains) are about 1²/₅*d.*, ⁹/₁₀*d.*, and ³/₅*d.* per Engl. M. respectively (7, 4½, and 3 pf. per kilomètre). To these fares must, however, be added a stamp-duty, included in the price of the tickets and varying from 5 pf. to 8 ℳ according to distance and class. On express-trains ('*Schnell-Züge*'; with three classes) and on through corridor-trains ('*D-Züge*', marked D in the time-tables; sometimes with no third-class carriages), there is an additional tax varying from 25 pf. to 2 ℳ. There is no reduction in the fare of return-tickets. No one is admitted to the platform without either a railway-ticket or a platform-ticket *(Bahnsteigkarte)*; the latter (10 pf.) may be obtained from the automatic machines placed for the purpose at all stations. The seats in the through corridor-trains are numbered and reserved like those of the American parlor-car, and may be obtained in advance at the stations of departure (no fee). Each ticket is available for four days and permits the journey to be broken once without any formality.

No Luggage is allowed free except smaller articles taken by the passenger into his carriage. The heavier luggage must be booked, and a ticket procured for it. The charge per 25 kilogrammes (55 lbs.) is 20 pf. up to 50 kilom. (31 M.), 50 pf. up to 300 kilom. (186 M.), and 1 *M* beyond 300 kilomètres. Trunks should be at the station at least $^1/_4$ hr. before the train starts. Luggage once booked, the traveller need not enquire after it until he arrives at his final destination, where it will be kept in safe custody (24 hrs. gratis), until he presents his ticket. When, however, a frontier has to be crossed, the traveller should see his luggage cleared at the custom-house in person. Porters are entitled to a fee, fixed by tariff, for carrying luggage to or from the cab. At most stations there is a left-luggage office for small baggage, where a charge of 10 pf. per day is made for each package.

The enormous weight of the trunks used by some passengers not unfrequently inflicts serious injury on the porters who handle them. Travellers are therefore urged to place their heavy articles in the smaller packages and thus to minimize the evil as far as possible.

Circular Tour Tickets ('Zusammenstellbare Fahrschein-Hefte'; see the 'Reichs-Kursbuch', Sec. 733) for prolonged tours are not issued for distances under 600 kilomètres (372 M.); those for distances up to 3000 kilom. (1860 M.) are valid for 60 days, for 3000-5000 kilom. (3100 M.) for 90 days, and beyond that distance for 120 days. The journey can be broken without any formality at any of the stations. These tickets (issued in the form of books of coupons) must be ordered one day before the beginning of the journey on special forms to be obtained at the railway-stations or at the city offices of the railways. The rate of fare is the same as for ordinary tickets. The tickets are available by all trains, though an extra charge is made for the use of the international 'Luxuszüge' (marked 'L' in the time-tables; 1st cl. only).

VII. Steamboats on the Rhine.

The passenger-service is carried on mainly by the united *Cologne and Düsseldorf Company,* the steamers of which are recognizable by their black and white funnels. The admirable saloon-steamers of this company accomplish the journey from Mayence to Cologne in $7^3/_4$ hrs., and that from Cologne to Mayence in $12^1/_4$ hrs., touching, in descending, at Biebrich, Coblenz, and Bonn only; in ascending, at Bingen also. The *Netherlands Steamship Co.* (funnels black below and white above), plying between Rotterdam and Ludwigshafen (Mannheim), serves mainly for the transportation of freight, but has also two good saloon-steamers for passengers (piers different from those of the other companies). Travellers must be prepared for a certain want of punctuality in the steamboat service, especially on Sundays and holidays, or when the water is low, or in going up stream when the water is unusually high, or in the autumn, when the hour of departure is often postponed on account of the morning mists. The first class on the steamer is known as the 'Saloon', the second class as the 'Fore-Cabin' ('Vorkajüte'). Saloon-passengers have, of course, the freedom of the whole steamer. The express-steamers carry saloon-passengers at somewhat higher rates than the ordinary steamers. Railway Circular Tickets, Cook's coupons, and the coupons of the Hamburg-America Line are good for the express-steamers, but holders of third-class tickets must pay an extra fare.

Passengers embarking at stations with piers must take tickets at the office on shore, as otherwise they must pay an extra fare of 50 pf.; those embarking at other stations should obtain them from the purser immediately on going on board. The charge for landing or embarking by small boat (not allowed after nightfall), including 110 lbs. of luggage, is 10 pf. The tickets are given up on leaving the ship. The fare from Mayence to Cologne by the express-steamer of the Cologne & Düsseldorf Company is 12 ℳ 40 pf. (return-ticket 16 ℳ 80 pf.); that by ordinary steamer is 10 ℳ 40 pf. (fore-cabin 6 ℳ 20 pf.; return 14 ℳ 20 or 8 ℳ 20 pf.). Return-tickets are good until the end of the year. The holder of a ticket costing not less than 2 ℳ is at liberty to break his journey, provided he signify his intention to the purser before the tickets are collected. Each passenger is entitled to 110 lbs. of luggage free. He may register his trunk for a fee of 10-30 pf.

Refreshments are provided on board the steamers, in the style of the larger hotels. Table d'hôte on the German steamers at 1 o'clock 3 ℳ, children half-price; ices 50 pf. extra. The wines are made a special feature in the commissariat.

Fall of the Rhine.

Height above the level of the sea —

	Feet			Feet			Feet
At Bâle.	800	At Mayence	265		At Cologne.	117
„ Kehl	433	„ Coblenz.	190		„ Düsseldorf.	87
„ Mannheim.	280	„ Bonn.	143		„ Emmerich.	33

Breadth of the Rhine.

	Yards			Yards			Yards
At Bâle.	190	At Coblenz	400		At Düsseldorf.	410
„ Mannheim.	430	„ Bonn	532		„ Schenkenschanz	
„ Mayence	492	„ Cologne	433		(Dutch front.).	910

Average Depth of the Rhine.

	Feet			Feet
Between Bâle and Strassburg.	3-12	At the Lurlei		76
„ Strassburg and Mayence	5-25	Between Bonn and Cologne.		10-30
„ Mayence and Bonn.	9-76	„ Cologne and Düsseldorf		12-66

VIII. Walking Excursions.

In spite of all the charm of the steamboat excursions, the real beauty of the Rhenish landscape unfolds itself almost more to pedestrians. The oftener the traveller breaks his journey the greater enjoyment he will derive from it. The Handbook contains more or less complete details about the chief excursions that may be made from the steamboat or railway stations. For tours of several days the so-called 'Höhenwege' or ridge-paths, following the crests of the hills, will be found specially enjoyable. They generally keep as far as possible from the highroads. The *Rheinische Verkehrs-verein* or *Rhenish Tourist Society* of Coblenz (p. 122) has marked all the paths on both sides of the river from Bingen and from Wies-baden to Bonn with a capital R ('Rheinhöhenweg'). Travellers who read German should procure the 'Rheinwanderbuch' by *Hans Hoitz* (90 pf.). — The *Eifelverein* or *Eifel Tourist Society* (p. 146) has marked the most attractive tourist-paths in three main directions (red angle, red triangle, and red circle) and has erected simple inns at the ends of the days' walks. Compare 'Eifelwanderungen', by *Hans Hoitz* (90 pf.). — *Schwarzwaldvereine* or *Black Forest Societies* (p. 385) have made considerable progress in laying out ridge-paths and in marking them on a uniform system (red rhombus). Two main routes traverse the entire district from Pforzheim to Bâle and from Pforzheim to Waldshut, and approaches have been made from all the important railway-stations. A third path skirts the E. side of the mountains from Pforzheim to Schaffhausen. Comfortable inns occur so frequently as to make it quite easy to adjust the day's trip to the traveller's powers.

IX. Motoring and Cycling Notes.

MOTOR CARS entering Germany are liable to pay a customs-duty of 150 ℳ, which is returned when the car quits the country. In populous districts the speed-limit is 9 M. (15 kil.) per hr.; other-wise there is no limit, but driving to the public danger, whatever the speed, is an offence. Lamps, brakes, and horns are imperative, but for local regulations (which vary) motorists should apply to the police. The rule of the road is to keep to the right in meeting, and to pass on the left in overtaking. Persons under 18 years of age are not allowed to drive automobiles or ride motor-bicycles. The cars of foreign visitors must display a special sign obtainable at the frontier custom-houses (fee 5 ℳ), and their owners must take out an official permission ('Erlaubniskarte'; up to 30 days 40 ℳ). The home-licence and chauffeur's certificate must be countersigned by a German consul and should be carried. It is best, however, to procure from the authorities at home an international licence, valid for one year and holding good in all countries recognizing the international agreement of Oct. 11th, 1909. This must be revised at the first frontier custom-house, and the cars must then display at the back, besides the official plate of their country, another indicating their nationality (GB for Great Britain, US for America). — Ravenstein publishes a road-book of Germany in two volumes, while the *Imperial Automobile Club* (Berlin) issues official touring maps. See also the bicycling maps mentioned at p. xviii.

CYCLING is very prevalent in the Rhenish districts, and there are suitable roads all the way from Holland to Bâle and the Lake of Constance. Among the most popular bits for wheeling are the left bank of the Rhine from Bonn to Bingen, the Rheingau, the valley of the Moselle, the road from Frankfort to Heidelberg, the Neckar valley and the W. slopes of the Black Forest, and the roads skirting the Haardt Mts. and the Vosges. Excursions in the Black Forest, the Vosges, or other mountainous districts make considerable demands on the strength and staying power of the rider, but some delightful rides downhill may be begun at the highest-lying railway-stations. Dangerous places are generally marked on the cycling maps mentioned below, but the cyclist should always be careful on roads unknown to him. Strong brakes and a good lamp for night-riding are indispensable. Some of the narrower and steeper streets in towns and villages are apt to be closed to the cyclist, and restrictions are also often made on the use of the wheel in public parks. In most cases a number-plate has to be attached to the bicycle, and the police have the right to demand the exhibition of the cyclist's club-ticket or passport.

No duty is levied at the frontier on bicycles accompanied by their riders, but a charge of 8-10 ℳ is made on crated machines, if they look new. Uncrated bicycles are carried as personal luggage when accompanied by the rider. On distances up to 100 kilomètres (62 M.), however, he may take a bicycle-ticket ('Fahrradkarte') at the lower rate of 20 pf.; he must then himself take his wheel to and from the baggage-car, after having attached to it the cycle-ticket (without the coupon), and must also transfer it from one train to the other, if carriages are changed *en route*. In Alsace and German Lorraine special compartments are provided for cyclists, with apparatus for suspending their machines.

The German steamers on the Rhine do not carry bicycles unless special tickets have been taken at the agencies beforehand. Passengers have themselves to deposit their wheels in the steerage, where they are generally left without anyone to look after them. The Dutch steamboat company makes no charge for bicycles, and moreover provides stands for them on the main deck.

The best **Cycling Maps** of the Rhenish districts are those issued by *L. Ravenstein* of Frankfort for Wiesbaden and Coblenz (3 ℳ), the neighbourhood of Wiesbaden (4 ℳ), the Environs of Frankfort (3 ℳ), Starkenburg (Valley of the Rhine, Odenwald, & Spessart; 4 ℳ), Upper Hesse (4 ℳ), and the Bavarian Palatinate & Rhenish Hesse (4 ℳ). — A series of cheaper maps (1½ ℳ each) for Central Europe is issued by *Liebenow & Ravenstein* of Leipzig. Those available for visitors to the Rhine are Nos. 84 (Cologne), 85 (Wetzlar), 98 (Prüm), 99 (Frankfort), 112 (Trèves), 113 (Mannheim), 127 (Strassburg), 140 (Colmar), and 141 (Freiburg). — The German volume of the Continental Road Book of the Cyclists' Touring Club (price 5s.) will be found useful.

X. Hotels.

The first-class hotels in the principal towns and watering-places throughout Germany are generally good and somewhat expensive; but it frequently happens that in old-fashioned hotels of unassuming exterior, particularly in places off the beaten track, the traveller finds more real comfort and much lower charges.

The average charges in the first-class hotels are as follows: room (including light and attendance) 3-5 $\mathcal{M}$, plain breakfast 1-1^1/$_2$ $\mathcal{M}$, dinner 3-5 $\mathcal{M}$, pension (*i.e.* board and lodging) 7-10 $\mathcal{M}$. In some of the most luxurious houses, and for extra accommodation, the charges are considerably higher. When not otherwise indicated, R. (room) in the Handbook is used to include light and attendance. At the larger hotels the price of the table d'hôte is often raised when no wine is ordered. Small gratuities are expected by the portier, boots ('Hausknecht'), chambermaid, and head-waiter ('Oberkellner'). The total amount of these may be reckoned at 10 per cent of the bill.

When the traveller remains for a week or more at a hotel, it is advisable to pay, or at least call for his account every two or three days, in order that erroneous insertions may be detected. Verbal reckonings are objectionable, except in some of the more remote and primitive districts where bills are never written. A waiter's mental arithmetic is faulty, and the faults are seldom in favour of the traveller. A favourite practice is to present the bill at the last moment, when mistakes or wilful imposition cannot easily be detected or rectified. Those who purpose starting early in the morning will do well to ask for their bills on the previous evening.

Hotel-keepers who wish to commend their houses to British and American travellers are reminded of the desirability of providing the bedrooms with *large* basins, foot-baths, plenty of water, and an adequate supply of towels. Great care should be taken that the sanitary arrangements are in good order, including a strong flush of water and proper toilette-paper; and no house that is deficient in this respect can rank as first-class or receive a star of commendation, whatever may be its excellencies in other departments.

In the height of the season it is advisable to order one's rooms in advance. To facilitate the ordering of rooms by telegram the International Society of Hotel Keepers, to which most of the proprietors of the larger hotels belong, has prepared a telegraphic code, a few of the terms of which are given below: — *alba*, room with one bed; *albaduo*, room with double bed; *arab*, room with two beds; *abec*, room with three beds; *belab*, two rooms with two beds; *birac*, two rooms with three beds; *bonad*, two rooms with four beds; *ciroc*, three rooms with three beds; *carid*, three rooms with four beds; *calde*, three rooms with five beds; *caduf*, three rooms with six beds; *casag*, three rooms with seven beds; *danid*, four rooms with four beds; *dalme*, four rooms with five beds; *danof*, four rooms with six beds; *dalag*, four rooms with seven beds; *dirich*, four rooms with eight beds; *durbi*, four rooms with nine beds; *kind*, child's cot; *sal*, sitting-room; *bat*, private bath; *serv*, servant's room. The day on which the accommodation is wished and the hour of arrival should also be stated: — *granmatin*, midnight to 7 a.m.; *matin*,

7 a.m. to noon; *sera,* noon to 7 p.m.; *gransera,* 7 p.m. to midnight. —
The length of the intended stay should also be indicated: — *pass,* one
night; *stop,* several days. The full name should be given in the signa-
ture. To countermand an order for rooms the word *cancel,* with the
sender's name, is sufficient.

XI. Post, Telegraph, and Telephone Offices.

Postal Rates. *Ordinary Letters* within Germany and
Austria-Hungary, 10 pf. per 20 grammes ($^2/_3$ oz.) prepaid; for
foreign countries 20 pf. (for the United States 10 pf., if sent by
direct steamer). *Registered Letters* 20 pf. extra. Letters by
Town Post, 5 pf. up to 250 grammes (9 oz.). — *Post Cards* 5 pf.,
for abroad 10 pf. Reply post-cards 10 pf., for abroad 20 pf. —
Printed Papers (Drucksachen), up to 50 gr. 3 pf., to 100 gr. 5 pf.,
to 250 gr. 10 pf.; for abroad 5 pf. per 50 grammes ($1^3/_4$ oz.).

Post Office Orders (Postanweisungen) within Germany, not
exceeding 5 *M,* 10 pf.; 100 *M,* 20 pf.; 200 *M,* 30 pf.; 400 *M,*
40 pf.; 600 *M,* 50 pf.; 800 *M,* 60 pf.; for Austria-Hungary 10 pf.
per 20 *M* (minimum 20 pf.). The charges for post-office orders
for foreign countries vary, and may be learned on application at
any post-office (for the United Kingdom 20 pf. per 20 *M,* for the
United States 20 pf. per 40 *M*).

Telegrams. The minimum charge for a telegram to Great
Britain or Ireland is 80 pf., to any other European country 50 pf.,
subject to which conditions telegrams are charged at the following
rates per word: Germany, Austria-Hungary, and Luxembourg 5 pf.;
Belgium, Denmark, Holland, and Switzerland 10 pf.; France 12 pf.;
Great Britain, Italy, Norway, Roumania, and Sweden 15 pf.; Greece
30 pf.; Turkey 45 pf.; other European countries 20 pf. Telegrams
to the United States cost from 1 *M* 5 to 1 *M* 60 pf. per word. —
Telegrams despatched and received within the same town are
charged 3 pf. per word (minimum 30 pf.). — Urgent telegrams,
marked D. (i. e. *dringend*), taking precedence of all others, pay
thrice the above tariff.

Telephones. The urban service costs 10-20 pf. per 3 min.,
the inter-urban service from 20 pf. to 2 *M.*

XII. Wines of the Rhine and Moselle.

On the banks of the Rhine from Mayence to Bonn, a distance
of 90 M., the cultivation of the vine may be seen in the greatest
possible perfection, the geniality of the climate (comp. p. xi) being
very favourable to the ripening of the grapes. While the palm must
be yielded to France for her red wines, no country in the world can
compete with the Rhenish Provinces in the vast variety and excellence of the white wines which they produce.

No error has been more prevalent than that the Rhenish and
Moselle wines possess an injurious acidity. Liebig on the contrary

affirms, not only that the exquisite bouquet of the Rhine wines is owing to the free acid which they contain, but that some of their most salutary properties arise from the tartar present in them. To this he attributes the immunity enjoyed by those who use the German wines from the uric acid diathesis. Many others who have investigated the subject entertain the same opinion. Another advantage possessed by Rhenish wines is the total absence of brandy, an ingredient with which the wines of Spain, Portugal, and Sicily are almost invariably fortified, to the utter destruction of their flavour, and the injury of the health of the consumer. That the addition of alcohol to wine is unnecessary for its preservation is proved by the fact that Rhine wines often retain their excellence for half-a-century, although they seldom contain more than eight or nine per cent of alcohol. The very property of keeping is indeed mainly attributable to the fact that the fermentation is more per-fect in Rhenish wines than in those of Spain and Portugal, where fermentation is checked by the addition of brandy. With the white wines of France the same object is effected by sulphuration. By these processes the richness and sweetness of new wine are artific-ially and unwholesomely retained.

The traveller who finds the table-wine of the hotels unpala-table, and whose eye wanders in bewilderment over the 'Wein-karte', is recommended to select a bottle of still Hock or Moselle at 3-4 ℳ per bottle, at which price the taste ought to be grati-fied. The hotel-prices of the high-class still wines, as well as of the sparkling wines, are often exorbitant.

The **Rheingau,** a district about 15 M. in length, produces the finest wines of the Rhine. Here is situated *Schloss Johannis-berg,* a most favoured spot, yielding a wine almost without rival. As the celebrated vineyards do not exceed 55 acres in area, little of this rare product falls to the share of the ordinary public. Moreover the first quality is only obtained in the finest seasons; the grapes are selected with the utmost care from the ripest bunches, not a drop of the precious juice being allowed to escape; the yield, under the most favourable circumstances, is therefore very limited. The various qualities of this wine are sold in the cask at Schloss Johannisberg by public auction. It is remarkable for raciness, del-icacy of flavour, and bouquet, rather than for strength. The other wines of the vicinity, distinguished by the name of *Johannisberg-Klaus,* and those yielded by the vineyards of Count Schönborn, are also highly esteemed. There is also 'Johannisberger' produced from the vineyards of the village of that name, but this is inferior to many of the other products of the Rheingau. In this neighbourhood are *Rüdesheim* and *Geisenheim,* both producing first-class wines. Bingen is a favourable district for strong wines; the hill behind it yields *Scharlachberger* (p. xxii). Below Bingen, on the opposite bank, is *Assmannshausen,* the red wine of which holds a high rank and in good vintages vies with Burgundy of the best class, being made from the same species of grape; but unfortunately, like the latter, it is often impaired by travelling. The *Marcobrunn* vineyard, between *Hattenheim* and *Erbach,* produces a white wine of exquisite flavour and bouquet. The wines, however, which compete most successfully with Johannisberger and trench closely upon its celebrity, are the *Steinberger,* produced from the carefully-cultivated vineyards on the hill at the back of Hattenheim, and the *Rauentaler Berg* (p. 251), the best vintages of which are unsurpassed in flavour and quality. *Hochheim,* situated on the Main, yields a wine of very superior quality, and has given the name of 'Hock' to the produce of the country generally.

The **Valley of the Rhine** below Bingen produces many pleasant and wholesome wines, but inferior to the above. Those of *Lorch, Enghöll, Steeg, Oberwesel,* and *Boppard* may be mentioned among the white. The Rheinbleicherte (*i. e.* 'bleich-rote' or pale red) of *Steeg, Oberwesel,* and *Bacharach,* and the light-red wines of *Salzig, Camp, Horchheim,* the *Kreuzberg* (near Ehrenbreitstein), and *Urbar* are also esteemed. Most of the wines grown below Coblenz are light-red. *Linz* produces excellent Rheinbleicherte.

Rhenish Bavaria yields a vast quantity of white wine, generally known as wine of the Haardt, or Palatinate. The best qualities are those of *Ruppertsberg, Deidesheim;* and *Forst,* after which rank those of *Ungstein, Dürkheim, Wachenheim,* and *Königsbach.* Good red wines are grown at *Gimmeldingen* and *Callstadt.* The inferior wines of this district usually have a coarse, earthy flavour.

Rhenish Hesse produces the excellent *Scharlachberger* above mentioned, next to which rank *Niersteiner, Oppenheimer, Laubenheimer,* and *Bodenheimer,* all pleasant wines, but less delicate than those of the Rheingau. *Liebfrauenmilch* ('Lait de Notre Dame') is a good sound wine which owes much of its reputation to the superior wines sold under that name, and to the quaintness of the name itself. The vineyards where it is grown (p. 452) are incapable of producing a tenth part of the wine usually so called. The flat vineyards of *Ingelheim,* between Mayence and Bingen, yield a good light-red wine.

The **Nahe** wines, like those of the Palatinate, possess considerable body, but little flavour. That of the *Scharlachberg* near Bingen (comp. p. xxi) is sometimes classed as a Nahe wine, and is the best of this group.

The **Valley of the Ahr** is the most northern point at which the grape is successfully cultivated. Its light and wholesome *'Ahrbleicherte'* are chiefly consumed in the neighbourhood of their growth. They are strengthening and astringent in their properties, and resemble Burgundy of an inferior class. The best are those of *Walporzheim, Ahrweiler,* and *Bodendorf.*

The **Moselle** wines are chiefly grown amidst rugged and sterile-looking slate rocks, and are distinguished by their delicate, aromatic flavour, though the inferior varieties are apt to be rather acid in bad years. The best are *Brauneberger, Ohligsberger,* and *Berncasteler Doctor,* which possess a delicious bouquet; and next to these may be placed the wines of *Zeltingen, Graach, Pisport,* and *Grünhaus.*

The **Saar** wines possess even less body than those of the Moselle, but surpass them in aroma. *Scharzhofberger* is a most excellent wine of this district.

Markgräfler, the wine of the Grand-Duchy of Baden *(Affental* best red wine), the wines of **Alsace,** the **Neckar** wines, and those of the **Bergstrasse** are almost entirely consumed in their respective districts.

The difference which exists among the products of the various vintages on the Rhine presents a marked contrast to the tolerably uniform quality maintained by the wines of Southern Europe The best wine-years of the last century in the Rheingau were 1806, 1811, 1822, 1834, 1846, 1857, 1862, 1865, 1868, 1884, 1886, 1889, 1893, 1895, 1897, 1900, 1904, and 1905. But even in these years the yield was by no means uniformly excellent in all parts of the Rhineland. The climatic conditions are not the same in all the districts; different years seem to suit the different kinds of vine; and the vineyards in the most favoured positions, where the grapes ripen soonest, often suffer the most severely from the early spring frosts.

Many of the inns on the Middle and Upper Rhine (especially in the smaller towns) have wine on draught, which, though not entered on the wine-list, is frequently better than the cheaper wines in bottle.

Sparkling Wines. The effervescing German wines were first manufactured at *Esslingen* (in 1826), *Heilbronn, Würzburg,* and *Mayence,* and afterwards at *Trèves, Coblenz,* and various other places. These wines, generally known in England as Sparkling Hock and Moselle, are distinguished from the French wines by the predominance of the flavour of the grape, and when obtained in unexceptionable quarters, are a light, pleasant, and wholesome beverage.

The process is precisely the same as that employed in the preparation of Champagne. The wine (which at the outset is an ordinary still wine, worth 1s. or 1s. 6d. per bottle) is bottled after the first fermentation is over; and, by the addition of a small quantity of sugar and exposure to a moderately warm temperature, a second fermentation and the generation of carbonic acid are produced. The bottles are then placed on racks with their corks downwards, where they remain a month or more, and are opened several times to allow the escape of the sediment.

At this stage of the process as many as 20-25 per cent of the bottles usually burst, while the contents of the survivors are much diminished. When the wine has thus been thoroughly clarified, the bottles are filled up, a small quantity of syrup (cognac and sugar) is added to give the requisite sweetness and body, and the final corking then takes place. The sparkling wine thus laboriously prepared for the market is worth more than double the original still wine from which it is manufactured. The inferior qualities are generally the most effervescent.

The traveller is cautioned against dealing with any but the most respectable wine-merchants, and should remember that excellence of quality is quite incompatible with lowness of price. As a pleasant and wholesome summer-beverage the Rhenish wines of the second and third class may be imported at a moderate price, the duty and carriage amounting to 4-5s. per dozen; but the higher class of Rhine wine, of which Marcobrunner may be taken as a sample, cannot be drunk in England under five or six shillings a bottle.

XIII. Rhenish Art
by
Professor Anton Springer.

In the valley of the Rhine we find that several different strata of civilization, if we may use the expression, had deposited themselves ere the rest of Germany had abandoned its primitive forest life. The lowest of these strata, were a section of them exhibited in geological fashion, would show an ante-Roman period, when the natives carried on a busy trade with the Mediterranean seaports and with Etruria. After Cæsar's campaigns a new stratum was gradually formed by the occupation of the country by Roman military colonists. This stratum was afterwards sadly contorted and broken by the storms of the barbarian migrations, and was at length almost entirely covered by that of the Frankish-Christian period, which began in the 7th century.

On Rhenish soil antiquarians will find frequent opportunities of tracing back the history of human culture to its earliest beginnings, while the ROMAN relics are so numerous and important as to arrest the eye of even the superficial observer. The *Peutinger Tabula*, the mediæval copy of a Roman map, now preserved at Vienna, shows the principal towns on the Rhine and also on the tributaries of its left side, together with the roads connecting them, and even the baths and other public buildings with which they were embellished. The Roman colonies on the Rhine, being chiefly the headquarters of the different legions, always presented a military character. Most of the existing monuments are accordingly votive stones and tombstones of soldiers. The artistic forms are, as a rule, somewhat primitive, while the subjects are frequently borrowed from the Oriental worship of Mithras. We also find that in some cases Gallic deities have been Romanized. The principal collections of Roman antiquities are at *Bonn, Cologne, Wiesbaden, Carlsruhe, Mannheim, Speyer, Mayence*, and *Trèves*. At Trèves, moreover, we obtain an admirable idea of the character of a very important Roman provincial town.

Trèves, the capital of Germania Inferior, and for a considerable time an imperial residence, did not merely possess buildings of practical utility like most of the other colonies, but was also embellished with some of the noblest decorative Roman structures ever erected north of the Alps. On the banks of the Moselle also, outside the town, rose a long series of villas, many of which were richly decorated with mosaics. Before the decline of the Roman supremacy CHRISTIANITY established itself on the banks of the Rhine. No churches of the earliest Christian epoch are however now extant except the nucleus of the cathedral of Trèves, and the decagonal (originally circular) church of St. Gereon at Cologne; its only relics are a number of tombstones at Trèves, and several monumental inscriptions.

In consequence of the barbarian migrations, the Roman-Christian culture was afterwards almost completely buried beneath a new stratum of German paganism, and the vast valley of the Rhine relapsed into its primitive rudeness, although at Cologne and Trèves the arts were not entirely extinct. The Austrian princes, however, were munificent patrons of the church, and the Bishops of Trèves and Cologne (*Nicetius* and *Charentinus*, about the middle of the 6th cent.) distinguished themselves by their zeal for church-building.

The artistic efforts of the Merovingian period, of which a few traces only are left, as in the *Cathedral* at *Trèves*, appear to have been very insignificant compared with those of **Charlemagne's** reign (768-814). In the prosecution of his numerous undertakings the great emperor was not merely stimulated by his zeal for the promotion of art, but by his ardent desire to revive the ancient glory of the Roman empire and to invest his capital with all the splendour of the ancient imperial residences, and particularly that of Ravenna. The Carlovingian art was entirely centred around the court of the emperor, and he was personally attended by a circle of scholars called his academy. Among the members of the academy was *Eginhard*, who in consequence of his surname Bezaleel has been supposed to have been familiar with art, but of whose labours in that sphere nothing certain is known. To him is attributed the building of the *Palace Chapel* at *Aix-la-Chapelle* (now the *Cathedral*), which is still in comparatively good preservation. It is obviously a copy of the court-chapel at Ravenna (San Vitale), but has been more judiciously and articulately designed, and has in its turn served as a model for later edifices, for which either its ground-plan (as at *Ottmarsheim* in Alsace), or its double row of columns in the interior of the rotunda (as in the case of *St. Maria im Capitol* at *Cologne* and the *Minster* at *Essen*), has been borrowed.

The magnificence of the palaces which the great emperor possessed on the banks of the Rhine was a favourite theme with the poets and prose-writers of the day. According to their accounts the *Palace* at *Ingelheim* was not inferior in splendour to that of Aix-la-Chapelle itself, but of that edifice there is no trace beyond a few fragments of walls and of columns which have been transferred to other buildings. The same variety of capitals is also seen in the *Church of St. Justin* at *Höchst am Main* founded under Abp. Otgar of Mayence (826-847). — During the later Carlovingian period the Rhineland again suffered severely from an irruption of barbarians. At this period the Normans took possession of the banks of the river and penetrated into its side-valleys; but civilization was now too far advanced to be seriously retarded by this catastrophe.

Endowed with a rich art-heritage handed down by antiquity, the Rhenish-Frankish tribes gradually overspread the country after the middle of the 10th cent., from which period down to the Reformation the development of Rhenish art is traceable without interruption.

In the EARLY MIDDLE AGES (10-12th cent.) Rhenish art differed materially from that of most other parts of Germany in being the product of an already cultivated soil, where ancient models were abundant, while in these other districts it was the growth of a soil previously untilled. On the banks of the Rhine were preserved fragments of Roman and early-Christian edifices; there the eye was familiar with architectural forms and mouldings; in the Rhenish towns were always to be found artificers possessed of considerable manual skill; and owing to the constant communication kept up with foreign places skilled labour could always be readily imported when necessary. Rhenish art was thus matured considerably earlier than that of Lower Saxony and Swabia. At the same time the features common to the whole of early mediæval art in the west recur in that of the Rhine also. The forms of worship having been well defined in the early-Christian period, the churches all present a certain uniformity of appearance. Like the early-Christian basilicas, the Rhenish churches of the 10th-12th cent, are of an elongated form; they possess aisles which are lower and narrower than the nave; and the altar is placed at the rounded extremity of the nave.

The Rhenish edifices also possess the characteristics of the **Romanesque Style,** which are common to the great majority of works of the 10th-12th centuries. In this style the pillars and columns are connected by means of round arches, the doors and windows also terminate in round arches, and the naves and aisles are either covered with flat roofs or with groined vaulting of rounded

form. The *Cubical Capital*, which was probably invented by
mediæval architects for the purpose of forming a harmonious connecting link between the column and the arch above, is also used
in the Rhineland, and the copings and mouldings of the Rhenish
buildings are the same as those employed in the contemporaneous
edifices of Western Europe. The Rhenish architecture, however, occupies an independent position of its own within the Romanesque
group. The character of the building-material (red sandstone), local
traditions, and the prevalent taste of the period all combine to impart to the Rhenish buildings a distinctive character which seldom
or never recurs in other countries. At an early period the use of
alternate courses of different colours came into vogue. Thus we
find arches faced with stone alternating with light-coloured brick,
the latter material having been taken from Roman ruins; and when
the architects had exhausted their supply of bricks, the art of
making which was unknown in Germany in the early middle ages,
they produced the same effect by the use of dark and light coloured
stones. The copings on pillars and walls were generally copied from
Roman models, and the ancient *Corinthian Capitals,* formed of a
wreath of leaves, were imitated with varying success (as indeed,
had also been the case in the Carlovingian epoch). The long-
established practice of art, and the wealth which the Rhenish towns
succeeded in amassing at an early period, enabled them gradually
to extend the dimensions of their churches, to develop the construction of vaulting earlier than elsewhere, and to impart to their
buildings a picturesque richness of effect. — The same conditions
were likewise favourable to the development of the GOLDSMITH'S
ART, and that of ENAMEL PAINTING. The Rhinelanders also attained
considerable proficiency in MURAL PAINTING at an early period,
but for the plastic art they displayed less aptitude.

As early as the 11th cent. the practice of art and of artistic
handicrafts seems to have become naturalized in the Rhenish towns
and in those of Lorraine. In all the larger towns extensive building
operations were undertaken, and at the same time a number of
handsome abbey-churches sprang up. At *Strassburg* a cathedral
was erected by *Bishop Werner;* at *Cologne* the archbishops *Heribert* and *Anno* exhibited much zeal for church-building; and at
Trèves the cathedral was extended by *Poppo.* The grandest monuments of German mediæval art, however, are the three CENTRAL
RHENISH CATHEDRALS of *Mayence, Speyer,* and *Worms,* examples
of the golden prime of a style which began and also ended earlier
here than in other northern districts. It was not till the Gothic
period that France and England fully realized their architectural
ideals, while the independent exertions of German masters had
already culminated in their Romanesque cathedrals. It has frequently been asserted that these cathedrals originally possessed flat

roofs only, and were not covered with vaulting till the 12th cent.; but recent researches prove that the vaulting of Mayence Cathedral dates from immediately after 1081, when the older wooden roof was destroyed by fire. It is also probable that the nave of Speyer Cathedral, in spite of its gigantic proportions, also received a stone vaulted roof soon after 1097. The charming *Abbey Church of Laach* proves that vaulted churches were easily and skilfully constructed in the first half of the 12th cent., notwithstanding the novelty of the style. While the pillars of this church are of uniform pattern and are placed at considerable intervals, those of the Central Rhenish cathedrals are placed much closer together, and those which bear the vaulting are differently shaped from those supporting the arcades.

Towards the end of the 12th cent., and for a considerable part of the 13th, COLOGNE was the chief cradle of Rhenish art. The sacredness of the city as the custodian of the highly revered relics of the Magi, combined with the wealth and the political power of its enterprizing citizens, not only led to the rebuilding of all the principal churches at this period, but was conducive to the general progress of architecture, and contributed to impart a rich and picturesque decorative character to the city itself. The architects do not seem to have aimed at grandeur of dimensions. The naves of the churches are usually small and insignificant, but the builders expended their utmost skill on the embellishment of the choirs. The apse, in combination with the rounded transepts, was regarded as the nucleus of the church, the other distinctive features of which consisted of the gable of the choir, the dome, and the towers. As an example of the picturesque effect of this arrangement we may mention the *Church of the Apostles* at Cologne when viewed from the Neumarkt. At the same time variety of ornament, richness of articulation, and pleasing effects of colour were also studied. Immediately under the roof runs a gallery, which is of some structural importance inasmuch as it lessens the dead weight of the wall, but is also effective in a decorative point of view as the small columns stand out in strong contrast to the dark background. Generally, indeed, the Rhenish masters appear to have devoted much attention to such effects of light and shade. Under the gallery runs a frieze consisting of dark slabs framed with light-coloured stone; the columns and half-columns are of a different material from the walls; and even the pilasters are composed of differently-coloured stones. In keeping with this picturesque character is the richness of the ornamentation. The architects were not satisfied with straight and simple lines. Their windows are either round or fan-shaped, and they are disposed in groups or enclosed within a pointed arch. The portals consist of archways resting on several columns; the space above the doors is filled with sculpture; and the façade is enlivened with narrow pillars and entwined arches. Buildings of this character, which are typical of the Rhineland, and occur in almost every town of any importance, are usually described as belonging to the TRANSITIONAL STYLE, as if the forms recurring in them were identical with those which pave the way for the Gothic. The term, however, is entirely missapplied, as it is impossible in the rich and handsome Rhenish churches of the 12th and beginning of the 13th cent. to discover the slightest germ of the Gothic style. The style may, however, be appropriately characterized as the final and most ornate manifestation of Romanesque architecture, a definition which is borne out by the general tendencies of Rhenish art. As an auxiliary of this style we may now mention the art of MURAL PAINTING, which was developed at an unusually early period, being diligently practised at several places on the Rhine in the second half of the 12th century. Most of these paintings were unfortunately covered with whitewash at a later period, but those still existing (at *Schwarz-Rheindorf*, opposite Bonn, the paintings of which resemble a symbolic poem, at *Brauweiler* near Cologne, in *St. Maria im Capitol* at Cologne, at *Boppard*, etc.) exhibit a rich and thoughtful style of composition, and show that the painters were skilled in drawing and even in the delineation of complicated action.

This prevalent branch of the Romanesque style, with its highly developed ornamentation, was not hastily abandoned by the Rhenish masters, and it was not till about the year 1250 that the **Gothic Style,** introduced from France, was completely nationalized in this part of Germany. The precise manner in which the Gothic architecture, with its spirited flying buttresses, lofty vaulting, and other members relieving the monotony of the walls, was introduced into the valley of the Rhine is unknown; but it was probably adopted simultaneously at several different points. At *Cologne* we observe in the church of *St. Gereon* an attempt to apply the new precepts to the old forms, and in the church of the *Minorites* we have a somewhat plain example of Gothic dating from the middle of the 13th century. In the *Liebfrauen-Kirche* at *Trèves* the Gothic forms were successfully adapted at an early period to an unusual ground-plan. The *Cistercian Church* at *Marienstatt* in Nassau is a fine example of the early-Gothic style, destitute as yet of all ornamentation, and to the same style belong the church of *Rufach* in Alsace and the western parts of *St. Thomas* at *Strassburg*. In the second half of the 13th cent. began the construction of the great GOTHIC CATHEDRALS. Those of *Cologne* and *Metz* were designed entirely in the Gothic style, while at *Strassburg* and *Freiburg* the earlier Romanesque beginnings were adapted to the new Gothic work. Goethe has contributed much to immortalize the name of *Erwin of Steinbach*, who is usually described as the originator of Strassburg Minster, but that master's actual share of the work seems to have been limited to the W. façade. The masters of the Strassburg as well as of the Cologne cathedral must have been thoroughly conversant with the details of French Gothic, but they were very far from being mere mechanical copyists. The façade at Cologne and the tower at Strassburg are entirely emanations of German imagination. In order, however, to convince himself of the independence of the German masters of the Gothic style the traveller must not confine his attention to the great cathedrals. Among the SMALLER GOTHIC CHURCHES he will discover frequent proofs of originality and not a few gems of architecture. Among these smaller churches we may mention the grave and dignified *Abbey Church of Altenberg*, near Cologne, and the *Collegiate Church of Xanten*, erected under the influence of Cologne masters; the superb *Church of St. Catharine* at *Oppenheim* and the ponderous *Cathedral of Frankfort* on the Central Rhine; and lastly, in Alsace, the *Church of St. George* at *Schlettstadt*, the *Church of SS. Peter and Paul* at *Weissenburg*, the church of *Nieder-Haslach*,and that of *Thann*, with its graceful tower. The numerous churches of the Mendicant and Dominican orders, some of which have nave and aisles of equal height, are generally too plain and monotonous to arouse much general interest.

The highest efforts of the Gothic architects in this part of Germany were devoted to the building of churches, but the Rhenish districts also contain SECULAR EDIFICES, including castles, town-halls, guild-houses, and private mansions, which present Gothic forms or at least Gothic characteristics. The eye, however, is less frequently struck by buildings of this class than by the churches, partly because well-preserved examples are now comparatively rare, and partly because in secular architecture generally there is usually less room for marked changes of style. Throughout the whole of the middle ages the dwelling-houses, for example, were constructed of timber, and the character of their ornamentation was rather determined by the nature of the material than by the fashion of the day. Even in the case of the stone houses the projecting upper stories frequently recall the style of their wooden predecessors. The architectural character of the palaces, châteaux, and castles, on the other hand, was necessarily determined by military considerations. As the requirements of both defensive and offensive operations were almost equally important during the 11th cent. and again during the 13th, the châteaux and castles retained the same forms for several centuries. Of Barbarossa's residence at *Gelnhausen,* an imperial palace of the Romanesque period, there still exist considerable ruins. The palace of the same emperor at *Hagenau* (1157) was entirely destroyed during the Thirty Years' War. Among the mediæval CASTLES those of Alsace are very numerous and important. The most considerable are the three *Castles of Rappoltsweiler*, that of *Hoh-Barr* near Zabern (1170), the *Hoh-Königsburg*, the *Wasenburg* near Nieder-bronn, and the *Lichtenberg* near Neuweiler, the last three belong-ing to the Gothic period. Most of the hills on the banks of the Rhine and its tributaries are also crowned with the ruins of mediæ-val castles, or others rebuilt in their original style. In most cases the pinnacled *Bergfried,* or keep, which was used both for pur-poses of attack and defence, is still standing; remains of the *Palas,* or dwelling-house, are also frequently preserved; and in many cases the outworks, gateways, and towers by which the approach to the castle was protected are still traceable. These ruins, however, which impart so picturesque a charm to the scenery of the Rhine, rarely possess much artistic value. The most interesting of the Rhenish castles is that of *Reichenberg,* near St. Goarshausen, with its three stories borne by columns.

The Gothic architecture is also notable for the richness of its PLASTIC ORNAMENTATION. The portals and the various niches and canopies are generally filled with statues, and the gables and other parts of the building adorned with reliefs. The finest specimens of Gothic statuary are to be seen on the *Portals* of the *Lieb-frauen-Kirche* at *Trèves* and the *Cathedrals of Strassburg* and *Freiburg*. The *Statues of the Apostles* in the choir of the *Cologne Cathedral* also afford evidence that the Gothic sculpture was some-times richly coloured. The same cathedral also contains the *Mon-ument of Archbishop Conrad von Hochstaden,* the finest specimen of bronze statuary of the Gothic period. The numerous tombstones of that period must also be examined by the student of the progress of Gothic sculpture, such as those of *Archbishop Siegfried, Peter Aspelt,* and *Johann von Nassau,* in the *Cathedral of Mayence,* and those of *Günther von Schwarzburg* and *Johann von Holz-hausen and his Wife* in the *Cathedral of Frankfort*. The best examples of late-Gothic sculpture, which afterwards degenerated into a mere handicraft, are to be found in the altars of carved wood.

Throughout the middle ages, however, Rhenish artists evinced more aptitude for the art of PAINTING than for that of sculpture. The stained glass at *Strassburg, Cologne,* and *Oppenheim,* and the remains of 14th cent. mural paintings at Cologne are not less val-uable than the easel-pictures of the 15th cent. which are still pre-served.

The COLOGNE SCHOOL OF PAINTING was the first of those which attained to any celebrity on German soil. The earliest master of the school known to us by name is *Meister Wilhelm,* who flourished at the end of the 14th cent., and to whose brush are attributed the faded mural paintings of the Hansa-Saal in the Rathaus of Cologne (now preserved in the Wallraf-Richartz Museum) and also a number of easel-pieces. There is, however, better authority for

attributing to *Meister Stephan Lochner* the execution of the *Dombild*, the finest German painting of the 15th century. This master,
who was a native of the district of Constance, and died in 1451,
has been successful in substituting figures of considerable spirit
and life for the traditional types of his predecessors, with their
emaciated arms, their undeveloped busts, and their childish expression of countenance, but he has failed to take the next step towards fidelity to nature by omitting to individualize his characters.
His female figures are exactly alike, and his male figures, though
divided into young and old, are also destitute of distinctive character. In his treatment of the drapery, weapons, gold trinkets, and
all other external accessories, however, Meister Stephan cannot be
reproached with the fault of monotony; in executing these details
he is scrupulously faithful to nature, and his task was doubtless
facilitated by his occasional use of the newly-invented art of oil-
painting. The Dombild, the *Madonna with the Violets* (preserved
in the Archiepiscopal Museum), and the *Madonna in the Arbour
of Roses* (in the Wallraf-Richartz Museum) are the most important
works of this school, the career of which somewhat resembled that
of the early-Flemish school under the leadership of Hubert van
Eyck. The Rhenish masters, however, were soon surpassed by their
Flemish contemporaries, and ere long entirely lost their independence. About the end of the 15th cent. the art of painting in the
Rhineland was at length thoroughly pervaded with Flemish influence. The new style, however, was least successfully imitated on
the Lower Rhine, and particularly at Cologne. A number of pictures of the end of the 15th and beginning of the 16th cent., mostly
found in churches of Cologne, have been collected by the brothers
Boisserée, and others. The drawing is stiff, the colouring gaudy,
and the expression harsh. These works are generally classed in
accordance with their subjects; and we thus frequently hear of the
'Master of the Lyversberg Passion', the 'Master of the St. Bartholomew', and other equally vague designations. The historian of art
will find abundant opportunity of studying this school in the
Wallraf-Richartz Museum of Cologne. One of the best masters of
the Lower Rhine was *Jan Joest* of Calcar, who painted the high-
altar-piece in the principal church there about 1505. Portrait-
painting was also practised with some success at this period by
Barthel de Bruyn, Johann von Melem, and others.

The UPPER RHENISH AND ALEMANNIAN SCHOOL OF PAINTING had
a more prosperous career than the Lower Rhenish. The masters
of this school also succumbed to Flemish influence, but they suc-
céeded in making a better use of what they had learned in the
Netherlands. At the head of the school was *Martin Schongauer*
of Colmar (d. 1491), a pupil of Roger van der Weyden, and more
famous as an engraver than as a painter. The engraver's art, in-

deed, fostered by the advance of scientific pursuits, was more rapidly and successfully developed than that of painting. The *Younger Holbein, Mathias Grünewald*, and *Hans Baldung Grien* were also members of this school, but as their training was not strictly Rhenish they are mentioned here only in passing. Holbein's famous 'Madonna of Burgomaster Meyer' is preserved at the palace of Darmstadt.

When, at a somewhat later period, the tide of the **Renaissance** overflowed the Rhineland, it met with little or no resistance. After a brief conflict with the Gothic architecture, which gave rise to the erection of a number of curious buildings in a mixed style, the Renaissance, introduced from France and Flanders, and possessing little in common with the genuine Italian Renaissance, became naturalized on the banks of the Rhine about the middle of the 16th century. This new style of art, however, never throve satisfactorily on Rhenish soil, partly because the Rhineland had ceased to be a great centre of civilization as it had been in the middle ages, partly because the sway of ecclesiastical princes is less favourable to the steady progress of art than that of hereditary sovereigns, and also because this unfortunate region was the theatre of numerous wars which of course paralysed all artistic effort. Although Renaissance art never took the form of a permanent and organic system, it has bequeathed to the Rhineland several works of great importance. Foremost among these is the *Castle of Heidelberg*, the most sumptuous example of German Renaissance, next to which we may mention the *Porch of the Rathaus of Cologne*, and the fragment of the *Rathaus of Jülich (Juliers)*. On the Upper Rhine, in the Palatinate, and in Baden we encounter a number of handsome châteaux and pleasing houses in the Renaissance style of the 16th century.

The history of the PLASTIC ART of the Renaissance period is traceable in the numerous tombstones of the 16th and 17th centuries, which are to be found not only in the large churches of the principal towns, but also in smaller and more remote places, such as *Simmern, Boppard*, and *St. Arnual* near Saarbrücken.

The dependence of the Rhineland on the Netherlands, which is often noticeable in the province of architecture, is still more obvious in the PAINTING of this period. Numerous Netherlands masters migrated to the German courts, and the Germans themselves imitated these foreign masters, even when they drew their inspirations from the Italians. In the second half of the 16th cent. the German masters fell under the influence of the Dutch school, and when French taste came to be in vogue they again yielded their homage to the fashion of the day. Many of these painters, even down to the 18th cent., such as *Roos, Juncker,* and *Seekatz*, possessed considerable natural ability and manual skill, but at the present day their works are well-nigh consigned to oblivion.

The most imposing of the Rhenish edifices of the 18th century are the palaces in the BAROQUE and ROCOCO STYLES, erected by the various petty Rhenish princes, temporal and spiritual, in imitation of the palace of Versailles, such as those of *Carlsruhe, Mannheim, Bruchsal, Brühl,* and *Bonn.*

At the close of the century the Rhenish principalities were swept away by the French Revolution, and with them were extinguished the last signs of the vitality of art. After the restoration of peace, however, a revival began to take place. The Boisserée collection (p. xxxii) was the means of bringing early-Rhenish art into very favourable notice and of inspiring the public with confidence in the capabilities of Rhenish artists. The 'Romanticists' were desirous that Cologne should be made the new centre of art and science, but in 1818 the university was founded at Bonn, and in 1819 the academy at DÜSSELDORF was re-established. The painter *Cornelius,* who was appointed director of the academy, and who usually spent the winter only at Düsseldorf (and the summer at Munich), exercised no great influence on the progress of Rhenish art. He was succeeded by *Wilhelm Schadow* (1827), under whose able guidance the Düsseldorf School was brought into the right track and secured the favour of the public. The chief subjects of the painters of this period are scenes from private life, melancholy, sentimental, and humorous, or poetical themes readily intelligible to the middle classes of society, and their style is generally pleasing. Some of the masters of this school, and particularly *C. F. Lessing,* have also chosen themes of the deepest national interest. Seventy years have elapsed since the Düsseldorf School first attained celebrity, and the public taste has undergone material changes since that period, but the industrious colony of painters on the banks of the Düssel still deservedly enjoys a high reputation. Lastly we may mention the school of art connected with the Städel Gallery at FRANKFORT, the academy of CARLSRUHE, forming a kind of offshoot of the Düsseldorf School, and (quite recently) DARMSTADT, at all of which modern German painting is taught and practised with considerable success.

I. NORTH PART OF RHENISH PRUSSIA.

1. From Brussels to Aix-la-Chapelle.

96 M. EXPRESS TRAIN in 3³/₄ hrs. (fares 16 fr. 20, 11 fr. 20, 6 fr. 50 c.);
to *Cologne* (139 M.) in 4³/₄-6 hrs. (fares 23 fr. 70, 15 fr. 80, 9 fr. 60 c.); to
(154 M.) *Düsseldorf* in 6¹/₂-7³/₄ hrs. (fares 27 fr., 18 fr. 30, 11 fr. 10 c.). From
Ostend to (217 M.) Cologne, viâ Ghent and Brussels, in 7-8 hrs. (6¹/₄ hrs. by
the North Express and the Ostend-Vienna Express); fares 33 fr. 70, 22 fr. 60,
13 fr. 70 c. Finest views between Louvain and Liège to the *right*. The
district between Liège and Aix-la-Chapelle full of interest. Through-
carriages from Brussels to Cologne. German custom-house at Herbestal.

From Brussels to (77¹/₂ M.) *Verviers* (Rail. Restaurant), with
the Belgian custom-house, see *Baedeker's Belgium and Holland.*

On an eminence near (82¹/₂ M.) *Dolhain*, a modern town, picturesquely situated in the valley of the *Vesdre* (Ger. *Weser*), stands the
ancient fortress of *Limburg*, with a modern château, the Gothic
Church of St. George, and the scanty relics of the ancestral castle
of the Dukes of Limburg. — The train ascends the valley of the

BAEDEKER's Rhine. 17th Edit.   1

Vesdre. 86 M. *Welkenraedt,* the last Belgian station, is the junction of a branch-line to Aix-la-Chapelle (Gladbach), viâ Bleyberg.
86³/₄ M. *Herbestal* (Rail. Restaurant, very fair), the first Prussian village, is the frontier station.

FROM HERBESTAL TO EUPEN, 3 M., railway in 12 minutes. — **Eupen** (*Reinartz,* very fair, R. & B. 2¹/₄-4, D. 1³/₄ ℳ), a town of 13,000 inhab., picturesquely situated on the Vesdre, has considerable manufactures of cloth and woollens. Light railways run hence to Dolhain (p. 1) and Aix-la-Chapelle (comp. p. 3). The railway goes on to Raeren (p. 12).

Beyond (89¹/₂ M.) *Astenet* the train crosses the valley of the *Göhl* by a handsome viaduct, 125 ft. in height. 91 M. *Hergenrath,* the station for the neutral district of Moresnet. About 2 M. to the W. rises the *Emmaburg* (p. 12).

The train next passes through a tunnel, reaches (94 M.) *Ronheide* (p. 12), and finally descends to (96 M.) *Aix-la-Chapelle.*

Aix-la-Chapelle.

Railway Stations. 1. *Central Railway Station* (Pl. D, 5), for all lines except those mentioned below. — 2. *Aachen-West,* to the W. of the town, for the local line to Moresnet and Welkenraedt, and also stopped at by the Gladbach-Düsseldorf and Maastricht-Antwerp trains. — 3. *Köln-Tor Station* (Pl. F, 1), for the Aix-la-Chapelle and Jülich railway.

Hotels. All the first-class hotels and the better second-class hotels have lifts, electric light, hot-air heating, etc. — *In the Middle of the Town:* *HÔTEL NUELLENS (Pl. b; C, 3, 4), Friedrich-Wilhelm-Platz 6, opposite the Elisenbrunnen, with garden and three dépendances (see below), R. from 3, B. 1¹/₂, D. at 1 p.m. 2¹/₂, at 7 p.m. 4¹/₂, pens. from 8 ℳ; *GRAND MONARQUE (Pl. a; C, 3), Büchel 51; *HENRION'S GRAND-HÔTEL, Comphausbad-Str. 18, adjoining the Corneliusbad (see below), with garden, R. 3-7, B. 1¹/₂, D. at 12.30 p.m. 2¹/₂, at 1.30 and 7 p.m. 4, S. 2¹/₂, pens. 8-12 ℳ; *HÔTEL DE L'EMPEREUR (Pl. d; C, 3), Edel-Str. 6, with garden and dépendance (see below), R. from 4, B. 1¹/₄, D. at 1.15 p.m. 3, pens. 7-15 ℳ; *MONOPOL (Pl. c; C, 3), Hölzgraben 11, R. 2¹/₂-3¹/₂, B. ³/₄, D. 2¹/₂, pens. 6-8 ℳ; DRAGON D'OR (Pl. g; C, D, 3), Comphausbad-Str. 7; DOM-HÔTEL (Pl. h; C, 3), Ursuliner-Str. 11, opposite the Elisen-Garten; KÖNIG VON SPANIEN (Pl. i; C, 4), Kleinmarschier-Str. 52, commercial, with restaurant, R. & B. 2 ℳ 80-3 ℳ 50 pf., D. incl. wine 2¹/₂, pens. 6 ℳ, well spoken of; KARLSHAUS (Pl. k; C, 4), see p. 4; HÔTEL-RÈSTAURANT ENGLISCHER HOF, Hartmann-Str. 17, near the Elisenbrunnen. — *Near the Central Station,* all with restaurants: *UNION HOTEL (Pl. l; D, 5), Bahnhof-Platz 1, R. 2¹/₂-6, B. 1, D. 3 ℳ; *HÔTEL DU NORD, Römer-Str. 3, R. 2¹/₂-5, B. 1, D. 3 ℳ; HÔTEL KAISERHOF (Pl. m; D, 4), Hoch-Str. 2 and Wall-Str. 65; INTERNATIONAL, Römer-Str. 11, R. 2¹/₂-4, B. 1, pens. 6-8 ℳ; Plainer: HÔTEL DÜREN, Bahnhof-Platz 4, R. 1¹/₂-2¹/₂, B. ³/₄, D. 1¹/₄-1³/₄, pens. 4¹/₂-6 ℳ, well spoken of.

Bath Establishments (also hotels, and open throughout the whole year). In connection with the 'Upper Springs' (p. 9): *Kaiserbad* (Pl. 36; C, 3), Büchel 26, well fitted up, *Neubad* (Pl. 38; C, 3), Büchel 34, *Quirinusbad* (Pl. 39; C, 3), Hof 7; cheaper; these three belong to the Hôt. Nuellens (see above). *Königin von Ungarn* (Pl. 37; C, 3), Edel-Str. 1, belonging to the Hôt. de l'Empereur. The following are supplied by the 'Lower Springs': *Rosenbad* (Pl. 40; C, 3), *Corneliusbad* (Pl. 35; C, 3), these two connected with Henrion's Grand-Hôtel (see above); *Comphausbad* (Pl. 34; C, 3), all three near the Kurhaus. Bath-houses at *Burtscheid,* see p. 11. — *Swimming Baths* (well fitted up), Adalbert-Steinweg 10, with restaurant. A new *Municipal Bath House,* with swimming pool, has been erected in the Elisabeth-Str.

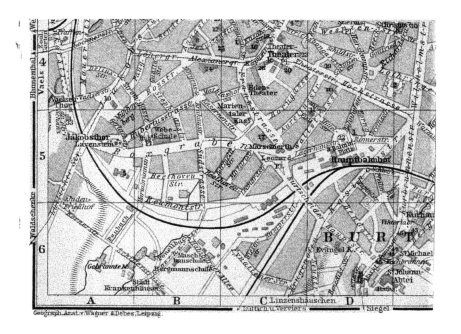

Geograph. Anst. v. Wagner & Debes, Leipzig.

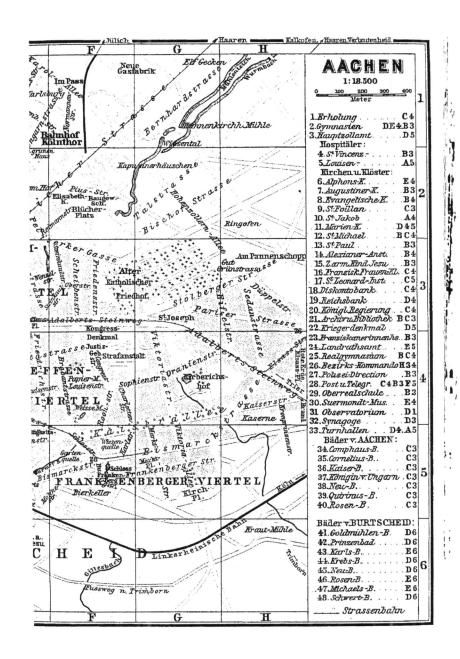

AACHEN

1:18.500

0   100   200   300   400
Meter

1. *Erholung* . . . . C 4
2. *Gymnasien* . . . . . DE 4 B 3
3. *Hauptzollamt* . . . . D 5
Hospitäler :
4. *St Vincenz* - . . . . B 3
5. *Louisen* - . . . . A 5
Kirchen u. Klöster :
6. *Alphons-K.* . . . . E 4
7. *Augustiner-K.* . . . . . . B 3
8. *Evangelische K.* . . . . . B 4
9. *St Foillan* . . . . C 3
10. *St Jakob* . . . . A 4
11. *Marien-K.* . . . . . . D 4 5
12. *St Michael* . . . . . B C 4
13. *St Paul* . . . . B 3
14. *Alexianer-Anst.* . . . . . B 4
15. *Z.arm.Kind Jesu* . . . . . B 3
16. *Franzisk.Frauen Kl.* . . . B 4
17. *St Leonard-Inst.* . . . . . C 5
18. *Diskontobank* . . . . . . C 4
19. *Reichsbank* . . . . D 4
20. *Königl.Regierung* . . . . C 4
21. *Archiv u.Bibliothek* B C 3
22. *Krieger denkmal* . . . . . D 5
23. *Franziskanerinnenhs.* . . B 3
24. *Landrathsamt* . . . . . E 5
25. *Realgymnasium* . . . . B C 4
26. *Bezirks-Kommando* H 3 4
27. *Polizei-Direction* . . . B 3
28. *Post u.Telegr.* C 4 B 3 F 5
29. *Oberrealschule* . . . . . B 3
30. *Suermondt-Mus.* . . . . E 4
31. *Observatorium* . . . . . D 1
32. *Synagoge* . . . . D 3
33. *Turnhallen* . . . D 4. A 5
Bäder v. AACHEN :
34. *Comphaus-B.* . . . . . C 3
35. *Cornelius-B..* . . . . . C 3
36. *Kaiser B.* . . . . C 3
37. *Königin v.Ungarn* . . . C 3
38. *Neu-B.* . . . . C 3
39. *Quirinus-B.* . . . . . . C 3
40. *Rosen-B.* . . . . . . C 3

Bäder v.BURTSCHEID :
41. *Goldmühlen-B.* . . . . D 6
42. *Prinzenbad* . . . . D 6
43. *Karls-B.* . . . . . . E 6
44. *Krebs-B.* . . . . D 6
45. *Neu-B.* . . . . D 6
46. *Rosen-B.* . . . . . . E 6
47. *Michaels -B.* . . . . . E 6
48. *Schwert-B.* . . . . . D 6

. . . *Strassenbahn*

Restaurants. WINE. *Kurhaus* (p. 9), D. 2½ ℳ; *Elisenbrunnen* (p. 9; also with rooms); *Grand Monarque*, see p. 2; *Karlshaus* (see p. 2; concerts); *Rethelstube*, Rethel-Str. 4; *Elbrechter Schenk* (Lucullus), Theater-Platz 5; *König von Spanien*, see p. 2; *Eulenspiegel*, Krämer-Str. 2, a quaint little establishment (also beer); *Pütz*, Edel-Str. 12; *Friderichs*, Elisabeth-Str. 6; *Erholung*, Friedrich-Wilhelm-Platz 7, with richly decorated rooms. — OYSTERS. *Lennertz*, Klostergasse 15 (Pl. B, 3). — BEER. *Elisenbrunnen* (see above); *Germania*, Friedrich-Wilhelm-Platz 8 and Wirichsbongard-Str. 5; *Spatenbräu*, Theater-Platz 1; *Wilhelmshallen*, Friedrich-Wilhelm-Platz 3, with large garden (concerts); *Karlshaus* (see above); *Vier Jahreszeiten* (also hotel), Kapuzinergraben 16, opposite the theatre: *Kaiserhof* (see p. 2), with a handsome concert-room (Kaiser-Saal), *Automatic Restaurants*, Kapuzinergraben 10 (Pl. C, 4) and Holzgraben 11 (Pl. C, 3).

Cafés. At the *Kurhaus* (see p. 9); at the *Elisenbrunnen* (p. 9); *Wiener Café*, Friedrich-Wilhelm-Platz 3; *Kaiser-Café*, on the ground-floor of the Hôtel Nuellens (p. 2); *Bristol*, Theater-Platz (concerts); at the *Lousberg* (see p. 11). — CONFECTIONERS. *Reul*, Hartmann-Str. 12; *Oellers*, Dahmengraben 7.

Cabs. — a. *Ordinary Cabs.* Per drive 1-2 pers. 70, each additional pers. 25 pf., with two horses 80 & 30 pf., trunk 30 pf. — To the Belvedere Inn on the *Lousberg*, 1-2 pers. 1 ℳ 50, each addit. pers. 25 pf., with two horses 2 ℳ & 30 pf. — By time: Each ½ hr. 1-2 pers. 1 ℳ 10, with two horses 1 ℳ 40 pf., each pers. addit. 25 pf. — Double fares at night.
b. *Taximeter Cabs.* Drive of 800 mètres for 1-2 pers. 70, each 400 m. more 10 pf.; same fares for 3-4 pers. for 600 & 300 m. and at night (1-2 pers.) for 400 & 300 m.; each pers. addit. 25 pf.; to the Lousberg 50 pf. (at night 1 ℳ) extra.

Electric Tramways traverse Aix-la-Chapelle and Burtscheid (10-20 pf.); comp. the Plan. Outside the town: to the *Osterweg* (Ronheide, Waldschlösschen, Karlshöhe), and *Moresnet*; to *Linzenshäuschen* and *Raeren* (p. 12) or *Eupen* (p. 2); to *Forsthaus Siegel* (these three lines run to the Aachener Wald); to *Haaren*, *Bardenberg* (Wilhelmstein, p. 15), and *Vaals* (three favourite resorts); to *Cornelimünster* (p. 12) and *Walheim* (p. 12); also to *Herzogenrath*, *Stolberg*, *Eschweiler*, *Vicht*, etc.

Post and Telegraph Office (Pl. C, 4; p. 4), Kapuzinergraben 19. For branch-offices, see the Plan.

Theatres. *Stadt-Theater* (Pl. C, 4; p. 4), performances in winter only; *Bernarts' Saison-Theater* (Pl. C, D, 3), Adalbert-Str. 20, with concert-room, garden, and restaurant; *Eden-Theater* (Pl. C, 4), Franz-Str. 45, varieties.

Visitors' Tax. For two months in summer, 12, 2 pers. 20, each additional person 5 ℳ (in winter 50 per cent less). — *Strangers' Enquiry & Intelligence Office* (Verkehrs- und -Auskunftsbureau), Friedrich-Wilhelm-Platz 14, adjoining the Elisenbrunnen (p. 9).

American Consul, *Pendleton King, Esq.*

English Church *(St. Alban's, or Empress Frederick Memorial Church)*, Couvent-Str.; services on Sun. at 8 (or 8.30) a.m., 11 a.m., and 6 p.m. Resident Chaplain, *Rev. A. R. Thorold Winckley, M. A.*, Augusta-Str. 17.

Aix-la-Chapelle (615 ft.), German *Aachen*, a very ancient town of 155,000 inhab. (including Burtscheid and Forst), the *Aquae Granni* of the Carlovingian period, lies in a fertile basin surrounded by gently sloping, wooded hills. It is a manufacturing town of some importance, with 120 cloth factories, 30 factories for needles and pins, 50 iron-foundries and machine-shops, etc. Already frequented as a health-resort by the Romans, as is proved

by the remains of their Thermæ (p. 9), Aachen was often the residence of the Frankish kings, and it became a favourite abode of
Charlemagne, who made it the capital of his dominions to the N.
of the Alps, and died here in 814. From the days of Charlemagne's
son, Louis the Pious, down to the accession of Ferdinand I. (1531)
Aix witnessed the coronation of 32 German emperors and kings,
and was called *par excellence* the free city of the Holy Roman
Empire and seat of royalty (*'urbs Aquensis, urbs regalis, regni
sedes principalis, prima regum curia'*). In the middle ages Aix-
la-Chapelle was the scene of many imperial diets and ecclesiastical
convocations, and in and after the 17th cent. several peace con-
gresses met here, the last in 1818. In 1794 the town was occupied
by the French, and in 1815 it passed to Prussia.

Externally this venerable imperial city has retained few relics
of her ancient history, and it is now practically a modern town.
The cathedral, the Rathaus, the Archives, a few relics of the
mediæval fortifications, now converted into promenades, such as
the restored *Marschier-Tor* (Pl. C, 5), the *Lange Turm* (Pl. A, 3;
adm. 20 pf.), and the *Pont-Tor* (p. 8), and the *Marienburg* (Pl. B, 1),
of the 16th cent., are the only remains of the old town.

The open space in front of the *Central Railway Station* (Pl. D, 5;
p. 2), built in 1905 from the plans of Mettegang, is embellished
with a *Warriors' Monument* (Pl. 22), by Drake (1872). — Passing
the Gothic *Marien-Kirche* (Pl. 11; D, 4, 5), a modern brick edifice
by *Statz* (1859), we reach the broad Theater-Strasse, and follow
it, to the left, to the Theater-Platz (Pl. C, 4), in the centre of
which stands the *Stadt-Theater*, erected in 1822-25 and enlarged
in 1901. Opposite (S.W.) are the *Government Buildings* (Pl. 20).
Adjacent is a *Telegraph Tower*, with an entrance to the handsome *Post Office* (Pl. 28; C, 4), in the Kapuzinergraben. The
Gothic *Karlshaus* (Pl. k, C 4; p. 2), at the corner of the Theater-
Platz and the Kapuzinergraben, serves as the meeting-place for
various Roman Catholic societies. In front of the theatre, on the W.,
is an equestrian statue of *Emperor William I.*, by F. Schaper
(1901), with allegorical reliefs on the pedestal. — Friedrich-Wilhelm-Platz and Elisenbrunnen, see p. 9. Passing the latter on
the left, we proceed through the Ursuliner-Str. to the cathedral,
which rises nearly in the centre of the town.

The *Cathedral, or **Minster** (Pl. C, 3), consists of two distinct
parts in different styles of architecture. The *Central Octagon*,
erected by Charlemagne in 796-804 as the court and national church
of his kingdom, and consecrated by Leo III., was adapted by Master
Odo from early Italian structures of the same kind and is the finest
example of the Carlovingian period. It is 48 ft. in diameter, is
surrounded by a sixteen-sided ambulatory, and terminates in a
cupola, 106 ft. high. The eight gables are of the beginning of the

13th cent., the fantastic roof is of the 17th. The octagon is surrounded by several *Chapels*, built in the 14th and 15th cent., and afterwards partly altered. On the W. side are the principal entrance and vestibule, surmounted by a modern Gothic bell-tower, with a pointed and slated roof. Adjoining the octagon on the E. is the lofty and elegant Gothic *Choir*, begun in the second half of the 14th cent., and completed in 1414.

Through the W. portal, the *Bronze Doors* of which were cast in the Carlovingian foundry at Aix about 804, or the adjacent side-door, we enter the VESTIBULE, where, on modern pillars, stand two late-Roman bronzes of the 3rd and 4th cent., *viz.* a brazen *Wolf* (or *She-Bear*) and a *Pine Cone*, both having once belonged to fountains. The pedestal of the pine cone dates from the 11th century. According to a mediæval legend, the devil helped in the construction of the church on condition that the first living being that entered the building should be sacrificed to him. The magistrates entered into the compact, but outwitted the devil by admitting a wolf into the sacred edifice on its completion.

The INTERIOR OF THE OCTAGON is borne by eight massive pillars, which separate the central space from the surrounding two-storied ambulatory. The lofty, round-arched openings of the upper story, or 'Hochmünster' (p. 6), are enlivened with a double row of columns, of unequal length, some of them in marble, others in granite, brought from Rome, Trèves, and Ravenna. Some of them were replaced by new ones in 1845, and the capitals are all new. In 1882 and 1902 the whole central structure was again brilliantly adorned with *Mosaics*, as of old. That on the vault of the dome, on a gold ground, representing Christ with the 24 Elders of the Apocalypse, was executed by *Salviati* at Venice from a 17th cent. copy of an old mosaic. On the walls below are figures of the twelve Apostles, two archangels, Mary and John the Baptist, with Charlemagne as founder and Pope Leo III. as consecrator of the church, all by H. Schaper. In the frieze below these has been reproduced the original inscription of eight verses. The columns are encased in cipollino. The decoration of the upper story with parti-colored marbles is also new. The tradition that the original burial vault of Charlemagne was below the flooring is now doubted, but a more careful investigation is about to be made. The large copper-gilt *Chandelier*, 13 ft. in diameter, was presented by Emp. Frederick I. about 1165. — The so-called *Ungarische Kapelle*, adjoining the octagon on the S. (to the right of the W. entrance), recently restored in the baroque style, contains the treasury (p. 6). — The oblong *Kreuz-Kapelle*, or *Chapel of St. Nicholas*, on the N.W. side, retains its Gothic architecture of the second half of the 15th century.

The egress leads to the late-Gothic CLOISTERS, which were restored in 1894; to the right is the late-Romanesque *Purgatory Chapel*, erected by Philip of Swabia after 1200, with a rich façade; the 'Quadrum' (court) contains a modern fountain by Prof. Frentzen and some old remains.

The CHOIR (adm., incl. the Hochmünster, 50 pf.) is remarkable for its light and elegant proportions. The thirteen windows (87 ft. high, 16 ft. wide) are filled with modern *Stained Glass,* representing scenes from the life of the Virgin (Assumption and Coronation designed by Cornelius), executed partly at Berlin, and partly at Cologne and Aix. On the pillars between the windows are statues of Charlemagne, the Virgin Mary, and the twelve Apostles, of 1430, recently coloured. In the centre hangs a piece of wood-carving (1524) above the empty *Tomb of Otho III.* (d. 1002). In front of the tomb is a *Reading Desk,* consisting of an eagle on a rich stand of open-work, cast in copper in the 15th century. To the right and left are *Winged Altars,* with paintings of the Cologne School (15th cent.). The *Pulpit,* adorned with copper-gilt plaques with embossed designs, precious stones, and late-Roman carved ivory (4th cent.), was a gift of Henry II. (d. 1024), but restored in the 17th cent.; it is protected by a wooden cover. The *High Altar* is a modern work from Schneider's designs (1876), in which several old columns have been incorporated. The golden *Antependium,* reconstructed in 1892, was a gift of Emp. Otho III.; it resembles the Pala d'Oro in St. Mark's, Venice, and is adorned with 16 repoussé reliefs of scenes of the Passion.

The HOCHMÜNSTER, or gallery of the octagon, contains the lately restored *Throne of Charlemagne,* composed of marble slabs, which was used during divine service by Charlemagne and his successors, and afterwards at the imperial coronations. The mosaic floor is modern. The *Balustrade* between the columns was probably cast in Charlemagne's foundry at Aix (p. 5), though some authorities think it came from the tomb of Theodoric at Ravenna. The *Ancient Sarcophagus,* in Parian marble, with the Rape of Proserpine in relief, preserved in the gallery of the Kreuz-Kapelle (p. 5), once contained the body of Charlemagne. When this was transferred to the reliquary mentioned below the sarcophagus was placed in a niche on the outside of the octagon, with a wooden figure of the emperor above it. — The *Karls-Kapelle,* which adjoins the Hochmünster on the N., dates from the second half of the 15th cent.; the *Anna-Kapelle,* on the S., was consecrated in 1449. The *Matthias-Kapelle,* also on the S., built in the latter half of the 14th cent., is used as a sacristy.

The rich *Cathedral Treasury (shown daily, except Sundays and festivals, 9-1 and 2-6 o'clock; ticket for 1-3 persons 3 ℳ, for each additional person 1 ℳ; apply to the sacristan, Domhof 2, preferably between 11.30 and 1; a single traveller will frequently find opportunities of joining a party) is contained in the Ungarische Kapelle mentioned at p. 5. The chief objects of interest are the following: 16. Sumptuous late-Romanesque silver *Marienschrein* or *Shrine of the Four Great Relics,* executed in 1220-38 (containing the 'robe of the Virgin, the swaddling-clothes of the infant Christ, the bloody cloth in which the body of John the Baptist was wrapped, and the linen cloth with which the Saviour was girded on the Cross', which are shown to the public gratis only once every seven years; last occasion in 1909); 47. Silver *Reliquary of Charlemagne (Karlsschrein)*, another magnificent late-Romanesque work, containing the relics of the great emperor, who was canonized in 1165; 18. *Bust of Charlemagne*, in gold and enamel, 14th cent.; 1. *Cross of Lothaire III.*, presented by that emperor (d. 1137), with a beautiful cameo of Augustus, dating from the first century of our era; 21. *Hunting Horn of Charlemagne*, of Oriental ivory work; several admirable *Gothic Reliquaries* and numerous mediæval vessels, in gold and silver, candelabra, and other curiosities. These objects are preserved in large glass cabinets, closed by doors, on the insides of which are paintings of the early-Flemish and early-Cologne schools.

To the W. of the cathedral, in the Fischmarkt, is the building for the **Archives** (Pl. 21; B, C, 3), handsomely fitted up in the interior, erected in 1886-89 on the site of the earliest town-hall of Aix (of 1267; since the 14th cent. called the 'Grashaus'), of which the façade had been retained; the statues of the seven electors are modern. A permanent *Selection of Documents* is shown on week-days, 12-1, free. A common staircase connects the Archives with the new *Library* (100,000 vols.), opened in 1897.

To the E., behind the choir of the cathedral, is the *Church of St. Foillan* (Pl. 9; C. 3), the oldest parish-church in the town. The present building, dating from the late-Gothic period, was rebuilt in the 17th cent. and restored in 1883-88. — The *Church of St. Michael*, or *Jesuits' Church* (Pl. 12; B, C, 4), built in 1618-28, contains a Descent of the Cross by Honthorst (1632). — The *Church of St. Paul* (Pl. 13; B, 3) contains the remains of frescoes of the 15th cent. and modern stained-glass windows.

To the N. of the cathedral is the MARKT-PLATZ (Pl. C, 3), with a *Fountain* and a poor statue of Charlemagne erected in 1620. Here is situated the *****Rathaus,** or *Town Hall* (Pl. C, 3), a handsome Gothic edifice, begun about 1333 on the site, and partly with the fragments, of the ancient Carlovingian palace, and completed, with the exception of the ornamentation, about 1370. After a partial restoration, the building was injured by a fire in 1883, by which the two towers, the *Markt-Turm* to the W. and the *Granus-Turm* to the E., were almost entirely burned down. Both belonged in large part to the ancient palace, and the latter served as a storehouse for the imperial archives and treasures. The subsequent thorough restoration, by G. Frentzen, was completed in 1903. On the façade are 54 statues of German emperors, and over the windows of the first floor is a frieze with 28 reliefs representing sciences, arts, trades, and manufactures. Below are coats-of-arms. The rear façade is embellished with statues of Alcuin, Eginhard, St. Benedict of Aniane, Wibald of Stavelot, and the burgomasters Gerhard Chorus and Johann von Punt, besides various coats-of-arms.

A flight of steps, erected in 1878, leads from the market-place to the *Vestibule* on the first floor, which is decorated with mottoes and the

armorial bearings of the guilds (ring for the custodian; adm. 50 pf.).
The reliefs on the *Portal* represent the coronation banquet of Rudolf I.
and the burghers of Aix-la-Chapelle taking the oath of allegiance after
the revolt of 1428; above is the Majestas Domini, with Charlemagne and
Leo III. — To the left is the COUNCIL HALL, containing portraits of
Frederick William III. (1817), Frederick William IV. (both by *Hensel*),
the emperors Leopold I., Charles VI., Charles VII. (by *J. van Kessel*,
1742), Francis I., William I. (*A. von Werner*, 1890), and Frederick III.
(*H. von Angeli*, 1889), the Empress Maria Theresa, Charlemagne (by an
unknown master of the 16th cent.), Pope Clement IX., and others. —
The staircase, added in 1848, is adorned with mural paintings of scenes
from local history, by *Prof. A. Baur*. The windows show the arms of
various local families who have held municipal office.

The **Kaisersaal,** a hall 144 ft. long and 60 ft. wide, with vaulting
borne by four massive piers, occupies the whole length of the upper
floor. The walls are decorated with eight *FRESCOES, the first four of
which are by *Alfred Rethel* (born at Aix 1816, d. 1859); the others, designed by him, were executed by *Kehren:* — 1. The Emp. Otho III. opening the burial-vault of Charlemagne; 2. Overthrow of the 'Irminsäule';
3. Battle with the Saracens at Cordova; 4. Conquest of Pavia in 774
(these by *Rethel*); 5. Baptism of Wittekind and Albion; 6. Coronation
of Charlemagne in St. Peter's at Rome; 7. Building of the Cathedral of
Aix-la-Chapelle; 8. Abdication of Charlemagne and Coronation of his
son Louis the Pious. The piers and vaulting bear polychrome ornamentation. The windows contain armorial bearings of the emperors; in the
oriel (the old chapel) are small stained-glass paintings with scenes from
the life of the Virgin and the apostles Philip and James the Younger,
by *Osterrath*. Fine echo.

The Gothic addition with the massive square tower on the W.
side of the Rathaus, between the Katschhof and the Klostergasse,
accommodates the *Municipal Administrative Offices*.

In the Templergraben, near the Templerbend Station, is situated
the Rhenish-Westphalian **Polytechnic School** (Pl. B, 2, 3), built
by *Cremer* in 1865-70, and now attended by 700 students. Adjacent are the *Chemical Laboratory* (1877-79) and the new *Architectural Building* (1908), the latter containing the Reiff Collection
of Art (Aix rooms of the 18th cent., etc.). In the Malteser-Str.
is the *Mining and Electric School*, completed in 1897. — In the
N.W. angle of the town is the old *Pont-Tor* (Pl. B, 2), of the
14th cent., lately restored and opened as a historical museum. Near
the new railway station in the Süsterfeld is the *Metallurgical
Institute* (1908).

The *Church of St. James* (Pl. 10; A, 4), a Romanesque edifice
with a handsome tower, built by Wiethase in 1877-82, is situated
in the S.W. corner of the town. — Farther to the S., beyond the
railway, are the new *School of Machinery, School of Mining,*
and *Hospitals*.

The celebrated warm SULPHUR SPRINGS of Aix, which were
known to the Romans, rise from the limestone-rock, and there are
also several chalybeate springs which have their source in the clay-
slate. Of the former the chief is the *Kaiserquelle* (132° Fahr.),
which rises on the 'Büchel' or slope of the market hill (Pl. C, 3),
and supplies the Kaiserbad, Neubad, 'Queen of Hungary', and Elisen-

brunnen. The *Quirinusquelle* (121°) rises in the bath-house of that name in the neighbouring 'Am Hof'. These two springs are called the 'Obere Quellen'. The 'Untere Quellen', as the *Rosenquelle* (117°) and *Corneliusquelle* (110°) are called, rise in the Comphaus-bad-Str., a little to the N.E. of the others. The baths of Aix-la-Chapelle are annually visited by about 4000 patients.

The **Elisenbrunnen** (Pl. C, 3, 4), as the drinking spring is named after the consort of Fred. William IV., is in the *Friedrich-Wilhelm-Platz*. The Doric colonnade connected with it, with a circular hall in the middle, was designed by *Schinkel* and erected in 1822-24. Two flights of steps descend to the 'Trinkhalle'. In the W. pavilion and the colonnade is a café-restaurant; in the E. pavilion is the Strangers' Enquiry Office (p. 3). — At the back of the colonnade is the *Elisen-Garten*, with another Trinkhalle, where a band plays from 7 to 8 a.m. and 12 to 1 p.m. during the season (adm. at these hours for non-subscribers 50 pf.). — The garden opens on the other side on the Ursuliner-Str., which is continued to the N. by the EDEL-STRASSE and the BÜCHEL, with several of the bath-houses mentioned on p. 3. The cellar of the *Königin von Ungarn* (Pl. 37, C 3; adm. 50 pf.) contains remains of an ancient Roman bath, which extended as far as the neighbouring streets, and was connected with an aqueduct coming from Burtscheid (p. 11). The discovery of stamps of the 6th legion ('Victrix') refers the building to between 70 and 120 A.D., when that legion was stationed on the Lower Rhine. The design of the fanciful *Bakauv Fountain*, by Krauss, erected in front of the Kaiserbad (Pl. 36; C, 3) in 1904, is based upon a local legend.

From the Friedrich-Wilhelm-Platz several streets, flanked with handsome shops, lead to the N.E to the COMPHAUSBAD-STRASSE, in which, opposite the bath-houses, stands the **Kurhaus** (Pl. D, 3), built in 1782 but recently much enlarged. It contains a large hall and concert room, a restaurant, and a reading room (open till 10 p.m.; adm. 50 pf., to concerts and festivals 1 ℳ). At the back of the Kurhaus, and facing the *Kur-Garten*, is the **Kursaal,** in the Moorish style, built by Wickop in 1863-64. Symphony concerts take place here weekly.

At the E. end of the Adalbert-Str. rises the *Church of St. Adalbert* (Pl. E, 3), founded by Emp. Henry II. in 1005 in honour of St. Adalbert, who was martyred in Prussia in 997. This building has been much altered at various dates, and was almost entirely rebuilt by Wiethase in 1873-76. — In the Kaiser-Platz, near the church, rises the *Kaiserbrunnen*, a tasteful fountain erected in 1879. — A little to the S., in the Richard-Str., is the Protestant *Christus-Kirche* (Pl. D, E, 4), by G. Frentzen. — Adjacent, Wilhelm-Str. No. 18, is the former *Palais Cassalette*, built by E. Linse in 1886, now containing the —

*Suermondt Museum (Pl. 30; E, 4). The chief attraction
of this museum is a collection of 180 valuable paintings of the
early-German, Flemish, and Spanish schools, presented to his
native town by *Herr Bartholomew Suermondt* (d. 1887), a well-
known connoisseur and patron of art. Various local antiquities and
objects of industrial art have been added to these. Open 10-1 (on
week-days in summer also 3-5); free on Sun. & Wed., other days
adm. 50 pf.; closed on Mon., except to strangers, who pay 1 *M.*

GROUND FLOOR. In Room I, to the right of the vestibule, is the
Berger Collection of Stoneware & Porcelain; adjacent is the reading-
room (II), with a *Collection of Engravings.* Adjoining the staircase is
Room III, the former banqueting-room, with the *Ceramic Collection*
(stoneware from Raeren, p. 12, etc.). — We then ascend a few steps,
pass through a room (IV) with an ethnographical collection, and reach
the collection of paintings. Cabinet V: No. 199. *Teniers the Younger*,
Hilly landscape; *A. Brouwer*, 149. Visit to the surgeon, 151. Peasants
dancing; 169. *H. Franck*, Ball in Venice. Cab. VI: 247. *Gerbr. van der
Eekhout*, Rabbi; 235. *Brekelenkam*, Fishwife; 301. *J. van der Meer
van Haarlem*, Dutch village; 302. *Sir Anthony More*, Margret Halseber;
329. *C. Saftleven*, Landscape with cattle; 241. *A. Cuyp*, Still-life; 265.
Heda, Luncheon. Cab. VII: 239. *A. Cuyp*, Church-interior; 254. *Govert
Flinck*, Portrait of a young lady; *Hondecoeter*, 279. Fieldfares, 280. Hawk-
ing gear; 236. *Brekelenkam*, The proposal. Cab. VIII: 289. *De Keyser*,
Portrait of a lady; 213. *Aertsen*, Market; 223. *P. de Bloot*, Dutch cottage;
233. *J. de Bray*, In praise of the herring. We now return to the vestibule
through the corridor parallel to the cabinets, which contains prehistoric,
Roman, and Frankish objects and architectural fragments.

FIRST FLOOR. The Vestibule and Room XIII (in front of us) contain
Lace, and a revolving stand with pages from psalters. Room XII (to the
left of R. XIII) is devoted to the *Textile Collection*, while Room XIV
(to the right) contains the *Works in Metal*, amongst which the cutlery is
especially noteworthy. Room XV, to the right of the vestibule, contains the municipal plate of Aix, and also two cartoons, several studies and
sketches, and an oil-painting (St. Boniface preaching) by *A. Rethel* (p. 8).
Room XVI contains works of the Flemish and Spanish schools: to the
left, 192. *F. Snyders*, Fowling with the owl; 174. *Jordaens*, Satyr and
boy; 183. *Rubens*, Fall of the Damned, an altered replica of the great
painting in Munich; to the right, 138. *Zurbaran*, St. Francis; 203. *C. de
Vos*, Portrait of a lady; by the steps, 184. *Rubens*, Cock and jewel. —
Room XVII. Modern Works: 489. *Lenbach*, Bismarck; 472. *P. Meyer-
heim*, Savages; 367. *Constable*, After the storm. Here also is a permanent exhibition of modern paintings, changed from time to time. —
Under the stairs: 204. *Paul de Vos* and *Th. van Thulden*, Boar-hunt; 227.
F. Bol, C. de Witt and family. — To the right of Room XVI is Room XIX,
with Gothic carvings, and old German and Netherlandish paintings.

SECOND FLOOR. In the vestibule are *Coins of Aix-la-Chapelle* (Cou-
mont bequest). — Rooms XXIII-XXXIII contain principally *Carvings,
Furniture*, and *Household Gear* of the Gothic, Renaissance, Baroque,
and Rococo periods, including the admirable Moest Collection of German
wood-carvings, which has raised this department of the museum to the
highest rank.

To the E., in the Adalbert-Steinweg, to the right, is a kind of
marble temple, erected from a design by Schinkel to commemorate
the Congress of Aix in 1818 (Pl. F; 3, 4). Adjoining it on the right
are the *Law Courts*, by Dieckhoff, while to the left is the turreted
Gothic *Prison* (Strafanstalt; Pl. F, 4).

Ornamental gardens extend from the Kaiser-Platz to the Pont-Tor. In the Hansemann-Platz (Pl. D; E, 2) is a monument to *David Hansemann* (1790-1864), the Prussian minister (1848), who established the Aix-la-Chapelle and Munich Fire Insurance Co. — Near it, in the Monheims-Allée, is the *Mariahilf Hospital* (Pl. D, 1, 2), with the pleasant grounds of the Stadt-Garten (closed 12-3), in which is a *Meteorological Observatory.* — On the *Salvator-berg* (Pl. C, 1), to the N.W., is a pilgrimage-church.

The **Lousberg** (860 ft.), a wooded eminence to the N.W. of the town (Pl. B, 1; cab, see p. 3), and rising 200 ft. above it, ascended in $^1/_4$ hr. from the Pont-Tor, is laid out in grounds and shady walks. The summit, on which rises a pyramid, commands a fine survey of the busy town and the wooded, undulating environs, as far as the outliers of the Eifel Mts.; to the E. lies the pretty *Soerstal*, with its numerous country-residences. Below the summit are the *Belvedere* (restaurant, with concerts) and a garden-pavilion of the 18th cent., transferred from Aix to this point and adorned with painting and carving (key at the restaurant).

Contiguous to Aix on the S.E. side, but for the most part beyond the Rhenish Railway and its viaduct (see p. 13), lies —

Burtscheid. — Baths (comp. plan at p. 2): **Karlsbad*, R. $2^1/_2$-$3^1/_2$, D. 3 ℳ; **Rosenbad*, péns. 6 ℳ; *Luisenbad*, R. 2-4 ℳ; *Michaelsbad; Prinzenbad; Schwertbad.* — Visitors' tax at the first four $2^1/_2$ ℳ, at the others $1^1/_2$ ℳ per week.

Burtscheid, now incorporated with Aix-la-Chapelle, has considerable manufactures of cloth and needles, and also contains frequented thermal springs. One of the chief of these is the *Victoriabrunnen* (Pl. E, 6; 140° Fahr.), where a band plays in summer every morning from 7 to 8 and also in the afternoon or evening. The *Kurhaus* was built in 1887-89 (good restaurant). On an eminence in the centre of the town rises the church of *St. John the Baptist* (Pl. D, E, 6), wich formerly belonged to a Benedictine abbey founded by Emp. Otho III. (d. 1002), but was rebuilt in 1730. The *Church of St. Michael*, with a lofty tower, also on the hill, was completed in 1751. In the modern N.E. quarter of Burtscheid, in the Zollern-Str. (Pl. E, 5), are the *District Offices*, containing wall-frescoes by Kampf (open free daily, 10-12.30), and the *Trinity Church.*

The **Frankenberg** (Pl. F, 5), past which an electric tramway runs, was once, according to the legend, a hunting-seat of Charlemagne, and is now in the centre of a new quarter of the town. The present building, lately restored, dates from 1637-53.

About $^3/_4$ M. farther to the E., beyond the railway, is the **Drimborner Wäldchen** (*Restaurant;* carr. $2^1/_2$ ℳ), which may also be reached by the electric tramway to Forst. The artificial ruin at the entrance is constructed of Gothic fragments; a Roman sarcophagus also may be seen here.

A favourite walk is to the *Paulinenwäldchen*, a grove taking its name from Napoleon's sister, 1 hr., by the Sandkaul-Str., the Crefelder-Str., and then to the left through the Soerstal (restaurant).

A pleasant excursion of about 2½ hrs. may be arranged as follows. By the electric tramway ('Osterweg'; p. 3) to the 'Waldschenke' station in the *Stadt-Wald*, or by the Verviers and Liège railway to *Ronheide* (p. 2), and then walk (½ M. and 1 M. respectively) to the **Karlshöhe** (*Restaurant*, good), and on viâ the *Kronprinzen-Rast* and the Osterweg to (3 M.) the view-tower (restaurant) and to the (2 M.) forester's house of *Linzenshäuschen* (restaurant). Thence we proceed through the Burtscheid woods to the forester's house of *Siegel* (restaurant), whence we take the electric tramway back to Aix. About ½ M. to the S.E. of Siegel is a Bismarck Tower (1907). — Another pleasant walk (1 hr.) leads from the Waldschenke or the Karlshöhe viâ *Heldsruh* and the *Vierländer-Steine* (at the junction of Prussia, Moresnet, Belgium, and Holland) to *Vaals* (electric tramway, see p. 3).

About 6 M. to the S.W. of Aix-la-Chapelle, on the hillside, stands the **Emmaburg**, an ancient (13th cent.) but lately restored castle, which is supposed to stand on the spot where, according to the legend, Charlemagne found his daughter Emma, whom he had banished from court along with Eginhard, his private secretary. It may be reached either from *Hergenrath*, the second railway-station towards Liège (p. 2), or by the electric railway (p. 3) to *Moresnet* (Casino), which is about 1 M. from the Emmaburg.

From Aix-la-Chapelle to Malmedy (51 M., in 2³/₄-3½ hrs.; fares 4 ℳ, 2 ℳ 60 pf.) and to St. Vith (57 M., in 3-3³/₄ hrs.; fares 4 ℳ 40, 2 ℳ 90 pf.). This line (see Map, p. 147) traverses the *Hohe Venn*, a hilly moorland forming the N.W. part of the Eifel (p. 145). — 1¼ M. *Rote Erde*, see p. 13. Near (5 M.) *Brand* are the water-works of Aix, with a main reservoir. — 7½ M. **Cornelimünster** (853 ft.; Post; 4000 inhab.), with the late-Gothic buildings of a suppressed *Abbey* (now a Roman Catholic seminary), in the picturesque valley of the *Inde*. The interesting abbey-church possesses one of the grave-cloths of Christ and other relics, said to have been presented by Louis the Debonair (shown every seven years). — We cross the Inde by a viaduct. — 10 M. *Walheim* (920 ft.), with a Gothic church, is the junction of a branch-line to Stolberg (p. 13). — From (13 M.) *Raeren* (1190 ft.), famous for its stoneware in the 16-17th cent., a branch-line runs to Eupen and Herbestal (see p. 2). 18½ M. *Roetgen* (1345 ft.); 24 M. *Lammersdorf* (1740 ft.); 27½ M. *Conzen* (1805 ft.).

30 M. **Montjoie** (1325 ft.; *Hôtel de la Tour*, R. 2-3, B. 1, D. 2-2½, pens. 5-7 ℳ; *Horchem*, R. & B. 2½-3½, pens. 4-6 ℳ, both very fair), a manufacturing town with 1865 inhab., lies about 1½ M. from the station, in a magnificent situation on both sides of the *Roer*, with a ruined *Castle* and the remains of an old watch-tower (the so-called *Haller*). The castle, known to have existed in 1217, passed to the duchy of Jülich in the beginning of the 16th century. It was considerably strengthened in 1543, after the storming by the Spanish troops of Charles V. In 1815 the duchy was added to Prussia. — Beyond Montjoie the railway commands a picturesque view of the town and the deep valley of the Roer, and then of the suppressed convent of *Reichenstein*. — From (34 M.) *Kalterherberg* (1788 ft.; Post) a road leads through the pretty valley of the Perlbach to (3½ M.) Montjoie. — 38½ M. *Sourbrodt*, on a barren moor, is the highest point of the line (1840 ft.). It is connected by a military railway with *Elsenborn*, a large military manœuvre ground. — 43 M. *Bütgenbach*. At (46 M.) *Weismes* (1585 ft.) the line forks, the left branch leading to St. Vith (p. 13), the right to —

51 M. **Malmedy** (1080 ft.; *Cheval Blanc*, very fair, R. 2-3, B. 1, D. 2 ℳ; *Grand Cerf*, R. & B. 3, D. 1¼-2 ℳ; *Hôt. de l'Europe*, R. 2-2½, B. ³/₄, D. 1½-2 ℳ), a town with 4800 inhab., in a picturesque valley, watered by the *Warche*. Malmedy is the chief town in that part of the territory of the 'immediate' Benedictine abbey of Stavelot-Malmedy (founded in 651) which fell to Prussia in 1815. Walloon is still the

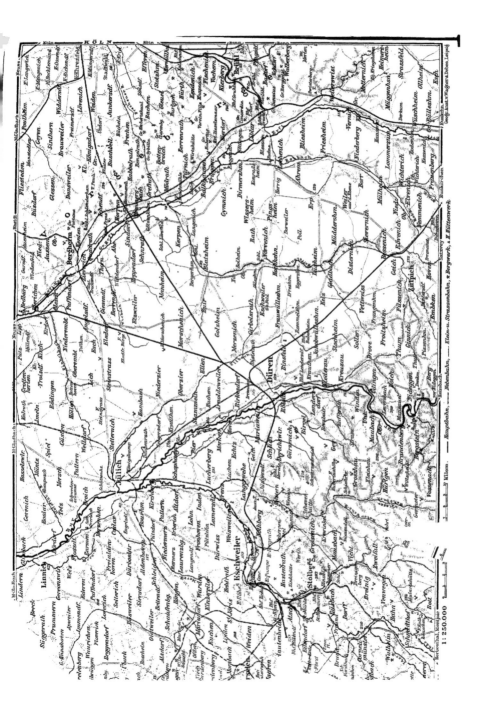

1 : 250.000

language of this district. The W. half of the territory belongs to Belgium. From Malmedy a diligence runs twice daily in 1¹/₄ hr. to (6 M.) **Stavelot** (950 ft.; *Hôtel d'Orange*, very fair; *Hôt. du Commerce*), a Belgian town of 8500 inhab., the parish church of which contains the valuable reliquary (13th cent.) of St. Remaclus, the Apostle of the Ardennes (d. 662).

The stations beyond Weismes (p. 12) on the St. Vith branch are (51 M.) *Montenau* and (54 M.) *Born*. — 57 M. **St. Vith** (1510 ft.; *Post*, very fair; *Etoile; Railway Hotel*), a town of 2200 inhab., also once belonging to Stavelot, has a church of the 15th cent. and is the junction of lines to Gerolstein (see p. 150) and Ulflingen.

2. From Aix-la-Chapelle to Cologne.

43¹/₂ M. Railway in 1¹/₄-2 hrs. (fares 5 ℳ 90, 3 ℳ 50, 2 ℳ 30 pf.; express fares 6 ℳ 40, 4 ℳ, 2 ℳ 55 pf.). ·

Aix-la-Chapelle, see p. 2. The train crosses a viaduct 308 yds. in length, and passes the castle of *Frankenberg* (to the left; see p. 11). At (1¹/₄ M.) *Rote Erde* the Malmedy line diverges to the S. (see p. 12). 3 M. *Eilendorf*. The train then passes through the *Nirmer Tunnel* (¹/₂ M.) and stops at (6 M.) *Stolberg Junction*, on the hill opposite which are the remains of a Roman villa. A short branch-railway and an electric tramway run hence to (2¹/₄ M.) **Stolberg** *(Scheufen; Zum Römer)*, a prosperous town with 15,000 inhabitants. Stolberg is the centre of one of the most important manufacturing districts in Germany, the numerous products of which are sent to every part of the world. The principal articles are zinc and lead; there are also iron-foundries, copperworks, and manufactories of pins, needles, mirrors, glass, etc. For the foundation of its prosperity it was indebted to French Protestant refugees, who established brass-foundries here in the 16th century. The old château, traditionally said to have once been a hunting-seat of Charlemagne, has been rebuilt and now belongs to the town.

Branch-railways run from Stolberg to several busy little towns.

⸿ · The train now traverses a picturesque district, with numerous coal-mines and foundries. Near Eschweiler it crosses the *Inde*, and passes through a tunnel.

8 M. **Eschweiler** *(Stürtz*, at the rail. station, very fair; *Wantzen; Hoerkens)*, a busy town of 23,600 inhab., picturesquely situated in a valley, with a castellated hospital. The forges, foundries, puddling-works, and factories in the immediate neighbourhood are very numerous. The coal-mines in this district are sometimes 1300 ft. deep and produce excellent coal.

Farther on, to the left, is the *Röthger Burg*, and still farther on, also to the left, near *Notberg*, rises a ruined castle with four towers. Among the hills to the right are several villages, including *Gressenich*, the ancient royal residence of *Crasciniacum*, near which are extensive mines of cadmium, iron, and lead-ore, once worked by the Romans, as proved by Roman coins found in them.

13 M. *Langerwehe* (Schützenhof), a village with 1800 inhab., near which are several large needle-manufactories.

The spurs of the *Eifel* are seen on the right. At the base of the wooded heights of the *Hochwald* on the right lies the village of *Merode*, 1¹/₂ M. from Langerwehe and 3 M. from Düren, with an old turreted château, dating in part from the 13th cent., formerly the seat of a wealthy family of Belgian counts. The train crosses the *Roer.*

19 M. **Düren.** — HOTELS.. *Mommer*, Eisenbahn-Str. 24, R. & B. from 2¹/₂ ℳ, with restaurant; *Schiller (Rheinischer Hof)*, Zehnthof-Str. 7, R. 2-2¹/₂, B. 1, D. 2 ℳ; *Kölner Hof*, Köln-Str. 21; *Drei Kaiser*, Kaiser-Platz 17, R. 1¹/₂-2¹/₂, B. ³/₄ ℳ. — *Railway Restaurant.*

Düren, a busy town of 30,000 inhab., with manufactures of cloth, paper, iron, etc., is situated on the *Roer* or *Rur* (pron. *Roor*) in a fertile plain. The most conspicuous object in the town is the Gothic tower of the church of *St. Anna.* Part of the mediæval town-wall, with its towers, still stands in the S.W. part of the Altstadt. To the W., in the Hoesch-Platz, are the handsome modern buildings of the *Theatre*, by K. Moritz (1906), and the *Museum*, by G. Frentzen (1905). The latter contains the municipal collections of antiquities, natural history, and paintings. The streets are embellished with numerous monuments. To the left of the railway are the buildings of the provincial *Lunatic* and *Blind Asylums.*

FROM DÜREN TO HEIMBACH, 18¹/₂ M., railway in 1¹/₄ hr. (fares 1 ℳ 50, 95 pf.). The railway ascends the valley of the *Roer.* Beyond (3 M.) *Lendersdorf* the castle of *Burgau* appears on the left. 4¹/₂ M. *Kreuzau;* 7¹/₂ M. *Untermaubach* (Stregg), with a mediæval château. — 12 M. **Nideggen** (*Heiliger*, near the castle, R. 2-3, D. 2¹/₂, pens. 5¹/₂-7 ℳ, with a large garden and fine view; *Heergarten, Heinen*, both well spoken of), with well-preserved town-walls and gates, is situated on a rock rising precipitously from the Roer, and is a favourite summer-resort. The station is at *Brück* (Nidegger Hof), 1¹/₂ M. from the village. The rock is crowned with a castle dating from the end of the 12th cent., enlarged in the 14th cent., and destroyed in the Thirty Years' War, which was once a favourite residence of the Counts and Dukes of Jülich. The keep is the largest of its kind in Germany; in the early-Gothic 'Palas' is the spacious Rittersaal. The Romanesque parish-church (12th cent.) was restored in 1898 and contains some old mural paintings. Good views from the Zülpicher Tor and the Effelslei. — 15¹/₂ M. *Blens.* — 18¹/₂ M. **Heimbach** (705 ft.; *Haus Schönblick*, R. 2-3¹/₂, D. 2¹/₂, pens. 5-7 ℳ, very fair; *Zur Talsperre; Eifler Hof*), prettily situated on the right bank of the Roer, with the small ruin of *Hengebach.* About 1 M. higher up, on the left bank, is the mouth of the discharge from the Urfttal reservoir (p. 147), which is here utilized by means of water-wheels and a power-house to generate an electric current of 34,000 volts for the use of the industrial establishments in the district of Aix-la-Chapelle and Düren. — The finest view of Heimbach is obtained from the Gemünd road, ascending to the S. in wide curves, past the (1¹/₂ M.) Trappist convent of *Mariawald*, and thence leading viâ *Wolfgarten* to (2 hrs.) *Gemünd* (p. 147).

FROM DÜREN TO NEUSS, 30¹/₂ M., railway in 1¹/₄ hr.; stations *Elsdorf, Bedburg, Harff, Grevenbroich, Capellen-Wevelinghoven. Neuss*, see p. 22.

FROM DÜREN TO JÜLICH, 9¹/₂ M., railway in 40 minutes. — **Jülich** or *Juliers (Dissmann; Quack)*, with 6000 inhab., the capital of the ancient duchy of that name, has belonged to Prussia since 1814. The

château dates from the 16th cent.; in the 'Hexen-Turm' is the municipal museum. Jülich is now also connected with Aix-la-Chapelle (17¹/₂ M.; 1¹/₄ hr.) by a direct line viâ *Aldenhoven* and *Würselen.* .
From Düren to *Euskirchen* and *Trèves*, see p. 147.

25 M. *Buir.* — 32 M. *Horrem* lies in the luxuriant vale of the *Erft*, which abounds with seats of the Rhenish noblesse. To the right are the châteaux of *Frenz* and *Hemmersbach* or *Horremer Burg.*

From Horrem a pleasant excursion may be made to (2¹/₂ M.) *Ichendorf* (good inn), and thence either viâ the old convent of *Königsdorf* (now a farm) to the station of Gross-Königsdorf (see below); or viâ Baron von Oppenheim's château of *Schlenderhahn* to (1¹/₂ M.) *Quadrath* and on past (1¹/₂ M.) *Bergheim* (Hôtel Weidenbach), a pretty little town on the Erft.

Narrow-gauge railways run from Horrem to (9¹/₂ M.) *Liblar* (p. 146), and viâ Ichendorf, Bergheim (see above), and Bedburg (p. 14) to (17 M.) *Ameln.*

The Erftal is quitted by the Königsdorf tunnel, 1 M. long. To the left, beyond (35 M.) *Gross-Königsdorf*, in the distance, is the village of *Brauweiler*, with an ancient Benedictine Abbey (1024), now a reformatory. The *Abbey Church*, an imposing late-Romanesque edifice with three towers, rebuilt in the 13th cent., contains a crypt of the 11th cent. and some interesting Romanesque sculptures. The frescoes on the vaulting of the chapter-house (scenes from the Epistle to the Hebrews) date from the 12th century. The cloisters are late-Romanesque.

As Cologne is approached the line traverses a fertile plain, studded with detached houses and factories. The hills to the right are spurs of the *Vorgebirge*, a low range which begins on the left bank of the Rhine between Cologne and Bonn. — 37¹/₂ M. *Lövenich.*

About 1 M. to the S.W. is the village of *Weiden*, with the best-preserved Roman tomb on this side of the Alps (3rd-4th cent. A.D.). It contains a sarcophagus, three busts, and two marble chairs (adm. 50 pf.).

41¹/₂ M. *Ehrenfeld*, a large and busy manufacturing suburb of Cologne.

43¹/₂ M. **Cologne**, see R. 10.

3· From Aix-la-Chapelle to Düsseldorf viâ Gladbach.

55¹/₂ M. RAILWAY in 1³/₄-3 hrs. (fares 7 ℳ 10, 4 ℳ 30, 2 ℳ 80 pf.; express fares 8 ℳ 10, 5 ℳ 30, 3 ℳ 30 pf.).

Aix-la-Chapelle, see p. 2. The trains start at the Central Station and call at (1¹/₄ M.) the Templerbend Station (comp. p. 2). — At (3¹/₂ M.) *Richterich* the *Maastricht Line* diverges to the left. The tall chimneys near (5¹/₂ M.) *Kohlscheidt* belong to coalmines (branch-line to Würselen, see above). About 1¹/₂ M. from Kohlscheidt rises the picturesque ruin of *Wilhelmstein* (restaurant). The train now descends into the pleasing and partly wooded valley of the *Wurm.* .

8 M. **Herzogenrath** *(Ritzerfeld; Prinz zu Schaumburg-Lippe),* French *Rolduc,* with an old castle. The suppressed *Abbey of Klosterrath* (now a school) crowns a height on the left.. The church, lately decorated by M. Göbbels, dates from 1209, and its crypt from 1108. — Branch-lines to *Stolberg* (p. 13) and to *Sittard.*

12¹/₂ M. *Palenberg,* with a Carlovingian chapel; to the left rise the châteaux of *Rimburg* and *Zweibrüggen.* From (15¹/₂ M.) *Geilenkirchen* (Harst) tramways run to Alsdorf and Tüddern. To the left is the château of *Trips.* — Between (20 M.) *Lindern* and (24¹/₂ M.) *Baal* the train crosses the valley of the *Roer* (p. 14).

27¹/₂ M. **Erkelenz** *(Schwarzer Adler),* a plush-making town with 5200 inhab., the picturesque ruins of a castle destroyed in 1674, and a late-Gothic Rathaus. The church of the 14th cent. has a new iron spire 270 ft. high. Monuments to Emp.William I. and Emp. Frederick. — 33 M. *Wickrath,* with a government-stud.

35¹/₂ M. **Rheydt** *(Jöbges; Reichshof),* with 40,200 inhab., manufactures silk, velvet, cotton, and machinery. It is the junction of the Gladbach-Roermond-Antwerp line and of the Left-Rhenish line viâ Gladbach and Neersen-Neuwerk to *Crefeld* (p. 35; 15 M., in 1 hr.) or to *Neuss* (p. 22; 17 M., in 1 hr.); and is connected by tramway with several neighbouring towns.

About 6 M. to the E. of Rheydt, reached viâ *Giesenkirchen* (tramway), is situated **Schloss Dyck,** the château of Prince Salm-Reifferscheid-Dyck, with a collection of armour and beautiful grounds (good inn, opposite the gate of the château). — *Schloss Liedberg,* 3 M. to the N. of Dyck, commands an extensive prospect.

38 M. **Gladbach.** — HOTELS. *Herfs,* R. 2-4, B. 1, D. with wine 3 *ℳ,* very fair; *Deutsches Haus, Europäischer Hof* (R. & B. 3-3³/₄ *ℳ), Rheinischer Hof,* these three nearer the station. — *Erholung Club,* with well-shaded garden (introduction needed). — *Tramways* run to the suburbs, to *Odenkirchen* viâ *Rheydt,* and to (5¹/₂ M.) *Hardt.*

Gladbach, known, to distinguish it from other places of the same name, as *München-Gladbach* (the epithet München, *i. e.* 'Mönchen' or monks, being derived from a Benedictine abbey, founded in 972 and suppressed in 1802), is an important manufacturing town of 60,700 inhab., and one of the centres of the Rhenish cotton, woollen, iron, and engine-making industries. Several important insurance societies also have their headquarters here. In front of the station is a *Bismarck Monument,* by Schaper. The early-Gothic choir of the *Münster-Kirche,* consecrated in 1275, is supposed to have been built by Meister Gerard (p. 46); the Romanesque crypt and the basement of the tower are of the 11th cent., the nave of the beginning of the 13th century. The treasury contains a fine late-Gothic portable altar and other interesting objects. In the Kaiser-Platz is a statue of *Emp. William I.* by Eberlein (1897). The *Town Museum* contains various antiquities and a historical textile collection (open on Sun. 3-4, Tues.-Sat. 10-12.30 & 3-5).

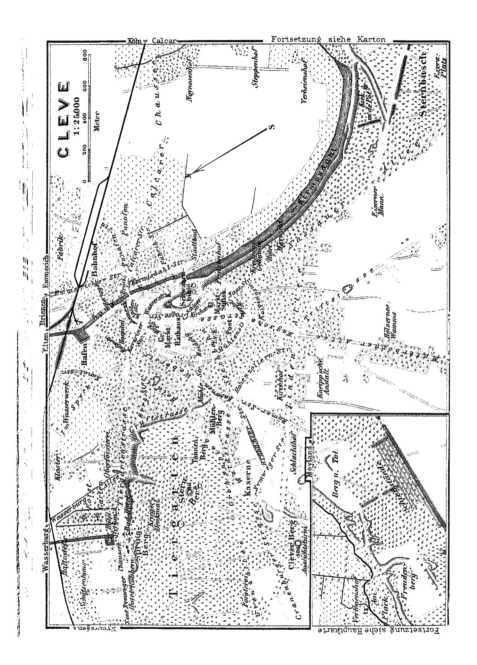

In the *Kaiser-Park* is the Kaiser-Friedrich-Halle, for concerts and theatrical entertainments, containing a statue of Emp. Frederick III. by Rutz and some mural paintings (staircase). — To the E. of the town is the large *Volks-Park*.

From Gladbach narrow-gauge lines run (viâ *Viersen*, p. 35) to *Dülken* and *Süchteln* (p. 35), to *Odenkirchen* viâ *Rheydt* (p. 16) and *Mülfort*, and to *Burgwaldniel* viâ *Beltinghoven* and *Hardt*.
From Gladbach to *Crefeld* and *Duisburg*, see R. 8.

The line now turns towards the E., traverses a flat, arable, and partly wooded tract, and leads to (41 M.) *Corschenbroich*, (43 M.) *Kleinenbroich*, and (48¹/₂ M.) *Neuss* (p. 22), the junction of the Cologne-Crefeld line. The train crosses the *Rhine* by an iron bridge of four arches, beyond which, to the left, opens a fine view of Düsseldorf. — 55¹/₂ M. *Düsseldorf*, see p. 28.

4. From Rotterdam to Cologne viâ Nymwegen and Cleve.

163¹/₂ M. EXPRESS TRAIN in 4³/₄-5¹/₂ hrs. (fares 13 florins 20 cents, 9 fl. 55 c., 6 fl.). [The Dutch florin, or guilder, worth 1s. 8d., is divided into 100 cents.] — Through-carriages from *Hoek van Holland* (p. xiv), in connection with the Harwich steamers, run to Cologne by this route in 5 hrs. — The l ne from Rotterdam to Cologne viâ *Breda*, *Boxtel*, and *Venlo* (153¹/₂ M.i; express in 5-5¹/₂ hrs.) joins ours at Kempen (p. 21; Prussian custom-house revision at *Kaldenkirchen*, Dutch at *Venlo*). — From Rotterdam to Cologne viâ *Emmerich*, see R. 5.

Rotterdam (Beurs Station), and thence to (72¹/₂ M.) *Nymwegen*, see *Baedeker's Belgium and Holland*. The Dutch frontier-station is (79¹/₂ M.) *Groesbeek*. — 82¹/₂ M. *Cranenburg*, with a brick church of the 14-15th cent. (restored in 1875-91), is the Prussian frontier-station, where luggage is examined.

89 M. **Cleve**. — HOTELS (all with gardens), *Kurhaus*, to the W. of the town, in the Tiergarten, R. 2¹/₂-4, B. 1¹/₄, D. 3-3¹/₂, S. 2, pens. 5-8 ℳ; *Maywald*, in the Nassau-Allée (p. 18), to the S. of the town, R. 3, B. 1, D. 3, pens. 6-8 ℳ, these two of the first-class (closed in winter). — *Styrum*; *Robbers*, with beer-restaurant, these two in the Tiergarten; *Loock*, opposite the post-office, R. 2-2¹/₄, B. ³/₄, D. 2¹/₄, pens. 5-6 ℳ, well spoken of; *Holtzem*, near the palace, R. 2-3, B. 1, D. 2¹/₄, pens. from 5¹/₂ℳ; *Rheinischer Hof*, at the station. — *Kneipp Institute* (Dr. Bergmann), to the S.W. of the town. — *Peters Wine Rooms*, Grosse-Str. 94 (also confectioner). — BEER RESTAURANTS. *Schagen*, Grosse-Str.; *Kaiser Friedrich*, Haagsche-Str. — POST OFFICE, Haagsche-Str. — MOTOR STAGE to Emmerich, see p. 24.

Cleve, Dutch *Kleef* (pop. 17,000), once the capital of the duchy of that name, is beautifully situated on the slope of a wooded hill, which at an early period formed the bank of the Rhine, and is much frequented by Dutch families in summer. The chalybeate spring is an additional attraction.

In the Emmericher-Str. is a monument commemorating the legend of the 'Knight of the Swan', so widely known from Wagner's opera of 'Lohengrin', which has been localized at Cleve. — On an

eminence in the middle of the town rises the *Palace* of the former
dukes, generally called the *Schwanenburg* (now a law-court and
prison), with the lofty *Schwanen-Turm*, erected by Adolph I. in
1439, on the site of a Roman tower. Some Romanesque portals have
been immured in the courtyard, and in the arcade is a Roman altar
of Mars Camulus found in the vicinity. Good views of the plain of
the Rhine are afforded by the tower and from the terrace in front
of the palace. Close by is a *Statue of the Elector John Sigismund* (d. 1619), by Bayerle, erected in 1859. — The *Rathaus*
contains a few antiquities (including some good Roman bronzes) and
some pictures. In the Kleine Markt is a *Monument to the Great
Elector*, erected in 1909 to commemorate the tercentenary of
Cleve's union with Prussia.

The Gothic *Stifts-Kirche*, an imposing brick edifice of 1341-56,
contains monuments of Counts and Dukes of Cleve, the finest those
of Adolph VI. (d. 1394) and Margaretha von Berg (d. 1425).

To the S.E. of the town lies the *Prinzenhof*, erected in 1664
by Prince Maurice of Orange (d. 1679), Governor of Cleve (appointed
by the Elector of Brandenburg). The Nassau Allée, with its old
lime-trees, extends along the hill-slope to the *Sternbusch*, whence
a road leads to the left to the *Hôtel-Pension Haus Freudenberg*
(very fair), formerly a hunting-lodge of Prince Maurice, 1½ M.
from Cleve, and thence to *'Berg und Tal'* (Hôt.-Pens. Sonder-
kamp), another summer-resort. — Towards the W. lie the hills
known as the *Tiergarten*, laid out with pleasant park-like grounds
(1654), which adjoin the road to Nymwegen. — The *Clever Berg*
(335 ft.; ¾ hr.), to the S. of the Tiergarten, commands one of the
most beautiful views on the Lower Rhine. In the foreground lies
Cleve, and farther off the villages of Qualburg and Bedburg,
Château Moyland, and the towns of Calcar, Xanten, Wesel, Rees,
Emmerich, etc.

At the village of *Brienen*, 2½ M. to the N. of Cleve, is a monument
erected in 1811 to *Johanna Sebus*, whom Goethe celebrated for her
heroism during an inundation of the Rhine. — The *Reichswald*, to the
S.W. of Cleve, a forest 17,000 acres in extent, covers the foot-hills of
the Vorgebirge (p. 15).

Branch-line to *Elten*, see p. 24.

FROM CLEVE TO DUISBURG VIÂ MOERS, 44 M., railway in ca.
2¾ hrs. (fares 4 ℳ 30, 2 ℳ 90 pf.). — At (5½ M.) *Till-Moyland*
is *Château Moyland*, an imposing brick building of the 15th cent.,
restored by Zwirner (1854 et seq.).

The owner of the castle, Baron von Steengracht, possesses the finest
private picture-gallery on the Lower Rhine, comprising good examples
of Frans Hals, Van Dyck, Van der Helst, Moreelse, Honthorst, Jan Steen,
Palamedes, Brueghel, Hobbema, and Wynants (adm. on application in
the court).

7½ M. **Calcar** *(Kuypers)*, a small town with 1900 inhab.,
was in 1490-1540 the seat of a school of wood-carving, which

derived its inspiration from Holland. It was also the birthplace of the celebrated Prussian General Seydlitz (1721-73), the conqueror at Rossbach, a handsome monument to whom, by Bayerle, adorns the market-place. The *Church of St. Nicholas*, a Gothic structure of the 15th cent., is a veritable museum of *Wood-carving, with its altars, choir-stalls, and candelabra. Its chief glory is the high-altar (1498-1500), with wings painted by *Jan Joest* of Haarlem, who worked at Calcar in 1505-8. By St. George's altar is a predella, with seven saints by *Heinrich Dünwegge*, and over St. Anne's altar is a Death of the Virgin by a Westphalian master of about 1460. The *Rathaus* (1436-45) and several brick houses with gables also deserve notice.

10¹/₂ M. *Appeldorn;* 12¹/₂ M. *Marienbaum*, with a pilgrimage-church.

16 M. **Xanten** (*Niederrheinischer Hof; Hövelmann zum König von Preussen*, R. & B. 2¹/₂ ℳ, very fair), a town of great antiquity, with 4000 inhab., is mentioned in the 'Nibelungenlied', as the birthplace of Siegfried the dragon-slayer. Xanten is also a station on the Wesel and Boxtel line (see p. 20).

The **Collegiate Church of St. Victor*, erected in 1263-1519, is a gem of Gothic architecture, illustrating the entire development of the style. The two Romanesque towers (215 ft. high) belonged to an earlier structure.

The interior is practically in its original state. The fine choir is enclosed by a screen of 1400. By the piers are lifesize statues of the 14-16th centuries. The choir-stalls date from ca. 1300. In front of the high-altar is a fine bronze candelabrum from Maastricht, in the form of an arch (1501). The high-altar, painted by *Bart. de Bruyn* (1534), contains a reliquary of 1129. Five other altars are adorned with elaborate wood-carving. The valuable tapestry and stained glass are of the 14-17th centuries. The sacristy contains some valuable ecclesiastical vestments, including those of St. Bernhard (11th cent.), while there are some fine reliquaries and ivory carvings of the 5-15th cent. in the treasury. In the picturesque cloisters are good late-Gothic and Renaissance epitaphs.

In front of the S. portal are large Stations of the Cross, dating from 1525-36. The passage under the *Chapel of St. Michael* (15th cent.) leads to the market-place, with the *Rathaus* (1786) and a Gothic house of the second half of the 15th century. The *Clever-Tor* (1393), lately restored, contains a good collection of Roman antiquities (adm. 50 pf.). — A fine view is afforded by the *Fürstenberg*, 1 M. to the S.E., on the slope of which lay the *Castra Vetera* of the Romans. It was founded by Augustus between B.C. 16 and 13, and was the headquarters of Roman operations on the Lower Rhine until its destruction by the Batavians in 71 A.D. (excavations made in 1906). — Steamer to *Wesel*, see p. 25.

22 M. *Menzelen* is the junction for the Wesel and Venlo line (p. 21). 23 M. *Alpen;* 25 M. *Millingen.* — 26¹/₂ M. **Rheinberg** (*Bienen; Börgmann*), an ancient place with 2800 inhab., is well-

2*

known for its 'boonekamp' bitters. It was besieged fifteen times between 1583 and 1703. The R. C. church contains a carved altar-piece of the Calcar School (1520). The Rathaus dates from 1449. On a hill about 4 M. to the S.W. lies *Kamp*, with an old Cistercian abbey. — 30 M. *Repelen*.

33½ M. **Moers** (*Königlicher Hof*, R. & B. 2½-3; D. 2½ *ℳ*, with wine; *Deutsches Haus*, both very fair), an active industrial town with 25,000 inhab., contains a *Château* of the old Counts of Moers, whose domains passed to Prussia in 1702. It is now town property and contains a historical museum. Moers is connected with Homberg (p. 35) by electric tramway.

From Moers a branch-line runs to *Crefeld* (special station; p. 35).

. 36½ M. *Trompet* (p. 35). — 39½ M. *Friemersheim*, and thence to (44 M.) *Duisburg*, see pp. 35, 36.

CONTINUATION OF MAIN LINE. 94½ M. *Pfalzdorf*, with 3000 inhab., founded along with the neighbouring villages of *Louisendorf* and *Bönninghardt* (p. 21) under Frederick the Great by Protestant emigrants from the Palatinate (Pfalz) in 1741.

97 M. **Goch** (*Hôt. Rademaker*), with 10,200 inhab., an important place in the middle ages, is also a station on the line from Boxtel to Wesel, traversed by the through-trains from Flushing to Berlin (London to Berlin in 21 hrs.). It possesses some noteworthy brick buildings, such as the Roman Catholic church of the 14-15th cent., the 'Steintor' of the end of the 14th cent., and the 'Haus zu den Fünf Ringen' of the 15th cent. (now a brewery).

FROM GOCH TO WESEL, 24 M., railway in ¾-1¼ hr. — 3 M. *Preussisch-Uedem;* 8 M. *Uedemerbruch;* 9½ M. *Labbeck.* — 12½ M. *Xanten* (see p. 19). — To the N. of (16 M.) *Birten* is a Roman amphitheatre. — 18½ M. *Büderich*, also a station on the Wesel and Venlo line (p. 21). — 24 M. *Wesel* (p. 24).

. The train crosses the *Niers.* 101½ M. *Weeze.* — 105 M. **Kevelaer** (*Posthaus*), a market-town with 7000 inhab., is annually visited by 100,000 pilgrims, attracted by a small miracle-working figure of the Virgin (1642), exhibited in the hexagonal Gnaden-Kapelle, a structure of 1654. The *Pilgrimage Church*, in front of which the chapel stands, is a modern Gothic edifice by Vincent Statz (1858-70), but it contains several old carved altars of the Franconian and Upper Saxon schools (15-16th cent.). The Gothic *Parish Church* contains a statuette of the Virgin of the Lower Rhenish school (15th cent.). Adjoining the vestibule are a Crucifixion, of the early 16th cent., and other groups from the Passion, of the 18th century.

. To the left lies *Wissen*, with the handsome restored château of Baron von Loë, and on the same side, farther on, is the château of *Haag*. We again cross the Niers.

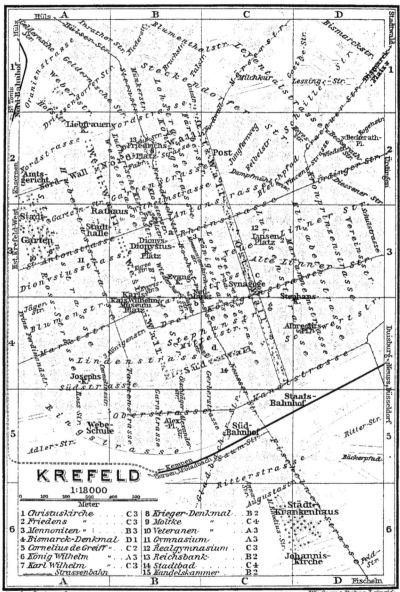

KREFELD

1:18000

Meter

1 *Christuskirche* . . . . C 3	8 *Krieger-Denkmal* . . B 2
2 *Friedens* " . . . . C 3	9 *Moltke* " . . C 4
3 *Mennoniten* " . . . B 3	10 *Veteranen* " . . A 3
4 *Bismarck-Denkmal* . D 1	11 *Gymnasium* . . . A 3
5 *Cornelius de Greiff* " . C 2	12 *Realgymnasium* . . C 3
6 *König Wilhelm* " . A 3	13 *Reichsbank* . . . . B 2
7 *Karl Wilhelm* " . C 3	14 *Stadtbad* . . . . C 4
Strassenbahn	15 *Handelskammer* . . B 2

Geograph. Anstalt von   Wagner & Debes, Leipzig.

110¹/₂ M. **Geldern** (*Hôtel Dahlhausen*), with 6500 inhab., once the capital of the Duchy of Guelders, has belonged to Prussia since 1713.

Our line here intersects the railway from *Venlo* and *Straelen* (old Gothic church with many art-treasures) to Wesel, Münster, Bremen, and Hamburg. Stations between Geldern and Wesel: 4 M. *Issum;* 7 M. *Bönninghardt* (p. 20); 10 M. *Menzelen* (p. 19); 12¹/₂ M. *Büderich*, on the left bank of the Rhine, which the railway crosses lower down. 17¹/₂ M. *Wesel*, see p. 24.

115¹/₂ M. *Nieukerk;* 117¹/₂ M. *Aldekerk.*

122¹/₂ M. **Kempen** (*Kempener Hof, Herriger,* R. & B. 2³/₄-3 ℳ; *Even*), first mentioned in 890 and incorporated as a town in 1294, contains 7000 inhabitants. The Rom. Cath. *Parish Church,* founded ca. 1200, restored in the 13-14th cent., and completed in 1464, is a Gothic edifice of tufa, with a Romanesque W. tower, a projecting choir, and an ambulatory. The high-altar and those of St. George, St. Victor (S. aisle), and St. Anthony (N. aisle) are adorned with paintings and carving (works of the Antwerp school of the 16th cent.). The fine choir-stalls (1493) and the sedilia (1486) were carved by Joh. Gruter. The organ-case dates from 1541. The *Castle*, with its three towers, which now contains the gymnasium, was built in 1396-1400 by Friedrich III. of Saärwerden, Archbishop of Cologne, and was restored in 1861-63. The *Kuhtor*, a brick building of the 14th cent., recently restored, contains the Municipal Collection of Antiquities (key at the Rathaus), including cabinets, wood-carvings of the 15-17th cent., portraits, weapons, and Roman and Frankish antiquities. *Thomas à Kempis* (1380-1471), supposed author of the 'Imitatio Christi', is commemorated by a bronze statue (by Piedbœuf; 1901) in the Kirch-Platz. — A branch-line runs to *Venlo* (and Rotterdam; see p. 17). Light railways to Kevelaer (p. 20) viâ Straelen and to *Viersen* (p. 35).

129¹/₂ M. **Crefeld.** — HOTELS. **Crefelder Hof* (Pl. b; B, 4), Hoch-Str. 60, R. 2¹/₄-7¹/₂, B. 1, D. 3 ℳ; **Herfs* (Pl. c; C, 3), Ost-Wall; **Beltz* (Pl. a; B, 3), cor. of the Rhein-Str. and Friedrich-Str., R. 2¹/₂, B. 1, D. 2¹/₂ℳ; *Europäischer Hof*, Kanal-Str. (Pl. C, D, 5, 4), R. & B. 3-3¹/₂, D. 1¹/₂-2 ℳ; *Bongartz's Grüner Wald* (Pl. d; C, 1), Hoch-Str. 8; *Stadt München*, Hoch-Str. 43, unpretending, but very fair. — RESTAURANTS. *Railway Restaurant,* good; *Brueren*, Rhein-Str. 81; *Reichshof*, Ost-Wall 140; *Ewige Lampe*, Ost-Wall, cor. of the Süd-Wall; *Wilder Mann*, Hochstr. 89.

ELECTRIC TRAMWAYS through the chief streets. — STEAM TRAMWAYS to *Linn* (p. 35), *Düsseldorf* (p. 28), *Uerdingen* (p. 35), *Hüls* (p. 35), etc.

Crefeld, with 128,000 inhab. (37,000 in 1850, 73,000 in 1880), an important railway-centre (see p. 35) and the seat of the chief silk and velvet manufactories in Germany, with a large harbour (at Linn, p. 35), is first mentioned by name in a document of 1166 and obtained municipal privileges in 1373. On the extinction of the Counts of Moers in 1600 it came into the hands of the Princes of Nassau and Orange, and in 1702 it fell by inheritance to the crown of Prussia. The foundation of its future prosperity was laid by the

Protestant and Mennonite refugees who found shelter here in the 16-17th centuries. The manufactories of Crefeld and its environs at present employ about 20,000 power and other looms and produce fabrics of an annual value of about 4,000,000*l.*, more than one fourth being exported to England and America.

The *Textile Academy* (Webe-Schule; Pl. A, 5) contains an interesting *Textile Museum,* and the rooms are decorated with frescoes by A. Baur, referring to the silk-industry.

In the West-Wall is the *Rathaus* (Pl. B, 3), with good frescoes (Battle of Arminius) by P. Janssen. — In the same street, farther to the S., is the *Emperor William Museum* (Pl. B, 4), completed in 1897 (open daily, except Mon., 10 to 1 and 2 to 4 or 5; adm. 50 pf., free on Sun. and Wed. afternoons).

On the staircase is a statue of Emp. William I., by *Eberlein.* — GROUND FLOOR (r.). Rhenish wood-carvings, pottery, furniture, weapons, glass, and china of the Lower Rhine (18th cent.); objects from E. Asia; library and graphic collections. — FIRST FLOOR. In the ante-room, The Blacksmith, a figure by *Const. Meunier.*(1896). In the other rooms furnitures and sculptures of the Italian Renaissance (Luca della Robbia; Donatello); majolica; modern paintings (portraits of Emp. William I., Leo XIII., and Bismarck, by *Lenbach;* Luna and Endymion, by *Hans Thoma;* pictures by *Kalckreuth, Dill, Von Volckmann, Monet, Gilsoul, La Touche,* etc.); sculptures by *Meunier, Rodin, Bartholomé, Maison, Von Stock,* and *Von Gosen.*

In the Nord-Wall are the *Chamber of Commerce* and the *Commercial School.* In the Kaiser-Friedrich-Platz are a *War Monument* (Pl. 8) and the new *Imperial Bank* (Reichsbank). — In the Ost-Wall are monuments in honour of *L. F. Seyffardt* (cor. of the Nord-Wall) and *Cornelius de Greiff* (Pl. 5; C, 2), the philanthropists, *Karl Wilhelm* (Pl. 7; C, 3), composer of the 'Wacht am Rhein' (1854), and *Moltke* (Pl. 9; C, 4). To the N.E., in the Bismarck-Platz, rises a bronze statue of *Bismarck* (Pl. 4; D, 1), by Eberlein.

On the Gladbach road, 3 M. to the S. of Crefeld, is a memorial of the battle of Crefeld, in which Ferdinand of Brunswick, one of Frederick the Great's generals, defeated the French on June 23rd, 1758. — The *Hülser Berg* (p. 35), 4 M. to the N. of Crefeld, is often visited thence.

131 M. *Oppum,* the junction for the line to Hochfeld and Duisburg (p. 35); 143 M. *Osterath.*

141 M. **Neuss** *(Krone; Brors),* mentioned as a Roman fortress in the annals of the Batavian war, under the name *Novaesium,* is one of the oldest towns in Germany. Pop. 30,500. In 1474 it was in vain besieged by Charles the Bold of Burgundy, and in 1586 it was conquered and treated with great severity by Alexander Farnese. It has considerable trade and industry. Near the rail. station is the new *Marien-Kirche,* in front of which is a fountain ('Marienborn') by Jos. Hammerschmidt. The *Quirinus-Kirche,* an interesting building in the transition-style, begun in 1209 by the master Wolbero and recently restored, is a basilica with nave and aisles, and with towers over the crossing and over

the W. end, which externally forms a second transept. Above the aisles run galleries, and some of the windows are peculiarly shaped. The rich ornamentation of the W. part of the building demands attention. The extensive crypt dates from the 11th century. The E. tower, which was re-erected after its destruction by fire in 1741, is crowned with a *Statue of St. Quirinus*, a Roman soldier who was converted to Christianity and became patron-saint of the town. — The late-Gothic *Rathaus* (1634-38), remodelled in the 'Empire' style at the close of the 18th cent., contains a large hall adorned with a series of historical paintings by Janssen. In the *Obertor*, a large gate-house of the 13th cent. at the S. end of the town (restored in 1906), with two towers, is a small collection of Roman antiquities. — Neuss formerly lay close to the Rhine, with which it is now connected by a short canal, ending in a busy harbour.

From Neuss to *Aix-la-Chapelle* and *Düsseldorf*; see R. 3; viâ *Neersen-Neuwerk* to *Rheydt* and *Viersen*, see pp. 16, 35; to *Düren*, see p. 14.

An electric tramway runs from Neuss viâ *Heerdt* to *Obercassel*, and across the bridge mentioned on p. 30 to *Düsseldorf*.

145 M. *Norf*. — 151 M. *Dormagen*, the Roman *Durnomagus*.

About 2¹/₂ M. to the E., on the Rhine, lies *Zons* (Mones zur Rotenburg), the Roman *Sontium*, a small town with numerous towers, which once belonged to Cologne. It is one of the best Rhenish examples of a mediæval fortified town. Motor-boat to Benrath, see p. 27. The Premonstratensian abbey of *Knechtsteden*, with a beautiful Romanesque church *(Gilbacher Dom)* begun in 1138 and restored after the fire of 1869, is situated 3 M. to the W.

154¹/₂ M. *Worringen*; perhaps the *Buruncum* of the Romans.

In a battle fought here in 1288 between the citizens of Cologne and the Brabanters under the Duke of Berg on one side, and the Archbishop of Cologne and the Duke of Guelders on the other, the struggle between the burghers and their archbishop was decided in favour of the former (comp. p. 45).

158¹/₂ M. *Longerich;* 162¹/₂ M. *Nippes*.
163¹/₂ M. *Cologne*, see p. 39.

5. From Rotterdam to Cologne viâ Emmerich and Oberhausen.

169 M. RAILWAY in 5-6¹/₂ hrs. (fares 13 fl. 20, 9 fl. 55 c., 6 fl.). The custom-house revision takes place at Emmerich (fast trains) or Elten.

Through-trains run from *Amsterdam* to Cologne (161¹/₂ M.) by this route in 5-6¹/₂ hrs. (fares 12 fl. 45 c., 9 fl., 5 fl. 85 c.). Comp. *Baedeker's Belgium and Holland.*

The STEAMBOAT Route on the Rhine from Rotterdam to Cologne viâ Arnhem (Cologne & Düsseldorf Co.) or viâ Nymwegen (Netherlands Steamship Co.), though offering some features of interest, is on the whole tedious. Comp. p. xv.

From Rotterdam (Maas Station) to (76¹/₂ M.) *Zevenaar*, the Dutch frontier-station, see *Baedeker's Belgium and Holland*. The German frontier-station is (81¹/₂ M.) *Elten*, with an abbey-church of the 13th century.

A BRANCH RAILWAY (6 M., in ³/₄ hr.), crossing the Rhine by a steam-ferry, runs from Elten to *Cleve,* whence it proceeds to Cologne on the left bank of the Rhine (see R. 4).

Our line remains on the right bank of the Rhine.

87 M. **Emmerich** (*Rheinischer Hof,* R. & B. 2¹/₂-3, D. 2 ℳ; *Hôt. Royal,* at the rail. station, R. & B. 2¹/₂-3, D. 1¹/₂ ℳ) is a clean Dutch-looking town with 12,600 inhabitants. At the upper end rises the Gothic spire of the *Aldegundis-Kirche,* at the lower is the *Münster-Kirche,* in the Romanesque style of the 11th and 12th centuries. The tower of the latter is of the 15th cent., while below the choir is a crypt of the 11th century. The carved choir-stalls date from 1486. Among the treasures of the sacristy is the 'Willibrordi Arche', a golden casket of the 8th century. The *Rat-haus* contains a collection of antiquities (open free on Sun., 11-12.30). — A steam-ferry (10 pf.) here crosses to the left bank of the Rhine, whence a motor-omnibus plies eight times daily (fare 60 pf.) to (¹/₄ hr.) *Cleve* (p. 17).

From (94¹/₂ M.) *Empel* a narrow-gauge railway runs to (3 M.) *Rees,* a small town on the Rhine.

108 M. **Wesel** (*Dornbusch,* R. 2¹/₂-3¹/₂, B. ³/₄, D. 2¹/₄ ℳ, very fair; *Kaiserhof,* near the station, R. 2-4, B. 1, D. 2 ℳ), a town with 23,200 inhab., situated at the confluence of the Rhine and *Lippe* and formerly strongly fortified. The *Berliner Tor,* a relic of the fortifications, erected in 1718-22 and restored in 1892, is adorned with sculptures and inscriptions. Near the rail. station is a marble monument to *Emp. William I.,* by Reinhold Begas (1907). The handsome *Rathaus,* lately restored, and embellished with seven modern statues on the façade, dates from 1390-96. Opposite stands a war-monument for 1870-71. **St. Willibrord's Church,* in the market-place, is the finest Gothic edifice on the Lower Rhine after St. Victor's at Xanten (p. 19). It was begun in 1424 and complet-ed as far as the choir goes in 1526. In 1882-96 the nave was added and the whole restored. The ornamentation of the gables deserves attention. The slender iron flèche is new. The interesting interior (sacristan, Grosse Markt 144), with its double aisles, is adorned with partly modern and partly ancient ceiling-paintings, while the vault-ing of the choir is a miracle of the stone-mason's art. A marble tablet records that Peregrine Bertie, Lord Willoughby d'Eresby, son of Richard Bertie and Catherine, Duchess of Suffolk, was born here in 1555. The exiles were Protestants, who had fled from the persecutions of Queen Mary, and were permitted by the magistrates of Wesel to take up their quarters in the church, then unused. — The *Lower Rhenish Museum,* in the Gold-Str., contains antiquities, weapons, and domestic utensils (adm. 50 c.). The *Mathena-Kirche,* begun in 1429, has an iron tower added in 1882. — In the *Exer-zier-Platz,* ¹/₂ M. from the station, is a *Monument* on the spot

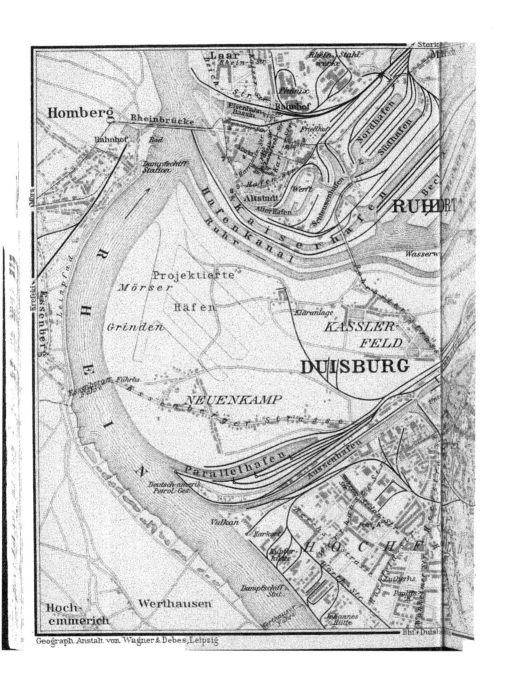

Laar

Rhein-Str.

Rhein. Stahl-werke

Sterk

Homberg

Rheinbrücke

Phönix

Bahnhof

Eisenbahn-Bassin

Bahnhof

Bad

Friedhof

Nordhafen

Südhafen

Dampfschiff-Station

Hafen

Werft

RUHRORT

Altstadt

Alter Hafen

Wasserw

Projektierte

Mörser

Häfen

Kläranlage

KASSLER-FELD

Grinden

DUISBURG

Essenberg Fährhs.

NEUENKAMP

Essenberger Strasse

Parallelhafen

Aussenhafen

Deutsch-amerik. Petrol-Ges.

Vulkan

HOCH-F

Kupfer-hütte

Dampfschiff Stat.

Hoch-emmerich

Werthausen

Johannes Hütte

Bhf. Duisb

Geograph. Anstalt von Wagner & Debes, Leipzig

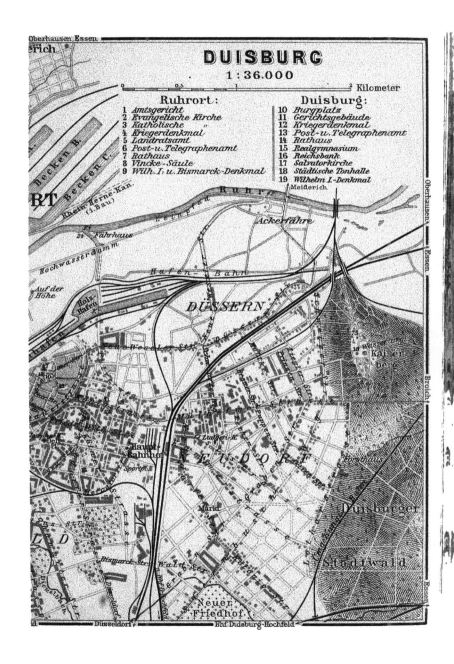

DUISBURG

1:36.000

0   0,5   1   2 Kilometer

Ruhrort:

1 Amtsgericht
2 Evangelische Kirche
3 Katholische „
4 Kriegerdenkmal
5 Landratsamt
6 Post-u. Telegraphenamt
7 Rathaus
8 Vincke-Säule
9 Wilh. I. u. Bismarck-Denkmal

Duisburg:

10 Burgplatz
11 Gerichtsgebäude
12 Kriegerdenkmal
13 Post-u. Telegraphenamt
14 Rathaus
15 Realgymnasium
16 Reichsbank
17 Salvatorkirche
18 Städtische Tonhalle
19 Wilhelm I.-Denkmal

where 11 Prussian officers of *Von Schill's Corps*, captured by the French in Stralsund, were shot in 1809.

. The river is spanned here by the large railway-bridge of the *Goch-Boxtel* and *Geldern-Venlo* lines (see pp. 20, 21). — A local steamer plies several times daily in summer from Wesel to *Xanten* (p. 19) in ¹/₂ hr.

The train crosses the Lippe and traverses a flat and bleak district. 110 M. *Friedrichsfeld;* 116 M. *Dinslaken.* — From (122 M.) *Sterkrade* a branch-line runs to (6 M.) Ruhrort (see below). We now pass the Gutehoffnungs-Hütte, one of the oldest iron and steel works in the district, and cross the *Emscher.*

124¹/₂ M. Oberhausen *(Rail. Restaurant,* very fair; *Hof von Holland, Central Hotel),* a town laid out in 1845, now contains 52,000 inhab. and is an important railway-junction, with railway-works, foundries, iron-furnaces, etc. For the lines to Hanover, Hamburg, etc., see *Baedeker's Northern Germany.* A branch-line runs viâ Meiderich to (5¹/₂ M.) Ruhrort (see below).

The train now crosses the *Ruhr.*

130 M. **Duisburg.** — HOTELS. In Duisburg: *Europäischer Hof,* Burg-Platz 11, R. 2, B. 1 ℳ, with wine-room; *Casino,* Casino-Str. 13, R. 2³/₄-5, B. ³/₄ ℳ, with fashionable restaurant; *Prinz Regent,* Universitäts-Str. 1, very fair, R. 2-4, B. 1, D. 1¹/₂ ℳ; *Berliner Hof,* König-Str. 103, near the rail. station, very fair, R. 2-5, B. 1, D. 1¹/₂-3 ℳ; *Kaiserhof,* König-Str. 44. — In Ruhrort: *Clevischer Hof,* Hammacher-Str. 30, R. & B. 3, D. incl. wine 3 ℳ, very fair; *Kaiserhof,* Friedrich-Platz 4; *Rheinischer Hof,* Fabrik-Str. 52.

TAXIMETER CABS for 1-2 pers., 900 mètres 70 pf., each 300 m. more 10 pf.; same fares for 3-4 pers. for 600 m. & 200 m., and for 1-4 pers. at night (10-7) for 450 m. & 150 m.

ELECTRIC TRAMWAYS. From the central railway-station through the town and Kasslerfeld to the Fabrik-Str. in *Duisburg-Ruhrort,* to *Duisburg-Meiderich,* to *Duisburg-Hochfeld,* and to the *Werthaus Ferry;* from the Friedrich-Wilhelm-Platz to the *Kaiserberg* (p. 26), *Monning, Speldorf,* and *Broich* (p. 35); from Duisburg-Ruhrort to *Homberg, Bruckhausen,* and *Duisburg-Meiderich.* — ELECTRIC RAILWAY from the König-Str. to *Kaiserswerth* and *Düsseldorf,* every 20 min. (see p. 33).

. *Duisburg,* combined in 1905 with *Ruhrort* and *Meiderich* to form one community, is one of the earliest settlements on the right bank of the Lower Rhine. Mentioned about 430 as a Merovingian 'Dispargum', it had become by the 11th and 12th cent. a favourite royal residence and a busy river-port. Ruhrort received its municipal charter in 1587. In the 13th cent. the district came into the possession of the Dukes of Limburg, passing afterwards to the Princes of Cleve, and in 1609 to the Elector of Brandenburg. The University of Duisburg, founded by the Great Elector in 1655, subsisted down to 1802. Both Duisburg and Ruhrort have made enormous strides both in trade and industry since the middle of the 19th cent., the population of the former rising from 15,000 in 1860 to 105,850 in 1905, while that of Ruhrort increased during the same period from 7000 to 37,000 (joint population now 216,000). Their combined harbours form probably the largest river-harbour in the world.

The chief exports are coal and coke, amounting in 1908 to 13,174,450 tons. The imports include iron-ore, chiefly from Sweden and Spain (5,577,907 tons in 1908); grain, flour, and mill-products from N. and S. America and Russia (695,697 tons in 1908); and timber from Russia, Sweden, and America (613,810 tons in 1908). The tug-steamers and barges of the great Duisburg ship-owners are met at every part of the Rhine.

From the Central Railway Station in Duisburg we follow the wide König-Str., passing the *Tonhalle* (Pl. 18; r.), the *War Monument* (Pl. 12; l.), and the *District Courts* (Pl. 11; r.). In the Schweden-Allée, the prolongation of the König-Str., is a *Bismarck Monument* by Prof. Reusch, erected in 1905. In the Burg-Platz (Pl. 10) is a fountain commemorating the geographer *Gerhard Mercator*, who lived in Duisburg in 1559-94 as the cosmographer of the Duke of Juliers. The *Salvator-Kirche* (Pl. 17), one of the finest Gothic churches of the 15th cent., recently well restored, contains some ancient mural paintings (Christus Salvator, St. Christopher, Angels) and the tombstone of Mercator. The interior of the *Rathaus* (Pl. 14), built in 1901, is finely decorated; the large Council Chamber is adorned with mural paintings by Claus Meyer and Willy Spatz, and contains a museum with globes and cartographical works by Mercator. The aula of the *Real-Gymnasium* (Pl. 15) contains a wall-painting by Prof. Keller, representing the reception of Blücher by the citizens of Duisburg on his return from Paris with the 'Victory' of Berlin (May, 1814). — About $^3/_4$ M. to the E. of the Central Railway Station (electric tramway, see p. 25) rises the *Kaiserberg*, commanding a beautiful view and surmounted by a water-tower and an equestrian statue of the Emperor William I. (Pl. 19) by Reusch. In the adjacent Stadt-Wald is the restaurant of *Monning*.

The **Harbour* extends from Wanheim, to the S. of the Hochfeld Railway Bridge (p. 36), to a point beyond Ruhrort on the N., while the harbours of Rheinhausen and Homberg (p. 35) practically form part of the same system. The whole district, $2^1/_2$ sq. M. in area, is thickly covered with industrial establishments.

The Duisburg district includes the *Hochfeld Harbour*, to the S. of the railway-bridge, built in 1867-74; the so-called '*Duisburger Rheinufer*', with the wharves of various large steel and iron factories; and the three *Duisburg Harbours*, adjoined by the premises of the German-American Petroleum Company.

The nucleus of the Ruhrort harbours consists of the so-called *Old Harbour*, at the entrance to which are a granite column (Pl. 8) to the memory of President Ludwig von Vincke (d. 1844) and· an obelisk (Pl. 9) with sculptures by G. Eberlein as a monument to Emperor William I. Adjacent is the *Shipping Exchange*, erected in 1901 (adm. 25 pf.). The Old Harbour is adjoined by the so-called *Sluice Harbour* (*Schleusenhafen*; 1837-42) and the *North* and *South Harbours* (1860-68). These in turn are enclosed by the *Kaiser Harbour* (1872-90) and the *Harbour Canal*, debouching at the confluence of the Rhine and the Ruhr. To the N. of the *Rhein-Brücke* (1907), connecting Ruhrort with Homberg (p. 35), is the so-called *Railway Basin* ('Eisenbahn-Bassin') communicating with the Rhine. Farther to the N. are blast-furnaces, rolling-mills, machine-shops, the foundries of the Phœnix Company, iron-works, and collieries. — At *Meiderich* are the steel-works of the Rhine Co.

On the left bank of the Rhine, $7^1/_2$ M. below Ruhrort (steamboat several times daily; also tramway), is the old town of **Orsoy** *(Jennes Hotel;* 2400 inhab.), which was formerly a fortress. The Roman Catholic church contains an important early-Flemish carved altar, with painted wings (ca. 1480-90).

From Duisburg to *Mülheim* and *Essen,* see R. 7c; to *Crefeld* and *Aix-la-Chapelle,* see RR. 8 & 3.

Near (134 M.) *Grossenbaum* is the château of *Heltorf,* the property of Count Spee, adorned with frescoes by masters of the Düsseldorf school. — $136^1/_2$ M. *Angermund;* 140 M. *Düsseldorf-Unterrath;* $142^1/_2$ M. *Düsseldorf-Derendorf* (see p. 28).

144 M. Düsseldorf, see R. 6.

Beyond Düsseldorf, to the left, rises *Schloss Eller.* Beyond (150 M.) *Benrath* (Hesse; Schloss Restaurant), among the trees to the right, stands a handsome royal château erected in 1756-71 by Elector Palatine Charles Theodore, with graceful rococo decoration in the interior (adm. 25 pf.; castellan in the right wing) and a fine park (open to the public). On the W. side of the park, $^3/_4$ M. from the château, is the starting-place of a motor-boat to Zons (p. 23; 30 pf.). — Beyond (155 M.) *Langenfeld* the train passes the château of *Reuschenberg* (left) and crosses the *Wupper;* beyond ($159^1/_2$ M.) *Küppersteg* the *Dhün* is crossed. The Rhine is approached near *Schloss Stammheim,* a château of Count Fürstenberg.

166 M. Mülheim-am-Rhein *(Hôtel Magdeburg; Brüsseler Hof),* a thriving manufacturing town with 50,800 inhab., which owes its prosperity to the hundreds of Protestants who migrated hither from Cologne in the early years of the 17th century. The equestrian statue of Emp. William I., by Buscher, was unveiled in 1898. A bridge-of-boats connects the town with the left bank (p. 70).

FROM MÜLHEIM TO IMMEKEPPEL, $18^1/_2$ M., railway in $1^1/_4$-$1^3/_4$ hr. — $5^1/_2$ M. **Bergisch-Gladbach** *(Bergischer Löwe),* a straggling town with 13,400 inhab., connected with Cologne by electric railway (p. 42). In the vicinity is the *Strundertalshöhe,* a popular resort. The Cistercian abbey of *Altenberg* (p. 36) lies 6 M. to the N. — 11 M. **Bensberg** *(Rheinischer Hof,* R. 2-$3^1/_2$, B. $^3/_4$ ℳ), a place of 11,100 inhab., possesses a château built by Elector Palatine John William in 1705, now a military school. In the woods, about 1 M. to the S., is the *Hôtel-Pension Bockenberg* (pens. 4-6 ℳ). — $18^1/_2$ M. *Immekeppel.*

From Mülheim to *Elberfeld* and *Barmen,* see R. 9.

Below Mühlheim the train intersects the old fortifications of *Deutz* (p. 70) and crosses the railway-bridge to (169 M.) *Cologne.*

6. Düsseldorf.

Railway Stations. *Central Station (Hauptbahnhof*, Pl. E 6; Restaurant, D. 2-2¹/₂ ℳ, good), for all trains. The *Derendorf Station* (Pl. E, 2, 3), to the N., and the *Bilk Station* (Pl. B, 8), to the S., are not stopped at by the fast trains.

Hotels. *PALAST-HÔTEL BREIDENBACHER HOF (Pl. a; C, 5), Allée-Str. 34, R. 3¹/₂-8, B. 1¹/₄, D. 5 ℳ; *PARK HOTEL (Pl. o; C, 4), pleasantly situated in the Cornelius-Platz, R. 4-12, B. 1¹/₂, D. 5 ℳ, two high-class hotels with good restaurants. — *HÔTEL ROYAL (Pl. f; D, 6), Bismarck-Str. 102, near the Central Railway Station, with wine-restaurant, R. 3¹/₂-8, B. 1¹/₄, D. 3-4 ℳ; *HÔTEL MONOPOL-MÉTROPOLE (Pl. h; D, 5), Kaiser-Wilhelm-Str. 2, with restaurant, R. 2¹/₂-5, B. 1¹/₄, D. 2-3 ℳ; *HÔTEL HECK (Pl. e; C, 5), Blumen-Str. 16, with a garden and glazed veranda, R. 3-6, B. 1¹/₄, D. 3 ℳ; HANSA HOTEL (Pl. m; D, 6), Bahnhofs-Platz, new; *RÖMISCHER KAISER (Pl. c; D, 6), Stein-Str., at the corner of Ost-Str., with wine and beer restaurant; MERKUR ('Düsseldorfer Bürgergesellschaft'), Schadow-Str. 40, R. 2-3, B. ³/₄, D. 1¹/₂-2 ℳ; KAISER-HOF, Kaiser-Wilhelm-Str., R. & B. 3¹/₂-5 ℳ, with restaurant; PRINZ ALEXANDER, Alexander-Platz; HÔTEL BRISTOL (Pl. g; D, 6), Wilhelms-Platz 12, with restaurant, R. 2¹/₂-5, B. 1, D. from 1¹/₄ ℳ; RHEINHOF, Breite-Str. 18, with restaurant; BAHNHOF-HÔTEL (Pl. l; D, 6), Wilhelms-Platz 11, with restaurant, R. 2¹/₂-5, B. 1¹/₄ ℳ; EUROPEAN HOTEL (Pl. b; B, 6), Friedrich-Str. 1, with restaurant, R. & B. 2³/₄-3¹/₄ ℳ. — Christian Hospices. NEANDERHAUS, Scheuren-Str. 8 (R. 1¹/₂-2 ℳ, B. 60 pf.) and Kloster-Str. 34 (Pl. C, D, 5).

Pensions. *Greeven*, Schumann-Str. 2, pens. 4-7 ℳ; *Krüsemann*, Feld-Str. 22 (4¹/₂-7 ℳ); *A. Müller*, Victoria-Str. 34 (4-7 ℳ); *Bierwirth*, Kaiser-Str. 28a (4¹/₂-6 ℳ); *Simons*, Stern-Str. 20a (4¹/₂-7 ℳ). — *Augusta-Haus* (for ladies), Stefanien-Str. 14 (3-4 ℳ).

Restaurants. WINE. At the above-named *Hotels; *Thürnagel*, Elberfelder-Str. 11 (Pl. C, 4, 5), D. 2, 3, & 4 ℳ; *Rebstock*, Grün-Str. 4, D. 2¹/₂ ℳ; *Alte Zeit*, Andreas-Str. 2; *Faccenda*, Königs-Allée 14; *Continental Bodega*, Königs-Allée 78. — BEER. At the above-named *Hotels; Kaletsch*, Königs-Allée 66; *Löwe*, Schadow-Str. 81; *Germania*, Bismarck-Str. 101; *Wittelsbacher Hof*, Königs-Allée 94; *Alt-Heidelberg*, Graben-Str. 14; *Schauspielhaus*, Breite-Str. 71.

Cafés. *Weitz*, Königs-Allée 70, with garden; *Bierhoff*, Breite-Str. 4, both with rooms for ladies; *Cornelius Café*, Königs-Allée 18; *Wittelsbach*, Königs-Allée 94, first floor; the two cafés in the *Hofgarten*, see p. 32.

Places of Amusement. *Tonhalle* (Pl. D, 4), Schadow-Str., with a good beer-restaurant (D. 1¹/₂-2 ℳ), garden, and concert-rooms (music three times a week, 70 pf.); *Flora* (Pl. B, 8), to the S. of the town, with palm-house (concert twice weekly; 50 pf.).

Theatres. *Stadt-Theater* (Pl. C, 4; p. 31); Allée-Str., for operas and dramas; performances between Sept. 15th and April 15th. — *Schauspielhaus* (Pl. B, 6; p. 32), at the corner of Kasernen-Str. and Karl-Theodor-Strasse. — *Lustspielhaus*, Kasernen-Str. 43. — *Apollo Theatre* (Pl. 2; C, 6), Königs-Allée 106, variety performances and operettas.

Baths. *Town Baths* (Pl. C, 6), entered either from the Grün-Str. or the Bahn-Str. — *River Baths* in the Rhine.

Cabs (taximeter and motor). Fare 70 pf. for 1-2 pers. per 800 mètres, for 3-4 pers. for 600 m., and at night (11-7) or outside the city limits for 400 m.; for 400 m., 300 m., or 200 m. more 10 pf. — Luggage 25 pf.

Tramways ply to the *Rhine Bridge* (p. 30), the *Flora* (see above), the *Zoological Garden* (p. 33), *Grafenberg* (p. 33), etc.; comp. the Plan. —
Electric Railways: from Graf-Adolf-Platz (Pl. B, 6) to *Obercassel* (p. 23), *Crefeld* (p. 21), and *Neuss* (p. 22); from the end of the Kölner-Str. (Pl. E, F, 5, 6) to *Benrath* (p. 27); from the corner of the Nord-Str. (Pl. C, 2) to *Kaiserswerth* (p. 33); from the Rathaus (Pl. B, 4, 5) to *Gerresheim* (p. 37), etc.

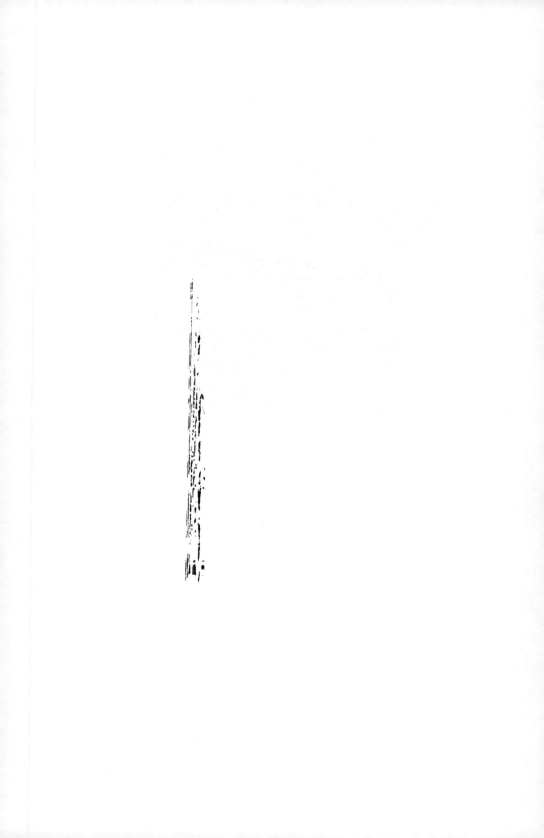

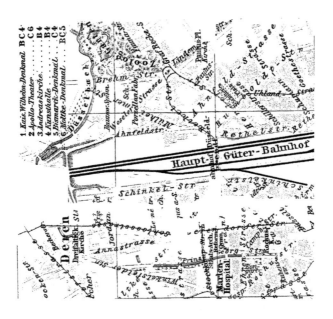

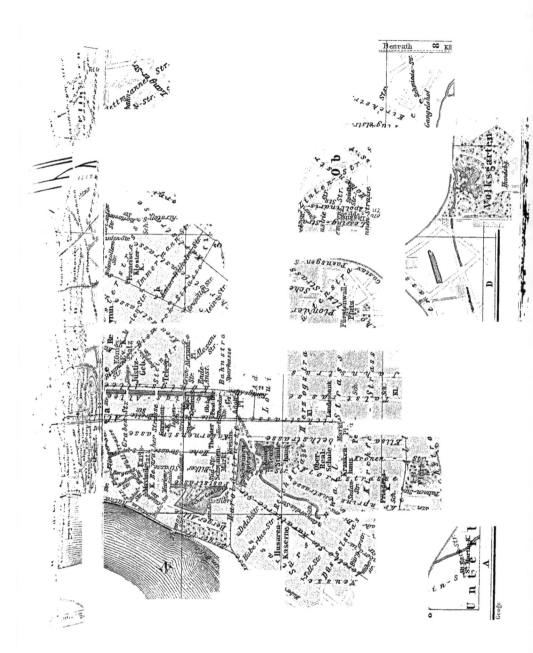

Local Steamers ply thrice daily to *Kaiserswerth* (p. 33) and *Uerdingen* (p. 35); to *Obercassel* (Pl. B, A, 5, 4) every ¹/₄ hr.

General Post Office (Pl. E, 5, 6), Wilhelms-Platz. — **Telegraph Office** (Pl. C, 5), Königs-Allée 56. — TOURISTS' ENQUIRY OFFICE, Graf-Adolf-Str. 91.

Exhibitions of Paintings. *Schulte,* Allée-Str. 42 (adm. 50 pf.); *Bismeyer & Kraus,* Bazar-Str. 4; *Paffrath,* Jacobi-Str. 14a. Large exhibition of pictures every 2 years in the *Palace of Art (Kunstpalast;* p. 32). — **Conservatorium of Music** (director, Prof. Panzner), Wahner-Str. 21.

British Consul-General, *Dr. F. P. Koenig;* vice-consul, *Herr F. N. Gütersloh.*

English Church, Prinz-Georg-Str. 60 (Pl. D 2); services on Sun. at 11 a.m. and 6 p.m. Chaplain, *Rev. A. Griffith,* Prinz-Georg-Str. 58.

Düsseldorf (90 ft.), with 312,000 inhab. (incl. suburbs), lies on the right bank of the Rhine at the influx of the *Düsselbach.* It is pleasantly laid out, with attractive gardens. First mentioned in a document of 1159, it was chosen at the beginning of the 16th cent. as a residence by the Dukes of Berg, and on their becoming extinct in 1609 it continued to be the residence of the Princes Palatine. It reached the acme of its prosperity under the splendour-loving *Elector John William* (1690-1716), who invited numerous artists to his court and established the picture-gallery. On his death the Princes Palatine transferred their seat to Mannheim. In 1767 Elector Charles Theodore founded the *Düsseldorf Academy of Art,* which was reorganized in 1819 and became one of the chief centres of German art (p. xxxiv). Recently Düsseldorf has become an important industrial and commercial town, with an extensive new harbour (to the S.W. of Pl. A, 6, 7).

In the heart of the older part of the town, with its narrow and irregular streets, once stood the old *Electoral Palace,* which, with exception of the tower (restored), was pulled down after a disastrous fire in 1872. In the Burg-Platz (Pl. B, 4), ca. 1 M. from the rail. station (Oberbilk-Rathaus tramway), stands the *Art-Industrial School,* built in 1882.

A little to the S. is the MARKET PLACE (Pl. B, 5), with the **Rathaus,** or *Town Hall,* built by *Heinrich Tüssmann* in 1570-73 (the W. wing in the French Renaissance style added in 1885). The council-room (open free on Sun. & Wed., 11-12.30) is embellished with modern historical frescoes by Baur, Klein-Chevalier, and Neuhaus. In front of the Rathaus rises an equestrian *Statue of Elector John William,* in bronze, by *Grupello* (1711). — In the neighbouring Bolker-Str. (No. 53) *Heinrich Heine,* the poet, was born in 1799 (d. 1856).

The **Church of St. Lambert** (Pl. B, 4), a Gothic edifice of the end of the 14th cent., with a tower partly Romanesque, contains at the back of the high-altar the *Monument* in marble of William V. (d. 1592) and John William III. (d. 1609), the last two Dukes of Cleve and Berg, erected in 1629. To the left of the altar is a late-Gothic Tabernacle.

The **Church of St. Andrew** (Pl. 3; B, 4), formerly the church
of the Court and of the Jesuits, completed in 1629 by *Deodat del
Monte*, and connected with the old Jesuit College now occupied by
the government-offices, contains the tombs of Count Palatine Wolfgang William (d. 1653) and Elector John William (p. 29), in the
choir. Altar-pieces by *Deger, Hübner*, and *W. Schadow.*

On the W. side of the old town, between the harbour and the
Rhine Bridge, extends the **Rhine Promenade**, completed in
1902, and bearing different names in its different sections (Berger-
Ufer, Rathaus-Ufer, Schloss-Ufer). In the Schloss-Ufer (No. 41)
stand the *Historical Museum* (Pl. B, 4), with local antiquities,
views of the town, plans, etc., and the *Löbbeke Museum* of natural
history, containing a collection of shells (both open free on Sun.
11-6, Wed. and Sat. 2-6, at other times 50 pf., closed on Mon.).

The ***Rhine Bridge** (Pl. A, B, 4; toll 5 pf.), built from the
designs of Prof. Krohn in 1896-98, spans the stream in two arches,
198 yds. in width and 75 ft. above the water-level. The gateways
at each end were designed by Prof. Schill; the central pier bears
a gigantic lion, the cognizance of Düsseldorf.

On the N. side of the old town rises the **Academy of Art**
(Pl. B, 4), an imposing Renaissance edifice by *Riffart*, completed
in 1881 (comp. p. 29). The principal façade, 520 ft. long, is turned
towards the Hof-Garten. On the groundfloor of the Academy are
the remains of the once famous PICTURE GALLERY, consisting of
Flemish and Italian works of the 17-18th cent., most of which were
removed to Munich in 1805 (open free on Sun., Wed., & Frid., 11-1).
The most valuable paintings are an Assumption by *Rubens* (ca.
1620) and Madonnas by *Cima da Conegliano* and *Giov. Bellini.*
The CABINET OF ENGRAVINGS (open daily 10-1 & 5-7; in the vacation,
Mon. & Wed. 10-12) also contains about 14,000 drawings and the
Ramboux collection of water-colours. The AULA, on the second
floor, is adorned with good frescoes (the Course of Human Life) by
Peter Janssen (d. 1908).

The old town is separated from the MODERN QUARTERS on the
E. side by the broad Allée-Strasse (Pl. B, C, 4, 5), in which rise
bronze statues of *Emp. William I., Bismarck,* and *Moltke.*

The **Kunsthalle** (Pl. 4; B, 4), erected in 1881 in the French
Renaissance style by *Giese* and enlarged in 1902, with a large mosaic
on the façade (Truth as the foundation of Art, after Fr. Röber),
contains an *Exhibition of Modern Paintings* (on sale) as well as
the **Municipal Gallery* of modern Düsseldorf masters. On the
staircase-walls are frescoes by C. Gehrts, representing the History
of Art. Adm. daily 9-6, 50 pf. (free on Wed., 9-6, and on Sat. &
Sun., 1-6); catalogue 30 pf.

A. Achenbach, Landscapes, Fish-market in Ostend; *O. Achenbach*,
Funeral at Palestrina and three Italian landscapes; *C. Begas*, Exposure

of Moses; *Ed. Bendemann,* W. Camphausen, the painter; *A. Besnard,* Portrait of a lady; *Von Bochmann,* Esthonian landscapes; *L. Bokelmann,* Funeral in N. Friesland; *W. Camphausen,* Frederick the Great; *M. Clarenbach,* Calm day; *Cornelius,* The Wise and Foolish Virgins, one of the earliest works, and one of the few oil-paintings executed by this master, begun in 1813, formerly in the possession of Thorvaldsen; *E. Dücker,* Coast-scene; *W. Firle,* Returning spring awakes new life; *E. von Gebhardt,* Jesus before Pilate, Nicodemus; *J. P. Hasenclever,* Wine-tasting, the master's last picture; *Th. Hildebrandt,* Wappers, the Antwerp painter; *J. Hübner,* Portrait of Prof. Keller; *E. Hünten,* Episode at the Battle of Gravelotte; *P. Janssen,* The monk Walter Dodde and the peasants of Berg before the battle of Worringen (p. 23); *G. Janssen,* The singer on the Rhine; *R. Jordan,* The first child; *A. Kampf,* Frederick the Great and his generals; *E. Kampf,* Scenes on the lower Rhine; *L. Knaus,* Card-players, Content with little; *F. von Lenbach,* Prince Bismarck; *K. F. Lessing,* Landscape with military scene; *A. Männchen,* Women breaking stones; *W. H. Mesdag,* Summer-evening in Scheveningen; *Kl. Meyer,* Merry musicians; *Munkácsy,* Study of a head; *L. Munthe,* Two winter-scenes; *F. Neuhaus,* Death of Count Helfenstein (1525); *J. Niessen,* Portrait of Schirmer; *A. Normann,* Norwegian fjord; *A. Rethel,* Philip of Swabia, Charles V.; *Th. Rocholl,* Stragglers; *J. Röting,* Portraits of W. Schadow and K. F. Lessing; *J. W. Schirmer,* Italian landscape, Dutch landscape, Twenty-six Biblical scenes; *A. Schrödter,* Don Quixote before Dulcinea of Toboso; *C. Sohn,* Tasso and the two Leonoras; *B. Vautier,* 'Little Obstinate', Peasant and broker, Chess-players; *H. Zügel,* Shepherdess, Going home. — *C. Janssen,* Woman breaking stones (marble group); *C. Meunier,* The mower, The ploughman (bronzes); *Rodin,* The age of brass (bronze), The last sigh (marble).

The **Museum of Industrial Art** (*Kunst-Gewerbe-Museum;* Pl. B, 4), a building in the Dutch Renaissance style by C. Hecker, on the N. side of the Friedrich-Platz, was built in 1896, with the exception of the W. wing, opened in 1906. It is open daily, except Mon., 10-5 (in winter 10-4), on Sun. & holidays 10-1 (adm. 50 pf.; free on Wed., Sat., & Sun.). Catalogue 50 pf.

The collections include textile fabrics, lace, embroidery, bindings, pottery, porcelain, works in iron, and wood-carvings. It also contains a good Japanese and Indian collection (2nd floor). The series of rooms fitted up in the old-German, Flemish, Oriental, and other styles is interesting.

The W. wing contains the *Provincial & Municipal Library* (open free 9-12.30 & 3-7; closed on Sat. afternoon & Sun.), containing a Heine collection.

On the E. side of the Allée-Str. is the handsome **Theatre** (*Stadt-Theater;* Pl. C, 4), built in 1874 by *Giese,* with statues (by Cl. Buscher; 1901) of *Mendelssohn,* who held the position of municipal director of music in Düsseldorf in 1833-35, and *Immermann* (d. 1840), the poet, under whose direction the old theatre enjoyed its first period of prosperity, on the façade. — Behind the theatre is the *War Memorial,* designed by Prof. Hilgers and erected in 1892. The inscription is by H. Sudermann, the dramatist.

To the S. of this point, in the Cornelius-Platz, rises the bronze *Statue of Cornelius* (Pl. C, 4), the eminent painter (b. at Düsseldorf, Kurze-Str. 15, in 1783, d. 1867), by *Donndorf,* erected in 1879. On the pedestal are figures of Poetry and Religion.

Farther on is the SCHADOW-PLATZ (Pl. C, 4, 5), which is embellished with a colossal *Bust of W. Schadow*, the painter (1789-1862), in bronze, designed by Wittig. — The hall of the *Real-Gymnasium* (Pl. C, D, 5), Kloster-Str. 7, is adorned with a handsome frieze by *Ed. Bendemann* (adm. 50 pf.). — In the KÖNIGS-PLATZ (Pl. C, 5) is the Protestant *Church of St. John*, in the Romanesque style, erected in 1875-81, and the *Justiz-Gebäude*, or court-house, the assize-room in which contains *Schadow's* last great oil-painting (Paradise, Hell, and Purgatory).

From the Cornelius-Platz the KÖNIGS-ALLÉE (Pl. C, 5, 6), embellished with a group of Tritons by *Fr. Courbillier* (1902), leads towards the S. To the right of it, and to the S. of the Benrather-Str., is the old drill-ground, with a group of handsome modern buildings, mostly in the baroque style. These include the *Bergisch-Märkisch Bank*, the *Gymnasium* (Pl. C, 6), the *Postmaster's Office (Oberpostdirektion)*, the *Steel Trust (Stahlwerksverband;* Pl. B, 6), with mural paintings by G. E. Pohle, the *Schauspielhaus*, and the Romanesque *Synagogue*. At the S. end of the Königs-Allée are the park-grounds of the *Schwanenspiegel* and *Kaiserteich*, with the **Provinzial-Ständehaus**, or *House of the Rhenish Estates* (Pl. B, 6, 7), built in 1879 in the Italian style by Raschdorff. The bronze group in front of it, by Tüshaus and Janssen (1897), represents the Rhine and its Tributaries. — In the Flora-Str. is the *Friedens-Kirche* (Pl. B, 8), which contains frescoes by Ed. von Gebhardt (open free on Mon., Wed., & Frid., 12-1; sexton, Flora-Str. 58). In the S. suburb (beyond Pl. C, 8) are the large *Hospitals*, built from plans by Radke in 1904-7.

The **Hof-Garten* (Pl. B-D, 3, 4; café-restaurants *Hofgarten-häuschen* and *Eiskeller*) was laid out in 1769, and was extended and altered by M. Weyhe in 1804-13. The well-kept grounds extend down to the Rhine on the W., and on the E. to the *Jägerhof* (Pl. D, 4), once a hunting-lodge of the electors (1760). The stables are tastefully adorned with carved wood-work. The *Pempelfort Garden*, mentioned by Goethe in his 'Campagne in Frankreich', now belongs to the *Malkasten* club of artists (Pl. D, 4). — Not far off is the modern *Church of St. Rock* (Pl. D, 3), a handsome Romanesque structure by Kleesattel.

On the N. the Hof-Garten is adjoined by the new **Kaiser Wilhelm Park** (Pl. A, B, 3-1), extending along the Rhine, on the former island of Golzheim. In the S. corner of the park is the handsome *Palace of Art* (p. 29), built in the S. German baroque style, with a handsome façade 145 yds. in length, a dome 151 ft. high, and a courtyard surrounded by arcades. Adjacent is a restaurant. Farther on, at the corner of the Crefelder-Str., is the *Hetjens Museum* (open 10-1 & 3-6, on Sun. 10-1, closed on Mon.; adm. 50, on Sun. 25 pf.), containing a good collection of Siegen, Raeren, and

other Rhenish pottery. Farther to the N. are the new buildings for the *Supreme Court* and the *Government Offices* (Pl. B, 2).

To the N.E. of the town, about 1¹/₂ M. from the Cornelius-Platz, and reached by tramway, lies the **Zoological Garden** (Pl. F, 1, 2; adm. 50 pf.; band on Wed. and Sun. afternoons), tastefully laid out. — At the end of Graf-Recke-Str. (Pl. F, 2) is the *Düsseltal Asylum* for homeless children, formerly a Trappist monastery, presented by the government to Count von der Recke in 1819, and fitted up by him for its present purpose.

The Grafenberger Allée (Pl. F, 3, 4; tramway) leads to the E. from Düsseldorf to (2¹/₂ M.) **Grafenberg** *(Restaurants Jägerhaus, Haardt, and Hirschburg),* with the reservoir of the water-works and the Provincial Lunatic Asylum. — To the N. is the much frequented **Stadt-Wald,** stretching as far as Rath and Gerresheim (electric railway, see p. 28), on the W. verge of which is the health-resort of *Waldesheim* (pens. 5-9 ℳ).

The ancient town of **Kaiserswerth** *(Rheinischer Hof),* with 2500 inhab., on the right bank of the Rhine, 5 M. from Düsseldorf (¹/₂ hr. by electric railway, p. 28), is the seat of a training school for Protestant Sisters of Charity, an extensive institution, with 250 branches in many different parts of Germany, founded by the benevolent *Pastor Fliedner* (d. 1864) in 1836. The old early-Romanesque *Church* of Kaiserswerth, a huge columnar basilica with transepts and four towers, dates from the middle of the 11th century. The choir is an elegant transition addition of about 1250, while the W. towers were rebuilt in 1874. The church contains an admirably executed *Reliquary* (1264), in which the bones of *St. Suitbertus,* a native of Ireland who first preached the Gospel here in 710, are preserved. From the *Königspfalz,* or Palace, of Kaiserswerth, the young Emp. Henry IV. was carried off in 1062 in a vessel belonging to his austere guardian Archbishop Anno. Emp. Frederick I. rebuilt the castle in 1174-84; from the 13th to the 15th cent. it was an object of strife between the Counts of Berg and Cleve and the Elector of Cologne, into whose possession it fell in 1464. In 1702 it was occupied by the French; after its capture by the imperial and Dutch troops the fortifications were blown up. The present extensive remains, which were fully exposed by excavations in 1899-1901, belong exclusively to the period of Frederick I. — Electric railway to Duisburg (9¹/₂ M.), see p. 25.

7. From Düsseldorf to Essen.

a. Viâ Kettwig.

22 M. RAILWAY in ³/₄-1 hr.

Düsseldorf, see p. 28. — 1¹/₄ M. *Düsseldorf-Derendorf* (p. 27); 3¹/₂ M. *Düsseldorf-Rath,* the junction for the line to Speldorf (see p. 34). — 7 M. *Ratingen* (E. Station), a town with 11,700 inhab., ancient walls and towers, and various industries, is mentioned in documents of the 9th cent. as Hrotinga. Farther on we traverse the deer-park of the Count of Spee. — 10 M. *Hösel,* a station in the midst of a forest, serving for various adjoining villages. About ²/₃ M. to the W. is Count Spee's château of *Linnep,* and in a pretty little valley about as far to the E. is the restaurant of *Schlieperhaus.* — The train threads the Hochstrass Tunnel. In entering the valley of the Ruhr we obtain a good view from the bridge.

13 M. **Kettwig** *(Schiesen,* very fair; *Jägerhof* and *Am Luftigen Restaurants,* both with views; *Berchem zum Ruhrtal,* on the

Ruhr) is a town of 6100 inhab., with manufactories of fine cloth. In the market-place, adjoining the church, is a monument to Emp. William I., with figures of Bismarck and Moltke. On the left bank of the Ruhr rises the *Hofmannsberg* or *Hausberg*, a hill seamed with quarries. In the woods are the old château of *Landsberg,* recently restored, and the *Hugenpoet,* belonging to Baron von Fürstenberg. Farther on in the direction of Werden is *Oefte,* the residence of Count von der Schulenburg.

From Kettwig to *Mülheim-an-der-Ruhr,* see p. 35.

16 M. **Werden** *(Deutscher Kaiser; Werdener Hof,* R. 2-3, B. 1 ℳ), an old town with 14,000 inhabitants. On the bridge over the Ruhr are statues of Emp. William I., Bismarck, and Moltke, all by Albermann. The Roman Catholic *Church,* once belonging to a Benedictine abbey founded about 796 by St. Ludgerus (d. 809), deserves notice. The foundations of the W. tower date from the 10th century. The crypt below the choir, containing the ancient stone coffin of St. Ludgerus, was constructed in the 9th and 11th centuries. The bulk of the church (1257-75) is in the transition style; the side-portals on the N. are particularly beautiful. The N. side-altar is adorned with paintings by Mintrop (d. 1870), who was born near Werden. The high-altar contains the relics of St. Ludgerus. The secular buildings of the abbey are now used as a reformatory.

Favourite view-points (with restaurants) near Werden are the *Platte* (on the opposite bank of the river), the *Pastoratsberg,* and (³/₄ M. farther on) the *Emperor Frederick Tower.*

A branch-line runs from Werden to (5¹/₂ M.) *Kupferdreh,* on the Steele & Vohwinkel Railway (p. 37).

17¹/₂ M. *Hügel.* On the hill is the *Villa Hügel,* belonging to the family Krupp, with extensive grounds. To the right rises the *Isenberg,* the summit of which (restaurant) affords an attractive view of the valley of the Ruhr. — Tunnel. 19 M. *Rellinghausen.*

22 M. *Essen,* see p. 35.

b. Viâ Speldorf and Mülheim-Eppinghofen.

25 M. RAILWAY in ³/₄-1¹/₄ hr.

From Düsseldorf to (3¹/₃ M.) *Rath,* see p. 33. Adjoining is the large Carthusian convent of *Hain* founded in 1891. — 6 M. *Ratingen* (W. Station; see p. 33); 8¹/₂ M. *Lintorf;* 16¹/₂ M. *Speldorf* (tramway to Duisburg, see p. 25). We cross the Ruhr to (18 M.) *Mühlheim-Eppinghofen* (see p. 35). 21 M. *Heissen.* — 23 M. *Essen* (Altendorfer-Strasse); 25 M. *Essen* (N. Station), see p. 35.

c. Viâ Duisburg and Mülheim-an-der-Ruhr.

27 M. RAILWAY in ³/₄-1¹/₂ hr.

From Düsseldorf to (14¹/₂ M.) *Duisburg,* see pp. 27, 26. Beyond Duisburg our line crosses the Ruhr. From (18¹/₂ M.) *Styrum* branch-lines run to (2¹/₂ M.) Oberhausen and (5¹/₂ M.) Ruhrort.

20 M. **Mühlheim-an-der-Ruhr** (*Retze*, R. 2-4, B. 1; D. $2^{1}/_{2}$-3 $\mathcal{M}$, very fair; *Dortmunder Hof*, plain) is a town with 93,600 inhab., numerous factories, and a considerable trade in coal. The larger of the two Protestant churches dates from the 13-15th centuries. Near the railway-station is the Friedrich-Wilhelms-Hütte, a large foundry. Mühlheim is connected by a suspension bridge and a railway bridge with the left bank of the Ruhr, on which lies the old château of *Broich*. In the vicinity is the *Stockfisch*, an open-air restaurant. A pleasant view is obtained from the *Kahlenberg*, 1 M. to the S.

A branch-railway ascends the valley of the Ruhr from Mülheim to ($8^{1}/_{2}$ M.) *Kettwig* (p. 34).

$20^{1}/_{2}$ M. *Eppinghofen*, the station for the E. part of Mühlheim. $25^{1}/_{2}$ M. *Essen-West*. — 27 M. **Essen** (*Rheinischer Hof, Royal, Park*, etc.), see *Baedeker's Northern Germany*.

8. From Gladbach to Crefeld and Duisburg.

$27^{1}/_{2}$ M. RAILWAY in 1-$1^{1}/_{2}$ hr. (fares 3 $\mathcal{M}$ 50, 2 $\mathcal{M}$ 50, 95 pf.).

München-Gladbach, see p. 16. — 3 M. *Helenabrunn*. — $5^{1}/_{2}$ M. **Viersen** (*Gansen; Dahlhausen*, both very fair), the junction of a line to Venlo (p. 17), a town with 27,600 inhab. and extensive manufactories of plush and velvet ribbons. The late-Gothic parish-church dates from the 15th century. The *Hohenbusch*, with a Bismarck Monument, commands an extensive view.

FROM VIERSEN TO MOERS VIÂ CREFELD, 25 M., railway with numerous ramifications. At ($1^{3}/_{4}$ M.) *Süchteln* the line forks, one branch running viâ *Vorst* and *St. Tönis* to the (11 M.) S. Station at Crefeld. The main line proceeds viâ *Süchtelnvorst* (junction for *Grefrath*), *Oedt, Schmalbroich, Kempen* (p. 21), and *St. Hubert*, to (13 M.) *Hüls*. Thence it goes on viâ *Inrath* to the (16 M.) N. Station and then to the (18 M.) S. Station at *Crefeld*, or viâ *Hülser Berg* (for the hill of that name), *Niep*, and *Capellen* to (25 M.) *Moers* (p. 20).

The Crefeld line next crosses the *Nord-Canal*, begun by Napoleon, but never completed, and the river *Niers*, and then traverses some drained marshland. 9 M. *Anrath*.

14 M. *Crefeld* (p. 21), the junction of lines to Moers (p. 20), to Rheydt (p. 16), to Cologne and Cleve (R. 4), and to **Homberg,** a busy industrial town and river-port, viâ *Uerdingen* and *Trompet* (p. 20). Homberg is connected with Ruhrort (p. 25) by an iron bridge traversed by a tramway. — $15^{1}/_{2}$ M. *Oppum* (p. 22); $17^{1}/_{2}$ M. *Linn*, with a river-harbour, belonging to Crefeld.

$18^{1}/_{2}$ M. **Uerdingen** (*Uerdinger Hof*, very fair), a commercial town on the *Rhine* (7800 inhab.), with extensive liqueur and sugar manufactories, is the junction of the line to Homberg and Ruhrort (see above). Tramway and local steamer to Düsseldorf (pp. 28, 29). — 23 M. *Friemersheim* is the junction of the railway from Cleve to

3 *

Duisburg (see p. 20). — 24 M. **Rheinhausen** has a harbour and iron-works belonging to Krupp.

The railway crosses the *Rhine*, by a bridge 1040 yds. long. — 25 M. *Hochfeld* (comp. p. 26). — $27^1/_2$ M. *Duisburg*, see p. 25.

9. From Cologne and Düsseldorf to Elberfeld.

From Cologne to Elberfeld, 28 M., railway in 1-$1^1/_2$ hr. — From Düsseldorf to Elberfeld, $16^1/_2$ M., in $^3/_4$-1 hr.

FROM COLOGNE TO ELBERFELD. *Cologne*, see p. 39. To (3 M.) *Mülheim - am - Rhein*, see p. 27; 8 M. *Schlebusch*. — $10^1/_2$ M. *Opladen* (Jansen; Tillmanns), an industrial town of 6200 inhab., on the *Wupper*, is the junction of lines to Düsseldorf and Remscheid.

FROM OPLADEN TO REMSCHEID VIÂ LENNEP, $20^1/_2$ M., railway in $1^1/_4$-$1^1/_2$ hr. This line affords opportunity for two attractive excursions to the territory of the former duchy of Berg. — 6 M. *Burscheid* (643 ft; Post), an industrial town with 6300 inhab., is the station for (2 M.) Altenberg, reached by road to *Strässchen* and thence by a red-marked footpath. — **Altenberg** *(Keller; Zum Bergischen Dom)* is a small town charmingly situated in the finest part of the wooded valley of the Dhün. The *Abbey Church* of Altenberg, known as the *Bergischer Dom*, was built in 1255-1379 for a Cistercian abbey founded by the brothers Adolf and Eberhard, Counts of Berg, in 1133, and was restored in 1910-11. It is a large cruciform edifice, resembling Cologne Cathedral, without towers, with a double-aisled choir, and a chevet of pentagonal chapels. The choir and nave contain a series of famous stained-glass windows (grisaille) of the 13-14th cent.; the large W. window shows saints under golden canopies (ca. 1380-88). In the choir are the tombs of the Counts of Berg, the finest being those of Gerhard I. (d. 1360) and Adolf VI (d. 1348). — To the W. is the *Chapel of St. Mark*, a gem of the transition style (1225), with paintings of the 13th century. — From Altenberg to *Bergisch-Gladbach*, see p. 27.

$12^1/_2$ M. **Wermelskirchen** (1014 ft.; *Bergischer Hof*), a manufacturing town with 15,900 inhab., is the starting-point for the excursion to Burg. We proceed by light railway to ($2^1/_2$ M.; fare 20 pf.) the *Remscheider Talsperre*, near a large dam and reservoir on the *Eschbach*. Here we change carriages and go on by another light railway, up the busy valley of the Eschbach, to ($4^1/_2$ M.; 40 pf.) the little town of **Burg** (1280 inhab.), consisting of *Unterburg* (300 ft.; Paffrath; Dortmunder Hof), situated at the confluence of the Eschbach and the Wupper, and *Oberburg*, perched on a rocky eminence 300 ft. above. We alight at the beginning of Unterburg and ascend the footpath, which joins the road in 20 minutes. Adm. to the castle 30 pf.; small guide 25 pf., with illustrations 1 *M*. — *Schloss Burg* (690 ft.), long the seat of the Counts of Berg, was founded ca. 1133 by Count Adolf, enlarged in the 15-16th cent., and carefully rebuilt on the old lines in 1890 et seq. The centre of the picturesque court is occupied by the massive square keep. To the right is the 'Palas', part of the original building. In front of it is a fountain by Courbillier (1903), and to the right is the entrance to the Schloss Restaurant (very fair). The 'Ritter-Saal', in the Palas, has been adorned with frescoes of scenes from local history, while the paintings in the Kemnate, or women's apartments, illustrate the life of the German châtelaine. In the upper story of the Palas is the *Local Museum*, including portraits, views, printed works, and antiquities. The frescoes in the chapel are by Willy Spatz. Fine view from the keep. From Burg to the Emp. William Viaduct, see p. 37.

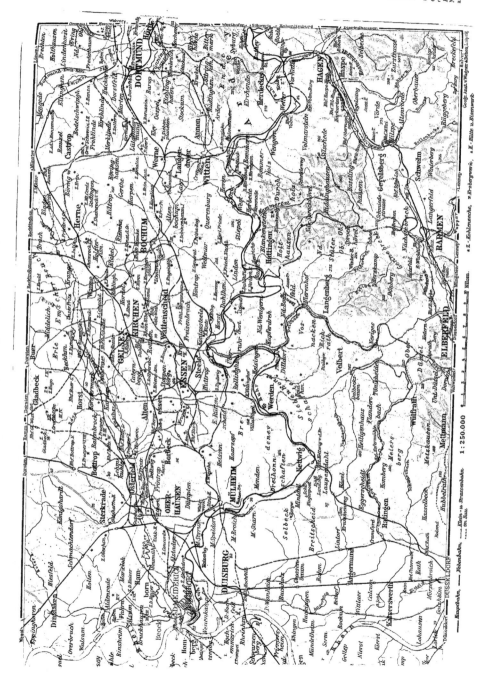

17^1/$_2$ M. *Lennep* (Kaiserhof, R. & B. 2^3/$_4$-3 $\mathcal{M}$), a cloth-making town of 11,600 inhab., is the junction for several lines. — 20^1/$_2$ M. *Remscheid* (1180 ft.; Weinberg; Kayser zur Krone), with 65,000 inhab., is an important centre for the manufacture of ironmongery.

13 M. *Leichlingen.* — 16^1/$_2$ M. *Ohligs*, the junction of the line from Düsseldorf to Solingen, Remscheid, and Vohwinkel.

Solingen (*Deutsches Haus*, very fair), with 45,500 inhab., is one of the most important seats of the manufacture of cutlery in the world. Solingen blades were famous in the middle ages.

Beyond *Schaberg*, the next station, the train crosses the valley of the Wupper by the imposing ***Kaiser-Wilhelm-Brücke** *(Emp. William Viaduct)*, the central arch of which is 560 ft. in span and 350 ft. above the river. Its total length is 1657 ft. The best view of it is obtained from the path descending into the valley from Schaberg station (^{1}/$_4$ hr.). Below is the Hôtel-Restaurant zur Bergischen Schweiz, and on the heights of the opposite bank is the Schloss Küppelstein Restaurant. About 1 M. upstream is *Müngsten*, while a pleasant forest-path leads downstream to (1 hr.) *Burg* (p. 36), crossing the Wupper by a bridge (5 pf.).

18^1/$_2$ M. *Haan.* — 21 M. *Gruiten*, and thence to Elberfeld, see below.

FROM DÜSSELDORF TO ELBERFELD. — 3 M. *Düsseldorf-Gerresheim*, with a fine church of 1236, is the junction for an alternative route to Elberfeld, which is not, however, traversed by express trains. — 5 M. *Erkrath;* 7 M. *Hochdahl*, with an iron foundry and remains of old fortifications.

At (10 M.) *Gruiten* (see above) we join the line from Cologne. — 12^1/$_2$ M. *Vohwinkel* (12,760 inhab.) is the junction of the line to (20 M.) *Steele*, an important coal-railway. Beyond (14 M.) *Sonnborn* the train crosses the *Wupper*, and calls at *Zoologischer Garten* and *Steinbeck*, two suburban stations of Elberfeld.

16^1/$_2$ M. *Elberfeld-Hauptbahnhof*, the chief station for **Elberfeld;** 17^1/$_4$ M. *Unter-Barmen;* 19^1/$_4$ M. **Barmen;** 20^1/$_2$ M. *Rittershausen.*

HOTELS IN ELBERFELD. *Weidenhof.(Pl. a; F, 4), R. 3-5, B. 1^1/$_4$, D. 3-3^1/$_2$ $\mathcal{M}$, with a good restaurant; *Europäischer Hof* (Pl. d; F, 4), with restaurant, R. from 3, B. 1, D. 2 $\mathcal{M}$, very fair; *Römischer Kaiser*, with restaurant, R. & B. 3 $\mathcal{M}$; *Kaiserhof* (Pl. e; G, 4); *Hôtel Bristol* (Pl. f; F, 4); *Trierer Hof*, Schlossbleiche 4 (Pl. F, 4), R. from 2, D. 1^1/$_2$-2 $\mathcal{M}$; *Union*, Schlossbleiche 22 (Pl. F, 3), commercial; *Monopol* (Pl. c; C, 3); *Kirstein* (Pl. b; F, 4), R. & B. 2^1/$_2$ $\mathcal{M}$. — HOTELS IN BARMEN. *Vogeler* (Pl. a; E, 4), R. 2^1/$_2$-4, B. 1, D. 2^1/$_2$ $\mathcal{M}$, good; *Schützenhaus* (Pl. b; E, 4), R. 2-2^1/$_2$ $\mathcal{M}$; *Central; Vereinshaus* (Pl. 27; E, 4), these two near the station.

RESTAURANTS at Elberfeld. At the hotels; also, *Ratskeller; Willemsen*, Königs-Str., with a garden; *Hofbräu*, Mäuerchen-Str.; *Altdeutsche Bierhalle*, Turmhof-Str. 15; *Himmelmann*,.Schwanen-Str. 26; *Café Holländer; Café Borussia*, Schlossbleiche; *Hansa Café*, Neumarkt (Pl. F, 3), with automatic service. — At Barmen. *Theatre Restaurant*, next door to the Hôtel Vogeler; *Stadthalle; Luftkurhaus* (p. 39).

CABS. For 1-2 pers. 50 pf. per drive; ^{1}/$_2$ hr. 1, 1 hr. 1^1/$_2$, each addit. ^{1}/$_2$ hr.. ^{3}/$_4$ $\mathcal{M}$; luggage 25-50 pf.; double fares at night and for first-class cabs. — *Electric Tramways*, see Plan. An *Elevated Tramway* (electric) connects Rittershausen, Barmen, Elberfeld, and (8 M.) Vohwinkel. — *Electric Railways* run from Elberfeld to (5 M.) *Ronsdorf*, and viâ Neviges and Velbert to (14 M.) *Werden* (p. 34); from Barmen viâ *Ronsdorf* and *Clarenbach* to (8 M.) *Remscheid* (p. 37), etc.

AMERICAN CONSUL, at Barmen, *George Eugene Eager;* Vice-Consul, *Chas. J. Wright.*
ENGLISH CHURCH SERVICE in the Lutheran Church.

The sister-towns of *Elberfeld* and *Barmen,* together with the just-mentioned and other suburban villages, now together form a single large manufacturing town, which fills the bottom and extends up the sides of the valley, and is intersected by the railway, the highroad (with a tramway-line), and the Wupper. They have risen to great importance since the middle of last century, now contain 323,000 inhab. (Elberfeld 167,000; Barmen, 156,000), and rank among the richest industrial towns on the continent. The chief products of their very numerous and extensive factories are cotton, calico, silk, ribbons, Turkey-red dyed goods, soap, candles, and chemicals. Since the introduction of power-looms the value of the cotton and silk manufactures has risen to upwards of $7^1/_2$ million pounds annually. The old parts of the towns are irregular and confined, but the modern portions contain many fine private buildings. Elberfeld contains many benevolent institutions, and is famous for its admirable system of poor-relief.

The finest part of **Elberfeld** is the quarter to the S. W., round the Königs-Str. (Pl. A-F, 3, 4), the Briller-Str. (Pl. E, 3, 2), and the Sadowa-Str. (Pl. D, 3). The principal public edifices are the *New Rathaus,* in the Neumarkt (Pl. F, 3); the *Zweite Reformierte Kirche* (Pl. 7; E, 3), designed by Zwirner; and the *Landgerichts-Gebäude* (Pl. 17; H, 4), or courts of law, with a picture of the Last Judgment by Baur in the principal hall. The *Old Rathaus* (Pl. 18; F, 3, 4) contains the municipal museum of art, with paintings and sculptures (open daily, except Mon., 10-1 & 2.30 to 5 or 7; adm. 50 pf.). In the Königs-Platz (Pl. F, 3) is a *War Monument* (Pl. 4) by Albermann, and in the Exerzierplatz (Pl. G, 2, 3) the *Gerechtigkeits-Brunnen* by Hoetger, a fountain crowned by the figure of Justice. In the Brausenwerther-Platz, the Neumarkt, and the Schlossbleiche are statues of *Emp. William I.* (Pl. 3; F, 4), *Emp. Frederick* (Pl. 2, F 3; both by Eberlein), and *Bismarck* (Pl. 1, F 4; by Brunow).

The *Hardt* (Pl. of Barmen, A, B, 3, 4), to the E., where there are a monument of St. Suitbertus, another war monument, and a Bismarck Tower, commands a pleasing view. A finer view is obtained from the *Königshöhe* on the *Kiesberg,* 2 M. to the S.W. of the town (restaurant and view-tower; Pl. B, C, 6). On the W. slope of the Kiesberg lies the *Zoological Garden* (Pl. A, 4, 5; railway-station, see p. 37). — To the W. are the promenades of the Kaiserhöhe on the *Nützenberg* (Pl. C, D, 3; restaurant), with a view-tower and the reservoir of the town water-works.

In **Barmen** the chief buildings are the *Protestant Church* (Pl. 16; C, 4), designed by Hübsch; the *Missionshaus* (Pl. C, 3), containing an interesting collection of curiosities from foreign countries (adm. 50 pf.); the *Stadt-Theater* (Pl. D, 4; 1905); and the *Ruhmeshalle* (Pl. 25; F, 4), or *Hall of Fame,* which contains

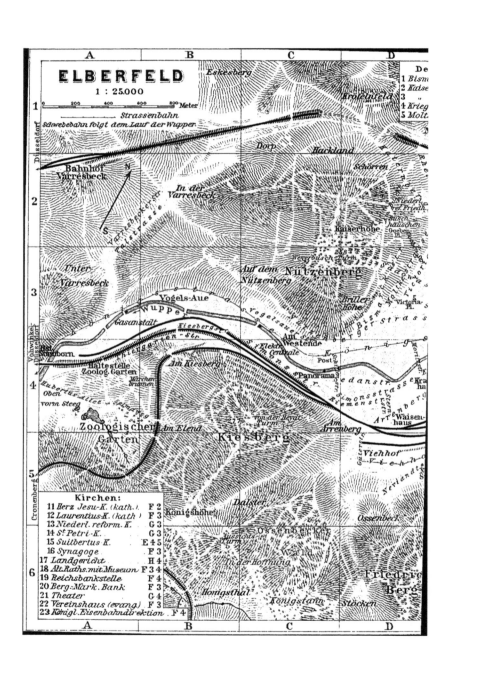

ELBERFELD

1 : 25.000

Strassenbahn

Schwebebahn folgt dem Lauf der Wupper.

Kirchen:

11 Herz Jesu-K. (kath.)   F 2
12 Laurentius-K. (kath.)   F 3
13 Niederl. reform. K.   G 3
14 St Petri-K.   G 3
15 Suitbertus K.   E 4 5
16 Synagoge   F 3
17 Landgericht   H 4
18 Alt.Raths.mit Museum   F 3 4
19 Reichsbankstelle   F 4
20 Berg.-Mark.Bank   F 3
21 Theater   G 4
22 Vereinshaus (evang.)   F 3
23 Königl.Eisenbahndirektion   F 4

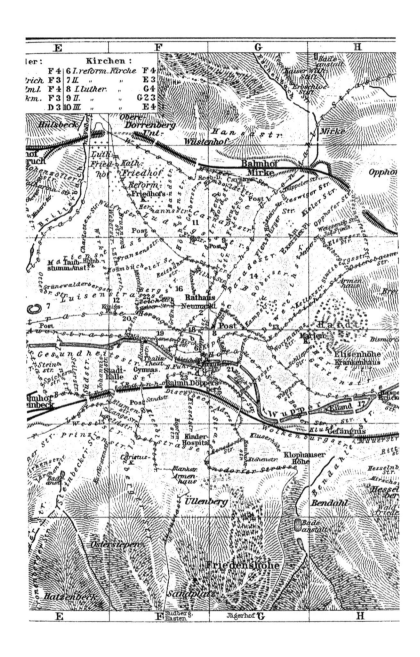

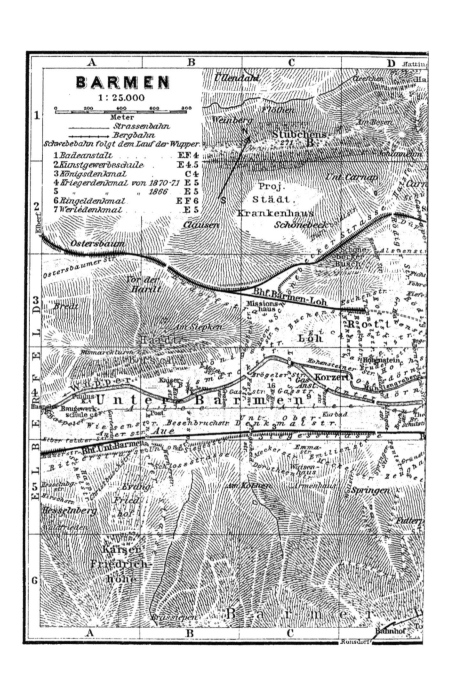

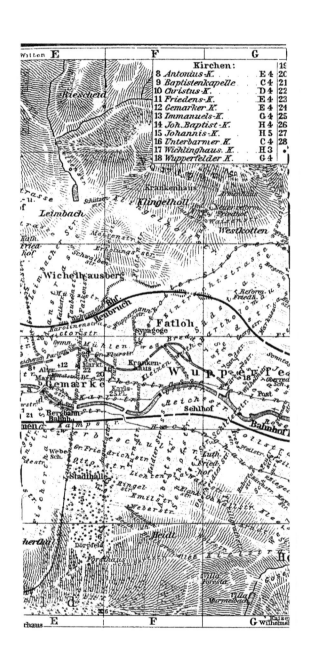

statues of Emp. William I., Emp. Frederick, and Emp. William II., as well as various collections. In front of the old Rathaus is a bronze *Statue of Bismarck.* The *Town Museum* (Pl. 19; E, 4) contains a collection of natural history and ethnography (open on Sun. 11-1 & 3-5, Wed. 2-5; adm. 10 pf.).

On the S. side are the *Town Hall* (Pl. E, 5; restaurant), the *War Monument* (Pl. 4), and monuments to *E. Rittershaus,* the poet (1834-97), and *F. W. Dörpfeld* (1824-93), the educationist, surrounded by pleasant grounds. Farther to the S. is the *Barmer Wald,* with the *Toelle-Turm* (Pl. D, 6), a belvedere (electric tramway in $1/_4$ hr., 30 pf.). Adjacent is the *Luftkurhaus,* a health-resort, with a restaurant. We may return to the E. through the shady *Murmelbach-Tal* (1 hr.) or proceed to the W., over the *Kaiser-Friedrich-Höhe* (Pl. A, 6), to (1 hr.) Elberfeld.

FROM ELBERFELD TO HAGEN, 15 M., in 1 hr. The line skirts the E. side of the valley of the Wupper. It then crosses the Wupper, quits the Duchy of Berg, and enters the County of Mark. The river anciently formed the boundary between the Franks and Saxons, and now separates the Rhineland from Westphalia. — 7 M. **Schwelm** (920 ft.; *Prinz von Preussen,* R. $1^1/_2$-$1^3/_4$, D. $1^1/_4$ *M*), a town with 18,500 inhabitants. Farther on the train passes through several cuttings. — $9^1/_2$ M. *Milspe.* Pleasing view up the valley of the *Ennepe,* which the train crosses by embankments and a viaduct, 100 ft. high. — $10^1/_2$ M. *Gevelsberg,* a town consisting of a long row of detached houses. The stream turns the machinery of numerous small iron-works, where scythes, sickles, and shovels are manufactured. At ($13^1/_2$ M.) *Haspe* are puddling-works and rolling-mills.

16 M. **Hagen** *(Hôtel Lünenschloss,* at the station; *Glitz; Monopol),* a manufacturing town with 85,000 inhab., is the junction for Bochum, Dortmund, Cassel, Siegen, and Siegburg (see p. 140); see *Baedeker's Northern Germany.*

Branch-lines also run from Elberfeld and Barmen to *Cronenberg, Ronsdorf, Lennep* (p. 37), *Remscheid* (p. 37), and many other manufacturing places of more or less importance.

10. Cologne.

Railway Stations. CENTRAL STATION (Pl. F, 4; *Restaurant,* D. from 2 *M; Official Tourist Office),* opposite the cathedral, for all the trains on the left bank of the Rhine and for most of the trains on the right bank. Most of the trains to Coblenz and Trèves also stop at the SOUTH STATION (Pl. C, 2; p. 72) and the WEST STATION (Pl. F, 1; p. 72). RIGHT RHENISH STATION at Deutz (Pl. E, 6), for branch-lines on the right bank of the Rhine and for a few of the express-trains on that bank. — *Porter* into the town: for packages not exceeding 55 lbs., 30 pf.; for each $22^1/_2$ lbs. more 10 pf.; double rates from 10 p.m. till 7 a.m. — *Cabs,* see p. 41.

Steamboat Quays. The steamers of the *Cologne & Düsseldorf Steamship Co.* (p. xvi) start from the Leystapel (Pl. D, 5), 10-12 min. from the cathedral and the central station; the fast steamers touch at the Trankgassen-Werft (Pl. F, 5), 3-4 min. from the central station, only on arriving in Cologne. The quay of the Dutch steamers (p. xv) is at the Franken-Werft (Pl. E, 5), 4 min. from the central station. — *Porter* into the town or to the railway-station: for hand-bag 10 pf., for trunk up to 55 lbs. 50 pf., up to 110 lbs. 80 pf., up to 330 lbs. 1 *M* 20 pf.

Hotels (advisable to order rooms in advance during the season). — *Near the Central Station and the Cathedral:* HÔTEL DU NORD (Pl. a;

E, 5), Franken-Platz 4, near the iron bridge, with railway-ticket, post, and telegraph office, and garden, R. from 3, B. 1¹/₂, D. 5, omn. ³/₄ ℳ; *Dom-Hôtel (Pl. i; E, 4), near the cathedral (comp. p. 52), R. 3-25, B. 1¹/₂, D. 4¹/₂ ℳ, with fine restaurant; *Hôtel Monopole ·(Pl. m; E, 4), Wallrafs-Platz 5, with café and restaurant, R. 3-10, B. 1¹/₄ ℳ; *Kölner Hof (Hôt. de Cologne; Pl. k, F 4), Bahnhof-Str. 5, with terrace and wine restaurant, R. 3-6, B. 1¹/₄ ℳ; *Savoy Hotel (Pl. o; E, 4), Domkloster 2, with good restaurant, R. 3-12, B. 1¹/₂, D. 4 & 5 ℳ; *Westminster Hotel (Pl. p; E, 4), Am Hof 24, R. 3-6, B. 1¹/₄ ℳ, with restaurant and winter-garden; Excelsior Hotel Ernst (Pl. e; F, 4), R. 3¹/₂-8, B. 1¹/₂, déj. 3¹/₂, D. 5 ℳ. All these are of the first class, with lifts, baths, electric light, and hot-air heating. — The following are also first-class, but less pretentious: Ewige Lampe & Europäischer Hof (Pl. g; F, 4), Komödien-Str. 2, with café-restaurant; St. Paul (Pl. s; F, 4), Unter Fettenhennen 19, with view of the cathedral, R. 2¹/₂-5, B. 1 ℳ, with restaurant; Continental (Pl. f; E, 4), Domhof 18, R. 2¹/₂-6, B. 1¹/₄, D. 3 ℳ; City Hotel, cor. of the Bahnhof-Str. and Marzellen-Str. (Pl. F, 4), R. from 3, B. 1¹/₄, D. 2-3 ℳ. — *Belgischer Hof (Pl. y; F, 4), Komödien-Str. 9, with a popular restaurant (Munich beer); *Mittelhäuser (Pl. l; F, 4), Marzellen-Str. 5, R. 3-5, B. 1¹/₄, D. 2¹/₂ ℳ. — Behind the Station: *Minerva (Pl. v; F, 5), Johannis-Str. 24, with beer-restaurant, R. 2¹/₂-5 ℳ; *Harm's Hôtel Terminus, Hermann-Str. 9 (Pl. F, 4, 5). — The following are still less pretentious, but the best of them are also fitted up with electric light, hot-air heating, etc.: Reichshof, Am Hof 18 (Pl. E, 4), Berliner Hof, Marzellen-Str. 19 (Pl. F, 4), with restaurant, R. 2-3 ℳ; Hôtel National (Pl. n; F, 4), Marzellen-Str. 1, R. & B. 3-4 ℳ; Hôtel Tils, Andreas-Kloster (Pl. F, 4), R. 2-3¹/₂, B. 1, D. 2¹/₂ ℳ; Fränkischer Hof, Komödien-Str. 32 (Pl. F, 4), with restaurant, well spoken of, R. & B. 2³/₄-4 ℳ; Bayrischer Hof, opposite the Museum (Pl. E, 4), plain but good; Alt-Heidelberg, Wallraf-Platz; Christliches Hospiz, Johannis-Str. 39 (Pl. & B. 1¹/₂-3 ℳ) and Johannis-Str. 77 (R. 1¹/₂-2³/₄ ℳ, B. 60 pf., pens. 3-4¹/₂ ℳ), both unpretending.

In the Middle of the Old Town: *Hôtel Disch (Pl. b; E, 4), Brücken-Str. 19, an old-established, first-class hotel, R. from 3 ℳ; Hôtel Langen, Salomonsgasse 13 (Pl. E, 4), commercial, with wine-restaurant; Kaiser-hof (Pl. u; E, 4), Salomonsgasse 11, R. 2-3, B. 1 ℳ, with beer-restaurant; Hôtel Löwenbräu, Hohe-Str. 90, with beer-restaurant; Hôtel Vander-stein Bellen, Heumarkt 20 (Pl. D, E, 5), with frequented wine-room (Moselle wines), R. & B. 2³/₄-3, D. (incl. wine) 2¹/₄ ℳ.

In the New Town: Kaiser Friedrich (Pl. h; C, 2), Salier-Ring 45, with lift, R. 2-6, B. 1, D. 1¹/₄-3 ℳ, well spoken of; Kaiser Wilhelm (Pl. w; G, 2), Kaiser-Wilhelm-Ring 43, R. 3-3¹/₂, B. 1 ℳ, both family hotels with wine and beer restaurants.

Pensions. Internationale (5¹/₄-6¹/₄ ℳ), Hermann-Str. 20 (Pl. F, 4, 5); Du Mont (4¹/₂-6 ℳ), Christoph-Str. 43 (Pl. F, 2); Helbach (4-6 ℳ), Bismarck-Str. 11, near the Stadtgarten (Pl. F, 2); Middendorf, Engelbert-Str. 67 (Pl. D, 2); Miss Oldfield, Blumen-Str. 3 (beyond Pl. H, 4, 5); Schreiner (4¹/₂-6 ℳ), Blumental-Str. 87 (beyond Pl. H, 4, 5); Schurmann, Gereonsmühlengasse 9 (Pl. F, G, 2).

Restaurants. Wine is usually ordered at the following, in addition to the Hotels-Restaurants indicated above. *G. Bettger & Co., Kleine Budengasse 6 (Pl. E, 4), a long-established house, with oyster-saloon; Peters, Severin-Str. 187 (Pl. B, C, 4), good Rhine wine; Beckmann ('Zum Treppchen'; D. 1¹/₄-2¹/₂ ℳ), Am Hof 38 (Pl. E, 4); Altdeutsche Wein-kneipe, Am Hof 14 (Pl. E, 4); Zur Kevvern Doos, Martin-Str. 26 (Pl. D, E, 4); J. J. Schoss, Am Hof 16; Nakatenus, Ludwig-Str. 5; Giffels, Hohenstaufen-Ring 21; Wirtz, Limburger-Str. 19 (Pl. E, 2); Continental Bodega (Southern wines), Hohe-Str. 127. The Roman Catholic Bürger-Gesellschaft (p. 64), with special rooms for non-members (entr. Appellhof-Platz 26), and the Civil-Casino (for members only) have both a reputation for their wine. — Beer is supplied at the following. *Fischer, in the arcade off the Hohe-Str. (Pl. E, 4); Bierstall, at the Belgische Hof (see

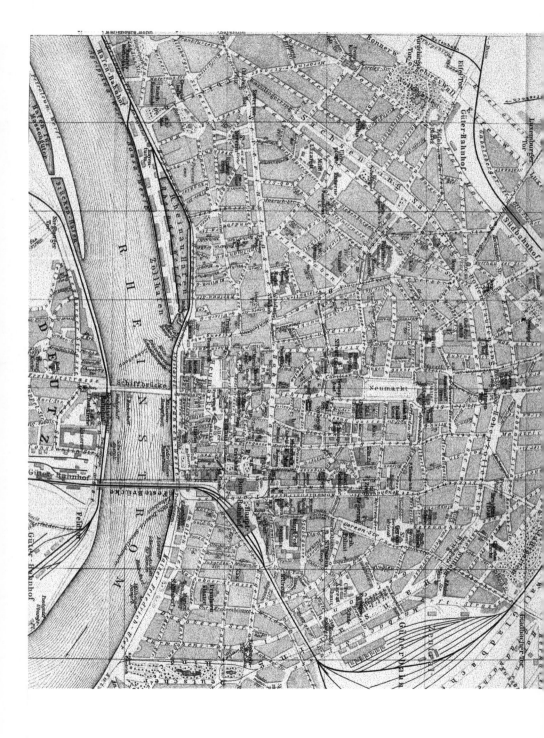

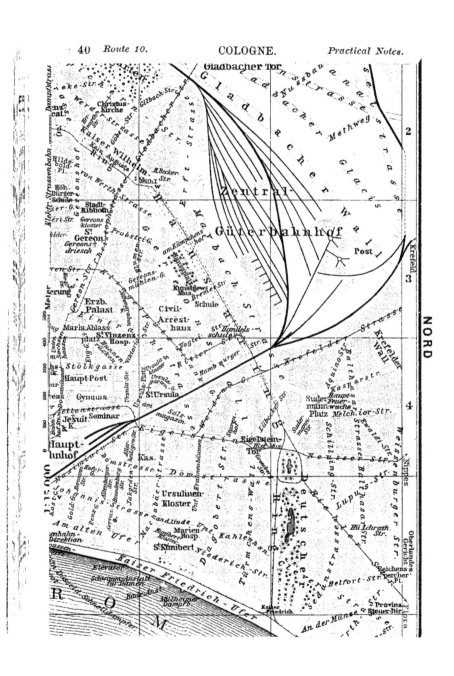

above), D. $1^1/_4$-$1^3/_4$ $\mathcal{M}$; *Stapelhaus* (Pl. E, 5; p. 62), at the Frankenwerft, with garden-terrace (military band); *Pschorrbräu*, Hohe-Str. 38; *Altes Praesidium*, Schildergasse 84 (Pl. E, 4, 3); *Kränkel*, Martin-Str. 24 (Pl. D, E, 4); **Opernhaus* (Pl. D, 2), a large garden-restaurant, with band, outside the Hahnen-Tor (p. 68); *Hansa-Haus*, Friesen-Platz 16 (Pl. F, 2). — COLOGNE BEER. *P. Jos. Früh*, Am Hof 12; *Päffgen*, Friesen-Str. 64; *Zum Bart*, Auf dem Brand; *Schreckenskammer*, Johannis-Str. 42; *Zur Zweipann*, Breite-Str. 17. — AUTOMATIC RESTAURANTS: Domkloster (at the Hôtel St. Paul, p. 40), Hohe-Str. 152, and Breite-Str. 50.

Cafés. *Monopole*, see p. 40; *Palant*, Hohe-Str. 117, at the corner of Minoriten-Str.; *Bauer*, Hohe-Str. 69, corner of the Perlenpfuhl; *Runge*, Hohe-Str. 9; *Café de l'Europe*, at the Hôtel Ewige Lampe, see p. 40; *Café Borussia*, Hohenzollern-Ring 66 (Pl. E, 2). *Damm's Tea Room*, Hohe-Str. 121, cor. of Minoriten-Str. (1st floor). — **Confectioners.** *Reichard*, Unter Fettenhennen 11 (Pl. E, F, 4); *Kaiser*, Breite-Str. 41; **Eigel*, Schildergasse 36 (Pl. E, 4, 3); *Esser*, Hohe-Str. 53.

Places of Recreation (mostly tramway stations, see p. 42). *Zoological Garden*, with frequented restaurant, see p. 70. Adm. 1 $\mathcal{M}$, on Sun. 50 pf.; concerts every afternoon in summer and every evening except Sun. (in winter on Sun., Wed., & Sat. afternoons only). Steamers, see p. 42. — *Flora Garden*, see p. 70. Adm. 1 $\mathcal{M}$, on Sun. 50 pf.; aquarium 25 pf.; good restaurant; concerts every afternoon. Steamers, see p. 42. — *Kurfürsten-Garten*, near the Zoological Garden, on the Rhine, at the corner of the Frohngasse, beside the quay of the Mülheim steamers (p. 42); band in the afternoon. — *Stadt-Garten* (Pl. F, 1), with restaurant. — *Volks-Garten* (Pl. A, 2, 3), with pretty grounds, concerts in summer, and a restaurant. — *Alteburger Mühle*, in Bayental (p. 67), on the Rhine, commanding a fine view. — *Stadtwald*, in Lindental, see p. 70.

Theatres. *Opera House* (*Opernhaus*, Pl. D 2; p. 68), for operas and ballets; *Schauspielhaus* (Pl. E, 3; p. 62), dramas and comedies; *Residenz-Theater* (Pl. F, 2), modern dramas, farces, and operettas; *Metropol-Theater* (Pl. E, 3), built by Perthel in 1906, for operettas; *Summer Theatre* in the Flora (see above). — Variety Theatres. *Reichshallen* (Pl. E, 3), also operettas and 'Kölner Hänneschen' in summer; *Apollo*, Schildergasse; *Skala-Theater*, Herzog-Str., near the Schildergasse.

Music. The *Gürzenich Concerts* (p. 59; seats in the body of the hall 6 $\mathcal{M}$, in the gallery $3^1/_2$ $\mathcal{M}$, main rehearsal 3 $\mathcal{M}$), twelve in winter and six in summer, have attained a European celebrity. — Two institutions which have earned a high reputation are the *Conservatorium of Music* (Pl. E, 3), Wolf-Str. 3, founded in 1851, and the *Männer-Gesangverein*, or Men's Vocal Society (p. 63).

Festivals. The Cologne *Carnival* is famous. Weekly after Jan. 1st the three chief carnival-societies hold burlesque meetings. A *Procession takes place on the Mon. before Shrove Tuesday; and on Shrove Tuesday there is a masked ball in the Gürzenich Hall (p. 59; early application for tickets necessary).

Sport. Race-meetings take place in April, Aug., & Oct. on the *Racecourse* of the Kölner Rennverein in the Neusser-Str. at Merheim. — *Grosse Sport-Platz*, also to the N. of the city, beyond the Zoological Garden, for cycling, tennis, football, and other sports. — *Boat House* of the Cologne Club, on the river, above Marienburg (p. 67).

Cab Tariff.

A. *Per Drive.* Persons:	1		2		3		4	
	$\mathcal{M}$	pf.	$\mathcal{M}$	pf.	$\mathcal{M}$	pf.	$\mathcal{M}$	pf.
Drive within Cologne and Deutz (bridge-toll there & back, 80 pf. extra) . . .	—	75	1	—	1.	25	1.	50
Zoological and Flora Gardens and Racecourse	1.	25	1.	25	1.	75	1.	75
B. *By Time.*								
For $^1/_2$ hr.	1	—	1	—	1.	50	1.	50
Each additional $^1/_4$ hr.	—	50	—	50	—	75	—	75

Luggage under 22 lbs. free; 22-55 lbs. 25 pf.; each addit. 55 lbs. or fraction 25 pf. — For drives to the suburbs 50 pf. additional is paid if the cab be not used in returning. Double fares from 11 p.m. to 7 a.m. (in summer 6 a.m.).

Taximeter Cabs. Drive of 800 mètres (ca. $\frac{1}{2}$ M.), 1-2 pers. 60 pf., each 400 m. extra 10 pf.; drive of 600 m. for 3-5 pers. (1-5 pers. outside the municipal district) 60 pf., each 300 m. extra 10 pf.; at night 400 m. for 1-5 pers. 60 pf., each 200 m. more 10 pf. In the case of motor cabs the fare is 80 pf. for 600, 500, or 400 m., with 10 pf. for each additional 300, 250, or 200 m. respectively. — Waiting, 10 pf. every 4 minutes. — Luggage as above.

Electric Tramways (fare 10-15 pf.; no transfers). The various lines are distinguished by numbers and coloured shields. No. 1 (blue & green): *Lindental* (comp. Pl. D, 1) - Cathedral (Pl. E, F, 4) - Deutz-*Kalk* (p. 70).— 2. (blue): *Lindental*-Cathedral-Deutz-*Mülheim* (p. 27).— 3. (yellow): *Ehrenfeld* (comp. Pl. F, G, 1)-Cathedral-Deutz-*Kalk*. — 4. (green and white) *Ehrenfeld*-Cathedral-Deutz-*Mülheim*. — 5. (white and red): *Ehrenfeld*-Neumarkt (Pl. D, E, 3)-*Chlodwig-Platz* (Pl. A, 4). — 6. (blue and red): *Bickendorf*-Ehrenfeld-Cathedral-Heumarkt (Pl. D, E, 5)-*Mannsfeld*. — 7. (red and yellow): *Cathedral*-Nippes-*Niehl* (comp. Pl. H, 4, 5). — 8. (yellow and white): *Neumarkt* (Pl. D, E, 3)-Melaten-*Müngersdorf* (comp. Pl. E, 1). — 9. (green): *Chlodwig-Platz* (Pl. A, 4) - Neumarkt-Cathedral-*Sechsig.* — 10. (red and green): *Zollstock*-Volksgarten (Pl. A, 3)-Neumarkt-Cathedral-*Nippes* (comp. Pl. H, 4, 5). — 11. (blue): *Merheim* (Racecourse, p. 41)-Cathedral-Heumarkt-*Bayental-Süd-Park* (p. 67). — 12. INNER LINE (Innenbahn; yellow): *Rosen-Str.* (Pl. B, C, 4, 5)-Neumarkt-Berlich (Pl. E, 3)-Hansaring-Kaiser-Friedrich-Ufer (Pl. H, 6) - *Zoologischer - Garten - Flora* (p. 70). — 14. RIVER BANK LINE (Uferbahn; green and white): *Rodenkirchen* (p. 74) - Marienburg (p. 67) - Agrippina - Ufer (Pl. A, 6) - Trankgasse (Pl. F, 5; Cathedral)-*Zoologischer-Garten-Flora* (p. 70). — 15. (red and yellow): *Neumarkt*-Zülpicher - Str. (Pl. C, 2, 1) - *Sülz* (Pl. B, 1). — 16. CIRCULAR LINE (Ringbahn; red): *Ubierring* (Pl. A, 5)-Rudolph-Platz (Pl. E, 2)-Hansaring-Riehler-Str. (Pl. H, 5)-Zoologischer-Garten (p. 70)-*Mülheimer-Schiff-Brücke* (p. 70). — 18. CIRCULAR LINE (Rundbahn; white): *Cathedral*-Heumarkt (Pl. E, D, 5)-Weissbüttengasse (Pl. C, 3, 4)-Barbarossa-Platz (Pl. C, 2)-Rudolf-Platz (Pl. E, 2)-Kaiser-Wilhelm-Ring (Pl. F, 2)-Gereonsdriesch (Pl. F, 3)-*Cathedral*. — 19. (white): *Neumarkt*-Berrenrather-Str. (Pl. B, 1)-*Sülz*. — 20. (yellow and green): *Nippes*-Schlachthof-Cathedral-Heumarkt-South-Station-Sülz-*Klettenberg*.

Steam Tramways. From the Schaafen-Str. (Pl. D, 2), viâ *Lindental, Benzelrath*, and *Mödrath*, to *Horrem* (p. 15) or *Blatzheim;* from the Barbarossa-Platz (Pl. C, 2) viâ *Brühl* (p. 83), to *Bonn* ('Vorgebirgs-bahn'; comp. p. 74). — **Suburban Electric Railways** run from the Museum (Pl. E, 4) viâ Deutz and Kalk to *Königsforst* (p. 70) and *Brück* (extension to *Porz* in construction) and from the Brücken - Rampe viâ Deutz and Mülheim to *Bergisch-Gladbach* (p. 27). — *Rheinufer - Bahn*, see p. 74.

Public Conveyances, starting daily in front of the Cathedral at 10 a.m. and 4 p.m., visit the chief sights of Cologne (tickets, 4 ℳ each, from Cook, Domhof 1, or at the hotels).

Local Steamers ply frequently between Cologne and *Mülheim* (p. 27; 10 & 5 pf.), starting from the Trankgasse Wharf (Pl. F, 5), and touching at the Zoological and Flora gardens (p. 70); also on summer-afternoons from the Holzwerft (Pl. D, 5) to *Marienburg* (p. 67; 20 pf., there & back 35 pf.). — Ferry to *Deutz* (Pl. D, 5, 6), 5 pf. & 3 pf.

Baths. The *Hohenstaufen-Bad* (Pl. D, 2), in the Hohenstaufen-Ring, is excellently fitted up, with large swimming - baths. *Dom-Bad*, Hohe-Str. 111a; *Ludwigs - Bad*, Hohe - Str. 53. — Baths in the Rhine, by the bridge - of - boats (also warm baths); in Deutz, near the bridge-of-boats, with swimming-baths.

Post and Telegraph Office (*Haupt-Postamt;* Pl. F, 1; p. 66), in the Dominikaner-Str.

Eau de Cologne. This celebrated perfume is said to have been invented by *J. M. Farina* of Domodossola in 1709, while another tradition asserts that it was first brought to Germany in 1690 by *Paul de Feminis.* The claim of the firms manufacturing it to the name of Farina is sometimes very indirect. The oldest firm is *Johann Maria Farina,* opposite the Jülichs-Platz (Obenmarspforten 23).

American Consul, *Mr. Hiram J. Dunlap;* vice-consul, *Mr. Chas. Lesimple.* — **British Consul,** *Herr C. A. Niessen,* Domhof 6 (also foreign banker).

English Church Service in the Chapel in the Hôtel du Nord Grounds, Bischofsgarten-Str. 3. Informations as to hours of service may be obtained from the local papers and at the hotels. Chaplain, *Rev. H. M. de Ste Croix.*

English Physician. *Dr. Prior,* Kaiser-Wilhelm-Ring 15. — **American Dentists.** *H. C. Merrill, W. H. Larrabee, & John W. Gale,* Hohenzollern-Ring 79; *Dr. Seeley,* Kaiser-Wilhelm-Ring 26; *Dr. Merckens,* Kaiser-Wilhelm-Ring 2. — **Chemists.** *O. Contzen* (Dom-Apotheke), Komödien-Str. 1; *H. Wrede,* Wallrafs-Platz 1 (both speak English).

Tourist Agents: *Thomas Cook & Son,* Domhof 1 (also foreign bankers). — The *Cologne Tourists' Enquiry Office* (*Kölner Verkehrsverein*), Margareten-Kloster 11, opposite the entrance to the cathedral, gives information (gratis), procures theatre-tickets, and performs various other useful services for strangers.

Collections and Objects of Interest.

*Cathedral (p. 46). The nave and transept are open the whole day, but walking about is forbidden during divine service, the hours of which vary (usually on week-days at 9 or 10 a.m. and 3 or 3.30 p.m.). Tickets to visit the choir (best light in the morning) and treasury ($1^1/_2$ ℳ each person) are sold by the 'Domschweizer', or attendants stationed in the cathedral. Hours of admission: from 1st May to 30th Sept. on Mon.-Frid. 10-11 a.m., 12.30-3, 3.30-7 p.m.; Sat. 10-11 a.m., 12.30-2.30 p.m.; Sun. 12-1.30, 6-7 p.m.; from 1st Oct. to 30th April Mon.-Frid. 10-11, 11.30-1, 3.30-5; Sat. 10-11, 11.30-1; Sun. 12-1 p.m. — Ascent to the upper gallery, the towers, etc., see. p. 52. — No fees need be given, and the services of valets-de-place are quite superfluous.

City Library (p. 64), Mon.-Frid. 10-1 & 4-8, Sat. 10-1.

Gürzenich (p. 59), 1-2 pers. 50 pf. each, a party 40 pf. each.

Industrial Art Library (p. 69), week-days 10-12 and 7-10.

Museum, Archiepiscopal (p. 52), week-days 9-6 (winter 10-4), adm. 50 pf., Sun. & holidays 10-2, adm. 30 pf.

Museum, Historical (pp. 68, 70), daily 9-5 (Oct.-March 10-4), Sun. 9-2; adm. free on Sun. & Wed., other days 50 pf.; closed during the Carnival and on the chief festivals.

*Museum of Industrial Art (p. 69), open as the Historical Museum; gratis.

Museum of Natural History (p. 62), open as the Historical Museum.

Museum, Prehistoric (p. 67), daily 9-1 (in winter 10-1); free on Sun. & Wed., other days 50 pf.

Museum, Rautenstrauch-Joest's Ethnographical (p. 67), daily 9-1 (in winter 10-1); adm. 50 pf., Sun. & Wed. free.

*Museum, Wallraf-Richartz (p. 52), open as the Historical Museum.

Pictures, Exhibitions of: Kölnischer Kunstverein, in the Wallraf-Richartz-Museum (p. 53); *Ed. Schulte,* Richartz-Str. 16 (Pl. E, 4; 50 pf.); *R. Lenobel,* Kreuzgasse 22 (Pl. E, 3; 50 pf.); *W. Abels,* Schildergasse 3.

*Rathaus (p. 58), open on same terms as the Gürzenich.

Römergang (p. 58), daily until 10 p.m. by electric light; adm. 25 pf.

Zoological Garden, see p. 41.

Principal Attractions (two days). 1st Day: *Cathedral* (p. 46), interior, and walk round the external choir-gallery; *Wallraf-Richartz-*

Museum (p. 52); *Hohc-Strasse* (p. 46); *St. Maria im Capitol* (p. 60); *Gürze-nich* (p. 59); *Rathaus* (p. 58); *Rheinufer* (p. 67). — 2nd Day: *Church of the Apostles* (p. 63); *St. Gereon* (p. 65); *Museum of Industrial Art* (p. 69); walk or drive in the *Ring-Strasse* (p. 67); *Zoological Garden* (p. 70) or *Stadtwald* (p. 70). The services of valets-de-place are quite superfluous. — A trip by trolley-car along the bank of the Rhine and the Ring-Str. (p. 67) is recommended. Afternoon excursions may be made to *Alten-berg* (p. 36), *Schloss Brühl* (p. 83), and *Weiden* (p. 15), but Sun. and holidays should be avoided for these.

Cologne (120 ft.; Ger. *Cöln* or *Köln*), the largest town in the Rhenish Province of Prussia, the residence of an archbishop, and one of the most important commercial places in Germany, is a fort-ress of the first class, with 510,000 inhabitants (four-fifths of whom are Roman Catholics), including a garrison of 8000 men and the incorporated suburbs. It lies on the left bank of the Rhine, across which a bridge-of-boats and an iron bridge lead to Deutz (p. 70). From a distance, and especially when approached by steamboat, the town with its numerous towers presents a very imposing appearance. Many of the narrow streets of the old part of the city contain interesting specimens of domestic architecture, dating from the 16th, 15th, and even the 13th century. The development of the town received a great impetus in 1881, when the adoption of a farther advanced line of fortifications literally doubled the area of the town-domain, and also in 1888 by the incorporation of the suburbs of *Bayental, Lindental, Ehrenfeld, Nippes,* and *Deutz. Kalk* and *Vingst* were incorporated in 1910. The harbour of Rheinau (p. 67) and the wharves constructed along the river in 1892-98 and extend-ing from Marienburg (p. 67) to below the Zoological Garden (p. 70; a distance of $5^{1}/_{2}$ M.) present a scene of great commercial activity.

History. Cologne was founded by the Ubii, at the time when they were compelled by Agrippa to migrate from the right to the left bank of the Rhine (B. C. 38), and by the érection of the *Ara Ubiorum* here it became the religious centre for the German peoples. In A. D. 51 Emp. Claudius, at the request of his wife Agrippina, founded here a colony of Roman veterans, which at first was called *Colonia Claudia Ara Agrip-pinensis,* afterwards shortened into *Colonia Agrippinensis,* and (by the 5th cent.) into *Colonia.* It was the seat of the Legate of *Germania In-ferior.* The Roman city-walls, probably constructed in the time of Claudius and renewed in the third century of our era, enclósed the rect-angle between St. Maria in Capitol (Pl. D, 4), the Cathedral (Pl. F, 4; Burgmauer, see p. 64), the Römerturm (Pl. F, 3; p. 64), and the S. end of the Kleine Griechenmarkt (Pl. C, 3). In 308 Constantine the Great began a stone bridge over the Rhine, which connected the city with the castle of *Divitia* (Deutz). This bridge was destroyed by the Normans in the 9th or 10th century.

From the end of the fifth century Cologne belonged to the kingdom of the Franks, and it was long occupied by the Ripuarian kings. Charle-magne raised the bishopric, which had been founded here in the fourth century, to an archbishopric, the first archbishop being the imperial chaplain *Hildebold* (d. 819), who built the oldest cathedral church, and presented to it a valuable library, which still exists in the cathedral. The archbishops soon began to lay claim to political as well as ecclesiastical power, and endeavoured to construe the privileges granted to them by the Emperor into unlimited jurisdiction over the city. In consequence of these pretensions they were continually at variance with the citizens, and their quarrels usually assumed the form of sanguinary feuds, particularly under *Anno II.* (1056-75), *Philipp von Heinsberg* (1167-91; p. 50), *Conrad von Hochstaden* (1238-61), *Engelbert von Falkenburg* (1261-74), and *Siegfried von Westerburg* (1275-97). The long contest was decided in favour of municipal independence by the battle of Worringen (1288; see p. 23), and the archbishops were compelled to transfer their residence to Brühl (p. 83), and afterwards to Bonn (p. 76). They retained, however, the highest jurisdiction and other rights, and the citizens continued to take the oath of allegiance, 'so long as they should be maintained in the rights and privileges handed down to them by their forefathers'. The conflicts carried on in the town itself, between different noble families or between the nobles and the guilds, were still more violent. It was not till 1396, when the guilds gained a decisive advantage, that there was a cessation of hostilities.

Its vigorous fund of vitality is shown by the fact that, in spite of all these troubles, Cologne was unquestionably one of the wealthiest and most prosperous cities in Germany at the end of the 15th century. Its commerce, especially its trade with London, where it possessed warehouses at the Guildhall, was of the greatest importance. At an early date Cologne became incorporated with the *Hanseatic League*, in which it contested the supremacy with Lübeck. The weights and measures of Cologne were in use in almost every Rhenish, Westphalian, and Dutch town. A fair held at Cologne at Easter attracted visitors from all parts of Europe, and even from beyond the sea.

In the course of its mediæval history Cologne may boast of having twice been a cradle of German *Art*. The first occasion was about the end of the 12th century, when the ecclesiastical enthusiasm shown by the acquisition of the relics of the Magi, and also the civic love of splendour found expression in a highly-developed style of ARCHITECTURE, calculated for picturesque effect (comp. p. xxviii). One after another the larger churches were remodelled, special attention being devoted to the choir. The best specimen of this period of architecture is presented by the *Apostel-Kirche*, as seen from the Neumarkt. During the 13th cent. the taste for building continued and led to a restoration of the *Cathedral*, in which, however, the traditional Romanesque architecture was abandoned for the new Gothic style, emanating from Northern France and then spreading rapidly throughout Europe. From the close of the 14th cent. onwards, Cologne enjoyed a second golden era of art, chiefly confined to the province of PAINTING (comp. p. xxxi). The municipal archives preserve the names of a great number of painters, but only in a very few instances can any of these be definitely attached to existing pictures. Among the best known are *Meister Wilhelm* (d. about 1380), *Stephan Lochner* (d. 1451; comp. p. 51), and the *Master of the Life of the Virgin* (flourished ca. 1460-90). — The taste for architecture was not extinct even at a later period. The porch of the *Rathaus*, for example, is an interesting specimen of the German Renaissance. Not only were old churches renovated, but occasionally new ones were built. Prior to 1801, when many of them were secularized, Cologne possessed more than 100 churches, which, of course, could be kept in repair only by constant care and attention. — In the province of SCIENCE, Cologne held by no means so high a place as in that of art. The university, founded in 1388, acquired, as the chief seat of the opposition to Humanism in the contest of Reuchlin with the Obscurantists (15-16th cent.), a wide but far from enviable reputation. It was suppressed at the close of the 18th century.

After the 16th century Cologne declined, at first gradually, and afterwards rapidly. In common with the rest of the Hanseatic towns its commerce lost its former importance. Continual internal discords, leading to the banishment in 1608 of the Protestants, who settled at Crefeld, Elberfeld, Düsseldorf, and Mülheim, proved very prejudicial to the interests of the city. It retained, however, its privileges as a free imperial city until its occupation by the French (6th Oct., 1794). By the peace of Campo Formio (17th Oct., 1797) it was incorporated with France. — It was not till after 1815, under Prussian rule, that Cologne began to revive. The rapid progress of its steamboat and railway systems, and the enterprise of the citizens, many of whom possess great wealth, have combined to make Cologne the centre of the Rhenish trade and one of the most considerable commercial cities in Germany. Since 1885 Cologne has enjoyed direct cargo-steamer communication with London, Copenhagen, St. Petersburg, and the German ports on the North Sea and the Baltic. Its chief industrial products are tools and machinery (p. 70), wire, chocolate, sugar, furniture, and glass.

a. Cathedral. Wallraf-Richartz Museum. Hohe-Strasse.

The *Cathedral, or *Dom* (Pl. E, F, 4), which justly excites the admiration of every beholder, and undoubtedly the finest Gothic edifice in Germany, stands on a slight eminence about 60 ft. above the Rhine, at the N.E. angle of the oldest part of the city (comp. p. 44), opposite the iron bridge and near the Central Station. It is predominantly a modern creation, but the original choir and unfinished nave have been absorbed in the present building, and early plans (see p. 50) have been followed to some extent in the new portions. As early as the 9th century an episcopal church (see p. 44) occupied this site, but in course of time the inhabitants regarded it as unworthy of the rapidly increasing size and prosperity of their city. The archbishop St. Engelbert first entertained the project of erecting a new church here, but in consequence of his untimely death in 1225 (see p. 50) it was never executed. His second successor *Conrad of Hochstaden* (see p. 50), after the old church had been severely injured by fire, at length laid the foundation-stone of the present structure on 14th Aug., 1248. The designer of this noble work is believed to have been *Meister Gerard,* to whom the Chapter made a grant in 1257 in recognition of his services.

The choir was the first part of the building proceeded with. The work progressed slowly, Gerard's successors, *Meister Arnold* and his son *Meister Johann,* being seriously hampered by the struggles between the archbishops and the citizens (see p. 45). On 27th Sept., 1322, the choir, which had been temporarily terminated by a lofty wall towards the W., was solemnly consecrated by *Archbishop Heinrich, Count of Virneburg.* The builder soon proceeded to lay the foundations of the N. and (in 1325) S. transepts, while at the same time the old church was gradually removed. In 1388 the nave was sufficiently advanced to be temporarily fitted up for service, and in 1447 the bells were placed in the S. tower. Subsequently the enthusiasm subsided, and by the end of the 15th century all hope of seeing the church completed was abandoned. The unfinished building was provided with a temporary roof about 1508, and in the 17th and 18th cent. the interior was decorated in the degraded style of the period. In 1796 the building was converted by the French into a hay-magazine.

Frederick William III., King of Prussia, at the suggestion of Sulpice Boisserée, caused it to be examined by the eminent architect Schinkel in 1816, and gave orders to preserve the building as it then was. Schinkel's pupil *Ernest F. Zwirner,* who succeeded to

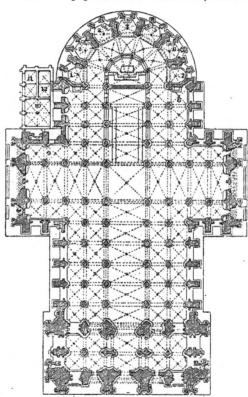

1. Engelbert Chapel. 2. Maternus Ch. 3. Ch. of St. John. 4. Ch. of the Magi. 5. Ch. of St. Agnes. 6. Ch. of St. Michael. 7. Ch. of St. Stephen. 8. Ch. of the Virgin. 9. Treasury. 10. Sacristy. 11. Chapter House. 12. Library.

the conduct of the work in 1833, was the first to form the project of completing the cathedral, an idea hailed with general enthusiasm. The foundation-stone of the new part of the building was laid by Frederick William IV. in 1842. After Zwirner's death (in 1861) he was followed as cathedral architect by *Richard Voigtel,* and in

1880, the completion of the cathedral was celebrated in the presence of the Emperor William I. The entire sum expended between 1842 and 1880 amounted to upwards of 900,000*l.*, the greater part of this amount being defrayed by government, the remainder by private subscriptions, societies, and the proceeds of a lottery. Since 1880 at least 450,000*l.* more has been spent on restoration and improvement.

The cathedral is a cruciform structure (see Plan, p. 47), the nave being flanked with double; and the transept with single aisles. Total length 570 ft., breadth 200 ft., length of transepts 282 ft., height of the walls 150 ft., height of the roof 201 ft., height of the central tower rising over the crossing 357 ft. The W. towers are 515 ft. in height. This enormous mass of masonry is enlivened by a profusion of flying buttresses, turrets, gargoyles, galleries, cornices, foliage, etc.

The *W. Façade*, which has been completed entirely in accordance with the still extant original designs of the 14th cent., with its two huge towers, is a superb example of strictly consistent Gothic workmanship. The towers consist of four stories, of which the three lower are square in form, while the fourth is octagonal, crowned with elegant open spires.

The largest of the *Bells* in the S. tower is the *Kaiser-Glocke*, which was cast in 1874 with the metal of French guns, and weighs 27 tons; 28 ringers were required to set it in motion. The next two in point of size, cast in 1447 and 1448, weigh 11 and 6 tons.

The *Principal Portal* is 96 ft. in height and 31 ft. in width; the side-portals 38 ft. high and 18 ft. wide; the central window 48 ft. high and 20 ft. wide. The portal of the S. tower was decorated in the beginning of the 15th cent. with excellent sculptures, probably by *Meister Conrad Kuyn*. The bronze doors were modelled by *Schneider* of Cassel, and cast at Iserlohn in 1891-92. — The arms of the transept are terminated by the N. and S. portals, which were completed in 1859, having been built entirely from Zwirner's designs, as the original plans were no longer extant. The *N. Portal* is executed in a simple style; the beautiful bronze *Doors, from the designs of *Mengelberg* of Utrecht, were cast at Stuttgart (1891). The *S. Portal*, with bronze doors after *Schneider's* designs (p. x), is elaborately decorated, and embellished with statues designed by *Schwanthaler*.

The *Choir*, completed in 1322, and flanked with seven chapels, is substantially a repetition of that of the cathedral of Amiens, but some of its details are even more perfect in form. In its lower parts it exhibits the simple and dignified forms of the early Gothic style, while in the upper parts the full magnificence of the consummated art is displayed.

The **Interior (admission, see p. 43), which is borne by 56 pillars, is 390 ft. in length. The nave is 48 ft. wide from the centre of one pillar to that of the one opposite, and 148 ft. in height; each of the inner aisles is 27 ft., each of the outer $22^1/_2$ ft. wide; each of the four aisles is 60 feet high. The area of the interior is 7400 sq. yds.

NAVE and TRANSEPT. The large stained-glass window above the W. portal was presented in 1878 by Emp. Frederick III., when Crown Prince. The five stained-glass *Windows in the N. (left) aisle, executed in 1508 and 1509, and presented by Archbishop Philipp von Daun-Oberstein, the town of Cologne, Archbishop Hermann of Hesse, and Count Philipp von Virneburg, are among the finest examples of the kind now extant. The subjects are: 1. Passion and Resurrection of Christ; below, St. Lawrence, Madonna and Child, and the donors. 2. Life of St. Peter, and Tree of Jesse; below, St. Sebastian and an archbishop. 3. Adoration of the Shepherds; below, SS. George, Reinold, Gereon, and Maurice, with Agrippa and Marsilius, the traditionary founders of Cologne. 4. Visit of the Queen of Sheba to Solomon, the Three Magi; below, St. Peter in the papal chair; the Archbishop of Cologne, the Madonna, and SS. Elizabeth and Christopher, patron-saints of Hesse. 5. Coronation of the Virgin, St. John the Evangelist, St. Peter, SS. Mary Magdalen and George, and the donor with his two wives. — The windows in the S. aisle and the transept are modern. Those in the S. aisle (presented in 1848 by King Lewis I. of Bavaria) and the first window of the S. transept (to the memory of Joseph von Görres, 1776-1848, 'catholicæ veritatis defensori generoso') were executed in Munich. The window above the S. Portal, presented by the Emp. William I., was executed in Berlin; that over the N. portal, commemorating the elevation of Archbishop von Geissel of Cologne (d. 1864) to the rank of cardinal, is of Cologne workmanship. — The old stained glass on the W. side of the N. Transept is from several ancient churches of Cologne, now demolished.

The statues on the pillars of the vestibule, the nave, and the transept represent prophets, apostles, and saints. — By a pillar of the S. transept stands a *Statue of St. Christopher*, about 10 ft. high, dating from the beginning of the 16th century. The first carved altar (1520) by the E. wall of this transept, in the late-Gothic style, is from the church of St. Maria ad Gradus (pulled down in 1817); the second altar is of Westphalian origin (15th cent.).

The CHOIR is separated from the nave by an iron railing. We enter by the N. (left) door. Consoles projecting from the 14 pillars of the central part, or *High Choir* proper, bear *Statues* of Christ, Mary, and the Apostles, dating from the 14th cent. and repainted in 1840. The nine frescoes in the spandrels, executed by Steinle in 1843, represent *Angel Choirs* in the ecclesiastical symbolic style; they are best seen from the gallery of the choir (p. 52). The carved-wood *Choir Stalls* and the mural paintings on the screens

behind them (concealed by silken tapestry) date from the middle
of the 14th century. — Brasses mark the burial-places of Archbishop von Spiegel (d. 1835) and Cardinal von Geissel (d. 1864);
in the adjoining vault repose Cardinal Paul Melchers (d. 1895), Cardinal Philip Krementz (d. 1899), and Hubertus Simar (d. 1902). —
The *High Altar*, restored in the original style in 1899, is surmounted by the old carved-wood 'Altar of St. Clara', with paintings
of scenes from the life of Christ; the wings, which were restored
in 1908-9, are an admirable and harmonious creation of Meister
Wilhelm (ca. 1370; comp. p. xxxi). — Above the triforium of the
choir is a series of admirable old *Stained Glass Windows*, representing the kings of Judah, etc. (ca. 1300). — The mosaic *Pavement* of the choir, of the ambulatory, and of the crossing was
executed from designs by Essenwein.

CHOIR CHAPELS. In front of the sacristy is the sarcophagus of
Archbishop Engelbert von der Mark (1364-68), with a fine figure
in sandstone.

1. The *Chapel of St. Engelbert* (first to the left, N. side) contained down to 1633 the remains of *Archbishop Engelbert von Berg*
(comp. p. 46), assassinated in 1225. The carved altar dates from the
16th century. The tomb of *Archbishop Anton von Schauenburg*
(d. 1561) is worthy of notice.

2. *Chapel of St. Maternus*. Tomb of *Archbishop Philipp von
Heinsberg* (d. 1191), with a good statue of the 14th century. The
form of this monument refers to the fact that the city-walls were
begun under this archbishop. The altar-piece is by *Barthol. de
Bruyn* (1548).

3. *Chapel of St. John*. Fine Tomb of *Archbishop Conrad von
Hochstaden* (d. 1261), founder of the cathedral, with the figure of
the deceased in bronze (restored in 1847), from the first half of the
15th century. Above the altar are mural paintings of the 14th century. Under glass is here preserved the original sketch of the W.
façade of the cathedral with the two towers in their completed form.
Part of this interesting design was found at Darmstadt in 1814,
the rest at Paris in 1816.

4. *Chapel of the Magi*, with a handsome railing by Mengeberg,
and frescoes (restored) and stained glass of the 14th century. Here
were formerly preserved the 'Bones of the Magi' or 'Three Kings',
which were brought by the Empress Helena to Constantinople. They
were afterwards taken to Milan, and in 1164 presented by Frederick
Barbarossa to Archbishop Reinald von Dassel, by whom they were
removed to Cologne. This is the origin of the three crowns in the
city's arms. The reliquary in which they are preserved is now in
the treasury (p. 51). The chapel contains a modern Gothic altar,
embellished with carvings (the Magi, etc.) of the 14th century. On
the S. side is the tomb of *Archbishop Ernest of Bavaria* (d. 1612).

The other electors of the House of Bavaria repose outside this chapel. — Opposite, at the back of the high-altar, is the tomb of *Archbishop Dietrich von Moers* (d. 1463).

5. *Chapel of St. Agnes,* with old stained-glass windows, restored in parts, and noteworthy mural paintings of the 14th cent., also restored. In the middle of the chapel is the Gothic *Sarcophagus of St. Irmgardis.*

6. *Chapel of St. Michael,* also with stained-glass windows pieced together from old fragments. Marble tombstone of *Archbishop Walram of Jülich* (d. 1349). Marble statue of the imperial general *Von Hochkirchen* (who fell at Landau in 1703), by the Florentine Fortini. — This chapel contains the celebrated **Dombild*, a large winged picture, painted by *Stephan Lochner* before 1450, representing the Adoration of the Magi in the centre, St. Gereon and St. Ursula on the wings, and the Annunciation on the outside.

This is doubtless the picture alluded to in Dürer's diary of his travels in the Low Countries, in which he mentions his paying two 'weisspfennige' to see the picture which *'Meister Steffen'* had painted at Cologne. Meister Stephan or Stephan Lochner was a native of Meersburg on the Lake of Constance, who seems to have settled at Cologne about 1442. In 1448 he was elected a municipal senator by his guild, and he died before the end of 1451. The picture which is of imposing dimensions, occupies an intermediate position between the ideal conceptions of mediæval times, and the modern realism introduced by the Dutch school. As the finest work of the Early German School, it has received great attention from connoisseurs, and justly occupies an important place in the history of art. It was in the Rathaus Chapel (p. 59) until the period of the French Revolution.

7. *Chapel of St. Stephen,* with frescoes and stained glass of the 14th cent. (restored). Stone sarcophagus of *Archbishop Gero* (d. 976), with a mosaic of the 10th cent., a relic of the old cathedral. Mural tomb of *Archbishop Adolf von Schauenburg* (d. 1556).

8. *Chapel of the Virgin* or *Small Choir of Our Lady* (properly speaking the last bay of the outer S. aisle). The altar, which was designed by Zwirner in 1856, is adorned with *Overbeck's Assumption.* On the S. wall is the so-called *Madonna of Milan,* a German work of the 14th century. — Near the altar is the monument of *Archbishop Frederick of Saarwerden* (d. 1414), consisting of a figure of the archbishop in bronze on a sarcophagus admirably decorated with figures of saints, the whole restored in 1847. — Tombstone of *Archbishop Reinald von Dassel* (d. 1167; see p. 50), upon which the marble statue of *Archbishop Wilhelm von Gennep* (d. 1362) was placed in 1842. Opposite is the sarcophagus of *Count Gottfried von Arnsberg* (d. 1368).

The **Treasury** (adjoining the sacristy on the left; adm., see p. 43) contains the golden *Reliquary of the Magi,* a costly specimen of Romanesque workmanship in the form of a basilica, probably executed in the years 1190-1200. It was seriously injured in 1794, when carried away for concealment from the French; and was unskilfully restored in 1807.

4*

The silver *Shrine of St. Engelbert*, in the style of the Renaissance, dates from 1633. — On the end-wall, to the left, are several ecclesiastical banners (banner of the Magi, 1897) and the so-called *Croy Epitaph*, a bronze relief of 1517, with the Adoration of the Magi. — On the entrance-wall, in the cabinet to the right: *Sword of Justice* (15th cent.), borne by the Electors of Cologne at imperial coronations in Frankfort. In frames are the so-called war-banner of Byssus, an embroidery ascribed to the 10th cent.; a processional cross (12-14th cent.); bishops' staves (8th, 14th, and 17th cent.); Gothic monstrance (14th cent.); Renaissance monstrance presented by Pius IX. in 1848; elaborate altar-cross (17th cent.); and vestments. In the cabinet to the left: Ten admirably-carved ivory tablets by Melchior Paulus (1703-33), with scenes from the Passion; reliquaries of the 15-17th cent.; *Osculum Pacis* in the Renaissance style, decorated with enamels, pearls, and precious stones; monstrance of the 17th cent., $19^1/_2$lbs. in weight, thickly set with precious stones; mitres. — The desk-case contains ancient printed works and MSS., including a MS. of the Gospels (11th cent.) and a Frankish breviary (12th cent.).

The former *Record Chamber*, to the right of the sacristy, contains a valuable collection of ecclesiastical ornaments in carved-oak cabinets.

The visitor should not omit to walk round the **Inner Gallery of the Choir* and those on the *Exterior of the Choir*, or to ascend the *S. Tower* (ascent from the outside, on the E. side of the S. transept; cards of admission 1 ℳ; parties formed about every 20 min.; on Sun. open from 9 or 10 to 2 only), as a better idea may thus be formed of the grandeur of the structure. The external gallery, or better still the open gallery of the tower, commands an extensive **View* over the sea of houses, the plain intersected by the Rhine, and the Seven Mts. in the distance.

In the garden on the terrace behind the choir are some architectural fragments, discarded in the process of restoration, which will serve to convey some idea of the colossal proportions of the edifice.

To the S. of the cathedral is the *Dom - Hôtel* (p. 40). The *Heinzelmännchen Fountain* (Pl. H B; E, 4), by E. and H. Renard (1900), in the adjoining street known as Am Hof, illustrates a local fairy tale, well versified by Kopisch.

The **Archiepiscopal Museum** (Pl. E, 4; adm., see p. 43), opposite the S. gate of the cathedral, is established in a chapel, formerly belonging to the Archiepiscopal Palace and re-erected in 1665. It contains a collection of ecclesiastical and other objects of mediæval art, sculptures, MSS., and paintings, of which the most valuable is the **Virgin with the violet* (first floor), belonging to the Priests' Seminary, by *Stephan Lochner* (p. 51). Also on the first floor is an exhibition of church vestments, ancient (7-16th cent.) and modern.

The W. end of the Dom-Kloster (Pl. F, 4), the space in front of the W. façade of the cathedral, commands the best view of the façade and the towers. The street named the 'Burgmauer', beginning here, marks the N. side of the Roman circumvallation (p. 44). — We cross the Wallrafs-Platz to the S.W., and reach the —.

*Wallraf-Richartz Museum (Pl. E, 4), built in the English Gothic style by *Felten* in 1855-61, and adorned with statues of eminent natives of Cologne. The central building faces the N., while at the back are two wings, including the handsome late-Gothic cloisters of the Church of the Minorites (p. 56). In the garden in front of the museum are (N.W.) a fragment of the E. side-portal of the *Pfaffentor* (p. 59), and (on the building) the pediment of a temple from the Roman Colonia. The bronze statues (by W. Albermann; 1900) represent *Herr Richartz* (d. 1861), a wealthy merchant who provided the funds for the museum-building, and *Canon F. Wallraf* (d. 1823), who bequeathed his collection of art to the town. — Adm., see p. 43. Printed guide (1909), 50 pf.; catalogue of the paintings (1906), 50 pf.

The GROUND FLOOR and CLOISTERS contain the **Collection of Antiquities.**

From the entrance-hall, in which, on the right and left of the staircase, are marble busts of Wallraf and Richartz, by *Bläser*, we descend to the —

LOWER CLOISTERS. The N. (front) wing contains Roman antiquities discovered at Cologne (1st-4th cent. A.D.). In the central cases are the contents of tombs, as originally found; between these, a tomb of masonry from the street of tombs at Aix-la-Chapelle. In Anteroom V. are mosaic pavements, including the *'Mosaic of the Sages', showing bust-portraits of seven Greek philosophers and poets (with the names Diogenes, Socrates, Aristotle, Chilon, Plato, Cleobulos, and Sophocles), found near St. Cecilia in 1844 (probably of the 4th cent.; some of the cubes are of glass). — In the W. wing (on the right) are Roman tombstones, including several with representations of the funeral feast (Nos. 86, 24, 25, 459), and the relief of a horseman (No. 96). At the end is an altar of Jupiter and Hercules Saxanus, from the valley of the Brohl. — The E. and S. wings are occupied by fragments of buildings and sculptures from mediæval and Renaissance churches and other buildings in Cologne, now pulled down. — We return to the entrance-hall and enter the —

UPPER CLOISTERS. Corner-room; to the right: 12. Colossal marble mask of Medusa, found in Italy. — To the left, in the *N. Wing:* Roman antiquities found at Cologne. The centre cabinets contain an admirable ***Collection of Ancient Glass*, mostly dating from the 2nd-4th cent. A.D., at which period Cologne was the centre of the glass industry. The vessels here are marked by their great diversity of form (negro heads, animals, etc.), colour, and ornamentation (filigree and bands, engraved and ground, enamel). On the walls are terracotta statuettes, lamps, and vases, besides a few sculptures. — *E. Wing*, Roman glass, so-called Barbotine goblets (terracotta with 'slip' ornamentation), bronze statuettes, small objects in metal, bone, jet, and amber; ornaments; writing implements in bronze; weapons; coins; prehistoric and Frankish antiquities. Sculptures: 654. Tragic mask; 555. Herma of Bacchus; 561. Female head (so-called Niobe); *626. Head of Athena Parthenos, after Phidias. — *S. Wing*. Greek and Roman vases; two mummies; drawings and engravings (changed from time to time). — *W. Wing*. Mediæval and Renaissance sculptures in wood and stone: large carved-oak *Altar (c. 1520), with scenes from the Passion (school of Calcar, p. 19); Virgin and Child, French work of 1300; marble figures from the old high-altar of the cathedral (1350); painted angels of the Cologne school (ca. 1530); single figures from altars of the Rhenish and Antwerp schools. — Between the windows: Watercolour copies of the frescoes in the chapter-room at Brauweiler (p. 15).

To the right on the groundfloor are five rooms with plaster casts; to the left are a room containing the model of the monument of Frederick William III. (p. 61) and another containing old mural paintings (Story of the Undutiful Son), from the Glesch House in the Hohe-Strasse. In the adjoining rooms is the *Kunst-Verein Exhibition of Pictures*, changed from time to time.

The STAIRCASE is adorned with *Frescoes by Steinle* (1860-61), illustrative of the history of art and civilization at Cologne.

On the one side the *Roman and Romanesque Periods:* Constantine the Great (324-337), Charlemagne (768-814) with Eginhard, Alcuin, and Paulus Diaconus, etc. Between the two emperors is St. Helena with her attendants. In the corner adjoining Charlemagne are the most famous archbishops of Cologne: St. Hildebold (p. 44) with the plan of the old cathedral, St. Bruno (d. 965) with the church of St. Pantaleon, Heribert (d. 1021) with the church of the Apostles, and Anno (p. 45) with the church of St. Gereon. Next to these is the Frankish queen Plectrudis (p. 60), with the plan of St. Maria im Capitol. — On the other side is the *Mediæval Period:* in the centre Albertus Magnus, the learned Dominican; on his right is Conrad of Hochstaden (p. 50); farther on are painters of Cologne (p. 45); then the two burgomasters welcoming a vessel of the Hanseatic League. — On the central wall the *Renaissance and Modern Period:* to the left, Rubens receiving the order for the altar-piece of St. Peter's church (p. 63); Winckelmann studying the Laocoon; in the centre the brothers Boisserée and Friedrich von Schlegel; to the right, Wallraf and Richartz, the founders of the museum. Here also is a fresco of the *Resumption of the Building of the Cathedral.*

The UPPER FLOOR contains the *Picture Gallery. Its most important section from a technical point of view is that containing the works of the Early Cologne School; but some excellent Dutch works of the 17th cent., two important canvases by Rubens, and the large Murillo acquired in 1898 will interest even the unprofessional visitor. The works of the Italian schools and the modern paintings are of less importance.

From the STAIRCASE (I) we enter the rooms to the right, containing the earlier paintings, and traverse them to the other end.

ROOMS II, IIa, and III. Cologne School (ca. 1350-1510). To the right: *Unknown Masters,* 1. Triptych, Crucifixion (about 1350), 4, 5. Annun-

ciation and Presentation in the Temple (about 1370), 2, 3. SS. John and Paul (about 1370). — *Meister Wilhelm* (about 1380), 8. Crucifixion, 9. Eight saints, 13. Virgin with a bean-blossom (now suspected, with some plausibility, to be a forgery of the first half of the 19th cent.); 36, 37. *Master of the Small Passion,* Annunciation (ca. 1400); *Meister Stephan Lochner* (d. 1451), **64. Madonna in an arbour of roses with angels, 65. SS. Mark, Barbara, and Luke, 66. SS. Ambrose, Cecilia, and Augustine, *63. Last Judgment. 367. *Westphalian Master* (about 1420), Crucifixion, with numerous figures. — *Master of the Life of Mary* (ca. 1460-90; so called from a series of pictures at Munich), *131. Crucifixion, with the Virgin, St. John, and Mary Magdalen, *134. Madonna and St. Bernard, 137. The Saviour, 138. St. Ægidius, 139, 140. Annunciation, *141. Descent from the Cross (1480; the wings, SS. Andrew and Thomas, are school-pieces). *Master of the Glorification of Mary,* 128. Glorification of the Virgin, 129. St. Anna with the Madonna and saints (view of Cologne from the harbour), 130. Four saints (view of Cologne from the land-side); *147-154. *Master of the Lyversberg Passion,* The Lyversberg Passion, a series of 8 pictures on a gold ground (formerly belonging to the Lyversberg family). — *Master of St. Severin* (ca. 1500; comp. p. 57), 189. Adoration of the Magi, 188. Last Judgment; *169. *Master of the Holy Kin-*

ship, The Kindred of the Madonna, on the wings SS. Rochus and Nicasius (right) and SS. Gudula and Elizabeth (left; after 1500). *Master of the Altar of St. Bartholomew* (ca. 1500; so called from the picture in Munich), *184. Altar-piece, a triptych: in the centre Christ appearing to the doubting Thomas, inside the wings, the Madonna with St. John, and St. Hippolytus with St. Afra; 183. Virgin and Child; 185. Altar of the Holy Cross, in the centre Christ on the Cross, on the wings John the Baptist and SS. Cecilia, Alexius, and Agnes.

Room IV. Various Schools (ca. 1400-1500). No. 426. *French Master,* The Holy Kinship; *Follower of Roger van der Weyden,* Descent from the Cross (triptych); 489. *Hieronymus Bosch,* Adoration of the Shepherds; 486. *Dutch School,* Holy Family; 488. *Gerrit von Haarlem,* Crucifixion; 422. *School of Dirck Bouts,* Story of Job; 359. *Master of Frankfort,* Madonna (triptych).

Room V. German Schools (15-16th cent.). No. 385. *A. Dürer* (studio-piece), Piper and drummer (belonging to the 'Job' painting mentioned on p. 297); *Lucas Cranach the Elder,* 403. Mary Magdalen, 404. Christ and St. John; 383. *M. Grünewald,* St. Anthony.

Room VI. Netherlandish Schools (16th cent.). No. 448 et seq. Large panel-paintings by the *Master of Linnich;* 492. *Jacob van Amsterdam,* Crucifixion; *442. *Master of the Death of Mary,* triptych, in the centre the death of Mary, inside the wings saints and donors (1515?); 478. *School of the Master of the Death of Mary,* Pietà (triptych); 437. *Herri met de Bles,* Portrait; 463. *Barend van Orley,* The Magi; 428. *Jean Bellegambe,* Holy Family; 499. *M. van Heemskerck,* Adoration of the Shepherds.

Room VII. Cologne School (16th cent.). *Barth. de Bruyn the Elder,* 249. Burgomaster Browiller, 264. Pietà, 251. Adoration of the Magi, 265. Crucifixion; *Anton Woensam of Worms,* 211. Holy Kinship, 212. Crucifixion; *B. de Bruyn the Younger,* 300, 301. Hermann von Wedich and his wife, 293. Adoration of the Magi (triptych). — We return to Room V, and thence enter (to the right) —

Room VIII. Italian Schools. On the end-wall are paintings of the early-Sienese school; also, 516. *Neri di Bicci,* 522. *B. Mainardi,* Madonna and saints. — 535. *Style of Boccaccio Boccaccino,* Portrait; *552. *Francesco Francia,* Madonna. — 534. *Seb. del Piombo,* Holy Family (original in Naples); 542. *Tintoretto,* Portrait; 543. *Paris Bordone,* Bathsheba; 573. *Mattia Preti,* Judith. — Also: 579. *Claude Lorrain,* Landscape with Cupid and Psyche. *577. *Murillo,* Vision of St. Francis of Assisi; the Saviour and the Virgin appear to the saint in the chapel of the Portiuncula, while angels strew roses on the altar in token that his prayer has been heard (painted after 1670 for the Capuchins of Seville and acquired in 1898 from Prince Alphonse of Bourbon). — We cross the hall to —

Room X. Flemish School (16-17th cent.). To the right, 680. *G. van Honthorst,* Adoration of the Shepherds; 617. *Corn. de Vos,* Family portraits. — 615. *Snyders,* Still-life; *606. *Rubens,* St. Francis of Assisi receiving the stigmata (painted ca. 1617 for the old Capuchin church at Cologne); 632. *D. Ryckaert III.,* Cobbler. — **604. *Rubens,* Juno and Argus, originally in the Palazzo Durazzo at Genoa (1611); 622, 623. *A. van Dyck*(?), Portraits of Jabach (p. 63), school-pieces. — *Jordaens,* 614. Prometheus, 612, 613. Portraits; 605. *Rubens,* Holy Family (probably by pupils; ca. 1636); 607. *A. van Dyck* (here ascribed to *Rubens*), Four negroes' heads (original in Brussels). — To the right is —

Room XI. Dutch Schools (16-17th cent.). To the right, 661. *Benj. Gerritsz Cuyp,* Camp-scene; 689. *M. J. van Mierevelt,* Portrait (1633); *673. *Jan van Goyen,* Landscape; *Jac. Gerritsz Cuyp,* 662. Children with a sheep (1638), 663. Portrait (1643). — *716. *Jan Steen,* Capture of Samson; 724. *Pieter Verelst,* Old woman; *647. *A. van Beyeren,* Breakfast; 649. *Terburg,* Portrait; 688. *J. van der Meer*(?), Dutch wharf. — 654, 655. *Corn. Janssens,* Portraits (1651); 668. *K. du Jardin,* Italian landscape.

ROOM XII (corner-room). Dutch paintings of the 17th cent. and other works, formerly in the possession of Fuchs, the sculptor: 629. *D. Teniers the Younger* (?), Temptation of St. Anthony; 711. *S. van Ruysdael*, Tavern by a river; 674. *Dirck Hals*, Genre-scene (1629); 727. *R. van Vries*, Landscape; 670. *G. van den Eeckhout* (?), Esther and Haman; 693. *J. M. Molenaer*, Peasant interior; 675. *W. C. Heda*, Still-life (1652); 712. *J. van Ruysdael*, Landscape; 666. *Dirck van Delen*, Prodigal Son.

We now reach the COLLECTION OF MODERN PAINTINGS (19th cent.), most of which are of the Düsseldorf and Munich schools.

ROOM IX' (Kaiser-Saal; to the right of R. XI, opposite the staircase): 784. *S. Meister*, Frederick William IV. as Crown Prince (1834); 828. *W. Camphausen*, King William saluted by his troops after the battle of Sedan, with Bismarck, Moltke, and Roon among his retinue (1872); 929. *F. A. von Kaulbach*, Emp. William II., in his uniform as an admiral.

ROOM XIII (straight on from R. X). To the right: 776, 774. *K. Begas*, Family of the painter (1821, 1826); 768. *Fr. Overbeck*, Patrons of art (cartoon designed by Cornelius); 586. *J. L. David*, Pericles by the dead body·of his son; 949-952. Studies by *Ingres*. — ROOM XIV. 841. *L. Rosenfelder*, Beside the coffin of Henry IV. in Speyer; 845. *Ed. Geselschap*, Musical party; 846. *R. S. Zimmermann*, The Schrannentag; 869. *O. Begas*, Caritas.

ROOM XV. To the right, 902. *Liezen-Mayer*, Queen Elizabeth signing the death-warrant of Queen Mary Stuart; 823. *A. Achenbach*, Departure of a steamer (1870); *859. *G. Richter*, Queen Louise (1879); 836. *B. Vautier*, Funeral-feast (1866); 813. *J. Schrader*, Cromwell by the sick-bed of his daughter; *Lessing*, 793. Monastery-court in winter (1828), 794. Landscape (1860); 789. *Ed. Bendemann*, Mourning Jews in exile (1832); 795. *J. W. Schirmer*, Italian landscape (1847); 826. *Henry Ritter*, The middy's scolding; 829. *Chr. Böttcher*, Summer-evening on the Rhine; 955. *C. Troyon*, Landscape (1841); 888. *F. Defregger*, The wrestling match (1870).

ROOM XVI. *A. Schreyer*, Wallachian diligence; 934a. *Robert Haug*, Skirmish; 924, 925. *J. Sperl*, Landscapes with figures by *W. Leibl*; 935. *W. Firle*, 'Forgive us our trespasses' (1898); 926a. *Fr. von Uhde*, Family concert; 931. *Fr. Neuhaus*, Frederick William I. and ·the Protestants of Salzburg; *W. Leibl*, 923. Portrait of Pallenberg, *921. Father of the painter (1866); 970. *Munkacsy*, Village-hero; 895. *Lenbach*, Leo XIII (1885); *R. Böcklin*, Castle on the sea captured by pirates (1886); *F. Stuck*, Portrait of the painter and his wife.

ROOM XVIa (upper cloister): 917. *K. Haider*, Schliersee maiden; 971. *Munkacsy*, Old woman; 906, 907. *Gabriel Max*, *922. *Leibl*, 889, 890. *Defregger*, Studies of heads; 876. *L. Knaus*, The empty dish; 930. *Schönleber*, Dutch coast; 918. *E. Grützner*, In the private library; 911, 912. *K. Seibels*, Landscapes with cattle; 955a. *Calame*, Mountain in a storm; no numbers, *J. Bretz*, Corn-sheaves; *F. Westendorp*, Béguinage at Bruges; *E. te Peerdt*, Park-scene, Winter-landscape; 925a. *Steinhausen*, The painter and his wife; 903a. *H. Thoma*, Summer happiness; *L. von Hofmann*, Surf; *G. Kuehl*, Cook laughing; 929a. *H. Zügel*, Under the willows; 938b. *Schreuer*, Carnival at Cologne; *E. Hardt*, Landscape on the Lower Rhine; *Neven du Mont*, Equestrian portrait; *M. Stern*, Nurses; *A. Schinnerer*, Mountain-festival.

The staircase between Rooms XIII and XIV ascends to the SECOND FLOOR, with a *Collection of Engravings* and another room containing modern pictures.

ROOM XVII. 913. *A. von Werner*, Moltke at Sedan; 854. *K. Becker*, The crowning of the poet Ulrich von Hutten; 887. *O. Schwerdgeburth*, Faust's Easter promenade; 892. *G. F. Deiker*, Boar-hunt; 963. *Nic. de Keyser*, ·After the battle of Worringen (p. 45); 867. *C. Piloty*, Galileo in his cell.

Adjoining the S. side of the Museum is the **Church of the Minorites** (Pl. F, 4), an early-Gothic building of simple but handsome proportions, probably built in 1220-60, and restored in 1860. The large window above the portal in the principal façade and the elegant spire, rebuilt in the 18th cent. in the style of the original, are specially striking. The fine sacristy has a round pillar in the centre. — In front of the church is a handsome bronze monument (1903) to *Adolf Kolping* (d. 1865), founder of the working-men's unions.

Between the Cathedral and the Museum, at the Wallrafs-Platz (p. 52), begins the narrow HOHE-STRASSE, or HOCH-STRASSE (Pl. E, D, 4), the busiest street in Cologne, which with its prolongations (Marzellen-Str. and Eigelstein to the N., Hochpforte and Severin-Str. to the S.) intersects the whole city from N. to S. and contains many attractive shops. The street is gradually being widened in accordance with a recent regulation which requires that all new buildings shall be set behind the present street-line. Immediately to the left is the *Stollwerckhaus*, a large office-building in a modern style, erected in 1907 from the plans of K. Moritz. To the right, near the centre of the street, is the *Königin-Augusta-Halle*, or *Passage*, an arcade with shops. Farther on, to the left, in the Augustiner-Platz, is a bronze *Statue of Bismarck*, by F. Schaper (1879).

In the Waidmarkt (Pl. C, D, 4), at the end of the Hochpforte, is the *Hermann Joseph Fountain*, by W. Albermann (1894), recalling a legend of Cologne. — Close by is the old church of —

St. George, consecrated in 1067, originally a plain Romanesque columnar basilica, with a crypt of the same character (now restored). The porch dates from 1536.

At the end of the Severin-Str. (tramway No. 9, p. 42), to the left, somewhat back from the street, is **St. Severin** (Pl. B, 4), which stands upon the site of a Christian church built as early as the 4th cent., and has been often destroyed. The present church was consecrated in 1237 and was thoroughly restored in 1880. The effective quadrangular tower was erected in 1393-1411 and was provided with a new spire in 1905-6; the nave was furnished with new vaulting in 1479; the baptismal chapel, adorned with stained glass, dates from 1505.

The sarcophagus of St. Severin with a roof-shaped lid, the excellent mountings of a door of the 12th cent., a copper-gilt reading-desk in the form of an eagle, and the Gothic choir-stalls will repay inspection. The *Master of St. Severin* (p. 54) takes his appellation from two early-Cologne pictures in the sacristy.

For the *Severins-Tor* and the *Ring-Strasse*, see pp. 68, 67.

b. The Old Town to the E. of the Hohe-Strasse.

Between the Hohe Strasse and the Rhine are situated several important buildings, not far from each other. Another relic of the

Roman period is also preserved here in the shape of the *Römer-gang*, a subterranean passage or drain constructed of massive blocks of tufa (adm., see p. 43). It is reached by a winding staircase in the restaurant 'Im Römer' (Unter Goldschmied 48; Pl. E, 4). The passage is about 7 ft. high and 4 ft. wide and has been explored for 120 yds. By the entrance are a few Roman remains.

A bronze *Statue of Field Marshal Moltke*, by Schaper, was erected in 1881 in the Laurenz-Platz (Pl. E, 4), a little to the S. — The Portalsgasse leads immediately to the left to the Rathaus-Platz.

The **Rathaus* (Pl. E, 4, 5; adm., see p. 43) stands on the sub-structions of a Roman stronghold (probably the Prætorium), of the arches of which some remains are still visible in the cellar. The oldest part of the building (14th cent.) is the central portion (with the Hansa-Saal), looking towards the Rathaus-Platz. In 1569-71 a *Portico* in the Renaissance style was built in front of this, from the plans of *Wilhelm Vernickel* (restored in 1881), bearing Latin inscriptions and reliefs (Samson; Daniel; Burgomaster Gryn's fight with the lion, see below). The handsome, five-storied *Tower* was built in 1407-14, from the proceeds of the fines imposed upon noble families in 1396. Most of the statuettes with which it was adorned have been replaced by modern substitutes. — The E. portions of the structure, facing the Altenmarkt, were erected in 1549-50; the façade, richly ornamented with reliefs and statues, was altered in 1591, but restored by Raschdorff in the original style in 1870.

The Löwenhof, built by *Lorenz* in 1540 in the Renaissance style, then newly introduced into Germany, is so named in reference to the tradition that Archbishop Engelbert sought the life of Burgomaster Gryn (1264), and threw the obnoxious citizen into a lion's den in his palace, from which, however, his intended victim contrived to escape unhurt.

The Muschel-Saal (shell-room), richly decorated in the rococo style in 1761, is adorned with tapestry executed by Vos from drawings by Wouverman, and formerly belonging to Elector Clement Augustus. — The Hansa-Saal, or Hanseatic Hall (90 ft. long, 24 ft. wide, 32 ft. high), on the first floor of the Rathaus, now used for meetings of the municipal council, is said to be that in which the first general meeting of the League took place on 19th Nov., 1367. The S. wall is entirely occupied by nine rich canopies, with large figures vigorously executed in stone, representing Pagan, Jewish, and Christian heroes (Hector, Alexander the Great, Cæsar; Joshua, David, Judas Maccabæus; Charlemagne, King Arthur, Godfrey de Bouillon); above these, but smaller, Charles IV., who fortified the town and presented it with the privileges of a market, as the figures on the right and left indicate. In the windows are the armorial bearings of the different imperial families of Germany, on the long wall those of forty-five patrician families of Cologne, on the ceiling those of the burgomasters of Cologne, from 1346 to the downfall of the independence of the city. The two upper series are the arms of the twenty-two guilds. — The *Propheten-Kammer*, now fitted up as a library, contains the new *Municipal Silver Plate*, consisting of magnificent table ornaments made in Cologne. — The former *Rats-Saal* is in the tower. The fine door, adorned with intarsia, was executed by *Melchior Reidt* in 1603; to the same period belong the stucco ceiling, ornamented with medallions of the emperors, and the door of the committee-room, transferred hither from the Arsenal. — The part of the building between the Hansa-Saal and the Rats-Saal has been adorned with modern carved panelling and mural paintings in the Gothic style.

In the RATHAUS-PLATZ, to the left, is the late-Gothic *Chapel* of the Rathaus, which formerly contained the Dombild (p. 51), and was consecrated in 1426. The spire is of graceful proportions; the sacristy dates from 1474. To the right is an edifice known as the *Spanish Building*, erected in 1611-17 after Flemish models, and restored in 1886.

On the right side of the Martin-Str., a little to the S. of the Rathaus, is the *Gürzenich (Pl. E, 4), with its pinnacles and turrets, built in 1441-52 at a cost of 80,000 florins, to serve as a 'Herren Tanzhaus' and banquet-hall on occasions when the Town Council desired to entertain distinguished guests with a magnificence worthy of the city. Besides the 'Gürzenich' property the Council purchased several other pieces of ground to form a site for this imposing building. The architect was *Johann von Büren*. The first grand festival was held here in 1475 in honour of Emperor Frederick III. In the 17th and 18th centuries the large saloon fell into decay, and was used as a magazine till 1857, when, after undergoing a thorough renovation at the hands of Jul. Raschdorff, it was restored to its original uses. This is the finest of the ancient secular edifices of Cologne.

Above the E. gateways are statues of *Agrippa* and *Marsilius*, the founder and the defender of Cologne in the Roman period, executed by Mohr, painted by Kleinertz in the ancient style, and erected in 1859 in place of the old ones, which had become injured by exposure to the weather.

Interior (adm., see p. 43). On the groundfloor is the former magazine, converted by Herr Weyer in 1875 into a fine EXCHANGE HALL (no adm. in the morning). The handsome STAIRCASE was added in 1890-91. — On the first floor is the spacious *FEST-SAAL (174 ft. long, 72 ft. broad), with a gallery, borne by twenty-two richly carved wooden columns. The modern stained-glass windows represent the armorial bearings of Jülich, Cleve, Berg, and Mark, the mediæval allies of Cologne, with St. Peter as the patron-saint of the city, two Imperial eagles, the arms of Cologne itself, those of six burgomasters of the period when the building was first erected, and those of the twenty-two guilds. The two large *Chimney Pieces* of the 15th century, richly carved with scenes from the history of the town, are worthy of inspection. The walls are adorned with a fine representation of the Procession on the completion of the cathedral in 1880, by *Camphausen*, the two *Röbers*, *Beckmann*, and *Baur*. — The ANTECHAMBER ('Kleine Gürzenich' or 'Isabellen-Saal') is adorned with mural paintings by Schmitz, representing the entry of the Empress Isabella in 1235, the legend of the Cologne wood-cutting expedition (*viz.* that Marsilius saved the town from a beleaguering enemy by sending out armed women against them on the pretext of felling wood), and the Festival of St. John (a symbolical washing away of the evil of the year in the Rhine, mentioned by Petrarch, who visited Cologne in 1333). — Concerts and ball, see p. 41.

The Martin-Str. ends at the *Lichhof* (Pl. D, 4), beside the church of St. Maria im Capitol. Immured in the N. side of the Platz is the main archway of the *Pfaffentor* (*Porta Paphia*; Pl. 'Pf.'), a fortification of the Roman period, and until 1826 preserved opposite

the W. side of the cathedral. It bears the inscription C. C. A. A.
(*i. e.* Colonia Claudia Ara Agrippinensis), below which the name of
Gallienus appears as that of the builder (259-268).

The church of *St. Maria im Capitol* (*Zint Märjen* in local
speech; Pl. D, 4), a cruciform edifice in the Romanèsque style, is
constructed on an imposing and somewhat peculiar plan. The choir
and transept terminate in semicircular apses with an ambulatory
round each, and impart to the E. end of the building the trefoil
shape, of which this is the earliest example
(ca. 1100). The vaulting of the aisles dates
from the beginning of the 12th cent., the upper
portion of the choir from the beginning of the

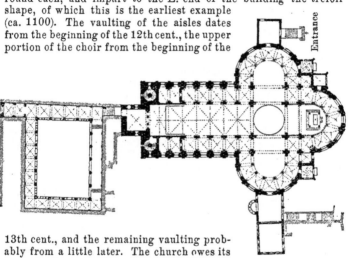

13th cent., and the remaining vaulting probably from a little later. The church owes its
name to the ancient tradition that this site
was once occupied by the Roman Capitol. The original edifice was
erected at least as early as 696 and is said to have been built by
Plectrudis, wife of Pepin of Héristal (d. 714) and stepmother of
Charles Martel.

The church, which has other entrances in the Marien-Platz and in
the Casino-Str. (No. 6), is not open for inspection until 12 noon. Best
light about midday.

The INTERIOR was decorated in 1870 with frescoes, begun by *Steinle*
(paintings in the apse), and completed by *Göbbels* from the designs of
Essenwein and *Klein*. — In the W. vestibule are some tombstones belonging to the Romanesque period. The richly sculptured organ-loft
(originally the rood-screen), which conceals the W. gallery, was brought
from Malines (1524). — At the beginning of the N. aisle is a painting
by *Hans Baldung Grien* (Death of the Virgin; 1521). — The modern
high-altar was designed by *Essenwein*. — The oaken door which leads
into the apse of the N. transept, decorated with very prominent reliefs,
dates from the foundation of the church. The S. (Hardenrath's) chapel
(of 1466) contains fine stained glass. In the Archive Room is a late-
Romanesque portable altar. — The fine CRYPT, with its nave and aisles,
its quadrangular chapels, and its side-chambers, corresponds with the

form of the choir. It contains the tomb of Plectrudis (12th cent.), and some ancient mural paintings. — The Romanesque CLOISTERS, beside the entrance in the Casino-Str., are quite built up.

We quit the Lichhof by the Gothic *Dreikönigen-Törchen* on the S. side. In the direction of the Rhine, Rheingasse No. 8, is the **Templars' Lodge** (Pl. D, 5), a handsome Romanesque edifice, with round-arched windows, niches, and corbie-stepped gables, dating from the 12th or the beginning of the 13th century. It was the family residence of the 'Overstolzen', a powerful family of mediæval Cologne, and was bought by the town in 1836 and judiciously restored. It is now used by the Chamber of Commerce. — A little to the S., in the Filzengasse, is the Protestant *Trinity Church* (Pl. D, 4, 5), in the early-Christian basilica style, designed by Stüler (1860). — For the church of *St. Maria in Lyskirchen* and the *Harbour*, see p. 62.

The street known as 'Am Malzbüchel' leads to the N.E. from the upper end of the Rheingasse to the HEUMARKT (Pl. D, E, 5), one of the largest squares in the town. Here rises the **Monument of Frederick William III.**, erected in 1878 to commemorate the liberation of the Rhenish provinces from French domination and their union with Prussia.

The colossal equestrian statue of the king on a lofty pedestal is surrounded by statues of the principal statesmen and warriors who coöperated with him in raising Prussia to the rank of a first-class power (Blücher, Stein, Arndt, Humboldt, etc.). The reliefs on the sides indicate the progress of the Rhenish provinces in science, art, commerce, and manufactures. The chief figure and the statues on one side are by *Bläser* of Cologne (1813-74), the rest by *Drake*, and others. The reliefs are by *Calandrelli*.

In the adjacent ALTENMARKT (Pl. E, 5) is a monumental *Fountain,* in the German Renaissance style, after a design by *Albermann* (1885). The chief figure is a statue of *Johann von Werth* (d. 1651), a famous cavalry general in the Thirty Years' War; the figures of a peasant and maiden at the sides refer to the tradition that he became a soldier on account of a love-disappointment.

The Zoll-Strasse leads from the Altenmarkt to the Rhine. In this street is the late-Romanesque church of **Gross St. Martin* (Pl. E, 5), probably founded by Abp. Bruno (p. 63) ca. 960. After the conflagration of 1150, the nave and aisles were rebuilt, and the massive E. portion, with its imposing tower (270 ft. high) surrounded by four corner-turrets, was taken in hand. The nave (completed about 1240) and the W. front show traces of French influence. Only half of the W. portico is now extant. The whole building has been restored by Nagelschmidt.

The INTERIOR (visitors ring at the screen; fee 50 pf. for 1-5 pers.; sacristan, Zoll-Str. 7a) has been decorated from the designs of *Essenwein.* The stained glass was executed in Innsbruck. To the left of the entrance are a marble font, adorned with lions' heads and foliage, said to have been presented by Pope Leo III. in 803, and the *Rood Altar* of

1509. The handsome *High Altar* and the side-altars are modern; beside the last altar in the N. aisle is the tomb of the titular bishop Hermann J. Schmitz, by Mengelberg (1902), with a picture in mosaic. Fine modern tiled pavement from designs by Kleinertz.

The Zoll-Str. ends at the **Stapelhaus** (Pl. E, 5), built in 1558-69 and restored in the original style in 1900-1. Besides a restaurant (p. 40) this edifice accommodates the municipal *Museum of Natural History* (adm., see p. 43), the entrance to which is in the Mautgasse.

On the *First Floor* are the Vertebrata, including a large collection of native birds, a collection of antlers, and various biological groups realistically arranged. — On the *Second Floor* are the less developed animals, the minerals and fossils, and an extensive collection of the mammalia and birds of E. Africa.

A large *Central Market* (Pl. D, 5) was opened in 1904 amid the quaint old lanes between the Heumarkt and the Rhine. — Farther up the river, in the street 'An Lyskirchen', is the ancient church of *St. Maria in Lyskirchen* (Pl. D, 5), rebuilt in the transition style at the beginning of the 13th cent. and embellished with ceiling-paintings and recently restored throughout (sacristan, An Lyskirchen 10).

Near this point are two bridges across the Rhine, *viz.* the old **Bridge-of-Boats** (*Schiffbrücke;* Pl. D, E, 6) and the **Iron Bridge** (Pl. E, F, 5), completed in 1910 and named *Hohenzollern-Brücke*. The latter (457 yds. long), built by Schwechten on the site of an older bridge (1855-59), accommodates four lines of railway and a roadway 52 ft. in breadth. It is adjoined by equestrian statues in bronze, of Frederick William IV. (by Bläser), William I. (by Drake), Frederick III. (by Tuaillon), and William II. (by Tuaillon). The first two of these were originally erected in 1867, the other two are new. The approach to the bridge on the left bank affords a good survey of the choir of the cathedral. A good view of the town is obtained by taking a walk over the iron bridge and back by the bridge-of-boats. — *Deutz*, on the right bank, see p. 70.

c. The Old Town to the W. of the Hohe-Strasse.

In the Brückengasse (on the right) is the late-Gothic church of *St. Columba* (Pl. E, 4), the kernel of which is a Romanesque columnar basilica. The church-treasury is rich. — In the Glockengasse, on the left, are the *Synagogue* (Pl. E, 4), built in 1859-61, and the *Schauspielhaus* (Pl. E, 3; p. 41), erected in 1872.

The Kreuzgasse and Antonsgasse lead hence to the S. to the convent and church of **St. Cecilia** (Pl. D, 3, 4), the latter a very ancient building, rebuilt as early as 950, and again in the 12th century, on which occasion parts of the edifice of the 10th cent. appear to have been retained. It contains a curious crypt, which is wrongly described as a remnant of the oldest episcopal church

.built by St. Maternus. Good Romanesque relief above the arch of the N. door. The interior has lately been restored; the painting of the choir dates from 1300, but the pictures in the apse and nave are modern. Opposite (N.E.) is the *Wolkenburg*, resembling the Gürzenich, the meeting-place of the *Männer-Gesangverein* (p. 41).

Adjoining St. Cecilia's is the church of **St. Peter** (Pl. D, 3), begun in 1524 and successfully restored in 1890-92 (entr. Sternengasse 72; sacristan No. 65).

The INTERIOR has been redecorated, with the aid of the old painting, — The choir contains a late-Gothic carved altar with good pictures on the wings (fee 50 pf.), and beautiful stained-glass *Windows of 1528 and 1530 (Bearing of the Cross, Crucifixion, Descent from the Cross). In the chapel to the right of the choir (but concealed by a mediocre altar-piece) is the *Crucifixion of St. Peter, by *Rubens*, recovered from Paris in 1814. This fine picture, one of the most vigorous works of the master, but repellent owing to its startling fidelity to nature, was painted by order of the Jabach family in 1638-40 in memory of Herr Eberhard Jabach, the well-known patron of art (d. 1636). It is shown by the sexton for the somewhat exorbitant fee of 1½ *M*. Behind the altar reposes Jan Rubens (d. 1587), the father of the painter.

At the back of the two churches last described is situated the spacious **Bürger-Hospital** (Pl. D, 3), occupying nearly a whole block. It may be inspected in the afternoon (small fee to the attendant). — To the N.W. are the Neumarkt and the Apostles' Church (see below).

At the E. end of the Sternengasse (No. 10, left side), near the Hohe-Str., is a handsome house in which *Rubens* is erroneously said to have been born. The house bears an inscription and a relief above the door in memory of the illustrious master; and on the opposite side is an inscription recording (correctly) that *Marie de Médicis*, widow of Henri IV. of France, died here in exile in 1642.

The church of **St. Pantaleon** (Pl. C, 3; now a Protestant garrison church) was founded by *Archbishop Bruno* (953-965), brother of Emperor Otho the Great. The substructure of the towers, with its two-storied additions, belongs to the 11th century. The towers were rebuilt in 1891. The choir dating from the beginning of the 13th cent., was reconstructed in the 14th; the reticulated vaulting of the nave was erected in 1622. Archbishop Bruno and the Empress Theophano (d. 999) are buried in the church. There are some remains of Romanesque mural paintings in the E. transept and the side-chapels. The elaborate late-Gothic rood-loft now serves as an organ-gallery. — The street known as Vor den Siebenburgen leads hence to the S.E. to the church of *St. Maria in der Schnurgasse* (Pl. B, 3, 4), an interesting baroque building completed in 1716, while the Mauritius-Steinweg runs N.W. to the *Mauritius-Kirche* (Pl. D, 2, 3), built by Vincenz Statz in the Gothic style in 1861-65.

In the N.W. angle of the NEUMARKT (Pl. D, E, 3), a square planted with trees, the largest in the old town, rises the ***Apostles' Church** (Pl. E, 2, 3), a late-Romanesque structure with double transepts, a square W. tower, and a dome over the E. crossing,

flanked by two slender turrets. The choir and the arms of the E.
transept end in the trefoil form (comp. p. 45) with three spacious
rounded apses, adorned with two series of niches and a miniature
gallery above them. The church, which occupies the site of a still
earlier edifice, was originally erected about 1036 as a flat-roofed
basilica. About a century later the aisles were vaulted, the pilasters
in front of the pillars introduced, and the W. tower completed. The
choir was added ca. 1200, and the nave was vaulted about the same
time. The dome, the choir, and the transepts are magnificently
adorned with mosaics on a gold ground, executed since 1895 from
designs by Kleinertz and Stummel.

The two horses' heads affixed to the upper story of a house on the
N. side of the Neumarkt (No. 10), at the corner of the Richmod-Str., are
connected by tradition with the miraculous awakening of Richmodis,
wife of Knight Mengis von Aducht, from a trance. Her husband declared
he would sooner believe that his horses could ascend to the loft of his
house than that his wife should return from the tomb. Scarcely had he
spoken the words, however, when the heads of his horses were seen looking
from the upper window. In all probability the heads formed part of
the armorial bearings of Nicasius von Haquenay, who built the house.

In the Schildergasse, to the left, at the corner of the Krebs-
gasse, are the *Police Headquarters* (Pl. E, 3), built in 1907 in a
Romanesque style.

The Richmod-Str. (tramway No. 12, p. 42) and its continua-
tions lead direct to the church of St. Gereon (p. 65). — From the
end of the Richmod-Str. the busy BREITE-STRASSE (Pl. E, 3, 4) leads
to the E. back to the Wallraf-Richartz Museum (p. 52) and the
cathedral. In it, to the left, at the corner of the Langgasse, is the
new office of the *Kölnische Zeitung* ('Cologne Gazette'), by Müller-
Erkelenz (1906), with sculptures by P. Breuer.

d. The N. Quarters of the Old Town.

The Burgmauer (p. 52), beginning at the Dom-Kloster (p. 52),
and the busy KOMÖDIEN-STRASSE (Pl. F, 4, 3) lead to the W. to the
imposing *Law Courts* (Pl. E, F, 3), erected in 1884-93 (new building, see p. 70). In the Appellhof-Platz is the building of the *Bürger-
Gesellschaft* (a Roman Catholic club), completed in 1901 (p. 40).
In the Zeughaus-Str., the continuation of the Komödien-Str., are
the *Arsenal* (1601; l.) and the *Government Building* (1830; r.). —
Farther on, to the left, at the corner of the Apern-Str. (which leads
to the Apostles' Church, p. 63), rises the so-called *Römerturm*
(Pl. F, 3), or *Clarenturm*, an ancient round tower inlaid with stones
of different colours. It formed the N.W. angle of the ancient Roman
town (comp. p. 44). The upper part, with battlements, is modern. —
The Steinfeldergasse leads hence to the Church of St. Gereon; on
the right is the GEREONSDRIESCH (Pl. F, 3), planted with trees, and
on the left the GEREONSKLOSTER, the square whence the church is entered. Opposite the entrance is the *City Library (Stadt-Bibliothek;*

Pl. F, 3), with the *Archives,* built in the Gothic style in 1894-97 (adm., see p. 43; 220,000 vols.; printed guide 60 pf.).

The church of *St. Gereon* (Pl. F, 3), dedicated to the 318 martyrs of the Theban legion, with their captain Gereon, who, according to the legend, perished here in 286 during the persecution of the Christians under Diocletian, is an edifice of very peculiar style (recently thoroughly restored). The long Romanesque choir is adjoined by a decagonal nave in the Gothic style, with a quadrangular vestibule. The original structure, circular in form, with ten niches resembling those of the Nymphæum of the 'Minerva Medica' at Rome, dates from the time of Constantine the Great (4th cent.).

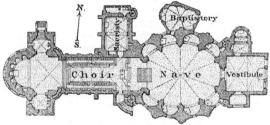

Archbishop Anno (d. 1075) added the choir and the spacious crypt. Towards 1190 the choir was rebuilt and the E. apse and towers added. In 1209-27 the round part of the church, having become dilapidated, was converted into the present decagonal nave, 154 ft. in height, 60 ft. in length, and 54 ft. in breadth, covered with groined vaulting, the eight shorter sides retaining the original niches. Other changes took place in the 14-15th cent., to which period belongs the vaulting of the choir and vestibule. The sacristan, who is generally to be found in the church in the morning (visitors knock), lives at Gereons-Kloster No. 4 (1-2 pers. 1 *M;* for more, 50 pf. each).

The VESTIBULE contains a few ancient tombstones. To the right is a small chapel added in 1897, with a Pietà by *J. Reiss.*

The INTERIOR, recently embellished with paintings by *Göbbels* after *Essenwein's* designs, presents an imposing appearance. In small chapels in the recesses of the nave, above which runs a gallery borne by short columns, are seen the stone sarcophagi of the martyrs, half built into the walls. Their skulls are arranged under gilded arabesques along the sides of the *Choir,* to which fifteen steps ascend. The carved choir-stalls date from the beginning of the 14th century. Above is some tapestry of the 18th cent., with scenes from the story of Joseph. The E. end of the choir is reached by seven steps more. — The *Sacristy,* in the purest Gothic style, dating from 1316, containing fine Gothic stained glass, and the octagonal *Baptistery* (adjoining the nave), with much-defaced mural paintings of the first half of the 13th cent., are also worthy of notice.

The CRYPT below the choir, with its three aisles borne by sixteen columns, dating (with the exception of the 12th cent. E. end) from the 11th cent., contains an interesting specimen of the art of that period:

viz. a *Mosaic Pavement*, the sections of which represent scenes from the lives of David and Samson, and the signs of the Zodiac. It was, perhaps, executed by Italian workmen, as similar scenes are very common in Italian churches. The fragments, which had got into disorder, were successfully restored and supplemented by the painter Avenarius in.1867-71.

The shortest route from the Gereonsdriesch (tramway No. 18, p. 42) to the Hansa-Platz and the *Museum of Industrial Art* (p. 69) is viâ the Klingel-Pütz and the Gereonsmühlengasse (Pl. F, G, 3). — On the left side of the Gereons-Str., which leads back to the cathedral, is situated the *Archiepiscopal Palace* (Pl. F, 3), whence the Hunnenrücken leads to the URSULA-PLATZ (Pl. F, G, 4).

St. Ursula (Pl. G, 4) occupies the site of a church of the 4th century. In the 11th cent. it existed as a flat-roofed basilica with galleries, but in the 13th cent. it received a vaulted roof. The square tower and early-Gothic choir (1287) also belong to the 13th century. The late-Gothic S. or fourth aisle was added in the 15th century. The entire edifice was restored in the original style in 1890-91.

The church is closed except during service, which ends about 10 a. m. (sacristan, Ursulagarten-Str. 1). — The N. aisle, near the choir, contains a monument, by *Johann Lenz*, erected in 1658 to *St. Ursula*, an English princess, who, according to the legend, when on her return from a pilgrimage to Rome, was barbarously murdered at Cologne with her 11,000 virgin attendants. The figure is in alabaster, with a dove at the feet. The bones of these virgin martyrs are preserved in cases, placed round the church. The legend is also illustrated by a series of old paintings, frequently retouched, on the side-wall on the left. Ten old pictures of the Apostles, to the left of the S. entrance, are painted on slabs of slate, one of them bearing the date 1224. Under the organ, by the pillar to the left, is a late-Gothic relief in stone, representing the Bearing of the Cross. Below is the sarcophagus of a child belonging to the family of the Frankish major-domo. — The GOLDENE KAMMER, or treasury (admission 1 ℳ), contains the fine late-Romanesque *Reliquary of St. Ætherius*, the *Reliquary of St. Ursula* (freely restored), several other reliquaries of the Gothic period, a carved rock-crystal chessman of the Carlovingian period, and Persian and late-Roman textiles.

The Marzellen-Str. leads hence to the Dom-Kloster (p. 52), passing the *Jesuits' Church* (Pl. F, 4), or *Church of the Assumption*, a late-Renaissance edifice (1618-29) on the site of an earlier building. The pulpit and high-altar are overladen with decoration; the communicants' bench is a masterpiece of workmanship in marble. The bells were cast with the metal of cannons taken by Tilly at Magdeburg, and presented by him to the church.

Just to the S.W. is the church of **St. Andreas** (Pl. F, 4), with a Romanesque nave (1223) and a raised Gothic choir (1414). It contains the fine brass-gilt late-Gothic 'Reliquary of the Maccabees' (with reliefs), the painted reliquary of Albertus Magnus (d. 1280; p. 54), a figure of St. Michael (15th cent.), and remains of frescoes (ca. 1330).

To the W. of the Jesuits' Church, in the street named 'An den Dominikanern', is the **Post Office** (Pl. F, 4), completed in 1893, an early-Gothic building with turrets at the corners. It is adorned with numerous statues. Inside are marble busts of Post-Master-

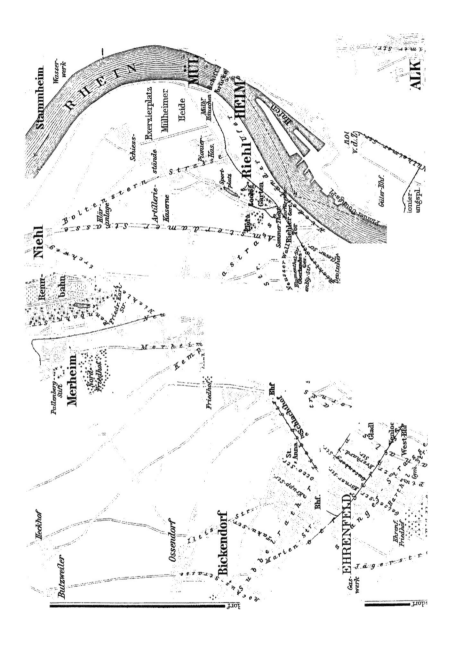

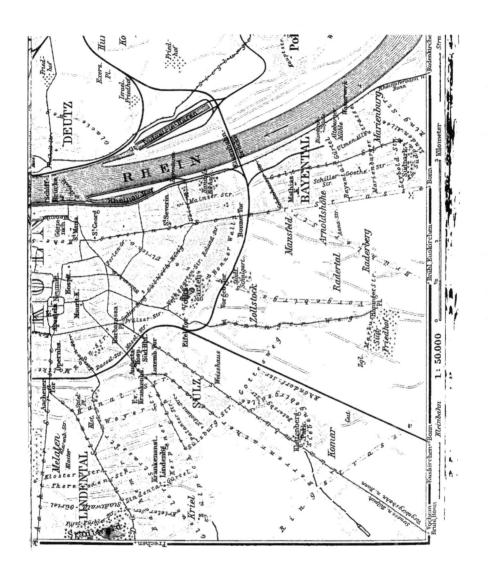

General Stephan (d. 1897) and Baron von Thurn-und-Taxis, the founder of the modern postal system (16th cent.). — Nearly opposite is the *Reichsbank*, or Imperial Bank, in an early-Gothic style (1897).

On the Rhine (Kaiser-Friedrich-Ufer; tramway No. 12, p. 42), near the N. end of the old town, is the church of **St. Cunibert** (Pl. G, 5), an excellent example of the transition style, consecrated by Archbp. Conrad in 1247 and restored in 1869-71. It is a vaulted basilica with two transepts and three towers.

The INTERIOR contains (in the choir and transepts) remains of good Romanesque mural paintings (restored by *Göbbels*), a picture of the school of *Meister Wilhelm*, and sculptures of the 14-16th cent. (Crucifixion). At the entrance to the choir is a fine colossal group of the Annunciation (late-Gothic; 1439). The choir has fine stained glass of the 13th cent. and encaustic mural paintings by *Welter* (1860). Fine modern organ.

e. The Ring-Strasse and the New Quarters of the City.

Tramways (Nos. 12, 16, and 18), see p. 42.

The most striking feature in the new town is the wide and handsome **Ring-Strasse,* or series of boulevards laid out since 1881, 3¹/₂ M. long, which completely encircles the old town and occupies the site of the old fortifications. Many of the streets expand into spaces laid out with flower-beds and trees. Fragments of the old city-wall and three mediæval gates are still extant, while the modern buildings are in many cases noteworthy.

At the S. end of the Ring-Strasse, on the new quay on the Rhine, stands the **Bayenturm** (Pl. B, 5) a square pinnacled tower of the 13-14th cent., now fitted up as a *Prehistoric Museum* (adm., see p. 43). Below the Bayenturm lies the *Rheinau-Hafen* (Pl. B, C, 5), a river-harbour, lined with warehouses, grain elevators, steam-cranes, and the like. Above the tower, on the Agrippina-Ufer, is the large *Harbour Railway Station*. Between the Agrippina-Ufer and the Römer Park stands the large **Commercial High School** *(Handels-Hochschule)*, built from Vetterlein's plans in 1905-7, the E. wing of which contains the *Museum of Trade and Industry* (open on week-days 2-5, adm. 50 pf.; free on Sun. & holidays, 10-2). Farther on is the new *Railway Bridge* (1910), with imposing gateways at each end. Beyond the bridge are the new quarter of the town called the *Bayental* and the villa-colony of *Marienburg*, with its handsome private residences and gardens. On the Oberländer Ufer are the massive *Bismarckturm* and the tower of the city water-works.

In the *Ubier-Ring* (Pl. A, 5), the S. section of the Ring-Strasse, are two notable new buildings in a baroque style: the *Royal Engineering School* (l.), built in 1901-4 by Schilling, and the *Rautenstrauch-Joest Museum* (r.), with ethnographical collections (1906; adm., see p. 43; guide 50 pf.). — On the right is the *Bottmühle* (Pl. B, 5), a tower surrounded by pleasure-grounds, formerly belonging to the fortifications. Beyond is the Stollwerck Chocolate Factory.

To the N. of the *Chlodwigs-Platz* (Pl. A, 4) is the handsome
Severins-Tor (Pl. A, 4), also a relic of the mediæval fortifications
(restored in 1895). — Adjacent is the church of *St. Severin* (p. 57).

From the Chlodwigs-Platz we follow the Carolinger-Ring to the
*Sachsen-Ring (Pl. B, 4, 3), both sides of which are occupied by
private villas and gardens. In the middle, opposite the new Gothic
Church of St. Paul (Pl. B, 3), is the *Ulrepforte*, a mediæval town-
gate, now connected with a cafe-restaurant. Farther on, on the
outside of a fragment of the old city-wall, is the *Ulre Monument*,
with an allegorical relief of the 14th cent. (restored in 1886), in
memory of the victory of the citizens over the soldiers of Abp.
Engelbert. — Several streets lead S.W. from the Sachsen-Ring to the
Volks-Garten (Pl. A, 2, 3; p. 41), with a lake and fountains. In the
Wormser-Platz (Pl. A, 3) is the *Luther-Kirche* (1905).

The *Salier-Ring* (Pl. B, C, 2), with the *Technical College*
(No. 32), leads to the Barbarossa-Platz (Pl. C, 2), a square adorned
with gardens and a fountain. In the *Hohenstaufen-Ring* (Pl. D, C, 2)
are the handsome *Hohenstaufen Baths* (p. 42). In the Zülpicher-
Platz, to the left, is the Roman Catholic *Herz-Jesu-Kirche*, by
Schmidt of Vienna (1892). To the N.W. is the Königs-Platz, with
a *Synagogue* (Pl. D, 1), erected in the Romanesque style in 1896-99.

In the short *Habsburger Ring* rises the **Opera House** (Pl.
D 2; p. 41), erected in the baroque style by *K. Moritz* (1900-1902).
The Atlantes in the vestibule are by Heller. The foyer is adorned
with paintings by Sascha Schneider (history of mankind). — Nearly
opposite, in the *Rudolfs-Platz*, an important tramway-centre, is
the **Hahnen-Tor** (Pl. E, 2), a massive town-gate of the early 13th
cent., with two towers, which has been restored and fitted up as a
Historical Museum of the City of Cologne (adm., see p. 43; visitors
ring). It contains chiefly objects and mementoes from the time
when Cologne was a free imperial city up to the end of the 18th
cent. (town-plans and views, banners, arms, Cologne stamps, dies,
and coins, and weights and measures).

We next reach the *Hohenzollern-Ring* (Pl. E, F, 2) and the
Kaiser-Wilhelm-Ring (Pl. F, 2). To the W. of the former is the
Rom. Cath. *Church of St. Michael* (Pl. E, 1), a large building in
the Lombard (early-Romanesque) style by E. Endler (1906). To the
W. of the Kaiser-Wilhelm-Ring lies the well-kept *Stadt-Garten*
(p. 41). In the square in front of it is the Protestant *Christus-
Kirche* (Pl. F, 2), by Hartel and Neckelmann, the interior of which
also deserves attention. In the gardens are a *Monument of Empress
Augusta* (1903) and farther on, on a rocky base surrounded by
a fountain-basin, a colossal bronze *Equestrian Statue of Emp.
William I.* (Pl. F, G, 2), 36 ft. high, by R. Anders (1897). On
the red granite base are seated figures of Father Rhine and Colonia.
— A little to the S.E. is the church of St. Gereon (p. 65).

In the *Hansa-Platz*, halfway down the *Hansa-Ring* (Pl. G, 3, 4), is a fragment of the old town-walls, known as the *Gereonsmühle.*

Adjacent stands the ***Museum of Industrial Art** (*Kunstgewerbe-Museum;* Pl. G, 3), erected in 1897-1900 by *Brantzky.* Adm., see p. 43; catalogue 50 pf.

Ground Floor. The glass-covered court is used for temporary exhibitions. From the vestibule we ascend the staircase on the right. — ROOM I. Mediæval ecclesiastical furniture and ornaments. In Case 1 are *Ivory Carvings, including the consecration-comb of St. Heribert (999-1021), Archbishop of Cologne, and an oriental ivory casket (13th cent.). The other cases contain carved caskets, enamels, embroideries, and metalwork. Wall 7, *Antependium from the church of St. Ursula (12th cent.; figures of saints of the 14th cent.). Gothic stained-glass windows (14-15th cent.). — ROOM II. Domestic furniture of the Gothic period (15th cent.). Also, figures of Justice (ca. 1510) and paintings on glass (Adoration of the Magi; 1474) from the Rathaus. — ROOM III. Early-Renaissance furniture, etc., from the Lower Rhine. Stained glass from the Carmelite church at Boppard (14th cent.) and from Altenberg (1505-32). — ROOM IV. Late-Renaissance room (Cologne); the wall-panelling and floor from the Spanish Building (p. 59). — ROOM V. Stoneware, tiles, and building-materials from the Lower Rhine. Stained glass of 1538 (Cologne). — ROOM VI. Cottage furniture and pottery (17-18th cent.). — ROOM VII. Industrial art of the Renaissance in Italy, France, and Spain. Wall 39. *Bronze door-knocker, by *Giovanni da Bologna.* Case 45. *Palissy Ware. Also, paintings on glass from Switzerland and Cologne (to the left, St. Catharine, by *A. Woensam*). — ROOM VIII. German furniture, metalwork, and ornaments of the High Renaissance period. *Stained Glass from Bâle, in the style of *Hans Holbein the Younger* (formerly at St. Blasien; 1528). — ROOM IX. Baroque furniture from Cologne, and blown-glass. Case 63. *Glass from Venice and Cologne.— GALLERIES X-XII. Iron and wood work from the late-Gothic period to the 17th century. In Gallery XII we may note the balcony-railing from Aix-la-Chapelle (1737).

First Floor. ROOM XIII (to the right). Dutch and Low German furniture (17th cent.). Dutch, German, French, Italian, and Swedish fayence (17-18th cent.). Stained glass from Cologne (17th cent.). — ROOM XIV. Furniture of the 18th century. Brussels tapestry by *Fr. van der Borcht* (ca. 1735). — ROOM XV. European porcelain of the 18th cent., the German potteries being especially well represented (*Cases 100 and 101, Höchst and Frankental porcelain). Wall 115. Sèvres porcelain. Case 91. Wedgwood and other English ware (18th cent.). Wall 108. Louis XVI. furniture. — GALLERY XXI. Cabinets 125-130. Book-bindings (14-18th cent.). Cabinets 131, 132. Cutlery and tools. Wall-cabinets 153, 154. Portions of the municipal silver-plate; modern porcelain and plaquettes. — ROOM XVI. Textile fabrics. — ROOM XVII. Oriental industrial art, including Chinese and Japanese porcelain and Indian metal-work, etc. On the walls, Oriental embroidery and textiles. — ROOM XVIII is used for temporary exhibitions. — Room XIX represents a Swiss room of the late-Renaissance period (1660). — GALLERY XX. Lace; furniture-ornaments in the Empire style (ca. 1800). — Gallery XXI is adjoined by the large PALLENBERG SALOON, fitted up from *M. Lechter's* designs at the expense of Herr Pallenberg (d. 1900). — GALLERY XXII. Embroideries; fans.

The first floor also accommodates the valuable **Library of Industrial Art,** including a collection of patterns (catalogues, 25 pf. & 2 ℳ). Adm., see p. 43 (entrance on the E. side of the building in the evening).

The new addition at the back of the museum, opened in 1910 and entered from the gallery of the glass-covered court, accommodates a valuable COLLECTION OF ECCLESIASTICAL ART, given to the city by Prebendary *Schnütgen.*

Farther on, on the right, is the *Commercial School* (1901), beyond which the Hansa-Ring is crossed by the railway.

The **Eigelstein-Tor** (Pl. G, 4), the N. fortified tower of the mediæval entrenchments, was restored in 1891, and is now fitted up, like the Hahnen-Tor (p. 68), as a *Historical Museum*, with models, views, portraits, and mementoes from the end of the 18th cent. on (adm., see p. 43). — The Ring-Strasse is terminated by the *Deutsche Ring* (Pl. H, 5), which is embellished with flower-beds, ponds, and fountains. At its E. end, facing the Rhine, on a massive granite base surrounded by shrubs, stands a bronze *Equestrian Statue of Emp. Frederick III.*, by Ad. Breuer (1903). — In the Riehler-Str. (Pl. H, 5) is the new building of the *Law Courts.*

The **Zoological Garden** (adm., see p. 43; tramways 12, 14, & 16, see p. 42; steamer, see p. 42), which lies about $^3/_4$ M. to the N. of the Deutsche Ring, is well laid out and contains a fine collection of animals. — Adjacent is the **Flora Garden** (adm., see p. 41), with a handsome winter-garden, a concert-room, a palm-house, and an *Aquarium*. On the S. side of the garden is the *Summer Theatre* (p. 41). — Beyond the Zoological Garden is the *Sport-Platz*, with cycling track, tennis courts, shooting ranges, and restaurant.

Along the Rhine, from this point to the Mülheim bridge-of-boats (p. 27), stretches the *Niederländer Ufer*, with large woodyards.

To the S.W. of the town (tramways Nos. 1 & 2, p. 42), is the suburb of Lindental, with many villas and a large hospital. Farther on is the **Stadtwald** *(Town Wood)*, a district 480 acres in extent, planted in 1895. In its S.E. part are the older park of the Kitschburg *(Haupt-Restaurant)* and the Big Pond (Grosser Teich); on the W. is a hill commanding a good view, and on the N., near the Aixla-Chapelle road (tramway No. 8, p. 42), is the pretty *Waldschenke.*

The extensive **Cemetery**, on the road to Aix-la-Chapelle, between the Hahnen-Tor (p. 68) and the Stadtwald, contains several fine monuments, including those of Canon Wallraf and Herr Richartz (p. 53), memorial monuments of the wars of 1866 and 1870-71, and a monument to the memory of French prisoners who died here.

On the right bank of the Rhine, opposite Cologne, lies **Deutz** (railway-station, see p. 39), the tête-de-pont of Cologne since the Roman period (see p. 44). It was incorporated with Cologne in 1888. The Roman Catholic *Church of St. Heribert* (Pl. D, 6), by Pickel, is in the Romanesque style and was finished in 1896. The treasury contains the sumptuous shrine of St. Heribert, of the year 1147. The town walls have recently been razed. — To the E. lies the industrial suburb of *Kalk* (now also incorporated with Cologne), with machine-shop, tool-factories, iron-foundries, and chemical works.

The **Königs-Forst** or *Royal Forest*, an extensive and undulating wooded district, intersected by many marked paths, is reached by the suburban railways mentioned at p. 42 (comp. the Map., p. 74).

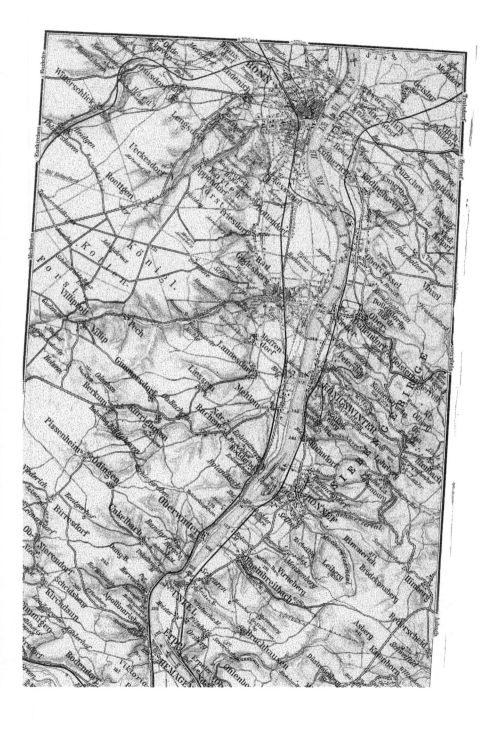

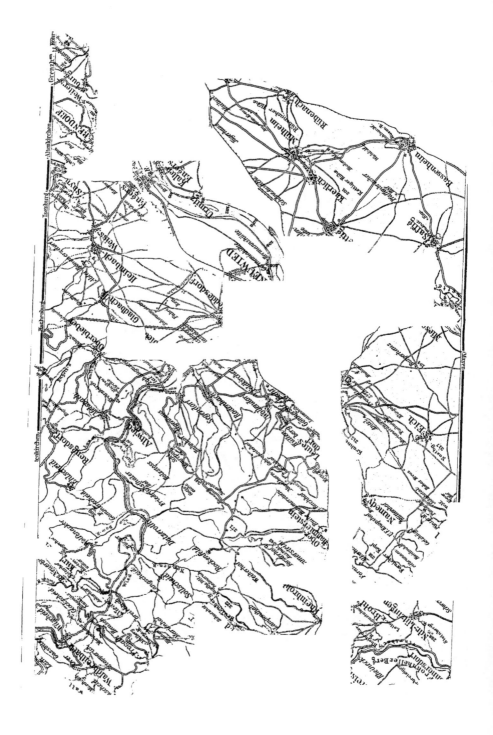

II. THE RHINE FROM COLOGNE TO COBLENZ. VALLEY OF THE LAHN. WESTERWALD.

11. From Cologne to Coblenz or Ehrenbreitstein by Railway.

Comp. Map, p. 74.

Travellers are entitled to break their journey once, and may afterwards proceed by the railway on either bank at their choice. The following are the recognized 'corresponding' stations: *Bonn* and *Beuel*, *Godesberg* and *Nieder-Dollendorf*, *Mehlem* and *Königswinter*, *Rolandseck* and
Honnef, *Oberwinter* and *Unkel*, *Remagen* and *Erpel*, *Sinzig* and *Linz*,
Nieder-Breisig and *Hönningen*, *Brohl* and *Rheinbrohl*, *Andernach* and
Fahr (or *Leutesdorf*), *Weissenthurm* and *Neuwied*. — Circular Tour tickets
entitle the holder to use the steamers (p. 85) also, but for a continuous
journey only, either up or down the river.

a. Railway on the Left Bank.

57 M. Railway in $1^{1}/_{2}$-$2^{3}/_{4}$ hrs. (fares 7 ℳ 40, 4 ℳ 40, 2 ℳ 90 pf.; express fares 8 ℳ 40, 5 ℳ 40, 3 ℳ 40 pf.). — Best views to the left. .

Cologne, see p. 39. After leaving the Central Station the train calls at the (2 M.) West Station and the (3 M.) South Station. — 7 M. *Kalscheuren*, the junction for the Eifel Railway (p. 146). — From the station at (10 M.) *Brühl* we obtain a view of the Royal Château on the right. (see .p. 84). — 13 M. *Sechtem;* $17^{1}/_{2}$ M. *Roisdorf,* with a mineral spring resembling that of Selters. On the right we observe the chain of hills known as the *Vorgebirge,* on the slopes of which are large market-gardens and deposits of lignite.

$21^{1}/_{2}$ M. *Bonn* (p. 75). The Protestant Church and the Cathedral tower are prominent to the left. Railway to Euskirchen, see p. 84.

26 M. *Godesberg,* see p. 86. — $27^{1}/_{2}$ M. *Mehlem,* see p. 90. The railway-station is $^{1}/_{4}$ M. from the river. Steam-ferry to Königs-winter, see p. 91.

At (30 M.) *Rolandseck* (see p. 92) the line runs close to the river. — $31^{1}/_{2}$ M. *Oberwinter* (p. 94). — We now obtain a fine retrospect of the Seven Mountains. — $36^{1}/_{2}$ M. *Remagen* (see p. 94), the station for the *Ahr Valley* railway (p. 104).

The train now crosses the *Ahr,* from the valley of which, on the right, rises the blunted cone of the Landskron. — 39 M. *Sinzig* (p. 110), on the right, with its handsome parish-church. — 42 M. *Niederbreisig* (see p. 110). — On the opposite bank come into view the château of Arenfels and (a little farther on) Rheinbrohl. $44^{1}/_{2}$ M. *Brohl,* see p. 112. — The train continues to skirt the Rhine. — 49 M. *Andernach,* see p. 112; branch-railway to *Mayen* and *Gerol-stein,* see pp. 152, 118. The train crosses the little *Nette,* passing on the right the lunatic asylum of *St. Thomas.* — 50 M. *Weissen-thurm* (p. 116), station for Neuwied (on the right bank of the river). — $51^{1}/_{2}$ M. *Urmitz,* see p. 116; $55^{1}/_{2}$ M. *Coblenz-Lützel.* — As we cross the *Moselle* by the iron bridge a view of the old Moselle Bridge, with the Emp. William Monument and the fortress of Ehren-breitstein beyond it, is obtained to the left.

57 M. *Coblenz,* see p. 121. — Continuation of the line to Mayence, see R. 29.

b. Railway on the Right Bank.

$56^{1}/_{2}$ M. Railway in $1^{1}/_{2}$-3 hrs. (fares 7 ℳ 20, 4 ℳ 30, 2 ℳ 90 pf., ex-press fares 8 ℳ 20, 5 ℳ 30, 3 ℳ 40 pf.). — Steam-ferry from Ehrenbreitstein to Coblenz, see p. 128. Tramway from Sayn to Coblenz, viâ Bendorf and Vallendar, see pp. 122, 128. From Vallendar *Local Steamers* also run to Coblenz 12 times daily, calling at Ehrenbreitstein. — Views to the right.

Cologne, see p. 39. The train crosses the Rhine Bridge to (2 M.) *Kalk* (South Station; p. 70), the junction of branch-lines to *Deutz* (p. 70) and to *Overath* (p. 140). 7 M. *Porz-Urbach.* At ($8^{1}/_{2}$ M.)

Wahn, to the left, is a large artillery-range. At (13 M.) *Troisdorf* (Kronprinz) the Cologne and Giessen Railway (p. 140) diverges to the left; our line turns towards the Rhine. Beyond (14 M.) *Friedrich-Wilhelms-Hütte,* with a large iron-foundry, the train crosses the *Sieg.*

18½ M. *Beuel* (p. 83), on the Rhine; tramway to Bonn, see p. 76. 21 M. *Oberkassel* (p. 87) is connected with the Left Rhenish Railway at Bonn by a steam-ferry.

Opposite (22½ M.) *Dollendorf* (p. 87), on the left bank, is Godesberg, with its ruined castle (p. 86). 24 M. *Königswinter* (p. 89).

25½ M. *Rhöndorf* (p. 91), at the S. base of the Drachenfels; 27 M. *Honnef* (p. 93), opposite Rolandseck; 29 M. *Unkel* (p. 95); 31 M. *Erpel* (p. 95), opposite Remagen. — 33 M. *Linz* (p. 111) lies opposite the mouth of the Ahr, above which rises the church of *Sinzig* (p. 110). 38 M. *Hönningen* (p. 111), with the château of *Arenfels* to the left; 40 M. *Rheinbrohl* (p. 113), opposite Brohl and the château of Rheineck. 43½ M. *Leutesdorf* (p. 113); 45 M. *Fahr-Irlich,* opposite Andernach. — The valley of the Rhine expands. The train crosses the little *Wied.* — 47 M. *Neuwied* (see p. 113).

50 M. *Engers* (p. 117), the junction for the Westerwaldbahn (Westerwald Railway).

FROM ENGERS TO SIERSHAHN, 13 M., railway in ca. ³/₄ hr. — The line crosses the Saynbach, and ascends the left bank of the stream.

2 M. **Sayn** (*Holler's Hôtel Friedrichsberg,* R. 1½-2¼, B. ³/₄, D. 1½-2, pens. 4½-5 ℳ; *Jägerhof,* belonging to the same proprietor, R. 1¼-1½, D. 1¼-1½, pens. 4 ℳ; *Hôtel-Restaurant Krupp),* at the confluence of the Brexbach and the Saynbach, with extensive iron-works belonging to the Krupp Co. and the château (rebuilt in 1848-50) and park of Prince Sayn-Wittgenstein-Sayn. The *Park* lies on the slope of the hill, on which are situated the ruins of the old *Castle* erected in the 10th cent. and destroyed in the Thirty Year's War, the ancestral seat of the once powerful Counts of Sayn. Below are the ruined castles of *Stein* and *Reifenberg.* — About 2 M. to the N.W. of Sayn, beyond the united villages of *Heimbach* and *Weiss,* are the ruins of the ancient abbey of *Rommersdorf,* with fine cloisters and chapter-house, erected about 1200, now the property of the Duke of Arenberg, and used as farm-buildings. In the valley of the Sayn, 3-3½ M. to the N. of Sayn, is the ruined castle of *Isenburg.*

The train now threads a tunnel and enters the valley of the Brexbach. — From (7½ M.) *Grenzau* a branch-line runs to (1¾ M.) **Höhr-Grenzhausen.** The station lies on the boundary between the two villages, in which earthenware, both useful and ornamental, has been manufactured for centuries. The Vienna Exhibition of 1873 brought the ware of this district into modern notice. There are several large factories near the station. The *Ceramic School,* with an interesting exhibition, and *Müllenbach's Inn* (very fair) are both in Höhr. — A tramway runs through the beautiful Ferbach Valley to (4½ M.) Vallendar (p. 74).

10½ M. *Ransbach,* with a whetstone factory. — A steep incline leads hence to (13½ M.) *Siershahn,* the junction of the Limburg and Altenkirchen line (p. 142).

52½ M. *Bendorf* (p. 117) is situated amidst orchards ½ M. to the E. of the line.

53¹/₂ M. **Vallendar** *(Rheinfahrt; Anker)*, a town with 4380
inhab., who carry on the manufacture of pottery, lies on an arm of
the Rhine opposite the island of *Niederwerth* (p. 117). On a height
above the town stands the Roman Catholic *Parish Church*, restored in 1839, with a tower of the 15th cent.; it contains some late-
Gothic church-plate. To the N., on the road to *Weitersburg*, are
the Vallendar Casino ('Monte Casino'; visitors admitted) and the
(³/₄ M.) 'Humboldt Bench', commanding an extensive view. On the
road to Höhr (p. 73), ³/₄ M. to the E., are the Romanesque towers
of the ruined nunnery of *Schönstatt*, with a cloth-factory in the
vicinity.

A little farther on a view is obtained of the mouth of the Moselle and the Emp. William Monument.

56¹/₂ M. *Ehrenbreitstein* (p. 128) lies at the foot of the precipitous rock on which the fortress is situated. — Continuation of
the line to Wiesbaden, see R. 30.

12. The Rhine from Cologne to Bonn.

STEAMBOAT (20¹/₂ M.) in 2¹/₄-3 hrs. (down 1¹/₄ hr.); fares 1 *M* 40, 85 pf.
— Besides the Railway of the Left Bank (described at p. 72) Cologne is
connected with Bonn by the VORGEBIRGE RAILWAY *(Vorgebirgsbahn)* and
the electric BANK OF THE RHINE RAILWAY *(Rheinuferbahn)*. The former,
22 M. in length (2¹/₄ hrs.), starts at the Barbarossa-Platz (Pl. C, 2) and
runs viâ *Hermühlheim, Vochem, Brühl* (p. 84), *Walberberg, Merten,
Waldorf, Bornheim,* and *Roisdorf* (p. 72) to its station in the Friedrichs-
Platz at *Bonn* (Pl. C, 2). The Rheinuferbahn, now the most popular
route (17¹/₂ M., in ³/₄-1 hr.), starts every ¹/₂ hr. (fares 1 *M* 30, 85 pf.). It
has three stations in Cologne (Trankgasse, Pl. E, F, 5; Ubier-Ring, Pl.
A, 5; and Marienburg, p. 67) and runs viâ *Rodenkirchen, Sürth, Godorf,
Wesseling* (junction of a branch to Brühl and Vochem), *Urfeld,* and *Hersel*
to the State Railway Station at *Bonn* (Pl. C, 3).

In the following routes *r.* and *l.* indicate the position of towns, and
other objects, with regard to the traveller *ascending* the river. — The
letters S., B., and R. affixed to names of places indicate respectively
steamer-landing, small-boat station, and railway-station.

The STEAMBOAT JOURNEY on this part of the Rhine is, it is true,
less varied than that on the narrower part of the river farther up,
but is by no means devoid of picturesque features. The lowland
here traversed by the river, known to geologists as the Kölner Bucht
or Bay of Cologne, is bounded on the W. by the 'Vorgebirge' (p. 72)
and on the E. by the hills of Berg. The stream averages about
¹/₃ M. in width, and is enlivened with numerous vessels. Its flat
banks are dotted with cheerful-looking villages. — As the steamer
leaves the landing-stage we enjoy a fine view of the majestic city
of Cologne, with its cathedral, numerous towers, and lofty bridge.
To the right is *Marienburg-Bayental* (S.), a residential suburb of
Cologne, with its lofty water-tower and Bismarck Tower (p. 67).

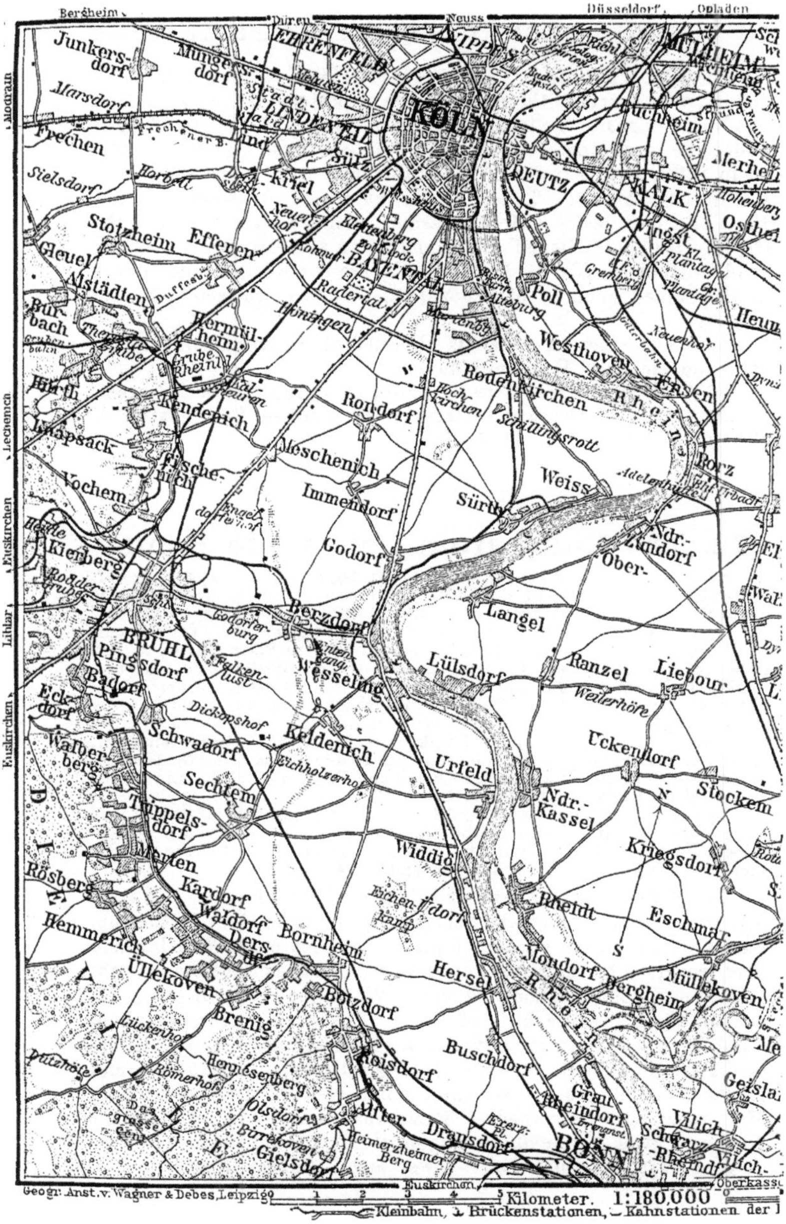

Junkers-dorf
Mungers-dorf
EHRENFELD
MÜLHEIM
Marsdorf
LINDENTHAL
Buchheim
KÖLN
Frechen
Merheim
Sielsdorf
Horch
Kriel
Sülz
DEUTZ
KALK
Ostheim
Stotzheim
Efferen
BAYENTHAL
Poll
Heumar
Gleuel
Altstädten
Raderthal
Westhoven
Ensen
Bur-bach
Hermül-heim
Hiningen
Rhein
Knapsack
Hurth
Kendenich
Rondorf
Bodenkirchen
Fische-
Porz
Vochem
Meschenich
Sürth
Weiss
Kierberg
Immendorf
Godorf
Ndr.-Dondorf
Ober-
BRÜHL
Berzdorf
Langel
Pingsdorf
Wesseling
Lülsdorf
Ranzel
Liebour
Badorf
Dickopshof
Eck-dorf
Schwadorf
Keldenich
Urfeld
Uckendorf
Walber-berg
Sechtem
Ndr.-Kassel
Stockem
Tüppels-dorf
Widdig
Kriegsdorf
Merten
Rösberg
Kardorf
Rheidt
Eschmar
Hemmerich
Waldorf
Bornheim
Uedekoven
Botzdorf
Hersel
Mondorf
Bergheim
Müllekoven
Brenig
Buschdorf
Rhein
Roisdorf
Gielsdorf
Alfter
Dransdorf
Graurheindorf
Vilich
BONN

Kleinbahn, Brückenstationen, Kahnstationen der

53¹/₂ M. **Vallendar** *(Rheinfahrt; Anker)*, a town with 4380 inhab., who carry on the manufacture of pottery, lies on an arm of the Rhine opposite the island of *Niederwerth* (p. 117). On a height above the town stands the Roman Catholic *Parish Church*, restored in 1839, with a tower of the 15th cent.; it contains some late-Gothic church-plate. To the N., on the road to *Weitersburg*, are the Vallendar Casino ('Monte Casino'; visitors admitted) and the (³/₄ M.) 'Humboldt Bench', commanding an extensive view. On the road to Höhr (p. 73), ³/₄ M. to the E., are the Romanesque towers of the rüined nunnery of *Schönstatt*, with a cloth-factory in the vicinity.

A little farther on a view is obtained of the mouth of the Moselle and the Emp. William Monument.

56¹/₂ M. *Ehrenbreitstein* (p. 128) lies at the foot of the precipitous rock on which the fortress is situated. — Continuation of the line to Wiesbaden, see R. 30.

12. The Rhine from Cologne to Bonn.

STEAMBOAT (20¹/₂ M.) in 2¹/₄-3 hrs. (down 1¹/₄ hr.); fares 1 ℳ 40, 85 pf. — Besides the Railway of the Left Bank (described at p. 72) Cologne is connected with Bonn by the VORGEBIRGE RAILWAY *(Vorgebirgsbahn)* and the electric BANK OF THE RHINE RAILWAY *(Rheinuferbahn)*. The former, 22 M. in length (2¹/₄ hrs.), starts at the Barbarossa-Platz (Pl. C, 2) and runs viâ *Hermühlheim, Vochem, Brühl* (p. 84), *Walberberg, Merten, Waldorf, Bornheim,* and *Roisdorf* (p. 72) to its station in the Friedrichs-Platz at *Bonn* (Pl. C, 2). The Rheinuferbahn, now the most popular route (17¹/₂ M., in ³/₄-1 hr.), starts every ¹/₂ hr. (fares 1 ℳ 30, 85 pf.). It has three stations in Cologne (Trankgasse, Pl. E, F, 5; Ubier-Ring, Pl. A, 5; and Marienburg, p. 67) and runs viâ *Rodenkirchen, Sürth, Godorf, Wesseling* (junction of a branch to Brühl and Vochem), *Urfeld,* and *Hersel* to the State Railway Station at *Bonn* (Pl. C, 3).

In the following routes *r.* and *l.* indicate the position of towns, and other objects, with regard to the traveller *ascending* the river. — The letters S., B., and R. affixed to names of places indicate respectively steamer-landing, small-boat station, and railway-station.

The STEAMBOAT JOURNEY on this part of the Rhine is, it is true, less varied than that on the narrower part of the river farther up, but is by no means devoid of picturesque features. The lowland here traversed by the river, known to geologists as the Kölner Bucht or Bay of Cologne, is bounded on the W. by the 'Vorgebirge' (p. 72) and on the E. by the hills of Berg. The stream averages about ¹/₈ M. in width, and is enlivened with numerous vessels. Its flat banks are dotted with cheerful-looking villages. — As the steamer leaves the landing-stage we enjoy a fine view of the majestic city of Cologne, with its cathedral, numerous towers, and lofty bridge. To the right is *Marienburg-Bayental* (S.), a residential suburb of Cologne, with its lofty water-tower and Bismarck Tower (p. 67).

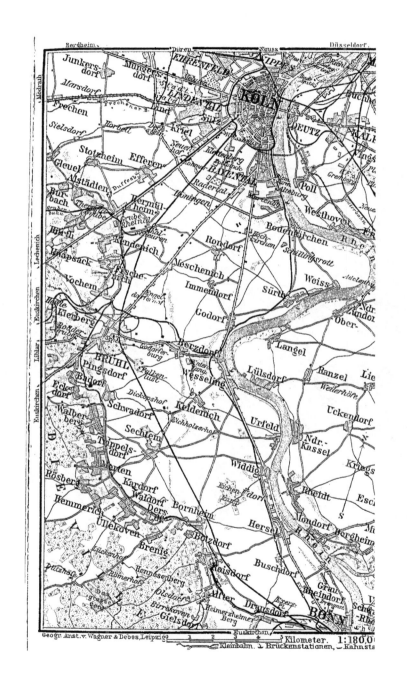

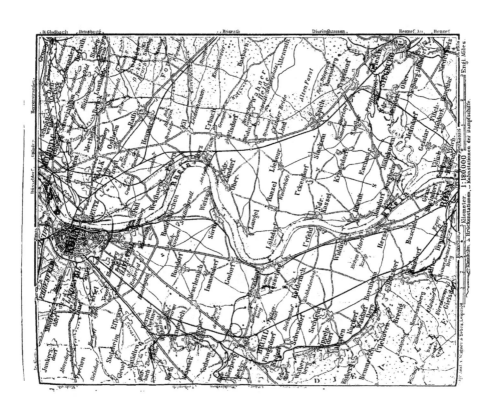

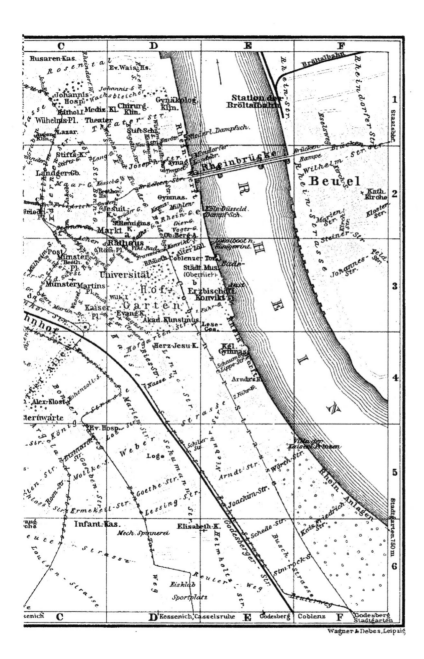

Wagner & Debes, Leipzig

Numerous industrial establishments are seen on both banks. To the right lies *Rodenkirchen*, with a machine-factory and dye-works. l. *Westhoven;* l. *Ensen;* l. *Porz* (S.), with foundry and cement-works. R. *Sürth;* r. *Godorf;* r. *Wesseling* (S.), with a new brick church; l. *Lülsdorf*, with a ruined castle; l. *Niederkassel;* r. *Urfeld;* r. *Widdig;* l. *Rheidt*, beyond a former island; r. *Hersel;* l. *Mondorf;* r. *Grau-Rheindorf*. To the left are the mouth of the Sieg and the church of *Schwarz-Rheindorf* (p. 83). On the hillside, farther inland, rises the suppressed Benedictine abbey of *Siegburg* (p. 140). Of the Seven Mts. the *Löwenburg* (comp. p. 98) is conspicuous, rising to the right of the Nonnenstromberg.

Before calling at *Bonn*, we enjoy a fine view of the handsome Rhine bridge.

13. Bonn.

Railway Stations. *Staatsbahnhof Bonn* (State Railway, Pl. C, 2), on the Left Bank Railway from Cologne to Mayence; *Staatsbahnhof Beuel* (comp. Pl. F, 1), on the Right Bank Railway from Cologne to Wiesbaden. *Rheinuferbahn Station*, adjoining the Staatsbahnhof Bonn; *Vorgebirgsbahn Station*, in the Friedrich-Platz (Pl. C, 2), these two for trains to Cologne (see p. 74). — **Steamer Wharves** of the *Cologne & Düsseldorf Co.* and the *Netherlandish S. S. Co.*, respectively above and below the Rhine bridge (Pl. D, E. 2); pier of the *Local Steamer to Königswinter*, below the Alte Zoll (Pl. E, 3).

Hotels. *On the Rhine:* *GRAND-HÔTEL ROYAL (Pl. b; D, 3), Coblenzer-Str. 11, a hotel of the first class, with a restaurant, a beautiful garden, and a view-terrace on the Rhine, R. 3½-8, with bath 8-15, B. 1½, D. 4, pens. 11-15 *M*. — RHEINECK (Pl. e; D, 2), at the pier, a good house of the second class, with terrace, R. 2½-4, B. 1, D. 2½ *M*; VATER ARNDT, near the latter; DISSMANN, by the bridge, R. & B. 2½-3½ *M*, both with restaurant; STADT BONN, Rheingasse 1. — *In the Town:* *GOLDNER STERN (Pl. a; D, 2), in the market-place, with ball-rooms and restaurant, first-class, R. 2½-6, B. 1, D. 3 *M*; RHEINISCHER HOF (Pl. f; C, 2), Stern-Str. 57, R. & B. 3 *M*; CENTRAL (Pl. c; C, 2), Wilhelm-Str. 1; TRAUBE, Meckenheimer-Str. 18 (Pl. B, 2, 3); BERGISCHER HOF, Münster-Platz 24, R. & B. 3 *M*; ROTE KANNE, in the market-place, clean. — *At the Railway Station:* CONTINENTAL (Pl. d; C, 3), Bahnhof-Str. 15a, R. 2-3, B. 1 *M*; WIENER HOF, Bahnhof-Str. 5, R. 2-4, B. 1 *M*; KRONPRINZ, Bahnhof-Str. 19, R. 2-2¼, B. ¾ *M*. — *In the Poppelsdorfer Allée:* No. 27, EVANGELISCHES HOSPIZ.

Pensions. *Mrs. Thomas*, Goeben-Str. 15; *Harling*, Hofgarten-Str. 4 (4½-8 *M*); *Schugt*, Erste Fährgasse 3, on the Rhine (4-6 *M*); *Rheingold*, corner of Rheinwerft-Str. and Theater-Str. (3-4½ *M*); *Beenken*, Marien-Str. 1 (5-7 *M*); *Neuerburg*, Lenné-Str. 8 (5-7 *M*); *Schniewind-Hesse*, Hohenzollern-Str. 28 (5-9½ *M*); *Rollins*, Baumschuler-Allée 29 (5-8 *M*); *Klusener*, Beethoven-Str. 4 (5-7 *M*); *Goeker*, Kaiser-Platz 11; *Concordia*, August-Str. 10 (4½-8 *M*).

Restaurants (at the hotels). Also *Perrin* (first-class), Wenzelgasse 50 (Pl. D, 2); *Schwarz*, Kaiser-Str. 15a; *Viehöfer*, Baumschuler Allée, at the corner of Meckenheimer-Str.; at the *Bonner Bürgerverein*, Kronprinz-Str. — **Beer.** *Kaiserhalle*, Martin-Str., cor. of the Kaiser-Platz; *Beethoven-Halle*, near the Rhine bridge; *Im Krug zum Grünen Kranze*, Coblenzer-Str. 27; *Zum Hähnchen*, Dreieck 3 (Pl. C, 2);

Sonne, Markt 24; *Alt-Heidelberg*, Münster-Platz; *Franziskaner*, near the Stern-Tor (Pl. C, 2, 3). — *Stadthalle* (open-air restaurant), see p. 80.

Cafés. *Kaiser-Café*, Kaiser-Platz 18 (Pl. C, 3); *Wiener Café*, Bahnhof-Str. 5. — **Confectioner.** *Müller*, Römer-Platz.

Bathing Establishments. *Victoria-Bad* (municipal bathing establishment), Franziskaner-Str.; *Dr. Pütz*, Kronprinzen-Str. 41 (also medicinal baths); on the *Rhine*, near the Alte Zoll, with swimming baths (40 pf.).

Tramways. From the Kaiser-Platz to the N. of the railway (Pl. C, 3): 1. Past the Railway Station viâ the Post-Str., Münster-Platz, Friedrich-Platz (Pl. C, 2), Friedrich-Str., and Rhine Bridge to the Right Bank Railway Station (p. 72) at Beuel (Pl. F, 2). 2. As above to the Friedrich-Platz, then viâ the Wilhelm-Str. to the Rheindorfer-Str. (Pl. C, 1). 3. As above to the Friedrich-Platz, then viâ the Market Place (Pl. C, D, 2), Coblenzer-Str., and Rheinweg to the Stadthalle (Pl. F, 5, 6). 4. From the Railway Station to Grau-Rheindorf (p. 75). — From the Poppelsdorfer Allée, to the S. of the Kaiser-Platz and beyond the railway: 5. Viâ the Kronprinzen-Str. and the König-Str. to the Argelander-Str. (Pl. C, 5, 6). 6. Viâ the Quantius-Str., the Meckenheimer-Str., and the Clemens-August-Str. to Poppelsdorf (Pl. A, B, 6). 7. From the Quantius-Str. viâ the Colman-Str. to Endenich (Pl. A, 4). — Steam Tramway from the corner of Kaiser-Str. and König-Str. (Pl. D, 4) to *Godesberg* (p. 86) and *Mehlem* (p. 90), every 1/2 hr. on week-days, every 1/4 hr. on Sun., in 20 and 30 minutes.

Cabs. Per drive in the town, 1-2 pers. 70 pf., each additional pers. 25 pf., box 10 pf.; per 1/2 hr. 11/2 ℳ. To *Godesberg* 3 or 4 ℳ, to *Kasselsruhe* (p. 83) 31/2 or 41/2 ℳ, each pers. more than two, 50 pf.

Post & Telegraph Office (Pl. C, 3), Münster-Platz.

Theatre (Pl. C, 1), open Oct.-April. — Concerts in the Beethoven-Halle, Brücken-Str. (Pl. D, 2; in winter only) and in the Stadthalle (p. 80). — Sportplatz (Pl. D, 6), with tennis-courts in summer and skating-rink in winter. — Enquiry Office, Kirch-Str. 5.

English Church Service in the University Church (p. 79) at 11 a.m.

Chief Attractions. Münster (p. 77); view from the Alte Zoll (p. 79); walk along the Rhine and across the bridge (p. 80); Provincial Museum (p. 80); Poppelsdorf (p. 82). — Château of Brühl (p. 84).

Bonn (154 ft), a town with 58,000 inhab. (incl. the incorporated suburbs, 80,000) and the seat of a university, is pleasantly situated on the W. bank of the Rhine at the point where the mountains recede and merge into the so-called 'Vorgebirge'. The imposing bridge over the Rhine, the Alte Zoll and its environs, the towers of the Cathedral, the Protestant Church, and the Schloss, the villas with their gardens on the Rhine, the University buildings at the lower end of the town, the Kreuzberg with its church in the background, and the handsome new Elisabeth-Kirche to the S., all conspire to make a very attractive picture.

Bonn, the *Bonna* or *Castra Bonnensia* of the Romans, was one of the 50 fortresses which Drusus (p. 267) erected along the Rhine in the year 10 B. C., and it was the headquarters of several legions. Excavations have proved that the Roman *Castrum* stood at the *Wichelshof*, to the N. of the town. In the middle ages Bonn was a place of little importance until 1273, when the Archbishop of Cologne transferred his residence and seat of government hither (comp. p. 45). The German kings, Frederick of Austria (1314) and Charles IV. (1346), were crowned in the Münster.

The Protestant tendencies of Hermann of Wied and Gebhard of

Waldburg, Archbishops of Cologne in the 16th cent., principally mani-
fested by the latter in his marriage with the nun Agnes of Mansfeld,
for which he was declared an apostate and banished from his Electorate,
brought Bonn into great trouble. In the Dutch War of Independence,
in the Thirty Years' War, and especially in the Spanish War of Succession, Bonn suffered repeatedly from sieges. That of 1689 was conducted by Elector Frederick III. of Brandenburg (King Frederick I.) at
the head of the imperial and allied troops. Marlborough and other
celebrated generals took part about the same time in the operations
against the town. The walls were levelled in 1717, in accordance
with the Peace of Rastatt. — Under the Electors of the 18th cent. Bonn
was very prosperous, and one of them in 1777 founded an *Academy*,
elevated to a *University* seven years later by Emperor Joseph II. On
7th Oct., 1794, the French marched into the town, and in 1797 the university was closed.

Under the French Bonn suffered much, and its population decreased
from 9500 to 7500, but since its recovery by the Prussians in 1814 and
the foundation in 1818 of the Frederick William University (4000 students)
it has gradually revived.

The Post-Str. leads direct from the *Railway Station* (Pl.
C, 3) to the Münster-Platz (see below). To the E. of the railway-station lies the KAISER-PLATZ (Pl. C, 3), the central point of
the tramway system, at the S. W. corner of which begins the
Poppelsdorfer Allée (p. 80). At the upper end of the square is
a marble statue of Emperor William I. by H. Magnussen (1906). To
the right rises the tower of the *Protestant Church* (Pl. D, 3), built
in 1866-71. We proceed to the left across the Martins-Platz,
passing the beautiful choir of the Münster, to the MÜNSTER-PLATZ
(Pl. C, 3).

The **Münster* (Pl. C, 3), a cruciform church with two choirs,
four small towers, and a lofty octagonal principal tower over the
crossing, is an imposing and picturesque example of the late-Romanesque style. The church formerly belonged to the Archdeanery of St.
Cassius and St. Florentius, and according to the legend was founded
ca. 310 by the Empress Helena, the mother of Constantine the
Great. After repeated destruction it was wholly rebuilt in the
11-12th centuries. The W. part of the crypt and the part of the
church above it date from the 11th, the choir from the second half
of the 12th, and the nave (one of the most important examples of
the transition style), the transept, and the chief tower from 1208-21.
A thoroughgoing restoration was made in 1883-1901.

The INTERIOR, which is entered from the Münster-Platz by the large
side-portal, is notable for its harmonious proportions. The general equipment, dating from the 18th cent., was rendered necessary by the damage
the church had received in the siege of 1689. The paintings are by
August Martin (1891-94). In the W. part of the nave is a kneeling bronze
figure of St. Helena, holding the Cross, cast at Rome in the middle of
the 17th century. Near the W. end of the N. aisle is the beautiful
Gothic tomb of Archbishop Engelbert von Falkenburg (d. 1275). In
the S. aisle is the Altar of the Nativity, an Italian work with elaborate sculptures of 1622. The choir contains interesting remains of
late-Romanesque mural paintings, freely restored in 1893-94. The
mosaic in the E. choir and the stained-glass windows are modern. —

In front of the choir-steps is the entrance to the *Crypt*, which is shown by the verger.

The ancient *Chapter House* adjoining the church on the S. is now the parsonage. The *Cloisters*, with pillars possessing beautiful capitals, date from the 12th cent. (entr. from the church or on the E. side, adjoining the choir). — In the street called 'Am Sürst' is a tasteful modern *Fountain*, with groups of children and geese. — The bronze statue of *Beethoven* on the W. side of the Münster-Platz is by Ernst Hähnel (1845).

The central point of the old town with its narrow streets, which stretches to the N.E. from the Münster-Platz to the Rhine, is the triangular MARKET PLACE (Pl. C, D, 2, 3). In the centre of it rises a *Fountain Column*, erected by the citizens in 1777 in honour of Maximilian Frederick, Elector of Cologne. The *Rathaus,* with its lofty flight of steps adorned with a wrought-iron balustrade of rococo pattern, was erected in 1737-38; the Council Chamber still retains its old decoration (white ornaments upon a greenish-blue ground). — A little to the N. is the late-Gothic *Church of St. Remigius* (15th cent.), formerly the *Minoriten-Kirche* (Pl. D, 2), with some modern paintings by Düsseldorf artists. — The *Jesuit Church* (Pl. C, 2), in the Bonngasse, is now used by the Old Catholics.

At No. 20 Bonngasse is the **Beethoven House** (Pl. C, 2), in which *Ludwig van Beethoven* (1770-1827) was born. The house has been restored to its original condition and is now fitted up as a Beethoven Museum (adm. 1 ℳ, on Wed. & Sun. 50 pf.).

The contents of the museum include numerous portraits of Beethoven, his family, and his contemporaries; his piano, quartet instruments, ear trumpets, scores, letters, etc. In the little garden are a bronze bust of him by Aronson (1905) and the original model for Klinger's ideal figure (1902). The garret in which he was born is in the back-building and has been preserved unaltered. Beethoven's father was a tenor-singer (d. 1792), and his grandfather (a native of Antwerp; d. 1773) band-master to the Elector. His mother, Maria Magdalena Keverich, was a native of Ehrenbreitstein. In 1787 Beethoven went to Vienna, which was his permanent home after 1792.

The **University Buildings** (Pl. D, 3), ca. 640 yds. in length and originally the *Electoral Palace,* occupy the S. side of the old town. The central portion, with its four towers, was begun by *Enrico Zuccali* in 1697-1703 and completed by *Robert de Cotte* in 1715-23. The two principal towers were rebuilt in 1895. The main entrance is in the street named 'Am Hof'. The vaulted portico leads to a large arcaded court. The *Lecture Rooms* on the ground-floor still retain their old stucco ceilings. The extensive E. wing contains the *Library* (355,000 vols., 1450 MSS.), adorned with numerous busts, and the collection of the *Art Historical Institute* (Italian and Netherlandish paintings of the 15-16th cent., and sculptures; open on Wed. and Sat. 11-1). Entrance in the Konvikt-

Strasse. — The old chapel of the Electoral Palace is now a Protestant place of worship (Church of England service, see p. 76).

Passing through the *Coblenzer-Tor* (1751-58), which intersects the E. wing of the university, and has its façade adorned externally with a figure of the Archangel Michael, we reach the *Coblenzer-Strasse* (see below). — Immediately to the left is the entrance to the **Alte Zoll** (Pl. D, E, 3), an old bastion on the bank of the Rhine, with a celebrated view of the Seven Mts. (seen hence to great advantage), Godesberg, the Rhine Bridge, Siegburg, and the hills of Berg. In the centre is a *Monument* to the poet *Ernst Moritz Arndt* (1769-1860), in bronze. The two French guns here were captured in the war of 1870. — An inclined plane descends from the Alte Zoll past the *Board of Mines*, an effective structure completed in 1904 in the baroque style of the Electoral period, to the Rhine wharf (p. 80).

Next to the Royal Hotel, No. 9 Coblenzer-Str., is the Civic Museum, in the former *Villa Obernier* (Pl. E, 3; open free on Sun. 11-2, Tues. to Sat. 11-1 and 3-5), containing a collection of modern pictures and a few sculptures, bequeathed to the town by Prof. Obernier (d. 1882).

Among the most notable contents may be mentioned: *A. Achenbach*, Rough sea; *O. Achenbach*, Castel S. Angelo and St. Peter's; *R. Tillmans*, Mourning widow; *José Benlliure*, Feast of the Madonna in Spain; examples of *H. Gude*, *E. Dücker*, *H. Deiters*, and *F. Fagerlin*. — On the second story is the extensive collection of the Old-Bonn Society, containing paintings, views, furniture, household gear, coins, etc. — In the annex is the exhibition, changed from time to time, of the Literature and Art Society. — Splendid view from the bow-windows.

On the W. side of the Coblenzer-Str., behind the University buildings, lies the **Hof-Garten** (Pl. D, 3), with its avenues of trees, laid out at the beginning of the 18th century. Close to the street, on the right, is a marble bust of *Karl Simrock* (1802-76), the poet and scholar, who was born at Bonn. On the S. E. side of the Hof-Garten stands the **Academic Museum of Art** (Pl. D, 3), containing one of the oldest collections of casts in Germany as well as some Greek originals (marble hermæ of Sophocles and Euripides, Aristophanes and Menander; small marble heads of a girl and a child; vases; and terracotta figurines). The museum is open free on Mon., Wed., & Frid., 3-5 (from Oct. to April 2-4), and is shown at other times by the custodian (central block, Hofgarten-Str.; fee).

In the Coblenzer-Str. (electric tramway, see p. 76), to the left, are numerous villas, with beautiful gardens, high above the Rhine. The *Collegium Albertinum (Erzbischöfliche Convict; Pl. D, E, 3), a large Gothic building, was erected in 1892 for the accommodation of Roman Catholic students at the University. Beyond the Erste Fährgasse are a handsome *Club House* (No. 35) and the *Royal Gymnasium* (No. 53). In the Zweite Fährgasse (Pl. E, 4)

are the former residence of the poet Arndt (No. 70) and the large
Mehlem Porcelain Factory. In the next cross-street (Wörth-Str.) is
the former *Royal Villa,* for royal princes studying in Bonn. Beyond
the Kaiser-Friedrich-Str. is the *Palace of Prince Adolphus of
Schaumburg-Lippe.*

The tramway (p. 76) runs hence to the left to the *Stadt-Garten* and the
Stadthalle, with concert-rooms, view-terrace, and restaurant, at the S.
end of the Rhine wharf. Close by are the dock of the Bonn and Oberkassel Ferry (*Trajekt;* p. 73) and the Bismarck Tower erected by the
students of Bonn.

Along the river-front of the town stretches the *Rhine Wharf*
(Pl. F 5-D 1), a broad quay $1^1/_4$ M. in length. The S. portion of
the wharf, under the terraced gardens of the houses in the Coblenzer-
Str., is laid out in promenades. At the Rhine Bridge are the
landing-places of the steamboats. Opposite the Cologne-Düsseldorf
dock are the terraces and gardens of the *Böselagerer Hof,* a noble's
palace of the first half of the 18th century.

The graceful **Rhine Bridge* (Pl. E, 2), built in 1896-98 from
the designs of *Prof. Krohn,* is, perhaps, the most beautiful in the
Rhenish provinces. It bestrides the river in three arches, the
central one of which has a span of 615 ft. (Upper Niagara Bridge
840 ft.), while the total length is 1415 ft. The fantastic and humorous plastic decoration of the bridge-towers represent scenes
from Rhenish life. An especially popular figure is the so-called
'Brückenmännchen' at the Beuel end of the bridge, who turns his
back on the community which refused to contribute toward its
building. Over the flight of steps ascending to the bridge from the
Rhine wharf is a seated figure of Julius Cæsar (comp. p. 117). The
bridge affords a fine view of Bonn and the Seven Mts. (toll 5 pf.). —
Beuel, see p. 83.

The N. end of the Rhine Wharf is overhung by the lofty terrace
upon which lie the *University Clinical Institutes* (Pl. D, C, 1).

In the S. W. part of the old town, beyond the railway, is the
Poppelsdorfer Allée (Pl. C, B, 4, 5), a broad, quadruple avenue
of old horse-chestnuts, leading to the Poppelsdorfer Schloss (p. 82).
— Passing through the first side-street on the right (Quantius-Str.;
electric tramway, see p. 76), we reach the —

*Provincial Museum (Pl. B, 3), No. 16, Colmant-Str., erected
in 1889-93, in the Italian Renaissance style and greatly enlarged
in 1909. It contains an extensive collection of Roman and mediæval
stone monuments, prehistoric, Roman, and Frankish antiquities,
a picture-gallery (the chief feature of which is the Wesendonk
collection), and a few mediæval works of art. The basement,
not yet opened, contains a collection intended for students. The
museum is open 10-1, free on Sun., Tues., and Thurs., on other days
50 pf.; in the afternoon (2-6; except on Sun, and holidays) 75 pf.
Visitors ring.

GROUND FLOOR.

In the vestibule is a Roman mosaic pavement found in Bonn, with the representation of a Gorgon's head. Room IX (entrance to the right of the ticket-office) contains tombstones of Roman soldiers (geographically arranged), the most noteworthy of which is *U 82. Monument of the centurion *M. Caelius*, who fell in the 'Bellum Varianum', the only stone monument extant relating to the battle in the Teutoburgian Forest (found in Birten near Xanten). — Room X (lighted from the ceiling). S. part: Tombstones of Roman civilians. Also groups of lions and a tomb from Weyden. — We now enter the lateral rooms on the right. Rooms XI-XIV contain Roman votive monuments, altars, inscriptions from buildings and monuments, and the like. Room XI. Objects from Upper Germania: Celtic deities from Wiesbaden, Castel, and Trèves; architectural inscriptions from Andernach and Liesenich; altars of Hercules Saxanus from the valley of the Bröhl. — Room XII. Altars from Lower Germania (Remagen, Bonn, Eifel). — Room XIII. Altars of the Deæ Matres. — Room XIV. Altars from Lower Germania (continued; Cologne, Worringen, Dormagen, Xanten): among these, *U 77. Large votive altar of the *Dea Victoria*, formerly misnamed the Altar of the Ubii, from the Alteburg near Cologne. — Room XV. Frankish Antiquities: early Christian and Merovingian tombstones (*14,189. with representation of a warrior); objects found in graves throughout the whole region of the Rhine; splendid gold trinkets; pottery of the Carlovingian period. — Room XVI. Small mediæval works of art: Rhenish pottery, works in ivory and metal. — We now retrace our steps through Room XV to Room X (N. part). Roman sculptures from Andernach, Oberpleis, etc.; in the centre, Gothic cross from Xanten, baroque altar from Bremm on the Moselle; Netherlandish tapestry of the 17th cent., representing the offering of Iphigenia. — We ascend the main staircase (by the entrance) to the —

UPPER FLOOR.

I. PREHISTORIC ROOM. Implements and vessels of the Flint and Bronze Periods. A glass-case contains the famous *Neandertal Skeleton*, i.e. the skull and bones of a man of the diluvial period, found in the Neander-Tal near Düsseldorf. — II. PREHISTORIC ROOM. Iron Period. Beautiful gold ornaments from Waldalgesheim, Weisskirchen, and Wallerfangen. — III. ROMAN TERRACOTTA ROOM, chronologically arranged: lamps, ordinary household vessels, and vessels of 'terra sigillata'. — IV. ROOM OF ROMAN WORKS IN METAL. Treasures found in graves, with bronze vessels, chronologically arranged. Pins. Abundant collection of bronze figures. Enamels. Small bronze implements. Iron weapons and utensils. — V. ROMAN GLASS ROOM. Roman earthenware from Rhenish factories, especially from a pottery at Cologne. Beautiful glass vessels (fragment of a Vas Diatretum, from Hohensülzen; painted glass bottle from Dürffental). Dishes of ground and engraved glass. Goblets. — On the STAIRCASE is a Collection of Coins.

Rooms VI-VIII contain the results of the excavations made by the Provincial Museum, in geographical order. Room VI. Objects found in Roman graves at Kreuznach, Cobern, Urmitz, and Andernach. — Room VII, Roman objects found at Niederbieber, Remagen, Bonn, and in the Eifel, including busts of emperors from Bonn and Niederbieber; *Objects of silver found at these two localities; rich trinkets of gold; jet ornaments. — Room VIII. Objects found at Cologne, Neuss, and Xanten. Results of the excavations of the Roman camps at Novæsium (p. 22) and Castra Vetera (p. 19). — We return to Room VII and thence enter Room XVII (lighted from the roof), containing mediæval and more recent sculptures: Crucifixion, from Trechtlingshausen; mosaic by Gilbert, Abbot of Laach; beautiful Renaissance tombstone of the Wiltberg family, 1571.

The side-rooms XVIII-XXVII contain the **Picture Gallery,** including the Wesendonk Collection. — Room XVIII (to the right) contains

Netherlandish paintings of the 15th and 16th centuries: 168. *Jan Mostaert,*
Triptych; three pictures by *Jan van Scorel.* — Room XIX. Netherlandish
and German Schools: 34. *P. Breughel the Younger,* John the Baptist
preaching, after P. Breughel the Elder; 141. *Master of the Holy Kinship,*
Christ and Mary; 187. *Unknown Master,* Altar-piece (about 1400); 49.
Lucas Cranach, Crucifixion; 250. *Schäufelein,* St. Jerome; 68. *Adam
Elsheimer,* Holy Women at the grave. — Room XX. Rhenish School:
137-140. *Master of St. Severin,* Representation from the legend of St.Ursula:
150-159. *Middle Rhenish Master,* Altar-piece from Bornhofen (Crown of
Thorns, Bearing of the Cross, Crucifixion, and Eight Saints). — Room XXI.
Flemish, French, and British Masters: 239. *Follower of Rubens,* Geometry;
233. *Sir Joshua Reynolds,* Portrait of a woman. — Room XXII. Italian
Schools (14-17th cent.): 123. *Lorenzo Monaco,* Saints; 121. *School of
Lorenzetti,* Madonna; 212. *School of Perugia,* Virgin adoring the Child;
62. *Domenichino,* Landscape; 35. *Bugiardini,* Madonna. — Room XXIII
(lighted from the roof). Italian and Spanish Masters: 167. *Moretto,*
Madonna; 336. *Zurbaran,* St. Francis; 289, 290. *School of Velazquez,*
Hunting-scenes. On the side-walls are large altar-pieces. — Rooms XXIV-
XXVI contain Dutch Masters of the 17th century. Room XXIV: 86. *Jan
van Goyen,* The Valkhof at Nymwegen; 281. *G. Terburg,* Portrait. —
Room XXV: 114. *S. Koninck,* Judas returning the thirty pieces of silver;
29. *Brekelenkam,* Vegetable-seller; 240, 241. *Ruysdael,* Landscapes. —
Room XXVI: 307. *Verheyden,* Poultry; 293. *A. van de Velde,* Ferry;
94. *In the style of Hobbema,* Landscape; 245. *Rachel Ruysch,* Flowers;
20. *Jan Both,* Italian landscape. — Room XXVII. Various Schools: 333,
334. *Januarius Zick,* Family portraits.

The Poppelsdorfer-Allée (p. 80) ends, $^3/_4$ M. from the Kaiser-Platz,
at the —

Poppelsdorfer Schloss (Pl. B, 5), formerly a residence of
the Electors, still in part surrounded by moats, erected in 1715-18
from the plans of Robert de Cotte, and completed in 1730-40. The
quadrangular ground-plan, with corner-pavilions and a terraced
central building on each of the four sides, encloses the circular court
with its arcades, round the top of which runs a beautiful wrought-
iron railing. The Schloss contains the *Natural History Collections*
of the University, with a noteworthy geological department (open
9 or 10 to 1, 30 pf.; free on Sun., 11-1, and Wed., 2-4). The *Botanical Garden* to the W., behind the palace, is open on Mon.,
Wed., & Frid. afternoon, the conservatories and palm-houses on Wed.
afternoon only. — Opposite the Poppelsdorf Schloss on the N.
rises the *Chemical Laboratory* (Pl. B, 5), in front of which is a
statue of *F. A. Kekulé* (1829-96), the chemist. Behind it are the
Anatomy Building, the *Physiological Institute,* and the *Agricultural Academy.*

To the S.W. of the Schloss the Clemens-August-Str. leads
past the *Wessel Porcelain Factory* (successor to the electoral
manufactury) and then past a street named after the little rococo
château of Sternberg (1750; Kirsch-Allée 34) to the (1 M.) —

Kreuzberg (410 ft.), a 'Mt. Calvary' crowned with a Franciscan
convict and a conspicuous white church (17th cent.). At the restoration made by Elector Clement Augustus in 1746-51 the chapel on

the E., containing the '*Holy Steps*', an imitation of the Scala Santa at Rome, was added to the church. In recollection of Christ's progress to the judgment-seat of Pilate and in deference to the sacred relics immured within it, the central flight of the triple staircase, consisting of 28 coloured marble steps, may be ascended only on the knees. Beautiful view from the tower.

The municipal **Kaiser-Wilhelm-Park**, on the *Venusberg*, to the S. of Poppelsdorf, is traversed by a number of pleasant walks and affords good views of the Rhine valley, the Seven Mts., and Godesberg (best by evening-light). It is reached by tramway to the end of the Argelander-Str. (No. 5, p. 76), whence steps and a winding road ascend to the monument to Emp. William I. Or we may take tramway No. 6 (p. 76) to the end of the Clemens-August-Str. and ascend to the left through the Melbtal. At the top is the *Hôtel-Restaurant Kasselsruhe*, with a concert-room. About 1/2 M. farther to the S. is the Bismarck Tower (view). To Godesberg, see p. 90.

The **Old Cemetery** (Pl. A, B, 2), 1/4 M. from the Sterntor, is the resting-place of many eminent men, chiefly professors at the university (Arndt, Simrock, Schlegel, Niebuhr, Schumann), and is also worthy of a visit on account of its handsome monuments, including a bronze memorial of the war of 1870-71, by Küppers. The *Chapel* in the middle of the cemetery, a late-Romanesque structure, built at Ramersdorf (p. 87) about the year 1200, was transferred thence to its present site in 1847.

On the right bank of the Rhine lies **Beuel** *(Hotel Schippers*, with an open-air restaurant, at the bridge; tramway No. 7, see p. 76), a small town that has grown rapidly since the construction of the bridge and has absorbed several adjoining villages. It contains many industrial establishments. In the Rhein-Str., below the bridge, is the station of the Bröl Valley Railway (Pl. E, 1), mentioned at p. 141. The Brücken-Str., with its prolongations, leads to the E. to (2/3 M.) the station (comp. Pl. F, 1) of the Railway of the Right Bank (p. 73). — *Finkenberg*, see p. 87.

About 1 M. from the tramway-station in the Rheindorfer-Str. in Beuel (Pl. F, 1) is the church of **Schwarz-Rheindorf**, which is one of the most notable Romanesque edifices in Germany, not only for the peculiarity of its two-storied construction, but also for the wealth of its mural decoration. The church was originally erected by Abp. Arnold von Wied of Cologne as a palace-chapel, in the form of a Greek cross, and consecrated in 1151. In 1173 Arnold's sister, the Abbess Hedwig of Essen, enlarged it for the uses of her Benedictine nunnery by a nave toward the W., which, however, was taken down at the beginning of the 19th century. The elegant miniature gallery which runs round the upper part of the church on the E., N., and S. sides shows traces of Lombardic influence, and has itself been frequently imitated in other Rhenish churches. The massive tower over the crossing rises in four sections. The main portal is in the N. transept. The mural paintings of the lower church, probably dating from before 1156, were restored in 1854. Those on the central vaulting, round the octagonal opening to the upper church, represent the Visions of Ezekiel (comp. p. xxviii), and those in the apses scenes from the New Testament, while in the niches of the N. and S. transepts are the figures of four kings. In the floor on the side next the nave is the brass of the founder (d. 1156), with an inscription of 1747. To the N. of this point is a winding staircase ascending to the upper church, where the nuns could attend mass without being visible to the congregation in the lower story. The mural paintings of the upper church, restored in 1875, are feebler efforts of the end of the 12th century. Visitors should ascend to the miniature gallery for the sake of the view. During a restoration of the church in 1902 a two-storied sacristy was built on its N. side.

The most brilliant example of the art of the Electoral period in Bonn is the Château of Brühl, halfway to Cologne, and reached by the railway (p. 72) in 20-26 minutes. Vorgebirge Railway, see p. 74.

  Brühl *(Railway Restaurant)*, a town with 6700 inhab. at the foot of the gentle slopes of the Vorgebirge (p. 72), was a stronghold of the Electors of Cologne from the end of the 13th cent. onwards. Opposite the station rises the —

  *Royal Palace, formerly that of the Electors, the most important building of the 18th cent. in the province of the Rhine. It was erected by Elector Clement Augustus in 1725-28 from the plans of Johann Conrad Schlaun, was afterwards sumptuously decorated by French and German artists, and was thoroughly restored in 1876-77. Comparatively simple in its external appearance, it offers in the interior admirable examples of the rococo style in all its forms of development, from the graceful flat decoration of the period of the Regency down to the severe and vigorous forms of the classical style. It is open on Sun. 11-6, on week-days 10-6 (in winter until 4); adm. 25 pf. Visitors apply on the right side of the court.

  Through the main entrance in the central structure we reach the flat-roofed porte-cochère, which opens to the right on the magnificent **Staircase*, constructed in 1740-48 under the influence of *Balthasar Neumann*, an architect of Würzburg. The great trophy on the N. wall and the other stucco ornamentations are by *Brillie* (1766); the allegorical ceiling-painting is by *Nicholas Stüber* (1732). The floor and steps are of marble. The wrought-iron balustrade and the lantern are both admirable specimens of their kind. On the upper floor, to the S., is the Salle des Gardes (see below), while to the N. are the former Rooms of the Electors, which were adorned in 1728-32 by *Michel Leveilly* in the elegant rococo style of the Regency, after designs by *François Cuvilliès*. The finest rooms are the Dining Room (which we enter first) and the State Bedroom (farther on), both in white and gold. — The Salle des Gardes *(Saal der Leibwache)*, fitted up in 1754 by *Johann Heinrich Roth*, with a ceiling-painting (apotheosis of Emp. Charles VII.) by *Nicholas Stüber* (1731), is in the latest rococo style. The adjoining Music Room and the rooms in the S. or Garden Wing were adorned by *Radoux*, *Renard*, *Brillie*, and others. The old bedroom is now fitted up as a drawing-room, while the last cabinet is used as the Emperor's bedroom. Most of the old furniture was sold in 1798, but the fine chimney-pieces and some leather hangings have been preserved. The extensive collection of portraits of princes belongs in part to the time of the Electors.

  The terrace on the S. side of the palace forms the approach to the extensive park, which is always open to the public. From the end of the central avenue we obtain a good view of the fertile Vor-

gebirge, the slopes of which contain lignite mines and bear the
marks of various industries.

To reach the town of Brühl, which lies to the N. of the palace,
we turn to the right at the railway-station. The Belvedere Hotel was
once one of the buildings belonging to the palace. The old parish
church, enlarged in 1885, contains a few paintings of the Early
Cologne School. The interior of the former Franciscan church was
altered in the rococo style in the 18th century.

FROM BONN TO EUSKIRCHEN, 21 M., railway in ca. 1 hr. (fares
1 ℳ 70, 1 ℳ 15 pf.). Beyond (3 M.) *Duisdorf* the train ascends
the valley of the Hardtbach, between the Hardt and the Vorgebirge.
5 M. *Impekoven;* 6 M. *Witterschlick;* 8 M. *Kottenforst,* in the
forest of that name (p. 90). — 10$^1/_2$ M. *Meckenheim* (Hähnchen), a
village of 1800 inhab., whence a pleasant walk may be taken along
the highroad viâ Gelsdorf and the Kalenborner Höhe to (8$^1/_2$ M.)
Altenahr (comp. p. 107). At the end of the walk an unexpected view
opens before us.

13$^1/_2$ M. **Rheinbach** (574 ft.; *Kauth; Rheinbacher Hof;
Wald-Hôtel,* 1$^1/_2$ M. from the railway-station, near the Stadt-
wald), a district town with 2250 inhab., mentioned in a document
of 762 under the name of 'Reginbach', possesses the remains of
some fortified towers and a late-Gothic parish-church (Roman
Catholic). In the wooded environs are numerous pleasant promenades
provided with benches. From the railway-station a marked path
leads to the (1 hr.) *Tomberg* (1037 ft.), a basaltic cone crowned
with an old castle, which existed at the beginning of the 11th
cent. and was destroyed in 1473. Half of the circular keep is still
preserved.

To the left extends the large Flamersheim Forest. 17 M. *Oden-
dorf;* 19$^1/_2$ M. *Cuchenheim.* — 21 M. *Euskirchen,* see p. 146.

---

14. The Rhine from Bonn to Remagen.

STEAMBOAT (comp. p. xv) in 1$^1/_2$-1$^3/_4$ hr. (down stream in 1 hr.); fares
90, 60 pf., return-fares 1 ℳ 30, 70 pf. (fare by express-steamer 1 ℳ 10,
return-fare 1 ℳ 70 pf.). Local steamer to *Königswinter,* calling at the
Stadthalle (p. 79) and Godesberg, six times daily in 40 minutes. — Abbreviations, see p. 74. — Railway of the Left Bank, see p. 72; of the
Right Bank, see p. 72.

The stretch between Bonn and Remagen is the beginning of
the most picturesque and famous portion of the Rhine (the 'Rhine
Gorge').

Left Bank.

The lofty tower of the Münster, the handsome residences on the river above *Bonn*, the long buildings of the University peeping from among the trees, and the grounds of the 'Alte Zoll' give the town a very attractive appearance when viewed from the steamboat.

The steamer next passes the Stadthalle (p. 79) and the Bismarck Tower.

Godesberg (S. & R.; see Map, p. 89). — HOTELS. On the Rhine: *Rhein-Hôtel Dreesen* (Pl. a), $^1/_3$ M. above the steamboat-pier, R. & B. $3^1/_2$-6, D. 3, pens. $6^1/_2$-11 ℳ, with a much-frequented garden-restaurant (concerts in the afternoon); *Schaumburger Hof* (Pl. b), $^1/_2$ M. below the pier, R. $2^1/_4$-3, B. $^3/_4$, D. 2-3, pens. 6-8 ℳ, with garden, very fair. — In Alt-Godesberg: *Royal* (Pl. c), Kurfürsten-Str. 3, of the first class, R. from 3, B. $1^1/_4$, D. 4, pens. 9-12 ℳ, with pleasant garden (closed Nov.-March); *Adler* (Pl. d), Coblenzer-Str., R. 3-6, B. 1, D. $2^1/_2$, pens. 7-10 ℳ, with wine-restaurant, good cuisine; *Kaiserhof* (Pl. e), Moltke-Str. 24, at the railway-station, with beer-restaurant, R. $2^1/_2$-$4^1/_2$, B. 1, pens. 6-10 ℳ.

PENSIONS. *Hôtel Godesberger Hof* (Pl. f), above the pier, with view-terrace, comfortably fitted-up, R. $2^1/_2$-12, B. $1^1/_4$, pens. 7-17 ℳ; *Villa Rosenburg*, Coblenzer-Str.; *Wilhelma*, Karl-Finkelnburg-Str. 19, pens. $5^1/_2$-12 ℳ; *Günther*, Kronprinzen-Str. 1, pens. 6-9 ℳ, all three of the first class; *Haus Lichtenstein*, Karl-Finkelnburg-Str. 14, pens. $4^1/_2$-$6^1/_2$ ℳ. — SANATORIA. *Godesberg Hydropathic* (*Wasserheilanstalt; Dr. Stably*), Kurfürsten-Str., next door to the Royal Hotel; *St. Vincenz Sonatorium*, Kronprinzen-Str. 2; *Dr. Schorlemmer's Sanatorium*, Rhein-Allée 37; *Dr. Müller's Schloss Rheinblick*, Waldburger-Str.; *Godeshöhe* (Dr. Bernard), to the W. of the town, with view.

RESTAURANTS (besides those at the hotels). *Railway Restaurant*, very fair; *Scheben* (Bodega); *Zum Godesberg* (Lindenwirtin), Friesdorfer-Str., frequented by the students of Bonn University. — In Godesberg-Friesdorf: *Restaurant Arndt-Ruhe* (p. 90; also bedrooms), with reminiscences of E. M. Arndt (p. 79).

CARRIAGES. Per drive for 1-2 pers. 1 ℳ, each additional person 25 pf.; first $^1/_2$ hr. one-horse $1^1/_4$ ℳ, two-horse $1^3/_4$ ℳ, each $^1/_2$ hr. following 1 or $1^1/_4$ ℳ, each addit. pers. 25 pf.; 1-4 pers. for 6 hrs. 9 or 12 ℳ. Trunk 10 pf.

TRAMWAY. Godesberg is one of the numerous stations on the steam-tramway from Bonn to Mehlem (see p. 76).

SMALL STEAMER from Bonn to Königswinter, see p. 85; landing-places 10 min. above and 10 min. below the Cologne and Düsseldorf pier. — MOTOR BOAT (from the Cologne and Düsseldorf pier): to *Königswinter*

Right Bank.

Beuel, connected with Bonn by a handsome bridge. — The *Finkenberg*, which is 1½ M. from the railway-station of Beuel, and the *Ennertberg* (518 ft.) at *Küdinghofen* consist of basaltic tufa, quarries of which are worked here.

About ¾ M. from the river is *Ramersdorf*, formerly a lodge of the Teutonic Order, now in the possession of Herr von Oppenheim, who has restored the building in a Gothic style.

As we approach Oberkassel, we observe a large cement-factory on the bank of the river.

Oberkassel (B. & R.; *Wolfsburg*, with veranda and garden, very fair), a pleasant little town with 2000 inhab., a Roman Catholic church of the 12-13th cent., a modern Protestant church, and the picturesque château of Prince Bernhard zur Lippe, dating from the 18th century. A monument commemorates the poet Gottfried Kinkel, who was a native of Oberkassel (1815-82). Footpaths lead to the *Steinerne Häuschen* (¾ M. from the railway-station), to the quarries of the *Rabenlei*, and to Heisterbach (p. 101; 2 M.). — Oberkassel is connected with Bonn by a railway-ferry (p. 79).

Nieder-Dollendorf (R.; *Rhein-Hôtel; Krone*), at the N.W. base of the Petersberg (p. 102), has an ancient parish-church, restored in the 18th cent., several half-timbered houses of the 16-18th cent., and Baron von Loë's château of Lungenburg, built in the 16th cent. and restored in 1869. Electric ferry to Godesberg.

From the railway-station of Dollendorf (p. 73) a steam-tramway (*Heisterbacher Talbahn*) runs six times daily up the Heisterbach Valley. 1¼ M. *Ober-Dollendorf*, with 2000 inhab. and an old church (restored in the 18th cent.), lies in a sheltered situation amid vineyards and orchards, between the slopes of the Petersberg and the Dollendorfer Hardt (807 ft.). 2¼ M. *Heisterbach* (p. 101); 3 M. *Wald-Station*, at the divergence of the route to the Rosenau and the Margaretenhof (Oelberg, Löwenburg; comp. p. 100); 3½ M. *Heisterbacherrott;* 4¼ M. *Grengelsbitze.*

Above Nieder-Dollendorf there are numerous villas between the road and the bank of the Rhine all the way to Königswinter.

Left Bank (Godesberg).

2 ℳ, there and back 4 ℳ; *Rolandseck* or *Honnef* 6, 8 ℳ; *Bonn* (Stadt-halle) 4¹/₂, 5 ℳ, (Rheingasse) 5, 6 ℳ. These fares are for 1-4 pers.; for each addit. pers. 25, 30, or 40 pf. Per hour 4 ℳ, for every ¹/₄ hr. more 50 pf. Handbag 10, trunk 30 pf. — ELECTRIC FERRY to Nieder-Dollen-dorf (p. 87).

TOURISTS' ENQUIRY OFFICE *(Verkehrsbureau)* at the railway-station. — VISITORS' TAX in summer (first 5 days free) 9 ℳ, for each member of a family 3 ℳ more. — MINERAL BATHS (see below), 1¹/₄-5 ℳ (7-1 & 3-6, Sun. 8-11). — RIVER BATHS, compare Plan.

Godesberg (195 ft.), founded as a watering-place at the end of the 18th cent. by the last Elector of Cologne, who caused its mineral spring to be enclosed by masonry, has been since the middle of the 19th cent. a favourite summer-resort of the wealthy merchants of the lower part of the Rhine valley. Of late it has increased with extraordinary rapidity and now contains 15,000 inhabitants. It con-sists of *Old Godesberg (Alt-Godesberg)*, to the W. of the railway, adjoining the basaltic hill called the Godesburg and the Marien-forster-Tal; of the streets and gardens extending on the E. side of the railway towards the Rhine; of the villages of *Rüngsdorf* and *Plittersdorf*, incorporated in 1901; and of *Friesdorf*, to the N.W., beyond the industrial quarter.

Along the Rhine, for a distance of 1¹/₄ M., extends the *Von-Sandt-Ufer*, a broad quay affording an admirable *View of the Seven Mountains, especially from the lofty terrace and from the new pleasure-grounds above the steamboat-pier (rfmts.). The *Rhein-Allée*, which leads inland from this point, is ³/₄ M. long and ends near the railway-station.

The older villas in Godesberg are distinguished by their luxuriant gardens. The Royal Hotel, the Hydropathic, and the Wendelstädt Villa, all three in the Kurfürsten-Str., are part of an electoral palace which was built about 1795. The *Kur-Park*, in the Coblenzer-Str., laid out in 1892, is the chief resort of visitors (good restaurant, concerts, summer-festivals, etc.). To the S.W. rises the *Draitsch*, an alkaline, chalybeate spring, with a bath-house and a Trinkhalle (1902). From the wooded park (Draitschbusch), on the slope beyond the spring, a fine view is obtained of the Godesburg and the Kotten-forst. Farther to the S. is the Wacholder-Höhe, with the *Château von der Heydt*, and its large park. In front of this, in the Elisabeth-Str., is the *Bismarck-Turm*, the *View from which is especially beau-tiful by evening-light. An attractive return-route leads viâ *Muffen-dorf*, which is embosomed in a forest of peach and other fruit trees.

The *Castle of Godesberg,** situated upon a basaltic cone 246 ft. in height, with approaches from the Burg-Str., from the Berg-Str. (opposite the Roman Catholic Church), and from the Truchsess-Str., occupies the site of a Roman and Germanic place of sacrifice, which afterwards became a Christian sanctuary. It was

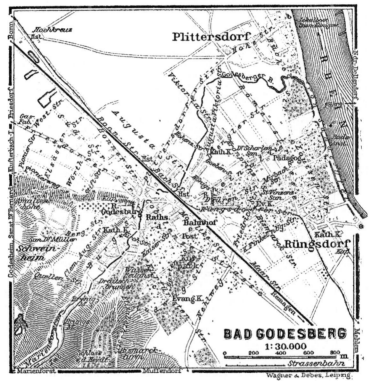

Right Bank.

Königswinter (S. & R.; comp. inset-plan on Map, p. 97). —
HOTELS. On the Rhine, all with views (some of them closed in winter):
*Grand-Hôtel Mattern (Pl. a), $1/_4$ M. from the pier, of the highest class,
with all modern comforts and good cuisine, R. 3-15, B. $1^1/_4$, D. 4, pens.
$8^1/_2$-15 ℳ; **Europäischer Hof* (Pl. c), R. 3-5, B. 1, D. 3, pens. 7-9 ℳ, with
large garden-restaurant, opposite the pier; **Düsseldorfer Hof* (Pl. e),
below the pier, R. 2-$4^1/_2$, B. 1, D. 3, pens. from $6^1/_2$ ℳ; *Berliner Hof* (Pl. b),
with garden-restaurant; *Monopol-Métropole* (Pl. d), R. $2^1/_2$-6, B. 1, D. 3 ℳ:
Union (Pl. f), R. 2-3, B. $3/_4$; pens. 5-7 ℳ; *Kölner Hof* (Pl. g), R. $1^3/_4$-3,
B. $3/_4$, pens. $4^1/_2$-6 ℳ, with popular restaurant; *Rheinischer Hof* (Pl. h),
R. & B. $2^1/_2$ ℳ, pens. 5 ℳ; *Germania* (Pl. i), R. 2-3, B. $3/_4$, pens. 5-6 ℳ;
Villa Bohnen (Pl. n), a hôtel garni. — In the TOWN: *Kaiserhof* (Pl. k),
Bahnhof-Str., R. $1^1/_2$-3, B. $3/_4$, pens. $4^1/_2$-6 ℳ, very fair; *Westfälischer
Hof*, Bahnhof-Str., R. 2-$2^1/_2$ ℳ; *Holländischer Hof* (Pl. m), Haupt-Str. 114,

Left Bank (Godesberg).

founded by the Electors of Cologne in 1210, was expanded in the 14th cent., and in 1583 was destroyed by the Bavarians. It is one of the most important examples of the art of fortification on the Lower Rhine. It includes a partly-preserved enceinte, a 'palas', and a circular keep 105 ft. in height, which commands a splendid panorama (10 pf.). The inn installed in the palas is very fair.

PROMENADES, with way-marks and numerous benches, intersect the royal *Kottenforst*, on the heights to the W. of Godesberg. The following attractive walk takes 2-2¼ hrs. Beyond the Draitschbrunnen we diverge to the right from the Löwenburg road, pass two mills, and reach (20 min.) the old convent-farm of *Marienforst*. We then ascend to the right through wood to (40 min.) the forester's house of *Venne* (255 ft.). Hence we return either by the so-called 'Schmale Allée', running to the N. of the forester's and passing the water-tower, the Viktors-Höhe, and Godesheim, or we may proceed 10 min. farther to the N., then descend by the winding 'Pionierweg' through the beautiful valley of the *Klufterbach*, and finally skirt the forest, enjoying beautiful vistas of the castle of Godesberg, to the Truchsess-Strasse. — The Drachen-Allée, which intersects the Schmale Allée, leads viâ *Annaberg* to *Kasselsruhe* near Bonn (p. 83) in 2 hrs. — From the forester's house of Venne we may reach the station of *Kottenforst* on the Bonn and Euskirchen railway (p. 85) in 2 hrs., or we may proceed viâ the *Schönwaldhaus* (restaurant) and *Villiprott* to Villip in 1½ hr. — About ½ M. farther on is the large and picturesque *Schloss Gudenau*, offering an excellent example of a lowland castle of the 17th century.

On the highroad to Bonn, near the railway-crossing, stands the *Hochkreuz*, a Gothic obelisk 33 ft. high, erected in 1349 by Walram von Jülich, Archbishop of Cologne, and restored by Zwirner in 1849. It is a station of the Bonn and Mehlem steam-tramway (p. 76).

Near **Mehlem** (R.; **Hôtel-Restaurant Villa Frieda*, R. 2½-3½, B. ¾, D. 2½, pens. 5-7½ ℳ; *Drachenfels*, on the Rhine, R. 2-2½, B. ¾, D. 2, pens. 4½-5 ℳ) the bank of the Rhine is studded with fine old country-houses surrounded by parks and gardens. The village, with its modern Romanesque church, lies ⅔ M. above the railway-station (steam-tramway to Bonn, see p. 76). The station is ⅓ M. from the Rhine. A steam-ferry and motor-launches ply to Königswinter (10 pf.). Motor-boat to Honnef and Rolandseck, see p. 92.

Right Bank (Königswinter).

R. 1³/₄-2 *ℳ; Lommerzheim,* Haupt-Str. 92, R. 1³/₄-2, B. ³/₄ *ℳ,* very good; *Hôtel-Restaurant Reinarz,* Haupt-Str. 122, R. & B. 2¹/₄ *ℳ,* unpretending. — Hotels at the Seven Mountains, see pp. 99-102.

WINE. *Bellinghausen,* on the Rhine, at the upper end of the town, with a garden-hall; *Winzer-Verein* or *Vintagers' Society,* near the Drachenfels railway (R. 1¹/₂, pens. 4¹/₂ *ℳ*). — CAFÉ AND CONFECTIONER: *Mies,* Haupt-Str. 67.

CARRIAGES. Carriage-and-pair from the station to the town or to the Petersberg Station, for 1-2 pers., 1 *ℳ;* from the tówn to the Petersberg Station, 1 *ℳ* 20 pf.; each pers. additional 20 pf., valise 10 pf., trunk 20 pf. (with one horse one-fifth less). — Drives in the environs, fares for 1-4 pers. (10 per cent extra for each pers. additional): to the *Drachenfels* 5¹/₂ *ℳ,* there and back within 3 hrs. 7¹/₂ *ℳ; Margaretenhof* 6 *ℳ,* there and back 8 *ℳ; Heisterbach* 5 *ℳ,* there and back 7¹/₂ *ℳ; Löwenburg* viâ Margaretenhof 8 *ℳ,* there and back (within 4 hrs.) 10 *ℳ,* viâ Heisterbach 10, there and back (5¹/₂ hrs.) 12 *ℳ; Petersberg* viâ Heisterbach 8 *ℳ,* the same, returning viâ Margaretenhof (5¹/₂ hrs.), 12 *ℳ; Rosenau* 7 *ℳ,* there and back 9 *ℳ; Honnef* 2¹/₂ *ℳ.* Drive through the Seven Mts. viâ Heisterbach, Petersberg, Margaretenhof, Löwenburg, and Honnef (8 hrs.), 16 *ℳ.*

STEAM FERRY to Mehlem (p. 90), starting above the steamboat-landing. — MOTOR BOAT (opposite the Kölner Hof) to *Rolandseck* 14-15 times daily viâ Mehlem, Rhöndorf, Honnef, and Grafenwerth (³/₄-1 hr.; fares 20-40 pf.). — SMALL STEAMER to *Godesberg* and *Bonn,* see p. 85. — MOTOR LAUNCH to Godesberg (Rhein-Str.), 1-4 pers. 1¹/₂ *ℳ,* each addit. pers. 20 pf.; Rolandseck 4 *ℳ* (40 pf.); Bonn (Stadthalle) 6 *ℳ* (60 pf.; return-fare 8 *ℳ*); Bonn (Rheingasse) 8 *ℳ* (80 pf.; there and back 10¹/₂ *ℳ*); per ¹/₂ hr. 2 *ℳ* (25 pf.).

MOTOR OMNIBUS (starting from the State Railway Station) along the Rhine to *Rhöndorf* and *Honnef,* 6 times daily (25, 40 pf.; p. 93). Ordinary omnibus 15-18 times daily (20, 30 pf.).

TOURISTS' ENQUIRY OFFICE *(Verkehrsverein),* Markt-Str. 6. — RIVER BATHS above the steamboat-landing.

Königswinter (165 ft.), a thriving little town with 4000 inhab., is the best starting-point for a visit to the Seven Mountains, at the foot of which it lies, and is consequently thronged by tourists in summer. A pleasant walk extends along the bank of the Rhine. At the upper end of the town are a *War Monument* and a monument to *Wolfgang Müller of Königswinter* (1816-73), the Rhenish poet. From the pier we traverse the town, passing the *Church* (1779) and the *District Court,* to the lower terminus of the *Drachenfels Railway* (p. 99). The station of the Railway of the Right Bank lies at the lower end of the town, and is passed by the road to the *Petersberg Railway* (p. 102).

Rhöndorf (R.). — HOTELS. *Bellevue,* on the Rhine, R. & B. 3, D. 2-2¹/₂, S. 1¹/₂, pens. 5-5¹/₂ *ℳ,* very fair; *Drachenfels,* Rhöndorfer Chaussée, pens. 5-6 *ℳ; Wolkenburg,* Löwenburger-Str. 2, R. & B. 2¹/₂, D. 1¹/₂, pens. 4-5 *ℳ,* with wine-room; *Traube; Thiesen.* — *Dr. Euteneuer's Hydropathic.* — MOTOR BOATS on the Rhine (tariff as at Königswinter, see above). — VISITORS' TAX as at Honnef (see p. 93).

Rhöndorf, at the foot of the Drachenfels, belongs to the parish of Honnef. It contains numerous villas. The two chief streets, the Haupt-Str. and the Löwenburger-Str., intersect in the middle of

6 *

Left Bank.

About $1^1/_2$ M. above Mehlem is the village of *Rolandswerth*, hidden from steamboat-travellers by the attractive island of *Nonnenwerth*, on which stands an old convent, rebuilt in the 18th cent. (now a girls' school, conducted by Franciscan nuns).

Rolandseck (S. & R.). — HOTELS. **Bellevue,* between the pier and the rail. station, .R. $2^1/_2$-5, B. 1, D. $3^1/_2$, pens. $6^1/_2$-9 $\mathcal{M}$, with garden-restaurant; *Decker,* in the same situation, R. 2-3, B. 1, D. $2^1/_2$, pens. 5-$6^1/_2$ $\mathcal{M}$, with garden; *Victoria,* R. $1^1/_2$-3, D. $2^1/_2$, pens. 4-$6^1/_2$ $\mathcal{M}$; **Hôtel Rolandseck,* $^1/_4$ M. below the steamboat-pier, with a large, much frequented garden-restaurant. — *Railway Restaurant;* magnificent view from the terrace; concert on Sun. and Thurs. (50 pf.).

MOTOR BOAT to Honnef and Königswinter, see p. 93. — Motor-launches may be hired for trips to Honnef (1-4 pers. 2 $\mathcal{M}$, each addit. pers. 20 pf.), Königswinter (4 $\mathcal{M}$; 40 pf.), Godesberg (6 $\mathcal{M}$; 60 pf.), or Remagen (5 $\mathcal{M}$; 50 pf.).

Rolandseck lies at the foot of the first considerable heights on the W. bank of the Rhine and is surrounded with numerous villas and gardens, extending along the wooded slopes at the back of the village. Leaving the station by the public grounds, and passing a view-pavilion on the hill, we arrive in 25 min. at the *Rolandsbogen,* or ***Roland Arch** (500 ft. above the sea-level), the last relic of the *Castle of Rolandseck* or *Rulcheseck,* perched on a basaltic rock, 344 ft. above the Rhine. Those who start from the Rolandseck Hotel pass under the railway and join the above-mentioned route. The legend that Roland, the paladin of Charlemagne, died here on finding that his betrothed Hildegunde was lost to him forever through having taken the vows in the convent of Nonnenwerth, is of modern origin. Picturesque view of the Seven Mts., best by evening-light.

About 5 min. farther on (reached direct from the Rolandseck Hotel in $^3/_4$ hr. by a well-shaded road) is the *Alter Vulkan Restaurant,* situated on the top of the **Rodderberg** (643 ft.), an ancient volcano, the crater of which is filled with loess (diluvial loam). In the hollow is the *Bruchhof.* — The descent to the railway-station of Mehlem takes 40 minutes.

Right Bank (Rhöndorf).

the village, beside the old church. Ascent of the Drachenfels, see p. 100; to the Löwenburg, see p. 103.

At the exit from the village the Clara-Str. leads to the left from the highroad to the new *Roman Catholic Chapel*, which contains the tombstone of the last Burggrave of Drachenfels (d. 1530). The road from Rhöndorf to Honnef is flanked by old elms and maples.

To the left lies the island of *Grafenwerth*, the upper end of which is connected with the bank by a causeway, constructed to increase the depth of the main channel. On Grafenwerth is the pier for —

Honnef (S. & R.). — We cross the island, which contains a frequented garden-restaurant, and ferry across to the right bank (bridge in construction). The ferry-dock is about ½ M. from the railway-station of Honnef.

HOTELS, nearly all with gardens. **Klein*, Haupt-Str. 31, pens. from 5 *M*; *Dell zum Siebengebirge*, pens. from 4½ *M*, both with restaurant and central heating; *Webel*, Haupt-Str. 62, R. 2-3, B. ³/₄, D. 2, pens. 5-6 *M*; *Wittler's Park-Hôtel*, Bahnhof-Str. 6, R. & B. 2½-3½, pens. 4½-6 *M*; *Kaiserhof*, Bahnhof-Str. 43, R. & B. 2-3, pens. 4-5 *M*; *Bahnhof-Hôtel*, at the railway-station, R. & B. 2½-3, D. 2, pens. 4½-6 *M*; *Hôtel Rheinau*. a new house on the Rhine Promenade, with view-terrace. — PENSIONS (all good and all with gardens). *Kurhaus* (p. 95), pens. 7 *M*; *Kercher*, pens. 5-8 *M*; *Schotten*, 5-6 *M* (these two for transient guests also); *Bischofshof* (5-6 *M*); *Erholung* (4½-6 *M*); *Giörtz*; *Villa Sanitas*; *Villa Wollschläger*; and numerous others. — GARDEN RESTAURANTS. *Carl Rüdesheim*; *Zum Schmelztal*. — CAFÉ & CONFECTIONER: *Dahlhausen*, in the market-place and in the Linzer-Strasse.

RIVER BATHS near the railway-station.

CARRIAGES. Drive in Honnef for 1-4 pers. 80 pf., with two horses 1 *M*; to *Rhöndorf* 1 or 1¼ *M*; to *Rolandseck Ferry* 1 or 1½ *M*; to *Königswinter* 1³/₄ or 2¼ *M*, there and back 2½ or 3½ *M*; to *Hohen-Honnef* (two horses) 1-2 pers. 4, 3-4 pers. 5 *M*; to the *Löwenburger Hof* 5½ or 7 *M*, there and back 8 or 10 *M*; to the *Margaretenhof* and *Sophien-hof* 6 or 8 *M*, there and back 8 or 11 *M*; round viâ *Löwenburg*, *Margaretenhof*, *Heisterbach*, and *Königswinter*, in 6 hrs., 10 or 13 *M*.

MOTOR OMNIBUS from Honnef (railway-station and market-place) up the valley of the *Schmelz* (p. 103) to the Restaurant Jägersruh (40 pf.), and thence to *Himberg* and *Aegidienberg* (1 *M*), and also in the other direction, to *Rhöndorf* and *Königswinter* (see p. 91).

MOTOR BOATS. From Königswinter to Rolandseck, calling at Honnef, see p. 92. To *Rolandseck* (p. 92), every ½ hr. (10 pf.); to *Königswinter*, 1-4 pers. 3, there and back 5 *M*; to *Bonn* 8½-10½, there and back 11½-14 *M*; each addit. pers. 40, 60, 80 pf., or 1 *M* 20 pf.

VISITORS' TAX (first 3 days free) for a week 1½, for the season 7½ *M* (families, 2 pers. 12, each addit. pers. 3 *M*).

Honnef (256 ft.), a scattered village with 6000 inhab., contains numerous villas, beautiful gardens, and shady avenues, and is one of the sunniest villages on the Rhine. Under the shelter of the wood-clad hills to the N. and E., spring here is generally 8-14 days ahead of other parts of the valley of the Rhine. The community consists of *Honnef* proper, on both sides of the main street, of a number of streets toward the Rhine (some of them not yet built up), of the hamlets of *Bondorf, Rommersdorf*, and *Rhöndorf* to the

Left Bank.

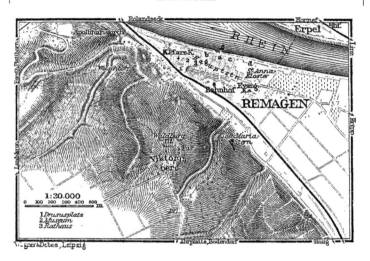

Oberwinter (R.; *Rhein-Hôtel; Post; Lorsen*), a village of 1500 inhab., has a large winter-harbour, Roman Catholic and Protestant churches, a half-timbered house of 1671, and numerous modern villas. — The **Retrospect hence is one of the finest on the Rhine. Rolandseck, the Drachenfels with its castle, the cliffs of the Wolkenburg, and the whole of the peaks of the Seven Mts., upwards of thirty in number, form a picture of incomparable beauty, while the lovely island of Nonnenwerth and the grand river itself constitute the foreground. On the right bank is the flattened summit of the Löwenburg, rising above Honnef. To the extreme right are the trachytic *Hemmerich* (1217 ft.), honeycombed with quarries, and the Grosse Leiberg (p. 95).

Farther up, the most conspicuous hills on the left bank are the *Birgeler Kopf* (577 ft.) and the basaltic *Dungkopf*, the latter separating the valleys of the *Unkelbach* and the Kalmuth (p. 97). Numerous villas are seen on the slopes.

Remagen (S. & R.). — HOTELS. On the Rhine: *Fürstenberg* (Pl. a), opposite the steamboat-pier, an old house of the first class, with much-frequented terraced garden, good cuisine and wine (beer-restaurant in the adjoining building), R. 2¹/₂-6, B. 1¹/₄, D. 4, S. 2¹/₂, pens. 8¹/₂-12¹/₂ ℳ (closed from Oct. 1st to April 30th); *Rhein-Hôtel* (Pl. b), R. 2-3¹/₂, D. 2¹/₂-3, pens. 5-8 ℳ; *Anker* (Pl. c); *Wacht am Rhein* (Pl. d), unpretending, all three also with garden-terraces. — At or near the Railway

Right Bank (Honnef).

N., and of *Beuel* and *Selhof* to the S.E. In the centre of Honnef is the market-place, abutting on the main street; here stands the Roman Catholic *Parish Church*, a late-Gothic building with nave and aisles of equal height, dating from the 12th and the 16-17th cent., and restored in 1860. The W. tower rises in five stages. In the choir are a ciborium of 1500 and a sandstone model of the Holy Sepulchre of 1508. In the main street is a *War Monument*, and to the left of it is the Kur-Garten, with the *Kurhaus*, a Trinkhalle, a covered walk, and a band-stand. The *Drachenquelle*, bored in 1898, is used for bathing as well as for drinking. Farther to the N. is the *Hölterhofstift*, a home for ladies; before we reach it, paths diverge on the right for the *Anna-Tal* and for the *Pappeln* (poplars), a favourite point of view, with benches (Breiberg, see p. 103). On the *Fuchshardt*, ³/₄ M. from the market-place (road rather steep; carriage, see p. 93), is the *Hohen-Honnef Sanatorium* (775 ft.; Dr. Weissen), an institution for sufferers from tuberculosis. Footpaths diverge from the road on the left for the view-points of *Rheingold* (rfmts.), *Mooshütte*, and *Augusthöhe* (787 ft.), going on thence to the Löwenburg (p. 103).

The *Grosse Leiberg*, a basaltic cone which commands an admirable view (1178 ft.), is reached from Honnef in 1 hr. by following the Schmelz-Tal road (p. 103) to the Jägersruhe and thence a footpath to the right.

The next village is *Rheinbreitbach* (Rheinbreitbacher Hof, pens. 3¹/₂-4 ℳ), situated about ³/₄ M. from the Rhine, at the foot of the *Virneberg*, in which copper and lead mines were formerly worked. The wire-rope railway leads to the basaltic quarries of the *Asberg*. The highroad goes on viâ *Scheuren* to Unkel.

Unkel (S. & R.; *Philipp*, formerly *Schulz*, with garden, view-terrace, and a memorial tablet to Freiligrath, pens. 4-5 ℳ, very fair), a wine-growing village with 850 inhab., lies close to the Rhine on a small plain interposed here between the river and the hills. A reef of basalt in the Rhine, known as the Unkelstein and formerly dangerous to navigation, has been removed by blasting. On the hill above are the farm-house of *Haanhof* and the manor-house of *Hoken-Unkel*.

Near Unkel the river contracts for a short distance to a width of barely 260 yds.

Erpel (R.; *Weinberg*, with garden-terrace, unpretending but good), a quaint village of 950 inhab., with a Romanesque church and a few attractive houses. A motor-ferry plies hence to Remagen (10 pf.).

Above Erpel rises the *Erpeler Lei* (666 ft. above the sea-level, 354 ft. above the Rhine), an abrupt basaltic cliff, commanding an extensive view. The ascent, which takes about 20 min. from the railway-station, follows the W. side.

Station: *Deutscher Kaiser* (Pl. e), R. & B. 3-4, pens. 5-6 *M*; *Victoria* (Pl. f), ¹/₄ M. from the railway-station, R. 1¹/₂-3, B. ³/₄, with large restaurant; *Hoersen*, R. & B. 2¹/₂-3 *M*; *Hof von Holland* (Pl. g), in the principal street, R. 2-2¹/₂, B. ³/₄, D. from 1³/₄ *M*. On the Victoria-Berg (see below), *Waldburg*, R. & B. 2-2¹/₂, D. from 1³/₄, very fair.

CARRIAGES. To the *Apollinaris-Kirche*, 80 pf., two-horse 1 *M*; to *Rolandseck* 3¹/₂ or 5 *M*, there and back in 7 hrs. 5 or 7¹/₂ *M*, whole day 7 or 10 *M*; *Laacher See* and back, 15 or 20 *M*; *Altenahr* 8 or 12 *M*, there and back 12 or 16 *M*; the *Victoria-Berg* (with two horses) 4, there and back 5 *M*.

MOTOR BOAT (starting from the Fürstenberg Hotel) downstream to *Rolandseck* (5, there and back incl. 1 hr.'s stay 7 *M*), *Rhöndorf* (7¹/₂ or 10 *M*), *Königswinter* (9 or 12 *M*), and to *Bonn* (15 or 20 *M*); upstream to *Linz* (3¹/₂ or 5¹/₂ *M*) and *Andernach* (15 or 20 *M*). These fares are for 1-5 pers.; each addit. pers. 30, 50, or 80 pf. more.

Remagen (213 ft.), a small town of 3500 inhab. and the chief shipping-place for Apollinaris water (p. 104), is of Celtic origin and was fortified by the Romans. It is mentioned as *Ricomagus* in the Peutinger Tabula (p. xxiv). Remagen once belonged, like Sinzig, to the duchy of Jülich; in 1624 it came into the possession of Pfalz-Neuburg.

At the lower end of the town is the *Roman Catholic Church*, a handsome modern Romanesque building, with an elegant choir and a central tower. The W. corner-tower and the elevated Gothic chapel in front (1246, with a tabernacle of the 15th cent.) belong to the old church. Some remains of the Roman castellum were found in the street to the W., below the terrace on which the church stands. The parsonage, to the E. of the choir, incorporates a Romanesque portal of the 11-12th cent., with enigmatic reliefs. Passing through the gate to the right and then turning to the left, we reach, at the street-corner (r.), a Gothic chapel of the 15th cent., fitted up as a small *Museum* (Pl. 2), containing Roman and Frankish antiquities found in or near Remagen (mostly casts; originals in Bonn, pp. 80, 81). In the cellar are fragments of the columns from the front of some large Roman building. The museum is open daily, 9-12 & 3-7 (25 pf.).

Beautiful views of the valleys of the Rhine and the Ahr and of the Eifel Mts. are afforded by the top of the **Victoria-Berg** (576 ft.; *Hôtel-Restaurant Waldburg*), which is reached in ¹/₄ hr. from the Drusus-Platz (Pl. 1), by a steep path ascending to the left on the other side of the railway, or in 20 min. from the point where the road is depressed to pass under the railway (¹/₃ M. to the S.E. of the station) by a broad and easier path. Finger-posts indicate the routes to the Landskron (p. 104; 1¹/₄ hr.) and to the *Ahrplatte* and other points of view.

Immediately below Remagen a road, diverging to the left from the highroad, ascends the steep clay-slate hill to the elegant Gothic four-towered **Apollinaris-Kirche**, erected in 1839-43 by *Zwirner* (p. 47), at the expense of Count Fürstenberg-Stammheim. This little church occupies the site of an ancient and much-frequented pilgrim-

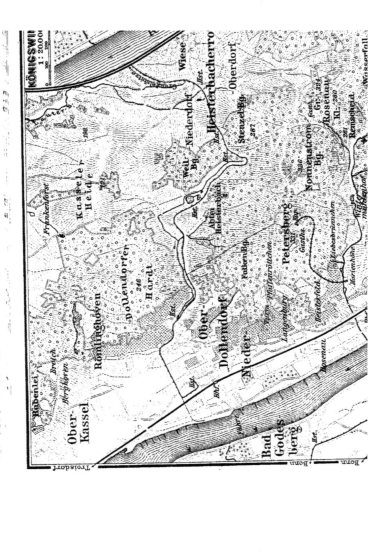

age-shrine. In 1164 Frederick Barbarossa is said to have presented the head of the highly-revered St. Apollinaris, Bishop of Ravenna, to Archbishop Reinald von Dassel of Cologne, who was in the act of conveying it to Cologne, together with the relics of the Magi (p. 50), when by some miraculous agency the vessel stopped in the middle of the river here, and refused to proceed until the head of the holy man had been safely deposited in a chapel on the Apollinarisberg.

The church is open daily from 7 a.m. to 8 p.m., on Sun. and holidays after 10 a.m. (admission, 30 pf.). The interior was adorned in 1843-51 by the Düsseldorf artists *Ernst Deger, Karl Müller, Andreas Müller,* and *Fr. Ittenbach* with large frescoes of scenes from the lives of the Saviour, the Virgin, and St. Apollinaris (transept). — The CRYPT contains the holy head, in a sarcophagus of the 14th cent.; the recumbent figure of the saint is modern. In the adjoining chapel is a painted crucifix carved in the 16th century.

Adjoining the church is a Franciscan convent. Beyond this are some gardens, through which we may ascend to the elevated spot bearing a statue of St. Francis (view).

Below Remagen, to the left of and above the railway, are several country-houses. To the N., on the hill opposite Unkel, is the conspicuous château of Herr A. von Guilleaume. On the highroad, 1 M. from Remagen, beyond the garden-gate of the little château of Marienfels, stands a *Roman Milestone*, bearing a Latin inscription placed on it in 1768, when the road was widened.

A road leads hence to the left, up the valley of the *Kalmuth*, to (1 M.) the farm of Herr M. von Guilleaume. Beyond this we may take a path to the left (blue and yellow marks), which brings us back to (1 hr.) Remagen viâ the forester's house of *Platthorn* and then down the highroad, past the Apollinaris-Kirche.

Railway from Remagen to *Adenau*, see p. 104.

15. The Seven Mountâins *(Siebengebirge)*.

One day suffices to explore the most interesting points in this district, unless the visit be for geological purposes. Walkers from *Königswinter* (p. 89) to the *Drachenfels* take ³/₄ hr.; thence to the *Great Oelberg* 1³/₄ hr.; thence along the *Nonnenstromberg* to the *Petersberg* 1 hr.; descent to *Heisterbach* 20 min.; back to *Königswinter* in ³/₄ hr., or to *Nieder-Dollendorf* in ¹/₂ hr. — From *Honnef* to the *Löwenburg* 1¹/₄ hr.; thence to the *Great Oelberg* 1¹/₄ hr., and viâ *Heisterbach* to *Königswinter* as above. In this case the Drachenfels is ascended last from Königswinter on foot or by the railway. — From *Dollendorf* we take the 'Talbahn' (p. 87) to *Heisterbach* (p. 101), ascend the *Petersberg* in 40 min., proceed thence to the *Great Oelberg* in 1¹/₂ hr., and so on as above, but in the reverse direction. — Carriage-tariffs, see pp. 91, 93.

RACK- AND -PINION RAILWAYS *(Zahnradbahnen)* ascend to the top of the *Drachenfels* (p. 99) and of the *Petersberg* (p. 102) in 10-12 min. (fare 1 ℳ, down 50 pf.). The station of the Drachenfels line is rather more than ¹/₄ M. from the steamboat-wharf or the station of the Railway of the Right Bank. The starting-point of the Petersberg line is ¹/₂ M. from the railway-station, and nearly 1 M. from the pier.

A DILIGENCE runs four times daily from Königswinter station to the Margaretenhof and Ittenbach (p. 101; 1 hr.; fare 1 ℳ). — HEISTERBACH VALLEY RAILWAY *(Heisterbacher Talbahn)* from the station of Dollendorf, see p. 87.

The *Verschönerungsverein für das Siebengebirge* (with its headquarters at Bonn) has done yeoman's service in constructing marked paths and in preserving points threatened by industrial exploitation. — Geologists who understand German should purchase *Laspeyres'* 'Siebengebirge am Rhein' (1901; 10 ℳ), with a geological map, published by Cohen at Bonn.

The *Seven Mountains,* which form the N.W. termination of the Westerwald district, extend along the Rhine for about 4¹/₂ M. from N. to S., with a breadth of 2¹/₂ M. Their peaks, cones, and ridges, mostly covered with forest, form a highly picturesque group from whatever part of the valley they are seen. The name is derived from the seven prominent summits of the *Drachenfels, Wolkenburg, Lohrberg, Grosse Oelberg, Nonnenstromberg, Petersberg,* and *Löwenburg.* These seven peaks are seen simultaneously only in the neighboorhood of Cologne; as Bonn is approached, the Löwenburg is hidden by the Nonnenstromberg. From Rolandseck we see two other summits, the *Geisberg* and the *Breiberg,* to the right of the Wolkenburg. The mass of the Siebengebirge consists of an older volcanic stratum of clastic or fragmental rocks (trachyte and tufa), 325-650 ft. in thickness and resting (at a height of 590 ft. above the sea) on the Devonian substruction of the region, and of a number of volcanic cones filled with basaltic lava (Oelberg, Nonnenstromberg, Petersberg, Löwenburg, etc.), which have broken through the clastic plateau at a later date. There are no streams of lava like those in the Eifel (p. 146). The soft and rounded forms of the hills are due partly to weathering and partly to the action of water, which percolated most easily into the loose tufa deposits.

ASCENT OF THE DRACHENFELS FROM KÖNIGSWINTER. The road passes near the station of the Railway of the Right Bank and coincides for some distance with that to the Margaretenhof (p. 101). At the Wintermühlenhof it turns to the right and leads past the villa of Hirschburg and round the W. slope of the *Hirschberg* (840 ft.; tower, with view of the valley enclosed by the Seven Mts.). We next cross the saddle between the Hirschberg and the Wolkenburg (where the road to the Oelberg diverges to the left; see p. 100) and pass a monument erected to *H. von Dechen* (d. 1889), the eminent geologist and explorer of the Seven Mts. Finally the road ascends in a curve to the terrace. — The shortest footpath (³/₄ hr.; also available for donkeys), either from the Right Rhenish station or from the river (comp. p. 91), passes the station of the mountain-railway (p. 99), various open-air restaurants, and the château of Drachenburg. A more attractive route (1 hr.) is that through the peaceful *Nachtigallen-Tal,* quitting the Drachenfels road where it turns to the left, 200 paces beyond the railway. The way through the Nachtigallen-Tal is that to the right, which leads through wood and joins the carriage-road higher up.

The RACK AND PINION RAILWAY (*Zahnradbahn;* p. 97) has a length of 1663 yds., with a rise of 837 ft. There are two intermediate stations: Drachenburg and Hôtel Burghof. Passengers with tickets for the Drachenburg are entitled to break the journey. — The prominent and ostentatious *Château of Drachenburg,* which crowns a spur of the Drachenfels, was built in 1879-85 by Tüshaus and Abbemal and is now owned by Herr von Simon. It is elaborately decorated within with mural paintings by Flüggen, Wagner, and Kirschbach (adm. 50 pf.). It stands in a deer-park, 40 acres in extent, in the S.E. part of which (open view) are a number of *Log Cabins,* rented as summer-quarters and each containing 2 or 3 rooms (full pension 8 *M;* meals taken at the château; particulars at the château). — A little to the E., in a small valley, is the *Hôtel-Restaurant Burghof* (R. & B. from 2, D. 2, pens. 5½-7 *M*).

The carriage-road and the railway end at the *Drachenfels Terrace,* about 100 ft. below the summit. Here stands a hotel (R. from 3, B. 1, D. 2½-4 *M*), with a veranda, a large open-air restaurant, and a post and telegraph office. Concerts are given on Wed. afternoon. On the side next the Rhine is a Gothic *Obelisk,* commemorating the patriotic spirit of the Rhinelanders in the years 1813-15.

The ancient castle of *Drachenfels (1066 ft.), or 'dragon's rock' (so called in reference to the dragon slain by Siegfried), 4-5 min. above the terrace, was re-erected by Arnold, Archbishop of Cologne, in 1147 and bestowed by him as a fief on the Cassius Monastery at Bonn in 1149. The keep is one of the rare examples of pure ashlar work in the district of the Rhine. From 1176 on the castle was in the hands of the Burggraves of Drachenfels whose race became extinct in 1530. The Elector of Cologne decreed its destruction during the Thirty Years' War. The stone for the cathedral of Cologne was furnished by the trachyte quarries of the Drachenfels ('Domkaul') from the 14th to the 19th century. As, however, they menaced the safety of the castle, they were purchased in 1836 by the Prussian Government, which also erected the retaining walls. The red wine grown on the S.W. slope is known as 'Drachenblut', or dragon's blood.

View. The summit commands one of the noblest prospects on the Rhine; to the E. are seen several of the seven peaks, S.E. the basaltic heights behind Honnef, among them the Breiberg, the Leiberg (p. 95), the Minderberg (near Linz), and the Hemmerich (p. 94), sloping down to the Rhine. Immediately below lie Rhöndorf, Honnef, Rheinbreitbach, Unkel, and Erpel; on the left bank Remagen and the Gothic church on the Apollinarisberg. In the background are the heights of the Volcanic Eifel: to the left the mountains round the Laacher-See; more to the right the ruin of Olbrück, the Hohe Acht, the Aremberg, and the Michelsberg, with its pilgrimage-church. More in the foreground are Oberwinter, the

islands of Grafenwerth and Nonnenwerth, the arched ruin of Rolandseck, and the Rodderburg. Opposite lies Mehlem. To the N.W. are Godesberg, the Kreuzberg, Bonn, and Cologne (in the distance).

> 'The castled crag of Drachenfels
> Frowns o'er the wide and winding Rhine,
> Whose breast of waters broadly swells
> Between the banks which bear the vine;
> And hills all rich with blossom'd trees,
> And fields which promise corn and wine
> And scatter'd cities crowning these,
> Whose far white walls along them shine,
> Have strew'd a scene which I should see
> With double joy wert *thou* with me.'
> *Byron* ('Childe Harold').

Ascent of the Drachenfels from Rhöndorf (p. 91), ³/₄ hr. The
steep footpath, indicated by a finger-post on the Löwenburg road, at the
exit from the village, leads past the *Kanzel* and the *Siegfriedshöhe*, and
ends at the veranda of the hotel.

To the N.E. of the Drachenfels rises the **Wolkenburg** (1085 ft.),
an andesite hill, also once crowned by a stronghold, which has long
since been demolished to make way for the extensive quarries which
have been worked here for centuries. No admission.

Ascent of the Great Oelberg from Königswinter, 2 hrs.
There is a road as far as the (3 M.) Margaretenhof, which is reached on foot in 1³/₄ hr. (diligence, see p. 98). The road crosses the
railway, as indicated at p. 98, and curves round into the Winter-
mühlen-Tal. To the left is the approach to the Petersberg Railway
(p. 102). Farther on we pass the *Wintermühlenhof*, where the
Drachenfels road diverges to the right. At the kilomètre-stone 1.7
the footpath and the new road to the Petersberg diverge to the left.
At kilomètre-stone 2.1 the footpath to the Rosenau (p. 101) also
diverges to the left. To the right is the *Ofenkaulberg*, with extensive subterranean quarries of tufa. At the Margaretenhof the
road crosses that coming from the Drachenfels and the Löwenburg
and goes on to Ittenbach (p. 101).

From the Drachenfels to the Great Oelberg (1¹/₂ hr.). The
carriage-road, which affords a series of charming views, diverges
to the right from the Drachenfels road in the saddle between the
Wolkenburg and the Hirschberg (595 ft.; see p. 98), about ³/₄ M.
from the Drachenfels. Walkers can save a little by taking the path
to the right at kilomètre-stone 1.8 above the Burghof Hotel, which
rejoins the road at (20 min.) the farm of *Elsiger Feld*. Footpaths
run parallel with the road farther on. Paths diverge for the Rosenau
(p. 101; left), for Rhöndorf (right), and (at a shelter-hut) for the
Löwenburg. — 40 min. (l.) Memorial to *B: Nasse* (d. 1906).

On the saddle (1095 ft.) between the *Lohrberg* and the top of
the Oelberg, where the Drachenfels road is joined by the roads
from Königswinter, Heisterbach, and the Löwenburg (p. 103), are
three good inns: the *Margaretenhof*, the *Sophienhof*, and the

Marienhof (prices in each case about the same; R. & B. $2^1/_2$, D. 2-$2^1/_2$, pens. 4-6 $\mathcal{M}$). When these are full, accommodation may be obtained at *Ittenbach*, 1 M. to the E.

At the cross-roads at the Margaretenhof are a cross with a relief of St. Margareta and the dragon (1641) and a finger-post showing the roads to the Oelberg, Petersberg, and Heisterbach. About 100 paces farther on (just short of kilomètre-stone 3.4) is another guide-post, indicating a footpath (r.) to ($^1/_2$ hr.) the top of the Oelberg.

The *Great Oelberg (1520 ft.; *Restaurant*, plain) affords the most extensive view on the lower Rhine. The whole wooded tract of the Seven Mts. lies like a map before the spectator; the Rhine glitters between the valleys which intersect its banks, and its course may be traced as far as Cologne, where the cathedral towers over the horizon-line. In the distance to the S. is the Taunus, and N.E. the heights near Düsseldorf. — The basalt quarries on the E. side of the Oelberg are interesting for the curious displacement of the basaltic columns, which are visible to a height of 100 ft.

From the Great Oelberg to the Petersberg (1 hr.) or to Heisterbach (1 hr.). In descending, a few minutes' walk from the top, we reach a finger-post on the path by which we ascended, indicating the way to Königswinter, Petersberg, and Heisterbach. After 10 min. this path joins the road from the Margaretenhof to Heisterbach (near the kilomètre-stone 2.7). From this road diverge, farther on, a footpath to Königswinter (short of kilomètre-stone 2.1) and a road (between kilomètre-stones 1.3 and 1.2) to the **Rosenau** (1060 ft.; *Hotel*, R. & B. $2^1/_2$, D. 2, pens. 5 $\mathcal{M}$, with view-terrace, very fair; foundations of an ancient castle). Above kilomètre-stone 1 the road forks. The left branch leads along the N. slope of the *Nonnenstromberg* (1105 ft.), finally in long windings which walkers may cut off, to ($1^1/_2$ M.) the Petersberg (p. 102). [Or we may follow the path over the top of the Nonnenstromberg.] The road to the right (short-cuts for walkers) runs in view of the *Stenzelberg* (945 ft.), with its extensive trachyte quarries, to Heisterbach. The trains of the *Heisterbach Valley Steam Tramway* (p. 87) stop when required at the point where the road reaches the Heisterbach Valley (Wald-Station, see p. 87). This point is 1 M. from the abbey by the road.

The venerable Cistercian Abbey of **Heisterbach** (495 ft.), enclosed by a circle of wooded heights known as the 'Heisterbacher Mantel', was founded in the 12th cent., suppressed in 1806, and almost entirely removed in 1809. Its abbey-lands now belong to Prince Bernard of Lippe. The gate (1750) still bears the arms of the abbey, a *Heister* (young beech) and a *Bach* (brook); at the side stand St. Benedict and St. Bernard as guardians. Of the magnificent abbey-church, erected in the transition-style in 1202-37, the end of the *Choir, with its slender basaltic columns, is alone extant, forming a singularly picturesque ruin. The upper arcade has stilted

round-topped arches, while the lower has been restored in the pointed Gothic style. In 1897 a memorial was erected to the monkish
author, Cæsarius von Heisterbach (d. 1240). The *Hôtel-Pension*
(R. $2^1/_2$-$3^1/_2$, B. 1, D. $2^1/_2$, S. 2, pens. 5-7 $\mathscr{M}$) has a much-frequented open-air restaurant. — The road passing Heisterbach descends
the valley to ($1^1/_2$ M.) *Dollendorf* (p. 87; railway-station and tramway-station).

FROM HEISTERBACH TO THE PETERSBERG (30-40 min.). Outside the
gate we follow the road ascending to the right till beyond the kilomètre-
stone 3.3, where the tramway crosses the road, and then ascend the footpath to the right (several finger-posts), which joins the road from the
Nonnenstromberg (see p. 101).

FROM HEISTERBACH TO KÖNIGSWINTER, $^3/_4$-1 hr. A well-trodden
path leads from the gate of the abbey to the left, and then along
the slope of the Petersberg, through wood and finally vineyards. [In
the reverse direction, we follow the Drachenfels road past the Right
Rhenish station to a point 35 paces beyond the railway-crossing,
where a finger-post on the left indicates the way to Heisterbach.]

FROM KÖNIGSWINTER TO THE PETERSBERG. Walkers generally
choose the route viâ Heisterbach (see above; $1^1/_2$ hr. in all). The
paths on the S. side of the hill are shorter. One of these ($^3/_4$ hr.)
begins at the starting-point of the Zahnradbahn and ascends to the
right, passing several crucifixes and Passion stations. Another
ascends to the left beyond the Wintermühlenhof (p. 100; 1 M. from
Königswinter) to the saddle between the Nonnenstromberg and the
Petersberg, where we reach the road mentioned at p. 101. — The
Zahnradbahn (rack-and-pinion railway; p. 97) is about $^1/_2$ M. from
the Right Rhenish rail. station. Close by is the hotel Im Kühlen
Grunde. The line is 1330 yds. in length and the average gradient
is 1 : 5 (maximum 1 : 4).

The top of the *Petersberg (1095 ft.), on which there is a
large and very fair *Hotel* (R. $2^1/_2$-5, B. $1^1/_4$, D. 3, pens. 6-10 $\mathscr{M}$),
with an open-air restaurant, affords, from the different points which
may be reached by a path skirting the margin of the extensive
plateau, various splendid views of the Rhine, the valley surrounded by the Drachenfels, Wolkenburg, Lohrberg, and Oelberg, and
to the N. of the Lower Rhenish plain with Cologne Cathedral and
of the Berg hills. At several points are remains of an early-
German stone-wall that surrounded the summit. About 1135 Walter
the Hermit established a convent on the Petersberg, the monks of
which migrated later to Heisterbach. The present chapel, near the
rack-and-pinion railway, dates from 1763.

Descending the road (short-cuts beyond the railway) we reach, at
kilomètre-stone 0.9, a point where the above-mentioned footpath to Heisterbach diverges to the left, while to the right is that to the Wintermühlenhof (p. 100). Farther on we skirt the Nonnenstromberg and reach
($^1/_2$ hr.) the Great Oelberg and Heisterbach road (p. 101) at a point $1^1/_2$ M.
from the Margaretenhof.

The Löwenburg is usually ascended from Honnef or Rhöndorf. From *Honnef* there are two roads: 1. the road (3 M.) viâ *Hohen-Honnef* (p. 95), which commands many good views; 2. the longer road (4½ M.) through the wooded *Schmelz-Tal* (motor-bus, see p. 93), then to the left through the *Einsiedler-Tal.* — Walkers (1½ hr.) may proceed to the left from the Hohen-Honnef road, as detailed at p. 95, to the August-Höhe, near which they regain the road, and then continue to the right through the woods on the E. flank of the Löwenburg; or they may traverse the Anna-Tal (p. 95) to the left to the *Breiberg* (1027 ft.; *View of the Seven Mts. from the Teufelstein) and then follow an undulating path which joins the Hohen-Honnef road 10 min. from the summit; or, finally, they may ascend to the right in the Anna-Tal, then proceed to the left to the road, cross it, and follow the footpath on the other side.

From Rhöndorf (p. 91) a road ascends through the narrow valley flanked on the N. by the heights of the Wolkenburg, the Schallenberg, and the Grosse Geisberg (1080 ft.), and on the S. by the broad Breiberg, to the (1½ hr.) top. — Walkers (1½ hr.) may take the path diverging to the *left* from the road, ¾ M. from the rail. station, which leads along the *Bolvershahn* and the *Schallenberg* to the *Kuckuckstein* (920 ft.), on the slope of the *Grosse Geisberg* (1063 ft.), and then viâ the *Jungfernhardt* to the road. [From the Schallenberg a path leads to the left to the Elsiger Feld, p. 100.] Or they may take the path leaving the road on the *right*, 250 yds. farther on, and proceed viâ the Breiberg (see above).

All these routes unite at the *Löwenburger Hof* (1160 ft.), a forester's house with a good open-air restaurant (D. 2 ℳ; also pension). A footpath ascends thence to (15-20 min.) the top of the **Löwenburg** (1493 ft.), a wooded peak of dolerite, crowned with a view-tower, marking the site of an ancient castle, the outer walls of which are still extant.

From the Löwenburg to the Great Oelberg. From the Löwenburger Hof a road, forming the continuation of the road from Honnef, leads towards the N. along the E. slope of the *Lohrberg* (1427 ft.). After 10 min. a finger-post on the left indicates the path to the summit of the Lohrberg, which may be reached in 10 min. (tower with view). The road reaches the Margaretenhof (comp. p. 100) in 25 min. more.

16. Valley of the Ahr.

The AHR rises at *Blankenheim* (p. 148) in the Eifel, 1520 ft. above
the sea, descends rapidly through a winding, picturesque, and generally
narrow valley, 55 M. in length, and falls into the Rhine (158 ft.) below
Sinzig (p. 110). Though usually the reverse of copious, it becomes a rush-
ing mountain torrent after heavy rain, sweeping down vast quantities of
débris, which has covered the greywacke rocks in the lower part of the
valley with deposits 35-40 ft. in thickness. In 1910 a terrible flood swept
away most of the bridges and caused the loss of eighty lives. — The
full-flavoured, dark-red wines produced by the vineyards of the Ahr are
still termed '*Ahrbleichert*', although the name signifies 'pale red wine of
the Ahr'. It was formerly customary, after pressing the grapes, to draw
off the juice immediately, before fermentation set in. The wine thus prepared was of a pink colour. The French plan of allowing fermentation
to begin before the separation of the juice from the skins has, however,
long been in vogue, and the dark-red colour is the result. The best
variety is that of Walporzheim (p. 106). The various *Winzervereine* or
Vintage Clubs maintain wine-rooms throughout the district.

FROM REMAGEN TO ADENAU, 26 M., railway in 2 hrs. (to Altenahr in about 1 hr).

Remagen, see p. 94. — The train describes a circuit round the
Victoria-Berg and enters the fruitful district at the mouth of the
Ahr, known as the 'Goldene Meil'. This is formed by the deposits of
this river, which have greatly contracted the channel of the Rhine.
— 3 M. *Bodendorf*, a village about $1^1/_2$ M. from Sinzig (p. 110), the
church of which is descried to the left. Farther on we obtain a
view to the left of the wooded hills on the right bank of the Ahr.

The train now skirts the **Landskron** (892 ft.), a lofty basaltic
hill, which may be ascended in $^1/_2$ hr. either from *Lohrsdorf* (at its
S. E. base, $1^1/_2$ M. from Bodendorf), from *Heppingen* (to the W.,
$1^1/_2$ M. from Neuenahr), or from Heimersheim (see below).

The castle on the summit (rfmts.), which commands an extensive
view, is said to have been founded in 1205 by Emp. Philip of Hohenstaufen, for the purpose of keeping in check the hostile Archbishop
Bruno of Cologne. It was destroyed by the French in 1677 and again
in 1682 by Elector William of Cologne. Later it came into the hands
of the Barons vom Stein, whose heirs still possess it. On the S.W. slope
is a *Chapel*, built over a basaltic grotto, the keys of which are obtained
at the castle. Near it is a quantity of massive basalt, overlying columnar basalt.

At the W. base of the Landskron are the *Heppinger*- and the
Landskroner-Mineralquelle, two refreshing springs, impregnated
with carbonic acid gas. The **Apollinarisbrunnen,** a similar
spring, situated a little farther up the valley, was discovered in
1851, and is exploited by the English *Apollinaris Company Limited*, which has made Apollinaris Water familiar throughout the
world (30 million bottles exported yearly). Special permission is
necessary for a visit to the extensive bottling works.

5 M. *Heimersheim* (Möhren, at the station). The village lies
$^1/_4$ M. from the station, on the right bank of the Ahr, and is entered

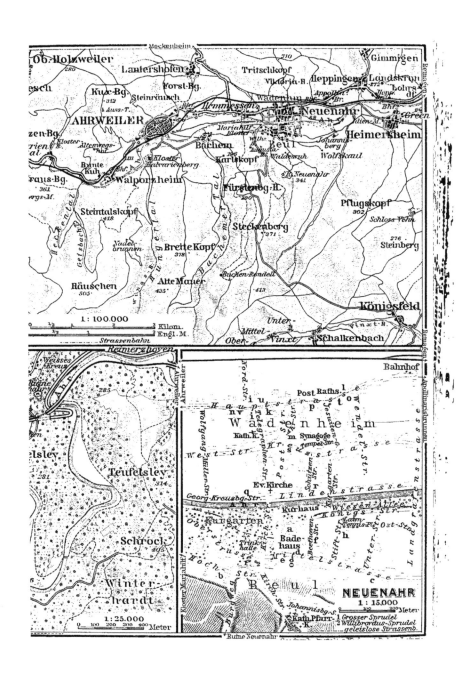

by a gateway of the 12th century. The small, but handsome church, with its octagonal tower over the centre of the transept, closely resembles that of Sinzig. Choir richly adorned. Stained glass of the early-Gothic period. Bearing of the Cross, in stone (1584). To reach (2 M.) Neuenahr walkers pass through the W. gate and take (10 min.) a footpath to the left.

$6^{1}/_{4}$ M. **Neuenahr.** — HOTELS (all houses of the first class have electric light, steam-heat, gardens, and terraces). On the right bank of the Ahr: *Kur-Hôtel* (Pl. a), in immediate connection with the Bath Establishment, first-class, with every modern comfort, R. $3\text{-}4^{1}/_{2}$, B. $1^{1}/_{4}$, D. 3, board $6^{1}/_{2}$ ℳ; *Victoria* (Pl. b), R. from 3, B. 1, D. 3, pens. 6-10 ℳ; *Concordia* (Pl. c), R. from $2^{1}/_{2}$, B. 1, D. $2^{1}/_{2}$, pens. $5^{1}/_{2}\text{-}8$ ℳ; *Heimes* (Pl. d), R. 2-3, B. 1, D. $2^{1}/_{4}$, pens. from $5^{1}/_{2}$ ℳ; *Fürstenberg* (Pl. e), R. & B. from 3, pens. from 5 ℳ; *Park Hotel* (Pl. f); *Goldener Anker* (Pl. g); *Mariahilf*, for Roman Catholics, pens. 3-6 ℳ; *Walburgisstift* (Pl. h), for Protestants, pens. $5\text{-}6^{1}/_{2}$ ℳ. — On the left bank of the Ahr, near the station: *Gr. Hôt. Flora* (Pl. i), with garden, R. $2^{1}/_{2}\text{-}3^{1}/_{2}$, B. 1, D. $3^{1}/_{2}$, pens. 7-10 ℳ; *Rheinischer Hof* (Pl. k), R. $2^{1}/_{2}\text{-}4$, B. $1^{1}/_{4}$, D. $3^{1}/_{2}$, pens. $7\text{-}9$ ℳ; *Kaiser Wilhelm* (Pl. r), with lift, R. $2^{1}/_{2}\text{-}7$, B. 1, D. $2^{1}/_{2}\text{-}3^{1}/_{2}$, S. $2\text{-}2^{1}/_{2}$, pens. 7-14 ℳ; *Karl Schröder* (Pl. n), R. $2^{1}/_{2}\text{-}4$, B. 1, D. $3^{1}/_{2}$, pens. 7-14 ℳ; *Hof von Holland* (Pl. o), R. 2-5, B. 1, D. 3, pens. 5-7 ℳ; *Bonn's Kronen-Hôtel* (Pl. l), R. 2-5, B. 1, D. $2^{1}/_{2}$, pens. 6-10 ℳ; *Palast-Hôtel* (Pl. m), R. $2^{1}/_{2}$, B. 1, D. 3, pens. 6-12 ℳ, with restaurant; *Traube* (Pl. p), R. $2^{1}/_{2}\text{-}4$, B. 1, D. 3, pens. $6^{1}/_{2}\text{-}8$ ℳ; *Hohenzollern* (Pl. q), on the Ahr, pens. $6^{1}/_{2}\text{-}9$ ℳ; *Germania* (Pl. s), R. 2-4, B. 1, D. 3, pens. $6^{1}/_{2}\text{-}8$ ℳ; *Kaiserhof* (Pl. t), R. 2-3, B. 1, D. $3\text{-}3^{1}/_{2}$, S. 2, pens. $6^{1}/_{2}\text{-}8^{1}/_{2}$ ℳ; *Hôtel Bristol* (Pl. u), R. $2^{1}/_{2}\text{-}4$, D. 3, pens. 7-10 ℳ; *Stern* (Pl. v), R. & B. $2^{1}/_{4}\text{-}3^{1}/_{2}$, pens. $5\text{-}6^{1}/_{2}$ ℳ; *Goldner Pflug*, R. 2-3 ℳ; *Reichsadler*, at the railway-station, R. & B. from 2 ℳ, these two for transient visitors. Private apartments and villas may also be procured.

CARRIAGES. From the station to the village, 1 pers. 60, each additional pers. 30 pf. Drive to *Altenahr* 5, with two horses 7 ℳ, there & back 10 & 13 ℳ, if the night is spent 14 & 18 ℳ; to the Laacher See 13 & 16, there & back 17 & 22 ℳ. — MOTOR OMNIBUS to Ahrweiler and Walporzheim.

POST & TELEGRAPH OFFICE, Haupt-Str., not far from the railway station.

VISITORS' TAX 24, the second member of a family 14, the third 10 ℳ; for non-patients 14 & 10 ℳ; per day 1 ℳ, half-day 50 pf. Baths $1^{1}/_{2}\text{-}6$ ℳ. — Bands play in the Kur-Park 6.30-8 a. m. and 5-7 p. m., and at the *Kurhaus* 8.30-10 p. m.

Neuenahr (302 ft.), a flourishing modern watering-place containing 3700 inhab. and visited by 25,000 patients yearly, consists of three formerly separate villages, viz. *Hemmessen* and *Wadenheim* (left bank) and *Beul* (right bank). On the left bank of the Ahr lie the railway-station, the town-hall, most of the hotels, the Roman Catholic church (1898-1900), and the Protestant church (1872). On the right bank, reached by various bridges, are the *Kurhaus*, erected in 1903-5, containing a restaurant, reading and other public rooms, a theatre, etc.; the *Kur-Hôtel* (see above); the *Bath Establishment* (with 100 baths of different kinds), built in 1898-99; and the *Kurhaus-Garden*, with its arcades. The water of the thermal springs (86-120° Fahr.), which were discovered in 1854, is alkaline and chiefly contains bicarbonate of soda, with an insignificant admixture of carbonate of magnesia, carbonate of lime, hydric phosphate, and lithia. The most important are the *Grosse Sprudel*, discovered in 1861, and the *Willibrordus-Sprudel* (120° Fahr.), discovered in 1904. The springs are beneficial in cases of chronic catarrh, derangement of the pulmonary and digestive organs, enlargement of the liver, diabetes, gall-stones, and rheumatism. — Attractive promenades extend down the right bank of the Ahr and up the left bank to Ahrweiler. — The old Roman Catholic church, on the S. side of Neuenahr, dates from the beginning of the 18th cent., the tower from the early middle ages.

The NEUENAHR FOREST *(Neuenahrer Wald)*, which covers the hills to the S. of the watering-place, is intersected in all directions by roads and paths. Favourite points on the edge of the forest are the open-air restaurants of *Waldesruh, Paradies-Garten,* and *Wilhelmshöhe.* Several paths (Burgweg, Kaiserweg) ascend to (40 min.) the basaltic hill (1120 ft.) crowned by the scanty ruins of the **Castle of Neuenahr.** The castle was built by the Counts of Are about 1226, and in 1353 came into the hands of the Knights of Roderberg, who afterwards assumed the title Count of Neuen-Are. It was destroyed in 1371 by Archbishop Siegfried of Cologne with the help of the inhabitants of Ahrweiler. The view from the belvedere (rfmts.) extends on the N. to Cologne and on the W. to the heights of the Eifel. — Other walks may be taken to the W. to *Bachem* (Himmelsburg Inn) and on to the Calvarienberg (see below); and to the E. to the *Johannisberg,* a hôtel-pension and open-air restaurant. Along the left bank of the Ahr to the *Victoria-Höhe* and back, ³/₄ hr.; to the top of the *Landskron* and back, 2 hrs.; to *Ahrweiler* ³/₄ hr.

8 M. **Ahrweiler** (340 ft.; *Stern,* R. 1¹/₂-2¹/₂, D. 2¹/₂ *M; Drei Kronen; Deutscher Hof)* is a thriving little town with 5450 inhab., surrounded by old walls and gates, and carrying on an active trade in wine. In the middle ages it belonged to the Electorate of Cologne, and was repeatedly besieged during the feud between the chapter of the cathedral, to which it adhered, and the deposed archbishops. In 1689 it was burned down by the French. The Gothic *Church of St. Lawrence,* founded in 1245, dates partly from the 14th and the late 15th cent., and was restored in 1901 and provided with a new spire. Above the town is the *Ehrenwall Sanitarium.* Pleasant walk from the station to the (¹/₂ M.) *Calvarienberg* on the right bank of the Ahr, crowned with a Franciscan monastery, dating from 1678 but occupied since 1838 by a girls' school managed by Ursuline nuns. Another walk may be taken from the Calvarienberg viâ the *Steintalskopf* (1370 ft.; shelter-hut) and through the *Geisbach-Tal* and *Hecken-Tal* to (1³/₄ hr.) Walporzheim.

The railway skirts the old walls of Ahrweiler on the S.

9¹/₂ M. **Walporzheim** (367 ft.; *St. Peter; St. Joseph* or *Winzer-Verein,* good wine at both), a place mentioned under the name of *Walpredeshoven* in a document of 893, and long celebrated for its wine. This village lies at the beginning of the narrower part of the Ahr Valley, which is well-suited for walkers as far as (2-2¹/₂ hrs.) Altenahr.

The railway and road now enter a rocky ravine, flanked by jagged and riven cliffs of slate; on the left rushes the Ahr, on the right rises an abrupt black wall of slate-rock, 200 ft. high, called the '*Bunte Kuh*'. At the top is a small inn, which commands an admirable view, especially by evening-light, and may be reached in ¹/₂ hr. either from Ahrweiler (past a chapel 'Deo' on the right) or Walporzheim.

The railway crosses and recrosses the stream. On the left bank, adjoining the road, are the ivy-clad ruins of the nunnery of *Marien-tal*, near the hamlet of that name (good wine at the inn).

From (12 M.) *Dernau* (Höning, at the rail. station; Kölner Hof, in the village) a path, affording good views, leads viâ the Heiligen-häuschen to (1 hr.) Mayschoss. — The valley again contracts, and the Ahr winds through a wild, rocky district. To the left lies the hamlet of *Rech*. The road follows the left bank of the stream, passing opposite the precipitous cliff on the top of which stand the fragments of the *Saffenburg* (845 ft.), captured by the French in 1702 and destroyed by the imperial troops in 1704. The railway crosses the river before and after the tunnel beneath the Saffenburg.

13¹/₂ M. *Mayschoss* (Inn of the Winzer-Verein, at the station). A bridge leads to the village, which lies on the left bank. A path, commanding beautiful views, ascends from the rail. station to the top of the *Schrock* (p. 108; 1¹/₄ hr.).

The railway once more crosses the Ahr. At the *Lochmühle* (¹/₂ M. from Mayschoss; Inn, very fair, R. 2-3, B. ³/₄, D. 2-3, pens. 4-5 ℳ) both the road and the railway enter a deep cutting through the projecting grauwacke cliffs of the *Gucklei* (627 ft.), which may be ascended by steps from this point. — We next pass the hamlets of *Laach* and *Reimerzhofen*, at the latter of which, 1 M. from the Lochmühle (beyond kilomètre-stone 25.5), pedestrians should ascend a path through the vineyards to the right to (¹/₄ hr.) the Weisse Kreuz (p. 108; paths through the vineyards are closed from the end of August till the middle of October). The railway crosses the river beyond Laach, but, after ascending a steep gradient, returns to the left bank by means of a bridge, 275 ft. long and 56 ft. high, and side by side with the road enters a short tunnel, by which the circuit of 1¹/₂ M. described by the valley is cut off. The river is again crossed before Altenahr is reached.

15 M. **Altenahr.** — Hotels. **Caspari* (Pl. a), R. 2-3, B. ³/₄, D. 2¹/₄-3¹/₂, pens. 5-7 ℳ; *Rheinischer Hof* (Pl. b), with garden on the Ahr, R. 2-2¹/₂, B. ³/₄, D. 2-3, pens. 5-6 ℳ, both ca. ¹/₄ M. from the station; *Post* (Pl. c), at the station, with small garden and view, R. & B. 2¹/₂, D. 2¹/₂, pens. 5-5¹/₂ ℳ, well spoken of; *Weisses Kreuz*, R. 1¹/₂-2, pens. 4¹/₂-5 ℳ. — *Restaurant of the Winzer-Verein*, at the rail. station.

Altenahr (548 ft.), with 900 inhab., situated amidst very picturesque scenery, is the final goal of most visitors to the Ahr Valley, and in summer, especially on Sundays, it is often unpleasantly crowded. The bridge, on the road from the station to the village, commands a lovely prospect, both upstream and downstream. The prettily-situated Romanesque church has a Gothic choir.

A broad path, beginning opposite the Hôtel Caspari (blue marks), ascends to (8-10 min.) the *Castle of Altenahr (892 ft.; adm. 50 pf.), the ruins of which are perched on a bold, jagged cliff, rising immediately above the village. This was the seat of the powerful Counts of Are in the 10th cent. and afterwards of the Counts of Hochstaden, of whom Conrad, Archbishop of Cologne, the founder of the cathedral of Cologne in 1248, was the last scion. The castle, then owned by the Elector of Cologne, fell into the hands of the French in 1672 and again in 1690, and was finally destroyed in consequence of the Peace of Utrecht (1714). — The best views of the castle are obtained from the *Weisse Kreuz*, on a rocky ridge to the N. of the castle, on the footpath between Reimerzhofen (p. 107) and Altenahr (the ascent begins with the broad path mentioned at p. 107) and from the *Schwarze Kreuz*, on the height on the right bank of the Ahr, opposite the castle on the S. (reached from the rail. station through the vineyards in $1/_4$ hr.). About 10 min. farther on is the *Teufelsloch*, a gap in the rocks, affording a view of the Ahr deep below.

The following attractive walk takes 3-3$1/_2$ hrs.: from the Altenahr bridge over the Ahr we follow the road to ($3/_4$ M.) *Altenburg* (see below), then take the cart-track to the left, which is joined in $1/_4$ hr. by the route from the Kreuzberg. In $1/_2$ hr. more we reach the top of the *Horn (1273 ft.; refuge-hut), and thence we go on, up and down, to (40 min.) the **Schrock** (1330 ft.; hut). Finally we descend viâ the *Teufelslei* (1030 ft.) to ($3/_4$ hr.) Reimerzhofen (p. 107) and follow the road back to Altenahr.

About 3 M. to the N. of Altenahr, on the road to Meckenheim, is the *Kalenborner Höhe* (1460 ft.; inn); and 4$1/_2$ M. to the N.W. of Altenburg and Kreuzberg (see below) is the *Hasenberg* (1550 ft.), near *Ober-Krälingen*. Near the latter, at *Vellen*, are the hill of *Hochthürmen* (1608 ft.) and the *Heidengarten*, both surrounded with basaltic blocks. — *Kirchsahr*, 2$1/_2$ M. to the W. of Krälingen, has a church with a good altar-piece of the early-Cologne school.

The railway crosses and recrosses the river near the hamlet of *Altenburg* (to the left; see above). On a bold eminence to the right, between the valleys of the *Vischelbach* and *Sahrbach*, rises the château of Herr von Böselager, below which lies the village of *Kreuzberg* (Wirz's Inn). Once more returning to the right bank, the train passes the village of *Pützfeld*, and reaches —

17$1/_2$ M. *Brück* (Linden), opposite the mouth of the *Kesselinger Tal.*

In the **Kesselinger-Tal,** with its fine rocky scenery, a road ascends to ($2/_3$ M.) *Denn*, where the path to the Hohe Warte (see p. 109) diverges to the S., and (2 M.) *Kesseling*. Here the road forks: to the right to *Weidenbach*, *Herschbach*, and (5$1/_2$ M.; about 3 hrs.' walk from Brück)

Kaltenborn (Langenfeldt's Inn); thence to the *Hohe Acht* (see below), ³/₄-1 hr. — The footpath leading to the S. from Denn, and ascending the **Denntal,** another valley with picturesque rocky scenery, is preferable. Farther on, it leads through meadows and fine woods to the *Hohe Warte* (2050 ft.; on the right) and past the forester's house of *Hohe Acht* (rfmts.) to the top of the *Hohe Acht* (see below; 3¹/₂ hrs.).

The river is crossed and recrossed. — 19¹/₂ M. *Hönningen.* Beyond *Liers* (3 M. up the Lierser-Tal rises the picturesque ruin of *Wenzberg*) we reach —

22 M. *Dümpelfeld,* where the highroad forks, the W. branch ascending the Ahr Valley, the S. branch that of Adenau.

The road that continues hence through the Ahr Valley leads by *Insul,* the picturesquely - situated (2 M.) *Schuld* (12 M. from Münstereifel, p. 147), the (2 M.) *Laufenbacher Hof* (Ahrtal Inn, very fair), and *Fuchshofen,* to the (¹/₂ M.) *Masholder Hof* and (³/₄ M.) *Antweiler* (Brenig), a hamlet lying ³/₄ M. to the N. of *Müsch,* on the road from Adenau to Blankenheim. — From the last two we may ascend in 1¹/₄ hr. to the top of the **Aremberg** (2044 ft.), a broad basaltic cone crowned with the ruins of the ancestral castle of the Dukes of Aremberg (key kept by the burgomaster at Antweiler).

The railway and highroad now quit the Ahr Valley, and ascend that of the *Adenauer Bach,* viâ *Nieder-Adenau* and *Leimbach.*

26 M. **Adenau** (950 ft.; *Eifeler Hof,* R. & B. from 2¹/₂, D. 1¹/₂-2 *M*; *Halber Mond,* similar charges; *Krone; Wildes Schwein,* R. & B. from 2 *M*), a district-town with 1750 inhab., on both banks of the stream. The parish-church, dating from the 11th cent., but subsequently completely altered, has a rectangular choir and a late-Gothic carved high-altar.

The following pleasant walk takes 4¹/₄ hrs. From the upper end of the town we proceed to the E. by the road up the *Exbach-Tal,* from which a footpath leads to the right (1³/₄ hr.) the basaltic **Hohe Acht** (2448 ft.), the highest summit of the Eifel. At the top are a view-tower and a restaurant. From the Hohe Acht a ridge-path ('Höhenweg', p. xvii) leads to (2 hrs.) the **Nürburg** (2225 ft.), surmounted by a ruined castle (mentioned as early as 943) and with the Graf Hochstaden Hotel (R. 1³/₄, B. 1, pens. 3¹/₂-4 *M*); fine panorama from the tower of the castle (key, 30 pf.). We descend to the Kelberg road and follow it back to Adenau.

DILIGENCE from Adenau once daily in 2 hrs. to (10 M.) *Kelberg* (Pauli, fair) and thence to *Utzerath* (5 M. in 1 hr.; p. 154).

From the rail. station of Adenau a road leads to the W. to (9-10 M.) Müsch and Antweiler (see above). Walkers save 2 M. by taking, beyond *Honerath,* the route viâ *Rodder.*

17. The Rhine from Remagen to Coblenz.

STEAMER in 3-3¹/₄ hrs. (downstream in 2 hrs.); fares 2 *M* 70, 1 *M* 55 pf. (return-fares 3 *M* 60, 2 *M* 5 pf.); express-fare 3 *M* 20 pf. (return 4 *M* 20 pf.). From Bonn to *Coblenz* in 4-5 hrs. (downstream in 2¹/₂-3¹/₄ hrs.); fares 3 *M* 70, 2 *M* 20 pf. (return 4 *M* 90, 2 *M* 90 pf.); express-fare 4 *M* 40 pf. (return 5 *M* 80 pf.). — Abbreviations, see p. 74. — Railway of the Left Bank, see p. 72; of the Right Bank, see p. 72.

Between Remagen and Coblenz the Rhine averages 1000 ft. in width, and the average fall is one foot in four.

7 *

Left Bank.

Between *Remagen* (p. 94) and Nieder-Breisig the Rhine describes a curve which the road and railway cut off.

Kripp, connected with Linz (p. 111) by a flying bridge, lies near the mouth of the *Ahr,* the deposits of which have here formed a fertile plain known as the *'Goldne Meil'* (comp. p. 104). Up the valley of the Ahr rises the conical summit of the Landskron (p. 104).

Sinzig (R.; see p. 72; *Deutsches Haus; Rheinischer Hof; Pension Villa Beauséjour*), probably the Roman *Sentiacum,* a very ancient town with 3600 inhab., still partly surrounded by walls, lies at the foot of the hills, 1 M. from the Rhine. It was once the site of a Frankish palace, afterwards an imperial residence, which latterly belonged to the Dukes of Jülich. The chief industries are the making of mosaic tiles and of bottles for the Apollinaris Spring Co. (p. 104). Picturesquely situated on a slight eminence rises the handsome *Parish Church,* which was consecrated in 1220, a charming example of the late-Romanesque style, the round arch predominating, with very slightly projecting transepts, square turrets at the sides of the choir, three apses, and an octagonal tower rising over the centre. The interior has been restored and decorated. The N. transept contains a winged picture on a gold ground, representing the Crucifixion and Ascension, and the Death of Mary, by an early Cologne master. Round the town are numerous villas, extending to the bridge over the Ahr. — To the W. opens the *Valley* of the *Hellenbach,* with its vineyards, through which we may proceed viâ *Westum* to (1¹/₄ hr.) *Heimersheim* (p. 104).

Nieder-Breisig (S. & R.; *Bender, Weisses Ross,* R. & B. 2, pens. 3¹/₂ ℳ), with 1370 inhab. and pleasant villas. Near the S. end of the village stands part of the *Tempelhof,* an old Templars' Lodge. About 1³/₄ M. higher up, a path ascends the wooded hill to the —
Château of Rheineck (594 ft.), erected in 1832 by Herr von Bethmann-Hollweg and decorated with frescoes by Steinle. The square tower, 65 ft. in height, on the S. side, is the only relic of the old castle, which was destroyed by the troops of the Electorate of Cologne in 1692. The knights of the castle became extinct in 1548. The burial-vault of the Bethmann family, on the path to

Right Bank.

Above *Erpel*, opposite Remagen, rises the *Erpeler Lei* (see p. 95). — *Kasbach* lies at the mouth of the brook of that name. *Linzhausen* (hotel, see below), practically forming part of Linz, is commanded by the ivy-clad ruins of *Ockenfels*.

Linz (S. & R.). — HOTELS. *Weinstock*, in Linzhausen (see above), ½ M. below the rail. station and the steamer-wharf, R. & B. from 3, D. 2, pens. from 5 ℳ, very fair; *Europäischer Hof*, similar charges, also good, these two with gardens on the Rhine; *Nassauer Hof*, Burgplatz, R. & B. 2½, D. 1¾ ℳ.

Linz, an old town, once belonging to the Electorate of Cologne, has 3600 inhab. and is an important shipping-port for basalt, which is extensively quarried in the neighbourhood (comp. below). Along the river-bank lie the loading-stages for the barges. The high-lying late-Romanesque *Church of St. Martin*, with a Gothic spire and other Gothic additions of the 16th cent., contains some old frescoes (restored) and an altar-piece of the early-Cologne school (1463), representing the Seven Joys of Mary (in the left gallery). To the S., opposite the choir, begins the ascent to the *Donatusberg* or *Kaiserberg*, reached from the Rhine in 20 minutes. At the top are a chapel and a bench (view).

Above Linz opens a ravine, containing the village of *Dattenberg*, with a modern church and a restored castle. Above the village is an interesting basalt-quarry, served by an aërial railway. The road to Dattenberg begins ³/₄ M. above Linz; that to the quarry diverges to the left, just short of the church. The vineyards on the slopes yield good red wine.

Farther up the river are *Leubsdorf* and *Ariendorf*, the former with an old château, with four circular corner-turrets.

On the slope we next observe the château of **Arenfels,** originally erected by Henry of Isenburg, and named by him after his wife, a Countess of Are. It was handsomely rebuilt in 1849-55 by Count Westerholt, under the directions of Zwirnér (p. 47; open to visitors on Wed.). The fine park is open daily, on application to the gardener.

Hönningen (R.; *Hôt. Schloss Arenfels*, R. & B. 2½, pens. 4½ ℳ), a village with 1370 inhab., a chemical factory, and a bath establishment (several mineral springs, strongly impregnated with carbonic acid).

About 1 M. to the S.E. of Hönningen is *Arienheller* (Kurhaus Jägerhof, R. & B. 2½, D. 1½, pens. from 5 ℳ), with a mineral spring discovered in 1897.

The quarry-railroad running past Arienheller ends at the *Mahlbergskopf* (1310 ft.), 4½ M. from Rheinbrohl. — On the hill above Arienheller we can easily trace the direction of the Roman Limes (Pfahlgraben), which reached the Rhine at Rheinbrohl.

Left Bank.

Nieder-Breisig (p. 110), contains sculptures by Begas. At the W. base of the hill, in the valley of the *Vinxtbach*, lies the hamlet of *Tal-Reineck*. The stream was the ancient *Abrinca* and formed the boundary between the provinces of Upper and Lower Germania, as it still does between the Middle and Lower Rhenish dialects. The name is a corruption of 'finis'.

At the mouth of the *Brohlbach* (p. 119) is **Brohl** (B. & R.; *Mittler*, on the Rhine, R. $1^1/_2$, B. 1, D. $1^1/_2$, pens. 4-$4^1/_2$ $\mathcal{M}$; *Könsgen*, at the rail. station; *Alte Post*, at the foot of the Diktberg), a busy village with a modern Roman Catholic church and a large harbour. It is the chief depôt for the tuffstone, trass, and phonolithic stone quarried in the Brohltal.

Above *Fornich* rises the *Fornicher Kopf* (1040 ft.), an extinct volcano commanding a wide prospect (ascent from Brohl in 1 hr.).

Namedy, beyond the railway and scarcely visible from the river, possesses a small Gothic abbey-church of the 14th cent. and an old mansion of the knights of Namedy, now transformed into a château.

On the small island of *Krummenwerth* rises the *Namedyer Sprudel* (motor-boat from Andernach), a geyser throwing its column of carbonic water, at intervals of 4 hrs., to a height of about 160 ft.

Beyond the wooded *Krahnenberg* (p. 114), the mountains confining the river recede.

Andernach (S. & R.). — HOTELS. On the Rhine: *Hackenbruch* (Pl. a), with view-terrace and baths, R. 2-3, B. 1, D. 3, pens. 6-7 $\mathcal{M}$; *Anker* (Pl. b), opposite the pier, also with terrace and baths, R. & B. $2^3/_4$-3, pens. 5-6 $\mathcal{M}$; *Rheinischer Hof*, above the Hackenbruch, R. 2-$2^1/_2$, B. $^3/_4$, pens. 4-5 $\mathcal{M}$, with restaurant; *Grosser Kurfürst*; *Schäfer* (Pl. e), on the Schänzchen, at the lower end of the town, R. 2-$2^1/_4$, B. 1, pens. $5^1/_2$-6 $\mathcal{M}$, with a frequented open-air restaurant. — In the town: *Hôtel Dahmen*, *Glocke* (Pl. g), R. $1^1/_2$-2 $\mathcal{M}$, both in the market-place, with restaurants. — OMNIBUS from the steamer-pier to the Krahnenberg railway 10 pf. — *Swimming Baths* in the Rhine (50 pf.).

Andernach, an ancient town with 7900 inhab., still to some extent surrounded by its old walls, was the Roman *Antunnacum*, one of the fifty forts of Drusus. Subsequently to the 6th cent., it is frequently mentioned as a royal Frankish residence. In the middle ages it was an Imperial town, but was taken by the Electorate of Cologne in 1496, when it lost its commercial importance. In 1688 it was burned by the French.

At the upper end of the town, near the Coblenzer-Tor, from a deep fosse, rise the ruins of the once fortified *Castle (Schloss)* of the Electors.

Near the pier is the *Rhein-Tor*, recently restored but gutted by fire in 1907; it contains a collection of antiquities. The street leads on to the *Rathaus*, a building of the latest Gothic period (1564).

Right Bank.

In the fertile plain at the foot of the hills lies **Rheinbrohl** (R.), a village with 2500 inhab. and two modern churches.

Nieder-Hammerstein (Zwick, well spoken of), yielding good wine.

Above *Ober-Hammerstein* rises a massive rock of grauwacke, crowned with the insignificant ruin of **Hammerstein.** Emp. Henry IV. resided in this castle for some time in 1105 when persecuted by his son Henry V., and here he kept the imperial insignia till their removal by his usurping successor. During the Thirty Years' War the castle was still of considerable importance.

Leutesdorf (R.; *Haus Löwenburg, R. 1-4, B. 1, D. 3, S. $2^1/_2$, pens. $5^1/_2$-$7^1/_2$ *M*, with view-terrace and garden), a village with 1750 inhab., is connected with Andernach by a flying bridge. Below it is an old Gothic church.

On the bank of the river lies the village of *Fahr* (R.); above, amid orchards, is the Romanesque *Feldkirche*. The village of *Irlich* lies near the mouth of the *Wied*, which the railway crosses. — The mountains confining the river now recede.

Neuwied (S. & R.). — HOTELS. *Wilder Mann (Pl. a), R. 2, B. 1, D. $2^1/_2$, S. $1^1/_2$ *M*; *Anker* (Pl. b), both on the Rhine; *Moravian Hotel* (Pl. c), frequented by English travellers, with restaurant; *Stelting* (Pl. d), these two in the town; *Bahnhofs-Hôtel* (Pl. e), R. & B. 2-$2^1/_2$ *M*. — *Alt-Reichskanzler Wine Room.* — Steam Ferry to Weissenthurm, 5 pf.

Neuwied, a pleasant and thriving town, with broad, well-built streets and several manufactories, was founded in 1653, on the site of the village of Langendorf, which had been destroyed in the Thirty Years' War, by Count Frederick of Wied-Neuwied, who invited numerous settlers, without distinction of religion or payment of money. The population (18,000) consists of Protestants, Roman Catholics, Moravian Brothers, Baptists, and Jews, who have lived together here in great harmony since that period. The Moravian Brothers or Herrnhuters, the 'Quakers of Germany', occupy a separate part of the town and form a kind of religious republic, having their own laws both for public and private life. The schools of Neuwied

Left Bank (Andernach).

At the lower end of the town is an imposing round *Watch Tower*, with an octagonal story above, adorned with a frieze of pointed arches, which was erected in 1451-68 and restored in 1880. A little farther on is the spot where the lava millstones, tufa, trass, and other volcanic products of the neighbourhood are shipped.

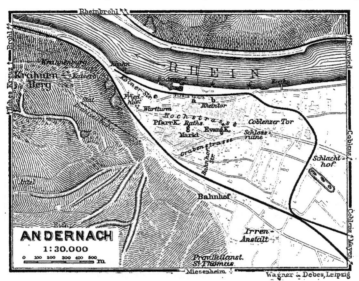

The R. C. *Parish Church*, about 200 paces inland from the watch-tower, is a fine late-Romanesque edifice (1206), with four stately towers. The still earlier choir, around which runs a gallery of small columns, dates from 1120. There is no transept. The interior has galleries over the aisles, and contains a late-Romanesque font and a large Gothic Deposition in the Tomb (in stone).

The foot of the *Krahnenberg* (p. 112) may be reached in about 10 min. either from the station or from the Rhine (past the choir of the parish-church). The ascent (20 min.) is somewhat steep (cable railway, hourly in the morning, half-hourly in the afternoon; fare 40, return-fare 50 pf.). At the top are the restaurants Krahnenburg and Kaiserburg (D. 1¼-2, pens. 4-4½ ℳ), which command beautiful views (best in the afternoon).

From the Krahnenburg a marked PATH leads along the ridge and through the Andernach Forest to the *Hohe Kreuz* and the *Hohe Buche* (Fornicher Kopf, see p. 112). Here the path forks, the right branch (red marks)

Right Bank (Neuwied).

enjoy a high reputation, and attract pupils even from England. *George Meredith* (1828-1909), for example, was educated here. — At the lower end of the town rises the spacious *Palace* of the Prince of Wied (early 18th cent.), with its fine park. The excellent collection of Dutch paintings in the palace is usually shown on application, in the absence of the family. A building adjoining the palace-gate contains a few *Roman Antiquities,* from a Pfahl-graben castle at Nieder - Bieber (see below), the most important being the silver eagle of a cohort and a memorial stone erected by the standard-bearers of the Victorienses in 246 A. D.

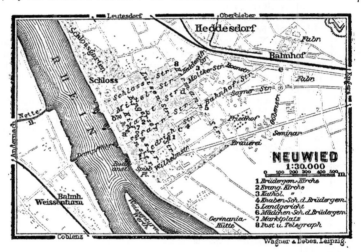

From Neuwied a STEAM TRAMWAY ascends the valley of the *Wied,* viâ *Heddesdorf* and the *Rasselstein Foundry,* to (2¹/₂ M.) *Nieder-Bieber,* with the late-Gothic Chapel of St. Boniface, containing the tomb of Archbishop Count Hermann von Wied (p. 76). The altar-piece, a paint-ing of the Annunciation after M. Schongauer's engraving in the Roman Catholic church of Neuwied, was placed here in 1905, when the chapel was restored. — From Nieder-Bieber the tramway ascends the valley of the *Aubach* to (4¹/₂ M.) *Ober-Bieber* (Wiedischer Hof), at the mouth of the *Wallbach.* In the valley of the Aubach, 2¹/₂ M. from Ober-Bieber, is the *Braunsberger Hof,* with a frequented garden-restaurant and a picturesque ruined castle. — From Ober-Bieber the road proceeds to (2¹/₂ M.) **Rengs-dorf** (930 ft.; *Richtmann,* very fair; *Post; Kaiserhof*), visited as a sum-mer-resort. The Pfahlgraben (p. 304) runs close by.

EXCURSION FROM NEUWIED TO MONREPOS AND ALTWIED. At the Rassel-stein Foundry (see above) walkers cross the stream, beyond which they traverse the pleasant park of *Nodhausen* (restaurant) to (1¹/₂ M.) *Segen-dorf* (Wolff). From Segendorf a road ascends in windings to (2¹/₂ M.)

Left Bank (Andernach).

leading to (3¹/₂ hrs.) Brohl (p. 112), while the left branch (blue) brings us to the Hôtel-Restaurant Waldfrieden (p. 120) and (3¹/₂ hrs.) Laach (p. 120).

Above Andernach the Rhine enters the Neuwied Basin, stretching hence to Coblenz. It owes its origin to a sinking in of the slate-mountains in the tertiary period and has been filled up in the diluvial era by the deposits of the river and its affluents as well as by the ejections from the volcanoes of the Eifel.

Opposite the château of Neuwied the *Nette* flows into the Rhine. Near its mouth is the *Netter Hof*, with mills, and above the *Netter-hammer Factory*. The twin summit to the W. is the Plaidter Hummerich (p. 118).

The railway-station of Weissenthurm (p. 72) lies below the village of that name, opposite Neuwied (ferry).

At the N. end of **Weissenthurm** rises a lofty square watch-tower (1370), the extreme point of the dominions of the Electors of Trèves, which here adjoined those of Cologne. Above the village stands an obelisk erected by the 'Sambre and Meuse army' to the French general *Hoche,* who died at Wetzlar in 1797.

Quarrying operations for procuring the pumice stone (comp. p. 117) led in 1898 to the discovery of two Roman camps above Weissenthurm. The one nearer the river, upwards of 400 yds. in circumference, was probably designed to protect the bridge constructed here by Julius Cæsar in 55 B.C. Bridge-piles were also found in dredging the river.

Urmitz, ³/₄ M. from the railway-station of that name (p. 72).

Kalten-Engers.

St-Sebastian-Engers.

Kesselheim.

Wallersheim.

Neuendorf.

As we approach *Coblenz* (p. 121) we enjoy a fine view of the Emp. William Monument, rising at the confluence of the Rhine and the Moselle, and of the Church of St. Castor. The steamboat stops below the bridge-of-boats connecting the town with Ehrenbreitstein.

Right Bank (Neuwied).

Monrepos, but the pedestrian may save a good deal by taking the foot-path to the left above Segendorf (green and white marks).

Monrepos (1045 ft.; 870 ft. above the Rhine), a château of the Prince of Wied, stands in a beautiful park and commands an extensive prospect of the Rhine valley and the Eifel (refreshments at the *Hahnhof*, to the W. of the château). Good points of view in the vicinity are the (10 min.) *Holzstoss* and the *Altwieder *Aussicht.* We reach the former in 10 min. by traversing the pretty beech-wood behind the château; for the latter we follow the road leading to the E. past the château and then take the third turning to the right (stone guide-post at a large oak). — Footpaths descend from the Altwieder Aussicht in 1/2 hr. to **Altwied** (*Wiedischer Hof; Kutscher's Inn,* where the key of the castle is kept), a village on the Wied 2 M. above Nieder-Bieber, commanded by the extensive ivy-clad ruins of the ancestral castle of the ancient Counts of Wied. — Altwied is about 2 M. from Rengsdorf (p. 115) viâ *Melsbach.*

Immediately above Neuwied are the *Germania* foundry and the *Hermannshütte,* the property of the Krupp Co. of Essen (p. 35). On both banks of the river here is dug up a peculiar kind of pumice stone conglomerate. It is cut into squares, mixed with mortar, and dried, and is much valued as a building material for inside walls.

Engers (R.; *Zur Römerbrücke,* on the Rhine, R. & B. 2¹/₄ ℳ; *Hôtel - Restaurant Fiegel,* at the railway - station), a village of 3000 inhab., with factories of artificial stone (comp. above). The handsome château, now a military school, was erected in 1758.

Near *Mühlhofen,* where the *Saynbach* falls into the Rhine; are several foundries. On the river is the hydropathic of *Rheinau.* On a hill in the background rises the ruined castle of *Sayn* (p. 73).

Bendorf (S. & R.; *Rheinischer Hof; Nassauer Hof*), a small town of 5700 inhab., with sanatoria for nervous patients and several factories, lies at some distance from the river.

The island of *Niederwerth,* with a village and an abbey-church of ca. 1500, conceals the town of *Vallendar* (R.; p. 73) and the village of *Mallendar,* both lying immediately on the river. On the hill above is the Kaiser Friedrich Aussichts-Turm. King Edward III. of England resided on the island of Niederwerth for a short time in 1337, and had several interviews with the Emp. Lewis and other princes. — Farther on are the château of *Besselich* (formerly belonging to the Knights Templar, now private property) and the village of *Urbar* high up on the hillside, surrounded with fruit-trees.

The fortress of Ehrenbreitstein rises above the town of *Ehrenbreitstein* (R.), which a ferry connects with the steamboat-wharf at Coblenz.

18. From Andernach and from Brohl to the Laacher See.

RAILWAY to *Kruft* (see below) or *Niedermendig;* thence on foot to the *Abbey of Laach* (from Kruft, viâ the Krufter Ofen, in $2^1/_4$-3 hrs., from Niedermendig in 1 hr.). — From Andernach viâ the Krahnenberg and Hohe Buche to Laach ($3^1/_2$ hrs.), see p. 114. — From Laach viâ *Wassenach* to *Bad Tönnisstein*, a station on the Brohl Valley Railway (p. 119), $1^3/_4$ hr.

FROM ANDERNACH TO NIEDERMENDIG (*Mayen, Daun, Gerolstein,* see p. 152), $9^1/_2$ M.; branch-railway in $^1/_2$ hr. (fares 90 or 60 pf.).

Andernach, see p. 112. — The railway diverges to the right from the Rhine Valley line. To the right is the provincial insane asylum of St. Thomas. — 4 M. *Plaidt;* the village (360 ft.; inn) has a handsome church. About $^3/_4$ M. to the S.W. is the *Rauscher-Mühle* (inn), in the valley of the brawling Nette (p. 116). In the vicinity are extensive tufa-quarries. On a rock rising abruptly from the Nette, 2 M. to the left, stands the ruin of *Wernerseck* (560 ft.), dating from 1400.

The hills which are now visible on both sides of the line are all extinct volcanoes: to the right are the *Nickenicher Weinberg* (735 ft.) and the *Krufter Ofen* (1538 ft.); to the left, the *Plaidter Hummerich* (968 ft.), with its saddle-like summit, and the *Korretsberg* (984 ft.).

6 M. **Kruft** (*Auer*), a village with 1900 inhab. and a large fish-hatchery. A pleasant road, soon contracting to a footpath, leads from the station to ($1^1/_4$ hr.) the Krufter Ofen (see above; view), whence we go on to Laach either direct (1 hr.) or viâ the Lydia-Turm (p. 120; $1^3/_4$ hr.).

Farther on, to the left, in the plain, is the *Frauen-Kirche,* or church of *St. Genoveva,* where according to the legend the saint was found by her husband Siegfried, Count Palatine of Hohensimmern (d. 754). The church contains monuments of a married couple (14th cent.), said to represent them. Numerous mineral springs bubble up in this neighbourhood, the water of which is now bottled and exported.

$9^1/_2$ M. **Niedermendig** (*Erholung,* R. & B. $2^1/_2$, D. $1^1/_2$ $\mathcal{M}$; *Gute Quelle, Post*), a village with 3500 inhab. and an old church recently enlarged, containing mural paintings of the 12th cent., stands upon a stream of basaltic lava (probably ejected by the Hochstein), which yields admirable material for millstones, paving-stones, etc. The quarries, which are more than 60 ft. under ground, and were probably once worked by the Romans, are almost all connected. The roof is supported by massive pillars left for the purpose. A guide (1 $\mathcal{M}$) precedes visitors with a torch; the inspection occupies an hour (overcoat desirable). The deserted gal-

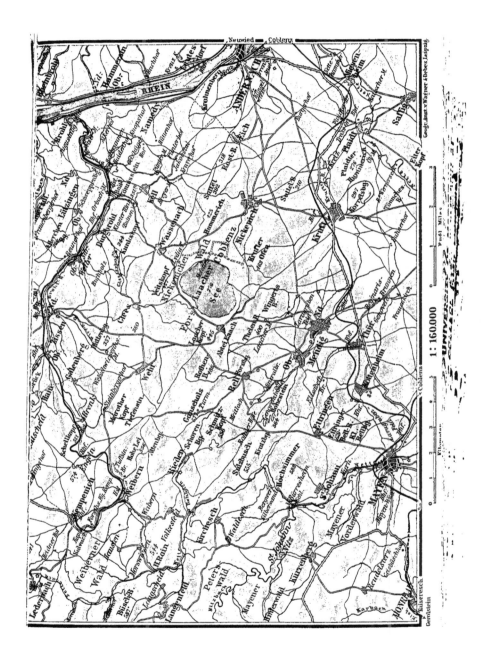

lcries are used as beer-cellars on account of their low temperature, to which the beer of Niedermendig chiefly owes its reputation. — Continuation of the railway to *Mayen* and *Gerolstein,* see p. 152.

From Niedermendig to Laach (p. 120), $3^{1}/_{2}$ M., by a dusty road. Carriages meet the trains (4 ℳ, with two horses 6 ℳ). The last part of the route, after the intervening hills have been crossed, affords a charming view of the lake and the fine abbey-church.

Brohl, see p. 112. — The narrow-gauge railway (to Tönnisstein 17 min., to Kempenich $1^{3}/_{4}$ hr.) ascends the **Brohltal,** a deep winding valley, enclosed by wooded mountains and embedded in a stream of volcanic mud 50-100 ft. in thickness. On both sides are numerous tufa-quarries, some of which are open, while others are driven like mining-shafts into the hill. — To the right, in the middle of the valley, rises the many-windowed castle of *Schweppenburg* (311 ft.), rebuilt in 1630 and owned by the Von Geyr family since 1716.

A side-valley, diverging here to the S., contains the *Heilbrunnen* or *Tönnissteiner Sprudel* (385 ft.), a mineral spring similar to the Kreuzbrunnen of Marienbad. The spring, which was known to the Romans (as evidenced by coins and vases), was reopened in the 16th cent. and has been exploited commercially since 1892.

$2^{1}/_{2}$ M. **Bad Tönnisstein** (460 ft; *Kur-Hôtel,* very fair, R. & B. $2^{1}/_{2}$-4, D. 2, pens. $5^{1}/_{2}$ ℳ), named from the ancient convent of St. Anthony (Antonius), was founded by the Electors of Cologne in the 17th cent. and has three carbonated alkaline springs and a park.

The line now crosses the Brohlbach and, traversing a tunnel, enters the broader part of the Brohl Valley. — $3^{1}/_{2}$ M. **Burgbrohl** (492 ft.; *Traube; Krone*), with an old castle, restored in the 18th century.

Beyond ($4^{1}/_{2}$ M.) *Weiler,* the ancient crater of the *Bausenberg* (1150 ft.) rises on the right; many pyroxene crystals are found in its lava. — 6 M. *Nieder-Zissen* (655 ft.; Mertens; Fuhrmann), with 1300 inhab., at the mouth of the Wirrbach-Tal.

From Nieder-Zissen a road leads past ($3/_4$ hr.) the volcanic basaltic peak of *Herchenberg* (1060 ft.), *Ober-Lützingen* (25 min.), and (25 min.) *Nieder-Lützingen* (820 ft.), to (40 min.) the castle of *Rheineck* (p. 110), where we reach the Rhine. — From Nieder-Zissen to *Neuenahr* (p. 104), about 12 M.

The next station is ($7^{1}/_{2}$ M.) *Ober-Zissen* (820 ft.), at the confluence of several brooks forming the Brohlbach. On a lofty phonolitic cone on the right, $2^{1}/_{4}$ M. from Ober-Zissen, appears the castle of **Olbrück** (1575 ft.), with an extensive view. The castle was destroyed by the French in 1689. The key of the tower is kept at Radermacher's Inn in *Hain,* the village below the castle (1 ℳ). — The railway now ascends more rapidly, with the *Hannebacher Lei* and the *Perlkopf* (1930 ft.) on the right. 10 M. *Brenk.* To the right rises the *Schellkopf* (1675 ft.). — 11 M. *Engeln,* the highest point of the line (1640 ft.), lies at the base of the *Engeler Kopf* (1880 ft.), a phonolitic hill. — At (12 M.) *Weibern* (1330 ft.) are quarries of hard grey tufa, long prized for building purposes. — 15 M. *Kempenich* (1880 ft.; Bergweiler), in a well-wooded district.

Visitors to the Laacher See quit the narrow-gauge line at Bad Tönnisstein (p. 119). The road thence ($1^3/_4$-2 hrs.) passes ($1/_2$ M.) the ruins of the (l.) Carmelite nunnery of *Antoniusstein*, and ascends viâ ($1^3/_4$ M.) *Wassenach* to (1 M.) the *Waldfrieden Hotel* (R. & B. 2 - $2^1/_2$, pens. 4-5 ℳ), on the upper margin of the Laach basin, at the point where the wood begins. Beyond the last houses of Wassenach and at the hotel are finger-posts pointing to the *Lydia-Turm*, commanding a wide prospect. On the right rises the wooded *Veitskopf* (1380 ft.), a volcanic peak with a double crater opening on the W., and abruptly-inclined lava-streams, containing numerous pyroxene crystals. The road to Laach descends to the W. bank of the lake and in 35 min. reaches the *Hôtel Maria Laach* (R. 2-3, B. $^3/_4$, D. $2^1/_2$, pens. 5-6 ℳ).

The **Laacher See** (900 ft.) occupies a nearly circular basin, $1^2/_3$ M. in diameter and 5 M. in circumference, and is about 175 ft. deep in the middle. It is the largest of the crater-like tarns of the Eifel (p. 146), and has obviously been a centre of volcanic activity. It is surrounded by six craters: the *Veitskopf* (two craters; see above), the *Laacher Kopf* (1508 ft.), the *Laacher Rotenberg* (1670 ft.), the *Thelenberg* (1328 ft.), and the *Krufter Ofen* (p. 118). Upwards of forty different streams of lava have been counted in the environs of the lake. The lake has no natural outlet, but the superfluous water flows off through an artificial shaft (re-opened and improved in 1842-44), which has reduced the superficial area by one-seventh.

On the S.W. bank rises the Benedictine Abbey of ***Laach,** founded in 1093 by Count Palatine Henry (d. 1095), which combines with the placid wood-girt lake to form a scene of idyllic beauty. The abbey was suppressed by the French in 1802, from 1863 to 1873 it was in the hands of the Jesuits, and in 1893 it was restored to the Benedictines. The *Church*, consecrated in 1156, with dome, transepts, two choirs, five towers, and crypt, is a noble example of the Romanesque style in its highest development. The beautiful *Porch* ('Paradies') in front of the W. façade belongs to the close of the 12th century. The vaulting in the interior deviates from the usual style in having its longitudinal sections in the nave no broader than those in the aisles (p. xxviii). In the W. choir is the monument of the founder, beneath a hexagonal canopy supported by columns, of which the two in front belonged to the Roman aqueduct through the Eifel Mts. The elaborate high-altar, in the E. choir, was presented to the abbey by Emp. William II. The other decorations are also modern.

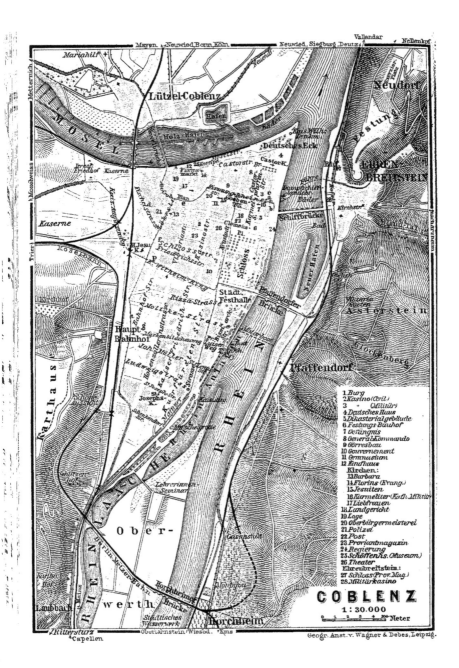

COBLENZ

1 : 30.000

Geogr. Anst. v. Wagner & Debes, Leipzig.

A pleasant excursion may be made from Laach viâ *Bell* (Daub's Inn, with key of the tower) to the (1¹/₄ hr.) view-tower on the **Gänsehals** (1873 ft.), commanding an extensive prospect of the Laacher See, the Pellenz, the mountains on the Rhine and the Moselle, and of Olbrück and the Seven Mts. to the N. From Bell viâ *Obermendig* (Spitzlay, plain), with the Elisabethbrunnen, to Niedermendig (p. 118) 1 hr. Interesting view to the right of the Ettringer Bellenberg (p. 152), the upper part of which resembles the section of a volcano.

19. Coblenz and its Environs.

The piers of the large STEAMBOATS are below the bridge-of-boats. — The RAILWAY STATION (restaurant, very fair) is at the foot of the Kartause, about 1¹/₄ M. from the piers (tramway, see below), and ¹/₂ M. from the Rhine Promenade. There is another station at *Ehrenbreitstein* (p. 128), for the trains of the Railway of the Right Bank. Railway Station at Coblenz-Lützel, on the left bank of the Moselle, see p. 72. — Hotel-omnibuses meet the trains at the central station, and also some of the steamers, but not the trains at Ehrenbreitstein.

Hotels. *On the Rhine:* *RIESEN-FÜRSTENHOF (Pl. a) & ANKER (Pl. c), opposite the steamboat-landing, two hotels (the latter closed in winter) belonging to the same proprietor, R. 3-6 (2-5), B. 1¹/₄, D. 2¹/₂-5, pens. 8-12 (7-10) ℳ; TRAUBE, Rhein-Str., R. 2-5, B. 1, D. 2-3, pens. 7-9 ℳ. — *In the Town:* *MONOPOL-MÉTROPOLE (Pl. f), at the corner of the Schloss-Str. and the Löhr-Rondell, R. 2¹/₂-6, B. 1, D. 3 ℳ, with restaurant, good wine; PALAST-PARK-HÔTEL (Pl. p), Kaiser-Wilhelm-Ring 54, R. 2¹/₂-4, B. 1, D. 3 ℳ, with restaurant, very fair; CENTRAL HOTEL (Pl. d), Fischel-Str. 32, R. 2-3¹/₂, B. 1, D. 2¹/₂ ℳ; WILDES SCHWEIN (Pl. e), in the Plan, R. 1¹/₂-4, B. 1, D. 2¹/₂ ℳ; HÔTEL DE TRÈVES, in the Clemens-Platz, next the theatre (Pl. 26), R. 1³/₄-2¹/₂ ℳ, with beer-restaurant; SCHEID, Münz-Str. 20, adjoining the Florins-Markt (p. 123), a good family hotel (R. & B. 2¹/₂ ℳ), with a frequented restaurant. — *At the Station:* HÔTEL BRISTOL (Pl. g); HANSA-HÔTEL (Pl. t), R. 2-3, B. 1 ℳ, with lift; BAHNHOFS-HÔTEL, R. 2-2¹/₄, B. 1 ℳ, all three with restaurants. — **Pensions.** *English Lodge (Villa Germania)*, Mainzer-Str. 98; *Hôtel Rheinhof*, at Pfaffendorf (p. 221), ³/₄-1 M. from the stations at Ehrenbreitstein and Coblenz, pens. 4¹/₂-5¹/₂ ℳ, with garden-restaurant.

Restaurants (besides those above-mentioned). WINE. *Carlton, Kaiser-Wilhelm-Ring 52, at the corner of the Bahnhof-Str., fashionable; *Fürstenhof*, at the Riese Hotel, with seats in the open air and a view of Ehrenbreitstein. — *Civil Casino* (Pl. 2), with a reputation for its wine; introduction by a member necessary. — BEER. **Städtische Festhalle* (p. 126; also wine); *Franziskaner Leistbräu*, *Franziskaner* (Munich Löwenbräu), both very fair, in the Goeben-Platz; *Münchner Kindl*, Schloss-Str. 34.

Baths. Warm, Russian, and Turkish baths in the *Residenzbad*, Castorpfaffen-Str. 8. — River-baths in the Rhine, attached to the bridge-of-boats (bath 50 pf.), and at the swimming-baths (also for ladies; warm baths) in the Rhine Promenade.

Post and Telegraph Office (Pl. 22), at the corner of the Clemens-Platz; also at the Central Railway Station.

Cabs. Within the town-limits (including Ehrenbreitstein; bridgetoll, see p. 128): per ¹/₄ hr., 1-2 pers. 70 pf., 3-4 pers. 1 ℳ; with two horses 1 ℳ, 1 ℳ 30 pf.; each ¹/₄ hr. additional, 50 pf., with two horses 60 pf. Double fare at night. *Luggage* from 33 to 55 lbs. 25 pf., up to 110 lbs. 50 pf. — Drive to the *Rittersturz* (p. 127) viâ the Laubach 4¹/₂ or 6, there and back with 2 hrs'. stay 6 or 8 ℳ; viâ the Kartause, 7 & 10, or 10 & 14 ℳ; fort of *Ehrenbreitstein* (p. 128), or to the top of the *Asterstein* (p. 129), 4 or 5, and back with 2 hrs.' stay, 5 or 7 ℳ.

Electric Tramways (running every 10-20 min.). 1. From the *Bridge-of-Boats* (p. 128) to the *Central Railway Station* and the *Schützenhof* and

thence to *Capellen* (p. 220; 20 min.; 35 pf., there & back 50 pf.). — 2. From
the *Goeben-Platz* to the *Schützenhof* and *Capellen* (20 min.; fares as in
No. 1). — 3. From the *Central Railway Station* viâ the Kaiser-Wilhelm-
Ring and the Pfaffendorf Bridge to *Ehrenbreitstein* (p. 128; 15 pf.) and thence
on to *Vallendar-Sayn* (p. 73). — 4. From the former *Mainzer-Tor* (p. 126)
viâ the Pfaffendorf Bridge to *Pfaffendorf* and *Niederlahnstein* (p. 221). —
5. From the *Plan* across the Moselle Bridge to *Neuendorf* (p. 116). —
6. From the *Plan* across the Moselle Bridge to *Metternich* (p. 152). —
7. From the *Church of the Sacred Heart* (p. 126) to *Moselweiss* (p. 162).

   Enquiry Bureau of the *Rheinischer Verkehrsverein*, Rhein-Str. 19
and at the Central Railway Station.

   English Church Service in the English Chapel, Görgen-Str., N.
end of Victoria-Str.

   Principal Attractions (½ day). Walk from the *Central Railway
Station* through the Markenbildchenweg to the Rhine Promenade (p. 126),
or (better) take the tramway to the Schützenhof and walk thence along the
Rhine Promenade to the Schenkendorf Monument, here turn to the left,
and proceed to the Städtische Festhalle, pass the Palace to the Goeben-
Platz, follow the Rhein-Str. to the Rhine Wharf, Church of St. Castor,
and Emperor William Monument, walk along the Moselle Wharf to the
Schöffenhaus, and proceed past the Moselle Bridge, viâ the Alter Graben,
to the Plan; thence return by tramway to the Rhine. Cross the Bridge-
of-Boats, ascend the Ehrenbreitstein or the Asterstein, and return viâ
the Pfaffendorf Bridge. — From the *Steamboat Landing* we follow the
Rhine Promenade to the Empress Augusta Monument and proceed viâ the
Mainzer-Str. (tramway) to the Städtische Festhalle, where we join the
route above described.

   Coblenz (200 ft.), at the confluence of the *Moselle* and Rhine, is
the capital of the Rhenish Province of Prussia, the seat of the civil
and military authorities, and the headquarters of the VIII. Army
Corps. Pop. 53,900; garrison 4700. Coblenz carries on an important wine-trade and manufactures large quantities of sparkling wine.
It claims to have the most beautiful situation and environs of any
of the larger Rhenish towns. On the right bank of the Rhine,
crowning a steep and rocky height, stands the massive fortress of
Ehrenbreitstein, while opposite, to the S., is the Pfaffendorfer Höhe,
with the fortifications of the Asterstein. To the S.W. rises the
Kartause, and to the N.W., beyond the Moselle, the low Petersberg,
both also with fortifications. Originally occupying a triangular
tract confined by the two rivers, the city, since the removal of its
fortifications in 1890, has gradually spread over the whole floor of
the valley between the Kartause and the Rhine.

   As the pure Latin form of its name *(Confluentes)* indicates, the town
was founded by the Romans, who erected a castellum at this point to
protect the passage of the Moselle. During the construction of the present
Central Railway Station important remains were discovered of the great
military road reconstructed by Aurelian (270-275), which came down
from the Kartause. The presence of numerous tombstones amid the flag-
stones of the road indicate that the population of Confluentes was more
civil than military. On the ruins of the Roman town there arose a
Frankish palatium, which Emperor Henry II. granted to the Archbishopric
of Trèves in 1018, with the rights of levying tolls and coining money.
As a member of the Rhenish Towns Confederation (p. 267) Coblenz
flourished greatly, but it remained under the jurisdiction of the archbishops, whose frequent residence it was from the 13th cent. onwards
(p. 124). In the Thirty Years' War it was captured by the Swedes, the

French, and the Imperialists, and in 1688 it was bombarded in vain by the French under Marshall Bouffiers. The last elector, *Clemens Wenceslaus* (b. 1739; son of Augustus III., King of Poland and Elector of Saxony), who left the Austrian military service for the church in 1761 and became archbishop in 1768, resided here almost exclusively (d. 1812 at Oberndorf near Augsburg). The town has much to be grateful for to this gifted prince, whose main interest lay in the secular welfare of his electorate rather than in the exercise of his ecclesiastical power, but nevertheless it received harsh treatment during the invasion of the Revolutionists in 1794 in consequence of his hospitality to the French émigrés. Strongly fortified by Prussia in 1815 et seq., Coblenz was accounted down to 1870 one of the most important military stations on the Rhine.

Coblenz originally lay wholly on the Moselle, clustering round the foot of a hill rising abruptly from the river and once crowned by the Roman castellum. On the highest point of this hill, partly on Roman foundations, rises the *Liebfrauen-Kirche (Church of Our Lady)*, or *Oberpfarr-Kirche* (Pl. 17), founded in 1182. The late-Romanesque nave and aisles date from 1242-59, the late-Gothic choir dates from 1404-31, and the beautiful reticulated vaulting of the nave from 1500. The limits of this original town toward the W., S., and E. are indicated by the concentric series of streets named the Alte Graben, the Plan, the Entenpfuhl-Strasse, and the Kornpfort-Strasse. These streets contain several old houses of the 17th-18th cent., with oriel windows, among which may be instanced the so-called *Four Towers (Vier Türme)* of 1689-91, which stand at the corner of the Alte Graben and the Löhr-Strasse. The last-named street, which is traversed by the tramway to the Central Railway Station (p. 121), follows the direction of the old Roman military road (p. 122).

The Alte Graben ends at the **Moselle Bridge,** erected by Elector Baldwin about 1344, and restored in 1440, which crosses the river in 14 arches. It commands a fine view downstream of Emp. William's Monument and of Ehrenbreitstein, and upstream of the Moselle hills rising beyond the railway bridge mentioned at p. 72. — The lofty turreted building adjoining the bridge is the ancient *Burg* (Pl. 1), or *Electoral Palace*, built in 1280-87, and partly reconstructed in the 16th-17th cent.; it is now municipal property. The entrance is in the Burg-Str., on the S. side.

A stone spiral staircase, dating from 1557, ascends to the first floor, on which is the *Municipal Picture Gallery* (open free on Sun. 11-1, at other times 25 pf.). The gallery contains works by Dutch masters of inferior importance and others by Coblenz painters, including examples by the various members of the *Zick* family (Johann, 1702-62; Januarius, 1732-97; Conrad, 1773-1836; Gustav, 1809-86).

In the N.E. corner of the oldest part of the town stands the *Florins-Kirche* (Pl. 14), a Romanesque pillared basilica of the last half of the 12th cent., with a Gothic choir of 1356 but having no transept. Since 1818 it has been used as a Protestant church. To the N. is the sexton's house, containing a Romanesque vaulted room which belonged to the refectory of St. Florin's abbey. In the Florins-

Markt are the so-called *Kaufhaus* (Pl. 12), built in 1479 as a town-hall, lately restored, and accommodating the collections of the 'Altertums-Verein', and the *Schöffenhaus* (Pl. 25), built in 1530 and fitted up in 1871 as a museum (prehistoric, Roman, and Frankish antiquities found in the environs; open free daily, 11-1). A flight of steps leads to the Moselle quay (good view of the pretty oriel window of the Schöffenhaus), along which we may descend to the Emperor William Monument (see below).

In the 18th cent. Coblenz began to extend towards the Rhine. The handsomest buildings facing the Rhine are all of very recent erection. Nearly opposite the bridge-of-boats (p. 128), on the site of an earlier building burned down in 1901, is the —

Royal Government Building (*Regierungsgebäude;* Pl. 24), erected in 1902-5 in the massive forms of the Rhenish variety of the Romanesque style, with a large S. tower, an elaborate main portal, and a lower N. tower. On the upper part of the central structure are figures in embossed copper of 'Ritter Georg' (Luther), Wine-growing, and Navigation. The most interesting features of the interior are the Staircase, the Accountant's Room, and the Council Chamber. The addition to the S. contains the residence of the District President. Somewhat back from the river, near which is the Royal Palace, is the new residence of the President of the Province (see p. 125).

A broad quay runs along the Rhine to the '*Deutsche Eck*', the point of land between the Rhine and the Moselle, so called from a former Teutonic Lodge ('Deutsch-Ordenshaus'; see p. 125). Upon this point rises the imposing **Monument of Emp. William I.,* erected in 1897 by the Province of the Rhine and designed by *Bruno Schmitz*. The copper equestrian figure of the emperor, 46 ft. in height, acccompanied by a Genius (30 ft. high) bearing the laurel-wreathed imperial crown, is by *Emil Hundrieser*. The whole is supported by an architectural basis of great merit. This is one of the most impressive purely personal monuments in the world, and dominates the landscape in all directions. A specially fine view of it is obtained from the steamers ascending the river.

The **Church of St. Castor,** founded in 836, lay originally outside the town, perhaps on an island in the Rhine. The present building, a Romanesque basilica with four towers, dating mainly from the 12th cent. and consecrated in 1208, has recently been well restored. It terminates in a semicircular apse adorned with a gallery of small columns and presents a picturesque appearance from the quay. The nave is roofed with rich Gothic groined vaulting, which was substituted in 1498 for the originally flat ceiling. To the right, in the choir, is the Gothic *Monument of Archbishop Kuno von Falkenstein* (d. 1388), while to the left is the less important monument of his great-nephew, *Archbishop Werner von Falkenstein.* — To the W. of the church stands the   .

Castor-Brunnen (*Br.* on Plan), erected in 1812 by the last French prefect in commemoration of the French campaign against Russia. The Russian general St. Priest with exquisite irony added the words: '*Vu et approuvé par nous commandant Russe de la ville de Coblence. Le 1. jan. 1814*'. — To the N.E., behind the church, on the side next to the Emperor William Monument, is the *Deutsch-Ordenshaus* (Pl. 4), the oldest settlement of the Teutonic Order in the Rhenish district, built in 1231 and fitted up for the reception of the government archives in 1900. It has an interesting Gothic portico and a small Romanesque chapel (open on week-days, 8-1).

The busy RHEIN-STRASSE leads from the river to the GOEBEN-PLATZ, in which rises a *Statue of General von Goeben* (1816-80), a distinguished commander in the wars of 1864, 1866, and 1871. The sculptor was *Fr. Schaper*. — The W. continuation of the Rhein-Str. leads to the small Jesuiten-Platz, which is flanked by the *Stadthaus* or *Oberbürgermeisterei* (Pl. 20), formerly a Jesuit College, a building of the end of the 16th cent. with a broad archway, and the *Jesuit Church* (Pl. 15), erected in 1609-15. A bronze statue in this square, by Uphues, commemorates *Johannes Müller* (b. in Coblenz 1801, d. in Berlin 1858), the physiologist. The Jesuiten-gässchen, skirting the Stadthaus, ends at the Entenpfuhl (p. 123).

The Post-Str. leads from the Goeben-Platz past the *Post Office* (Pl. 22), to the CLEMENS-PLATZ, which is embellished with an *Obelisk*, commemorating the construction in 1791 (by the Elector Clemens Wenceslaus) of the first aqueduct supplying the town with water. The *Stadt-Theater* (Pl. 26), on the W. side of the square, was built by Clemens Wenceslaus in 1786. — On the S.E. side of the square is the new *Residence of the President of the Province*. The road to the E. leads to the Rhine Promenade (p. 126).

To the S. of the Clemens-Platz extends an open space, known as the 'Parade-Platz', planted with lime-trees and flanked on the left side by the former electoral stables (now artillery-barracks) and the palace.

The **Palace,** a large building with a lofty Ionic portico, was erected in 1778-86, from the designs of the French architects *Ixnard* and *Peyre;* for Clemens Wenceslaus (p. 123), and occupied by him till 1794. The building suffered considerably from the French occupation, but was restored by Frederick William IV. of Prussia in 1842-45 from plans by Stüler. In 1850-58 it was occupied by the Prince of Prussia (afterwards Emp. William I.) when military governor of the Rhine province and Westphalia. The Empress Augusta annually spent a part of spring and autumn here until her death in 1890.

The ROYAL APARTMENTS are open 10-12 & 2-6 (in winter till 4; adm. 25 pf.; visitors ring for the castellan in the lower corridor of the N. wing). The ceiling-painting (Night and Morning) in the *Reception Room* is one of the chief works of Januarius Zick (p. 123). The *Gobelins Room* contains tapestry said to have been presented by Louis XVI. to Frederick the Great. In the *Electors' Room* are portraits of Electors of Trèves, from 1511 on (that of the last, Clemens Wenceslaus, by Tischbein); also memorials of various kinds from the period of the electors and later. — The *Palace Chapel*, in the N. wing, has served since 1854 as a Protestant garrison-church.

Beyond the approach to the Pfaffendorf Bridge (p. 128), on the left side of the street, rises the *Städtische Festhalle* (1901; p. 121), with a café-restaurant on the groundfloor, concert-rooms, and extensive wine-cellars. To the right is the *Barbara Fountain (Brunnen)*, designed by Schreyögg and erected in 1907 as a war-monument. Behind it, on the site of the former town-walls, begins the KAISER-WILHELM-RING, flanked by several public buildings: to the right, the *Office of the Post Master*, the *Municipal Real-Gymnasium*, and the *People's Bank (Volksbank)*; to the left, the Protestant *Christus-Kirche* and the *Kreishaus*, both erected from the plans of Prof. Vollmer. Beyond these, in the Löhr-Str., is the Roman Catholic *Church of the Sacred Heart (Herz-Jesu-Kirche)*, with its five towers, built in 1900-6 by Ludwig Becker in the Romanesque style.

Beyond the Festhalle, where the old Mainzer-Tor formerly marked the limits of the town, begin the new quarters of the town, with many attractive villas, the *Church of St. Joseph* (1896-98), and the wide MAINZER-STRASSE (electric tramway, pp. 121, 122) as the main artery of traffic. The side-streets on the left lead to the Rhine Promenade.

The **Rhine Promenade (Rhein-Anlagen)*, a creation of the Empress Augusta, extends up the river to the S. of the Rhine Quay (p. 124) for a distance of $1^1/_2$ M., commanding a view of the Pfaffen-dorf Bridge, the Ehrenbreitstein, the Pfaffendorfer Höhe, and the crowded river. The first part of it skirts the lofty wall of the Palace garden. To the left, beyond the bridge, to which a flight of iron steps ascends, is a column commemorating its construction, while to the right is a bust of the patriotic poet, *Max von Schenkendorf* (b. 1783), who died at Coblenz in 1817. Farther on, to the right, are numerous villas surrounded with gardens. To the left, beside the bathing establishment at the end of the Moltke-Str., is the wharf of the motor-ferry to Pfaffendorf (p. 128). To the right is the street named the 'Markenbildchenweg', which leads to the ($^1/_2$ M.) Central Railway Station (comp. p. 121). Adjoining is the *Trinkhalle*, with numerous seats in the open air (rfmts.), a favourite resort on Thurs. and other days when the band plays. It also contains various relics. An inscription records the enthusiastic reception which the King and Queen of Prussia received here in July, 1870, after the events at Ems which led to the outbreak of war with France. Opposite the end of the island of Oberwerth is the tasteful *Monument to Empress Augusta*, the seated marble figure and the reliefs by K. F. Moest, and the architectonic background by Bruno Schmitz

(1896). On the island of *Oberwerth,* which is connected with the Rhine Pomenade by a causeway, are an exercise-ground for pontoniers, a group of villas, the old Manor House, and a Roman Catholic seminary. — Behind the Augusta Monument runs the Mainzer-Strasse. In it, about $^1/_2$ M. farther on, is the *Schützenhof,* an open-air restaurant, whence the Hohenzollern - Str. runs direct to the Central Railway Station (tramways, see pp. 121, 122).

The grounds end at the point where the Berlin and Metz railway crosses the arm of the river between the island of Oberwerth and the mainland by an embankment. The **Horchheim Railway Bridge,** which spans the wider arm of the river, between Oberwerth and the E. bank, was constructed in 1877-79 and is 1300 ft. long. It consists of three wide brick arches and of two iron arches, each with a span of 350 ft. It is also open to pedestrians, who enjoy from it an admirable *View in all directions.

The bridge reaches the E. bank $1^1/_2$ M. above the bridge-of-boats at Coblenz. — The railway-station of *Horchheim* (p. 221) is situated at the upper end of the village, $^1/_2$ M. from the bridge.

Beyond the embankment, about 2 M. from the former Mainzer Tor (p. 126) by the Mainzer-Str., is the mouth of the small valley of the *Laubbach,* with the buildings of an abandoned hydropathic (restaurant). A road, ascending to the left at the entrance to the valley leads viâ the *Geisenköpfchen* in 25 min. to the Rittersturz, which may also be reached in $^1/_4$ hr. by a shorter footpath diverging to the left. The ***Rittersturz** (545 ft.; restaurant), a hill laid out with promenades, commands a beautiful view of Coblenz and Ehrenbreitstein (downstream) and of Lahneck, Marksburg, and Stolzenfels (upstream).

The walk may be prolonged to the S., either to the right to the top of the Kühkopf (see below), or to the left along the slope to the (25 min.) ***Dommelberg,** with a platform commanding a view resembling that from the Rittersturz. Three prehistoric stone circles on the slope of the Dommelberg point to the existence in this neighbourhood of a Celtic settlement.

The summit of the **Kühkopf** (1260 ft.) is reached from the Rittersturz in $^3/_4$ hr. by following the above-mentioned path through wood, finally crossing the Hunsrück road. It commands an extensive view of the Rhine and the Moselle, with the volcanic summits of the Eifel (left). — From the Kühkopf we reach Capellen in 1 hr. by returning to the Hunsrück road, following it to the right for a short distance, and then diverging to the left by the road (guide-post) passing Schloss Stolzenfels (p. 220). A surprising number of Celtic and Roman remains have been discovered on the 'Pastors-Pfad' (path from Capellen to Waldesch), which crosses the last-mentioned road. Among these are the foundation-walls of a temple of Mercury; the hand of the colossal statue, with tortoise and serpent, is preserved in Schloss Stolzenfels. — Winningen (p. 162) is reached from the Kühkopf viâ the forester's house at *Remstecken* in $1^1/_2$ hr.

The **Kartause** (so named from an ancient Carthusian monastery), a hill rising to the W. of the *Central Station,* is crowned by fortifications. On its N. slope is the picturesque *Cemetery,* where repose the remains of *Max von Schenkendorf* (p. 126), *Karl Baedeker* (1801-59; on the slope above the chapel), and *Gen. von Goeben* (p. 125).

Ehrenbreitstein and Asterstein.

Ehrenbreitstein is reached either by one of the bridges or by the *Steam Ferry* (fare 5 pf.) starting every 10 min. from the Rhine Quay opposite the Rhein-Str. and landing on the other side near the railway station. Those who want to catch a train will find the ferry safer than the bridge-of-boats, which is often opened for passing ships. A *Motor Ferry* (p. 126; 5 pf.) plies every $^1/_4$ hr. from the Rhine Promenade to Pfaffendorf.

Electric Tramway from the Central Railway Station at Coblenz to Ehrenbreitstein, see p. 121. Others run from Ehrenbreitstein to Vallendar, Bendorf, and Sayn (p. 73) and to Arenberg (p. 129) every 20 minutes. From Pfaffendorf to Niederlahnstein, see p. 122.

Two bridges connect Coblenz with the right bank of the Rhine. The chief traffic follows the **Bridge-of-Boats** *(Schiffbrücke)*, which begins at the Altstadt part of the Rhine Quay. Communication from the Neustadt is effected by the **Pfaffendorf Bridge,** which crosses the stream in three iron arches, each of 320 ft. span, and ends at a point between Ehrenbreitstein and *Pfaffendorf.* This was constructed in 1862-64 for the railway but is now used by carriages and pedestrians. Both bridges command beautiful views. The bridge-toll on each is 2 c. (one-horse carr. 22, two-horse 29 pf.).

Ehrenbreitstein, a small town with 5300 inhab., is situated in a valley between the Ehrenbreitstein and Asterstein, extending along the base of the latter, past the large winter-harbour, to the Pfaffendorf bridge. — To reach the railway-station and the fortress of Ehrenbreitstein we turn to the left into the *Hof-Strasse.* Here, to the left, is the *Kurfürsten Hotel* (with restaurant), once occupied by M. de La Roche, chancellor of the electorate of Trèves, to whom Goethe paid a visit in 1774 (memorial tablet). The tramway-station is close by. Farther on, to the left, is the *Railway Station* of the Right Bank (pp. 74, 217), while to the right is the large *Dikasterial-gebäude* (court of justice), erected as an Electoral Palace in 1747-50 and now used as a barrack and provision magazine (Pl. 27).

A visit to the fortress of Ehrenbreitstein from Coblenz takes $1^1/_2$-2 hrs. (carr., see p. 121). About 200 yds. beyond the railway-station we diverge to the right from the road descending the Rhine and ascend the hill (20 min.), where, at the last gateway, the cards of admission are issued from April 1st to Nov. 15th (50 pf.). Visitors are conducted to the point of view by a sergeant. Foreign officers are not admitted.

The **Fortress of Ehrenbreitstein** rises opposite the influx of the Moselle, 385 ft. above the Rhine, on a precipitous rock, which is connected with the neighbouring heights on the N. side only. The present fortress, built in 1816-26 by General von Aster, succeeds a very ancient stronghold of the Electors of Trèves, which

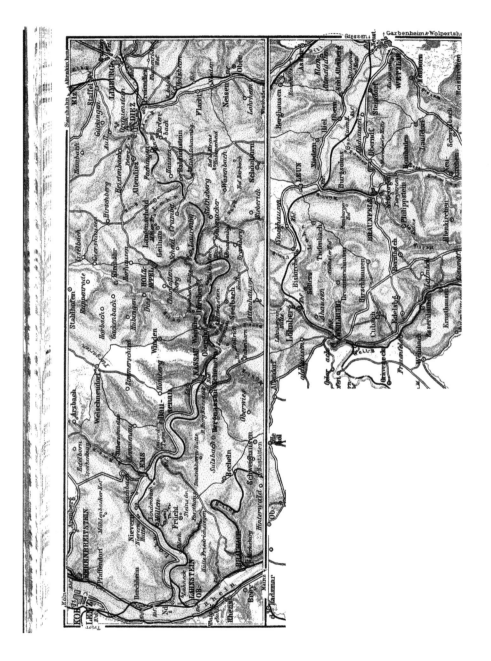

played an important part in the Thirty Years' War, and was taken
by the French in 1799 after a gallant resistance. The *View embraces the fertile valley of the Rhine from Stolzenfels to Andernach,
and the volcanic peaks of the Eifel (p. 145). In the foreground,
far below, are the Rhine and Moselle, and between them the Emp.
William Monument and the triangular town of Coblenz.

Fort Asterstein, situated on the hill to the S. of Ehrenbreitstein, also commands a fine view. It may be visited from Coblenz
in 1¹/₄ hr.; no permission is necessary. From the bridge-of-boats
we proceed in a straight direction to the end of the Kirch‑Str.
and follow the road to the right below the Villa Schützenburg.
Where the road turns to the left, a shorter route (20 min.) ascends
by the steps to the right, crosses the road which leads up from the
'Promenade', and again ascends by steps. Halfway up, the *Café
Rheinlust*, and beyond it the *Luisenturm* are passed. We then
follow the road to the summit, where there is an *Obelisk* in memory
of the war of 1866. The road continues, past the Victoria-Garten
(restaurant) and then descends to Pfaffendorf.

The road which ascends the valley at the back of the Ehrenbreitstein
(electric tramway in 20 min.; see p. 128) leads by *Niederberg* to (2¹/₂ M.)
Arenberg, usually known as *Roter Hahn*, a village with a pilgrimage-
church, a 'Herz-Jesu' chapel, a 'Mount of Olives', a Grotto of Lourdes, and
so on. — The road diverging to the right beyond Arenberg crosses the hill
(view), passes the 'Jägerhaus' (rfmts.), and leads to (4¹/₂ M.) Ems (p. 130).

20. Ems and the Valley of the Lahn.

RAILWAY (continuation of the Moselle Railway, p. 161) from *Coblenz*
to (72 M.) *Giessen* viâ Niederlahnstein, Ems, and Wetzlar in 2³/₄-4 hrs.
(fares 9 ℳ, 5 ℳ 70, 3 ℳ 70; express fares 10 ℳ, 6 ℳ 70, 4 ℳ 20 pf.); to
(10¹/₂ M.) *Ems* in ¹/₂-³/₄ hr. (fares 1 ℳ 45, 90, 55 pf.). — The *Steamboat
Station* for Ems is Oberlahnstein (p. 221).

The LAHN rises in the S. part of Westphalia, turns to the W. at
Giessen (about halfway to its mouth), and winds through the unstratified
limestone and graywacke formations of the Rhenish schistous district
(between the Taunus and the Westerwald; comp. p. 219). Its fall is rapid.
The scenery of the Lahntal vies with that of the most beautiful of the
other side-valleys of the Rhine. The features of interest include hills
rising to a height of 800 ft. above the floor of the valley, picturesque
little towns, and numerous old churches, ruined castles, and chateaux.
Nassau, Dietz, Limburg, and *Weilburg* are the most picturesque points.

Coblenz, see p. 121. The train crosses the Rhine by the bridge
mentioned at p. 127, and passes through a cutting on the landward
side of Horchheim (comp. p. 221).

3 M. *Niederlahnstein* (p. 221; Railway Restaurant), the junction
of the Railway of the Right Bank (p. 217). — The train now skirts
the Allerheiligen-Berg (p. 221) and crosses the *Lahn*. On the left
lies the old *Hohenrhein Foundry* (now wire-works), where the
Oberlahnstein branch-railway diverges (p. 223). Part of the river
has been canalized. Numerous locks have been constructed to meet

the rapid fall of the stream, which amounts tó 10 ft. in a distance
of half-a-mile. The navigation, however, formerly important for
the transport of the iron ore of the Weilburg district, is now insignificant. — 6 M. *Friedrichssegen,* the station for the lead and
silver mines of the same name, which lie about $1^1/_2$ M. to the E. —
$8^1/_2$ M. *Nievern,* with a large foundry.

$10^1/_2$ M. **Bad Ems.** — HOTELS (the large ones with modern con-
veniences generally open in summer only; hotel-omnibuses at the station).
On the right bank of the Lahn: *Hôtel d'Angleterre* (Pl. a), Römer-Str. 46,
at the lower end of the promenade, with large garden, and dépendance
Park Villa, Victoria-Allée 6, R. 3-8, B. $1^1/_2$, D. 4, S. 3, pens. 9-15 ℳ, with
lift and private baths; *Royal Kurhaus*, Römer-Str. 1, R. from 3, B. $1^1/_4$,
D. $3^1/_2$-4, S. $2^1/_2$, pens. from 8 ℳ, with lift and baths (see p. 132); *Hôtel des
Quatre-Saisons et de l'Europe* (Pl. c), Römer-Str. 5, R. 3-6, B. $2^3/_4$, D. $3^3/_4$,
S. $2^1/_2$, pens. from 8 ℳ, with lift and baths (see p. 132); *Vier Türme* (Pl. d),
in the grounds of the Kurhaus, same management and prices; *Darmstädter
Hof* (Pl. e), near the bridge, with café and open-air restaurant; R. from 3, B. $1^1/_4$,
D. $3^1/_2$, pens. 8-10 ℳ, with lift; *Hôtel Bristol* (Pl. f), Römer-Str. 45,
opposite the Vier Türme, R. 2-5, B. 1, D. $2^1/_2$-3, pens. 6-10 ℳ; *Stadt
Wiesbaden*, opposite the Wandelbahn; *Schützenhof*, opposite the Vier
Türme; *Löwe* (Pl. i), Lahn-Str. 1, R. 2-3, B. 1, D. 2, pens. 6-8 ℳ, open
the whole year, with steam-heating and a very fair beer-restaurant;
Weisses Ross (Pl. k), Lahn-Str. 6, R. 2-3, B. 1, pens. 6-7$^1/_2$ ℳ, also with
very fair beer-restaurant; *Monopol-Métropole* (Pl. l), Römer-Str. 18, R. 2-4,
B. 1, D. 2-2$^1/_2$, pens. $5^1/_2$-9 ℳ, with attractively fitted-up restaurant;
Promenade, near the bridge, with café and open-air restaurant; *Weil-
burger Hof* (Pl. n), Graben-Str. 59, R. $1^1/_2$-2$^1/_2$, B. $^3/_4$, D. 2, pens. 5-6$^1/_4$ ℳ;
Hof von Holland (Pl. o), Lahn-Str. 21, R. from 2, B. $^3/_4$, pens. 5-8 ℳ;
Hôtel-Pension Soltau (Pl. p), Römer-Str. 91, R. 2-3, B. 1, pens. $5^1/_2$-8 ℳ.

On the left bank (cooler than the right bank): *Römerbad* (Pl. q;
p. 132), corner of the Mainzer-Str. and the Badhaus-Str., R. 3-10,
B. $1^1/_4$, D. $3^1/_2$-4, pens. 8-16 ℳ, with lift and garden; *Hôtel Gutten-
berg* (Pl. r), Mainzer-Str. 5, R. 3-4$^1/_2$, B. $1^1/_4$, D. $3^1/_2$-4, pens. from 8 ℳ,
with lift, garden, and restaurant; *Villa Bella Riva* (Pl. s), Villen-
Promenade 15, at the Kaiser-Brücke, R. 3-6, B. $1^1/_4$, D. $3^1/_2$-4, pens. 8-
12 ℳ, with large garden; *Schloss Balmoral & Villa Diana*. — *Hôtel
de Flandre*, opposite the station, with garden; *Hôtel-Pension Schloss
Johannisberg* (Pl. v), Wintersberg-Str. 1, R. 2-3, B. 1, D. $2^1/_4$, pens. 6-8 ℳ,
well spoken of; *Hôtel Royal* (Pl. w), Malberg-Str. 4, R. 2-3, B. 1, D. 2,
pens. $5^1/_2$-7 ℳ; *Hôtel de France* (Pl. x; Jewish), Bahnhof-Str. 1, R. $2^1/_2$-8,
B. 1, D. $3^1/_4$, pens. $6^1/_2$-10 ℳ.

There are also numerous LODGING HOUSES, some of which are very
comfortably fitted up, especially in the Villa Promenade. The more remote houses are of course the least expensive. Breakfast is provided at
all of these, but dinner more rarely.

RESTAURANTS and CAFÉS, besides those at the above-named hotels:
Kursaal (p. 132), with café and tables in the Kur-Garten; *Villa Beriot*,
with a garden, on the left bank of the Lahn; *Alemannia*, near the station;
also several in the environs (*Rottmannshöhe, Schweizerhäuschen*, etc.).

CABS. Drive within the precincts of the town, one-horse cab, 70 pf.,
two-horse cab, 1 ℳ; per hr. 3 or $4^1/_2$ ℳ; to Kloster Arnstein and back
$10^1/_2$ or 15 ℳ; to Kemmenau and back $7^1/_2$ or 11 ℳ; to Ober-Lahnstein
$7^1/_2$ or 11, there and back $9^1/_2$ or 14; to Nassau and back $6^1/_2$ or 10 ℳ.
— MOTOR BOAT from the lower end of Ems up the Lahn to Nassau, with
numerous stopping-places.

VISITORS' TAX, after a stay of 7 days, for 1 pers. 18 ℳ, each addit.
member of the same family 9 ℳ. Day-ticket, 50 pf., or, on special oc-

casions, 1 *M.* — *Baths:* 1-3 *M.* — For drinking the waters at the royal springs a ticket ('Brunnenkarte'; 6 *M*) is necessary.

POST AND TELEGRAPH OFFICE, Römer-Str. 24a, near the Wandelbahn.

BOOKSELLERS. *Kirchberger*, Colonnaden 15, and in the Nassauer Hof (also money-changer); *Pfeffer*, Lahn-Str. 33.

ENGLISH CHURCH SERVICE in the *English Church*, on the left bank.

Ems (260 ft.), a small town with 7000 inhab., mentioned for the first time as a warm bath in a document of 1172, is prettily situated on both banks of the Lahn, in a narrow valley enclosed by wooded rocky heights. It consists of a street of lodging-houses on the right bank of the river, the original *'Bad Ems'*; of a new

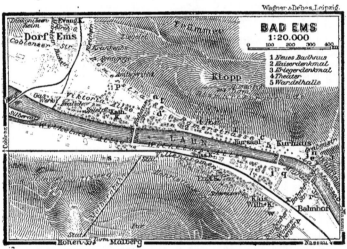

quarter on the left bank, named *'Spiess-Ems'*, at the base of the Malberg; and of *'Dorf Ems'*, or the old village, at the lower end of 'Bad Ems'. The *English Church* is on the left bank (see Plan).

The warm alkaline-muriatic springs (containing 2 per cent of carbonate of sodium, 1 per cent of common salt, and a varying amount of free carbonic acid) are among the most renowned in Europe. They are especially efficacious in pulmonary, intestinal, and female complaints. The older springs were always the property of the State, which has also acquired (1902 and 1908) the more recent springs bored by private enterprize. The height of the season is from the middle of July till the end of August, and the annual number of visitors exceeds 12,000. About $3^{1}/_{2}$ million bottles of the water are exported annually. The pastilles made of the salts are also largely used.

The KUR-GARTEN, which is generally thronged with visitors from

7 to 8.30 a. m. and when the band plays in the afternoon (4-5.30 p. m.), extends along the right bank of the Lahn for $^3/_4$ M. It is connected with the left bank by two bridges, one of which is covered. In the middle of the grounds stands the *Kursaal*, built in 1839 and containing reception rooms, a reading room, and a restaurant (p. 130; band, 8-9.30 p. m.). At the upper end of the Kur-Garten, a marble slab in the ground indicates the spot, where, on 13th July, 1870, King William gave his memorable answer to the French ambassador Benedetti. To the W. of the Kursaal is a marble statue of *Emp. William I.* (Pl. 2) by Professor Otto. At the lower end of the park is the bath-house of the *Four Towers (Vier Türme;* p. 130), built at the beginning of the 18th century. Hard by is the *Roman Catholic Church.*

In the Römer-Str., which skirts the N. side of the Kur-Garten, is the **Royal Kurhaus** (p. 130), erected at the end of the 18th century, and frequently enlarged since then. It is connected with the Kursaal by an iron colonnade. The left wing contains the *Kesselbrunnen* (115° Fahr.), the *Erste Krähnchenbrunnen,* the *Zweite Krähnchenbrunnen* or *Fürstenbrunnen* (103°), and the *Kaiserbrunnen* (83°; the pleasantest to drink). In a lateral corridor are the *Gargling Rooms,* the *Victoria-Quelle* (85°), and the *Stahl-Quelle.* A separate pavilion in the court contains the *Wilhelms-Quelle* (113°). — The bath-house in connection with them is joined by covered passages with the *Hôtel des Quatre-Saisons et de l'Europe* (p. 130).

On the left bank of the Lahn, near the Gitter-Brücke, lie the *Römerbad* (Pl. q; p. 130), with the Römer-Quelle (112° Fahr.), and the so-called *New Bath House (Neue Badhaus;* Pl. 1), with baths supplied from the copious *Neue Quelle,* or *New Spring,* which was enclosed in 1850 (122°). From this point the *König-Wilhelms-Allée* descends along the bank of the river, passing the *Russian Church* and the *Kaiser-Brücke,* to the *Silberau* (restaurant), where the Lahn is crossed by *Remy's Brücke,* the lowest of the four bridges of Ems. The so-called 'Villen-Promenade' is more attractive. Beginning at the New Bath House, it crosses the railway near the station of the wire-rope railway (see below), then passes the Hôtel Bella Riva and leads through wood to the open-air restaurant of *Lindenbach* (rail. station) and to the ($^3/_4$ hr.) *Rottmannshöhe* (restaurant).

Near the Kaiser-Brücke is the station of the *Wire-Rope Railway* to the top of the wooded **Malberg** (1096 ft.; fare 85, down 50 pf., up & down 1 ℳ 5 pf.). Pedestrians reach the top in $^3/_4$ hr. by beautiful walks either on this (W.) side or on the E. side, passing the English Church (p. 131) and the *Schweizerhäuschen.* At the top are a view-tower and the *Hohen-Malberg Restaurant.* — On the summit of the *Winterberg,* $1^1/_2$ M. to the E. of the Malberg, is a

tower, built on the foundations of an old Roman tower belonging to the Pfahlgraben (p. 304) which formerly stood here.

A shady path, affording a view of the Allerheiligen-Kirche (p. 221), leads to the S.W. from the Malberg to (³/₄ hr.) the village of **Frücht** (890 ft.), which contains the burial-vault of the famous Prussian minister Baron Stein (1757-1831; see p. 134). The epitaph contains a tribute to the strong and upright character of the statesman. Frau Eppstein at Frücht (house No. 26) keeps the keys of the chapel (gratuity). — From the vault we may proceed to the left, viâ the much-frequented *Oberlahnsteiner Forsthaus*, to (1 hr.) the rail. station of Hof-Zollgrund (p. 223); or we may take a pretty woodland path to the right leading to (1¹/₂ hr.) Braubach or (finally by the marked Höllensteg) to the Marksburg (p. 223). — Another popular return-route from Frücht leads viâ the *Schweizer-Tal* to *Miellen* and the railway-station of *Nievern* (1 hr.; p. 130).

On the right bank of the Lahn, immediately above the highroad, towers the abrupt *Bäderlei*, or '*Sieben Köpfe*', a jagged rock of slate crowned with the *Concordia-Turm* (865 ft.; rfmts.), a viewtower. We reach the summit in ³/₄-1 hr. by following the Graben-Str., above the Kurhaus, and then ascending by the stony footpath passing the war-monument (Pl. 3) and the *Mooshütte*, or by the broad road to the right farther on. The *Bismarck Promenade*, diverging to the left at the beginning of the latter, leads round the Pfahlgraben to the (³/₄ hr.) Bismarck Tower on the *Klopp*, whence we descend to Dorf Ems (fine views).

The *Kemmenauer Höhe*, or *Schöne Aussicht*. (1440 ft.; restaurant), 1¹/₂ hr. to the N. of Ems (reached by a path ascending to the left from the upper end of the Graben-Str. through a small lateral valley), is one of the highest points to the N. of the Lahn, and commands an extensive view of the valley of the Rhine, the Taunus, and the Eifel Mts. In the foreground, far below, is the *Sporkenburg;* to the right are the two singular-looking *Arzbacher Trachytköpfe*. A similar view towards the E. is obtained from a point 1 M. to the N. of the village of *Kemmenau*, on the way to Montabaur (p. 142).

The RAILWAY TO WETZLAR ascends along the left bank of the winding Lahn. From (13 M.) *Dausenau* a bridge crosses the river to the town of that name (Nassauer Hof, R. 1¹/₂-2, pens. 4¹/₂-6 *ℳ*), on the right bank, still surrounded by old walls. The church (restored in 1884) dates from the 13th, its vestibule from the 15th century. — Near Nassau we cross the Lahn.

15¹/₂ M. (from Coblenz) **Nassau.** — HOTELS. *Müller*, at the station; *Krone, Hôtel Nassau*, both in the Amts-Str.; *Bellevue*, prettily situated on the left bank of the Lahn, R. & B. 2-2¹/₂, pens. 4-5 *ℳ*, very fair. — *Union Brewery*, with garden.

Kurhaus Bad Nassau (open in winter also), on the road to Ems.

Nassau (290 ft.), a small town (2300 inhab.), believed to have existed as early as 790 under the name of *Nasonga*, is prettily situated on the right bank of the Lahn (which is here crossed by a suspension-bridge), and is much frequented by summer-visitors. It was the birthplace of the celebrated Prussian minister *Baron Stein* (see above). The *Schloss*, though modernized, dates from 1621, and now belongs to the Countess von der Gröben. In 1815 Stein caused

a Gothic tower to be added to commemorate the war of independence (1813-15), and it now also bears a tablet in memory of 1870-
71 (admission on Mon., Wed., & Frid., 9-11 & 2-6; visitors deposit
a donation for a charitable purpose in a box at the entrance). The
small *Schloss-Park* is open to the public daily, except Sun., 8-12 a.m.
and 2-7 p.m.

On the opposite bank of the Lahn rises a wooded eminence
(ascended from the station in 25 min.), crowned by the ruined
Castle of Nassau, erected in 1101 by Dudo IV. and Drutwin IV.,
Counts of Laurenburg (p. 135), whose descendants henceforth assumed the name of Nassau; it has been suffered to fall to decay
since the end of the 16th cent. (key of tower at the restaurant).
Lower down on the same hill are the ruins of *Burg Stein* ($^1/_2$ M.
from the suspension-bridge), the ancestral seat of the Barons Stein,
the earliest mention of which is in 1158, and which was inhabited
down to the end of the 17th century. The projecting rock in front of
it bears a *Monument to Stein,* consisting of a highly characteristic
statue in marble, by Pfuhl of Berlin, beneath a Gothic canopy of
red sandstone, 66 ft. in height, inaugurated in 1871. In his right
hand the great minister holds a scroll with the date 11th June, 1807,
in allusion to his memorial regarding the reorganization of the
Prussian state. The terrace affords a survey of the valleys of the
Lahn and Mühlbach.

The rocks of the *Hohe Lei,* reached from Nassau in $^3/_4$ hr. (path at
places destitute of shade), command a beautiful view, including the
monastery of Arnstein. In returning we may proceed viâ *Weinähr* to
the Gelbach-Tal (p. 135) and thence walk over the ridge to Obernhof
(p. 135). — Other walks may be taken to the pavilion on the *Nassauer
Berg* ($^3/_4$ hr.); to the pavilion on the *Hahnkopf;* to the *Mühlbach - Tal*
and *Kaltbach - Tal;* and on the left bank of the Lahn to *Kloster Arnstein* (see below).

Beyond Nassau the railway follows the right bank of the Lahn,
and is soon carried through a series of tunnels. Before and beyond
the second a glimpse is obtained on the right of *Burg Langenau*
(3 M. from Nassau, 1 M. from Obernhof), built in 1244, the ancient
seat of an Austrian family, the Rhenish branch of which became
extinct in 1603. The watch-tower and external walls are well preserved; within the latter farm-buildings have been erected. — Beyond
the castle, on the opposite bank, rises the **Kloster Arnstein,*
with its church of the 12th cent. (enlarged in 1359, restored in 1885,
damaged by a fire in 1909) and other buildings, picturesquely situated
on a wooded eminence. A castle of very ancient origin which once
stood here was converted by the last Count of Arnstein or Arnoldstein
into a Premonstratensian monastery in 1208 (suppressed in 1803).
It is most easily visited from Obernhof (p. 135). On leaving the
station we turn to the right, and after 300 paces we follow the path
to the left, indicated by a finger-post, to ($^3/_4$ M.) Arnstein (refreshments at the Kloster-Mühle).

A picturesque path leads hence to (4¹/₂ M.) Nassau, viâ *Hollrich,* where the path forks, the left branch leading viâ *Berg-Nassau,* and the right (somewhat shorter) along the Lahn.

Near (18¹/₂ M.) **Obernhof** (315 ft.) are lead and silver mines. The station is on the left bank and the village (Kloster Arnstein Inn) on the right bank of the Lahn (bridge). A fine point of view, on the sharp ridge between the valleys of the Lahn and the Gelbach (reached in 20 min., by an easy but shadeless path), is known as the *Goethe-Punkt,* from a visit made to it by Goethe in 1814.

The line now passes through a long tunnel, beyond which the valley contracts. Then a long curve. High up, on the slope of the left bank, is situated the '*Alte Haus*', a solitary fragment of wall belonging to the old nunnery of *Brunnenburg.*

23 M. **Laurenburg** (325 ft.), with silver-smelting works, a small château, and the ruins of the ancestral residence of the Counts of Nassau, who were originally Counts of Laurenburg (comp. p. 134). This castle is first mentioned in 1093 and was already a ruin in 1643.

The picturesque *Rupbach-Tal* debouches at Laurenburg. — From Laurenburg a road leads viâ the village of (25 min.) *Scheid* to (20 min.) *Geilnau,* with a mineral spring, in the valley of the Lahn, which here describes a wide bend. Fine view in descending.

Beyond the *Kramberg Tunnel* the train stops at (26 M.) **Balduinstein** (355 ft.; *Noll*); the imposing ruins of the castle of that name on the right, built in 1319, rise in a narrow ravine behind the village. A steep footpath (25 min.) and a good road (2 M.; carriages generally at the station in summer) leads through the village to the castle of **Schaumburg** (915 ft.), situated on a wooded basaltic peak to the right and first mentioned in 1194. It was once the seat of the princes of Anhalt-Schaumburg, who became extinct in 1812, and is now the property of the Prince of Waldeck and Pyrmont. The oldest parts of the present building date from the 18th cent.; the modern part, in the English-Gothic style, was erected for Archduke Stephen, who was the lord of the manor from 1850 to 1867. Picturesque view from the tower (adm. 20 pf.). Fine park. At the foot of the castle is the *Waldecker Hof,* a fair inn (with pension). — We descend at first through wood, and then through the village of *Birlenbach* to (3 M.) Diez.

28¹/₂ M. *Fachingen* (375 ft.; Anker) derives importance from its mineral water, of which a large quantity is annually exported.

30 M. **Diez** (365 ft.; *Oranien*, at the station, with garden, R. 2-4, B. 1, pens. 4¹/₂-7 *ℳ; Hof von Holland,* an old-established house; *Victoria,* R. & B. 2¹/₂ *ℳ*, very fair; *Rail. Restaurant*), with 4400 inhab. and large marble-polishing works, picturesquely situated on the left bank of the Lahn, at the confluence of the Aar (railway to Schwalbach and Wiesbaden, see pp. 264, 263). It is commanded by an old *Castle* of the Counts of Diez and Nassau, now a house of correction. The old *Bridge* (altered) across the Lahn is supported by piers

erected on two others belonging to an earlier bridge (destroyed in 1552). The old *Peters-Kirche*, on a hill on the right bank, was restored in 1846. — To the N. of Diez is the *Hain Promenade* (views), with a monument to Emp. Frederick, a restaurant, and a Trinkhalle (1 M. from the rail. station). Farther on is *Schloss Oranienstein*, erected in 1676, now a Prussian military school.

Above Diez the valley expands into the 'Limburg Basin', which stretches as far as Runkel. The railway cuts off the two large curves formed by the river in this basin.

32¹/₂ M. **Limburg.** — HOTELS. *Preussischer Hof* (Pl. a; B, 3), Obere Graben-Str. 19, cor. of the Bahnhof-Str., R. from 2¹/₄, B. ³/₄, D. 2 *M; Nassauer Hof* (Pl. b; B, 3), Neumarkt 3, R. 1¹/₂-4, B. ³/₄, D. 2 *M; Bayrischer Hof* (Pl. c; A, 3, 4), Obere Schiede, these three all near the rail. station and very fair; ALTE POST (Pl. d; B, 3), Neumarkt, R. 2, B. ³/₄, D. 1¹/₂ *M*, with a frequented beer-restaurant. — *Wiener Café*, Graben-Str. 23. — Comp. the Plan, p. 138.

Limburg on the Lahn (400 ft.), an old town with 9300 inhab., which belonged in the middle ages to the Counts of the Lahngau (who became extinct in 1407) and then to the Elector of Trèves (1420-1803), is now the seat of a Roman Catholic bishop. It is situated on the *Lahn*, which is crossed here by a bridge constructed in 1315.

From the rail. station we proceed past the *Protestant Church* (Pl. A, B, 4) and through the Bahnhof-Str. to the Neumarkt (Pl. B, 3), with a memorial fountain for 1870-71. Farther on in the same direction is the Kornmarkt (Pl. B, 3), at the beginning of the old town, the narrow streets of which still contain some picturesque gabled houses. From the Kornmarkt the short 'Domtreppe' (finger-post) ascends to the —

   *****Cathedral** (Pl. C, 2), with its seven towers, the *'Basilica St. Georgii Martyris erecta 909'*, which rises conspicuously above the river. It was founded by Conrad Kurzbold, the powerful Salic Count of the Niederlahngau, remains of whose *Castle* adjoin the church. The present structure (sacristan opposite the entrance; fee), a remarkably fine example of the Transition style (late-Romanesque), erected in 1213-42, was skilfully restored in 1872-78. The ground-plan shows the 'centralizing' tendencies of the Rhenish architects of the period. The interior has galleries, arcading, and richly articulated surfaces. The mural paintings of the 13th cent. have been freshened up. The church contains a font of the 13th cent., and a monument (also 13th cent.) to the founder (d. 948), with a recumbent figure. The stained glass is modern. — The valuable treasury of the cathedral, preserved in the *Parish Church (Stadt-Kirche;* Pl. C, 3), next door to the bishop's residence, is shown on Wed., 11-12 and 3-6 (1-5 pers. 3 *M*, at other times 6 *M;* apply to the dean).

Visitors should cross the *Bridge* (Pl. B, 1) to the bath-houses

on the right bank, for the sake of the beautiful view of the cathedral
and the castle.

From Limburg to *Au* viâ *Altenkirchen* and to *Hachenburg*, see
pp. 141, 142.

From Limburg to *Wiesbaden, Höchst*, and *Frankfort*, see R. 39 d.

Fine retrospect of the cathedral as the train leaves Limburg.
The banks of the Lahn become flatter for a short distance. To the
left lies *Dietkirchen*, with one of the oldest churches in the country,
built before 801, on a rocky hill rising abruptly from the river.
On the Lahn, $1^1/_4$ M. farther up, are the village and old castle of
Dehrn (steamboat from Limburg in summer). — 34 M. *Eschhofen;*
$35^1/_2$ M. *Kerkerbach,* junction for Dehrn and Heckholzhausen.

$36^1/_2$ M. **Runkel** (390 ft.; *Zur Lahnbahn,* unpretending but
good), an ancient town with 1100 inhab., situated on both banks of
the Lahn, is commanded by an extensive old castle of the Princes of
Wied, dating from about 1159, perched on a rocky height, and now
occupied by the local authorities. On the hill opposite lies the village of *Schadeck*, with an old castle (10 min. from the station;
pretty view). The vineyards on the steep banks of the Lahn above
Runkel are the last in this region; they have recently been replanted
and now produce a Moselle wine ('Riesling').

Near ($38^1/_2$ M.) *Villmar* (395 ft.; Basting) are considerable
marble quarries. The *Bodenstein,* on the left bank of the river,
bears a sandstone statue, 8 ft. high, of Conrad I. (911-918), by
L. Cauer. — 43 M. *Aumenau* (410 ft.) and ($45^1/_2$ M.) *Fürfort* are
shipping-points for the ironstone and slate found in the district.
At Fürfort are large chemical works, and near it rises the ruined
castle of *Gräveneck.* After a succession of tunnels, bridges, and
viaducts, the train reaches —

$50^1/_2$ M. **Weilburg.** — HOTELS. *Nassauer Hof*, at the railway-
station, R. $1^1/_4$-$2^1/_4$ *M; Deutsches Haus, Traube,* both in the old town and
pretty fair, R. & B. $2^1/_2$ *M.* — *Moser's Wine Rooms*, in the market-place.

Weilburg (453 ft.), a small town with 3800 inhab., known to
have existed as early as 906, was the seat of the Counts of Nassau
in 1195-1355 and of the Princes of Nassau-Weilburg in 1355-1816.
The lower town, near the stone bridge over the Lahn, was laid out
at the end of the 17th century. The old town (formerly walled) and
the *Château* (571 ft.) crown a rocky ridge descending abruptly on
three sides to the winding Lahn. The château, rebuilt in 1543-49
and dating in its present form from 1675-1719, now belongs to the
Grand-Duke of Luxemburg, son of Adolphus, Duke of Nassau, who
lost his throne in 1866. The interior, lately restored, is shown for
a fee. The court is picturesque. On the terrace, which commands
a good view of the Lahn valley, is a bronze statue of Duke Adolphus
(d. 1905) by Emil Cauer. The *Stadt-Kirche,* near the château, built
in 1707-11, contains the family vault of the ducal family.

To the S. is the entrance to the pretty **Weiltal,** up which a railway runs viâ (2¹/₂ M.) *Freienfels,* (4 M.) *Essershausen,* (5¹/₂ M.) *Ernsthausen,* (6¹/₂ M.) *Weilmünster,* and (8 M.) *Rohnstadt,* to (10 M., in ca. 1 hr.) *Laubus-Eschbach.* From Freienfels, with a ruined castle, a pleasant walk may be taken to *Philippstein,* with the picturesque ruins of a castle, and to *Braunfels* (see below); from Laubus-Eschbach we may walk to (2³/₄ hrs.) *Neu-Weilnau* (p. 310) viâ *Emmershausen* and the upper Weiltal. — About 3 M. to the N.W. of Weilburg, on a steep basaltic hill, rises the ruin of *Merenberg* (key at the village-school; 20 pf.).

52 M. *Löhnberg* (450 ft.), with an old castle; 56 M. *Stockhausen* (465 ft.). In the neighbourhood are several iron-mines.

58 M. *Braunfels* (484 ft.; Bahnhofs-Hôtel, unpretending) is the junction of a narrow-gauge line (20 min.; fares 50, 30 pf.) which runs to the S. to (2¹/₂ M.) the small town (1600 inhab.) of **Braunfels** (895 ft.; *Schloss-Hôtel,* with a terrace, R. 2-3, B. 1, D. 2¹/₂, pens. 5-7 *M ; Bellevue; Hôt. Böhme; Solmser Hof,* plain; several pensions), the residence of the Prince of Solms-Braunfels, whose extensive **Schloss,* dating in part from the late-Gothic period, contains interesting old armour, pictures, trophies of the chase, and other curiosities (adm. 50 pf.). Pleasant grounds; fine view from the tower.

60 M. *Burgsolms.* From (61 M.) *Albshausen* (484 ft.; Deutscher Kaiser) we may walk in ¹/₂ hr. to the suppressed Premonstratensian abbey of *Altenberg,* with its fine early-Gothic church (end of 13th cent.).

64¹/₂ M. **Wetzlar.** — HOTELS. *Herzogliches Haus* (Pl. a; B, 1), in the Butter-Markt, 1¹/₄ M. from the station, R. & B. 3 *M,* very fair; *Hôtel Kaltwasser* (Pl. b), *Kessel* (Pl. c), R. & B. 2¹/₂-3¹/₂ *M,* both near the station. — Wine at *Ortenbach's Luncheon Rooms,* Hausergasse. — *Town Baths,* Bahnhof-Str.

Wetzlar (500 ft.), with 12,000 inhab., lies on both banks of the Lahn, at its confluence with the *Dill,* and consists of the modern new town near the railway and of the picturesque old town on the heights of the left bank. It was a free imperial town from 1180 to 1803, and from 1693 to 1806 it was the seat of the *Reichskammer-Gericht* or imperial court of justice (comp. p. 139). An unusual charm is imparted to Wetzlar by the reminiscences of the youthful Goethe, who practised here before the Reichskammer-Gericht in 1772 and selected it as the scene of his 'Sorrows of Werther'.

The most conspicuous building is the *Cathedral* (Pl. B, 1), a huge, richly articulated, and very picturesque edifice. The oldest part on the W., consisting of the so-called 'Heidenturm', with the Romanesque portal, dates from the beginning of the 12th century. The choir, which is essentially Gothic, the transept, and the adjoining bays of the S. aisle date from the 13th cent., while the N. side was erected partly in the 14th. When the church was converted into a Gothic edifice in the 14-15th cent., the two low Romanesque towers of basalt were left standing within the large towers of red

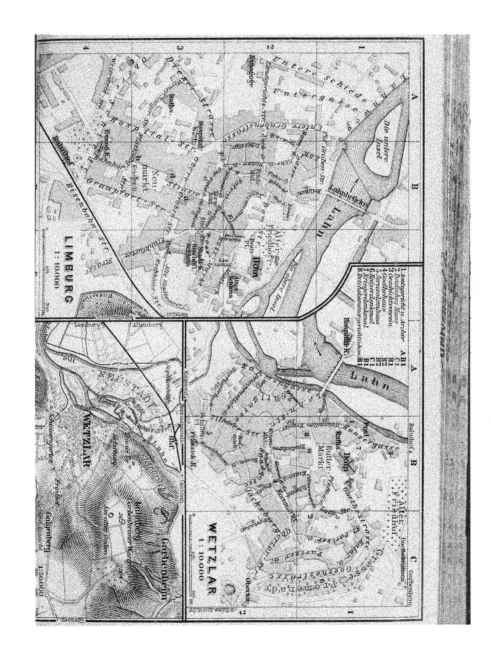

LIMBURG
1 : 10000

WETZLAR
1 : 10000

1. Landgericht u. Amtsger.   AB1
2. Deutsches Haus   C1
3. Geschichtsverein   B1
4. Goethehaus   B2
5. Jerusalemhaus   C1
6. Kaiserdenkmal   B1
7. Kriegerdenkmal   B1
8. Reichskammergerichtsarchiv. B1

sandstone, of which one was left unfinished, while the other received its slate roof in 1561. The sculptured portals to the S. and W. of the towers were added in the 14th century. The building, which had suffered severely from the effects of wind and weather, was repeatedly repaired during the 19th cent., and in 1904-1910 the whole structure underwent a thoroughgoing restoration from plans by Stiehl. In the interior a handsome screen separates the nave of the cathedral, used by the Protestants, from the choir, used by the Roman Catholics. The verger lives on the terrace to the N., on which stands a *War Monument.*

The building with the imperial eagle in the Butter-Markt, to the S. of the cathedral, was the earliest seat of the Reichskammer-Gericht (Pl. 8; B, 1). From 1756 to 1782 it met in the Herzogliches Haus (now a hotel, p. 138). In the Entengasse is a Gothic house of the 13th century. Goethe lived first in the Gewandgasse (No. 11) and then in the Kornmarkt (No. 11). — The Pfaffengasse leads from the Butter-Markt to the *Deutsches Haus* (Pl. 2; C, 1), or Lodge of the Teutonic Order, which was the residence of Herr Buff, the manager of the estates of the Order, and the father of the Charlotte of 'Werther'; it still contains a room with a few memorials of her, including some letters from C. W. Jerusalem, secretary to the Brunswick embassy, who was the original of Goethe's 'Werther' (key kept by the verger of the cathedral). The house where the young Jerusalem shot himself, in the Schiller-Platz, near the *Franciscan Church* (Pl. 5; B, 2), contains a few reminiscences of him. — Outside the Wöllbacher Tor is the *Goethe-Brunnen* (Pl. C, 1), shaded by a venerable lime-tree, a favourite resort of Goethe, with a replica of Trippel's bust.

The *Museum of the Historical Society (Geschichtsverein;* Pl. 3, B 1), Hausergasse 30, contains prehistoric remains, old weapons and banners, memorials of Goethe, and so forth. — At the Hauser-Tor is the building of the *Archives* of the Reichskammer-Gericht (Pl. 1; A, B, 1), finished in 1806 contemporaneously with the abolition of the court, and containing the 'indivisible remainder' of the state-papers which were (with this exception) distributed among the German states.

To the S.W. of Wetzlar rises the ruined castle of *Kalsmunt* (12-13th cent.; key kept by Herr Waldschmidt, Schiller-Platz, 10 pf.). At the foot of the hill is the *Schützen-Garten.*

A broad road ascends on the left bank of the Lahn to (1¹/₂ M.) *Garbenheim,* the Wahlheim of 'Werther', with a memorial erected in 1849. The traveller may return by the *Bismarck Tower,* commanding a fine view. — On the slope of the *Stoppelberg* (1315 ft.; view-tower), 3 M. from Wetzlar, lies the pleasant village of *Volpertshausen,* in a house in which (now a school) the ball described in 'Werther' took place.

To the W. of the town, near the Altenberg road, is a memorial of the victory won by Archduke Charles of Austria over the French under Jourdan on June 15th, 1796.

In the Dill valley, about 1¼ M. to the N. of Wetzlar station, is the ruin of *Hermannstein*. — To *Ehringshausen* and thence to the *Diana-burg* and *Greifenstein*, see p. 144.

From Wetzlar to *Cologne* or *Giessen*, see R. 21.

21. From Cologne to Frankfort viâ Wetz-lar and Giessen. The Westerwald.

143 M. RAILWAY in 4½-7½ hrs. (fares 17 ℳ 20, 10 ℳ 40, 6 ℳ 90 pf.; express fares 19 ℳ 20, 12 ℳ 40, 7 ℳ 90 pf.); to (104 M.) *Giessen* in 3-5 hrs. (fares 13 ℳ 30, 8 ℳ, 5 ℳ 30 pf.; express fares 15 ℳ 30, 10 ℳ, 6 ℳ 30 pf.).

From Cologne to (13 M.) *Troisdorf*, where the Right-Rhenish line diverges, see p. 72. Beyond Troisdorf the line crosses the *Agger*, on the bank of which, to the right, is the *Friedrich-Wil-helms-Hütte*, a large iron-foundry.

15½ M. **Siegburg** (*Stern*, R. & B. 2½-3, D. 3 ℳ, very fair; *Felder*, at the station, R. & B. 2½, D. 1½ ℳ), an industrial town of 16,100 inhab., with a royal ammunition factory and other industrial establishments, lies on the right bank of the *Sieg*, on the slope of the basaltic *Michaelsberg*. On this hill, in 1064, St. Anno, Abp. of Cologne and guardian of Emp. Henry IV., erected a Benedictine Abbey, which was not suppressed till 1803. The buildings, restored after repeated destruction in the 17-18th cent., were converted into a reformatory in 1879 and were purchased by the town in 1908. The crypt of the abbey-church dates from the time of St. Anno, the choir is late-Gothic. The Roman Catholic *Parish Church*, with its six-storied W. tower, early-Gothic choir, and late-Gothic vaulted nave, has lately been freely restored. The contents of its treasury, mainly from the old abbey, include several portable altars and seven richly adorned reliquaries of the 12-15th cent., including that of St. Anno (d. 1075).

FROM SIEGBURG TO HAGEN, 66 M., railway in 4½ hrs. — The rail-way ascends the industrial valley of the *Agger*, crossing the river several times. Beyond (1¼ M.) *Driesch* we proceed through the Lohmarwald to (4½ M.) *Lohmar* (Hermanns; Knipp). — 5½ M. *Donrath;* 8½ M. *Wahl-scheid;* 10 M. *Bachermühle;* 12½ M. *Overath* (branch-line to Kalk, p. 72); 13 M. *Vilkerath*. — 16½ M. *Ehreshoven*, with the château of Count Nessel-rode. In the vicinity are important copper, zinc, and silver mines. 20 M. *Engelskirchen* (Guillaume; Kauert), with large spinning-mills, lies at the mouth of the industrial valley of the *Leppe*, which a branch-railway ascends. — 23 M. *Ründeroth* (Baumhof, very fair), below the confluence of the *Wiehl* with the Agger, has 3600 inhab. and several foundries, puddling-works, and iron-mines. — 25 M. *Osberghausen*, the junction of a branch-line viâ Wiehl to (15 M.) Waldbröl (see p. 141). — From (27½ M.) *Dieringhausen* a branch-line continues to follow the valley of the Agger to *Derschlag* and *Olpe*. — From (51 M.) *Brügge* a branch-line runs to (4½ M.) *Lüdenscheid* (Post, R. 2-2½, D. 1½-2½ ℳ), a manufacturing town of 29,300 inhabitants. — 66 M. **Hagen**, see p. 39.

FROM SIEGBURG TO BEUEL (p. 83; 7 M.) runs a branch of the Bröl-Tal Railway (see p. 141).

Beyond Siegburg (view of the the Seven Mountains to the right), the train crosses the *Sieg,* and ascends the valley of the river, over 38 bridges and through 12 tunnels, to Betzdorf and Siegen. — 20 M. *Hennef* (Laa; Nasshoven) is the junction of the Bröltal Railway (p. 83) to (29 M.; 20 M. from Hennef) *Waldbröl* and to (24 M.) *Asbach.*

On the *Bennauer Kopf* at Asbach are important quarries of columnar basalt. — The BRÖL-TAL, which the Waldbröl line ascends, is very picturesque. At *Allner,* where the Bröl joins the Sieg, is a château of the 16-18th cent., remodelled in 1875-6. Other stations are *Bröl, Ingersauelermühle, Herrnstein, Feldhoferbrücke* (Linke, very fair, a favourite summer-resort), and *Schönenberg.* — From Waldbröl a branch-line runs to Wissen (see p. 143).

Beyond Hennef we see the just-mentioned château of *Allner,* adjoining the wood to the left. Farther on, also to the left, are the monastery of *Bödingen,* surrounded by vineyards, and the château of *Attenbach.*

22$^1/_2$ M. *Blankenberg* (Honrath, with a view-terrace, very fair), founded by the Counts of Sayn. ca. 1180 and afterwards in the possession of the Dukes of Berg, once held a municipal charter but is now a mere hamlet (200 inhab.). Its ruined castle (destroyed at the end of the 17th cent.) is perched upon a narrow and precipitous ridge and forms, with the ivy-clad town gates and walls, a very picturesque example of a mediæval fortification. — Beyond a tunnel a retrospect is obtained of the monastery of *Merten* on the hill to the right, with its Romanesque church.

27$^1/_2$ M. **Eitorf** *(Prinz Carl;* very fair; *Station Hotel).* The wooded hills enclosing the valley now increase in height. — 31 M. *Herchen* (Station Hotel). Two tunnels are passed through. Near *Windeck,* with the castle of that name on the hill to the left, the railway and highroad pass through a deep cutting. — 36$^1/_2$ M. *Schladern* (Klever). A new channel has here been constructed for the Sieg, while the old one has been left dry for a distance of 2 M. — Tunnel.

41 M. **Au,** the junction for Limburg (see below).

FROM AU TO LIMBURG VIÂ ALTENKIRCHEN AND SIERSHAHN, 55 M., railway in 3$^1/_2$-4 hrs. (fares 7 *M,* 4 *M* 20, 2 *M* 80 pf.). — The railway ascends the valley of the Sieg, traversing the *Westerwald,* a rugged plateau chiefly of Devonian formation, intermixed with diluvial and tertiary strata and basaltic cones. 3 M. *Breitscheid.* Tunnel. 5$^1/_2$ M. *Ober-Erbach.*

8 M. **Altenkirchen** (787 ft.; *Luyken,* Rathaus-Str., R. 1$^3/_4$-2$^1/_2$, B. $^3/_4$-1 *M,* with garden; *Weissgerber; Bahn-Hôtel),* an in-dustrial village of 2250 inhab. on the *Wied,* with iron and lead mines, formerly the capital of the countship of Sayn-Wittgenstein-Altenkirchen, is the junction for the railway to Limburg viâ Ha-damar (see p. 142). In 1796 the French under Kleber here defeated

the Austrians under Prince Ferdinand of Wurtemberg; and a memorial has been erected to the French general Marceau.

We descend the valley of the Wied viâ *Neitersen*, *Seifen*, *Puderbach*, and *Raubach*, the last with a large paper-mill. 24 M. *Dierdorf*, with a château of Prince Wied and an old park. Beyond *Marienrachdorf* we reach (19¹/₂ M.) *Selters* (850 ft.), the junction of a narrow-gauge railway to Hachenburg (see below). We next ascend the valley of the Holzbach.

33 M. *Siershahn* (955 ft.), the junction of the line to Engers (p. 117). 35 M. *Wirges*, with large glass-works; 35³/₄ M. *Dernbach.*

38 M. **Montabaur** (755 ft.; *Schlemmer zur Goldenen Krone; Post*), a quaint little town with 3700 inhab., was refounded in 1217 by the Elector Dietrich of Trèves on the site of an earlier settlement, and named 'Mons Tabor'. The former electoral château (915 ft.), rebuilt in 1687-1709, is now occupied by the district-authorities. — Branch-line to Westerburg (see p. 143).

41¹/₂ M. *Goldhausen.* — 44¹/₂ M. *Wallmerod*, also a station on the Montabaur and Westerburg line, is situated in a forest-district and known to have existed as early as the 13th century. In the vicinity is the château of *Molsberg*, with its large park, belonging to Count von Walderdorff. — The train now descends into the valley of the Lahn viâ *Nieder-Erbach* and *Staffel*. To the left we obtain an admirable view of Limburg Cathedral. We cross the Lahn to *Freiendiez.* — 55 M. *Limburg*, see p. 136.

FROM ALTENKIRCHEN TO LIMBURG VIÂ HACHENBURG, 40¹/₂ M., railway in 2¹/₂ hrs. (fares 5 ℳ 10, 3 ℳ 20, 2 ℳ 5 pf.). The train ascends past *Ingelbach* and *Hattert* and commands a splendid retrospect to the right, extending as far as the Seven Mountains.

9¹/₂ M. **Hachenburg** (1245 ft.; *Krone*, a long-established house, simple but very fair, R. 1¹/₂-2¹/₂, D. 1¹/₂ ℳ; *Nassauer Hof*), a small town of 1800 inhab. with a château of Prince Sayn, built in the 13th and restored in the 17th century. The grounds of the château afford fine views. — Branch-railway to Selters, see above.

On the *Nister*, in a pleasant wooded district about 2¹/₂ M. to the N.W., is the Cistercian convent of **Marienstatt**, established in 1215 as an offshoot of Heisterbach (p. 101). The beautiful early-Gothic church resembles the mother-church in the ground-plan, especially in the choir, but otherwise has been completed in a severe Gothic style, with vaulting and buttresses but without ornamentation (see p. xxix). In the N. aisle is the monument of Count Gerhard II. of Sayn (d. 1493).

12¹/₂ M. *Korb*, the station for the summer-resort of *Marienberg* (1590 ft.; Ferger), which lies 3¹/₂ M. to the E.; 14¹/₂ M. *Erbach;* 19¹/₂ M. *Langenhahn*, with the ruined castle of *Weltersburg.*

23 M. **Westerburg** (1312 ft.; *Löwe*, very fair), with 1450 inhab., the capital of the independent countship of Westerburg-Leiningen, consists of a lower and modern town in the valley of the Schafbach, and of an older and upper town on a basaltic cone, crowned

with the château of Count Leiningen. — From Westerburg branch-
-railways run to (30 M.) Herborn (p. 144) and to (16 M.) Montabaur
(p. 142).

25 M. *Willmenrod;* 27¹/₂ M. *Wilsenroth,* with basalt quarries.
— 30¹/₂ M. *Frickhofen.* About 1¹/₂ M. to the E. is the *Dornburg*
(1300 ft.), a basaltic cone with a perpetual formation of ice beneath the
boulders, which, however, is being destroyed by the removal of the
loose stones from the surface. In the vicinity is Fischer's Hotel. —
At *Niederzeuzheim* the train reaches the valley of the Elbbach, which
it now descends. — 33¹/₂ M. **Hadamar** (423 ft.; *Stahl; Nassauer
Kof,* R. & B. 2 *M*), a town of 2400 inhab., was the seat of the Count
of Nassau-Hadamar in 1606-1711. The castle is now a gymnasium. —
36 M. *Elz;* 37¹/₂ M. *Staffel* (p. 142); 39¹/₂ M. *Freiendietz* (p. 142).
40¹/₂ M. *Limburg,* see p. 136.

CONTINUATION OF MAIN LINE. 44¹/₂ M. *Wissen,* junction for
Morsbach and Waldbröl. A little farther on, on the opposite bank
of the Sieg, rises the old château of *Schönstein,* the property of
Prince Hatzfeld. — 47 M. *Niederhövels.*

52 M. **Betzdorf** (*Deutsches Haus; Breidenbacher Hof,* both
very fair), with 4700 inhab., lies on the Sieg. The railway forks
here, the left branch running to *Siegen* (see *Baedeker's Northern
Germany),* the right to Giessen. A branch-line runs to (6 M.) *Daaden*
(Schmitz), 2 M. to the S. of which, at *Friedewald,* is the château of
Count von Hachenburg, a fine Renaissance edifice of 1582, judiciously
restored in 1895 (court shown on application at the 'Wachtstube').

The line to Giessen ascends the valley of the *Heller* to (57 M.)
Herdorf (branch-line to Unterwilden), *Neunkirchen* (59 M.), and
(63 M.) *Burbach,* crosses the watershed between the Heller and
the *Dill* near (66 M.) *Würgendorf,* and threads its way through
the *Hickengrund.* 69¹/₂ M. *Nieder-Dresselndorf;* 74 M. *Haiger,*
a quaint place with a late-Gothic church, in which some old mural
paintings have been brought to light. — The line next enters the
valley of the *Dill,* the chief affluent of the Lahn.

77 M. **Dillenburg** (755 ft.; *Kurhaus,* R. & B. 2¹/₂-3, D. 1³/₄,
pens. 5-7 *M; Neuhoff,* R. 1¹/₂-2, B. ³/₄, D. 1¹/₂ *M; Schloss-Hôtel,*
at the Wilhelms-Turm, with terrace, pens. from 4 *M,* very fair), a
picturesque town of 5000 inhab., on the Dill, with iron mines, a
mining school, and tanneries. The *Protestant Church* (1501) contains some princely tombs. In the Oranien-Platz is a statue of
Bismarck (1898). The *Wilhelms-Turm,* 130 ft. high, was erected
in 1872-75 on the site of the ruined castle of Dillenburg, in which
William of Orange, the liberator of the Netherlands, was born in
1533, and contains some reminiscences of him (open 5-6 p.m. in
summer, 30 pf.). Adjacent is the *Wilhelms-Linde,* a lime-tree

under which William received the Netherlandish ambassadors in 1568. Good views are obtained from the Adolfshöhe, the Bismarck Temple, and other pleasant points in the environs.

A BRANCH RAILWAY ascends the *Dietzhölz-Tal* to (10 M.) *Strass-Ebersbach* (Schmitt), whence the Wilhelms-Warte on the *Sasenberg* (1/2 M.) may be visited.

81¹/₂ M. *Herborn* (670 ft.; Ritter; Metzler), an industrial place with 4000 inhab., on the Dill. The old castle is now a seminary. Branch-lines run to Driedorf-Fehl (Marienberg), Westerburg (p. 142), and *Nieder-Walgern.* — 85 M. *Sinn.* On (4 M.) a hill to the right is the ruin of *Greifenstein* (1370 ft.), with a chapel of 1683-94, restored in 1885. — 89¹/₂ M. *Ehringhausen.*

A pleasant excursion may be made to the W., through wood, to (1 hr.) the *Dianaburg* (1350 ft.; view; rfmts. at the forester's), a shooting-lodge of Prince Solms-Braunfels. Thence we may proceed to the N. to (1¹/₂ hr.) the village of *Greifenstein* (ruin, see above) and (1¹/₂ hr. more) *Sinn.*

At (95¹/₂ M.) *Wetzlar* the line enters the valley of the *Lahn,* and unites with the Lahn Railway (see p. 138).

The train crosses the Hessian frontier at (100 M.) *Dutenhofen* and joins the Cassel and Frankfort line. The ruins of *Gleiberg* and *Vetzberg* are seen on the left.

104 M. **Giessen** (*Grossherzog von Hessen,* R. 2-3 ℳ; *Victoria; Prinz Karl; Schütz; Kuhne; Rail. Restaurant*), situated on the Lahn, is mainly of modern origin, and contains 36,000 inhabitants. It is the seat of a university, founded in 1607, which is attended by about 1100 students. For a fuller account of Giessen and the rest of this route, see *Baedeker's Northern Germany.*

About 6 M. to the N. E. of (114 M.) *Butzbach* rise the considerable ruins of the castle of *Münzenberg* (690 ft.), destroyed in the Thirty Years' War (view).

120 M. **Nauheim** (470 ft.; *Kaiserhof,* R. from 3¹/₂ ℳ; *Métropole,* R. 3-10 ℳ; *Bristol; Prince of Wales,* and many others; visitors' tax 20 ℳ), a town with 5000 inhab., pleasantly situated on the N. E. slope of the Taunus Mts. (p. 300), possesses warm saline springs, impregnated with carbonic acid gas, which attract 30,000 patients annually. At the W. end of the *Kur-Park* is the handsome *Kurhaus,* with a fine terrace overlooking the extensive grounds.

The train skirts the Gradierhäuser ('evaporating-houses'), crosses a lofty viaduct, and reaches —

122 M. **Friedberg** (430 ft.; *Hôtel Trapp,* R. & B. 2¹/₂ ℳ; *Weith; Restaurant Felsenkeller,* with view), with 9000 inhab., which was once a free imperial town. The Gothic *Stadt-Kirche,* built in 1260-1350, was restored in 1896-1901.

The Taunus Mts. rise to the right. Beyond (134¹/₂ M.) *Vilbel* (p. 299) the *Nidda* is crossed. 136¹/₂ M. *Bonames;* 138 M. *Eschersheim-Heddernheim;* 141 M. *Bockenheim,* three suburbs of Frankfort.

143 M. **Frankfort,** see p. 279.

22. The Volcanic Eifel.

The Eifel is a mountainous plateau, seamed with deep rocky ravines, situated between the Moselle, the Rhine, and the Roer, about 45 M. in length, and 25 M. in breadth. Geologically it consists substantially of folded and early stratified layers of Devonian rocks, such as grauwacke sandstone, slate, fossiliferous marl, and

coral. In the S. part of the plateau (see below) these formations
were disturbed by volcanic action at so recent a period, that (as in
Auvergne) the craters with their walls of slag and the streams of
lava which issued from them are still clearly discernible. Among
the most characteristic volcanic features are the depressions amid
the scoriaceous sand, lava, and tufa, generally now occupied by
lakes (the so-called 'Maare'). These were formed, not by continuous
volcanic action, but by single explosions of gas and steam. The
numerous mineral springs are also more or less due to volcanic
action. The valleys are deep and often of great beauty. The general
bleak aspect of the plateau has lately been considerably modified
by afforestation. — The E. part is called the *Hohe Eifel*, near
Adenau and Kelberg, and comprises the Hohe Acht (2410 ft.; p.109),
the Nürburg (2180 ft.; p. 109), the Aremberg (p. 109), and the
Erensberg (2265 ft.); the W. part is the *Schneifel* (*i.e.* Schnee-
Eifel), in the neighbourhood of Prüm (p. 150); and the S. part is
the picturesque *Vorder-Eifel*, or *Volcanic Eifel*, extending as
far as the Rhine (Laacher See, p. 120), and embracing Gerolstein,
Daun, Manderscheid (p. 157), and Bertrich (p. 168).

The bracing air of the Eifel has made it a very popular summer-resort.
The hotels are usually clean and comfortable. The best headquarters
are at *Kyllburg, Manderscheid,* and *Daun.* The *Eifel-Verein* (*Eifel
Club;* 13,000 members) has opened up many pretty and formerly inac-
cessible valleys and has done good service in marking paths. For the
'Höhenwege', see p. xvii. — Comp. the guide *(Eifelführer)* issued by the
Eifel Club (15th edit., Trèves, 1909; 3 *M*) and *Dr. von Dechen's 'Geo-
gnostischer Führer durch die Vordereifel'* (2nd edit., 1886; 8 *M*). A pleasant account of the district is afforded by 'In the Volcanic Eifel', by
Katharine and *Gilbert Macquoid* (illus.; 1896).

a. Railway from Cologne to Trèves.

112 M. RAILWAY in $3^1/_4$-$5^1/_2$ hrs. (fares 14 *M* 20, 8 *M* 50, 5 *M* 60 pf.,
express 16 *M* 20, 10 *M* 50, 6 *M* 60 pf.); to (69 M.) *Gerolstein* in $2^1/_4$-$3^1/_2$ hrs.
(fares 8 *M* 70, 5 *M* 50, 3 *M* 50 pf., express 9 *M* 70, 6 *M* 50 pf., 4 *M*).

Cologne, see p. 39. As far as (7 M.) *Kalscheuren* the line
follows the direction of the Left Rhenish Railway (R. 11a); it then
turns to the right, and intersects the *Vorgebirge* (p. 81). $9^1/_2$ M.
Kierberg (315 ft.), 1 M. to the W. of Brühl (p. 83).

$13^3/_4$ M. *Liblar*, junction for light railways to Horrem (p. 15),
and to Brühl (p. 83) and Vochem. The village lies $^3/_4$ M. to the
W., on the light railway to Euskirchen (see p. 147). To the S. of
it is the château of *Gracht*, rebuilt in 1698 and much altered in
1850-53. — $17^1/_2$ M. *Weilerswist* (405 ft.), the station for *Gross-
Vernich*, on the *Erft*, the valley of which the train ascends; 21 M.
Derkum (490 ft.).

25 M. **Euskirchen** (492 ft.; **Joisten*, in the market-place,
R. & B. $2^1/_2$, D. with wine $2^1/_2$ *M*; *Kaspari; Traube; Post*, at
the station), a growing town of 12,000 inhab., with cloth and other
factories. The Rom. Cath. *Church of St. Martin*, of the 13-14th

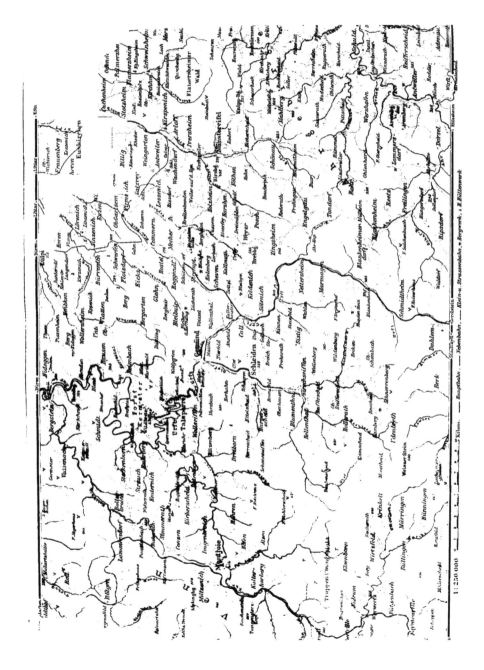

cent. (restored in 1899), has a lofty tower and contains a Gothic ciborium and a carved high-altar of 1500. The *Rathaus,* restored in 1901, dates from the 14th century. Three towers of the old fortifications are still standing. — Euskirchen is the junction of railways to Bonn (see p. 85), Düren, and Münstereifel, and of light railways to Liblar and several other points.

FROM EUSKIRCHEN TO DÜREN, 18½ M., railway in ca. ³/₄ hr. — 6 M. **Zülpich** *(Kölner Hof),* an ancient town (2150 inhab.), the Roman *Tolbiacum,* a station on the Roman road from Trèves to Cologne. The handsome Romanesque church of *St. Peter* dates from the 11th and 12th centuries. The romantic old castle (14th cent.) and the four 15th cent. gates are also noteworthy. — 18½ M. *Düren* (see p. 14).

FROM EUSKIRCHEN TO MÜNSTEREIFEL, 8½ M., railway in ca. ³/₄ hr. — **Münstereifel** (918 ft.; *Hillebrand,* R. & B. 2¼-2½, D. 1½-2, pens. 1-5 ℳ, very fair; *Post,* R. 1¾ ℳ), a small town (2800 inhab.) on both sides of the *Erft,* offers, with its old towers and gates (14th cent.), its ruined *Castle* (13th cent.), its churches, and its private houses of the 16-18th cent., an unusually attractive picture of olden times. From the railway-station we enter the town by a new gateway at the Schlacht-haus-Turm and reach, in a straight direction, the market-place, with the Rom. Catholic *Parish Church,* a late-Romanesque basilica of the 12th cent. (restored in 1876-93), with a square central tower and two circular side-towers with octagonal tops. Inside are an admirable early-Gothic wooden figure of the Virgin, four large marble epitaphs of the 16-17th cent., and Gothic sedilia with a reliquary above them. The crypt, part of which is much older than the church, has double aisles and contains a fine monument of 1335. In the clergy-house are several ecclesiastical portraits of the 16th cent. and an early-Cologne altar-piece of the second half of the 15th century. The Markt-Str. leads hence to the E. across the Erft to the former *Jesuit Church* (17th cent.), the 'Collegium' of which is now a school. The most noteworthy of the town-gates are the *Orchheimer-Tor* (S.) and the *Werther-Tor* (N.). — About 6 M. to the S.E. of Münstereifel (beyond *Rodert*) rises the basaltic *Michelsberg* (1930 ft.), with a pilgrimage-chapel and fine view. Other pleasant excursions may also be made from Münstereifel.

The train now leaves the diluvial district of the lower Rhine, ascends to the W. through the valley of the *Veybach,* and enters the N. part of the Eifel, where the Devonian formations are overlain by sandstone. To the right rises the picturesque old castle of *Veynau* (14-15th cent.). 30 M. *Satzvey* (700 ft.), also with a castle; 34 M. *Mechernich* (980 ft.; Bleiberg, R. & B. 2-2½ ℳ; Russischer Hof), a village of 3600 inhab., with extensive lead-mines (worked by the Romans) and foundries, one of the tall chimneys of which is 440 ft. high. Beyond (37 M.) *Scheven* we thread a tunnel and enter the valley of the *Urft.*

39½ M. *Call* (1235 ft.; Post or Nesgen), a village with forges. Remains of a Roman aqueduct are visible near the station.

FROM CALL TO HELLENTAL, 10½ M., railway in 1 hr. (fares 90, 55 pf.). — 3½ M. **Gemünd** (1110 ft.; *Bergemann,* with garden, very fair; *Klaphacke*), at the junction of the *Urft* and *Olef,* is the best starting-point for a visit to the *Urfttal Reservoir (Urfttalsperre),* constructed to afford water-power for the manufacturing district of Aix-la-Chapelle and Düren and filling up the valley of the Urft for a distance of 5½ M., with a width varying from 100 yds. to ½ M. (depth 100 ft.). We walk or drive (omn. 50 pf.) to (2½ M.) *Pulvermühlen* (Wald-Hôtel), whence motor-boats ply (fare 1 *M*, there & back 1¹/₂ *M*) in 40 min. to the *Sperrmauer* or *Dam* (Talsperre Restaurant, very fair) at the end of the picturesque artificial lake. This enormous structure almost challenges comparison with the Nile Dam at Assuân, which it exceeds in height (170 ft.) and width (18-180 ft.), though it is much inferior in length (250 yds.; Nile Dam 2150 yds. long, 130 ft. high, and 23-98 ft. thick). The best view of the dam is obtained from the *Wildbret-Hügel*, climbed from the Talsperre Restaurant in ¹/₂ hr.

The railway now ascends the busy valley of the *Olef.* — 5¹/₂ M. *Olef.* — 7¹/₂ M. **Schleiden** (1310 ft.; *Kölner Hof*, R. 1¹/₂-2, B. 1, D. 1¹/₂-2, pens. 4-5 *M*, very fair; *Schleidener Hof*), with 660 inhab., two ancient churches, and a modern château. — 10 M. *Blumental* (hotel), a little above which rise the imposing ruins of the castle of *Reifferscheid*, mentioned as early as 975, the ancestral seat of the Princes and Counts of Salm-Reifferscheid-Dyck. — 10¹/₂ M. *Hellental* (Schinck, very fair), picturesquely situated on the Olef.

42¹/₂ M. *Urft* (1330 ft.; Schneider). Opposite, on the right bank, lies *Dalbenden*, with two 18th cent. houses and a fragment of a Roman aqueduct. The old Premonstratensian abbey of *Steinfeld*, founded in the 10th cent. and now a school, lies 1 M. to the S.W. (not visible); the fine Romanesque church has Gothic cloisters and interesting tombstones. — 45¹/₂ M. *Nettersheim* (1475 ft.), with limestone quarries.

49¹/₂ M. *Blankenheim* (1630 ft.), which lies 2¹/₂ M. from the station (diligence thrice daily; Kölner Hof, R. & B. 2¹/₂-3 *M*), is situated in a narrow valley to the E., with the picturesque ruins of the ancestral castle of the knights of Blankenheim, built in the 12th century. The remains of a large Roman villa were discovered here in 1894. The *Ahr* (p. 103) rises at Blankenheim, where its sources are enclosed by a wall.

The line continues to ascend, until beyond (52 M.) *Schmidtheim* (1815 ft.), with an old château of Count Beyssel, it crosses the watershed between the Urft and the *Kyll* (Meuse and Moselle), the valley of which it descends. — 57¹/₂ M. *Jünkerath* (1415 ft.; Kreisch; Hattenrath; Eifler Hof), with large iron-works, is also the station for *Stadtkyll*, 3 M. to the W. About ¹/₄ M. below the station are some relics of the Roman castle of *Icorigium*. — 60 M. *Lissendorf* (1355 ft.). The train now enters the Volcanic Eifel properly so called.

63¹/₂ M. **Hillesheim** (1285 ft.; *Kloep*, R. & B. 2¹/₂-3, D. 1³/₄-2 *M; Fasen*, both very fair), a small town with 1200 inhab. and quaint old houses, 2 M. to the E. of the station. The (1 M.) *Kyller Höhe* commands a beautiful view.

The *Casselburg* (p. 149) may be ascended from Hillesheim station in 1¹/₄ hr. We descend the valley of the Kyll to (20 min.) *Niederbettingen* and (¹/₂ hr.) *Bewingen*. We then take the footpath to the left, beyond the signalman's hut, and ascend to (¹/₂ hr.) the top.

FROM HILLESHEIM TO ADENAU by road, 17¹/₂ M. The best plan is to leave the road at (3 M.) *Kerpen*, with a ruined castle, and proceed to (1¹/₂ M.) *Niederehe* (Schmitz), with an old convent-church containing interesting monuments. Thence by a footpath, along the stream, to the *Nohner Mühle*, the ruin and waterfall of *Dreimühlen*, and *Ahütte* (Fasen).

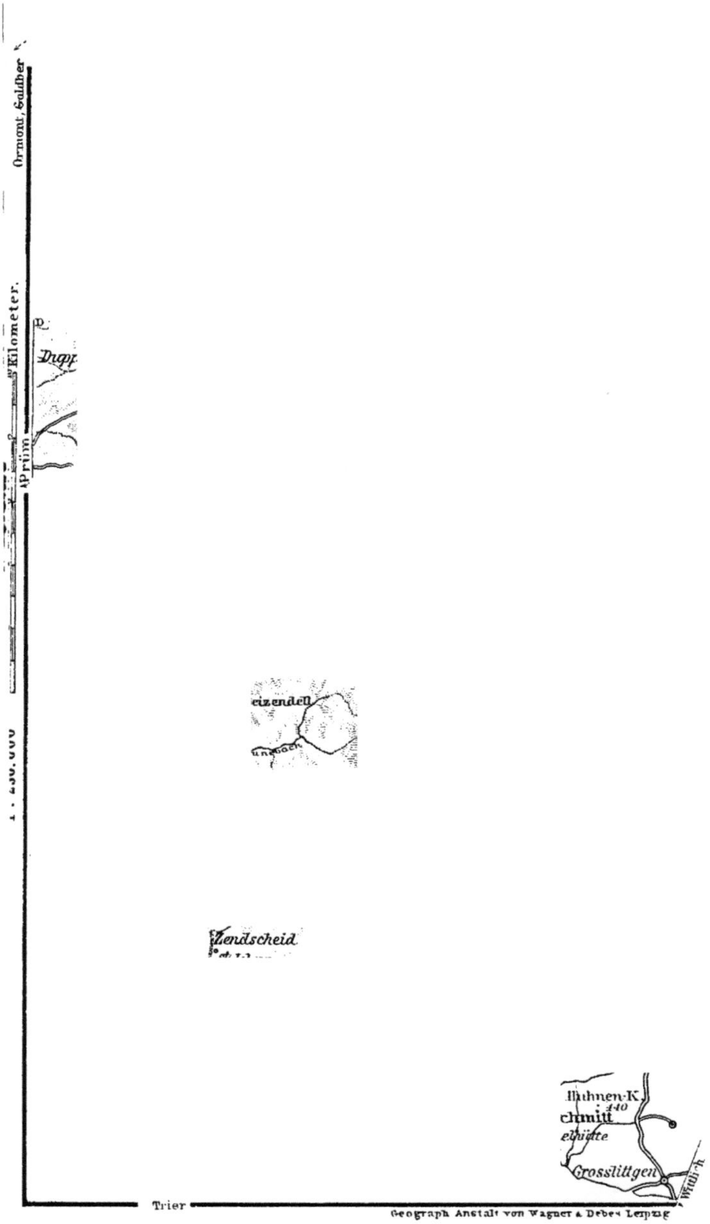

Ormont-Gouldber

1 : 200,000

3 Kilometer.

Prüm

Dlop

eizendell

Izendscheid

Huhnen-K

440

clmitt

eBiste

Grosslittgen

Trier

Geograph. Anstalt von Wagner & Debes, Leipzig.

1 : 250,000   Kilometi

At *Leudersdorf*, 1¹/₄ M. to the W., are the remains of a Roman villa. From Ahütte we follow the valley of the *Ahbach* to (¹/₂ hr.) the picturesque ruin of *Neu-Blankenheim*. Hence we ascend by a path to the right (E.) to the (¹/₂ hr.) Nohn road, follow this to *Kirmudscheid*, and either take the road to the right viâ *Wirft* and *Honnerath* or proceed viâ *Barweiler*, *Wiesenscheid*, and the *Nürburg* to *Adenau* (p. 109).

The most interesting part of the line begins below Hillesheim. The valley, which is fertile and well-cultivated, is enclosed by precipitous and partly-wooded limestone rocks of most picturesque forms. To the right of the village of **Pelm** (Britz; Bahnhofs-Hôtel: station on the Andernach railway, 1¹/₄ M. to the N.E. of Gerolstein; see p. 155), famed for its 'Gerolsteiner Schlossbrunnen' waters, rises a wooded hill (1590 ft.) crowned with the ruined *Casselburg* (ascent by the road from Pelm station in 20-25 min.), once the ancestral castle of the knights of Kastelberg. The main tower, 164 ft. high, commands a splendid view of the Kylltal and the Eifel. The key is kept at the forester's opposite (rfmts.).

The *Papenkaul* (p. 150) may be reached from the forester's house in 40 min.; near it is a stalactite cavern, known as the *Buchenloch*, in which some colossal fossilized bones were lately found (p. 180). From the Papenkaul we descend to Gerolstein in ¹/₄ hr., passing the lime-tree mentioned at p. 150. — Road to *Daun*, see p. 150.

The valley of *Gees*, to the S.E. of Pelm, abounds in fossils.

69 M. Gerolstein. — The *Railway Station* (restaurant) lies on the right bank of the Kyll, the village on the left. — HOTELS. *Heck*, Haupt-Str. 69, in the highest part of the town, ¹/₂ M. from the railway station, with garden extending up the slope of the Schlossberg, R. 2¹/₄-2¹/₂, D. 2, S. 1¹/₂, pens. 4¹/₂-5 ℳ, very good; *Post*, Haupt-Str. 124, R. & B. 2¹/₂-3 ℳ; *Gerolstein*, unpretending. — *Eifeler Hof*, at the railway station, R. & B. 2¹/₂, D. 1³/₄ ℳ.

Gerolstein (1230 ft.), the junction of the branch-lines to Andernach and Coblenz (p. 121) and to St. Vith (see p. 150; carriages changed in both cases), is geologically one of the most interesting points of the Eifel. Visitors will be struck not only by the picturesque volcanic formations, but also by the innumerable fossils in the limestone of the middle Devonian period. The best-known of the numerous mineral springs are the *Florabrunnen*, the *Sprudel*, and the *Hansabrunnen*, the water of which is freely exported. The village, containing 1560 inhab., stretches from the Kyll bridge up the slopes of the *Schlossberg*, the top of which may be reached in ¹/₄ hr. by passing the church and turning to the left. On the summit (395 ft. above the valley) are the ruins of a castle, built by Gerhard von Blankenheim in 1115 and destroyed in 1694, which afford a view of the limestone rocks of the Munterlei and the Auburg on the opposite side of the valley. The view of the valley itself is obscured by the smoke of the numerous railway trains. — By the approach to the castle are finger-posts indicating the routes to the wooded *Heiligenstein* (1663 ft.; bench with view of the Schlossberg, 10 min.) and (r.) to the volcanic *Dietzenlei* (2030 ft.), rising in the Gerolstein wood, 3 M. to the S., near Büscheich.

The best view of Gerolstein itself is obtained a few paces beyond a large and venerable lime-tree, on the footpath to the *Munterlei,* reached in 5 min. from the Kyll bridge by crossing the railway.
The view from the (20 min.) flag-staff, higher up, is more extensive
but less picturesque. Still farther up is the *Papenkaul* (1745 ft.;
20 min.), a fine crater, from which a narrow stream of lava descends by a grassy valley on the N. side into the Kylltal (from the
Papenkaul to the Casselburg $^1/_2$ hr.; red way-marks; see p. 148).

FROM GEROLSTEIN TO ST. VITH, 36$^1/_2$ M., by the 'Hohe-Venn-Bahn',
railway in ca. 2$^1/_2$ hrs. — The chief intermediate station is (15 M.) **Prüm**
(1395 ft.; *Goldener Stern,* R. 1$^1/_2$, pens. 4$^1/_2$-5 $\mathcal{M}$; *Kaiserhof*), situated on
the brook of that name, at the S. end of the *Schneifel,* anciently the
seat of a Benedictine abbey founded by the Merovingians in 720, and
once in the enjoyment of political independence, but suppressed by the
French in 1801. Pop. 2700. The two-towered church, containing the tomb
of Lothaire I. (d. 855), dates from the 16th century. In the environs are
beautiful woods with paths. About 5 M. to the N. of Prüm lies *Schönecken*
(Rondé), in a charming situation, with the ruins of a castle. — 27 M.
Bleialf. — 36$^1/_2$ M. *St. Vith* (p. 13).

Walkers should choose the OLD ROAD FROM GEROLSTEIN TO DAUN
(10 M.), which diverges to the right from the new road at the upper end
of *Pelm* (p. 149). It ascends rapidly and soon reaches its highest point
at (1$^1/_2$ M.) *Kirchweiler* (Schlömer), whence it goes on between the *Erres-
berg* (2297 ft.) to the N. and the **Scharteberg** (2267 ft.) to the S., the
latter even more distinctly recognizable than the former as an extinct
volcano and well worth a visit. The circular crater is surrounded with
blistered masses of slag. About 100 ft. below the summit begin the lava-
streams which descend towards the N., S., and E. The last of these
is traceable by the occasional protrusion of the rock through its superficial covering, and may be examined in the quarries worked in it in the
direction of *Steinborn,* where a transverse section of two streams lying
one above the other is exposed to view. The lowest stratum consists of
porous and but slightly cleft basaltic lava; above it lies slag, 3-4 ft. in
thickness; next comes a layer of rapilli (small round nodules of lava)
and volcanic sand; and finally, next the surface, basaltic lava again. A
little farther to the S. is the **Nerother Kopf** (2120 ft.), a hill of slag
crowned with a ruined castle and containing a picturesque grotto. —
Beyond Kirchweiler the hilly road to Daun next passes *Steinborn,* where
there is an aërated mineral spring (to the left the *Felsberg,* to the right
the *Rimmerich,* two craters with lava-streams), and *Neunkirchen.*

To the right, beyond Gerolstein, are the steep crags of the
Munterlei (see above) and the castle-like rock of *Auburg.* At *Lis-
singen* (r.) are two castles, adjoining each other and still occupied.
— 74 M. *Birresborn* (1100 ft.; Krone), a village of 1000 inhab.
on the right bank of the Kyll, connected by a stone bridge with the
railway-station on the left bank. About 1$^1/_4$ M. above the village
is situated the *Mineral Spring of Birresborn,* the strongest and
best-known of the carbonic acid springs of the Eifel.

76$^1/_2$ M. *Mürlenbach* (1050 ft.: Krumpen, very fair), a village
(800 inhab.) with the ruins of a castle founded by the Merovingians
and rebuilt in the 17th century. — 78 M. *Densborn* (1210 ft.),
with two ruined castles. The limestone-rocks are now succeeded
by variegated sandstone. The line traverses a pleasant wooded
tract, and passes the villages of *Usch* and *Zendscheid.* 82$^1/_2$ M.

St. Thomas, with a suppressed Cistercian nunnery, the fine church
of which, erected in the transition style about 1225, contains some
mediæval tombstones. The train passes through a tunnel.

84$^1/_2$ M. **Kyllburg** (comp. Plan and Map, p. 154). — Hotels.
Eifeler Hof (Pl. a), $^1/_2$ M. from the station, first-class, with view-ter-
race, R. & B. 2$^1/_2$-3$^1/_2$, D. 2, pens. 4$^1/_2$-6$^1/_2$ *M; Stern* (Pl. b), R. 1$^1/_4$-1$^3/_4$, B.
$^3/_4$, pens. 4$^1/_2$-5 *M; Géronne-Surges*, similar prices, all three in the town;
Post, at the railway-station, R. 1$^1/_2$-2 *M*, B. 60 pf., D. 1$^1/_2$, pens. 4-4$^1/_2$ *M*.

Kyllburg (890 ft.), with 1100 inhab., picturesquely situated on
and at the base of a hill, surrounded by the Kyll and rising about
490 ft. above it, is one of the most frequented points of the Eifel.
From the station we follow the road to the left as far as the Kyll
bridge and then, at the tunnel, the steep street to (10 min.) the
above-mentioned hotels. Hence the Hoch-Strasse leads to the left
to the Stifts-Kirche, while to the right a steep 'Route de Calvaire',
passing the small Protestant church, ascends to ($^3/_4$ M.) the *Mariensäule*, a tower affording a fine view of Kyllburg and Malberg. The
Hoch-Strasse goes on along the ridge, passing the entrance to the
Hahn Promenade (see below) and an old watch-tower (10 min.). The
Abbey Church (*Stifts-Kirche*; 1195 ft.) is a fine Gothic building
of 1276, without aisles. The choir contains fine stalls and stained-
glass windows, executed in 1534 from designs after Dürer. The
adjoining cloisters (entered from the second door to the right of
the main portal) and the chapter-house, to the E. of the cloisters,
date from the 14th century. Pleasant promenades (accessible from
the Hoch-Str.) run, at three different levels, through the woods on
the *Hahn*, the S. slope of the hill (2 M.; benches). Another, the
Ringpfad, runs along above the left bank and is reached by crossing
the bridge and diverging after 5 min. to the right from the road.
The road goes on to ($^3/_4$ M.) the *Wilsecker Linde*, which affords a
good view of the wooded valley of the Kyll and the hill crowned by
the abbey-church. By keeping to the right at every turn beyond this
we reach the Ringpfad, which may be followed back to the town.

On a height above the Kyll, 1 M. to the W. of Kyllburg, is the village
of *Malberg*, commanded by a château incorporated with an old castle (view).

Road from Kyllburg to (15 M.) *Manderscheid*, viâ Oberkail and Eisenschmitt, see p. 160. A pleasanter route is afforded by the footpath, which
diverges to the left 1 M. beyond the Kyll bridge and runs viâ Kyllburgweiler, Seinsfeld, and Corneshütte to (5$^1/_2$ hrs.) *Bettenfeld* (see p. 159),
3 M. by road from Manderscheid.

The train now passes through a short tunnel and crosses the
Kyll. The brook here describes a circuit, which the railway cuts
off by means of the *Wilseck Tunnel*. — 88 M. *Erdorf* (765 ft.;
Reissdörfer) is the junction for a branch-line to *Bitburg* (3$^1/_2$ M.,
in $^1/_4$ hr.).

The Road to Bitburg crosses the Kyll. Immediately beyond the bridge
a road leads to the right to (2 M.) *Fliessem* (Leonardy), passing a little
to the E. of (1$^1/_2$ M.) *Odrang*, with the remains of a Roman villa with
several fine Roman mosaic pavements (fee to the keeper).

Bitburg (1008 ft.; *Post*, R. & B. $2^1/_2$ ✳, very fair; *Junggeburth*) was the *Bedae Vicus* of the Romans, and a station on their road from Trèves to Cologne, several of the milestones of which have been found in the neighbourhood. Pop. 2800. The *Kobenhof*, the house of Kob von Rüdingen, dates from 1576. To the N., on the Prüm road, is an old *Castle*.

The line continues to follow the picturesque wooded valley, bounded by sandstone-rocks. The brook now becomes navigable for rafts. Tunnels and bridges follow each other in rapid succession, and numerous mills are passed. At *Hüttingen* is a picturesque waterfall, 16 ft. high. 93 M. *Philippsheim* (645 ft.), the station for ($1^1/_2$ M.) *Dudeldorf*, with an old castle. 95 M. *Speicher;* the village, with important potteries, lies on the hill, $1^1/_2$ M. to the E. 97 M. *Auw*, with a pilgrimage-church, erected in 1708-46. — $101^1/_2$ M. *Daufenbach*, with sandstone-quarries. — $104^1/_2$ M. *Cordel* (475 ft.; Thiel), with large quarries, where hundreds of flint-axes have been found, is frequented as a summer-resort. To the right of the station rises the ruined castle of *Ramstein* (560 ft.; $^3/_4$ hr.), erected in the 14th century. — 107 M. *Ehrang* (see p. 170) lies at the junction of the Kylltal with the valley of the Moselle.

112 M. **Trèves,** see p. 175.

b. Railway from Andernach to Mayen and Gerolstein.

$58^1/_2$ M. RAILWAY in $3^1/_4$-4 hrs. (fares 4 ✳ 50 pf., 3 ✳). — From Coblenz to Mayen, 23 M., branch-line (in $1^1/_4$ hr.; fares 1 ✳ 80, 1 ✳ 25 pf.) viâ *Metternich*, *Rübenach*, (8 M.) *Bassenheim* (with a restored castle), *Ochtendung*, *Kerben*, *Polch*, and *Hausen*. Travellers for Gerolstein change carriages at Mayen.

From Andernach to ($9^1/_2$ M.) *Niedermendig*, see p. 118. — $12^1/_2$ M. *Cottenheim* (785 ft.; Eich; May), with millstone-quarries. To the right is the *Mayener Bellenberg*, beyond which rises the *Ettringer Bellenberg* (1405 ft.), a broken-down crater, which was the source of the lava-stream in the quarries of Mayen (p. 153). To the left rises the *Hochsimmer* (1820 ft.), with a tower commanding a wide view.

$14^1/_2$ M. **Mayen.** — RAILWAY STATIONS: *Mayen-Ost* (870 ft.), the main station, 1 M. from the market-place; *Mayen-West* (880 ft.), nearly $^1/_2$ M. from the market-place.

HOTELS. *Kohlhaas*, Markt-Platz, R. $1^1/_2$-$2^1/_4$, B. $^3/_4$, D. $1^3/_4$-$2^1/_4$, pens. 5 ✳, very good; *Müller*, Markt-Platz 9, R. $1^1/_2$, B. $^3/_4$, D. $1^1/_2$-2, pens. $4^1/_2$-5 ✳, also very fair. — *Kur-Hôtel*, situated $1^1/_4$ M. to the N.W., in the valley of the Nette, a favourite summer-resort, pens. $4^1/_2$-5 ✳.

Mayen (780 ft.), a district-town with 13,500 inhab., is of Celtic origin, and in the Roman period was an important station on the military road from Trèves to the central part of the Rhine valley. At a later date it was the capital of the Maifeld and the seat of the 'Gaugraf', and from the 13th cent. on it belonged to the Electorate of Trèves. It was then surrounded by walls and towers, part of which are still standing. The town lies in a hollow at the beginning of the narrower part of the Nette Valley, and is a convenient centre for excursions. In the S.W. part of the town, picturesquely situated on a hill above the market-place, is the *Genoveva-Burg,* erected in 1280, apparently on the site of the old residence of the Counts Palatine, to which the foundations of the S. tower probably belong. Down to 1798 it was the seat of the local representative of the Elector of Trèves, but it is now private property and has been greatly altered. The Roman Catholic *Parish Church* is conspicuous for the spiral and twisted form of its steeple; the W. part of the church is Romanesque (12th cent.), while the nave and choir are late-Gothic. The *Coblenzer-Tor* or *Brücken-Tor,* on the E. side of the town, contains the collections of the Historical Society, including prehistoric relics and objects from the Roman and Frankish settlements and graves of the vicinity. — The quarries of basaltic lava to the N. of the Ost-Bahnhof (E. Railway Station) furnish a much-prized material for millstones, pavements, and stairways.

A prehistoric castle of the late stone age was discovered in 1907, about ¹/₂ M. from the E. Railway Station.

A good road, passing under the railway-viaduct, leads to the N.W. from Mayen up the deep and wooded valley of the Nette (with several open-air restaurants) to the Kur-Hôtel (p. 152) and the (4¹/₂ M.) turreted *Château of Bürresheim,* situated at the confluence of the Nette and the Nitz. The huge and well-preserved structure, dating from the 12-17th cent., now belongs to the Count of Renesse-Breitbach. — An extensive view is obtained from the *Hochsimmer* (p. 152), which is reached from Mayen viâ the Kur-Hôtel and St. Johann in 1¹/₂ hr.

Diligences ply once a day from Mayen to (8¹/₂ M., in 2¹/₄ hrs.) *Virneburg* (Müller) viâ *Cürrenberg;* and to (10¹/₂ M., in 2¹/₂ hrs.) Münster-Maifeld (p. 163).

The train skirts the town, with its numerous towers, crosses the valley of the Nette by a viaduct 115 yds. long, passes the station *Mayen-West,* and then penetrates the watershed between the Nette and the *Elz* by means of tunnels.

21 M. **Monreal** (970 ft.; *Kircher,* R. & B. 1¹/₂ ℳ; *Lunnebach*), charmingly situated in the valley of the Elz, has two ruined castles, the *Resch* and *Monreal.* The latter, the more important of the two, dates from 1229. The chapel in the cemetery contains some interesting remains of old frescoes.

Fine retrospect of Monreal as we proceed. — 25 M. *Urmersbach,* in the *Stellbach-Tal.* — 26¹/₂ M. **Kaisersesch** (1490 ft.; *Post,* R. 1¹/₂ ℳ; *Schwan*) lies ²/₃ M. from the station. In the wood, near the latter, may be distinguished the broad embankment of a Roman military road, almost parallel with which are a moat and rampart, extending across the whole Eifel district. — Excellent slates are quarried near Kaisersesch.

From Kaisersesch to Cochem (p. 165), 8 M., diligence twice daily in 2 hrs. (in the other direction 2¹/₂ hrs.). The road passes *Landkern,* with the small *Dreifaltigkeits-Kapelle* ('Chapel of the Trinity'), containing an ancient column, with curious reliefs of the Trinity, the Crucifixion, and the Virgin with her dead Son. Farther on the road joins the *Endert-Tal* and passes near the *Winneburg* (p. 165).

The railway ascends beyond the *Wolfsberg* (1835 ft.) to (30 M.) *Laubach-Müllenbach* (1575 ft.), with a view extending on the S.W. over the Vorder-Eifel, and on the S. over the hills of the Moselle to the Hunsrück. — 33 M. *Uersfeld*. — 36 M. **Ulmen** (1435 ft.; *Bahnhof-Hôtel*, R. $1^1/_2$-$2^1/_4$, B. $^3/_4$, D. $1^1/_2$-2 $\mathcal{M}$; *Franzen; Schlags*), on the *Ulmener Maar*, with a ruined castle and a high-lying church. — 39 M. *Utzerath* (1515 ft.); diligence to Adenau, see p. 109.

42 M. *Darscheid* (1620 ft.; Häs). A picturesque walk may be taken through the *Lehwald* to ($2^3/_4$ M.) Mehren (p. 156) by follow-ing the Daun road from the rail. station for 6-8 min. and then turn-ing to the left. Or we may diverge to the right from the Mehren road after 2 M., turn to the left again almost at once, and cross the bleak summit of the *Hardt* to ($^1/_2$ hr.) the Weinfelder Maar (p. 155; comp. the Map). The view from the Hardt resembles that from the Mäuseberg (p. 155).

The line now descends, through beautiful woods, along the *Förmerich* or *Firmerich* (1615 ft.), an extinct crater, into the valley of the *Lieser*.

44 M. Daun. — HOTELS. In Ober-Daun: **Schramm*, in an open situation, R. $1^3/_4$-2, B. $^3/_4$, D. 2, S. $1^1/_2$, pens. $4^1/_2$-$5^1/_2$ $\mathcal{M}$, with electric light, baths, and good cuisine; opposite, *Gandner*, R. & B. 2, D. $1^1/_2$ $\mathcal{M}$. — In Unter-Daun: *Hommes*, an old-established house, R. & B. from $2^1/_4$, D. $1^3/_4$, pens. $4^1/_2$-5 $\mathcal{M}$; *Dauner Hof, Eifler Hof*, near the station. — *Bath-ing House* at the Gemünder Maar (p. 155; key kept at Daun).

CARRIAGE to Manderscheid or Lutzerath, 12 $\mathcal{M}$. — DILIGENCE twice daily to ($10^1/_2$ M.) Manderscheid and ($9^1/_2$ M.) Gillenfeld.

From the *Railway Station* (1310 ft.; omnibus) the road to the left leads through Unter-Daun to Ober-Daun; the footpath to the right crosses an iron bridge (Städter-Brücke) and leads direct to Ober-Daun.

Daun, a town of Celtic origin, with 1100 inhab., lies pictur-esquely on the *Lieser*, on the slope of a small hill which is crowned with the remains of the old *Schloss* of the Counts of Daun, a cel-ebrated family, several members of which distinguished themselves in the Austrian service. The still partly-preserved circumvallation encloses the former fiscal office (Renthaus) of the Elector of Trèves, dating from the 17th cent. (now a forester's house) and the small Protestant church (1863), the approach to which is opposite the Burgomaster's Office (Bürgermeisterei). At the District Office (Land-ratsamt), on a piece of Roman pavement, stands a large cast-iron figure of Bacchus (1591), brought from the convent of Howen near Zülpich and said to be a reproduction of a Roman stone statue. In the courtyard of the Schramm Hotel is a Roman tombstone. The Roman Catholic *Parish Church* in Unter-Daun is one of the oldest in the Eifel, its vaulting dating from the 15th century. To the right of the entrance is a hatchment of a Count Daun, dating from

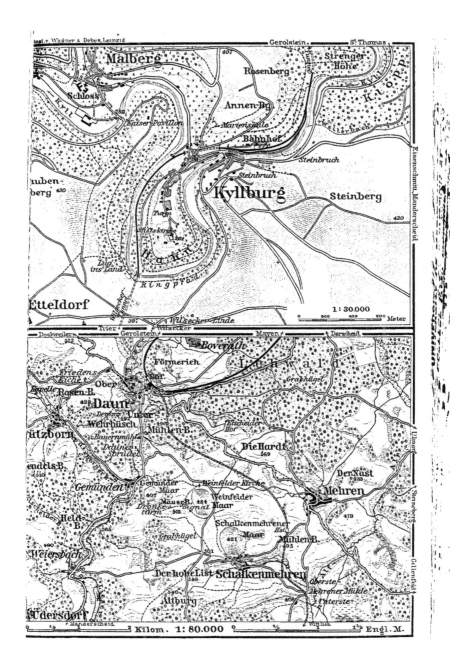

1741. — From the Schramm Hotel and also from the Hommes Hotel paths ascend to the promenades on the *Wehrbüsch* (1615 ft.), a lava hill, crowned with a war monument. To the N.W. of Ober-Daun, and to the left of the road to Dockweiler (finger-post pointing to Pützborn, then to the right), is the wooded lava ridge of the *Warth* (1690 ft.), another fine point of view. — About $^2/_3$ M. to the S. of Daun, on the Manderscheid highroad (see below), rises the *Dauner Sprudel*, a strong chalybeate spring charged with carbonic acid gas. Adjacent is the well-equipped *Sophien-Bad* (bath 60 pf.-1$^1/_2$ $\mathscr{M}$).

FROM DAUN TO WITTLICH 22$^1/_2$ M., railway in 1$^1/_4$-1$^3/_4$ hr. — The line crosses the Lieser-Tal, to the E. of Daun, by a lofty viaduct. 3 M. *Schalkenmehren* (p. 156); 7 M. *Gillenfeld* (p. 156); 10 M. *Eckfeld* (p. 156); 11$^1/_2$ M. *Manderscheid-Pantenburg* (p. 157); 13 M. *Laufeld;* 16 M. *Hasborn;* 18$^1/_2$ M. *Plein.* — 22$^1/_2$ M. *Wittlich* (p. 170).

The Gerolstein train ascends the valley of the Lieser to (46 M.) *Rengen*, then runs through wood, and reaches its highest point (1860 ft.) beyond (50$^1/_2$ M.) *Dockweiler-Dreis* (Meyer's Inn, at Dreis, very fair). The Dreiser Weiher is a dried up Maar (p. 146), with emanations of carbonic acid gas. We then descend through a pretty wood-girt valley to (53$^1/_2$ M.) *Hohenfels*, in a volcanic basin. The towers of the Casselburg now become visible to the left, beyond the Kylltal; to the right is the building of the Gerolstein Schloss-Brunnen. 57 M. *Pelm.* — 58$^1/_2$ M. *Gerolstein* (see p. 149).

c. Walk from Daun to Kyllburg viâ Gillenfeld and Manderscheid.

FIRST DAY. By the *Dauner Maare*, the *Mäuseberg*, and *Mehren* to the *Pulvermaar*, 3 hrs.; to *Gillenfeld*, $^1/_2$ hr.; viâ the *Belvedere* to *Manderscheid*, 2$^3/_4$ hrs. — SECOND DAY. Over the *Mosenberg* to *Bettenfeld*, 1$^1/_2$ hr.; to *Eisenschmitt*, 1$^1/_2$ hr.; thence to *Kyllburg*, 7$^1/_2$ M. Railway to Gillenfeld and Manderscheid, see above.

We follow the Manderscheid road (from which, beyond the Dauner Sprudel, diverge to the left first the old, and then the new road to Schalkenmehren) to the village of *Gemünden* (1 M.), which lies to the right on the *Lieser*. A finger-post indicates the way (to the left) to the (8 min.) *Gemünder Maar (1335 ft.), the smallest but most beautiful of the crater-lakes of Daun. It lies in a partly-wooded basin, and is about 18 acres in area and 125 ft. in depth. On its bank is a monument to Moltke. A good footpath (finger-post) leads hence through a coppice, with picturesque views of the Maar and Daun, to the (25 min.) tower ('Dronke-Turm') on the **Mäuseberg** (1840 ft.), which commands a fine view of the Volcanic Eifel, with the Mosenberg to the S.W., the Moselle hills to the S., and the Nürburg and Hohe Acht to the N. From the trigonometrical signal on the highest point, a little to the E., we look down on the solitary *Weinfelder Maar* (1590 ft.), another of these crater-lakes, 42 acres in area and 170 ft. in depth, and on

the *Weinfelder Kirche*, the only relic of the village of Weinfeld,
now used as a burial-chapel. — From the signal we may regain
Daun in $^3/_4$ hr. by descending the path to the Weinfelder Kirche
and then following the road (short-cut by old road).

To the S. E. of the Weinfelder Maar lies the *Schalkenmehrer
Maar* (1380 ft.), the third of the lakes of Daun, 55 acres in area
and 70 ft. in depth, which we reach from the signal in 8 min. by
descending the slope of turf. On the S. bank of the lake, which is
drained by the *Alfbach* (p. 168), is the village of *Schalkenmehren*
(Michels), in a patch of fertile soil.

By proceeding from the Weinfelder Kirche towards the E. across
the ridge between the two Maare, passing, halfway, under the new
Wittlich railway (p. 155), we reach (2 M.) the village of **Mehren**
(*Herbrand, Zur Post*, R. & B. $1^1/_2$-$1^3/_4$, pens. $3^1/_2$-4 $\mathcal{M}$), situated
on the highroad to Bertrich (p. 168), $4^1/_2$ M. to the S. E. of Daun
and $1^1/_4$ M. from Schalkenmehren ($^1/_2$ M. from the railway-station
between these two villages).

Near *Steineberg*, about $1^1/_4$ M. to the N.E. of Mehren and 2 M. from
Darscheid (p. 154), is the *Ringwall*, an extensive prehistoric burial-ground
commanding a fine view (best from the platform at the top).

The new railway descends along the right bank of the *Alf*. The
highroad crosses ($^1/_2$ M.) the stream and then reascends through
wood. About 4 M. from Mehren we take the Gillenfeld road to the
right, and diverge by a footpath to the left to the **Pulvermaar*
(1350 ft.), the most beautiful and, after the Laacher See (p. 120),
the largest of the crater-lakes of the Eifel, 95 acres in area and
245 ft. deep, situated in a basin fringed with woods. The hills
(ca. 230 ft.) on its banks consist almost entirely of volcanic sand,
which appears as a black powder in the water of the lake. On the
S. side rises the *Römersberg* (1565 ft.), a considerable rock composed of slag. From this point to Strotzbüsch, see p. 169; to
Lutzerath (p. 169), $4^1/_2$ M.

About $1^1/_2$ M. to the W. of the Pulvermaar lies the village of
Gillenfeld (1335 ft.; *Zillgen*, R. $1^1/_2$, B. $^3/_4$, pens. 4-5 $\mathcal{M}$, very
fair; carriages for hire), a station on the railway from Daun to
Wittlich (p. 155), rebuilt after various conflagrations. [From
Schalkenmehren we reach Gillenfeld in $1^1/_2$ hr. by crossing the Alf
at the Mehrener Mühle and passing the village of *Saxler*.]

At *Strohn*, 2 M. to the S. of Gillenfeld, the valley of the Alf cuts
into the lava-deposits of the *Wartgesberg* (1562 ft.), one of the largest
volcanic hills of the Eifel. It is undoubtedly a crater, though its form
is not easily recognized as such.

FROM GILLENFELD TO MANDERSCHEID, 6 M. (carr. 8-10 $\mathcal{M}$; railway, see p. 155). After about 1 M. the road leads for a short
distance through wood, affording a view of the small *Holzmaar*
(1395 ft.) to the right. 2 M. *Eckfeld*, a station of the Daun and
Wittlich Railway. — Near (1 M.) *Buchholz*, at Hoffmann's Inn,

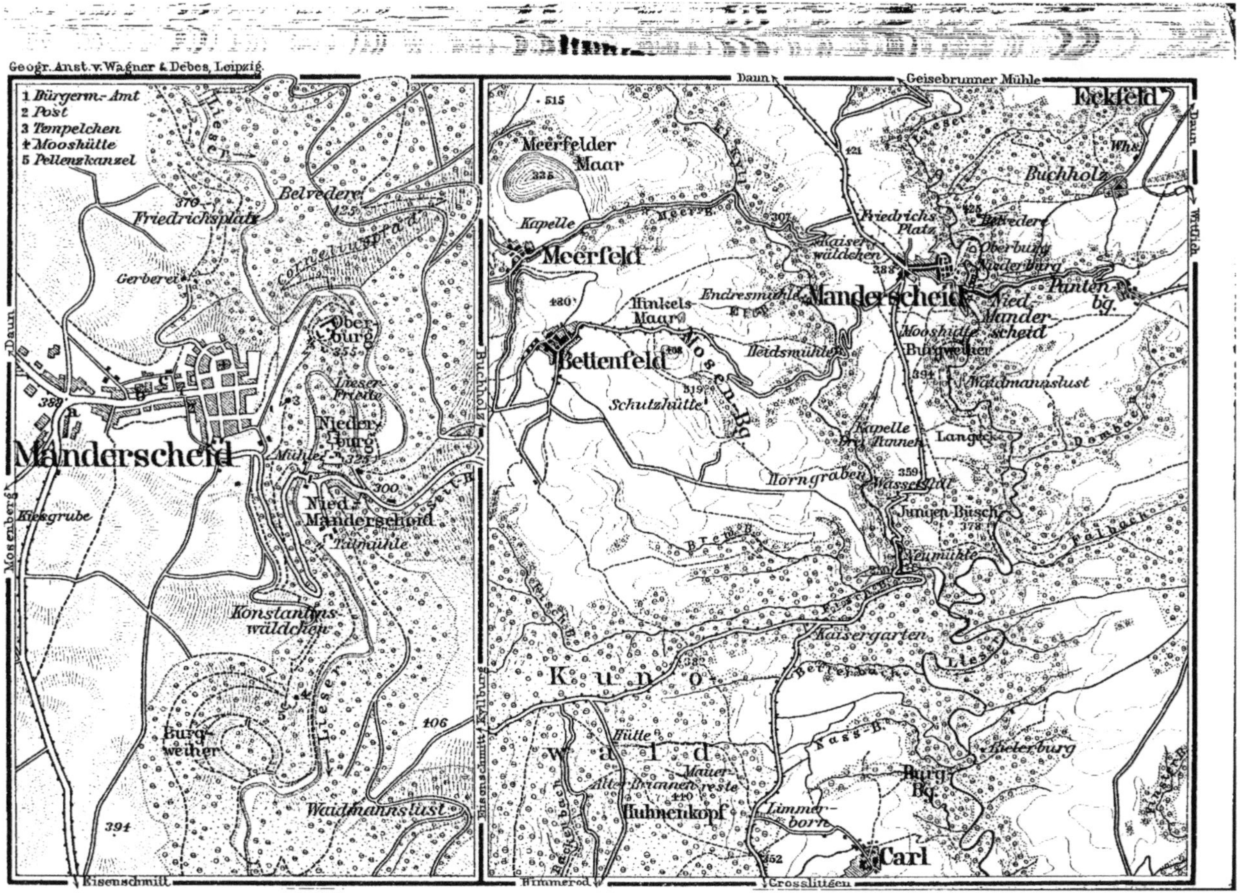
Geogr. Anst. v. Wagner & Debes, Leipzig.
1 Bürgerm.-Amt
2 Post
3 Tempelchen
4 Mooshütte
5 Pellenzkanzel
Manderscheid
Friedrichsplatz
Belvedere
Gerberei
Oberburg
Niederburg
Nied. Manderscheid
Kiesgrube
Konstantinswäldchen
Burgweiher
Waidmannslust
Lieser
Buchholz
Daun
Mosenberg
Eisenschmitt
Geisebrunner Mühle
Meerfelder Maar
Meerfeld
Kapelle
Bettenfeld
Hinkels-Maar
Mosen-Bg.
Schutzhütte
Heidsmühle
Endresmühle
Horngraben
Kaiserwäldchen
Friedrichs Platz
Eckfeld
Wittlich
Pantenbg.
Langeck
Jungen-Busch
Neumühle
Kaisergarten
Kuno
Wald
Hütte
Mauerreste
Alter Brunnen
Huhnenkopf
Limmenborn
Carl
Burg Bg.
Kielerburg
Himmerod
Grosslittgen
Eisenschmitt, Kyllburg

a footpath diverges to the right, which is joined 10 min. farther on
by another path coming from the church of Buchholz. Here we
again turn to the right and after a walk of 10 min. more through
trees reach the *Belvedere* (p. 158). Thence we follow the route
described below to (20-25 min.) Nieder-Manderscheid, whence the
road ascends to (1 M.) Manderscheid.

ROAD FROM DAUN TO MANDERSCHEID, 10^1/$_2$ M. Walkers using
the Lieser path take 3-3^1/$_2$ hrs. — As indicated at p. 155 the
highroad passes above Gemünden. 2^3/$_4$ M. *Weiersbach,* where we
are joined on the left by a road coming from (2^1/$_4$ M.) Schalkenmehren (p. 156). We now ascend, quitting the valley of the Lieser,
and passing (l.) the beginning of the road to Trittscheid. 4 M.
Uedersdorf. The masses of lava which the road traverses probably
owe their origin in part to a volcano which culminated in the
Weberlei (1530 ft.), a slag-hill to the S.E. of Uedersdorf and near
the Kleine Kyll. 5^1/$_2$ M. *Bleckhausen.* To the right we have a
fine view of the three summits of the Mosenberg (p. 159). The
road enters Manderscheid on the W. — Walkers leave the highroad
^{1}/$_2$ M. to the S. of Weiersbach and follow the road to Trittscheid.
Beyond the bridge over the Lieser they take the marked 'Lieser
Path' (Lieser-Pfad) to the right, which crosses to the right bank of
the stream beyond the *Geisebrunner Mühle,* 1^1/$_2$ M. from Weiersbach. About ^{1}/$_2$ hr. farther on, below the Friedrichs-Platz, it joins
the promenades of Manderscheid (see below).

Manderscheid. — HOTELS (often crowded in summer; none of
them with view of the castles). *Müllejans* (Pl. a), in an open position
at the W. end of the town, R. & B. 2-3, D. 1^3/$_4$-2, S. 1^1/$_4$ *M.,* very fair;
Zens (Pl. b), in the town, R. & B. 2^1/$_2$-3, D. 1^3/$_4$-2, pens. 5-6 *M.,* very
fair; *Hubert Heid* (Pl. c), pens. 4^1/$_2$-5 *M.;* M. *Heid;* *Fischer.*

CARRIAGES (one-horse): to Mosenberg 5, Eisenschmitt 8, Daun 8,
Wittlich 9-10, Gillenfeld 6, Bertrich 15, Kyllburg 14 (viâ Himmerod 16),
viâ Neroth to Gerolstein 12 *M.* — AUTOMOBILES may be ordered by telephone from the Electric Works in Eisenschmitt (p. 160); to Kyllburg for
3 pers. 17^1/$_2$ *M.*

The STATION of Manderscheid-Pantenburg, on the Daun and Wittlich
Railway (p. 155), lies about 3 M. to the E. of Manderscheid.

Manderscheid (1275 ft.), a village and frequented summer-resort
with 800 inhab., lies on the E. margin of an upland plain about
300 ft. above the deep and winding valley of the Lieser. With its
ruined *Castles* and the jagged slate-rocks rising precipitously from
the valley, it forms a wonderfully romantic picture from which
ever side it is viewed. The Counts of Manderscheid traced their
descent back to the 9th century. A fraternal quarrel between the
Lords of the Ober-Burg and those of the Nieder-Burg resulted in
the former falling in the 12th cent. into the hands of the Electors
of Trèves, who rebuilt it. The younger line at the Nieder-Burg
did not become extinct till 1780. The Upper Castle now belongs
to Count Brühl, the Lower Castle to the Eifel-Verein. Paths afford-

ing good views and provided with numerous benches have been constructed in the valley and round the castles.

The following walk takes $1^1/_2$-2 hrs. At the Post Office (Pl. 2) we diverge to the right from the main street, turn to the left at the dairy (where the wide sweep of the road to Nieder-Manderscheid begins), and reach the *Tempelchen* (Pl. 3), situated to the W. of the castles (view best by evening-light). [The path to the right leads to the Konstantins-Wäldchen (see below).] We then follow the ridge to the *Ober-Burg* or Upper Castle (1165 ft.), the lofty keep of which is still preserved, although the interior is in ruins. At the entrance to the castle is a finger-post indicating the way (on the left) to the Grafenweg, Corneliuspfad, and Belvedere (see below). The path to the right leads viâ Lieserfriede, crosses the stream by a wooden foot-bridge, and keeps to the right (to the left to the Belvedere, see below) to *Nieder-Manderscheid* (720 ft.), where the key for the *Nieder-Burg* or Lower Castle is obtained at Steffens's Inn (25 pf. each person). The fortifications extended down to the valley and commanded the passage of the river. The highest point (1066 ft.) is crowned by a donjon, which has been made accessible. — From Nieder-Manderscheid we ascend again to Manderscheid, either by the road (20 min.) or by a footpath ($^1/_4$ hr.). On regaining the above-named dairy we may make a détour to the *Konstantins-Wäldchen*, which affords a fine view of the castles from the S. This détour may be extended to the *Mooshütte* (Moss Hut; Pl. 4) and the *Pellenz-Kanzel* (Pl. 5), high above the pond called the Burgweiher (there and back $^1/_2$ hr.).

The following walk ($2^1/_2$ hrs.) is also pleasant. At the *Bürgermeisteramt* (Pl. 1), or Mayor's Office, we diverge to the left from the main street, turn to the left again beyond the tannery, and reach (10 min.) the view-point named the *Friedrichs-Platz*. Hence we descend in zigzags to the Lieser (route to the Geisebrunner Mühle and Weiersbach, see p. 157), cross the foot-bridge to the left bank, and ascend to the right, partly by logging roads, through fine beech-woods to the (50 min.) *Belvedere* (1395 ft.), which commands, especially by morning-light, a superb view of Manderscheid, the castles, and the three summits of the Mosenberg. The stump of a column of a Roman villa on the Mosenberg commemorates the visit of King Frederick William IV. in 1833. A steep zigzag path, known as the Corneliuspfad (see below), descends hence to the Ober-Burg. An easier path, indicated by a finger-post a few paces beyond the Belvedere, leads to (10 min.) the Buchholz road (p. 156) and then descends to the right to ($^1/_4$ hr.) Nieder-Manderscheid. Coming in the reverse direction we leave the road $^1/_4$ hr. from the Nieder-Manderscheid bridge and ascend to the left beyond a wayside shrine. — A visit should also be paid to the pavilion named the *Waidmannslust* (there and back $1^1/_2$-2 hrs.), which is reached by passing the garden of the Steffens Inn and then ascending by a logging track marked in green. The view is not inferior to that from the Belvedere. To the W. towers the Mosenberg, to the N. in the distance the Nerother Kopf. We descend to the Burgweiher and ascend along it to the W., to the Mooshütte in the Konstantins-Wäldchen.

The excursion to the Mosenberg, the best-preserved of the Eifel craters, takes in all 3-3½ hrs. We take the Bettenfeld road, diverging to the right from the Wittlich road near the Hôtel Mülle-jans, and descend the valley of the *Kleine Kyll*, cutting off the large curves by footpaths to the left. At (20 min.) *Heydsmühle* (970 ft.; garden-restaurant) we cross the stream and continue to follow the road to (1 M.) the point where it bends to the S.E. Here we diverge to the left, cross a meadow toward the wood, and ascend to the left, finally skirting some cliffs of slag to the (20 min.) refuge-hut on the *Mosenberg (1705 ft.). This hill has four craters, with their axes running from N. to S.; but the northernmost of these, contain-ing the marshy *Hinkelsmaar*, to the N. of the Bettenfeld road, is not visible from this point. The second crater is occupied by the *Mosenberger Maar* (1535 ft.), a pond 226 yds. in diameter and 13 ft. deep. The two southernmost craters are separated by a saddle of slag. We descend to this (no path) and advance to the S. margin of the crater, which has been broken by a huge stream of basaltic lava. We follow an overgrown path along the N. margin of the lava, which is now covered with brushwood, and finally de-scend abruptly to the right through wood to the (40 min.) *Horn-graben*, where the end of the stream of lava has been disclosed by an old quarry. A few minutes farther on a foot-bridge crosses the stream, which here forms a small waterfall, while circular pot-holes have been hollowed in its bed by whirling stones. On the left bank we ascend to the left to (½ hr.) the Kyllburg road, by which we return to (½ M.) Manderscheid.

The WALK FROM MANDERSCHEID TO KYLLBURG takes 7-7½ hrs. From Manderscheid to the (1 hr.) Mosenberg, see above. From the refuge-hut a footpath descends to the N.W. into the crater, soon after joining the road which leads to (1 M.) the village of **Bettenfeld** (inn), which had already come into sight at the top of the hill. It lies at the S. base of the ridge which surrounds the large *Meerfelder Maar* (55 ft. deep), a good view of which is obtained from the top of the hill 8 min. to the N. of the village. The S. half of the Maar has been drained and is now a meadow. About ½ M. to the S.W. of Bettenfeld, at the point where the road to Meerfeld turns to the right, a blue-marked footpath diverges to the S.W. and leads in a straight direction through wood, crossing two transverse paths, to (¾ hr.) the *Salm-Tal*. To the right lies (1½ hr.) the *Cornes-Hütte*, an old iron-work which has been converted into a saw-mill. We cross a small bridge, pass a stone cross, ascend rapidly through wood, and then by a more level path crossing a transverse road (finger-post), and reach (¾ hr.) *Oberkail* (p. 160). Or from the Cornes-Hütte we may proceed viâ *Seinsfeld* and *Kyllburgweiler* to Kyllburg (see p. 151). — Another attractive walk is afforded by the yellow-marked forest-path which leads to the S. from Bettenfeld across the *Rotenbusch*, farther on crossing the Kyllburg road (comp. below), and going on to (2 hrs.) Himmerod.

The ROAD FROM MANDERSCHEID TO KYLLBURG (15$^1/_2$ M.) continues to follow the plateau, then descends in windings to the valley of the *Kleine Kyll*, crosses this stream by a bridge 970 ft. above the sea, and passes the (2$^1/_2$ M.) *Neumühle*, finely situated near the mouth of the *Fischbach* amid scenery that is at once picturesque and imposing. [The Neumühle may also be reached from Manderscheid in 1 hr. by the path which leads from the Mooshütte into the lower valley of the Lieser.] The road then winds up the left bank of the Fischbach and at the 'Kaiser-Garten', 3$^1/_2$ M. from Manderscheid, divides, the left branch leading viâ Gross-Littgen and Minder-Littgen to Wittlich (p. 170), the right one to Kyllburg. The latter leads through wood and passes (1$^1/_4$ M.) a finger-post pointing to the left to Himmerod (see below; 2$^1/_4$ M.) and to the right to Bettenfeld (p. 159; 4$^1/_2$ M.). From this point it descends to (3$^1/_2$ M.) —

8 M. **Eisenschmitt** (1055 ft.; *Wagner-Jung*, R. & B. 2-2$^1/_2$, D. 1$^1/_2$-2, pens. 4-4$^1/_2$ ℳ, well spoken of; *Müller*), a village of 600 inhab., with an old iron-factory now converted into electricity works and a mill. It lies in the green and wood-girt valley of the *Salm*, which geologically belongs to the red sandstone district extending all the way to the Moselle (see p. 161). Many attractive walks may be taken in the neighbourhood. About $^3/_4$ M. up the valley is the shooting-lodge of *Bergfeld*, built in 1891 and belonging to Herr von Galen. About the same distance down the valley is the old foundry of *Eichelhütte* (1015 ft.), now a cloth-factory, where the Huels Hotel offers pleasant summer-quarters (pension 4$^1/_2$-5 ℳ; old park). About 1 M. farther on, on the road to Gross-Littgen, are the imposing ruins of the Benedictine abbey of *Himmerod (988 ft.; two plain inns), founded in 1139 by St. Bernhard of Clairvaux and broken up in 1802. The convent-farm is now in the possession of Count Kesselstatt, who has cleared out the ruins (adm. 30 pf.). The lofty portal of the large baroque church (1735-50) is in good preservation. The cloisters, dating from the 16th cent., are in the Gothic style.

The road to (7$^1/_2$ M.) Kyllburg (diligence once daily in 2 hrs.) ascends from Eisenschmitt in sweeping curves, which may be avoided by shorter footpaths. At the top, where the road to Gross-Littgen diverges to the left, lies (1$^1/_4$ M.) *Schwarzenborn* (1390 ft.; Timpen), and 3 M. farther on is **Oberkail** (1280 ft.; *Eifeler Hof*), a village of 800 inhab. on the Kailbach, with the scanty remains of a castle of the Counts of Manderscheid-Oberkail and a church of 1787. Farther on we pass fragments of the Roman walls, which once extended S.W. from this vicinity to Bitburg, and then descend to —

15$^1/_2$ M. *Kyllburg* (see p. 151).

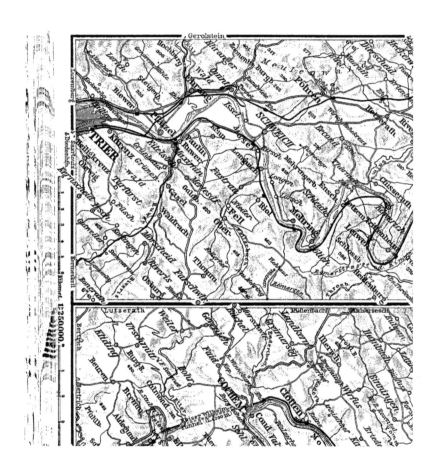

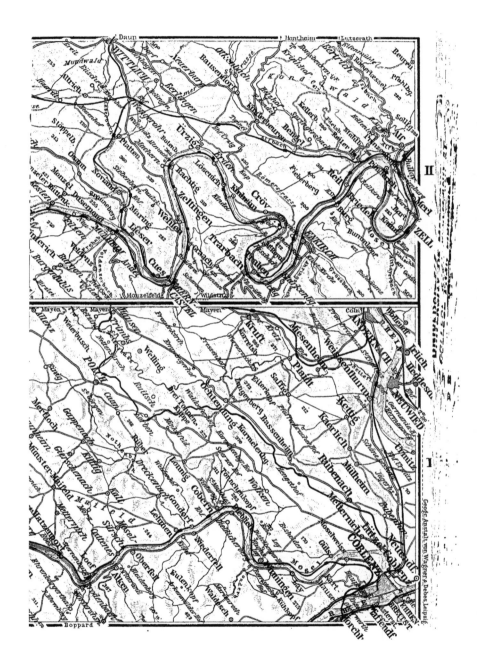

ROAD FROM MANDERSCHEID TO WITTLICH, 12¹/₂ M. (railway, see p. 155). — As far as the Kaiser-Garten, see p. 160. The road continues to follow the ridge. 7 M. *Gross-Littgen* (P. Hubert), a considerable village where the road to Eisenschmitt diverges (see p. 160; viâ Himmerod 6 M.). About 2¹/₂ M. farther on, beyond *Minder-Littgen*, the road begins to descend gradually, affording an extensive prospect of the mountains of the Moselle-district. A footpath to the left avoids the windings of the road, but a more attractive path is that diverging to the left at Minder-Littgen and leading viâ the Pleiner Mühle (see p. 170). — *Wittlich*, see p. 170.

23. From Coblenz to Trèves. The Moselle Valley Railway (Moseltalbahn) from Bullay to Trèves.

STATE RAILWAY (*Mosel-Bahn*), 69 M., in 2-3¹/₄ hrs. (fares 8 ℳ 70, 5 ℳ 50, 3 ℳ 50 pf.; express fares 9 ℳ 70; 6 ℳ 50 pf., 4 ℳ). This railway quits the river beyond Bullay (p. 167), but we may change carriages here and finish the journey by the MOSELTAL-BAHN (see p. 171), a narrow-gauge railway on the right bank (not included in the 'circular tour' tickets). — When the river is high enough STEAMBOATS (119 M.) ply four times weekly in summer from Coblenz to Trèves in 2 days, spending the night at *Trarbach*. The descent from Trèves to Coblenz takes 12-13 hrs. Fares for the ascent 9 ℳ 40 or 6 ℳ 20 pf., descent 9 ℳ 40 or 7 ℳ. The steamboat-pier at Coblenz lies between the bridges over the Moselle; that at Trèves is near the Brücken-Tor (Pl. A, 4).

The letters R.B. and L.B. denote the right and left banks with reference to the traveller descending the river. The places to which the mileage is prefixed are railway-stations.

The best roads for cyclists are alternately on the right and left banks: from Coblenz to Treis R.B., then to Alf L.B., Bullay to Trarbach R.B., Traben to Kinheim L.B., Kindel-Berncastel-Thörnich R.B.; from there L.B., in dry weather, along the Moselle, otherwise viâ Becond and the Hohe Kreuz Inn to Schweich; thence R.B. to Trèves.

The **Moselle** (Lat. *Mosella*) rises in the S.W. part of the Vosges district (p. 531), describes a wide curve through the plateau of Lorraine, and enters German soil at Novéant, after a course of 125 M. About 60 M. farther on it reaches, at Trèves, the Rhenish Slate District (p. 219), which even in the tertiary epoch was so thoroughly worn down that it was covered by a layer of sandstone, extending into the Eifel district. Between Trèves and Coblenz the river has carved out a deep channel for itself through the plateau and forms numerous, often loop-like curves, which makes it travel 120 M. in a distance of 60 M. as the crow flies. The river has itself broken through some of the narrower barriers at a very early period, so that dry loops or bows of the old bed may still be recognized beside the present channel. The hills are lower than those of the Rhine but bear as many picturesque castles. The smiling villages on the banks often contain quaint old timbered houses. The Moselle wines have long been famous for their delicate bouquet (see p. xxiii). The first vines were planted ca. 280 A.D., in the time of Emp. Probus, and thus antedate those of the Rhine. A little later a Roman poet, *Decimus Magnus Ausonius* (circa 309-92), celebrated the praises of the Moselle and its 'fragrant Bacchus' in a poem entitled 'Mosella'. From the middle ages till the close of the 18th cent. the whole district belonged to the Electorate of Trèves, with the exception of a few 'enclaves' which were in the hands of Reformed rulers and are still mainly peopled by Protestants. *Schloss Eltz, Cochem, Marienburg, Traben-Trarbach, Berncastel*, and *Trèves* are the most attractive spots on the whole river.

Coblenz, see p. 121. The train skirts the base of the Kartause (p. 152). To the right are the convent of Marienhof and the Kemperhof Orphanage; behind, on the left bank of the Moselle, is Metternich (p. 152). — Above (2 M.) *Moselweiss* we cross to the left bank (views). — 2¹/₂ M. *Güls* (Zillien, very fair), a prettily-situated village with 2000 inhab., in an orchard-like district. *Lay,* a village on the right bank.

5 M. **Winningen** *(Schwan,* on the river, with garden-restaurant, R. & B. 2¹/₂ ℳ, very fair; *Goldener Adler Wine Room),* a market-town with 1900 inhab., once belonging to Baden (1560-1794) and hence forming one of the Protestant 'enclaves' mentioned above. Wine is much grown in the environs.

Pleasant walks viâ the *Distelberger Hof* (inn) to (¹/₂ hr.) *Blumslay,* and up the *Conder-Tal,* on the right bank (ferry), to *Remstecken* and the (1¹/₂ hr.) *Kühkopf* (p. 127), etc.

Farther up the river the left bank consists of precipitous rocks, called the *Winninger* and *Coberner Ulen,* producing the best flavoured wine of the Lower Moselle. — On the opposite (r.) bank lies *Dieblich* (inn), with a handsome church.

L. B. (9¹/₂ M.) **Cobern** *(Simonis,* R. & B. 2-2¹/₂, D. 2 ℳ, very fair), commanded by two castles of the Knights of Cobern, the last of whom was executed at Coblenz in 1536 as a disturber of the public peace. The rail. station lies ²/₃ M. above Cobern, near Gondorf (see below).

- A steep footpath ascends through the vineyards (the path with the pilgrimage-stations is longer, but easier) to the (¹/₂ hr.) picturesque *Niederburg.* It is, however, preferable to ascend direct to the (35 min.) Oberburg, following (20 min.) the finger-post pointing to the right at a bend in the road (fine view of the Niederburg and the valley). Within the *Oberburg,* or *Altenburg,* is the ***Chapel of St. Matthias** (key obtained from J. Reif, Scheidergasse 7, in the village), a hexagonal edifice measuring 53 ft. from angle to angle. It is the most elegant work of the late-Romanesque style in the Rhineland, dating from 1230 and probably inspired by the church of the Holy Sepulchre at Jerusalem, which had lately become known through the Crusades. The central portion rises above the rest, and is borne by six columns. The elaborate decorations are executed in a masterly style. The chapel was restored in 1894, and the old painting has been renewed.

There is also an interesting Romanesque church (recently restored) at *Lonnig,* a village 2¹/₂ M. to the W. of Cobern.

Farther up, on the same (l.) bank, lies *Gondorf* (Haupt, R. & B. 2, pens. 4 ℳ, very fair), with the *Tempelhof,* a recently restored Gothic castle, and an old château of the Counts and Princes Von der Leyen, now intersected by the railway. The village is mentioned as early as 871 under the name of *Condravia,* and on account of the numerous Roman and Frankish tombs found here is supposed to have been the Roman harbour of *Contrua.*

On the opposite bank lie *Niederfell* (Anker) and *Kühr.*

L. B. (10¹/₂ M.) *Lehmen* (Zum Sternenburg), with a castellated manor-house. The river is bordered here with precipitous crags.

R. B. *Oberfell*. — L. B. (13 M.) *Cattenes*, at the mouth of a ravine containing numerous mills.

R. B. *Alken* (Burg Thurant), an old place with mediæval houses and fortifications, now comes suddenly into view. On the hill above it rise the towers of the old castle of *Thuron*, or *Thurant*, built by Count Palatine Heinrich about 1200, and a frequent object of quarrel between the Counts Palatine and the Electors of Cologne and Trèves. It was besieged by the two Archbishops in 1246-48, when 600,000 gallons of wine are said to have been consumed by the assailants. The chroniclers relate that, on this occasion, the traitorous 'Burgvogt' was hurled across the valley by a catapult into the enemy's camp and arrived there without scathe — a happy escape commemorated by a chapel on the *Bleidenberg* (view). — 15 M. *Loef* (Sternburg) is the station for —

R. B. **Brodenbach** (*Post*, R. 1¹/₂-2, D. 1¹/₂-2 ℳ, with garden, very fair), pleasantly situated at the base of lofty wooded hills, just below the mouth of the *Ehrenbach-Tal*. Up this valley runs the road to Halsenbach and St. Goar (see pp. 191, 226), passing near the *Ehrenburg, the finest ruin on the Moselle (trip there & back 1¹/₂-2 hrs.).

The Ehrenbach valley is narrow and ravine-like at first, but expands about ¹/₂ M. from the river and contains a number of mills. Near the first of these a footpath diverges to the left between two rocks and leads past a (3 min.) point of view to the (¹/₂ hr.) *Ehrenburg*, situated on an isolated peak. A vaulted, winding carriage-way leads to the foot of the two round towers, which command a beautiful panorama (unpleasant stair). The castle came into the hands of the Barons vom Stein (p. 134) in 1798, and is still owned by their heirs. Key and rfmts. at the keeper's. — From the Ehrenburg to *Boppard*, 2¹/₂ hrs.; see p. 191.

An attractive but much longer excursion may be made to the ruin of *Waldeck* (p. 191). We follow the road up the Ehrenbach-Tal to *Morschhausen* and (5 M.) *Beulich*, whence a footpath leads to the ruin (3 hrs. from Brodenbach).

An overhanging cliff is now passed on the left bank, beyond which the valley of the Moselle expands.

16¹/₂ M. **Hatzenport** and *Boes* (*Traube* or *Kranz*, moderate and very fair), two long contiguous villages, above which rises an old church. The railway-station is ³/₄ M. above Hatzenport.

About 3¹/₂ M. to the N.W. (diligence from Hatzenport twice daily) lies **Münster-Maifeld** (815 ft.; *Sonne*, R. 1³/₄-2, B. ¹/₂, D. 1¹/₂ ℳ, very fair; *Maifelder Hof*, plainer), an ancient town with 1700 inhab., from the 6th cent. onwards the chief place in the *Meginovelt*, or *Megingau*, which extends hence to the Rhine. The conspicuous *Church*, formerly belonging to an abbey, is the successor of a basilica of St. Martin, said to have existed here as early as 633. The front with its two round towers, resembling a fortress, dates in plan from early in the 12th cent.; the choir is in the transition-style of 1225-30; the nave, in the early-Gothic style, was followed by the transepts and the curious elevated chapel in the building between the towers; but the whole was finally completed in the developed Gothic style in the course of the 14th century. Attention

11*

should be paid to the statue of the Virgin (ca. 1350), to the ciborium of about 1450, and to the tombs of Kuno von Eltz (d. 1536) and his wife. — Schloss Eltz (see below) is 3 M. from Münster-Maifeld by road; diligence to Polch (p. 152) twice daily in 1 hr.

L.B. (18 M.) *Burgen,* at the foot of the hill on which rises the massive tower of *Bischofstein,* erected in 1270. An attractive route leads hence viâ *Lasserg* and *Neuhof* to (1^1/$_2$ hr.) Schloss Eltz, ending with a charmingly unexpected view of the castle (see below). The village of *Burgen* lies on the opposite bank, at the mouth of the *Beybach-Tal* (p. 191), in which, 7 M. farther up, is the ruin of Waldeck.

19^1/$_4$ M. **Moselkern** *(Burg Eltz,* with garden, very fair, R. 1^1/$_2$-2^1/$_4$, B. ^{3}/$_4$, D. 2, pens. 4^1/$_2$-5 *ℳ; Balmes),* at the mouth of the *Elz.*

In the narrow, tortuous valley of the Elz, 3^1/$_2$ M. above Moselkern, lies *Schloss Eltz,* one of the best-preserved mediæval castles in Germany, the excursion to which takes 3-3^1/$_2$ hrs. (viâ Burgen, see above, 3^1/$_2$-4 hrs.). The road from Moselkern ascends the left bank of the Elz for 1 M., and then crosses to the right bank. Beyond the mill (inn) we follow a path to the left along the garden-fence, cross the mill-stream by a small bridge, and (10 min.) follow the slope of the hill to the left, finally crossing a bridge. The castle, the ancestral residence of the Counts of Eltz, is situated upon a lofty rock and forms a most romantic picture with its lofty gables, turrets, and towers. The different parts of the château, which has never been destroyed, date from the 12-16th centuries. Visitors are admitted to the court only. To see the interior, which has been restored in mediæval simplicity, permission must be previously obtained from the Countess of Eltz, who lives at Vukovár in S. Hungary. — Opposite Schloss Eltz are the ruins of *Trutz-eltz,* or *Baldeneltz,* erected by Archbishop Baldwin of Trèves to command the castle, with the counts of which he carried on a protracted feud. The best view of Eltz and Baldeneltz is obtained farther up, at the mission-cross on the road to Wierschem and Münster-Maifeld. To the right, at this point, diverges the road to Lasserg and Burgen (see above).

Farther up the Elztal (no path) is the imposing ruined castle of **Pyrmont,** which is reached from Münster-Maifeld viâ *Pillig* in 1^1/$_2$ hr. The Elz forms a fall here. Above the castle lies (^{3}/$_4$ hr.) the lonely *Schwankirche* (1475; restored in 1880), a pilgrim-resort. The key of the church is kept in the adjacent inn. Thence to (1^1/$_2$ hr.) Carden (see below) viâ *Brohl* or *Forst.*

20^1/$_2$ M. *Müden* (inn), on the left bank, opposite the entrance of the pretty *Lützer-Tal.*

23 M. **Carden** *(Brauer,* on the Moselle, R. & B. 2^1/$_2$, D. 1^1/$_2$ *ℳ)* is a village with 700 inhab., below which is a cave where St. Castor (see p. 124) is said to have dwelt in the 4th century. The present *Church,* once part of an abbey, was erected in 1183-1247 on the site of an earlier one founded by the saint. The choir and transept are late-Romanesque, the nave early-Gothic. The interior contains an interesting terracotta group of the Magi (high-altar) and other late-Gothic sculptures. Of the late-Gothic *Cloisters* nothing remains except one walk. To the N. is the Romanesque *Chapter House.* To the E. of the church, near the railway, is the *Tithe House,* an

interesting specimen of a Romanesque secular building of the 12th cent., with fine windows; it was restored in 1894. The *Burghaus*, at the lower end of the village, is a Renaissance structure of 1562.

R.B. **Treis** *(Wildburg*, R. & B. 2 ℳ, well spoken of; *Krone)*, with 1400 inhabitants. In the valley behind it are the ruins of the *Wildenburg* and *Schloss Treis*. The old church is of the late-Gothic period, the new church was built in 1830. — From Treis a road leads over the hill to (4¹/₂ M.) Bruttig (p. 166). Another ascends the *Flaumbach-Tal* to (5¹/₂ M.) the convent of *Engelport* (recently restored) and (23 M.) Kirchberg (p. 190).

24 M. *Pommern*, at the mouth of the *Pommerbach*, in the valley of which are the ruins of the nunnery of *Rosental*, founded in 1170. — 27¹/₂ M. *Clotten* (Sehl, good wine), with 1900 inhab., a late-Gothic church (afterwards enlarged), and the ruins of the castle of *Coraidelstein*.

29¹/₂ M. **Cochem.** — Hotels. *Union*, near the landing-stage, ¹/₂ M. from the station, R. 1 ℳ 70-2 ℳ 70, B. 80 pf., D. 2¹/₄-2¹/₂, pens. 5¹/₂-6¹/₂ ℳ, with view-terrace; *Zum Landsknecht*, R. & B. 2¹/₂, pens. from 4¹/₂ ℳ, with popular wine-room and terrace, on the river, very good; *Stadt Köln*, Ravené-Str., between the steamboat-landing and the railway-station, R. 2, B. ³/₄, D. 2, S. 1¹/₂, pens. 4¹/₂-5 ℳ, with garden-restaurant (Munich beer); *Schloss-Hôtel*, Schloss-Str., with views; *Hôtel-Restaurant Kemp*, on the Moselle, R. & B. 2-2¹/₂, pens. 4 ℳ, with view-terrace (Munich and Pilsen beer); *Germania; Stadt Coblenz; Zum Kaiser*, with popular beer-room, all on the Moselle.

Motor Launch to Senheim. — Diligence to (8¹/₂ M.) Kaisersesch (p. 153) twice daily.

Cochem (282 ft.), a district-town with 3800 inhab., at the entrance of the *Endert-Tal*, is one of the prettiest places on the Moselle, especially as seen from the right bank. Adjoining the picturesque Endert-Tor is a timber house of 1625.

Burg Cochem, on the hill to the S. (1 M. from the station; reached from the pier viâ the Zollgasse and Schloss-Str.), an old imperial castle, was given in pledge to the Archbishops of Trèves by King Adolf of Nassau in 1294 and was destroyed by the French in 1689. It was rebuilt in 1868-78 for Herr Ravené (d. 1879) by the Berlin architect Raschdorff, with the aid of ancient plans and views. The principal tower is adorned with a huge figure of St. Christopher, in mosaic. Visitors apply for admission in the restaurant at the entrance (1-4 pers. 1 ℳ, each extra pers. 25 pf.); the sumptuously decorated rooms are shown only when the proprietor is not in residence.

On the right bank, opposite Cochem, lies *Cond* (good wine at the Traube); fine view from (¹/₂ hr.) the 'Conder Tempelchen'.

In the Endert-Tal, on a hill about 3 M. from Cochem, rises the tower of the *Winneburg*, the most ancient seat of the Metternich family, destroyed by the French in 1689. The road to Kaisersesch (p. 153) ascends the Endert-Tal. A pleasanter route is to ascend viâ Cochem Castle to the *Lescher Linde* (view), go thence by the *Lescher Hof* to *Faid*, and return viâ the Winneburg.

As we leave Cochem we have a view of the castle to the left. The train then passes through the *Cochemer* or *Ellerer Berg* to Eller (see below) by means of the *Emperor William Tunnel* ($2^2/_3$ M. long, taking 4-6 min. to traverse), the excavation of which through the clay-slate occupied $3^1/_2$ years (1874-77).

The Moselle sweeps round the Ellerer Berg in a winding curve of $12^1/_2$ M. in length, which the steamer takes $2^1/_2$ hrs. to traverse in ascending and $1^1/_2$ hr. in descending.

At *Sehl* (left bank), 1 M. above Cochem, a fine retrospect is enjoyed of Cochem, its castle, and the Winneburg. — L.B. *Ebernach*, once a priory, now a lunatic asylum.

R.B. *Valwig* is noted for excellent wine.

L.B. *Nieder-Ernst* and *Ober-Ernst*. Between them a modern church with two towers. Above the sharp bend which the river makes here, about 3 M. above Cochem, lies —

R.B. *Bruttig* (Friedrichs, unpretending), a small town with quaint old houses (*e.g.* the Schunk House of 1659). The church contains some Gothic sculptures from the old church. Petrus Mosellanus (d. 1524), the grammarian, was a native of Bruttig.

R.B. *Fankel*, lying somewhat inland. — L.B. *Ellenz* (Dehren, very fair).

R.B. *Beilstein* (Lipmann, R. $1^1/_2$-$2^1/_2$, pens. $4^1/_2$-6 ℳ), a quaint little town nestling at the foot of the rocks, is overlooked by the old imperial castle of the same name, which afterwards belonged to the Electors of Trèves, and then to the Counts (now Princes) of Metternich-Winneburg; it was destroyed in 1688.

L.B. *Poltersdorf.* — R.B. *Briedern.* — R.B. *Mesenich* (Anker).

R.B. *Senheim* (Schneiders), with a high-lying church. Route hence viâ the König to Bullay, $2^1/_2$ hrs.

L.B. *Senhals* (Henrichs, Deis, both very fair); omnibus twice daily to ($3^3/_4$ M.) Eller (see below). Farther on, *Nehren*, and the manor-house of *Lehmen*, with its old tower.

L.B. **Ediger** (*Löwen-Friedrichs*, R. & B. $2^1/_4$-$2^1/_2$, D. $1^1/_2$, pens. $4^1/_2$-5 ℳ), surrounded with old fortifications and possessing numerous mediæval buildings and a late-Gothic church (with a monstrance of 1522). There are extensive vineyards here. — An omnibus runs hence five times daily to ($1^1/_4$ M.) the station of Eller (see below).

The Emp. William Tunnel (see above) ends at the base of the wooded *Calmond*, in the pretty valley of the *Eller*.

33 M. *Eller* (Friedrichs, clean), with old manor-houses. Above it, on the right bank, are the ruins of Stuben (p. 167), from which a pleasant walk may be taken along the Moselle to Bremm, where we cross the stream, traverse the Petersberg, and descend to Neef ($1^1/_2$-2 hrs.).

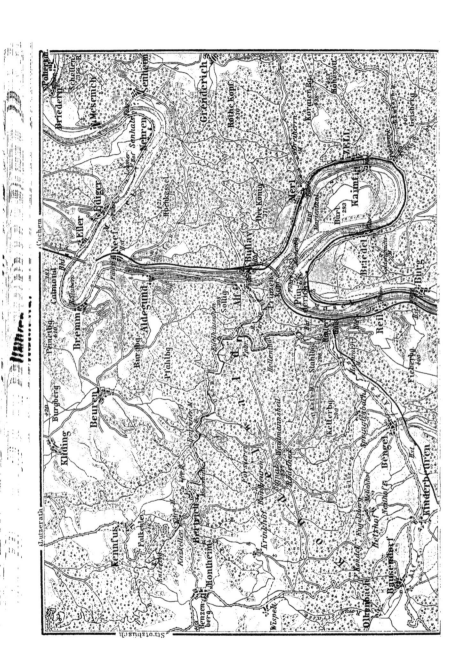

The train crosses the Moselle and passes through a tunnel under the *Petersberg,* round which the river describes a curve 2 M. in length. At the W. end of the peninsula are situated the ruins of the monastery of *Stuben,* founded in the 12th cent. and suppressed in 1788. The baroque altar in the chapel on the Petersberg was brought from this convent. Farther up, on the left bank, is *Bremm,* the late-Gothic church of which, lately repainted, has elaborate reticulated vaulting and a Romanesque tower. Then *Aldegund,* with an old church and a handsome modern one. — 34 M. *Neef,* with an old manor-house.

36¹/₂ M. **Bullay** (*Marienburg,* R. 1³/₄-2, B. ³/₄, D. 1³/₄-2¹/₄, pens. 4¹/₂-5¹/₂ ℳ, very fair; *Rail. Restaurant,* with a view-terrace, very fair), on the right bank, the station for *Alf* and the baths of *Bertrich* (p. 168) on the opposite bank and the junction of the Moselle Valley Railway to Trèves viâ Zell and Berncastel (station 220 yds. from that of the State Railway; comp. p. 171).

From the Bullay station we may reach the 'Vierseenplatz' (Four Lakes View) on the *König* (iron finger-post by the roadside near the station) in about ¹/₂ hr. Beautiful view of the Marienburg and the Moselle country, superior to that from the Marienburg itself. Descent in ¹/₂ hr. to Merl. [Interesting walk from Alf or Bullay to the Marienburg, Kaimt, Zell, Merl, König, Bullay: 3 hrs.]

The road to Alf turns to the right at the station of Bullay, passes under the railway, and leads past the station of the Moselle Valley line to (7-8 min.) the village of *Bullay,* the parish-church of which contains a Renaissance altar of 1618. The ferry to Alf starts here. Carriages have to make a détour and cross the double iron lattice-bridge (of which the higher level supports the railway, the lower the ordinary roadway) leading to the foot of the *Marienburg* (p. 168), which is ascended hence by a good footpath to the left in 20 min. (path to the right to the Waldfrieden, see below).

Alf. — HOTELS. *Post,* R. 1³/₄-2³/₄, B. ³/₄, D. 2¹/₂, pens. 5-6 ℳ, very fair, with garden; *Burg Arras,* R. & B. 2-2¹/₂, pens. 4 ℳ. — *Pension Nollen,* 4¹/₂-5 ℳ, very fair; *Pens. Waldfrieden* (see below), R. 2-2¹/₂ ℳ, pens. 4-6 ℳ, very fair.

DILIGENCE to (7 M.) Bertrich (p. 168) viâ Alf thrice daily in 1¹/₄ hr., starting from the railway-station of Bullay (fare 90 pf.); also *Omnibus* several times a day (1 ℳ); diligence to (13¹/₂ M.) Lutzerath (p. 169) every morning. — CARRIAGE to the Marienburg and back 4 ℳ; to Bertrich, with one horse 5 ℳ, with two horses 7 ℳ.

Alf, a village with 1700 inhab., well suited for a stay, lies at the mouth of the picturesque valley of the *Alf,* on the left bank of the Moselle, opposite Bullay. Near the modern early-Gothic church are sculptures and iron reliefs of the 16th cent., found in digging the foundations. — The road from Alf to the Marienburg (2 M.) ascends behind the Pens. Nollen to the *Pension Waldfrieden* (see above; view), passes the view-tower (fine panorama) on the *Prinzenkopf* (20 pf.), and then follows the narrow ridge (fine view on both sides).

The ***Marienburg** (673 ft.; *Restaurant & Pension*, very fair), with the ruins of a castle said to have once existed here, or of the nunnery erected on the same spot in 1146, is one of the finest points on the Moselle. The view embraces the wooded and vine-clad slopes of the Moselle, the smiling villages on its banks, the summits of the Hunsrück and the Eifel, and two detached reaches of the river, resembling lakes.

Pleasant walks may be taken from the Marienburg to Merl (p. 171), to the S.E., and over the *Barl* (928 ft.) to Kaimt (p. 171). The descent to Alf may also be made viâ Burg Arras: we follow the road round the Prinzenkopf to (1 M.) the Alf, Reil, and Bengel road, which soon passes the 'Schöne Aussicht' (l.); we then leave the 'Poetenweg' to the left and proceed to the right through wood to Burg Arras; and finally descend to the 'Fabrik Alf' and thence through the valley to Alf (see below; 1¹/₄ hr. in all). From the 'Schöne Aussicht' a path leads to the S. along the ridge to the chapel on the *Reiler Hals* (view), whence we may descend to Pünderich Station (p. 171).

The road from Alf to Bertrich (5¹/₂ M.) at first ascends the romantic *Valley of the Alf*, between the *Sollig* and the *Prinzenkopf*, and then, at (1¹/₂ M.) the 'Fabrik Alf' (now a rope-walk), ascends the valley of the *Uessbach*. At the top of the hill lies *Burg Arras*, said to have been built by Abp. Robert of Trèves in 938 for a charcoal-burner and his two sons, who had distinguished themselves by their courage in the destruction of a band of Hungarians. It was restored in 1902. — Wine and refreshments may be obtained at the *Beurener Mühle*, 4 M. from Alf. Just short of Bertrich the so-called *Römerkessel* opens to the right, a small valley formed by an arm of the Uessbach, which was drained on the construction of the road.

Bertrich. — HOTELS (all well spoken of). *Pitz*, connected with the Kurhaus, R. 2¹/₄-4¹/₂, B. 1, D. 3, pens.5-9 ℳ (S. extra), closed Oct. to April; *Drei Reichskronen; Adler; Kurfürst*, R. 1¹/₂-3 ℳ, B. 80 pf., pens. 4¹/₂-6 ℳ; *Dhein*, R. 1¹/₂-2, B. ³/₄, D. 2, pens. 5-7 ℳ; *Dillenburg*, R. 2-2¹/₂, B. ³/₄, D. 2-2¹/₂, pens. 5-5¹/₂ ℳ; *Zum Kurplatz*, R. 1¹/₂-2, B. ³/₄, pens. 4¹/₂-5¹/₂ ℳ; *Central Hotel* or *Westfälischer Hof*, R. from 1¹/₂, B. ³/₄, D. 2, pens. 4¹/₂-5 ℳ; *Römerbad*. — *Villa Meduna*, R. 2-6, weekly 10-36, B. 1 ℳ; *Haus Arndt* (family pension), pens. 5¹/₂-7¹/₂ ℳ; *Marienhöhe*, 1¹/₄ M. from the village, pens. from 4 ℳ. — Popular *Bierhalle* in the Kurhaus; *Restaurant Schweizerhaus*, in a high situation. — VISITORS' TAX, 1 pers. 10, a family 20 ℳ.

CARRIAGE to Alf and Bullay 5, with two horses 6 ℳ, there and back 6 and 8 ℳ; two-horse carr. to Pulvermaar 12, to Manderscheid 14. to Daun and back 22, to Daun and the Belvedere near Manderscheid 24 ℳ.

Bad Bertrich (540 ft.), a small watering-place with 500 inhab., delightfully situated in the secluded valley of the Uessbach, and visited annually by 2000 patients, may be described as a kind of modified Carlsbad, the alkaline waters of which (90° Fahr.) are specially efficacious in gout, rheumatism, and nervous, liver, and intestinal complaints. The springs were known to the Romans and belonged from the 15th cent. on to the Electors of Trèves, who restored the baths. The *Kurhaus* was built by Elector Clemens

Wenceslaus (p. 123) in 1780, the *New Bath House* in 1908-9. The Roman relics now in the garden of the bath-etablishment were found in the Römerkessel (p. 168). Pleasant walks have been laid out in all directions (chart of way-marks at the well in the main street).

The road to Lutzerath through the valley of the *Uess* crosses that stream about ¹/₂ M. from the Kur-Garten. To the left, beyond the bridge, is the *Elfen-Mühle* (restaurant). About 50 paces farther on we cross a bridge to the left and reach the *Käskeller* ('cheese-cellar'), a grotto composed of basaltic columns, each formed of 8 or 9 spheroids, resembling Dutch cheeses. Near it is a *Waterfall*, (often dry in summer), crossed by a graceful bridge. A basaltic stream of lava is visible in several places in the bed of the Uessbach.

Pleasant walks may be taken from the Käskeller to the (1 hr.) *Enters-burg* (view-tower); to the (1¹/₂ hr.) *Rödelheck* (1585 ft.; refreshments at the adjacent forester's), which commands an extensive panorama, and thence across the ridge to the E. to the (¹/₂ hr.) *Reinhardslust;* to (3³/₄ M.) *Pünderich* (see below); and to (3 M.) *Springirsbach* (p. 170).

If we follow the path marked with red crosses, which diverges from the road to Lutzerath beyond the Elfen-Mühle, we reach (in 40 min.) the **Falkenlei** (1360 ft.), a semi-conical hill, the S.E. side of which is a precipice 170 ft. in height, exhibiting the geological formation of the interior. At the bottom lie solid masses of lava; at the top scoriæ and slag. Numerous caves and clefts have been formed in the rock, in which the temperature seldom exceeds 48° Fahr. The rocks are thickly covered with yellowish red moss and lichens. The summit (shelter-hut) affords an extensive view of the volcanic peaks of the Eifel; the highest are the Hohe Acht (p. 109), the Nürburg (p. 109), with a tower on its summit, and the Hohe Kelberg (2130 ft.); to the W. the prospect is circumscribed by the long isolated ridge of the Mosenberg (p. 159), a little to the left of which rises the Nerother Kopf with its ruin (p. 150).

As the starting-point for a VISIT TO THE EIFEL (R. 22), Bertrich is better adapted for drivers (carr., p. 168) than for walkers, as the first part of the route is rather featureless. From the Elfen-Mühle the road ascends to the left to (2¹/₂ M.) *Hontheim*, and then follows the ridge to the right to (3 M.) *Strotzbüsch*. From Strotzbüsch we may follow the road for about 2 M. more and then proceed to the left viâ the *Römersberg* to the (¹/₃ M.) *Pulvermaar* (p. 156). — Walkers may descend to the N. from the Falkenlei to *Kennfus* and follow the highroad thence to (3³/₄ M.) *Lutzerath* (Maas, very fair), which is about 4¹/₂ M. from the Pulvermaar.

The STATE RAILWAY to Trèves does not follow the upper valley of the Moselle but traverses the Vorder-Eifel (p. 146) by way of the Wittlich valley. Beyond Bullay the train crosses the Moselle by the double bridge mentioned at p. 167, and penetrates the *Prinzen-kopf* (p. 168) by a curved tunnel, 480 yds. in length, which emerges upon the river above Pünderich (p. 171). The railway is next carried along the hill by an imposing viaduct.

38¹/₂ M. *Pünderich*, the station for the village on the right bank, 1¹/₄ M. farther down (p. 171; ferry), and junction for a branch-railway which ascends the left bank viâ Reil, Burg (r.b.), and En-kirch (r.b.; comp. p. 171) to *Traben* (6¹/₂ M. in ¹/₂ hr.; p. 171).

Beyond Pünderich the train quits the valley of the Moselle, and enters the *Alftal* by means of another tunnel (530 yds.) through the *Reiler Hals.* To the right is seen the church of the old canonry of *Springirsbach,* founded in 1107, but rebuilt in the Italian style of the 18th century. Adjacent is Nicolay's Inn. To the N. is the beautiful *Kondelwald,* traversed by a path along the Signal to Bertrich (p. 168). — 41¹/₂ M. *Bengel.* Beyond *Kinderbeuren* (Wirtz) we thread a tunnel.

44 M. *Uerzig,* 2 M. from the village of that name on the Moselle (p. 172), to which an omnibus runs twice daily.

The train now descends into the valley of the *Lieser.*

From (47 M.) *Wengerohr* branch-lines run to *Berncastel* (p. 173; 9¹/₂ M., in ³/₄ hr.) and to (2¹/₂ M., in 10 min.) *Wittlich,* whence an extension goes on to Manderscheid and Daun (see p. 155).

Wittlich (540 ft.; *Well* or *Wolf,* in the market-place, R. 1¹/₂- 2, B. 1, D. 2-2¹/₂, pens. 5-7 *M; Rebstock,* R. & B. 2¹/₂-3¹/₂ *M; Traube,* at the rail. station, R. 1¹/₂-2, B. 1 *M),* an old town with 5500 inhab., prettily situated on the Lieser, received its municipal charter in 1291. Its environs are picturesque, and both wine and tobacco are raised in the vicinity.

Pleasant walks may be taken to the N.E. to (20 min.) the *Affenberg* (945 ft.; view; Philippsburg Restaurant) and the *Grünewald;* to the S. to (20 min.) a *Roman Villa* (discovered in 1904) and to (³/₄ hr.) the *Wald-frieden Restaurant* in the *Mundwald* (view); and to the N. up the right bank of the Lieser, past the *Basten-Mühle* (with old giants' cauldrons in the river-bed), to (1¹/₄ hr.) the *Pleiner Mühle,* situated at the mouth of a romantic gorge, through which a path leads to (¹/₂ hr.) Minder-Littgen (p. 160).

The Trèves railway crosses the Lieser. To the right lie the hamlet of *Bürscheid,* the village of *Altrich,* and the *Haardter Höfe.* Beyond the watershed between the Lieser and the *Salm* we reach —

52 M. *Salmrohr,* 2 M. from which is the pilgrimage-resort *Eberards-Clausen,* an old abbey with an interesting church (carved altar of the second half of the 15th cent.). — 57 M. *Hetzerath* (630 ft.; Paltzer), 4¹/₂ M. from Clüsserath (p. 174).

59 M. *Föhren.* We now obtain a good view of Trèves, to the left. — 61¹/₂ M. *Schweich* (Restaurant Max), 1 M. from the station, on the Moselle, is connected with the right bank by a bridge (Moselle Valley Light Railway, see p. 175). The train then passes through the tunnel of *Issel,* 850 yds. in length. — 63¹/₂ M. *Quint,* with iron-works, is named from its position 5 Roman miles from Trèves ('ad quintum'). About 1¹/₄ M. up the valley of the Quintbach is the summer-resort of *Kaiserhammer* (560 ft.).

65 M. *Ehrang* (Heimann), a village with 3500 inhab., on the old Roman road, is a station on the Eifel railway (p. 152) and is also connected with Trèves by a branch-line (5 M.) passing *Biewer* and *Pallien* (p. 183). The Moselle railway crosses the river by a stone arched bridge.

69 M. **Trèves,** see p. 175.

Moselle Valley Railway *(Moseltalbahn)* from Bullay to Trèves.

63 M. MOSELLE VALLEY LIGHT RAILWAY on the right bank from Bullay to Trèves, in 4 hrs. (fares 5 *M*, 3 *M* 20 pf.; to Trarbach 1 *M*, 65 pf., to Berncastel 2 *M* 10, 1 *M* 45 pf.; return-tickets, good for 45 days, at a fare and a half). The station at Bullay is 220 yds. from that of the State Railway (see p. 167). Observation-cars are attached to the trains, and refreshments may be obtained in summer. — The stations for places on the left bank are indicated in the text by the letters L.B.

The Moselle Valley Railway presents an uninterrupted succession of charming landscapes, which the traveller can enjoy all the more owing to the moderate speed of the train (12-15 M. per hour). The first station beyond Bullay is —

2 M. *Merl* (Cröff, well spoken of). At the lower end of the village rise the 'Eisturm', belonging to the former fortifications, and the Severinsturm, a clock-tower of the destroyed church of that name,

3 M. Zell (*Fier*, with terrace; *Kaiserhof*, R. $1^3/_4$-$2^3/_4$, B. $^3/_4$. pens. 4-5 *M*, also with terrace, well spoken of), a district-town with 2700 inhab., including the suburb of *Koray* on the N. Remains of its old fortifications still exist. The interesting old *Electoral Château* was built in 1543. Handsome new *Town Hall*. Fine view from the *Hochcollis* (E.) and from the *Bummkopf*. — Opposite, on the left bank (ferry), lies *Kaimt*, whence a path leads along the base of the Barl to (1 hr.) the Marienburg (p. 168).

$5^1/_2$ M. *Briedel* (Schneider, pens. $3^1/_2$-4 *M*), with a castle, commands a good view of the Marienburg.

$7^1/_2$ M. *Pünderich* (Schneider; Lutz) is connected by a ferry with the left bank, where a steep path ascends to the Marienburg in $^1/_4$ hr. Also on the left bank, $1^1/_4$ M. from the ferry, is the station of the railway mentioned at p. 169, the viaduct of which is visible.

$8^1/_2$ M. *Reilkirch* is the churchyard of the village of *Reil*, which lies a little higher up on the opposite bank and is a station on the branch-line from Pünderich to Traben (p. 169).

10 M. *Burg;* 12 M. *Enkirch* (Anker; Steffensberg, both very fair), named *Ankaracha* in the earliest documents (908), has 2350 inhab. (mainly Protestants) and picturesque timbered houses. The R. C. church, in the Gothic style, is outside the village. Good wine is raised on the Stephansberg. — On the left lie *Kövenich* and *Litzig*.

The railway hugs the cliffs surmounted by the scanty remains of the *Starkenburg*, once a stronghold of the Counts of Sponheim, whose sway extended from the Hunsrück to the Moselle. In 1331 the Countess Laurette von Starkenburg detained Archbishop Baldwin of Trèves in captivity here for an attempted infringement of her rights, until he paid a large ransom for his liberation.

15 M. **Trarbach**, at the mouth of the Kautenbach-Tal, is connected by an iron bridge (toll 5 pf.) with **Traben** on the opposite

bank, with which it has formed one town since 1904. Pop. 5500
mostly Protestants. Traben is the terminus of the branch of the
State Railway mentioned at p. 169.

HOTELS. At Traben: *Clauss-Feist*, new, with steam-heating and
terraced garden, on the Moselle, ca. ¹/₄ M. from each of the rail. stations,
R. & B. 2¹/₂-4, D. 2¹/₂, S. 1¹/₂, pens. 5-7 ℳ. — At Trarbach: *Adolf*, at
the station of the Moselle Valley Railway, with veranda on the Moselle,
R. 2-3¹/₂, B. ³/₄, D. 1¹/₂, S. 1¹/₄, pens. 4¹/₂-5¹/₂ ℳ; *Brauneberg*; *Traube*. —
RESTAURANTS. *Brückenschenke*, on the right bank, a quaint establishment, with view-terrace (good wine); *Berncasteler Doctor*. — *Casino*,
at Trarbach, good wine (introduction required).

Trarbach, first heard of under the name of Travendrebach in
1143, and *Traben*, mentioned as Trabanna in a document of 840,
passed into the possession of the Counts of Pfalz-Zweibrücken in
1560. The former was devastated by fire in 1857 and the latter
in 1870, but both have been rebuilt. The Protestant church of
Trarbach contains some mediæval monuments; the gymnasium
dates from 1573. The important wine-trade of the sister-towns is
evidenced by the large cellerage buildings. — On the hill above
Trarbach (reached in 20 min.) is the ruin of the *Gräfinburg*, built,
according to the legend, by Countess Laurette von Starkenburg with
the ransom of Archbishop Baldwin (see p. 171). On the *Trabener
Berg* (892 ft.), round which the river sweeps in a bold curve, are
traces of the fortress of *Montroyal*, constructed by Louis XIV.
in 1686, but demolished in 1697 in pursuance of the Treaty of
Ryswyck.

At Trarbach opens the *Kautenbach-Tal*, a valley enclosed by wooded
and rocky slopes, in which, ³/₄ M. from the Moselle bridge (omn. 4 times
a day in summer), is the small **Wildbad Trarbach**, with thermal baths
prescribed in cases of gout. About 1¹/₂ M. farther up is the older *Bad
Wildstein* (Käss's Inn, R. & B. 2³/₄, D. 2¹/₂, pens. 5¹/₂-7 ℳ), supplied from
the same springs. — We may follow the valley to the village of *Longkamp*
(p. 189) and descend through the Tiefenbach-Tal (p. 173) to Berncastel (in
all 3¹/₂ hrs.; carr. 15 ℳ), or we may ascend the hill above the older Bad
for ¹/₄ hr., proceed through wood for ¹/₂ hr., and then (guide-post) descend
to (1 hr.) Berncastel direct.

At Trarbach begins the district of the 'Upper Moselle', which
produces the 'Zeltinger Schlossberg', 'Berncasteler Doctor', 'Brauneberger', and other highly-prized varieties of Moselle wine.

The Moselle Valley Railway continues to follow the right bank.
On the left bank lies *Rissbach*.

17 M. *Wolf*, with a large Protestant orphanage. The ruins on
the hill are those of a monastery.

18 M. (L.B.) **Cröv** (*Zur Gräfinburg*, unpretending but good)
possesses an interesting half-timbered house with two oriel-windows.

Beyond *Kindel* we reach (20¹/₂ M.) *Lösenich*, which is also the
station for *Kinheim*, on the left bank. — 22 M. *Erden* (Erdener
Treppchen, R. & B. 2¹/₂ ℳ), noted for its wine.

22¹/₂ M. (L.B.) **Uerzig** (*Post*, very fair; *Selbach*), a place of
some importance, which once possessed an independent jurisdiction

and has long been known for its wine. It is 2 M. from the station
mentioned at p. 170. On the Michaelslei, above Uerzig, is a tower
built into the red sandstone rock, formerly a castle.

23³/₄ M. *Rachtig.* On the left bank lies *Machern*, once a
nunnery.

24¹/₄ M. **Zeltingen** *(Post*, with garden, pens. 4-5 ℳ) is celebrated for its wine. The whole of the slopes from Rachtig to Berncastel are covered with vineyards, the best those on the *Schlossberg.*

26 M. (L.B.) *Wehlen.* — 27 M. *Graach* (Velten). Adjacent to
the church is a former convent. The *Martinshof*, or *Josephshof*,
the *Himmelreich*, and the *Kirchlei* all produce esteemed varieties
of wine.

28 M. **Berncastel.** — HOTELS. At Cues, on the left bank of the
Moselle: **Drei Könige*, near the bridge, with fine view, R. & B. 2¹/₂-4,
D. 2¹/₂, S. 1¹/₂ ℳ; *Zur Moselbrücke*, R. & B. 2-2¹/₂ ℳ. — On the right
bank, in Berncastel: *Post*, a little above the bridge, R. & B. 2¹/₄-2¹/₂,
D. 2, S. 1¹/₂ ℳ, with view-terrace, very fair; *Römischer Kaiser*, op-
posite the bridge, R. & B. 2¹/₄-3, D. 1¹/₂-2 ℳ, with restaurant, well
spoken of; *Burg Landshut*, R. & B. 2-2¹/₂ ℳ; *Schloss-Hôtel* (see below),
R. & B. 3, D. 2 ℳ. — Good wine at the *Casino* (introduction necessary).

Berncastel (360 ft.), a prosperous and picturesquely situated
place with 4500 inhab., is connected with *Cues* on the left bank by
an iron bridge and now forms one municipality with it. The quaint
old town is for the most part crowded into the narrow valley of
the Tiefenbach (see below). In the market-place are the *Rathaus*,
containing three ancient drinking-cups, and the old *Pillory*. At the
upper end of the town, on the river, are the new *District Offices.*
A sunny path ascends to (20 min.) the ruined electoral castle of
Landshut, which commands a beautiful view (key of the tower at
the adjacent Schloss-Hôtel; 20 pf.). — *Cues* is the terminus of the
branch-railway from Wengerohr mentioned at p. 170 (station straight
on from the bridge). It was the birthplace of the learned Cardinal
Nicolaus Cusanus (d. 1464), who founded *Cues Hospital* and bequeathed to it his library. The hospital owns several of the vineyards in the neighbourhood.

Berncastel carries on a large trade in wine; and the vineyards
which cover both banks produce some of the finest vintages of the
Moselle. Especially prized varieties are 'Berncasteler Doctor' (raised
on the N. side of the Tiefenbach-Tal) and 'Badstub'.

The **Tiefenbach-Tal,** through which runs the road viâ the Hunsrück to Kirchberg (p. 190), vies with the valley of the Ahr (p. 103) in
the grandeur of its rock-formations. There is a waterfall near a chapel,
1 M. from Berncastel; and from this point we may proceed to the right,
through a lateral valley, to (³/₄ hr.) *Monzelfeld* (view) and (1 hr.) *Veldenz*
(p. 174). — From Berncastel to Trarbach, see p. 172.

30 M. *Andel.*

31¹/₂ M. *Mülheim* (Bottler), an ancient village with 800 inhab.
and an important wine-trade, lies at the entrance to the picturesque

Veldenz Valley, with *Burg Veldenz* and the villages of *Veldenz* (Bottler) and *Tal Veldenz.* The Veldenz valley forms the lower part of a prehistoric 'bow' of the Moselle, the neck of which has been penetrated by the river at Dusemond (comp. p. 161). — Opposite Mülheim, on the left bank, lies **Lieser** *(Baum),* a well-built wine-growing village near the mouth of the brook of that name, with a modern château. It is a station on the branch-line from Wengerohr to Berncastel (p. 170).

33 M. *Dusemond* (Plunien, well spoken of). — Next come *Neu-Filzen* and *Filzen.*

34 M. (L.B.) *Kesten* (Licht) lies at the foot of the *Brauneberg* (p. xxiii). On the hill lies *Monzel.* From Kesten a footpath leads over the Brauneberg to (1^1/$_4$ hr.) Pisport (see below).

35^1/$_2$ M. *Winterich.* The hills of *Ohligsberg* and *Neuberg,* on the other bank, produce excellent wine. The rocky slopes of the *Geierslei* approach close to the river.

37^1/$_4$ M. (L.B.) *Minheim,* at the apex of a sharp curve in the river.

38 M. *Niederemmel,* the station for *Pisport* (Hain), the Roman *Pingontius Portus,* which lies on the left bank and has been for centuries famous for its wine. Pisport is 5 M. from *Salmrohr* (p. 170) viâ *Clausen.* Above Pisport, on the left bank, lies *Ferres,* the *Boveriis* of ancient charters.

42 M. **Neumagen** *(Neumagener Hof; Kaiserhof;* 1650 in-hab.), the Roman *Noviomagus,* where Constantine had a castle, mentioned by Ausonius. Extensive excavations made in 1877-85 showed that the castle was enclosed by a rampart 11^1/$_2$ ft. thick, 275 yds. in circumference, and strengthened with 16 circular towers. Many Roman tombstones (now at Trèves, p 181) were used in the foundations. — Neumagen is also the station for *Dhron* or *Thron,* a village noted for its wine, which lies 1^1/$_4$ M. distant, in the valley of the Dhron, a stream abounding in fish.

. From Neumagen a road ascends the Dhron valley, viâ *Papiermühle, Licht,* and *Berg,* to (10 M.) *Thalfang* (p. 189).

43^1/$_2$ M. (L.B.) *Trittenheim,* with a handsome church, the birth-place of Johann Trithemius, the historian (d. 1516). — The carriage-road on the hills on the opposite bank, between the valleys of the Moselle and the Dhron, follows the line of an ancient Roman road (fine view at a point 2^1/$_4$ M. above the new Trittenheim bridge).

The train runs along a viaduct skirting the river. 45^1/$_2$ M. *Leiwen;* 47^1/$_4$ M. *Köwerich.* On the left bank lies *Clüsserath,* at the mouth of the *Salm.*

49^1/$_2$ M. *Thörnich.* Then *Detzem* ('ad decimum', *i.e.* the tenth Roman milestone from Trèves). On the left bank come successively *Ensch, Schleich,* and *Pölich,* where remains of a Roman villa have been excavated. — 53 M. (L.B.) *Mehring* (Post), with 1600 inhab. and iron mines.

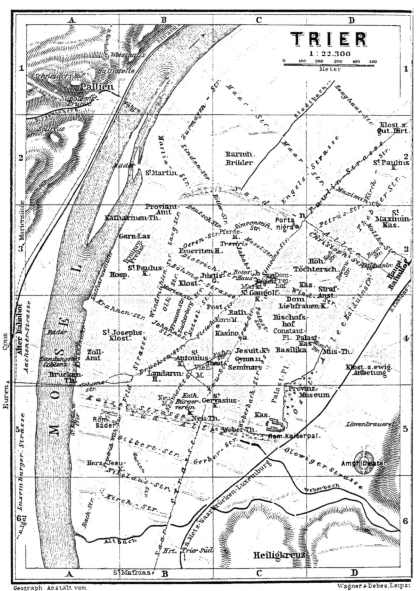

TRIER

1 : 22.300

Geograph. Anstalt von

Wagner & Debes, Leipzi

55 M. *Riol,* situated a little inland, on the side of the hill, is the *Rigodulum* of Tacitus, where the Roman general Cerealis conquered the Treveri, and took their leader Valentinus prisoner, A.D. 70. — 56 M. *Longwich,* prettily situated.

57 M. (L.B.) *Schweich* (p. 170). The Moselle here makes a bend, which the railway and the road avoid. — 58 M. *Kenn.*

60 M. *Ruwer* (Longen), with 1100 inhab., lies at the base of the *Grüneberg* (famed for its wine) and at the mouth of the picturesque Ruwer-Tal, up which runs the railway to Hermeskeil (p. 189). The first two stations on this line are ($1^1/_4$ M.) *Grünhaus* (with a château) and (2 M.) *Casel,* both noted for their wine.

Nearly opposite Ruwer, on the left bank, is *Pfalzel,* a village of Roman origin, with 2900 inhab., where Adela, daughter of King Dagobert I., founded a nunnery in 655.

63 M. *Trèves.*

24. Trèves.

Railway Stations. MAIN RAILWAY STATION (*Hauptbahnhof;* Pl. D, 3), for trains in all directions with the exception of those of the *Moselle Valley Narrow Gauge Railway (Moseltal-Kleinbahn),* the station of which lies 220 yds. to the N. The *South Railway Station* (p. 193), at Löwenbrücken, and the *West Railway Station,* on the left bank of the Moselle, are for local traffic only.

Hotels. *PORTA NIGRA (Pl. n; C, 3), in an open situation opposite the Porta Nigra, with lift and pleasant veranda, R. 3-$7^1/_2$, B. 1, D. 3 ℳ; *HÔTEL DE TRÈVES (Pl. a; C, 4), Brot-Str. 24, R. 3-10, B. 1, D. 3 ℳ, both these of the first class with excellent restaurants and baths; *RÖMERTOR, Simeons-Str. 10, opposite the Porta Nigra, new, R. 2-5, B. 1, D. $1^1/_2$-3 ℳ; ANKER (Pl. c; B, 4), cor. of Metzel-Str. and Johannis-Str., R. & B. from $2^3/_4$, D. $1^1/_2$-2 ℳ, with lift and restaurant; POST (Pl. e; C, 4), Kornmarkt, R. 2-6, B. 1, D. $2^1/_2$ ℳ, well spoken of; DOM-HÔTEL (Pl. b; C, 3), Markt, R. & B. 3-5 ℳ, with restaurant; HÔT. KURFÜRST (Pl. k; B, 5), Kaiser-Str. 30, R. & B. 2, D. $1^1/_2$ ℳ, with restaurant. — Near the rail. station: REICHSHOF, R. 2-$3^1/_2$, B. 1 ℳ, with restaurant, very fair; BAHNHOFS-HÔTEL, R. 2-3 ℳ, with restaurant; HÔTEL DU RHIN, R. 2-3 ℳ.

Restaurants. WINE. *Zur Steipe, in the Rote Haus (p. 177), first class; Joh. Baden, Fleisch-Str. 6; Hubertus, at the rail. station. — BEER. Kaiserhof and Baur, both in the Fleisch-Str., with gardens; Im Römer, Brot-Str. 2; Franziskaner, Nagel-Str., with garden; Victoria, Bahnhof-Str., corner of Roon-Str. (also rooms at all of these). — The Casino (Pl. C, 4), in the Kornmarkt, the Katholischer Bürgerverein (Pl. B, 5), Viehmarkt, and the Treviris (Rom. Cath. house of call) are three clubs, which enjoy a reputation for their wine; strangers require an introduction from a member, but the last two have also public restaurants.

Baths. Warm Baths, Brot-Str. 46, and St. Martinsbad, Zurlauben (Pl. B, 2). River Baths in the Moselle (Pl. A, 3).

Electric Tramways. Green Line: from the Main Railway Station (Pl. D, 3) viâ the Nord-Allée, Market, and Neu-Str. to St. Matthias's (comp. Pl. B, 6; p. 183). — Red Line: as above to the Market, and thence by the Fleisch-Str. to the Moselle Bridge (Pl. A, 4), and down the left bank to Pallien (Pl. A, 1). — White Line: from the Municipal Cemetery, viâ the Paulin-Str. (Pl. D, 2), Market, and the Moselle Bridge to Euren (Pl. A, 4, 5).

Cabs. I. Zone. Per drive within the town, including *Amphitheatre, St. Maximin, St. Paulin,* and *St. Martin,* for 1 pers. 50, 2 pers. 60 pf.;

each additional pers. 25 pf. more. — II. Zone *(Bellevue,* to the entrance at the foot of the hill, *St. Matthias's, Pallien),* 1 pers. 75 pf., each addit. person 25 pf. III. Zone *(Napoleons-Brücke, Schneider's Hof,* and *Weisshaus),* 1 pers. 1¹/₂ *M,* each addit. pers. 50 pf. Longer drives according to bargain. — By time, for each ¹/₄ hr., 1-2 pers. 50, 3-4 pers. 75 pf.

Post and Telegraph Office (Pl. B, C, 4), Fleisch-Str. 59.

Chief Attractions (1 day). Porta Nigra; Market; Cathedral; Church of Our Lady (Liebfrauenkirche); Basilica; Provincial Museum; Roman Palace; Amphitheatre; views from the Amphitheatre and the Weisshaus (p. 183). — Excursion to Igel, see p. 183.

Trèves (405 ft.), Ger. *Trier,* on the right bank of the Moselle, with 48,200 inhab. (6000 Protestants), said to be the oldest town in Germany, was a settlement founded by Augustus in the territory of the Treveri, a tribe of Gauls that had been conquered by Cæsar. This *Augusta Treverorum,* invested with the rank of a colony by Vitellius, was by the middle of the 1st cent. a thriving town, the population of which, judged by the size of the walls, has been estimated at 50-60,000. During the 4th century it was frequently the residence of the Roman Emperors. The numerous relics of that age in the vicinity are among the finest on this side of the Alps. In the 5th cent. Trèves suffered repeated destruction at the hands of the Franks. Christianity gained a foothold here at an early period. Agricius of Antioch was elected first Bishop of Trèves in 314, and for nearly 15 centuries the town continued to be the residence of the bishops, archbishops, and electors. The most prominent of these were Count Baldwin (1307-54) of Lützelburg, the brother of Emp. Henry VII., who established the temporal power of the archbishopric, and Count Richard of Greiffenklau (1511-31), a stubborn opponent of the Reformation. In 1802, after the storms of the French Revolution, the bishopric was re-established. By the Peace of Paris in 1814 the city passed to Prussia. Trèves is the centre of the trade in Moselle wines, and the choicest vintages of the Moselle, Saar, and Ruwer districts are offered for sale at its annual spring auctions. Its leather and tobacco industries are also important.

The surrounding vine-clad hills and wooded heights, and the rich plain in which the town with its red sandstone walls and numerous towers is situated, are strikingly picturesque.

'Trevir metropolis, urbs amœnissima,
Quæ Bacchum recolis, Baccho gratissima,
Da tuis incolis vina fortissima
Per dulcor!'

From the *Railway Station* (Pl. D, 3) we proceed in a straight direction, passing the *Baldwin Fountain,* commemorating the above-named archbishop (to the left the Baldwin-Str., leading to the Museum), to the —

*Porta Nigra (Pl. C, 3), a well-preserved town-gate of the Roman period (second half of the 3rd cent. A. D.), 118 ft. long, 75-95 ft. high, and 52-69 ft. in depth. It consists of three stories, with two gateways, 23 ft. in height, and is constructed of huge blocks of lias sandstone, blackened with age and fastened with iron braces instead of mortar. In the 11th cent. the structure was converted into a church, provided with an apse on the E. side, and named after St. Simeon, a Greek hermit (d. 1035) who had lived in the E. tower. In 1817 all the later additions were removed except the apse at the E. end, and in 1876 the original Roman structure was thoroughly disclosed. On the N.E. side of the gate a portion of the old Roman wall (comp. p. 182) has been brought to light.

The opening of the Porta Nigra was closed by portcullises and defended by two towers. If the enemy succeeded in storming the gate he found himself in a small enclosed court, secured on the side next the tower by a barricade and exposed to a raking fire from all parts of the gatehouse. — Admission daily in summer, 9-11; at other times on application to the custodian of the Roman Palace (p. 181). Entrance on the W. side.

The Simeons-Str., in which No. 19, the House of the Magi (Dreikönigenhaus; 12th cent.) deserves attention, leads to the S. from the Porta Nigra to the MARKET PLACE (Pl. C, 3). An ancient *Column* here, supposed to date from 958, was renewed in 1723, and is surmounted by a cross with the Lamb of God. The *Petersbrunnen*, a beautiful Renaissance fountain, was erected in 1595. Behind it rises the late-Gothic spire of the *St. Gangolphs-Kirche*. The **Rotes Haus** (Pl. C, 3), to the right, a late-Gothic building of 1450, was formerly the *Rathaus* and had an open arcade on the groundfloor (wine-room, see p. 175). The upper rooms contain a Municipal Museum, including objects of art bequeathed by Prof. F. X. Kraus, historical relics and views, and costumes and household-gear from the districts of the Moselle and Saar (open free, on Sun. 11-1, at other times for a fee). The addition erected in the Renaissance style in the 17th cent. bears the inscription: 'Ante Romam Treviris stetit annis MCCC', referring to a mediæval tradition that Trèves was founded by Trebeta, son of the Assyrian king Ninus. — In the Dietrich-Str. (Pl. B, C, 3; beside No. 5) is the so-called *Franken-Turm* or *Propugnaculum*, dating from the early Romanesque period and said to be the oldest domestic building in Germany.

To the E. of the Market Place lies the DOMFREIHOF, a small square with a *Statue of Emperor William I.*, in bronze, by F. von Miller, erected in 1893.

The ***Cathedral** (Pl. C, 4), the nucleus of which was a quadrangular basilica erected in the 4th cent. probably as a market, is one of the oldest churches in Germany. This basilica, which was of the same breadth as the present edifice, extended from the second pillar from the W. entrance to the E. apse. In the centre stood four huge granite columns, connected by arches, some remains of which lie in the cloister-garden. The ancient edifice was partly destroyed by the Franks, but was restored in the original style by *Bishop Nicétius* (528-66). It was afterwards again devastated by

the Normans, and restored by *Archbishop Poppo* (1016-47) and
his successors, who increased its size by an addition of one-third
at the W. end, in the style of the original Roman edifice, and also
built an apse. The E. apse was added by *Bishop Hillin* (1152-69).
The vaulting of the nave and aisles dates from the 13th cent.; the
octagonal, dome-roofed treasury was not built till the 18th. — The
various periods at which the structure has been built are all clearly
visible on the N. exterior; the Roman work consists of red sandstone and bricks, that of Archbishop Poppo is partly of brick and
partly of limestone. A thorough restoration of the whole exterior
of the building has lately been completed.

The INTERIOR (open 10-2 & 3-6; verger's house behind the cathedral,
No. 4) was newly decorated in 1907. By the removal of the stucco several
Roman arches and Frankish capitals have been exposed to view. In the
W. apse is the monument of an archbishop of the 14th cent. (perhaps

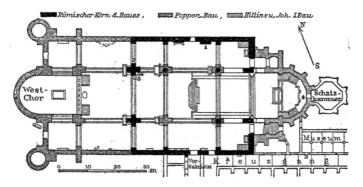

Baldwin, brother of Henry VII.), beneath which is a white marble font.
The *Pulpit* (ground-plan, 5), adorned with reliefs of the Beatitudes, the
Last Judgment, the Sermon on the Mount, the Resurrection (above the
steps), and the Five Senses (round the foot), dates from 1572. In the
vaults repose 26 archbishops and electors. The finest monuments are
those of *Johann III*: (*von Metzenhausen*, d. 1540; restored in 1898), and
Elector Richard III. (*von Greiffenklau*, p. 176), both in the N. aisle
(ground-plan, 1 & 2). The two monuments are excellent specimens of
the German Renaissance at its zenith, both in their general plan and
in the conception and execution of the decoration and figures. — The
choir-screens, the steps with statues of Constantine and St. Helena, and
the imposing high-altar (ground-plan, 4) date from 1652-1700. — The
Treasury (adm. on week-days at 11.30-12, by tickets procured from the
verger, 1 ℳ) contains the Shrine of St. Egbert, a small enamelled altar
of the 10th cent., and several Romanesque reliquaries of the 11th and
12th cent., with the heads of the Apostle Matthias and the Empress
Helena, a nail from the Cross, etc., a late-Romanesque censer, and some
richly-bound Gospels of the 9-13th centuries. — In a room above the
cloisters is preserved the 'Holy Coat' without seam, exhibited at rare
intervals, and attracting vast crowds of pilgrims.

On the S. side of the cathedral are the beautiful *Cloisters* of the 13th cent. (shown by the verger). They are adjoined by the sacristy, built in 1900 by W. Schmitz, and an early-Gothic double-chapel.

In other rooms opening off the cloisters is the *Cathedral and Diocesan Museum* (open on Mon., Wed., and Frid., 11-1, in winter on Sun. 11.30-1, adm. 30 pf.; entrance at No. 3, on the ground-plan). Room I. Roman and Romanesque remains from the old Cathedral, including a Roman mosaic floor and some Romanesque sculptures and wall-paintings. Room II. Gothic and Renaissance sculptures, with statues from the portal of the Liebfrauen-Kirche. On the upper floor are a chapel and two rooms with ecclesiastical ornaments, lace, manuscripts, and smaller antiquities.

To the S. of the cloisters is the *Liebfrauen-Kirche* (Pl. C, 4), one of the most interesting early-Gothic churches in Germany, begun after 1227, probably in imitation of the abbey-church of Braisne near Soissons, and lately restored. It is in the form (approximately) of a circle (54 yds. long, 42 yds. broad, 115 ft. high), intersected by a vaulted cross-structure, and supported by 12 slender pillars. The principal *Portal* is richly decorated with sculptures, symbolical figures of the Old and New Testament, etc.

The INTERIOR (closed 12-2; verger at Liebfrauen-Str. 2) is remarkable for its harmonious proportions. The figures of the Apostles painted on the pillars in the 15th cent. are visible all at once from a slab of slate in the pavement, about 8 paces from the entrance. The choir is frescoed with scenes from the life of the Virgin by *Ehrich* and *Döringer* (1895-97). The modern high-altar is by V. Statz. The altar to the right of the choir contains the mummy of Bishop Theodulf, who died in the 6th century. Adjacent on the left is a St. Sebastian ascribed to *Guido Reni* (closed). To the left of the choir, adjoining the tombstone of Carl von Metternich (1636), is an altar, recently gilded, with alabaster reliefs of 1610. Numerous monuments to various other canons are distributed about the walls of the church. — The sacristy has an interesting old side-door with exquisite carved foliage and contains the portrait-monument of Johann Segensis (d. 1564).

Adjacent is the *Bischofshof*, the residence of the bishops. Opposite is the *Palace of the Count of Kesselstatt*.

The **Town Library**, at the *Gymnasium* (Pl. C, 4; open on week-days 8-1; adm. 50 pf.), contains numerous rare printed works and several valuable manuscripts.

Important among the printed books are the Bible of Fust and Gutenberg of 1450, and the Catholicon of 1460. One of the most interesting MSS. is the *Codex Aureus*, containing the four Gospels, presented by Ada (d. 809), a reputed sister of Charlemagne, to the Abbey of St. Maximin. It is illuminated with allegorical paintings, and the binding is superbly adorned with jewels and a cameo of uncommon size, probably representing the family of Constantine. The *Codex Egberti*, dating from about 970, is perhaps the finest extant specimen of the art of illumination at that period. The *Liber Aureus* contains documents of the convent of Prüm, ranging from the 9th to the 11th century, and admirably illustrating the advance of the illuminator's art. Several letters of Luther, one from Blücher on the death of Queen Louisa, etc., are also interesting. — The *Ante-Chamber* contains portraits of Electors of Trèves, and others. — The *Reading Room*, in the Renaissance style, is the old Jesuit Library.

The *Trinity*, or *Jesuits'*, *Church* (Pl. C, 4) is decorated with stained glass from Munich and wall-paintings by Steffgen. On the right is the monument by Albermann (1907) to the Jesuit poet Friedrich von Spee (1591-1635), known for his enlightened opposition to the persecution of witches.

Bounding the Constantins-Platz on the E. are the **Palace Barracks** (Pl. C, D, 4), formerly, in the 17th cent., the palace of the Electors, with late-Renaissance portals in the court, sculptures on the façade, and a baroque staircase dating from 1701, on the side towards the Palast-Platz. The building includes the old Roman Basilica, now the Protestant church (verger beside the guardhouse; fee).

The *Basilica (Pl. C, 4), built entirely of brick, probably in the reign of the Emp. Constantine (306-337), served originally for the administration of justice and for commercial purposes, like the similar ancient Roman structures at Rome itself and elsewhere. Early in the middle ages it was the seat of the governors appointed by the Frankish sovereigns, and in 1197 it was made over to the archbishops. In 1846-56 it was restored and consecrated as a Protestant church. The imposing interior, terminating in an apse at the N. end, is lighted by a double row of windows. The basilica is 225 ft. long, 100 ft. wide, and 98 ft. high.

The N.W. side up to the lower row of windows, the apse, and the lofty arch between the nave and the apse are all antique. The S. façade and the E. side, on the other hand, are almost entirely modern. Below the floor was a hypocaust, or heating-apparatus. The main entrance at the S. end, with its three doors, was preceded by a portico; while there was a smaller entrance in the N. part of each of the sides. — Over the altar is a tabernacle with four columns of yellow African marble, presented to Frederick William IV. by the Khedive of Egypt.

From the Palace Barracks we pass through an opening in the town-wall and reach the —

*Provincial Museum (Pl. C, 5), a handsome Renaissance building in red sandstone, erected in 1885-89, and extended on the W. in 1905. It contains an extensive collection of antiquities (giving a good idea of the importance of the Roman Trèves), some mediæval and later works, a number of pictures, and a collection of art-industrial objects. Open free in summer on Sun. & Wed., 11-1, and on other days, at the same hours, for a fee of 50 pf.; at other times adm. is obtained for a fee of 75 pf. Short guide 20 pf.; illustrated catalogue, 1 ℳ 60 pf.

Ground Floor. — From the Central Hall (I) we enter, to the left, Room II, containing *Pre-Roman Antiquities:* objects of the early stone period from the Buchenloch cave at Gerolstein (p. 149); Italic bronze vessels of the 6th and 5th cent. B.C. from pre-Roman graves in the districts of the Nahe and the Saar. — Room III. *Roman Mosaic* found in Trèves, with Bacchus and the Seasons. Model of the Hermæ basin in Room A. We now enter the new building. Room A. Sixty *Hermae,* with portraits, popular types, and heads of divinities, from the curbing of a fish-pond at Welschbillig (3³/₄ M. to the N.W. of Cordel, p. 152). — Room B. *Architectural Fragments and Monuments* from Trèves and environs: Statue of Juno enthroned; columns of coloured marble; Jupiter column;

small marble group of Jupiter, Juno, and Minerva. — Room C. *Roman
Tombs from Neumagen* (p. 174), dating from about 100-250 A.D. and
illustrating the costumes and daily life of the ancient dwellers on the
Moselle. Among these may be mentioned the *Tomb Monument of the
Emperor Albinius Asper*, with numerous traces of painting; *Funeral
Altar* with a frieze of sea-monsters; *Relief* of a school, with a schoolmaster between two youths reading from a scroll of parchment, and a
boy who comes to greet them; *Ships* laden with wine-casks, one of them
complete except for a few alterations, and another interesting for the
characteristic head of the helmsman; large *Monument* with scenes from
the Circus, on the back of which, as on the others, should be noticed
the vari-coloured rosettes; large *Pediment*, with a family group. — On
the wall, plaster-casts of the reliefs on the *Igel Monument* (p. 183), a
full-size reproduction of which (in cement) forms the centre of the collection in the court. — Room D. *Mediaeval and Modern Sculptures in
Stone.* *Renaissance Canopy*, of fine workmanship, from the Liebfrauen-
Kirche (1531); Romanesque relief from the Neu-Tor in Trèves. — Room E.
Roman Grave Monuments from the environs of Trèves; Roman milestones.
We return to the old building. — Room V. *Roman Grave Monuments*,
etc., found in Trèves, among them an inscription from a monument
dedicated to *L. Caesar*, the adopted son of the Emperor Augustus. —
Room VI. *Mosaic* with victorious charioteers; *Sarcophagus* with a representation of Noah's Ark; numerous *Christian Inscriptions;* reproduction of the wooden coffin of St. Paulin (d. ca. 350). — Room VII.
Remains of a heating-apparatus, mills, locks, and other technical objects
from the Roman period. — We return to Room IV, which contains Coptic
fabrics and recent acquisitions.

    First Floor. Room XIV. *Roman Mosaic*, probably from about
300 A.D., found during the erection of the Museum (upwards of one-third
is lost), representing Muses teaching wise men (Homer between Ingenium
and Calliope, Thamyris, [Ac]icarus and Polymnia, Aratus and Urania,
Cadmus and Clio, Agnis and Euterpe), famous poets and writers (Livy,
Virgil, Cicero, Menander, Ennius, Hesiod), the Months with their gods,
the Signs of the Zodiac, and the Four Seasons. — Room XV (to the left).
Roman Antiquities found at Trèves. Antique marble columns; *Torso
of Cupid;* *Torso of Amazon*, based on the same original as the Mattei
Amazon in the Vatican; torso of an athlete; smaller objects from the
Roman Baths, particularly combs and hair-pins; *Mural Paintings;* mosaics
with Muses, animals, and sages. — Room XVI. *Antiquities found in
the Environs of Trèves. Mosaics* from the Roman villa at Oberweis.
Among the *Mosaics* from Trèves should be noticed the philosopher
with the sun-dial; *Coins* and *Bronzes* from the temple ruins at Möhn;
terracottas from the environs of the temple at Thronecken; plans of
Roman buildings. — Room XVII. Bronzes. — Room XVIII. Earthenware
vessels and lamps. — Room XIX. *Objects from Roman Tombs.* — Room XX.
Roman Drinking Cups with inscriptions; terracottas; fine *Collection
of Glass, Rings* and *Gems;* Sigillata vessels. — Room XXI. *Objects from
Roman Graves* in the S. cemetery of Trèves. — Room XXII. *Collection
of Coins;* Celtic and Roman coins; counterfeit dies; Roman coins minted
at Trèves, in chronological order; coins of the Electors of Trèves. —
Room XXIII. *Frankish Antiquities:* weapons, glass, and ornaments.
    Room XXIV. In the cabinets: ivory carvings; enamelled reliquaries;
Limoges enamels (cup by *N. Laudin*); bronze dish of the 12th cent.
with representation of the Good Samaritan. On the walls a number of
pictures, mostly of the Rhenish and Netherlandish schools (largely copies)
and a piece of tapestry of the 15th cent. (Christ and the Apostles). —
Room XXV. Collection of Rhenish stoneware; majolica and porcelain;
large collection of glass (16-18th cent.).

    The *Roman Palace* (Pl. C, 5), at the S. end of the Ost-Allée,
to the right, and entered also from the Palast-Platz, forms a pic-

turesque group of ruins, part of which is 65 ft. high. In the middle
ages the building was used alternately as a church and as a fortress.
The rubbish in the interior accumulated to such an extent, that
one of the windows was once used as an entrance to the town. —
Visitors ring at the entrance.

The best-preserved part of the edifice is a *Rectangular Room*, with
three apses, at the S.E. end, formerly lighted by two rows of arched
windows, and heated by channels for hot air, many of which are still
visible. — To the right and left of this chamber stood two *Towers*, one
of which is still extant and commands a fine view of the ruins and of
the town (ascent by a steep spiral staircase). — At the N.W. end, where
the excavations are still in progress, various circular and square rooms
and subterranean passages have been brought to light. — The keeper
(50 pf.) has also the key of the Porta Nigra (p. 176).

Beyond the railway tracks, a shady road, passing the Union
Brewery on the left, ascends to the E. to ($^1/_4$ M.) the **Amphitheatre**
(Pl. D, 5), situated among vineyards, and freely open to the public.
This arena, with a diameter from N. to S. of 76 yds., and from E.
to W. of 53 yds., was capable of accommodating 7-8000 spectators.
(That at Verona held 20,000 spectators, the Colosseum at Rome
40-50,000.) The E. half is built into the rocky side of the hill,
while the W. is raised to the same level by artificial means. At the
N. and S. ends are gateways, each with three openings, that in the
centre leading to the arena, and those at the sides to the seats for
spectators. There are also two entrances for the public on the W.
side. The dens for the wild beasts are still traceable adjacent to
the arena, under which run subterranean passages intersecting in
the middle. The amphitheatre was probably built in the reign of
Trajan or Hadrian. — The later Roman wall ran along the top of
the W. semicircle and was continued on the N. to the Porta Nigra,
on the S. almost to St. Matthias's. — The garden-restaurant of the
Löwen-Brauerei, outside the N. entrance of the Amphitheatre,
affords an excellent view of Trèves by morning-light.

Adjoining the Kaiser-Str. are the **Roman Baths** (Pl. A, 5),
an imposing structure of the 4th cent. A. D., 564 ft. in length, excavated in 1877-85 (adm. 25 pf.; plan 10 pf.). The principal façade
was turned towards the N. The masonry above the level of the
ground has almost entirely disappeared, though at the beginning of
the 17th cent. it was preserved up to the second story. At the N.W.
end of the excavation is the rectangular *Frigidarium* (cold baths;
A on the plan); to the S. of this are the cruciform *Tepidarium*
(warmer baths; B) and the cruciform *Caldarium* (warm baths; C);
to the E. is the heated swimming-basin.

Adjacent is the **Moselle Bridge** (Pl. A, 4; tramway, see
p. 175), with eight arches, most of the buttresses of which are of
Roman origin. The second and seventh buttresses from the town-
side were blown up by the French in 1689, and restored in 1729.
The bridge is 620 ft. long. — On the left bank of the Moselle is

the *West Railway Station (Westbahnhof)* mentioned at p. 175, and on the height above is a conspicuous *Column of the Virgin* ('Mariensäule').

The best *View of Trèves in the afternoon is obtained from the hill on the left bank of the Moselle above the village of *Pallien* (Pl. A, 1; tramway, see p. 175; roads, see Pl. B, 1). At the land-ing-place of the ferry is a board indicating the way to the *Café Bellevue*. Beyond the Napoleons-Brücke, carrying the Aix-la-Chapelle road over the ravine of the Sirzenicher Bach, a path ascends to the right to *Schneider's Hof* and the **Weisshaus,** with a pretty park and a restaurant (cab, see p. 175). About $1^1/_2$ M. higher up is the *Kockelsberg* (restaurant), commanding an admir-able view.

From the Weisshaus a marked path leads over the hill, passing the cross known as the *Toter Stadrat* (938 ft.), into the valley of the Biewer. It then goes on by the *Cave of St. Genoveva* (656 ft.) to the ruined castle of Ramstein and ($3^1/_2$ hrs.) Cordel (p. 152).

About $^3/_4$ M. to the S. of Trèves is situated the venerable **Church of St. Matthias** (comp. Pl. B, 6; tramway, see p. 175), dating in its present form from the 12th cent., with alterations made in the 16th and 18th cent., and containing the sarcophagus of the Apostle (a favourite resort of pilgrims). Beside it is a Roman cem-etery. — In the N. E. suburb (tramway, see p. 175) is the *Church of St. Paulin*, originally a Gothic building, but destroyed by the French in 1674, and restored in the baroque style in the second quarter of the 18th cent. and adorned with frescoes. In the vicinity is a spot marked by a *Cross*, where some of the early Christians suffered martyrdom at the hands of the Romans. Near it is the venerable *Abbey of St. Maximin*, now a barrack (Pl. D, 3).

Our survey of Roman Trèves should be completed by an ex-cursion to the village of *Igel* (railway, see pp. 184, 193), which contains one of the most remarkable Roman relics on this side of the Alps, the so-called ***Igel Column.** The monument, which is adorned with numerous reliefs, is a square column, 75 ft. in height and $16^1/_2$ ft. broad at the base, and was erected as a funeral mon-ument of the family of Secundini, probably about 200 A. D.

The inscription informs us that it was erected to SECUNDINIUS SECURUS and PUBLIA PACATA, along with other kinsmen, by their children, LUCIUS SECUNDINIUS AVENTINUS and SECUNDINIUS SECURUS. — Of the numerous reliefs the most interesting are those of scenes from the life of the family, which appears in them as an eminent representative of the com-merce and industry of Roman Trèves. On the *South Side*, facing the street: below the pediment, Four figures engaged in selling cloth; below, Kitchen scene and a household meal with attendants serving wine; in the main field are the builders of the monument, holding out their hands in farewell, with Hermes as the guide of departed souls to the left; below, scene in a counting-house. On the *East Side*, below the pediment, Payment of dues. On the *North Side*, above the main field, Train of pack-mules; in the podium, Departure of a ship with bales of merchandise. On the *West Side*, below the pediment, a carriage passing a milestone;

presentation of hares, fish, and other offerings ; on the podium, carriage and similar scenes to those on the N. side. The other reliefs are of mythological content, and their relation to the family history is not clear. — Plaster casts in the Provincial Museum, see p. 181.

The church on the hill behind the monument commands a fine view of the valleys of the Moselle and the Saar (best by evening-light). At Igel is the Willmerstedt Inn.

Excursion to Luxembourg.

RAILWAY from Trèves to (32 M.) Luxembourg in 1-1¹/₂ hr. (fares 4 ℳ 10, 2 ℳ 60, 1 ℳ 10 pf. ; express fares 4 ℳ 60, 3 ℳ 10, 1 ℳ 35 pf.). — The official currency of Luxembourg is the same as that of Belgium (francs and centimes), but German money is in more common use. For a fuller description of Luxembourg, see *Baedeker's Belgium & Holland*.

The railway follows the right bank of the Moselle to (4¹/₂ M.) *Karthaus* (p. 186), crosses the river, passes (7 M.) *Igel* (with the Igel Column, p. 183, to the right), and reaches the Luxembourg frontier, here formed by the *Sauer (Sure)*. — 9¹/₂ M. *Wasserbillig*, on the right bank of the Sauer, the first station in Luxembourg, is the junction of a line ('Prinz-Heinrich-Bahn') ascending the Sauer valley to *Echternach, Bollendorf,* and *Diekirch* (see *Baedeker's Belgium and Holland*). [The Prussian village of Bollendorf (Barreau's Inn, very fair) lies on the left bank and is a good start-ing-point for visits to the fantastic rocky scenery of Luxembourg. A Roman villa was unearthed here in 1907.] — The stations be-tween Wasserbillig and Luxembourg are unimportant. Before reach-ing the latter we cross the *Pulvermühlen-Tal* by a viaduct 275 yds. long and 100 ft. high.

32 M. **Luxembourg.** — HOTELS. In the Old Town, ³/₄-1¹/₄ M. from the station : *Grand-Hôtel Brasseur* (Pl. a ; B, 2), Rue de l'Arsenal 2, R. 4-6, B. 1¹/₂, D. 4, omn. 1 fr. ; *Hôtel Continental* (Pl. b ; B, 2), Rue de l'Arsenal, R. from 3, B. 1¹/₄, D. 3 fr. ; *Hôtel de Cologne* (Pl. c ; B, 2), Ave. de la Porte Neuve 11, R. 2¹/₂-6, B. 1¹/₄, D. 3 fr. ; *Hôtel de Luxem-bourg* (Pl. f ; C, 3), Ave. de l'Eau, with restaurant, R. 2¹/₂-3, B. 1 fr. ; *Hôtel de l'Ancre d'Or*, Place Guillaume 7 (Pl. C, 3), R. 2-2¹/₂, B. 1, D. 2¹/₂ fr. — Near the Railway Station (930 ft.): *Hôtel Clesse* (Pl. d ; C, 5), with restaurant, R. 3-5, B. 1¹/₄, D. 3 fr. ; *Hôtel Staar (Hôt. de la Gare)*, well spoken of ; *Terminus*, R. 2 fr. — Several CAFÉS in the Place d'Armes (Pl. B, 3). — BEER. *Hofbräuhaus*, Rue Notre-Dame (Pl. B, C, 3), at the corner of the Rue de l'Athénée, D. 1¹/₂-2 fr.

TRAMWAYS from the railway-station through the town (20 c.).

Luxembourg (1065 ft.), formerly the seat of the Counts of Lux-embourg or Lützelburg, a family of whom the German Emperor Henry VII. (1398-13) was a member, came into the possession of Burgundy in 1443, and in 1477 passed to the Low Countries. It was an important fortress and was frequently besieged and captured by the Spaniards and the French. In 1815 the duchy became con-nected with Holland through a personal union with the Dutch king, and down to 1867 the town was a fortress of the German Con-federation. Since 1890 it has been the capital of the independent

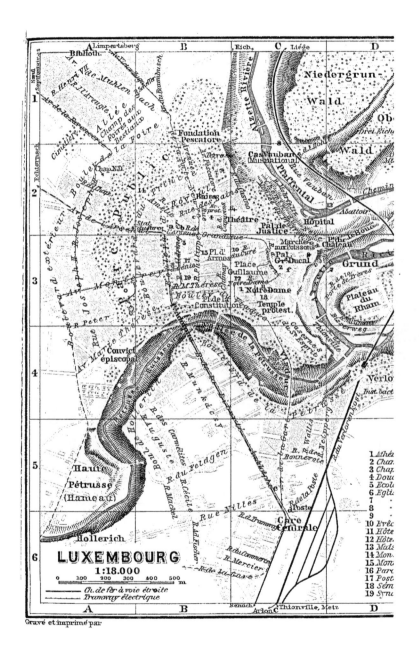

LUXEMBOURG

1:18.000

0   100   200   300   400   500   m

Ch. de fer à voie étroite
Tramway électrique

Gravé et imprimé par

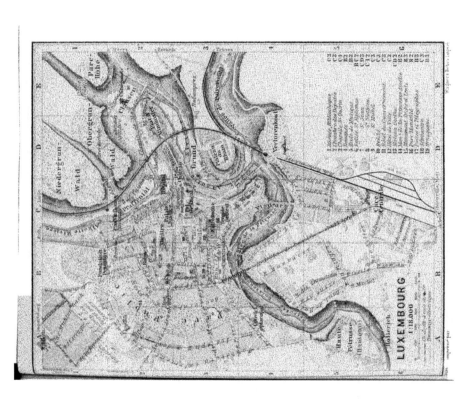

LUXEMBOURG
1:18.000

grand-duchy of Luxembourg and now contains 21,000 inhabitants. The *Upper Town (Oberstadt)*, or Luxembourg proper, occupies a rocky tableland bounded on three sides by the deep valleys of the *Pétrusse* and the *Alzette*. In this narrow ravine, about 600 ft. below, lie the busy *Unterstädte* or lower portions of the town, consisting of *Pfaffental* (Pl. C, 1, 2), *Clausen* (Pl. E, 2), and *Grund* (Pl. D, 3). The view of the town, with its variety of mountain and valley, gardens and rocks, groups of trees and huge viaducts, is singularly striking and has been graphically described by Goethe in his 'Campagne in Frankreich'. The fortifications have been razed.

From the railway-station (Gare Centrale; Pl. C, 6) we may proceed to the N. by the Avenue de la Gare (tramway) to the old *Viaduct* (Pl. C, 4), which is 1150 ft. long, or we may bear to the N.W. and follow the Avenue Adolphe and the Boulevard de la Liberté to the *Pont Adolphe* (Pl. B, 4, 3), a bridge 692 ft. long, 52 ft. in breadth, the central arch of which has a span of 280 ft. Both viaducts cross the valley of the Pétrusse high above the bed of the stream (fine view).

Both routes lead viâ the *Place de la Constitution* (Pl. B, 3) to the central point of the city, the *Place Guillaume* (Pl. C, 3), which is embellished with a *Statue of William II.*, King of the Netherlands, by Mercié. Here also stands the *Hôtel de Ville* (Pl. 12; C, 3). — The Gothic cathedral of *Notre Dame* (Pl. C, 3) has a fine Renaissance portal (1621) and a baroque organ-loft.

A little to the N.E. of the Place Guillaume lies the *Granddacal Palace* (Pl. C, 3), a handsome building with two oriel-windows, erected in 1580, and recently altered and enlarged. — The old *Vauban Barracks* (Pl. C, 2), in the suburb of Pfaffental, not far from the *Alzette Bridge*, with its two well-preserved towers (17th cent.), contain the *Musée National*, with Roman and Frankish antiquities (open on Mon. & Wed., 2-5) and a Natural History Collection (open on Tues. & Thurs., 2-5).

A pleasant walk may be taken through the *Park*, passing the monument to Princess Amalie (Pl. 14; B, 2), to the terrace on the left of the Eich road (Pl. B, 1), which affords a striking view of Pfaffental.

From Luxembourg to Remich, 17 M., branch-railway in ca. 1³/₄ hr., passing (11 M.) *Bad Mondorf* or *Mondorf-les-Bains*, a watering-place with saline thermal baths (68° Fahr.). — Remich *(Hôtel des Ardennes; Hôtel de la Poste)*, a small town with 2500 inhab., lies on the slopes rising from of the Moselle, connected by a bridge (4 pf.) with the Prussian bank. — To the railway-station of *Nennig* (p. 193) 1¹/₄ M. (diligence 5 times daily).

From Luxembourg to Diedenhofen (p. 193), 20 M., railway in ¹/₂-³/₄ hr.

25. From Trèves to Saarbrücken. Valley of the Saar.

55 M. RAILWAY in 1¹/₂-2¹/₂ hrs. (fares 7 ℳ 10, 4 ℳ 30, 2 ℳ 40 pf.; express fares 8 ℳ 10, 5 ℳ 30, 2 ℳ 90 pf.). — *Electric Railway* from Luisental to Saarbrücken, see p. 204.

Trèves, see R. 24. The line follows the course of the *Saar.* Numerous coal-mines, iron-foundries, steel-works, glass-works, and chemical manufactories are passed. — 1¹/₂ M. *Trier Süd;* 4¹/₂ M. *Karthaus* (p. 193), on the right bank of the Moselle.

5¹/₂ M. **Conz** (265 ft.; *Post*), with 3300 inhab., at the confluence of the Saar and the Moselle, is the Roman *Contionacum,* whence several imperial edicts were dated. A few remains of the imperial villa mentioned by Ausonius (p. 161) are still recognizable near the church. There was a bridge over the Saar here in the Roman period; the present structure dates from 1782. Conz is also united with Trèves by a special branch-line (5 M.) passing the stations of *Zewen* and *Euren.* — 8 M. *Canzem.*

In prehistoric times the river between Trèves and Saarburg described a number of long loops, now left dry by subsequent changes in the river-course (comp. p. 161). The lateral valley to the E., near (10 M.) *Wiltingen* (with Roman remains), in which lie *Scharzhof* and *Ober-Emmel,* celebrated for their wines, was one of these ancient river-loops, which joined the Moselle at Conz, while the present river-course bends to the W. The celebrated vineyards at *Okfen* and *Wawern* lie to the E. and W. in another of these loops ending at (12 M.) *Schoden.*

14¹/₂ M. *Beurig* is the station for —

Saarburg (*Post,* very fair, with garden and view; *Saarburger Hof*), picturesquely situated on the left bank of the river in a basin, and commanded by the considerable ruins of a castle of the Electors of Trèves; a tunnel leads under the castle to the town. Pop. 2100. The Gothic *Church of St. Lawrence* was erected in 1856. The *Leuk,* which here unites with the Saar, forms a waterfall, 60 ft. high, near the 'Post'. The *Pavilion,* on the height to the S., opposite the castle, commands a fine view of the Saar valley (to Castel), the Kammerforst, and the Saargau (W.). Another picturesque view of the town is obtained from the road to Okfen, on the right bank of the river, about 1 M. below the bridge.

17 M. *Serrig* (510 ft.) is the best starting-point for a visit to the *Klaus* or chapel of *Castel,* rising on a precipitous rock on the left bank.

From the station we descend in 5 min. to the Saar, cross it by boat, and descend the left bank to the hamlet of *Staadt.* Here we ascend a side-valley. In 4 min. we reach a point where the direct route to (¹/₂ hr.) the Klaus diverges to the left. We, however, keep to the right, in order to procure the key at (¹/₂ hr.) the village of *Castel,* which is 8 min. from

Kleinbahnen
Echternach
Geograph. Anstalt von Wagner & Debes, Leipzig
Simmern
TRIER
Euren
Zewen
Conz
Waldrach
Osburg
Thalfang
Erbeskopf
Steinkopf
Sandkopf
Reinsfeld
Hermeskeil
Schöndf.
Pellingen
Obermennig
Wiltingen
Schoden
Ockfener B.
SAARBURG
Beurig
Irsch
Serrig
Freudenburg
Taben
Weiten
Mettlach
Besseringen
Teufelskopf
Weiskirchen
Wadern
Lockweiler
Losheim
Wahlen
Britten
Nunkirchen
Brotdorf
Büdingen
Hilbringen
Merzig
Reimsbach
Bettingen
Lebach
Dirmingen
Eppelborn
Tholey
Theley
Marpingen
Uchtelfangen
Illingen
Wiesbach
Beckingen
Nalbach
Diefflen
Dillingen
Saarwellingen
Rehlingen
Pachten
Roden
Wallerfangen
SAARLOUIS
Fraulautern
Schwarzenholz
Quirscheid
Hülzwlr.
Ensdf.
Lisdorf
Schwalbch.
Guichenbch.
Bous
Püttlingen
Wadgassen
Hostenbach
Völklingen
Busendf.
Differten
Ludweiler
Burbach
Malstatt
St. JOHANN
SAARBRÜCKEN
St. Arnual
St. INGBERT
Sulzbach
Dudweiler
Friedrichsth.
Bildst.
Neunkirchen
Kreuzwald
Lauterbach
Stieringen-Wendel
Forbach
Kerbach
Kleinblittersdf.
Grossblittersdf.
Bolchen
Oberhomburg
St. Avold
Kochern
SAARGEMÜND
Metz
Birkenfeld
St. Wendel
Ottweiler
Neunkirchen
Zweibrücken
Kaiserslaut.
Kilometer 1:500.000
Engl Miles.

the Klaus. The **'Klaus',** on a bold rock overhanging the Saar, is a chapel restored in 1838 by Frederick William IV., in which he deposited the bones of the blind king John of Bohemia, who fell at Crécy in 1346; the modern sarcophagus is of black marble. The chapel stands in a park. Fine views of the valley of the Saar and of Saarburg, which may be reached from Serrig by a pleasant walk along the left bank of the river in 1 hr.

At (20^1/$_2$ M.) *Taben* the bold forms of the wooded and riven hills of the Saar valley are especially picturesque. The village, on the left bank (bridge), has some old abbey-buildings. On the height above is *St. Michael's Chapel,* commanding a fine view. — 24^1/$_2$ M. *Saarhölzbach.*

26 M. **Mettlach** (550 ft.; *Zur Saar,* very fair; *Schwan*), with 1530 inhab. and the imposing buildings (1737-71) of a suppressed Benedictine abbey, originally founded in the 8th cent. by St. Ludvinus, and now occupied by the extensive earthenware-factory of *Villeroy & Boch* (2000 workmen), who have other works at Merzig and Wallerfangen (p. 188). The modern parish-church contains a reliquary of the 12th cent. and other valuable objects from the old treasury of the abbey. The 'Museum' at the factory (open on week-days 10-12 & 3-5) contains specimens of the very tasteful productions of the works since their establishment in 1810, and also numerous pieces of ancient and modern pottery of all kinds. Most of the pretty park, with the ruined choir of the early-Romanesque *Chapel of St. Ludvinus* (remodelled in the Gothic style), is accessible to the public. Fine view from the *Pavilion* (^{1}/$_2$ M.; restaurant). Near the iron bridge across the Saar is a bronze bust of the founder of the factory. On the left bank lies *Keuchingen,* an artisan colony.

From the Pavilion (see above) a pleasant forest-path ascends to (^{3}/$_4$ hr.) the ruined castle of **Montclair** (1060 ft.), destroyed in 1350 by Elector Baldwin of Trèves (key kept by the park-keeper at Mettlach). — On the left bank of the Saar, opposite the N. point of the Montclair hills, rises the **Clef** (1475 ft.; rfmts. on Sun.), reached from Keuchingen in 1^1/$_2$ hr. by a white-marked path ascending to the left from the highroad. The hill was once fortified as the key to this district.

Beyond Mettlach the train tunnels through the heights of Montclair (see above), round which the Saar makes a considerable circuit:

30^1/$_2$ M. **Merzig** (570 ft.; *Hôtel Hoffmann, Trierscher Hof,* both very fair), an industrial town with 7500 inhab., on the wooded right bank of the Saar, is of ancient origin *(Marciacum)*. The *Roman Catholic Church,* a late-Romanesque (transitional) basilica of the end of the 12th cent., with a lofty dome over the crossing, round-arched windows, and pointed arcades, was restored in 1887-88. The Gothic *Protestant Church* was built in 1865. The *Rathaus* dates from 1625. About 1 M. lower is a large *Lunatic Asylum,* behind which rises the *Galgenberg* (view).

A light railway runs to *Büschfeld* (on the Wemmetsweiler and Nonnweiler railway, p. 189).

32 M. *Fremmersdorf;* 35 M. *Beckingen,* the station for *Ret-lingen,* on the left bank (bridge), whence the ruin of *Siersberg* may be reached in ³/₄ hr. — 38 M. *Dillingen* (595 ft.; Schmitt), with 6750 inhab. and large armour-plate works, is the junction for the Niedtal line to *Busendorf* (Metz, Diedenhofen; p. 199), and for a branch-line in the Primstal to (8 M.) *Primsweiler,* a station on the railway from Wemmetsweiler to Nonnweiler (p. 189).

40¹/₂ M. **Saarlouis** (600 ft.). From the rail. station, which is situated in the manufacturing town of *Fraulautern* (Kaiserhof; 5750 inhab.), a narrow-gauge branch-line runs to (2 M.) the district-town of *Saarlouis* (Rheinischer Hof; Zwei Hasen), which contains 8300 inhab. and lies on the left bank of the Saar. It was formerly a fortress, constructed in 1680-85 by Vauban for Louis XIV., but is now used as a military depôt only. The Rathaus contains tapestry presented by Louis XIV. Near the market-place is a fine war monument, by Wandschneider (1910). — About 2 M. to the N. (light railway) is *Wallerfangen,* prettily situated, with a park and the fayence manufactory of Messrs. Villeroy & Boch (p. 187).

The line now makes a bend to the left, round a loop of the Saar. 42¹/₂ M. *Ensdorf,* connected with Saarlouis by tramway; 45 M. *Bous* (610 ft.), junction of the branch-line from Metz to Saarbrücken mentioned at p. 203. 49 M. *Völklingen* (625 ft.; Rheinischer Hof; Kaiserhof), with 13,600 inhab. and a large foundry, is another junction of the above-mentioned branch-line. — 51 M. *Luisental* (650 ft.); 53 M. *Burbach-Malstatt* (p. 204), with a large foundry.

55 M. *Saarbrücken* (see p. 204).

26. The Hochwald and the Hunsrück.

THE HUNSRÜCK, the S.W. part of the Rhenish slate mountains (p. 219), bounded by the Rhine, the Moselle, the Saar, and the Nahe, consists of an undulating schistose plateau intersected by isolated ranges of harder rock, mixed with quartz and running from S.W. to N.E. In a narrower sense the name is restricted to the triangle between the Rhine and the Moselle, while the whole S.W. district is known as the *Hochwald,* the E. part as the *Soonwald.* — The *Verein für Mosel, Hochwald, und Hunsrück,* with its seat in Trèves, has issued a detailed guidebook (7th edit., Kreuznach, 1908; 3 *M*).

FROM TRÈVES TO TÜRKISMÜHLE, 47 M., railway in 3 hrs. (fares 3 *M* 70, 2 *M* 40 pf.). — *Trèves,* see p. 175. The train descends the valley of the Moselle to (3 M.) *Ruwer* (p. 175), then ascends the valley of the Ruwer, skirting the slopes of the wine-growing Grüneberg, and passing *Grünhausen* and *Casel* (see p. 175). — 6 M. *Waldrach* (525 ft.; Thilmany). To the left opens the valley of the Riveris, from which a Roman aqueduct, still in part recognizable, led to Trèves. — We continue to ascend the valley of the Ruwer at a somewhat steep gradient, passing numerous bridges and cuttings. 8¹/₂ M. *Sommerau* (640 ft.), commanded by a ruined

castle; 11 M. *Pluwig* (765 ft.); 15 M. *Lampaden;* 17 M. *Hentern,*
with the remains of a Roman villa. — 18 M. *Zerf* (Seiler), 1 M.
from the railway-station of which is the prettily situated village
of *Nieder-Zerf* (Nikolas Schneider), whence we may walk through
the wood to (7 M.) Saarburg (p. 186). — 22¹/₂ M. *Schillingen;*
24¹/₂ M. *Kell* (1445 ft.; Lang), with 1000 inhab., in the Errwald.
We cross the watershed between the Moselle and the Nahe (1710 ft.).
— 29¹/₂ M. *Reinsfeld.*

33 M. **Hermeskeil** (1975 ft.; *Wagner,Wommer,* in the village;
Otten, at the railway-station), the principal place in the Hochwald,
with 2200 inhab., is the junction of a line to Simmern and Bingerbrück (see below and p. 192).

We now descend the wooded valley of the Löser viâ (36¹/₂ M.)
Bierfeld, pass through a tunnel leading into the valley of the
Prims, and cross a viaduct. 38 M. *Nonnweiler,* the junction of
a branch-line to Büschfeld (p. 187). 40 M. *Otzenhausen* (Meyer);
43¹/₂ M. *Sötern.* — 47 M. *Türkismühle,* see p. 206.

The *Hunnenring,* on the hill 2¹/₂ M. to the N. of Otzenhausen, with
a circumference of nearly 1 M., is the largest and best-preserved of the
prehistoric fortresses in the Rhineland. It consists of loose blocks of
sandstone and is highest on the N. side (60 ft.), where it was most exposed to attack. On the S. side, where the hill falls off rapidly, there is an
outer rampart, ca. ¹/₂ M. in length. Within the circumvallation is a spring.
— From the Hunnenring viâ *Züsch* to Hermeskeil is a walk of 1³/₄ hr.

FROM HERMESKEIL TO SIMMERN, 46 M., railway in 3 hrs. (fares
3 ℳ 50, 2 ℳ 30 pf.). — *Hermeskeil,* see above. After passing the
two small stations of *Rascheid* and *Pölert* we cross the valley of
the Rossbach by a viaduct. — 8 M. *Dhronecken* (1295 ft.), with a
ruined castle; 10 M. *Thalfang* (1475 ft.; Johannes; Post), a village with 560 inhab., a Protestant church of the 13th cent., and a
modern Roman Catholic church. — 13 M. *Deuselbach,* the starting-
point for an ascent of the *Erbeskopf* (2677 ft.), the highest point
of the Hochwald (1¹/₂ hr.). At the top is a tower commanding a
wide view. In the woods about 2¹/₄ M. to the E. (red-marked footpath), is the forester's house of *Hüttgeswasen,* with the good
Gethmann Inn, much frequented in summer (R. & B. 2¹/₄, pens.
4¹/₂ ℳ). This lies on the road from Birkenfeld (7 M.; p. 206) to
Morbach (7 M.; see below). — We cross the valley of the Sieben-
born by a viaduct and then thread a tunnel. At *Hoxel* we cross
the valley of the Hachenbach by another lofty viaduct. — 19¹/₂ M.
Morbach (1415 ft.; Hochwaldhof; Mettler-Thomas), with 1200 inhab., in a wooded neighbourhood. About ¹/₄ M. to the S. lies the
ruined choir of the Gothic Chapel of St. Cuno. Viâ Bruchweiler
and Kempfeld to (2¹/₂ hrs.) the Wildenburg, see p. 208.

23¹/₂ M. *Hinzerath* (Hector), 1 M. to the N. of which is the
Stumpfe Turm (1844 ft.), a Roman watch-tower 35 ft. in height,
restored in the middle ages and commanding a wide view.

The Moselle road diverges from the Hunsrück road about $^1/_4$ M. to the W. of the Stumpfe Turm and leads to ·the village of *Longkamp* (Post), whence we may go on through the Tiefenbach-Tal to ($4^1/_2$ M.) Berncastel, or through the Kautenbach-Tal to (6 M.) Trarbach (see p. 172).

From Hinzerath a forest-path leads to the S.E. over the Graue Kreuz (2280 ft.) to ($1^3/_4$ hr.) *Bruchweiler* (p. 208).

$31^1/_2$ M. *Büchenbeuren* (1380 ft.; Schüler), in a wooded district (to Kirn, see p. 208). To the left are the hills of the *Idarwald*. — 33 M. *Sohren.* — 39 M. **Kirchberg** (1400 ft.; *Kleinschmidt; Bellevue*), a small town of 1200 inhab., $^2/_3$ M. to the S. of the railway-station and near the site of the Castle of Dumnissus, on the Roman road from Bingen to Trèves. In the middle ages it belonged to the Counts of Sponheim and afterwards to the Palatinate. The town is circular in shape and is enclosed by an old moat. To Ravengiersburg, see below. — 43 M. *Unzenberg.*

46 M. **Simmern** (railway-station, 1148 ft.; *Vollrath*, at the railway-station, R. $1^1/_2$-2, D. $1^1/_2$ *M; Post*, R. $1^1/_2$-3, D. $1^1/_2$-2 *M; Goldenes Lamm*, R. 2, D. $1^1/_2$-2 *M*, these two in the Markt-Str.), a district town of 2400 inhab., the chief place of the Hunsrück, is first mentioned in a document of 847. From 1358 to 1794 it was in the possession of the Counts Palatine, a collateral line of whom (Pfalz-Simmern) formed an independent duchy from 1410 to 1598. The *Château*, rebuilt in the middle of the 18th cent. after its destruction by the French in 1689, is now occupied by the district court and prison. In the market-place is the Protestant *Church of St. Stephen*, a late-Gothic building of the 15th cent., remodelled in 1716, and recently restored throughout. The nave and aisles are of equal height; the choir has no aisles. The church contains some tombs of the Palatine Princes (p. xxxiii), the most important of which is that of Duke Reichard (d. 1598) and his first wife, Juliane von Wied (d. 1575), adorned with reliefs from the Old and New Testaments. A flight of steps leads from the market-place to the upper town (the so-called *Römerberg*) and to the *Roman Catholic Church*, dating from 1749-52. — About $^3/_4$ M. to the W. is 'Auf dem Schmiedel', a Protestant educational establishment.

At the village of *Sargenroth*, $4^1/_2$ M. to the S. of Simmern, lies the *Nunkirche* (1430 ft.), a pilgrimage-chapel of the early middle ages. The adjacent Bismarck Tower (key at Sargenroth) commands¯ an extensive prospect. Thence we may proceed to the W. to (2 M.) *Ravengiersburg* (Engelmann), with a late-Romanesque abbey-church with some late-Gothic details, and recently restored. From this point we may go on viâ Rödern to ($4^1/_2$ M.) Kirchberg (see above).

FROM BOPPARD TO SIMMERN, 33 M., railway in. $2^1/_2$ hrs. (fares 3 *M* 10, 2 *M* 05). *Boppard* (210 ft.), see p. 224. The construction of the railway is of interest, and the first part ·is worked on the rack-and-pinion system, with a gradient of 1:16.5. The line turns into the Mühltal and runs at a slow pace along the· slope high above the floor of the valley. After threading a tunnel, it skirts the face of the Kalmutwand on retaining·walls, then sweeps to the

S., penetrates the Rauhe-Berg by two tunnels, and crosses the
Hubertus-Tal by a viaduct 164 yds. long and 165 ft. high. Another
viaduct takes it across the Rauschenloch, beyond which it passes
through two more tunnels. Views of the wooded valley are obtained
from every point.

3¹/₂ M. *Buchholz*, on the Roman road leading from Bingen to
Coblenz; the village lies 1¹/₂ M. to the W.

From the station of Buchholz a pleasant walk may be taken to
Boppard through the *Fraubach-Tal* (³/₄ hr.; paths marked by red arrows).
More picturesque routes are the forest-path through the *Josephinen-Tal*
and past the forester's house of *Kreuzberg* (1¹/₄ hr.; red disks) and the
path above the railway-track viâ the ridge of the *Kalmut* and the *Elfenlei*
(1³/₄ hr.; yellow signs). — To reach the Moselle we proceed to the village of *Buchholz* and pass (after 25 min.) about ¹/₂ M. to the left of
Windhausen. In 7 min. more we reach *Herschwiesen*, and about 25 min.
beyond this point follow the footpath leading to the left to the *Ehrenburg*. About 1¹/₂ M. farther on we reach *Brodenbach* (see p. 163). A
pleasant détour may be made to the château of *Schöneck*, which crowns
a wooded knoll about ³/₄ M. to the S. of Windhausen (view of the ruins
of *Rauschenschloss* in the background). Thence we go on through the
narrow *Ehrenbach-Tal* ('Klamm') to Brodenbach (2¹/₂ hrs.).

Beyond this point the train is connected with an ordinary loco-
motive. The line runs through the woods. — 5¹/₂ M. *Fleckertshöhe* (1445 ft.), at the intersection of the Castellaun highroad and
the Roman road.

From the station a broad forest-path (blue marks) ascends to (³/₄ hr.)
the **Fleckertshöhe** (1742 ft.), which affords an extensive view, including
the Seven Mountains, the Hochwald, and the Taunus. At the top is the
restaurant Zur Schönen Aussicht (also pension). — From Boppard (p. 224)
the Fleckertshöhe is reached in 2 hrs., either by following the Castellaun
highroad as far as the kilomètre-stone marked 7.4 and then diverging
to the left by a path through or skirting the pine-woods; or by crossing
the park of Marienberg and taking the path to the right through the
wood just short of the churchyard (indicated by blue arrows). — From
the Fleckertshöhe we may descend through meadows and woods viâ *Weiler*
to Bad Salzig (p. 226) in 1 hr.

7¹/₂ M. *Ehr.* — 9¹/₂ M. *Halsenbach* (1550 ft.), 1¹/₂ M. to the
S.E. of the village. The station lies near the intersection of the
roads from Boppard to Castellaun and from St. Goar to Brodenbach. About 1¹/₂ M. to the S., in the direction of Castellaun, rises
the *Lamscheider Sauerbrunnen*, a carbonic mineral spring, the
water of which is exported.

The station of Halsenbach is 8 M. from St. Goar viâ Hungeroth (see
p. 226) and 9¹/₂ M. from Brodenbach viâ *Liesenfeld, Nieder-* and *Ober-
Gondershausen, Beulich,* and *Morschhausen* (see p. 163). — From Ober-
Gondershausen (3 M. from the station of Halsenbach) a field-path runs
to the S. to (³/₄ hr.) the *Schmausen-Mühle* (inn), in the deep, wooded
valley of the *Beybach*. We may then descend this valley, passing the
Rabenlei, to (³/₄-1 hr.) the imposing ruin of **Waldeck**, the ancestral
seat of the Counts of Boos-Waldeck. Thence we ascend a forest-path
to the S. towards *Dorweiler* (which, however, we leave some distance to
the right) and continue to follow it viâ *Mannebach* and *Uhler* to (2¹/₂ M.)
Castellaun (p. 192). — Or we may ascend to the N. to *Beulich* and
follow the Moselle road to (2¹/₂-3 hrs.) Brodenbach (p. 163).

The next stations are *Leiningen, Pfalzfeld,* and *Lingerhahn*.

24 M. **Castellaun** (railway-station, 1125 ft.; *Schwan*, R. & B. 2, D. 1¹/₂ *ℳ; Frankhäuser*), a small and ancient town with 1500 inhab., belonged to the Counts of Sponheim from the 9th to the 14th cent. and afterwards to the Palatinate (see below). The village lies on a height 200 ft. above the station and is surrounded with woods. The castle, conspicuously situated on a rock above the town, was destroyed by the French in 1689.

Beyond Castellaun the train ascends to *Bell* (1525 ft.) and then descends through the *Külz-Tal* viâ *Alterkülz*, *Külz*, and *Keidel‑heim*, finally crossing the Simmerbach and threading a tunnel to —

33 M. *Simmern* (see p. 190).

FROM SIMMERN TO BINGERBRÜCK, 28¹/₂ M., railway in 2 hrs. (fares 2 *ℳ* 30, 1 *ℳ* 45). *Simmern*, see p. 190. — 4 M. *Argental* (1610 ft.), the highest point of the Hunsrück railway; 6 M. *Ellern* (1485 ft.).

8 M. *Rheinböllen* (1275 ft.; Railway Restaurant), the starting-point for an attractive day-trip through the *Soonwald*. The village (Schwan), with 1400 inhab., lies ³/₄ M. from the railway-station, on the road to Bacharach (p. 236).

About 2 M. to the S. of the railway-station rises the **Hochsteinchen** (2145 ft.), with a tower commanding a splendid *View. Other excursions may be made to (1¹/₂ hr.) *Tiergarten*, a forester's house and pension in a beautiful pine-forest; to (³/₄ hr.) the *Opeler Berg* (2035 ft.), surmounted by a trigonometrical signal and commanding an extensive view; to (³/₄ hr.) the forester's house of *Opel;* to (1 hr.) the *Weissenfels* (1772 ft.), with a wide view; to (¹/₂ hr.) the forester's house of *Neupfalz;* and to (1 hr.) *Stromberg* (see below).

9¹/₂ M. *Rheinböller Hütte* (1210 ft.; Zur Eisenhütte), with the large Puricelli foundry. On the hill to the right is the shooting-lodge of Karlsburg, belonging to Herr Puricelli. — 12 M. *Strom-berg-Neuhütte*, another large foundry. — We descend the *Gulden-bach-Tal* to —

15 M. **Stromberg** (770 ft.; *Post*, in the market-place; *Becker*, Haupt-Str., R. & B. at both 2¹/₄ *ℳ*), a small town with 1100 in-hab., situated on the old Roman road from Bingen to Trèves and formerly belonging to the Palatinate. The railway-station lies between lofty limestone cliffs, partly in the former bed of the Guldenbach, for which a new channel has been blasted. To the S. rises the Schlossberg, surmounted by the *Fastenburg,* a castle destroyed in 1689, the enceinte of which enclosed the town (inn at the top in summer). On the rock opposite the station on the W. is the château of *Goldenfels*, which was defended in 1793 for a whole day against 600 French soldiers by a Prussian lieutenant at the head of 37 men (memorial stone, shown on request).

At (17 M.) *Schweppenhausen* (635 ft.) begins the region of the vine. 18¹/₂ M. *Windesheim;* 20¹/₂ M. *Heddesheim*, whence a pleasant walk may be taken to (1¹/₄ hr.) Kreuznach viâ the view-point known as the 'Hungriger Wolf'. — On the sandstone hills to the right, beyond the Guldenbach, we descry the so-called *Eremitage*, a small convent hewn in the solid rock and occupied down to the beginning of the 19th century. At (23 M.) *Kloninger's Mühle* the train leaves the valley of the Guldenbach and runs to the N. to (24¹/₂ M.) *Langenlonsheim.* We here reach the Nahe Railway, which we follow to (28¹/₂ M.) *Bingerbrück* (see p. 214).

27. From Trèves to Metz viâ Diedenhofen.

64 M. RAILWAY (*Prussian State Railway* to Sierck, *Alsace & Lorraine Railway* thence to Metz) in 2-3 hrs. (fares 8 ℳ 10, 4 ℳ 90, 3 ℳ 30 pf.; express fares 9 ℳ 10, 5 ℳ 90, 3 ℳ 80 pf.).

The railway, a prolongation of that described in R. 23, ascends the valley of the Moselle above Trèves. — 1¹/₂ M. *Trier Süd.*

4¹/₂ M. **Karthaus** (445 ft.; *Gasthof zum Bahnhof*) is the junction of the Saarbrücken and Luxembourg lines (see pp. 186, 184). Adjoining the rail. station is an old Carthusian convent, now in the hands of the Franciscans, who have rebuilt the baroque church. Below the bridge at Conz (p. 186) the train crosses the *Saar*, affording a view of the pretty valley of that stream. 7¹/₂ M. *Wasserliesch*, ¹/₂ M. to the S. of Igel (p. 183); 13 M. *Wellen.* Near (14¹/₂ M.) *Nittel* the train passes through a tunnel. 18 M. *Wincheringen;* 23 M. *Palzem.* On the right, close to the Moselle, the château of *Thorn;* farther on, to the left, the château of *Bübingen.*

25 M. *Nennig.* The station is at the village of *Wies*, 1¹/₄ M. from the village of *Nennig*, at the S. end of which are the remains of a Roman villa, excavated in 1853, containing a remarkably fine *Mosaic Pavement, 49 ft. long and 33 ft. broad (now protected by a wooden covering; fee). It is nearly as large as the Mosaic of the Athletes in the Lateran at Rome, and surpasses that celebrated work in artistic execution. The principal scene represents a combat of gladiators, and is surrounded by seven medallions with animals, fencers, and musicians. — A charming walk may be taken from Nennig to Sierck.

29 M. *Perl* (Sons-Mersch Hotel), the last Prussian station; fine view from the Hammelsberg. — 32 M. **Sierck** (*Hôtel de Metz*, very fair), a small and ancient town with 1300 inhab., picturesquely situated on the right bank of the Moselle, and commanded by the ruins of a castle of the Dukes of Lorraine. About 6 M. to the N. E. is *Schloss Meinsberg* or *Mensberg*, popularly known as *Schloss Marlborough*, from its occupation by the great British general in 1705. — 36 M. *Mallingen;* 38¹/₂ M. *Königsmachern.*

43¹/₂ M. **Diedenhofen**, Fr. *Thionville* (*Hôtel Terminus*, at the station; *St. Hubert; Post*), a town of 13,000 inhab., is the

BAEDEKER's Rhine. 17th Edit. 13

centre of the iron industry of Lorraine and the junction of railways to Trèves, to Luxembourg, to Metz, and to Longuyon viâ Fentsch. The station lies on the right bank of the Moselle, the town on the left bank, to which a stone bridge crosses. The *Tour aux Puces* or *Floh-Turm* (Flea Tower), to the right of the bridge, is the oldest building in the town and contains a small historical collection (view; key at the hôtel de ville). The fortifications were rased in 1903, and new streets have been laid out on their site. — Besides the important railways mentioned above, Thionville is also the junction of branch-lines viâ (28 M.) *Teterchen* (p. 203) to (43¹/₂ M.) *Beningen* (p. 203) or to (44 M.) *Völklingen* (p. 203), and to (16 M.) *Bad Mondorf* (p. 185).

47 M. *Ueckingen*, with blast-furnaces; 49 M. *Reichersberg;* 51 M. *Hagendingen;* 53 M. *Maizières*, with blast-furnaces; 57¹/₂ M. *Woippy*, the scene of the last sally of the besieged French army on Oct. 7th, 1870; 60 M. *Metz-Nord* (Pl. A, 1). The train now crosses the Moselle, passes the station of *Metz-Schlachthaus*, crosses a small arm of the river, and enters the chief station of (66 M.) *Metz*.

Metz. — HOTELS. At the Railway Station: *Hôtel Royal* (Pl. g; C, 6), Kaiser-Wilhelm-Ring 23, very fair, R. 2-4, B. 1, D. 2-3 *M,* with restaurant; *Elsässer Hof,* at the W. end of the Kaiser-Wilhelm-Ring, with beer-restaurant, well spoken of. — In the Old Town: **Grand-Hôtel* (formerly Hôt. de l'Europe; Pl. a, C 4), Priester-Str. 4, first-class, R. from 2¹/₂, D. 3 *M; Grand-Hôtel de Metz* (Pl. b; C, 4), Priester-Str. 3, similar prices; *Englischer Hof* (Pl. d; B, 4), Korn-Str. 4, by the cathedral, R. 2-4, B. 1, D. 2¹/₂-3 *M; Hôtel de France* (Pl. c; C, 4), Kammer-Platz 25 (French); *Hôtel du Nord* (Pl. e; B, 4), Steinweg 4, with beer-restaurant and summer-theatre; *Post*, Priester-Str. 38, R. from 2, B. 1 *M*, well spoken of, with restaurant; *Rheinischer Hof*, Esplanaden-Str. 26, R. 1¹/₂-1³/₄ *M*, with restaurant. — *Evangelisches Hospiz*, Nanziger-Str. 4, cor. of the Mozart-Str. (Pl. A, 6), R. 1¹/₂-3 *M*.

CAFÉS. **Kaiser-Pavillon* (also restaurant), on the Esplanade (Pl. B, 5), with view; *Grand-Café Windsor*, Römer-Str. 9; *Turc, Schacht*, both in the Esplanaden-Str.; *Central* (French), Parade-Platz. — WINE RESTAURANT. *Moitrier*, Kapellen-Str. 2, cor. of the Römer-Str. WINE ROOMS. *Fritz zur Traube*, Tuch-Str. 1; *Mosella*, Priester-Str. 18; *Bodega* (American Bar), Priester-Str. 23. — BEER. **Braustübl*, Post-Str. 15 (Pl. C, 5); *Neues Münchener Kindl*, Bischof-Str. 11 (Pl. B, C, 5); *Löwenbräu*, Goldkopf-Str. 6 (Pl. C, 4); *Klosterhof*, Klein-Pariser-Str. 6; *Germania*, Römer-Allée 10 (Pl. B, 5); *Bürgerbräu*, Esplanaden-Str. 1, Kaiser Wilhelm-Platz, with garden; *Hofbräu*, Bank-Str. 1; *Franziskaner*, Kammer-Platz 55; *Restaurant* in the Central Railway Station, D. 2 *M*. — AUTOMATIC RESTAURANTS, in the *Römer-Str., Römer-Allée*, and elsewhere.

TRAMWAYS. 1 (white signs). From Moulins (comp. Pl. A, 2) viâ the Französische-Tor (Pl. A, 1), Parade-Platz (Pl. C, 4), and the Central Railway Station to Sablon. — 2 (blue signs). From the Outer Diedenhofener-Tor (Pl. B, 1) to the Französische-Tor and then as in No. 1. — 3 (yellow signs). From the North Railway Station (Metz-Nord; see above) viâ the Diedenhofener-Brücke (Pl. B, 2) to the Parade-Platz and then viâ the Neumarkt (Pl. C, 5) and the Central Railway Station to Montigny (comp. Pl. A, 6). — 4 (green signs). From the North Railway Station to the Neumarkt as in No. 3 and then viâ Mazellen-Platz (Pl. D, 5) to the East Cemetery at Plantières (comp. Pl. D, 6). — 5 (red signs). From Queuleu viâ Mazellen-Platz (Pl. D, 5) to the Neumarkt and then to Montigny as in No. 3.

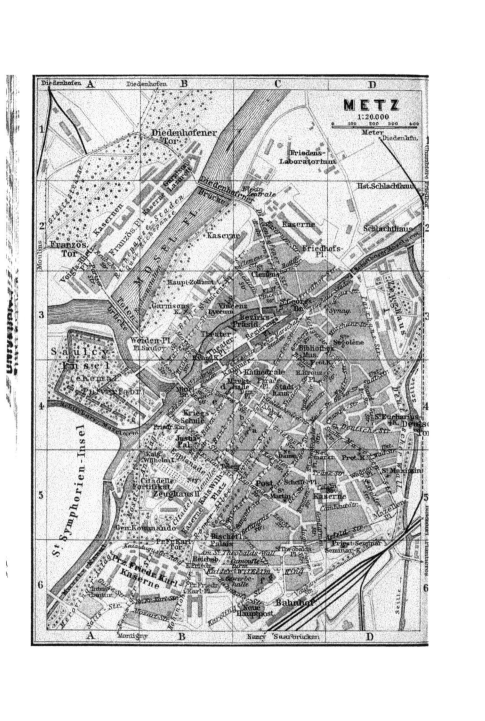

Cabs. *Taximeter Cabs.* For 1-2 pers. per 1000 mètres 50 pf., each addit. 500 mètres 10 pf.; 3-4 pers. per 750 mètres 50 pf., each addit. 375 mètres 10 pf.; at night, 1-4 pers. per 500 mètres 50 pf., each addit. 250 mètres 10 pf. Each box 20 pf. — *Ordinary Cabs.* To or from the rail. station 1 *M*, each pers. additional 20 pf.; per ¹/₂ hr. for 1-2 pers. 1 *M* 20 pf., 1 hr. 2 *M*, each pers. addit. 20, 40 pf.

Tourists' Enquiry Office *(Verkehrsverein)*, in the Pavilion, Kaiser-Wilhelm-Platz (Pl. B, 5), open on week-days, 8.30-12 & 2-6. — **Vosges Club** *(Vogesenklub)*, Post-Str. 15.

Post Office (Pl. C, 5) in the Martins-Platz; new building in progress at the Central Railway Station (Pl. C, 6). — **Telegraph Office** (Pl. B, C, 5), Esplanaden-Str. 10.

Metz, the fortified capital of German Lorraine and the headquarters of the 16th army-corps, with 54,000 inhab. (75,000 with the suburbs), much more than a half of whom are Germans, and a garrison of 25,000 men, lies in a wide basin on the *Moselle*, which, at the lower end of the town, is joined by the *Seille* on the right. Its origin antedates the Roman era. As *Divodurum* it was the chief town of the Gallic tribe of the *Mediomatrici*, whose name in a shortened form (Mettis) became that of the town. It was the seat of a bishop in the 4th cent.; became afterwards the capital of the kingdom of Austrasia; and in 870 passed into the possession of Germany. In the 14th cent. Metz became a free city of the German Empire. In 1552 it was taken by the French, and successfully maintained by them against Charles V. By the Peace of 1648 it was ceded to the French, who refortified it in the 17-18th cent. from the plans of Vauban and Cormontaigne. In 1871 it was again incorporated with the Empire of Germany. The town is surrounded by a ring of strong forts, and new advanced forts have been erected at a distance of 6 M. Great alterations have taken place since the inner walls were pulled down, and various new quarters have arisen, extending on the S. to the villages of *Montigny* and *Sablon*, and on the E. (beyond the Seille) to *Plantières* and *Queuleu*. The interior of the old town has also been greatly changed by new buildings.

The *Central Railway Station* (Pl. C, 6), built by Kröger of Berlin in the round-arched style, with a massive clock-tower, was opened in 1908. The Bahnhof-Str. and the wide Kaiser-Wilhelm-Ring, with its green lawns, occupy the site of the old ramparts and moat. The *Camoufle Tower* here is a mediæval structure. The *Equestrian Statue of Emp. Frederick*, by Dorrenbach, was unveiled in 1909. The *Prinz-Friedrich-Karl-Tor* (Pl. B, 5, 6), built in 1851 and named *Porte Serpenoise* after a mediæval gate on the same site, once formed the main entrance to the fortress. Farther to the W. is the handsome *Residence of the Commandant (General-kommando;* Pl. B, 5). — The only remnant of the old *Citadel*, built in the 16th cent. and razed in 1800, is a provision magazine. The other military structures all date from the 19th century. The Merovingian church of *St. Peter* (7th cent.), in the court of the

13 *

fortress, and a *Chapel of the Templars* (ca. 1200) are survivals of the old quarter of the town that lay on the site of the citadel.

The *Esplanade (Pl. B, 5), with its avenues of chestnuts and limes, its flower-beds, its statues, and its beautiful view, is the most charming part of Metz. On the E. side, adjoining the Kaiser-Wilhelm-Platz, stands a *Statue of Marshal Ney* (1769-1815), by Pêtre (1855). Farther on is an *Equestrian Statue of Emp. William I.*, by Ferd. von Miller (1892), with reliefs of the battle of Gravelotte and of the entry of the Crown Prince Frederick William in 1886. In other parts of the grounds are several figures of animals by Fratin and a fountain nymph by Charles Pêtre. The view from the parapet (Café Kaiser-Pavillon, p. 194) embraces several branches of the Moselle and the fortified heights on the left bank: to the W., Fort C. Alvensleben on the hill above Plappeville, Fort Friedrich Karl on the ridge of St. Quentin (with a Bismarck Tower on its slope); to the left the village of Scy with its church; farther on to the left, in the valley of the Moselle, Ars with its foundries, and in the distance on the right bank the high hill of St. Blaise, which is now included in the external line of the fortifications (p. 195). — The garden adjoining the Esplanade on the N., laid out by Marshal Boufflers in 1668, is adorned with a fine bronze statue by Ferdinand von Miller (1898) of General Field Marshal Prince Frederick Charles of Prussia, the conqueror of Metz in 1870. The *Court of Justice (Justizpalast;* Pl. B, 4) was begun in 1776 as a residence for the royal governor, but was diverted to its present use in consequence of the Revolution. — Broad flights of steps descend to the new *Kaiserbrunnen* and to the pleasure-grounds which extend along the Moselle to the S. as far as Montigny.

The *Priester-Strasse* and *Römer-Strasse*, running to the N. from the Esplanade and the Kaiser-Wilhelm-Platz, are the chief seats of business. The Fabert-Str., continuing the Priester-Str., ends at the Parade-Platz (Pl. C, 4), between the cathedral and the *Stadthaus* (1771). The square is adorned with a *Statue of Marshal Fabert* (1599-1662), a native of Metz, who distinguished himself in the campaigns of Louis XIV.

The *Cathedral (Pl. C, 4; *St. Stephen*), the finest edifice in the town, is a magnificent Gothic structure, begun under the influence of the Rheims school of architecture in the second half of the 13th century. The lofty nave was completed before 1392, the choir dates from 1486-1522. A thoroughgoing restoration, under the superintendence of *Tornow*, was taken in hand in 1875. The S.W. façade, with its huge window (78 ft. high and 42 ft. wide), was provided in 1895-1903 with a Gothic portal in place of the previous baroque one; among the elaborate sculptures is the Prophet Daniel (r.), with the features of Emp. William II. The Liebfrauen-Portal, at the angle of the S. side, was added in 1880-85 and is also richly sculptured. Since 1906 the restoration has been in charge of *Dombaumeister Schmitz*. The interior (open to visitors on week-days only, after 10.30 a.m. and after 3 p.m.) produces a very harmonious effect. Its total length is 404 ft., its breadth 101 ft. (across the transepts 154 ft.). The fine stained-glass windows in the S. aisle date from the 13th cent.; those in the nave are of the 14th and 15th cent.; those in the transept and the choir are of the 15th and early 16th cent.; and several others are modern. Seven steps lead from the S. aisle to a chapel that was originally the choir of the independent church of Notre-Dame-la-Rotonde. The chapel of the Sacrament, farther on, has rich vaulting. In the N. aisle is an old Roman bath, supposed to be from the Roman baths of Metz and formerly used as a font. The crypt contains tombs of 14th cent. bishops. The tower is 295 ft. high (110 steps to the first gallery, 105 more to the huge bell called the *Mutte*, and 78 thence to the highest gallery); it commands a wide view.

On the Moselle island to the N.W. of the cathedral are the *Provincial Offices (Bezirks-Präsidium;* Pl. C, 3), formerly the French prefecture, built in 1806. In the second court is the new building of the *Provincial Archives*, containing documents of Charlemagne, Lewis the German, Otho I., Frederick Barbarossa, and several popes (open 9-12 & 3-6). In the Theater-Platz is the *Theatre* (18th cent.), in front of which is a monumental fountain. Fine view of the cathedral. A *Protestant Church*, in the Romanesque style, has been built at the S. extremity of the island. — On the opposite bank of the river rise the *Church of St. Vincent* (Pl. B, C, 3), a structure of the 13-14th cent., with a façade of 1768-86, and the Prot. *Military Church* (Pl. B, 3), in the Gothic style, with a tower 318 ft. in height.

From the N. E. corner of the Parade-Platz the Birnbaum-Str. leads to the N. to the *Municipal Library (Stadt-Bibliothek;* Pl. C, 3) and the *Municipal Museum, both installed in an old Carmelite convent (Bibliothek-Str. 2). The library (open 10-4, Sat. 10-1; closed on Sun.) contains documents of the 13-17th cent., MSS. with miniatures, and old books printed at Metz (from 1482 on). The Museum (open free on Sun. 11-1 and 2-4 and on Wed. 2-4; at other times for a fee) contains Gallo-Roman antiquities, a few mediæval objects, a natural history collection, and a number of good pictures, all (unfortunately) shown under very unfavourable conditions.

Ground Floor. In the Ante-Chamber are some Renaissance carvings. STONE ROOM. Nos. 30 et seq., Gravestones from the Gallo-Roman town of Vicus Soliciæ (Soulosse; *e.g.* No. 37, Man and his wife in their shop); 26. Master and his servant, relief from a large sepulchral monument; 13, 9, 10, parts of other elaborate grave monuments; 304. Victory from Sablon, reproduction of a work of Italic-Greek origin recognized through coins bearing a similar design; 170. Isis, in the Pergamenian style, but (like the Victory) executed in Metz stone; Mithras altar; Altars of the

Gallic deities Sucellus and Nantosvelta in Roman garments; 294. So-called Merten Column in four sections, with reliefs; opposite, 463-466. Remains of a Christian marble sarcophagus of the 4th cent., in which the body of Emperor Lewis the Pious was laid (p. 253). In the annex: Part of a stone screen from St. Peter's (p. 195); oaken ceiling with fantastic paintings from the beginning of the 13th century.

Upper Floor. Rooms I-III and the glass-cases in the following rooms contain small prehistoric and Roman antiquities, a carved ivory tablet (10th cent.), and coins of Metz. — In Room IV begins the picture gallery. To the left, Netherlandish paintings: 111. Small landscape; 60. *Pieter van Boel*, Fruit; 74. *Adrian van Ostade*, Merry company. To the right: 115. *Corot*, Shepherd; 126. *Delacroix*, Bearing of the Cross. — Room V, to the right, Netherlandish portraits: *103. *Rembrandt*, Old man (1633); *94, *95, Portraits by *Jacques Gerhardt Cuyp* (1649); 77. Portrait on copper; 93. *P. Moreelse* (1631), 106. *P. Lesire* (1656), Portraits; 104, 96. Old Copies after Rembrandt and Van Dyck. Also French portraits: 40. Portrait from the 16th cent.; 122, 177. Portraits by *N. Largillière* (17th cent.); 99. *J. B. Greuze*, Portrait of a boy; to the left, 47. *Rigaud*, Louis XIV. — Room VI, to the right: 159. *Franç. Boucher*, Rustic family. By the entrance to the following room: 102. Portrait of Charles IX. of France, in Limoges enamel. — Room VII. Lorraine painters previous to 1870: 120. *Thomas Devilly*, Retreat from Russia; 270. *E. Bracht*, Moorland.

In the Geisberg-Str., to the N. of the Library, is an old municipal grain-magazine of the 16th cent., now used as a commissariat-store.

The Bibliothek-Str. ends on the E. at the Trinitarier-Str., which runs to the N., past the *Hôtel St. Livier* (a mediæval patrician's dwelling), to the early-Gothic *Church of St. Segolene* (Pl. D, 3), a building of the beginning of the 14th cent., rebuilt in 1897 and provided with two towers. The S. end of the Trinitarier-Str. abuts on the Heilige-Kreuz-Platz (Pl. C, 4), the highest ground in the town. Here, and also to the S., in the Judengasse, the St. Ludwigs-Platz, and sundry other streets, are many interesting old houses.

We cross the bridge between the Goldschmied-Str. and the Deutsche-Str. (Pl. C, D, 4), over a filled-in arm of the Seille, and proceed to the E., passing the *Church of St. Eucharius* (12-15th cent.), to the —

*Deutsche Tor (Pl. D, 4), a highly effective fortified gate on the Seille, along which the old E. ramparts of the city ran. The two towers next the town date from the 13th century. The roadway, expanded in 1892 by the street to the S. and the bridge, is now closed. The strong external towers date from the 15th cent.; their battlements were added in the 19th century. The court and internal chambers are fitted up as a museum, with objects found on the demolition of the citadel (p. 195), other stone monuments of Metz, old views and plans of the town, relics of 1870, seals, coins, costumes and household utensils of Lorraine, and so on (fee).

Farther down the Seille part of the mediæval fortifications has been preserved. Beyond the rail. station of Schlachthaus (Pl. D, 2; p. 194) we reach the *Chambière Cemetery*, with a monument to the French soldiers who died at Metz in 1870.

FROM METZ TO PAGNY, 12¹/₂ M., railway in ¹/₂-³/₄ hr. (fares
1 ℳ 60, 1 ℳ 10, 70 pf.). — Soon after leaving Metz, we pass on
the left *Fort St. Privat*, now *Prinz August von Württemberg*,
and then the tree-girt château of *Frescati*, where the capitulation
of Metz was signed on Oct. 27th, 1870. Close by is a huge shed
for military air-ships. A little farther on, the train crosses the
river. — 5 M. *Ars-sur-Moselle*, with iron-works, lies at the beginning of the valley of the *Mance*, up which runs the road to
(21¹/₂ M.) Gravelotte (p. 202). On the hill is the *Kronprinz Fort*.
In the Moselle valley, between Ars and *Jouy-aux-Arches* (fair inn
at the N. end of the village), on the right bank, are situated extensive remains of a *Roman Aqueduct* erected ca. 100 A. D., which
brought water to Metz from the source of the Gorze (a distance of
15 M.) and here crossed the Moselle in an arched bridge, ³/₄ M. long
and 60 ft. high. Seven of its arches and one pier are still standing
at Ars, and 10 arches at Jouy. On the hill of *St. Blaise* (1195 ft.),
above Jouy, is the *Graf Haeseler Fort*. — 7 M. *Ancy*, on the
Moselle. — 8¹/₂ M. *Novéant*, the German frontier-station, lies at
the entrance to the valley of the *Gorze* (p. 201). A new bridge
crosses the Moselle to Corny, the headquarters of Prince Frederick
Charles during the investment of Metz. — 12¹/₂ M. *Pagny* is the
French frontier-station. Thence to *Nancy* and *Paris*, see *Baedeker's
Northern France*. From Pagny a railway runs viâ Arnaville,
Chambley (14¹/₂ M.), and *Mars-la-Tour* (p. 201) to Conflans-Jarny.

FROM METZ TO AMANWEILER, 10 M., railway in 36 min. (fares
1 ℳ 40, 85, 50 pf.). The railway skirts the suburb of Montigny,
crosses the Moselle, and stops at (3¹/₂ M.) *Longeville*, at the foot
of the hill of St. Quentin. At (8 M.) *Moulins* (electric railway, see
p. 194) it reaches the valley of *Moutveau*, which it ascends viâ
(6 M.) *Châtel-St-Germain* to (10 M.) *Amanweiler* (*Amanvillers;*
hotel opposite the railway-restaurant), 1³/₄ M. from St. Privat(p. 203).
From Amanweiler to Verdun, see *Baedeker's Northern France*.

FROM METZ TO DILLINGEN, 37¹/₂ M., railway in 2 hrs. — 2¹/₂ M.
Vantoux-Vallières; 4¹/₂ M. *Nouilly*, with the battlefield of Aug. 14th,
1870 (see p. 200); 6 M. *Failly;* 20 M. *Anzelingen;* 24¹/₂ M. *Busendorf* (p. 188). — 37¹/₂ M. *Dillingen*, see p. 188.

The Battle Fields of August 14th, 16th, and 18th, 1870.

The three excursions require a day each, but it is quite practicable
to combine the visits to the battlefields of Aug. 16th and 18th by using
a motor-car or a bicycle and by taking the railway to Novéant and back
from Amanweiler. Readers who understand German will find more details in the guidebooks and maps sold at the booksellers (25 pf.-2 ℳ).
The military visitor will find 'Taktische Wanderungen' by *Lieutenant
Colonel Liebach* indispensable (3 ℳ). A commemorative ceremony is
held yearly on Aug. 15th in the ravine between Gravelotte and St. Hubert,
and the graves are decked with flowers. — Carriages or motor-cars are
best procured through the Tourists' Enquiry Office (p. 195).

The BATTLE OF AUGUST 14TH marks the first act in the bloody struggle as a result of which the French army was cooped up in the fortress of Metz. Towards midday the German advance guard had come into touch with the enemy on its retreat from Saarbrücken. About 3.30 p.m. the German General von der Goltz began the attack with parts of the VII. Army Corps. The chief bone of contention was the line passing through *Colombey* and *Nouilly*, two villages which have given the German name to the battle, while the French call it the *Battle of Borny*, after the headquarters of Marshal Bazaine. Colombey was taken about 5 p.m. and successfully maintained against superior forces, while to the N. the I. Army Corps under Manteuffel advanced toward Nouilly. By 9 p.m. the French had been forced back under the guns of the fortress and their strategic retreat, begun in the morning, had been so delayed that the German army now surrounding the S. side of Metz was able to overtake them two days later. The losses of the Germans amounted to 222 officers and 4784 men, those of the French to 3608 officers and men.

CIRCULAR DRIVE. Those who visit the battlefields by carriage proceed viâ Plantières, Borny, Grigy, Ars-Laquenexy, and Aubigny to Colombey, then go on viâ Lauvallière and Noisseville to Nouilly, and return viâ Vantoux (20 M. in all).

WALKERS take the railway to *Peltre* (p. 203). Thence they ascend viâ *Mercy-le-Haut* and *Ars-Laquenexy* to (1½ hr.) *Aubigny*, the point at which General von der Goltz began his advance. It has a château and a monument to the 45th Infantry. In ¼ hr. more we reach *Colombey*, the château of which still lies in ruins. Adjoining the park is a large Military Cemetery, with a fine monument to the 13th Infantry. From the cemetery we proceed to the N. along the *Toten-Allée* ('Avenue of the Dead'), passing numerous monuments, then take the road to the right, and follow the pine-walk diverging to the left to (½ hr.) *Lauvallière*. By following the road farther to the W. we reach the tavern of *Amitié*, to the right of which is a monument to the I. Army Corps, commanding a survey of the whole battlefield. About ½ M. to the N. lies the village of *Noisseville*, which was again the centre of violent contests on Aug. 31st and Sept. 1st, when Bazaine made a determined but ineffectual attempt to break through the German lines. About ¾ M. to the S. is the large French monument, with a bronze group by E. Hannaux, a native of Metz. At *Nouilly* (p. 199) we regain the railway, by which we return to Metz.

The battlefields of August 16th and 18th lie to the W. of Metz, on the roads to Verdun. On Aug. 15th the III. Prussian Army Corps, under General von Alvensleben II., crossed the Moselle in the night and advanced as far as *Gorze*.

At about 10 p.m. on AUGUST 16TH the III. Army Corps surprised the retreating French army at *Flavigny* and *Vionville*. Both these places were captured at about 11.30 a.m.; but farther advance was impossible in the face of the superior numbers of the French troops. Several cavalry charges were made to repel the French attacks. Among these was the famous charge of the 7th Cuirassiers and the 16th Uhlans (Bredow's Brigade), which dis-

Battle of Aug. 18 th, 1870.
Positions at 6 p.m.
(Right wing of the French flanked by the
Guards and the 12 th, Corps. — — Posit.
of the French at the beginning. — — Posit.
of the Germans at the ceasing of the battle

Battle of Aug. 16 th, 1870.
Positions in the evening
(ceasing of the battle)

Battle of Aug. 14 th, 1870.

☐☐☐ Posit^{ns} at the beginning of the battle.

---- Positions occupied by the Germans towards the end of the battle.

persed two regiments of French infantry and four gun-batteries and
has been celebrated by Freiligrath in his 'Todesritt'. No less
bloody was the struggle to the W. of Vionville at *Tronville* and
Mars-la-Tour, where the X. Army Corps (under General von Voigts-
Rhetz) made its attack about 3 p.m. and managed to maintain its
position against the overwhelming superiority of the French, with
the aid of various costly attacks of the Dragoon Guards. About
6.45 p.m. the finest cavalry engagement of the whole war took place
here. Six regiments of French cavalry were dispersed by twenty-
one squadrons of the Rheinbaben division. After it had lasted
nearly twelve hours darkness put an end to the battle, in the final
stages of which 67,000 Germans with 222 guns were opposed to
138,000 French with 476 guns. In spite of their numerical superiority the French did not succeed in regaining their lost ground or in
opening the road to Verdun. Their losses amounted to 879 officers
and 16,128 men, those of the Germans to 711 officers and 15,079 men.

To visit the battlefields we proceed by railway to *Novéant* (p. 199)
and go on thence by omnibus to (¹/₂ hr.) **Gorze** *(Hôtel-Restaurant Ha-
billon,* carriages to hire; *Hôt. Sanssouci).* The drive round the battlefields leads viâ Flavigny and Vionville to Mars-la-Tour and returns to
Gorze viâ Vionville and Rezonville (15 M. in all).

Walkers take 4-5 hrs. for a satisfactory survey of the battlefields,
or (if Mars-la-Tour be included) 7-8 hrs. At the upper end of Gorze
we ascend to the left, then take the footpath diverging to the right,
which passes the farm of St. Thiébault and ascends to (³/₄ hr.) the hill
of *Flavigny,* on which are various monuments to German regiments. We
then proceed to the left to (¹/₄ hr.) the *Friedrich-Karl-Stein,* which
commands an extensive view. In the direction of Rezonville we descry
a monument occupying the spot where King William, on the evening of
Aug. 17th, gave the orders for the battle of the following day. We next
descend to (¹/₂ hr.) **Vionville**, where there are two other German monuments. The road to (3¹/₂ M.) Mars-la-Tour passes more monuments and
then crosses the French frontier. In **Mars-la-Tour** *(Café du Commerce)*
are a French monument and the monument of the German Dragoon Guards,
while a little farther on, to the right, is that of the 16th Infantry.
Near the church are a monument to Joan of Arc and a 'Musée Militaire'
with relief-plans of the battles. Near the railway-station (p. 199) is the
interesting French monument by Bogino. — Proceeding to the E. from
Vionville, we pass a spot where enormous numbers of soldiers were buried
and the so-called 'Denkmalsbank' (a memorial bench), and reach (2¹/₄ M.)
Rezonville, the chief point d'appui of the French and retained by them
until the close of the battle. Memorial tablets indicate the houses in which
King William, Bismarck, and Moltke spent the night of Aug. 18-19th.
About ³/₄ M. to the N., on the 'Römer-Strasse', which now forms the
frontier, are monuments to the 3rd and 16th Hussars and to the Bredow
brigade. — From Rezonville we may either proceed viâ Gravelotte to
(6 M.) the railway-station of Châtel (p. 199) or return to Gorze by the
road to the S., passing two other German monuments.

The **Battle of August 18th** decided the fate of the French army
and the fortress of Metz. Bazaine had withdrawn his forces in the
direction of Metz and had taken up a strong position on the hill at
the farther side of the valley of the Mance, extending from Point-
du-Jour to St. Privat. As the Germans were ignorant how far the

French line extended to the N., the IX. Prussian Army Corps (under General von Manstein) began the battle towards midday by a frontal attack near *Vernéville.* General von Steinmetz then ordered the VIII. Corps (under General von Goeben) to advance at *Gravelotte* and the VII. Corps (under General von Zastrow), farther to the right, to advance also. The attacking parties suffered terrible losses, but in the face of the strong French position were unable to gain any considerable advantage except the capture of the farm of St. Hubert below Point-du-Jour, which was effected in the afternoon by parts of the VIII. Corps. The troops of the Corps of Guards and of the XII. (Royal Saxon) Guards, which at first had been arranged in echelon formation, consequently diverged to the N.E. and captured *Ste. Marie-aux-Chênes* about 3.30 p.m., after which the Guards (about 5 p.m.) made a sanguinary but ineffectual attempt to storm *St. Privat.* A second attempt at 7.30 p.m., preceded by a heavy cannonade and the outflanking of the French right wing by the Saxons at *Roncourt,* was more successful. The French broke up in confusion. Their left wing, however, at Point-du-Jour, maintained its position against the attack delivered under cover of darkness with the aid of the II. Army Corps and did not retire upon Metz until the morning. The number of Germans engaged in the battle amounted to 230,000, that of the French to 180,000. The Germans lost 899 officers and 19,260 men, the French 609 officers and 11,700 men.

CARRIAGE DRIVE viâ Moulins and Rozérieulles to Gravelotte, then viâ Vernéville and Ste-Marie-aux-Chênes to St. Privat, returning viâ Amanweiler and through the Montveau valley (27^1/$_2$ M. in all). From Amanweiler we may also use the railway.

WALKERS, starting at the railway-station of *Ars* (p. 199), on the Gravelotte road, ascend the valley of the Mance to the Protestant chapel and then take the footpath, to the right, which climbs the ravine and (^{1}/$_4$ hr.) crosses the bare ridge in the direction of the new *Feste Kaiserin.* At *St. Hubert* (inn) it reaches the Metz and Verdun road. The fort (no admission) occupies the height of *Point-du-Jour*, which, during the battle, was the chief point d'appui of the French left wing. At St. Hubert itself and in the ravine below are several German monuments. From St. Hubert we ascend to (^{1}/$_2$ hr.) —

Gravelotte (*Cheval d'Or, Poste*, both very fair), which formed the centre of the right wing of the German position, consisting of the 7th and 8th Prussian Corps. At the E. end of the village is a large soldiers' cemetery, to which most of the graves scattered over the plain have been removed. Adjoining is a large *Memorial Colonnade, with an Angel of the Resurrection in bronze-gilt by L. Cauer, busts and medallions of the German leaders and generals round Metz, and memorials of the fallen (1905). On the road to Rezonville, opposite the Cheval d'Or, is a *Military Museum*. The parish-church has been rebuilt since the war.

In the middle of the village the road divides, both branches leading to Verdun. On that to the right (N.) lies the farm of *Mogador*, near which (l.) is a rock with an inscription, marking the spot whence Emp. William witnessed the battle; it affords a good survey of the opposite heights, then occupied by the French. *Malmaison*, the next farm on this road, was occupied by the 9th Prussian Corps d'Armée, the lines of which extended along the road diverging to the right as far as (3 M.)

Vernéville. Near Vernéville, to the right of the road to Chantrenne, are monuments to the 9th Rifles (*Jäger*) and the 36th Infantry. To the W. (road leading to the left in the village) is a column erected by the 18th Division.

On the road from Vernéville to (3 M.) *Amanweiler* (p. 199) is the monument of the 9th Regiment of Field Artillery, which surprised the French corps stationed at Amanweiler about 11.30 a.m., but became in its turn the object of the concentrated French cannonade. Farther on are various monuments which indicate the line of attack followed by the right wing of the Corps of Guards. A finger-post shows the way to (20 min.) the monument of the Hessian Division, which was combined with the 18th Prussian Division to form the 9th Army Corps. The monument stands near the railway from Amanweiler to Verdun, on the French frontier, which here projects in the form of a triangle. — The road from Vernéville to (4 M.) Sainte-Marie-aux-Chênes (see below) leads across French territory, passing through *Habonville* and near *St. Ail.*

Amanweiler, where we regain the railway, lies $1^3/_4$ M. to the S. of **St. Privat,** the chief point d'appui of the French right wing. Here there are an extensive *Military Museum* (adm. 40 pf.; café in the same building), with plans of battles, panoramas, and relics, and also two memorial monuments. There are other German monuments at the N. end of the village. The keeper of the graves at St. Privat has the key of the conspicuous view-tower, to the S.W. of the village, which was erected as a general monument to the German Guards.

To the W. of St. Privat, on the road to (2 M.) *Ste-Marie-aux-Chênes,* are monuments to various regiments of the Guards. In the village is a French monument. — At *Roncourt,* $^3/_4$ M. to the N. of St. Privat, is the König-Albert-Haus, a museum with relics of the Saxon troops.

28. From Metz to Bingerbrück viâ Saarbrücken and Neunkirchen. Valley of the Nahe.

137 M. RAILWAY in $4^1/_3$-$6^1/_3$ hrs. (fares 17 ℳ 10, 16 ℳ 40, 9 ℳ 90 pf.; express fares 19 ℳ 10, 18 ℳ 40, 10 ℳ 40 pf.). — Saarbrücken is also connected with Metz (50 M., in $2^1/_2$ hrs.) by a branch-railway viâ Courcelles, Teterchen, and Völklingen.

Metz, see p. 194. The train skirts the suburb of Queuleu. — $4^1/_2$ M. *Peltre,* the starting-point for a visit to the battlefield of Aug. 14th, 1870 (p. 200).

8 M. *Courcelles-an-der-Nied,* the junction of a branch-railway up the valley of the Nied to *Teterchen* (p. 194), where it unites with a branch-line from Diedenhofen and goes on to join the Saarbrücken and Trèves railway at Bous or Völklingen (p. 194). — $13^1/_2$ M. *Remilly,* junction of the Saarburg and Metz line (p. 492); 18 M. *Herlingen;* $21^1/_2$ M. *Maiweiler;* $24^1/_2$ M. *Falkenberg;* $27^1/_2$ M. *Tetingen;* 31 M. *St. Avold,* an industrial place with 3500 inhab. and a garrison of 2500 men; $34^1/_2$ M. *Oberhomburg,* on the Rossel.

From (38 M.) *Beningen* branch-lines run to the N. to *Hargarten* and *Teterchen* (see above), and to the S. to *Farschweiler, Hundlingen,* and Saargemünd (p. 489).

40 M. *Kochern.* — 43 M. *Forbach* (Karsch), a town with 8600 inhab. and large papier maché works, is dominated by the Schlossberg, which is crowned with a view-tower and a ruined castle. The

small museum contains antiquities found in the neighbourhood. In the distance, to the right, rises the Spicherer Berg (p. 205). — Beyond (45 M.) *Stieringen* the train crosses the *Saar*.

50 M. **Saarbrücken.** — RAILWAY STATION (Pl. E, 2; Restaurant, very fair), in St. Johann, on the right bank of the Saar.

HOTELS (lifts, electric light, and hot-air heating in the larger houses). In St. Johann: *Rheinischer Hof* (Pl. a; E, 3), Bahnhof-Str. 43, ¹/₂ M. from the station, R. 3-5¹/₂, B. 1, D. 3 *M; *Messmer* (Pl. b; E, 2), Victoria-Platz, near the station, with good wine-room ('Malepartus'), R. 2¹/₂, B. 1, D. 2¹/₂ *M; *Grand-Hôtel Schwan* (Pl. c; E, 2), Kaiser-Str. 44, near the station, R. 2¹/₂-3¹/₂, B. 1, D. 2¹/₂, S. 1³/₄ *M*, with restaurant; *Hôtel-Restaurant Terminus* (Pl. d; E, 2), Reichs-Str. 19, opposite the station, R. 2¹/₂-5, B. 1, D. 2 *M*, Munich and Pilsen beer; *Kaiserhof* (Pl. e; E, 2), Victoria-Str., with restaurant; *Korn* (Pl. f; E, 2); *Bristol* (Pl. g; E, 3), Sulzbach-Str., with restaurant and garden. — In Saarbrücken: *Monopol* (Pl. i; E, 3), Hohenzollern-Str., with restaurant. — In Burbach: *Hôtel-Restaurant Reichshof*. — BEER at the *Neue Münchener Kindl*, by the New Bridge, with view-terrace, and at the *Alte Münchener Kindl*, Victoria-Str., both in St. Johann. — *Schloss-Café*, by the New Bridge in St. Johann (also confectioner). — *River Baths* above the old bridge.

ELECTRIC TRAMWAYS from the railway-station of St. Johann to Saarbrücken, either direct across the New Bridge, or viâ Malstatt-Burbach and the Kaiser-Wilhelm-Brücke. Cars also run to the Schanzenberg, St. Arnual (p. 205), Luisental (p. 188), Friedrichstal (p. 205), and other points in the environs.

Saarbrücken (597 ft.), on the left bank of the Saar, formerly the residence (1381-1793) of the Counts and Princes of Nassau-Saarbrücken, was in 1909 combined with the sister-towns of *St. Johann* and *Burbach-Malstatt*, on the right bank, to form a single municipality with ca. 100,000 inhabitants. It is the centre of the Saar coal-district, which, extending on the E. to the Bavarian Palatinate and on the S. to Lorraine, produces 11 million tons annually. Five-sixths of the coal-pits are owned by the State. St. Johann is entirely modern, dating its importance from the construction of the railway, which does not touch Saarbrücken. The towers of the *Railway Station* (Pl. E, 2) still show traces of the French bombardment of Aug. 3rd, 1870. From the station the Reichs-Str. (passing the *Bergwerks-Direction*, or Royal Mining Office; Pl. 3) and the Victoria-Str. lead to the *Neue Brücke* (Pl. E, 3), the central and busiest of the three bridges connecting the banks of the Saar. Below the bridge on the right bank of the Saar is the large harbour, with ingenious apparatus for loading the barges which carry coal on the canalized Saar. — In the Kaiser-Wilhelm-Platz is the Protestant *Church of St. John* (Pl. F, 3), built in the Gothic style in 1894-98, with a tower 266 ft. in height. Opposite is the *Rathaus* (Pl. E, F, 3), erected by Hauberisser in 1897-1900, containing an elaborate banquet-hall with wall-paintings by Wrage. Hard by is the *Roman Catholic Church* (Pl. F, 4), an edifice of the 18th century. — In the Markt-Passage (Pl. E, F, 4) is the new *Saar Museum*, containing industrial and natural history collections (adm. on Sun. 11-6, 25 pf., Wed. 2-6, 50 pf.).

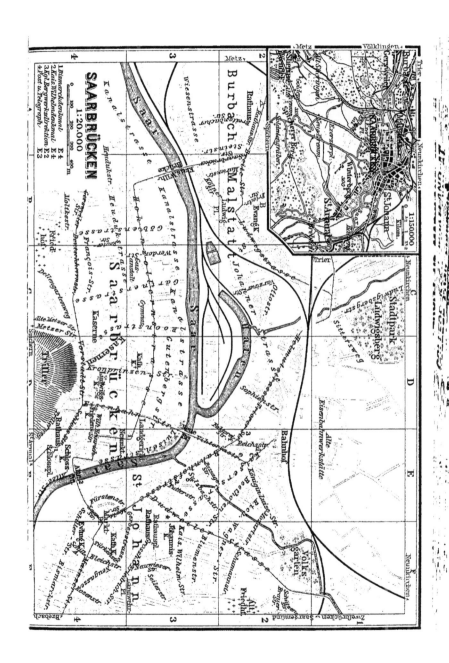

The *Alte Brücke* (Pl. E, 4; Old Bridge), built in the 16th cent. on the same spot as the earlier mediæval and Roman bridges, is adorned with an equestrian statue of William I., by Donndorf (1904). The bridge commands a fine view of Saarbrücken, with the Winterberg, St. Arnual, and Halberg to the left.

On the left bank we proceed past the *Schloss-Kirche* (Pl. E, 4), which contains some monuments of the princes, to the Schloss-Platz. The banquet-hall of the *Rathaus* (Pl. E, 4; 18th cent.) contains paintings by A. von Werner, presented to the town by Emp. William I., commemorating the events of July 19th to Aug. 9th, 1870 (see below). In front of the *Château*, which was burned down by the French in 1793 and has been restored in a somewhat makeshift manner, stands a *Bismarck Monument*. — A narrow road leads from the Schloss-Platz to the *Triller* (Pl. D, 4), an eminence with gardens (fine view). — The *Ludwigs-Kirche* (Pl. D, 4) dates from 1762-75.

On the heights of *Spicheren*, about 3 M. to the S. of Saarbrücken, on 6th Aug., 1870, a sharp engagement took place between the Prussians and French, in which the latter, although numerically superior, were obliged to retreat. A visit to the battlefield occupies 3-4 hrs. (carr. ca. 12 ℳ). The Metz road (Pl. C, 4) is followed, passing on the right, just outside the town, the old drill-ground (Lulustein), which is often heard of in the annals of the military operations of 1870. About $1/_4$ M. farther on, to the right, is the *Ehrental*, a military cemetery with numerous monuments. $3/_4$ M. '*Neue Bremm*' Inn; $1/_2$ M. '*Goldene Bremm*' Inn, near which is the unpretending *Spicherer Berg Hotel*. On the left rises the **Spicherer Berg** (330 ft. above the road; ascent in 20 min.), with its steep and scantily-wooded slopes, a strong position in which the French had intrenched themselves. The Germans began the attack from the right and left side of the road, and from the *Winterberg* (see below). Numerous monuments mark the battlefield. The loss of the Prussians amounted to 223 officers and 4648 men, that of the French to 249 officers and 3829 men.

A good survey of the battlefield, as well as a fine view of the Saar valley, is obtained from the tower of victory on the **Winterberg** (1005 ft.), a hill to the N.E. of the Spicherer Berg. At its base passes the electric railway to St. Arnual. — At **St. Arnual**, 2 M. to the S.E. of Saarbrücken, is a *Church* (1270-1315) in the best Gothic style, with remarkably fine font and pulpit, and interesting monuments of the Counts of Nassau-Saarbrücken. Opposite is the *Halberg*, with the modern château of the late Freiherr von Stumm (p. 206).

Saarbrücken is the junction for the Metz & Bingerbrück, Trèves & Strassburg (RR. 28, 25, & 67), Saarbrücken, St. Ingbert, Homburg, & Neustadt (R. 60), and Saarbrücken, Zweibrücken, & Landau (R. 62) railways, besides various branch-lines.

The Bingerbrück line ascends the valley of the *Sulzbach*. $52^1/_2$ M. *Dudweiler* (760 ft.; Nassauer Hof), a town of 19,500 inhab., with coal-pits and coke-furnaces. About $1^1/_2$ M. to the E. is the so-called 'Burning Mountain' ('Brennende Berg') a seam of coal that has been smouldering for 200 years. — 55 M. *Sulzbach* (855 ft.), with 21,000 inhab. and coal-pits; 57 M. *Friedrichstal* (970 ft.), with coal-pits and glass-works. We then thread the Bildstock tunnel. $59^1/_2$ M. *Reden* (925 ft.).

62 M. **Neunkirchen** (845 ft.; *Halberg,* near the bridge, R.
2-3, B. $^3/_4$, D. with wine 3 $\mathcal{M}$; *Post,* near the station) is a town of
33,000 inhab., with coal-pits and large iron and steel works, which
have been owned by the Stumm family for over a century. In front
of the works rises a statue, by Schaper, of *Freiherr von Stumm-
Halberg* (d. 1901), who greatly extended the operations of the firm
and did much to increase the welfare of his 5000 workmen.

Neunkirchen is also connected with Saarbrücken ,by another line
(16 M.), passing several small stations.

The train now quits the Saar coal-district and threads the
Wiebelskirchen Tunnel. 65$^1/_2$ M. *Ottweiler* (860 ft.; Kaiserhof),
a town with 6100 inhabitants. On the hill to the left is a Protestant
Normal School. — 68 M. *Niederlinxweier.*

71$^1/_2$ M. *St. Wendel* (970 ft.; Knoll), a district-town of 5600
inhab., appears in history as early as the 7th century. The Roman
Catholic parish church, a Gothic building (13-14th cent.) with aisles
of equal height with the nave, contains a late-Gothic pulpit of 1462
and the grave of St. Wendelinus (behind the Gothic high-altar).

About 7$^1/_2$ M. to the W. (diligence daily in 1$^1/_2$ hr.), at the foot of
the *Schaumberg* (1835 ft.), a volcanic hill commanding a fine view, is
the small town of **Tholey** *(Eckert),* with 1180 inhab., formerly the seat
of an early-Gothic Benedictine abbey founded in the 7th cent., the early-
Gothic church of which is still in existence. Numerous Roman antiquities have been found in the environs.

74$^1/_2$ M. *Hofeld;* 76 M. *Namborn.* At (78$^1/_2$ M.) *Wallhausen*
we cross the watershed (1263 ft.) between the Nahe and the *Blies,*
a tributary of the Saar. 80 M. *Türkismühle* (1194 ft.), on the Nahe,
the junction of a branch-line to Hermeskeil and Trèves (p. 189).

The line now traverses the pretty valley of the *Nahe,* with its
vineyards. The Nahe wines are similar to those of the Bavarian
Palatinate. — 81$^1/_2$ M. *Nohfelden,* with an old keep. — From (84 M.)
Birkenfeld-Neubrücke (1115 ft.) a branch-line diverges to (3 M.)
Birkenfeld (1315 ft.; *Post,* R. 1$^3/_4$-2$^1/_2$ $\mathcal{M}$; *Neue Post,* both very
fair), the capital (2200 inhab.) of the principality of Birkenfeld, now
belonging to the Grand Duchy of Oldenburg, with a ruined castle
(11th cent.) of the Counts of Sponheim. It is of pre-Roman origin and
is first mentioned in a document of the end of the 10th century. —
From Birkenfeld a highroad leads to Hüttgeswasen (p. 189), passing,
about halfway (3$^1/_2$ M.), the *Hambacher Sauerbrunnen.*

Beyond Birkenfeld the construction of the line is interesting.
Before reaching Kirn-Sulzbach we cross 20 bridges and thread
10 tunnels. — 85 M. *Hoppstätten;* 87 M. *Heimbach;* 89 M. *Nohen:*
91 M. *Kronweiler;* 91$^3/_4$ M. *Sonnenberg.* To the right, in a side-
valley, is the picturesque ruin of *Frauenburg.* 94 M. *Enzweiler.*

95 M. **Oberstein.** — Hotels. *Central,* at the rail. station; *Post,*
R. & B. 2$^1/_2$-3 $\mathcal{M}$; *Stark,* R. & B. 2$^1/_2$ $\mathcal{M}$, both these at the new bridge.
with restaurants: *Bach,* above the Neue Schloss (p. 207). — *Railway
Restaurant.* with view, very fair.

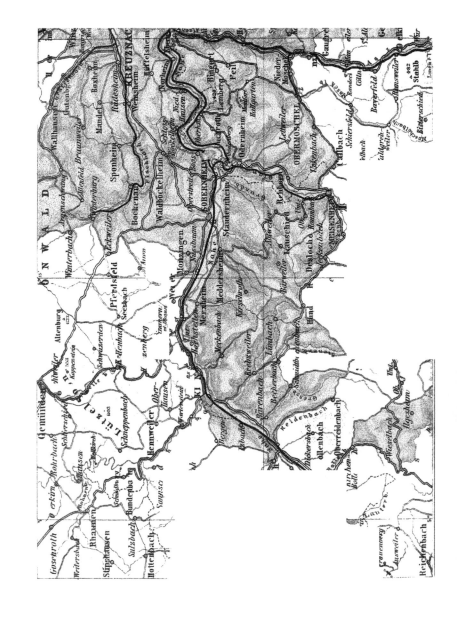

TRAMWAY from the railway-station to ($2^1/_4$ M.) *Idar* in 20 minutes. — DILIGENCE from Idar to ($7^1/_2$ M.) *Kempfeld* (p. 208) in $1^3/_4$ hr.

Oberstein (870 ft.), a town of 9700 inhab., situated on both sides of the Nahe, at the mouth of the *Idarbach*, is one of the finest points in the valley of the Nahe. The precipitous cliffs, 400 ft. in height, which confine the town within narrow limits, are crowned with two ruined castles of the Barons of Oberstein, who became extinct in 1670. The best way to the castles (there and back $1^1/_2$ hr.) is the 'Burgweg', ascending to the right beyond the 'Post'. By this route we first reach the *Neue Schloss* (restaurant), and then, beyond a hollow containing a War Monument (1870-71), the **Alte Burg*, crowning the steep porphyry cliffs above the town. About 5 min. higher is a pavilion commanding a very extensive view. We may now return by the *Protestant Church*, curiously built into the face of the rock about halfway down (200 ft. above the Nahe), and said to have been erected in the 12th cent. by an Oberstein with his own hands, as an atonement for fratricide; it was restored in 1482. The sexton lives close by. The Gothic *Roman Catholic Church* lies on the right bank of the Nahe, near the railway-station.

Along with the little town of Idar, which lies in the Idar-Tal 2 M. to the N., Oberstein forms the centre of the interesting *Agate Industry*, which dates back to the middle ages and now employs about 2000 workmen. The polishing mills extend along the banks of the Idarbach. Most of them are driven by water-power, in which case the workmen lie prone and press the agates to be polished with all their strength against the huge revolving millstones. Some of the mills, however, are now worked by steam or electricity. Agates were formerly found here in abundance, but their place is now taken mainly by stones of a similar character from Brazil, the East Indies, Australia, and New Zealand. The process by which the colourless agates are converted into onyxes, sardonyxes, etc., by the addition of colouring matter, was known to the ancients and has been in use here since 1830. — **Idar** (985 ft.; *Schützenhof; Fürstenberg*) has 5700 inhab., and a Gewerbehalle, or industrial hall, in which the polished stones are sold at officially-regulated prices. Idar and Oberstein contain more than 100 goldsmiths, occupied in setting the stones in metal.

From Idar an attractive excursion ($2^1/_2$-$2^3/_4$ hrs.) may be made by following the road up the valley viâ *Hettstein* and *Obertiefenbach* to (6 M.) the *Katzenloch*, where the Idarbach breaks through the hills in a ravine upwards of 1 M. long, at the upper end of which are a large saw-mill and an inn. From the lower end of the gorge a marked path leads to the right to ($1/_2$ hr.) the **Wildenburg** (2230 ft.; forester's house and inn), situated on a lofty quarzite rock, with a prehistoric stone-wall (view). A short-cut diverges to the right from the road $3/_4$ M. above Obertiefenbach. — About $1^1/_2$ M. to the N. of the Wildenburg is the village of *Kempfeld* (1670 ft.; Fuchs), and $3/_4$ M. farther on in the same direction is *Bruchweiler* (Kling), whence a road leads to (6 M.) Morbach (p. 189) and a footpath to Hinzerath (p. 189).

On leaving Oberstein we cross a bridge and obtain a view, to the left, of the *'Fallen Rock'*. Beyond this we thread a tunnel and cross another bridge. 97$^1/_2$ M. *Nahbollenbach*. — 100 M. *Fischbach* (Post), at the mouth of the valley of that name.

A pleasant walk may be taken through the Fischbach-Tal, viâ (5$^1/_2$ M.) *Herrstein* (Hey), to *Mörschied*, whence we may go on through woods to (1$^3/_4$ hr.) the *Wildenburg* (p. 207).

102$^1/_2$ M. *Kirn-Sulzbach*. The valley now expands. — 104$^1/_2$ M. **Kirn** (595 ft.; *Stroh*, at the station, R. & B. 2$^1/_4$-2$^1/_2$, D. with wine 2$^1/_2$ $\mathscr{M}$, with garden, very fair; *Lamm; Post*), a small town of 7000 inhab., with tanneries and cloth-mills, was the seat of a Roman settlement, and reappears in history in the 9th century. From the 10th cent. onward it was the seat of the Gaugrafen and Rheingrafen, from whom it passed in the 18th cent. into the hands of the Princes of Salm-Kyrburg. The old Protestant church, originally a Roman basilica, with a Gothic choir of the 15th cent., contains a fine tabernacle and several tombs of the Rheingrafen. Adjacent is an old Piarist convent of the 18th cent. (now used as a school). Above the town to the E. is a modern Rom. Cath. church. The ruin of *Kyrburg*, which crowns the vine-clad porphyry hill to the N.W. of the town, is reached from the rail. station in 20 min. (restaurant).

Kirn lies at the mouth of the *Hahnenbach-Tal*, up which runs the road to (17 M.) Büchenbeuren (p. 190), passing several agate-polishing works. To the N.W. of Kirn (1$^1/_2$ M.) is the ruin of **Steinkallenfels**, clinging to the rocks like a swallow's nest. On a wooded height in the background rises the white château of **Wartenstein,** with its numerous windows. The finely situated ruin of *Schmidburg*, 4$^1/_2$ M. to the N., belonged to the Electors of Trèves. From Wartenstein we may proceed viâ *Oberhausen* to Dhaun (see below), where a pleasant route leads either viâ Johannisberg (see below) or through the woods to (3$^1/_2$ hrs.) Kirn.

The train next passes through a tunnel. On an eminence to the left stands the church of *Johannisberg*, which contains ancient tombstones of the Rheingrafen.

Farther down the imposing rocky gorge of the *Kellenbach* opens on the left, and the ruins of *Schloss Dhaun* appear in its background. — 108 M. *Martinstein* (Goldener Hirsch; Railway Hotel), curiously built on a rock, with its church on an eminence surrounded by a fine group of trees. The station is at the upper end of the village.

*Schloss Dhaun, the seat of a branch of the Rheingrafen which became extinct in 1750, was erected in the 12th cent., and greatly extended in 1729. It is now in the possession of the Simon family of Kirn. This strikingly-picturesque castle is situated 2$^1/_4$ M. from Martinstein and 3$^1/_2$ M. from Kirn (see above; carriage 7$^1/_2$ $\mathscr{M}$). A relief over one of the doors, representing an ape giving an apple to a child, commemorates the incident that a child of one of the Counts was carried off by an ape, but fortunately recovered. Magnificent view of the valley of the Nahe as far as the Lemberg, of the Simmer-Tal, and of the dark ravines of the Soonwald. Admission, including fee to attendant, 30 pf. Near the entrance is an inn. — We may return to Martinstein from Dorf Dhaun viâ Johannisberg.

Wallhausen Bingen

Bhf.
Rennbahn

1 Bismarckplatz
2 Cauers Atelier
3 Elisabethquelle
4 Fausthaus
5 Kasino
6 Nikolauskirche
7 Pauluskirche
8 Post u. Telegraph
9 Reichsbank
10 Schule
11 Viktoriaquelle
12 Wilhelmskirche

Kahlenberg
Wahlsbg.
Steinweg
Hopfgarten
Ziegelei

Neustadt

Holzmü.

Glashütte
Heidenmauer

Wiesenbg.

Bhf.
Fabr.
Elterbach
Gut
Röm.
Mosaikboden

Schl.
Viktoriasee
Fabr.
Strateg. Bahn

H. St.
Lohrer M.

Kauzenberg
159

Altstadt

Lohrer Kopf
Schützenhs.

Agnesienberg

Radeförth
Mannheimerstrasse

Bahnhof Bad

12

KREUZNACH

Kaiserau

Hühnerkopf
Heinrichsruh

Salinenstr.

Diakonissen-
haus
Friedhof

Lohrerhof
240 Lambertskopf
Karl Küh.
Viktoria
Stift
165

Teufelskopf
Johannasruh

Dachskopf 271
Taunuskopf
Jagdhs.
Baumshütte
Oranienbg.

Ziegelei

H a a r d t
Oertels-
hütte
Karlshalle
Grafenstein
Tempel

Kaiser
Kopf
Hektorskopf
Elisabethhütte
Monau
Kuhberg

Schinzenkopf
217
Delte
Forsths.

Tempel-
berg

Steinkopf
Marxhas
Fels
Gradier
Werke
Theodorshalle

Dreispitz
Uhukopf
Raben
Kopf
Ottoslust
Traisen
Nöllbg.
Heinrichs
Kopf
Hint.

Nahe

Götzenfels
Bastei
Felseneck

Löchen B.
Rotenfels
227
Wilhelmsfels
279

Nahe
Strateg. Bahn
Bhf.

Rheingrafensteiner
Hof

322
Gans

Schloss
Rheingrafenstein

Bad Münster
a. Stein
Kuhs.

Münsterg.

Ebernburg
Dkm.
Burg
R. Rheingrafenstein
Hüttental
Forsths.
Spreitel

Speckerbrücke
Emmasruh
Haidberg
285

Kaiserslautern-Neustadt Altenbaumburg

Geogr. Anst. von Wagner & Debes, Leipzig

110$^1/_2$ M. *Monzingen* (Dick's Hotel, fair), with quaint old houses with oriel windows, lies to the left, on the vine-clad slopes, which produce the best wine of the Nahe valley.

From Monzingen a road leads through the *Hoxtal* to the pleasant health-resort of *Waldfriede* (1320 ft.; pens. 4-5 *M*), whence various excursions may be made.

113$^1/_2$ M. **Sobernheim** (500 ft.; *Goldner Adler; Caesar*) is a small and ancient town, partly enclosed by a wall. Pop. 3500. It possesses a late-Gothic church, an old *Maltese Chapel* adjoined by a former lodge of the order (now a school), and some quaint old houses.

115$^1/_2$ M. **Staudernheim** (460 ft.; *Salmen*, very fair) lies on the right bank of the Nahe, connected with the station by a five-arched bridge. Branch-railway to *Odernheim*, see p. 454.

On leaving Staudernheim, we observe on the right, beyond the Nahe (20 min. to the E. of Staudernheim), the ruins of **Disibodenberg,** a Benedictine (subsequently Cistercian) abbey named after the Irish bishop Disibodus, the first propagator of Christianity in this district, which was annexed during the Reformation by the Dukes of Zweibrücken and is now private property.

Little is left of the buildings beyond the foundations. The abbey-church, consecrated in 1143, was an imposing edifice with pillars; the vaulting of the choir, which was composed of nave and aisles, was borne by imbedded columns. The secular portions of the monastery are in the Gothic style of the 13th century. Adjoining the church were the cloisters, and to the right of them the chapter-house. Farther to the W. was the residence of the abbot, and to the E. was the refectory, of which the gable-walls are still standing. The custodian shows a number of Gothic fragments from the old building, which are collected in a vault. The ruins afford a good survey of the valleys of the Nahe and its affluent the *Glan* (p. 462). The descent to Odernheim (p. 454) takes $^1/_4$ hr.

118 M. *Wald-Böckelheim* lies 2 M. to the N. of the station (diligence thrice daily). Burg-Sponheim (p. 214) is about 1$^1/_2$ M. from the village. — On the left, 1 M. from the station, rises an abrupt rock, crowned with the ruins of *Böckelheim*, destroyed by the French in 1688, in which the Emp. Henry IV. was kept prisoner by his son Henry V. in 1105 (comp. pp. 113, 217). — From (121 M.) *Niederhausen* the *Lemberg* may be ascended in 1$^1/_4$ hr. (p. 211). — We thread two tunnels. The Rotenfels appears on the left, the bridge of the strategic railway (p. 454) and the Ebernburg on the right. The train now passes through a cutting and reaches —

125 M. **Münster am Stein.** -- HOTELS (all with baths). *Schmuck's Kurhaus Hotel*, by the Kur-Park, with dépendance, R. 3-5, B. 1$^1/_4$, D. 3$^1/_2$, S. 2$^1/_2$, board 6-8 *M*; *Park Hotel*, with two villas, R. 2-6, B. 1$^1/_4$, D. 4, S. 2$^1/_2$-3, pens. 7$^1/_2$-12 *M*, both these with gardens and closed from Oct. to the end of April; *Hôtel-Pension Baum*, R. 2$^1/_2$-5, B. 1$^1/_4$, D. 2$^1/_2$, S. 2, pens. 7-10 *M*; *Hôtel-Pension Zipp*, at the station, R. 2-3, B. 1, D. 2$^1/_2$, pens. 6-7 *M*, with garden; *Englischer Hof, Schwan*, good, cheaper. — Numerous private hotels. — *Railway Restaurant*, very-fair.

TRAMWAY viâ Theodorshalle and Karlshalle to Kreuznach, see p. 212. — CARRIAGE to the Ebernburg 2$^1/_2$, there and back 4 *M*.

VISITORS' TAX for 1 pers. 12, 2 pers. 17, 3 pers. 20, 4 pers. 23, 5 pers. 26 ℳ. Adm. to the Kur-Garten 40 pf. The season lasts from May to September.

Münster am Stein (370 ft.), the junction for the Alsenz Railway (R. 58a) and for the so-called strategic railway to Staudernheim (p. 209), Meisenheim, and Homburg (R. 58b), is a village of 1000 inhab., situated on the left bank of the Nahe, opposite the mouth of the Alsenz and surrounded on three sides by steep cliffs. It possesses salt-springs, and has of late years acquired importance as a watering-place (5000 patients annually). The waters of the principal salt-spring (87°) are conducted directly to the baths. The well-shaded Kur-Garten contains a restaurant. Adjoining are the Evaporating Houses (Gradierhäuser). The new Protestant church is a handsome building in the Romanesque style.

The *Rheingrafenstein (770 ft.), a picturesque cliff of porphyry, here rises 425 ft. almost perpendicularly from the Nahe. We cross the river by the ferry near the saline springs, and ascend the *Hutten-Tal* (restaurant) by a path which leads to the ruin in 1/2 hr. (the highest point is reached by a flight of stone steps ascending through the rocks). The boldly situated ruined castle, built in the 12th cent., once the residence of the 'Rheingrafen' (Rhenish counts), was blown up by the French in 1689.

Finger-posts indicate the way from the Rheingrafenstein to the (1/2 hr.) *Gans* (1056 ft.), an indented ridge of porphyry commanding an extensive view, embracing Bingen, the Hunsrück, and the Donnersberg. About 3/4 M. to the E. is the *Schlösschen Rheingrafenstein* (918 ft.), and about 1/4 M. farther on is the *Rheingrafensteiner Hof* (inn), whence a road leads to the little temple on the Kuhberg (see p. 214).

Opposite the Rheingrafenstein, to the W., about 1/2 hr. from the Münster am Stein station, rises the *Ebernburg (590 ft.). We cross the bridge (toll 3 pf.) and ascend to the right, passing several inns (near the station of *Ebernburg*, p. 453). About half-way up is a *Monument to Sickingen and Hutten*, by K. Cauer, erected in 1889. In the pinnacled building at the top is a popular garden-restaurant (closed in winter). Fine prospect of the environs.

From 1448 onward the Ebernburg was in the possession of the Herren von Sickingen, the most celebrated of whom, *Franz von Sickingen*, was born here in 1481. Undaunted by the fulminations of the Imperial Chamber, this doughty knight carried on numerous private feuds and afforded asylum to many men who were under the ban of the Empire. Foremost among these ranks Ulrich von Hutten, whose letters to Charles V, to the German noblesse, were written at the Ebernburg ('der Gerechtigkeit Herberge'). Under Hutten's influence Sickingen planned to introduce the Reformation into the central Rhenish district by force and to abolish all the ecclesiastical principalities, but he was overcome by the united strength of the Elector Palatine, the Elector of Trèves, and the Landgrave of Hesse. A few weeks after his death (p. 462) the Ebernburg was captured and destroyed by these princes. The castle was fortified by the French in 1689, but was again dismantled at the Peace of Ryswyck (1698). In 1750 the ruin passed to the Palatinate.

The **Rotenfels** (1035 ft.), a barren red porphyry cliff towering to the N. of the Ebernburg, is ascended from Münster in $^1/_2$ hr. and from Kreuznach in 1 hr. (comp. p. 214). At the highest point, which commands a wide view of the valleys of the Nahe and the Alsenz, extending to the Landsberg, is a mountain-indicator. The view from the Bastei (950 ft.), 7 min. farther on, is more picturesque.

A charming excursion from Münster am Stein may be made through the *Hutten-Tal*, and finally through beautiful woods, to the (1$^1/_4$ hr.) **Altenbaumburg** *(Restaurant)*, an extensive ruined castle destroyed by the French in 1689, the ancestral seat of the ancient 'Raugrafen', and formerly called the *Boymeneburg*, or *Croneburg*. — Those who are not forced to catch a train at (25 min.) *Altenbamberg* (p. 453) may proceed viâ the *Schäferplacken* and *Fürfeld* to (1$^1/_4$ hr.) the *Ibener Kapelle*, a fine specimen of Gothic, restored in 1886. Thence they may return to (2$^1/_2$ hrs.) Kreuznach viâ Hackenheim. — The ruined château of *Montfort* (destroyed in the 15th cent.) may be reached from Münster, by the villages of *Ebernburg* and *Bingert*, in 2 hrs. (rfmts. at the *Montforter Hof*). — The ***Lemberg** (1312 ft.), which rises precipitously from the Nahe, near Bingert (1$^3/_4$ hr. from Münster), commands an extensive panorama. The descent may be made to the (20 min.) *Duchroth-Oberhausen* station (p. 454) or by the bridge of Oberhausen and through wood, finally traversing the *Trumbach-Tal*, to (1$^1/_4$ hr.) stat. *Niederhausen* (p. 209).

The train crosses to the right bank (view of the Rheingrafenstein), skirts the river and the Gans (p. 210), and passes the Karlshalle (p. 214) and the Badeviertel (p. 213).

127$^1/_2$ M. **Bad Kreuznach.** — There are two stations: 1. *Stadt Kreuznach* (p. 214), $^2/_3$ M. from the town, which is stopped at by a few trains only; 2. *Bad Kreuznach*, on the E. side of the island on which the baths are situated. Hotel-omnibuses and cabs (p. 212) await the arrival of the trains. — Comp. plan on the Map, p. 209.

Hotels. The best for patients who are making a long stay are those on the Badewörth and in the 'Badeviertel', all provided with baths, gardens, and so on. They are closed in winter. *GRAND-HÔTEL ROYAL & ENGLISCHER HOF (Pl. a), Kurhaus-Str. 24, R. 2-20, B. 1$^1/_4$, déj. 2$^1/_2$, D. 3$^1/_2$-4, S. 2$^1/_2$, pens. 8-15 ℳ, with lift, central heating, terrace, and small park; *KURHAUS (Pl. b), next door, R. 2$^1/_2$-5, B. 1$^1/_4$, D. 3$^1/_2$, S. 2$^1/_2$, pens. 7-11 ℳ, with lift, terrace, and garden; *ORANIENHOF (Pl. c), Oranien-Str. 4, at the S. end of the Badeviertel, $^1/_4$ M. from the Kur-Park, R. 3-12, B. 1$^1/_4$, déj. 2$^1/_2$, D. 3$^1/_2$, S. 2$^1/_2$, pens. 8-15 ℳ, with baths, lift, terrace, and small park. — *HÔTEL DU NORD (Pl. d), Friedrich-Str. 2, with lift, R. 2$^1/_2$-6, B. 1$^1/_4$, D. 3, S. 2-2$^1/_2$, pens. 7-12 ℳ; *EUROPÄISCHER HOF (Pl. e), Salinen-Str. 55, R. 3-6, B. 1$^1/_4$, D. 3, S. 2, pens. 7$^1/_2$-12 ℳ; KAUZENBERG (Pl. f), Kurhaus-Str. 20, R. 2$^1/_2$-4, B. 1$^1/_4$, D. 3, pens. 6$^1/_2$-9 ℳ; DHEILSCHMIDT, Salinen-Strasse. — *For Transient Guests.* BERLINER HOF (Pl. g), Bismarck-Platz 4, in the old town, R. & B. 2$^1/_2$-4 ℳ; PFÄLZER HOF, Post-Str. 14, R. 2$^1/_2$-5, D. 2-3 ℳ, with steam-heating and garden; TAUBE ('Täubchen'), Hoch-Str. 46, R. 1$^3/_4$-2$^1/_2$, with restaurant, these two in the new town on the left bank of the Nahe. — Numerous lodging-houses and pensions. Prices are highest between June 15th and August 15th.

Restaurants. *Heilquelle*, Ross-Str., near the small Bade-Brücke; *Park Restaurant, Bellevue*, near the Kur-Park bridge; *Kaiserau*, above the island, at the foot of the Kauzenberg (p. 214); *Pflug*, near the railway-station (good wine).

Cabs. Drive in the town, 1-2 pers., with one horse 80 pf., with 2 horses 1 ℳ 20 pf.; 3-4 pers. 1 ℳ 20 and 1 ℳ 50 pf.; per hour, in the town 2 or 3 ℳ, outside the town 2$^1/_2$ or 3$^1/_2$ ℳ; to the Theodorshalle 1$^1/_2$ and 2, or 2 and 2$^1/_2$ ℳ. Carriages to the following places and back, with 2 hrs. stay: ℳ—

	1-horse ℳ pf.	2-horse ℳ pf.		1-horse ℳ pf.	2-horse ℳ pf.
Rheingrafenstein.	7.50	9.—	Münster (without returning) . . .	2.—	3.—
Rheingrafenstein viâ Münster . .	9.—	12.—	Ebernburg, Alten-baumburg, or		
Rheingrafenstein, Münster, and the			Eremitage . . .	6.—	9.--
			Lohrer Mühle . .	5.—	7.--
Ebernburg . . .	10.—	13.50	Rotenfels	9.--	12.—
Münster.	4.--	6.—	Sponheim	7.---	10.50

Electric Tramways run every ½ hr. in the morning and every ¼ hr. in the afternoon between the Altstadt (Central Railway Station) and the Neustadt (Stadthaus) viâ the Old Nahe Bridge (30 pf.), and also through the Kreuz-Str., passing the Kur-Park bridge, to Karlshalle, Theodors-halle, and Münster am Stein (p. 210; 30 pf.). — **Light Railways** to Wall-hausen and Winterburg, see p. 214.

Visitors' Tax, for one pers. 18 ℳ, for each addit. member of a family 6-7 ℳ; single ticket admitting to the grounds of the Kurhaus 75 pf. *Bath Office* in the Kurhaus.

Post and Telegraph Office (Pl. 8), in the Neustadt, on the left bank of the Nahe.

English Church, see p. 213; services during the season.

Kreuznach (340 ft.), a town of 24,000 inhab., with a consider-able trade in wine, large cellars for sparkling wine, tobacco factories, and tanneries, lies on both sides of the Nahe, which here forms the island of Badewörth and separates the Altstadt and the 'Bade-viertel' on the right bank from the Neustadt and the Kauzenberg on the left bank. To the N. E. of the Altstadt are the remains of a Roman castellum and the so-called *Heiden-Mauer* ('Heathens' Wall), while to the S.W. of the Neustadt are some relics of a Roman villa. The Carlovingian palatium of *Cruciniacum* was erected on the site of the Roman castle in 819. In 1065 the place fell into the hands of the Bishops of Spires, and in 1241 it passed to the Counts of Sponheim. In 1290 *Crucenach* received a muni-cipal charter. Incorporated with the Palatinate in 1565, Kreuznach suffered severely from the Spaniards and the Swedes during the Thirty Years War and from the French in 1689. Its reputation as a watering-place dates no farther back than the second quarter of the 19th century. Its powerful saline springs, formerly exploited only for the making of salt, are especially efficacious in scrofula, gout, sciatica, and the like. The water contains traces of bromine, iodine, and radium. The annual number of visitors amounts to 8000.

From the *Main Railway Station* we first enter the ALTSTADT, the principal streets of which are the Mannheimer-Str. and the Kreuz-Str., intersecting each other at right angles. The former passes the Bismarck-Platz, with the *Bismarck Brunnen* (Pl. 1), a fountain with a bronze statue by H. Cauer (1897). The Public School (*Volksschule;* Pl. 10), in the Kreuz-Str., contains the mu-nicipal collection of Roman and mediæval antiquities. In the grounds on the Nahe is a bust of the poet G. Pfarrius, who celebrated the beauties of the Nahe valley. — To the S. of the Altstadt lies the

BADEVIERTEL or Bath Quarter, the chief streets of which are the Salinen-Strasse and the König-Strasse. In the Salinen-Str. are the *Kreisgebäude (District Offices)* and (at the corner of the Rheingrafen-Str.) the interesting studio of the *Cauers*, a well-known family of sculptors (Pl. 2), including Emil Cauer (1800-67) and his sons and grandsons. The Elisabeth-Strasse, intersecting the two streets above named, crosses the narrow right arm of the Nahe and leads to the Kur-Park.

The Mannheimer - Str. ends at the picturesque *Old Nahe *Bridge*, which leads across the lower end of the Badewörth to the Neustadt. The wider parts of the bridge above the piers are occupied by small houses. Farther down the river is the new *Kaiser - Wilhelm-Brücke*, which leads across the Marien-Wörth to the left bank. On the *Marien-Wörth* is an hospital managed by Franciscan monks.

On the BADEWÖRTH, adjacent to the Old Nahe Bridge, is the Protestant *Church of St. Paul (Paulus-Kirche; Pl. 7)*, erected on the site of a church of the 14th cent. destroyed in 1689, the elegant Gothic choir of which was fitted up in 1863 as an English chapel. Adjoining St. Paul's is a marble statue, by Emil Cauer, of *Dr. Prieger*, who first called attention, in 1817, to the properties of the Kreuznach springs. The chief rendezvous of visitors is the *Kur-Park*, at the S. end of the island, containing the *Kur-Haus* (Pl. b) of 1840, the *Bath House* of 1872, and the large *Inhalatorium* of 1895, all well equipped. The *Elisabeth-Quelle* (Pl. 3), containing bromine and iodine, and rising from the porphyry rock at the S. end of the island, is used for drinking and is connected with a covered walk.

On the left bank of the Nahe and on both sides of the Ellerbach lies the NEUSTADT. Here stands the Roman Catholic *Church of St. Nicolas* (Pl. 6), formerly belonging to a Carmelite convent, begun in the late-Romanesque style of the middle of the 13th cent. and practically finished in the early-Gothic style in the 14th cent., though there are some late-Gothic additions of the 15th century. The ceiling of the nave is supported by massive round pillars. A trapezoidal archway leads from the nave to the broader choir, which formerly contained the seats of the monks. In the choir are interesting tombstones of the Counts of Sponheim, Dhaun, and Waldeck (14-15th cent.). To the N. of the church, in the Eiermarkt, is a monument by Robert Cauer, commemorating *Michel Mort,* a butcher of Kreuznach, who sacrificed his life in the battle of Sprendlingen (1279) to save his prince, Johann von Sponheim. A small house (Pl. 4) at the corner of the Karl-Str., near the Kaiser-Wilhelm-Brücke, is pointed out as the residence of Dr. Johann Faust, the humanist, who was born about 1485 and became a schoolmaster at Kreuznach through Franz von Sickingen. From 1509 onwards he led a reckless and unsettled life and so has come to be regarded in popular legend as a master of the black arts and in league with the devil.

On the right bank of the Ellerbach, 148 ft. above the Nahe, rises the *Kauzenberg* or *Schlossberg*, with the ruins of a castle of the Counts of Sponheim, destroyed by the French in 1689 and now private property. The view embraces the valley from Rheingrafen- stein to Bingen. A lion hewn in stone brought here from Dhaun, is another memorial to Michel Mort (p. 213). The vineyards on the S. slope yield a somewhat fiery wine. — Paths, with picturesque views, lead hence by the wooded *Haardt* to the Rotenfels (p. 211).

A fine *Roman Mosaic Pavement*, 32 ft. long and 24¹/₄ ft. wide, be- longing to a villa, was discovered in 1893, in a very fair state of pre- servation, on the Hüffelsheim road, behind the Schlossberg, ³/₄ M. from the old bridge (p. 213). It represents combats of wild beasts and gladia- tors (adm. 30, Sun. 10 pf.).

From the 'Badeviertel' the prolongation of the Salinen-Str. leads past the Oranienhof Hotel and the *Victoria-Stift*, a charity hospital for children, to the salt-works of *Karlshalle*. On the Nahe is the *Stadt-Park*, with the Stadt-Quelle and the Oranien- Quelle. Farther on, beyond the bridge, we reach the salt-works of *Theodorshalle*, halfway to Münster am Stein. All these springs furnish the bathing-houses of Kreuznach with an inexhaustible supply of water. A factory has been erected for the extraction of radium. The old Kur-Haus is now a home for officials.

A fine view, from the S., of Kreuznach and the valley of the Nahe as far as the Niederwald is obtained from the conspicuous little temple on the *Kuhberg*, which is reached by the shadeless Rheingrafensteiner-Str. in 20 minutes. From the Kuhberg to the Rheingrafensteiner Hof (¹/₂ hr.), see p. 210. In the Ring-Str. is the *Rhenish Deaconesses' Institute*. — On the way to Hachenheim is the *Cemetery*, which contains several monuments by members of the Cauer family and a figure of Germania as a memorial of 1871.

FROM KREUZNACH TO WALLHAUSEN, 5¹/₂ M., tramway in ¹/₂ hr. (start- ing from the Holzmarkt) viâ *Roxheim.* — About 1¹/₂ M. beyond Wall- hausen is *Dalberg*, with the ruins of the ancestral seat of the family of that name. Farther on are (3 M.) the *Weissenfels* (view; 1¹/₂ hr. from Stromberg, p. 192) and *Argenschwang*, with a ruined castle.

FROM KREUZNACH TO WINTERBURG, 11 M., tramway in 1-1¹/₄ hr. (also starting from the Holzmarkt) viâ *Rüdesheim* and *Weinsheim*. — 6 M. **Burg-Sponheim**, with the ruined castle of the Sponheim family. About 1 M. off is the village of *Sponheim*, with the fine Romanesque church (1123) of the former Benedictine Abbey, of which the learned Johannes Trithemius (p. 174) was abbot in 1484-1506. It has lately been restored. — 8¹/₂ M. *Bockenau*. — 11 M. *Winterburg*, a convenient starting-point for a visit to (6 M.) the *Altenburg* (2044 ft.; Waldfriede; view-tower) and (9 M.) the ruined castle of *Koppenstein* (view).

On leaving the main station of Kreuznach the train crosses the Nahe. 128 M. *Kreuznach-Stadt* (p. 211); 130¹/₂ M. *Bretzenheim*, 1¹/₂ M. to the S. of the Hermitage (p. 193); 137 M. *Langenlonsheim* (292 ft.; Berliner Hof), junction of the Bingerbrück and Simmern line (p. 193); 133¹/₂ M. *Laubenheim;* 135 M. *Münster*.

137 M. *Bingerbrück* (275 ft.), see p. 245.

IV. THE RHINE FROM COBLENZ TO MAYENCE. FRANKFORT. TAUNUS.

29. From Coblenz to Mayence.

Railway on the Left Bank.

57 M. RAILWAY in 1½-3 hrs. (fares 7 ℳ 30, 4 ℳ 40, 2 ℳ 90 pf.; express fares 8 ℳ 30, 5 ℳ 40, 3 ℳ 40 pf.). — Views to the left.

Railway on the Right Bank, see R. 30. The tickets are available on either bank (see p. 71). The following are the recognized corresponding stations: *Capellen* and *Oberlahnstein; Rhens* and *Braubach; Spay* and *Osterspay; Boppard* and *Camp; St. Goar* and *St. Goarshausen; Niederheimbach* and *Lorch; Bingen* and *Rüdesheim; Mayence* and *Wiesbaden* (or *Mainz-Kastel*). — *Steamboat*, see RR. 31 & 33. — S., affixed to the name of a place, indicates that it is also a steamboat-station.

Coblenz, see R. 19. Beyond Coblenz a view of the upper Rhine bridge and the fortress of Ehrenbreitstein is obtained to the left. The line skirts the river nearly the whole way and affords good views of the opposite bank. — 3 M. *Capellen* lies at the foot of the castle of *Stolzenfels* (p. 220). Opposite are Oberlahnstein and the castle of Lahneck. After passing the Königsstuhl, which rises to the left, the line intersects the old village of (5½ M.) *Rhens* (p. 222). Farther up, on the opposite bank, is Braubach with the Marksburg.

12½ M. *Boppard* (S.; p. 224). On the opposite bank, farther on, are the convent of Bornhofen and the castles of Sterrenberg and Liebenstein (p. 227); still farther up, beyond (15½ M.) *Salzig* (p. 226), are Wellmich and the Mouse (p. 227). — 17½ M. *Hirzenach* (p. 226).

21 M. *St. Goar* (S.; p. 228). The station lies on a height at the back of the town. On the opposite bank is St. Goarshausen with the Cat (p. 229). Farther on, after passing a tunnel, we obtain a view of the Lurlei to the left. We then thread two other tunnels, beyond which is (25½ M.) *Oberwesel* (S.; p. 230). We next have a view on the left of the ruin of Gutenfels, Caub; and the Pfalz (p. 235).

30 M. *Bacharach* (S.; p. 234); 32 M. *Niederheimbach* (p. 236); 35 M. *Trechtingshausen* (p. 238). On the opposite bank, Lorch and Assmannshausen successively come in sight. At Bingerbrück the wider part of the valley is entered. Comp. Map, p. 246.

38 M. *Bingerbrück* (see p. 245) lies on the left bank of the Nahe, about ¾ M. from Bingen, and nearly opposite the *Mouse Tower* (p. 227). Travellers bound for Kreuznach, Saarbrücken, and Metz (R. 28), Simmern (pp. 193, 192), etc., change carriages here. Steam-ferry to *Rüdesheim*, see p. 240.

The train now crosses the Nahe. To the left, a view of the Niederwald and the ruined castle of Ehrenfels (p. 239).

38½ M. *Bingen* (S.), see p. 243. The line now skirts the base of the Rochusberg, then begins to leave the river, and enters the plain of the Rhine, which is covered here with shifting sands and

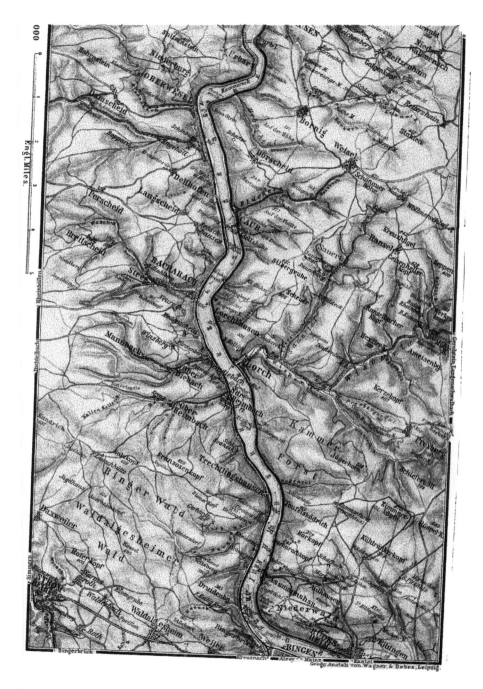

pine-woods. The line to Alzey (R. 59) diverges to the right. —
41 M. *Gaulsheim* (p. 248). — 44 M. *Gau-Algesheim* is the junction
for the so-called strategic railway to *Kreuznach* and *Münster am
Stein* (15 M.).

46 M. **Ingelheim,** station for the two villages of *Nieder-
Ingelheim* (Hirsch; Krone) and *Ober-Ingelheim* (395 ft.; Lamm),
each $^2/_3$ M. distant and both noted for their good red wine. The
Selztal Railway connects them with *Frei-Weinheim* (S.; p. 249), on
the Rhine, and with other villages farther up the valley. Nieder-
Ingelheim, with 3700 inhab. and a few factories, was once the site
of a celebrated palace of Charlemagne (768-84), to adorn which
mosaics, sculptures, and other works of art were sent from
Ravenna by Pope Hadrian I. It was burned down in 1270, restored by Charles IV. in 1354, and again devastated in the Thirty
Years' War and in 1689. A few remains of the palace-chapel are
incorporated in the transept and choir of the Protestant *Church of
St. Remigius*. An excavation of the palace has been in progress
since 1909.

The Selztal Railway ascends in a sweeping curve to (2 M.) Ober-
Ingelheim (3500 inhab.), which has some relics of its old fortifications and a handsome Protestant church of the 13th century. It
was at Ingelheim, on Dec. 31st, 1105, that the archbishops of
Mayence and Cologne dethroned Emp. Henry IV. — The *Waldeck*
(760 ft.), $^1/_2$ hr. above Ober-Ingelheim, commands one of the finest
views of the Rheingau; a Bismarck Tower was erected on the summit in 1903.

49 M. *Heidesheim.* To the right is a large House for Idiots.
From (52$^1/_2$ M.) *Budenheim* the *Lenneberg* (p. 277) may be ascended
in $^1/_2$ hr. — 55 M. *Mombach.* To the right are the hills of Rhenish
Hesse; to the left, on the opposite bank, lies Biebrich (p. 252).

57 M. **Mayence,** see R. 36.

30. From Ehrenbreitstein to Wiesbaden.
Railway on the Right Bank.

58$^1/_2$ M. RAILWAY in 1$^3/_4$-2$^3/_4$ hrs. (fares 7 $\mathcal{M}$ 30, 4 $\mathcal{M}$ 40, 2 $\mathcal{M}$ 90 pf.;
express 8 $\mathcal{M}$ 30, 5 $\mathcal{M}$ 40, 3 $\mathcal{M}$ 40 pf.). — Break of journey, see p. 71. —
Views to the right.

The line from Trèves and Coblenz (Moselle Railway) joins ours at
Niederlahnstein (carriages changed). Travellers bound for Kastel (Mainz)
or Frankfort (R. 37a) need not go viâ Wiesbaden, as a direct line to
these towns diverges beyond *Biebrich-West* (p. 219; Map, p. 246).

Ehrenbreitstein (Coblenz), see R. 19. — After leaving the station,
which lies at the foot of the fortress of Ehrenbreitstein (p. 128), the
train passes to the left of the old railway bridge and runs at the
back of Pfaffendorf (p. 128), affording a fine view (r.) of the city and

14 *

the fortifications of the Kartause. — Passengers who start from Cologne (Central Station, p. 39) cross the handsome railway bridge (p. 128) at the island of Oberwerth and join our line at Nieder-lahnstein (see below).

2½ M. *Horchheim* (p. 221). — 4 M. *Niederlahnstein* (p. 221), the junction of the Lahn railway (R. 20). In the opposite direction, passengers bound for Coblenz change carriages here.

The line crosses the *Lahn*. View of Capellen and Stolzenfels to the right, and of Lahneck to the left.

4½ M. *Oberlahnstein* (S.; p. 221). On the left bank are the Königsstuhl and the village of *Rhens* (p. 222).

7 M. *Braubach* (S.), with the *Marksburg* (p. 223). Narrow-gauge line hence to Nastätten (Zollhaus), see p. 223. To the right is *Niederspay*, and farther on, on the same bank, *Oberspay*.

10 M. *Osterspay* (p. 223). Passing the small village of *Filsen*, we now obtain a view of Boppard, beautifully situated on the opposite bank.

13½ M. *Camp* (S.; p. 227), a little above which are the pil-grimage-church and convent of *Bornhofen*, at the foot of the ruined castles of *Sterrenberg* and *Liebenstein* (the 'Brothers', p. 227). Local steamer to Boppard, see p. 224.

17½ M. *Kestert* (p. 227). — 21 M. *St. Goarshausen* (p. 229). Narrow-gauge line hence to Nastätten (Zollhaus), see p. 231. Op-posite lies the picturesque little town of St. Goar, with the extensive ruins of Rheinfels.

The train now passes through a tunnel under the *Lurlei* (p. 231), and through another under the *Rossstein*. On the opposite bank lies Oberwesel, commanded by the Schönburg.

28 M. *Caub* (S.; p. 233), above which rises the ruin of *Guten-fels*. In the middle of the Rhine is the curious old château of the *Pfalz*. Higher up the river, on the opposite bank, lies the vener-able town of Bacharach, overshadowed by the ruin of Stahleck. The train intersects the village of (30 M.) *Lorchhausen*. On the left bank are seen the ruin of Fürstenberg and the village of Rhein-diebach.

32 M. *Lorch* (S.; p. 237). On the opposite bank, farther up, is Niederheimbach, commanded by the round tower of the Heimburg; then the slender tower of the Sooneck, the ruin of Falkenburg, the Clemens-Kapelle, and the picturesque modernized castle of Rhein-stein.

36½ M. *Assmannshausen* (S.; p. 246) is the starting-point of a rack-and-pinion railway to the *Niederwald* (p. 241).

A little higher up, at the so-called 'Binger Loch' (p. 246), the stream becomes very rapid. The train passes below the ruin of *Ehrenfels*, opposite which lie the island with the Mouse Tower and (below the mouth of the Nahe) Bingerbrück, with the Elisenhöhe.

On the opposite bank of the Nahe is Bingen, with the ruin of Klopp and the view-tower on the Rochusberg.

39 M. *Rüdesheim* (S.; p. 240), the station for the Niederwald (p. 241). On the left rises the Brömserburg. Opposite is the Rochusberg, with its chapel (p. 245). The train traverses the vineyards of the Rheingau. Comp. Map, p. 246.

41¹/₂ M. *Geisenheim* (S.; p. 248). — 44 M. *Oestrich-Winkel* (p. 249); the station is at *Mittelheim*, between these two places. Tho the left is Schloss Vollrads. From Winkel to Johannisberg is an easy ascent of ³/₄ hr. (see p. 248).

46¹/₂ M. *Hattenheim* (p. 249). On the hill to the left is Hallgarten; to the N. E., on the slope of the *Bos*, is the Steinberg; to the right is Schloss Reichardtshausen. — 49 M. *Erbach* (p. 250).

50 M. *Eltville* (S.; p. 250); route to *Schlangenbad*, see R. 35b. 52 M. *Niederwalluf* (S.; p. 251), where the train begins to quit the river; 54¹/₂ M. *Schierstein* (p. 252).

56 M. *Biebrich-West* (S.; p. 252). On the opposite bank rise the towers of Mayence. The train turns inland to the left, running parallel for some distance with the Taunus line, and soon reaches —

58¹/₂ M. **Wiesbaden** (see p. 253).

31. The Rhine from Coblenz to Bingen.

STEAMBOAT in 4-5 hrs., downstream in 2¹/₄-3 hrs. (fares 3 ℳ 90, 2 ℳ 30 pf., return-fares 5 ℳ 20, 3 ℳ 10 pf.; express-steamer 4 ℳ 70, return 6 ℳ 20 pf.); from St. Goar to Bingen in 2-2¹/₄ hrs., downstream in 1-1¹/₄ hr. (fares 2 ℳ, 1 ℳ 20 pf., return-fares 2 ℳ 80, 1 ℳ 60 pf.; express-steamer 2 ℳ 40, return 3 ℳ 30 pf.). — The letters S., B., and R. affixed to the name of a place signify, respectively, steamboat-pier, small-boat landing-place, and railway-station.

RAILWAY on the *Left Bank*, see R. 29; on the *Right Bank*, from Ehrenbreitstein to Wiesbaden, see R. 30. — Along the left bank runs an excellent road (to Boppard 14 M., to Bingen 40 M.).

The large white posts on the banks indicate the distance from Kastel-Mayence in kilomètres. As their position is also shown on the accompanying map of the Rhine, the traveller will easily ascertain his exact whereabouts with their aid.

Between Coblenz and Bingen the Rhine flows through the so-called *Rhenish Schist Plateau (Rheinische Schiefergebirge)*, a broad upland plateau of graywacke and schistose rock, intersected by seams of quartz and limestone. The S. part of this geological district includes the Taunus on the E. and the Hunsrück on the W., while to the N., beyond the line of the Lahn and the Moselle, it comprises the Westerwald on the E. and the Eifel on the W. The river-valley forms a deep rift through the hills, sometimes, rather unexpectedly, cutting through the folds of its strata at right angles. This, *e.g.*, is the case below Oberwesel and again near Bingen.

Left Bank.

Coblenz, see p. 121. The steamer passes through the bridge-of-boats connecting Coblenz with Ehrenbreitstein (see p. 128). To the right are the new Government Buildings (p. 124), the Schloss (p. 125), and numerous villas. On the heights above the town are the fortifications of the *Kartause* (p. 127). We pass under the *Pfaffendorf Bridge* (p. 128). A little farther on is the large island of *Oberwerth,* connected with the left bank by a causeway and with the right bank by the *Horchheim Bridge* (p. 127), under which the steamer steers. The wooded hill, just below Capellen, is the *Kuhkopf* (p. 127).

Capellen (R.). — HOTELS. **Bellevue,* with garden, R. 2-3¹/₂, B. 1, D. 3, pens. 5¹/₂-7¹/₂ *ℳ; Stolzenfels,* at the lower end of the town, with shady garden-terrace, R. 1¹/₂-3, B. 1, D. 2¹/₂-3, pens. 5-7 *ℳ; Lahneck,* R. 1¹/₂-2, B. ³/₄, pens. from 4¹/₂ *ℳ,* well spoken of.
MOTOR BOAT to Oberlahnstein (20, 10 pf.), starting above the station.
ELECTRIC TRAMWAY to Coblenz, see p. 121.

Capellen (197 ft.), consisting of a single row of houses on the landward side of the railway-embankment, lies at the foot of the wooded hill which bears the château of Stolzenfels. The château is approached by a winding road of easy ascent (¹/₄ hr.), crossing a viaduct. Beyond the *Klause* (stables), a drawbridge is crossed.

The royal **Castle of Stolzenfels** (505 ft.) was built by Frederick William IV. in 1836-42 from the designs of *Schinkel.* It occupies the site of a fortress of the 13th cent., the pentagonal tower of which (110 ft. high) has been retained. It is open to visitors from 10 to 12 (on Sun. 11 to 12) and from 2 to 7 (in winter 2-4; adm. 25 pf.). A magnificent view is enjoyed from the corner-turret on the right side of the court. The interior is embellished in the romantic taste of 1840. The frescoes on the outside wall, above the garden-colonnade, are by *Lasinsky,* those in the chapel by *E. Deger* (1853-57), and those in the Kleine Rittersaal, by *Stilke* (1842-46). The other objects of interest include arms and armour, drinking vessels, old pictures, and various small works of art.

About 2 M. above Stolzenfels a path diverges to the right from the Schlossweg, leading to the *Augusta-Höhe* and (¹/₂ M. farther) the top of the *Hasenberg,* two points (refuge-huts) commanding a fine view of the valley of the Rhine (there and back 1³/₄-2 hrs.).

About 1¹/₄ M. above Capellen, among tall trees near the highroad, is the *Königsstuhl* ('king's seat'), erected in 1376 by the Emp. Charles IV. on the site of an ancient meeting-place of the Electors. At the end of the 18th cent. it had fallen to decay but in 1843 it was rebuilt, partly out of the old materials. The structure is octagonal in shape, 22 ft. in diameter, and 18 ft. in height.

The first historical mention of the Königsstuhl occurs in 1308, when Henry of Lützelburg was elected emperor. In 1400 the four Rhenish electors here elected Count Palatine Rupert III. as emperor in the stead of the Bohemian King Wenzel, whom they had deprived of the imperial crown at a meeting held the previous day on the opposite bank of the Rhine.

Right Bank.

Ehrenbreitstein, see p. 128. Below the fortress of *Asterstein* (p. 129) lies the picturesque village of *Pfaffendorf,* connected with the left bank by the iron bridge mentioned at p. 128.

The vineyards of *Horchheim* (R.; Holler's Garden Restaurant) produce good red wine. The rail. station lies at the upper end of the village. — The fertile strath between Horchheim and the mouth of the Lahn has been marred by the intrusion of factory-chimneys.

Niederlahnstein (R.; *Douqué,* on the Lahn, $^3/_4$ M. from the rail. station, with garden, R. & B. $2^1/_2$-3, pens. 4-$5^1/_2$ $\mathscr{M}$, good cuisine; *Wochner,* at the station, unpretending), on the right bank of the Lahn (4300 inhab.), is the junction of the Railway of the Right Bank, the line to Coblenz and Trèves, and the Lahn railway (RR. 30, 20). From the road ascending the Lahntal a path diverges to the left, passing several shrines, to ($^1/_2$ hr.) the memorial church on the top of the *Allerheiligen-Berg,* which commands fine views of the valleys of the Lahn and the Rhine. — Below Niederlahnstein, at the mouth of the Lahn, stands the solitary late-Romanesque *Church of St. John,* rebuilt in 1906 and connected with a Benedictine nunnery. The Lahn is crossed near its mouth by a railway-bridge, and by another for the road-traffic (toll 2 pf.).

A little way from the Rhine, on a rocky hill above the Lahn, rises the picturesque castle of **Lahneck,** with its pentagonal tower, once owned by the Electors of Mayence. It is mentioned for the first time in 1224, was destroyed by the French in 1689, and was restored since 1860. It was on seeing this ruin in 1774 that Goethe composed his exquisite 'Geistes-Gruss'.

Oberlahnstein (S. & R.). — The pier of the Cologne and Dusseldorf steamboats is 200 yds., that of the Dutch boats 400 yds. from the State Railway Station. — HOTELS. *Lahneck,* $^1/_2$ M. from the railway-station and the pier, with garden and view; *Breitenbach,* well spoken of, R. $1^1/_2$-2, B. $^1/_2$, pens. 4-6 $\mathscr{M}$; *Weiland,* opposite the railway-station, R. $1^1/_2$-2, B. $^3/_4$, pens. 4-$4^1/_2$ $\mathscr{M}$. — MOTOR BOAT to Capellen 14-20 times daily. — LIGHT RAILWAY to Braubach and Nastätten (see p. 223), starting at the upper end of the town, 7 min. from the State Railway Station.

Oberlahnstein (197 ft.), a thriving town with 8000 inhab., a machine-shop, and an iron-foundry, formerly belonging to the Electors of Mayence, is mentioned in a charter of 890. Several towers recall the former fortifications. *Schloss Martinsburg* at the head of the town, containing an interesting court, once a residence of the Electors of Mayence, dates from 1394; the new part was built in 1712. The *Rathaus* (restored in 1901) is a noteworthy late-Gothic half-timbered edifice, with a prehistoric collection. The *Protestant Church,* at the foot of the town, was built in 1872-75. Ober-

Left Bank.

Just below the Königsstuhl is the building of the *Rhenser Mineralquelle,* a mineral spring rising in the bed of the Rhine, which was known in the 17th cent. and re-discovered in 1857. A new shaft was sunk on the bank to a depth of over 1100 ft. in 1892-95.

Above the Königsstuhl ($^3/_4$ M.) lies the quaint little town (1500 inhab.) of **Rhens** (*Königsstuhl,* with garden, on the river), still partly surrounded by the walls and fosses constructed in 1370 by Archbishop Frederick III. of Cologne. On the highroad, near the S. gate, are several old half-timbered houses. Outside this gate lies the prettily situated old *Parish Church.* There is also a modern church, in a tasteful Gothic style. A finger-post indicates a path over the hill to ($1^1/_4$ hr.) Boppard (comp. below). — We next pass the small village of *Brey,* surrounded by fruit-trees.

[See opposite]

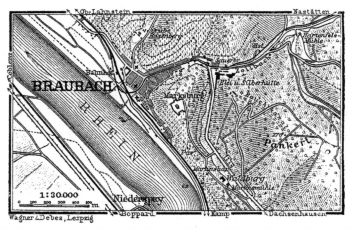

Farther up are the villages (R.) of *Niederspay* (with a modern brick church in the Transition style) and *Oberspay* (Rindsfüsser). On the promontory to the right, round which the Rhine sweeps to the W., stands a half-ruined chapel, the only relic of the village of *Peterspay.* — On the hill to the right stands the *Jacobsberger Hof,* a farmhouse 525 ft. above the Rhine, whence a hill-road leads to (3 M.) Rhens (see above), cutting off the circuit of 6 M. formed by the river. The vineyards on the slopes, known as the *Bopparder Hamm,* produce excellent wine.

Right Bank (Oberlahnstein).

lahnstein is the steamboat-station for Ems (p. 130), which may be reached hence either by the main line viâ Niederlahnstein (p. 221), or by the older line (slow trains only) on the left bank of the Lahn.

In the fertile strath above Oberlahnstein, with its numerous orchards, is the *Victoria-Brunnen,* the mineral water of which is extensively exported.

Braubach (S. & R.) — HOTELS (all near the railway-station). *Kaiserhof,* with garden and view-terrace, R. 2-3, B. ³/₄, pens. 4¹/₂-5 ℳ, very fair; *Rheinischer Hof,* in a quiet situation, with garden, R. 1¹/₂-2, B. ³/₄, pens. 4-4¹/₂ ℳ, well spoken of; *Deutsches Haus,* well spoken of, with beergarden; *Nassauer Hof,* R. 1¹/₂, B. ³/₄, pens. 4-4¹/₂ ℳ.

Braubach, an ancient town with 2800 inhab. (mainly Prot.), is first heard of in a document of 933 and came finally into the hands of the Landgraves of Hesse, who introduced the Reformed doctrine in 1525. At the pier is a war-monument by Bodo Ebhardt (1903).

FROM OBERLAHNSTEIN VIÂ BRAUBACH TO NASTÄTTEN, 20¹/₂ M., narrowgauge railway in 2 hrs. The line follows the Railway of the Right Bank to Braubach (comp. p. 217), and thence ascends the *Zollbach* to *Hof-Zollgrund* (hence viâ the Oberlahnsteiner Forsthaus to Ems, 1¹/₂ hr.; see p. 133). Beyond a bold viaduct it mounts in curves (views to the right) to *Dachsenhausen* (1250 ft.). Fine survey from the *Heisebäumchen* (1345 ft.), ¹/₂ M. to the S. of the station. — Thence the railway descends to *Winterwerb,* whence we may walk viâ *Hof Erlenborn,* the *Dachskopf* (1500 ft.), and *Hof Neuborn* to (2 hrs.) Camp or (2 hrs.) Bornhofen (p. 227). The descent continues viâ *Gemmerich* and *Ehr* to *Marienfels* (705 ft.; with a mineral spring), in the fertile *Mühlbach-Tal.* We then ascend the last-named valley to the S.W., viâ *Miehlen* (725 ft.). — *Nastätten,* see p. 231.

Above Braubach, and reached either by road or footpath in ¹/₂ hr. (guide-posts), rises the ***Marksburg,** 490 ft. above the river, the only old fortress on the Rhine which has escaped destruction.

In 1437 Count Philip of Katzenelnbogen founded a chapel in the castle and dedicated it to St. Mark, after whom the castle has since been named. It belonged to Hesse-Darmstadt from 1479 to 1803, and was then used by the government of Nassau as a state-prison. Since 1900 it has been the property of the Society for the Preservation of German Castles, by whom the interior has been restored in the 15th cent. style (tickets of admission, 40 pf., at the restaurant at the entrance). The castle contains a good collection of armour, weapons, and warlike costumes. The tower (view) was heightened in 1905 after old pictures of the castle.

On the saddle to the S. is the ancient *Chapel of St. Martin* (mentioned in 1242), recently decorated in the 15th cent. style. — The conspicuous chimneys belong to the Braubach lead and silver mines. Mining was carried on here by the Celts before the Roman period.

Opposite Oberspay, ¹/₂ hr. above Braubach, opens the *Dinkholder-Tal,* with a chalybeate spring *(Dinkholder Brunnen)* resembling those of Schwalbach. Walkers may ascend the valley, cross the ridge, and descend on the other side to Camp (p. 227).

On the wooded height above *Osterspay* (R.; Müller) stands the château of *Liebeneck,* belonging to the Baron von Preuschen.

Left Bank.

Boppard (S. & R.). — HOTELS. On the Rhine, with view-terraces: *Spiegel* (Pl. a), R. 2-5, B. 1, D. 2½-3, pens. 5½-8 ℳ, an old-established house; *Bellevue & Rhein-Hôtel* (Pl. b), R. 2-5, B. 1, D. 2½-3, pens. 5-9 ℳ; *Hirsch* (Pl. c), R. 2-3½, B. 1, D. 2½, pens. 5-7 ℳ; *Ackermann* (Pl. d), R. 2½-3, B. 1, D. 2, pens. 5-7 ℳ; *Rebstock*, next door, pens. 4-4½ ℳ, well spoken of; *Salm* (Pl. f), at the lower end of the town, pens. 4-5 ℳ; *Krone* (Pl. g), plain but well spoken of. — In the town: *Lange* (Pl. h), opposite the post-office, pens. from 4½ ℳ, Munich beer; *Bahnhofs-Hôtel* (Pl. i), plain but well spoken of. — *Mühlbad*, at the lower end of the town, a family hotel, pens. 5-9 ℳ, with large garden (closed in winter). — Wine at the *Winzer-Verein*, Christgasse. — PENSIONS. *Frl. König*, Mainzer-Str. 39, pens. 4½-7 ℳ; *Frl. Gerlach*, Simmerner-Str. 11a, pens. 4½-7 ℳ; *Frau Winkelmann*, Mainzer-Str. 15, pens. 4-6 ℳ; *Henzler*, in the Mühltal (p. 226), pens. 30-35 ℳ per week. — *Marienberg Hydropathic Establishment* (p. 226), pens. 7½-13½ ℳ, with lift and central heating (Dr. Höstermann).

LOCAL STEAMER to Camp (p. 227), in connection with all trains on the railway of the right bank. — *Floating Bridge* across the Rhine.

Boppard (210 ft.), the ancient *Bodobriga*, founded by the Celts, was afterwards fortified by the Romans and used as a depôt for their 'slingers' ('Balistarii Bodobricæ'). The old town is still partly surrounded by the mediæval fortifications. Numerous villas have sprung up in the environs. Pop. 5800.

The handsome *Parish Church*, in the late-Romanesque style, founded early in the 12th cent., and rebuilt about a century later, is remarkable for the peculiar 'Norman' vaulting of the nave. The contemporary painted decoration of the interior was carefully restored in 1894-95; the decoration of the choir is modern. — The *Carmelite Church* (1318), nearer the railway-station, in the pointed style, contains a tombstone of the 7th cent. (by the third pillar), carved stalls of the 15th cent., and old mural paintings.

On the Rhine, near the flying bridge, rises the old *Castle* of the Archbishops of Trèves, with a tower, now occupied by law-courts. Beside the moat, behind the castle, are considerable remains of a *Wall* constructed of Roman concrete ('opus spicatum'), and probably dating from the reign of Valentinian I. (364-375 A.D.). When complete it was 10 ft. thick and 26 ft. high, and was strengthened with towers at the angles and 24 semicircular towers along its sides; it enclosed the interior of the town, in the form of a rectangle 1000 ft. long by 500 ft. wide. The original positions of the four gates, each exactly in the centre of one of the sides, are indicated by tablets on the houses No. 78 Ober-Str. (W.), 47 Ober-Str. (E.), 12 Kronengasse (N.), and 7 Kirchgasse (S.).

The suppressed *Franciscan Monastery* with its church, at the upper end of the town, has been converted into a seminary for Roman Catholic teachers. — Knights Templar of Boppard are mentioned among the crusaders at the siege of Ptolemaïs (1191), and fragments of their *Lodge (Tempelhof)*, with round-arched windows, lie in a

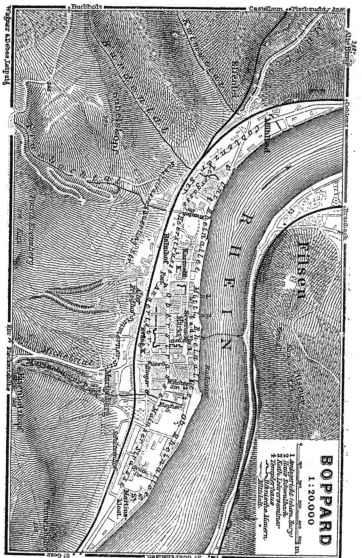

Left Bank (Boppard).

neighbouring side-street. — The old monastery of *St. Martin,* a little farther up the river, is now a reformatory for children.

The Hunsrück Road, which crosses the railway near the *Protestant Church* (1851), leads to the S. to the buildings (1738) of **Marienberg** (295 ft.), formerly a Benedictine nunnery, and now a hydropathic establishment (p. 224). The terrace in front affords a good view. The cloisters in the inner court contain tombs of the nuns. The old park, 9 acres in extent, is open to the public.

The numerous attractive walks in the ENVIRONS OF BOPPARD are indicated by guide-posts and coloured marks (guidebook of the Verschönerungs-Verein, 50 pf.). — The *Kreuzberg* (774 ft.; restaurant) may be ascended in ³/₄ hr. by footpaths through the Fraubach-Tal, or by the more picturesque route through the Michels-Tal and Josephinen-Tal.

Below Boppard, near the Mühlbad (p. 224) and ¹/₃ M. from the rail. station, opens the *Mühltal,* a valley enclosed by wooded hills, along the S. slope of which runs the Hunsrück Railway. On the road, 1 M. up the valley, is the *Pension Henzler* (p. 224). The 'Tempel', seen on the hill to the right, is the outlook of the **Alte Burg** (815 ft.), reached by a path ascending to the right, near the Pens. Henzler. At the top of the hill the path forks, the left branch leading to the Vierseen-Platz, the right to the Alte Burg. From the *Vierseen-Platz,* or 'place of the four lakes' (995 ft.; restaurant), four apparently unconnected parts of the Rhine are visible. A path descends hence past the *Jacobsberger Hof* (p. 222) to (1³/₄ hr.) *Rhens* (p. 222).

On the other side of the Mühltal the Kronprinzen-Weg leads from the Pens. Henzler to Boppard viâ the *Elfenlei.* — From the pension we may ascend the valley, passing a *Fish Breeding Establishment* (50 min. from Boppard; restaurant) and traversing fine woods, to (2¹/₂ hrs.) *Winningen* (p. 162). — From Boppard to the Moselle, see p. 191.

Hunsrück Railway and *Fleckerts-Höhe,* see pp. 190-192.

The valley now begins to contract again. At the mouth of a side-valley appears —

Salzig (R.; *Traube,* well spoken of), a village of 1600 inhab., embosomed in orchards of cherry-trees. In good years the value of the cherry-crop, mostly exported to Holland and England, amounts to 10,000*l.* About ³/₄ M. up the valley are the *Baths of Salzig (Bad Salzig),* with saline springs (65° and 82° Fahr.) which are efficacious in cases of catarrh, gall-stones, gout, and rheumatism. The equipments include a comfortable hotel, a bath-house, and a covered promenade. — Farther up we skirt the cliff named *Plobus.*

Hirzenach (R.; Traube, R. 1¹/₂-2, D. 1¹/₂, pens. 3¹/₂-4¹/₂ *M*). A handsome building, once a deanery, and the tasteful early-Gothic church (ca. 1170), belonged to the Abbey of Siegburg. — At the foot of the wooded *Prinzenstein* (view-pavilion) are the extensive buildings of the *Werlau Mines* (lead and silver).

Below the ruined castle of Rheinfels (p. 228), which comes into sight on the right, opens the attractive *Valley of the Gründelbach,* through which ascends the road to the Hunsrück (to Hungenroth 7 M.; thence to the rail. station of Halsenbach, 1¹/₄ M. more; comp. p. 191).

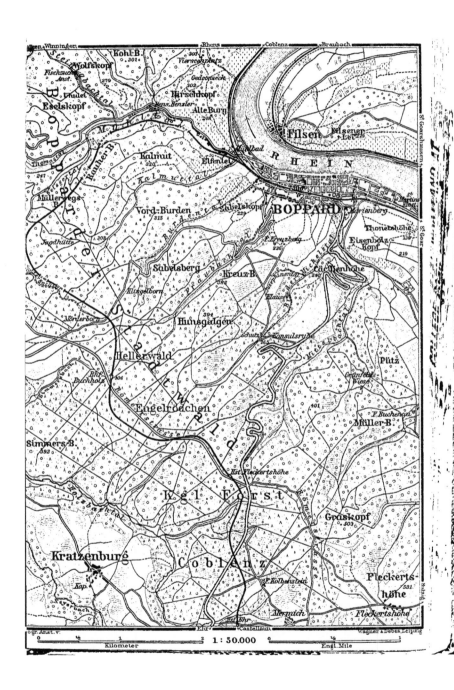

Right Bank.

Opposite Boppard rises the *Filsener Lei* (750 ft.), which the river sweeps round in a bold curve. On the bank, 600 yds. from the landing-place of the flying bridge (p. 224), lies the village of *Filsen*, whence the view-pavilion on the Filser Lei is reached in 20 minutes. We turn to the right in the village, pass through an archway and by several shrines, and reach a small chapel, whence we ascend to the right through brushwood. We may descend in 50 min. to Camp or viâ Liebeneck to Osterpay.

Camp (R. & S.; *Anker*, R. & B. 2-2$\frac{1}{2}$, D. 1$\frac{1}{2}$, pens. 4-4$\frac{1}{2}$ *M*), a village with 1800 inhab., frequented as a summer-residence. The name is derived from an earthen mound on the hill, which has been assumed to mark the site of a Roman camp (campus), though it probably dates only from the Thirty Years' War. The *Wilhelmshöhe*, to the S., is a good point of view.

A road shaded with walnut-trees and skirting vineyards leads along the bank from Camp to the ($\frac{3}{4}$ M.) convent of —

Bornhofen (*Hôtel Marienberg*, R. & B. 2$\frac{1}{4}$-3, D. 2$\frac{3}{4}$-4, pens. 4$\frac{1}{2}$-5$\frac{1}{2}$ *M*, very fair; *Morbach zum Liebenstein*, R. & B. 2-2$\frac{1}{2}$, pens. 4-4$\frac{1}{2}$ *M*), with a Gothic church erected in 1435, a great resort of pilgrims. — On a bold rocky eminence above the convent stand the twin castles of —

Sterrenberg and **Liebenstein,** better known as *The Brothers*, connected by a sharp chine of rock. The castles were held as early as the 12th cent. as a fief of the empire by the Knights of Boland, and in 1317 came into the possession of the Electors of Trèves. Sterrenberg, the higher ruin, is of great extent and commands a charming view. It is separated from Liebenstein by a moat and a massive wall, known as the 'Streit-Mauer' (wall of combat) in reference to the legend according to which the castles belonged to two brothers who loved the same maiden and came within an ace of a fratricidal duel.

Immediately beyond *Nieder-Kestert* (R.; Stern) the Rhine bends sharply to the S.E. The river becomes more rapid, and the gravelly banks in its channel disappear.

Ehrental, a little farther up, is a small village inhabited by miners who work the lead-mines in the vicinity.

Wellmich (Adler), with a small Gothic church, is commanded by the castle of *Thurnberg*, or *Deurenburg*. This stronghold, completed in 1363 by Archbishop Kuno von Falkenstein, was derisively called the **Mouse** *(Maus)* by the Counts of Katzenelnbogen in contradistinction to their 'Cat' (p. 229). It has been rebuilt by its present owner and commands a fine view.

St. Goar (S. & R.). — HOTELS (all with view-terraces). **Schneider*, R. 2-4, B. 1¹/₄, D. 3, pens. 6-8 ℳ, with central heating; **Lilie* (closed from the middle of Oct. to 1st April), R. 2-5, B. 1, D. 3, S. 2, pens. 6-10 ℳ, both these in the Rhine Promenades, at the lower end of the town; **Rheinfels*, R. 2-5, B. 1, D. 3, S. 2, pens. 5-8 ℳ, oppos e the steamboat-pier. — *Goldener Löwe*, Rhein-Promenade 1, R. 1¹/₂-2¹/₂, B. ³/₄, pens. 4¹/₂-6 ℳ; *Rose*, Heer-Str. 29, also at the lower end of the town, R. 1¹/₂-3, B. ³/₄, pens. 4-5 ℳ; *Traube*, R. 1¹/₂-2, B. ³/₄, pens. 4-4¹/₂ ℳ; *Jägerhaus*, R. & B. 1³/₄-3, pens. 4 ℳ, both at the steamboat-pier; *Zur Schönen Aussicht*, Heer-Str. 175, R. 1¹/₂-3, B. ³/₄, pens. 4-4¹/₂ ℳ. — On the road to Oberwesel: *Keutmann*, opposite the Loreley, ³/₄ M. from the railway-station and the steamboat-pier, R. 2, D. 1¹/₂, pens. 4-4¹/₂ ℳ. — *Rheinlust*, a garden-restaurant on the hillside above the town; *Volk*, on the Rhine (Munich beer).

STEAM FERRY to St. Goarshausen (p. 229), 10 pf.

ENGLISH CHURCH SERVICE in July and August.

St. Goar, a town with 1600 inhab. and a large harbour, owes its name and origin to St. Goar, who preached the gospel here in the middle of the 6th century. From the 13th cent. onward it was the capital of the lower county of Katzenelnbogen (comp. p. 231), which fell to the line of Hesse-Rheinfels in 1567. With the fortress of Rheinfels, crowning the hill above, it was considered the strongest place in the middle part of the Rhine valley.

The *Protestant Church*, in the market-place, below the railway-station, was originally a collegiate foundation of 1137 and was rebuilt in 1444-69. The crypt and choir are still Romanesque. The interior contains an excellent late-Gothic pulpit in stone and the admirable Renaissance monuments of the Landgrave Philip (d. 1583) and his countess (in a private chapel). The interesting mural paintings of the 15th cent. were freed of whitewash and restored in 1907. — The *Roman Catholic Church*, at the lower end of the town, is adorned with an old stone effigy of St. Goar, and an inscription.

The castle of **Rheinfels** (adm. 20 pf.), rising at the back of the town, 375 ft. above the Rhine (¹/₄ hr. from the pier), is the most imposing ruin on the river. It was founded by Count Diether III. of Katzenelnbogen (d. 1276), a friend of the Emp. Frederick II., and a new Rhine-toll was established here. In 1692 it was successfully defended by the Hessian General von Görz against the French General Count Tallard. In 1758 the castle was surprised and taken by the French, who kept a garrison in it till 1763. Thirty years later it was basely deserted by the Hessian commandant, and fell into the hands of the French revolutionary army (1794). Three years afterwards it was blown up. In 1843 the ruins were purchased by Emp. William. The interior contains little worthy of note; view limited. — The path to the castle leads under the railway and passes the churchyard-wall, on which is the *'Flammensäule'*, a rough sandstone obelisk of pre-Roman origin, 5 ft. in height.

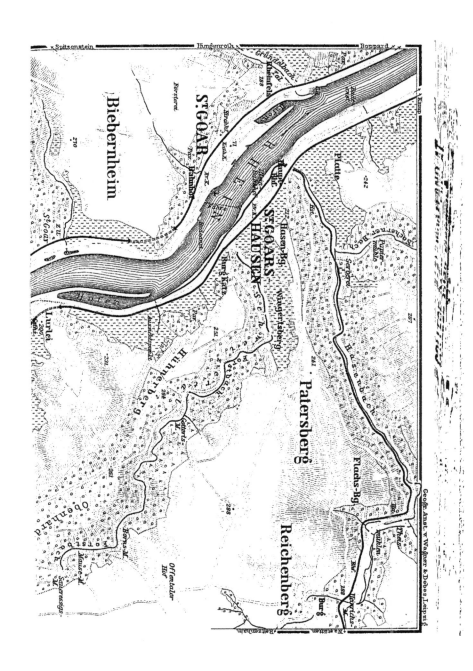

Right Bank.

St. Goarshausen (R.; *Adler*, very fair; *Nassauer Hof;* ferry to St. Goar, see p. 228; *English Church Service* in July & Aug.) is a small town with 1660 inhab., the upper part of which is so confined between the river and the hill that a bulwark of masonry, on which two watch-towers are situated, had to be built at an early period to protect the town against inundations. The Protestant church was finished in 1863.

Above St. Goarshausen to the S., about halfway up the hill, rises the castle of *Neu-Katzenelnbogen,* commonly called the **Cat** *(Katz)*, erected in 1393 by Count Johann of Katzenelnbogen, whose family became extinct in 1479. It then belonged to the Hessian princes, and was destroyed by the French in 1806. The present owner has built himself a house in a harmonious style on the old foundations (no admission). — At the foot of the hill opens the rocky *Schweizer-Tal* or *Swiss Valley,* traversed by a road passing under the railway.

The LURLEI (see p. 231; there & back 2$1/2$ hrs.) is most conveniently visited by following the Schweizer-Tal road, past the (1$1/4$ M.) *Gotterts-Mühle,* to the top of the hill, where we turn to the right by a field-path (guide-post). The summit of the Lurlei (hotel) commands an admirable view of the deep Rhine valley. For the descent we may choose either the steep path with steps reaching the road at the ($1/4$ hr.) tunnel, or the easier path ($1/2$ hr.) through the vineyards, which reaches the St. Goarshausen road near the entrance of the winter-harbour. The latter path, however, is closed in autumn. — A footpath leads from the Lurlei to the ($1/4$ hr.) pavilion on the *Hühnerberg* (866 ft.), commanding a view of the basin of St. Goar (another path also from the guide-post above the Gotterts-Mühle).

EXCURSION TO REICHENBERG, 3$1/2$ M. We either take the narrow-gauge line mentioned below, or follow the path leading through the *Hasenbach-Tal,* a valley which opens a little below St. Goarshausen. The footpath diverges to the right from the road through the valley, and rejoins it near Reichenberg. A pleasant way back is viâ the village of *Patersberg* (1125 ft.), on the brink of the vine-clad slopes above the Swiss Valley, or past the *Offentaler Hof* (best view of the castle of Reichenberg), to the S., and then through the Swiss Valley.

The castle of *Reichenberg,* erected in 1284 by Count Wilhelm I. of Katzenelnbogen, rebuilt in 1319, and during the Hessian supremacy the residence of the governor of the lower county (p. 231), was at length sold in 1818 for the sake of the building materials. Fortunately, however, it escaped demolition, and is still a grand and picturesque ruin with a lofty tower (p. xxxi). It is now the residence of Prof. Wolfgang von Oettingen. The approach to the court is striking. Here, on the right, rises the imposing *Herrenhaus,* or dwelling-house, which originally consisted of three stories. The dividing beams have been broken away, the early-Romanesque capitals of the columns date from a much older building. The granite columns to the right and left of the entrance to the *Tower* are said to have been brought from Ingelheim (p. 216); they are parts of the same shaft, which has been sawn through the middle. The tower commands a view of the neighbourhood. A second tower to the E., connected with the other by a lofty curtain-wall, is half destroyed. Fee to the guide, $1/2$-1 *ℳ.*

Left Bank (St. Goar).

The *Spitzenstein* (1316 ft. above the sea, 1106 ft. above the Rhine) commands a beautiful view. It is reached from St. Goar in 1¹/₄ hr. by the road (p. 232) leading past the Rheinfels to (¹/₂ hr.) *Biebernheim*, which may also be reached in 20 min. by a zigzag path from the rail. station. We continue to follow the road to (40 min.) the *Drei Buchen* ('Three Beeches'), a good point of view, near which is a finger-post (l.) indicating the way to (10 min.) the shelter on the Spitzenstein. The descent may be made viâ *Niederburg* to (1 hr.) Oberwesel (see below), or viâ *Urbar* to the Rhine opposite the Lurlei and so back to St. Goar.

A little above St. Goar is the narrowest (about 220 yds.) and deepest (76 ft.) part of the river. The famous echo of the Lurlei, returned by the lofty cliffs on both sides, is not audible from the steamer or amid the noise of the day, but may be successfully wakened in the quiet of early morning or late evening.

The steep rocks of the *Kammereck*, to the right, are penetrated by three railway-tunnels.

As we approach Oberwesel, a ridge of rocks, known as the '*Seven Virgins*', is visible when the river is low. It is said that these rugged masses were once seven fair maidens of the Schönburg, who were condemned by the river-god for their prudery to this metamorphosis.

· **Oberwesel** (S. & R.). — *Hôtel-Restaurant Gertum*, opposite the steamboat-pier, R. & B. from 2¹/₂, D. 1¹/₂-3 *M*; *Goldener Pfropfenzieher*, at the lower end of the village, somewhat back from the road, with garden, R. 1¹/₂-2¹/₂, B. ³/₄, D. 2-2¹/₂, pens. .5 *M*, very fair; *Deutsches Haus*, on the highroad, with garden, R. & B. 2¹/₄ *M*; *Diedert*, plain.

Oberwesel, an old town with 2900 inhab., named *Vosavia* in Peutinger's map of Roman roads (p. xxiv), and once a free town of the empire, was afterwards ceded by Henry VII. (1308-13) to his brother, Archbishop Baldwin of Trèves. Its churches, walls, and towers (14th cent.), over which frown the ruins of the Schönburg, render Oberwesel one of the most picturesque spots on the Rhine.

At the S. end of the town rises the conspicuous *Frauen-Kirche*, or *Church of Our Lady*, a fine Gothic edifice in red sandstone, erected in 1307-31 and lately restored. At variance with the usual Gothic custom, the buttresses are inside, the result being to give an air of almost forbidding plainness to the exterior. ..

Right Bank (St. Goarshausen).

FROM ST. GOARSHAUSEN TO ZOLLHAUS, 27¹/₂ M., narrow-gauge railway in about 3 hrs. The line ascends the *Hasenbach-Tal* (p. 229; station) to (3 M.) *Reichenberg* (700 ft.; Crämer), whence there is a fine view of the castle (¹/₂ M.). — At (6 M.) *Bogel* (1180 ft.) we reach the edge of the plateau between the Rhine and the Lahn. — The line then descends into the *Mühlbach-Tal* (p. 223).

10 M. **Nastätten** (820 ft.; *Guntrum*, very fair) is the junction of the line to Braubach (p. 223). — 14 M. *Holzhausen auf der Heide* (1275 ft.) is situated on the road from Ems to Schwalbach and Wiesbaden (the so-called Báder-Strasse), whence a footpath, diverging to the left about 1 M. to the S.W. of the station, leads through wood to the (1 M.) *Alteburg*, a Roman entrenched camp.

21 M. **Katzenelnbogen** (915 ft.; *Hôt. Bremser*, very fair), on the *Dörsbach*, lies at the base of a porphyry cliff crowned by the ancestral castle of the Counts of Katzenelnbogen, who since the 11th cent. extended their sway over the district between the Rhine and the Lahn (the 'lower county') and over the now Hessian province of Starkenburg (the 'upper county'). On the death of Philip, the last count, in 1479, his possessions passed to the Landgrave of Upper Hesse. In 1815 all the lower county on the right bank of the Rhine became Prussian.

25 M. *Hohlenfels* is dominated by the ruins of the castle of that name (940 ft.), beside which is a more recent castle, now occupied as a plain but good inn. — 27¹/₂ M. *Zollhaus*, see p. 264.

On the left rise the imposing rocks of the *Lurlei,* or *Loreley,* 430 ft. above the Rhine. The well-known legend of the fairy who had her dwelling on the rock, and, like the sirens of old, enticed sailors and fishermen to their destruction in the rapids at the foot of the precipice, has long been a favourite theme with the poet and the painter. Heine's beautiful ballad (1823) and Silcher's music have combined to lend it a worldwide popularity. According to Marner, a poet of the 13th cent., the Nibelungen treasure lies hidden beneath the 'Lurlenberg'. The name means rock ('Lei') of the 'Luren', or mountain-imps who raise the teasing echo. — At the foot of the Lurlei is a large winter-harbour.

Opposite Oberwesel rises the *Rossstein*, a rocky point penetrated by a tunnel and confining the Rhine to a channel 220 yds. in width. The stream bends sharply to the left (S.).

Left Bank (Oberwesel).

INTERIOR (entrance on the N. side; sexton's house in the market-
place). The *Screen* between the choir and nave dates from the 14th century. The *High Altar*, of 1331, is adorned within by delicate wood-carving and outside by painted figures of saints. The late-Gothic retable
and the painting of the choir (1897) are modern. By the side-altars and
in the aisles are several *Paintings of the Lower Rhenish School;* that
at the N. side-altar has a representation of the nave of the church. On
the piers of the nave are interesting *Mural Paintings* of the 15-16th centuries. At the W. end of the N. aisle is the old retable of the high-
altar, a notable example of the Rhenish late-Renaissance (1625; restored
in 1907). In the N. chapel and in the nave are several *Tombs of the
Knights and Counts of Schönburg* (16-17th cent.; see below). By the
W. wall is the late-Gothic monument of Canon Lutern (d. 1505).

The Gothic *Church of St. Werner,* partly resting on the town-
wall, on the side next the Rhine, was (like the church of the same
name at Bacharach, p. 236) built about 1301. — At the lower end of
the town is the handsome *Ochsen-Turm*, with its lofty pinnacles.

Upon the hill lies the late-Gothic *Church of St. Martin,* with
its castle-like tower. The interior contains a Renaissance pulpit
(1618), a coloured and gilt group of St. Anna and the Virgin (Gothic),
and a small winged altar with reliefs of the Passion, the Ascension,
and the Last Judgment (the sacristan lives at No. 223, near the choir).

The route to the *Spitzenstein* (1½ hr.; p. 230) ascends to the left
near the Ochsen-Turm, just outside the town-wall. — A pleasant walk
may be taken along the Rhine to (3½ M.) *St. Goar* (p. 228).

Above Oberwesel rise the modern château (Herr von Osterroth)
and the picturesque old ruin of **Schönburg,** with its four huge
towers. The castle, erected in the 12th cent. and destroyed by the

[See opposite]

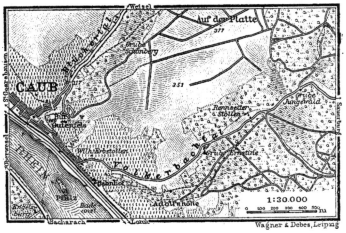

1:30.000

Wagner & Debes, Leipzig

[See opposite]

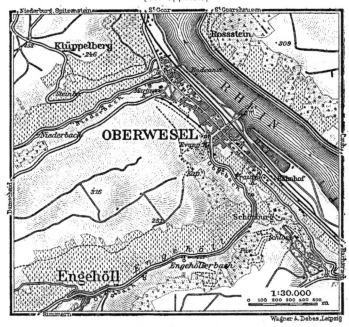

Right Bank.

Caub (R. & S.; *Zur Pfalz*, at the station; *Zum Grünen Wald*; *Adler*, R. 1½-2 ℳ; wine at the *Turm*), an ancient town with 2370 inhab., still partly surrounded with mediæval fortifications, is important on account of its productive subterranean slate-quarries and as a wine-growing centre. The *Church*, dating from the 12th cent. and partly modernized in 1770, has, with the exception of the choir, been used by the Protestants ever since the Reformation. An attractive promenade along the town-walls, built over in the 18th cent., is reached from beside the square tower. A large *Statue of Blücher*, by Schaper, erected in 1894, shows the field-marshal pointing out to his soldiers the way over the Rhine (comp. p. 236). A tablet on the 'Stadt Mannheim' marks his headquarters from Dec. 31st, 1813, to Jan. 2nd, 1814.

At the back of the town rises the castle of **Gutenfels,** with its lofty square pinnacled tower, named *Cube* in the middle ages, which was sold together with the little town of Caub by the Knights

15*

Left Bank (Oberwesel).

French in 1689, was the cradle of a once mighty race which became extinct in 1719. In 1615 it was the birthplace of Count Frederick Hermann of Schönburg, better known as Marshal Schomberg, who fought under the Prince of Orange, and in 1668, when in the French service, compelled the Spaniards to acknowledge the House of Braganza. On the revocation of the Edict of Nantes, he was obliged to quit the French service, and under the Elector of Brandenburg became minister of state, and governor of Prussia; he finally passed over to England with the Prince of Orange, and fell at the memorable battle of the Boyne in 1690. The castle now belongs to Messrs. Rhinelander of New York. About ¹/₂ M. from the station, on the road ascending from the Frauen-Kirche, a footpath diverges to the right (10 min.). We ring at the entrance to the castle (fee). — On the W. side, a pleasant path descends into the rocky *Engehöll* valley, which yields an excellent wine. From the village of Engehöll (wine at Schneider's) to Oberwesel, 2¹/₄ M.

Just before reaching Bacharach we pass the island called the *Bacharacher Werth*. The channel of the river, here known as the 'Wilde Gefährt', is crossed by a reef.

Bacharach (S. & R.). — HOTELS. **Herbrecht* (late *Wasum*), at the station, with a view-terrace, 4 min. from the steamboat-pier, R. 2-3, B. 1, D. 2¹/₂ (on Sun. 3), S. 1¹/₂. pens. 5-7 *M.* — In the town: *Altes Haus*, R. & B. 2, pens. 3¹/₂-4 *M.* — Wine at *Bastian's* and at *Jeiter & Müller's* (both with views).

Bacharach, an ancient town with 1900 inhab., mentioned as *Bachercho* in 1019 and as *Bagaracha* in 1140 and belonging to the Elector Palatine down to 1803, lies at the entrance to the *Steeger-Tal*, above which, to the left, rises the ruin of St. Werner's church. The old town-walls, with their three-sided towers at intervals of 100-150 paces, afford a good example of mediæval fortifications. Bacharach was noted for its wine at an early period, and down to the 16th cent. was one of the greatest wine-marts on the river. Pope Pius II. caused a cask of 'Bacharach wine' to be brought to Rome annually, and the town of Nuremberg obtained its freedom in return for a yearly tribute to Emp. Wenzel of four tuns of the same wine.

Along the Rhine runs a long esplanade, laid out as pleasure-grounds. A walk should also be taken along the old wall, against which lean the houses on the river-side of the town.

In the Markt-Platz, where the road through the Steeger-Tal diverges from the main street of the town, rises the Protestant *Church of St. Peter,* or Templars' Church, a highly interesting late-Romanesque edifice of elegant proportions, dating from the beginning of the 13th cent. and recently restored. It includes a round choir originally decorated in polychrome, two round E. towers, and

Right Bank (Caub).

of Falkenstein to the Palatinate in 1277. The building has recently been restored. The Earl of Cornwall, who was elected King of Germany in 1257, is said to have become enamoured here of the beautiful Countess Beatrix of Falkenstein, whom he married on the death of his first wife in 1269. The castle is reached in 10-15 min. by a path leading through the Blücher-Tal and over the landslip of 1876.

At the mouth of the *Volkenbach-Tal*, below the station, is the *Wilhelm Erbstollen*, a slate-quarry worked since 1837, to which visitors are admitted 9-12 and 1-5 (tickets at the office). — The road ascending the valley, past the *Rennseiter Stollen*, leads to the (1½ hr.) *Sauerburg* (p. 239). — The *Adolfshöhe* (20 min.) and the *Dürscheider Weg* (20 min.) are view-points near Caub.

Above Caub, on a ledge of rock in the middle of the Rhine, rises the *Pfalz,* or *Pfalzgrafenstein*, a hexagonal building, founded by Emp. Lewis the Bavarian (1314-47) and well preserved externally and internally. It has a pentagonal tower covered with an unsightly roof, numerous turrets and jutting corners, loopholes in every direction, and one entrance only, situated about 6 ft. above the rock, and reached by means of a ladder. On the S. side is seen the lion of the Palatinate as bearer of the escutcheon of the ancient lords of the castle. The interior (keys kept by a boatman at Caub, who ferries visitors to the building; fee 75 pf.) is uninteresting.

[See opposite]

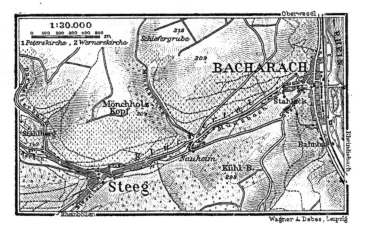

Left Bank (Bacharach).

a square W. tower. Under this last is a fine early-Gothic porch.
A little to the N. of the church is the *Altes Haus Inn*, a tasteful
example of half-timbered architecture (1568), restored in 1897.

On a slight eminence (ascent on the S. side of the church of
St. Peter) stands the graceful *Church of St. Werner*, erected in
1293 in the Gothic style in the form of a trefoil, partly restored in
the 15th cent., but now a ruin, one-third of the original building
having been destroyed. The delicate tracery of the windows should
be noticed. It was erected to commemorate the canonization of St.
Werner, a boy who, according to tradition, was murdered by Jews
in 1286, and whose body was landed here after having miraculously
floated up the stream from Oberwesel. Above the church (10 min.
walk) rises the castle of Stahleck (see below).

The *Steeger-Tal*, at the back of the town, affords a pleasant walk;
it is sometimes called the *Blücher-Tal* from the fact that Blücher after
his passage of the Rhine on 1st Jan., 1814, pursued a body of French
troops through this valley towards the Hunsrück. After about 1 M. we
reach the village of **Steeg** (Hütwohl). By passing to the left of the
church, ascending to the right by (10 min.) the Leinerts-Weg (beyond the
old tower), and following the (¼ hr.) road to the right, we reach the
'Schönblick', a good point of view. The road goes on to Rheinböllen
(p. 192). — On the hill above the right branch of the valley rises the
ruined castle of **Stahlberg,** which like those of Stahleck and Fürstenberg (see below) once belonged to the Counts Palatine. It is reached by
a climb of 20 minutes.

From Steeg a ridge-path ('Höhenweg'; see p. xvii) leads to the *Lausch-
Hütte* and the *Ernst-Ludwig-Turm*.

Above Bacharach rises the once strongly-fortified castle of
Stahleck, the extensive ruins of which extend down to the valley.
It was destroyed by the French in 1689. The date of its erection is
unknown. Hermann of Stahleck became Count Palatine of the Rhine
in 1142 but was deposed by Emp. Frederick I. in 1155 (comp. p. 331).

On a rocky eminence, above the village of *Rheindiebach*, rise
the ruins of **Fürstenberg,** made over to the Palatinate in 1243
as a fief of Cologne. In 1292, when Adolph of Nassau was on his
way to be crowned at Aix-la-Chapelle, the garrison of the castle
had the audacity forcibly to detain the vessel of the king for the
purpose of levying toll. In 1321 the castle was taken by the Emperor Lewis the Bavarian from his opponent Frederick the Fair,
and presented to his consort Margaret of Holland. In 1689 it was
destroyed by the French.

The brook entering the Rhine here formerly separated the domains
of the Electors of Mayence and the Palatinate. — In its valley lie the
villages of *Oberdiebach* and *Manubach*, both noted for their wine.

Niederheimbach (R.; Rheinischer Hof), a long village, commanded by the massive tower of *Hoheneck*, or **Heimburg,** a
castle of the 13th and 14th cent., recently restored, next comes in

Right Bank.

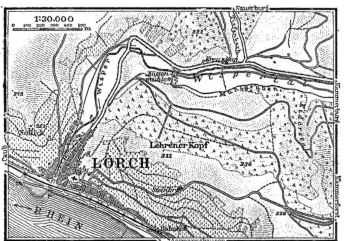

Wagner & Debes, Leipzig

At the mouth of the *Retzbach*, nearly opposite the castle of Stahleck (p. 236), is the hamlet of *Lorchhausen*, with a modern Gothic church.

Opposite the Fürstenberg, on the right bank of the *Wisper*, which falls into the Rhine just below Lorch (comp. p. 239), stands the ruined castle of **Nollich** (580 ft. above the Rhine), mentioned in 1110. The rugged cliff on its W. slope is called the *'Devil's Ladder'*, of which a legend records that a knight of Lorch with the assistance of mountain-sprites once scaled it on horseback, and thus gained the hand of his lady-love. The Wisper-Tal is unenviably known for the keen 'Wisper Wind', which blows through it towards the Rhine.

Lorch (R. & B.; *Krone*, with garden, R. & B. 2-2¹/₂, pens. 4¹/₂-5 *M*, good wine of its own growing; *Schmidt*, at the upper end of the town), a small town with 2200 inhab., mentioned in a charter as early as 832, has always been reckoned as belonging to

Left Bank (Niedcrheimbach).

view. At the island named the *Lorcher Werth* the Rhine is nearly
$1/2$ M. wide.

The valley of the Rhine now slightly contracts. On the right
rises the slender tower of **Sooneck,** commanding the entrance to
a ravine. The castle, which was erected by Archbishop Willigis of
Mayence about 1010, was destroyed by Emp. Rudolph of Hapsburg,
but rebuilt in the 14th century. The ruin was restored in 1834 by
Emp. William I. and now belongs to Emp. William II.

On an eminence beyond *Trechtingshausen* or *Trechtlingshausen* (R.; Weisses Ross, interesting visitors' book) rises the
Reichenstein, or **Falkenburg,** dismantled by Rudolph of Hapsburg as a robbers' stronghold in 1282, refortified by Elector Lewis
of the Palatinate in 1290, and finally destroyed by the French in
1689. The castle (restored) is now private property. At the foot of
the hill is the entrance to the *Morgenbach-Tal.*

The Morgcubach-Tal to a distance of about 1 M. is one of the most
romantic lateral valleys of the Rhine. Just above the mill (inn), where
the most picturesque view is enjoyed, a path to the left ascends in $3/4$ hr.
to the Schweizerhaus (p. 247).

On a mound formed by the detritus brought down by the Morgenbach stands the venerable *Klemens-Kapelle,* a small late-Romanesque edifice, with late-Gothic choir-stalls. It is supposed to have
been built by the knights of Waldeck to ensure the souls' peace of
the robber-knights put to death by Rudolph of Hapsburg.

Farther on, halfway up the hill, rises the castle of *Rheinstein*
(p. 247).

Just above *Bingerbrück* (p. 245) the *Nahe* unites with the Rhine.
The steamers do not touch at Bingerbrück. Over *Bingen,* on the
opposite bank of the Nahe, rise the Klopp and the Rochusberg, with
its view-tower (see p. 243).

Right Bank (Lorch).

the Rheingau. In the middle ages it was a favourite residence of noble families. The lofty Gothic *Church of St. Martin*, of the 13-15th cent., which possesses the finest bells in the Rheingau, was entirely restored in 1871-74. The high-altar with rich late-Gothic carving of 1483, a fine late-Gothic font of 1464, and the monument of the knight *Joh. Hilchen von Lorch* (d. 1548) merit inspection. The inscription on the last records that Hilchen distinguished himself against the Turks, and as field-marshal in 1543-44 against the French. His house, a handsome Renaissance building of 1546-48, adorned with scupturing, is situated on the Rhine about the middle of the village. In front of the church is a fine stone Crucifix of 1491.

The road through the *Wisper-Tal (comp. p. 237) to Langen-Schwalbach ($20\frac{1}{2}$ M.; carriage with one horse 20, with two horses 30 ℳ; there and back 25 or 35 ℳ) leads by (6 M.) the *Kammerberger Mühle* (inn), the ruins of *Rheinberg* and *Kammerburg*, and the ($2\frac{1}{4}$ M.) *Lauken-Mühle* (inn) to ($2\frac{1}{4}$ M.) the ruin of *Gerolstein*, the finest point in the valley. About $1\frac{1}{2}$ M. farther on, beyond the *Greulings-Mühle*, the road quits the Wisper-Tal and enters the *Fischbach-Tal*. After passing the ($\frac{1}{2}$ M.) *Riesen-Mühle* it reaches the long valley of the *Dornbach*, which it follows to a point beyond (3 M.) *Ramschied*. Near Ramschied a saline spring is passed on the left. We now ascend in windings, cross the old Rheingau road ('Hohe Strasse'; 1585 ft.), and descend to ($4\frac{1}{2}$ M.) *Schwalbach* (p. 264).

In the valley of the *Sauer*, which unites with the Wisper $1\frac{1}{4}$ M. above Lorch, is the **Sauerburg**, $3\frac{3}{4}$ M. from Lorch and $2\frac{1}{2}$ M. from Caub, once in the possession of the Sickingen family, and destroyed by the French in 1689 (recently restored). In the churchyard of *Sauertal*, below the castle, is the tomb of the last Sickingen, who died in poverty in 1836. — The Rheinhöhen-Weg (p. xvii) leads past the Sauerburg.

Opposite Trechtingshausen opens the *Boden-Tal*, at the mouth of which are the vineyards that yield the Bodentaler wine, mentioned as early as 1107. A zigzag path ascends hence through wood to the top of the *Teufelskädrich* (1365 ft.).

At *Assmanshausen* (p. 246) the Rhine suddenly contracts (*'Binger Loch'*). In the middle of the river rises the *Mouse Tower*. Nearly opposite Bingerbrück, below the *Rossel*, is the ruin of *Ehrenfels*, about halfway up the Niederwald. See R. 32.

32. Rüdesheim and the Niederwald.
Bingen. Assmannshausen.

A visit to the *Niederwald*, on foot, may be made from either Rüdesheim or Assmannshausen in 2¹/₂-3 hrs., or, with the aid of the mountain-railways (Zahnradbahnen) in 1¹/₂-2 hrs. The ascent from Assmannshausen has the advantage of presenting the views in an increasing ratio of interest. For *Bingen* and the Rochusberg 3 hrs. should be allowed, while the *Rheinstein* may be visited from either Assmannshausen or Bingen in 1¹/₂-2 hrs. The combination forms a day of unusual interest. Bingen should be visited in the afternoon so as to have the sun behind us as we look towards the Niederwald. — A SMALL STEAMER of the Niederwald Railway Co. plies from mid-April to the end of Sept. 6-7 times a day between Rüdesheim, Bingen, Assmannshausen, and Rheinstein (fares 50 & 35 pf.). At both Rüdesheim and Bingen it starts from the dock of the Cologne and Düsseldorf steamers.

Rüdesheim. — STEAMBOAT PIERS. The pier of the *Cologne and Düsseldorf Co.* is in the middle of the river-front, ¹/₃ M. from the State Railway Station (p. 218) at the lower end of the town and 300 yds. from the Niederwald Railway Station (see below); the piers of the *Dutch Company* and the local boats for *Bingen* and *Assmannshausen* are nearer the State Railway Station. — *Steam Ferry Boat* to Bingerbrück starting from the State Railway Station (passage under the railway) every 20-30 min. (20, 10 pf.).

HOTELS. *Darmstädter Hof, at the steamboat-piers, R. 2-4, B. 1-1¹/₄, déj. 2¹/₂, D. 3¹/₂, S. 2¹/₂, pens. 7¹/₂-12 ℳ; *Jung, at the State Railway Station, R. 2¹/₂-5, B. 1¹/₄, D. 3, pens. 6¹/₂-10 ℳ (closed Nov. to Feb.), both these with baths, garden-terraces, and wine of their own growing; *Rheinstein, at the steamboat-piers, R. 2-4, B. 1¹/₄, D. 3, S. 2-3, pens. 6¹/₂-8 ℳ, with garden-terrace and wine of its own growing (closed Oct. 15th to April 15th); *Bellevue, between the State Railway Station and the steamboat-piers, R. 2-4, B. 1, D. 3, pens. 6-10 ℳ, with baths and restaurant. — *Rheinischer Hof*, *Ehrhard*, *Massmann*, R. & B. 2¹/₂-6, D. 1¹/₂-3 ℳ, these three also at the piers and very fair. — *Hôtel-Restaurant Winzerhaus*, Ober-Str. 1, behind the Hôtel Jung, with wine-room (Metternicher Hof); *Weil*, near the State Railway Station, R. & B. 2¹/₂-3¹/₂ ℳ, with restaurant. — *Traube*, R. 1¹/₂-2¹/₂ ℳ; *Lill*, R. 1¹/₂-2 ℳ; both in the Rhein-Str.; *Hohenzollern*, Germania-Str., near the piers.

RESTAURANTS AND WINE ROOMS at the *Hotels* and at the *State Railway Station*; *Rheinhalle*, close to the rail. station, on the Rhine (closed in winter); *Old German Wine Room*, D. (12-2) from 2 ℳ, at the station of the Zahnradbahn; *Joh. Müller*, Drosselgasse 5 (also rooms to let).

BATHS. Two establishments on the Rhine.

CARRIAGE (with two horses) to the Niederwald Monument and back (1-4 pers.) 6 ℳ; returning viâ Assmannshausen 12 ℳ. The view-points on the Niederwald are accessible to walkers only.

NIEDERWALD RAILWAY (rack-and-pinion system), ascent in 12 min (fare 1 ℳ 5 pf.; descent 50 pf.); round-trip tickets, also available for the Assmannshausen Railway, 1 ℳ 55 pf. The station is at the upper end of the town. Omnibus connection in summer with the State Railway Station.

BOATS to Bingen, 1-10 pers. 1 ℳ; Bingerbrück, 1-5 pers. 2 ℳ; to Assmannshausen 1-6 pers. 3 ℳ; to Rheinstein and Assmannshausen 5 ℳ. Each additional pers. 10 pf.; trunk 10 pf.

Rüdesheim (255 ft.), a district-town of 5000 inhab., with large 'champagne' cellars and an extensive wine-trade, lies in a sunny situation at the S. base of the *Niederwald* (p. 241). It is mentioned in a document of 864, and its celebrated wine can boast the longest

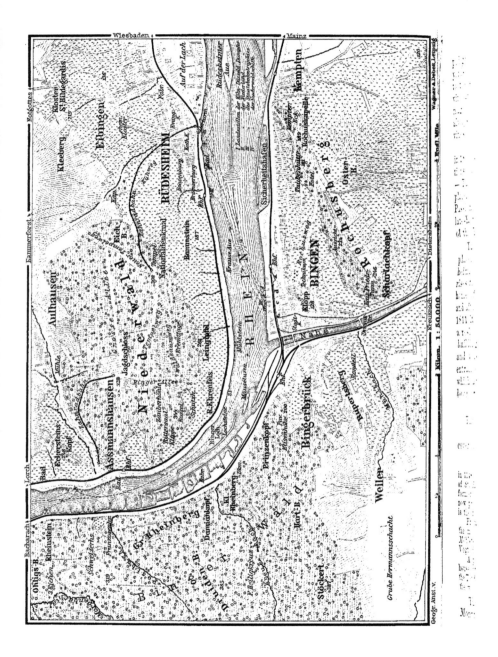

pedigree in the Rheingau. The best sorts are yielded by the vineyards behind the town, called the *Hinterhaus*, the *Rottland*, close
to the station, and those of the *Rüdesheimer Berg* (the terraced
vineyards to the W. of the town). According to tradition Charlemagne observed from his palace at Ingelheim (p. 216) that the snow
always melted first on the Rüdesheimer Berg, and therefore caused
vines to be brought from Tramin (near Botzen) and planted here.

At the upper end of the town are the *Protestant Church*, built
in 1855, and the late-Gothic *Adlerturm*, a relic of the old fortifications. Adjacent is the station of the Niederwald railway (p. 240).
— The Gothic *Church of St. James* (Rom. Cath.), in the market-
place, built about 1390-1400, has interesting paintings from the
Passion on the vaulting (of a slightly later date), and contains a
late-Renaissance altar (ca. 1590) and two Renaissance monuments
of the Brömsers of Rüdesheim (1543 and 1567).

The *Vorderburg*, a fragment of a square tower near the market-
place, 33 ft. in height, is a relic of one of the three castles of Rüdesheim. — At the lower end of the town, near the Rhenish station,
rises the *Brömserburg*, or properly the *Niederburg*, the ancestral
home of the Knights of Rüdesheim, who became extinct in 1548,
and afterwards in the hands of the Archbishops of Mayence. Since
1811 it has belonged to the Counts Ingelheim, who fitted it up as
a residence. It is now leased to a club. It is an unadorned ashlar
building of three stories, 108 ft. long, 82 ft. wide, and 62 ft. high,
and was formerly crowned with a projecting gallery. The main
entrance is at the S.W. angle. The lower part of the walls, within
which are staircases and passages, is 8-13 ft. thick. — The *Ober-
burg*, or *Boosenburg*, behind the Brömserburg, was entirely rebuilt
in 1868, with the exception of the keep.

The *Brömserhof*, a mansion of the 16-17th cent. (now a charitable institution), in the Obergasse (No. 6), has a pointed tower
covered with slates and contains ancient frescoes (1558).

On the slope of the hill, 1/2 M. to the N.E. of Rüdesheim, lies *Eibingen*
(446 ft.; Fendel's Tavern), with the old nunnery of that name, founded
in 1148 and secularized in 1803; a little to the N. is the new nunnery
of *St. Hildegard* (1901). Farther to the N.E., on the hillside, is the
former Capuchin convent of *Notgottes (Agonia Domini)*, founded in 1621,
now private property. About 3/4 M. to the E. (21/4 M. from Rüdesheim)
is the former monastery of *Mariental*.

From Rüdesheim to the ruin of *Ehrenfels* (p. 246), 1/2 hr. Opposite
the mouth of the Nahe, close to the right bank of the Rhine, is the
Mühlstein, a quartz rock with a cavity containing the heart of Niklas
Vogt (d. 1836), the historian (comp. p. 249).

A pleasant walk may be taken to the N.W. to (11/2 hr.) the forester's
house of *Kammerforst* (1520 ft.; restaurant with rooms, pens. 4 M), near
the Teufelskädrich (p. 239). From Kammerforst a broad path leads through
the wood to *Lorch.* Comp. Map, p. 216.

The ***Niederwald** (1080 ft.), with its conspicuous National
Monument and its beautiful views, marks the upper end of the nar-

rower part of the Rhine valley just as the Seven Mountains (p. 98) do the lower. Geographically it belongs to the W. Taunus, which reaches the Rhine at this point. The geological formation is gray-wacke and clay slate; and the weathered débris of these rocks on the slopes makes an excellent soil for the vine. The top is clothed with oaks and beeches.

FROM RÜDESHEIM TO THE NIEDERWALD MONUMENT. The *Rack-and-Pinion Railway* (p. 240) ascends gently through vineyards to the terminus (Jung's Garden Restaurant, very fair), about 3 min. from the monument. — The *Road* (2¹/₄ M.) ascends in a wider sweep. — *Walkers* reach the monument in ³/₄ hr. either by a path (closed when the grapes are ripe) through the vineyards to the N. of the railway-station (finger-post at Jung's Hotel) or by the 'Kühweg', passing the Roman Catholic church.

The *National Monument on the Niederwald, erected in commemoration of the unanimous rising of the German people and the foundation of the new German empire in 1870-71, stands upon a projecting spur of the hill (985 ft. above the sea-level; 740 ft. above the Rhine), opposite Bingen. It was begun in 1877 from the designs of *Johannes Schilling* of Dresden and was inaugurated in 1883 in the presence of the Emperor and other reigning princes of Germany. The huge basis is 82 ft. high, while the noble figure of *Germania, with the imperial crown and the laurel-wreathed sword, an emblem of the unity and strength of the empire, is 34 ft. in height. The principal relief, on the side of the pedestal facing the river, symbolizes the 'Wacht am Rhein'. It contains portraits of King William of Prussia and other German princes and generals, together with representatives of the troops from the different parts of Germany, with the text of the famous song below; to the right and left are allegorical figures of Peace and *War, while below are Rhenus and Mosella, the latter as the future guardian of the W. frontier of the empire. The fine reliefs on the sides of the pedestal represent the departure and the return of the troops. — The ter-race in front commands an admirable *Survey of the entire Rhein-gau. At our feet, on the left bank of the Rhine, lies Bingen, with its large harbour and the castle of Klopp, overtopped by the Rochus-berg; the broad river with its verdant islands winds through the charming landscape; villages, country-houses, and farms border both banks (esp. numerous on the right bank); in clear weather the Melibocus (p. 319) is visible to the S.E. beyond the plain of the Rhine; to the S. we have a glimpse of the vine-clad valley of the Nahe, breaking through the hills between Bingen and Bingerbrück; beyond rises the distant Donnersberg (p. 456).

A finger-post immediately behind the custodian's house indicates the 'Waldsaumweg', leading to (25 min.) the 'Rossel' (p. 243).

The 'Tempelweg', beginning at the railway-station, leads past the back of the monument to (1 M.) the Jagdschloss.

From Assmannshausen (p. 246) the railway (Zahnradbahn; p. 246) ascends through the Assmannshäuser-Tal and sweeps round to the Jagdschloss. — The road continues to follow the valley and passes *Aulhausen.* — *Walkers* ($^3/_4$ hr.) diverge to the right from the road at a small shrine (guide-post) about $^1/_5$ M. from the church, cross the Zahnradbahn, and ascend the winding path, finally passing through the W. enclosing wall of the Jagdschloss preserve.

The **Jagdschloss** (1076 ft.), an old shooting-lodge, belongs to government, but has been rented to a hotel-keeper of Assmannshausen (R. 2-3, B. 1, D. 2-3, pens. in the 'Logierhaus' opposite from $5^1/_2$ ℳ). Picturesque silvan walks in the neighbourhood.

From the Jagdschloss the 'Tempelweg' (see above) leads direct to the Monument in 20 minutes. Walkers should select the path leading by the Rossel. Passing the 'Logierhaus' on the left, they reach in 10 min. the *Zauberhöhle* or 'magic cave', with three apertures commanding views, through clearings in the wood, of the Klemens-Kapelle, with the Falkenburg, the castle of Rheinstein, and the Schweizerhaus.

About 5 min. walk farther on is the **Rossel (1130 ft. above the sea, 866 ft. above the river), an artificial ruin on the highest point of the Niederwald, commanding a beautiful prospect: to the left, Bingen, Hesse, and the valley of the Nahe, with the Donnersberg in the background (to the left); to the right the wooded heights of the Hunsrück (Soonwald). Far below, the Rhine rushes through the Binger Loch, past the ruin of Ehrenfels. On the right, in the immediate vicinity, rises Rheinstein, with the Schweizerhaus; farther down stands the tree-girt Clemens-Kapelle, beyond it the Falkenburg. — The *Klippe,* a point of view to the W. of and below the Rossel, commands a picturesquely framed view of the valley of the Rhine, and is most conveniently visited from the Zauberhöhle before ascending to the Rossel.

A finger-post at the foot of the Rossel indicates the 'Waldsaumweg', leading E. to (25 min.) the National Monument (p. 242). Halfway is the *Eremitage,* an open blockhouse with a picturesque view of Bingen and the Nahe. At the stone-bench, 5 min. farther on, we keep to the right.

From Rüdesheim we cross to ($^1/_4$ hr.) Bingen, on the left bank, either by one of the steamers of the Rhine Co. or by the local boat mentioned at p. 240.

Bingen. — HOTELS. On the Rhine Quay: **Hôtel Victoria* (Pl. a), nearest the station, R. 2-5, B. $1^1/_4$, déj. 2, D. 3, S. $2^1/_2$, pens. 6-10 ℳ, with large restaurant, garden, view-terrace, and wine of its own growing; **Starkenburger Hof* (Pl. b), at the lower end of the town, $^1/_4$ M.

from the Bingerbrück Railway Station, newly equipped, R. 2-4, B. 1, D. 2¹/₂, peñs. 6-10 *M*, with café-restaurant and terrace; .*Weisses Ross & Goethehaus* (Pl. c), below the Hôtel Victoria, R. & B. 3-4, D. 1³/₄-2¹/₂, pens. 5-8 *M* (closed Nov. to March); *Distel* (Pl. d), R. 1³/₄-2¹/₂, B. ³/₄, D. 1³/₄-3¹/₂, pens. 5-6¹/₂ *M*, with pretty garden; *Deutsches Haus*, R. 1³/₄-3, B. ³/₄, D. 1¹/₂-2, pens. from 5 *M*, very fair; *Göbel*, R. 1³/₄-2¹/₂, B. ³/₄, D. 1³/₄-2¹/₂ *M*, also very fair; *Karpfen*, R. 1¹/₂-2¹/₂, B. ³/₄, D. 1-2 *M*, plain but good. — In the Town: *Goldner Pflug*, Kapuziner-Str. 12, near the market-place; *Hilsdorf*, in the Speise-Markt, R. & B. 2¹/₂-3, D. from 1¹/₄ *M*, plain but good, with café-restaurant. — *Hôtel Rochusberg* (p. 245), R. 1¹/₂-2¹/₂, B. 1, D. 2¹/₂, pens. 5-6 *M*, omnibus from the station 50 pf., with a garden-restaurant (closed Oct. to April). — At Bingerbrück (p. 245): *Mohrmann*, R. 2-2¹/₂ *M*, above the station.

ELECTRIC TRAMWAYS. No. 1. From *Bingen Railway Station*, past the Ferry Station, to *Bingerbrück*. — No. 2. From *Bingen Railway Station* viâ *Büdesheim* to *Dietersheim*.

BOATS. To the Mouse Tower, 1-2 pers. 1¹/₂ *M*, each additional pers. 25 pf.; to Assmannshausen, 1-6 pers. 3 *M*; to Rheinstein and Assmannshausen, with 2 hrs'. stay at the former, 5 *M*. — BATHS in the Rhine.

CARRIAGES. To the Rochus-Kapelle and back, one-horse, 1-2 pers. 3¹/₂, 3-4 pers. 4 *M*; two-horse 1-2 pers. 4, 3-4 pers. 5 *M*; to the Scharlachkopf and back, one-horse 4 or 5 *M*, two-horse 5 or 6 *M*; to Rheinstein and back, 4 or 5, & 5 or 6 *M*.

RAILWAY STATION (*Restaurant*, with veranda), at the upper end of the town, see p. 216. — *Steamboat Piers* (Pl. I, II, & IV), for the Cologne-Düsseldorf and Dutch steamboats, and also for local boats of the Niederwald Railway Co. (p. 240), all on the Rhine Quay.

Bingen (250 ft.), a Hessian district-town with 10,000 inhab., lies at the confluence of the *Nahe* and Rhine, above the Binger Loch (p. 246), the difficult navigation of which made the place an important river-port. The name is of Celtic origin. The Romans erected a castle here, at the point whence their military roads to Cologne and Trèves diverged, and in 70 A.D. they defeated the rebellious Gauls in the battle of Bingium. In the middle ages it was a free town of the empire, but it soon passed, with the Rheingau, into the hands of the Elector of Mayence. During the Thirty Years' War it was repeatedly captured, and in 1689 it was almost totally destroyed by the French. The recent prosperity of the town is testified by its new winter-harbour, quays, and embankments. It is the seat of the *Rhenish Technical College* (900 students), of a *Technical and Industrial School*, and of a *Commercial School*. The late-Gothic *Parish Church*, in the Altstadt, near the Nahe, is of the 15th cent., with a Romanesque crypt of the 11th, but it has been modernized. The Gothic font dates from the 15th century. The old *Rathaus* is now the district court.

Above the town, on the site of the ancient Roman fortress, rises the castle of **Klopp**, which has been restored and extended since 1854. It now accommodates the municipal offices. The tower and terrace afford a beautiful view. The tower contains a collection of antiquities (adm. 20 pf.). The Graben-Str., the Schloss-Str., and the Rochus-Str. (beyond the Hôtel d'Angleterre) ascend to it from the Rhine. Emp. Henry IV. was seized here at Christmas, 1105, by his treacherous son (afterwards Henry V.), who carried him captive to the castle of Böckelheim (comp. pp. 209, 217).

Behind Bingen rises the **Rochusberg,** the ascent of which takes 1¼ hr., there and back, and, combined with visits to the *Rochus-Kapelle* and the *Scharlachkopf*, about 1¾ hr. by carriage. The routes thither are all provided with guide-posts. Like the Niederwald, on the opposite bank of the Rhine, the Rochusberg belongs to the Rhenish slate-district, and it is also interesting to botanists. From the castle of Klopp we may proceed direct viâ the Mariahilf-Str. and the Rupertus-Str. At the top we reach the *Hôtel Rochusberg* (p. 244), with a veranda, commanding a fine view, and thence we follow the road on the margin of the wood (or through the woods, below, passing a round dovecot), which leads to the chapel in 8 min. more. The *Rochus-Kapelle* (340 ft. above the Rhine), a chapel on the E. brow of the Rochusberg, was built in 1677 in memory of the plague of 1666, struck by lightning and burnt to the ground in 1889, and rebuilt of red Main sandstone in 1889-94 in a late-Gothic style from plans by Meckel. At the festival of St. Roch (first Sunday after 15th Aug.), charmingly described by Goethe, thousands of persons congregate here and celebrate certain solemnities, to which open-air dances, music, and feasting form a lively sequel. — The *Kempter Eck*, 4 min. to the N.E. of the chapel, commands a view over the whole of the Rheingau (p. 247).

From the Hôtel Rochusberg a shady path leads to the W. in 20 min. to the **Scharlachkopf** (807 ft.), the highest point of the Rochusberg, the S. slopes of which, extending to the district of Büdesheim (p. 455), yield the generous *Scharlachberger* wine. A fine view of the Nahe Valley, the Taunus, and the Rheingau is obtained from the *Kaiser-Friedrich-Turm* on the top, 69 ft. high.

Near its mouth the Nahe is crossed by a *Railway Bridge,* also used as a roadway. The old *Bridge* ('Drusus-Brücke'), with its seven arches, ½ M. farther up, is built on the foundations of a Roman bridge, and has been repeatedly restored. Below the bridge is an underground Romanesque chapel. — Above the old bridge the Hunsrück road ascends to the *Rondell*, a fine point of view.

On the left or Prussian bank of the Nahe, on the *Rupertsberg*, lies **Bingerbrück** (hotel, see p. 244), a village with 2800 inhab., which sprang up on the construction of the Rhine and Nahe railways. A Benedictine nunnery, formerly situated on the Rupertsberg, was destroyed by the Swedes in 1632.

The *Elisenhöhe* (830 ft.; pavilion), reached from Bingerbrück station in ½ hr., commands a fine view of the Rheingau and the Niederwald. — Other good points of view are the *Prinzenkopf* and farther on, the *Damiankopf*, between Bingerbrück and Rheinstein. — From the Damiankopf a path leads to the *Schweizerhaus* (Vaitsberger Hof, Burg Rheinstein, see p. 247) in ¾ hr. Two other paths (finger-posts) lead to the left from the road along the Rhine to (1¼ hr.) the Schweizerhaus, one diverging about 1 M. from Bingerbrück, the other (and more attractive) about 1 M. farther on.

16 *

On a quartz-rock in the middle of the Rhine (forming the upper end of the Binger Loch reef, see below) is situated the **Mouse Tower,** built early in the 13th cent., probably for the exaction of river-tolls, and reconstructed in 1856. The legend according to which the cruel Bishop Hatto of Mayence (914) caused a number of poor people, whom he compared to mice bent on devouring the corn, to be burned in a barn during a famine, whereupon he was pursued to this island by hordes of mice and devoured alive, is first heard of in the 14th cent. and is perhaps due to a popular misunderstanding of the name (old German *Mûsturm =* arsenal). A flag on the tower indicates that the passage of the Binger Loch is open for vessels descending the river.

On the opposite (right) bank of the Rhine, halfway up the Nieder-wald, amid the terraced vineyards of the Rüdesheimer Berg, rises the ruined castle of **Ehrenfels,** erected about 1210 by Philipp von Bolanden, 'Vizedom' of the Rheingau (comp. p. 248), the frequent residence of the Archbishops of Mayence in the 15th cent., much damaged by the Swedes in 1635, and finally destroyed by the French in 1689. The two towers are connected by a lofty wall on the side exposed to attack, facing the hill.

The valley of the Rhine here contracts suddenly and forms the *Binger Loch,* at the point where the river, on reaching the Rhenish Slate Hill District, has penetrated a bar of hard quartz rock. There used to be a fall here. Down to the 10th cent. the rapids formed an insuperable barrier for the navigators of the river. Repeated attempts were made to widen the navigable channel, especially in the 13th and 17th cent., but the removal of the dangerous reef had to wait for the technical skill of the 19th century. The last extensive series of blasting operations took place in 1890-1900. Even to-day the channel is little more than 100 yds. in width. The total fall between Bingen and Assmannshausen is about 9 ft., equivalent to nearly 1 : 1000.

Assmannshausen. — The Station of the Railway of the Right Bank is at the upper end of the village, the Steamboat Pier at the lower end of the village.

Hotels (all on the Rhine). **Krone,* R. 2-2$^1/_2$, B. 1, D. 2-3, pens. 5$^1/_2$-6 $\mathcal{M}$ (a marble bust on the outside of the house commemorates the visit of the poet Ferdinand Freiligrath in 1844; the hotel-registers contain the names of numerous poets and artists); *Park-Hôtel,* a new building next door, belonging to the same proprietor; **Anker,* R. 2-2$^1/_2$, B. 1, D. 2$^1/_2$, pens. 5-5$^1/_2$ $\mathcal{M}$. — *Rhein-Hôtel,* at the lower end of the village, opposite the pier, R. & B. 2$^1/_2$-3$^1/_2$, D. 1$^1/_2$-3, pens. 5$^1/_2$-7 $\mathcal{M}$, very fair; *Rheinstein,* at the upper end of the village; *Reutershan,* R. 1$^1/_2$-2$^1/_2$, B. $^3/_4$ $\mathcal{M}$; *Germania,* at the station, R. 1$^1/_2$-2 D. 1-1$^1/_2$ $\mathcal{M}$.

Zahnradbahn, or *Rack-and-Pinion Railway,* to the top of the Nieder-wald; the station is at the E. end of the village, near the church.

Assmannshausen (260 ft.), a village with 1000 inhab., 3 M. below Rüdesheim, is celebrated for its full-bodied and high-flavoured

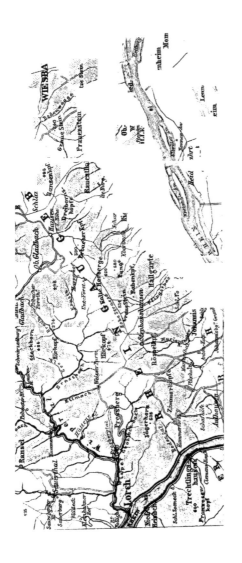

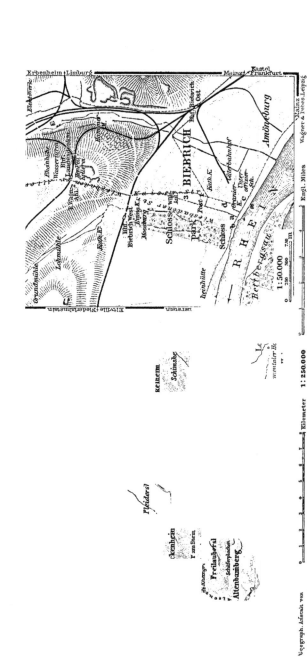

red wine, which grows on the sunny N. slopes of the side-valley behind. From the pier we reach the main street by the archway above the Anker Hotel; from the rail. station of the Right Bank we reach the Niederwald Railway by passing the Germania Hotel. About ¼ M. below the village is *Bad Assmannshausen*, with a warm alkaline spring (90°), containing lithia, which was known as far back as the Roman period. It is efficacious in gout and rheumatism. The Kurhaus is surrounded by some noble trees.

A motor-launch (30 pf., there & back 50 pf.) maintains communication with the left bank of the Rhine, where, halfway up the hill and 260 ft. above the river, stands the picturesque castle of *Rheinstein. An easy path ascends to it from the wharf in 10 minutes. It was formerly called the *Vaitzberg*, or *Vautsberg*. Its origin is unknown, but it is mentioned as early as 1279, and after 1348 was a residence of Kuno von Falkenstein, Archbishop of Trèves, since whose time it has frequently appeared in history. In 1825-29 Prince Frederick of Prussia caused the castle to be restored in the mediæval style; it now belongs to Prince Henry of Prussia. Rheinstein is a very interesting example of a mediæval castle, of which the massive battlemented towers called the 'Bergfriede', the 'Herrenhaus' or 'Palas', and the substantial 'Schildmauer' on the side exposed to attack are well represented. A good collection of armour and antiquities is shown in the interior (adm. 1 ℳ, two or more pers. 50 pf. each). The chapel contains the tombs of Prince Frederick (d. 1863) and his son George (d. 1902).

On the road and railway on the left bank, ³/₄-1 M. below Rheinstein. are the *Clemens-Kapelle* and the *Falkenburg* (see p. 238). — Bingen is 2¹/₂ M. distant by road. Attractive forest-paths lead over the ridge to the S. of Rheinstein to (1¹/₂ hr.) Bingerbrück (comp. p. 245), passing the *Schweizerhaus* (inn) and the *Vaitsberger Hof.* Or from the Schweizerhaus we may proceed viâ the *Drei Eichen* ('Three Oaks') to the valley of the Morgenbach (p. 238).

33. The Rhine from Bingen to Mayence.

STEAMBOAT (comp. p. xv) in 2-2¹/₂ hrs., downstream in 1³/₄ hr. (fares 1 ℳ 60, 95 pf., return-fares 2 ℳ 10, 1 ℳ 25 pf.; express steamer 1 ℳ 90 pf., return-fare 2 ℳ 50 pf.). — Steamboat-pier at Bingen, see p. 244. — The steamboat-station for Wiesbaden and for passengers going on to Frankfort by the Railway of the Right Bank is at *Biebrich* (comp. p. 277); agents at Wiesbaden, see p. 256. — Abbreviations, see p. 74.

Railway of the Left Bank, see R. 29; of the Right Bank, see R. 30.

In the basin of Mayence, the northernmost portion of the plain of the upper Rhine, the Rhine comes into contact with the Taunus, a projection of the Rhenish Slate Hills, which forces the river to make a sharp bend towards the W. The fall of the river decreases to 1:7800 (or ca. 5 inches per mile); and it reaches the majestic width of 650-880 yds. Its channel is split up by numerous long and narrow islands. The S. slopes of the Taunus, facing the river, are among the warmest and most fertile regions in Germany. A small strip of it, near Biebrich, has belonged from time immemorial to the Counts of Nassau. The W. part of the district, beginning at Nieder-Walluf, forms the **Rheingau,**

a famous wine-growing district, which used to belong to the Archbishops
of Mayence and was enclosed by the '*Gebück*', a densely woven and
almost impenetrable belt of trees. The culture of the vine here goes
back to the pre-Carlovingian era and attained its present dimensions as
early as the 13th century. The wine-growers were 'freemen' of the empire and were under the care of an archiepiscopal official ('Vizedom'),
but lost their privileges after the Peasants' Rebellion of 1527. The
district passed to Nassau in 1803 and to Prussia in 1866. The left bank
of the Rhine between Bingen and Mayence is Hessian.

Bingen (S. & R.), the *Scharlachkopf*, the vine-clad *Rochusberg*,
and the *Rochus-Kapelle*, see pp. 244, 245. The steamer crosses the
river, calls at *Rüdesheim* (S. & R.), and steers along the right bank,
where the more important localities are situated.

On the slopes of the left bank lie the villages of *Kempten* (p. 455)
and *Gaulsheim* (R.; p. 216).

1. **Geisenheim** (S. & R.; *Frankfurter Hof,* on the highroad,
R. & B. 2³/₄-4, D. 1¹/₂, pens. 4¹/₂-6 ℳ, an old and well-known
house; *Deutsches Haus,* at the pier, R. 2¹/₂-3, pens. 4-5 ℳ), a
pleasant little town with 3900 inhab., mentioned in history as early
as 779, and now boasting of a number of country-houses. The late-
Gothic *Church,* completed in 1518, has a conspicuous portal, and
open towers of red sandstone added by Hoffmann in 1838; the
interior was modernized in 1745-52. The adjoining tower (100 ft.
high) belongs to a factory of sparkling wine. In front of the *Rathaus* is a venerable lime-tree. At the upper (E.) end of the town
are a new Romanesque church and the mansions of *Counts Ingelheim*
and *Schönborn.* At the W., or lower, entrance to the town is the
villa *Monrepos* of Herr von Lade, with its interesting orchards,
now the property of the state and maintained as a pomological and
viticultural museum. Near the station is the *Œnological and
Pomological Academy,* a government-institution for the scientific
instruction of wine and fruit growers. Behind rises the red *Rote-
berg,* the slopes of which produce the best Geisenheim wine.

To the right we have a fine view of Ingelheim (p. 216). — The
large building on the bank to the left is a factory for the making
of printing and lithographing machines.

1. **Schloss Johannisberg,** a conspicuous point in the landscape, picturesquely situated on a vine-clad eminence, 340 ft. above
the Rhine and 607 ft. above the sea, may be reached in ³/₄ hr. either
from Geisenheim, viâ *Johannisberg im Grund* (Kauter's Tavern),
or from Winkel (p. 249). Near Johannisberg im Grund, at the foot
of the Johannisberg, lies the '*Klause*', the remains of a nunnery
founded about 1150, and suppressed in 1452. — The extensive
château was erected in 1757-59 by the Prince-Abbot of Fulda, on
the site of an old Benedictine monastery founded by Archbishop
Ruthard ca. 1090. In 1802, on the suppression of the Abbey of Fulda
(which had purchased the Johannisberg from Mayence in 1716), the
castle became the property of the Prince of Orange; in 1807 it was

presented by Napoleon to Marshal Kellermann, and in 1816 it was conferred by the Emp. of Austria as an imperial fief on Prince Clemens of Metternich, who did not fully recognize the sovereignty of the Duke of Nassau till 1851. The famous vineyards (p. xxi), in area about 55 acres, are most carefully cultivated. Visitors are not admitted to the interior of the château, though they may usually enjoy the striking view from the terrace in front. The *Chapel* of the château, consecrated in 1130 and modernized in the 18-19th cent., contains the tomb of *Nik. Vogt* (p. 241). — To the E. of the château, on the Winkel road, is the villa of Hr. von Mumm of Frankfort.

A few minutes to the N.W. of the Schloss lies **Dorf Johannis-berg** (*Zum Schloss Johannisberg,* very fair). On the *Hanselberg,* to the W. of the village, is the Villa Bauer. Farther to the N.W., amid wood, is the old convent of *Mariental* (p. 241).

l. **Winkel** (*Rheingauer Hof,* Haupt-Str. 21, R. & B. 2-2$^1/_2$ *ℳ*) and *Mittelheim* (R.; old Romanesque church) together form one long street and contain 2500 inhabitants. Near the Rhine is the *Graue Haus,* a stone structure of the 9th cent. and unquestionably one of the oldest dwelling-houses in Germany. At the W. extremity is situated the country-house of the *Brentanos,* often visited by Goethe and still containing memorials of him (comp. Bettina von Arnim's 'Correspondence of a Child').

r. *Frei-Weinheim* is the steamer-station for Ingelheim (Selztal Railway; p. 216).

At (l.) **Oestrich** (R.; *Schwan,* on the Rhine, very fair) the in-habitants of the Rheingau formerly swore fealty to each newly-elected Archbishop of Mayence (comp. p. 248). The village (2700 in-hab.) with its projecting crane, and the Johannisberg in the back-ground, affords a pleasant picture.

On the slope behind Oestrich lies **Hallgarten** (656 ft.; *Kremer,* plain), in the midst of vineyards; near it is the well-preserved château of *Vollrads,* probably erected in 1362 by a member of the *Greiffenklau* family, in whose possession it still is. Above Hallgarten (1 hr.) rises the *Hallgarter Zange* (1900 ft.; inn), with a view-tower, whence various attractive walks may be taken (numerous guide-posts). — From the Zange an attractive walk may be taken viâ the *Mapper Hof,* with remains of the Gebück (p. 248) and a romantic little ruin, to Schlangenbad (p. 265). Another follows the wooded valley of the *Ernstbach* to (2$^1/_2$-3 hrs.) the Wisper-Tal, reached at a point $^3/_4$ M. below the *Lauken-Mühle* (p. 239). Or we may go on from the Mapper Hof viâ the *Erbacher Forsthaus* to Gerolstein, in the Wisper-Tal (p. 239). Other paths lead W. along the ridge from the Zange, passing *Stephanshausen* (1085 ft.; Gute Quelle) to (3 hrs.) Kammerforst (p. 241) or Johannisberg. All these routes are provided with finger-posts.

Before reaching (l.) **Hattenheim** (*Hôtel-Restaurant Ress,* on the Rhine, R. 1$^1/_2$-2$^1/_2$, pens. 4$^1/_2$-7 *ℳ*, with garden, very good; wine at the Winzerverein's; beer at *Noll's*), a village of 1300 inhab., with extensive cellars for the storage of wine. We have a view of *Schloss Reichardtshausen,* with its large park.

A road leads inland from Hattenheim to the (2¹/₄ M.) once celebrated Cistercian Abbey of **Eberbach** (restaurant at the entrance), founded in 1116, erected into an abbey by St. Bernard of Clairvaux in 1131, and situated in one of those sequestered valleys which this order always selected for their monasteries. ('Bernardus valles, montes Benedictus amabat, oppida Franciscus, celebres Ignatius urbes.') The Abbey (adm. 10-50 pf.), secularized in 1803, and now a royal domain and partly used as a prison, was built at various periods from the 12th to the 15th century. The Romanesque *Abbey Church*, consecrated in 1186 and restored in 1868, contains a number of **Monuments*, most of them of abbots of the 12-18th centuries. The Gothic monument which encloses the tombs of Gerlach, Archbishop of Mayence (d. 1371), and Adolph II. of Nassau (d. 1474), particularly deserves inspection. The *Library* and *Archives*, above the sacristy, probably occupy the original quarters of the abbots; and above the *Chapter House* is the early-Gothic *Dormitory*, altered in the 18th century. The *Refectory* was rebuilt in 1720. The lay brothers' house (the W. wing) has been known as the *Abtbau* since the restorations of 1709. The *Infirmary* (so-called old church; to the E., beyond the brook), which is in the transition style, is now occupied by wine-presses. The vaults below these buildings are used as wine-cellars. Important wine-auctions take place here in May.

Close to the abbey is the celebrated **Steinberg** vineyard, 60 acres in area, which was planted by the monks of Eberbach and is enclosed by a wall. The vines are tended with great care, and their produce is esteemed at least as highly as the wines of the Johannisberg. The **Bos** (an old word for 'hill'), an eminence close to the monastery, 880 ft. above the sea-level, with a refuge-hut, commands a good view of the vineyard. — To the E. of the Eberbach valley, conspicuously situated on a hill, is the extensive *Lunatic Asylum of Eichberg.*

Between Hattenheim and Erbach lie the islands of *Sandau*, connected with the left bank, and *Westphalen'sche Au*, or *Rheinau*. To the left of the road between these villages is the *Marcobrunnen* ('boundary-well'), near which are the vineyards yielding Marcobrunner, one of the most highly prized Rhenish wines, and chiefly belonging to Count Schönborn. The different-coloured posts indicate the limits of the various properties; the white posts mark the lands belonging to government.

l. **Erbach** (R.; *Engel*, in the market-place, R. & B. 1¹/₂-2¹/₂ *ℳ*, with garden, good wine), mentioned in history as early as 980, is partly concealed from the steamboat-passenger by the long island of *Rheinau*. At the W. end of the village is the château of *Reinhartshausen*, the property of Prince Frederick Henry of Prussia, containing good old Italian and Netherlandish paintings, acquired from the collection of Princess Marianne of the Netherlands (d. 1883; open from April to Oct., 10-6; adm. 1 *ℳ*).

l. **Eltville** (S. & R.). — HOTELS. *Reisenbach, Bahnhof-Hôtel*, both at the station, with restaurants, R. 2-2¹/₂ *ℳ*. — Beer at *Cratz's*, in the town. — The pier is ¹/₄ M. from the railway-station, where also the steam-tramway to *Schlangenbad* (p. 264) starts.

Eltville or *Elfeld* (290 ft.), with 4000 inhab., large sparkling wine factories, and many garden-girt villas, was known in the middle ages as *Altavilla* and was once the capital of the Rheingau. The German king Günther of Schwarzburg resigned his dignity here in

1349, when besieged and hard pressed by his opponent Charles IV. (p. 289). In the 15th cent. Eltville was often the residence of the Archbishops of Mayence, when they were at odds with the burghers of Mayence.

Near the pier are the formerly archiepiscopal institutions of *St. Peter* and *St. Victor*, which now, like the *Martins-Turm*, the last relic of the town-gates, belong to Count Eltz. — The *Castle*, erected in 1332-50 by Baldwin, Archbishop of Trèves, then administrator of the archbishopric of Mayence, was destroyed in 1635, with the exception of the keep, the bailey, and the moat. — The Gothic *Church*, built in 1353, contains a canopy of the 15th cent., a font of 1517, and several Renaissance tombs. Outside the N. wall is a Mt. Calvary of 1520.

The *Lichtenstern House*, in the main street, is a notable Renaissance structure of 1670 (upper story rebuilt). In the garden is a late-Gothic dwelling-house, formerly known as the *Sanecker Hof*. — The *Frühmesserei* is designated by a tablet as the house where the brothers Bechtermüntze established a printing-press about 1460 (probably with the aid of their kinsman Gutenberg, p. 275).

The island opposite the town, called the *Eltviller Au*, is occupied by a large farm.

About $2^1/_2$ M. to the N.W. of Eltville (omn. twice daily in $^1/_2$ hr.) lies the large village of **Kiedrich** (440 ft.; *Engel*, very fair; *Krone; Burg Scharfenstein*), with some quaint half-timbered houses. The Gothic church of *St. Valentine* (14-15th cent.), restored in 1857-74, with a pulpit of 1493 and other works of art, and the chapel of *St. Michael*, erected in 1440-44 in the ornate late-Gothic style, restored in 1845-58, merit a visit. Near Kiedrich is the *Gräfenberg*, one of the most celebrated vineyards of the Rheingau; it is crowned by the castle of *Scharfenstein* (view), which was erected by the Archbishops of Mayence at the close of the 12th cent., dismantled by the Swedes in 1632, and finally by the French in 1682. The *Virchow-Quelle*, a mineral spring rising near Kiedrich, resembles the Wiesbaden springs, but its temperature is much lower (75°). — Kiedrich is $1^1/_2$ M. from Eberbach (p. 250) viâ Eichberg.

The following WALK of 2 hrs. may be recommended. The highroad is quitted 1 M. from Eltville, and the vineyards ascended by a footpath to the left (partly closed during the vintage); on reaching the summit of the plateau, we turn again slightly to the left; (25 min.) the **Buben-häuser Höhe** (880 ft.), commanding a magnificent view of the entire Rheingau, with the town of Eltville in the foreground. About $^3/_4$ M. farther to the N., on the summit of the hill, is situated **Rauental** (856 ft.; *Rheingauer Hof*, with garden, R. & B. 2 *M*, very fair; *Nassauer Hof; Goldener Engel; Restaurant of the Winzerverein*), a village with an ancient church (15th cent.), and celebrated for its wine. On the slope of the hill on the N. side of Rauental a shady promenade leads to Schlangenbad (p. 265) in 1 hr.

Beyond Eltville several more villas are passed, the most conspicuous of which are *Burg Crass*, with a garden-restaurant, *Villa Rheinberg*, and the *Steinheimer Hof*, the last belonging to the Grand-Duke of Luxembourg.

1. **Niederwalluf** (S. & R.). — HOTELS. *Schwan*, on the Rhine, with garden and view, much frequented by visitors from Mayence and Wies-

baden, R. 2½-3½, B. 1, D. 2½, pens. 6 *M*; *Zur Schönen Aussicht*, at the station. — *Rheineck Sanatorium* (Dr. Hirte), for nervous and other sufferers, pens. 6-10 *M*. — Motor-ferry to Budenheim, 15 pf.

Niederwalluf, a place with 1300 inhab., mentioned as early as 770, lies at the mouth of the *Waldaffa* or *Walluf*, near the ancient E. boundary of the Rheingau (p. 247). — An attractive road leads hence to (2½ M.) *Neudorf* (p. 264).

On the opposite bank of the Rhine is *Budenheim* (p. 217).

l. **Schierstein** (R.; *Seipel's Hotel Sonneneck*, R. 1½-2 *M*, B. 80 pf., with garden; *Drei Kronen*, R. 1½-2½, B. ³/₄ *M*), an old village, with a manufactory of sparkling wine and a river-harbour, stands in the midst of a vast orchard. — About 1½ M. inland is the ruin of *Frauenstein*, with the village of that name (Goldenes Ross); ³/₄ M. to the S.E. of the latter is the *Spitze Stein* (835 ft.; p. 263), with extensive view.

The steamer next passes the isle of *Rettbergs-Au*, opposite which lies Biebrich. In the distance is the Taunus.

l. **Biebrich** (S. & R.). — Hotels. *Kaiserhof* (Pl. a), R. 2-5, B. 1 *M*, with view-terrace; *Nassauer Hof & Krone* (Pl. b), with garden-restaurant, much frequented by excursionists from Wiesbaden, both near the pier and the electric tramway terminus; *Bellevue* (Pl. c), 3 min. above the pier, R. 1½-2½, B. 1 *M*; *Zur Eintracht* (Pl. d), Mainzer-Str., ¼ M. from the pier. — *Café-Restaurant Bavaria*, Kaiser-Str. 58. — *River Baths* on the Rettbergs-Au.

Electric Tramway from the steamboat-pier to Wiesbaden (Beausite), Mayence, and Schierstein (see p. 256).

Railway Stations. *Biebrich-West* (p. 219), at the N.E. entrance of the Schloss-Park; *Biebrich-Ost* (p. 262), connected with the steamboat-pier by electric tramway. There are also subsidiary stations at the *Wald-Strasse* and *Landes-Denkmal*.

Local Steamer to Mayence, see p. 266; pier below those of the large steamers.

Biebrich (280 ft.), a town of 19,000 inhab., with cement, aniline dye, roofing paper, and soap factories, iron foundries, and gypsum works, is the steamboat-station for Wiesbaden. At the upper end of the town is a *School for Non-Commissioned Officers*, and at the lower is the former *Palace* of the Dukes of Nassau, now in the possession of the Grand-Duke of Luxembourg, a long baroque edifice, begun in 1699-1706 and completed about the middle of the 18th century. The extensive *Park* contains a splendid chestnut avenue and other fine trees. The *Moosburg*, a miniature castle in the park, built in 1806 in the mediæval style, occupies the site of the imperial palace of *Biburk*, where Lewis the German resided in 874 (no admission). — From Biebrich to Wiesbaden, see p. 262.

Below Biebrich lies *Amöneberg*, the first Hessian village, with cement, fertilizer, and chemical works. The steamboat next passes between two islands, the *Ingelheimer Au* (restaurant in the hunting-lodge), now connected with the mainland to form the winter-harbour of Mayence (p. 271), on the right, and on the left the *Peters-Au*, over which passes the *Kaiser-Brücke* (p. 262). On the Peters-Au

WIESBADEN

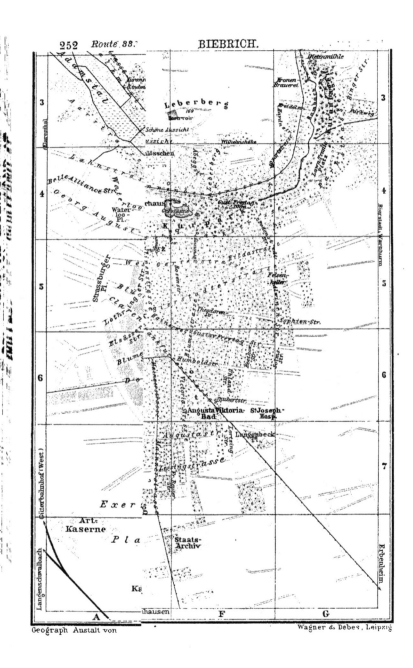

the Emp. Louis the Pious, son and successor of Charlemagne, expired in 840. His body was conveyed to Metz (p. 198).

r. **Mayence,** see R. 36. The pier of the Dutch steamers is just below the Rhine bridge, that of the Cologne and Düsseldorf Co. a little above it.

34. Wiesbaden.

Railway Station (Pl. D, E, 8), with frequented *Restaurant, in the S. part of the city. No hotel-omnibuses meet the trains. Cabs, see p. 255. — The STEAMBOAT STATION is at Biebrich (see p. 252; tramway No. 1, see p. 252).

Hotels (most of the first-class houses have recently been rebuilt or enlarged and are provided with all modern comforts, thermal and other baths, terraces, and gardens. *NASSAUER HOF & *HÔTEL CECILIE (Pl. a, g; E, 4), R. from 4, B. 1¹/₂, déj. 3¹/₂, D. 4¹/₂, pens. from 10 ℳ, with fashionable restaurant; ORANIEN (Pl. f; E, 5). a dépendance of the Nassauer Hof, Bierstädter-Str. 2a; *HÔTEL ROSE (Pl. c, l; E, D, 4), Kranz-Platz 7, an old-established house, R. 4-10, B. 1¹/₂, déj. 3, D. 4¹/₂, pens. from 10 ℳ; *HÔTEL WILHELMA (Pl. v; E, 4), at the corner of Sonnenberger-Str. and Wilhelm-Str., with terrace and good restaurant, R. 4-8, B. 1¹/₂, déj. 3¹/₂, D. 4¹/₂, S. 3¹/₂, pens. 12-18 ℳ; *PALAST-HÔTEL (Pl. n; D, 4), Kranz-Platz 5, R. 4¹/₂-12, B. 1¹/₂, déj. 3, D. 4¹/₂, S. 3, pens. 12-19¹/₂ ℳ, with good restaurant; *KAISERHOF (Pl. t; F, 6), Frankfurter-Str. 17, cor. of the Victoria-Str., with a large garden and a swimming-bath connected with the *Augusta-Victoria-Bad* (p. 258), R. 4-15, B. 1¹/₂, D. 5, S. 3¹/₂, pens. from 12 ℳ; *QUISISANA (Pl. q; F, 4), Park-Str. 5, R. 4-10, B. 1¹/₂, déj. 3, D. 4, pens. 10-16 ℳ, a family hotel with good restaurant; *HÔT. DU PARC & BRISTOL (Pl. v; E, 5), Wilhelm-Str. 30, R. 3-15, B. 1¹/₂, déj. 2¹/₂ ℳ; *VIER JAHRES-ZEITEN (Pl. b; E, 4), Kaiser-Friedrich-Platz 1, cor. of the Wilhelm-Str., R. from 4, B. 1¹/₂, déj. 3¹/₂, D. 5, S. 3¹/₂, pens. from 10 ℳ; *ALLÉE-SAAL (Pl. c; E, 4), Taunus-Str. 3, R. 4-8, B. 1¹/₄, D. 4, S. 2¹/₂, pens. 10-14 ℳ; *SENDIG'S EDEN HOTEL, Sonnenberger-Str. 8, R. 4-8, B. 1¹/₂, D. 4, S. 2¹/₂-3, pens. from 10¹/₂ ℳ, with good restaurant; *MÉTROPOLE (Pl. u; E, 6), Wilhelm-Str. 8, with restaurant, R. 3-6, B. 1 ℳ 40 pf., déj. 2¹/₂, D. 3¹/₂, pens. 8-12 ℳ; *ASTORIA HOTEL (Pl. o; E, F, 4), R. 2-6, B. 1¹/₄, déj. 3, D. 3¹/₂ & 4, S. 2-2¹/₂, pens. 7-12 ℳ, a family hotel with restaurant; *IM-PÉRIAL (Pl. i; F, 4), R. 3-6, B. 1¹/₂, D. 3¹/₂, S. 2, pens. 8-11 ℳ; *VILLA ROYALE (Pl. r; F, 4), R. from 3, B. 1¹/₂, pens. from 7 ℳ, these three in the Sonnenberger-Str.; *ENGLISCHER HOF (Pl. d; D, 4), Kranz-Platz 11, R. 3-7, B. 1¹/₄, D. 3¹/₂, S. 2¹/₂, pens. 9-13 ℳ; *AEGIR (Pl. z; E, 6), Thele-mann-Str. 5, R. from 3¹/₂, B. 1¹/₄, D. 4, S. 2¹/₂, pens. from 8¹/₂ ℳ; *VIC-TORIA (Pl. x; E, 6), Wilhelm-Str. 1, R. 3-6, B. 1¹/₂, D. 4, S. 2¹/₂, pens. 8-12 ℳ; *CONTINENTAL (Pl. e; D, 4), Langgasse 36, R. 3-6, B. 1¹/₄, D. 3-3¹/₂, pens. 8-12 ℳ; *BELLEVUE (Pl. y; E, 5), Wilhelm-Str. 26, R. 3-6, B. 1¹/₄, D. 4, S. 2¹/₂, pens. from 9 ℳ; *RESIDENZ-HÔTEL, Wilhelm-Str. 3, R. from 3, B. 1¹/₂, D. 3¹/₂, S. 2¹/₂, pens. 8-12 ℳ; *NIZZA (Pl. o; F, 6), Frankfurter-Str. 28, adjoining the Augusta-Victoria-Bad, R. 3-6, B. 1¹/₄, D. 3, pens. 8-12 ℳ; FURSTENHOF, new, Sonnenberger-Str. 12a, opposite the Kurhaus, R. from 3, B. 1¹/₄, D. 3¹/₂, S. 2, pens. 8-12 ℳ; *GRETHER'S HÔTEL ST. PETERSBURG (Pl. h; E, 5), Museum-Str. 3, R. 2¹/₂-5, B. 1, D. 3 ℳ; *RHEIN-HÔTEL (Pl. r; E, 6), Rhein-Str. 16, cor. of the Rheinbahn-Str., R. 2¹/₂-4, B. 1, déj. 2, D. 3, S. 2, pens. 7¹/₂-9 ℳ, with restaurant; *MINERVA (Pl. m; E, 6), Rhein-Str. 9, cor. of the Kleine Wilhelm-Str., R. 2¹/₂-5, B. 1, déj. 1¹/₂, D. 2¹/₂, S. 1¹/₂, pens. 6-10 ℳ.

DAHLHEIM (Pl. d; D, 3), Taunus-Str. 15, R. 2¹/₂-3¹/₂, B. 1, D. 2¹/₂, S. 1¹/₂, pens. 6-8 ℳ, with restaurant; NATIONAL, Taunus-Str. 21, with restaurant; HÔTEL DE L'EUROPE (Pl. w; D, 4), Langgasse 32, with restaurant,

R. 3-4, B. 1, déj. 1¹/₂, D. 3, pens. 7-9 *M*; Hôtel Biemer, Sonnenberger-Str. 11, R. from 3, pens. from 7 *M*; Frankfurter Hof, Webergasse 37, with restaurant; Fuhr (Pl. *g*; E, 3), Geisberg-Str. 3, R. & B. 3-5, D. 2, pens. 5-7 *M*, with restaurant; Westfälischer Hof, Schützenhof-Str. 3, with thermal baths and garden, R. & B. 3-6, D. 2¹/₂, pens. 6¹/₂-10 *M*; Savoy (Pl. *s*; D, 4), Bären-Str. 3, with thermal baths, Hebrew; Hahn, Spiegelgasse 15, R. 2-2¹/₂, B. 1, pens. 6¹/₂-8 *M*.

The following hotels are mainly frequented by passing travellers: *Taunus Hotel (Pl. i; E, 6), Rhein-Str. 19, R. from 2¹/₂, B. 1¹/₄, D. 1³/₄-3 *M*, with frequented restaurant and café; *Grüner Wald (Pl. k; D, 5), Markt-Str. 10, R. 2-4, B. 1, pens. 5¹/₂-8 *M*, with restaurant; Hôtel Weins, Bahnhof-Str. 7 (Pl. D, 6), with garden; Einhorn, Markt-Str. 32; Vogel, Rhein-Str. 27, R. 2-3, B. 1, D. 1¹/₂-2 *M*, with restaurant; Union, Neugasse 7 (Pl. D, 5), R. 2, B. ³/₄ *M*, with the Zauberflöte Restaurant; Burghof, Langgasse 21; Belgischer Hof, Spiegelgasse 3, with wine-room. — Near the railway-station, in the Nikolas-Str. (Pl. E, 6, 7): No. 1, Hansa-Hôtel, new and very good; No. 16, Reichspost, R. 2-3, B. 1, with restaurant; No. 25, Krug, R. 2-2¹/₂, B. 1 *M*, with restaurant; No. 37, Berg. In the Goethe-Str. (Pl. D, E, 7): No. 16, Neue Adler, very fair. — Christliches Hospiz, Rosen-Str. 4 (Pl. F, 5; R. 2¹/₂-7, B. 1, D. 2, S. 1¹/₂, pens. 6-10 *M*) and Oranien-Str. 53 (Pl. D, 7; R. 2-3¹/₂, B. ³/₄, D. 1³/₄, pens. 4³/₄-6¹/₄ *M*); Hospiz zum Heiligen Geist (R.C.), Friedrich-Str. (Pl. D, 5).

Outside the town (adapted for summer-quarters), all with open-air restaurants: Neroberg (803 ft.; Pl. B, C, 1; p. 261); Bahnholz (865 ft.; to the N. of Pl. E 1; p. 261; one-horse carriage 4, two-horse 5 *M*), R. 2-3, D. 2, S. 1¹/₂, pens. 5-8 *M*; Waldeck (N.W. of Pl. A, 2, 3), Aar-Str., in the Adams-Tal (p. 261), Wilhelmshöhe, on the Bingert (p. 260), 10 min. above Sonnenberg. — *Hôtel-Restaurant Taunusblick*, see p. 262.

The numerous so-called **Bath Houses**, as distinguished from the hotels with baths, though themselves offering some hotel accommodation, are all well spoken of (bath included in the pension-price). *Schwarzer Bock, Kranz-Platz 12 (Pl. D, 4), R. 3-8, B. 1¹/₄, D. 3, pens. 8¹/₂-13¹/₂ *M*; *Adler (Pl. p; D, 4), Langgasse 42, R. 3-5¹/₂, B. 1, D. 3, S. 1¹/₂, pens. 7¹/₂-10 *M*; Kaiserbad (Pl. k; E, 4, 5), Wilhelm-Str. 42, R. 2¹/₂-5, B. 1¹/₄, D. 3, S. 2, pens. 7¹/₂-10¹/₂ *M*; Römerbad (Pl. m; D, 4), Kochbrunnen-Platz 3; Schützenhof (Pl. s; D, 5), Schützenhof-Str. 4, with restaurant; Kölnischer Hof, Kleine Burg-Str. 6, R. 3-7, B. 1¹/₄, D. 3-3¹/₂, S. 2-3, pens. 8-12 *M*; Pariser Hof, Spiegelgasse 9, R. 2¹/₂-3¹/₂, B. 1, D. 2, pens. 6-8 *M*; Bender, Häfnergasse 12, R. 3-5, pens. 5-8 *M*; Weisses Ross, Kochbrunnen-Platz 2, R. 3-6 *M*; Goldenes Kreuz, Spiegelgasse 6. — *Private Hotels* and *Hôtels Garnis*, in the Taunus-Str., the Geisberg-Str., the Kranz-Platz, and so on.

Pensions (mostly near the Kur-Park, Pl. E, F, 4, 5). *Villa Hertha* (Miss Rodway), in the Dambach-Tal, near the springs (4¹/₂-8 *M*). In the Sonnenberger-Str.: *Winter*, No. 14 (8-12 *M*); *Rupprecht*, No. 17 (6¹/₂-10 *M*); *Villa Lengerke*, No. 22. Leberberg: *Villa Credé*, No. 1; *Windsor*, No. 4 (6-9¹/₂ *M*); *Villa Oranienburg*, No. 7; *Villa Frank*, No. 8 (6-10 *M*). Abegg-Str.: *Villa Albion*, No. 3; *Villa Miranda*, No. 8. Garten-Str.: *Villa Roma*, No. 1 (6-12 *M*); *Violetta*, No. 3; *Villa Olanda*, No. 18 (6-12 *M*). Frankfurter-Str.: *Hôtel-Pension Primavera*, No. 8 (7-12 *M*); *Villa Humboldt*, No. 22 (6-10 *M*). Taunus-Str.: *Hôtel-Pension Ritter*, No. 45; *Thuringia*, No. 49 (7-12 *M*); *Hôtel-Pension Intra*, No. 51. Luisen-Str.: *Guhl*, No. 22, and many others. At Wiesbaden an arrangement should always be made as to the length of notice required from visitors leaving a pension.

Restaurants. *Kurhaus (p. 257), with good wine, D. or S. 2¹/₂-4¹/₂ *M*; *Carlton, Wilhelm-Str. 6, well fitted up (concerts at midday and in the evening), D. 4, S. 2¹/₂-3 *M*; *Foyer Restaurant, in the royal theatre, S. from 3¹/₂ *M*, all these of the first class. — *Schmid's Weinstube*, Spiegelgasse 4; *Ratskeller*, in the Rathaus (p. 259; entrance from the Markt-Str.; good wine, also beer; D. 1¹/₂-3 *M*); *Meier*, Luisen-Str. 12. — Good **Wine Rooms** (fitted up in the Old-German style), with cold viands:

Pohl, Michelsberg 10; *Rheingauer Winzerstube*, Bahnhof-Str. 5. Southern wines: *Continental Bodega*, Wilhelm-Str. 16. — **Beer.** *Taunus Hotel*, see p. 254; *Café-Restaurant Métropole*, see p. 253; *Ratskeller*; *Mutter Engel*, Langgasse 52, D. 1¹/₂-3 *M*; *Hôtel de l'Europe* (p. 253), with terrace; *Grüner Wald* (p. 254); *Deutscher Keller*, at the Rhein-Hôtel (p. 253); *Poths*, Langgasse 11; *Hansa-Hôtel*, *Schützenhof*, see p. 254. — VEGETARIAN RESTAURANT: *Zur Gesundheit*, Schiller-Platz 1. — *Automatic Restaurants*: Markt-Str. 19a, Rhein-Str. 29, etc. — *Open-Air Restaurants* outside the town, see pp. 260, 261, 262.

Cafés. *Café Hohenzollern*, Wilhelm-Str. 10 (also beer); *Berliner Hof*, Taunus-Str. 1, cor. of Wilhelm-Str., with garden (also beer); *Taunus Hotel* (p. 254). — *Tea Room* in the Hôtel Rose (p. 253), well fitted up (music 4.30 to 5.30 p.m.). — **Confectioners.** *Café Blum*, Wilhelm-Str. 40; *Lehmann*, Grosse Burg-Str. 14.

Visitors' Tax, after a stay of more than 4 days: (a) *For a year*, 1 person 50 *M*, each additional member of the family 25 *M*; (b) *For six weeks*, 20 *M*, each addit. coupon 10 *M*; (c) *For 10 days*, 6 *M*, each addit. coupon 3 *M*; (d) *For a day*, 1¹/₂ *M*. A charge (for a year 15, for six weeks 10 *M*) is also made for the care of the glasses in the Trinkhalle (p. 258). — The **Kurverwaltung** (office in the Kurhaus) will supply visitors with any information they may desire.

Sanatoria (Kuranstalten). *Dietenmühle*, Park-Str. 44 (Dr. Waetzold); *Dr. O. Dornblüth*, Garten-Str. 11; *Kurhaus Friedrichshöhe* (Dr. Friedländer), Leberberg 14; *Lindenhof* (Dr. van Weenen), Walkmühl-Str. 43; *Bad Nerotal* (Dr. Stehr & Dr. Plessner), Nerotal 18; *Dr. Schütz*, Villa Panorama. — Besides the above-mentioned, there are several other establishments for affections of the stomach, victims of the morphia habit, maladies of the eyes, etc.

Theatres. *Royal Theatre* (Pl. E, 4; comp. p. 257), for opera, drama, and ballet (closed in July and August); *Residenz-Theater*, Luisen-Str., on the site of the old Artillery Barracks (Pl. D, 6), for modern plays, farces, and so on; *Walhalla* (Pl. D, 5), Mauritius-Str. 1a; *Volks-Theater*, Dotzheimer-Str. 5, these two for vaudeville.

Concerts in the *Kurhaus* daily, 4-5.30 and 8-9.30 p.m.; also in summer at the *Kochbrunnen*, 6.30-8 a.m. (50 pf., 10 tickets 3 *M*; free to subscribers to the Kurhaus). — **Orchestral Concerts** in winter in the *Kurhaus* (every Frid. from Nov. to Feb.; 5, 4, 2 *M*) and at the *Royal Theatre* (six symphony concerts). The *Verein der Künstler und Kunstfreunde* gives concerts of chamber music in the Victoria Hotel.

Exhibitions of Pictures. R. *Banger*, Luisen-Str. 4; *Aktuaryus*, Taunus-Str. 6, adm. at both 1 *M*; *Nassauischer Kunstverein*, in the Museum (p. 259), open free.

Cab Tariff (double fares from 11 p.m. to 6 or 7 a.m.).	One-h. *M* pf.	Two-h. *M* pf.
Drive in the town:		
1-2 persons	—.80	1.—
3-4 persons	1.—	1.20
By time: per hour within the town, 1-4 pers. . .	2.—	3.—
- - - beyond - - - - . .	2.80	4.—
Russian Chapel	1.70	2.—
Neroberg or Fasanerie	2.40	3.—
Biebrich	3.—	4.—
Fischzucht (p. 261)	3.50	4.50
Platte and back, with stay of 1 hr.	7.—	10.—
Schwalbach and back (1 day)	15.—	18.50
Eppstein and Königstein, and back (1 day)	25.—	32.—

Trunk 20 pf., smaller articles free. — To or from the railway-stations 20 pf. extra.

Taximeter Cabs (recognized by their red wheels; double fares at night): 1-2 pers. for 800 mètres 60 pf., each additional 400 m. 10 pf.;

3-4 pers. for 600 m. 80 pf., each addit. 300 m. 10 pf.; trunk 25 pf. (extra charges outside the town).

Motor Cabs: 1-4 pers. for 600 mètres 70 pf., each additional 200 m. 10 pf.; outside the town and at night, 1-4 pers. for 450 m. 70 pf., each additional 133 m. 10 pf.; outside the police-district (if the carriage is not used for return) for 300 m. 70 pf., each additional 100 m. 10 pf. Waiting, 10 pf. every 2 minutes. Trunk 25 pf.

Electric Tramways (transfers issued). 1. (with yellow board): From the *Railway Station* (Pl. E, 8) either viâ the Wilhelm-Str. (Kurhaus) and Kochbrunnen to *Beausite* (Pl. B, 1, 2; near the Neroberg railway), or viâ the Rondel (Pl. D, 8) and Adolfshöhe (p. 262) to *Biebrich* (bank of the Rhine; branch-line to Schierstein), and on viâ Amöneburg to *Mayence* (Stadthalle). — 2. (red board): From the *Railway Station* (Pl. E, 8) viâ the Moritz-Str. (Pl. D, 7, 6), Kirchgasse, and Kranz-Platz to *Sonnenberg* (p. 260). — 3. (blue board): From the *Railway Station* (Pl. E, 8) viâ the Schloss-Platz (Pl. D, 5) to *Unter den Eichen* (Pl. A, 1; p. 261). — 4. (green board): From the *Railway Station* (Pl. E, 8) viâ the Ring-Kirche (Pl. B, C, 6) to the *Emser-Strasse* (Pl. B, C, 4; going on in summer afternoons to *Unter den Eichen*). — 5. (white board): From the *Ring-Kirche* to the *Infantry Barracks* (Pl. B, 8). — 6. (white board): From the *Kurhaus* (Pl. E, 4) to *Biebrich-Ost* (p. 277) and *Mayence* (Stadthalle). — 7. (blue board): From the *Museum* (Pl. E, 5) viâ the Friedrich-Str. (Pl. D, 5) to *Dotzheim* (comp. Pl. C-A, 6; p. 263). — 8. (blue board): From *Dotzheim* viâ the Museum (Pl. E, 5) to *Bierstadt* (comp. Map, p. 261).

Post and Telegraph Office (Pl. E, 6), Rhein-Str. 25.

U. S. Consular Agent, *Mr. John B. Brewer.*

English Church *(St. Augustine's),* Frankfurter-Str. 3; services at 8 and 11 a.m. and 5 p.m. (summer 6 p.m.). — **American Church Service,** in the Rathaus (p. 259), on Sun. (during the season) at 5 p.m.; pastor from Frankfort.

Tourist Agents. *Schottenfels,* Theater-Kolonnade; *Engel,* Wilhelm-Str. 46. — **Photographer,** *J. Benade,* Taunus-Str. 37.

Wiesbaden (385 ft.), a town of 106,000 inhab., is situated at the S. base of the Taunus and has been celebrated as a watering-place for centuries. It lies, amid orchards and vineyards, in a wide basin, surrounded by wood-clad heights and opening towards the S. Its warm springs, its mild climate (mean annual temperature 51° Fahr.; annual rainfall 22 inches), its attractive environs, its good hotels, and the great number of excellent sanatory establishments of every kind have made the town the leading international watering-place of Germany. Its springs are especially beneficial in cases of rheumatism, gout, neuralgia, and other nervous affections, as well as for chronic dyspepsia and excessive obesity. The annual number of visitors amounts to 200,000. The season lasts from April to October and is at its height in May and June. The springs, however, are frequented throughout the year. The hotels and bath-houses are adapting themselves more and more to winter-patients, and the charges are then lower.

Wiesbaden, the Roman *Aquae Mattiacorum,* was one of the Roman forts to defend the frontier of the Main and may have existed as such from the time of Drusus. It was already a considerable settlement in the beginning of the first century of our era (canabæ, see p. 267). This was probably destroyed by the Mattiaci in 69-70 A.D., but had again attained prosperity at the end of the century as the chief place of the *Civitas Mattiacorum.* In the reign of Domitian the Wiesbaden castle was still one of the advanced defences of Maycnce, but Hadrian removed the garrison (Cohors II. Rætorum) to the Saalburg (p. 304). Pliny (Hist. Nat. xxxi. 2) refers to the warm springs in the following words: '*Sunt Mattiaci in Germania fontes calidi trans Rhenum, quorum haustus triduo fervet*'. — In the Frankish period and later 'Wisibada' appears as the capital of a district called 'Königssundra-Gau'. It was the capital of the Counts of Nassau-Idstein and Nassau-Usingen from 1355 onwards, and of the duchy of Nassau from 1816 to 1866.

The *Railway Station* (Pl. E, 8), a handsome sandstone building with a roof of shining green tiles and a clock-tower 131 ft. in height, was built from plans by Prof. Klingholz and opened in 1906. In front of it passes the new Ring-Strasse. To the left, in the Kaiser-Friedrich-Ring, is the *Landeshaus* (Pl. D, 8) or House of the Provincial Diet, completed in 1906. The new Kaiser-Str. (Pl. E, 7, 6) occupies the site of the old railway-stations.

The lime-shaded Wilhelm-Strasse (Pl. E, 6, 5, 4), the Corso and main thoroughfare of Wiesbaden, is flanked with hotels, attractive shops, and the Museum (p. 259). To the right it is adjoined by the Wilhelms-Platz (Pl. E, 5, 6), with a bronze *Statue of Bismarck*, by Herter (1898), and by the Anlagen, or public pleasure-grounds, of the *Warme Damm* (Pl. E 5), in which rises Schilling's *Monument to Emp. William I.* (1894). — The **Royal Theatre** (Pl. E, 4) was built in 1892-94 by *Fellner & Hellmer* (new foyer by *Genzmer*, 1902). To the S. of it stands a *Monument to Schiller* by Uphues (1905), and to the E. are two columns of the old Kurhaus.

Towards the end of the Wilhelm-Str., to the left, lies the Kaiser-Friedrich-Platz (Pl. E, 4), adorned with a bronze *Statue of Emp. Frederick III.* by Uphues (1897). — On the right is the Kursaal-Platz (Pl. E, 4), embellished with flower-beds and two fountains, and flanked by spacious Doric *Colonnades*, which serve as a bazaar. In the new colonnade is the entrance to the Royal Theatre (see above). Above the old colonnade is a bronze bust of the poet *Bodenstedt*, who died at Wiesbaden in 1892.

On the E. side of the Kursaal-Platz stands the ***Kurhaus** (Pl. E, 4), erected in 1905-7 from the plans of Friedrich von Thiersch, and perhaps the most imposing structure of the kind in Germany. It is 420 ft. in length, while its widest part, in the middle, is 211 ft. deep and is surmounted by a dome 69 ft. in height. The W. façade, with its massive Ionic portico and unadorned wings, has been skilfully adapted to the pseudo-classical style of the colonnades, while the more elaborate E. façade, with its terraces and wing-pavilions, forms an appropriate transition to the grounds of the Kur-Park. The rooms of the interior are fitted up with great sumptuousness. The office (comp. p. 255) is at the main entrance (adm. before 1 p.m. 1 ℳ).

The Central Part of the structure is occupied by the *Promenade Hall*, the columns of which, of red Swedish granite with bases and capitals of bronze, contrast vigorously with the light-coloured walls of

Italian and Belgian marble. The cupola is adorned with twenty figures
of dancing women. — The SOUTH WING contains the *Large Concert Hall*,
with gilded Corinthian columns, a coffered ceiling in blue and gold, elaborate ornamentation with numerous figures, gold lattice-work, and a
Latin inscription in gold letters on the bluish-green frieze; the *Conver-
sation Room*, in the style of Louis XIV.; the *Gaming Room;* the *Reading Room;* and (on the S. side) the *Garden Saloon* or *Shell Room*, with
large arched windows, a mosaic of shells, charming reliefs by A. Storch,
and frescoes by Fritz Erler. — In the NORTH WING are the *Small Concert Room*, which is modelled on the old Kursaal and contains the marble
columns and the candelabra with which it was adorned; the tasteful *Wine
Restaurant*, with its panelling of light-coloured cherry-wood and its
graceful columns and pilasters: and the quaint *Beer Saloon*, the panelling, chimney-piece, and ceiling of which consist of majolica.

The **Kur-Park* (Pl. E, F, 4, G, 4, 3), with its large pond and
fine old trees, is a favourite afternoon promenade. A fountain with
a jet 100 ft. in height plays in the pond every afternoon. In the
open gardens is a good statue of *Gustav Freytag* (by Schaper,
1905), who lived in Wiesbaden from 1879 till his death in 1895.
On the Blumen-Wiese are lawn-tennis courts. — To the S.E. of the
Kur-Park lies the handsomest residential quarter of the town, with
numerous attractive villas and gardens, especially in the Park-
Str., Rosen-Str., and Blumen-Str., and the *Augusta-Victoria-Bad*
(Pl. F, 6), a handsome Renaissance building erected in 1890-94
(visitors admitted; 1 ℳ).

From the N. end of the Wilhelm-Str. the SONNENBERGER-STRASSE
(Pl. E, F, 4; comp. p. 260) leads to the E., passing between the Kur-
Park and the slope of the Leberberg, with its numerous villas. On
the hill above the Sonnenberger-Str. is the *Paulinen-Schlösschen*
(Pl. E, 4), built in 1843 for the widow of Duke William and now
owned by the town. The TAUNUS-STRASSE (Pl. E, D, 4, 3), also
beginning at the N. end of the Wilhelm-Str., leads to the N.W.,
past the grounds of the Kochbrunnen, in the direction of the Nero-
Tal (comp. p. 260). To the right diverges the Geisberg-Str., off
which opens the Dambach-Tal (Pl. E, 3), containing a monument
to the chemist *Karl Remigius Fresenius* (d. 1897), founder of a
famous chemical laboratory at Wiesbaden.

The grounds round the Trinkhalle at the **Kochbrunnen** (Pl.
D, E, 4) are mainly resorted to in the early morning (concerts, see
p. 255). The spring, which rises below the pavilion, is the combined
outpour of 15 hot springs, which rise within an area of a few square
yards and yield about 5000 gallons per hour; from these the adjacent bath-houses are supplied. The water has a natural temperature
of 156° Fahr. and contains 8.76 per cent of solid matter, chiefly
chloride of sodium. A charge of 20 pf. is made for each glass. In
addition to the Kochbrunnen, there are no fewer than 23 bathing-
springs, the chief of which are the *Schützenhof-Quelle* and the
Adler-Quelle.

In the KRANZ-PLATZ (Pl. D, 4), behind the Kochbrunnen, is a

marble *Hygieia Group.* The Langgasse (Pl. D, 4, 5), which issues
from the Kranz-Platz, and the first cross-street to the left, the
Untere Webergasse, are the main streets of the old part of the town.
In the former a new *Municipal Bath House* is to be erected.

On the slope of the Heidenberg, to the W. above the Langgasse,
stretches the so-called *Heidenmauer* ('heathens wall'; Pl. D, 4), a
line of Roman masonry, 65 ft. long, 15 ft. high, and 9 ft. thick. It
was probably part of the defences erected under Diocletian soon
after 300 A.D.

☛ The royal (formerly ducal) **Palace** (Pl. D, 5), on the W. side
of the Schloss-Platz, was built by *Goerz* in 1837-40, and renovated
in 1883. Visitors are admitted daily from 10 to 4 or 6 (adm. 25 pf.).
The interior is adorned with statues by *Schwanthaler*, frescoes by
Posse, and pictures by modern masters. In front of the palace is
a bronze statue, by Schott (1908), of *Prince William of Orange*,
the founder of the independence of the Netherlands (1533-84). Adjacent is the '*Wilhelms-Heilanstalt*', or military hospital (1871).

Opposite the palace stands the **Rathaus** (Pl. D, 5), erected in
1884-87 by *Hauberrisser* in the German Renaissance style. On
the balcony above the flight of steps are statues of four civic virtues.
In the basement is the Ratskeller (p. 254). — The *Markt-Kirche*
(Pl. E, 5; Prot.), built of polished bricks in 1853-62, has five towers
(the principal nearly 300 ft. high). The adjoining *School for Girls*
was built by Genzmer (1901).

The **Museum** (Pl. E, 5), Wilhelm-Str. 20, occupying a building erected by *Zais* in 1813-17 as a palace for the crown-prince,
contains the municipal picture-gallery, collections of antiquities and
natural history specimens, and a library. The rooms are small and
badly lighted, and a new building is in contemplation. The Museum
is open free daily, with the exception of Sat., 10-1 & 3-5 (in winter
11-1 only).

The **Picture Gallery** is on the groundfloor to the right (catalogue
40 pf.). — Rooms I-III. Old Masters. Dutch School: *Joos van Craesbeeck,
Pieter de Ring, Phil. Wouwerman, Em. de Witte, W. van de Velde the
Younger, Jan Wynants*, etc. Flemish School: *F. Snyders, B. Bruyn*,
Copy of *Rubens*' Battle of Amazons. German School: *L. Cranach, Hans
Schäufelin, Angelica Kauffmann.* — Rooms IV-VI. Modern pictures by
*Gerh. Janssen, L. Knaus, Count L. von Kalckreuth, K. F. Lessing, M.
Liebermann, F. Piloty, Scholderer, Hans Thoma, W. Trübner, Len-
bach*, etc.; also modern plaquettes and medals.

··· The **Collection of Antiquities** is on the groundfloor to the left.
Most of the objects were found in Nassau. In the Ante-Room and
Rooms I-V: Prehistoric objects (in R. I carved bones, etc., from the caves
near Steeten on the Lahn) and Roman antiquities, as in other Rhenish
collections. In R. II: Bronze door from Mayence; triangular bronze tablet,
with a relief of Jupiter Dolichenus, from Heddernheim. R. III: Jupiter
Column from Schierstein, erected by a legionary in 221 A.D. R. IV: Model
of the Roman thermæ discovered in 1903 to the W. of the Kochbrunnen.
R. V: Inscription in bronze-gilt letters, in honour of Caracalla (213 A.D.),
from the fortress on the Pfahlgraben at Holzhausen (p. 231). R. VI: Objects

found in Alemannian and Frankish tombs (ca. 350-800 A.D.). In RR. VII and VIII: Mediæval and modern objects, locks, mountings, bronzes, glass, porcelain, earthenware, ecclesiastical sculptures, local costumes of Nassau; in the middle, tombstones of Diether III. (p. 228) and Diether IV (d. 1315), Counts of Katzenelnbogen.

The first floor contains a NATURAL HISTORY COLLECTION.

The LIBRARY (daily, except Sun., 10-1 & 3-8), in the upper story, contains 160,000 printed volumes and many valuable old MSS. Among its treasures are a Portion of an astronomical calendar of 1447, being the earliest printed work by Gutenberg to which a date can be assigned, and the Mayence Catholicon of 1460 (comp. p. 275).

The *Waterloo Monument* in the Luisen-Platz (Pl. D, 6) commemorates the Nassovians who fell in the struggle with Napoleon in 1815. On the N. side of this square stands the Roman Catholic *Church of St. Boniface*, built by *Hoffmann* in 1844-49, and containing pictures by *Steinle* and *Rethel*. — To the W. the Rhein-Str. ends at the Protestant *Ringkirche* (Pl. B, C, 6), a noteworthy edifice by *Otzen*, in the late-Romanesque style, consecrated in 1894 (sacristan, An der Ringkirche 3; fee 50 pf.). — From this point the Kaiser-Friedrich-Ring leads in a crescent back to the railway station (p. 257).

The *Old Cemetery* (Pl. C, 3) contains a mausoleum of the Duchess Pauline (d. 1856), with sculptures by Drake, and other handsome monuments. — *New Cemetery*, see p. 261. — The *South Cemetery (Südfriedhof)*, on the road to Erbenheim, was opened in 1909.

ENVIRONS OF WIESBADEN.

By following the SONNENBERGER-STRASSE (Pl. E, F, 4; tramway) and footpaths skirting the *Rambach*, we reach ($1/2$ hr.) *Sonnenberg* (Nassauer Hof; Café Altdeutsches Haus), a village inhabited by workmen. To the right, halfway up the hill, is a Roman Catholic church. Farther on, to the left, near the tramway-terminus, is a castle, dating from the 12th cent., which once belonged to the Counts of Nassau and was destroyed by the French in 1689 (tavern at the top). The tower (116 steps) commands a pretty view. From the ruins a road leads to the N.E. to the (20 min.) *Bingert* (945 ft.; view), which is marked by three trees. — Higher up the valley is the *Stickel-Mühle*, a garden-restaurant, a little beyond which is the charmingly situated village of *Rambach* (770 ft.).

From Rambach we may ascend (1 hr.) the *Kellerskopf* (1558 ft.; rfmts.; view-tower, 10 pf.), which rises to the N. The descent may be made to ($3/4$ hr.) *Niedernhausen* (p. 310).

The most popular open-air resort near Wiesbaden is the charming **Nero-Tal** (Pl. B, C, 2, 1), with its pleasure-grounds, villas, and views of the Greek Chapel and the vineyards of the Neroberg. The tramway (No. 1, p. 256) follows the Echo-Str., which skirts the pleasure-grounds. The terminus adjoins the *Café-Restaurant Beausite* (Pl. B, 2) and the station of the *Neroberg Cable Tramway* (train every $1/4$-$1/2$ hr. in summer; fare 25, down 15, up and down 30 pf.).

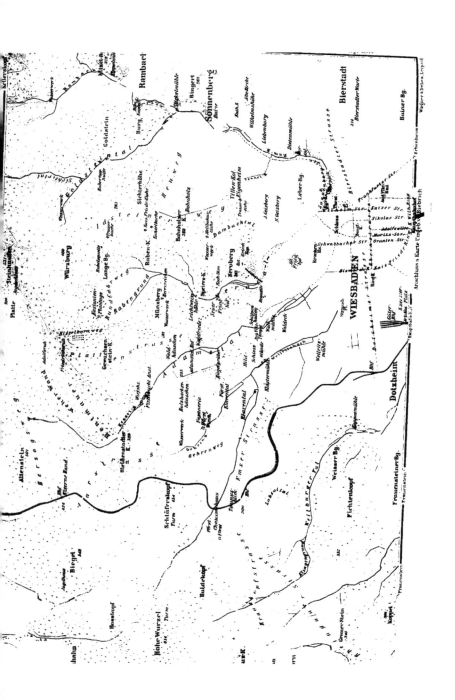

The road to the Neroberg ascends to the *Platter-Strasse*, passing a large quartzite quarry, and the insignificant Leichtweiss
Cavern (see below). Walkers take $1/_4$ hr. from the Beausite by a
steep zigzag path and the pleasant 'Philosophenweg'.

The *Neroberg (800 ft.; Pl. B, C, 1), a favourite resort, is surmounted by a frequented *Hôtel-Restaurant* (p. 254) and by a tower
(10 pf.) affording a fine view of the Taunus, with the Rhine valley
and the Odenwald to the S.E., the towers and bridge of Mayence to
the S. (beyond the Biebrich water-tower). The whole hill is covered
with fine beech-trees, interspersed with a few gnarled old oaks.

To the S. E., a few minutes below the summit, is situated the
Greek Chapel (Pl. C, 1; 607 ft.), erected as a mausoleum for the
Duchess Elizabeth Michailowna, a Russian princess (d. 1845). This
is reached from the Neroberg-Str. station of the tramway in 10 min.;
but pleasanter routes (20-25 min.) lead by the Kapellen-Str. (Pl. D,
3, 2), lined with villas, or through the *Dambach-Tal* (p. 258; Pl.
E, D, 3, 2). The chapel is covered by five domes, all gilded and
surmounted by Russian double crosses. The highest cross is 180 ft.
from the ground.

The interior is entirely of marble. A rich altar-screen *(Ikonostasis)*,
with numerous figures of saints on a golden ground, painted in Russia,
separates the body of the chapel from the choir, to which the priests
and their attendants alone have access. The beautiful *Monument of the
Duchess* is by Emil Hopfgarten (d. 1856). Except during the Sun. service (11-1; in summer only), the chapel is shown by the sacristan, who
lives near the Russian cemetery (1 ℳ, several persons 50 pf. each).

Pleasant walks extend past the *Reservoir* and the (35 min.)
Trauerbuche to the (1$1/_4$ hr.) Platte. Other paths lead to the
Spëierskopf ($1/_4$ hr.), the *Felsengruppe* (20 min.), the *Leichtweiss
Cavern* (see above), and past the *Melibocus Oak* to the *Hôtel-
Restaurant Bahnholz* (p. 254), with its terraced garden (views).

The **Platte** (1657 ft.), a hill to the N. of Wiesbaden, with a
shooting-lodge of the Grand-Duke of Luxembourg, built in 1824,
is frequently visited for the extensive view (finest by evening-light).
At the entrance are figures of two stags. In the interior is a fine
collection of antlers (adm. 1 ℳ, for a party 50 pf. each). Inn adjacent. Besides the above-mentioned footpath and the Nero-Tal road,
the Platte is reached by the Platter-Str. (Pl. A, 1), which leads
past the Old and New Cemeteries (1$1/_2$ hr.).

By the terminus of the electric tramways Nos. 3 & 4 (p. 256)
is the popular resort known as **Unter den Eichen** (Pl. A, 1),
with the garden-restaurants *Café Orient* and *Schützenhallen*. Hard
by, in the wood, is the *New Cemetery*. To the N.W. is the charmingly situated *Augusta Victoria Temple*. Thence we may walk
through the *Adams-Tal* to the ($1/_2$ hr.) *Waldhäuschen* (garden-
restaurant) and the (10 min.) *Fish Breeding Establishment* ('Fisch-
zucht'), to which visitors are admitted by the keeper (restaurant).

We may return by the Platter-Str., or, crossing this road, by a footpath through the *Kiefernwald* (pine-woods), the pretty *Rabengrund,* and the Nero-Tal.

About 2 M. to the W. of Wiesbaden, to the right of the old Schwalbach (Ems) road, lies the nunnery of *Klarental* (rfmts.), founded in 1296 by King Adolph of Nassau and his consort Imagina of Limburg, and dissolved in 1559. A little farther up is a building formerly used as a *Pheasantry (Fasanerie),* with an old park. A shady footpath leads hence to the (¹/₂ hr.) Chausseehaus.

The railway-stations of **Chausseehaus** (950 ft.), named after a forester's house ¹/₂ M. above it (with the *Hôtel-Restaurant Taunusblick*), and of *Eiserne Hand* (comp. p. 263) are starting-points for various delightful walks, indicated by finger-posts and coloured way-marks. About 1¹/₂ M. to the N. of both stations is the *Schläferskopf* (1483 ft.), and about 3 M. to the N.W. is the *Hohe Wurzel* (2028 ft.), both with view-towers.

FROM THE CHAUSSEEHAUS TO SCHLANGENBAD, 3¹/₂ M. (occasional omnibus-service). At the Hôt. Taunusblick the road diverges from the old Schwalbach road, and thence ascends to the W. through wood and meadow, with fine views of the Rhenish plain. After passing *Schloss Hohenbuchau,* on the right, we reach the village of **Georgenborn** (1188 ft.; carr. from Wiesbaden 11, with two horses 13 ℳ). A few minutes beyond the village, to the left, is the *Hôtel-Restaurant Hohenwald* (pens. 4¹/₂-5 ℳ, R. & B. 2¹/₂ ℳ), with a view-terrace. Thence a footpath diverges to the right for the Hohe Wurzel (see above). The road makes a wide bend (shorter paths should be avoided) past the *Empress Augusta Temple,* with a view of Rauental and Schlangenbad, down to *Schlangenbad* (p. 265).

Wiesbaden is connected with **Biebrich** (p. 252; 3 M. to the S.) by the Biebricher-Strasse (Pl. D, 8), with its chestnut avenue, and by the WIESBADENER ALLÉE, which connects with the Biebricher-Str. beyond the railway (comp. carton on the Map of the Rheingau, p. 246; tramway No. 1, p. 256). On the Biebricher-Str. lie the *Adolfshöhe* and *Rheinhöhe,* two garden-restaurants. To the left, at the railway-crossing (stat. Landesdenkmal, p. 263), is the *Biebrich Water Tower* (view extending to the Niederwald). Beyond the crossing, to the left, is the sparkling wine factory of *Henkell & Co.,* a modern building by Bonatz (1909; shown to visitors 10-12 & 2.30-4, except Sat. afternoon). To the right are the Richard Wagner Park and the so-called *Landes-Denkmal* (1907), dedicated to the last duke. Those who use the electric tramway should alight at the 'Schloss-Park' station and walk through the park to the Rhine (¹/₄ hr.).

From Wiesbaden to Mayence.

6 M. Railway in 13-18 minutes. — Tramway, viâ Biebrich, see p. 256.

The train passes (2 M.) *Biebrich-Ost* (p. 252) and then crosses the Rhine and the isle of Petersau (p. 252) by the *Kaiser-Brücke.* This bridge, built after designs by Schwechten and opened in 1904, is 997 yards long and spans the river at a height of 31 ft. above high-water mark. Amöneburg (p. 252) lies below the bridge on the right bank. — 6 M. *Mayence* (Central Station), see p. 265.

35. Schwalbach and Schlangenbad.

a. From Wiesbaden to Schwalbach and Limburg.

RAILWAY to *Langen-Schwalbach* in 1 hr. (fares 1 *M* 20, 80 pf.). As far as Dotzheim an alternative route is offered by tramway No. 7 (p. 256). — Railway from Langen-Schwalbach to Limburg in 1³/₄ hr. (fares 1 *M* 70, 1 *M* 15 pf.). — Comp. Map, p. 246.

The railway crosses the Biebrich and Schierstein roads. 1¹/₄ M. *Landesdenkmal* (p. 262). To the left we have a view of Mayence and the plain of the Rhine. To the right are the Neroberg and the Platte. — 2¹/₂ M. *Waldstrasse*. — 4¹/₂ M. *Dotzheim* (635 ft.), with a machine-factory. About 2¹/₄ M. to the W. is the *Spitze Stein* (p. 252). The line now leads through wood. — 7 M. *Chaussehaus* (950 ft.), see p. 262. — The line now skirts the E. slope of the Schläferskopf (p. 262). 9¹/₂ M. *Eiserne Hand* (1390 ft.), on the top of the Taunus, whence we may walk in a N.E. direction to the Platte (p. 261) viâ the *Altenstein* (1643 ft.) in 1¹/₄ hr., or proceed to the S.W. to the Hohe Wurzel (p. 262), or (finally) ascend the Schläferskopf (p.262). — The line descends into the valley of the *Aar*. 10¹/₂ M. *Hahn-Wehen* (1140 ft.); 12 M. *Bleidenstadt*, with a church (l.), the spire of which has been shattered by lightning.

15 M. **Schwalbach.** — The RAILWAY STATION (940 ft.) is about 1 M. from the Kursaal, on the road descending the Aar valley. Omnibuses (30 pf.) and carriages await the trains.

HOTELS (most of them closed in winter). *Alleesaal*, Neue-Str. 1, with dépendances, *Villa Grebert* and *Villa Gartenlaube*, in a large and shady garden, R. 3¹/₂-20, B. 1¹/₂, D. 4¹/₂, pens. from 12 *M*; *Herzog von Nassau*, Neue-Str. 6, R. 3-10, B. 1¹/₂, D. 4, S. 3, pens. 8-14 *M*, with garden; *Hôtel Métropole*, Reit-Allée 2, with four dépendances, R. 3-10, B. 1¹/₂, D. 4¹/₂, S. 3, pens. 8-15 *M*; *Quellenhof & Post-Hôtel*, Brunnen-Str. 53; *Victoria*, Neue-Str. 2, with café-restaurant and confectioner's, R. 2¹/₂-4¹/₂, B. 1¹/₂, D. 3, S. 2, pens. 7-12 *M*; *Continental*, Bad-Weg 3; *Taunus*, Brunnen-Str. 45, R. 2-6, B. 1¹/₄, D. 3, pens. 8-14 *M*; *Wagner*, Coblenzer-Str. 18, R. 2-8, B. 1, D. 2¹/₂, pens. 7-10 *M*; *Russischer Hof*, Adolf-Str. 36, very good; *Berliner Hof*, Brunnen-Str. 33; *Stadt Coblenz*. — Some of the *Lodging Houses* ('Kurhäuser'; with or without board) are very comfortably fitted up. In July and the first half of August the prices are highest and it is advisable to secure rooms in advance.

RESTAURANTS. *Kursaal*, D. 2¹/₂ *M*; *Dietrich* (at the Berliner Hof); *Bibo (Löwenburg)*, with a few bedrooms, Brunnen-Str. 4, D. 2 *M*, Bavarian beer; *Weidenhof*, Kirch-Str. 2, D. 1¹/₂ *M*, Munich beer, very fair; *Malepartus*, Brunnen-Str. 43, also rooms, Bavarian and Bohemian beer.

POST AND TELEGRAPH OFFICE, Rhein-Str. 1.

BATHS in the *Königliches Badhaus*, Brunnen-Str. 20 (7 a.m. till 1 p.m., baths 1-4 *M*, mud-bath 5-7¹/₂ *M*). At the *Lindenbrunnen*, 1 *M* 20 to 3 *M* 50 pf. per bath. — VISITORS' TAX, per week 5, for the season 15 *M*, every additional member of a party 10 *M*; '*Trinkkarte*' for drinking the waters 3¹/₂ *M*; *Daily Tickets* for admission to the Kurhaus 50 pf. — MUSIC in the morning and afternoon, at the Stahlbrunnen, the Weinbrunnen, and the Trinkhalle alternately. *Reunions* (dancing, etc.) Wed. and Sat. evenings in the Kurhaus.

CARRIAGES. One-horse 2¹/₂, two-horse 4 *M* per hour, afternoon 3 and 5 *M*; to *Eltville* 9¹/₂ and 15 *M*. — *Donkeys* 2 *M* per hour.

ENGLISH CHURCH *(Christ Church)*, Frankfurter-Str.

Schwalbach, officially styled *Langen-Schwalbach* (1033 ft.), with 3000 inhab., is situated in a side-valley of the Aar, surrounded by woods and meadows. It has been known for at least 300 years and in the 17-18th. cent. rivalled Spa as a fashionable watering-place. The annual number of visitors is now upwards of 7000, including many foreigners. The water (48-53° Fahr.), strongly impregnated with iron and carbonic acid, is used both internally and externally and is especially efficacious in anæmia, nervous affections, and female complaints generally. The earth used in the mud-baths is found in the immediate vicinity.

The two principal springs, the *Stahlbrunnen* in one of the valleys, and the *Weinbrunnen* in the other, are separated by a low ridge laid out with pleasure-grounds. A handsome *Kursaal,* with a restaurant, a reading-room, etc., was opened in 1879. Farther up, beyond the pond near the Weinbrunnen, there are extensive lawn-tennis courts, the Royal *Moorbadehaus (Mud Baths),* and (farther on) the *Golf Club* and the links.

WALKS in the pleasure-grounds and adjacent woods. Also to the (¹/₄ hr.) *Paulinenberg;* the *Platte* (1330 ft.), the summit of which, with a fine view, may be reached in 15-20 min. more; and the *Bräunchesberg,* with a pavilion commanding a good view of the town and the valley of the Aar. — From Schwalbach the highroad leads to (4¹/₂ M.) *Schlangenbad* (p. 265); the top of the intervening saddle may also be reached by a shady path through wood.

A road, known as the 'Bäder-Strasse', leads viâ *Kemel* (1696 ft.), *Holzhausen auf der Heide* (p. 231), *Singhofen,* and *Nassau* (p. 131) to (23¹/₂ M.) *Ems* (p. 130). A good road (also a favourite of cyclists) leads from Schwalbach down the picturesque *Valley of the Wisper to (20 M.) *Lorch* (p. 239).

The railway continues to follow the pretty valley of the Aar. — 15¹/₂ M. *Adolphseck* (Otto), with a picturesque ruined castle; 19¹/₂ M. *Hohenstein* (780 ft.; Burg Hohenstein, very fair), with the picturesque ruins of a stronghold destroyed in 1647. Several small stations. — 26¹/₂ M. **Zollhaus** *(Railway Hotel),* with a large cement factory and the *Johannisbrunnen,* is the junction for the narrow-gauge line to Nastätten (pp. 231, 223; St. Goarshausen, Oberlahnstein). *Burg-Schwalbach,* with a ruined castle (restaurant), 1¹/₄ M. to the S.E., and the romantic ruin of *Hohlenfels* (p.231) may also be visited from Zollhaus. — 28¹/₂ M. *Hahnstätten* (465 ft.; Nassauer Hof, unpretending but very fair), with iron-ore deposits (siderites). — 29¹/₂ M. *Oberneisen;* 31 M. *Flacht.* To the right is the ruin of *Ardeck.* — 33¹/₂ M. *Diez,* see p. 135. — 36 M. *Limburg,* see p. 136.

b. From Eltville to Schlangenbad.

LIGHT RAILWAY in 35 minutes. — Carriage from Wiesbaden to Schlangenbad and back 12, with two horses 14 *M.*

Eltville, see p. 250. — 2 M. *Neudorf* (495 ft.; Krone), in the valley of the *Waldaffa.* Road to Niederwalluf, see p. 252. — The small station of Rauental lies at the point of divergence of the road to ($^3/_4$ M.) the village of Rauental (p. 251). To the right lies *Tiefental* (inn), an ancient convent (1173), suppressed in 1803.

Schlangenbad. — HOTELS, all with restaurants and most of them closed in winter (between the middle of June and the middle of Aug. rooms must be engaged beforehand). *Royal Bath Houses (Königliche Kurhäuser: *Nassauer Hof*, with veranda and good restaurant, *Berliner Hof*, *Schweizerhaus*, *Oberes*, *Mittleres*, & *Unteres Kurhaus*, and *Gesell-schaftshaus*), R. at these 2-18, B. 1$^1/_4$, D. 3$^1/_2$ M. — *Hôtel Victoria, R. 2$^1/_2$-15, B. 1$^1/_4$, D. 3, pens. from 8 M; *Russischer Kaiser, R. from 3-10, B. 1$^1/_2$, D. 3$^1/_2$ M, these two in the Rheingauer-Str., near the Bath Houses. — Less pretending: *Waldfrieden*, on the Wiesbaden road, on the edge of the forest, R. 2-6, B. 1, pens. 7-12 M; *Pariser Hof*, Rheingauer-Str. — There are also numerous lodging-houses and apartments to let.

VISITORS' TAX, per week 3, for the season 12 M. — BATHS, 1$^1/_2$-2 M. — CONCERTS 3-4 times daily.

CARRIAGES, two-horse 5 M, one-horse 3$^1/_2$ M per hour; to Schwalbach 4 or 6, to Wiesbaden 12 or 9 M. — DONKEY, per hour, 1 M 50 pf.

ENGLISH CHURCH SERVICE in summer.

Schlangenbad (985 ft.), charmingly situated in a narrow green and wooded valley, belongs to the group of so-called 'indifferent' springs, while it is also valued for the ozone of its pine-woods. The springs (80-87° Fahr.) are admirable for nervous affections, female complaints, and diseases of the assimilative organs. The annual number of visitors amounts to 2500. The *Upper Bath House* occupies the site of one erected in 1694 by the Landgrave Karl of Hesse-Cassel, then lord of the soil; the *Central Bath* dates from the 18th cent.; the well-equipped *Lower Bath House* was completed in 1868. The *Schlangen-Quelle* and *Marien-Quelle* are used for drinking.

The environs afford a great variety of shady walks: *e.g.* to the *Wilhelmsfelsen;* viâ the *Hôtel-Restaurant Hohenwald* (p. 262) and *Georgenborn* (p. 262) to the *Chausseehaus* (p. 262); to the *Graue Stein* (1115 ft.) and *Frauenstein* (p. 252); to the *Hohe Wurzel* (p. 262); to the *Hansenkopf* (near the *Rheingaublick*) and the *Wilde Frau;* viâ *Hausen* to the *Hallgarter Zange* (p. 249; 2$^1/_2$ hrs.).

36. Mayence.

Railway Stations. The CENTRAL RAILWAY STATION (Pl. E, F, 1; *Restaurant*) for trains in all directions. Hotel-omnibuses meet the trains. — The station of *Mainz Süd* (Pl. A, 3, 4; *South Mayence*), which is connected with the Central Station by a tunnel under the Kästrich and the citadel, 1300 yds. long, is chiefly for local traffic. — STEAMBOAT PIER, see p. 253.

Hotels. *Near the Rhine* (many with views): *HÔTEL DE HOLLANDE (Pl. c; D, 5), Rhein-Str. 77, opposite the Stadt-Garten, R. from 3 M (some with private baths), B. 1$^1/_2$, D. 4 M; *HÔTEL DU RHIN (Pl. a; D, 5), Rhein-Str. 63, with the Carlton Restaurant, R. 2$^1/_2$-15, B. 1$^1/_4$, D. 3$^1/_2$ M; HÔTEL D'ANGLETERRE (Pl. b; D, 5), Rhein-Str. 87, R. 2$^1/_2$-8, B. 1$^1/_4$, D. 3$^1/_2$ M, these three of the first class; STADT COBLENZ (Pl. h; C, 4), Rhein-Str. 49, with good wine-restaurant, R. 2$^1/_2$-4 M; GERMANIA (Pl. g; C, 4), Rhein-Str. 43, with restaurant, R. & B. 2$^1/_2$-4 M, well spoken of. — *In the Town* (commercial): KARPFEN (Pl. k; C, 4), in the Brand, R. 2-3$^1/_2$, B. 1, D. 2$^1/_2$ M; LANDSBERG (Pl. l; D, 4, 5), Löhr-Str. 29, with wine-re-

staurant, R. $1^1/_2$-$2^1/_2$ $\mathscr{M}$; Hôtel zur Post (Pl. m; C, 4), Brandgasse 14,
R. $1^1/_2$-$2^1/_2$, B. $^3/_4$ $\mathscr{M}$. — *Near the Central Station:* Central Hotel (Pl. d;
F, 2), Bahnhofs-Platz 8, with restaurant, R. 2-4, B. 1 $\mathscr{M}$; Mainzer. Hof
(Pl. o; E, F, 2), cor. Bahnhof-Str. and Parcus-Str., with restaurant, R.
2-4 $\mathscr{M}$; Bahnhof-Hôtel (Pl. e; F, 2), Bahnhofs-Platz 6, with wine-restau-
rant, R. 2-$3^1/_2$ $\mathscr{M}$; Pfälzer Hof (Pl. n; E, 2), Münster-Platz 5, cor. of
the Bahnhof-Str., with restaurant; Taunus Hotel (Pl. i; E, 2), Bahnhof-
Str. 17, with restaurant, R. 2-3 $\mathscr{M}$; Rheingauer Hof (Pl. t; F, 2), Schott-
Str. 5 (Pl. F, 2), R. & B. $2^1/_2$-4 $\mathscr{M}$; Pfeil & Continental (Pl. f; E, 2),
Bahnhof-Str. 15, cor. of the Parcus-Str., R. 2-3 $\mathscr{M}$, B. 80 pf.; Goldene
Krone (Pl. s; E, F, 2), Bahnhof-Str. 12; Weis (Pl. q; E, 2), Bahnhof-
Str. 2; Richter's Eisenbahn-Hôtel, at the right exit of the railway sta-
tion, these four unpretending.

Restaurants. Wine. *Casino zum Gutenberg*, Grosse Bleiche 29;
Rheingauer Weinstube, Dominikaner-Str. 8; *Scharhag*, Triton-Platz (Pl.
D, 3). — Wine and Beer. *Concerthaus* (see below), Grosse Bleiche 65;
Ratskeller, Alte Universitäts-Str. 11, behind the theatre; *Stadthalle*
(p. 271), Rhine Promenade, with view-terrace, much frequented in summer.
Beer. *Wocker*, Gutenberg-Platz; *Heiliger Geist* (p. 271), Mailands-
gasse, near the Rhein-Str., with an 'old-German' room with guild insignia
and armour; *Kötherhof*, Schiller-Platz; *Schöfferhof*, Schuster-Str. 22;
Hohenzollern, Kaiser-Str. 98, near the Rhine; *Rodensteiner*, Kaiser-Str. 16.
Beer-rooms of the *Rheinische Brauerei* and the *Actien-Brauerei*, both
in the Bahnhofs-Platz. — **Confectioners.** *Janson*, by the main entrance
of the cathedral; *Müller*, Gutenberg-Platz 11.

Cabs (double fare from 10 p.m., in winter from 9 p.m., to 7 a.m.).	One-horse cab		Two-horse cab	
	1-2 pers.	3-4 pers.	1-2 pers.	3-4 pers.
	$\mathscr{M}$ pf.	$\mathscr{M}$ pf.	$\mathscr{M}$ pf.	$\mathscr{M}$ pf.
Per drive within the gates .	—.50	—.70	—.70	—.90
Per hour	2.—	2.30	2.40	2.90
Per $^1/_2$ hr.	1.—	1.30	1.30	1.60
Each $^1/_4$ hr. more	—.40	—.50	—.60	—.70

Each box 20 pf.; smaller articles free.

Electric Tramways (comp. plan; fares 10-15 pf.). From the *Central Station* to *Kastel* (p. 277), to *Weisenau*, to *Mombach*, to *Gonsenheim*,
and to *Kostheim*; also a circular line, passing the cathedral and returning
to the station. From the Rhein-Str. ('Stadthalle', Pl. D 5; every $^1/_2$ hr.) viâ
Kastel, *Amöneburg*, and *Biebrich* (p. 252) to *Wiesbaden* (comp. p. 256). —
Steam Tramways. 1. From the *Rhein-Str.* ('Fischtor'; Pl. C, 4) viâ
the Grosse Bleiche, Münster-Platz, Binger-Tor (Pl. E, 1), the Cemetery,
and Zahlbach to *Hechtsheim*; 2. From the *Rhein-Str.* viâ the Binger-Tor,
the Cemetery, Gonsenheim, and Lenneberg to *Finthen* (p. 277).

Small Steamboats. 1. Steam-ferries to the station at *Kastel* (p. 277)
from the *Eiserne Tor* (Pl. C, 5); fares 10 or 6 pf. — 2. To *Biebrich* (p. 252)
hourly in summer, starting near the *Stadthalle* (Pl. D, 5) and calling at
the *Kaiser-Tor*; fare 40 pf., there and back 50 pf. — 3. To *Kostheim*.

Theatre (Pl. D, 3; p. 275), from the middle of Sept. to the middle
of April daily. — **Music** (in summer), on Sun., Wed., Frid., and Sat.
afternoons in the Esplanade (p. 271); on Sun., Tues., and Thurs. evenings
in the Stadthalle (p. 271); military music in the Schiller-Platz (p. 275),
on Sun., Wed., and Frid., 12-1. — Orchestral concerts in the 'Concerthaus' of the 'Liedertafel' (Pl. E, 4).

General Post & Telegraph Office, Bahnhof-Str. (Pl. E, 2). —
Tourists' Enquiry Office *(Verkehrsbureau)*, Bahnhof-Str. 7 (Pl. E, 2).

Baths. *Apollo Bad*, Bilhildis-Str. 5; *Institut für physikalische Heil-
Methode*, Neubrunnen-Str. 8. — *River Baths* in the Rhine (comp. Plan).

Chief Attractions (one day). Cathedral (p. 271); the Rhine Promenade, with view from the Rhine Bridge (p. 271); Collection of Roman
Antiquities and the Gutenberg Museum in the Palace (pp. 268-270). View
from the Stephans-Kirche (p. 276) or from the Anlage (p. 276).

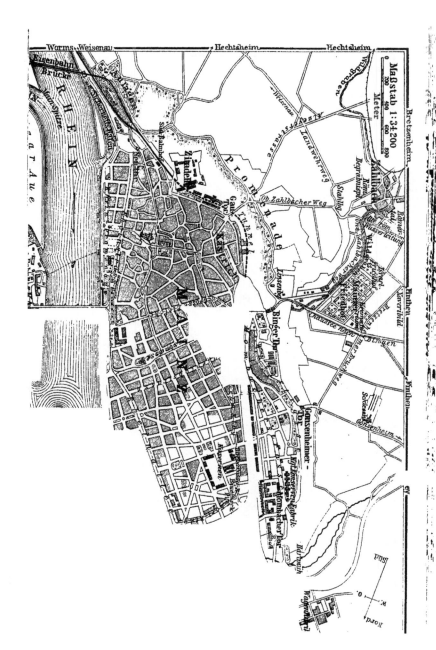

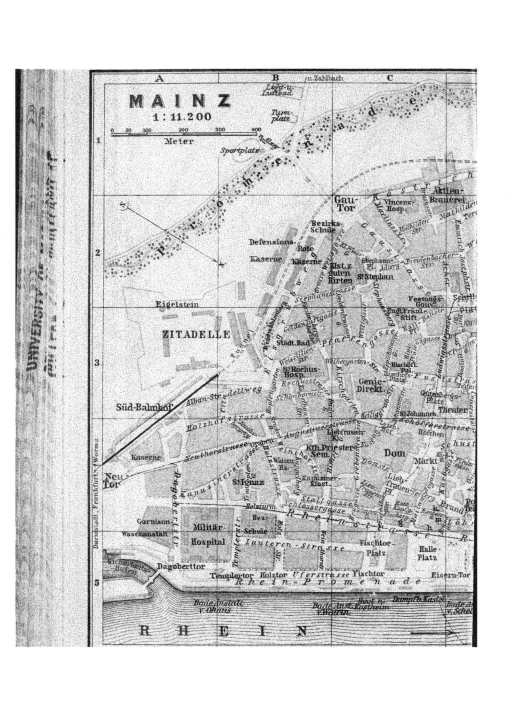

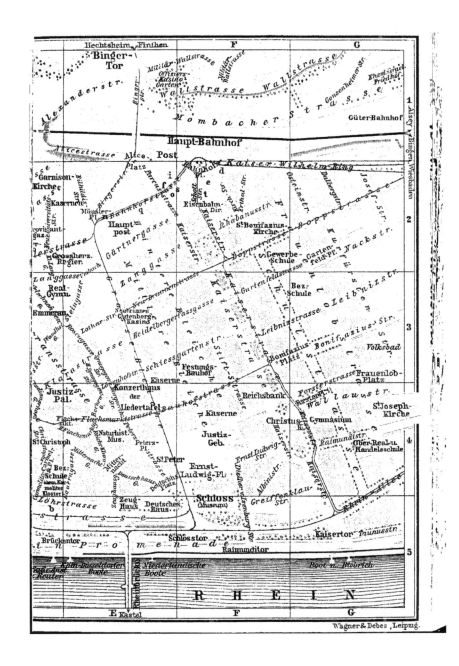

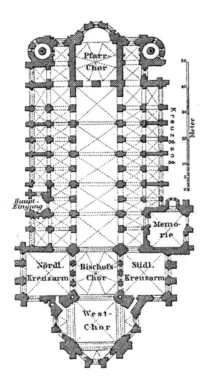

Mayence, German *Mainz* (270 ft.), the seat of a bishop, and a strongly fortified town with 110,000 inhab. ($^1/_3$ Prot., 3400 Jews), including the suburbs and a garrison of 8000 soldiers, is pleasantly situated on the left bank of the *Rhine,* opposite and below the influx of the *Main,* and is connected with *Kastel* (p. 277) on the opposite bank by a bridge (p. 271). The old town was formerly limited by its fortifications, but since 1871 a new town almost twice as big has grown up outside them. Large new harbours were built in 1880-87. In 1905 the demolition of the entire circumvallation was taken in hand. Mayence is one of the headquarters of the trade in Rhine wine and it is also well known for its leather goods and artistic furniture. Market-gardening is extensively carried on in the environs.

The town and its most ancient name *(Mogontiacum)* are of Celtic origin. Between B. C. 14 and B. C. 9 *Drusus,* the son-in-law of Augustus, established a camp here, on the tableland outside the Gautor (Pl. C, 2), and this speedily attracted a colony of native residents, Roman traders, and veterans *(canabae).* Mayence became the seat of the legate, or governor, of *Germania Superior,* and thenceforward served as the base for the Roman campaigns in Central Germany. Domitian, who extended the Roman supremacy on the right bank of the Main as far as the Taunus and the Wetterau (83-89 A. D.), probably built the first bridge across the Rhine (afterwards repeatedly restored) and constructed the *Castellum Mattiacorum* (the present Kastel) to defend it.

Authentic accounts prove that Christianity flourished at Mayence in the fourth century (about 368), and the town afterwards became a bishopric. Under St. Boniface (or Winfried, d. 755), the apostle of Central Germany, the see was raised to an archbishopric and made the seat of the primate of Germany. This prelate, the son of an English wheelwright, was so little ashamed of his parentage that he assumed a pair of wheels as his armorial bearings, which are retained to this day in the arms of the city. In 1254 Arnold Walpod (d. 1268), a citizen of Mayence, founded the *League of the Rhenish Towns.* Mayence became the centre and leader of this powerful association, which ere long was strengthened by upwards of a hundred other towns, from Bâle to the N. Sea. Such was the commercial prosperity of the town at that period that it was called the 'Goldene Mainz'. Two centuries later, however, it lost most of its extensive privileges in consequence of a violent attack made upon it by Archbishop Adolf of Nassau in 1462, on which occasion 500 citizens were killed, and the most influential banished. Thenceforth the once independent city was ruled by the archbishops. Under *Elector Albert of Brandenburg* (1514-45), who was at first inclined to the new learning, art and literature flourished for a period. The university of Mayence, founded in 1477, boasted of such distinguished men as Nicholas Vogt, John von Müller, Bodmann, and George Forster among its members, but it was suppressed by the French in 1798.

In 1552 Margrave Albert Alcibiades of Brandenburg ravaged the town. In the Thirty Years' War it was captured by the Swedes (1631), the Imperialists (1635), and the French (1644). The strong fortress fell once more into the hands of the French in 1688, but was recaptured in 1689. On 21st Oct., 1792, the French republicans under Custine entered the town almost without a blow, but it was retaken the following year by the Prussians. In 1797 it was ceded to France by the Peace of Campo Formio, and became the capital of the Department of Mont Tonnerre. In 1803 the archbishopric was secularized. In 1816 Mayence was assigned to the Grand Duchy of Hesse and in the following year it was made a bishopric. The *Fortress* of Mayence belonged to the German Confederation down to 1866. Its importance as the terminus of Rhenish navigation has passed to Mannheim and Frankfort.

The KAISER-STRASSE (Pl. F, 2, 3), embellished with trees and flower-beds, occupies the site of the old N. fortifications and extends from the central railway-station to the Rhine. At its other end rises the dome of the Christus-Kirche (see below). We, however, turn to the right on leaving the station and follow the *Bahnhof-Str.* (Pl. E, 2) to the small MÜNSTER-PLATZ (Pl. E, 2). The Schiller-Str., in which is the *Erthaler Hof* (1735), now the *Government Buildings*, leads hence to the right (S. E.) to the Schiller-Platz (p. 275), while the Grosse Bleiche runs to the N.E. towards the Rhine.

The GROSSE BLEICHE (Pl. E, 2, 3, 4) is the principal old street in the town. On the N. side of it (No. 15) is the former *Stadion'sche Hof* (1728-33). In a small square to the left is the *Neue Brunnen*, an obelisk with river-gods and lions below (1726; lower part renewed in 1877). On the right, at the E. end of the street, is the *Church of St. Peter* (Pl. E, 4; 1748-56), notable for its bold vaulting. The charming rococo decorations and the frescoes are by Appiani of Milan.

In the ERNST-LUDWIG-PLATZ (Pl. F, 4), formerly called the Schloss-Platz, are the new *Court of Law* (Justiz-Gebäude), by Bonartz, and other monumental buildings in course of erection. The Ernst-Ludwig-Str. leads to the Protestant *Christus-Kirche* (Pl. F, G, 4), which was completed in 1903 and is surmounted by a conspicuous dome, 262 ft. in height.

The former **Electoral Palace** (Pl. F, 4, 5), an imposing Renaissance building of red sandstone, begun in 1627 and hastily finished in 1675-78, was enlarged by the addition of the N. wing in 1751-52 and has undergone an extensive process of restoration in 1903-10. It contains the municipal antiquities and art-collections and the Roman-Germanic Central Museum. The collections are open free on Sun., 10-1 and 2-5, and Wed., 2-5 (in winter 2-4), closed on Mon.; at other times (10-1 & 2-5, on Sat. 10-1 only; in winter closed on Sat. and in the afternoon) cards of admission (50 pf.) must be obtained. The Picture Gallery is also closed on Sun. afternoon. Entrance, Ernst-Ludwig-Platz 15. Library and Gutenberg Museum, see p. 270.

On the groundfloor is the *Museum of Antiquities, chiefly of objects found in or near Mayence. The number and variety of the Roman and Frankish objects will astonish the beholder.

The VESTIBULE contains the original models of *Thorvaldsen's* statue of Gutenberg (p. 275) and *Scholl's* statue of Schiller (p. 275), and a model of the pile-work of the Roman bridge (p. 267). — In the ANTE-ROOM are Roman architectural fragments, and mediæval and modern iron work. — To the right are THREE ROOMS, with prehistoric antiquities (from the flint and lake-dwelling period down to the first century of our era), objects found in German tumuli, and articles imported from Etruria.

We first enter the PAVILION in the court-yard, containing the *Roman, Frankish, and Mediaeval Inscriptions* and the larger *Sculptures*. By the entrance is the *Jupiter Column, found in 1904 at Mayence and dating from the reign of Nero. It is adorned with reliefs and has been re-erected in three sections. Adjacent is a reproduction of it. Of the bronze statue of Jupiter which the column bore nothing is left except one foot and the thunderbolt (in the main room). On the ground beside the column are the remains of the triumphal arch erected by Dativius Victor in the 3rd cent. A. D. Right end-wall: Roman sculptures, including remains of the so-called 'Giant Columns' (Jupiter-Ziu with the earth-demon), stone sarcophagi, and the like. In the middle are several so-called 'Four God Stones', used as pedestals for the giant columns, among which may be mentioned No. 22 a., erected by the 'vicani Mogontiacenses vici novi'. Beyond the third window on the left are Roman tombstones: 241, 242. Children's tombstones, with affecting inscriptions; between these, 247. Tomb of a slave, showing the symbol of death; to the right, 223, 224, 221. Tombs of Roman knights; to the left, *232. Tomb of Blussus, a sailor, with reliefs of the deceased with his wife and child and of his ship; soldiers' tombstones with reliefs, including 202 a, 222, 169, 167. (Eagle-bearers), and 176. Signum-bearer; to the left, 246 a. Tombstone of the shepherd Jucundus, with fine reliefs and a metrical inscription in which the Main is referred to as 'Moenus'; 228 a. Richly-decorated tombstone of a military tribune of the time of Tiberius. Roman milestones and building-stones with the stamps of Roman legions. Between the windows are Roman pottery and brick-stamps. — The last section contains Frankish Christian gravestones and architectural fragments from Ingelheim (p. 216). — Beside the end-wall: Mediæval sculptures; figures from the portal of the Liebfrauen-Kirche, pulled down in 1804; reliefs (1317) of the seven electors, Emp. Lewis of Bavaria, and St. Martin, from the old Kaufhaus; to the right, archway, window, etc., from the old Fisch-Turm (ca. 1200).

We now return to the ante-room and pass the staircase leading to the picture-gallery and the Gutenberg Museum (p. 270), adjoining which are piles from the Roman bridge, a Roman mosaic floor, and amphoræ. We then enter —

Room I, containing mediæval and later objects (earthenware, wax seals, weapons, glass, etc.). — Room II, straight on, is the chief room. To the left of the entrance and in the middle of the room are Roman, to the right, Alemannian and Frankish antiquities. We first inspect the *Roman Section.* By the first window: Objects from the Roman civil cemetery at Mayence (3rd cent. A. D.); in the window-niche, skeleton of a woman with a wig, in the original leaden coffin; towards the middle of the room, *Goblet in perforated work ('vas diatretum') and bottle with chased Bacchic scenes. In the first large case by the second window are the *Contents of a Roman shoemaker's workshop, with sandals, leather, and tools, found in 1857 in the Schiller-Platz. In the window-niche, two bronze water-spouts in the shape of lions' heads; writing materials, stamps, military diplomas, votive weapons, etc. In the second and third cases are ornaments, rings, household utensils, surgical instruments, weapons, etc. By the window, rings, hair-pins, and mirrors. The fourth case contains terracottas, lamps, etc. In the last window-niche are fibulæ, etc. In the middle of the room, under glass: funeral urns of legionaries. Farther on, to the right, Bronze female head; small votive chariot with charioteer, in bronze-gilt. In the long central case, tools and weapons, keys, locks, trumpets. Between the pillars on the left are bronze statuettes, bronze vessels, portions of armour, and a large array of helmets. — The *Frankish* antiquities occupy the right side of the room. The cabinets contain an extensive collection of weapons, ornaments, utensils, and glass. By the first window, under glass: gold rings of the bronze period; Roman hand-mirror; mediæval ivory carvings and ornaments, including a gold enamelled fibula, of the 11th century. — Room III. contains the remainder of the Frankish and Alemannian antiquities. At the entrance is the tomb of a Frankish woman (from Oberolm); in the first central case, a glass drinking-horn; by the first window, belt-buckles and ornaments; by the second window, Carlovingian swords and lance-heads.

The first floor of the main building (staircase, see p. 269) contains the **Municipal Picture Gallery,** which is temporarily displayed in three rooms (catalogue 20 pf.).

The AKADEMIE-SAAL, built in 1775 and adorned with ceiling-paintings by *Januarius Zick,* contains the Italian and Netherlandish works, including examples by *G. de Lairesse, J. M. Molenaer, Franz Francken the Elder, P. de Vos, Salomon van Ruysdael* (95. Spring-landscape, *137. River-landscape), *Cornelis Bega, Jan Livens, Thomas Wyck, Jan van Goyen, Claes Berchem, Cornelis Decker, P. Neefs the Elder, Dirk Hals, D. Teniers the Younger, Jacob Jordaens* (*389. Christ among the Scribes, 1663), *Philip de Champaigne, Eusebio Ferrari* (217-219. Winged Altar, St. Jerome, Adoration of the Holy Child, Tobias and the Angel), *Guercino, Guido Reni, Giovanni Battista Tiepolo*, and others.   An astronomical clock of the 18th cent. should also be noticed. — The WEISSE SAAL ('White Room'), with a fine rococo ceiling, contains modern German paintings by *Philip Veit,   W. Lindenschmit the Younger, Flüggen, A. Achenbach, Baisch, Bracht, A. Burger, Eduard Grützner, Eduard Harburger, Leibl, Schönleber, Adolph Schreyer, Vautier, Zügel,* and others.   Also a cycle of water-colours by *F. J. Becker.* — The ROTE SAAL ('Red Room'; adjoining) contains early-German paintings by *Hans Baldung Grien* and *H. L. Schäufelin;* an old copy of *Dürer's* Adam and Eve at Madrid; German paintings of the 17-18th cent., including examples of *Seekatz, Christopher G. Schütz, J. H. Roos, J. L. E. Morgenstern, Raphael Mengs, Johann Kaspar Schneider* (Scene on the Rhine, with a view of the Taunus, 1789); French paintings of the 18th cent., by *Nicolas Mignard, J. M. Nattier, H. Rigaud,* and *Antoine Pesne,* chiefly portraits.   Old views of Mayence, portraits of governors of the town, and the like.

The *Municipal Library,* the **Gutenberg Museum,** and the *Collection of Coins* occupy the first and second floors of the W. wing.

The LIBRARY (open on Mon., Tues., Thurs, & Frid. 9-1, Wed. & Sat. 9-4; reading-room also 2-5 or 2-6) consists of about 200,000 vols., including 4500 incunabula, and 1200 MSS. from the 8th cent. onwards. The reading-room contains portraits of nineteen electors.

The *Gutenberg Museum* (open free daily, 10-4 or 10-6) is connected with the library. The anteroom contains documents relating to Gutenberg, writings referring to the invention of printing, and memorials of the Gutenberg festivals of 1837, 1840, and 1900. — On the staircase are *Sutter's* designs for the procession of 1900; also a model of ancient Mayence, by *N. Göbel.* — Two rooms on the second floor contain an exhibition illustrating the history and development of printing, book-illustration, etc. In the cases by the windows are specimens of early printing by Gutenberg, Fust, and Schöffer, and a selection of the most important works to the present day.

The COINS (12,000 specimens) include a full set of those of Mayence, from the Merovingian time down to the overthrow of the electoral sway.

The whole of the S.E. wing is devoted to the ***Roman-Germanic Central Museum.** It contains, besides a number of originals, admirable reproductions of all the important antiquities found in Germany and the neighbouring countries down to the 10th cent. and affords a unique survey of the civilization of those days. On the groundfloor are the prehistoric, on the first floor the Roman-Germanic, and on the second the Merovingian-Carlovingian objects.

Opposite the Electoral Palace, to the S.E., is the *Palace of the Grand-Duke* (Pl. E, 5), formerly a *Lodge of the Teutonic Order*, built in 1731-39 in the baroque style. Adjacent is the *Arsenal*, which was erected by Elector Philip Charles in 1738-40.

A little to the S.W. is the **Museum of Natural History** (Pl. E, 4), occupying the ancient church of the Reiche Clara Convent (open as the Municipal Picture Gallery, see p. 268). It contains an extensive ornithological section, ethnographical collections from the South Sea Islands, a collection illustrating the fauna of the Mediterranean, entomological and geological collections, etc. — Adjacent is the handsome new building of the *High School for Girls (Höhere Mädchenschule)*.

A handsome **Esplanade** (Pl. A-G, 5), 4¹/₂ M. long, 100 yds. broad, and planted with trees, has been constructed along the Rhine, beginning on the S. at the railway-bridge mentioned at p. 276; it extends on the N. past the extensive harbour to the Ingelheimer Au (p. 252). — Opposite the arsenal, at the spot where the old Roman bridge once stood (p. 267), the Rhine is spanned by an iron **Bridge** (Pl. E, 5; toll 4 pf.), erected in 1881-85 from designs by *Thiersch*. Of the five arches the central one has a clear span of 334 ft., and the others of 321 ft. and 282 ft. The bridge commands a fine panorama. *Kastel*, see p. 277.

The *Stadthalle* (Pl. D, 5) is a modern building in the Renaissance style, with a large hall, used for balls, concerts, and public meetings. Café-Restaurant, see p. 266; view of the Rhine from the terrace. Near it, Rhein-Str. 59, is the so-called *Iron Tower* ('Eiserne Turm'), and farther up the river is the so-called *Wooden Tower* ('Holzturm'; Pl. B, 4), two fragments of the old fortifications, dating respectively from the 13th and the 15th century. — In the Mailandsgasse, near the Iron Tower, is the old *Church of the Holy Ghost* (13th cent.), now a restaurant (p. 266).

The centre of the old town of Mayence is occupied by the market-place, in which are some quaint old houses (*e.g.* No. 13, 'Zum Boderam') and a fountain erected in 1526 by Elector Albert of Brandenburg (perhaps from the designs of P. Flötner). On the W. side stands the imposing —

*Cathedral (Pl. C, 4; *St. Martin's*). A cathedral is mentioned as having existed at Mayence as early as 406, and a new building with a baptistery, was erected by Bishop Sidonius in the 6th century. A Romanesque church was built under *Archbishop Willigis* (975-1011), but it was burned down on the very eve of its consecration in 1009. It was restored by *Abp. Bardo* in 1036, but was again destroyed by fire in 1081. On its re-erection the building received a vaulted roof (see p. xxviii). In 1159 the church served as a fortress during the struggle between *Abp. Arnold* and the citizens. The upper part was yet again destroyed by fire in

1191. Between that date and 1243 were erected the W. transept, the main choir, the octagonal dome, the Memorie or chapter-house (p. 274), and the cloisters. Gothic side-chapels were added after the close of the 13th cent., and the cloisters were wholly remodelled in 1397-1405. The wooden spire of the main W. tower was replaced in 1774 by a stone steeple in the Gothic style, by J. F. Neumann the Younger of Würzburg (p. 469). In the French period the church was used as a magazine and barracks, but in 1814 it was repaired and restored to its sacred uses. A thorough restoration of the E. part of the building was carried out in 1858-79, under the superintendence of *Laske, Wessiken,* and *Cuypers.* The middle tower was rebuilt in the Romanesque style in 1875, while the crypt under the E. choir and the two side-towers were renewed in harmony with the extant remains.

In consequence of all these vicissitudes the church possesses great value in the history of architecture. The groups of towers at the E. and W., especially the picturesque W. tower (270 ft.) above the cross, present an imposing appearance, somewhat injured, however, by the numerous additions. The lower portions of the E. round towers probably belong to the building of Willigis or Bardo. The transept, with its three huge windows, the W. choir (above which is an equestrian statue of St. Martin), and the three W. apses with their rich decoration of round-arched frieze and dwarf-galleries, show the flamboyant forms of the Transition period. All the additions, except the Memorie, are Gothic in style. The decoration of the interior shows the mark of each century in turn. — Comp. the ground-plan, p. 267.

The MAIN ENTRANCE, which is reached between some of the houses in the market-place, is in the N. aisle. The two brazen doors were executed by order of Archbp. Willigis in 988, as the Latin inscription on the border of the valves records, and are the oldest in Germany after those of Aix-la-Chapelle. On the upper panels are inscriptions, engraved in 1135, enumerating the privileges granted to the town by Archbishop Adalbert I., out of gratitude for his liberation from the hands of Henry V. — There are other entrances in the E. façade in the Liebfrauen-Platz, with interesting capitals at the S. portal, and in the S. transept, opening from the Leich-Hof. The cathedral is open daily, 8-9 and 9.30-12 a.m., and 2-6 p.m. The verger, who lives in the Leich-Hof, shows the W. choir, Memorie, cloisters, crypt, and St. Gothard's Chapel (fee $1/2$-1 $\mathcal{M}$); he also shows the rest of the church outside the usual hours (Sat. not after 4 p.m., on Sun. 5-7 p.m. only).

The INTERIOR, the vaulting of which is borne by 56 pillars, is 122 yds. long, 50 yds. broad, and 90 ft. high in the nave. The slender pillars are separated by very narrow openings, and each alternate one is provided with a ressaut from which the vaulting

springs. The W. choir, nave, and aisles have been painted dark
blue and richly decorated, the dome of the W. choir and the nave
being adorned with paintings designed by *Ph. Veit*. The subjects
of the latter are (in the dome) scenes from Old Testament history
referring to the sacrifice of Christ, and (in the nave) scenes from
the life of Christ. The red sandstone and the grey limestone of
the walls have been restored to light by the removal of the whitewash. — The most interesting feature of the interor consists in the
numerous *Tombstones it contains, ranging from the 13th to the
19th cent. (comp. p. xxxi). We begin to the right of the principal
entrance.

N. Transept. Monuments of the *Von Gablentz* family (1592) and
of *Dean von Breidenbach* (d. 1497). The font dates from 1328, the
altar from 1601. The handsome *Portal* of the St. Gothard Chapel (p. 274),
in the transition-style, formerly belonged to the Church of the Holy
Ghost (p. 271).

N. Aisle. By the 1st pillar, *Renaissance Monument of *Albert of
Brandenburg, Elector of Mayence and Archbishop of Magdeburg* (the
statue, of Kelheim stone, admirably executed), 1545; adjacent is his
tombstone, by the same pillar. The chapel opposite contains a Crucifixion of 1563. — By the 2nd pillar, *Monument of *Elector Sebastian
von Heusenstamm* (d. 1555); by the 3rd pillar, *Elector Daniel Brendel
von Homburg* (d. 1582); on the 5th pillar, *Elector Wolfgang von Dalberg*
(d. 1601), all three also in the Renaissance style. Opposite the 5th pillar,
in the chapel of the Virgin, which was restored and embellished with
painting and stained glass in 1875, is the tomb of *Bishop Ketteler*
(d. 1877). — In the adjoining St. Magnus Chapel are an Entombment in
stone and numerous reliefs in marble. The Raising of Lazarus, by the
pillar, is a masterpiece of late mediæval wood-carving (15th cent.). By
the 8th pillar on the E. is a monument erected to St. Boniface in 1357;
till 1829 it was in the church of St. John (colouring renewed). By the
9th pillar, *Monument of Elector Conrad III. of Daun* (d. 1434), Gothic. —
The Chapel of St. Barbara contains an early-Gothic winged altar-piece
and is adorned with mural paintings by Settegast; the Chapel of
St. Victor has a baroque altar, dating from 1622. — On the wall of
the E. choir, opposite, is the baroque monument of *General Count
Lamberg* (d. 1689).

A flight of 19 steps ascends hence to the Pfarrchor, or E. Choir,
the floor of which has been raised about 8ft. by the restoration of the
crypt. It contains a modern canopy and altar. To the right in the —

Nave, by the 10th pillar, *Elector Peter von Aspelt* or *Aichspalt*
(d. 1320), leaning with his right hand on Henry VII. and with his left
on Lewis the Bavarian, the two emperors crowned by him; adjoining
him, King John of Bohemia, also crowned by him. Several other monuments of archbishops and electors. By the 6th pillar on the N. side,
Elector Diether von Isenburg, 1482. Opposite is the *Pulpit*, executed
in stone at the end of the 15th cent., with a modern covering in wood.
By the 4th pillar on the N. side, *Albert of Saxony*, administrator of
the archbishopric, 1484, with a simple and noble figure of the youthful
prince. Opposite (S. side), *Elector Berthold von Henneberg*, 1504,
probably by Tilman Riemenschneider, one of the finest late-Gothic
monuments in the cathedral. By the 2nd pillar on the S., *Elector
Jacob von Liebenstein*, 1508, late-Gothic. The tomb of *Elector Uriel
von Gemmingen* (d. 1514), opposite, is the earliest tomb showing the
transition from Gothic to Renaissance.

S. Aisle. The Chapel of All Saints (1317) contains an altar in the
Renaissance style, presented in 1604 by Phil. Cratz von Scharfenstein,

afterwards Bishop of Worms. In the Chapel of St. John are a Renaissance altar presented by Canon Fried. von Fürstenberg (d. 1607), and a winged altar-piece in carved work on a gold ground representing the Twelve Apostles and the Coronation of the Virgin, 1517. The adjoining Chapel of St. Lawrence and St. Michael's Chapel have some fine stained glass (modern), and an altar of 1662 in the Renaissance style. — To the left of the handsome entrance-portal (14th cent.) to the 'Memorie' and cloisters (see below) is a *Slab* (16th cent.; built into the wall) bearing an inscription to the memory of *Fastrada* (or Fastradana), the third wife of Charlemagne; she died at Frankfort in 794, and was buried there in the church of St. Alban, destroyed in 1552.

The S. Transept contains several monuments to prelates of the 18th century. A fine head of Saturn on the monument of *Canon von Breidenbach-Bürresheim* (1743), and the noble Gothic *Monument of Archbp. Conrad II. von Weinsberg* (d. 1396), adjoining the W. choir, are noteworthy. Over the door opening on the Leich-Hof (p. 272) is a Romanesque relief.

The Bischofschor, or W. Choir, separated from the transepts by galleries of 1682, contains rococo *Choir Stalls, erected in 1767. In the dome are the paintings already mentioned (p. 273).

From the S. aisle the portal above noticed (to the right, the old Romanesque portal) leads into the **Memorie,** erected in 1243, and roofed with wide groined vaulting. This was the old chapter-house, and owes its name to the memorial services held in it annually. By the W. wall (r.) is the episcopal throne in stone. Adjacent are several monuments of the years 1536, 1550, and 1558. — The Gothic *Chapel of St. Nicholas*, to the S. of the Memorie, dates from the 14th cent. and has been restored in the original style.

The **Cloisters** also contain several monuments. On the S. wall is *Schwanthaler's Monument to Frauenlob*, a female figure decorating a coffin with a wreath, erected by the ladies of Mayence in 1842 to Count Heinrich von Meissen (d. 1318), surnamed *Frauenlob* (women's praise), 'the pious minstrel of the Holy Virgin, and of female virtue'. At the end of this wall are six seated figures of the Apostles (late-Romanesque) from the buttresses on the garden-side. At the beginning of the E. wall is a Gothic relief, with groups of saved and lost souls. Near it is an older tombstone of Frauenlob, erected in 1783, a copy of the original of 1318. The cloisters, which afford a good view of the church-towers, also contain sculptured fragments from other churches of Mayence, some of great beauty and interest.

A gloomy chamber to the S. of the cloisters contains fine Renaissance *Choir Stalls and tapestry of the 14-17th centuries.

Between the N. transept of the cathedral and the Markt, partly concealed from view by surrounding buildings, is the *Chapel of St. Gothard*, a double church with aisles, a characteristic Romanesque building, erected in 1135-8. It originally formed the chapel of the archiepiscopal palace (entrance from the N. transept, p. 273). The dwarf-gallery on the exterior (comp. p. 83) and the pillars and columns within deserve notice.

A little to the W. of the Leich-Hof (p. 272) is the Prot. *Church of St. John* (Pl. C, 3), which occupies the site of the old baptistery. — A little way off, in the Augustiner-Str., is the *Liebfrauen-Kirche* (Pl. B, C, 4), of 1768-76, with rococo decoration and ceiling paintings by Januarius Zick. In the Kapuzinergasse is the *Church of St. Ignatius* (Pl. B, 4), a baroque building of 1763-74.

Near the cathedral is the Gutenberg-Platz (Pl. C, D, 3),

which is embellished with a **Statue of Gutenberg,** the inventor
of printing, designed by *Thorvaldsen,* and erected in 1837. The
inscription at the back by Ottfried Müller runs thus: —

> *Artem quae Graecos latuit, latuitque Latinos,*
> *Germani sollers extudit ingenium.*
> *Nunc, quidquid veteres sapiunt sapiuntque recentes,*
> *Non sibi, sed populis omnibus id sapiunt.*

Owing to the obscurity which envelopes the inventor of printing,
and to the fact that he had several contemporaries of the same name
as himself, there is some difficulty in identifying him. Native and
foreign writers, however, of the 15th cent. agree in naming as the inventor JOHANN GÄNSFLEISCH, surnamed GUTENBERG from his mother's
name, who was born in Mayence about the end of the 14th cent., at the
former *Hof Gutenberg,* Christoph-Str. 2 (Pl. D, 4), and not, in spite
of the tablet, at the Hof zum Gänsfleisch, Emmeran-Str. 23 (Pl. D, 3).
After a stay in Strassburg, Gutenberg seems to have established himself
in his native city in 1444. The earliest book printed by him from
moveable types to which a certain date can be assigned belongs to the
year 1447 (p. 260), though the fragment 'Vom Weltgericht', preserved
in the Gutenberg Museum (p. 270), and the 27-line fragment of Donatus,
now in the Bibliothèque Nationale at Paris, are earlier. His first work
of importance was the 42-line Bible (1450-1455?). *Johann Fust,* who
had assisted Gutenberg in this work, afterwards separated from him,
and established a new printing-office in partnership with *Peter Schöffer.*
Gutenberg's subsequent career; his connection with the 36-line Bible,
the types of which were in the hands of Albrecht Pfister of Bamberg
from 1461 onwards; and the question whether Gutenberg printed the
Mayence Catholicon (1460), the earliest long work in Italic characters,
are all points still veiled in obscurity. After a residence in Eltville
(p. 250), the date and duration of which are uncertain, Gutenberg died
in Mayence in 1467 or 1468, and was buried in the Franciscan church,
which was burned down in 1793. — Gutenberg's alleged first printing-
office, at the *Hof zum Jungen,* Franziskanergasse 3, and those of Johann
Fust and Peter Schöffer at the *Hof zum Humbrecht,* Schuster-Str. 20, and
the *Schöffer-Hof,* Korbgasse 3, are all indicated by memorial tablets.

Opposite the monument is the *Theatre,* erected in 1833 and
rebuilt in 1910. — In the Schuster-Strasse, one of the chief business
streets, which runs off the old market-place, is the Gothic *Church
of St. Quentin* (Pl. D, 4; 15th cent.), and near it the *Church of
St. Christopher,* in the early-Gothic style. Between them is the large
Pensioners' Hospital and opposite is the *Knebel'sche Hof* (No. 2),
with a rich oriel in the Renaissance style. — From the Schuster-
Str. the Stadionerhof-Str. leads to the W. to the *Dalberger Hof*
(1715-18), now occupied by law-courts (Justiz-Palast; Pl. D, E, 3, 4),
and to the *Church of St. Emmeran* (Pl. D, 3), a tasteful late-Gothic
building, erected in 1450 and restored in 1881 (old ceiling-paintings).

The SCHILLER-PLATZ (Pl. D, 2), which is planted with chestnut-
trees and embellished with a bronze *Statue of Schiller,* by Scholl
(1862), is bounded on the S. by the *Osteiner Hof* (1747), now the
residence of the Military Governor and of the Commandant, and on
the W. by the *Bassenheimer Hof* (1756; with café-restaurant), the
Barracks, and the *Military Casino* or *Schönborner Hof.*

The broad Emmerich-Joseph-Str. leads hence to the W. to a
flight of 76 steps ascending to the *Mathilden-Terrasse* (Pl. D, 2),

which affords a view of the town and environs. Below the terrace
are the vaults (sparkling wine) of Kupferberg & Co. On the *Kästrich.*
(Castrum) a new and well-built quarter of the town has sprung up
since the explosion of a powder-magazine here in 1857.

On one of the highest points in the town (85 ft. above the level
of the Rhine) rises the early-Gothic *Church of St. Stephen
(Pl. C, 2), erected in 1257-1328 and restored after the explosion in
1857. It consists of nave and aisles of equal height, with a choir
at each end. The octagonal *Tower*, 170 ft. high, commands a beautiful view of the city and the Eigelstein (280 steps; visitors ring
near the flying buttress to the right of the N. door of the tower).

The INTERIOR contains altar-pieces by *Veit* to the right and left of
the E. choir; behind the high-altar are a late-Gothic tabernacle of 1500
and four exquisite brass altar-columns of 1509. — The treasury contains
a vestment of St. Willigis, a chasuble, said to be of Sicilian origin
(ca. 1000), dalmatics of the 15th cent., a censer of the 10th cent., and
other interesting objects. — The late-Gothic *Cloisters*, dating from 1449,
entered from the right aisle, are remarkable for their tasteful vaulting
and windows. The door in the E. wall leads to the Stephan-Strasse.

The Stephan-Str. leads from the church to the S.E. to the 'Eis-
grubweg', where the *Windmühlenberg* (Pl. B, 3), an eminence
planted with lime-trees, commands one of the finest views of the
cathedral, between the houses. — Beyond the Alarm-Bastion is the
entrance to the citadel.

The **Citadel** (Pl. A, 3; adm. by cards, obtainable at the office
of the Commandant, see p. 275; 20 pf.), which occupies the site of
the Roman castrum, dates from the 17th century. In its S.W. corner rises the *Drusus-Turm* or *Eigelstein,* a dark mass of concrete,
40 ft. in height, said by tradition to have been erected by the Legions in honour of Drusus (p. 267), who was killed in B. C. 9 on
his retreat from the Elbe. The monument was once much higher
than at present, and probably had an outer casing of masonry. In
1689 it was furnished with a spiral staircase in the interior. Fine
panorama from the top.

The **Anlage** (restaurant; music, p. 266), or public promenade,
on a slight eminence outside the *Neutor* (Pl. A, 4; tramway), on
the S. side of the town, occupies the site of the electoral château
of *Favorite* (removed in 1793). — The *Railway Bridge,* built in
1862, which here crosses the Rhine near its junction with the Main,
consists of four arches, each about 131 yds. in span. It commands
an admirable view of both rivers and of the town.

The **Wall-Strasse** (Pl. E, F, G, 1) begins behind the Central
Station, beyond the viaduct which carries the Binger-Str. over the
railway, and ascends the hill, commanding a view of Biebrich, Wiesbaden, the Taunus, and the Rheingau. — Near the *Mombacher-Tor*
are the large *Military Stores Factory,* and the *Cavalry Barracks*
(distinguished by a gilded horse from the former electoral stables).

Outside the Binger-Tor (Pl. E, 1; steam-tramway, see p. 268) lies the *Cemetery*, which was once the burial-ground of the Roman legions and of the earliest Christian church (St. Aureus). In the new part is a large crematorium. — About ¹/₂ M. farther on, on a hill to the right of the village of *Zahlbach*, are the remains of a Roman **Aqueduct**, of which 60 concrete pillars, some of them 23 ft. high, are still standing. By this channel a supply of water for the use of the Roman castle was conducted from the Königsborn (see below).

The steam-tramway to Finthen diverges to the right from the Zahl-bach road near the cemetery, traverses the orchards and market-gardens of *Gonsenheim* (p. 455), passes the villa-colony of **Lenneberg** *(Schloss-Hôtel)* or *Leniaberg*, and then ascends to *Finthen (Fontanae)*, on the road to Bingen, 5 M. from Mayence. — From Finthen we proceed to the N. viâ (¹/₄ M.) *Königsborn* (inn), with the spring that furnished the main supply of the Roman aqueduct (see above), to the (1¹/₂ M.) **Forsthaus Ludwigshöhe** (restaurant & pension) on the *Leniaberg*, with view-tower, and to (3 M.) *Budenheim* (p. 217). A pleasanter route is offered by the direct wood-path from station Lenneberg to (25 min.) the Ludwigs-höhe. On the hill is the château of Waldhausen (1909).

37. From Wiesbaden or Mayence to Frankfort.

The Wiesbaden line is part of the through-route from Cologne to Frankfort on the right bank of the Rhine (140 M.; express train in 3³/₄-4¹/₂ hrs.). The Mayence line is part of the main line between the same cities on the left bank (138 M.; express in 3³/₄-4 hrs.; fares in each case 17 ℳ 20, 11 ℳ 40, 6 ℳ 90 pf.). Connection with the Rhine steamers is equally convenient on either route. — Comp. Map, p. 300.

a. From Wiesbaden to Frankfort.

25¹/₂ M. RAILWAY *(Taunusbahn;* opened in 1839) in ³/₄-1¹/₄ hr. (fares 3 ℳ 40, 2 ℳ, 1 ℳ 35 pf.; express fares 3 ℳ 90, 2 ℳ 50, 1 ℳ 60 pf.).

Wiesbaden, see p. 253. — 1¹/₂ M. *Biebrich-Ost* (p. 252) is the station for passengers who wish to transfer to the Rhine steamers. Tramway to the wharf in 6 min. (10 pf.); trunks and valises, trans-ported on special cars, 25 pf. each. — Numerous factories are passed. To the right we see the Rhine, with the Petersau and the Kaiser-Brücke (p. 252).

5 M. **Kastel** *(Anker)*, a suburb of Mayence on the right bank of the Rhine, with 8700 inhab., has been fortified ever since the Roman period (Castellum Mattiacorum). The station is situated close to the bridge over the Rhine. Tramway to Mayence, see p. 266; cab 1 ℳ, with two horses 1¹/₂ ℳ (bridge-toll extra).

The railway skirts the spurs of the Taunus at some distance from the *Main*, which is only occasionally visible.

8 M. **Hochheim** (405 ft.; *Kaiserhof*, with restaurant), a small town with 3700 inhab., celebrated for its wines. The most esteemed is yielded by the vineyards of the old *Domdechanei* (deanery). The sparkling 'Hock' made at Hochheim (whence the name), is much prized, and is largely exported to England (comp. p. xxiii).

At (12 M.) *Flörsheim* (Hirsch), a village on the Main, omnibuses

18*

and carriages are in waiting to convey travellers to the (1½ M.) baths of **Weilbach** (sulphur and lithia springs). The village of *Weilbach* (1000 inhab.) lies ³/₄ M. to the N. of the baths. Pleasing view from the '*Kanzel*' (pulpit), a hill with four trees, ½ M. above *Diedenbergen*, and 3 M. to the N. of Weilbach.

16 M. *Hattersheim.* The white Hofheim Chapel (p. 310) and the Meisterturm can be seen on the nearer spurs of the Taunus. 18 M. *Sindlingen-Zailsheim.*

20 M. **Höchst.** — HOTELS. *Schmitt*, Humboldt-Str., at the railway-station; *Casino*, Casino-Str., R. & B. 2-2½ ℳ; *Hirsch, Nassauer Hof*, both in the Haupt-Strasse. — WINE at the *Schöne Aussicht*, also rooms.

Höchst am Main (290 ft.), a Roman frontier-fortress in the time of Augustus, belonged to the Electorate of Mayence from 1352 to 1801 and was once the seat of a celebrated porcelain factory (1740-94). It is now a thriving town of 15,800 inhab., with iron and brass foundries, large aniline and alizarine dye-works (2500 hands; also medical preparations), and other factories. The Rom. Cath. *Church of St. Justinus*, on the lofty right bank of the Main, beyond the Haupt-Str., a 9th cent. basilica, many times rebuilt, has a Gothic choir added in 1443. The *Statue of Bismarck* (1899) is by Alois Mayer. A palace of the Electors of Mayence here, built in the 15-16th cent., was destroyed by the Frankforters in 1634, but the tower and the moat still remain. The building is now private property. Behind it is the *Rote Haus*, which in the 18th cent. was a summer-residence of the Electors.

From Höchst to *Königstein*, see p. 306; to *Soden*, see p. 309; to *Eppstein* and *Limburg*, see pp. 309, 310.

25½ M. *Frankfort*, see p. 279.

b. From Mayence to Frankfort.

23½ M. RAILWAY in 36-75 min. (fares 3 ℳ 10, 1 ℳ 90, 1 ℳ 25 pf.; express fares 3 ℳ 60, 2 ℳ 40, 1 ℳ 50 pf.).

Mayence, see p. 265. The train starts at the central station, runs under the citadel to the S. station (*Mainz Süd*), and crosses the Rhine by the bridge mentioned at p. 276.

3 M. *Gustavsburg-Kostheim.* Gustavsburg was made a fortress by the Swedes in 1633 and is now a manufacturing suburb of Mayence, with large machine-shops. Kostheim lies on the opposite (right) bank of the Main. — 5½ M. *Bischofsheim* (p. 313); 8 M. *Rüsselsheim* (Rüsselsheimer Hof), with Opel's large motor-car works; 10 M. *Raunheim;* 15 M. *Kelsterbach.* We have a view of the Taunus to the left. 17 M. *Schwanheim;* 20 M. *Goldstein*, junction of the Sachsenhausen line. — The line now traverses the Frankfort 'Stadtwald'. 21¼ M. *Frankfurt-Niederrad*, also a station on the 'Waldbahn' (p. 299). We cross the Main.

23½ M. *Frankfort* (Central Station; p. 279).

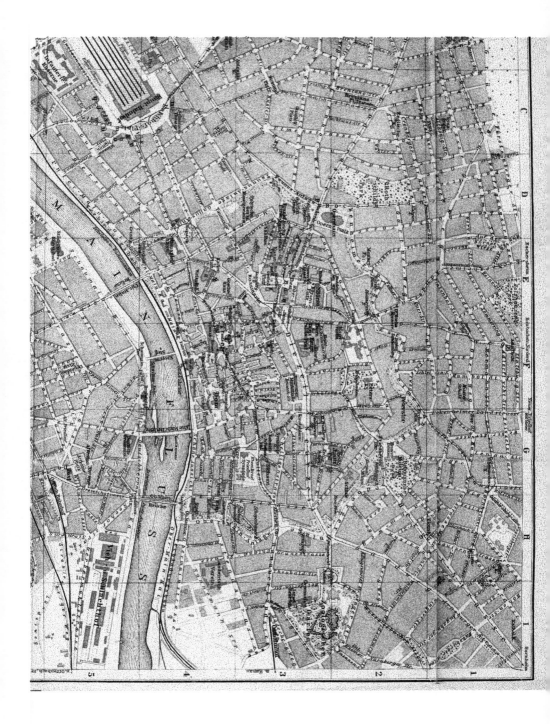

38. Frankfort.

Railway Stations. The CENTRAL STATION (*Haupt-Bahnhof;* Pl. C, 4, 5), with a good restaurant (D. from 12 to 2 p.m. from 2 ℳ) and baths (1 ℳ). No hotel-omnibuses meet the trains. Cabs, see p. 280; an extra fare of 20 pf. is paid for the luggage-cabs. Tramway, see p. 280. Trunks may also be forwarded to the city by the express Company ('Paketfahrgesellschaft'). — OST-BAHNHOF (Pl. I, 3), for local trains to Hanau and viâ Hanau to the Odenwald (p. 326). — The *Süd-Bahnhof* in *Sachsenhausen* (Pl. F, G, 6) and the *Offenbach Station* (Pl. G, H, 5) have little interest for strangers. — *Official Tourist Bureau* at the Central Station; *International Sleeping Carriage Co.*, Kaiser-Str. 17.

Hotels. *At the Central Station.* *HÔTEL D'ANGLETERRE (Pl. c; C, 4), R. from 4, B. 1¹/₂, D. from 6, S. 4¹/₂ ℳ; *CARLTON HOTEL (Pl. n; C, 4), R. from 4, B. 1¹/₂, déj. 3¹/₂-4¹/₂, D. 6, S. 4¹/₂ ℳ. Both these houses are of the very first class, with all modern comforts, private baths, and fashionable restaurants. — *HÔTEL DE RUSSIE (Pl. k; C, 5), R. 3-7, B. 1¹/₄, déj. 3, D. 4¹/₂ ℳ; *HÔTEL BRISTOL (Pl. v; C, 4, 5), with restaurant, R. 3-7, B. 1¹/₂, déj. 2-2¹/₂, D. 3-4, S. 3 ℳ; *CONTINENTAL (Pl. m; C, 5), R. 2¹/₂-7, B. 1¹/₄, D. 2¹/₂-3¹/₂, S. 2¹/₂-3¹/₂ ℳ. — *GRAND-HÔTEL NATIONAL (Pl. l; C, 5), with restaurant, R. 2¹/₂-5, B. 1¹/₄, déj. 2¹/₂-3¹/₂, D. 3-3¹/₂ ℳ; *MONOPOL-MÉTROPOLE (Pl. t; C, 5), R. 2¹/₂-6, B. 1¹/₄, déj. 2¹/₂, D. 3-3¹/₂ ℳ, with wine-restaurant; *SAVOY HOTEL (Pl. o; C, 5), Wiesenhütten-Str. 42, R. from 2¹/₂, B. 1¹/₄, D. 3-3¹/₂ ℳ. — *DEUTSCHER KAISER & KAISERHOF (Pl. h; C, 5), Wiesenhütten-Platz; HÔTEL ROYAL (Pl. x; C, 4' 5), Kronprinzen-Str., R. 2-4, B. 1 ℳ, with restaurant; GERMANIA (Pl. q; C, 5); PRINZ HEINRICH (Pl. u; C, 5), Scharnhorst-Str., R. 2-5, B. 1 ℳ, with wine and beer restaurant; VIER JAHRESZEITEN (Pl. w; C, 5), Scharnhorst-Str. 33 (commercial), R. & B. 2¹/₂ ℳ, with restaurant; STADT FRANKFURT (Pl. r; C, 5); STUTTGARTER HOF (Pl. y; C, 5), Kronprinzen-Str. 59, with restaurant, R. 2-4, B. 1 ℳ; STADT COBLENZ (Pl. j; C, 5), Gneisenau-Str. 17, R. 2-2¹/₂, B. 1 ℳ; BASELER HOF (*Christliches Hospiz*), Wiesenhütten-Platz (Pl. C, 5), R. 2-5, B. 1, D. 1¹/₂-2 ℳ. — *In the Town.* *FRANKFURTER HOF (Pl. a; E, 4), Kaiser-Platz, R. 4-10, with bath from 9, B. 1¹/₂, déj. 4¹/₂, D. 5-6, S. 4¹/₂ ℳ, with fashionable restaurant and railway-office; ESPLANADE HOTEL (Pl. b; D 4), Gallus-Anlage 2, newly opened, with restaurant and garden, R. from 4, with bath from 9, B. 1¹/₂, déj. 4, D. 5-6, S. 4, pens. from 12 ℳ, these two of the highest class; *HÔTEL IMPÉRIAL (Pl. p; D, 3), Opern-Platz, with restaurant, R. 3¹/₂-8, B. 1¹/₂, déj. 3-4¹/₂, D. 3-4¹/₂ ℳ; *SWAN (Pl. d; E, 3), at which the peace of 10th May, 1871, was concluded, Theater-Platz, cor. of the Steinweg, R. 3¹/₂-10, B. 1¹/₄, D. 3¹/₂ ℳ; *UNION (Pl. f; E, 3), Steinweg 9, R. 2¹/₂-8, B. 1¹/₄, D. 3 ℳ; HÔTEL WESTMINSTER (Pl. z; E, 3), Theater-Platz 3, with the Falstaff Restaurant (p. 280); PARISER HOF (Pl. e; E, 3), Schiller-Platz 5, R. 2¹/₂-6, B. 1¹/₄, D. 2-3¹/₂ ℳ. — HÔTEL DREXEL (Pl. i; G, 3), Grosse Friedberger-Str. 18, commercial; CENTRAL HOTEL (Pl. g; E, 4), Bethmann-Str. 52.

Pensions. *Mrs.Emerson,* Park-Str. 6 (Pl. D, 1); *Miss White,* Kettenhofweg 78 (Pl. C, 2, 3); *Miss Sharp,* Wolfsgang-Str. 70 (Pl. D, 1); *Pfaff,* Guiolett-Str. 21 (Pl. C, 3), pens. 6-12 ℳ; *Villa Germania,* Bockenheimer Land-Str. 64 (Pl. C, 2), pens. 6-10 ℳ; *Pens. Métropole,* Bockenheimer Land-Str., corner of Wiesenau (Pl. C, 2), pens. 6-9 ℳ; *Westend,* Wiesenau 53 (Pl. C, 1, 2), pens. 6-8 ℳ; *Kehrmann,* Beethoven-Str. 7 (Pl. B, 2), pens. 6-10 ℳ; *Oranien,* Beethoven-Str. 71, cor. of the Bockenheimer Land-Str. (Pl. B, 2), pens. 5-15 ℳ; *Terminus,* Hohenzollern-Platz 14 (Pl. B, 3, 4), pens. 5-8 ℳ; *Villa Métropole,* Gärtner-Weg 24 (Pl. D, E, 2), pens. 4¹/₄-7 ℳ; *Barth,* Niedenau 52 (Pl. C, 3), pens. 5-8 ℳ; *Vorster,* Linden-Str. 17 (Pl. C, 2, 3), pens. 5-8 ℳ.

Restaurants. WINE. *Buerose, Goethe-Str. 29 (Pl. E, 3); *Kaiserkeller, Kaiser-Str. 29 (1st floor), D. 2¹/₂-3¹/₂ ℳ; *Ratskeller (p. 287); *Malepartus, Grosse Bockenheimer-Str. 30 (Pl. E, 3); Wolf, Börsen-Platz 5 (Pl. E, 3) and Bahnhofs-Platz, opposite the Schumann Theatre

(p. 283); *Bernhard*, Grosser Kornmarkt 10 (Pl. E, F, 4), with 'old-German' drinking-room on the upper floor. — The restaurants in the *Palm-Garten* (p. 293) and in the *Zoological Garden* (p. 294; D. 2½-3½, S. 2 ℳ) are much frequented on summer-evenings. — BEER. *Kaiserkeller*, Kaiser-Str. 29, *Tannhäuser*, Kaiser-Str. 71, and others in the same street (Pl. D, 4); *Alemannia* (Münchner Hofbräu), Schiller-Platz 4; *Kaiser-garten*, Opern-Platz 2a (Pl. D, 2, 3), with garden, much frequented in summer, D. 1-2 ℳ; *Falstaff* (in the Westminster Hotel); *Kaiserhof*, Goethe-Platz 5 (Pl. E, 3; Pilsen beer, Vienna cuisine); *Zum Faust*, in the Schauspielhaus (p. 284); *Löwenhof* (Löwenbräu), Zeil 54 (Pl. F, 3); *Fürstenberg*, Bibergasse 8 and Börsen-Platz; *Elsässer Taverne*, Biber-gasse 10 (Pl. E, 3); *Stadt Ulm*, Schäfergasse 9; *Löwenbräu* ('Braustübl'), Grosse Bockenheimer-Str. 2; *Pilsener Bierhalle*, Börsen-Platz 9; *Dom Restaurant*, cor. Dom-Str. and Braubach-Str. (Pl. F, 3). *Automatic Restaurants* in the Zeil, Kaiser-Str., etc.

Cafés. *Buerose*, Bahnhofs-Platz 12; *Hauptwache* (p. 284); *Café Bauer* (Haus Bavaria), Schiller-Str. 2, with mural paintings by H. Thoma; *Bristol*, Schiller-Platz 5; *Astoria*, cor. of Kaiser-Str. and Gallus-Anlage; *Milani*, Schiller-Platz; *Kursaal*, in the gardens at the Friedberger-Tor. — **Confectioners.** *F. R. Bütschly*, Kaiser-Str. 23; *A. Bütschly*, Goethe-Platz, with ladies' café; *Johner*, Goethe-Str. 25; *H. Kurtz*, Steinweg 4 ('Frankfurter Brenten'); *De Giorgi*, Liebfrauen-Str. 3 (chocolate); *Ashby's Tea Rooms*, Goethe-Platz 3; *Kakaostube (Cocoa Rooms)*, Kaiser-Str., cor. of the Rossmarkt.

Cabs. There are two cab-zones, the first embracing the main part of the town.

a. TAXIMETER CABS (distinguished by the tall white hats of the dri-vers). First zone: 1-2 pers. for 800 mètres 50 pf., each addit. 400 mètres 10 pf; 3-4 pers. for 600 mètres 50 pf., each addit. 300 mètres 10 pf. Second zone: 1-2 pers. for 600 mètres 50 pf., each addit. 300 mètres 10 pf.; 3-4 pers. for 400 mètres 50 pf., each addit. 200 mètres 10 pf. (the latter charges also hold good for 1-4 pers. at night, *i.e.* from 11 p.m. to 6 a.m.). — For every 4 min. waiting 10 pf., for 1 hr. 1½ ℳ.

b. ORDINARY CABS (from 11 p.m. to 6 a.m. double fares).	1-2 pers. ℳ pf.	3 pers. ℳ pf.	4 pers. ℳ pf.
Drive in the 1st Zone	— 60	— 80	1 —
Drive in the 2nd Zone	1 —	1 20	1 40
½ hr. in the town	1 —	1 20	1 20
1 hr. in the town	1 80	2 —	2 —
Every additional 10 minutes	— 25	— 30	— 30

c. MOTOR CABS. For 1-4 pers. for 600 mètres (at night for 400 m.) 50 pf., each addit. 300 mètres (at night 200 m.) 10 pf. For every 2 min. waiting 10 pf., for 1 hr. 3 ℳ.

Luggage, 25 pf. for each article over 22 lbs.

Electric Tramways. 1. From the *Bockenheimer Warte* (Pl. A, 2) viâ the Feuerbach-Str. (Pl. C, 2, 3) to the *Central Railway Station (Haupt-Bahnhof;* Pl. C, 4, 5). — **2.** From *Bockenheim* (Railway Station) viâ the Land-Strasse (Pl. B, C, 2), the Zeil (Pl. F, 3), and the Berger-Str. to *Bornheim* (Pl. I, 1). — **3.** From the *Bockenheimer Warte* (Pl. A, 2) viâ the Opern-Platz (Pl. D, 2, 3) and the Zeil to the *East Railway Station (Ost-Bahnhof;* Pl. I, 3; Zoological Garden). — **4.** From *Bockenheim* (Schönhof) viâ the Land-Strasse (Pl. B, C, 2), Opern-Platz (Pl. D, 2, 3), Untermain-Brücke (Pl. E, 5), and the Schul-Str. to *Sachsenhausen* (Offenbach Station; Pl. G, 5). — **5.** From the *Palm Garden* (Rossert-Str.; Pl. B, 1) viâ the Reuterweg (Pl. D, 1, 2), Opern-Platz (Pl. D, 2, 3), Untermain-Brücke, and the Schweizer-Str. (Pl. E, F, 5, 6) to *Sachsenhausen* (Offenbach Railway Station; Pl. G, 5). — **6.** From the *Palm Garden* (Rossert-Str.; Pl. B, 1) viâ the Reuterweg (Pl. D, 1, 2) and the Zeil to the Wittelsbacher Allée (Pl. I, 2; Zoological Garden). — **7.** From *Eckenheim* (beyond Pl. G, 1; Cemetery) viâ the Konstabler-Wache (Pl. G, 3) and the Obermain-Brücke (Pl. H, 4) to *Sachsenhausen* (comp. Pl. G, 6). — **8.** From the Cemetery (beyond Pl. G, 1) viâ the Friedberger-Land-Strasse (beyond Pl. G, 2), the Hauptwache (Pl. E, 3), and the Schweizer-Str. (Pl. E, 5, F, 6) to the *Ziegelhüttenweg* (beyond Pl. F, 6). — **10.** From *Bornheim* (beyond Pl. I, 1) viâ the Berger-Str. (Pl. I, 1, H, 2) and the Zeil (Pl. F, 3) to the *Central Railway Station* (Pl. C, 4, 5). — **11.** From the *Bornheimer-Land-Strasse* (Pl. H, 1) viâ the Oeder-Weg (Pl. F, 1, 2) and the Schiller-Str. (Pl. E, 2, 3) to the *Rebstöcker-Strasse* (beyond Pl. A, 5). — **12.** From the *Central Railway Station* (Pl. C, 4, 5) viâ the Hauptwache and the Eschenheimer-Tor (Pl. E, 2) to *Nordend* (Rohrbach-Str.; beyond Pl. H, 1). — **13.** From the *Gutleut-Strasse* (Pl. B, C, 6, 5) viâ the Hauptwache to the *Eschen-heimer-Land-Strasse* (Pl. E, 2, 1; Holzhausen-Str.). — **15.** From the *East Railway Station* (Pl. I, 3; Zoological Garden) viâ the Zeil and the Central Railway Station to *Niederrad* (beyond Pl. D, 1). — **16.** From the *Central Railway Station* (Pl. C, 4, 5) viâ the Untermain-Brücke (Pl. E, 5) and Oberrad (beyond Pl. I, 5) to *Offenbach* (beyond Pl. I, 5, 6). — **18.** From *Bockenheim* (Schönhof; beyond Pl. A, 1) viâ the Central Railway Station and the Rathaus (Pl. F, 4) to the *East Railway Station* (Pl. I, 3). — **18a.** From *Bornheim* (School; beyond Pl. I, 1) viâ the Sandweg (Pl. I, H, 1, 2) and the Rathaus (Pl. F, 4) to the *Central Railway Station* (Pl. C, 4, 5). — **19.** From *Bornheim* (School; beyond Pl. I, 1) viâ the Sandweg, the Offenbach Railway Station (Pl. G, 5), the Garten-Str. (Pl. E, D, 5, 6) and the Central Railway Station to the *Palm Garden* (Rossert-Str.; Pl. B, 1). — **20.** From *Bockenheim* (Schönhof) to *Rödelheim*. — **22.** From *Bornheim* (Saalburg-Str.; beyond Pl. I, 1) to *Seckbach*. — **23.** From the *Schauspielhaus* (Pl. E, 4) to *Heddernheim* (beyond Pl. E, 1). — **24 & 25, Electric Railways** from the *Schauspielhaus* (Pl. E, 4) to *Oberursel (Hohe Mark)* and to *Homburg* (see pp. 305, 300).

Baths. *Städtisches Schwimmbad* (Pl. G, 3), Allerheiligen-Str. *River Baths* in the Main (comp. Pl. F, 4, G, H, 4, and C, D, 5).

Theatres. *Opera House (Pl. D, 2, 3; p. 292); *Schauspielhaus* (Pl. E, 4; p. 284); *Residenz-Theater*, Neue Zeil 80 (Pl. G, 3). — VAUDEVILLE and CIRCUS in the *Schumann Theatre* (p. 283).

Concerts. The *Museums-Gesellschaft* gives 12 orchestral concerts in the Saalbau (p. 292) on Frid. evenings and Sun. afternoons in.winter, and also ten evening concerts of chamber-music.

Post & Telegraph Office, in the Zeil (Pl. F, 3; p. 284).

Frankfort Tourists' Association *(Frankfurter Verkehrsverein)*, Bahnhofs-Platz 8, opposite the Central Station.

Collections and Objects of Interest.

Art Exhibitions. Frankfurter Kunstverein (p. 292), open week-days 9.30-6, Sun. and holidays 10.30-1, 1 ℳ; *Hermes*, Rossmarkt 15; *Bangel's Gemäldesäle*, Kaiser-Str. 66; *Schneider's Kunstsalon*, Rossmarkt 23; *Katharinenhof*, Katharinenpforte 6 (Pl. E, 3); *Joseph Baer & Co.*, Hoch-Str. 6 (Pl. E, 2), incunabula, bindings.

Bethmann's Museum (p. 294), open week-days 10-1 and 3-5, free on Sun. and holidays and in winter 11-1.

Cathedral (p. 288): the interior is best visited on week-days in the morning 10-11.30, in the afternoon after 2; the tower is open 7-7, in winter 9-4, 25 pf., free on Wed. and Sat. afternoons.

Goethe's House (p. 285), open 8-1 and 3-6, Sun. and holidays 8-1, in winter 9-6 and 9-1; fee 1 ℳ.

Libraries: *Stadtbibliothek (Town Library;* p. 291) open Mon. to Frid. 10-1 and 4-8, Sat. 10-1; the manuscripts, incunabula, and bindings may be seen in the Reading Room on week-days 10-12, Sun. and holidays 11-1. — *Library.of the Museum of Art and Industry* (p. 291), open Tues. to Sat. 10-1 and 6-9, in winter on Sun. also 10-1. — *Rothschild Library*, Untermain Quay 15, open week-days 11-1 and 4-8, on Sun. 10-1.

Manskopf Museum of Musical History, Wiesenhütten-Str. 18 (Pl. D, 5), with the permission of the owner only.

Municipal Gallery (p. 299), open as the Städel Art Institute (see p. 282).

Museum of Art and Industry (p. 291), open Tues. to Sat. 10-1 and 3-5, Sun. and holidays 10-1, also on the first Sun. in the month 2-4; free on Sun. and Wed., at other times 50 pf.

Museum of Ethnology (p. 293), open free daily 10-1.

Museum, Historical (p. 289), open 10-3, free on Sun., Tues., Wed., and Frid., at other times for a fee of 50 pf.

Palm Garden (p. 293), 1 ℳ; concerts 4-6 and 7.30-10 p.m.

Römer (p. 286), open Mon. to Sat. 8-7, on Sun. and holidays 8-1, in winter 9-6 and 9-1, 50 pf.; free on Mon. and Wed. 10-1.

Senckenberg Natural History Museum (p. 293), open free Wed. 3-5 (2-4 in winter), Frid. and Sun. 11-1; Tues. & Thurs. 10-1, Sat. 3-5 (2-4 in winter), 50 pf.

Städel Art Institute (p. 295), open free on Tues., Thurs., Frid., & Sat. 10-1, Wed. 11-4, Sun. 11-1; at other times for a fee of 1 ℳ. Engravings and drawings, Tues. to Sat. 11-1 & 5-7 (closed on Thurs. afternoon).

Synagogue (New; p. 291): open except Sat. and festivals 10-12 and 2-4, upon application to the castellan.

Zoological Garden (p. 294): 1 ℳ.

British Consul: *Sir F. Oppenheimer*, Consul General, Bockenheimer Land-Str. 8; *C. F. Gardner*, Vice-Consul. — **American Consul**: *Frank D. Hill*, Consul General, Schiller-Str. 20; *Char. A. Risdorf*, Vice-Consul.

English Church *(Victoria Memorial)* in the Staufen-Str. (Pl. C, 2); services at 8 and 11 a.m. and 6 p.m.; Chaplain, *Rev. Stuart Hall*, Fichard-Str. 49. — American Church Service, Sun. at 11 a.m. in the Hôtel Impérial, Opern-Platz.

Chief Attractions (1½-2 days): the Kaiser-Strasse, Rossmarkt, Goethe-Platz, Schiller-Platz, and the Zeil; the Altstadt (Old Town), with the *Cathedral*, the *Historical Museum*, the Old Main Bridge, the *Römer* and *Goethe's House;* towards evening walk to the *Palm Garden*, passing the Opera House. *Städel Art Institute* (p. 295). — Mail Coach Circular Drive, starting at the Central Railway Station at 9.30 a.m., 2.45 p.m., and 5.30 p.m. (fare 4 ℳ).

Frankfort-on-the-Main (300 ft.), with 370,000 inhab. (230,000 Protestants, 115,000 Roman Catholics, and 25,000 Jews), formerly a free town of the Empire, lies in a fertile plain bounded by mountains, on the right bank of the navigable *Main*. For many centuries it has been one of the most important commercial cities in Germany, lying at the point of convergence of the great trading routes (now represented by the railways) from Hesse, Thuringia, Franconia, Swabia, and the lands of the Rhine. Its money-market is nearly as influential as that of Berlin. The whole appearance of the city betokens the generally diffused well-being of its inhabitants. The old part of the town contains many houses of the 15-18th cent., as well as public buildings. The town is surrounded by '*Anlagen*', or public grounds, with tasteful houses and gardens, laid out on the site of the fortifications removed in 1806-12. The most fashionable quarter is the West End, between the Taunus Promenades, the Bockenheim High Road, and the Victoria-Allée. New streets now cover the whole district of the old 'Free State', extending to the suburbs of *Bornheim* on the N.E. and *Bockenheim* on the N.W., incorporated in 1877 and 1895 respectively. On the left bank of the Main lies the suburb of *Sachsenhausen*, connected with Frankfort by four stone bridges and an iron suspension-bridge. Two railway-bridges cross the river at the lower end of the city, where an industrial quarter has sprung up, with machine-shops, an iron foundry, and chemical works. Frankfort is the headquarters of the XVIII. Army Corps and seat of the supreme district court.

Frankfort is first mentioned in 793 as the seat of the royal residence ('Pfalz') of '*Franconofurd*' (ford of the Franks), and in 794 Charlemagne held a convocation of bishops and dignitaries of the empire here. After the erection of a new palace (p. 287) by Lewis the Pious in 822 the town soon reached such a high degree of prosperity that at the time of the death of Lewis the German (876) it was already looked upon as the capital of the East Frankish Empire. From the time of Henry, son of Conrad III. (1147), and of Frederick Barbarossa (1152) onwards most of the German sovereigns were chosen at Frankfort, and in 1356 it was recognized by the Golden Bull of Charles IV. (p. 288) as the permanent seat of the elections. After 1562 Frankfort, in spite of the older claims of Aix-la-Chapelle (p. 4), became also the place of coronation of the emperors (Maximilian II. in 1562, Francis II. in 1792). In 1333 Frankfort had become practically independent of the royal power, and in the 16th cent. it was officially recognized as a 'free imperial town'. Its fairs, sanctioned by the emperors in 1240 and 1330, maintained their importance down to the 19th century. It was also the headquarters of the German book-trade down to the end of the 18th century. On the dissolution of the Empire in 1806, Frankfort was made over to Karl von Dalberg, Primate of the Rhenish Confederation (previously Archbishop of Mayence), and in 1810 it became the capital of the grand-duchy of Frankfort. From 1815 to 1866 it was one of the four free cities of the German Confederation and the seat of the Diet. In 1848-9 the great Constitutional Assembly of Germany held its sittings in the church of St. Paul. Since 1866, when it passed to Prussia, the population of the city has been quadrupled. The canalization of the Main (1886 et seq.) and the construction of the harbours have made Frankfort an important terminus of the goods-traffic on the Rhine.

a. Kaiser-Strasse and Zeil.

The **Central Railway Station** (*Hauptbahnhof;* Pl. C, 4, 5), a large and handsome building by Eggert and Frantz (1883-88), is one of the finest and most convenient stations on the Continent. It is richly adorned with allegorical sculptures (Genius of Steam, Electricity, Agriculture, Industry, etc.), by Herold and other artists.

The large Bahnhofs-Platz (Pl. C, 4, 5), in front of the station, is one of the chief centres of the tramway system, lines 10, 12, 13, 15, 18, & 18a running hence to the interior of the city (comp. pp. 280, 281). It is fringed by various hotels (see p. 279), and at its N. end stands the *Schumann Theatre* (p. 281), erected in 1904-5, with a group of horse-tamers, in copper, by Uphues, between its towers.

The wide *KAISER-STRASSE* (Pl. C, D, E, 4), with its fashionable shops, substantial office-buildings, restaurants, and places of amusement, is now the gayest and busiest street in the city. At the point where this street crosses the Gallus Promenade is a *Clock Tower* (*Uhrturm;* Pl. D, 4). To the right is a *Monument to Bismarck*, executed in copper by Siemering from a design by Mantzel (1908); by the side of the Great Chancellor is a horse bearing a figure of

Germania and trampling the Dragon of Discord under foot. — A little to the S. is the **Schauspielhaus** or *Theatre* (Pl. E, 4), built in 1900-2 after designs by *H. Seeling.* It holds 1200 spectators. The sculptured figures and reliefs on the façades are inspired by Goethe's 'Dichtung und Wahrheit'; the 'Dichtung' group on the main façade and the reliefs on the S. façade are by *Varnesi,* while the 'Wahrheit' group and the reliefs on the N. façade are by *Haus-mann.* The sculptures in the pediment are by *Klimsch.* The prominent gilded dome, 169 ft. high, is surmounted by a copper statue 10 ft. in height, representing Frankfort as Protector of the Arts, after *Herold.* The fountain in front of the building is by Haus-mann (1910). Restaurant on the terrace (Zum Faust), see p. 280.

The Kaiser-Str. then leads viâ the Kaiser-Platz, with its tasteful fountain, to the Rossmarkt (Pl. E, 3), in the W. half of which rises the *Monument of Gutenberg,* erected in 1858, a fine group on a large sandstone pedestal, designed by Ed. von der Launitz. The central figure with the types in the left hand is Gutenberg, on his right Fust, on his left Schöffer (comp. p. 275). On the frieze are portrait-heads of fourteen celebrated printers, with Caxton among them. In the four niches beneath are the arms of the four towns where printing was first practised: Mayence, Frankfort, Venice, and Strassburg. Round the base are figures representing Theology, Poetry, Natural Science, and Industry. Among the handsome new buildings are the premises of the *Diskonto-Gesellschaft* (E.) and of the *Germania Insurance Co.* (N.). — The Goethe-Platz (Pl. E, 3), which adjoins the Rossmarkt on the N., is embellished with Schwan-thaler's *Monument of Goethe* (1844), with reliefs of scenes and figures from Goethe's poems.

Adjoining the Rossmarkt on the N.E. side is the Schiller-Platz (Pl. E, 3), with the old *Hauptwache,* built as a guard-house in 1729 and now a café (p. 280), and a *Statue of Schiller,* by Diel-mann (1863). — To the S. rises the *Katharinen-Kirche* (Pl. E, F, 3), built in 1680, with numerous old tombs (one of 1378) and modern stained-glass windows (verger, Katharinen-Pforte 11). The neighbouring *Liebfrauen-Kirche* (Pl. F, 3; R.C.), a late-Gothic church of the 15th cent., also contains interesting tombstones (one, in the left aisle, of 1322). — From the Schiller-Platz the Grosse Eschen-heimer-Str. (see p. 292) runs to the N.

The Zeil (Pl. F, G, 3), once the chief street of Frankfort, is somewhat less brilliant as to its shops than the Kaiser-Str., but also contains a number of tasteful modern buildings. To the left is the handsome *General Post Office* (Pl. F, 3), built by Ahrens and Prinzhausen in 1892-94 and adorned with groups in copper by Hausmann. The monument to Emp. William I. in the court is by Krüger (1895). The Zeil is continued by the Neue Zeil, in which, to the left, are the *Police Headquarters (Polizei-Präsidium;*

Pl. G, 3), behind which are the *Law Courts (Justiz-Palast;* Pl. G, 2, 3), a German Renaissance structure by Endell (1884-89). — Friedberg Promenade (Anlagen) and Zoological Garden, see p. 294.

b. The Old Town. Streets on the Right Bank of the Main.

The Old Town (Altstadt), to the S. of the Zeil, corresponds more or less closely to the town of the 12th cent., the W. and N. limits of which are still indicated by the Hirschgraben, Holzgraben, and Baugraben. The picturesque maze of tortuous lanes is, however, now beginning to give place to wide new thoroughfares.

At Grosse Hirchgraben 23 is the **Goethe House (Pl. E, 4),* where the poet was born (28th August, 1749) and spent his boyhood (adm., see p. 281). The house was purchased by the '*Freie Deutsche Hochstift'* in 1863, and has been restored to the condition in which it was after the alterations made in 1755 (see 'Dichtung und Wahrheit').

The GROUND FLOOR (ticket-office on the right) contains the dining-room and kitchen. The former was also the room of *Catharina Elisabeth Goethe* (1731-1808), Goethe's mother. — On the staircase are the 'Roman Views' mentioned in 'Dichtung und Wahrheit'.

FIRST FLOOR. The three rooms towards the street were the quarters of Royal-Lieutenant Count Thorene, who occupied Frankfort with the French army in 1759. The 'Karl August Room' (l.) was occupied for several days in 1779 by the Duke Charles Augustus of Weimar, when visiting Goethe's parents. — Towards the court is the music-room.

SECOND FLOOR. The middle front-room contains the picture-gallery of the poet's father, *Councillor Johann Caspar Goethe* (1710-82), arranged as it was in 1755. To the left is his study, from the corner-window of which he could watch the goings-out and comings-in of his son. To the right is the bedroom of the poet's parents, and beyond is the room in which their illustrious son *Wolfgang* was born. — At the back is the room of Goethe's sister *Cornelia* (1750-77).

THIRD FLOOR. The middle front-room was the young Goethe's study, where he created Götz, Clavigo, Werther, and the beginning of Faust. In the adjoining room to the left is his puppet-theatre.

The archway in the court leads to the **Goethe Museum**, containing reminiscences of the poet's boyhood and also of his later relations with his native town. On the walls are portraits of Goethe, his family, and others. The museum is to be enlarged by a collection of the pictures executed for Count Thorene by Frankfort artists and is to be transferred to a new building next door to the Goethe House. — The rooms above the museum contain the *Goethe Library* of the Deutsche Hochstift (see above), a specialized collection of the classical period of German literature, with Goethe as its centre (20,000 vols.).

In the PAULS-PLATZ (Pl. F, 4) is the *Church of St. Paul* (bell to the right; 20 pf.), a rotunda built in 1833, where the German parliament of 1848-49 held its meetings. In front of it is the *Union Monument (Einheits-Denkmal;* 1903), 'dedicated to the champions of German union in the years of preparation, 1815-63'. On the S. side of the square are additions to the Römer (Goldener Schwan, façade of the new Rathaus; comp. p. 287).

The central point of the Old Town is the RÖMERBERG (Pl. F, 4), or market-place in front of the Römer, which was the scene of those

public rejoicings after the election of an emperor so graphically
described by Goethe in his autobiography. The *Justitia Fountain*
in the centre, erected in 1543, and adorned with a stone figure of
Justice in 1611, was completely renewed in 1887 and furnished with
a figure in bronze. While the coronation banquet was being held
in the Römer this fountain ran with red and white wine, and an
ox was roasted whole in an adjoining booth.

The *Römer (Pl. F, 4) is the name now applied to the *Municipal Offices*, which consist of a group of twelve separate old houses
(some of which abut on the Pauls-Platz) and of the equally extensive

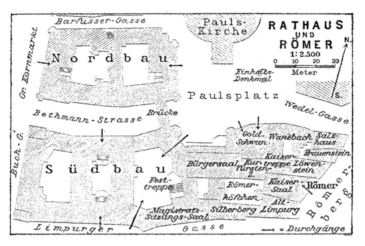

new Rathaus (adm., see p. 282). Three of the houses in the Römerberg were supplied in 1896-98 with new late-Gothic façades, with
lofty gables, from the plans of *M. Meckel*. These are the *Haus zum
Römer*, properly so called, fitted up in 1405 as a town-hall, with
large halls on the groundfloor; the so-called *Alt-Limpurg*, to the
left of it, at the corner, the seat in the 17th cent. of the influential
patrician guild of that name; and the *Haus Loewenstein*, to the
right. The *Haus Frauenstein*, to the right of the Loewenstein,
formerly the headquarters of another patrician society, has a painted
façade in the taste of the 18th century. The *Salzhaus*, at the
corner of the Wedelgasse, has its end-façade in carved wood. The
Haus Wanebach, Wedelgasse 3, is a characteristic timber structure of the 16th cent., with a small and picturesque court; it was
restored in 1888-90. The façade of the *Goldener Schwan*, Pauls-
Platz 1, dates from 1731. Beyond the court, in the Limpurger-

gasse, is the *Haus Silberberg*, restored in 1898. — The **New Rathaus** was erected in 1900-1903 from the plans of *Von Hoven* and *Neher*. The *'Südbau'*, extending on the W. to the Buchgasse, with its lofty tower (230 ft.), is in the German Renaissance style; the smaller *'Nordbau'*, which is connected with it by a bridge over the Bethmann-Str., is in the baroque style. The façades are freely adorned with sculpture, partly allegorical, partly reliefs of national types and portraits of Frankfort worthies of the 17-19th centuries.

The fine vaulting of the gateway in the Haus Silberberg and the winding staircase in the court of the Alt-Limpurg (1607) deserve attention. — From the front hall the handsome *Kaiser-Treppe* (1742) ascends to the left to the **Kaisersaal** (adm., see p. 282), where the new emperor dined with the electors and showed himself from the balcony to the people assembled on the Römerberg. The hall, which is covered with tunnel-vaulting in wood, was completed in 1411, repeatedly restored, and thoroughly renewed in 1838-53. It is embellished with portraits of the Emperors, by *Veit, Bendemann, Lessing, Rethel, Steinle,* and other artists. Above the portrait of Charlemagne is the Judgment of Solomon by Steinle (1844). —We next enter the **Wahlzimmer** ('Kurfürsten-Zimmer'; election-room), remodelled in 1731-32, where the electors met to deliberate on the choice of an emperor. — The inscription in the vestibule ('Eyns mans redde, ein halbe redde, man sal sie billich verhoren bede') dates from 1442.

The New Rathaus, containing the administrative offices, the board of works, the court of trade, the office of the City Treasurer, and so on, is also entered from the above-mentioned front hall. The grand staircase ('Festtreppe') ascends to the large **Bürgersaal,** adjoining the Wahlzimmer and containing a marble statue of Emp. William I., by Kaupert (1891). On the groundfloor is the *Ratskeller* (p. 279).

The S. side of the Römerberg is bounded by the **Nicolai-Kirche** (Pl. F, 4), an elegant church of the 13th cent., with one aisle only (N.), and a massive tower adjoining the choir. It was altered in the late-Gothic style in 1450 and restored in 1842-45. Altar-piece, a Resurrection by *Rethel.*

A little to the S. of the Römerberg is the old Fahr-Tor, to the left of which, at the corner of the quay, rises the *Rententurm,* a relic of the old fortifications erected in 1455. Adjacent is the **Saalhof** (Pl. F, 4) probably occupying the site of an imperial palace of that name ('aula regia') which was built by Charlemagne. The palace was rebuilt in 1717 and 1842; the only old part is the Romanesque chapel.

On the Main, a little lower down, is the Roman Catholic **Church of St. Leonhard** (Pl. F, 4), begun in 1219, probably on the site of the royal grange, and created a collegiate church in 1317. It has a late-Gothic choir built in 1434, while the whole was completed in 1507 and restored in the 19th century. The outer aisles possess galleries. The two Romanesque towers of the choir belonged to the original structure. On that to the N. is seen the imperial eagle, said to have been bestowed by Lewis the Bavarian on the abbey for services rendered to him in defiance of the papal ban.

INTERIOR (entr. in the N. aisle). The 'Salvator-Chörlein', or chapel to the left of the choir (1503), is notable for its vaulting with the detached ribs. The two Romanesque portals in the left aisle formed the entrances to the church before its extension. Over that to the E. is an old relief. Ancient mural paintings, including a Last Judgment (restored) above the triumphal arch. The Madonna to the right of the choir is by *Steinle*. At the entrance to the side-chapel, is a Last Supper by *Holbein the Elder* (predella of the altar-piece mentioned at p. 290).

The street called the ALTER MARKT (Pl. F, 4) leads from the Römerberg towards the E. to the cathedral. At the corner, on the right, is the house *Zum Grossen Engel*, of 1562. To the left, Markt No. 44, is the *Steinerne Haus*, a castle-like Gothic building (1464), with round-arch frieze and corner-turrets, a statue of the Virgin, and a fine vaulted gate. A side-street to the left leads to the *Nürnberger Hof*, of which a Gothic archway is the only remnant. A monument in the small Hühner-Markt commemorates the local poet Friedrich Stoltze (d. 1891). — In the narrow court of Markt No. 30 are two carved friezes representing the Fall and the Prodigal Son (16th cent.). Nearly opposite is the *Tuchgaden*, where the guild of butchers offered a draught of honour to the emperor when proceeding after his coronation from the cathedral to the Römer. Farther on, Markt No. 5, is the *Goldene Wage*, first mentioned in 1323, rebuilt in 1450, and restored in 1899, with a rich façade and a fine stucco ceiling on the upper floor (for adm. apply at the old furniture shop). Opposite is the *Haus zum Rebstock*, with a picturesque court.

The *Cathedral or *Dom (St. Bartholomew; Rom. Cath.; Pl. F, 4), originally founded by Lewis the German about 870 and reconsecrated in 1239, is the oldest church in the city. The short Gothic nave and aisles date from 1235-39, the choir was rebuilt in 1315-38, and the unusually long transept was erected in 1346-53. The cloisters were added in 1348-1477; the W. tower, begun in 1414-15, was left unfinished. The *Wahlkapelle* (Election Chapel) dates from 1355, having apparently been erected in connection with the Golden Bull (p. 283); the late-Gothic *Scheidkapelle* in the S. aisle, from 1487. The church was injured by a fire in 1867, but was restored in 1869-81 by the architect *Denzinger*. On that occasion the vault of the nave was raised and the cloisters and tower were completed. The crowning of the tower with an octagonal cupola surmounted by a spire is from the designs of the architect *Hans von Ingelheim* (1483), which had been discovered in the municipal archives.

Interior. Visitors ring for the verger at the N. portal (closed 11.30-2; comp. p. 281; good light necessary). — In the N. transept are the Tombs of Johann von Holzhausen (d. 1393) and Rudolph von Sachsenhausen (d. 1370). — The chapel adjoining the choir on the left contains a terracotta group of the Death of Mary, presented in 1480. The beautiful five-light window was executed by Dixon, after an ancient design from Cologne. — In the chapel to the right is a Resurrection, converted into an altar in 1855. Adjacent are a canopy (modern figure of the Virgin) and a fine terracotta ciborium (15th cent.). — By the S. portal is the tomb of Andreas Hirde (1518), with a relief of the Mocking of Christ. — The frescoes in the transept, by *Steinle* and *Linnemann*, represent events from the history of the town: the Council of Frankfort (794); Reconciliation of Otho I. and his brother Duke Henry (941); Conrad III. and St. Bernard of Clairvaux (1147); Burial of Günther von Schwarzburg (1349); Capistrano preaching repentance (1434); Albert Achilles of Brandenburg carried into the meeting of the electors (1486); Coronation of Maximilian II. (1562); and the Imperial Procession to the Römer. — The coronation of the emperors used to be solemnized by the Elector of Mayence beneath the crossing, originally before the altar that stood here until 1711.

The CHOIR is generally closed. The choir-stalls date from 1354. Above them are ancient frescoes, representing the life of St. Bartholomew, dating from 1407. The tabernacle to the left dates from the early 15th century. To the right is a Descent from the Cross by *Van Dyck*. Beside the high altar, to the right of the entrance to the *Wahlkapelle* (election chapel), stands the beautiful monument of the German king, *Günther von Schwarzburg*, who died in 1349 at Frankfort, where he had taken refuge from his opponent Charles IV. The armorial bearings around it belong to the families who erected the monument. The original inscription is in old-German, the new one in Latin.

The frescoes in the NAVE, by *Steinle* and *Linnemann*, represent the patrons of the church and other subjects. — The *Scheidkapelle* (p. 288), with stained-glass windows after ancient designs, contains representations of the Seven Works of Mercy, executed from *Steinle's* designs. — The TOWER commands a fine view (adm., see p. 281). The chamber at its base is painted as a vestibule or 'Paradise'.

On the outside of the N. wall of the choir is a large Crucifixion, executed in tufa in 1509 for the Frankfort patrician Jacob Heller. — The house Dom-Platz No. 4, to the E. of the cathedral, bears a small relief of *Luther*, in memory of the tradition that on his journey to Worms he preached a sermon here.

To the S., Weckmarkt 1, are the **Municipal Record Office** (*Archiv;* Pl. F, 4), built in 1874-77 from designs by *Denzinger*, and the old *Leinwandhaus* (or Drapers' Hall), dating from the end of the 14th cent., restored in 1892 and again in 1902. The upper story of the former contains the historical archives, while the lower story and the entire Leinwandhaus are devoted to the —

*Municipal Historical Museum (adm., see p. 282; 'Guide' 20 pf.). An extension of the building and a re-arrangement of its contents are in contemplation.

ROOM I. (*Entrance Hall* of the Archive Building). Municipal banners (16-18th cent.), civic uniforms and flags of Frankfort; instruments of torture; stained glass of the 14-15th cent.; 'Giant's Column' from Heddernheim. On the walls, tombs from the old St. Peter's Cemetery (p. 293) and railings from the old Judengasse, etc. — To the left, ROOM II. Costumes of citizens and Frankfort official costumes; doll's house (1748); local costumes from the neighbourhood of Frankfort; peasant's room from Hesse. — ROOM III. Greek, Italian, and Egyptian antiquities; N. European stoneware; objects from lake-dwellings in Switzerland; objects from tumuli in the vicinity of Frankfort. — ROOM IV. Objects from tumuli in the vicinity of Bad Nauheim; and Frankish antiquities. — ROOM V. Roman antiquities, mostly from Heddernheim; Mithras-reliefs; ancient helmets, weapons, ornaments, utensils; Roman mosaic (Helios). — ROOM VI. Armour and weapons. — In the PASSAGE leading to the Leinwandhaus are smaller weapons and stained glass.

ROOM VII. On the ceiling, two large eagles from a canopy used at coronations; eagles from the fountain on the Römerberg (p. 286); guild-

banners, guild-signs, tavern-signs; stove-tiles; sleighs of the 18th cent.;
an early type of velocipede. — CHAPEL (formerly the Debtors' Prison;
'Haus der Geduld'). Old choir-stalls; stained glass (13th cent.); Easter
ass (15th cent.). — Through the corridor to the right we reach ROOM VIII,
which contains *Paintings by early-German masters (15-16th cent.), etc.
On the main wall to the right are 15 sections of a large altar-piece (the
Passion) painted in the studio of *Hans Holbein the Elder* in 1501 for
the former Dominican church. 2nd Central Section: *Lower Rhenish
School*, Series of paintings (end of the 15th cent.), from the Carmelite
church. 3rd Section: Old copy, by *Jobst Harrich* of Nuremberg, of
Dürer's celebrated Assumption, which was painted in 1509 for Jacob
Heller, purchased in 1614 by Elector Maximilian of Bavaria, and destroyed
by fire at Munich in 1674 (the wings are the original productions of
Dürer's studio). 4th Section: *Hans Baldung Grien*, Baptism of Christ.
On the rear wall: *M. Grünewald*, SS. Cyriac and Lawrence (grisaille);
Franconian School, Presentation in the Temple (16th cent.). In this
room are also chests and cabinets (15-17th cent.), church statuary (*e.g.*
two Madonnas by *T. Riemenschneider*), small examples of ecclesiastical
art (12-16th cent.), albums (17-18th cent.), and patents of nobility (18-19th
cent.). — Through the corridor to the right we reach ROOM IX. Ecclesiastical paintings and utensils (processional crosses, monstrances, vestments; 14-18th cent.). Portraits of citizens of Frankfort (17-18th cent.).
— ROOM X. Pewter, copper, and brass work (16-19th cent.); coloured
terracotta bust (a Duke of Würtemberg?; 16th cent.). Cabinet 1: Inlaid
furniture; Cab. 2: Musical instruments (16-19th cent.). — We turn back
to the CORRIDOR. The glass-cases contain articles connected with the
Jewish ritual, guild paraphernalia, the old standard weights and measures
of Frankfort when a free city, etc. — STAIRCASE: Old views and plans
of Frankfort (16-18th cent.).

First Floor. The cabinets in the CORRIDOR contain masonic insignia,
views of Frankfort, seals, coins, etc. Among the old documents is the
'Golden Bull' (see p. 283). — ROOM XI. Iron-work; German stoneware
and fayence; guild bowls and goblets; table-service by *Wenzel Jamnitzer*
of Nuremberg; Höchst porcelain. — We return through the corridor to
ROOM XII. 1st Cabinet: French stove in the 'Empire' style; room from
the Neue Kräme in the style of Louis XVI.; ivory carvings; paintings
by Frankfort artists (17-19th cent.). 2nd & 3rd Cab.: Paintings, including (beside the first window in Cab. 3) several Madonnas of the *Early
Cologne* and *Rhenish Schools*. In the window-cases are watches (18-19th
cent.), snuff-boxes, and trinkets (17-19th cent.). — ROOM XIII. Glass
(15-19th cent.). 1st Cab.: Views of Frankfort, including a Panorama of
Frankfort in 1811, by *Morgenstern;* miniatures. 2nd Cab.: Room from
the Kruggasse.

To the S.E. of the cathedral, in the Fahrgasse, is the late-
Gothic *Haus zum Fürsteneck* (No. 17). — From the S. end of the
Fahrgasse we enjoy a picturesque retrospect of its quaint old houses,
with their projecting stories (16-17th cent.). Hence the **Old Bridge**
(Pl. G, 4), constructed of red sandstone, crosses the Main. It is
mentioned in a document of 1222, but has been restored several times restored. The middle of the bridge is embellished with a *Statue of
Charlemagne* (1843). Near it is a mediæval iron cross, with a
figure of Christ. The presence of the cock which surmounts it is
explained by the tradition that a cock became the victim of a vow
made by the architect to sacrifice to the devil the first living being
that crossed the bridge. — For *Sachsenhausen*, see p. 295.

The quay flanked with lofty houses, which extends along the

right bank of the river, is called the *Schöne Aussicht* (Pl. G, 4).
A tablet on No. 17 indicates the house in which the philosopher
Arthur Schopenhauer (1788-1860) lived in 1843-59. At the upper
end, the *Upper Main Bridge*, built in 1878 by Lauter, crosses
the river. In front of it are a *Bust of Lessing*, in marble, by
Kaupert, and the —

Town Library (*Stadt-Bibliothek;* Pl. H, 4), built by *Hess*
in 1820-25, with a Corinthian portico, and altered and enlarged in
1891-93 by *Wolff*. On the attic stories of the wings are eight
statues of prominent citizens of Frankfort; and in the pediment is
a fine group by *Schierholz*.

In the INTERIOR, at the foot of the staircase, is a marble *Statue of
Goethe*, by P. Marchesi (1838), besides which there are busts of other
Frankfort celebrities. The ceiling-painting is by *F. Kirchbach.* — The
library contains 335,000 volumes. In the *Reading Room* is an exhibition
of valuable MSS., printed works, bindings, etc. (catalogue 10 pf.). Hours
of admission, see p. 281.

At the back of the Library, Lange-Str. No. 4, is the *Hospital
of the Holy Ghost.* In the grounds adjoining the Rechnei-Graben
(pond; Pl. H, 3, 4) is a *Bust of Schopenhauer* (see above), erected
in 1895. From the Rechnei-Graben the Rechneigraben-Str. leads
to the W. to the Börne-Platz, in which is a *Synagogue* (1881), adjoining the old Jewish cemetery. At the N.W. corner of the square
diverges the Börne-Str. (Pl. G, 3), formerly the Judengasse, the
dingy houses of which have been removed with the exception of the
old *House of the Rothschild Family* (No. 26, to the right).

Farther on is the old *Synagogue*, by Kayser (1860). The Börne-
Str. joins the Fahrgasse (p. 290), which leads into the Zeil (p. 284).

c. Northern Part of the Inner Town.

From the S.W. corner of the Rossmarkt (p. 284) the Grosse
Gallus-Strasse (Pl. E, 3, 4) leads to the old *Taunus Gate*. To the
left is the house (No. 19) in which *Bismarck* lived when Prussian
ambassador to the Diet in 1852-58. — At the end of the street we
turn to the right into the NEUE MAINZER STRASSE, in which, to the
left (No. 49), stands the building of the *School of Industrial Art*
(Kunstgewerbe-Schule) and the —

*Museum of Art and Industry (*Kunstgewerbe-Museum;*
Pl. D, 3), a collection of considerable value, enriched in 1904 by
the addition of the W. Metzler Collection. Adm., see p. 282;
illustrated catalogue 50 pf.

ROOMS I & II. *Modern Art.* Wall-panels with landscapes in inlaid
wood, by C. Spindler of Alsace; French and German medals; show-case
by Plumet and Selmersheim, with acquisitions from the Paris Exhibition
(1900); show-case by Pankok (1905); book-bindings.
Room III. *Textile Art* (woven fabrics, embroidery, laces). Adjacent
is Room XVIII, with varying exhibitions. — R. IV. *Mediæval and Gothic*

Art. *Limoges, champlevé (13-14th cent.), and painted enamel (by Nardon and Jean Pénicaud, ca. 1500); goldsmith's work; ivory carvings; *Books with miniatures; aquamanile in the form of a cock; gilded bronze triptych with Adoration of the Magi, a Rhenish work of ca. 1400; embroidered tapestry, with savage men and women; Gothic choir-stalls from Damme in Oldenburg; German wood-carvings of the 16th century. — R. V. *Italian Renaissance.* *Majolica, bronzes, chests, carvings, Venetian glass, marble fountain in the style of Desiderio da Settignano. — RR. VI & VII. *German and Netherlandish Renaissance.* Furniture (intarsia cabinet, S. German cabinets); silver-mounted ebony drug-chest from Augsburg; *German pottery and glass; Dutch furniture (17th cent.); Dutch, German, and French fayence; book-bindings of the 15-18th centuries. — R. VIII. *Art of the 18th Century.* Furniture and wood-carvings (carved cabinet from Liège, S. German console-table); porcelain from Meissen (table-set in the form of a temple, by Kändler, ca. 1750), *Höchst (p. 278), Frankental, and Nymphenburg. — R. IX. *Oriental Work.* *Apothecary's vessel from Damascus (12th cent.); Persian and Turkish tiles and fayence; Persian glass; Chinese porcelain; Japanese ceramic ware, lacquer-work, and sword-guards. — R. X. *Linel Collection.* Dutch lacquered cabinet; bronze-mounted furniture; *Frankental and Meissen porcelain; *Book-bindings; intarsia reliefs by N. Haberstumpf (Eger, 1714). — R. XI. *Metal Work* in gold, silver, pewter, bronze, and wrought-iron; *Domestic Altar from Mayence with elaborate marquetry (ca. 1720; the silver reliefs modern); leaden relief of the Entombment by Raphael Donner. — R. XII. *Small Objects of Ancient Art.* Vases, Tanagra figurines, bronze implements; reproductions of silver-ware. — R. XIII. (to the right of R. I.). *Medals and Plaquettes of the Renaissance.* — RR. XV-XVII (adjacent) contain a collection of casts and the library. — R. XIV. Panelled *Room from the Haus Fürsteneck* (p. 290; ca. 1615).

Farther on, at the intersection of the Mainzer-Str. with the Junghof-Str. (Pl. D, 3), are the *Bank of Trade and Industry* (l.), the *Imperial Bank* (r.), and the *Frankfort Bank* (l.). — In the Junghof-Str. are the *Saalbau*, by H. Burnitz, for concerts and balls (Nos. 19, 20), the *Deutsche-Vereins-Bank* (No. 11), and the *Frankfort Art Union* (*Kunstverein;* No. 8; adm., see p. 281). The Junghof-Str. ends at the Rossmarkt (p. 284).

Near the old *Bockenheimer Tor* rises the magnificent *Opera House* (Pl. D, 2, 3), designed by *Lucae* (d. 1877), and opened in 1880. It can accommodate 2000 spectators. The sculptures in the pediment in front are by *Kaupert,* those at the back by *Rumpf.* Most of the mural paintings in the interior and the drop-scene, representing the Prologue to Faust, were executed from cartoons by *Steinle;* the proscenium-frieze is by *O. Donner von Richter.* — Opposite the Opera House, in the Taunus Promenade, is a *Monument to Emp. William I.,* by Buscher, erected in 1896.

Near by is the **New Exchange** (*Neue Börse;* Pl. E, 3), built by *Burnitz* and *Sommer* in 1879, with a handsome Renaissance hall (business-hours 12-2). The N.E. and W. galleries contain a *Commercial Museum* (adm. 50 pf.).

The circular *Eschenheimer Turm* (Pl. E, F, 2), erected in 1400-28, is the finest of the few ancient tower-gateways of the city now extant. — In the Grosse-Eschenheimer-Strasse, which leads to the Schiller-Platz (p. 284), is the old *Thurn and Taxis Palace*

(Pl. F, 3; No. 26), dating from the beginning of the 18th cent. and occupied by the German Diet in 1816-66. Since 1908 it has been the seat of the **Museum of Ethnology** (*Museum für Völkerkunde;* adm., see p. 282), containing extensive collections from Africa, Asia, America, and the South Sea Islands. The anthropological Section also deserves particular notice.

The Protestant **Church of St. Peter** (Pl. F, 2), built and fitted up in the Renaissance style that prevailed in N. Germany at the period of the Reformation, was erected from plans by Grisebach and Dinklage in 1893-95. The tower is 255 ft. in height. The interior repays a visit (50 pf.). — On the terrace behind St. Peter's is a *War Monument,* erected to the memory of the natives of Frankfort who fell in 1870-71, by *Eckhardt.* — To the S. is the old *St. Peter's Cemetery,* containing the tomb of Goethe's mother (p. 285) and an ancient group of the Crucifixion.

d. The Outer Quarters of the City.

The Promenades (p. 282) encircling the old town are embellished with statues of eminent and patriotic citizens of Frankfort.

The most important street of the N.W. quarter of the town is the Bockenheimer Land-Strasse (Pl. D-A, 2; tramways, see p. 280), which begins at the old Bockenheimer Tor, between the Opera House and the Emperor William Monument (p. 292). In this street, to the right, is the old Rothschild Park, and farther on is the entrance to the *Palm Garden (Pl. B, 1; adm., see p. 282), a park opened in 1869, with some old palm-trees, conservatories, beautiful flower-beds, a pleasure pavilion, a restaurant, and playgrounds. The artificial rocky hill commands a good view of the Taunus.

The *Bockenheimer Warte* (Pl. A, 2; tramway terminus, see p. 280); ca. 1¹/₂ M. from the centre of the city, marked the limit of the free imperial district down to 1866. The town of Bockenheim belonged to the electorate of Hesse.

The new quarter of the city, to the S.W. of the Palm Garden and the Bockenheimer Land-Strasse, contains a number of imposing public buildings. Thus at Victoria-Allée No. 7 stands the —

Senckenberg Natural History Museum (Pl. A, 2), built by L. Neher in 1904-07 and connected by arcades with the *Senckenberg Library* and the *Jügel-Stiftung* (an academy for sociology and commercial science; 1901) on the one side, and with the laboratory of the *Physikalische Verein (Physical Society)* on the other. The Natural History Society, founded in 1817, is named in honour of the physicist and naturalist, Johann Christian Senckenberg (d. 1772), who bequeathed to the city a hospital, a medical institute, his collections, and his library. The museum is one of the most important in Germany. Admission, see p. 282.

GROUND FLOOR. In the court at the back are the skeleton of a
Diplodocus (a gigantic antediluvian lizard from Wyoming) and other
huge fossil animals such as the *Zeuglodon* (the earliest known form of
the whale). In the transverse room to the right, containing the fossils
of vertebrate animals, is an *Ichthyosaurus*, with a perfectly preserved
skin. — MAIN FLOOR. The two wings contain the vertebrate animals,
including a group of *Gorillas*. In the transverse room are five compartments with groups of forest-animals from Germany and a group
from German East Africa. — UPPER FLOOR. To the left are marine
fauna, insects, and the like; to the right is the section of anatomy and
evolution.

The Victoria-Allée is continued by the long HOHENZOLLERN-
PLATZ (Pl. A, B, 3, 4), which sweeps round in a curve to the left
and is laid out as a park. In it are the *Offices of the Postal
Authorities* ('Oberpostdirection'; 1907), the municipal *Festhalle*
(Pl. A, 3, 4), built from plans by Thiersch at a cost of one-and-a
half million marks, the *Goethe Gymnasium* (1897), and the *Church
of St. Matthew* (1905). The Hohenzollern-Str., continuing the
Hohenzollern-Platz, ends at the Bahnhofs-Platz (p. 283).

In the N.E. quarter of the city the following points of interest
may be mentioned. In the grounds outside the Friedberger-Tor
(Pl. G, 2) is the *Hessen-Denkmal* (Pl. G, 2) or *Hessian Monument*,
erected by King Frederick William II. of Prussia to the Hessians
who fell in 1792 in the attack on Frankfort, then occupied by the
French. — *Von Bethmann's Museum* (Pl. G, 2; adm., see p. 281)
contains one of the most popular pieces of modern sculpture, viz.,
*Ariadne on the panther (1814), the masterpiece of J. H. Dannecker.
— The **Zoological Garden** (Pl. I, 2, 3; adm., see p. 282; tramways, see p. 280), the oldest in Germany after that at Berlin, having
been opened in 1858, includes an assembly hall, a restaurant, and
a salt-water aquarium. In the square in front of the Zoological
Garden is the *Schützenbrunnen*, commemorating the 'Schützen-
feste', or national rifle competitions, held at Frankfort in 1862
and 1887.

The **New Cemetery,** on the Eckenheimer-Land-Strasse (comp. Pl.
G, 1; tramway No. 7, p. 280), contains a number of well-executed monuments. Thus on entering by the columned gate we see to the left the
grave of *A. Schopenhauer*, the philosopher (d. 1860), and to the right
that of *Marianne von Willemer* (d. 1860), the friend of Goethe (comp.
p. 299). The arcades on the E. side contain the vaults of some of the
old families of Frankfort. To the left is that of the *Von Bethmann
Family* (key kept by custodian, 50 pf.),containing a relief by Thorvaldsen
to the memory of a young Herr von Bethmann who died in 1812 of an
illness caused by his exertions on the occasion of a fire at Baden, near
Vienna. On the N. side is the *Mausoleum* of the Elector William II.
of Hesse (d. 1847) and his wife the Countess Reichenbach, by Hessemer
(closed). Close by are monuments to the memory of the soldiers and
insurgents who fell at the barricades in 1848.

To the E. of the New Cemetery is the JEWISH CEMETERY (open daily
except Sat.; entr. to the S., outside the Christian Cemetery). It contains
several tombs of the Rothschild family, including the large marble sarcophagus of Karl von Rothschild, who died at Naples in 1855.

e. Sachsenhausen.

On the left bank of the Main lies the suburb of **Sachsenhausen** (p. 282), said to have been founded by Charlemagne, and assigned by him as a residence to conquered Saxons. Beside the old bridge over the Main (p. 290), is the *Deutsch-Ordenshaus* (Pl. G, 5), or House of the Teutonic Order, erected in 1709. A little to the E. are the large *Cattle Market and Slaughter House.* To the right is the *Church of the Magi (Drei Königs-Kirche;* Pl. F, 4), rebuilt in 1877-81.

Farther down the river, on the handsome Schaumain Quay, is the *Städel Art Institute (Pl. E, 5), founded by *Johann Friedrich Städel,* the banker, who bequeathed to it his collection of art and his entire fortune. The handsome building, in the Italian Renaissance style, was erected from designs by Oskar Sommer in 1874-78. Through purchase and bequest the gallery has become one of the most important in Germany in the field of ancient art. It contains unusual treasures not only of the early-Netherlandish work of the 15th cent., but also of the Dutch art of the 17th cent., including, especially, *Rembrandt's* Blinding of Samson. Among other recently acquired works are *Rubens's* Aged Statesman and the Torgau Princes' Altar by *Cranach the Elder,* both works of the first rank. Among the numerous paintings of the Italian Schools of the 15-16th cent. the brilliantly-coloured masterpiece of *Moretto* is conspicuous. The modern section affords a good survey of the Romantic School ('Nazarenes'), the head of which, *Overbeck,* worked in Rome in 1810 et seq., while *Steinle* (d. 1886) was its last important representative. Ample material also exists for the study of the earlier Düsseldorf School. Modern art, too, is represented by admirable examples. — Admission, see p. 282. Short catalogue of the gallery 50 pf.; elaborate catalogue, 1st vol. (old masters) $2^{1}/_{2}$ *M,* 2nd vol. (later masters) 1 *M;* illustrated edition in one volume 12 *M.*

GROUND FLOOR. — To the left of the Vestibule are the exhibition-room for the Graphic Arts, the *Drawings* (ca. 13,000) and the *Engravings* (ca. 64,000), and the *Library.* To the right are the *Plaster Casts,* a few Greek vases, and some *Original Sculptures.* At the back are three rooms containing German paintings of the early 19th cent., chiefly of the Düsseldorf School (the so-called 'Classicists'), and a few more modern works.

Among the original sculptures may be mentioned, No. 99, a painted terracotta Altar of 1511 from Gubbio, with the colouring partly renewed (in the side-room to the left of the Plaster Cast Room). — Among the best of the German paintings are: 437. *C. F. Lessing,* John Huss before the Council of Constance; 453. *A. Achenbach,* Storm at sea; *Lessing,* 438. Ezzelino da Romano, 441. Venerable oak; 429. *Ludwig Richter,* Italian landscape; 447. *Jacob Becker,* Shepherd struck by lightning; *Joseph A. Koch,* 404-406. Landscapes with historical representations;

19*

539. *A. Schreyer*, Wallachian vehicle; 442. *A. Zimmermann*, Scene in the Tauern (1851); 585. *H. W. Mesdag*, Danger (1886).

The First Floor contains the Picture Gallery. On the stair-case is *Tischbein's* celebrated painting of 'Goethe in the Roman Cam-pagna' (1789). The *Dome Room (Kuppelraum)*, containing a bust of Städel, views of Frankfort, and the like, divides the rooms into two sections. The rooms to the W. contain the Netherlandish and German works of the 15-17th cent. and the Italian paintings of the 14-16th cent., those to the E. the later Italian and Spanish paint-ings and the German works of the 19th century.

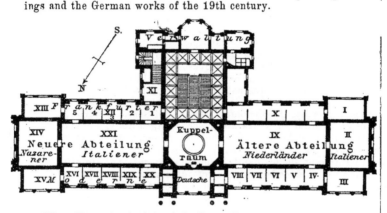

West Half, to the left of the Dome Room.

Room IX (lighted from the ceiling). *Netherlandish School of the 17th Century.*

To the left: *173. *Frans Hals*, Portrait of a man (1638); *149. *A. Brouwer*, Bitter medicine; 307. *A. Cuyp*, Flock of sheep; 217. *P. Janssens*, Lady at a wrtting-table; *157a. *David Teniers the Younger*, Con-sultaiion; *174. *Frans Hals*, Portrait of a woman, companion-piece to No. 173; 181. *School of Rembrandt*, Parable of the Labourers in the Vineyard; 217a. *Jan Vermeer*, The geographer; 177. *Jan Verspronck*, Portrait of a woman; 143. *P. Franchoys*, Portrait of a man; 197. *B. Fa-britius*, Half-length portrait of a youth; *241. *Jan van Goyen*, Haarlemer Meer; No number, *Rubens*, **Aged statesman, of the master's best period (a gift from the Kann Collection, 1907); **642. *Rembrandt*, Blinding of Samson or Triumph of Delilah, realistically rendered in the taste of the period, but masterly in composition and execution (dated 1636; acquired in 1905 from the Schönborn Gallery in Vienna); 127. *Rubens*, King David playing the harp; *245. *Sal. van Ruysdael*, Dutch canal; *Rembrandt*, *182. Margaretha van Bilderbeecq (1633), 183. David before Saul (ca. 1633); 639. *P. Aertsen*, Christ and the Woman taken in adultery.

Cabinets VII-IV (entrance through Cabinet VIII, p. 297) and the Cabinet Series X (p. 297) contain the smaller works of the Netherlandish School of the 17th century.

*215. *Jan Steen*, Tavern-scene; *148, *147. *A. Brouwer*, Operations on peasants; *205b. *A. van Ostade*, Pig-killing (1637); *David Teniers* *the Younger*, 151. Pasture, 152. St. Jerome, 153. The smoker, 157c. Amoretti in the workshop of an alchemist, 157d. Peasants dancing; 93. *Master of the Death of the Virgin*, Winged altar-piece (Pietà, St. Veronica, and Joseph of Arimathæa; 1524).

Corner Room III. *Netherlandish School of the 15-16th Centuries.*

**98. *Jan van Eyck*, 'Madonna of Lucca' (formerly in the possession of the Duke of Lucca); *Master of Flémalle*, *103. St. Veronica, *104. Madonna and Child, *102. Trinity (grisaille; parts of a large altar at Flémalle), 105. Penitent Thief (a fragment of a large Crucifixion); *97. *Dirck Bouts*, Vision of Emperor Augustus; 99. *Petrus Cristus*, Virgin and Child (1457); *100. *Roger van der Weyden*, Virgin with SS. Peter, John the Baptist, Cosmas, and Damian (ca. 1450); 108. *Gerard David*, St. Jerome before the Cross; 108a. *Dirck Bouts*, Madonna and Child; 110. *Gerard David*, Annunciation; 107. *H. Memling*, Portrait of a man; 113. *Q. Matsys*, Portrait of a man.

Room II (lighted from the ceiling): *Italian Works of the 15-16th Centuries.*

11. *Botticelli*, Profile por ra of a woman; 7. *Fra Angelico da Fiesole*, Madonna enthroned, with angelic musicians; no number, *Palma Vecchio*, *Jupiter and Callisto, of the master's first period (acquired in 1907); 12. *Botticelli*, Madonna; 32. *Antonello da Messina*, St. Sebastian; 33, 34. *Carlo Crivelli*, Annunciation, parts of a large altar-piece (in the Brera at Milan); 43a. *Titian* (?), Portrait of a man; *45. *Moretto*, Madonna with the four church-fathers, Gregory, Jerome, Ambrose, and Augustine; 20. *Lombard School*, St. Catharine; 13. *Bartolomeo Veneto*, Half-length of a girl; 14a. *Angelo Bronzino*, Portrait of a lady; 22a. *Correggio*, Madonna of Casalmaggiore.

Corner Room I, to the S. of the Dutch Room (p. 296), contains *Italian Works of the 14th Century* (1. Barnaba da Modena, Madonna; 19. Macrino d'Alba, Triptych). Cabinet Series X contains *Netherlandish Paintings of the 17th Century.* To the N. is the —

Section of the *German Painters of the 16th Century* (Cabinet VIII and the room adjoining it on the right).

*655. *Lucas Cranach the Elder*, So-called Princes' Altar from Torgau ('Torgauer Fürstenaltar'), an admirable early work (1509), representing the Holy Kinship; the figures on the wings are portraits of (l.) Frederick the Wise of Saxony and his family and (r.) his brother John with his family (acquired 1906); 95, 96. *Barthold Bruyn the Elder*, Man and wife; *T. Riemenschneider*, *Statue of the Madonna, an admirable work in sandstone; 81. *Master of Frankfort*, Winged altar; *Hans Baldung Grien*, 73. Witches' Sabbath (1523), 73a. Christmas Eve; 72. *Swabian Master*, Portrait; 83. *A. Dürer*, Job's wife pouring water on him to alleviate his sufferings (from the Jabach Altar); *71. *Hans Holbein the Younger*, Portrait of Sir George of Cornwall, with a carnation in his hand.

East Half, to the right of the Dome Room.

Room XXI (lighted from the ceiling). *Italian and Spanish Masters of the 17-18th Centuries.*

No number, *G. B. Tiepolo*, *Patron-saints of the Grotta Family (ca. 1754; acquired 1908); *Tiepolo*, 652. Character, 50. Scipio; *Velazquez*, 58. Infanta Margarita, afterward consort of Emp. Leopold I., *57. Half-length of Cardinal Gaspar Borgia (d. 1645; marked by delicacy of psychological characterization and vigorous colouring); 51. *Belotto*, Venetian view; 52, 53. *Canaletto*, Venetian scenes; 59. *Mass. Stanzioni*, Susanna at the bath; no number, *Guercino* (?), Madonna and St. Anthony; 56. *P. Batoni*, Allegory of the Arts.

Room XIV (lighted from the ceiling). *German School of the Early 19th Century.*
454. *Alfred Rethel,* Daniel in the lions' den; *Steinle,* 444. Tiburtine Sibyl, 444b. Mary Magdalen at the Sepulchre; 413. *Fr. Overbeck,* Triumph of Religion in the Arts; 455. *Rethel,* Emperor Maximilian's guardian angel (fresco); *416. *Philip Veit,* Introduction of the Arts into Germany through Christianity (a fresco from the old building, transferred to canvas), a masterpiece of the Nazarene art. — 430. *Maurice von Schwind,* The 'Sängerkrieg' at the Wartburg (1846). — 414. *F. W. von Schadow,* The Wise and Foolish Virgins; 439. *C. F. Lessing,* Rest in the forest.

Rooms XV-XX, adjoining Room XXI on the N., contain *Modern Works of Various Schools.*
Corner Room XV. 644. *Claude Monet,* Country-house; 2. *A. Sisley,* Bank of the Seine; no number, *Ch. Fr. Daubigny,* Fruit-garden; 662. *J. B. C. Corot,* Summer-landscape; 462a. *C. Troyon,* Cattle; 23. *Chintreuil,* Landscape; no number, *G. Courbet,* *Wave; *V. van Gogh,* Peasant's farm. — Cabinet XVI. *3. *M. Liebermann,* Court of the orphanage at Amsterdam; *620. *Leibl,* Peasant and his wife; 25. *G. Moreau,* Pietà; 664. *G. Courbet,* Entrance to the village. — Cabinet XVII. *Lenbach,* 458n. Moltke, 458t. Bismarck; no number, *Waldmüller,* Rustic lovers (1863); *K. Spitzweg,* *6. Hermit, 612. Trout-stream. — Cabinet XVIII. *458a. *A. Feuerbach,* Lucretia; 530. *Böcklin,* Villa by the sea; *4. *W. Trübner,* Negro reading a newspaper; 35. *J. F. Millet,* Portrait; 691. *Lenbach,* Gladstone. — Cabinets XIX & XX. 11. *H. Baisch,* Pasture; 535. *H. Zügel,* Sheep; 458g. *J. Wenglein,* Bavarian landscape; 33. *Ed. Schleich the Elder,* Harvest-day; 1. *P. W. Keller-Reutlingen,* Mill at Bruck; 21. *A. Stäbli,* Rainy landscape.

The rooms adjoining Room XXI on the S. are devoted to the *Frankfort Painters* from the 17th cent. to the present day.
Cabinet Series XII. — Cabinet 2. Painters of the 17th cent., including *Lingelbach, Mignon,* and *Roos.* — Cabinet 3 contains examples by the 18th cent. painters *Seekatz, Urlaub, Pforr, Radl, Schütz,* and *J. L. E. Morgenstern.* — With Cabinet 4 we begin the 19th cent.: works by *Karl Morgenstern, Dielmann,* and *Burnitz* (583. Wood-scene at Cronberg, 457b. On the Nied at Frankfort). — Cabinet 5 contains paintings by *A. Burger* (525. Family worship) and *W. A. T. Steinhausen.*
Room XIII. Modern Frankfort painters. *Hans Thoma,* 22. Portrait of himself, 588. Eve, *587. Landscape; 10. *Fr. Böhle,* River-landscape; 623. *O. Röderstein,* Old woman reading; 52. *W. Trübner,* Amorbach Convent; no number, *A. W. Goebel,* Beggar-woman and child. — We return to the beginning of Cabinet Series XII and here turn to the left into —
Cabinet XI. *Altheim,* 632. Supper, 648. After grievous toil; *O. Scholderer,* 646, 618. Still-life, 657, 666. The artist and his wife.

We ascend the staircase to the left to the Cabinets on the Second Floor.
In the first three cabinets are water-colours by *Eduard von Steinle* (1810-86; after 1839 teacher at the Städel Institute of Frankfort):

Cabinet 1. 'The Beatitudes', studies for mural paintings at the Castle of Rheineck; the best of these (on the entrance-wall) are 507. Moses, 508. Good Samaritan, and 505. Christ and Mary Magdalen. — Cabinet 2. Drawings; 575-578. The Seasons. — Cabinet 3. 564. The Cardinal Penitentiary; *568. The return of Geneviève; *570, 571. Snow-white and Rose-red; *569. 'He who is lucky wins the bride'. — Cabinet 4. *Steinle,* 444d. Comfort, 444c. Fiddler; 412. *F. Pforr,* Count of Hapsburg; 418.

Ph. Veit, Abbé de Noirlieu; 411. *J. D. Passavant*, St. Eustace. — Cabinet 5. 458h, 458i, 458k. *Schirmer*, Landscapes; 444a. *Steinle*, Engraver; 424. *C. Rottmann*, Reggio, with Mt. Ætna. — Cabinet 6. 470. *P. von Cornelius*, Last Judgment, study for the painting in the choir of the Ludwigs-Kirche at Munich; 637, 636. *P. Becker*, Views of Marburg.

With the Städel Institute is connected the *Kunstschule* or *School of Art*, founded by Philip Veit and now containing fine studios. Under the same administration stands also the new —

Municipal Gallery (*Städtische Galerie;* Pl. D, 6), opened in 1909 at No. 71, Schaumain Quay. It is intended to supplement the Institute by a collection of sculptures of all epochs and of modern paintings, especially by Frankfort masters. The sculptures occupy the *Liebig Haus*, a villa bequeathed to the town by Baron Liebig together with his collections, and a newly-built annex. A building for the paintings is being erected in the grounds of the villa. — Admission, see p. 281.

Sculptures. ANTIQUE COLLECTION of the well-known archæologist, A. Furtwängler, who died in 1907; also numerous heads and torsos; in the annex, *Athena by *Myron* (a Roman copy of the 1st cent. B.C.). — EARLY CHRISTIAN ART. Results of the K. M. Kaufmann Expedition to Egypt. — MEDIAEVAL AND RENAISSANCE ART. Among the German woodcarvings may be mentioned St. George by *Syrlin the Elder* (15th cent.) and the large Mount of Olives by a *Swabian Master*. Among the Italian works are the Assumption by *Andrea della Robbia* (in the annex) and a bronze plaquette of the Duke of Piombino. The Pietà in sandstone (14th cent.) is a work of the Franco-Burgundian School.

The **Paintings** include examples by *Hans Thoma* (11 paintings), *Wilhelm Trübner* (6 paintings), *Peter Burnitz, Victor Müller, Anton Burger, Otto Scholderer, Hugo von Habermann, Albert von Keller, Leo Putz, Wilhelm Leibl, Max Slevogt, Franz Stuck, Heinrich Zügel, Fritz von Uhde, Ludwig Dill, Peter Backer*, and *Fritz Böhle*.

Exhibitions of recent acquisitions are held from time to time.

In the S.W. part of Sachsenhausen we may mention the *Hippodrome* (Pl. D, 6), opened in 1899, the *Royal Institute of Experimental Therapeutics*, and the *Town Hospital*. — In the Hühner-Weg (Pl. H, 6) is the *Willemer-Häuschen* (adm. 20 pf.), and $1^1/_2$ M. to the E., on the Main, near Oberrad (tramway), stands the *Gerbermühle*, celebrated through Goethe and Marianne von Willemer (1814; comp. p. 294).

Excursions in the FRANKFURTER STADTWALD *(Frankfort City Forest)* are best accomplished with the aid of the 'Waldbahn', which starts at Sachsenhausen (Untermain-Brücke, Pl. E 5) and the Offenbach Local Station, Pl. G 5) and traverses the forest in three directions. The stations within the forest are *Forsthaus* (restaurant), *Neu-Isenburg, Niederrad* (near the racecourse), and *Schwanheim* (p. 278). — The old *Sachsenhauser Warte*, reached by the Darmstadt highroad in 25 min., commands an extensive view (adm. on application to the Head Forester).

At *Heddernheim*, now incorporated with Frankfort, a station of the railway to Giessen (p. 144), and also of the electric railways to Homburg and Oberursel (Hohe Mark; see p. 300), is the so-called Heidenfeld, where the remains of the Roman castle of *Nida*, dating from the time of Domitian, have been laid bare. — At *Vilbel*, two stations farther on (p. 144), the remains of a Roman bath have been found in the nursery-gardens of Messrs. Siesmayer. There is also a carbonic spring here.

39. The Taunus.

The name **Taunus,** in the wider sense, applies to the whole of the mountainous region between the Main, the Rhine, and the Lahn, but is usually restricted to the southern mountains of that district, extending from Nauheim on the E. to Assmannshausen on the W. Behind a narrow and fertile strip of lower hilly ground the densely wooded mountains rise somewhat rapidly from the plain of the Rhine and Main, forming an abrupt termination to the slate mountains of the Rhine (p. 219). Geologically, the range consists of clay-slate, with grauwacke on the N. The highest points are the *Great Feldberg* (2887 ft.), the *Little Feldberg* (2710 ft.), and the *Altkönig* (2615 ft.). Numerous warm springs rise at the base of the range, between Wiesbaden and Nauheim.

One and a half or two days suffice for a glimpse at the most interesting spots in this district: Railway from Frankfort to *Homburg*, where the night is spent, ¹/₂-³/₄ hr. Next morning, ascent of the *Feldberg* in 3¹/₄ hrs., either viâ the *Saalburg* or direct; descent viâ the *Altkönig* to *Königstein*, 2 hrs.; thence by *Falkenstein* to *Cronberg* 1¹/₂ hr.; or by the *Rossert* to *Eppstein* in 3¹/₂ hrs. Those who devote a single day to the *Feldberg* generally start from Cronberg or Königstein. — All routes and paths in the Taunus are marked with colours which are explained by 'Central Tablets' posted at the crossings and in the charts (1 ℳ 25 pf.) published by the 'Taunus Club'. *Cronberg* and *Königstein* are the chief resorts for winter-sports. There are information-offices for visitors at all the larger places.

CYCLISTS may make a pleasant tour by riding from Homburg to (3¹/₄ M.) Oberursel, (3 M.) Cronberg, (2¹/₄ M.) Königstein, (3¹/₂ M.) Fischbach, and (1¹/₂ M.) Eppstein. The distance from Königstein to Höchst is about 6¹/₄ M.; the portion before Soden (3 M.) takes careful riding.

a. From Frankfort to Homburg.

12 M. RAILWAY in 28-43 min. (fares 1 ℳ 60, 1 ℳ, 65 pf.). Direct through-trains also run five times daily from Wiesbaden to Homburg in 67 min., viâ Höchst and Rödelheim (see below).

Frankfort, see p. 279. — 2 M. *Bockenheim* (p. 293), the N.W. suburb of Frankfort, with iron-foundries and factories for the production of machinery, furniture, and tinware. — We cross the *Nidda.* 4¹/₄ M. *Rödelheim,* junction of the Cronberg line (p. 305) and of a junction line to *Höchst* (p. 278); 7¹/₂ M. *Weisskirchen.* — 9¹/₄ M. *Oberursel* (Schützenhof, very fair; Bär; Frankfurter Hof), an old town (781) of 6100 inhab., with a cotton-mill, machine-shops, a copper rolling-mill, and a high-lying Gothic church of the 15th century. Oberursel is also a station of the electric railway from Frankfort to the Hohe Mark (ascent of the Feldberg, see p. 308). — 12 M. *Homburg.*

FROM HEDDERNHEIM (FRANKFORT) TO HOMBURG, 7 M., electric railway every ¹/₂ hr., in connection with tramway No. 23 (p. 281; through-carriages from Frankfort in ³/₄ hr.; fare 65 pf.). — *Heddernheim,* see p. 299. During the whole journey, the Taunus Mts., with the Altkönig and Feldberg in the middle, are visible to the left. — 2 M. *Bonames;* 4¹/₂ M. *Nieder-Eschbach;* 6 M. *Ober-Eschbach.* At (6¹/₂ M.) *Gonzenheim* we pass under a viaduct and across the Usingen line (p. 305). — At (7 M.) *Homburg* the cars stop in the market-place.

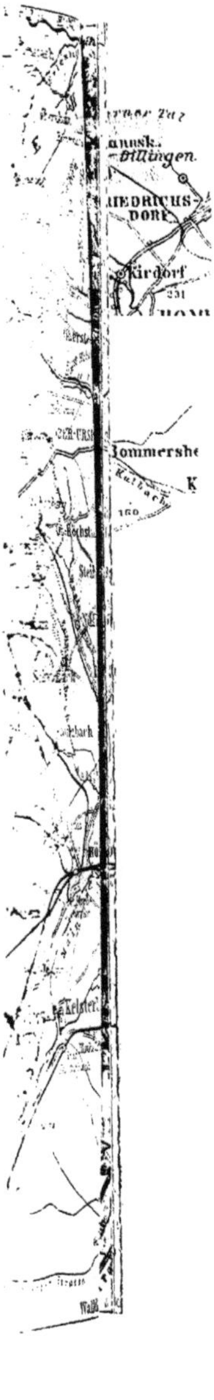
Billingen.
Kirdorf
231
160

Homburg. — RAILWAY STATION (Restaurant, very fair), $^3/_4$ M. from the Kur-Haus.

HOTELS (the larger ones with every modern comfort, closed in winter). *Ritter's Hôtel du Parc* (Pl. a; B, 2), Kaiser-Friedrich-Promenade 69, R. from $3^1/_2$, B. $1^1/_2$, déj. 3-4, D. 5-6$^1/_2$, S. 4-5, pens. 11-20 $\mathcal{M}$; *Hôtel Victoria* (Pl. b; B, 2), Luisen-Str. 91, R. from 5, B. $1^1/_2$, D. 5-6$^1/_2$, pens. 10$^1/_2$-20 $\mathcal{M}$; *Grand-Hôtel* (Pl. c; B, 2), with its dépendance Villa Fürstenruhe; *Hôtel Augusta* (Pl. d; B, 2), R. from $3^1/_2$, B. $1^1/_2$, déj. 4, D. 5, S. $3^1/_2$, pens. 10$^1/_2$-17 $\mathcal{M}$; *Bellevue* (Pl. c; B, 2), Ludwig-Str. 16, R. from $3^1/_2$, B. $1^1/_2$, déj. 3, D. 5, S. 3-4, pens. 10$^1/_2$-16 $\mathcal{M}$; *Métropole* (Pl. f; B, 2), Ferdinands-Platz 19, R. from $3^1/_2$, B. $1^1/_2$, déj. 3, D. $4^1/_2$, S. 3, pens. 10$^1/_2$-18$^1/_2$ $\mathcal{M}$; *Savoy* (Pl. g; B, 2), Kisseleff-Str. 9, R. from 3, B. $1^1/_2$, déj. 3, D. $4^1/_2$, pens. 10-14 $\mathcal{M}$; *Hôtel Minerva* (Pl. h; B, 2), Kaiser-Friedrich-Promenade 47, R. from 3, B. $1^1/_2$, D. 4, pens. 10$^1/_2$-16 $\mathcal{M}$; *Braunschweig*, Luisen-Str., a Hebrew house of the first class. — *Adler*, Luisen-Str. 22, open all the year round, R. 3-5, B. $1^1/_4$, déj. $2^1/_2$, D. 3, S. $2^1/_2$, pens. 8-12 $\mathcal{M}$, with restaurant; *Bristol*, Kisseleff-Str.; *Stephanie*, Ludwig-Str.; *Kaiserhof* (Pl. k; B, 2), Luisen-Str., with very fair restaurant, D. $1^3/_4$-$2^1/_2$ $\mathcal{M}$; *Hôtel-Restaurant Windsor* (Pl. l; B, 2), Schwedenpfad 8, R. from 3, B. $1^1/_4$-$1^1/_2$, pens. from $8^1/_2$ $\mathcal{M}$; *Hôtel d'Angleterre* (Pl. m; B, 2), Luisen-Str., R. 3-4, B. $1^1/_1$, D. 3, pens. 7-9 $\mathcal{M}$. — Second-class (recommended to passing travellers): *Strassburger Hof* (Pl. n; B, 2), Thomas-Str.; *Schützenhof* (Pl. o; A, B, 2), Auden-Str. 1; *Frankfurter Hof* (Pl. q; A, 1), Elisabethen-Str. 19; *Goldene Rose*, Luisen-Str. 26. — There are also many private hotels, pensions, and sanatoria.

MUSIC in summer, 7.30-8.30 a.m., by the Springs; at 3.30-5 and 8-10 p.m. in the Kur-Garten. Also a theatre, concerts, and balls.

VISITORS' TAX: 1 pers. 20 $\mathcal{M}$, 2 pers. 30 $\mathcal{M}$, 3 pers. 38 $\mathcal{M}$, 4 pers. 44 $\mathcal{M}$, each addit. pers. 6 $\mathcal{M}$; for those staying not more than a week, 3, 12, 16, 20, 3 $\mathcal{M}$; day-ticket 50 pf., after 7 p.m. on week-days 1 $\mathcal{M}$; adm. to see the Kur-Haus, 25 pf.

POST OFFICE, Luisen-Str., opposite the Kurhaus (Pl. B, 2).

CARRIAGE with one horse from the station to the town, 1-2 pers. 70 pf., 3-4 pers. 1 $\mathcal{M}$, box 20 pf. By time: $^1/_4$ hr. one horse 1-2 pers. 60 pf., 3-4 pers. 90 pf., two horses 1 $\mathcal{M}$; $^1/_2$ hr. 1 $\mathcal{M}$ 30, 1 $\mathcal{M}$ 70 pf., and 2 $\mathcal{M}$; to the Gothic House 2, $2^1/_2$, and 3 $\mathcal{M}$ 20 pf.; to the Saalburg and back $6^1/_2$, $7^1/_2$, and 9 $\mathcal{M}$ 10 pf.; to Königstein with two horses 15 and 18 $\mathcal{M}$.

ELECTRIC TRAMWAY from the *Central Station* every 10-20 min. to *Dornholzhausen* (20 pf.), and to the *Saalburg* ($^1/_2$ hr.; 55 pf.; in winter on Sun. only), with branch-lines to the *Gothic House*, in the Grosse Allée, and to *Kirdorf*.

ENGLISH CHURCH (Pl. B, 2; *Christ Church*), Ferdinands-Str., near the railway-station, with 500 sittings; Sun. services during summer at 8 a.m., 11 a.m., and 3.30 p.m. Daily Matins at 8.45 a.m. Chaplain, *Rev. G. F. Seaton, M. A.* — *Presbyterian Services* in the Schlosskirche at 11.30 a.m. and 7.15 p.m. in July and August.

Homburg vor der Höhe (630 ft.), a town with 14,000 inhab., situated amid the spurs of the Taunus Mts., was the residence of the Landgraves of Hesse-Homburg from 1622 to 1866, and is one of the most popular watering-places in the Rhineland (over 14,000 visitors annually, one-third of whom are English). It was a favourite resort of King Edward VII. (d. 1910).

In the Luisen-Strasse, the chief thoroughfare of the town, in the heart of the visitors' quarter, lies the —

Kurhaus (Pl. B, 2), built in its present form in 1860-62 by the Belgian architect Cluyssenaer, at the expense of the brothers Blanc, of Monte Carlo. The interior, remodelled in 1907, contains a number of very handsome apartments, such as the Conversations-Saal, the Concert Room, the Gaming Room, the 'Goldsaal', and the *Restaurant (D., at 1.15 p.m., 3 *M*). The terraces at the back are a favourite resort in fine weather, and the corridors of the ground-floor afford a sheltered promenade during rain. — Adjacent, to the

Wagner & Debes, Leipzig.

S.E., is the *Theatre.* — In the Kur-Garten, behind the Kurhaus, to the right, is the *Kurhaus-Bad* (1902).

Crossing the Kaiser-Friedrich-Promenade and passing marble busts (Pl. 11 & 12; B, 2) of the Emp. Frederick and the Empress Victoria (by Uphues), we reach the fine **Kur-Park,** which is about 125 acres in extent. Broad walks lead hence to the right to the *Lawn Tennis Courts* (Pl. C, 2; international tournament in Aug.), the *Solsprudel* (Pl. 7, C 2; used for bathing only), and the *Whey Cure Institute* (Molkenanstalt), much frequented in the afternoon (café). In various parts of the grounds rise the aërated chaly-beate and saline SPRINGS, which are especially efficacious in chronic stomach troubles, constipation, and adiposity. The most important are the *Stahlbrunnen* (Pl. 8) and the *Luisenbrunnen* (Pl. 6; both very rich in iron), the *Kaiserbrunnen* (Pl. 3), and the *Elisabeth-brunnen* (Pl. 2), the most popular of all, which has been used since 1622 and is more saline than the Rakoczy spring at Kissingen. Near the two adjacent 'Trinkhallen' are well-kept flower-beds, a palm-house, and the band-stand. The *Chalalongbrunnen* (Pl. 1), with a building erected by the King of Siam, was bored in 1907. The *Landgrafen-Brunnen* (Pl. 4), 500 ft. deep, is the richest in salt. The *Kaiser-Wilhelm-Bad* (Pl. C, 2), built by L. Jacobi in 1887-90, contains 52 admirably equipped bathrooms and inhalation rooms (bath-hours 7-1 and 4-6, Sun. 8-12). In front of it is a statue of Emp. William I. (Pl. 13), by Gerth (1905). — Behind the Elisabeth-brunnen are the *Golf Links.* — In the Ferdinands-Str., leading from the Kaiser-Friedrich-Promenade to the Luisen-Str., is the *English Church* (Pl. B, 2; services, see p. 301).

At the W. end of the town rises the **Schloss** (Pl. A, 2), which was erected, partly of stone from the Saalburg, by Landgrave Frederick II. in 1680-85, was rebuilt in 1820-40, and was fitted up in 1866 for the use of the royal family of Prussia. From the Dorotheen-Str. we traverse the upper garden and pass through the portal (to the right the dwelling of the castellan) into the upper court, in which rises the *Weisse Turm*, 174 ft. high and dating from the 14th cent. (adm. 25 pf.; extensive view). Above the central gateway is the front half of an equestrian statue, and opposite to it a bust of the landgrave, who, under the leadership of the Great Elector, decided the victory of the Brandenburgers over the Swedes at Fehrbellin in 1675 by the spirited charge of his cavalry. In the N.E. corner is a Roman portico from Brauweiler (p. 15), re-erected here in 1901. Adm. to the interior of the palace, June to Sept. 11-5, April, May, Oct., & Nov. 1-3, 50 pf., Sun. 25 pf. The church at the E. corner of the Schloss contains the burial-vault of the Landgraves. — The *Lower Palace Garden*, with its large pond, to the W. of the Schloss, is open to the public.

To the S.E. of the Schloss is the Prot. *Church of the Redeemer* (*Erlöser-Kirche;* Pl. A, 2); to the N.E. is the handsome new *Stadt-Brücke*, leading to the old town, past some old towers.

WALKS. Besides the Kur-Park mentioned at p. 302, the traveller may also visit the *Hardt* or *Hardtwald*, adjoining it on the N.E.; from the lower palace-garden the Grosse Allée leads to ($^1/_2$ hr.) the *Gothic House* (restaurant), a shooting-lodge built in 1823, and to the *Grosse Tannenwald;* the *Wildpark* (restaurant) with its numerous deer, $^1/_4$ hr. from the Gothic House; the *Goldgrube* (1595 ft.), 1 hr. from the Gothic House.

An Expedition to the Saalburg may be made by the electric tramway (p. 301). Beyond (1¹/₄ M.) **Dornholzhausen** (725 ft.; *Scheller*, R. 2-4, B. 1, D. 2, pens. 5-6 ℳ, very fair; *Deutsches Haus*, unpretending), a favourite summer-resort, the tramway ascends rapidly to the (3³/₄ M.) terminus. Walkers from Dornholzhausen follow a path indicated by yellow marks, which leads straight on to the Saalburg (*Hôtel-Restaurant Saalburg*, very fair) in 1 hr.; or they may follow the blue-marked path viâ the Luther-Eiche to the *Herzberg* (1930 ft.; view-tower) and thence a path indicated by green marks in 1¹/₂-1³/₄ hr.

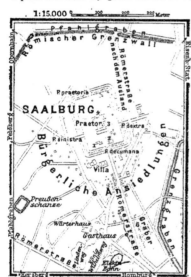

The *****Saalburg** (1388 ft.), a Roman castellum of the 2nd and 3rd cent. A.D., excavated in 1868 and reconstructed since 1897 on the lines indicated by the foundations, was one of the forts belonging to the *Pfahlgraben (Limes)*, a line of intrenchments constructed to protect the Roman territory in S.W. Germany. It extended from Kelheim on the Danube to Miltenberg on the Main, and from Krotzenburg (above Hanau) to the Taunus, and finally to Ems (p. 130) and Rheinbrohl (p. 113), a distance in all of 340 M. (guide, by H. Jacobi, 60 pf.).

The castellum, which was surrounded by a civil settlement, is 725 ft. long and 482 ft. wide. At the main gate, the *Porta Decumana*, is a modern bronze statue of Emperor Antoninus Pius (138-161). This gate opens on the *Retentura*, or rear-camp, with the large *Horreum* (Pl. 2) or storehouse (now the Saalburg Museum) to the right and the *Quaestorium* (Pl. 1) or administrative offices (with a post office) to the left. The middle of the fort is occupied by the *Praetorium*. In front is the winter drill-hall, now containing reproductions of catapults and ballistæ. In the inner court are two fountains and two storehouses for weapons and armour, that to the right containing the Limes Museum (Pl. 3). At the back is the *Sacellum* (Pl. 4), or military temple, with modern bronze statues of Hadrian (117-138) and Alexander Severus (222-235), of whose altars votive stones were discovered. The N. part of the fort contains the fore-camp *(Praetentura)*. The gate *(Porta Praetoria)* faces the Pfahlgraben. The *Saalburg Museum* and the *Limes Museum* (open 9-6.30; adm. 30 pf.) contain more than 15,000 objects, such as broken weapons, fragments of pottery, tools, cooking utensils, and ornaments. In the Limes Museum is a relief of Mommsen (d. 1904), the distinguished historian. In the hall to the right of the Sacellum is a model of a watch-tower. — The Roman military road leading to the S. from the camp was flanked, in the customary fashion, by tombstones. On it is the *Mithras Sanctuary* (Pl. 5). The *Mortuary House* (Pl. 6), re-erected a little to the left, on the ancient foundations, contains a few sepulchral relics (key kept by the custodian of the Saalburg; fee).

At the *Dreimühlborn*, ¹/₂ M. to the N.E. of the Saalburg, to the right of the Oberhain road, and also at the *Drususkippel*, some remains

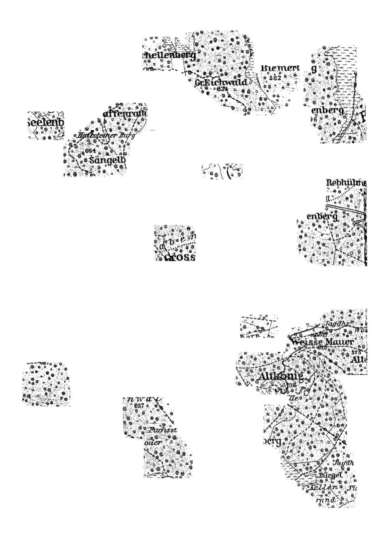

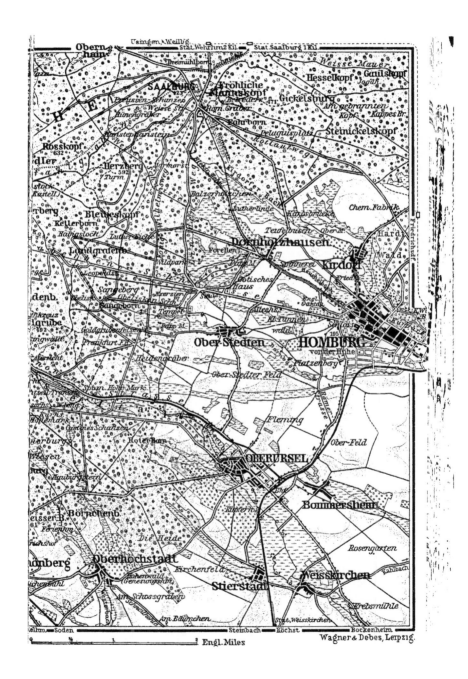

Engl. Miles

Wagner & Debes, Leipzig.

of Germanic-Roman open-air forges have been preserved. — A road, leaving the Usingen road to the right, about 250 yds. beyond the fort, descends viâ the *Lochmühle* (restaurant) to (20 min.) the *Saalburg* station (see below).

About ¹/₄ hr. to the E., beyond the mortuary house, rises the *Fröhliche Mannskopf* (1580 ft.; belvedere), the path to which is indicated at first by red, then by blue marks. The blue-marked path goes on to the *Gickelsburg* (1535 ft.), with remains of an ancient circular fortification, and the *Pelagius-Platz*, where it rejoins the red-marked path *(Rotlaufweg)*, by which we may return through the Hardtwald to Homburg.

FROM HOMBURG TO USINGEN, 14¹/₂ M., railway in about 1 hr. — 2¹/₂ M. *Seulberg.* — 3 M. *Friedrichsdorf* (Adler; Weisser Turm, a restaurant above the town), founded by Huguenots in 1687, is a small industrial town, formerly belonging to Hesse-Homburg, with 1360 inhabitants. A branch-line runs hence to (11 M.) *Friedberg* (see *Baedeker's Northern Germany).* — Beyond (4¹/₂ M.) *Köppern* we ascend the pretty *Köpperner-Tal*, skirting the *Erlenbach.* — 7¹/₂ M. *Saalburg*, the station for the Saalburg (p. 304); 8¹/₂ M. *Wehrheim* (1017 ft.); 11 M. *Anspach*, the station for (5 M.) *Neu-Weilnau* (p. 310) and (5 M.) *Schmitten* (p. 310; diligences to both). — 14¹/₂ M. *Usingen* (955 ft.; Adler), a small town with 1900 inhab., residence of the Princes of Nassau-Usingen from 1659 to 1774.

b. From Frankfort to Oberursel *(Hohe Mark)*, Cronberg, or Königstein. Feldberg.

FROM FRANKFORT TO OBERURSEL, 8¹/₂ M., electric railway in 35 min. (fare 50 pf.; to the Hohe Mark 70 pf.). The cars start at the Schauspielhaus (Pl. E, 4). — Intermediate stations: 3¹/₂ M. *Eschersheim;* 4 M. *Heddernheim* (see p. 299); 5¹/₂ M. *Niederursel;* 7 M. *Weisskirchen;* 8 M. *Bommersheim.* Just short of Oberursel we pass the power-house of the line. — *Oberursel* (State Railway Station), see p. 300. The electric railway goes on to the *Hohe Mark* (p. 308; 2³/₄ M.).

FROM FRANKFORT TO CRONBERG, 10 M., railway in about ³/₄ hr. (fares 1 ℳ 40 pf., 90, 55 pf.). — 4¹/₂ M. *Rödelheim* (p. 300); 7 M. *Eschborn;* 7³/₄ M. *Nieder-Höchstadt.*

10 M. **Cronberg.** — *Railway Station* (935 ft.), ¹/₃ M. below the village. — HOTELS. *Kaiser Friedrich, R. 2¹/₂-6, B. 1¹/₄, pens. 6-10 ℳ; *Frankfurter Hof*, with paintings by Frankfort artists in the dining-room; *Schützenhof*, all with gardens and views. — *Hahn's Restaurant*, at the station, very fair.

Cronberg (1015 ft.), a small town with 3000 inhab., lies picturesquely on a hill with numerous villas belonging to a colony of Frankfort painters and surrounded by orchards and chestnut-groves. The hill is surmounted by a *Castle* (1095 ft.) of the 13th cent. and by a *Château* of the 16th (restored). These belonged to the Knights of Cronberg, who became extinct in 1704. About ¹/₂ M. to the N.E. is *Schloss Friedrichshof*, built in 1889 for the Empress Frederick (d. 1901), and now (like the castle and château) owned by her daughter, Princess Frederick Charles of Hesse. The Victoria Temple, to the N.W. of the park, commands an extensive view.

At the entrance to Cronberg is a 'Central Tablet' (p. 300). —
The road to (2 M.) Falkenstein (diligence thrice daily; also omnibus)
follows the main street of the village. After about 1 M. the road
to Königstein (see below) diverges to the left. Walkers take the
footpath through the woods to the right, immediately beyond this
road, and in 20 min. more reach the village of —

Falkenstein (ca. 1310 ft.), with a convalescent home for
officers and two hotels (the *Frankfurter Hof* and the *Taunus
Inn*). The wooded hill to the W. is crowned with the ruin of *Burg
Falkenstein* (1465 ft.), the path to which (12 min.) is indicated by
a finger-post at the upper end of the village. This castle, the ancestral seat of Archbishop Kuno of Trèves, was erected in the
14th cent. on the site of the ancient fortress of Nüring, and was
destroyed in 1688. Fine view from the tower (key at the village).
From Falkenstein to Königstein, 1¹/₄ M.

The road from Cronberg to (3 M.) Königstein (motor-omnibus,
meeting all trains, 60 pf.) is at first identical with that to Falkenstein (see above). — From Soden to Königstein, see p. 309.

From (Frankfort) Höchst to Königstein, 10 M., light railway
in ³/₄-1 hr. (through-carriages from Frankfort by certain trains);
best views to the right. — From Frankfort to (5¹/₂ M.) *Höchst*, see
p. 278. — Farther on fine views of the Taunus range (r.) are obtained, and later (l.) of the Hofheimer Kapelle and the Meisterturm
(p. 309). Chief stations: 4¹/₂ M. (from Höchst) *Münster* (560 ft.);
5¹/₂ M. *Kelkheim-Fischbach* (p. 310), the latter 1¹/₂ M. to the
N.W., near the Staufen and the Rossert; 8 M. *Schneidhain* (900 ft.;
p. 310). — We pass below the S. side of the castle.

10 M. **Königstein**. — The *Railway Station* (1115 ft.) lies about
¹/₃ M. below the town. — Hotels. *Grand-Hôtel Königstein*, Sodener
Chaussée, ¹/₂ M. from the railway-station, on the edge of the wood, of
the first class, R. 4-8, B. 1¹/₂, déj. 3¹/₂, D. 4-4¹/₂, S. 3¹/₂, pens. 11-15 ℳ,
with garden, terraces, and view; *Park-Hôtel & Kur-Garten*, in the town,
R. 3-5, B. 1¹/₄, D. 2¹/₂, S. 1¹/₂, pens. 7-9 ℳ, with restaurant and large garden;
Hôtel Colloseus, with garden, closed in winter, R. 2¹/₂-5, B. 1¹/₄, D. 3,
pens. from 6¹/₂ ℳ. — *Procasky*, R. & B. 2¹/₂-3¹/₂, D. 1¹/₂, pens. 5-6 ℳ, with
garden and restaurant; *Bender*, R. 1¹/₂-2¹/₂, B. ³/₄, pens. 4¹/₂-6¹/₂, also with
garden and restaurant. — *Kurhaus Taunusblick*, pens. 6-10 ℳ; *Dr. Ame-
lung's Kuranstalt; Hydropathic Establishment* (Dr. Thewalt). Also numerous pensions (*Miss White*, Villa Stella, Altkönig-Str. 6) and lodging-
houses. — *Visitors' Tax*, 1 pers. 5, families 8-10 ℳ.

Carriages (with one or two horses): to Cronberg 2¹/₂ & 3¹/₂ ℳ; Soden
3¹/₂ & 4¹/₂ ℳ; Rote Kreuz 4¹/₂ & 7 ℳ; ascent of the Feldberg and back
10 & 15 ℳ. — *Automobile Omnibus* to Cronberg, see above.

Königstein (1190 ft.), a picturesquely-situated little town with
2500 inhab. and many villas, is one of the most beautiful points in the
Taunus region. Just outside the village, to the E., is the *Château* of
the Grand-Duchess Dowager of Luxembourg and Duchess of Nassau,
rebuilt about 1858. On the slope of the hill is the *Villa Roth-*

schild. At the N. end of the town is the castellated *Villa Andreae.*
On the hill to the W. are the extensive ruins of the *Castle of Königstein* (1310 ft.), which was blown up by the French in 1796. This
stronghold is mentioned in history for the first time in 1225; in
1581 it came into the possession of the Electors of Mayence, whose
armorial bearings are still to be seen over the entrance. The vaults
and casemates are still partly preserved. Fine view from the tower.
The castle is reached by taking the road to the left, ³/₄ M. from
the railway-station, which brings us in 4 min. more to the main
street, from which we diverge 4 min. later at the finger-post.

    Excursions. From the E. end of the town we may ascend to
(20 min.) the view-tower on the *Hartenberg.* The village of
Mammolshain, prettily situated ¹/₂ hr. farther on, amid fruit-trees,
lies 20 min. above *Crontal* (p. 309). — A path, indicated by green
marks, leads from the E. end of the town to (35 min.) *Burg Falkenstein* (p. 306). — From the N. end of the town a road leads through
the pretty *Billtal* to (1¹/₄ M.) Dr. Thewalt's Hydropathic (p. 306),
the fish-hatchery, and the Stoltze-Plätzi; 2¹/₄ M. farther on is
Ruppertshain, with a sanatorium for consumptives, 1 M. above
which lies the summer-resort of *Eppenhain.* Near the latter is the
Rossert (p. 310). — From Königstein to *Eppstein*, 5 M., see p. 310.

    The ascent of the **Grosse Feldberg** (2885 ft.; p. 300) from
Königstein takes 2¹/₄ hrs. We first take the Limburg road, then
turn to the right and follow the Reifenberg road, passing the *Seelenborn* and leading to the inn at the *Rote Kreuz.* From this point
we may proceed to the right either by the road or by a red-marked
footpath, crossing the saddle to the N. of the *Kleine Feldberg*
(2710 ft.), and so reach the top in ³/₄ hr.; or we may take the blue-
marked path to the left, passing the foundations of a Roman fortress, and reach the top in 1 hr. Walkers, however, will do better
by taking the road to the right at the *Rommberg*, 20 min. from
Königstein; then, at the point (¹/₂ hr.) where this road bends to the
right, they should take the first footpath to the left, which ascends
somewhat abruptly, passing the Kleine Feldberg and joining the
above-mentioned footpath on the right. The summit of the Grosse
Feldberg consists of a barren plateau of quartz; on it are three
Hotels and a view-tower 98 ft. high (adm. 20 pf.). The dining-room
of the oldest inn contains some pictures by Frankfort painters.
About 3 min. to the N. of the tower is a huge block of quartz, 10 ft.
in height and nearly 39 ft. in breadth, which is mentioned in a
document of 1043 as the '*Brunhildenbett*'.

    We may return viâ the *Altkönig* (2618 ft.), 1 hr. to the S.E. of
the Grosse Feldberg, which is surmounted by an interesting Germanic fortification of the 1st cent. before the Christian era. From
the hotels we follow the black rectangles and in ¹/₄ hr. reach a finger-
post with several arms. Hence we proceed to the left to (25 min.)

‚the *Fuchstanz* (2192 ft.), a clearing with a summer-restaurant, whence a red-marked path leads to the left to the summit. The fortification consists of a double girdle-wall of loose stones, respectively 1518 yds. and 1070 yds. in circumference. The S.W. side of the outer ring is adjoined by a rectangular rampart. — From the Altkönig to Falkenstein (red way-marks), ³/₄ hr.

ASCENT OF THE FELDBERG FROM FALKENSTEIN (1³/₄ hr.). A road (white marks) ascends gradually from the head of the village to (2 min.) a sign indicating a path (left) to the *Hattensteiner Schlag* and the (³/₄ hr.) *Fuchstanz* (see above), and thence to the top. — A red-marked path leads to the right from the upper end of Falkenstein viâ the *Streng-Hütte* to the *Altkönig.* — The path from the Altkönig to (35 min.) the Fuchstanz is marked at first with yellow (path to Oberursel), then with green marks.

FROM OBERURSEL (p. 300; 3 hrs.). The road, popularly known as the Kanonen-Strasse, ascends along the left bank of the stream. In 1 hr. we reach the *Hohe Mark* spinning-mill (fair restaurant), the terminus of the electric railway (p. 305), beyond which the route is indicated by brown marks. In about 1 hr. more (about 100 yds. before a wide curve of the road) we ascend a few steps to the right and follow the path (finger-posts) to the (20 min.) *Buchborn.,* a fresh spring. Thence we proceed straight on, crossing the Kanonen-Strasse and skirting the intrenchment, to the Schieferbruch, which is within ¹/₂ hr. of the top.

FROM HOMBURG (3¹/₄ hrs.). We take the road at the (¹/₂ hr.) *Gothic House* (p. 303), and follow the straight '*Elisabethen-Schneise*' (route marked with yellow crosses). At the (2¹/₄ hrs.) *Sandplacken*, with an inn and a finger-post, the Feldberg route diverges to the left (50 min.). A finer path (green crosses) diverges to the left ¹/₄ M. from the S.W. exit of the Schloss-Garten, on this side of the bridge, and leads past the *Frankfurter Forsthaus* and the *Hohe Mark* (see above). — From the SAALBURG (p. 304) a yellow-marked path leads along the other side of the Pfahlgraben to (2 hrs.) the Sandplacken. Or we may take the green-marked path leading from the Saalburg Hotel over the Herzberg (p. 304).

FROM CAMBERG (p. 310; 4¹/₂ hrs.). We follow the white marks to (25 min.) the wood. In the wood we diverge to the right after 12 min. and eventually reach (35 min.) its S. margin, where we have a fine view of Steinfischbach and the Feldberg. We may now either proceed to the left to (25 min.) the *Tenne* (inn; wide view), and thence go on viâ *Reichenbach*, in the valley of the Ems, or (white way-marks) we may proceed viâ *Steinfischbach* (Anker), *Reinborn*, *Wüstems*, and *Oberems* to the Limburg and Frankfort highroad and follow this till we reach the Idstein route to the Feldberg (see below).

FROM IDSTEIN (p. 310; 3¹/₂ hrs.; red way-marks). We at first follow the wood-walks, obtaining a fine view of the Glaskopf, the Grosse Feldberg, and the Kleine Feldberg from the hill near (1 hr.) *Heftrich.* A little to the S. of this point are the scanty remains of the *Alteburg*, one of the forts on the Pfahlgraben (p. 304). From Heftrich we follow the road to (2¹/₄ M.) *Cröftel;* here we take the footpath·to the right, which crosses the Limburg and Frankfort highroad 5 min. short of *Glashütten* (inn) and leads to the Rote Kreuz (p. 307).

FROM WIESBADEN we use the railway to *Niederhausen* (p. 310) and then follow the road viâ (1¹/₄ M.) *Ober-Josbach* to (1¹/₂ M.) *Ehlhalten* (Krone), in the valley of the *Schwarzbach*. From here we ascend the road to (2¹/₄ M.) *Schlossborn* and go on thence through beautiful woods to the (1 hr.) Königstein and Camberg (Frankfort and Limburg) highroad, which we reach about ²/₃ M. to the S.E. of *Glashütten* (see above). We then follow footpaths leading to the S. and E. round the *Glaskopf* (2254 ft.), passing the *Seelenborn* (p. 307), and finally bringing us to (1 hr.) the *Rote Kreuz* (p. 307), 40 min. from the summit.

c. From Frankfort to Soden.

10 M. RAILWAY in $^1/_2$-1 hrs. (fares 1 ℳ 40, 85, 50 pf.).

From Frankfort to *Höchst*, see below. — Thence by a short branch-line viâ *Sulzbach* to —

Soden. — HOTELS. *Kurhaus*, R. from 2$^1/_2$, D. 3, pens. from 7 ℳ; *Hôtel Colloseus*, R. 2-6, D. 3, pens. from 6$^1/_2$ ℳ; *Europäischer Hof*, R. 2$^1/_2$-5, B. 1$^1/_4$, D. 3, pens. 6-10 ℳ; *Russischer Hof*, R. 2-4, B. 1, D. 1$^3/_4$-3 ℳ; *Uhrich, Adler*, the last two suited for passing tourists.

CARRIAGE per hour 3 ℳ, to Königstein 3$^1/_2$, to Cronberg 4$^1/_2$, to the top of the Feldberg 20 ℳ.

VISITORS' TAX for 1 pers. 14, for 2 pers. 20, for each addit. pers. 5 ℳ.

Soden (490-655 ft.), a village with 1900 inhab., lies at the foot of the Taunus Mts., in the sheltered valley of the *Sulzbach*. On the Königstein road, which intersects the town from S.E. to N.W., are most of the hotels and the pleasant *Kur-Park*, with the *Kurhaus*, the *Bath House* (admirably fitted up), and the *Inhaling House*. The baths are visited by about 2500 patients annually. The numerous warm SPRINGS contain salt, iron, and carbonic-acid gas, and are chiefly prescribed for heart and bronchial affections and mild diseases of the lungs. The *Milchbrunnen, Warmbrunnen, Solbrunnen*, and *Champagner-Brunnen*, which are chiefly used for drinking, rise in the Quellen-Park, in the so-called Haupt-Strasse.

WALKS. To the *Drei Linden* (820 ft.; blue way-marks), a good point of view, near Neuenhain (see below); to the *Altenhainer-Tal* (red marks), $^1/_2$ hr. to the N.W.; to the *Sodener Wäldchen*, etc.

FROM SODEN TO CRONBERG, 3 M. The road diverges to the W., at the lower end of the Kur-Park. About $^1/_4$ M. from Soden there is a finger-post indicating the footpath and the carriage-road (yellow marks) to (2 M.) *Crontal*, which possesses two saline springs, and to Cronberg.

FROM SODEN TO KÖNIGSTEIN, 3 M. The road ascends past (1 M.) *Neuenhain* (790 ft.), where there is another chalybeate spring used for sanatory purposes. It finally winds down to *Königstein* (p. 306).

d. From Frankfort to Eppstein and Limburg.

46$^1/_2$ M. RAILWAY in 1$^1/_2$-2$^1/_4$ hrs. (fares 4 ℳ 10, 2 ℳ 60, 1 ℳ 65 pf.).

Frankfort, see p. 279. 6 M. *Griesheim;* 8$^1/_2$ M. *Höchst*, see p. 278. The line describes a curve and crosses the Kastel & Wiesbaden railway. 12$^1/_2$ M. *Kriftel.*

13$^1/_2$ M. **Hofheim** (445 ft.; *Krone*, R. 1$^1/_2$-3, pens. 3$^1/_2$-4$^1/_2$ ℳ, very fair; *Pfälzer Hof*), an early Roman settlement, is now a pleasant village of 3300 inhab., at the entrance to the *Lorsbacher-Tal*, a grassy valley, enclosed by wooded slopes and watered by the *Schwarzbach.*

Pleasant walks lead to the ($^1/_2$ hr.) *Hofheimer Kapelle* (750 ft.) and on to the ($^1/_4$ hr.) *Meisterturm* (958 ft.; key at Hofheim, open on Sun.; restaurant in summer), which affords a survey of the extensive valley of the Main, the Taunus Mts., the Bergstrasse, and the Mts. of the Palatinate.

The line ascends the Lorsbacher-Tal and crosses the Schwarzbach several times. 16$^1/_2$ M. *Lorsbach*, a prettily-situated village.

19¹/₂ M. **Eppstein.** — *Hôtel-Restaurant Oelmühle, below the
village, at the mouth of the Fischbach-Tal, R. 2-3, B. 1, D. 1³/₄, S. 1¹/₂,
pens. 6-6¹/₂ℳ, with large open-air restaurant; Hôtel Seiler & Kurhaus Bergfriede, at the station; Kaiser-Tempel (see below), R. & B. 2¹/₂, D. 1¹/₂, pens.
5 ℳ, with large garden-restaurant; Hänsel, 1 M. to the W. of the station.

Eppstein (605 ft.), a straggling little town with 1150 inhab.,
lies in the *Lorsbacher-Tal*, above the mouth of the *Fischbach-
Tal* and below those of the *Draisbach-Tal* and *Goldbach-Tal*.
On a precipitous rock above the place rises the picturesque *Castle*
of the same name, mentioned in history as early as 1120, the ancestral
seat of a celebrated family, five members of which were archbishops
and electors of Mayence between 1060 and 1305. It is now the
property of Prince Stolberg-Wernigerode. Good views are obtained
from the (¹/₄ hr.) *Malerplätzchen* and the (¹/₂ hr.) *Kolossal-Bank*.

On a (25 min.) projection of the *Staufen* is the *Kaiser-Tempel*
(hotel, see above). Fine view. On the summit of the Staufen (1480 ft.;
³/₄ hr. to the E.; yellow way-marks) are a private villa and a belvedere.

The **Rossert** (1690 ft.), which is easily reached from Eppstein in
1 hr. by a path (yellow marks) ascending the valley and then by a road
to the left, commands a fine view of the valleys of the Rhine and Main.
Below the summit is a refuge-hut, shaded by trees (rfmts. on Sun.). From
the Rossert to Königstein 1³/₄ hr., see p. 307.

Immediately below Eppstein the Königstein road ascends the *Fischbach-Tal* to (1³/₄ M.) *Fischbach* (730 ft.; p. 306). Thence we cross (blue
way-marks) a lofty plateau to (2¹/₄ M.) *Schneidhain* (p. 306), whence a
light railway runs to (1¹/₂ M.) *Königstein* (p. 306).

Beyond Eppstein the train passes through a tunnel. — From
(23 M.) **Niedernhausen** (850 ft.; Hôt. Villa Sanitas, in Königshofen, pens. 3-4¹/₂ ℳ) a branch-line runs to *Auringen-Medenbach,
Igstadt, Erbenheim,* and (12¹/₂ M.) *Wiesbaden* (in ¹/₂-³/₄ hr.).

28 M. **Idstein** (872 ft.; Lamm, Merz, pens. 3¹/₂-5 ℳ), a town
of 3400 inhab., with many old houses, was once the residence of a
branch of the Nassau family. The château, re-erected in the 16-
17th cent., is to be restored; the church, richly adorned with marble,
dates from 1667. The Grosse Feldberg (p. 307) may be ascended
hence in 3¹/₂ hrs. — 31 M. *Wörsdorf*. — 34 M. *Camberg* (700 ft.;
Gutenberger Hof, pens. 3-4¹/₂ ℳ), a little town with 2400 inhabitants. Ascent of the Feldberg, see p. 308.

About 9 M. to the E. lies Neu-Weilnau (1280 ft.; Zur Schönen Aussicht,
pens. 4-6ℳ), in the prettiest part of the wooded valley of the Weil. Opposite
is Alt-Weilnau (1293 ft.), with a ruined castle. — From Neu-Weilnau a
yellow-marked path leads viâ Treisberg to (3 M.) Schmitten (1510 ft.; Ochs,
pens. 4ℳ), frequented by consumptives. Diligence to Anspach, see p. 305.

36¹/₂ M. **Nieder-Selters** (538 ft.; Caspary), formerly belonging to the Electorate of Trèves.

Nieder-Selters has been celebrated since the 16th cent. for its mineral
waters, in which carbonate of soda and salt are agreeably blended,
widely known under the erroneous name of 'Seltzer Water'. The buildings of the spring are near the station.

39 M. *Oberbrechen;* 41 M. *Niederbrechen;* 45 M. *Eschhofen*
(p. 137).

46¹/₂ M. *Limburg on the Lahn,* see p. 136.

V. GRAND DUCHIES OF HESSE (RIGHT BANK OF THE RHINE) AND BADEN.

40. From Frankfort or Mayence to Mannheim and Heidelberg.

a. Viâ Lampertheim to Mannheim *(Carlsruhe).*

50¹/₂ M. RAILWAY from Frankfort to Mannheim in 1¹/₄-2¹/₄ hrs.; ordinary fares (no first class) 3 ℳ 90, 2 ℳ 60 pf., express fares 7 ℳ 50, 4 ℳ 90, 3 ℳ 10 pf.

From Frankfort to (3¹/₂ M.) *Goldstein,* see p. 278. The line traverses the plain watered by the Rhine and the Main, consisting geologically of alluvial detritus and forming the northernmost portion of the valley of the Upper Rhine. — 9¹/₂ M. *Walldorf;* 10¹/₂ M. *Mörfelden.* — 16 M. *Dornberg* is the junction for the Mayence and Darmstadt railway (p. 313). 18¹/₂ M. *Dornheim;* 20¹/₂ M. *Leeheim-Wolfskehlen.* — 21¹/₂ M. *Goddelau-Erfelden* is the junction for the Darmstadt and Worms railway (p. 318). 23¹/₂ M. *Stockstadt,* on the Rhine; 25¹/₂ M. *Biebesheim.*

28 M. **Gernsheim** *(Post; Zum Bahnhof),* a small and busy town on the Rhine, with 4100 inhab., mentioned in history as early as 773 and destroyed by Mélac in 1689. It contains a monument to Peter Schöffer, one of the inventors of printing (p. 275), who was born here. — 30¹/₂ M. *Gross-Rohrheim.* 33 M. *Biblis,* with a handsome church with two towers, is the junction for Worms (p. 318). 36 M. *Bürstadt,* junction of the Bensheim and Worms railway (p. 321). — 39 M. **Lampertheim** *(Rebstock; Schwan),* the junction of a branch-line to Worms, is a town with 8900 inhab.

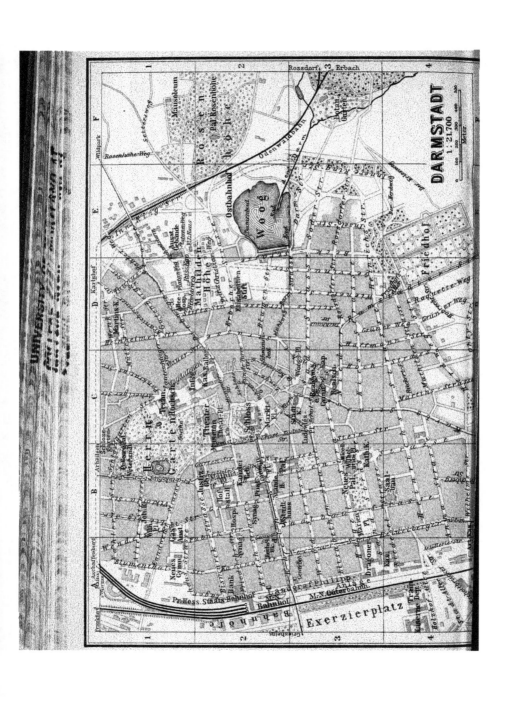

and a large new church. Our line divides here, the right branch leading by *Waldhof* to the (47 M.) Neckar suburb of Mannheim, while the left passes *Waldhof* and *Käfertal* and crosses the Neckar to the central station at (50¹/₂ M.) *Mannheim* (p. 342). Continuation of the railway to *Carlsruhe,* see p. 346.

b. Viâ Darmstadt to Heidelberg and Mannheim.

From Frankfort to *Darmstadt* (16¹/₂ M.) railway in ¹/₂-1 hr. (fares 2 ℳ 20, 1 ℳ 40, 90 pf.;. express fares 2 ℳ 70, 1 ℳ 90, 1 ℳ 15 pf.). From Mayence to *Darmstadt* (21 M.) railway in ³/₄-1 hr. (fares 2 ℳ 60, 1 ℳ 70, 1 ℳ 15 pf.; express fares 3 ℳ 10, 2 ℳ 20, 1 ℳ 40 pf.). From *Darmstadt* to *Heidelberg* or *Mannheim,* 38 M., in 1-2 hrs. (fares 4 ℳ 70, 3 ℳ, 1 ℳ 95 pf.; express fares 5 ℳ 20, 3 ℳ 50, 2 ℳ 20 pf.). Best views to the *left* (E.).

FROM FRANKFORT TO DARMSTADT. Beyond the imposing sand-stone bridge over the Main a branch-line diverges to the left to Offenbach and Hanau, and farther on the Mayence and Mannheim lines diverge to the right (p. 278). On the hills to the left is the *Sachsenhäuser Warte.* 2¹/₂ M. *Frankfurt-Louisa.* — The following stations are for the most part some distance from the unimportant villages after which they are named. The railway from Mayence to Darmstadt passes beneath our line shortly before we reach (16¹/₂ M.) *Darmstadt.*

FROM MAYENCE TO DARMSTADT. Starting from the central station (p. 265), the train runs under the citadel to the *S. Mayence* station *(Mainz Süd),* and crosses the Ludwigshafen railway (p. 446) and the Rhine. 2¹/₂ M. *Gustavsburg-Kostheim* (p. 278). 5 M. *Bischofsheim* is. the junction for the Frankfort Railway (p. 278) and for the junction-line across the Main to *Kastel* (Wiesbaden). 10 M. *Nauheim.* From (12¹/₂ M.) *Grossgerau* a branch-line runs to *Dornberg,* the junction of the line to Mannheim viâ Lampertheim (p. 312). — 13¹/₂ M. *Kleingerau;* 16¹/₂ M. *Weiterstadt.* — 21 M. *Darmstadt,* where carriages are usually changed..

Darmstadt. — RAILWAY STATIONS. 1. *Central Station,* consisting of the former Main-Neckar Station (Pl. A, 2; Restaurant), on the W. side, and the former Ludwigsbahnhof (Restaurant on the 1st floor, with attractive terrace; D. from 1¹/₂ ℳ), on the N. side of the Bahnhofs-Platz, also for the Odenwald line. A new Central Railway Station is in construction ¹/₃ M. to the W. — 2. *East Station* (Ostbahnhof; Pl. E, 2), on the Odenwald Railway.

HOTELS. *Traube* (Pl. a; B, 2), Luisen-Platz 6, rebuilt in 1908, R. 3-9, B. 1¹/₄, D. 3 ℳ; *Britannia* (Pl. d; B, 2), Rhein-Str. 35, rebuilt in 1907, R. 3-6, B. 1¹/₄, D. 3¹/₂-4 ℳ; *Hess* (Pl. h; B, 2), new building, with a large restaurant, R. from 2¹/₂ ℳ, these three all very fair, with elevators and baths; *Railway Hotel,* at the Ludwigsbahnhof. — *Hôtel Köhler* (Pl. c; A, 3), Rhein-Str. 48, R. 2-8, B. 1, D. 2-3 ℳ, well spoken of; *Prinz Heinrich* (Pl. f; A, 2), Bleich-Str. 48; *Prinz Karl* (Pl. e; C, 3), Karl-Str. 1. — *Pension Gaulé,* Heinrich-Str. 62, pens. 4-7 ℳ.

RESTAURANTS (in addition to those in the hotels). *Casino Restaurant,* Neckar-Str. 1, cor. of the Rhein-Str. (in the house of the 'Vereinigte Gesellschaft', wine and beer); *Wiener Café,* Rhein-Str. 28; *Sitte,*

Karl-Str.; *Saalbau* (Pl. B, 4), with garden and concerts; *Automatic Restaurant*, Rhein-Str. 12. — *Fürstenhalle* (wine and luncheon rooms), Elisabethen-Str. — Cafés. *Ernst Ludwig*, Rhein-Str. 12; *Wiener Café*, see p. 313; *Eichberg*, Rhein-Str. 16 (also confectioner); *Schloss-Café*, Rhein-Str. 2.

Baths. *Merz*, Martin-Str. 22; *Marien-Bad*, Landgraf-Philipp-Anlage 62. — Swimming Baths in the *Woog* (Pl. E, 2); *Hallenschwimm-Bad* (Pl. D, 2), in the Mühl-Str. (public).

Cab with one horse for 10 min., for 1-2 pers. 70, with two horses 1 ✻; for 1/2 hr. 1 & 11/2 ✻; for 3/4 hr. 11/2 & 2 ✻; for 1 hr. 2 & 21/2 ✻. Each additional person 20 pf. more. From cab-stand to the railway-stations 1/2 ✻. Double fares at night (10-6). — From the stations 10 pf. extra.

Electric Tramways (see plan) ev. 71/2-15 min. in the town, 10 pf.; outside ev. 1/4-1/2 hr., 15 pf. — Steam Tramway to *Griesheim* (p. 318; comp. Pl. C, B, A, 2); and to *Eberstadt* (p. 319; comp. Pl. B, A, 2, 3, 4) and *Arheilgen* (comp. Pl. B, 2, 1).

Theatre (*Hof-Theater;* Pl. C, 2), closed in summer.

Art Exhibition in the *Kunst-Verein*, Rhein-Str., cor. of the Bahnhofs-Platz. — Tourists' Enquiry Office *(Verkehrsbureau)* in the waiting-room (Wartehalle) in the Ernst-Ludwig-Platz (Pl. C, 2). — Post Office, Luisen-Platz (Pl. B, 2).

British Chargé d'Affaires, *F. D. Harford, Esq.*

English Church Service in the Palace Chapel on Sun. from Oct. to June, at hours announced in the local paper for Saturday.

Darmstadt (480 ft.), the capital of the Grand-Duchy of Hesse, with 83,000 inhab., a town with broad streets and tasteful pleasure-grounds, was, though dating from the 11th cent. and the residence of the Landgraves of Hesse-Darmstadt since 1567, a place of no importance down to the close of the 18th cent., being wholly over-shadowed by the adjoining trading-centres Frankfort and Mayence. In spite of the fact that the building operations of Lewis I. (1790-1830) and his successors imported to it a more substantial appearance, it still maintained the character of a quiet official town. It was not until the last quarter of the 19th cent. that the rapid development of its industry transformed it into a centre of animated traffic. Iron-foundries, boiler-factories, and machine-shops are its chief industrial establishments, while its chemical and pharmaceutical works are also important. Under the Grand-Duke Ernest Lewis, who succeeded to the throne in 1892, Darmstadt became an advanced post of 'applied art', through the activity of the architects J. Olbrich (d. 1908), K. Hofmann, A. Messel (d. 1909), Pützer, and Wickop, and the sculptors and craftsmen Habich, Behrens, and Scharvogel. The Grand-Ducal School of Art ('Lehratelier'), with its ceramic department, and the manufacture of artistic furniture have a considerable reputation.

From the *Central Railway Station* (Pl. A, 2) the Rhein-Strasse, the main street of the town, leads to the E. to the Palace. From this the Neckar-Str. diverges to the right, and in the latter, immediately to the right, adjoining No. 1 (somewhat back from the street), is the *Industrial Museum (Gewerbemuseum;* open free daily, 11-1). Farther on, to the right, is the *Stadthaus,* beyond which is the square called the LUISEN-PLATZ (Pl. B, 2). In the centre of this square is a *Bronze Statue of Grand-Duke Lewis I.* by Schwanthaler (1844), borne by a red sandstone column 140 ft. in height. In the interior of the column a staircase of 172 steps ascends to the top, which commands a view of the whole town (fee 50 pf.). On the left side of the square, which is also adorned by two monumental fountains by Olbrich (1908), is the *Kanzleigebäude* (1777), while to the right are the *Ständehaus* (House of the Estates) and the *Old Palace* (1804). — In the Mathilden-Platz, close by, are a handsome fountain and a bust of *Abt Vogler* (1779-1814), the teacher of Weber and Meyerbeer. At its N. end are the old *Courts of Law (Justizgebäude)*, adjoined by the *New Courts* by Hofmann, added in 1905.

The **Grand-Ducal Palace** (Pl. C, 2), begun in the 15th cent., was largely rebuilt by the Landgrave George I. at the end of the 16th cent.; the portals, finished after the landgrave's death, are a good specimen of the German Renaissance. The bulk of the building was erected in 1716-27, by *Rouge de la Fosse*. The tower contains a chime of bells (1671). — A flight of steps ascends from the Markt-Platz to the first floor, containing the *Library*, which consists of about 503,000 vols., 4000 MSS., and numerous typographical curiosities (open on week-days, 11-12).

On application at the steward's office (first door to the right in the 'Kirchenhof'; 50 pf.), visitors are conducted by an attendant to the *Assembly Rooms* and *Imperial Rooms*, which are shown daily, 3-4 (in winter, Tues. & Frid. only; Sun. 11-1). They are decorated in the rococo and 'Empire' styles and contain various collections. The chief treasure is the celebrated **Madonna with the family of Burgomaster Meyer of Bâle**, by *Holbein the Younger*, painted in 1526. A skilful restoration by *A. Hauser* (1888) has removed much of the repainting of some of the heads, and the work again shines with its original glory.

In the square in front of the Palace (Pl. B, C, 2) stands a bronze *Equestrian Statue of Lewis IV.* (d. 1892), by Schaper. On the N. side of the square is the New Museum, in front of which stands the *War Monument* for 1870-71, by Herzig.

The ***Museum** (*Landesmuseum;* Pl. B, C, 2), built in 1901-6 from the designs of A. Messel, now contains the art and other collections formerly preserved in the Grand-Ducal Palace, and also collections of natural history. The picture-gallery includes several interesting examples of the early German (Stephan Lochner) and the Netherlands (Rembrandt, Rubens) schools and a large array of drawings by Arnold Böcklin; the collection of industrial art, the specimens of early-mediæval ivory-carvings and enamels, also merits inspection. Open free on Sun. & holidays, 10-1, and on Wed.; 3-5 (winter 2-4); on Tues., Thurs., & Sat., 11-1, 1 *M.* Illustrated catalogue (1908), 1½ *M.*

To THE RIGHT OF THE VESTIBULE. *Industrial Art* of the 16-18th cent., *Antiquities, Ethnographical Collection,* and *Casts.*

Room I. *Industrial Art* of the 16-18th cent., including admirable specimens of goldsmith's work of the German Renaissance. — In the glass-roofed Court (II) and adjoining corridor are a Roman mosaic pavement, from Vilbel (p. 299), and a select *Collection of Prehistoric, Ancient, and Frankish Antiquities.* — From the glass-roofed court we enter the groundfloor rooms (Court III), in which are the *Scientific Archaeological Collection* and the *Ethnographical Collections.* — IV. The large hall in the E. wing contains the *Plaster Casts;* the *Cabinet of Coins and Medals* is on the first floor of the tower.

To the Left of the Vestibule. *Weapons and Armour,* *Ecclesiastical Art, Sociology, Domestic Interiors,* and *Small Objects of Art.*

Room I. *Weapons & Armour*, including a richly damascened suit said to have belonged to Philip the Generous (16th cent.), inlaid guns and pistols, large ballista; and mediæval shields. — The second door in the N. wall admits to the —

II. *Mediaeval Ecclesiastical Rooms,* which open off a court containing tombstones and coats-of-arms. The *Romanesque Room,* on the N. side, exhibits smaller examples of Rhenish and other early-mediæval art, including elaborately ornamented reliquaries, small altars, ivory carvings, etc. — In the *Church Room* (adjoining on the W.): Romanesque portal of stone, admirable stained-glass windows (choir 13th cent., nave and sacristy 15th cent.), and wood-carvings of the Gothic period. — We return through the armour room to the S.W. staircase, leading to the —

III. *Museum of Social History,* in the lower story of the W. wing. This comprizes costumes of the 16-18th cent., musical instruments, Hessian military relics, specimens of rustic art in Hesse, etc. — On the upper stories of the W. wing are the —

IV. *Reproductions of Mediaeval Rooms* and the *Small Art Collections.* Friedberg Room with furniture, plastic decorations, altars of the 15th century. Gothic works in silver and ivory, and a *Crucifixion and other works by Tilman Riemenschneider; Italian room, with old portals and ceiling, containing plaquettes and majolica (Della Robbia work); Nuremberg room of the 16th cent., with shooting-guild targets; finely panelled room from Chiavenna (ca. 1580). Upper Floor: Late-Gothic room from Tyrol; panelling of 1625, from the Upper Rhine; small plastic works of the 16-18th centuries.

Straight on from the Vestibule are the collections in the main building. I. On the groundfloor is the *Zoological Department,* systematically and geographically arranged. — II. The entresol accommodates the *Mineralogical and Geological Collections,* with fine fossils.

III. On the upper floor is the **Picture Gallery.**

Early German Schools. Room 63 (lighted from the ceiling) and Cabinets 71-74. — Room 63 contains 15th cent. altar-pieces from the Middle Rhine: *School of Meister Wilhelm,* Crucifixion with saints; *Stephan Lochner,* *Presentation in the Temple (1447); G. Pencz,* Portrait; *L. Cranach the Elder,* Saints. — In the cabinets: Ortenberg Altar, from the Middle Rhine (ca. 1410); *Master of the St. Bartholomew Altar,* Madonna and saints; *G. David,* Madonna with angelic musicians. — *Hans Holbein the Younger* or *Ambrosius Holbein,* *Portrait of a young man (1515); Cranach the Elder,* Madonnas, Portraits of Cardinal Albrecht von Brandenburg, Archbishop of Mayence, and others.

Netherlandish Schools (Room 64 and Cabinets 67-70). — R. 64. *Neuchatel,* *Portrait of a physician; portraits, Biblical scenes, and genre paintings by *B. Fabritius, G. Flinck,* and other pupils of Rembrandt; *Jacob Backer,* *Full-length of an old woman; *Rubens,* *Diana hunting; landscapes by *Aert van der Neer, Bril, Momper,* and others. — In the cabinets: *Rembrandt*, **Scourging of Christ (1658); *D. Teniers the Younger*, *Portrait of an officer; works by *Ruysdael, Potter, Porcellis, Kalf, Gabron, P. de Hooch*, and *Adriaen van Ostade; P. Brueghel the Elder*, *Dance beneath the gallows - tree (1568); *Gonzales Coques*, Portraits; *Patinir*, Rest on the Flight into Egypt.

ITALIAN AND FRENCH SCHOOLS. Rooms 65 & 66. *Titian*, *Portrait (1565); *Paolo Veronese*, Venus and Adonis; *G. B. Moroni*, Carthusian monk; several excellent works of the 17-18th cent., by *C. Dolci, Feti, Cortona, Sassoferrato, Batoni*, and others. — Examples of *Rigaud, La Joue, Robert, Ary Scheffer*, etc.

MODERN GERMAN SCHOOLS (17-20th cent.). Room 82 (with relief from the Parthenon frieze). *Lessing, Becker, Radl, Lucas*, Landscapes; *Steinbrück*, Genoveva; *Enhuber*, Bavarian court of justice; *Hofmann*, Gethsemane; *Noack*, Religious disputation between Luther and Zwingli at Marburg; *Lenbach, Hauber, Lampi*, Portraits. — The two cabinets (75 & 76) are mainly devoted to Frankfort and Darmstadt artists of the 17-19th cent.: *Flegel, Roos, Junker, Schütz, Fiedler, Seekatz*, etc. — Rooms 81 and 80 contain landscapes by *Schirmer, Morgenstern, Schleich, Röth, Munthe, Thoma*, and *Lugo; Bracht*, *Shores of oblivion; *Lenbach*, Portrait of Herr von Liphart; genre-works by *Henseler, Raupp, Uhde, Männchen*, and *Hoelscher; Bautzer*, *Hessian peasants, *Rustic bride; *Feuerbach*, *Iphigeneia (1862); works by *Heinz Heim, L. von Hofmann*, and *W. Trübner*. — In Cabinet 77 are examples of *Koch, Schwind, Kobell, Kaufmann, Bürkel, Achenbach*. — In Cabinets 78 & 79 are *Drawings by Böcklin (the gift of Baron Max von Heyl).

Opposite the entrance of the gallery is the approach to the *Cabinet of Engravings*, in the three rooms of which are exhibited selections (periodically changed) from the large collection of engravings, wood-cuts, and drawings.

Between the Museum and the *Theatre* (Pl. C, 2) are good *Statues*, by Scholl, of the landgrave *Philip the Generous* (d. 1567) and his son *George I.* (d. 1596), founder of the grand-ducal family.

In the HERRN-GARTEN (Pl. B, C, 1), behind the theatre, an ivy-clad hill marks the resting-place of the *Landgravine Henrietta Carolina* (d. 1774), 'femina sexu, ingenio vir' according to the inscription on the urn dedicated to her by Frederick the Great. To the N.W. is the *Goethe Monument* (1903), with a fine bronze figure of a youth and reliefs by L. Habich. On the N. edge of the Herrn-Garten is the *Prince George Palace*, containing a collection of porcelain and fayence of the 18th cent. (50 pf.). — To the E. of the Herrn-Garten is a *Technical Academy* ('Technische Hochschule'; Pl. C, 1), which was founded in 1836 and now has 80 professors and 2000 students. The new buildings for physics and engineering are by Pützer and Wickop.

In the *Markt* (Pl. C, 2) stands the *Rathaus*, a simple Renaissance building of 1600. In the Kirch-Str., to the S.E., is the *Stadtkirche* (Pl. C, 3), with a Gothic choir (1500) and the elaborate Renaissance monument of Landgrave George I. — To the S.W. is the Ludwigs-Platz, with the *Bismarck Fountain*, by Pützer and Habich (1906); to the S.E. are the *Real-Schule* and the *Gymnasium*, founded in 1627.

In the Wilhelminen-Platz (Pl. B, 3) is the modern *Roman Catholic Church* (usual entrance at the S.E. angle), containing the

well-executed marble sarcophagus of the Grand-Duchess Mathilde
(d. 1862), by *Widnmann*. — On the N. side of the Platz is a monument by Habich (1902) to the Grand-Duchess Alice (the daughter
of Queen Victoria; d. 1878); on the W. side is the *New Palace of
the Grand-Duke*, built in 1865, in the Italian Renaissance style.

To the E. of the town, above the *Alice Hospital* (Pl. D, 1;
station of the electric tramway), rises the **Mathildenhöhe** (Pl. D,
E, 1, 2), with the new *Russian Chapel*. The Mathildenhöhe is occupied by the villas of an *Artists' Colony ('Künstler-Kolonie')*, with
the *Ernst Ludwig House* (1901), and by numerous other villas.
Here also are the *Exhibition Building ('Ausstellungsgebäude';
1908)* and the *Hochzeit-Turm*, a tower 160 ft. in height, erected in
honour of the second marriage of the Grand-Duke, with a sumptuous
interior decoration and commanding a fine view (adm. 20 pf.). All
these buildings were erected under the superintendence of Olbrich.
In the Alexandra-Weg is a monument to *Gottfried Schwab* (d. 1903),
the poet, who was a native of Darmstadt. Farther on, adjoining
Olbrich's Garden, is a handsome fountain, designed, like the Schwab
monument, by Habich. — Farther to the E., beyond the Odenwald
Railway (*E. Station*, see p. 313), is the **Rosenhöhe** (Pl. F, 1, 2),
with the *Palace* of the same name, and the *Grand-Ducal Mausoleum*, containing the remains of the Grand-Duke Lewis IV. (d. 1892)
and his wife, Princess Alice of England (d. 1878). The *Tomb of
the Princess Elisabeth, who died when a child, is by *Rauch* (1831).

To the S.E. of the town stretches a new VILLA QUARTER, with buildings by Hofmann, Wickop, Messel, and other architects (tramways at
Ohly-Str. and Schliesshaus-Str.). Farther to the W. in the Ohly-Str. is
the new Protestant *Paulus-Kirche*, by Pützer (1907), in the tympanum
of the main portal of which is a large Crucifixion by Robert Cauer.
Opposite is the new building of the *National Mortgage Bank* ('Landes-
hypothekenbank'), by Meissner (1908).

ENVIRONS OF DARMSTADT. Pleasant walks may be made in the extensive woods round the town. — Electric tramway from the Ernst-
Ludwigs-Platz (Pl. B, C, 2) every 1/2 hr. (in the afternoon every 1/4 hr.) to
the *Fasanerie*, on the edge of the wood; thence on foot to (20 min.) the
hunting-seat of *Kranichstein*, and (1 1/4 hr.) the forester's house of *Ein-
siedel* (hotel-restaurant). — To the S. rises the *Ludwigshöhe* (795 ft.;
40 min. from the Böllenfall-Tor tramway terminus), with view-tower and
restaurant. To the S.E., opposite the Ludwigshöhe, is the *Dommerberg*
(948 ft.), with a monument to Bismarck; farther to the S.E. lies *Nieder-
Ramstadt-Traisa* (p. 327; tramway projected).

FROM DARMSTADT TO WORMS, 27 1/2 M., railway in 1-1 1/2 hr. — 6 M.
Griesheim, with an artillery-range and camp (steam-tramway); 8 1/2 M.
Wolfskehlen; 10 M. *Goddelau-Erfelden*, the junction of the Frankfort
and Mannheim line (p. 312), which coincides with the Worms line as far
as (20 1/2 M.) *Biblis*. 23 1/2 M. *Hofheim (im Ried)*, the junction of the
Bensheim and Worms line (p. 321). We cross the Rhine by means of
an iron bridge to (25 1/2 M.) *Worms-Rhein*. The train makes a circuit
round the N. side of the town. — 27 1/2 M. *Worms* (p. 448).

FROM DARMSTADT TO MANNHEIM, 38 1/2 M. (Riedbahn). To *Goddelau-
Erfelden*, see above; thence to *Mannheim*, see p. 312.

From Darmstadt to Eberbach, see R. 41b.

The next station on the way to Heidelberg is (18 M. from Frankfort) *Darmstadt South Station*, for *Bessungen*, since 1888 a suburb of Darmstadt, with two gardens belonging to the Grand-Duke. — Near this point begins the *Bergstrasse*, an ancient road skirting the fruit and vine clad W. slopes of the Odenwald (to which the name 'Bergstrasse' is sometimes applied in a wider sense), and leading to Heidelberg. — 21 M. *Eberstadt* (Traube; Darmstädter Hof), 1 M. to the E. of the station. A branch-line runs hence to (1¼ M.) the busy little town of *Pfungstadt* (Strauss, with garden), with 6500 inhab. and a well-known brewery. — On the hills to the left rises the ruined castle of *Frankenstein* (1300 ft.), commanding a fine view (inn). The chapel contains tombs of the 16-17th centuries. — 25 M. *Bickenbach* (384 ft.).

FROM BICKENBACH TO SEEHEIM, 3 M., branch-railway in ¼ hr. — 1 M. *Alsbach* (Krone, pens. from 3½ ℳ; Sonne, both plain). Above, to the right, ½ hr. from Alsbach and ¾ hr. from Zwingenberg (see below), is *Burg Bickenbach* or the *Alsbacher Schloss* (775 ft.), with an embattled tower. From this point we may ascend the Melibocus in ¾ hr., or follow the winding 'Herrenweg' (blue and white marks) to the (2 hrs.) Auerbacher Schloss, or walk on to (1 hr.) Jugenheim.

2 M. **Jugenheim** (530 ft.; *Goldene Krone & Alexander-Bad; Post; Deutsches Haus; Schloss-Hôtel*, pens. 4-6 ℳ), a favourite summer-resort, with pleasant villas. About 1 M. to the S.E. is the château of *Heiligenberg* (710 ft.), the residence of Prince Lewis of Battenberg (fine views in the park). On the way to it we pass a ruined convent, near which are some (immured) gravestones of the 15th cent. and the 'Cent-Linde', an old lime-tree marking the site of a 'Centgericht' or Court of a Hundred. On an eminence to the W. are a conspicuous golden cross, erected by the Empress Mary of Russia (d. 1880) to her mother, the Grand-Duchess Wilhelmina (d. 1836), and the Mausoleum of Prince Alexander of Hesse (d. 1888).

2½ M. **Seeheim** (450 ft.; *Hufnagel*, very fair; *Victoria*), where there is a grand-ducal summer-château, the garden of which is open to the public. Above Seeheim rises the ruined castle of *Tannenburg* (1115 ft.), destroyed in 1399; it is scarcely visible from below.

27½ M. **Zwingenberg** (318 ft.; *Löwe*, with garden; *Anker*, R. 1¼-2 ℳ), an old town with 1650 inhab., lies at the foot of the wooded *Melibocus* or *Malchen* (1690 ft.), the highest point of the Bergstrasse and entirely of granite. On the summit is a tower, erected in 1772 (small gratuity; rfmts).

The ASCENT OF THE MELIBOCUS, often combined with that of the Felsberg (p. 323), may be made from Alsbach, Zwingenberg, Jugenheim, or Auerbach. Paths all marked; carriage to the top 10-12 ℳ. — FROM ALSBACH (1¼ hr.; yellow marks) we may ascend either viâ the castle (see above) or by another path more to the E. — FROM JUGENHEIM (1½-1¾ hr.) we proceed to the mouth of the *Balkhäuser-Tal* and then take either the old route (r.; blue and red marks) viâ the *Leserberg* or the new route (l.) viâ *Robertsruhe*. The two routes unite (¾ hr.) near the Kattenberger Schneise. — FROM ZWINGENBERG (1¼ hr.) the steeper route leads to the E. from the '*Löwe*' and ascends the hill; after 8 min. the path follows the water-conduit to the right, leads through a small fir-wood over the *Luzieberg*, and in 25 min. more regains the carriage-road, which is furnished with direction-posts. — FROM THE AUERBACHER SCHLOSS (¾-1 hr.; yellow marks) we follow the 'Herrenweg' to the 'Notgottes-Sattel', and then ascend direct.

29 M. **Auerbach.** — Hotels. *Krone,* a good old house rebuilt in 1907, R. 1³/₄-2, B. ³/₄, pens. 4¹/₂-5¹/₂ *M; Park Hotel,* R. 1³/₄, B. ³/₄, pens. 3-4 *M,* both with gardens; *Bauer; Traube.* — Lodgings (R. from 7 *M* per week). — Beer at the *Schützenhof.* — Carriage-tariff at the hotels.

Auerbach (330 ft.), a picturesque village of 2500 inhab., mentioned as early as 795, is a favourite summer-resort, and affords good headquarters for excursions in the W. part of the Odenwald. Good wine is produced in the neighbourhood, the best quality being called Rottwein.

The **Auerbacher Schloss* is situated on an eminence (1135 ft.; inn) to the N.E. of the village, whence footpaths ascend on the S. and W. sides of the hill in ¹/₂-³/₄ hr. The carriage-road leading through the Hochstätter-Tal skirts the S. and E. sides. Said to have been founded by Charlemagne, the castle appears after 1257 as a fortress of the Counts of Katzenelnbogen, held at first as a fief of the monastery of Lorsch (see below), and then of the Electorate of Mayence. The present building dates from the 15th cent.; in 1674 it was blown up by Turenne. The view from the towers is less extensive but more picturesque than that from the Melibocus. — A little to the W., below the Notgottes-Sattel, the foundations of the ancient *Capelle zur Heiligen Not Gottes* were discovered in 1892, and the site of the altar marked by a new crucifix. From Auerbach the 'Neue Weg', which diverges to the left from the path to the castle at the upper end of the village, leads thither in ³/₄ hr.

Environs. One of the prettiest points near Auerbach is the **Fürstenlager,** a small château built during the 18th cent. by the Landgraves of Hesse, and enlarged by Lewis I. (p. 315), with charming grounds. Coffee and milk may be had at the château. It may be reached by the road in 20 min. from the 'Krone' inn, or (pleasanter) by following the path to the right indicated by the finger-post opposite the inn. — The walk from the Auerbacher Schloss to the Fürstenlager is also pleasant: we follow the broad road to the E. as far as the (exhausted) mineral spring in the *Hochstätter-Tal* (refreshments at the forester's), pass the mill, and turn to the W. to the *Neun Aussichten* ('nine views'), a clearing in the wood, where nine different picturesque views are obtained through the nine forest-paths which converge here. Farther on we reach the Fürstenlager (1¹/₄ hr. in all). — About ¹/₂ hr. to the E. of the Fürstenlager lies *Schönberg* (p. 324).

30¹/₂ M. **Bensheim** (330 ft.; *Reuter's Hotel,* at the station, R. 1¹/₂-2, B. ³/₄ *M,* very fair) is a busy town (8200 inhab.) in a picturesque situation at the entrance of the *Lauter-Tal,* through which the road ascends to Schönberg and Reichenbach (p. 324). It dates as far back as the 8th century, and till 1802 belonged to Mayence. The two churches, Roman Catholic and Protestant, are modern.

From Bensheim to Worms, 14 M., railway in about ³/₄ hr. — 3 M. **Lorsch** (4400 inhab.; *Hôtel Hartmann),* on the *Weschnitz,* with ruins of a monastery *(Laureshamense Monasterium),* founded in 763 on an island in the Weschnitz and afterwards removed to its present site. In 788 Charlemagne assigned it as a place of banishment to Tassilo, Duke of Bavaria, who had been condemned to death as a traitor. To the E.

of the Markt-Platz, ¹/₄ hr. from the station, is the *Michaels-Kapelle*
(adm. 50 pf.), which is now recognized as the monastery-portal erected
by Lewis the Younger, the son of Lewis the German, about 880 in the
style of a Roman triumphal arch. This building, now used as a chapel,
is one of the most elegant and best-preserved specimens of the architecture of the period. The two stories are separated by a leaf-pattern
frieze resting on four composite columns. The upper story is adorned
with an arcade of nine triangular-headed arches resting on Ionic pilasters.
The flat surfaces of both stories are covered with a rough kind of mosaic
work, in alternate squares of white and red. The interior has been
much modernized. Lewis the German and his son, and Kunigunde, wife
of Emp. Conrad I., are interred at Lorsch. Their stone coffins seem to
belong to the Carlovingian era. The Nibelungen-Lied represents the
vaults at Lorsch as the burial-place of Siegfried and Queen Ute (mother
of Chriemhilde). Beyond the chapel are some portions of the nave of
the convent-church, which was consecrated in 1130.

8 M. *Bürstadt* (p. 312); 10¹/₂ M. *Hofheim im Ried*, and thence to
Worms, see p. 318.

Near (33¹/₂ M.) **Heppenheim** (328 ft.; *Halber Mond*, R. 2-3,
B. ³/₄, pens. 4¹/₂-5 ℳ, with garden and large restaurant; *Darmstädter Hof;* 6300 inhab.), to the left of the road, rises the *Land-
berg*, a hill crowned with three trees, where the provincial tribunals
were held in the middle ages. The new domed church at Heppenheim occupies the site of one said to have been founded by Charlemagne.

The ruin of **Starkenburg** (965 ft.) is reached by a good path from
Heppenheim in ¹/₂ hr. It was erected in 1064 by an abbot of Lorsch,
captured by the Swedes and Spaniards in the Thirty Years' War, and
besieged in vain by Turenne in 1674. It gives its name to a province of
Hesse. Fine view from the lofty square tower. — Branch-line to Lorsch
(3¹/₂ M.; see above).

The train now enters the dominions of Baden. 35 M. *Laudenbach.* Beyond (36¹/₂ M.) *Hemsbach* we cross the small *Weschnitz.*

39¹/₂ M. **Weinheim.** — HOTELS. *Pfälzer Hof*, a well-known
house, with large garden, R. 2-2¹/₂, pens. 4¹/₂-5¹/₂ ℳ; *Vier Jahreszeiten*,
in the town, R. 1¹/₄-1¹/₂, pens. 3¹/₂-4¹/₂ ℳ; *Prinz Wilhelm*, at the station,
R. 1¹/₂-2 ℳ.

Weinheim (355 ft.), a town of 12,500 inhab., with tanneries and
manufactures of agricultural machinery, lies at the union of the
Gorxheim and *Birkenau* valleys. It once belonged to the Abbey
of Lorsch, and is of ancient origin, though owing to its destruction
during the Thirty Years' War and in the devastation of the Palatinate in 1689, there are few old buildings of any importance. A
few towers belonging to the former fortifications, the *House of the
Teutonic Order (Deutsch-Ordens-Haus*, ca. 1770; now a custom-
house), and the Gothic *Rathaus* are the only relics of its former
prosperity. The Gothic towers of the *Roman Catholic Church*
and of the *Berkheimsche Schloss* are modern, as also the *Roden-
stein-Brunnen* in the Bahnhof-Strasse. — To the E. rises the old
castle of *Windeck* (722 ft.), with its round 'Bergfried' tower (p. 247),
mentioned as early as the 12th cent., and later the property of the
Palatinate, commanding a beautiful view. Above it towers the

Wachenberg (1320 ft.), with an imposing new tower. — Pleasant
walks may also be taken to the *Fuchsen-Mühle* (garden-restaurant)
in the *Birkenauer-Tal*, the *Gorxheimer-Tal*, the *Kastanienwald*,
the *Geiersberg* (1120 ft.), the *Hirschkopf* (1145 ft.), etc.

FROM WEINHEIM TO HEIDELBERG, 10½ M., steam-tramway in 1¼ hr.
along the Bergstrasse. 2 M. *Lützel-Sachsen* (Traube), known for its red
wine; 2½ M. *Gross-Sachsen* (Zähringer Hof; also rail. stat., see below);
3½ M. *Leutershausen;* 5½ M. *Schriesheim* (*Deutscher Kaiser*), commanded by the ruins of the *Strahlenburg* (670 ft.; inn). Then past the
former stronghold of *Schauenburg* to (7½ M.) *Dossenheim*, with quarries
of red porphyry. — 8½ M. **Handschuchsheim** (*Badischer Hof; Bach-
lenz; Siebenmühlental;* electric tramway, see p. 330), with a ruined castle of
the 16th cent. and a Gothic church. — The line intersects Neuenheim, passes
over the new Neckar bridge, and reaches its terminus in the *Bismarck-
Platz* at (10½ M.) *Heidelberg* (p. 329).

FROM WEINHEIM TO MANNHEIM, 10½ M., steam-tramway viâ *Käfertal* (p. 313).

Railway from Weinheim to Fürth, see p. 325.

43 M. *Gross-Sachsen* (see above). — 46 M. **Ladenburg** (*Bahnhofs-Hôtel; Rose*), the Roman *Lopodunum*, with the early-Gothic
church of *St. Gallus*, some quaint old houses, and a gate-tower
(N.). The Neckar is crossed here.

48 M. *Friedrichsfeld*, where the lines to Heidelberg and Mannheim separate. A branch-line runs hence to (4½ M.) *Schwetzingen*
(p. 341).

54½ M. **Heidelberg**, see p. 329. — 54 M. **Mannheim**, see
p. 342.

41. The Odenwald.

The **Odenwald**, a wooded mountain-district lying between Darmstadt and Heidelberg and extending on the E. as far as the Main, is
about 25 M. in breadth. Orographically it stands in the same relation
to the Haardt (p. 457) as the Black Forest to the Vosges (comp. p. 383).
The Odenwald presents the appearance of a sloping plateau, on the W.
side of which the older strata (granite, syenite, red sandstone) are in
evidence, while the main mass of the range is formed of variegated
sandstone overlying these. This variegated sandstone nowhere reaches
the Rhine valley, except on the S., where the Neckar has hollowed out
its lateral valley. The W. verge rises somewhat steeply from the plain
of the Rhine; its fertile and well-cultivated slopes are known as the
Bergstrasse (p. 319). The 'Hintere Odenwald', essentially a wooded
district, is less prosperous. The highest points are the *Katzenbuckel*
(2055 ft., see p. 341), the *Neunkircher Höhe* (1985 ft., see p. 324), the
Krehberg (1965 ft., see p. 324), the *Tromm* (1860 ft., see p. 326), the *Melibocus* (1690 ft., see p. 319), and the *Felsberg* (1645 ft.; p. 323).

The *Odenwald Club* has constructed paths, erected belvederes at
various points, and issued a map (1 ℳ 80 pf.) and a guidebook (by
Windhaus and Anthes; 2½ ℳ).

a. Western Portion.

ONE DAY: From *Jugenheim* viâ the *Felsberg* and *Lindenfels* to *Fürth*
(p. 326), 6 hrs.

TWO DAYS. First day, as above to *Lindenfels*. Second day: by the
Tromm to *Waldmichelbach* 3½ hrs., thence by *Ober-* and *Unter-Schön-
mattenwag* to *Hirschhorn* 4 hrs., or viâ *Schönau* to *Neckarsteinach* 5 hrs.

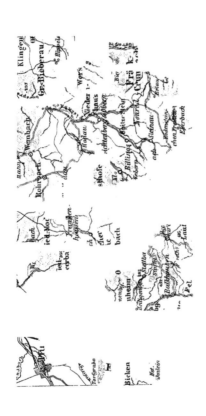

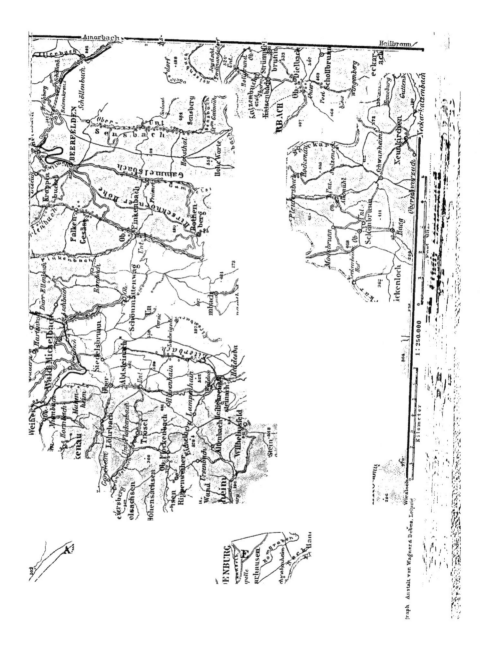

Graph. Anstalt von Wagner & Debes, Leipzig

From *Jugenheim* (p. 319) to the Felsberg (1¹/₂ hr.; route indicated by a white 'F'). · Beyond the château of *Heiligenberg* (see p. 319) we ascend to the right through the grounds, and, at the finger-post indicating the way *('Wilhelminenweg')* to the Felsberg, turn to the left round the hill, whence a pleasing glimpse of the Melibocus is obtained. We next ascend along the edge of the wood (view of the Auerbacher Schloss) to the *Staffeler Kreuz* (Kuralpe Inn), and then to the right (somewhat steeper) to the **Felsberg** (1645 ft.; *Hôtel Felsberg*, very fair, R. 1¹/₂, pens. 4 ℳ). The view to the E. (best enjoyed from the Ohly-Turm; 10 pf.) embraces a great part of the Odenwald, and extends to the Spessart. — A rough cart-track (finger-posts behind the hotel) leads to (5 min.) the *Altarstein*, a cubical block of syenite, bearing traces of an attempt to hew it into lengths for a huge architrave. About 5 min. lower down, in a small gully, is the *Riesensäule*, a column of the same material, 30 ft. in length and 3-4¹/₂ ft. thick, with a notch 1¹/₂ inch deep in the middle. There is no doubt that an old Roman quarry once existed here, which perhaps also furnished the columns for the well at Heidelberg Castle (p. 336). The *Felsenmeer* ('sea of rocks'), on the side of the road, below the Riesensäule, consists of blocks of syenite scattered in huge and confused masses, covering an area of 500 paces by 200. — A path, indicated by yellow rectangles, descends past the Felsenmeer to Reichenbach (p. 324) in less than ³/₄ hr.

FROM THE MELIBOCUS (p. 319) TO THE FELSBERG is a walk of nearly 1¹/₂ hr. The path (yellow rectangles) ascends on the E. side of the hill (to the right the 'Neunkrümmweg', see below) to the saddle separating the Balkhäuser-Tal from the Hochstätter-Tal, and then follows the N.W. flank of the Felsberg.

ASCENT OF THE FELSBERG FROM AUERBACH (p. 320), 2-2¹/₂ hrs. One path (to the left as we quit the village; red and white marks) leads viâ *Hochstätten*, another (yellow marks on the upper part of it) viâ the *Fürstenlager* (p. 320). The return should be made by the picturesque path leading towards the Melibocus (see above; yellow rectangles) until we reach the Neunkrümmweg. We then follow the latter, on the height above the Hochstätter-Tal, to the Notgottes-Sattel (p. 319), and then the 'Herrenweg' (yellow; p. 319) to the (1¹/₂ hr.) Auerbacher Schloss.

FROM THE FELSBERG TO LINDENFELS VIÂ THE NEUNKIRCHER HÖHE, 3¹/₂ hrs. This is the route usually chosen by tourists. We take the above-mentioned cart-track to the *Altarstein,* but diverge to the left before reaching this and follow the yellow way-marks to *Beedenkirchen,* taking care to go straight on beyond the church, and not to the right (to Lautern). Beyond Beedenkirchen guide-posts indicate the route to (ca. ¹/₂ hr.) *Brandau* (1040 ft.), whence a public vehicle plies twice daily to Ober-Ramstadt (8 M.; see p. 327). From Brandau to Neunkirchen we may either take the direct path (white way-marks) in 1¹/₂ hr; or choose the longer route (1³/₄-2 hrs.) viâ *Lützelbach* (inn, very fair), near which, to the left of the road to Klein-Bieberau (red and blue way-marks), is a lofty precipice known as the *Wildfrauhaus.* — At **Neunkirchen** (1680 ft.; *Grüner*

Baum, very fair) a monument commemorates Herr Ohly, the founder of the Odenwald Club.

A path indicated by white marks descends from Neunkirchen and then ascends through wood to the (¹/₂ hr.) 'Weinweg' (see below), whence it again descends to the (¹/₂ hr.) ruin and farm of *Rodenstein* (p. 327).

An easy path (red way-marks) ascends from Neunkirchen to the (¹/₂ hr.) top of the **Neunkircher Höhe** (1985 ft.), the highest point in the Hessian Odenwald, with a view-tower ('Kaiser-Turm'; 95 ft.; 20 pf.) commanding an extensive survey as far as the Haardt, Taunus, Vogelsberg, and Spessart. A path (red rectangles), rough at first, descends hence to the S. to the road and (35 min.) *Winterkasten* and thence, passing the view-tower on the *Litzelröder,* to (35 min.) *Lindenfels* (p. 325).

Amongst the other paths radiating in all directions from the Neunkircher Höhe one (yellow marks) leads to the S.W. to (³/₄ hr.) *Gadernheim* (see below); and another (also yellow) to the N.E. viâ *Freiheit* (a little beyond which, to the left, above, is the *Wildweibchenstein*) to (1¹/₂ hr.) *Rodenstein* (p. 327) and (³/₄ hr.) *Nonrod.* From the latter path, about 20 min. from the Neunkircher Höhe, the *Weinweg* (see above; red and yellow triangles) diverges to the left and leads through wood to the (1¹/₄ hr.) saddle above Nonrod (fine view) and thence to (1¹/₂ hr. more) *Gross-Bieberau* (p. 327).

HIGH ROAD FROM BENSHEIM TO LINDENFELS, 11 M., motor-omnibus twice daily in summer in 1 hr. The road ascends the valley of the *Lauter* to (1³/₄ M. from Bensheim) **Schönberg** *(Sonne; Traube),* a village with a château of Prince Erbach-Schönberg. Fine view from the garden of the château and from the village-church. — Thence we proceed viâ *Wilmshausen* and *Elmshausen* to (2¹/₂ M. farther) **Reichenbach** (625 ft.; *Traube),* a village of 1600 inhab., with a war-monument and a fountain in the market-place formed of hewn blocks of syenite from the Felsberg (p.323). The way to the (1 hr.) Felsberg, past the monument, to the right, is indicated by a guide-post.

The road now ascends the gradually contracting valley, past the ultramarine works of *Lautern,* to (2¹/₂ M.) *Gadernheim* (1155 ft.; Rettich's Inn) and, past Schmidt's Inn, to (1¹/₄ M.) *Kolmbach* (1340 ft.), and finally crosses the *Kolmbacher Höhe* (1475 ft.; fine view) to (3 M.) Lindenfels.

A shorter footpath (1¹/₄ hr.; yellow rectangles) diverges to the right from the Lindenfels highroad to the E. of Reichenbach, and joins the road leading to Count Erbach's farm of *Hohenstein.* At the (¹/₂ M.) *Hohe Stein,* a quartz crag projecting from the woods (beside which is a memorial stone to Prince Alexander of Bulgaria), we diverge once more to the left, and, beyond *Unter-Raidelbach,* we rejoin the highroad at a point between Gadernheim and Kolmbach.

Knoden, where the key of the view-tower on the hill (1755 ft.) is to be obtained at Reinig's Inn, lies ¹/₂ hr. to the S. of the farm of Hohenstein, 1¹/₂ hr. to the E. of Schönberg (first red and blue, then red marks), and ³/₄ hr. to the S.W. of Gadernheim (first blue, then red marks). About ³/₄ M. to the S. of Knoden (blue way-marks) is the wooded *Krehberg* (1965 ft.).

Lindenfels. — Hotels *Victoria & Pension International*, Bensheimer-Str. 32, outside the town to the N., in an open situation, R. 1³/₄-2¹/₄, B. ³/₄, pens. 4-5¹/₂ ℳ. — In the town: *Hessisches Haus*, with shady garden; *Odenwald*, R. 1¹/₂-2, B. ³/₄, pens. 4¹/₂-5 ℳ; *Traube, Darmstädter Hof*, to the S., both plain. — Diligence to Reichelsheim (p. 327).

Lindenfels (1170 ft.), a favourite summer-resort (1600 inhab.), the finest point in the Odenwald, with a modern Prot. church and an older Rom. Cath. church, is picturesquely situated on an eminence. It is surrounded by the remains of old fortifications and is commanded by a large ruined *Château* (1310 ft.), formerly the property of the Palatinate. — On the beautiful wooded hill 1 M. to the E. is the *Ludwigshöhe*, a small wooden temple commanding a fine view. Towards the E., the prospect is more extensive from a point ¹/₄ hr. higher up. — Attractive views are also obtained from the *Karolinen-Tempel*, ¹/₂ hr. to the N.W. of Lindenfels, in the 'Buch', above the Kolmbach and Gadernheim road and the large syenite-polishing works of Kreuzer & Böhringer, and from the 'Bismarck-Warte' (tower) on the *Litzelröder*, reached in 20 min. by a path diverging from the Bensheim road opposite the Hôt. Victoria.

From Lindenfels to Heppenheim, about 9 M., pleasant footpath (red and white way-marks). We take the path descending to the left at the last house before the gate of the château, and then the third path on the right. Beyond *Eulsbach* we climb to the top of the hill on the other side of the valley and at the beginning of the wood turn to the left to (³/₄ hr.) *Erlenbach* and (¹/₂ hr.) *Mittershausen*, a little beyond which we strike the highroad from Fürth to Heppenheim. Following this over the saddle, we then take the path through the meadows on the left to (³/₄ hr.) *Kirschhausen* and in ³/₄ hr. more reach Heppenheim (p. 321). A guide-post just beyond Kirschhausen indicates the route to the right to the Starkenburg (p. 321).

From Lindenfels to Fürth, highroad, see p. 326. A shorter footpath (red rectangles) descends to the S. from Lindenfels, enters the (10 min.) wood to the left, (25 min. farther) crosses a fir-clad eminence (avoid the path to the left here), and reaches Fürth in 10 min. more.

From Weinheim to Fürth, 10 M., branch-railway in about 1 hour. — *Weinheim*, see p. 321. The train passes the station *Birkenauer Tal* and ascends the picturesque valley, which is watered by the *Weschnitz*. — 2¹/₂ M. *Birkenau*, a village with 1900 inhab., possesses a Prot. and a Rom. Cath. church, and a château and park of Baron von Wambolt. — 3¹/₂ M. *Reissen*. — 5¹/₂ M. *Mörlenbach* (Krone), with 1050 inhabitants.

From Mörlenbach to Wahlen, 10 M., railway in ca. 1 hr. — 2 M. *Weiher*; 5 M. *Kreidach*; 6 M. *Waldmichelbach* (see below); 7 M. *Unter-Waldmichelbach*; 7¹/₂ M. *Aschbach*; 8¹/₂ M. *Affolterbach*. — 10 M. *Wahlen*.

Waldmichelbach (1215 ft.; *Starkenburg*, pens. 3¹/₂-5 ℳ; *Odenwald*, pens. 3¹/₂-4 ℳ), a picturesquely situated little town (pop. 2000), and a capital centre for excursions. Fine view from the *Schimmelberg* (1640 ft.), 1 hr. to the N.W. (blue and white marks), near *Stallenkandel* on the highroad, 3 M. from Zotzenbach (p. 326; blue marks). — To Hirschhorn (p. 340), 12¹/₂ M., a diligence plies once a day from Waldmichelbach viâ *Schönmattenwag* (Hirsch Inn at *Unter*-Schönmattenwag), *Heddesbach*, and *Langental*.

Another path, marked by white diamonds, leads from Waldmichelbach to (1 hr.) *Siedelsbrunn* (Morgenstern). Thence we may continue to
follow the same path viâ *Ober-Absteinach, Unter-Absteinach*, the *Eichel-
berg* (1730 ft.), the *Schriesheimerhof*, and the *Hochstrasse* to (6¹/₄ hrs.)
Heidelberg. Or we may take the path indicated by blue marks to
(3¹/₂ hrs.) *Heiligkreuz-Steinach* (Löwe), whence another (red marks) leads
to (1 hr.) *Schönau* (p. 340) and *Neckarsteinach* (p. 339).

7 M. *Zotzenbach*, ¹/₂ M. from the village of that name. — 8 M.
Rimbach (*Deutscher Kaiser*, very fair) is a village with 1800 inhabitants. — 9¹/₂ M. *Lörzenbach-Fahrenbach*. — 10 M. **Fürth**
(620 ft.; *Adler*, R. & B. 1³/₄-2, D. 1¹/₂ ℳ), with 1550 inhab., 4¹/₂ M.
by road from Lindenfels (p. 325) viâ *Krumbach*, and about 3 M.
by the footpath (red rectangles).

Paths ascend from Rimbach (white triangular way-marks) and from
Fürth (red rectangles) to the S.E. to the (1¹/₂ hr.) top of the **Tromm**
(1860 ft.), which commands an extensive view (belvedere on the top; key
at the *Inn zur Schönen Aussicht*). We then proceed to the S. (red rectangles), passing several hovels, and at the point where the path enters
an oak-plantation descend to the right to *Gadern*. Hence the route leads
through a pleasant valley to (1¹/₄ hr.) *Waldmichelbach* (p. 325).

b. Eastern Portion.

RAILWAY FROM FRANKFORT TO EBERBACH, 66 M., in 3-4 hrs. — FROM
DARMSTADT TO WIEBELSBACH, 17¹/₂ M., in 1 hr.; at Wiebelsbach the two
lines unite.

Frankfort, see p. 279; departure from the E. Station. — 3 M.
Mainkur. About 2 M. to the N., on the hill, is *Bergen* (Zur Schönen
Aussicht, a garden-restaurant), a favourite resort of the Frankforters.
To the N., on the road to Vilbel (p. 299), are the *Bergener Warte*
(view) and the battlefield where Marshal Broglie defeated the Prussians under the Duke of Brunswick in 1759. — To the right, on
the other side of the Main, are the village and château of *Rumpen-
heim*. — 6 M. *Hochstadt-Dörnigheim;* 8¹/₂ M. *Wilhelmsbad*,
another favourite resort of the Frankforters, near which is a Bismarck column (1905).

10 M. *Hanau*, W. station; 11 M. *Hanau*, E. station (Restaurant), the junction for the express-trains from Frankfort and Stuttgart to Berlin. **Hanau** (*Adler*, R. from 2¹/₂, B. 1, D. 2¹/₂ ℳ),
situated near the confluence of the *Kinzig* and the Main, is a pleasant-
looking town with 31,600 inhab. and flourishing manufactures of
trinkets and tobacco. In the Neustädter Marktplatz is a monument
to the brothers *Grimm*, who were born here (1785 and 1786). On
the Main lies the château of *Philippsruhe*, belonging to the Landgrave of Hesse.

The Odenwald railway now crosses the Main. — 13 M. *Klein-
Auheim;* 14 M. *Hainstadt*. — 17¹/₂ M. *Seligenstadt*, a small town
with 4600 inhab., owes its name to a celebrated Benedictine abbey
founded about 828 by Eginhard, the biographer of Charlemagne.
The church has been entirely modernized in appearance, and few

traces of the original building have been left. The ruins of the
imperial residence date from the 13th century.

23¹/₂ M. *Babenhausen*, the junction of the Darmstadt and
Aschaffenburg railway. The Protestant church, an edifice in the
Transition style with a late-Gothic choir and aisle, contains some
interesting monuments of the Counts of Hanau and a late-Gothic
carved altar of 1518. — 26 M. *Langstadt;* 28 M. *Klein-Umstadt;*
30¹/₂ M. *Gross-Umstadt;* 33 M. *Wiebelsbach-Heubach* (see below).

Darmstadt, see p. 313. Beyond (2¹/₂ M.) the *E. Station* (p. 318;
branch-line to Grosszimmern) the line traverses extensive woods. —
5¹/₂ M. *Nieder-Ramstadt-Traisa* (Kurhaus, Post, Löwe, at Ram-
stadt; Darmstädter Hof, Hessischer Hof, at Traisa), a 'garden-city',
with many villas belonging to Darmstadt merchants (comp. p. 318).
We skirt the little *Modau*. — 7¹/₂ M. *Ober-Ramstadt* (Wiener's
Inn; to Brandau, see p. 323); 10 M. *Zeilhard*. — 12¹/₂ M. *Reinheim*
(528 ft.; Darmstädter Hof), an old town with 1900 inhab., on the
Gersprenz, is the junction for *Offenbach* (23¹/₂ M., in 2-2¹/₂ hrs.;
see *Baedeker's Southern Germany*) and for Reichelsheim.

FROM REINHEIM TO REICHELSHEIM, 11 M., railway in about 1 hr.
The line follows the busy *Gersprenz-Tal*. — 2 M. **Gross-Bieberau**
(530 ft.; *Post*), with 1700 inhab., whence several footpaths lead viâ the
Neunkircher Höhe to Lindenfels in 3-4 hrs. One of these passes the village of *Lichtenberg* (inn), with a Renaissance château (886 ft.; 1570-80),
now used as a hydropathic (view). — 5 M. *Brensbach* (560 ft.; Post). —
7 M. *Nieder-Kainsbach* (580 ft.) is the station for **Fränkisch-Crumbach**
(*Hörr zum Rodenstein*), a market-town ³/₄ M. to the S.W., with a château.
To the S.E. of Nieder-Kainsbach, overlooking the *Kainsbacher-Tal*, is the
(1¹/₂ M.) ruined castle of *Schnellerts* (see below). — 11 M. **Reichelsheim**
(755 ft.; *Schwan*, very fair; *Engel*, R. & B. 1¹/₂-2, pens. 3-4 ℳ; *Adler*), a
prettily-situated village, commanded by the ruin of *Reichenberg* (1075 ft.).
In a sequestered hilly and wooded region, ³/₄ hr. to the N.W. of this
point, rises the ruined castle of **Rodenstein**, from which, according
to the popular legend, when a war is about to break out, the Wild
Huntsman and his train gallop with fearful din to the castle of Schnellerts
(see above). — From Reichelsheim to *Lindenfels* (p. 325), 5 M. (diligence
daily).

15¹/₂ M. *Lengfeld* (660 ft.; Krone). At the top of the *Otzberg*
(1205 ft.; 40 min.), round which lies the little town of *Hering*, is
the old castle of that name, with a massive tower (extensive view).

17¹/₂ M. *Wiebelsbach-Heubach*, where the line unites with that
from Frankfort (see above).

36¹/₂ M. (from Frankfort) **Höchst** (520 ft.; *Post*, very fair;
Burg Breuberg), a town with 1900 inhab., lies in the valley of the
Mümling, which the train now ascends to Erbach.

About 2¹/₂ M. lower down the pleasant Mümling-Tal (diligence twice
a day) lies *Neustadt* (Zum Ochsen), above which rises the imposing,
partly ruined castle of *Breuberg* (1000 ft.; restaurant). — A marked path
leads from Neustadt to (2¹/₂ hrs.) *Wörth*.

38 M. *Mümling-Grumbach;* 40¹/₂ M. *König* (Büchner), with

a high-lying church; 42 M. *Zell-Kirchbrombach.* The valley contracts. To the right, farther on, is Schloss Fürstenau (see below).

45 M. **Michelstadt** (680 ft.; *Hôtel Friedrich*, R. 2-3, B. $^3/_4$,
pens. 4-6 ℳ, with garden; *Löwe; Alt-Deutscher Hof; Fürstenauer
Hof*), a town with 3400 inhab., mentioned in history as early as
741, lies in one of the prettiest parts of the Mümling-Tal. The
late-Gothic *Parish Church* contains monuments of the Counts of
Erbach and an old library. The *Rathaus* (1484) and some other
buildings are interesting examples of timber-architecture. The
Market Fountain dates from 1541. A few relics of the old fortifications still exist. Near the station is *Dr. Gigglberger's Hydropathic Establishment.* — About $^1/_4$ M. to the N. of the station is
Schloss Fürstenau, partly built before 1270, with four towers and
a shady park, which has been the seat of the Counts of Erbach-
Fürstenau since the 14th century. About $^1/_4$ M. to the W., at the
beginning of the village of *Steinbach*, are the remains of an interesting convent-church, founded by Eginhard (p. 326) in 827. The
nave, the apse, the smaller apse of the N. transept, and the crypt are
preserved (key kept by the door-keeper of the château). — Marked
paths lead to many fine points of view in the environs, such as the
Hermannsberg, the *Adalbertshöhe*, and the *Lärmfeuer* (990 ft.;
$^3/_4$ hr. to the W.).

From Michelstadt a road ascends to the E., passing *Dorf Erbach*
and (4$^1/_2$ M.) Count Erbach's shooting-box *Eulbach*, with its fine deer-
park, to (7$^1/_2$ M.) Amorbach. In the park of Eulbach the remains of a Limes
fort (p. 304) discovered here and at *Würzberg*, 3 M. to the S., have been
re-erected. — **Amorbach** (545 ft.; *Post*, R. 1$^1/_2$-2$^1/_2$, B. $^3/_4$, pens. 4$^1/_2$-
6 ℳ; *Badischer Hof*, R. 1$^1/_4$-1$^1/_2$, B. $^3/_4$-1, pens. 4-4$^1/_2$ ℳ), a town with
2260 inhab., is the junction of railways to Aschaffenburg and to Walldürn and Seckach. It is the residence of Prince Leiningen, and contains
a suppressed Benedictine abbey of the 17-18th cent., the buildings of
which are now used by him as offices. The library (1790) and the cloisters
are noteworthy. The abbey-church, originally Romanesque but remodelled
in 1742-47, is now Protestant. The interior is tastefully decorated in the
rococo style, with stucco-work by J. M. Feichtmayer and ceiling-paintings by M. Günther. The organ is a very fine one. The town contains
some interesting secular buildings, such as the convent-mill. The *Gott-
hard-Ruine* commands a view of seven valleys.

From Amorbach a diligence runs daily to (13 M.) Kailbach (p. 329),
viâ *Ernsttal* (Prinz Ernst, R. 1$^1/_2$-2$^1/_2$, B. 1 ℳ), 1$^1/_2$ M. from which is
Wald-Leiningen, a modern château in the English-Gothic style, with a
deer-park. Pedestrians should select the red-marked path viâ (1$^1/_2$ hr.)
the *Wildenburg* (or *Wildenfels*), one of the most important ruins in the
Odenwald, about 1$^3/_4$ hr. from Ernsttal. A pleasant walk may also be
taken from Kailbach or Ernsttal along the old Roman 'Limes' (red way-
marks), viâ *Eduardstal* and *Reisenbach* to *Mülben*, and thence (blue
diamonds as way-marks) viâ *Katzenbach* and the *Katzenbuckel* (p. 341)
to Eberbach.

From Amorbach to Miltenberg, 5$^1/_2$ M., railway in $^1/_2$ hr. — 1$^3/_4$ M.
Weilbach (Engel).

5$^1/_2$ M. **Miltenberg** (425 ft.; *Riese*, R. & B. 2$^1/_2$-3, pens. 4-5 ℳ;
Rose, near the station; *Linde*, by the bridge), a busy little town with 4500
inhab., charmingly situated on the *Main*, with extensive quarries of red
sandstone and a modern bridge. The old *Castle* of the Electors of May-

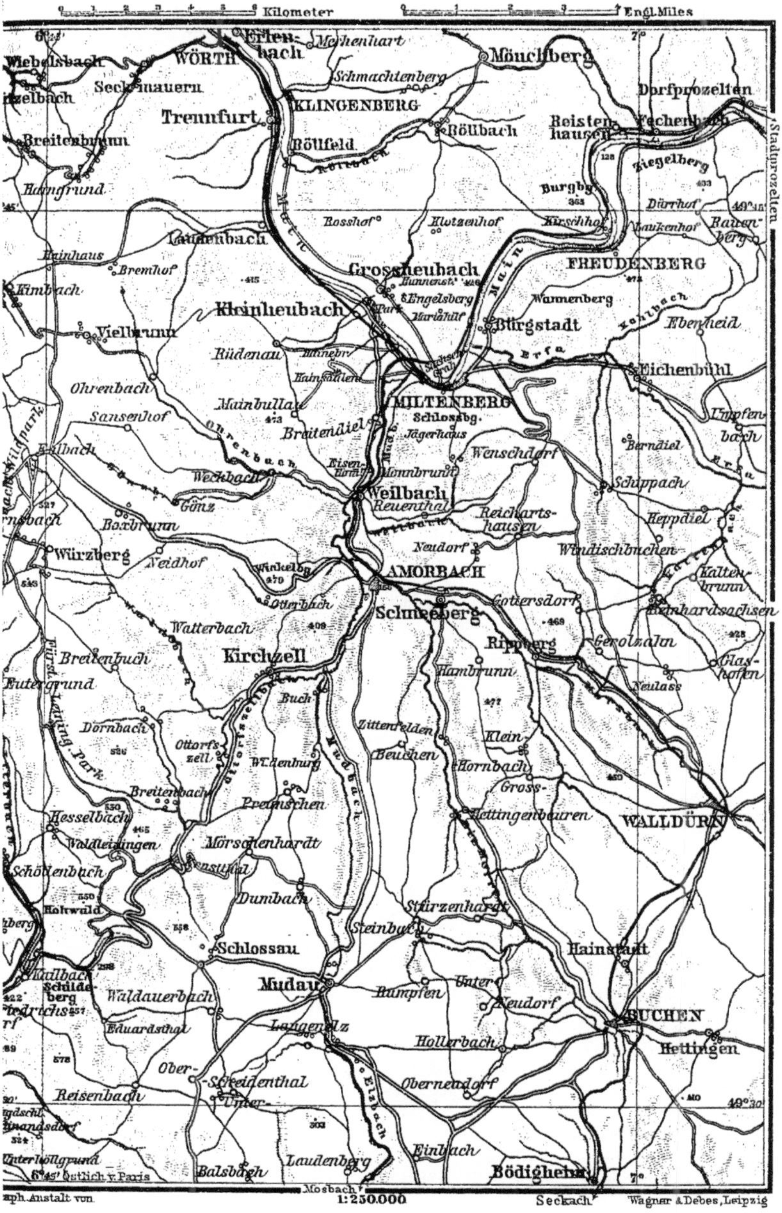
Kilometer
Engl. Miles
WÖRTH
Erlenbach
Mechenhart
Mönchberg
Seckmauern
Schmachtenberg
Dorfprozelten
Trennfurt
KLINGENBERG
Reistenhausen
Fechenbach
Röllbach
Breitenbrunn
Röllfeld
Ziegelberg
Hainigrund
Burgberg
Dürrhof
Stadtprozelten
Rosshof
Klotzenhof
Kirschhof
Laukenhof
Rauenberg
Laudenbach
Main
Hainhaus
Bremhof
Grossheubach
FREUDENBERG
Kimbach
Engelsberg
Wannenberg
Kleinheubach
Mariahilf
Bürgstadt
Ebenheid
Vielbrunn
Rüdenau
Erfa
Eichenbühl
Ohrenbach
MILTENBERG
Mainbullau
Schlossbg.
Sansenhof
Breitendiel
Jägerhaus
Umpfenbach
Wenschdorf
Berndiel
Weckbach
Mud
Mönnbrunn
Schippach
Eisenhammer
Weilbach
Reuenthal
Boxbrunn
Reichartshausen
Heppdiel
Würzberg
Neudorf
Windischbuchen
Neidhof
Winkelbg.
AMORBACH
Kaltenbrunn
Otterbach
Schneeberg
Gottersdorf
Reinhardsachsen
Watterbach
Rippberg
Gerolzahn
Breitenbuch
Kirchzell
Hambrunn
Glashofen
Neulass
Buch
Dornbach
Zittenfelden
Ottorfszell
Beuchen
Klein
Hornbach
Breitenbach
Preunschen
Gross
Hesselbach
Hettingenbeuren
WALLDÜRN
Waldleiningen
Mörschenhardt
Schöllenbach
Dumbach
Stürzenhardt
Steinbach
Hainstadt
Schlossau
Mudau
Unter
Neudorf
Kailbach
Schloss-berg
Waldauerbach
Rumpfen
BUCHEN
Eduardsthal
Langenelz
Hollerbach
Hettingen
Ober-Scheidenthal
Unter-
Oberneudorf
Reisenbach
Elzbach
Einbach
Laudenberg
Balsbach
Bödigheim
6°45' Östlich v. Paris
7°
49°30'
49°45'
Mosbach
1:250.000
Seckach
Wagner & Debes, Leipzig

ence, built in the 13-15th cent. and destroyed by Albert of Brandenburg in 1552, has been recently restored (private property). The town contains several curious timber-dwellings (*e.g.* the 'Riese' Inn) and gate-towers. — Lower down the river, on the right bank, lies the Franciscan monastery of *Engelsberg* (view), and opposite it is *Kleinheubach*, with a château and park. In the woods, to the W. of Miltenberg, are the so-called *Heunen - Säulen* ('columns of the Huns'), twelve gigantic columns of syenite, the remains of a quarry of the Roman period, which appears to have been suddenly abandoned. — From Miltenberg to *Aschaffenburg*, see *Baedeker's Southern Germany*.

47 M. **Erbach** (720 ft.; *Odenwald*, very fair; *Schützenhof; Adler*, R. & B. $1^1/_2$-$2^1/_4$, pens. 3-4 ℳ), a town with 2980 inhab., situated in the Mümling-Tal, is the principal place in the dominions of Count Erbach. The *Schloss*, rebuilt in the Renaissance style in the 16th cent. on the site of a very ancient castle, and frequently restored, contains an interesting collection of armour, fire-arms, valuable stained glass of the 13-17th cent., Greek and Etruscan vases, and other antiquities (the upper rooms, containing the antiquities, closed in winter; catalogue 50 pf.). In front of the Schloss is a statue of *Count Franz von Erbach* (d. 1823), the founder of the collections. In the chapel is a stone *Sarcophagus* of the 13th or 14th cent. which once held the remains of Eginhard (d. 840; p. 326) and his wife Emma (d. 836), brought from the church of Seligenstadt in 1810 (fee 75 pf.).

The train now crosses the Mümling and gradually ascends the E. side of the valley, high above the river. Near ($51^1/_2$ M.) *Hetzbach* (968 ft.) it traverses the *Himbächel Viaduct*, 820 ft. long and 145 ft. high. From Hetzbach a branch-line runs to. the little industrial town of *Beerfelden* (1300 ft.; Traube, R. $1^1/_2$, pens. 4 ℳ), 3 M. to the S.W., whence the picturesque *Gammelsbacher-Tal* stretches down to the Neckar. — Our line penetrates the *Krähberg* (1798 ft.) by a tunnel 2 M. long and follows the winding course of the *Itter*. $54^1/_2$ M. *Schöllenbach;* $57^1/_2$ M. *Kailbach* (Hôtel-Pension Stahl; p.328); $61^1/_2$ M. *Gaimühle* (to the Katzenbuckel $1^1/_4$ hr.: see p. 341). — 66 M. *Eberbach*, see p. 340.

42. Heidelberg and the Valley of the Neckar. Schwetzingen.

The **Railway Station** (365 ft.; *Restaurant*, very fair, D. 1 ℳ 70 pf.- 2 ℳ 20 pf.) is on the W. side of the town. The quick trains alone have through-carriages. The Neckar-Tal line has a second station at the *Karlstor;* see p. 339.

Hotels. *Near the Station:* *Hôtel de l'Europe (Pl. a), in the Leopold-Str., with a fine garden, R. 4-8, B. $1^1/_2$, D. 4, pens. 9-15 ℳ; *Grand-Hôtel (Pl. g), Rohrbacher-Str. 11, also with a fine garden, R. from 3 ℳ; *Victoria (Pl. f), Leopold-Str. 6, with veranda and garden, R. $3^1/_2$-6, B. $1^1/_4$, D. 4, pens. from 9 ℳ; Schrieder (Pl. b), at the station, with restaurant, R. 2-4, B. $1^1/_4$, pens. from 6 ℳ; Métropole-Monopol (Pl. m), Leopold-Str. 22, R. $2^1/_2$-6, B. $1^1/_4$, D. 3, pens. 6-9 ℳ. — Darmstädter Hof (Pl. i), near the Bismarck Garden, very fair, R. $2^1/_4$-$3^1/_2$, B. 1, D. $1^3/_4$-3, pens. 6-8 ℳ. — The following have beer-restaurants: *Lang (Pl. l), Rohr-bacher-Str. 13, near the station, R. 2½-3½, B. 1, D. 2½, pens. 6-7½ ℳ; Bayrischer Hof (Pl. h), Rohrbacher-Str. 2, near the station, R. 2-5, B. 1, pens. from 6 ℳ, well spoken of; Heidelberger Hof, Wrede-Platz (p. 333); Hôt. Harrer & Pens. Beau-Séjour, Leopold-Str. 32 & 39, well spoken of; Reichspost (Pl. e), next the post-office, R. 2¼-3½, B. 1 ℳ, very good.

In the Town (³/₄-1 M. from the station): *Prinz Karl (Pl. c), in the Kornmarkt (p. 334), an old-established house of the first class, R. from 3, B. 1½, D. 4, pens. from 8½ ℳ. — With beer-restaurants: Ritter (Pl. k; p. 333), R. 2½-3½, B. 1 ℳ, very fair; Badischer Hof, Haupt-Str. 113; Silberner Hirsch, in the market-place, wine from the cask, R. 1½-3, B. ³/₄ ℳ; Prinz Max, Marstall-Str., R. 1¼-2, B. ½ ℳ; Holländischer Hof *(Christliches Hospiz),* by the old bridge, R. 1½-2½, B. ³/₄ ℳ, both plain. — Hôtels Garnis: Perkeo, Haupt-Str. 75, to the W. of the Lud-wigs-Platz, R. 2-3, B. ³/₄ ℳ; Roter Hahn (see below), Haupt-Str. 44; Kaiserhof (see below), in Neuenheim, Brücken-Str. 37, R. 1½-3 ℳ.

On the Hill, behind the Castle: *Schloss-Hôtel (p. 337), command-ing a fine view, first-class, mainly frequented by foreigners, R. 4-12, B. 1½, D. 5, pens. 10-18, omn. 1½ ℳ; Bellevue, belonging to the same company, R. 3-7, B. 1¼, D. 3½, omn. 1½ ℳ, both with fine view, closed in winter; Schlosspark-Hôtel & Pension, Wolfsbrunnenweg 12, a little higher up. — *Kohlhof (p. 338), reached from the station by cab in 1¼ hr.

On the right Bank of the Neckar: Scheffelhaus (p. 339), R. 2, B. ³/₄, pens. 5½-6½ ℳ.

Pensions. *Pension Internationale & Anglaise* (English), Neuen-heim, Berg-Str. 40. In the Leopold-Str. ('Anlage'). No. 51a, *Silvana* (pens. 4-5 ℳ); No. 30, *Continentale* (pens. 5-8 ℳ); No. 24, *Flora* (pens. 4½-6½ ℳ). *Schildecker,* cor. Plöck-Str. and Theater-Str.; *Alt-Heidelberg,* Rohrbacher-Str. 29 (pens. 5-6 ℳ); *Primosole,* Gaisberg-Str., entrance from Ried-Str. (pens. 4½-7 ℳ); *Kleinecke,* Wilhelm-Str. 5; *Quisisana,* Blumen-Str. 9 (English; pens. 4-6 ℳ); *Karlstor,* Haupt-Str. 248, by the Karls-Tor (p. 334; pens. 4-5 ℳ).

Restaurants, with beer and wine. *Artushof,* in the Hotel Lang (see above); *Perkeo (see above), D. from 1¼ ℳ; *Ritter* (see above); *Roter Hahn* (see above); D. 1½ ℳ); *Kaiserhof* (see above); *Stadthalle* (p. 338); *Rodensteiner,* Haupt-Str. 118 and Sandgasse; *Luxhof,* Haupt-Str. 24; *Hohenzollern,* Haupt-Str.; *Automatic Restaurant,* Haupt-Str. 71. — **Wine Rooms.** *Goldene Gerste,* Haupt-Str. 93; *Badische Weinstube* (restaurant), Haupt-Str. 11; *Pfälzer Hof,* Haupt-Str. 127; *Goldene Sonne,* Haupt-Str. 170. — **Open-air Restaurants.** *Stadtgarten,* in the Leopold-Str., music in the evening; *Bremeneck,* in the new Schloss-Str., beside the Cable Railway; *Schloss-Restaurant (p. 337), D. 2-3 ℳ; *Schiff,* beyond the new bridge; *Waldhorn* (Scheffelhaus; see above).

Cafés. *Café Impérial,* Wrede-Platz; *Häberlein,* Leopold-Str. 35, both in the Anlage (p. 333); *Theatre Café,* Theater-Str. 2a.

Cabs (all with two horses). For a drive within the town: 1-2 pers. 1 ℳ, 3-4 pers. 1 ℳ 30 pf.; between 10 p.m. and 6 a.m. double fares; each heavy box 25 pf. — *By time:* ½ hr. for 1-2 pers.. 1 ℳ 20, for 3-4 pers., 1 ℳ 60 pf.; each addit. ¼ hr., 60, 80 pf. — To the *Castle* (direct) 1-4 pers. 2½ ℳ, there and back 4 ℳ; *Schloss-Hôtel* 3 ℳ 30 pf., there and back 4 ℳ; *Castle* and *Molkenkur* 5, there and back 6 ℳ: *Castle, Molkenkur,* and *Wolfsbrunnen* 7 or 8 ℳ; *Castle, Molkenkur,* and *Königstuhl,* 12 or 14 ℳ; *Kohlhof,* 10 or 12 ℳ.

Electric Tramway. From the Central Railway Station viâ the Bismarck-Platz, the Haupt-Str., the Kornmarkt (station of the Cable Railway), and the Karls-Tor (p. 334) to Schlierbach (p. 339); from the Schlachthaus (Slaughter House) viâ the Bergheimer-Str., Bismarck-Platz, and Neuenheim to Handschuchsheim (p. 322); from the Central Railway Station to the Cemetery (p. 339); from the Central Railway Station to Wiesloch (p. 346).

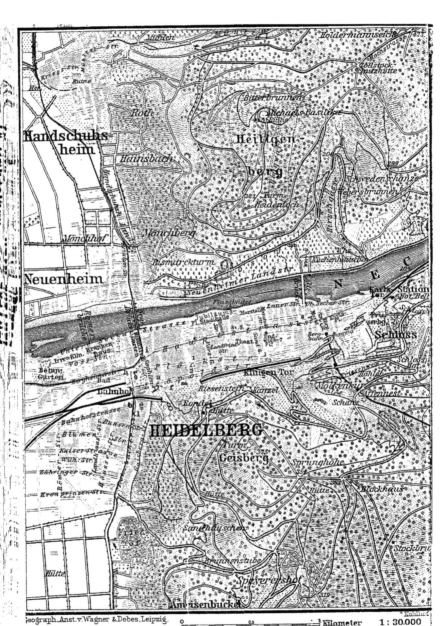

0   0.5   1 Kilometer   1 : 30.000

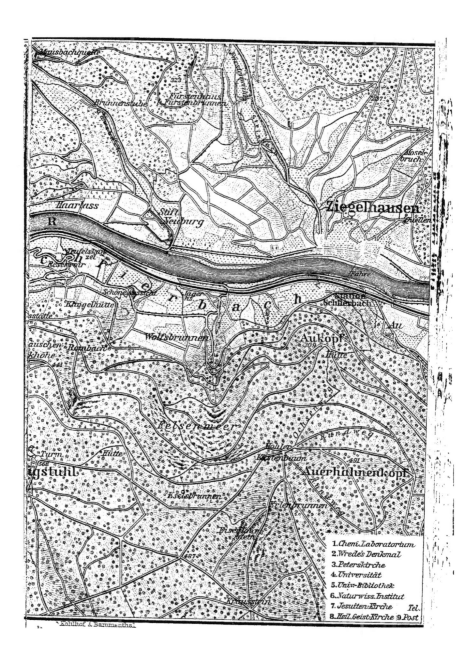

1. Chem. Laboratorium
2. Wrede's Denkmal
3. Peterskirche
4. Universität
5. Univ-Bibliothek
6. Naturwiss. Institut
7. Jesuitten-Kirche   Tel.
8. Heil.Geist-Kirche 9. Post

Cable Railway (with electric motive power) from the *Kornmarkt* (p. 334) to the *Castle* (p. 334; 35 pf., there and back 50 pf.) and to the *Molkenkur* (75 pf., there and back 1 ℳ 5 pf.), every 10 min. in 3-6 min. ; from the Molkenkur to the *Königstuhl* (p. 338), every 20 min. in 10 min. (75 pf., there and back 1 ℳ 5). As far as the castle the line runs almost wholly through a chilly tunnel.

Post and Telegraph Office (Pl. 9), opposite the station. — **Tourists' Enquiry Office** *(Verkehrsverein)*, Haupt-Str. 77, entrance from the Bienen-Str. (open on week-days 9-1 & 3-7). — **Baths.** Bergheimer-Str. 47 (swimming-baths); *River Baths*, between the bridges.

English Church, Plöck-Str. 46 (300 seats); services at 8 a.m., 11 a.m., and 5.30 p.m. Chaplain, *Rev. Dr. H. McDonald*, Werder-Str. 28.

Principal Attractions (3½-4½ hrs. ; guide unnecessary). We proceed from the rail. station through the Leopold-Str. to *St. Peter's* and by the Schloss-Str. to the *Castle* (½ hr.). Or we may take the tramway to the Kornmarkt and the cable-railway to the Castle. An inspection of the Castle takes 1 hr. We next walk (20 min.) or take the cable-railway to the *Molkenkur*. We then descend viâ the Kornmarkt (½ hr.) and the Heilig-Geist-Kirche to the *Old Neckar Bridge*, and follow the right bank to the *New Bridge*, which crosses to the station (¾ hr.). — In summer the Castle is often illuminated soon after dark; it is best seen from the right bank of the Neckar between the two bridges (cab 8 ℳ).

Heidelberg, with 50,000 inhab. (17,500 Rom. Cath.), is situated on the *Neckar*, at the point where that river debouches from the Odenwald in the plain of the Rhine. Few towns can vie with it in the beauty of its environs and its historical interest. Conrad of Hohenstaufen, who became Count Palatine of the Rhine in 1155, selected Heidelberg as his principal residence, and under him and his successors the insignificant little place soon became a town of considerable importance. The extension and completion of the castle in the 16-17th cent. is one of the high-water marks of German art; its destruction by the French in 1688-9 and 1693 reminds us of the weakness of the German Empire after the Thirty Years' War. Heidelberg continued to be the capital of the Palatinate for nearly five centuries, until Elector Charles Philip, owing to ecclesiastical differences with the Protestant citizens, transferred his seat to Mannheim in 1721. Since 1802 Heidelberg has belonged to Baden.

The old town of Heidelberg is squeezed in between the castle-hill and the Neckar, and consists mainly of the so-called *Haupt-Strasse*, a street about 1¼ M. long. The newer residential quarters are built on the W. slope of the Geisberg and in the valley, partly in the district of *Bergheim*, which, like Neuenheim (p. 338), dates back to the Roman period. In this quarter are the *Railway Station* and the *Post & Telegraph Office* (Pl. 9), opposite each other. On the river are several *Medical Institutes* and the *Botanical Garden* of the University, and lower down the river are factories.

From the *Railway Station* we may approach the Haupt-Str. (tramway, p. 330) viâ the *Bismarck-Platz*, from which the *Bismarck Garden* (with a marble bust of the chancellor by Donndorf) extends to the left to the new bridge (p. 338); or we may turn to the right and follow the Leopold-Str., with the Anlage (see p. 333).

In the Haupt-Str., to the left (No. 97), is a baroque house of
1712, containing the **Municipal Collections** *(Städtische Sammlungen;* Pl. 'St. S.'). These are open daily, 9-1 & 3-6 (from Sept.
16th to April. 30th, 10-1 & 2-4); adm. 40 pf., Sun. 20 pf.

GROUND FLOOR. Room 10 (to the right). Reproductions and casts from
the Haus zum Ritter (p. 333); in the court to the right (Rooms 14-17), and
behind to the left (Rooms 9 & 9a), Christian and Roman stone monuments.

FIRST FLOOR. The front building contains the *Palatine Section.*
Room 19. Renaissance chimney-piece (perhaps from the Otto-Heinrichs-
Bau); engraved portraits and documents of the Palatine Electors down
to Lewis V. (d. 1544). Rooms 20-21. Similar objects from the time of
Elector Otho Henry (d. 1559) to Frederick V. (d. 1632) and Charles (d. 1685);
Liselotte of Orleans (d. 1721); old printed works (Heidelberg, 1485).
Rooms 22-23. Frankental Porcelain. Room 24. Electors after 1685;
medals and coins of the Palatinate. Room 25. Weapons and armour.
— Right Wing. Rooms 26-30. *Prehistoric, Primitive, and Roman Ob-
jects*, principally from the systematic excavations in the vicinity of
Heidelberg (1898-1907). — Left Wing. Room 31. Heidelberg engravings,
broadsides, and pamphlets illustrating the history of the Palatinate.
Rooms 32-33. Ecclesiastical antiquities and paintings, including works
by Lucas Cranach the Elder and the Younger. Rooms 34-35. Posselt
Gallery, containing chiefly Netherlandish works of the 17-18th cent.; in
Room 35 also is a small cabinet of engravings in the style of Louis XVI.

SECOND FLOOR. Ante-room (37). Portraits of the later Electors.
Room 38. Grand-Dukes of Baden; works of the painters E. Fries, D.
and K. Fohr, and K. Rottmann, who were all born in or near Heidelberg
about 1800. Rooms 39 & 40. Portraits of students and professors, etc.
Rooms 41-44. Representations of *Heidelberg Castle* of earlier and later
date. Room 45. Views of *Heidelberg* and municipal antiquities.

Farther on is the LUDWIGS-PLATZ, with the University Buildings
(Pl. 4), dating from the beginning of the 18th cent., and an *Equestrian
Statue of Emperor William I.*, by Donndorf. The **University,**
the famous *Ruperto-Carola,* and after the universities of Prague
and Vienna the oldest in Germany, was founded in 1386 by Elector
Rupert I. Its period of greatest prosperity was in the latter half
of the 16th and the beginning of the 17th cent., when, under Electors Otho Henry, Frederick III., and Frederick IV., it was the
centre of 'Humanism', and the chief Reformed seat of learning in
Germany. During the stormy times of the Thirty Years' War and
the devastation of the Rhenish Palatinate by the French it survived
with difficulty. It is indebted for its modern development to Charles
Frederick of Baden, who in 1804 provided it with eminent professors
and scientific collections. The aula was restored in 1886, the five-
hundredth anniversary of the foundation of the university (apply
to the janitor).

A few steps to the S.E. of the University stands the *Jesuit
Church* (Pl.-7), a baroque structure of 1709-50, decorated with
polychrome ornamentation in 1873. To the S.W., in the Plöck-Str.,
is the *University Library* (Pl. 5), erected in a modern Renaissance
style by F. Durm in 1905.

The library contains 400,000 vols., about 4000 MSS., 3000 papyri, and
3200 ancient documents. It is open on week-days 11-1 and on Wed. also

3-5; the catalogue-room is open daily, except Sat. & Sun., 5-6. Scarcely
one-third of the MSS. in the famous Bibliotheca Palatina, which was
transferred to Rome after the capture of Heidelberg by Tilly, have been
returned. (Thirty-eight were restored in 1814, and eight hundred and
thirty-eight in 1816, including some original MSS. of Luther.) A number
of documents and MSS. (many with miniatures, including the 'Manesse'
Minnesänger MS. of the early 14th cent.) are exhibited in one room. For
admission to this and the other rooms, visitors should apply to the janitor.

Opposite the library rises the *Peters-Kirche* (Pl. 3; Prot.), originally erected at the end of the 15th cent., but rebuilt in 1865-70,
with a modern pyramidal tower, several monuments, and two paintings by Hans Thoma (in the aisles).

At the Peters-Kirche ends the Leopold-Strasse (the so-called
'Anlage'), the shady promenades of which offer to walkers a more
attractive route than the Haupt-Str. from the railway-station to
the centre of the town. It passes three monuments. In front of the
Victoria Hotel is a bust of the local poet, *K. G. Nadler* (d. 1849).
Farther on, in the Wrede-Platz, to the left of the street, adjoining
the Chemical Laboratory (Pl. 1), is a bronze *Statue of the Bavarian
Field Marshal Prince Karl von Wrede* (Pl. 2; born at Heidelberg in 1767) by Bugger (1860). Then to the right, opposite the
Märzgasse, is a bronze statue of *Robert Bunsen*, the chemist, who
taught at Heidelberg from 1852 to 1889, by H. Volz (1907). To
the right, opposite the Peters-Kirche, and on the other side of the
railway, are the *Klingen-Tor* (see also p. 338) and a bust of *Karl
Metz* (d. 1877), the founder of the German volunteer fire-brigade
system. From this point the street, known as the '*Schlossberg*',
ascends to the entrance of the Schloss-Garten at the Elisabeth-
Pforte (20 min; see p. 335).

Beyond the Ludwigs-Platz the Haupt-Str. continues to run
towards the E. In the Market Place (380 ft.) rises the Gothic
Heilig-Geist-Kirche (Pl. 8; sacristan, Augustinergasse 9), erected
at the beginning of the 15th cent. under King Rupert (see below).
In 1705 the nave was separated from the choir by a wall, in order
that the Roman Catholics might worship in the latter (now used by
the 'Old Catholics'), while the Protestants retained the nave. The
choir contains the tomb of King Rupert and his wife Elizabeth,
sister of the first Elector of Brandenburg. — Opposite the church,
to the S., is the *Gasthaus zum Ritter* (Pl. k), erected in 1592 in
the style of the Otto-Heinrichs-Bau (p. 335), almost the only house
which escaped destruction in 1693. It was judiciously restored in
1905. — Opposite the choir, on the E. side of the market-place, is
the *Rathaus* (1703), containing a new hall adorned with paintings
by Lindenschmit. — A few paces to the N., viâ the Steingasse, is
the old *Neckar Bridge* (p. 338).

The last of the side-streets to the right of the Market Place is
the *Oberbadgasse*, at the upper end of which begins the Schloss-
Strasse (p. 335), leading to the castle. — The station of the Cable

RAILWAY TO THE CASTLE (p. 331) is in the neighbouring *Kornmarkt*, beside the 'Prinz Karl' Hotel. — PEDESTRIANS cross the Kornmarkt diagonally to the right, and ascend the BURGWEG, which leads in 12 min. (long vaulted gateway near the top) to the great balcony (p. 336). A footpath diverges to the left from the Burgweg, leading along the Friesenberg. — A fourth route to the castle is to take the tramway to the E. end of the town near the *Karls-Tor* (built in 1775-81), and thence ascend the *Friesenberg* (to the right) on foot, proceeding at the top either to the left by the Karmeliter-Wäldchen, or to the right along the castle-hill.

The **Castle (640 ft.), situated on the 'Jettenbühl', a wooded spur of the Königstuhl, may possibly have been founded by *Conrad of Hohenstaufen* (d. 1195; see p. 341), but more probably by *Count Palatine Lewis I.* (1214-31). A more imposing building was erected by *Rupert III.* (1398-1410), who was elected Roman king at Rhens in 1400. The castle and the fortifications were enlarged by the electors *Frederick I.* 'the Victorious' (1449-76), and *Lewis V.* (1508-44). The palatial parts of the edifice were afterwards erected by the electors of the 16th and 17th cent., particularly *Otho Henry* (1556-59), *Frederick IV.* (1583-1610), and *Frederick V.* (1610-21), King of Bohemia (husband of Elizabeth†, daughter of James I. of England). In 1622, when Heidelberg was taken by Tilly during the Thirty Years' War, the castle escaped almost uninjured. It was afterwards restored by *Charles Lewis* (1632-80). After the death of *Charles,* the last Protestant Elector (in 1685), Louis XIV. preferred a claim to the Palatinate, and began the cruel and destructive war which involved the Castle of Heidelberg and so many others in one common ruin. On 24th Oct., 1688, the town and castle capitulated to *Count Mélac,* the French general, who spent the following winter here. On the approach of the German armies, however, he determined to evacuate the place, and on 2nd March, 1689, he caused the fortifications to be blown up. These were subsequently restored, but in 1693 the imperial commander surrendered the place to the French almost without a blow, and Marshal de Lorge completely destroyed the castle and much of the town. The *Electors Charles Philip* (1716-42) and *Charles Theodore* (1742-99) made some attempts to render the castle once more habitable; but in 1764 it was struck by lightning and finally reduced to the ruinous condition in which we see it at present. Farther decay is prevented by careful preservation and (where necessary) restoration, and visitors may help this good cause by joining the *Heidelberger Schlossverein* (annual subscription 3 ℳ).

From the terminus of the funicular railway (p. 331), at the top

---

† Her daughter Sophia was married at Heidelberg in 1658 to Ernest Augustus, afterwards Elector of Hanover, and became the mother of George I. of England.

DAS HEIDELBERGER SCHLOSS

1:2000

0 10 20 30 40 50 60 70 80 90 100

Meter

Burgweg

Stückgarten

Bосdl.

Elisabethpforte

Schlosswindend.

Karlsschanze

Dicker
Turm

Gr. Fass-
Gebäude

Garass-
Gebäude

Grosse Batterie.

Altan

Englischer
Bau

Alles
Ballenhaus

Bibliotheck-
bau

Friedrichsbau

Kapelle

Fräulzin-
Saalbau

Rupprechtsbau

Frauenzim-
merbau

Sprengthurm.

Zichbrunnen.

Oeconomie

Neuhaus

Aelu-
eckiger
Turm

Otto Heinrichs-
bau

Ludwigs-
bau

Apo-
theker-
Turm

Rückenbau

Gesprengter
Turm

Kelter.

Gr. Wartturm.

Apothekerbrunnen

Brückenhaus

Friesenberg

Koniferengarten

Musik-
Pavillon

Restauration

G r o s s e   T e r r a s s e

Grosse
Grotte

nach dem Schlosshotel

Scheffeltэrrasse

of the Schloss-Strasse (p. 333), we pass through the W. entrance
of the Castle (comp. the Plan; guide superfluous) into the Schloss-
Garten, laid out in 1808 on the ruins of the fortifications. The
paths to the left, of which the second passes through the *Elisabeth-
Pforte,* erected by Frederick V. in 1615 in honour of his consort
(see p. 334), lead to the *Stückgarten,* an old bastion, which, together
with the corner-tower, the so-called *Dicke Turm,* defended the
castle on the W. side. A tablet here commemorates the visits of
Goethe and Marianne von Willemer ('Suleika'; comp. p. 294) in 1814
and 1815. Between the Dicke Turm and the Friedrichs-Bau (p. 336)
is the plain *Englische Bau,* or *Elisabethbau,* which also was
erected by Frederick V.

We now cross the *Bridge* over the S. moat of the Castle, pass
under the *Great Watch Tower,* and enter the **Schlosshof,* or
castle-yard, the focus of the whole structure. Almost all the architectural ornamentation of the castle was lavished on the inner façades
abutting on the court, as the external walls served chiefly for purposes of defence. The irregular grouping of the buildings reveals
at once the lack of any systematic plan in their construction. This,
however, is directly responsible for the picturesqueness of the general
effect, which is farther enhanced by the clinging ivy and the verdant
trees. The two most interesting buildings are the Otto-Heinrichs-
Bau, on the E., and the Friedrichs-Bau, on the N., both constructed
of red Neckar sandstone, with sculptures and details in yellowish
sandstone from Heilbronn.

The **Otto-Heinrichs-Bau,* begun in 1556, the finest example
of the German early-Renaissance style, rises in three stories, partly
of the Ionic and partly of the Corinthian order, with a strong em-
phasis on the horizontal lines. The lower story, with the Kaiser-
saal to the left and the Elector's Rooms to the right (with columns,
consoles, portals, and a mantelpiece), is of considerable elevation.
The two upper stories, the first containing the large dining-hall,
are each not more than half as high. The top ends in two small
gables. The whole façade is richly adorned with beautiful sculptures, all recently restored. The cornice of the portal, to which a
double flight of steps ascends, is supported by male and female
figures. Above it is the bust of the founder, the Elector Otho Henry,
with armorial bearings and inscription. In the niches of the façade
are a number of statues, all having a symbolical meaning after the
fashion of the Renaissance. In the four lower niches are Joshua,
Samson, Hercules, and David; in the middle niches, allegorical
figures of Strength, Justice, Faith, Charity, and Hope; in the upper
niches, Saturn, Mars, Venus, Mercury, Diana, Apollo, and Jupiter,
or the seven gods of the planets. In the window-arches are medal-
lion-heads of eminent men of antiquity. The designer of this beautiful
building, in which Netherlandish individuality and Italian skill are

combined with German richness of form, is still uncertain. The plastic ornamentation was executed first under the superintendence of *Master Antoni*, of whom we know nothing further, and afterwards (from 1558 on) by *Alexander Colin* of Malines (b. 1526), who, however, went to Innsbruck in 1562 to work on the Monument of Emp. Maximilian.

The *Friedrichs-Bau*, erected in 1601-7 from *Joh. Schoch's* designs and restored in 1898 et seq., is an imposing building in the late-Renaissance style, and consists of three stories (Doric, Tuscan, and Ionic), surmounted by Corinthian pediments. It is simpler and less elegant in its forms than the Otto-Heinrichs-Bau, but more perspicuous in its architectonic proportions. The vertical lines are strongly emphasized, while the massive columns taper towards the top. In the niches are 16 statues of Charlemagne, Otho of Wittelsbach, and the Counts Palatine down to Frederick IV. These are replicas of the admirable originals executed by *Sebastian Götz* of Coire (1604-7). — Between the Otto-Heinrichs-Bau and the Friedrichs-Bau is the *Gläserne Saalbau* or *Neue Hof*, erected by Frederick the Wise in 1549, and showing a quaint mixture of Gothic and Renaissance forms.

A vaulted passage (at Pl. K) leads under the Friedrichs-Bau to the *Balcony*, constructed in 1610, which commands a beautiful view (the back of the Friedrichs-Bau is here seen to advantage). The footpath (*Burgweg*; p. 334) to the town begins at the base of this platform.

Adjoining the Friedrichs-Bau on the left is the so-called *Bandhaus* or *Königs-Saal*, erected by Lewis V. for the ladies of the court ('Frauenzimmer-Bau'), but afterwards altered. Farther back is the *Library* or *Archives*, usually called the *Alte Bau*, and farther on the *Ruprechts-Bau*, a simple Gothic structure erected by Rupert III., the upper part rebuilt by Lewis V. The imperial eagle with the arms of the Palatinate recall the election of Rupert to the sceptre of the Roman kingdom. Over the entrance is a garland of roses borne by two angels; the half-open pair of compasses is a sign that the building is commended to the care of the Holy Virgin.

Opposite is a covered *Draw Well* ('Ziehbrunnen'), with four columns of syenite (from the Felsberg, p. 323), which once adorned the palace of Charlemagne at Ingelheim, and were brought here by Count Palatine Lewis V.

Adjacent is the office in which tickets are issued for admission to the **Interior**: charge, 1 pers. 1, 2 pers. 1½ *M*, 3 or more pers. 50 pf. each; for the 'Great Tun' alone, each pers. 10 pf.; for the upper rooms of the Friedrichs-Bau, 50 pf. each (extra).

Visitors are first conducted to the groundfloor of the RUPRECHTS-BAU (see above), where the original sculptures of the Otto-Heinrichs-Bau and the Friedrichs-Bau are preserved; on the first floor is a fine Renaissance chimney-piece by Conrad Forster, court-sculptor to Elector Frederick II. — Thence they are led through the lower rooms of the LIBRARY and the dungeon to the casemates of the ENGLISCHE BAU (p. 335) and to the DICKE TURM (p. 335); the last should be ascended for the sake of the view. They then return to the court by the KÖNIGS-SAAL (p. 336), which has been restored for student-festivals.

In the FRIEDRICHS-BAU visitors are admitted to the Chapel and to the upper rooms (adm., see p. 336), which are architecturally interesting and have been redecorated.

To the left of the Friedrichs-Bau is the entrance to the CELLAR (Pl. K; adm., see p. 336), containing the famous *Heidelberg Tun*, a monster cask capable of holding 49,000 gallons. The present tun was constructed in 1751 by the Elector Charles Theodore, as the successor to two others, the first of which was erected in 1591 by the Count Palatine Casimir, the second by the Elector Charles Lewis in 1662 and restored by Charles Philip in 1728. By the tun stands a grotesque wooden figure of Perkeo, court-jester of Elector Charles Philip.

We next cross the court to the OTTO-HEINRICHS-BAU (p. 335; Kaisersaal), and then pass to the left into the GLÄSERNE SAALBAU and to the octagonal tower, which may be ascended (128 steps). Finally, crossing the court once more, we visit the KITCHENS ('Küchen-Bau') and the GESPRENGTE TURM (see below; fine view from the platform).

We leave the court by the Great Watch Tower, cross the moat (p. 335), and turn to the left in the garden. The *'Gesprengte Turm'* (blown-up tower), or *Kraut-Turm*, at the S.E. angle of the castle, is of masonry so solid that, when the French blew it up in 1693, one-half became detached and fell in an unbroken mass into the moat, where it still remains. The tower is 79 ft. in diameter, the walls 19 ft. thick. It was near this spot that Matthison composed his fine 'Elegie in den Ruinen eines alten Bergschlosses', an imitation of Gray's 'Elegy in a Country Churchyard'. — A few paces farther on is the *Schloss Restaurant* (p. 330; band in the afternoon).

The **Great Terrace* to the N.E., constructed in 1613, commands beautiful views of the castle itself and of the town. A *Statue of Victor von Scheffel* (1826-86) was erected here in 1891. — The plantation of coniferæ on the *Friesenberg* (p. 334), below the terrace, contains many rare trees.

Behind the terrace is the *Schloss-Hôtel* (p. 330; 735 ft.), and a little higher up is the *Hôtel Bellevue* (p. 330); fine view from the terrace.

About 1½ M. farther to the E. is the **Wolfsbrunnen** (590 ft.; *Restaurant*), once a favourite resort of Frederick V. and his wife Elizabeth, and celebrated in a sonnet of Martin Opitz, who was a student at Heidelberg in 1619. According to tradition, the enchantress Jetta was here killed by a wolf, whence the name. In the vicinity is the reservoir supplying the water for the town-aqueduct. We may then proceed, enjoying a series of pleasant views, to (1½ M.) *Schlierbach* (p. 339), and cross the Neckar to *Ziegelhausen* (p. 339), where boats are always ready to take walkers back to Heidelberg by the river.

The ROUTE TO THE MOLKENKUR (20 min.; finger-posts; railway in 3 min., see p. 331) ascends the steps opposite the Gesprengte Turm, passes through a small gate, and reaches the road which passes at the back of the castle (finger-post). We may now either ascend by the road or by the zigzag footpath. If we follow the latter, we may after a few minutes either diverge by the 'Friesenweg' to the right or continue to follow the zigzag path.

The *Molkenkur (985 ft. above the sea-level; 345 ft. above
the castle) is a restaurant (rooms also) which commands an admirable view, and is the only point from which the castle is seen
from above.

A few yards beyond the Molkenkur is the terminus of the Cable
Railway, where four roads meet (finger-post). That on the left descends
to the Schloss; the next ascends to the Wolfsbrunnen (p. 337) and
(20 min.) the *Bismarck-Höhe (1445 ft.; view-tower); the one straight on
ascends to the Königstuhl (see below), while that to the right descends to
Heidelberg, which it reaches at the *Klingentor* (p. 333). From the last,
after ½ M., a road ('Speyerershof-Weg') diverges to the left and ascends
in 5 min. to a *Bench*, commanding an excellent view of the upper part
of the town and of the Schloss. A few paces farther on is the Kanzel
('pulpit'), a small projecting platform, with a parapet, affording a survey
of Heidelberg and the plain. The Rondell (800 ft.), reached hence in
5 min., an open space in front of a covered seat, is also a charming
point of view. From the Rondell a broad path (indicated by a guide-
post 'nach dem Bahnhof') leads by the 'Sieben-Linden' and the Wolfs-
höhle to Heidelberg, emerging at the Victoria Hotel. — Immediately
beyond the Rondell is a footpath ascending to the top of the (20 min.)
*Geisberg (1230 ft.), the tower on which commands one of the finest
views near Heidelberg. — About 1 M. from the Geisberg is the *Speyerers-
hof* (965 ft.; inn), a favourite point for a walk. Thence to the Heidelberg
station about 1¾ M.

The Königstuhl (1865 ft.; restaurant) is reached from the Molkenkur by a shady path ('Plättlesweg') in ¾ hr., or by the carriage-road in
1 hr. Mountain-railway (Bergbahn), see p. 331 (runs in winter also). Adjacent is the Rodelbahn or Toboggan Slide. The tower on the top,
95 ft. in height (lift), commands a view extending to the Merkur at Baden.
— About 1 M. to the S. of the Königstuhl, beyond the new University
Observatory, is the Kohlhof (1580 ft.; *Hotel, with 100 beds, baths,
electric light, etc., R. 2-4, B. 1, D. 3, S. 2, pens. 6-12 ℳ), a health-resort
with pleasant shady promenades. The tower at the *Posseltslust* (1580 ft.),
7 min. to the S.W., commands a good view.

The Old Bridge over the Neckar (see p. 333), constructed
by Elector Charles Theodore in 1786-88, is embellished with a
statue of the Elector and allegorical groups at each end. About
1300 yds. lower down is the handsome New Bridge, erected in
1877 (electric tramway, see pp. 330, 331). Both bridges command
beautiful views. Between the two bridges, on the left bank, is the
Stadthalle, a large hall with a restaurant.

On the right bank of the Neckar are the Neuenheim Road, with
many villas, and the suburb of *Neuenheim* (Schiff, with garden),
near the New Bridge. The first road beyond the latter ascends to
the right to the Philosophenweg, a beautiful walk extending
along the slope of the *Heiligenberg*, and commanding a splendid
view of the town and of the plain of the Rhine as far as the Haardt
Mts. The pleasantest way back is through the small lateral valley
of the *Hirschgasse*, past the well-known students' tavern and duel-
ling-place of that name (1 hr. in all; mostly without shade).

Those who have time should not fail to ascend from the Philosophenweg (beyond the quarry to the left), passing the Bismarck
Tower (1903), to the (¾ hr.) *Heiligenberg, the ancient *Mons*

Piri, encompassed by a double girdle-wall of stone, dating from the prehistoric era. On the S. summit (1250 ft.) is a view-tower, commanding an admirable survey of Heidelberg, the Castle, the valley of the Neckar, and the Bergstrasse. Adjacent is the *Heidenloch,* an old cistern. On the N. summit (1455 ft.), 10 min. farther on, are the remains of the Romanesque *Abbey Church of St. Michael* (12th cent.) and the foundations of an earlier church established about 880. We descend through the Siebenmühlen-Tal to Handschuchsheim (see p. 322); or we may follow the white way-marks, pass the Zollstock, and reach (1¹/₄ hr.) the tower and the *Weisse Stein* (1805 ft.).

The road ascending the river to Ziegelhausen passes the restaurant *Waldhorn* (p. 330), which affords an admirable view of the castle. — Farther on, 1¹/₂ M. from the Old Bridge, is the convent (secularized) of *Neuburg* (Stiftsmühle Restaurant). Beyond it is the village of *Ziegelhausen* (comp. p. 337; Adler, very fair), a favourite resort of the Heidelbergers (ferry over the Neckar, 2 pf.).

The Heidelberg **Cemetery,** on the slope of the Geisberg (p. 338), to the S. of the railway-station, contains the tombs of Gervinus (d. 1871), Bluntschli (d. 1881), and other eminent professors. At the S. end is a *Crematorium.* — Tramway, see p. 330.

The Valley of the Neckar from Heidelberg to Neckarelz.

RAILWAY TO NECKARELZ, 31¹/₂ M., in 1-1¹/₂ hr. (fares 4 ℳ, 2 ℳ 50, 1 ℳ 65 pf.; express fares 4 ℳ 50, 3 ℳ, 1 ℳ 90 pf.). — Besides the ordinary trains, there are in summer eight (on Sun. fourteen) local trains every day to *Neckargemünd* (fares 10-20 pf.; tickets obtained in the train), calling at *Karlstor, Jägerhaus, Schlierbach,* and *Kümmelbacher Hof* (fine view). — When the state of the Neckar permits, a STEAMBOAT plies once or twice daily from Heidelberg to *Neckarsteinach* (up 2 hrs., down 1 hr.); fares 1 ℳ, 60 pf. On Friday it goes on to (13 hrs.) Heilbronn.

The train passes from the main railway-station to (2 M.) the *Karlstor Station* by a long tunnel under the castle-hill. The abbey of *Neuburg* and the village of *Ziegelhausen* (see above) are seen to the left, on the right bank of the river. — 3³/₄ M. *Schlierbach* (Restaurant and Pension Völker; tramway to Heidelberg, see p. 320).

6 M. **Neckargemünd** (405 ft.; *Pfalz,* with garden on the Neckar, R. 2-3, B. ³/₄, pens. 4¹/₂-6 ℳ; *Hirsch,* R. 1¹/₂-2, pens. 3-4¹/₂ ℳ; *Menzer's Greek Wine Room*), a pleasant little town with 2200 inhab., at the point where the Neckar is joined by the *Elsenz,* the valley of which is ascended by a railway to Neckarelz viâ Meckesheim (see p. 341). Walks may be taken to the *Bockfelsen,* the *Tilly-Stein,* and the castle of *Reichenstein.*

The Neckartal Railway crosses the Neckar, penetrates a tunnel leading into the valley of *Schönau,* and reaches —

10 M. **Neckarsteinach** (420 ft.; *Harfe,* with garden on the river, R. & B. from 2³/₄, pens. from 4¹/₂ ℳ; *Schiff,* R. 1¹/₄-1¹/₂ ℳ, B. 60 pf., pens. 3¹/₂-4 ℳ, with a terrace; *Schwalbennest,* opposite

the station, R. $1^1/_2$, pens. 4 ℳ), a small town with 1600 inhab., in a highly picturesque situation, once the seat of the valiant race of the Steinachs, who became extinct in 1653. The church contains numerous monuments of the family, several of whom bore the surname of Landschaden ('land-scourge'), perhaps from the perpetual feuds in which they were engaged. The four old castles still bear testimony to their power. A path leads viâ the *Vorderburg*, the *Mittelburg* (restored in the mediæval style and surrounded with a park by its present proprietor, Baron von Dorth), and the *Hinterburg*, to ($^1/_2$ hr.) *Burg Schadeck*, or the *'Swallow's Nest'*, which frowns above a lofty precipice. A good view of the pleasing valley of the Neckar is obtained from the tower. A pleasant walk from the Swallow's Nest follows the 'Mittlere Bergweg' to ($^3/_4$ hr.) Neckargemünd.

In the *Steinach-Tal*, 3 M. above Neckarsteinach, lies **Schönau** (585 ft.; *Löwe;* 2000 inhab.), with the ruins of a Cistercian convent, founded in 1136. The old refectory is now the Protestant church. — From Schönau to Waldmichelbach, see p. 326.

On the left bank of the Neckar, on a wooded eminence, rises the castle of *Dilsberg* (1090 ft.), unsuccessfully besieged by Tilly during the Thirty Years' War. At the beginning of the 19th century it was used as a state-prison, particularly for Heidelberg students, and the rigour of the confinement is shown by the story that one day when some strangers, visiting the castle, desired to see the cells, they were told by the officer in command that he could not oblige them, as the prisoners were then making a tour in the Odenwald and had taken the keys with them.

$12^1/_2$ M. *Neckarhausen.* — 14 M. **Hirschhorn** (430 ft.; *Zum Naturalisten*, R. $1^1/_2$-2, B. $^3/_4$, pens. 4-5 ℳ; *Erbach-Fürstenauer Hof*), a small town with 2200 inhab., the most picturesque point in the lower valley of the Neckar. Above the town ($^1/_4$ hr.) and connected with it by walls is the handsome and loftly-situated old *Castle* of the once powerful, but now extinct barons of Hirschhorn or Hirzborn. The interior (remodelled in 1583-86) contains remains of Gothic windows and some old frescoes (13th cent.?). A path with steps descends to the Gothic church of a monastery erected by the Hirschhorns in 1406, containing eight monuments of the 15-16th centuries. The *Ersheimer Kapelle*, rising above the river on the left bank (ferry), a late-Gothic building of 1517, also contains monuments of the Hirschhorns. — Two tunnels are passed through.

$19^1/_2$ M. **Eberbach** (430 ft.; *Bohrmann's Hôtel zur Krone*, R. $1^3/_4$-3, B. $^3/_4$, pens. $4^1/_4$-$5^1/_2$ ℳ; *Leininger Hof*, R. $1^1/_2$-$2^1/_2$, B. $^3/_4$, pens. 4-$4^1/_2$ ℳ, these two very fair, with gardens; *Rail. Restaurant*), an old town with 6100 inhab., belonging to the Prince of Leininingen and carrying on a brisk trade in timber. The Neckar is here crossed by a bridge. The old *Castle*, above the town, has been restored. Pleasant wood-walks in the vicinity. — From this

point we may in 2 hrs. (finger-posts) ascend the **Katzenbuckel**
(2055 ft.), the highest of the Odenwald Mts., either viâ *Burghalde-
Emichsburg* or (somewhat longer) viâ *Waldkatzenbach* (Adler).
The mountain is composed of sandstone, through which diorite
protrudes at the top. The tower commands a fine view of the valley
of the Neckar, Wurtemberg as far as the Swabian Alb, and the
Black Forest. We may descend to *Zwingenberg* (see below) in
1³/₄ hr. — Railway to Erbach, Höchst, and Darmstadt (or Frankfort), see R. 41b.

Beyond Eberbach the train passes *Stolzeneck,* on the left bank,
the ruins of a castle of the 13th century. — 25¹/₂ M. **Zwingenberg** (480 ft.; *Schiff,* an old hostelry, R. 1-1¹/₂, pens. 3-4 ℳ), on
the right bank, lying close to the river, is commanded by a picturesque castle of the Grand-Duke of Baden, which was rebuilt in
1594-95, and has lately been restored and rendered habitable. Five
of the eight towers are still preserved. The chapel contains some
mediæval wall-paintings. The Katzenbuckel may also be ascended
hence (2¹/₂ hrs.), the best route leading through the romantic *Wolfsschlucht,* behind the castle.

27¹/₄ M. *Neckargerach* (Krone), on the left bank. On the hill
above are the ruins of the *Minneburg,* which was destroyed in the
Thirty Years' War. The valley now expands. On the left bank is
the *Reiherhalde,* so called from the flocks of herons (Reiher) which
have established themselves here. A little above *Obrigheim,* on
the left bank, is the ruin of *Dauchstein.* At *Diedesheim* the river
is crossed by a bridge-of-boats. Near (28 M.) *Binau* the train passes
through a tunnel ¹/₂ M. in length.

31¹/₂ M. **Neckarelz** (505 ft.; *Klingenburg,* very fair, R. 1¹/₂-
2¹/₂, B. ³/₄, pens. 5-6 ℳ; *Löwe; Rail. Restaurant*), on the right
bank, at the influx of the *Elz* into the Neckar, contains a late-Gothic
lodge of the Templars. Opposite the town rises the *Neuburg.*

Neckarelz is the junction for the MECKESHEIM AND NECKARGEMÜND
LINE (comp. p. 339), by which we may return to *Heidelberg* (32 M., in 2 hrs.).

From Neckarelz to Würzburg and to Heilbronn viâ Jagstfeld, see
Baedeker's Southern Germany.

FROM HEIDELBERG TO SPEYER, 16 M., railway in 1¹/₄ hr. (fares
1 ℳ 50, 70 pf.). — 3 M. *Eppelheim;* 4¹/₂ M. *Plankstadt.*

5¹/₂ M. **Schwetzingen** *(Hôtel Hassler,* at the station, R. 1¹/₂-
2¹/₂, B. ³/₄, D. 2 ℳ; *Hirsch; Adler),* a pleasant little town with
6800 inhab., attracts numerous visitors from Heidelberg. The
Schloss (¹/₄ hr. from the station), erected by Elector Charles Lewis
in 1656, and destroyed by Mélac in 1689, but afterwards restored,
was the residence of the electors at the beginning of the 18th century. The gardens (117 acres) were laid out by Elector Charles
Theodore in the middle of the 18th cent. in the style of the grounds
at Versailles and embellished with statues, temples, artificial ruins,

a mosque with lofty minarets, and other objects in the taste of the period. In 1775 the beautiful old avenues were surrounded with grounds in the English style. The fountains play daily from the middle of April to the middle of October. A walk round the whole of the gardens takes about two hours ('Guide', 50 pf., at the entrance). — *Hebel*, the poet (p. 432), is buried in the old churchyard.

. Schwetzingen is the junction of the Speyer line with that from Mannheim to Carlsruhe (p. 346), and of a branch to Friedrichsfeld (p. 322). All the express-trains of the Cologne and Bâle line stop here. — The Speyer line passes (10 M.) *Thalhaus* and crosses the Rhine by a bridge of iron pontoons near (13 M.) *Altlussheim.*

Speyer, see p. 468. The *Rhine Station* (14 M.) is near the cathedral; the *Principal Station* (16 M.) is reached in 10 min. more.

43. Mannheim and Ludwigshafen.

Railway Stations. The *Central Station* (restaurant) lies on the S. side of the town (Pl. D, 5). A second station for the line to Lampertheim and Frankfort or Mayence (R. 40a), and the stations for the steamtramways to Weinheim (p. 321), Heidelberg (p. 329) and Feudenheim lie near the Neckar Bridge (Pl. D, 2).

Hotels. *Park Hotel (Pl. p.; D, 5), Friedrichs-Platz, R. 3½-6, B. 1¼, D. 3½ ℳ; *Pfälzer Hof (Pl. a; C, 4), Parade-Platz, a long-established house, also of the first class, R. 3-5, B. 1¼, D. 3½ ℳ. — National (Pl. e; D, 5), Lehn, both at the Central Railway Station; Victoria, O 6, No. 7; *Deutscher Hof (Pl. c; C, 4), R. 2-3½, B. 1 ℳ; Kaiserhof (Pl. d; D, 4), these two commercial.

Restaurants. *Arkadenhof, Fürstenberg,* both in the Friedrichs-Platz (Pl. D, E, 4, 5), near the Festhalle; *Festhalle* (p. 345); *Kaiser-Ring, Friedrichshof,* L 15, Nos. 12 & 15, at the Railway Station; *Weinberg,* D 5, No. 4 (Pl. C, 4), *Thomasbräu,* P 3, No. 14 (Pl. D, 4), in the centre of the town; *Leinweber* (wine), D 5, No. 2 (Pl. C, 4); restaurant in the *Stadt-Park* (military music on summer afternoons). — Cafés. *Central,* P 5, No. 1; *Bristol,* D 2, No. 4; *Börse,* E 4, No. 12.

Cabs. *From the Station to the Town:* 1 pers. 80 pf., 2 pers. 1 ℳ, 3 pers. 1 ℳ 20, 4 pers. 1 ℳ 40 pf. — *By time:* per ½ hr., for 1-2 pers. 1½, 3 or more pers. 2 ℳ; per hr. 2 or 2½ ℳ, etc. By night half as much again. *Luggage:* 22-55 lbs., 20 pf.; 56-110 lbs., 30 pf.; over 110 lbs., 40 pf. — Taximeter Cabs: 1-2 pers., for 600 m. 80 pf., every 200 m. more 10 pf., and so on. Fares at night 50 per cent. higher.

Electric Tramways. From the Central Railway Station (Pl. D, 5) round the N. side of the inner town, and to the station at Ludwigshafen (Pl. A, 4); from the Waldhof (to the N. of the Neckar-Gärten, Pl. C, 1) to Ludwigshafen (Aniline Factory, Hemshof, Friesenheim; Pl. A, 4); from the Gontard-Platz (Pl. C, D, 6) to Käfertal (Pl. F, 2); from the Jungbusch quarter (Pl. B, C, 2, 3) to the Slaughter House (Pl. F, 6); from the Rhein-Str. (Pl. B, 3) to Neckarau (Pl. E, 6).

Steam Ferry (Pl. B, 5) to Ludwigshafen, every 5 minutes.

Steamboat (p. xv). The landing-place (Pl. B, 5) is below the bridge over the Rhine. Steamboat to Mayence, viâ Worms, in 4 hrs.

Theatres. *Hof-Theater* (p. 344); *Festhalle* (p. 345; comedy & operettas); *Apollo Theatre,* G 6, No. 3 (Pl. C, 3); *Saalbau,* N 7, No. 7 (Pl. D, 4), these two for vaudeville.

Tourists' Enquiry Office, in the Kaufhaus (Pl. 10), Bogen 57.

Post Office (Pl. C, 4), Parade-Platz; another office at the Central Station.

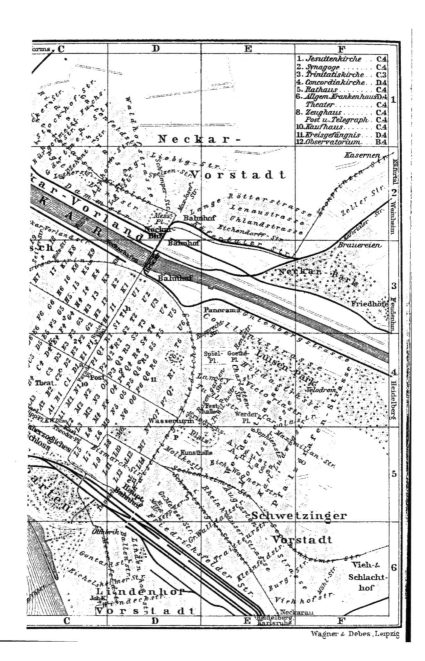

Wagner & Debes, Leipzig

British Consul, *Dr. Paul Ladenburg.* — **American Consul,** *Samuel II. Shank, Esq.*

Rhine Baths, above the bridge.

Mannheim (310 ft.), a town with 200,000 inhab., situated on the right bank of the Rhine, near the confluence of the Neckar and connected by a bridge with *Ludwigshafen* (p. 345), was founded in 1606 by Elector Palatine Frederick IV. The castle he then built was destroyed along with the infant town in the Thirty Years' War, and again by the French in 1689. When, owing to ecclesiastical differences, Elector Charles Philip (1716-42) transferred his residence from Heidelberg to Mannheim in 1720, the latter enjoyed a period of prosperity that lasted until Charles Theodore (1742-99), the next elector, in his turn removed the court to Munich in 1778. Since 1802 Mannheim has belonged to Baden. For its more recent importance Mannheim is indebted to the development of the Rhine navigation, of which it is the terminus, and of the railways. It is now the most important commercial town of the Upper Rhine, coal, grain, petroleum, rice, and coffee being the staple commodities. A considerable manufacturing industry (chemicals, machinery, etc.) has also sprung up. — Mannheim is the most regularly built town in Germany, being divided into 136 square sections like a chess-board. The blocks of houses are distinguished by letters and numerals, only those outside the Ring-Strasse being named.

The **Grand-Ducal Palace** (Pl. C, 4, 5), a spacious building in the baroque style, was erected in 1720-29 and 1749-60 and thoroughly restored in 1896-1903. It contains three courts and has a façade 656 ft. long. In the central court are a handsome *Monument to Emp. William I.*, by Eberlein (1894), and two *Monumental Fountains* by the same sculptor (1898), representing the Rheingold and the legend of the Rhine. In front of the E. and W. wings are bronze statues of *Charles Frederick* of Baden (1728-1811) and *Charles Lewis* of the Palatinate (1617-1680), both by Johann Hoffart (1907). The *Interior of the palace is adorned with fine plaster-work and tapestry. Besides the apartments of the Grand-Duke the castle contains also several collections. The Collection of Antiquities and Casts is open free in summer on Sun., 11-1 and 3-5; the Cabinet of Natural History on Sun., 11-1 and 3-5, and on Wed., 3-4; the Picture Gallery on Sun. & Wed., 11-1 and 2-4 (in winter in the afternoon only); at other times for a fee of $^1/_2$-1 $\mathcal{M}$.

The central structure (entr. in the S. angle of the court) contains the **Antiquarian Collections.** — VESTIBULE. Mediæval sculptures in stone; arms of the 17-19th centuries. — ROOM I. Vases, terracottas, bronzes, marble sculptures, cinerary urns from Greece and Italy. — ROOM II. Vases; Germanic antiquities (chiefly from the district of the Palatinate) of pre-Roman, Roman, and early-Germanic origin. — ROOM III. Stone monuments of the Roman period. — We return through the entrance-hall to ROOM IV, which contains the recent acquisitions. — ROOM V. Costumes; porcelain. — ROOM VI. Etchings, medals, documents, and so on. — ROOM VII. Ethnographical collection.

The E. wing (entrance in the court, near the monument) contains a **Collection of Casts,** after the antique. — In the same wing (entr. from the Karl-Theodor-Platz) is the **Natural History Cabinet,** in six rooms in the baroque style.

On the upper floor of the E. wing are the **Public Library** (11-1; 60,000 Vols.), in a fine hall, richly decorated in the rococo style, and the **Grand-Ducal Picture Gallery,** founded in 1803 with the collection (catalogue 50 pf.) of Charles Frederick. At the end of the corridor we turn to the left into the Gallery. Rooms VI. and VII. Early German works (Birth and Death of the Virgin, two altar-wings by *M. Wolgemut?*) and examples of a more modern period (including landscapes by *F. Kobell;* d. 1799). — Rooms IV. and V. Italian works of the 17-18th cent. and landscapes by *Gaspard* and *Nicolas Poussin.* — Rooms I-III. A few good paintings of the Netherlandish Schools, including examples of *A. van Ostade, S. van Ruysdael, Phil.* and *Pieter Wouverman, Rubens* (*Isabella Brant, his first wife), *D. Teniers the Younger,* and *Snyders.*

Opposite the central court, L 1, No. 1 (Pl. C, 4), is the **Museum of Local History** *(Stadtgeschichtliches Museum),* open free on Sun. and Wed. 3-5 (in winter 2-4); at other times, 1-2 pers. 1 *M.*

The *Palace Garden* (Pl. B, C, 4, 5), the *Städtische Anlagen,* and the *Town Park* (Pl. B, 4) are pleasant resorts.

The *Theatre* (Pl. C, 4) was built in 1776-79. Schiller's first pieces, the 'Robbers', 'Fiesco', and 'Cabal and Love', were performed here with the coöperation of Iffland and partly under his own direction (1782-84). *Schiller's Monument,* by Cauer, in front of the theatre, was erected in 1862. Adjacent, on the right and left, are statues of *Iffland* (d. 1814), a distinguished actor and poet who began his career at Mannheim, and *Von Dalberg* (d. 1806), intendant of the theatre in 1779-1803, both by Widnmann. — The *Church of the Jesuits* (Pl. 1; C, 4), with an elaborately adorned façade, was built in 1733-56. The former *Zeughaus* or *Arsenal* (Pl. 8; C, 4) was built in 1777-78. In front of it is a bronze statue of *Moltke,* by Uphues (1902). Adjacent is the large *Kurfürst-Friedrich-Schule* (1904-6). In the Parade-Platz (Pl. C, 4) is the *Rathaus* (Pl. 10), built in 1736-46 as a 'Kaufhaus' and remodelled in 1903-10. In the same square is a curious monument by Grupello (p. 29), representing 'Time's Changes' (1741); the fountain-figures are by Hoffart (1894). — In the Speise-Markt (Pl. C, 3, 4) is a monument of 1771, referring to the foundation of Mannheim. — By the old Rhein-Tor is a *War Monument,* by Volz (1896). — In the Kaiser-Ring, near the Central Station, is a *Bismarck Monument* by Hundrieser (1900). Farther to the N., at the beginning of the E. extension of the town, is the *Water Tower (Wasserturm;* Pl. D 4), behind which is the attractive Friedrichs-Platz (Pl. D, E, 4, 5), with its handsome buildings. To the right stands the *Städtische Kunsthalle* (Pl. D, 5; entrance in the Moltke-Str.), designed by H. Billing (1907) and accommodating the MUNICIPAL PICTURE GALLERY (open free on Tues., Wed., Frid., and Sat. 10-1 & 2-4, on Sun. 11-1 & 2-4, at other times for a fee of 50 pf.). It contains a number of good modern pictures by A. and O. Achenbach, E. Aman-Jean,

Courbet, Daumier, Dill, Feuerbach, Géricault, Hoelzel, Lavery, Leubach, Ed. Manet (*Execution of Emp. Maximilian of Mexico), Spitzweg, Thoma, Trübner, and others. The Kunsthalle also accommodates the periodical exhibitions of the Kunstverein. — To the left of the Friedrichs-Platz is the *Städische Festhalle* (Pl. E, 4), called the Rose Garden, erected in 1899-1903 in the modern baroque style by Prof. Bruno Schmitz; it contains the huge Nibelungen-Saal, with a frieze in relief representing the legend of Siegfried, and the smaller, richly adorned Musen-Saal (adm. on week-days 2-4, Sun. 1-2, 50 pf., at other times 1 *ℳ* each). — The Ring-Str. leads hence to the N., passing Moest's monument to the statesman *A. Lamey* (1816-96), to the *Panorama* (Pl. E, 3; 50 pf.). This stands close to the Neckar, which is spanned a little to the W. by the *Friedrichs-Brücke* (Pl. D, 3), constructed in 1890-91.

The spacious **Harbours* (Pl. A, B, 4, 3, 2, 1), at the mouth of the Neckar below the town, have been greatly extended since 1897 and now cover an area of 240 acres. They are admirably equipped with the docks, warehouses, railway connections, and so forth, that are required to deal with the important trade of the town (p. 343). The most important of the series is the *Mühlau-Hafen* (Pl. A, 1-3), opening off the Rhine and connected with the Neckar by a canal. No less than 6,810,000 tons of freight were handled at Mannheim Harbour in 1907. A motor-boat, starting from the Rhein-Brücke (see below) and the Friedrichs-Brücke (see above), makes a circuit of the harbours twice daily (fare 90 pf.).

The **Rhine Bridge** (Pl. B, 5), built in 1865-68, and a steam-ferry connect Mannheim with Ludwigshafen. The former, used by the railway, tramway, and foot-passengers, has handsome portals designed by *Durm* and adorned with groups of figures by *Moest*.

Ludwigshafen. — RAILWAY STATION, near the Rhine (Pl. A, 4); trains to *Neustadt*, etc., see p. 463; to *Worms*, see pp. 448, 447; to *Speyer*, see p. 472. Passengers to or from Mannheim change carriages.

HOTELS. *Deutsches Haus*, cor. of Ludwigs-Str. and Kaiser-Wilhelm-Str., R. 2½-3½, B. 1, D. 2½ *ℳ*; *Pfälzer Hof*.

RESTAURANTS. *Gesellschaftshaus*, opposite the Roman Catholic Church, with garden and baths; *Hein's Brewery*, Kaiser-Wilhelm-Strasse.

Ludwigshafen, an important commercial and manufacturing town with 90,000 inhab., belonging to Bavaria and begun in 1843, was originally only the *tête-de-pont* of Mannheim. The new churches, in the Romanesque and Gothic style, are well worthy of inspection. The former (Rom. Cath.) contains frescoes by Süssmeier. At the rail. station is a monumental fountain. — Above the town is the Luitpold Harbour, opened in 1897. — Branch-line to (8 M.) *Dannstadt*.

FROM LUDWIGSHAFEN TO GROSSKARLBACH, 14½ M., railway in 2-2¾ hrs. Stations: *Friesenheim* (tramway, see p. 342), *Oppau, Edigheim, Frankental* (p. 447), *Hessheim, Heuchelheim, Dirmstein, Laumersheim*.

44. From Mannheim to Röschwoog (Strass-burg, Metz) viâ Schwetzingen, Carlsruhe, and Rastatt.

61¹/₂ M. RAILWAY. To (38 M.) *Carlsruhe* in ³/₄-1³/₄ hr. (fares 4 *M* 70, 3 *M*, 1 *M* 95 pf.; express fares 5 *M* 20, 3 *M* 50, 2 *M* 20 pf.).

The line, known as the *Rhine Valley Railway ('Rheintal-Linie')*, is somewhat uninteresting. Immediately after leaving Mannheim, and again at Schwetzingen, we see on the left the mountains near Heidelberg. 2 M. *Neckarau*, an industrial suburb of Mannheim; 5 M. *Rheinau*, with a large harbour.

8¹/₂ M. *Schwetzingen*, see p. 341.

The line now traverses pine-forests; on the right the Palatinate Mountains are visible nearly the whole way. — Beyond (13¹/₂ M.) *Hockenheim* we catch sight of Speyer Cathedral, across the Rhine. 15 M. *Neulussheim;* 19¹/₂ M. *Waghäusel*, where the Baden insurgents were signally defeated in 1849; 20¹/₂ M. *Wiesental.*

25 M. *Graben-Neudorf*, junction of the Bruchsal and Germersheim railway (p. 347), is connected with Carlsruhe by a local line also. — 28¹/₂ M. *Friedrichstal;* 31 M. *Blankenloch;* 34 M. *Hagsfeld.*

38 M. *Carlsruhe* (p. 347). The train enters the station from the E.

The 'Strategic Railway' from Carlsruhe to Rastatt and Röschwoog was opened in 1895. — To the left rise the mountains of the Black Forest. — 46 M. *Durmersheim* (p. 348); 48 M. *Bietigheim;* 49¹/₄ M. *Oetigheim.*

52 M. *Rastatt*, see p. 355.

Beyond the bridge over the Murg (p. 355) the strategic line diverges to the right from the main line. 56 M. *Wintersdorf.* We cross the Rhine by a bridge 640 yds. long. 59¹/₂ M. *Roppenheim.*

61¹/₂ M. *Röschwoog*, see p. 472.

45. From Heidelberg to Carlsruhe.

33¹/₂ M. RAILWAY in ³/₄-1¹/₂ hr. (fares 4 *M* 30, 2 *M* 70, 1 *M* 75 pf.; express fares 4 *M* 80, 3 *M* 20 pf., 2 *M*).

Heidelberg, see p. 329. 2¹/₂ M. *Kirchheim;* 3¹/₂ M. *Leimen;* 5 M. *St. Ilgen;* 6³/₄ M. *Walldorf-Nussloch.* 8 M. *Wiesloch*, junction for local railways to Meckesheim (12 M.; p. 341) and Waldangelloch (10 M.). The village is ³/₄ M. from the line. — 12 M. *Roth-Malsch;* 13¹/₂ M. *Mingolsheim.* On the right is *Kislau*, formerly a hunting-seat of the Prince-Bishops of Speyer, and now a penitentiary.

15 M. **Langenbrücken** (360 ft.; Ochs; Sonne), a small village with sulphur-baths (Amalienbad); 17¹/₂ M. *Ubstadt.*

20¹/₂ M. **Bruchsal.** — HOTELS. *Bahn-Hôtel Friedrichshof*, with garden-restaurant, R. 2-6 *M; Keller*, R. 2-3, B. ³/₄ *M*, these two near the station; *Post*, Kaiser-Str., with wine-restaurant, very fair. — RESTAU-RANTS. **Railway Restaurant*, at the back of the station; *Hohenegger*, with garden. — *Local Railways* to several places in the environs.

Bruchsal (370 ft.), a town with 14,900 inhab., was once the residence of the Bishops of Speyer. Turning to the left from the station, we follow the Bahnhof-Str. to the right and then the Schloss-Str. to the left and in ¹/₄ hr. reach the **Schloss*, built in 1722-70 (restored in 1904) by J. B. Neumann (architect of the Würzburg Palace), with a fine staircase, state apartments in the most elegant rococo style (shown for a gratuity), adorned with stucco-ornamentation by J. M. Feichtmayer and frescoes and oil-paintings by Zick (1754), and an old garden. The *Church of St. Peter* contains the burial-vault of the last bishops. — Bruchsal is the junction for the Wurtemberg line; comp. *Baedeker's Southern Germany*.

FROM BRUCHSAL TO GERMERSHEIM, 16 M., railway in ³/₄-1¹/₂ hr. Sta-tions: 2¹/₂ M. *Karlsdorf;* 5¹/₂ M. *Graben-Neudorf* (p. 346); 8¹/₂ M. *Hutten-heim;* 11 M. *Philippsburg*, once an imperial fortress, but razed by the French in 1800; 13 M. *Rheinsheim*. The train then crosses the Rhine. — 16 M. *Germersheim*, see p. 472.

On the Michaelsberg, near (23¹/₂ M.) *Unter-Grombach*, stands the old *Michaels-Kapelle* (855 ft.; restaurant and view). On a hill near (26 M.) *Weingarten* rises the tower of the ruin of *Schmalenstein*.

31 M. **Durlach** (380 ft.; *Karlsburg; Friedrichshof; Amalien-bad*, ¹/₄ M. from the station), a small town with 12,000 inhab., the residence of the Margraves of Baden-Durlach from 1565 to 1715, was almost entirely burned down by the French in 1688. The *Turmberg* (840 ft.; cable-railway to the summit 25 pf., up & down 30 pf.) commands a splendid view.

From Durlach to *Pforzheim* and *Wildbad*, see R. 54a.

33¹/₂ M. *Carlsruhe*.

46. Carlsruhe.

The RAILWAY STATION (Pl. E, 3; restaurant) is on the S. side of the town. On the W. side of the town there is a small station ('Mühl-burger Tor'; Pl. B, 2) for the trains to Maxau (p. 354) and the local trains to Leopoldshafen and Graben-Neudorf (p. 346). A new main station is being built to the S. of the Lauterberg (Pl. D, 5).

Hotels. *Near the Station:* *GERMANIA (Pl. a; D, 3), at the corner of the Krieg-Str. and Karl-Friedrich-Str., B. 1¹/₄, D. at 1 p.m. 4, pens. from 9¹/₂ *M;* *VICTORIA (Pl. i; E, 3), Krieg-Str. 22, R. 2¹/₂-6, B. 1, D. 2-4, pens. 6¹/₂-10 *M;* MONOPOL (Pl. m; E, 3), with beer-restaurant; FRIEDRICHS-HOF (Pl. e; D, 3), Karl-Friedrich-Str. 7, with wine and beer rooms, very fair, R. & B. 2³/₄-3¹/₂), D. 1¹/₂-2¹/₂ *M;* HÔTEL LUTZ (Pl. l; E, 3), R. 2-3, B. ³/₄, D. 1¹/₂-2¹/₂ *M;* GRÜNER HOF (Pl. d; E, 3), very good; NATIONAL (Pl. n; E, 3); KYFFHÄUSER (Pl. o; D, E, 3), Kreuz-Str. 19. — *In the Town:* *HÔTEL GROSSE (Pl. c; D, 2), in the Markt-Platz, R. 2¹/₂-6, B. 1¹/₄, D. 3, pens. 7-10 *M;* *ERBPRINZ (Pl. b; D, 2), Kaiser-Str. 90a, with Vienna café. R. 2³/₄-6, B. 1 *M*. very fair; ROTES HAUS (Pl. g; D, 2), Wald-Str. 2, well spoken of. — **Hotels Garnis.** PARK HOTEL (Pl. p; D, E, 3), Kreuz-Str. 37, with café-restaurant, R. from 2, B. 1, D. 1³/₄-2¹/₄.

Restaurants. WINE. *Erbprinz*, sec p. 347, on the first floor: *Künstlerhaus*, Karl-Str. 44 (Pl. C, 3), D. 2-3¹/₂ *M* (also beer); *Krokodil* (Pl. k; C, 2, 3). Wald-Str. 63, D. 1¹/₂-2 *M*, very fair; *Vier Jahreszeiten*, Hebel-Str. 21 (Pl. D, 2, 3), D. 1¹/₂ *M*; *Friedrichs-Hof*, see p. 347; *Odeon*, Kaiser-Str. 213 (Pl. C, D, 2), near the General Post Office. — CAFÉS. *Bauer*, Lamm-Str. 7d (Pl. D, 2, 3); *Hildenbrand*, Wald-Str. 8 (Pl. C, 2, 3), D. 1³/₄ *M*. — BEER. *Krokodil* (see above); *Moninger*, Kaiser-Str. 142, cor. Karl-Strasse. — GARDEN RESTAURANT, *Stadtgarten* (p. 354), D. 2-3 *M*. — AUTOMATIC RESTAURANT, Kaiser-Str. 201.

Electric Tramways (comp. the plan). From the market-place through the Kaiser-Str. to the River Harbour (Rheinhafen) on the W., and to Durlach on the E. From the Central Railway Station to the Cemetery (Friedhof), to the City Hospital (Städtisches Krankenhaus), and so on.

Steam Tramways. 1. From the *Mess-Platz* (Pl. D, 3, 4) viâ Ettlingen (p. 355) to *Herrenalb* (p. 388) or to *Pforzheim* (p. 385). — 2. Through the *Krieg-Str.* (Pl. B-E, 3) to (9¹/₂ M.) *Durmersheim* (p. 346) on the W., or to the E. to (10 M.) *Spöck*.

Cabs. For ¹/₄ hr. 1-2 pers. 70 pf., 3 and more pers. 90 pf.; second, third, and fourth ¹/₄ hr. 60 or 70 pf.; each additional ¹/₄ hr. 50 or 60 pf. Extra fares for the suburbs. Double fares at night (9-6). Hand-luggage free: each trunk 20 pf.

Post & Telegraph Office (Pl. 30; C, 2), Kaiser-Str. 217.

Theatres. *Court Theatre* ('Hoftheater'; Pl. 12, D 2), five times a week. The theatre is closed from July to September. — *Summer Theatre* in the Stadt-Garten (p. 354). — *Colosseum*, Wald-Str. 16, a variety-theatre.

Badischer Kunstverein (Pl. 22, D 2; *Art Union*) containing a changing collection of modern pictures, chiefly by artists of Carlsruhe (open daily, except Frid., 11-1 & 2-4; 50 pf.).

Baths. *Städtisches Vierordtsbad* (Pl. D, 4), with swimming-bath; *Friedrichsbad*, Kaiser-Str. 136, with swimming-bath. — *In the Rhine*, at Maxau (p. 354), to which special trains convey bathers in summer.

Tourists' Aid Association *(Verein zur Hebung des Fremdenverkehrs)*, in the Rathaus.

British Chargé d'Affaires, *F. D. Harford, Esq.* (Darmstadt).

English Church Service in the Chapel of the almshouse ('Pfründnerhaus'; Pl. B, 2), Stephanien-Str. 98, fortnightly at 11 a.m.

Chief Attractions (¹/₂ day). Karl-Friedrich-Strasse (p. 349); Kaiser-Strasse (pp. 349, 354); Schloss-Platz (p. 349); Kunsthalle (p. 350).

Carlsruhe or *Karlsruhe* (380 ft.), the capital of the Grand-Duchy of Baden (140,000 inhab., including a garrison of 4000 men), situated 6 M. from the Rhine, on the W. outskirts of the Hardtwald, owes its origin to the Margrave Charles William of Baden-Durlach (1709-38), who transferred his residence hither in 1715 (comp. p. 360). The plan of the old town resembles a fan, the streets radiating from the palace, but the new streets on the W., S., and E. are less regular in plan. Carlsruhe has considerable industrial importance, its principal manufactures being railway rolling stock, furniture, and plated goods. River-harbour, see p. 354.

The development of modern German architecture may be very distinctly traced in Carlsruhe. The palace and the other older buildings are in the French style prevalent at the beginning of the 18th century. The structures of the next period exhibit the simple and harmonious classical forms introduced by *Friedrich Weinbrenner* (1766-1826), an architect who received his training in Rome. His principal successors were *Hübsch* (1795-1863) and *Eisenlohr* (1805-54), who erected many handsome buildings in the modern Romanesque (round-arched) style, and long determined the tone of Carlsruhe architecture. The stately edifices erected in recent years by *Berckmüller* (d. 1879) and *Durm* form a fourth period, together

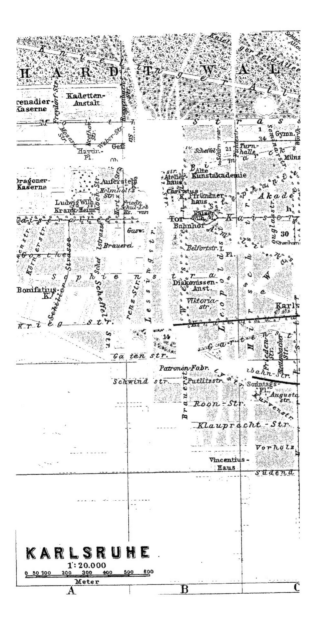

KARLSRUHE

1 : 20.000

0 50 100 200 300 400 500 600
Meter

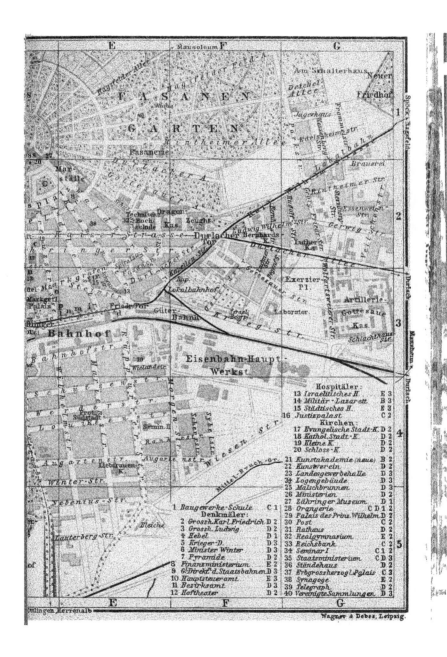

Wagner & Debes, Leipzig.

with the still more modern buildings (in the Kaiser-Str. and elsewhere) by *Curjel & Moser, Billing, Ratzel,* and others.

The *Grand-Ducal School of Art,* founded at Carlsruhe in 1853, has contributed not a little to the development of the German school of land-scape-painting. Its first director was the classical painter *J. W. Schirmer* (1807-63), of Düsseldorf, a disciple of Lessing, who was succeeded by *Hans Gude* (1864-80). The present director is *Hans Thoma* (b. 1839).

To the W. of the *Railway Station* (Pl. D, E, 3) stand a bronze statue of *Winter* (Pl. 6; d. 1838), the minister, designed by Reich (1855), a *War Monument* (Pl. 5) in memory of 1870-71, by Volz, and other monuments.

At the entrance to the KARL-FRIEDRICH-STRASSE (Pl. D, 3, 2) is a memorial *Fountain* (Pl. 25) by Lang, with marble figures by Moest. In the Rondell-Platz, farther on, rises an *Obelisk* ('Ver-fassungssäule'; Pl. D, 3) with a medallion of Grand-Duke Charles (1811-18); on the right is the *Margrave's Palace,* by Weinbrenner.

On the left side of the MARKET PLACE (Pl. D, 2) is the *Rathaus* (Pl. 31), built in 1821, in front of which are two colossal bronze figures of Baden and Carlsruhe, by Hirt (1900). On the right is the *Protestant Church* (*Stadtkirche;* Pl. 17), with a Corinthian portico (1817), the burial-church of the grand-ducal family. Both these edifices are by Weinbrenner. The fountain with a *Statue of the Grand-Duke Lewis* (1818-30; Pl. 3) is by Raufer. The Pyramid (Pl. 7), to the N. of it, marks the grave of Margrave Charles William (p. 348). At this point the Karl-Friedrich-Str. is intersected by the KAISER-STRASSE (Pl. B-F, 2), one of the main arteries of traffic, flanked with handsome modern houses and attractive shops, and running through the centre of the town from E. to W.

In front of the palace, in the centre of the Schloss-Platz, is a bronze *Statue of the Grand-Duke Charles Frederick* (Pl. 2; d. 1811), by Schwanthaler (1844). — The **Palace** or *Schloss* (Pl. D, 1), erected in 1750-82 from *L. Retti's* designs, is in the form of a semicircle, and surmounted by the *Bleiturm* (138 ft.), which affords an extensive view. The interior is shown by the castellan (8-12 & 2-6; 50 pf.). — The E. wing contains the *Zähringen Museum* (Pl. 27; D, 1), a collection of art-objects and curiosities connected with the ducal house, and also the *Ducal Stables* (*Mar-ställe;* open 12-4). — On the W. side of the Schloss-Platz is the *Theatre* (*Hof-Theater;* Pl. 12), erected in 1851-53, by *Hübsch.*

Arched passages in the wings of the Schloss lead to the **Palace Garden** (*Schloss-Garten;* Pl. D, 1), embellished with fountains, sculptures, etc. Among the sculptures are a small monument to *Hebel* (Pl. 4; p. 432), a *Victory* by Rauch, and a group of *Her-mann and Dorothea.* The garden extends into the *Hardtwald* (p. 354) and the *Wild-Park.*

Behind the Court Theatre is the **Botanic Garden** (Pl. D, 1, 2; closed on Sat. and Sun., and from 12 to 2 on other days), with a *Winter Garden* (open on Mon., Wed., and Frid., 10-11.45 and 2-4).

Adjacent is the *Hall of Art* (*Kunsthalle;* Pl. D, 2), built by *Hübsch* (1836-45) in the modern Romanesque style, with a new wing (1896) by *Durm* and an addition on the N. side for the *Thoma Museum* and the earlier schools, opened in 1909. The entrance is in the Hans-Thoma-Str. (formerly the Linkenheimer-Str.). The collections are open to the public on Wed. and Sun. (also Frid. in summer), 11-1 and 2-4; at other times for a gratuity.

Ground Floor. To the right are casts, modern models, and original works. Room III contains pictures. — Hence we turn to the left into the THOMA MUSEUM, containing numerous works (paintings, drawings, sketches, and studies) by *Hans Thoma*, exhibited in three rooms and a vaulted hall. The last, known as the 'Kapelle', is entered from the middle room on the left through a vestibule, with a bust of Thoma by Hildebrand, and contains eleven large paintings of scenes from the life of Christ (1907-8). The decoration of the rooms is also by Thoma.

The grand-ducal *PICTURE GALLERY* was founded under Philip I., Margrave of Baden (1479-1533) but did not become important till the time of the Margravine Caroline Louise (d. 1783), who acquired the chief Netherlandish and French works. The early-German paintings come mainly from the Von Hirscher Collection. The schools of Düsseldorf, Munich, and Carlsruhe are well represented in the modern section, while the development of Anselm Feuerbach in particular is admirably illustrated here.

STAIRCASE. Frescoes by *Schwind* (1840): Consecration of Freiburg Cathedral by Duke Conrad of Zähringen. 542. *Dietz*, Destruction of Heidelberg. — The allegorical paintings in the lunettes are by *Schwind* and *Gleichauf.*

First Floor. FIRST CORRIDOR (to the right): Copies after classical masters. — CABINET 1: 988, 1049. *L. Dill*, Moorland; 1030. *L. Schmid-Reutte*, Crucifixion. — CABINET 2: *1018. *W. Leibl*, Memento mori (a skull); *W. Trübner*, *1006. Gigantomachia, 899. 'Cæsar before crossing the Rubicon'; *K. Haider*, 977. Approaching thunderstorm, 1053. Thunderstorm in spring; *911. *H. Schroeder*. Landscape.

ROOM I: *J. W. Schirmer:* 613-616. Landscapes with the parable of the Good Samaritan; 612. Approaching thunderstorm. *K. F. Lessing:* 533. Crusaders in the desert; 534. Dispute between Luther (left) and Dr. Eck (right) at Leipzig in 1519 in presence of Duke George of Saxony and Prince Barnim of Pomerania (dated 1867); 1019. *H. Lessing*, Portrait of his father, K. F. Lessing. — ROOM II: 667. *Schmitson*, Horses in the Pushta; 543. *F. Dietz*, Gustavus Adolphus lying in state; 619. *A. Achenbach*, Steamer colliding with an iceberg.

CABINET 3: 564. *J. B. Kirner*, Distribution of prizes in the Black Forest; 525. *W. Lindenschmitt the Elder*, Battle of the Teutoburgian Forest. — CABINET 4: 989. *Fr. Fehr*, Twilight; 1130. *U. Hübner*, Summer day. — CABINET 5: *Poetzelberger*, 1055. River-scene, 932. The farewell; 791. *Fr. Adam*, After the battle of Wörth (p. 474); *1134. *G. Courbet*, The rocks of Etretat (Normandy). — CABINET 6: 893. *Ed. von Steinle*, St. Luke painting the Virgin; *509. *Overbeck*, Raising of Lazarus. — CABINET 7: Landscapes by *K. Rottmann* and *H. Gude*.

ROOM III: 548. *J. Scholtz*, Wallenstein's banquet; 632. *F. A. von Waldenburg*, Swiss landscape; 577. *W. Sohn*, Question of conscience; 570. *Tidemand*, Norwegian genre-scene; 836. *B. Vautier*, Visiting the squire's room.

ROOM IV: *959. *L. Dill*, Flooded sage-fields in the Po valley; 968. *Lugo*, Erlenbruck near the Titisee (p. 418); 1023. *Steinhausen*, St. Paul growing blind; 934. *H. Zügel*, Pasturing sheep; 935. *Count Kalckreuth*, Thunder-clouds; 874. *Bokelmann*, Holstein village on fire; 969. *Hasemann*, Spinning-room in the Black Forest.

Room V: 574. *Riefstahl*, Funeral in Appenzell; 931. *B. Kampf*, Volunteers of 1813 receiving the benediction; 797. *Defregger*, The young painter; 554. *F. Keller*, Margrave Lewis William of Baden at the battle of Salankemen (1691); 802. *Klaus Meyer*, Infant school; 637. *H. Gude*, Norwegian harbour of refuge; 801. *Kallmorgen*, Rhine in flood at Carlsruhe; 880. *Herm. Baisch*, Rain on the Lower Rhine; *Schönleber*, 771. Dutch village, 819. Scene on the Neckar, 1112. View of Laufenburg on the Upper Rhine (p. 438); 963. Scene on the Neckar.

Room VI: 958. *Böcklin*, Poverty and Care; *A. Feuerbach*, 549. Silenus and youthful Bacchus (1847), *550. Colossal figure of Poetry, from the Venetian period of the master (1856), 1031. Flower-girl of Carlsruhe (1854), 1032. Nanna Risi (1861), 822. Portrait of himself (1878), 946. Portrait of himself (1852), 823. Flowers, *813. Plato's Symposium (1867-69), *551. Dante and the noble ladies of Ravenna (1858), *416. Small copy of Titian's Assumption at Venice (1855); 983. *E. A. Walton*, Sun-dial; *Walter Crane*, Rape of Persephone; 789. *J. A. Koch*, Historical landscape; 976. *Fr. Stuck*, Florentine woman (half-length); *521. *M. von Schwind*, Ritter Kurt's Bridal Procession (Goethe), a humorous composition in the old-German manner, bearing the motto, 'Widersacher, Weiber, Schulden, ach! kein Ritter wird sie los' (Of foes, women, and debts, alas! no knight can get rid).

Room VII: 19-21. Cartoons by *Schnorr von Carolsfeld*.

Second Corridor (Print Room): 547. *Vischer*, Berthold IV. of Zähringen at the battle of the Adda. — Cabinet 8: 298. *Berchem*, Mountain-gorge, with the history of the Disobedient Prophet (I. Book of Kings, xiii, 24). — Cabinet 9. Water-colours and drawings. *Fr. Boucher*, 691, 692. Designs for Nos. 479 and 480 (see p. 352), 1070. Recumbent nude girl; 824. *Feuerbach*, Sketch of his 'Concert' (now at Berlin); 857. *M. von Schwind*, Contest of the minstrels at the Wartburg (sketch of his fresco in that place); 855. *J. A. Koch*, Landscape, with figures by Carstens.

Third Corridor. Nos. 858, 859, & 790 are water-colours, illustrating the costumes of Baden peasants in the procession in honour of the silver-wedding of the Grand-Duke Frederick I. (1881), painted by *Tuttiné* and *Issel*. 722-747. *J. W. Schirmer*, Representations from Genesis. Cartoons by *Schnorr von Carolsfeld*.

The Addition of 1909 contains in its upper story (above the Thoma-Museum) the Netherlandish French, and Italian works. — Room I: 213. *Snyders*, Still-life; *Teniers the J.*, 193. Supper in a barn, 194. Physician; 344, 345. *Hondecoeter*, Poultry; 773. *J. van Kessel*, Wood-scene; 186. *J. Jordaens*, Moses smiting the rock; 177. *Rubens*, Family-portrait.

Cabinet 1: *260. *Jan Steen*, Young couple in a garden; 269, 270. *P. van Slingelandt*, Domestic scenes; 301. *Karel du Jardin*, Shepherdess; *262. *J. Ochtervelt*, Love-suit; *Caspar Netscher*, 264. Death of Cleopatra (1673), 265. Concert; *235. *B. van der Helst*, Young Couple (1661); 250. *Saftleven*, Surgical operation; 256. *Brekelenkam*, Dealer of oranges; 239. *Flinck*, Portrait; *361. *J. D. de Heem*, Festoon of flowers and fruit; 356. *Cl. W. Heda*, Still-life; *W. van Aelst*, 350. Still-life, 351. Thistle; *238. *Rembrandt*, Portrait of himself (ca. 1645); 772. *P. Lastman*, The Apostle Philip baptizing the Moorish chamberlain.

Cabinet 2: 251. *Saftleven*, Job; 323. *Wouwerman*, The broken milk-pot; 318. *Jan Both*, Italian evening-scene; *A. Brouwer*, 191. Dentist, 192. Sleeping peasant; *A. van Ostade*, 244, 245. Peasant-scenes, 246. Writer, 247. Smoker, 248. Draught-players; *G. Dou*, *266. Cook at a window, 267. Lace-maker; 259: *Pieter de Hooch*, Woman and girl in a room overlooking a garden; 335. *J. van Ruysdael*, Wood-scene; 333. *A. van der Neer*, Moonlight-scene; 276. *W. van Mieris*, Joseph and Potiphar's wife; 279. *E. H. van der Neer*, Lute-player; *Jan van der Heyde*, 339. Canal in Holland, 340. Dutch market-place (both with figures by Lingelbach); *261. *Gabriel Metsu*, Declaration of love (1661); 380. *Jan van Huysum*, Flower-piece; 252. *J. M. Molenaer*, Country wedding.

Cabinet 3. French Paintings. *495-499. *J. S. Chardin*, Still-life pieces; 468. *Ph. de Champaigne*, Portrait; 473. *N. de Largillière*, Mme. Adélaide of France (daughter of Louis XV.) as Flora; *479, 480. *Fr. Boucher*, Pastoral scenes; 474, 475. *H. Rigaud*, Portraits.

ROOM II. Italian Schools. 460, 461. *Salv. Rosa*, Landscapes, with figures; *449. *Michelangelo da Caravaggio*, Laughing Toper; 453. *Franc. Albani*, Ariadne and Dionysus; 436. *Giulio Romano*, Rape of the Daughters of Leucippe; 440. *Bronzino*, Florentine nobleman; 420. *Piombo*, Vision of St. Anthony of Padua(?); 455, 456. *Sassoferrato*, Madonna; 403. *Niccolò da Foligno*, Crucifixion, with Pope Gregory the Great below (1468; from a church-banner); *404. *Vittore Pisano*(?), Adoration of the Holy Child; 427. *Andrea Solario* (Giov. Pedrini?), Madonna and Child; 409. *Lor. di Credi*, Holy Family.

The **Second Floor** of the annex contains the old Dutch and early-German works. — ROOM I. 808. *Jan Brueghel the E.*, Temptation of St. Antony; *Fr. Francken the Y.*, 171. History of the Prodigal Son, 172. The Israelites after crossing the Red Sea; *188. *Jacques Fouquières*(?), View of Heidelberg (1620); 155. *L. van Leyden*(?), Adoration of the Magi; *148. *Jan van Mabuse*, Coronation of the Virgin; 158. *N. Neuchatel*, Portraits of a married couple (1561); *164. *Ad. Elsheimer*, St. Lawrence; 162. *Hans von Aachen*, Match-making; 152. *Jan van Hemessen*, Loose company.

CABINET 1: 130. *G. Pencz*, Jörg Herz, master of the Nuremberg Mint (1545); *Hans Holbein the Y.*, 64. Bearing of the Cross (1515), 65. St. Ursula (1522), 66. St. George, 67. Erasmus; *Hans Baldung Grien*, 87. Margrave Christopher I. of Baden, 88. Margrave Christopher I. and his family kneeling before the Virgin and St. Anna (1511), 90. St. Joseph and the Madonna (fragment of an Adoration of the Child; 1539); 97. *Hans von Kulmbach*, Winged altar-piece; *L. Cranach the Elder*, 107, 108. Madonna and Child, 109. Judgment of Paris, 119, 120. John and Frederick the Wise, electors of Saxony (1525), 121. Luther in his shroud, 122. Portrait, 123. Madonna and Child (the last three are studio-pieces).

CABINET 2: *Schäufelin*, 84. Crucifixion (1515), 85. Presentation of Jesus; *Burgkmair*, 70. The dead Christ, 71-73. Saints; *Bernhard Strigel*, 59. Pietà, 60. Mocking of Christ, 61. Annunciation, 62. Christ washing St. Peter's feet; *Barth. Zeitblom*, 42. St. Virgil, bishop of Salzburg, and St. Lawrence, 43. SS. Maurice and Sebastian, 44. Priest bestowing the blessing; *993, *994. *M. Grünewald*, Bearing of the Cross, Crucifixion, two masterpieces (ca. 1518) from the church of Tauberbischofsheim.

ROOM II: *Multscher*, 32. Death of the Virgin, 33. Crucifixion (ca. 1460); *Schongauer*, 36. Coronation of the Virgin, 37. Visitation; 48. *Upper Swabian School*, 'Landenberg Altar' (ca. 1500), with Crucifixion in the centre and SS. Pelagius and Conrad at the sides.

The CABINET OF ENGRAVINGS contains *Hans Baldung Grien's* sketchbook, etc.

Near the Kunsthalle, in the Hans-Thoma-Str., is one of the entrances to the *Botanic Garden* (p. 350). Beside it is a bust of the architect *Hübsch* (p. 349). Farther on, to the right, is a bronze *Statue of Prince William of Baden* (1829-97), by *Volz* (1901).

Two buildings at the W. end of the BISMARCK-STRASSE contain the *School of Art* (*Kunst-Akademie;* Pl. B, 2; see p. 349). In the Platz in front of it is a bust of the poet *Victor von Scheffel* (see p. 354), by Volz (1892).

The Riefstahl-Str. and the Westend-Str. lead to the S. from the Industrial School, passing *Christ Church* (Prot.; 1900) and a *Monument to Wilhelm Lübke* (1826-93), the historian of art, to the square in front of the Mühlburger-Tor, which is embellished with a bronze *Equestrian Statue of Emp. William I.*, by Ad.

Heer (1896). — Near the Tor are the Old-Catholic *Church of the Resurrection* (*Auferstehungskirche;* Pl. A, B, 2), in the early-Gothic style, by Schäfer (1897), the office of the *Carlsruhe Life Insurance Co.,* the *Supreme Court* (Pl. B, 2), and other public buildings. In the Gutenberg-Platz, on the W. side of the Nelken-Str. (Pl. A, 2, 3), is the *Marktbrunnen,* a monumental fountain by Ratzel (1908). — In the Stephans-Platz, to the S., behind the large *Post Office* (Pl. 30; C, 2), is the *Stephan Fountain* (1905), by Billing and Binz. To the N. of the post-office, at the corner of the Akademie-Str. and Karl-Str., stands the *Palais Prinz Max.*

On the N.W. side of the FRIEDRICHS-PLATZ (Pl. D, 2, 3) is the *Roman Catholic Church* (Pl. 18), a domed building by Wein-brenner (1814). On the N. is a row of arcades; and on the E. side are the *Central Offices of the Baden Railways* (Pl. 9; D, 3).

On the S. side of the square is the imposing building of the **United Grand-Ducal Collections** (*Vereinigte Sammlungen;* Pl. 40, D 3), with its conspicuous central portion somewhat re-sembling a triumphal arch, erected by *Berckmüller* in 1865-71. The four marble figures are by *Steinhäuser.* In front is a marble group of Orestes and Pylades by the same artist. The staircase is adorned with frescoes by *Keller* and *Gleichauf.* Adm. free on Sun. and Wed., 11-1 and 2-4; at other times for a fee (50 pf.).

GROUND FLOOR. At the foot of the staircase are a gilt statue of Jupiter, from the Rastatt Palace, and a Renaissance fountain from Sulz-burg (ca. 1600). Straight in front are the larger stone monuments and the stairs leading up to the library (p. 354). — In the E. wing (left) are the *Mineralogical, Geological, and Zoological Collections.*

In the W. wing (right) are the ANTIQUARIAN AND ETHNOLOGICAL COL-LECTIONS. ROOM I. *Egyptian Antiquities* and **Greek Vases and Terra-cottas* (catalogue 2 ℳ). In the middle (No. 1), large and beautiful red-figured amphora (on the front, Orpheus in the Underworld; on the back, Bellerophon and the Chimæra); in front, to the left, (No. 3), black-figured amphora (on the front, Birth of Athena); to the right (No. 7), red-figured hydria (Judgment of Paris; Bacchic scenes), of exquisite workmanship. Case 13. Stone and clay figures from Cyprus; on the exit-wall, Tanagra figurine; *Coptic Textiles* (5-6th cent. A.D.). — ROOM II. To the right and left of the entrance, Roman Mithras Reliefs from Neuenheim (No. 16) and Osterburken (No. 118). *Maler Collection of Bronzes,* including Greek and Etruscan *Helmets, armour, and shields; girdles, vessels, and Etruscan mirrors; statuettes (in glass-case 188, *504. Figure of a youth): in the glass-case by the column, Etruscan tripod (No. 414); 1859. Cist from Palestrina (ca. 250 B.C.; in the corner by the window). Exit-wall: *Marble Sculptures of Italic Provenance* (*Torso of Cupid). — ROOM III. The first section contains *Germanic Antiquities:* prehistoric, Roman (some beautiful terra sigillata vessels), and Alemannian-Frankish objects (4-8th cent.). In the second section is the *Ethnographical Collection,* consisting mainly of objects from Japan, China, Africa (especially Tunis), and Mexico.

MEDIÆVAL AND LATER COLLECTIONS. ROOM IV. *Weapons* from the armoury of the margraves, chiefly Turkish spoils of war captured by Margrave Lewis William (1691; p. 360). — ROOM V (a flight higher; opened by the custodian). Modern weapons and flags. *Collection of Baden Costumes.* — ROOM VI. *Art-Industrial Collection:* stove-tiles, cabinets, musical instruments, church-utensils, carvings, stained glass, coins and medals. — We return to the staircase, and thence pass through one of the doors opposite the entrance into the hall containing the — COLLECTION OF LARGER STONE MONUMENTS: Roman inscriptions, sarcophagi, votive altars, milestones, chiefly from Baden; remains of a Roman monument of victory, found near the Roman castellum in Schlossau; Romanesque portal of the abbey-church at Petershausen (12th cent.).

THE NATIONAL LIBRARY, on the Upper Floor, contains 200,000 volumes and a handsome reading-room (open Sun. 11-1, week-days 10-1 & 6-8). Here also is the *Grand-Ducal Cabinet of Coins.*

Behind the building just described lies the *Erbprinzen-Garten,* with a bronze group of nymphs by *Weltring* (1891). The **Palace of the Crown Prince** (Pl. 37; D, 3), in the Krieg-Str., was erected in the late-Renaissance style by *Durm* in 1891-96. It is at present occupied by Grand-Duke Frederick II.

In the E. half of the KAISER-STRASSE (p. 349), at the corner of the Kronen-Str., rises the *Synagogue* (Pl. 38; E, 2), built by Durm. Farther on, to the left, is the **Polytechnic School** (*Technische Hochschule;* Pl. E, 2), erected by *Hübsch* in 1836 and enlarged by *Fischer* in 1863. This institution is the oldest of the kind in Germany (founded 1825). Adjoining the main building are the *Aula,* added by Durm in 1898, and the *Electric, Physical,* and *Botanical Institutes.* — At the end of the Kaiser-Str. is the new Roman Catholic *Church of St. Bernhard,* by Meckel.

About ¹/₂ M. from the Durlacher-Tor (tramway) are the *Luther-Kirche* (l.; Pl. G, 2) by Curjel & Moser, and the *Schloss Gottesaue* (r.; Pl. G, 3), erected in 1583-99, now an artillery-barrack.

To the N.E. the Karl-Wilhelm-Str. leads from the Durlacher-Tor to (³/₄ M.) the handsome **New Cemetery,** in which repose the statesman *Karl Mathy* (d. 1868) and the poet *J. Victor von Scheffel,* a native of Carlsruhe (1826-86).

The ***Stadt-Garten** (Pl. D, 4, 5; adm. 20 pf.) is a favourite haunt of the 'Carlsruher'. In front of its entrance is a bronze *Statue of Bismarck,* by Moest (1904). Adjoining the Vierordts-Bad is the *Hygieia Fountain,* by Hirt (1909). There is a restaurant in the *Festhalle.* In the S. part of the park are a small *Zoological Garden (Tiergarten)* and the *Lauterberg,* an artifical hill 125 ft. high, with the reservoir of the town waterworks and an artificial ruin (view).

Among pleasant resorts for walking are the *Hardtwald* (Pl. A, B, C, 1), with the Schützenhaus, an open-air restaurant on the Eggenstein road (1¹/₂ M.), and the *Wild-Park,* tickets for which are obtained at the Hofzahlamt, Schloss-Platz 1 (50 pf.). The latter contains the modern Gothic mausoleum of the grand-ducal family.

FROM CARLSRUHE TO LANDAU. 25 M., railway in 1¹/₂ hr. — 1¹/₄ M. *Mühlburgertor.* — 2¹/₂ M. **Mühlburg,** with the *River Harbour* of Carlsruhe (1898-1901), connected with the Rhine by a canal 2000 yds. in length. — 4 M. *Knielingen;* 6¹/₄ M. **Maxau** (*Rheinischer Hof;* baths, see p. 348), where we cross the Rhine by a bridge-of-boats: then *Maximiliansau;* 8 M. *Wörth* (p. 472); 12 M. *Langenkandel;* 17 M. *Winden,* where the line joins the Palatinate railway (p. 464). — 25 M. *Landau,* see p. 463.

47. From Carlsruhe to Baden-Baden.

23 M. RAILWAY in 1-1¹/₂ hr. (fares 3 ℳ, 1 ℳ 80, 1 ℳ 15 pf.; express fares 3 ℳ 50, 2 ℳ 30, 1 ℳ 40 pf.). Good views of the Black Forest to the left (E.) as the train nears Rastatt. — Carriages are generally changed at Oos (comp. below).

Carlsruhe, see p. 347. — The train crosses a viaduct spanning the Alb, the strategic railway to Rastatt and Alsace, and a goods railway. To the right are *Beiertheim* and the two towers of the church of *Bulach.* To the left are wooded hills.

4¹/₂ M. **Ettlingen** *(Hirsch, Sonne,* both very fair, with gardens; *Krone),* with 8600 inhab., possesses large shirting, velvet, and paper manufactories (paper has been made here since 1482). A pretty path leads hence viâ the *Redoute* (1055 ft.) to *Schlutten-bach* (1115 ft.) and thence to the platform on the *Steinig* (1310 ft.; 1³/₄ hr.). Ettlingen is also a station on the Albtal railway (p. 387) and on the steam-tramway from Carlsruhe to Pforzheim (p. 348).

6 M. *Bruchhausen.* — From (9¹/₂ M.) *Malsch* a picturesque road leads to (9 M.) Herrenalb (p. 388), viâ *Freiolsheim, Moos-brunn,* and *Bernbach.* — 12 M. *Muggensturm.*

15 M. **Rastatt** (390 ft.; *Railway Hotel,* at the station, 10 min. from the town; *Schwert; Kreuz,* in the market-place), a town with 14,400 inhab., burned by the French in 1689, but soon afterwards rebuilt by the celebrated Imperial general Margrave Lewis of Baden (d. 1707), was the residence of the Margraves till the line became extinct in 1771. The large *Palace* is conspicuous for its high tower.

In one of the apartments the peace between France and Austria, which terminated the Spanish War of Succession, was signed on 6th May, 1714, by Prince Eugene of Savoy and Marshal Villars. A congress held here in 1797-99 between Austria and Germany on the one side and France on the other led to no result, and at its close Roberjot and Bonnier, two of the French delegates, were barbarously murdered by Austrian hussars in an adjacent wood, but at whose instigation it was never discovered. — The Baden revolution began at Rastatt in 1849 with a mutiny of the soldiery, and it was also terminated here by the surrender of the fortress to the Prussians after a siege of three weeks.

From Rastatt to *Gernsbach* and *Forbach,* see pp. 391-393; strategic line to *Carlsruhe* and *Alsace,* see p. 346.

The train now crosses the *Murg,* and reaches —

20¹/₂ M. **Baden-Oos** (410 ft.; *Golf; Stern, Engel,* both un-pretending), with the Baden golf-links (international tournaments in the end of July and beginning of August) and a huge shed for an air-ship. From this point a branch-line ascends the valley of the Oos, passing *Badenscheuern* or *Baden-Weststadt* (good wine at the Anker) to (23 M.) *Baden-Baden.*

From Baden-Oos to *Freiburg* and *Bâle,* see RR. 50, 51, 53.

48. Baden-Baden and Environs.

Arrival. The RAILWAY STATION (500 ft.; Pl. A, 1) is on the N.W. side of the town, 15-20 min. from most of the hotels. *Cab* ('*Packdroschke*'; at the first exit on the left): $1/_4$ hr. for 1-2 pers. 80 pf., for 3-4 pers. 1 $\mathcal{M}$ 40 pf.; for $1/_2$ hr. 1 $\mathcal{M}$ 40 or 2 $\mathcal{M}$ (to Lichtental 1 $\mathcal{M}$ 50 or 2 $\mathcal{M}$); at night (9-6) 50 per cent more; for each article of luggage over $22^1/_2$ lbs. 30 pf. — *Omnibus* to Lichtental, see p. 358; *Electric Tramway* (in construction), see p. 359. — *Porter* from or to cab 5 pf. for each article of luggage; for carrying a trunk into the town 30-60 pf., more than one 20-40 pf. each; light articles 10-20 pf. each.

Hotels (generally good). The larger houses are usually closed from Nov. until the beginning of March. — *HÔTEL STEPHANIE (Pl. b; C, 4), two houses in an open situation on the right bank of the Oos, opposite the Lichtentaler-Allée, surrounded with gardens, no pension rates; *HÔT. DE L'EUROPE (Pl. f; B, 3), Kaiser-Allée 2, in a fine situation opposite the Kur-Park and the Trinkhalle, R. from 4, B. $1^1/_2$, D. 5, pens. from 12 $\mathcal{M}$; *HÔT. MESSMER (Pl. a; B, 3), Werder-Str., near the Conversationshaus, with three dépendances and a large garden, for many years a resort of the Emperor William I., R. 4-8, B. $1^1/_2$, D. 5, pens. from 12 $\mathcal{M}$; *HÔTEL REGINA, similarly situated, with garden, R. from 4, D. $4^1/_2$ $\mathcal{M}$; *HÔTEL D'ANGLETERRE (Pl. e; C, 3), Sophien-Str. 2, by the Promenaden-Brücke, with garden, R. $3^1/_2$-6, B. $1^1/_2$, D. $4^1/_2$, pens. 10-14 $\mathcal{M}$; *HOLLÄNDISCHER HOF (Pl. h; C, 3), Sophien-Str. 14, in the Leopold-Platz, with the *Pension Beauséjour* (Pl. i; C, 3) and garden, R. from 4, pens. from 11 $\mathcal{M}$; *BELLEVUE (Pl. d; C, 5), in an open situation near the 'Gönner-Anlage' (p. 363), with garden, R. from $3^1/_2$, pens. from 11 $\mathcal{M}$; *COUR DE BADE ('Badischer Hof'; Pl. n, B 2), Lange-Str. 47, at the entrance to the town, with thermal baths and garden, open in winter also; *HÔTEL DE RUSSIE (Pl. k; B, 2), Kaiser-Allée 4, with garden, R. 4-12, B. $1^1/_2$, D. 5, pens. from 10 $\mathcal{M}$; *VICTORIA (Pl. g; C, 3), Leopolds-Platz, also open in winter, R. $2^1/_2$-7, pens. 9-16 $\mathcal{M}$, with café-restaurant. — *HÔTEL DE FRANCE (Pl. l; B, 2), Luisen-Str. 32, with garden, open in winter also, R. from 3, B. $1^1/_2$, D. 4, pens. $8^1/_2$-14 $\mathcal{M}$. — *PARK HOTEL, Fremersberg-Str., in a fine, lofty position, overlooking the Lichtentaler-Allée, R. 3-8, B. $1^1/_4$, D. 4, pens. $9^1/_2$-14 $\mathcal{M}$; *ZÄHRINGER HOF (Pl. m; B, 2), Lange-Str. 44, with thermal baths and large garden, reaching to the Schloss-Str., R. 3-6, B. $1^1/_2$, D. $3^1/_2$, pens. 8-12 $\mathcal{M}$.

The following houses are somewhat less expensive and almost all of them open in winter: *PETER'S HÔTEL HIRSCH (Pl. t; B, C, 2), Hirsch-Str. 1, cor. of Lang-Str., with baths and lift, R. $2^1/_2$-5, B. $1^1/_4$, D. 3, pens. $7^1/_2$-10 $\mathcal{M}$. — *TERMINUS (Pl. o; A, 1), R. 2-5, B. $1^1/_4$, pens. 7-10 $\mathcal{M}$; *VILLE DE BADE ('Stadt Baden'; Pl. p, A 1), with restaurant, R. 2-4, B. $1-1^1/_4$, D. 3, pens. 6-8 $\mathcal{M}$; BAYRISCHER HOF (Pl. q; A, 1), Lange-Str. 92, with restaurant, garden, and covered terrace, R. 2-4, B. $1-1^1/_4$, pens. 6-8 $\mathcal{M}$, these three near the station and convenient for passing travellers. *PETERSBURGER HOF (Pl. s; C, 3), Gernsbacher-Str. 12, with restaurant; *DREI KÖNIGE (Pl. u; C, 3), Lange-Str. 13 and Luisen-Str. 10, with restaurant and covered terrace, R. $3^1/_2$-$6^1/_2$, pens. 8-12 $\mathcal{M}$; *STADT PARIS (Pl. z; C, 3), Sophien-Str., near the Friedrichsbad, with lift and wine-room, R. $2^1/_2$-$4^1/_2$, B. $1^1/_4$, D. 3, pens. 7-9 $\mathcal{M}$; *STADT STRASSBURG (Pl. w; C, 3), Sophien-Str. 26, with restaurant and covered terrace, R. $2^3/_4$-6, B. $1^1/_4$, D. 3, pens. 8-12 $\mathcal{M}$; *RÖMERBAD, Bäder-Str. 1, opposite the Friedrichsbad, R. $2^1/_2$-3, B. 1, D. 3, pens. $6^1/_2$-$8^1/_2$ $\mathcal{M}$; STAHLBAD, Lichtentaler-Str. 27, R. $2^1/_2$-$4^1/_2$, B. 1, pens. $6^1/_4$-$8^1/_2$ $\mathcal{M}$, well spoken of; GERMANIA (Pl. y; C, 4), Ludwig-Wilhelm-Platz, beside the Protestant Church; MÜLLER, Lange-Str. 34, R. 2-$4^1/_2$, B. $1^1/_4$, D. 3-$3^1/_2$, pens. $6^1/_2$-$9^1/_2$ $\mathcal{M}$; GOLDENES EINHORN, Lange-Str. 7, with restaurant, both well spoken of. — CENTRAL HOTEL, Jewish, R. $2^1/_2$-5 $\mathcal{M}$.

Among the less pretentious hotels may be mentioned: BOCK (Pl. B;

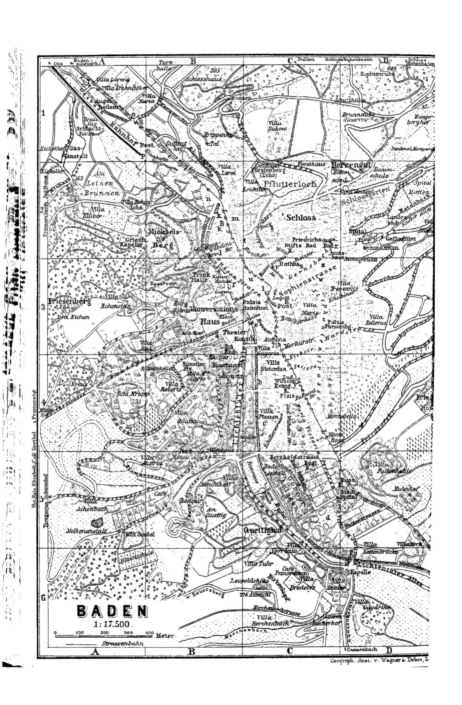

BADEN

1:17.500

B. 2), Lange-Str. 45, backing on the Promenade, R. 2-3, pens. 5-7 ℳ: Hôtel-Pension Baldreit, Küfer-Str. 5, near the market-place; Salmen, Löwe, Geist, R. 1¹/₂-2¹/₂ ℳ, with beer-rooms, all in the Gernsbacher-Str.; Grüner Baum, Markt-Platz 22, with beer-room; Schweizerhof, near the Ville de Bade, R. 2-4, B. 1 ℳ, with restaurant.

Outside the town: Friesenwald, Werder-Str. 32, on the Beutig (pens. 6-8 ℳ), Gretel (a sanatorium), *Kaiserin Elisabeth, and Hôtel-Restaurant Panorama (Pl. C, 6), Lichtentaler-Allée 32 (R. 2-3¹/₂, B. 1¹/₄, déj. 2, D. 2¹/₂-3, pens. 7-10 ℳ; large garden), see p. 364; *Hôtel Früh (R. 2¹/₂-6, pens. 6¹/₂-10 ℳ) and Hôtel Kordmattfelsen, see p. 368; a little lower down, *Kurhaus Schirmhof, in a beautiful situation, well-managed, R. 2¹/₂-6, B. 1, D. 3, S. 2, pens. from 7 ℳ. — Pension Waldeneck, Fremersberg-Str. 40. — Gunzenbacher Hof (Pl. C, 6; pens. 6¹/₂-8 ℳ), very fair, see p. 364. — Zur Morgenröte and Waldschlösschen, see p. 367. — *Inns at Lichtental*, see p. 364.

Pensions. *Alléehaus (Pension Augusta Victoria)*, Lichtentaler Allée 10 (pens. 7-12 ℳ); *Alsen*, Gernsbacher-Str. 49; *Villa Bellavista*, Yburg-Str. 35 (6-9 ℳ); *Blücher*, Gernsbacher-Str. 76 (5¹/₂-8 ℳ); *Fürst Bismarck*, Schützen-Str. 11 (6¹/₂-15 ℳ); *Villa Diana*, Gernsbacher-Str. 5; *Glover*, Bismarck-Str. 9 (from 7 ℳ); *Hansa*, Bismarck-Str. 11a (pens. 6¹/₂-10 ℳ); *Heeser*, Moltke-Str. 3 (5¹/₂-7¹/₂ ℳ); *Hohenstein*, Friesenberg-Str. 6 (5¹/₂-8 ℳ); *Kalender*, Kronprinzen-Str. 2 (R. 2¹/₂, pens. from 7 ℳ); *Kloss*, Sophien-Str. 38 (pens. 5-8 ℳ); *Luisenhöhe (Bazoche)*, Werder-Str. 12 (R. 2-12, pens. 8-18 ℳ); *Villa Marguerite*, Seufzer-Allée 6 (pens. 6-10 ℳ); *Nagel*, Luisen-Str. 22; *Schneider*, Schiller-Str. 15, near the Lichtentaler Allée. R. from 1¹/₂, pens. 6-9 ℳ; *Villa Sans-Souci*, Yburg-Str. 9 (pens. from 5 ℳ); *Villa Salenius*, Yburg-Str. 3 (pens. 6-8 ℳ); *Vincenti*, Bismarck-Str. 1. — **Sanatoria.** *Quisisana (Dr. Becker & Dr. Mayer)*, Bismarck-Str. 19 (pens. from 8 ℳ); *Dr. Emmerich's Sanatorium*, Quettig-Str. 2, for nervous patients; *Sanatorium of Dr. Frey and Dr. Dengler*, Hohenlohe-Str., for heart and nervous patients; *Dr. Heinsheimer*, Leopold-Str. 23; *Dr. H. Lippert*, Ludwig-Wilhelm-Str. 11; *Dr. Burger's Sanatorium*, Maria-Victoria-Str. 12, for internal complaints; *Dr. Ebers's Sanatorium (Friedrichshöhe)*, Bernhard-Str. 30; *Ludwig-Wilhelm-Stift* (for ladies; pens. 5¹/₂-6¹/₂ ℳ), see p. 361. — *Swedish Medical Gymnastics* (Kellgren System), Berthold-Str. 6.

Restaurants. In addition to the above-mentioned hotels: *Conversationshaus, of the first class, D. 4¹/₂-7 ℳ (wine, etc., cheaper at the uncovered tables); *Goldenes Kreuz, Lichtentaler-Str. 13, near the Leopolds-Platz, much frequented, D. 1¹/₂-2 ℳ; *Zur Post*, with an 'old-German' wine and beer room, Lichtentaler-Str. 4; *Bayrischer Hof* (see p. 356); *Krokodil*, Mühlengasse 4, between Nos. 25 and 27 in the Lange-Str., very fair, D. 1³/₄-2¹/₂ ℳ; *Stadt Paris, Stadt Strassburg* (also hotels, see p. 356), Sophien-Str.; *Löwenbräu*, Gernsbach-Str. 11, with small garden and terrace, D. 2 ℳ; *Bletzer*, Lichtentaler-Str. 35; *Sinner's Saalbau*, Lichtentaler-Str. 44, and numerous others.

Cafés and Confectioners' Shops. *Conversationshaus*, see above; *Café Palais, in the former Palais Hamilton (Pl. C, 3; p. 362), with beautiful garden, first-class; *Rumpelmayer*, Augusta-Platz (Pl. C, 3), first-class, with small garden; *Villa Sorrento* (Pl. C, 5, 6), Lichtentaler-Allée 14; *Augusta-Bad* (p. 359); *Panorama* (with rooms, see above), above the Lichtentaler-Allée, see p. 364; *Zabler*, Lichtentaler-Str. 12, with garden. *Tea Room*, Alléehaus (see above), Lichtentaler-Allée 10. — There are also several good cafés and milk-gardens in the environs, such as the *Gunzenbacher Hof* (p. 364); *Molkenanstalt*, Quettig-Str. 9; *Gretel*, see p. 363.

Cabs (two horses; 'Packdroschken' at the railway station, see p. 356). 1. Drive by time: ¹/₄ hr. 1-2 pers. 1 ℳ, 3-4 pers. 1 ℳ 70; ¹/₂ hr. 1 ℳ 80 and 2 ℳ 30; ³/₄ hr. 2 ℳ 50 and 3 ℳ 30; 1 hr. 3 ℳ 50 and 4 ℳ 50 pf. (in winter ¹/₄ hr. 80 pf. and 1 ℳ 50; ¹/₂ hr. 1 ℳ 50 and 2 ℳ; ³/₄ hr. 2 ℳ 30 pf. and 3 ℳ; 1 hr. 3 and 4 ℳ); each additional ¹/₄ hr., irrespective of the number of pers., 70 pf. Cabs discharged beyond the cab-radius, which includes the whole of the town shown in our plan, with the exception of the hills to the S.W. of the Greek Chapel and Schloss Krupp and the hills to the N.E., are entitled for the return to an extra fare of 50 pf. (1-2 pers.) or 80 pf. (3-4 pers.). — To Lichtental 1 ℳ 60 or 2 ℳ 20 pf.; to the pensions Schirmhof, Korbmattfelsenhof, Kaiserin Elisabeth, or Waldschlösschen, 2½ or 3½ ℳ.

Fares at night (9-6) 50 per cent. more. Each article of luggage above 22½ lbs. 40 pf.

b. DRIVES (1-4 persons).

Under Class I carriages may be kept for 1½ hr.; under Cl. II, 2 hrs.; under Cl. III, 3 hrs.; under Cl. IV, 4 hrs.; under Cl. V, 6 hrs.; under Cl. VI, 9 hrs.; and under Cl. VII, 12 hrs.

		ℳ	pf.
I.	Viâ the Neue Schloss to Teufelskanzel and back	6	—
	Viâ the Greek Chapel to the Korbmattfelsenhof and back	5	—
	Viâ the Jagdhaus-Strasse to the Waldsee and back	5	—
II.	To the Fish Breeding Establishment or the Seelach 5, there and back	6	—
	To the Geroldsauer Mühle 4, there and back	5	—
	Jagdhaus 6, and back viâ the Fremersberger Hof, or vice versâ	7	—
	Circular drive by the Yburg road, the Seelighöfe, and the 'Verbindungs-Weg' to Lichtental, and back to Baden	7	—
III.	To the Geroldsau Waterfall 6, there and back	8	—
	To the Alte Schloss 6, there and back	8	—
	To the Alte Schloss and back viâ Ebersteinburg, or vice versâ	10	—
IV.	To Ebersteinburg and back	12	—
	To the Fish Breeding Estab. and Eberstein and back	13	—
	Viâ Oos to the Favorite and back	10	—
	To the Yburg and back	13	—
	To the Fremersberg-Turm and back	12	—
V.	To the Fremersberg-Turm and thence back viâ the Katzenstein and the Jagdhaus	14	—
	To the Fish Breeding Estab. and Schloss Eberstein and back viâ Gernsbach	16	—
	To the Fish Breeding Estab. and Gernsbach and back	13	—
	To the Alte Schloss, Ebersteinburg, Teufelskanzel, and by the new road below the Mercurius-Turm to Müllenbild and back, or vice versâ	16	—
VI.	The same, including Gernsbach *or* Schloss Eberstein	20	—
	The same, including Gernsbach *and* Schloss Eberstein	23	—
VII.	Viâ Geroldsau to the Plättig (20 ℳ), Sand (22 ℳ), and the Hundseck, and back to Baden	24	—
	Viâ Geroldsau to Bühler-Tal and the Gertelbach-Schlucht, and back viâ Bühl and Steinbach or vice versâ	23	—
	Return viâ Sand and the Plättig	28	—

Electric Tramway from *Baden-Weststadt* (p. 355) to *Lichtental,* viâ Lange-Str. (railway-station) and Lichtentaler-Str. (fares 10-20 pf.).

Motor Omnibus (from April to September; intermediate fares). 1. From the *Kurhaus* (p. 362) viâ Lichtental to the *Geroldsau Waterfall* (p. 365) 4 times daily, 1 ℳ; to Lichtental 60 pf. — 2. From the *Goldenes Kreuz* (p. 357) viâ Lichtental and the Fish Breeding Estab. (p. 365) to *Gernsbach* (p. 392), 3-4 times daily, 1½ ℳ (some cars run viâ Schloss Eberstein, p. 392). — 3. From the *Kurhaus* viâ the Korbmattfelsenhof (p. 368) to *Schirmhof* (p. 357), once daily, 80 pf. — 4. From the *Railway Station* viâ the Café Zabler, Schwanenwasen, the Plättig, and Sand to the *Hundseck* (p. 390), twice daily, 3 ℳ 20 pf.

Omnibuses or **Brakes** (*Gesellschaftswagen;* main station near the Conversationshaus). 1. From the *Ludwig-Wilhelm-Platz* (Pl. C, 4), viâ the Leopolds-Platz, Lange-Str., and the Railway Station to *Baden West-stadt* (Badenscheuern, p. 355), 22 times daily, 20 pf. — 2. From the *Kurhaus* viâ the Sophien-Str. and the Zähringer-Str. to the *Alte Schloss* (p. 365) twice daily, 1¹/₂ *M.*, there and back 2 *M.* — 3. From the *Railway Station* (40 pf.) viâ the Leopolds-Platz (20 pf.) to *Lichtental* (p. 364) 7 times daily. — 4. From the *Kurhaus* viâ Lichtental to *Seelach* (p. 364), thrice daily (in summer 4 times), 1 *M*, there and back 1¹/₂ *M.* — 5. From the *Kurhaus* viâ Lichtental to the *Fish Breeding Estab.* (p. 365) twice daily, 1 *M*, there and back 1¹/₂ *M.* The morning omnibus starts from the railway-station. — 6. From the *Kurhaus* viâ the Fish Breeding Estab. to *Schloss Eberstein* (p. 392), once daily, 2 and 3 *M.* — 7. From the *Kurhaus* viâ Lichtental to the *Geroldsau Waterfall* (p. 365), twice daily, 1 *M.* — 8. From the *Kurhaus* viâ the Plättig and Sand to the *Hundseck* (p. 390), once daily, 3 and 5 *M.* — 9. From the *Theater-Platz* viâ the Yburg-Str. to *Yburg* (p. 368; return viâ the Korbmattfelsenhof and the Werder-Str.) twice daily, 2 and 2¹/₂ *M.* — 10. From the *Kurhaus* viâ the Werder-Str. and the Korbmattfelsenhof (4 times daily; 70 pf.) to the *Jagd-haus* (p. 368; return through the Jagdhauser-Allée), twice daily, 1¹/₂ and 2¹/₂ *M.* — 11. From the *Kurhaus* to the *Schloss Favorite* (p. 366), once daily, 2 and 2¹/₂ *M.* — 12. From the *Kurhaus* to the *Mercurius* (p. 367), once daily, 2 and 3 *M.* — 13. From the *Kurhaus* to the *Fremersberg-Turm* (p. 368), once daily, 2 and 2¹/₂ *M.* — Intermediate fares on all these lines.

Visitors' Tax (compulsory after 4 days' stay). Tickets of admission to the Conversationshaus (p. 357) and grounds (sold at the Enquiry Office, see below) are necessary for afternoon and evening concerts (4-5 & 8-10 p.m.; the morning concert, 7-8 a.m., is free): for one day, 1 pers. 1¹/₂ *M;* for ten days, 1 pers. 8 *M*, each additional person 4 *M* more; for one month 20 & 10, for a year 50 & 25 *M.* Monthly ticket for drinking the waters 2 *M*, single glass 10 pf. — *Balls* every Saturday during the season. *Orchestral Concerts* at special prices once a month.

The **Season** proper lasts from April to October and is at its height from June to August. The mild climate and health-giving air also attract numerous visitors out of season; the Friedrichs-Bad, the Trinkhalle, the smaller hotels, and several of the larger ones are open in winter.

Baths. **Friedrichs-Bad* (p. 361), open from April 16th to Oct. 15th from 6.30 a.m. to 6.30 p.m.; other months from 7 or 8 a.m. to 6, 5, or 4 p.m.: ordinary baths 1 *M* 20 pf.-1¹/₂ *M*, general vapour baths, swimming-basins, and douches (1¹/₂-2 hrs.) 1 *M* 80-2¹/₂ *M*, bath 'de luxe' (Salonbad) 5-10 *M.* **Augusta-Bad* (p. 361); *Darmstädter Hof* (Pl. r; C, 3), Gerns-bacher-Str. 5 (bath from 30 pf.), also rooms and pension. *Air and Swimming Baths* (Pl. C, 5), on the right bank of the Oos.

Baths Office (*Grossherzogliche Kommission der Badeanstalten),* in the Grossherzogliche Amtshaus (Pl. C, D, 2). — **Municipal Baths Committee** (*Städtisches Kurkomitee),* in the Conversationshaus.

Theatre. From June to Sept. performances on Mon., Wed., Frid., and Sat., in winter on Wed. only.

Races at *Iffezheim* (3 M. to the N.W. of Oos, p. 355), at the end of August and the beginning of September.

Post and Telegraph Office (Pl. C, 3), Leopolds-Platz 12.

Enquiry Office (*Verkehrsbureau),* Städtisches Palais, Luisen-Str. 1.

Tourist Agency Offices. *F. W. Schick,* Sophien-Str. 5; *F. Trapp,* Hirsch-Str. 2.

English Church (*All Saints'),* Berthold-Str. 5, close to the Grand-Hôtel Bellevue; Sun. services at 8.30 a.m., 11 a.m., and 7 p.m. Chaplain, *Rev. T. Archibald S. White, M. A.,* Lange-Str. 33. — *Church Lending Library.*

Physicians (all speak English). *Dr. Schliep,* Kaiser-Wilhelm-Str. 2; *Dr. Dengler,* Kapuziner-Str. 1 (comp. p. 357); *Dr. Auerbach,* Lichtentaler-Str. 13.

Baden (600 ft.), or *Baden-Baden* (to distinguish it from the Baden near Vienna and that in Switzerland), lies at the entrance of the Black Forest, among picturesque, well-wooded hills, in the delightful valley of the *Oosbach*. It vies with Heidelberg and Freiburg in the beauty of its situation, and is one of the most popular watering-places in Europe, being rivalled in Germany by Wiesbaden only. The population is 21,500 (chiefly Roman Catholics) and the number of visitors is over 75,000 annually.

The efficacy of the waters was known to the Romans, who called it *Aquae Aureliae*. For six centuries Baden-Baden was the seat of the Margraves of Baden, of whom Hermann II. (d. 1130) first resided in the old castle. The new castle, above the town, was erected by the Margrave Christopher (1475-1527), but both town and castles suffered so much during the Thirty Years' War and the war of the Palatinate (1689), that the Margraves transferred their residence to *Rastatt* in 1706. The modern reputation of Baden as a sanatorium dates from the beginning of the 19th century. The first 'Conversationshaus' was opened in 1808, and the gaming-table, which was immediately set up, became a favourite resort of European wealth and fashion. The suppression of public gambling in 1872, however, has given Baden-Baden more of the character of a health-resort.

The OLD TOWN, with its narrow streets, is situated on the right bank of the Oosbach, and extends up the slope of a spur of the Battert, the summit of which is crowned by the grand-ducal château. Farther to the S. rises the Gothic —

Pfarrkirche or **Stiftskirche** (590 ft.; Pl. C, 2; open till noon and again after 2 p.m.), erected in the 7th cent., raised to the dignity of an abbey-church in 1453, destroyed by fire in 1689, repaired in 1753, and restored in the original style in 1866. The choir contains interesting *Monuments* of the Margraves of Baden, from Bernhard I. (d. 1431) downwards, notably those of Bishop Frederick of Utrecht (d. 1517), brother of Christopher I. (bronze monument in a Gothic niche, to the left), and of Margrave Lewis William (colossal tomb, on the right). The lower part of the W. tower is Romanesque. — Opposite the W. portal lies the *Rathaus* (Pl. C, 3), formerly the Jesuits' College and then the Conversationshaus (1809-24).

Adjacent to the church, on the S.E. slope of the Schlossberg, are the *Hot Springs (Thermalquellen)*, the chief of which have been united in two channels, the *Hauptstollen* and the *Kirchenstollen*. They yield about 110,000 gallons per day, and vary from 111° to 147° Fahr. in temperature. The efficacy of the water is chiefly due to its high natural temperature, the solid ingredients, chiefly chloride of sodium, amounting only to three per cent. There are also slight traces of arsenic. The *Büttquelle*, below the Rathaus, is strongly impregnated with radium. Close to the springs are the two chief bath-houses, in which the springs are put to their fullest use.

The **Friedrichs-Bad** (Pl. C, 2; p. 359) is an imposing sand-stone edifice by *Dernfeld* (1869-77), embellished with statues, busts, and medallions. In summer it is reserved for gentlemen, in winter it is used by ladies also. Its admirable equipments comprise hot and cold plunge-baths, sitz-baths, electric baths, baths for bathing in company, vapour and douche baths, Turkish baths, swimming-baths, and apparatus for curative gymnastics and massage.

Visitors are admitted to view the interior of the Friedrichs-Bad and the Augusta-Bad (see below) after 6 p.m. (fee 50 pf.).

On the E. the Friedrichs-Bad is adjoined by the **Kaiserin-Augusta-Bad,** a handsome Italian Renaissance building, erected by *Durm* in 1891-92 and adorned with sculptures by *Hör*. It is reserved for ladies, but is open in summer only. The handsome staircase is adorned with a bust of Empress Augusta by *Moest* and a frieze by *Gleichauf*. The general equipments resemble those of the Friedrichs-Bad.

Between these two bath-houses are the remains of *Roman Baths* (open 11-12, 10 pf.; steps lead down from the Augusta-Bad). — To the N. of the Platz is the *Institut zum Heiligen Grab*, with a church.

To the E. of the Augusta-Bad are the *Spital-Kirche,* used by the Old Catholics, and the *Old Cemetery (Alte Friedhof;* Pl. D, 2), now transformed into a promenade and containing a fine crucifix by Niclaus Lerch of Leyden (1467) and a late-Gothic 'Mount of Olives' with stone figures. To the left, at the foot of the Schloss-berg, are the *Landes-Bad* (Pl. D, 2), for poor patients, and the *Inhalatorium*. To the right are the *Ludwig-Wilhelms-Stift,* a home for ladies (p. 357), and *Dr. Ebers's Sanatorium* (higher up; p. 357).

The **Neue Schloss** (Pl. C, 2; 675 ft.), on the hill to the N. of the town, is most conveniently reached viâ the Schloss-Str. and Burg-Str., ascending from the Pfarrkirche (p. 360). It was founded in 1479, enlarged in 1530 and 1570-80, seriously damaged in 1689, and partly restored. In 1842 it was fitted up as a summer-residence for the Grand-Duke. The Schloss is open all day, 8-12 a.m. and 2-6 p.m. (50 pf., for a party 20 pf. each). The W. gateway, with its Gothic vaulting, leads into the court (bell to the left for the castellan), on the E. side of which is the handsome Renaissance château. It contains a number of handsome saloons and the apartments of the Grand-Duke, adorned with several good modern pictures, carving, family-portraits, etc. The winding-staircase (ca. 1575) in the Dagobert-Turm is interesting. The curious subterranean vaults with stone and iron doors were perhaps once used as dungeons. — The tasteful *Garden*, with a bronze bust of Grand-Duke Frederick I., and a view-terrace, on the S. side of the Schloss, is always open (entrance at the N.E. angle of the Schloss; steps descend to the town).

The chief resorts of visitors are in the new quarters and the beautiful *Pleasure Grounds,* extending along the left bank of the

Oos, which flows for a long distance through an artificial channel. The busiest point is the Conversationshaus.

The **Conversationshaus** or *Kurhaus* (525 ft.; Pl. B, 3), designed by *Weinbrenner*, erected in 1824, and considerably enlarged in 1854, is 125 yds. in length and is preceded by a portico of 8 columns.

The INTERIOR is gorgeously fitted up by Parisian masters. Immediately within the colonnade is the GREAT SALOON, where the band plays in the evening in unfavourable weather. To the left are the so-called LANDSCAPE SALOON, the ITALIAN SALOON, and the FLOWER SALOON; to the right the RENAISSANCE SALOON. The NEW SALOONS, opened in 1854, are fitted up in the Renaissance style of Louis XIII. and Louis XIV. — In the N. wing of the building are the well-stocked reading-rooms. The S. wing contains the restaurant (p. 357).

The band which plays on the 'Kaiser-Promenade' (formerly the Promenade-Platz), in front of the Conversationshaus, always attracts a large assemblage of the fashionable world, and on fine Sunday afternoons the grounds are crowded with visitors from Strassburg, Carlsruhe, and other neighbouring places. The short avenue leading to the Leopolds-Brücke is flanked with fashionable shops.

A few paces to the N. of the 'Kaiser-Promenade' is the **Trinkhalle** (Pl. B, 3), designed by *Hübsch*, and erected in 1839-42. It is most frequented from 7 to 8 in the morning, when the band plays and the waters are drunk. The relief in the tympanum, by *Reich*, represents the nymph of the springs administering health to sufferers of every kind. The frescoes in the arcades, by *Götzenberger*, illustrate legends of the Black Forest.

On the S. side of the Promenade is the **Theatre** (Pl. B, 3), built by *Derchy* in 1861, and richly fitted up from designs by *Couteau*. — Between the Conversationshaus and the Hôtel Messmer (p. 356) ascends the Werder-Str., in which, to the right, is the studio of *Professor J. von Kopf*, the sculptor (d. 1903), to which visitors are admitted in summer on Tues. & Thurs. 3-6, and on Sun. 11-12 and 3-6. — The *Kunsthalle* (Pl. B, C, 3), behind the theatre, contains an exhibition of pictures (open 10-6, 50 pf.; Sun. & holidays 11-6, 20 pf.; free to holders of Kurhaus tickets). Near it are the *International Club* and a handsome new *Exhibition Building* (*Kunstausstellungsgebäude*, Pl. B, 4; open 10-6, Sun. 11-6, 1 *ℳ*). Farther on, in the Lichtentaler-Allée, is a marble bust of the *Empress Augusta*, by Kopf (1894). — In the Kronprinzen-Str., farther up the hill, is the *Künstlerhaus* (Pl. B, 4), with the studios of several painters.

Crossing the Leopolds-Brücke we see immediately to the left the former *Palais Hamilton*, bought by the town in 1900, with a pretty garden (café-restaurant, see p. 357).

The palais contains the *Archducal Picture Gallery* (open 10-12.30, on Sun. 11-12.30), founded by Herr Louis Jüncke (d. 1900) who presented 100 pictures by German, Spanish, French, and Italian painters of the 19th century. In the same building (entr. from the Insel-Str.) are the *Municipal Historical Collections*, open free on Sun. 11-12.30, Tues. & Thurs. 10.30-12.30, and Sat. 3-5 (in winter on Sun. & Thurs. only).

The LEOPOLDS-PLATZ (Pl. C, 3), close by, is embellished with a bronze *Statue of Grand-Duke Leopold* (d. 1852). On the right is the *Post Office*. — The SOPHIEN-STRASSE, to the E. of this Platz, is bordered with trees. In the Stephanien-Str., which diverges to the S., is the handsome *Synagogue.* — In the new S. quarter of the town, in the Ludwig-Wilhelm-Platz, are the Gothic *Protestant Church* (Pl. C, 4), by Eisenlohr, and the **English Church** (Pl. C, 5). The latter contains some good stained-glass windows, a fine candelabrum presented by the Empress Augusta, and a lectern given by the Grand-Duchess of Baden. In the Lichtentaler-Str. is the *Russian Church* (Pl. C, D, 5), with a gilded dome. — On the S.W. slope of the Friedrichshöhe lie the *Cemetery (Friedhof;* Pl. D, 4) and the new *Crematorium.*

On the Michaelsberg rises the **Greek Church** (685 ft.; Pl. B, 2), erected in 1863-66 from designs by *Klenze* of Munich in memory of a son of the Roumanian prince Michael Stourdza, who died at Baden in 1863, in his 17th year. The roof and dome are gilded; the interior, which contains the tombs of the family, is sumptuously decorated with gold, marble, and paintings. Key at the house No. 2; fee 50 pf. (service on Sun., 10-11). — A little to the S. is the *Château of Baron Venninger-Ullner* (Pl. B, 3), built by Oppler in a mediæval style. — Farther up is the **Friesenberg** (940 ft.), the pretty forest-paths on which afford beautiful views; it is reached by following the Werder-Str. (p. 362) or the Beutig-Str., or direct from the Greek church. — The Beutig-Str. is continued to the *Cross on the Beutig* (770 ft.; Pl. A, 4), opposite which is the *Villa Meineck.* Farther on, to the left of the road, is the *Hôtel-Café Gretel*, and still farther on, $1^1/_4$ M. from the Conversationshaus, is the *Hôtel Kaiserin Elisabeth* (comp. p. 357). — Pretty paths lead from the Friesenberg to the *Waldsee* (655 ft.), in the valley of the *Michelbach,* which stretches to the N. between the Friesenberg and Fremersberg (p. 368) and joins the valley of the Oosbach below the Baden railway-station.

ENVIRONS OF BADEN.

The most attractive walk in the vicinity of Baden is the *Lichtentaler Allée (Pl. B, 3, 4, C, 5, 6), ascending the left bank of the Oosbach, and much frequented in the afternoon by pedestrians, equestrians, and carriages. The fine old trees are surrounded with flower-beds and shrubberies. On the left, beyond the brook and the tennis-courts, is the *Gönner-Anlage*, ornamental grounds with a handsome fountain (1909), while to the right, on the slope of the hill, are gardens and villas. About $1/_4$ M. from the theatre, beside the Allée-Haus (No. 10), the roads to the Fremers-berg and the Yburg (p. 368) diverge to the right; and $^1/_2$ M. farther on the road to Gunzenbach (Pl. D, 6) also runs off to the right.

Following the above-mentioned Fremersberg road and then turning to the left, we may reach the *Sauersberg* (845 ft.: view), in $^1/_2$ hr., and the *Molkenanstalt* or *Whey Cure Establishment* (refreshments) in 10 min. more. — The *Gunzenbach-Tal*, with a prettily situated garden-restaurant and the *Gunzenbacher Hof* (pension; Pl. C, 6), is interesting to mineral-ogists. At the entrance to the Gunzenbach-Tal a guide-board indicates the way to the *Leopoldshöhe*, above the *Hôtel-Café Panorama* (p. 357), commanding a fine view. — Paths lead from the Allée and from the Gunzenbach-Tal to the top of the *Caecilienberg* (see below).

About $1^1/_2$ M. from the Conversationshaus we reach —

Lichtental. — Hotels (all with gardens and restaurants). *Bär; Ludwigsbad*, with a chalybeate spring; *Löwe*, R. $1^1/_2$-$2^1/_2$, B. $^3/_4$, D. $2^1/_4$, pens. 5-7 ℳ; *Goldnes Kreuz*, similar charges. — *Pension Haase; Erholungsheim*, a sanitarium. — *Caecilienberg Beer Garden.*

Tramway and Omnibus to Baden, the Fish Breeding Establishment, etc., see p. 358.

Lichtental (610 ft.), formerly called *Unter-Beuern* and now incorporated with Baden-Baden, takes its name from the *Nunnery of Lichtental*, which was founded in 1245 by Irmengard, grand-daughter of Henry the Lion and widow of Hermann V. of Baden. It lies to the right, just beyond the bridge, and near it are a *War Monument* and the *Protestant Church*, with its two towers. The convent, taken by the Margraves of Baden under their special protection, has escaped the devastations of war and the ravages of time, and is still occupied by 16 or 18 Cistercian nuns. The *Church*, which has no aisles, contains the 14th cent. tomb of the foundress (d. 1260), by Wölfelin von Rufach. Adjoining the church and con-nected with it by an archway is the *Toten-Kapelle* (mortuary chapel), built in the Gothic style in 1288, and restored in 1830. It contains tombstones of Margraves of Baden-Durlach, and two altar-pieces (retouched) of the Upper Rhenish School (1496). The *Orphan Asylum*, within the precincts of the convent, was founded by the wealthy and benevolent London tailor *Stulz* (p. 371), who was afterwards ennobled.

The pine-clad *Caecilienberg* (755 ft.), immediately behind the nunnery, a spur of the *Klosterberg* (1360 ft.), affords pleasant walks and charming views. Higher up rises the new *Parish Church*.

On the **Seelach** (900 ft.), on the E. side of the Gerolsau (ascended from the nunnery in $^1/_2$ hr.; road to the right of the parish-church, foot-path to the left), stands a villa in the mediæval style, adjoining which is a restaurant with a view-terrace (omn., see p. 358). — The broad road ascends, skirting the Baden aqueduct, to ($1^3/_4$-2 hrs.) the *Scherrhof* (2225 ft.), whence the top of the *Badener Höhe* (p. 390) may be reached by foot-paths in $1^1/_2$ hr.

From Lichtenthal the road, which is destitute of shade, ascends the Beuerner-Tal, passing several houses and hamlets, to **Ober-Beuern** *(Waldhorn).* — The valley now contracts and trees become

more numerous. About 1½ M. from the convent the road divides, the main branch, to the left, proceeding by Müllenbach to Gernsbach and Schloss Eberstein (comp. pp. 368, 392). To the right, on the branch leading to Gaisbach and Forbach (p. 393), is the *Gaisbach Fish Breeding Establishment* (the '*Fischkultur*'; 875 ft.; fair inn and restaurant; adm. to breeding-ponds 20 pf.), situated in a cool and shady nook of the valley, and a favourite point for excursions from Baden (omnibus and automobile, see p. 358).

Near Lichtental, on the S.W. (to the right at the Löwe Hotel), opens the **Geroldsau**, a pretty grassy valley watered by the *Grobbach*, and fringed with wood, where (¼ hr.) the *Geroldsauer Mühle* (open-air restaurant) and the straggling village of *Geroldsau* (740 ft.; Auerhahn; Hirsch) are situated. A road a little beyond the Auerhahn inn (1¾ M. from the nunnery) leads to the right from Geroldsau by *Malschbach* (860 ft.) to *Neuweier* (p. 369; 6 M. from Lichtental). We, however, follow the road to the left. A footpath, more picturesque than the road, diverges to the right from the latter 250 yds. beyond the bridge over the Grobbach, and ascends the right bank of the stream. About 2¾ M. from the Lichtental nunnery we reach the pretty *Geroldsau Waterfall* (990 ft.; restaurant; motor-omnibus, see p. 358).

From the Geroldsau Waterfall to SCHWANENWASEN and PLÄTTIG (1¼-2 hrs.; carriage from Baden-Baden in 3 hrs., and motor-omnibus in 1¼ hr., see p. 358). The road soon (¾ M.) forks. The branch to the right crosses the *Grobbach* and ascends round the *Lanzenkopf* to (4½ M.) the top of the *Schwanenwasen* (p. 389). The Ober-Plättig (p. 389) lies about 2 M. farther on. — Walkers may follow the carriage-road (or they may skirt the stream by a footpath which rejoins the road ¼ hr. farther up), but beyond the bridge, at the (7 min.) first sharp curve, they should quit the road and ascend the 'logging road' to the left for 8 min., then take the footpath to the left, which crosses a road in ¼ hr., rejoins the same road 5 min. later, follows it for 7 min., then ascends to the right past the *Grobbach Falls* to (8 min.) another bifurcation. The arm to the right leads to (8 min.) the Schwanenwasen, that to the left to (¾ hr.) the Plättig.

TO THE BADENER HÖHE, 2 hrs. At the fork, ¾ M. from the Geroldsau Waterfall, carriages take the branch to the left, which remains on the right bank of the Grobbach and ¾ M. farther on turns once more to the left into the valley of the *Urbach*. Just below the influx (l.) of the (¾ M.) *Grimbach*, the road crosses the Urbach and then ascends its valley in numerous windings to the *Herrenwieser Sattel* (2895 ft.), whence the road to the Badener Höhe leads to the left. — Walkers should choose the road (2¼ M. from the waterfall) ascending the valley of the *Grimbach;* 1 M. farther on is a footpath to the right, skirting the *Falls of the Grimbach* and crossing two cart-tracks. At the (20 min.) top we follow the road to the left for 8 min. and then the path to the right. The latter crosses another road beside a solitary house and leads to (½ hr.) the *Badener Sattel* (2907 ft.), whence a path runs to the right to (½ hr.) the Badener Höhe (p. 390).

The ALTE SCHLOSS (1 hr.; comp. Pl. C, 2, D, 2, 1, and the Map; omn., see p. 358) is reached by a carriage-road ascending at first through meadows and orchards and afterwards through fragrant pine-woods. Walkers should, however, ascend the Schloss-Str. (p. 361), and above the Schloss-Garten follow the short-cuts avoiding the curves of the road. About halfway is the *Sophienruhe* (1145 ft.), a projecting rock with a pavilion, beyond which is a fresh spring. (The path diverging to the left at the next bend leads to the Kellersbild, see below.) — From the station we take the Leopold-Str., passing the Schiesshaus (comp. Pl. A, B, 1), and then follow the direction-posts (40 min. to the Schloss).

The *__Alte Schloss Hohenbaden__ (terrace, 1330 ft.; *Restaurant with fixed tariff and shady seats in the open air) is an extensive structure situated on a buttress of the *Battert*, the walls of which probably date in part from the 3rd cent., when the Romans constructed some fortifications here. From the 11th cent. until the construction of the Neue Schloss (p. 361) it was the seat of the Margraves. The so-called Rittersaal dates from the end of the 14th century. Since its destruction by the French in 1689 the castle has been a complete ruin, but the tower has been rendered accessible by steps (10 pf.). The **View from the top embraces the valley of the Rhine from Speyer to a point far beyond Strassburg (not itself visible); in the foreground lies the charming valley of Baden, with its bright villas, its light-green woods of beech and oak, and its sombre pine-forests; to the S. is the Black Forest with the Badener Höhe (morning light most favourable).

Finger-posts on the terrace in front of the Schloss, and behind it, opposite the inner entrance, indicate the way to the summit of the *Battert* (1855 ft.), round which towards the S. rise the precipitous **Felsen** ('rocks'), a number of fantastically-cleft masses of porphyry. The *Felsen-Brücke*, 20-25 min. from the Schloss, commanding a magnificent view, is the finest point. An easier route leads from the castle-terrace by an almost level path along the base of the Felsen. At the ($^3/_4$ M.) fork we turn to the right and after 10 paces to the left to (1 M.) Ebersteinburg; or we may continue by the path to the right ('Teufelskanzel and Merkur') and rejoin the old Gernsbach road (see p. 367). — The road from the Schloss to Ebersteinburg leads along the N. side of the Battert.

About 2 M. to the N.W. of the Alte Schloss, on the *Hardberg*, is the *Dreiburgen-Blick*, affording a view of the Alte Schloss, the Yburg, and the Ebersteinburg. It may be reached from Baden viâ the *Kellersbild* (see above) or viâ Badenscheuern.

From the Alte Schloss at Baden and from Ebersteinburg pleasant paths lead through the woods (comp. Map at p. 364; the paths eventually quit the woods) to (6 M. from Baden; 1 M. to the S.W. of the station of Kuppenheim) the **Favorite** (430 ft.; motor-omnibus, see p. 359), a château of the Grand-Duke, erected in 1725, in the rococo style, by the Margravine Sibylla Augusta, widow of the Margrave Lewis William (d. 1707), who after the death of her husband superintended the education of her sons for nineteen years, and then retired to this spot. The interior (50 pf., for a party 20 pf. each) is decorated in the taste of the period and contains a valuable collection of porcelain. Small restaurant.

The ROUTE FROM BADEN TO EBERSTEINBURG ($2^1/_2$ M.) is by the old Gernsbach road (Pl. D, 2), ascending the valley to the E. between the Battert and the Mercurius. Walkers should choose the pleasant footpath to the Teufelskanzel, diverging to the right about $^1/_2$ M. from the Old Cemetery (p. 361), at the *Morgenröte Inn*. Farther on is the *Waldschlösschen Inn*. Near the saddle of the hill (1225 ft.; *Wolfsschlucht Inn*) are two rocks known as the *Teufelskanzel* (r.; 1245 ft.) and *Engelskanzel* (l.; 1280 ft.), both affording good views. At the inn the roads cross; that to the right leads through wood to the Mercurius and the Müllenbild (see below; pleasant return-route over the Friedrichshöhe, see below). The Ebersteinburg road leads to the left. A little farther on is a finger-post, also on the left, indicating the way to the romantic *Wolfsschlucht,* through the woods of which we may ascend to the village of Ebersteinburg.

From the village of *Ebersteinburg* (1400 ft.; Krone, R. 2-4, D. $2^1/_2$, pens. 5 $\mathcal{M}$; Hirsch) we ascend in 10 min. to the top of the isolated eminence which bears the ruins of the castle of *Ebersteinburg,* or the *Alt-Eberstein* (1605 ft.; restaurant). Fine view from the tower (10 pf.). The castle stands on Roman substructures, and the present edifice dates from the 10-14th centuries. It was once the seat of the Counts of Eberstein, and afterwards belonged to the Margraves of Baden. Visitors should be familiar with Uhland's ballad of the Count of Eberstein and the Emperor's daughter.

The MERCURIUS, the highest mountain near Baden, may be ascended in $1^1/_2$ hr. by one of several different routes. The carriage-road (brakes, see p. 359) diverges on the above-mentioned saddle of the hill to the right from the old Gernsbach road, passes near the Teufelskanzel, and leads to the top in long windings in less than an hour. — The shortest route starts from the Scheiben-Str. in Baden (Pl. C, D, 3), and crosses the *Friedrichshöhe* (985 ft.). At the top of this hill is the reservoir of the Baden water-works, near which is the *Karlshof Restaurant*, with a garden commanding a fine view. We keep straight on, through wood (numerous finger-posts). The easiest ascent quits the old Gernsbach road above the Morgenröte Inn (see above) and leads to the right over the *Maisenköpfle* (1120 ft.). From Lichtental we mount to the left by the Kreuz Inn, leaving the *Schaafberg* (1050 ft.) to the right, and then ascend the *Falkenhalde*. — The summit of the **Mercurius,** or *Grosse Staufen* (2205 ft.), is occupied by a restaurant and a tower, which commands a very extensive view. The mountain derives its name from a Roman vôtive stone found here, now preserved in a small niche made for its reception. — The above-mentioned carriage-road passes near the summit of the Mercurius, skirts the W. slope of the *Kleine Staufenberg* (2050 ft.), and at the Müllenbild joins the new road to Gernsbach (p. 368). Pedestrians may reach Gernsbach from the Mercurius in 1 hr.

viâ Staufenberg (see below), by taking the path to the E. at the bifurcation of the roads on the *Binsenwasen* (1695 ft.; finger-post).

FROM BADEN TO GERNSBACH (p. 392) by the new road viâ
Lichtental and Beuern (p. 364), $6^1/_2$ M. About $^3/_4$ M. from the
Fish Breeding Establishment the hamlet of *Müllenbach* is reached,
after which the road ascends very circuitously (pedestrians effect a
saving by proceeding straight on from the inn) to the *Müllenbild*
(1255 ft.; $4^1/_2$ M. from Baden), where it is joined on the left by the
road from the ($2^1/_2$ M.) Mercuriusberg. It then divides into two
branches, that to the left descending to ($2^1/_2$ M.) Gernsbach, and
that to the right leading along the hill to (3 M.) Schloss Eberstein
(p. 392; omn., see p. 358). — The old road (6 M.) as far as the
saddle (1225 ft.) between the Teufelskanzel and the Engelskanzel
is described on p. 367. Fine view of the Murgtal in descending. On
the right, after about $1^1/_4$ M., where the road again ascends a little, is
the *Neuhaus*, a solitary inn. The road then descends and in 10 min.
makes a sharp bend to the right into the valley; $^1/_4$ hr. *Staufenberg*,
where strawberries are largely cultivated; $^1/_2$ hr. farther on *Gernsbach* (p. 392; $3^3/_4$ M. from the saddle). Pedestrians proceed straight
on at the bend and descend along the edge of the wood (40 min.).

To THE FREMERSBERG, carriages (omn., see p. 359) either follow
the Werder-Str. and Moltke-Str., passing the *Hôtel Kaiserin Elisabeth;* or they may leave the Lichtenberger-Allée by the Fremersberg-Str. (Pl. B, 5; p. 364), which diverges to the right, and in little
more than $^1/_2$ M. passes a group of houses known as *Tiergarten*.
About $^1/_2$ M. farther on the two routes unite, beside the *Hôtel Früh*
and the *Hôtel Korbmattfelsenhof*. The road then forks, the left
branch leading to the *Korbmattfels* (1700 ft.) and the Yburg (see
below), and the right through wood to (3 M.) **Fremersberg**
(1730 ft.; *Inn;* view-tower). — Pedestrians ascend from Baden in
$1^3/_4$ hr. by an attractive route past the *Waldsee* (p. 363). We return
by the ($1^1/_4$ M.) *Jagdhaus* (800 ft.; omn., p. 359), with a frequented
restaurant (also pension) commanding a fine view of the Rhine valley
and Strassburg Minster, to ($3^3/_4$ M.) Baden.

To THE YBURG, another favourite excursion (5 M.; omn., see
p. 359). The road ascends from the Allée-Haus (p. 364) among
gardens (view), skirts the E. slope of the *Korbmattfels* (see above),
traversing fine woods, and reaches (4 M.) the shelter on the *Lache*
(1490 ft.), a narrow saddle, where numerous paths diverge. Hence
to the Yburg, about 1 M. The ancient **Yburg** (1695 ft.; *Inn*, very
fair) was, like the Ebersteinburg, once a Roman watch-tower. Wide
view from the tower (10 pf.) of the Black Forest Mts. and the Rhine
valley, best in the morning. From the Yburg to *Steinbach* (p. 369),
$4^1/_2$ M. A road and footpath descend to the Hôtel zum Korbmatt-
felsen (see above) in $^3/_4$-1 hr.

From Baden-Baden to *Forbach,* see p. 393.

49. From Baden-Baden to Strassburg.

35 M. RAILWAY in 1-2¹/₂ hrs. (fares 5 ℳ 10, 3 ℳ 20, 2 ℳ 5 pf.; express fares 5 ℳ 60, 3 ℳ 70, 2 ℳ 30 pf.). Finest views to the left. — Comp. *Map*, p. .

Baden-Baden, see p. 356. — 2¹/₂ M. *Baden-Oos*, see p. 355. — To the left rise the Black Forest Mts.; in the foreground the *Yburg* (p. 368). 4¹/₂ M. *Sinzheim*. — Near (7 M.) **Steinbach** (*Stern*, pens. from 4 ℳ; 2100 inhab.), on a barren hill to the left, is a statue of *Erwin*, the architect of Strassburg Cathedral (p. 480), supposed to have been a native of Steinbach (d. at Strassburg, 1318). A road leads hence to the E. to (6 M.) the *Yburg* (p. 368). In the valley of the *Steinbach*, about 2 M. from the station of the name, lies the village of *Neuweier* (605 ft.; Lamm, very fair), with an ancient castle and excellent wine ('Mauerwein'). Hence to Baden, viâ Malschbach (p. 365), 6 M.; to the Yburg 4¹/₂ M. — *Affentaler*, one of the best red wines of Baden, is produced around (1¹/₂ M.) *Affental* (Auerhahn), to the S.E. The *Schartenberg* (1710 ft.) is ascended from Affental in ³/₄ hr.

10 M. **Bühl** (445 ft.; *Badischer Hof*, R. 1¹/₂-2¹/₂ ℳ; *Rabe*, R. & B. 2 ℳ; *Stern*, R. 1¹/₂-2 ℳ, these two very fair), a thriving place with 3400 inhab., at the mouth of the *Bühler-Tal* (p. 389). The new Gothic church has a handsome pierced spire; the old church, with a tower dating from the 16th cent., is now the Rathaus. On the hill to the S.E. rises the ruined castle of *Alt-Windeck* (1235 ft.; 1¹/₄ hr.), with two towers, once the seat of a powerful race which became extinct in 1592 (inn; view).

A steam-tramway plies from Bühl to (24 M.) *Kehl* (p. 370) in 2 hrs. — About 6 M. to the N.W. of Bühl lies *Schwarzach*, with a late-Romanesque abbey-church of the 12th cent. (well restored).

Local railway up the *Bühler-Tal* to *Obertal*, and road thence to the *Sand*, *Plättig*, etc., see p. 388.

11¹/₄ M. *Ottersweier* (Adler; Sonne), with 2400 inhabitants.

15 M. **Achern**. — HOTELS. *Post*, well managed, R. 1¹/₂-2, pens. 6 ℳ; *Adler*, R. 1³/₄-3 ℳ, well spoken of. — BEER at the *Engel* and the *Rössle* (also confectioner's, with rooms). — BATHS in the Acher, 20 pf. CARRIAGES at the station and hotels according to tariff: to Allerheiligen 16 ℳ; Brigittenschloss 12 ℳ; Breitenbrunnen 16 ℳ.

Achern (470 ft.), a thriving little town with 4600 inhab., lies at the mouth of the Kappeler-Tal. The market-place is adorned with a monument of the *Grand-Duke Leopold* (d. 1852). The *Lunatic Asylum of Illenau*, near Achern, accommodates about 500 patients.

Branch-railway from Achern through the Kappeler-Tal to *Ottenhöfen* (Allerheiligen), see p. 395.

At *Sasbach* (Linde), 1¹/₂ M. to the N. of Achern, the French Marshal Turenne fell in 1675 during an engagement with the imperial General Montecuccoli. The granite obelisk was erected by the French government in 1829.

About 3½ M. to the E. of Achern is the *Erlenbad* (now a seminary for lady-missionaries), whence we may go on to (3 M.) the ruins of *Neu-Windeck* or *Laufer Schloss*, perched on a precipitous rock above the village of *Lauf* (diligence from Achern). From Lauf by *Neu-Windeck* or *Glashütte* and by a path viâ the *Breitenbrunnen Kurhaus* (p. 390) to the top of the *Hornisgrinde* (p. 390), 3-3½ hrs. — The **Brigittenschloss** (or *Hohenroder Schloss;* 2500 ft.), picturesquely situated 7½ M. to the E. of Achern, is insignificant as a ruin, but commands a noble prospect. Halfway the road passes through *Sasbachwalden* (845 ft.; Stern, well spoken of; Rebstock), a beautifully-situated village, above which is the *Gaishöhle*, with waterfalls (inn).

18½ M. *Renchen* (Sonne; Engel), with 2100 inhab., at the mouth of the *Renchtal*, with a monument to H. J. von Grimmels-hausen, the author of 'Simplicissimuss', who died here in 1676.

22½ M. **Appenweier** (450 ft.; *Railway Hotel*), a village with 1700 inhabitants. The railways to Kehl and Strassburg and to *Oppenau* (see p. 398) diverge here from the main line (R. 50; carriages generally changed).

The Strassburg line traverses the plain of the *Kinzig*, which falls into the Rhine at Kehl. 25½ M. *Legelshurst;* 27½ M. *Kork.* — To the right is *Fort Bose.*

31 M. **Kehl** (460 ft.; *Blume*, R. from 1 ℳ 60 pf., D. 2½ ℳ; *Salmen,* near the station; American Consul, *W. J. Pike*), a small Baden town (3000 inhab.), was erected by the French as a tête-de-pont of Strassburg in 1688. Since the bombardment of Strass-burg in 1870 Kehl has been largely rebuilt. Excellent baths on the Rhine below the bridges.

Steam-tramway to Bühl, see p. 369. Another runs in 1¼ hr., viâ (8½ M.) *Altenheim* (branch to *Offenburg,* see p. 371), *Ichenheim,* and *Meissenheim,* to (15½ M.) *Ottenheim* (station 1¼ M. from the Rhine bridge), where it joins the Lahr tramway (p. 371). — In the graveyard of Meissenheim rests Friederike Brion (d. 1813), Goethe's early love (see p. 472). 'Ein Strahl der Dichtersonne fiel auf sie, so reich, dass er Un-sterblichkeit ihr lieh'.

At Kehl the Rhine is crossed by two iron bridges (p. 488). The train traverses the lower of these, with a view (on the right) of the new Strassburg harbour and the Sporen-Insel. — Beyond (33½ M.) *Neudorf* it enters the large station of (35 M.) *Strassburg* (p. 475).

50. From Baden-Baden to Freiburg.

66½ M. RAILWAY in 1¾-4 hrs. (fares 8 ℳ 40, 5 ℳ 10, 3 ℳ 30 pf.; ex-press fares 9 ℳ 40, 6 ℳ 10, 3 ℳ 80 pf.).

From Baden-Baden to (22½ M.) *Appenweier,* see R. 49. — The line now runs parallel with the mountains of the Black Forest. In the distance to the left rises the castle of *Staufenberg* (1256 ft.), founded in the 11th cent. by Otho of Hohenstaufen, Bishop of Strass-burg, and now the property of Prince Max of Baden. It is much visited (1½ hr.) for its splendid view from (24 M.) *Windschläg,* the next station, viâ (3 M.) *Durbach* (720 ft.: Ritter: Linde).

27¹/₂ M. **Offenburg.** — Hotels. *Railway Hotel*, with garden, R. 2-3¹/₂, B. 1, D. 1¹/₂-2¹/₂ ℳ; *Offenburger Hof*, R. 1³/₄-2¹/₂, B. ³/₄, D. 1¹/₄-2 ℳ, both very fair; *Ochs*, R. 1¹/₂-2¹/₂, D. from 1¹/₂ ℳ; *Schwarzer Adler*, R. 1¹/₂-2 ℳ; *Sonne*, good wine, the last three in the town. — *Railway Restaurant*. — Steam-tramway to Altenheim, see p. 370.

Offenburg (530 ft.), a busy town on the *Kinzig*, with 15,400 inhab., was a free imperial town in the Middle Ages; in 1330 it was pledged to the Bishop of Strassburg, in the beginning of the 16th cent. it became 'the capital of the district of *Ortenau*, from 1701 to 1771 it belonged to the Margraves of Baden, and till 1805 it was again Austrian. It contains a statue of *Sir Francis Drake*, 'the introducer of the potato into Europe, 1586', by Friederich, a monument with the bust of the naturalist *Oken* (d. 1851), and a modern Gothic *Protestant Church* in red sandstone with an open-work tower. Offenburg is the junction for the Black Forest railway (p. 401). — A pleasant excursion may be made to the E., viâ *Zell*, to (2¹/₂ hrs.) the top of the *Brandeckkopf* (2270 ft.; view-tower).

We cross the *Kinzig*. On a hill to the left rises *Schloss Ortenberg* (p. 401). 33 M. *Nieder-Schopfheim;* 35¹/₂ M. *Friesenheim.*

38¹/₂ M. *Lahr-Dinglingen* (530 ft.; comp. Map, p. 401), the junction of a branch-line to (2 M.) **Lahr** (550 ft.; **Sonne; Krauss*), an industrial town with 14,800 inhab., in the *Schutter-Tal*. Lahr contains a venerable *Abbey Church*, a modern *Roman Catholic Church*, and an old *Rathaus*. In the Kaiser-Str., beyond the *Christus-Kirche*, is the *Stadt-Park*, containing the municipal collections and library and monuments to Bismarck and the poet Eichrodt (1827-92). Near the old *Storchen-Turm* are the remains of a so-called 'Wasserschloss' of the 12th cent. (*i.e.* a castle protected by water).

A Steam Tramway runs from Lahr to *Dinglingen* and (7¹/₂ M.) *Ottenheim* (comp. p. 370), and in the other direction, up the *Schutter-Tal*, to (3 M.) *Reichenbach* and (4¹/₂ M.) *Seelbach*. From Reichenbach a road leads to the E., viâ *Hohen-Geroldseck*, to *Biberach* (see p. 402).

41¹/₂ M. *Kippenheim* (530 ft.; Anker), a market-town, lying ¹/₂ M. from the station, was the birthplace of *Stulz*, the rich tailor (p. 364), and possesses a monument to him. — The castle of *Mahlberg*, on a basaltic hill to the left, above the small town of that name (595 ft.; Prinz), was once the seat of the old Baden governors. In the middle ages it belonged to the Hohenstaufen family.

From (44 M.) **Orschweier** (545 ft.; *Krone*) a narrow-gauge railway runs viâ *Grafenhausen* and *Kappel* to (5 M.) the *Rhine* (opposite Rheinau, on the left bank, whence there is a steam-tramway to Strassburg); and, in the other direction, through fine woods, to *Ettenheim* (Deutscher Hof), *Münchweier*, and the (5 M.) small baths of *Ettenheimmünster*.

A melancholy interest attaches to Ettenheim as the spot where the Duc d'Enghien was arrested by order of Napoleon on the night of 13th March, 1804, to be shot at Vincennes six days later.

46 M. *Ringsheim* (view from the *Kalenberg*, 1020 ft.; ³/₄ hr.). Between (48 M.) *Herbolzheim* and (49¹/₂ M.) *Kenzingen* the line crosses the *Bleiche*. Farther on it crosses the *Elz* twice. Above *Hecklingen* are the ruins of *Lichtenegg*, once a seat of the Counts of Tübingen. To the W. is the *Leopold Canal*, which conveys the Elz into the Rhine.

53 M. **Riegel** (590 ft.), the station for the *Kaiserstuhl Railway*, which runs to (¹/₂ M.) the small town of *Riegel* (Kopf, pens. 3¹/₂-4¹/₂ ℳ), where it forks, one branch skirting the E., the other the N. and W. slopes of the *Kaiserstuhl-Gebirge*, a basaltic and vine-clad hill-district about 42 sq. M. in area, which rises from the plain in upwards of 40 peaks between the Dreisam and the Rhine.

KAISERSTUHL RAILWAY. The E. branch of the railway runs viâ *Bahlingen, Nimburg, Eichstetten,* and *Bötzingen* to (8 M.) *Gottenheim* (p. 381). From Bötzingen a road ascends viâ (¹/₂ M.) *Ober-Schaffhausen* (Krone; Bad) to (1 hr.) the saddle between the *Eichelspitze* (1290 ft.) and the *Neunlindenberg* (1825 ft.), whence we may ascend the *Totenkopf* (1835 ft.; view), the highest point of the Kaiserstuhl. We may descend viâ the stud-farm of *Liliental* to (1¹/₄ hr.) Ihringen (p. 381). — The stations on the N. and W. branch are more interesting. 2¹/₂ M. **Endingen** *(Hirsch; Pfauen)*, a small town (3000 inhab.) with a Rathaus of the 16th cent., is a good starting-point for a walk through the Kaiserstuhl-Gebirge. From (6 M.) *Sasbach* (Löwe) we may visit (¹/₂ hr.) the extensive ruin of *Limburg* (880 ft.; view), the birthplace of Rudolph of Hapsburg (1218). On the Rhine, 1¹/₄ M. from (8 M.) *Jechtingen,* is the ruin of *Sponeck* (inn). 9¹/₂ M. *Burkheim* (Adler); 11 M. *Rothweil;* 13 M. *Achkarren;* 15¹/₂ M. *Breisach* (p. 381).

54¹/₂ M. *Köndringen.* On the hill (³/₄ hr.) is the ruined castle of *Landeck.* — 57 M. **Emmendingen** *(Post,* very fair; *Sonne),* a town with 7500 inhab. and two modern churches. Beyond it, on a hill to the left, are (3 M.) the extensive ruins of the *Hochburg,* dismantled in 1689 by order of Louis XIV.

The train now crosses the canalized *Elz.* 60 M. *Kollmarsreuthe.* — 61 M. *Denzlingen;* branch-line to Elzach, see p. 414.

The *Glotterbach* is then crossed, the pretty wine-growing valley of which (motor-omnibus from Denzlingen), with the scattered farms of *Unter-Glottertal* and *Ober-Glotterial,* extends to the foot of the Kandel. In a side-valley, 5 M. from Denzlingen, are the chalybeate baths of *Glotterbad.* — Near Freiburg (left) stands the watchtower of the ruined castle of *Zähringen,* once the seat of a powerful race, which became extinct in 1218 on the death of Count Berthold V. We now pass a large prison (left) and reach —

66¹/₂ M. *Freiburg* (*Railway Restaurant).

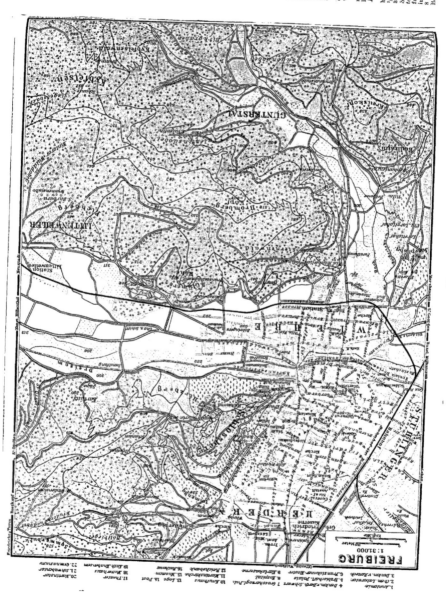

FREIBURG 1:31000

51. Freiburg and its Environs.

Hotels. *Near the Station:* *ZÄHRINGER HOF (Pl. a), in an open situation, opposite the station, an old-established house, R. from 3, B. 1¹/₄, D. (at 1 p.m.) 4, pens. from 9 ℳ; *HÔTEL DE L'EUROPE (Pl. b), to the N. of the station, also in the grounds of the Bahnhof-Str., R. 2¹/₂-4¹/₂, B. 1¹/₄, D. 3-3¹/₂, pens. 7¹/₂-10¹/₂ ℳ; *NATIONAL (Pl. d), to the S. of the railway-station, R. 2¹/₂-6, B. 1¹/₄, D. 3¹/₂, pens. from 7¹/₂ ℳ; *HÔTEL VICTORIA, Eisenbahn-Str. 54, next door to the post office, R. 2¹/₂-3¹/₂, B. 1¹/, D. 3, pens. 7-9 ℳ; HÔTEL CONTINENTAL ZUM PFAUEN (Pl. e), Friedrich-Str. 61, with garden-restaurant, R. 2-4, B. 1, D. 3¹/₂, pens. 6-9 ℳ; ROSENECK, Fahneuberg-Platz, beside the Hôt. de l'Europe, R. 2-3, B. 1, D. 2¹/₂, pens. 6-8 ℳ; HÔTEL-RESTAURANT ZUR POST, Eisenbahn-Str. 35, opposite the post office, well spoken of, R. & B. 3, D. 1¹/₂-1³/₄ ℳ. The following are unpretending: BAHNHOF-HÔTEL, Bismarck-Str. 3; HÔTEL-RESTAURANT SALMEN, to the S. of the station, Berthold-Str. 50, R. 1³/₄-3, D. 1¹/₂ ℳ; HIRSCH, Berthold-Str. 10. — *In the Town:* *RÖMISCHER KAISER (Pl. h), Kaiser-Str. 120, by the Martins-Tor (p. 379), R. 2-10, B. 1, D. 2¹/₂ ℳ; ENGEL (Pl. c), Engel-Str. 3, near the Minster, R. 2¹/₂-3 ℳ; DOM-HÔTEL ZUM GEIST (Pl. g), Münster-Platz 5, opposite the W. portal of the Minster, R. 1¹/₂-3, D. 1¹/₂-2¹/₄ ℳ, these two good and long-established houses, with wine-restaurants; ZUM KOPF (see below), R. 2-2¹/₂, B. ³/₄ ℳ; FREIBURGER HOF, Kaiser-Str. 130, to the S. of the Martins-Tor; *PARK HÔTEL HECHT (Pl. k), Werder-Str. 4, opposite the Allée-Garten, with restaurant, R. 2-4, B. 1, pens. 7-8 ℳ; HÔTEL-RESTAURANT GASS, Garten-Str. 6, to the E. of the Allée-Garten, very fair, R. 1¹/₂-2¹/₄, B. ³/₄, pens. 5 ℳ; HÔTEL-RESTAURANT HOHENZOLLERN, Günterstal-Str. 57, at the Wiehre Railway Station, well spoken of. The following are unpretending: WILDER MANN (Pl. f), Salz-Str. 30, fair; BREISGAUER HOF, Kaiser-Str. 137; MARKGRÄFLER HOF, Gerberau 22; DEUTSCHER KAISER, Günterstal-Str. 38, cor. of Konrad-Str.; PRINZ HEINRICH, Günterstal-Str. 41; EVANGELISCHES HOSPIZ, Hermann-Str. 8, R. 1¹/₂-2 ℳ.

Pensions. *Beau-Séjour*, Werder-Str. 8 (5-8 ℳ); *Bellevue*, Günterstal-Str. 59 (pens. 5-8 ℳ); *Frau Utz*, Friedrich-Str. 37, cor. of the Katharinen-Str. (4¹/₂-7 ℳ); *Schlossbergblick*, Ludwig-Str. 33 (4¹/₂-7 ℳ); *Villa Minerva*, Günterstal-Str. 56 (5¹/₂-7 ℳ).

Restaurants & Cafés. *Museum (Café Schauz: Pl. 15), Kaiser-Str. 61 (D. 1³/₄-2¹/₂ ℳ); *Zum Kopf, Engel-Str. 5, to the N. of the Minster, founded in 1770, with garden; *Zum Martinstor, close to the gate of the same name (p. 379), wine upstairs, beer downstairs; *Alte Burse*, Berthold-Str. 5, at the University; *Wiener Café*, near the war-monument; *Rommel's Schlösschen*, above the Schwaben-Tor (view). — **Wine.** *Briem*, Schiff-Str. 5; *Hummel*, Münster-Platz 22; *Binz*, Kaiser-Str. 134; *Dattler*, Schlossberg 1 (p. 379), with view.

The *STADT-GARTEN, with good restaurant and a large hall for concerts, is a favourite summer-resort. Ticket for one day 20 pf., for a week 1 ℳ; adm. to concerts in the afternoon and evening, 30-60 pf.

Baths at the *Marienbad, Marien-Str. 4. *Swimming Baths* at the municipal establishment on the Dreisam and at the Lorettoberg, also for ladies, with garden-restaurant. Special 'Bathers' Trains' run to the *Rhine Baths* at the bridge of Alt-Breisach (p. 381).

Cabs. Per ¹/₄ hr., one-horse, for 1-2 pers. 80 pf., 3-4 pers. 1 ℳ, two-horse, 1, 1¹/₂ ℳ; ¹/₂ hr. 1 ℳ or 1 ℳ 50′, and 1 ℳ 50 pf. or 2 ℳ; each additional ¹/₄ hr. ¹/₂ ℳ, two-horse 1 ℳ more. Each article of luggage above 22¹/₂ lbs. 80 pf. From 9 p.m. (in winter 8.30) to 7 a.m. (8) double fares. — To the *Schlossberg* (Kanonen-Platz), one-horse 4-4¹/₂; *Loretto*, 2¹/₂-3 ℳ; *Günterstal*, 2-2¹/₂ ℳ; *Kybburg*, 3-3¹/₂ ℳ; two horses 50 per cent more, return fare ¹/₂-1¹/₂ ℳ more. For a circular drive (with two horses, return-fare included) comprising Loretto, Waldsee, Littenweiler, Ebnet, Karthaus, 8 ℳ; Schlossberg, St. Ottilien, Karthaus, 10 ℳ; Luisenhöhe, Horben, Bohrer-Restaurant, Günterstal, 12 ℳ, etc.

Motor Omnibus in summer thrice daily from the Johannis-Kircho at Wiehre (p. 379) viâ Kybburg to the Bohrer Restaurant on the Schau-ins-Land (p. 380; 1³/₄ hr.; 3 ℳ), and thence, viâ Halden and Notschrei, to Todtnau (p. 431; 50 min. more; 1¹/₂ ℳ).

Electric Tramways (10 pf.) from the station to the Schwarzwald-Str. (red sign C); to the Wiehre station (white sign B), and also (changing cars at the Kaiser-Str.) to the Rennweg, on the N., and the Loretto-Str., on the S. (yellow sign A); to the Wonnhalde-Str. (Rebhaus, 15 pf.) and Günterstal (20 pf.; green sign D).

Post and Telegraph Office (Pl. 14), Eisenbahn-Str. 58.

Strangers' Enquiry Office *(Verkehrsverein)*, Rotteck-Str. 9, near the new theatre (Seeing Freiburg Trip, daily at 9 a.m., 3 ℳ).

English Church *(SS. George & Boniface)*, Thurnsee-Str. 59, beyond the Dreisam; services at 8 (H. C.), 11, and 5.30. Chaplain, *Rev. J. H. Selmes, M. A.*, Bromberg-Str. 36.

Principal Attractions. The traveller should follow the Eisenbahn-Str. from the station through the town as far as the Kaiser-Str., then turn to the right, follow the Salz-Str. to the Schwaben-Tor, and ascend the *Schlossberg*, a walk of 25 minutes. On the way back we cross the Karls-Platz to the *Minster* and *Kaufhaus*, traverse the Kaiser-Str. *(Fountains, War Monument, Ludwigs-Kirche)*, and return to the station. The best *View is obtained from the *Lorettoberg* by evening-light (1-1¹/₂ hr.).

Freiburg (880 ft.), situated in the *Breisgau*, 11 M. from the Rhine, vies with Baden and Heidelberg in the beauty of its environs. The mountains of the Black Forest, the picturesque hills in the vicinity, the populous and fertile plain, bounded by the vine-clad Kaiserstuhl, and the lovely valley of the Dreisam, all combine to render the situation highly attractive. The streets are supplied with streams of pure water from the *Dreisam*, which gives them an agreeable freshness in summer, and the town is surrounded with a girdle of pretty promenades and villas.

The town owes its origin to *Duke Berthold II. of Zähringen*, who founded it about 1091, and it remained in possession of his successors till the line became extinct in 1218. For over 400 years, beginning with 1368, Freiburg belonged to the House of Hapsburg; it suffered much in the Thirty Years' War; it was taken by the French in 1677, fortified by Vauban, and confirmed to them by the Peace of Nymwegen in 1678; by the Peace of Ryswyck in 1697 it was given back to Austria, but it was captured by Villars in 1713, after an obstinate defence. It was again restored to Austria by the Peace of Rastatt in 1714, plundered and to a great extent destroyed by the French in 1745, and then, after the destruction of the fortifications, once more made over to Austria by the Peace of Aix-la-Chapelle in 1748. The **Breisgau**, a hereditary possession of the house of Austria, of which Freiburg was the capital, was annexed to Baden by the Peace of Pressburg in 1806, and the town thus restored to the representatives of the house of Zähringen.

Freiburg is the chief city of the upper Rhenish province of Baden, and since 1456 has been the seat of a university, now attended by about 2600 students, and since 1827 of an archbishop. Population, including the suburbs of *Zähringen* and *Herdern* (N.), *Wiehre* and *Günterstal* (S.), *Haslach* and *Stühlinger* (W.), about 76,300, of whom 20,000 are Protestants and 1000 Jews. Silk, cotton, pottery, buttons, machinery, etc., are largely manufactured in and around the town, which also carries on a trade in wine and is the chief market for the productions of the Black Forest.

The railway-station is connected with the town by the EISEN-BAHN-STRASSE, which passes the monument of *Rotteck*, the historian (d. 1840; Pl. 3). Crossing the Rottecks-Platz, with the *Pfründhaus* (almshouse) and the *Villa Colombi* (containing the municipal picture-gallery), we reach the FRANZISKANER-PLATZ, in which is a statue of the Franciscan *Berthold Schwarz* (Pl. 4), the alleged inventor of gunpowder (1300; at Freiburg). Here stands also the Gothic *Church of St. Martin* (Pl. 11), with a new tower and part of the ancient cloisters. Opposite is the *Rathaus* (16th cent.), adorned with frescoes, and connected by an archway over the Turm-Str. with the newer portion, which was used until 1894 as the university. The relief on the S. oriel window, representing a unicorn-hunt (1543), should be noticed. The interior is shown by the care-taker (to the right in the court; on the left are the municipal collections of sculpture and of coins, open free on Sun. 11-12.30). — Close by, Berthold-Str. 17, is the present *University*, formerly a Jesuit convent. A new building, by Ratzel and Billing, has been erected in 1906-1911 a little to the S., in the Belfort-Str. To the N.E. of this is the imposing new *Stadt-Theater* (1910), by R. See-ling. To the S. are the new *University Library* (Univ. Bibliothek), a Gothic edifice by Schäfer, and the **Allée-Garten,** embellished with an artificial waterfall.

A little to the E. of the Franziskaner-Platz runs the broad KAISER-STRASSE, the main street of the town, which it intersects from N. to S. In the centre rises an old *Fountain* of the late-Gothic period, embellished with a number of old and modern figures. To the S. of it is a modern fountain (1807), with a statue of Berthold III., the law-giver of Freiburg (1120). To the N., in the same street, is another modern fountain (1868), with a statue of Archduke Albert VI., founder of the University. — No. 51, on the E. side of the street, is the *Basler Hof*, now a government office, with a handsome frescoed façade of the 15-16th centuries. — A little farther to the N. is the War Monument, p. 378.

The Münster-Str., diverging from the Kaiser-Str., leads straight to the W. portal of the Minster, in front of which rise three lofty *Columns* (1719) bearing statues of the Virgin, St. Alexander, and St. Lambert, its patron-saints.

The ***Cathedral** or **Minster** is one of the finest Gothic build-ings in Germany, and has justly been admired from a very early period. The church, which is constructed entirely of dark-red sand-stone, was begun at a period when the Gothic style had not as yet become naturalized in Germany. We accordingly find that the tran-sept with the side-towers (Pl. 8 & 9), the oldest part of the edifice (shaded on the ground-plan), dating from the 12th cent., is in the Romanesque style. The nave was begun before 1250, and the diffi-culty found in bringing the new Gothic forms into harmony with

the older style is clearly illustrated in the two E. bays, adjoining
the earlier transept. The completion of the nave (after 1260) was
accomplished by some younger architect of marked ability, who
also added the final stories and spires to the side-towers, and about
1270 began the main tower, which was carried above the bell-
chamber before 1301. The construction of the choir was begun in
1354 by *Johannes of Gmünd,* but it was not completed till the
beginning of the 16th cent. (1513). The Renaissance portico of the
S. transept was added in the 17th century.

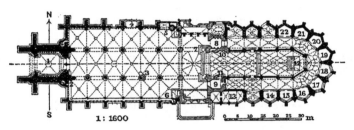

1 : 1600

The most artistic part of the whole building is the **Tower*
(380 ft. high), the earliest and most perfect of its kind. The three
bold and simple stories at once reveal their structural significance;
the massive square basement, the lofty octagonal bell-tower, and
the airy pyramid of perforated masonry, which the octagon, both
in form and ornamentation, serves harmoniously to connect with the
square base. When viewed corner-wise the entire tower has the
appearance of an uninterrupted pyramid. — The four knightly
figures on the buttresses are supposed to be the last members of
the Zähringen family. On the buttresses to the right and left of
the W. portal are carved standard-measures for loaves of bread,
bricks, etc., along with the dates, the earliest of which is 1270.

The *Portico* (Pl. 1) is richly adorned with allegorical sculptures
of varying excellence; some of the female figures are specially fine.
The colouring was renewed in the 17th cent. and again in 1889.

On the *Central Pillar* of the portal is the Madonna and Child; on
the sides are representations of the Annunciation and Visitation (right)
and Adoration of the Magi (left), also of Judaism overthrown (right)
and the Church triumphant (left). In the pediment over the portal is
pourtrayed the farther history of the Saviour down to his return at the
Last Day. In the niches are angels and Biblical and allegorical figures.
— On the right of the portico are the Foolish Virgins, the Seven Liberal
Arts, and SS. Catharine and Margaret. On the left are the Wise Virgins, the Heavenly Bridegroom, Abraham, John the Baptist, Mary Magdalen, Zacharias with the angel, and finally Wantonness (a nude female
form) and Worldliness (a fashionable youth, with a rose-crowned goblet).

Among the other sculptures on the exterior of the Minster may be
mentioned a Romanesque bishop at the S. portal, the Death of the Virgin
above the S. choir-door, and the Creation (14th cent.) above the N. choir-door.

The *Interior* (410 ft. long, 98 ft. wide, 88 ft. high), consisting
of nave and aisles, transept, choir, and ambulatory, produces an im-
pression of greater antiquity than the contemporaneous cathedral
of Strassburg, which it resembles in several particulars (*e.g.* in the
fine rose-windows inserted in square frames at the W. end of the
aisles). The progress of the construction (see p. 376) may be traced
in the increasing elegance, from E. to W., of the capitals in the
blind arcades of the aisles. The late-Gothic choir terminates in a
wreath of chapels, so arranged that the central axis of the cathedral
is occupied by a pier. The church has been restored since 1880.
It is open daily after 9.30 a.m. (the sacristan, Münster-Platz 29,
admits visitors to the choir; fee 50 pf.).

Nave. On the central column of the portal is a fine early-Gothic
Madonna. By the pillars are two angels and the twelve Apostles. The
Pulpit (Pl. 3), executed by *Jerg Kempf* in 1561, is said (erroneously)
to be hewn out of a single block of stone; the portrait of the artist
is introduced under the steps. — The arch at the intersection of the
nave and transept is embellished with a fresco by *L. Seitz* (1877), representing the Coronation of the Virgin.

Aisles. The windows contain good stained glass, chiefly of the
14th cent., but largely re-arranged in modern times and patched with
glass from other churches. Two of the windows are modern. — N. Aisle
(left). The so-called Grafen-Kapelle (Pl. 4), by *J. Kempf* (1558), had no
entrance from the interior of the cathedral until 1829. Tombs with modern marble statues of archbishops of Freiburg. The sculptured groups
in the Chapel of the Eucharist (Pl. 5) are by *Xav. Hauser* (1805). — S.
Aisle. To the right of the Sepulchral Chapel (Pl. 6; 14th cent.; exterior
1578) is the tomb of a knight (14th cent.), said to mark the grave of the
last Zähringer (p. 372).

Transepts. The Renaissance arcades, removed to their present position in 1789, were originally erected in 1580 by *H. Böringer*, as screens
between the choir and transepts. The carved wood-work of the side-
altars are in the Gothic style. That on the N. (Pl. 7), with the Adoration of the Magi by *J. Wydynz* (1505), is the finest. — In the S. transept is the entrance to the Sacristy (Pl. 13). The curious Romanesque
frieze with scenes from the mediæval bestiaries, at the S. entrance to the
ambulatory (beneath the S.E. tower, Pl. 9), should be noticed. In the
passage is a Romanesque relief representing Samuel anointing David.

Choir. On the wall (right) a monument of *General de Rodt* (Pl. 11;
d. 1743); on the left, tombstones of a Count and Countess of Freiburg
(Pl. 10; 14th cent.); farther on, modern statues of the last scions of the
Zähringen family, by *Xav. Hauser* (19th cent.). — The *High-Altar-Piece*
(Pl. 12) is the chief work of *Hans Baldung Grien* (1511-16): in the centre,
Coronation of the Virgin with the Apostles on each side; on the left
wing, Annunciation and Visitation; on the right wing, Nativity and
Flight into Egypt; below, a carving of the Adoration of the Magi; on
the outside, SS. Jerome and John the Baptist (left) and SS. Lawrence
and George (right). On the back is a Crucifixion, with portraits of the
painter and of the donors below.

Choir Chapels. The stained glass (first half of the 16th cent.) is
damaged; in some cases the originals have been replaced by copies, and
several of the windows are entirely modern. — 1st Chapel (Pl. 14). Winged
altar-piece (early 16th cent.): in the centre SS. Augustine, Anthony, and
Rochus, SS. Sebastian and Christopher on the wings; as antependium, a
wall-tapestry of 1501, with the Adoration of the Shepherds. Another portion of this tapestry in the Snewlin Chapel. — 2nd (University) Chapel
(Pl. 15). *Holbein the Younger*, *Altar-piece (Nativity, Adoration of the

24*

Magi, Donors), painted about 1520, brought hither from Bâle after the Reformation, and restored in 1866. Next to it, the Portrait of Mich. Küblin, dated 1600 (covered). Near it are memorial stones to former professors. — The so-called Dettinger Chörlein (Pl. 16) contains an altar of 1615. In the second Imperial Chapel (Pl. 19) are the remains of the so-called 'Snewlin Altar-piece', by *Hans Baldung Grien*, with the Baptism of Christ and St. John in Patmos. — The next of Böcklin Chapel (Pl. 20) has a Romanesque *Crucifix* in silver-gilt (11th cent.). — The Locherer Chapel (Pl. 22) contains an interesting carved altar-piece, by *J. Sixt* (1524), representing the Madonna, with her protecting robe outspread, and SS. Anthony and Bernard.

TOWER (Pl. 2; open 5.30 a.m. to 6 p.m.). Entrance in the church to the right of the portal; 328 steps to the highest platform; ticket, 20 pf., obtained at the top. The clock was made by Schwilgué in 1852 (comp. p. 482); the oldest of the bells dates from 1258.

⁕ The TREASURY (open on Mon., Wed., & Frid. 10-12 a.m.; cards of admission, obtained at Alb. Schleinzer's, Münster-Platz 23, 2 ℳ, for 3-5 pers. 5 ℳ) contains goldsmiths' and silversmiths' work of the 13-18th cent. and some pictures (including *Lucas Cranach*, Christ with the Virgin and St. John; 1524).

Opposite the S. portal of the Minster are the plain *Archiepiscopal Palace*, and the **Kaufhaus,** or *Merchants' Hall* (Pl. 10). The latter was completed in 1532. In front is a vaulted round-arched portico, resting on five pillars, and above it are a balcony and two oriels, with painted arms in relief; on the outer wall, four small statues of Emperors of Germany.

A little to the S. of the Kaufhaus is the *Theatre* (Pl. 17), in the former Augustine Church. The adjacent convent now contains the *Municipal Collection of Antiquities*, comprising a few Roman and numerous mediæval antiquities from the neighbourhood of Freiburg (open free on Sun., 10-1; at other times, 20 pf.). — In the Salz-Str., which runs from the Kaiser-Str. to the Schwaben-Tor (p. 379), are the *Grand-Ducal Palace* (Pl. 7) and the *Municipal Collection of Prehistoric Antiquities* ('Sammlung für Urgeschichte').

In the N. part of the Kaiser-Str. (p. 375), opposite the *Infantry Barracks* (Pl. 9), built by the Austrian Government in 1776, rises a large **War Monument** *(Siegesdenkmal)*, by *Moest*, erected in 1876 to the 14th German Army Corps and its leader, General von Werder. — A little farther on is the Prot. **Church of St. Lewis** (*Ludwigs-Kirche; Ev. Kirche* on Plan), in the Romanesque style, erected in 1829-38 with materials from the ruined abbey-church of Thennenbach. — In the Albert-Str., diverging to the left farther on, and in the adjacent streets are the various buildings of the *Medical and Scientific Faculties* of the university, and the *Botanic Garden* (Sautier-Str. 2). — To the E., in the Karl-Str., lies the *Old Cemetery* (Alte Friedhof); the vestibule of the chapel contains a Dance of Death, of the 18th century. At Karl-Platz 35 (near the *Stadt-Garten*, p. 373) are the collections of the *Kunstverein* or *Art Society* and the *Municipal Collection of Domestic Utensils from the Black Forest* (open free on Sun., 11-1; at other times, 20 pf.).

The Kaiser-Str. ends, to the S., at the **Martins-Tor** (Pl. 20), restored and provided with a turreted roof in 1901. On the wall is represented St. Martin sharing his cloak with a beggar. — Passing through the Gerberau, to the E. of the Martins-Tor, and skirting a bit of the old town-wall, we reach the **Schwaben-Tor** (Pl. 21; restored in 1901), on which is an ancient fresco, representing a Swabian peasant driving a wagon laden with wine.

From the Schlossberg-Str., which runs hence to the left, a broad path to the right leads to the *Schlossberg, once defended by three Vauban forts, destroyed by the French in 1745. The ruins are surrounded with pleasure-grounds. Hard by is the so-called 'Kanonen-Platz' (famous view of the Minster), whence promenades lead to the Burg-Str. and to the Stadt-Garten (p. 373), while roads lead along the hill to the N. to the Immen-Tal and to the E. to St. Ottilien (see below). Farther up is the *Ludwigshöhe* (1235 ft.), commanding a fine view (best in the morning). To the N., on the 'Saltpetre Rock', is a *Bismarck Column,* erected by the students (1900). — Guide-posts indicate the path to the *Hohe Brücke,* the highest point of the Schlossberg ('Mond'; 1490 ft.), with the (¹/₄ hr.) *Feldberg-Blick.*

From the Hohe Brücke footpaths lead to the N.E. viâ the *Silberbrunnen* to (1¹/₄ hr.) *St. Ottilien* (1515 ft.), with a chapel and inn, also reached by roads from the Immen-Tal and the Kanonen-Platz. — Thence we may proceed to the (1³/₄ hr.) *Rosskopf* (2425 ft.), with an iron belvedere, and to the castle of *Zähringen* (p. 372; 2¹/₂ hrs.). — From the Immen-Tal a path leads to the N. to the *Jägerhäusle* (1080 ft.; gardenrestaurant). The hill of *Hebsack,* to the W., commands a fine view of Freiburg.

To the W. of the railway-station lies the new suburb of **Stühlinger,** reached by a viaduct, 185 yds. in length, crossing the line between Berthold-Str. and Sedan-Str., and commanding a view of the hills to the E. The conspicuous *Herz-Jesu-Kirche,* with its two towers, dates from 1892-97.

At the S. end of the Kaiser-Str. the *Kaiser-Brücke,* decorated with statues of emperors, spans the Dreisam. On the left bank an attractive residential suburb, with two new churches and an *English Chapel,* has sprung up at **Wiehre.** Near the R. C. church, at Tal-Str. 12, is the *Municipal Museum of National History and Folk Lore.* The station of Wiehre (p. 416) lies about ¹/₂ M. from the Kaiser-Brücke. Electric tramway, see p. 373.

On the other side of the railway, to the S.W., 1 M. from the bridge, rises the **Lorettoberg** (1090 ft.), with a chapel dating from 1657, and a view-tower (inn). View best by evening-light. — At the foot of the Lorettoberg, on the margin of the Bodlesau, is the health-resort of *Rebhaus,* surrounded by pleasure-grounds (pens. 6¹/₂-16 ℳ). Electric tramway, see p. 374.

The *Schönberg (2120 ft.), to the W. of the Lorettoberg, reached from Freiburg in about 2 hrs. viâ the village of *Merzhausen* and the

Jesuiten-Schloss (inn), or from the station of Uffhausen (p. 382) in 1½ hr., affords the best panorama of the Black Forest chain. Near the Schöneberger Hof is the ruined *Schneeburg.*

From Wiehre a shaded path leads by the small reservoir and the '*Franzosen-Schanze*' (Glümershöhe) in ½ hr. to the **Waldsee**, with a good garden-restaurant. Thence to Littenweiler (p. 416), 1½ M.

Between the Lorettoberg on the W. and the *Bromberg* on the E. lies the charming *Günters-Tal* (tramway and cabs, see pp. 373, 374). At the entrance to the valley footpaths diverge to the left from the road, and lead along the wooded slopes of the Bromberg. The electric tramway ends about 2 M. from the Kaiser-Brücke (p. 379) at **Günterstal** *(Schauinsland; Hirsch; Zum Kybfelsen)*, with an old convent, now an orphanage. About ¾ M. farther on is the *Kybburg Hotel* (very fair; pens. from 7 ℳ), whence we may return through the beautiful pine-forests on the S.W. side of the valley, viâ the (½ hr.) *Luisenhöhe* (Inn, pens. from 5 ℳ) and the Lorettoberg, to Freiburg. Attractive paths lead through the woods, both from the entrance of the Günters-Tal, near the *Villa Mitscherlich*, to the S.E., and to the E. from Günterstal to the *Kybfels* (2750 ft.; view), 7½ M. from Freiburg.

The ***Schau-ins-Land,*** or *Erzkasten* (4220 ft.; comp. Map, p. 416), the nearest of the higher mountains of the Black Forest, commanding a view resembling that from the Blauen (p. 428), may be ascended in 4½ hrs. (automobile, see p. 373). The route leads by *Günterstal* (electr. tramway, see p. 374), beyond which we follow the road through the picturesque valley watered by the *Bohrerbach*, passing the Kybburg Hotel, to the *Bohrer Restaurant*, 2¼ M. from the terminus of the electric tramway. The carriage-road then ascends by the *Sägendobel* (8 M.; gradient 3 : 7). Walkers remain in the valley for ¼ hr. more, then ascend to the left, by the new 'Haibrains-Weg', cutting off the first great bends of the road, follow the road for about ¼ hr. more, and then avoid a curve by another footpath. The *Rathaus*, a small but good inn, 2 hrs. from the Bohrer Restaurant, lies 10 min. below the summit. The descent may also be made viâ the Rappeneck to the Kappeler-Tal (p. 416).

The Schau-ins-land is rich in minerals (argentiferous lead and zinc-blende) for the extraction of which a tunnel has been made through the mountain to a distance of 1¼ M. The S. end of the tunnel is in the *Hofsgrund*, about ¼ hr. to the S.E. of the summit, and the N. end at the head of the Kappeler-Tal, whence a suspension-railway, nearly 4½ M. long, brings the ore down to the works to be treated.

About ¾ hr. to the S. of the summit is the *Halde* (3840 ft.), a popular health-resort, with a good inn (pens. from 5 ℳ). Thence to the *Notschrei* (p. 416), ¾ hr.; from it direct to the Feldberg (p. 422), 2½ hrs. — The Belchen (p. 430) lies 3½ hrs. to the S.W. of the Schau-ins-Land (see p. 423).

52. From Freiburg to Colmar.

27¹/₂ M. RAILWAY in 1¹/₄ hr. (fares 2 ℳ 50, 1 ℳ 35 pf.).

The line traverses the *Mooswald,* a marshy tract, crosses the *Dreisam Canal,* and turns to the W., between the undulating slopes of the *Tuni-Berg* on the left, and the volcanic *Kaiserstuhl* (p. 372) on the right. 4¹/₂ M. *Hugstetten* (670 ft.; Kreuz). — 7¹/₂ M. *Gottenheim* (635 ft.; Adler; Deutscher Kaiser) is the S. terminus of the railway skirting the E. side of the Kaiserstuhl (p. 372). — 9¹/₂ M. *Wasenweiler;* 11¹/₄ M. *Ihringen* (635 ft.; Hirsch; Ochs), with noted vineyards.

14¹/₂ M. **Breisach** or *Alt-Breisach*; *Deutscher Kaiser* or *Post; Salmen,* both very fair), the Roman *Mons Brisiacus,* a picturesque old town, with 3600 inhab., lies on and at the foot of a rock rising abruptly to a height of 260 ft. above the Rhine; it was an important fortress, regarded as the key of S. Germany. After 1331 it belonged to Austria; in 1638 it was taken after a long siege by the Swedes under Bernhard von Weimar; after his death (1639) it was garrisoned by the French until 1697. After varying fortunes it was restored to Austria in 1714, and destroyed by the French in 1793.

On the highest point in the town (745 ft.) rises the *Minster of St. Stephen,* a cruciform edifice, recently restored. The choir (supported by an open substructure), the S. tower, and the W. half of the nave are Gothic, dating from the 14th cent.; the transept and N. tower are Romanesque. In the interior are a beautiful rood-loft of the latter part of the 15th cent., and a large Gothic winged altarpiece (Coronation of the Virgin) in carved wood (1526). Two large pictures in the choir by Dürr, 1851. The treasury contains some interesting works of art. Fine view from the terrace, including the Black Forest, Jura, and Vosges and extending in clear weather to the Alps. — In the '*Schloss-Garten*' (Wihler's Restaurant) is a tower erected in honour of Colonel Tulla (d. 1828), an officer of engineers. To the S. rises the *Eckardsberg,* with fragments of an old fortress. — A pleasant walk may be taken across the bridge-of-boats to the left bank of the Rhine (Restaurant zur Rheinbrücke), which commands a fine view of the town, the Black Forest, and the Vosges.

KAISERSTUHL RAILWAY to *Burkheim* (Sponeck), etc., see p. 372.

The railway now crosses the Rhine by means of an iron bridge. — 16 M. *Neu-Breisach,* a small town (3500 inhab.) and fortress, constructed by Vauban in 1703, and taken by the Germans in 1870, after a siege of eight days. — 22¹/₂ M. *Sundhofen.* — 27¹/₂ M. *Colmar,* see p. 496.

53. From Freiburg to Bâle.

38¹/₂ M. RAILWAY in 1-2 hrs. (fares 4 ℳ 80, 3 ℳ, 1 ℳ 95 pf.; express fares 5 ℳ 30, 3 ℳ 50, 2 ℳ 20 pf.).

Freiburg, see p. 372. — The train skirts the vine-clad W. spurs of the Black Forest. Stations *Uffhausen* (for local trains only; fare 10 pf.), *St. Georgen*, and *Schallstadt*.

9¹/₂ M. **Krozingen** (*Badischer Hof*, at the station) is the junction for a branch-line viâ (1¹/₄ M.) *Ober-Krozingen*, (3 M.) *Staufen* (p. 430), *Grunern* (4¹/₂ M.), and (5¹/₂ M.) *Ballrechten-Dottingen*, to (7 M.) **Sulzburg** (1115 ft.; *Hirsch; Schwarzwald*), a town with 1230 inhab. and a church belonging to a Benedictine abbey founded in 995. The environs are prettily wooded, and good wine is grown on the Kastelberg. A pretty road leads from Sulzburg to (2¹/₂ M.; cab 2 ℳ) *Bad Sulzburg* (1515 ft.; Kurhaus, very fair), situated 6¹/₂ M. from Badenweiler (p. 425), by a pleasant route through the wood. Ascent of the Belchen from Bad Sulzburg, 4-4¹/₂ hrs., see p. 430.

The Belchen (p. 430) is visible on the left. The small town of (13 M.) **Heitersheim** (740 ft.; *Kreuz;* 1300 inhab.), once the seat of the Master of the Maltese Order, is ³/₄ M. from the station. — 15 M. *Buggingen*.

18¹/₂ M. **Müllheim.** — HOTELS. *Bahnhof-Hôtel*, at the station, with garden and restaurant, R. 1¹/₄-2, B. ³/₄ ℳ, very fair. — *Löwe, Schwan, Post*, in the town, similar charges. — *Railway Restaurant*. — Steam-tramway to *Badenweiler*, see p. 424. Travellers arriving late are recommended to pass the night at Müllheim, as the hotels at Badenweiler are often full.

Müllheim (760 ft.) is a thriving little town of 3160 inhab., lying on the hillside, 1¹/₄ M. from the station, and extending for about 1¹/₂ M. up the valley of the *Klemmbach*, through which runs the road to Badenweiler. It has new Prot. and Rom. Cath. churches, and is noted for the Markgräfler wine produced in the neighbourhood. — Branch-railway to *Mülhausen*, see p. 500.

19¹/₄ M. *Auggen* (Bär), with a handsome church; 21¹/₂ M. *Schliengen* (790 ft.). — The line now approaches the Rhine, which is here divided by islands into several arms. Best views to the right. 23¹/₂ M. *Bellingen;* 26 M. *Rheinweiler;* 28 M. *Kleinkems.* — The line winds along the hillside above the river. Three short tunnels pierce the '*Isteiner Klotz*', a limestone cliff with new fortifications, to (30 M.) *Istein*, a picturesque village with a château of Baron Freystedt. 31 M. *Efringen-Kirchen.* — Beyond (33¹/₂ M.) *Eimeldingen* (875 ft.) the train crosses the *Kander;* fine view. 35 M. *Haltingen* is the junction for a branch-line to *Kandern* (p. 429).

36 M. *Leopoldshöhe*, whence branch-lines diverge to the right to *St. Ludwig* (p. 501) and to the left to *Lörrach* (p. 433). The-

train now crosses the *Wiese*, and stops at the station of (38½ M.)
Klein-Basel (Railway Restaurant, very fair; Schrieder; Bayrischer
Hof), ³/₄ M. from the Rhine-bridge and connected with the central
station at Bâle (3 M.) by a junction-line.

Bâle. — Hotels. *Trois Rois*, on the Rhine; *Univers*, *Euler*,
Schweizerhof, *National*, *Victoria*, St. *Gotthard - Terminus*, *Bristol*,
Jura, near the central station. — In the town: *Hôt. de l'Europe; Métro-
pole; Bauer au Rhin; Wage; Storch.*

Bâle or *Basel* (870 ft.; pop. 129,470), a busy commercial place,
is first mentioned in 374 as *Basilea*. In the middle ages it was a
free city of the empire, and in 1501 it became a member of the
Swiss Confederation. The *Minster* was erected in the Transition
style after 1185, and was consecrated in 1365. The towers and the
adjoining cloisters date from the 15th century. Extensive view
from the *Pfalz*, a terrace on the Rhine behind the Minster. The
Museum (open daily, fee 1 fr.), in the street leading from the Minster
to the bridge, is chiefly valuable for its collection of paintings and
drawings by *Holbein the Younger* (b. at Augsburg 1497, d. at
London 1543), who lived at Bâle in 1515-26 and 1528-32. There
are also a number of good works by modern painters, including
several by *Böcklin* (1827-1901), who was a native of the place.
The *Historical Museum* in the old Barfüsser-Kirche is very interesting. Bâle contains several other interesting buildings, such
as the *Rathaus* of 1508-21, and the *Spalen-Tor*, built in 1400,
formerly one of the town-gates. For farther details, see *Baedeker's
Switzerland.*

54. The Black Forest *(Duchy of Baden)*.

Of all the wooded districts of Germany, none presents so beautiful and varied landscapes as the *Black Forest* or *Schwarzwald*.
From Durlach and Pforzheim on the N., where it is separated from
the Odenwald by the 'Bruchsaler Senke', it extends to the S. for
about 100 M., approaching so closely to the Swiss Jura as to leave
only a narrow rift for the passage of the Rhine. Its breadth varies
from 14 M. on the N. to 38 M. on the S. Like the Odenwald and
Haardt, the Black Forest and the Vosges form, as it were, the
halves of a huge flattened vault, which has collapsed along its
longer axis. The steeper face of the Black Forest is thus turned
towards the W., where it is seamed with narrow and often ravine-
like valleys, hollowed out by the copious rainstorms hurled against
it by the W. winds. A long series of detached spurs form the foot-
hills towards the plain. The main massif, much corrugated and
furrowed, especially near the Feldberg, by ancient glaciers, forms
a genuine mountain-range. On the E. side, with its wider valleys
and gentler hills, it slopes gradually to the valleys of the upper

Neckar and the Danube, both of which lie about 800 ft. higher than the plain of the Rhine. — The Black Forest consists mainly of granite and gneiss, frequently intersected by veins of porphyritic rock. On the N. its solid mass is overlain by a broad covering of variegated sandstone, while there is also a narrower strip of the same formation to the E. This N. or Lower Black Forest, culminating in the *Hornisgrinde* (3825 ft.; p. 390), is separated by the Kinzig-Tal from the higher crystalline portion, or S. Black Forest, of which the *Feldberg* (4900 ft.; p. 422), the *Herzogenhorn* (4650 ft.; p. 423), and the *Belchen* (4640 ft.; p. 430) are the highest mountains. The 'Freiburger Bucht' forms an isolated breach in the mountain-wall, protected by the ruined volcanic mass of the Kaiserstuhl (p. 372). — The lower heights are covered with fragrant pine-forests, rising from a mossy carpet variegated with ferns, berry-bearing plants, and other shrubs. At about 3250 ft. trees become sparser; and above 3950 ft. grass and mountain-pine alone are found. Compared with the Vosges and the Odenwald, the Black Forest is notable for the copiousness of its water-supply, even on its most elevated plateaus. The dark hue of its lakes (Mummel-See, p. 390; Wildseen, pp. 387, 391; Titisee, p. 418; Schluchsee, p. 424) is due to the numerous bogs. The veins of ore in the crystalline rocks have nearly all been exhausted (comp. p. 380). Its thermal springs have been used as baths for centuries. Nearly half of its surface is covered with woods; and a large proportion of its inhabitants are consequently employed in wood-cutting and lumbering. The foot-hills towards the Rhine and the lower-lying valleys produce large quantities of wine and fruit. In some of the remoter valleys, especially in the S. part of the Forest, the women still wear their national costume on Sundays.

The so-called 'Schwarzwaldhäuser' ('Black Forest Houses'), many of which are still extant, usually occupy isolated positions in the midst of the fields and meadows. They generally lean against the hillside in such a way that the attic-story, used as a barn, may be driven into across a bridge. The upper part of the house is of wood. The thatched roof projects so as to shelter the galleries running round the upper story.

Tour of twelve days from Baden. 1st. Alte Schloss at Baden-Baden, Ebersteinburg, Gernsbach, Neu-Eberstein, and back (RR. 48, 54d). — 2nd. Geroldsau, Sand, and Hundseck, 5 hrs. (pp. 365, 389, 390). — 3rd. Hornisgrinde, Ruhstein, and Allerheiligen, 6 hrs. (pp. 390, 391). — 4th. Kniebis, Rippoldsau, and Wolfach, 9½ hrs. (pp. 400, 409, 408; drive from Rippoldsau if desired). — 5th. Railway to Hornberg, walk thence to (5 hrs.) Triberg viâ Althornberg (pp. 402, 403). — 6th. Brend, Gütenbach, and Kandel, 9½ hrs. (pp. 412-14). — 7th. Waldkirch; railway to Freiburg (pp. 414, 372). — 8th. Railway through the Höllen-Tal to the Titisee; ascent of the Feldberg (pp. 416-19), 4 hrs. walking. — 9th. (Herzogenhorn, p. 423), St. Blasien, Höchenschwand, 5½ hrs. (pp. 435, 436). — 10th. By the Albstrasse to Albbruck (p. 437); railway to Wehr (pp. 438, 433). — 11th. Wehra-Tal to Todtmoosau (pp. 433, 434), viâ Gersbach and Hohe Möhr to Zell (p. 432), railway to Schönau (p. 431). — 12th. Belchen (pp. 429, 430), Blauen, and Badenweiler, 9 hrs. (pp. 428, 427). — If needs must, the chief points (Baden-Baden, Allerheiligen, Triberg, Freiburg. Höllen-Tal, Feldberg, and Badenweiler) can be visited in five days.

Inns. Good inns are found practically everywhere, and all have telephones. Living, even in the remotest districts, is no longer so remarkably cheap as formerly. The following is the average scale: R. $1^1/_2$-$2^1/_2$ $\mathcal{M}$, B. 60 pf. to 1 $\mathcal{M}$, D. $1^1/_2$-$2^1/_2$ $\mathcal{M}$, pens. from 4 or 5 $\mathcal{M}$. In engaging rooms beforehand it is always necessary to follow up the preliminary letter or telegram with a second, definitely accepting the terms offered by the landlord.

The *Black Forest Clubs (Schwarzwald-Vereine)* of Baden and Wurtemberg (annual subscription respectively 5 $\mathcal{M}$ & 3 $\mathcal{M}$) have greatly facilitated pedestrian excursions throughout the entire district, by making footpaths, erecting guide-posts, etc. The so-called HÖHENWEGE or *Ridge Paths* are very attractive (comp. p. xvii).

CYCLISTS find excellent roads, not only in the valleys but also in the more elevated regions of the Black Forest, though, of course, the gradients are often steep. MOTORING is also steadily on the increase. — *Omnibuses* and *Coaches* are numerous.

The WINTER SPORTS of the Black Forest are focussed on the Feldberg, which was the first great centre of ski-running in Germany; but they are also practised at many other points. Suitable ski routes are marked with red flags or stakes. Most of the mountain-inns are open in winter. The headquarters of the Ski Club are at Freiburg.

a. From Carlsruhe to Pforzheim and Wildbad viâ Durlach.

33 M. RAILWAY in $2^1/_4$ hrs. (fares 4 $\mathcal{M}$, 2 $\mathcal{M}$ 50, 1 $\mathcal{M}$ 65 pf.).

From Carlsruhe to ($2^1/_2$ M.) *Durlach*, see p. 347. — The train traverses the fertile valley of the *Pfinz*. 4 M. *Grötzingen;* 6 M. *Berghausen;* $7^1/_2$ M. *Söllingen;* 9 M. *Kleinsteinbach;* $10^1/_2$ M. *Wilferdingen* (Krone); $12^1/_2$ M. *Königsbach;* 15 M. *Ersingen;* 17 M. *Ispringen.*

19 M. **Pforzheim.** — HOTELS. *Nusser zur Post*, R. from $2^1/_2$, B. 1, D. $2^1/_2$ $\mathcal{M}$; *International; Schloss; Schwarzer Adler, Goldener Adler, Ohlert, Bahnhofs-Hôtel*, all near the railway-station; *Hydropathic.* — *Railway Restaurant.*

Pforzheim (805 ft.), a thriving manufacturing town, with 59,300 inhab., lies at the confluence of the *Enz*, the *Würm*, and the *Nagold*. The manufacture of gold and silver wares carried on here employs upwards of 12,000 workmen. Close to the station is a monument to the Emperor William I. The *Schlosskirche* (12-15th cent.) contains a number of monuments of the Margraves of Baden of the 16th century. In the Karl-Friedrich-Str. is a *Statue of Margrave Ernest* (1535-58), the founder of the now extinct Baden-Durlach-Ernestine family.

From Pforzheim to Wildbad viâ the *Büchenbronner Höhe* (2005 ft.) $6^1/_2$ hrs.; beginning of the so-called 'Höhenweg' (p. xvii).

Steam-tramway from Pforzheim to Carlsruhe, see p. 348. — A branchline connects Pforzheim with Mühlacker, where it joins the Bruchsal line to Stuttgart. — Railway to Calw, Tübingen, and Constance, see *Baedeker's Southern Germany.*

The Wildbad railway continues to follow the pleasant, grassy valley of the *Enz*, which now contracts. 21 M. *Brötzingen;* $22^1/_2$ M. *Birkenfeld.*

25¹/₂ M. **Neuenbürg** *(Bär; Sonne)*, a picturesquely-situated little town, with 2400 inhab., is commanded by a *Schloss* (now occupied by public offices), erected by Duke Christopher of Wurtemberg (1650-68), on a wooded height encircled by the Enz. Adjoining the Schloss, which was restored in 1658 and 1735, is a ruined castle of the 12-13th centuries.

The train crosses the Enz, passes under the Schlossberg by a tunnel, and again crosses the stream. 28 M. *Rotenbach*, with a large saw-mill; 29¹/₂ M. *Höfen;* 31 M. *Calmbach* (Sonne, very fair, R. 1¹/₂-2, B. ³/₄ ℳ).

33 M. Wildbad. — HOTELS. *Königliches Bad-Hôtel* (Pl. a), with lift, R. 3¹/₂-15, B. 1¹/₂, D. 3¹/₂ ℳ; *Klumpp* (Pl. b), R. from 3¹/₂, B. 1¹/₂, D. at 1 p.m. 3¹/₂-4, S. 2¹/₂, pens. from 10 ℳ; *Bellevue* (Pl. c), united with the Klumpp, both with lift, same charges; *Post* (Pl. d), with lift, R. 2¹/₂-5, B. 1¹/₄, D. 3, pens. 7-12 ℳ; *Villa Concordia* (Pl. h); *Russischer Hof* (Pl. e), with lift and restaurant, R. 2¹/₂-5, B. 1¹/₄, D. 3, pens. 6¹/₂-10 ℳ; *Pfeiffer zum Goldenen Lamm* (Pl. g), R. 2¹/₂-3¹/₂, B. 1, D. 2¹/₂, pens. 6¹/₂-8¹/₂ ℳ; *Graf Eberhard*, in the Kur-Platz; *Schmid zum Goldenen Ochsen* (Pl. f); *Goldenes Ross* (Pl. i), R. 2-3¹/₂, pens. 6-7¹/₂ ℳ; *Löwe* (Pl. k): *Sonne* (Pl. l); *Stern*, Haupt-Str. 74; *Weil* (Hebrew); *Zur Eisenbahn* (Pl. m); *Schwarzwald* (Pl. n); *Kühler Brunnen*, with garden-restaurant, these four by the station. — *Pension Villa Montebello* (Pl. o), with dépendances, pens. 8-10 ℳ. — Also numerous *Hôtels Garnis* and lodginghouses, the best being those above the Anlagen (Kerner-Str. and Olga-Str.). — RESTAURANTS. *Bad-Hôtel; Graf Eberhard*, D. 1 ℳ 80 pf.; *Schmid*, etc. (see hotels).

POST & TELEGRAPH OFFICE at the station. — CAB (one-horse) 1 ℳ per ¹/₄ hr.; to or from the station 1, with two horses 2 ℳ. — *Swimming Bath*, Olga-Str. (60 pf.), with curative gymnastic apparatus. — *Visitors' Tax* (first two days free) 4 ℳ per week, 12 ℳ per month. — *Kur-Verein*, König-Karl-Str. 178. — ENGLISH CHURCH *(Holy Trinity);* service in summer.

WIRE-ROPE RAILWAY to the top of the *Sommersberg* (2395 ft.), ¹/₂ M. long, with a maximum gradient of 52 per cent. The cars start at the Russischer Hof (Pl. e). Fare, up 70 pf., down 50 pf., up & down 1 ℳ; to the Panorama-Weg 35 pf., thence to the top 50 pf. At the top is a *Hôtel-Restaurant*, with view.

Wildbad (1380 ft.), a celebrated watering-place (3700 inhab.), situated in a narrow, pine-clad ravine on both banks of the *Enz*, possesses warm alkaline springs and is frequented both in summer and winter. The main street, with the baths and hotels, lies on the right bank, while the station is at the lower end of the town on the left bank. In the *Kur-Platz* are the *Stadt-Kirche*, erected in 1746, the handsome *Kurhaus* or *Bad-Hôtel*, and the large *Badgebäude* ('Alt-Wildbad'), with its admirably equipped baths (shown from 1.30 to 3.30 p.m.). The *Springs* (90-100° Fahr.), which rise in the baths themselves, are very efficacious in the relief of gout and rheumatism (upwards of 16,000 patients annually). There are five well-arranged public baths for men and three for women (1¹/₂ ℳ), and 50 private baths (2¹/₂-6 ℳ). Farther on is the *Katharinenstift*, with baths for the poor. A bridge leads hence to the *König-Karls-Bad*, an elaborate Renaissance building with thermal and vapour

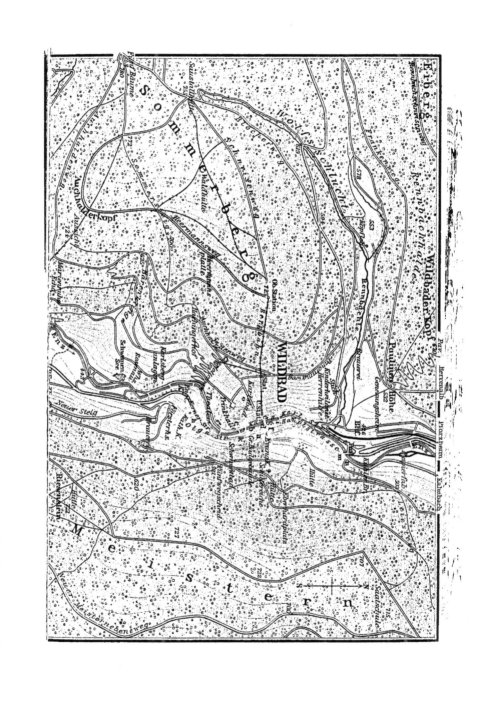

ıths and reading-rooms. Close by stands the *Trinkhalle,* with a
ınd-pavilion in the centre. On the right bank, in the Anlagen, is
e *Theatre.*

There are pleasant walks and grounds on both banks of the Enz
ıove the village (*i.e.* to the S.). On the left bank is the *Rosenau
estaurant;* on the right bank is the (1 M.) *Windhof Hotel* (D.
/₄ *ℳ*). — Good views are obtained from the *Panorama-Weg*
ıilway, see p. 386) and the *Charlotten-Weg,* both on the E. side
the *Sommersberg.* — From the upper station (2428 ft.), of the
ire-rope Railway (p. 386) two level walks lead through the woods.
ıe *Heermanns-Weg,* to the extreme left, runs viâ the *Heermanns-
latte* to the (¹/₂ hr.) *Fünf Bäume* (see below), while the *Schneissen-
'eg* (also to the left) leads to the (20 min.) *Saustall-Hütte,* whence
₂ may descend to the right viâ the *Blöcher-Weg* to (¹/₂ hr.) the
il. station, or to the Soldaten-Brunnen (¹/₂ hr.; see below).

EXCURSIONS. A road ascends the Enztal viâ the (3 M.) *Kälber-Mühle,*
th the pumping-station of the great reservoir supplying 50 parishes in
ɜ N. portion of the Black Forest (Wurtemberg), to (7¹/₂ M.) *Enzklösterle*
394) and (10¹/₂ M.) *Gompelscheuer* (Lamm); thence to (11 M.) Kloster-
·ichenbach (p. 394). — From the Bellevue Hotel the *Höhenweg* (p. xvii)
ccnds viâ the *Fünf Bäume* (1-1¹/₄ hr.; comp. above) in 2¹/₂ hrs. to the
ɔrnsee or *Wildsee* (2980 ft.), and thence to the (³/₄ hr.) *Kaltenbronn*
ɔoting-lodge (2820 ft.; rustic inn; road to Reichental, see p. 393) and
the (¹/₂ hr.) *Hohloh* (3250 ft.), crowned by a view-tower (72 ft. high).
·scent viâ the *Latschig* to *Forbach* (p. 393), 2 hrs. — From the railway-
ıtion a beautiful wood-path (approach to the Höhenweg; no inn) as-
ɩds viâ (1¹/₄ hr.) the *Soldaten-Brunnen* (see above), the (³/₄ hr.) ruin of
hmannshof, the (20 min.) forester's house of *Dürreych,* and (2¹/₄ hrs.) the
ufels-Mühle (p. 388) to (1¹/₂ hr.) *Gernsbach* (p. 392). — Viâ the (1¹/₂ hr.)
ach-Mühle to (³/₄ hr.) *Dobel* (p. 388) and (1 hr.) *Herrenalb,* see p. 388.

From Carlsruhe and Ettlingen or from Gernsbach to Herrenalb.

From Carlsruhe, 16 M., ELECTRIC RAILWAY (Albtalbahn) in about
hr. (fares 1 *ℳ* 35, 90 pf.).
From Gernsbach, 7¹/₂ M., DILIGENCE daily in 2 hrs., and MOTOR OM-
us twice daily in summer in 40 min. (fare 1¹/₂ *ℳ;* comp. p. 392). Car-
ɟe-and-pair 12 *ℳ.*

The ELECTRIC RAILWAY, starting at the Fest-Platz, near the
ıtral railway-station (Pl. D, 3, 4) in Carlsruhe, runs viâ *Rüppur*
ʹ5 M.) *Ettlingen* (p. 355), where it enters the industrial valley
ʹhe *Alb.* — From (7 M.) *Busenbach* a branch-line runs viâ Itters-
ʹh to Pforzheim (21¹/₂ M.; p. 385). — Beyond (12 M.) *Marxzell,*
ʹhe mouth of the *Maisenbach,* the Albtal contracts. — 13¹/₂ M.
auenalb (Klosterhof), with the dilapidated buildings of a convent,
ınded in 1138 and suppressed in 1803. At the Steinhäusle we
ʹss the boundary of Wurtemberg. — 16 M. *Herrenalb.*

The ROAD FROM GERNSBACH (p. 392) TO HERRENALB ascends to
N.E. (fine retrospects), crosses the Wurtemberg boundary, and
ʹches (3 M.) *Loffenau* (1050 ft.; Adler), a long village with a

new red sandstone church. Thence we may ascend the (1³/₄ hr.)
Teufelsmühle (2975 ft.; refuge-hut; from Herrenalb, see below). —
From Loffenau the road ascends to the (2¹/₂ M.) *Käppele* (1745 ft.),
and then descends to (2¹/₂ M.) Herrenalb. A considerable saving
is effected by taking the footpath which diverges to the left (finger-
post) about 100 paces beyond the church of Loffenau, and by following the old road (l.) from Käppel.

Herrenalb. — Hotels. **Post* or *Ochse,* R. 1¹/₂-4, pens. 6-9 ℳ;
Falkenstein, R. 2-6, B. 1¹/₄, D. 3-3¹/₂, pens. 6-12 ℳ; *Sonne,* R. 2-5, B. 1,
D. 2¹/₂, pens. 6-10 ℳ; *Stern,* R. -4, B. 1¹/₄, D. 2-3, pens. 6-9 ℳ; *Bellevue,*
R. 1¹/₂-4, B. ³/₄, D. 2¹/₂, pens. 5²/₈ ℳ; *Kühler Brunnen,* pens. 5 ℳ, very
fair. — *Kurhaus Herrenalb* (Dr. Mermagen), a hydropathic establishment, pens. 60-70 ℳ weekly; *Kur-Anstalt & Sanatorium Hummelsburg,*
with baths. — *Private Apartments.* — *Visitors' Tax,* 4-8 ℳ (first 4 days
free). — *Conversationshaus,* with reading and entertainment rooms, on
the left bank of the Alb.

Herrenalb (1200 ft.), a village with 1300 inhab., on both banks
of the Alb, is frequented on account of its equable and somewhat
moist climate (7000 visitors annually). The once celebrated Benedictine abbey, founded in 1148, was destroyed by the Swedes in
1642. The steward's offices are now incorporated in the Kurhaus.
The *Church,* almost wholly rebuilt, contains the tomb of the Margrave Bernhard of Baden (d. 1431), with a recumbent figure. The
remains of the 'Paradise', or W. ante-church (12th cent.), contain
tombs of the abbots. — The wooded heights around Herrenalb
afford many pleasant walks. A particularly attractive view is obtained from the pavilion on the *Falkenstein* (1425 ft.), a huge
granite rock rising from the valley to the N. (20 min.; ascent to
the W. of the Hummelburgshöhe).

Excursions (comp. indicator in the Conversationshaus). To the
Teufelsmühle (2975 ft.), 2 hrs. We pass the cemetery and ascend the
valley to the S.W., finally crossing the stream to the Loffenau saw-mill.
Hence we ascend viâ the saddle of the *Risswasen* (1855 ft.) and the *Grosse
Loch* (2540 ft.) to the refuge-hut on the Teufelsmühle. — To the S.E. to
Gaistal, up along the slope of the Axtlo, and along the crest to the
S. to the (3¹/₂ hrs.) *Hohloh* (p. 387; descent to Kaltenbronn 25 min.). —
To the W. to the *Bernstein* (2264 ft.), 1¹/₂ hr. — To the N.W. viâ *Bern-
bach* to the view-tower on the *Malberg* (2005 ft.), 2 hrs.

From Herrenalb to Wildbad (p. 386), 10¹/₂ M. The road runs viâ
Dobel (Sonne, pens. from 4¹/₂ ℳ, very fair; extensive view from the *Signal,*
2370 ft., ¹/₄ M.) and the *Eyach-Mühle* (1570 ft.). Shorter footpaths through
the woods. — Motor-omnibus to *Höfen,* see p. 392.

c. From Bühl through the Bühler-Tal to the Sand (Plättig) and Hundseck, and to Allerheiligen viâ the Hornisgrinde and the Ruhstein.

From Bühl to *Obertal,* 3³/₄ M., branch-railway in 22 min.; thence
omnibus every morning to the *Gertelbach-Tal* (80 pf.), *Wiedenfelsen*
(1 ℳ 80), *Sand* (2 ℳ 20), and *Hundseck* (2 ℳ 50 pf.). Families with luggage should hire from Bühl (or even from Baden-Baden; motor-omnibus,
see p. 359): to the Wiedenfelsen (2 hrs.) 14 ℳ, Sand (2¹/₂ hrs.) 16, Plättig
16, Hundseck 18 ℳ. — On Foot: from Obertal to the Sand or direct to

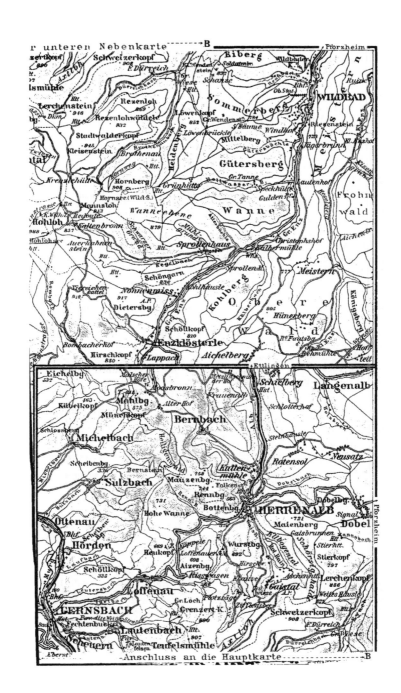

new red sandstone church. Thence we may ascend the ($1^3/_4$ hr.)
Teufelsmühle (2975 ft.; refuge-hut; from Herrenalb, see below). —
From Loffenau the road ascends to the ($2^1/_2$ M.) *Käppele* (1745 ft.),
and then descends to ($2^1/_2$ M.) Herrenalb. A considerable saving
is effected by taking the footpath which diverges to the left (finger-
post) about 100 paces beyond the church of Loffenau, and by following the old road (l.) past Käppel.

Herrenalb. — HOTELS. **Post* or *Ochse*, R. $1^1/_2$-4, pens. 6-9 ℳ;
Falkenstein, R. 2-6, B. $1^1/_4$, D. 3-$3^1/_2$, pens. 6-12 ℳ; *Sonne*, R. 2-5, B. 1,
D. $2^1/_2$, pens. 6-10 ℳ; *Stern*, R. 2-4, B. $1^1/_4$, D. 2-3, pens. 6-9 ℳ; *Bellevue*,
R. $1^1/_2$-4, B. $^3/_4$, D. $2^1/_2$, pens. 5-8 ℳ; *Kühler Brunnen*, pens. 5 ℳ, very
fair. — *Kurhaus Herrenalb* (Dr. Mermagen), a hydropathic establishment, pens. 60-70 ℳ weekly; *Kur-Anstalt & Sanatorium Hummelsburg*,
with baths. — *Private Apartments*. — *Visitors' Tax*, 4-8 ℳ (first 4 days
free). — *Conversationshaus*, with reading and entertainment rooms, on
the left bank of the Alb.

Herrenalb (1200 ft.), a village with 1300 inhab., on both banks
of the Alb, is frequented on account of its equable and somewhat
moist climate (7000 visitors annually). The once celebrated Benedictine abbey, founded in 1148, was destroyed by the Swedes in
1642. The steward's offices are now incorporated in the Kurhaus.
The *Church*, almost wholly rebuilt, contains the tomb of the Margrave Bernhard of Baden (d. 1431), with a recumbent figure. The
remains of the 'Paradise', or W. ante-church (12th cent.), contain
tombs of the abbots. — The wooded heights around Herrenalb
afford many pleasant walks. A particularly attractive view is obtained from the pavilion on the *Falkenstein* (1425 ft.), a huge
granite rock rising from the valley to the N. (20 min.; ascent to
the W. of the Hummelburgshöhe).

EXCURSIONS (comp. indicator in the Conversationshaus). To the
Teufelsmühle (2975 ft.), 2 hrs. We pass the cemetery and ascend the
valley to the S.W., finally crossing the stream to the Loffenau saw-mill.
Hence we ascend viâ the saddle of the *Risswasen* (1855 ft.) and the *Grosse
Loch* (2540 ft.) to the refuge-hut on the Teufelsmühle. — To the S.E. to
Gaistal, up along the slope of the Axtlo, and along the crest to the
S. to the ($3^1/_2$ hrs.) *Hohloh* (p. 387; descent to Kaltenbronn 25 min.). —
To the W. to the *Bernstein* (2264 ft.), $1^1/_2$ hr. — To the N.W. viâ *Bern-
bach* to the view-tower on the *Malberg* (2005 ft.), 2 hrs.

FROM HERRENALB TO WILDBAD (p. 386), $10^1/_2$ M. The road runs viâ
Dobel (Sonne, pens. from $4^1/_2$ ℳ, very fair; extensive view from the *Signal*,
2370 ft., $^1/_4$ M.) and the *Eyach-Mühle* (1570 ft.). Shorter footpaths through
the woods. — Motor-omnibus to *Höfen*, see p. 392.

c. From Bühl through the Bühler-Tal to the Sand (Plättig) and Hundseck, and to Allerheiligen viâ the Hornisgrinde and the Ruhstein.

From Bühl to *Obertal*, $3^3/_4$ M., branch-railway in 22 min.; thence
omnibus every morning to the *Gertelbach-Tal* (80 pf.), *Wiedenfelsen*
(1 ℳ 80), *Sand* (2 ℳ 20), and *Hundseck* (2 ℳ 50 pf.). Families with luggage should hire from Bühl (or even from Baden-Baden; motor-omnibus,
see p. 359): to the Wiedenfelsen (2 hrs.) 14 ℳ, Sand ($2^1/_2$ hrs.) 16, Plättig
16, Hundseck 18 ℳ. — ON FOOT: from Obertal to the Sand or direct to

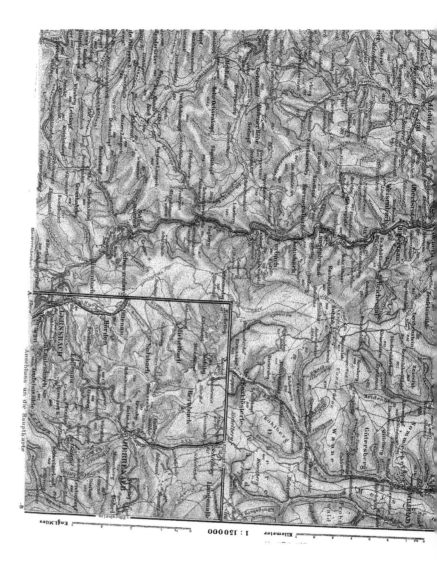

the Hundseck, $2^{1}/_{2}$ hrs.; ascent of the Hornisgrinde from the Hundseck, $2^{1}/_{4}$ hrs. (from Baden-Baden, see pp. 365, 390); thence to Ruhstein 3-$3^{1}/_{2}$ hrs., and to Allerheiligen $1^{3}/_{4}$ hr. more.

Bühl, see p. 369. The railway ascends the industrial **Bühler-Tal,** or valley of the *Bühlott.* From ($1^{1}/_{4}$ M.) *Kappelwindeck* we may reach the ruin of *Alt-Windeck* (p. 369) in 1 hr., viâ *Riegel,* and then follow paths through wood to the ($2^{1}/_{4}$ hrs.) Hundseck (p. 390). — $2^{1}/_{2}$ M. *Altschweier;* 3 M. *Bühlertal* (Grüner Baum; Engel). — $3^{3}/_{4}$ M. *Obertal* (Badischer Hof; Wolf) is the terminus.

The road forks here, the left arm leading to the *Schwanenwasen* (2115 ft.; Kur-Hôtel, R. from 2, D. $2^{1}/_{2}$ ℳ; motor-omnibus from Baden-Baden 3 ℳ, p. 359), the right to the Sand and Plättig. We follow the latter. About 1 M. from Obertal a road diverges on the right for ($1^{1}/_{2}$ M.) *Buchkopf,* a summer-resort. Farther on ($1/_{3}$ M.), on the right, is the *Schindelpeter Inn,* and to the left is a picturesque footpath ascending viâ the *Falkenfels* and *Fohrenfels* to the ($1^{1}/_{4}$ hr.) Plättig (see below). The road continues to ascend the valley of the Wiedenbach, and beyond a sharp curve (3 M. from Obertal), where a footpath for the (40 min.) Sand diverges to the left, makes a bend and reaches the *Kurhaus Wiedenfelsen* (2270 ft.; R. $1^{1}/_{2}$-4, B. 1, D. 3-$3^{1}/_{2}$, pens. 5-8 ℳ), which commands a beautiful view down the valley.

Walkers take the narrow road which diverges to the right about $1/_{3}$ M. beyond the Schindelpeter Inn, and leads in 20 min. to the Hôtel-Restaurant Gertelbach (R. $1^{1}/_{2}$-$2^{1}/_{2}$, D. $2^{1}/_{2}$, pens. $4^{1}/_{2}$-6 ℳ), at the mouth of the ***Gertelbach Schlucht.** An easy footpath ascends through the picturesque ravine, at the (35 min.) head of which is a guide-post indicating the route to the (40 min.) Hundseck (p. 390). We, however, turn to the left and reach the (5 min.) road, $1/_{4}$ M. from the Kurhaus Wiedenfelsen.

About $1/_{4}$ M. beyond the Kurhaus the road again curves to the N. (to the right is the above-mentioned path to the Gertelbach Schlucht), and, after passing the *Bärenfels* (Schwarzwald-Hôtel Bärenstein, R. from 2, pens. from $6^{1}/_{2}$ ℳ), it reaches its highest point (2715 ft.) at the **Sand** ($4^{1}/_{3}$ M. from Obertal, $1^{1}/_{2}$ M. from Wiedenfelsen). The **Kurhaus Sand* (R. 2-$3^{1}/_{2}$, D. 3, pens. 7-9 ℳ), the oldest of the many summer-resorts in this part of the Black Forest, is situated at the intersection of the roads from the Bühler-Tal to the Murgtal and from Baden to the Hundseck viâ the Plättig. — About 1 M. to the N. is the **Plättig** (2546 ft.; **Kurhaus,* pens. 6-8 ℳ), known also as *Ober-Plättig* to distinguish it from *Unter-Plättig,* a forester's house $1/_{2}$ M. to the N.E. Hence to Baden-Baden viâ the Geroldsau Waterfall, 11 M., see pp. 365-363.

On the Murgtal road, $1^{1}/_{2}$ M. to the E. of the Sand, lies the small village of Herrenwies (2490 ft.; **Kurhaus,* R. from 2, D. 3, pens. 6-8 ℳ), in an upland plain watered by the *Schwarzenbach.* The road descends the valley of that stream to (5 M.) *Raumünzach* (p. 393).

The road leading to the S. from the Sand passes the (1 M.)

Hundseck (2900 ft.; *Kurhaus*, R. 2-4, D. 3, pens. 6½-10 ℳ),
on the road leading from Bühl viâ the Windeck to *Hundsbach*
(Kurhaus, unpretending) and the Raumünzach-Tal.

Pleasant forest-paths radiate from all these summer-resorts. From
the Plättig (in 1¼ hr.) and the Sand (in 1 hr.; less from Herrenwies) we
may ascend to the tower (100 ft. high) on the **Badener Höhe** (3287 ft.),
which commands a most extensive panorama. We may then descend to
the N., viâ the falls of the *Grimbach*, to (1¾ hr.) the Geroldsau Fall
(p. 365); or viâ the Scherrhof to Lichtental (p. 364); or, skirting the
Seekopf (3284 ft.), we may proceed to the E. to the *Herrenwieser See*
(2720 ft.; 4½ acres) and return to the S.W. along the slope to (2½ hrs.)
Herrenwies. — The **Mehliskopf** (3310 ft.; view-tower) may be ascended
from the Sand or the Hundseck in ¾ hr.; and the **Hohe Ochsenkopf**
(3460 ft.; view-tower) in 1 hr. from Herrenwies.

From the road to Bühl viâ the Windeck the 'Höhenweg' (p. xvii)
diverges opposite the Hundseck Kurhaus and leads in 50 min. to the
cross-roads at the *Kurhaus Untersmatt* (3050 ft.; very fair). A
guide-post here indicates the routes to Breitenbrunnen and Achern
(right) and (straight on) to the Hornisgrinde (2½ M.; after ½ hr.
we diverge to the right from the road; footpath to the tower, ½ hr.
more). The route viâ *Breitenbrunnen* (2655 ft.; Inn, R. 1¼-3,
pens. 4½-7 ℳ), a summer-resort 1½ M. to the S.W., on the road
to Achern (8 M.; carr. 10-14 ℳ), is not much longer than the direct
route. We follow the cart-road immediately to the left of the inn,
cross the (20 min.) bed of a torrent (usually dry), and in 40 min.
more reach the summit of the Hornisgrinde.

The bare and marshy summit of the **Hornisgrinde** (3820 ft.), on
which a new tower 82 ft. in height and a refuge-hut have been erected,
is the highest point in the N. portion of the Black Forest. The
view is extensive, but frequently shrouded in mist: to the E. the
Swabian Alb and the cones of the Höhgau; S. the heights of the
Black Forest and beyond them the Alps; S. W. the Kaiserstuhl and
Vosges; W. the vast plain of the Rhine; nearly opposite rises the
spire of Strassburg Minster, and on a mountain in the foreground
the extensive ruins of the Brigittenschloss; N. the mountains around
Baden. Guide-posts indicate the numerous routes from this point.

FROM THE HORNISGRINDE TO ALLERHEILIGEN (4 hrs.; 10¼ M.; to
the Ruhstein, 6¼ ℳ, viâ the Höhenweg, p. xvii). The path descends
to the S. to (20 min.) the **Mummelsee** (3385 ft.; 7½ acres), a
gloomy little lake, surrounded by pine-clad mountains, and popularly
believed to be inhabited by water-sprites *(Mümmelchen)*. By the
Seebach, the brook issuing from the lake on the S., is an *Inn* (pens.
5-7 ℳ).

From the Mummelsee we may descend in ¾-1 hr. to the *Wolfsbrunnen*
Inn on the Ottenhöfen and Ruhstein road (p. 396). The 'Elsa-Weg', one
of the approaches to the Höhenweg, descends viâ the *Hohfelsen* to Vorder-
Seebach (p. 396) and (1¾ hr.) Ottenhöfen.

Following the road, we reach in 20 min. the two huts on the
mountain-saddle at the *Seibelseckle* (3140 ft.), on the road from

Schönmünzach to the Mummelsee (p. 390). A stone here marks the boundary between Wurtemberg and Baden. Numerous guide-posts. Our route ('bessere Weg nach Wildsee', $2^3/_4$ M.) leads to the S., skirting the *Schwarzkopf* (3520 ft.) and the *Altsteigerskopf* (3585 ft.), to (1 hr.) a refuge-hut (3350 ft.), 360 ft. above the picturesque and isolated *Wildsee*. After $^1/_4$ hr. more we cross a broader path and follow the footpath straight on through wood to (1 M. farther). —

Ruhstein (2995 ft.; *Klumpp's Inn*, R. $1^3/_4$-$2^1/_2$ M., D. 2 M 80, S. 1 M 60 pf., pens. $5^1/_2$-7 M, often quite full in summer), situated at the highest point of the road from Achern to the Murgtal (see below), on the saddle between the Alte Steigerskopf and the Vogelskopf, 6 M. from Ottenhöfen, $10^1/_2$ M. from Baiersbronn, and $15^1/_2$ M. from Freudenstadt (p. 392; motor-omnibuses, see pp. 392, 395, 410).

The Höhenweg (p. xvii) ascends from Ruhstein to the *Vogelskopf* (3390 ft.), then follows the frontier to the ($1^1/_2$ hr.) *Schliffkopf* ($3^1/_2$ M.; p. 397), and in another $1^1/_2$ hr. reaches the *Zuflucht* ($4^1/_2$ M.; p. 397).

FROM RUHSTEIN TO ALLERHEILIGEN, $1^3/_4$ hr. (level forest-route, with views). Beyond the frontier, 2 min. to the W. of Ruhstein, where the Wolfsbrunnen (p. 396) road bends to the right, we turn to the left, keeping again to the left at the next fork. After $^1/_2$ hr. we cross the *Bosensteinereck* (2725 ft.) and skirt the *Melkereikopf* (3333 ft.). After $^1/_2$ hr. more, at the point where a path to (20 min.) Allerheiligen strikes off to the right, the road descends gradually to the left into the valley of the Gründenbach (p. 396). Farther on it bends to the right and reaches the ($^1/_2$ hr.) saddle known as 'Bei St. Ursula' (p. 396), $^1/_4$ hr. from Allerheiligen.

Walkers may also take the path which diverges to the right from the Höhenweg (p. xvii) at ($^1/_4$ hr.) the Vogelskopf and crosses the Melkereikopf. This rejoins the Ruhstein route in $^3/_4$ hr., a little short of the above-mentioned footpath to Allerheiligen.

d. The Murgtal from Rastatt to Baiersbronn and thence to Freudenstadt. From Schönmünzach to the Hornisgrinde.

From Rastatt to *Forbach*, $16^1/_2$ M., RAILWAY in $1^1/_2$-$1^3/_4$ hr. — ROAD from Forbach to (6 M.) *Schönmünzach* and (13 M.) *Kloster-Reichenbach* (diligence twice daily). RAILWAY thence to (2 M.) *Baiersbronn* and ($7^1/_2$ M.) *Freudenstadt* in $^3/_4$ hr. — From Baiersbronn a road ascends the valley of the Murg to ($10^1/_2$ M.) *Ruhstein;* diligence to Obertal twice daily in 1 hr.; motor-omnibus twice daily in summer (once daily from Freudenstadt, p. 410) to Ruhstein in 50 min. (fare 2 M; comp. p. 395). — Ascent of the *Hornisgrinde* from Schönmünzach on foot, $4^1/_2$ hrs.; thence to *Allerheiligen* viâ Ruhstein 4 hrs. ($8^1/_2$-9 hrs. in all).

Rastatt, see p. 355. The railway ascends the right bank of the *Murg.* — $2^1/_2$ M. *Kuppenheim* (Ochs), a small town with 2000 inhab., on the left bank of the Murg, which is here spanned by an iron bridge. The *Favorite* (p. 366) lies 1 M. to the S.W.

The valley now begins to contract. — $5^1/_2$ M. *Rotenfels* (Ochs),

with a small château of Princess Sophia of Lippe-Detmold. —
6¹/₄ M. *Gaggenau* (Grüner Hof), with considerable iron-works;
8 M. *Hördten.*

10 M. Gernsbach. — *Railway Station* below the town, on the
right bank of the Murg.

HOTELS. In the Town (on the left bank of the Murg, near the bridge):
Goldener Stern, an old-established house, R. 1³/₄-2¹/₄, D. 2³/₄, pens. 5-6¹/₂ ℳ ;
Krone, R. 1¹/₄-2, pens. from 4 ℳ, these two very fair. — To the S. of
the Town (near the station of Scheuern, see p. 393): *Pfeiffer's Bad-Hôtel*,
with garden and baths of all kinds, R. 2-4, pens. 5-8 ℳ. — *Lodgings*
obtained by application to the 'Kur-Komitee'.

CARRIAGES (no tariff, previous arrangement recommended). To or
from the station, with two horses 1¹/₂, with one horse 1 ℳ. — To Schloss
Eberstein, with two horses 6 ℳ, with one horse 4 ℳ; to Baden direct, 9
or 7 ℳ; to Baden viâ Schloss Eberstein, 12 or 8 ℳ; to Herrenalb, 18 or
12 ℳ; to Wildbad, 30 or 20 ℳ.

MOTOR OMNIBUS to Baden-Baden, see p. 359; to (2 hrs.) Wildbad
twice daily in summer viâ Loffenau, Herrenalb, Dobel, Höfen, and Kalm-
bach (fare 3¹/₂ ℳ, in the reverse direction 5 ℳ).

Gernsbach (525 ft.), on the *Murg*, is an ancient and thriving
little town, with 2700 inhab., and frequented as a summer-residence.
It is one of the chief seats of the Black Forest timber trade, especially for the export of pine-logs to the shipbuilders of the Lower
Rhine and Holland. The 'Murgtal-Schiffer-Gesellschaft' is a com-
pany which has existed for centuries and owns 16,000 acres of forest
('Schifferwald' as distinguished from 'Herrschaftswald' or private
property). The *Rathaus*, with its corner-oriel, built in 1617 (re-
stored in 1886), is a good example of the Renaissance style. The
Protestant Church, with a choir of 1462, contains the tombs of a
Count and Countess of Eberstein (16th cent.). The *Roman Catholic
Church* is a late-Gothic building.

From Gernsbach to *Herrenalb*, see p. 387. The attractive ascent
(2³/₄ hrs.) of the *Teufelsmühle* (p. 388) may also be made from the station of Scheuern (p. 393) viâ the Fechtenbuckel or viâ Scheuern and the
Rockertfels.

From the road ascending the valley of the Murg, at the upper
end of Gernsbach, a road diverges to the right to (1¹/₂ M.) **Schloss
Eberstein* (1015 ft.), mentioned in the 13th cent., afterwards
destroyed, and in 1798 rebuilt under the name of '*Neu-Eberstein*'.
Walkers may choose the path diverging 5 min. farther on, at the
Klingel-Kapelle, and ascend by the cliff of *Grafensprung* (view-
temple). The castle is delightfully situated on a wooded hill, high
above the Murg, and commands an extensive view. It contains
ancient relics, weapons, paintings, etc. (rfmts. at the steward's).
Horticulturalists will be interested in the fine fuchsias.

— A footpath descends to the S. from the castle to Obertsroth (p. 393).
— Pedestrians may reach (7¹/₂ M.) Baden from Schloss Eberstein in
2³/₄ hrs. by the road mentioned at p. 368, viâ Müllenbild, and Lichtental.
Carriages take 1¹/₂ hr. Motor-omnibus, see p. 359. The road leads through
fine woods.

The RAILWAY next reaches the stations of ($10^1/_2$ M.) *Scheuern* (Stern; Auerhahn), *Obertsroth* (11 M.; Blume, very fair, pens. $4^1/_2$-7 $\mathcal{M}$), the village of which name is on the left bank of the Murg, and (12 M.) *Hilbertsau*, on the right bank, to which also the highroad here crosses. — $12^1/_2$ M. *Reichentaler-Strasse* is the station for the village of *Reichental* (1330 ft.; Auerhahn), $2^1/_2$ M. to the E.

A pleasant road leads from Reichental viâ *Kaltenbronn* (p. 387) and past the *Hohloh* (r.; p. 387) and the *Kälber-Mühle* (p. 387) to ($5^1/_2$-6 hrs.) *Wildbad*. The footpath viâ the *Hornsee* (p. 387) is shorter.

13 M. **Weisenbach** (635 ft.; *Grüner Baum*, pens. $4^1/_2$-5 $\mathcal{M}$, very fair) has a modern Gothic church, saw-mills, etc.

Beyond Weisenbach the railway crosses the Murg to the left bank, while the highroad continues to follow the right bank. As far as Schönmünzach the valley is wild and beautiful. The rocks are granite. The brown stream flows below amid grey rocks and green meadows, while the slopes are richly wooded with pines, firs, and a few beeches. The railway, partly hewn in the rock, vies with the Schwarzwald Railway in boldness of construction (see p. 405). There are seven tunnels and two large viaducts on the short stretch from Weisenbach to Forbach.

14 M. *Au.* The valley becomes narrower and wilder. Beyond a large wood-pulp and paper mill we reach (15 M.) *Langenbrand* (870 ft.; Ochs), also station for *Bermersbach* (see below), $3/_4$ M. to the S.W. — The train recrosses the Murg to the station of ($16^1/_2$ M.) *Forbach-Gausbach*, the present terminus of the railway. *Gausbach* (1000 ft.; Waldhorn, very fair; Linde) lies on the right bank of the Murg, which the highroad here crosses to —

Forbach (1090 ft.; *Friedrichshof*, pens. $4^1/_2$-$6^1/_2 \mathcal{M}$; *Grüner Hof*, pens. 4 $\mathcal{M}$; *Krone* or *Post*), a thriving village (1800 inhab.), with a modern church, the finest point in the valley. It is a favourite resort from Baden-Baden.

The DIRECT ROUTE FROM BADEN-BADEN TO FORBACH (12 M.) follows the new road at the Fish Breeding Establishment (p. 365; $4^1/_2$ M. from Baden) to ($1/_2$ M.) *Gaisbach* and ($1^1/_4$ M.) *Schmalbach* (1325 ft.), beyond which we take the path through the woods, indicated by finger-posts, surmounting the *Rote Lache* (2290 ft.; refuge-hut), to ($4^1/_2$ M.) *Bermersbach* (1360 ft.; Blume, very fair) and *Forbach*.

FROM FORBACH TO HERRENWIES, 4 hrs., viâ the 'Höhenweg' (p. xvii). About $1/_2$ M. above Forbach we leave the road for the zigzag path to the right, which ascends through fine woods to ($2^1/_2$ hrs.) the Herrenwieser See (p. 390), and thence in $3/_4$ hr. viâ the Seekopf to the Badener Höhe (p. 390). — Viâ the *Hohloh* and *Kaltenbronn* to *Wildbad*, see p. 387.

Beyond Forbach the Murgtal, although more secluded, continues grand and beautiful, especially when viewed downstream at the saw-mills on the *Holderbach*, $1^1/_4$ M. from Forbach. About $2^1/_2$ M. farther on, at the village of *Raumünzach* (1305 ft.; Grüner Baum), the river of that name falls into the Murg.

About $1/_2$ M. above the confluence the Raumünzach is augmented by the *Schwarzbach*, which forms a picturesque waterfall below the 'Fall-

25*

brücke'. *Hundsbach* (p. 390) lies 2 hrs. farther up the valley of the Raumünzach. — A road leads through the valley of the Schwarzbach to (5¹/₂ M.) *Herrenwies* (p. 389).

6 M. (from Forbach) **Schönmünzach** (1500 ft.; *Post*, R. 1¹/₂-2¹/₂, pens. 5-7 *M*, very fair; *Waldhorn*, R. 1¹/₄-3, pens. 4¹/₂-7 *M*; *Schiff*, unpretending but very fair), the first village in Wurtemberg, contains glass-works, and is a favourite summer-resort. The *Schönmünzach* falls into the Murg here. To the Hornisgrinde, see p. 395. Numerous walks in the woods. Carriage to the Seibelseckle 14, to Ottenhöfen 20, to Allerheiligen 28 *M*.

A woodland-path diverging after 7 min. from a road to the right, about ¹/₄ M. above Schönmünzach, ascends to the (40 min.) *Schloss Inn*, on the site of the former castle of Rauenfels (view). Thence a footpath descends to the (¹/₄ hr.) *Saw Mill*, beyond which we have another fine view. — Among the hills to the W. lies the (1¹/₂ hr.) *Schurm-See* (2580 ft.). Thence to *Hundsbach* (p. 390), 1¹/₂ hr.

The Murg, 1¹/₄ M. beyond Schönmünzach, penetrates a precipitous wall of rock, beyond which the valley loses its wild character, as granite gives place to gneiss. On the height to the left lies *Schwarzenberg*. For about 1¹/₄ M. the road runs among the houses of *Hutzenbach* (Bär; Krone). From (1¹/₄ M.) *Schönegründ* (inn) a road leads to the N. by *Besenfeld, Urnagold,* and *Gompelscheuer* (p. 387) to (10¹/₂ M.) *Enzklösterle* (Waldhorn, very fair), and thence to *Wildbad* (p. 386).

The next village in the Murgtal is (6³/₄ M. from Schönmünzach) **Kloster-Reichenbach** (1705 ft.; *Sonne*, R. 1¹/₂-2, pens. 4¹/₂-5 *M*, very fair), with a suppressed Benedictine abbey, founded in 1082; the church (restored) is a flat-roofed Romanesque basilica with a portico.

From Kloster-Reichenbach a branch-railway, partly on the rack-and-pinion system, ascends the Murgtal to (2 M.) **Baiersbronn,** a little below the village of that name (1910 ft.; *Ochs*, R. 1¹/₄-1³/₄ *M*; *Bahnhof-Hôtel*, R. 1¹/₄-2 *M*), situated on the old road. Thence it proceeds up the valley of the *Forbach*, passing the (3³/₄ M.) foundries of *Friedrichstal* and *Christophstal*, to (5¹/₂ M.) the town station and (7¹/₂ M.) the central station of *Freudenstadt* (p. 410).

The MURGTAL ROAD (comp. also Map, p. 397) first follows the branch-line just mentioned, crosses (1¹/₄ M. from Kloster-Reichenbach) the Murg, and ascends the left bank. Beyond the confluence of the Forbach the road from (³/₄ M.) Baiersbronn, after crossing the railway, the Forbach, and the Murg, unites with our road. About 4¹/₂ M. from Reichenbach, at the straggling village of *Mitteltal* (Tannenburg, Lamm, both very fair), a road leads to the left by the *Elbach-Tal* to the (4¹/₂ M.) *Rossbühl*, joining the road described at p. 399, near the Schwedenschanze. About 1¹/₂ M. farther up the Murgtal, into which several brooks descend from the Kniebis, are the *Schwan Inn* and the hamlet of *Tannenfels*, in the woods opposite which is the ruin of that name. We now soon reach the first houses of *Obertal* (Sonne, Adler, both very fair), whence a road leads to the left through the valley of the *Rechte Murg* to (1¹/₂ M.) *Buhlbach* (2040 ft.; Inn zur Glashütte, very fair) and thence through wood to the (4¹/₂ M.) Rossbühl (p. 399).

The road in the Murgtal continues to ascend, forming long windings, to its highest point at (6 M.) the *Ruhstein* (p. 391).

FROM SCHÖNMÜNZACH TO THE HORNISGRINDE. Two roads ascend the *Schönmünzach*, the Baden road on the left bank, and the Wurtemberg road on the right. Following the latter, which diverges at the Schiff Inn, beyond the bridge, we reach (3 M.) *Zwickgabel* (inn), cross the brook, and ascend to the right along the *Langenbach*, which unites at Zwickgabel with the Schönmünzach. The road then passes (1^1/$_2$ M.) *Vorder-Langenbach*, and at (2^1/$_4$ M.) *Hinter-Langenbach* (Auerhahn, kept by the forester, R. 1-1^1/$_4$ $\mathcal{M}$, B. 70 pf.) ascends to the left. About ^{1}/$_4$ M. farther on is a way-post, indicating the route to the (3^3/$_4$ M.) Wildsee (p. 391) and (12 M.) Allerheiligen. The road now ascends more rapidly to the (3 M.) *Seibelseckle* (p. 390), on the frontier of Baden, beyond which it descends to the road from Baiersbronn to Ruhstein and Ottenhöfen, which it reaches beside the (2^1/$_4$ M.) Wolfsbrunnen Inn (p. 396).

The Hornisgrinde may be ascended from the Seibelseckle either by a route diverging to the right from the last-mentioned road and passing the *Mummelsee* (p. 390; 'Höhenweg', p. xvii), or by the direct path beginning opposite the log-cabins and leading to the N.W. (to the tower, ^{3}/$_4$ hr.). *Hornisgrinde*, see p. 390.

e. From Achern viâ Ottenhöfen to Ruhstein or Aller-heiligen.

From Achern to *Ottenhöfen*, 6^3/$_4$ M., RAILWAY in 40 minutes. — MOTOR OMNIBUS thence to (7^1/$_4$ M.; 1 hr.) *Ruhstein* once daily in summer (fare 2^1/$_2$ $\mathcal{M}$); continuation to Baiersbronn and Freudenstadt, see p. 410. — From Ottenhöfen on foot to *Allerheiligen*, 1^3/$_4$-2^1/$_4$ hrs.; from Allerheiligen to Oppenau 2^1/$_2$ hrs., to Rippoldsau 5 hrs.

Achern, see p. 369. The railway ascends the *Kappeler-Tal*, a pleasant green dale watered by the *Acher* (to the left on the hill, the *Brigittenschloss*, p. 370). — 1^1/$_4$ M. *Oberachern.* — 4^1/$_2$ M. *Kappelrodeck* (725 ft.; Löwe; Ochse), commanded by the château of *Rodeck* (965 ft.), dating from the 8th cent., and lately altered and restored, with fine grounds and views (for adm. apply to the gardener).

FROM KAPPELRODECK TO ALLERHEILIGEN, 4^1/$_2$ hrs., by a path through wood, commanding fine views. This route, steep at first, leads under the château of Rodeck to (^{1}/$_2$-^{3}/$_4$ hr.) the *Käferwaldkopf* (1530 ft.; view), the rocks of the (^{1}/$_2$ hr. farther) *Bürstenstein*, and (2 hrs.) the *Allerheiligensteig*, which begins at Lautenbach. Thence we follow the ridge viâ the *Sohlberg* (p. 397).

6^3/$_4$ M. **Ottenhöfen** (1020 ft.; *Engel ; Linde ; Pflug ; Wagen*, all very fair, R. 1^1/$_4$-2 $\mathcal{M}$), the terminus of the railway, a prettily-situated village, forming suitable headquarters for a number of pleasant excursions. The road forks here, the left branch leading to Seebach and Ruhstein, the right to Allerheiligen.

The ROAD FROM OTTENHÖFEN TO RUHSTEIN (Baiersbronn) continues to ascend the valley of the Acher, crossing to the left bank

at *Hagenbruck,* below the *Bosenstein.* From the hamlet of
Vorder-Seebach (1280 ft.; Hirsch) a road leads to the left through
the wooded *Grimmerswalder - Tal* to (4¹/₂ M.) Breitenbrunnen
(p. 390). [From this road, after 8 min., diverges the Elsa-Weg,
leading to (2 hrs.) the Mummelsee (p. 390).] From the *Adler Inn*
at **Hinter-Seebach,** a little farther on, a steep path leads past
the Scherzen-Fels and the Bosensteinereck (on the Ruhstein road,
p. 391) to (2¹/₄ hrs.) Allerheiligen. Our road turns to the left at
Achert, 3 M. from Ottenhöfen (the steep old road, 4 M. to Ruhstein,
keeps to the right), crosses the Acher, and 1¹/₄ M. farther on reaches
the *Wolfsbrunnen Inn* (2200 ft.; to the Mummelsee 1 hr.; see
p. 390; guide-post). Thence it ascends in curves, commanding extensive views, to (2³/₄ M.) *Ruhstein* (p. 391).

The ROAD FROM OTTENHÖFEN TO ALLERHEILIGEN (6 M.; carr.
6-8 ℳ) ascends the *Unterwasser-Tal* towards the S. to the (2¹/₄ M.)
Erbprinz Inn. Here the new road describes a wide curve in the
valley towards the left, while the old road ascends the steep slope
on the right, the two re-uniting at (2¹/₄ M.) the saddle named 'Bei
St. Ursula' (p. 391). Fine retrospects from the new road; 1 M. from
the Erbprinz a way-post shows the route to the Edelfrauengrab viâ
the Blöchereck. From the saddle (short-cut by steps to the right)
the road descends in windings to (³/₄ M.) Allerheiligen.

FROM OTTENHÖFEN TO ALLERHEILIGEN by the *Edelfrauengrab* and
the *Blöchereck* (2¹/₄ hrs.), a very attractive walk. In front of the church
we turn to the left, then follow the footpath immediately to the right,
and the road to the left higher up, which diverges from the road to
Allerheiligen at a point about 300 yds. beyond the church. After 10 min.
we follow the middle road in a straight direction, traverse the pretty
Gottschläg-Tal (Edelfrauengrab Inn, pens. 4-5 ℳ), cross the brook several
times, and finally ascend by steps to the (20 min.) **Edelfrauengrab**
('grave of the noble lady'), a small grotto to which a romantic legend
attaches. The environs are very picturesque, especially the path ascending beyond this point past numerous pretty cascades, to the (1 hr.)
Blöchereck. Farther on the path leads through wood and soon reaches
the road; ³/₄ hr. *Allerheiligen.* The pretty footpath from the Blöchereck,
skirting the Schwabenkopf to the saddle, is ¹/₄ hr. longer. — Travellers
coming from Seebach (p. 390) may diverge to the left at *Hagenbruck*
(p. 395), beyond the Kreuz Inn, ¹/₂ M. before reaching Ottenhöfen.

*Allerheiligen (2035 ft.; *Mittenmaier's Inn,* R. from 2, B. 1,
D. 3, S. 2, pens. from 6 ℳ, very fair), with the ruins of a Præmonstratensian abbey, founded by the Duchess Uta of Schauenburg in
1196, and partly destroyed by lightning in 1803, is one of the most
frequented spots in the Black Forest. The church was a Gothic
edifice with polygonal side-choirs to the E. of the transept and a
square tower over the crossing.

Immediately below the convent is a rugged cleft in the rocks,
through which the *Gründenbach* is precipitated into the valley
beneath in a series of falls, 270 ft. high in all, called the **Bütten-
stein Falls** or *Büttenschröffen.* The waterfalls and their picturesque accessories are seen to most advantage in ascending, and by

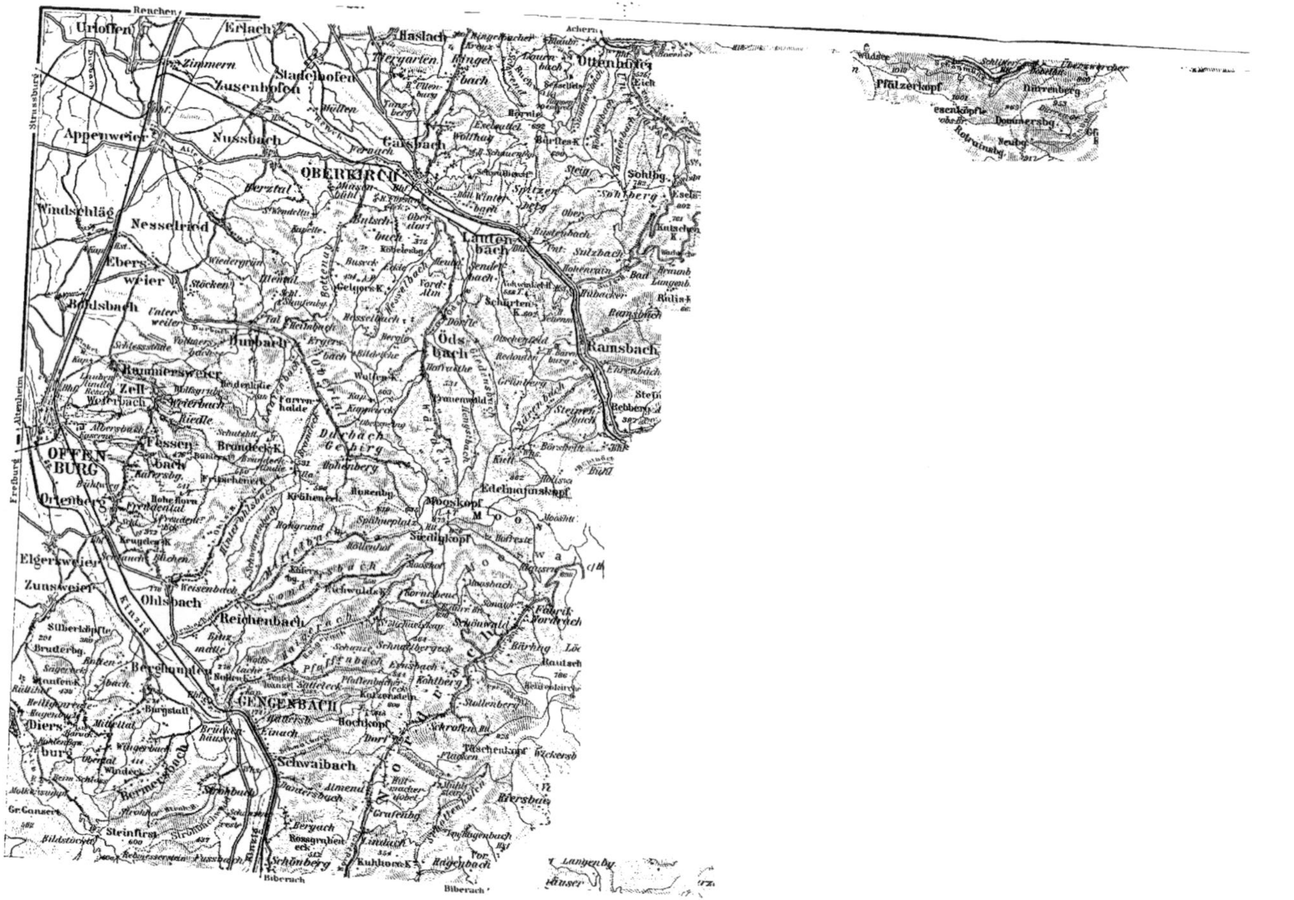

Renchen
Urloffen
Erlach
Zimmern
Stadelhofen
Zusenhofen
Appenweier
Nussbach
OBERKIRCH
Haslach
Tiergarten
Ringelbach
Gaisbach
Ottenhöfen
Achern
Windschläg
Nesselried
Ebersweier
Bohlsbach
Durbach
Rammersweier
Zell
Weierbach
Riedle
OFFENBURG
Fessenbach
Ortenberg
Elgersweier
Zunsweier
Ohlsbach
Reichenbach
Kinzig
Berghaupten
GENGENBACH
Diersburg
Schwaibach
Strohbach
Schönberg
Biberach
Lautenbach
Ödsbach
Ramsbach
Mooskopf
Edelmannskopf
Brandeck K.
Durbach Gebirg
Hohenberg
Schöllkopf
Mooswald
Schönwald
Nordrach
Kohlberg
Hochkopf
Lindach
Kuhhorn K.
Rugenbach
Steinfirst
Gr. Gansert
Pfälzerkopf
Dürrenberg
Donnersbg.
Strassburg
Altenheim
Freiburg
Alpirsbach

evening light. The best way of approaching them is, accordingly, to take the footpath to the 'Luisenruhe, Engelskanzel, and Teufelsstein', which diverges to the right of the barn, opposite the new Logierhaus, and leads through wood to the (1/2 hr.) road at the foot of the falls (1665 ft.). We then ascend the path to the (1/2 hr.) inn.

Way-posts at the above-mentioned view-point Luisenruhe indicate paths leading viâ the picturesque *Sohlberg* (2570 ft.; p. 398) to (3 hrs.) *Oberkirch* (p. 398), and viâ the *Braunberg* (2150 ft.) to (2 hrs.) *Sulzbach* (p. 398).

The **Rote Schliffkopf** (3465 ft.) may be ascended in 1¼ hr. from Allerheiligen by a path diverging to the right on the left bank 150 yds. above the ruin near the bridge (guide-post). We turn to the right on quitting the wood and in 1 hr., at the refuge-hut on the *Steinmäuerle* (3280 ft.), reach the 'Höhenweg' (p. xvii) which here skirts the Wurtemberg frontier. On the (10 min.) summit is a view-platform. — The Höhenweg leads hence to the N. (good views) to the (1¼ hr.) *Ruhstein* (p. 391), while to the S. from the Steinmäuerle it leads viâ the Schwabenschanze to (4 M.) the *Zuflucht* (see below). The steep path descending to the S.E. from the Steinmäuerle passes the (¼ hr.) source of the Rechte Murg (2875 ft.), and in ½ hr. more joins the road from Buhlbach (p. 394) to Kniebis, which we follow to the right (short-cuts for walkers) to the (½ hr.) view-platform beside the Zuflucht Inn at the Schwabenschanze (see below).

FROM ALLERHEILIGEN TO OPPENAU, 7 M. The carriage-road, which affords the shortest and best route, diverges to the right from the Ottenhöfen road a few min. beyond the ruin, crosses the brook, and descends in windings to (1¾ M.) the foot of the waterfalls. Once more crossing the stream, it passes (½ M.) the *Wasserfall Inn* (R. 1½-2, pens. 4-5 ℳ), and follows the right bank of the *Lierbach* (as the Gründenbach is now called), high on the slope of the hill. Near Oppenau, 1 M. beyond the *Taube Inn* (p. 398), the Kniebis-Strasse and the road to (3 M.) Antogast (p. 399) diverge to the left. — *Oppenau*, see p. 398.

FROM ALLERHEILIGEN TO RIPPOLDSAU OVER THE KNIEBIS, 5 hrs. Below the new Logierhaus we take the path which diverges to the left at a finger-post ('Zur Zuflucht'), crosses the Oppenau road, and ascends, crossing a wide woodcutters' path, through pine-woods. In ¼ hr. more we reach another woodcutters' path (2405 ft.), which leads along the slope of the Schliffkopf (see above) to (¼ hr.) the *Friedrichs-Brücke* (2520 ft.), spanning the Hirschbach, and thence along the *Schurkopf* or *Schauerkopf* (3205 ft.), finally (¾ hr.) narrowing to a footpath (numerous guide-posts). Farther on we come to the Wurtemberg frontier and to the 'Höhenweg' (p. xvii), descending on the left from the Schliffkopf (see above). Immediately afterwards we see the *Röschenschanze* or *Schwabenschanze* ('Swabian intrenchment'), an ancient earthwork (3170 ft.; belvedere) on the highest point of the *Rossbühl* (p. 399). About ¼ M. farther on we reach the *Kurhaus Zuflucht* (3140 ft.), on the road from Oppenau to Rippoldsau and Freudenstadt; and 2¼ M. to the S.E. is the *Alexanderschanze Inn* (p. 400; the Höhenweg is not advisable in wet weather), where the Oppenau road joins that from Griesbach to Freudenstadt. Thence to *Rippoldsau*, see p. 400.

f. From Appenweier to Oppenau and the Baths in the Renchtal.

RAILWAY from Appenweier to *Oppenau*, 11 M., in $^3/_4$-1 hr. — ROAD from Oppenau viâ *Peterstal* to *Griesbach*, 7$^1/_2$ M.: diligence thrice daily in 1$^3/_4$ hr. There are also horse-omnibuses, and carriages may be ordered in advance from the hotels at the Renchtal baths. From Griesbach to *Freudenstadt* viâ the Kniebis, 13 M.

Appenweier, see p. 370. The train approaches the Renchtal. 2$^1/_2$ M. *Zusenhofen.* — 5$^1/_2$ M. **Oberkirch** (625 ft.; *Schwarzer Adler*, R. 1$^1/_2$-2, pens. 4-5 *M*, well spoken of; *Linde*, R. 1$^1/_2$-2$^1/_2$, pens. 4$^1/_2$-5$^1/_2$ *M*, both with gardens), situated in an extremely fertile district on the slope of the hill, at the entrance to the narrower Renchtal. Pop. 3500.

About 1 M. farther on, beyond the Rench, to the right of the line, is the ruined castle of *Fürsteneck*. A road ascends on the left bank of the Rench from Oberkirch to *Oedsbach*, whence the Moosturm (p. 401) may be reached in about 3 hrs. About 2$^1/_4$ M. to the N.E. of Oberkirch lie the ruins of *Schauenburg*, whence a fine view is obtained; *Von Haber's Höllhof*, $^3/_4$ M. to the E., is another good point of view. — Viâ the Sohlberg to Allerheiligen, see p. 397. — To the N. of Oberkirch are the villages of (1 M.) *Gaisbach* (Lamm) and (3 M.) *Ringelbach* (Salm), both noted for their wine.

7$^1/_2$ M. *Lautenbach* (705 ft.; Schwan, very fair; Kreuz; Stern), with a late-Gothic church (1471-83) containing an interesting screen and stained-glass windows. The tower was added in 1898. Hence to the Moosturm viâ Oedsbach, ca. 3 hrs. Ascent of the *Schärtenkopf* (1975 ft.) 1$^3/_4$ hr.; the descent may be made to Hubacker.

8$^1/_2$ M. *Hubacker* (fair inn) is the station for **Sulzbach,** a small bath 1$^1/_4$ M. to the N. (R. 1$^1/_2$, pens. from 5 *M*) with a saline spring (70° Fahr.). From Sulzbach a road, soon splitting into two arms, passing respectively to the E. and W. of the *Kutschenkopf* (2495 ft.) and the *Eselskopf* (2630 ft.), leads to (5 M.) Allerheiligen (p. 396). Walkers should choose the E. arm viâ the *Braunberg*, 2 hrs.

11 M. **Oppenau.** — HOTELS. *Hôtel Post*, with garden, pens. 4-6 *M*; *Goldener Adler*, also a posting-house, pens. 4$^1/_2$-5 *M*; *Ochs*, pens. 3 *M* 80 pf.; *Hirsch*. — *Taube*, with mineral baths, 1$^1/_2$ M. from Oppenau, on the road to Allerheiligen (p. 396), pens. from 4$^1/_2$ *M*, well spoken of.

CARRIAGE to Antogast 5, Freiersbach or Peterstal 7, Griesbach 10 *M*; to the waterfall at Allerheiligen 7, to the convent 10 *M*. — DILIGENCE, see above.

Oppenau (885 ft.), a busy little town, with 2000 inhab., is frequented as a summer-resort. In the market-place is a *War Monument*. — A conspicuous belvedere near the town commands an excellent view; it is reached in 20-25 min. by passing the N. side of the church.

From Oppenau to the *Moosturm* (p. 401), about 2 hrs. We follow the Renchtal road (p. 399) for 6-8 min., then turn to the right (way-post) and ascend to Kutt.

. Close by the Oppenau station the highroad divides, the right (S.) branch being the Renchtal road (p. 398), and the left (E.) arm being the Rossbühl Road, formerly known as the Kniebis road. The latter passes through Oppenau. Immediately beyond the town the road to (4 M.) *Antogast* (1585 ft.; *Huber), with chalybeate baths, charmingly situated in the pretty *Maisach-Tal*, and known as *St. Arbogast* in the 16th cent., diverges to the right, and crosses the Lierbach; the road in a straight direction leads to Allerheiligen (p. 396). Footpath to (1¹/₄ hr.) Griesbach (see p. 400).

The road diverging to the left from the Antogast road gradually ascends (in ³/₄ hr. footpath to the left, returning in ¹/₂ hr. to the road again), and finally traverses some fine woods (in ¹/₂ hr. footpath to the left) to the summit of the **Rossbühl** (3170 ft.), on which, to the left, is the *Schwabenschanze* (p. 397). It then makes a wide curve, past the *Schwedenschanze* (on the right), to the *Zuflucht Inn* (p. 397).

———

The road continuing to ascend the valley of the Rench (diligence, see p. 398) passes through a small part only of Oppenau, and leads southwards to the baths of Freiersbach, Peterstal, and Griesbach. 1¹/₄ M. *Ibach* (985 ft.). — 2 M. *Löcherberg* (Pflug).

A carriage-road, commanding fine views, gradually ascends from Löcherberg through a fertile valley viâ the *Harmersberg* to (4¹/₂ M.) *Ober-Harmersbach* (p. 401). — A slightly longer route to Zell, viâ Nordrach, diverges to the right from the above-mentioned road, about 2¹/₄ M. from Löcherberg. This route divides after 20-25 min. into two arms, which, however, reunite 20-25 min. farther on, at *Fabrik Nordrach* or *Nordrach Colonie* (1475 ft.; Dr. O. Walther's Establishment for Consumptives, pens. 10 ℳ), so-called from a disused glass-factory. Fine pine-woods. Walkers may also reach this point in 2¹/₄ hrs. by a path diverging to the right at the second bridge in Ibach and passing the Bühler Eck. — About 3¹/₂ M. down the valley of Nordrach lies its chief village **Nordrach** (*Linde*, pens. 4-5 ℳ, very fair), whence the *Hochkopf* (2015 ft.; fine views) may be ascended (descent to the W. to Gengenbach, p. 401). The road continues to follow the Nordrach valley to (3¹/₂ M.) *Zell* (p. 401; omnibus twice daily).

Farther on in the Renchtal, 2¹/₄ M. from Löcherberg, is **Bad Freiersbach** (1260 ft.; *Meyer's Hotel*, with baths, pens. from 5 ℳ, very fair), with chalybeate springs, situated in a pretty dale, enclosed by lofty hills. Then (³/₄ M.) —

5 M. (from Oppenau) **Peterstal**. — Hotels. *Bär; Hirsch; Schlüsselbad.* — *Bad Peterstal*, at the upper end of the village, well equipped, R. 2-4, B. 1¹/₄, D. 2¹/₂, pens. 6³/₄-8¹/₂ ℳ, closed in winter; visitors' tax 2¹/₂ ℳ per week. — Numerous private apartments. .

Peterstal (1295 ft.), the most important of the small baths in the Renchtal, occupies a sheltered situation, embellished with well-kept grounds. The four springs contain iron and carbonic-acid gas. The baths, which were known in the 16th cent., are frequented by about 1500 patients annually.

A pleasant route leads to the S.E. from the Bear Hotel in Peterstal through the *Freiers-Tal* and past the ($\frac{1}{4}$ hr.) village of *Freiersbach* to the ($1\frac{1}{4}$ hr.) saddle of *Freiersberg* (1875 ft.) to the E. of the *Grosse Hundskopf*, and thence down the valley of the *Wildschapbach* to ($1\frac{1}{2}$ hr.) *Schapbach* (p. 408). [From the saddle the 'Höhenweg' leads to the left to ($\frac{3}{4}$ hr.) the Glaswaldsee-Blick (p. 408).] — The route diverging by the side-valley to the S., beyond the village of Freiersbach, crosses the ($\frac{1}{4}$ hr.) brook and reaches the ($1\frac{1}{2}$ hr.) saddle *Littweger Höhe* (2770 ft.; Höhenweg, see below), to the W. of the Grosse Hundskopf, whence, following the guide-posts, we may descend the *Rankach-Tal*, passing the Bear Inn, to ($1\frac{1}{2}$-$1\frac{3}{4}$ hr.) *Ober-Wolfach* (p. 408). Thence to the railway-station of Wolfach, $\frac{3}{4}$-1 hr. more.

A pleasant footpath leads from Peterstal to *Antogast* in 2 hrs. At ($\frac{1}{2}$ hr.) the hamlet of *Döttelbach*, on the roadside, we ascend through the archway.

The Renchtal now turns to the N.E. In $\frac{3}{4}$ hr. we reach —

$2\frac{1}{2}$ M. (from Peterstal) **Griesbach** (1665 ft.; **Kurhaus, Adlerbad, Tannenhof*, R. $1\frac{1}{2}$-4, pens. $5\frac{1}{2}$-10 $\mathscr{M}$; *Linde*), possessing a chalybeate spring, which has been highly valued for 400 years, and pine-cone, mud, and other baths. About 1800 patients annually. Pleasant grounds surround the village, and the ($\frac{3}{4}$ hr.) Haberer Turm commands a good view.

A footpath leads from GRIESBACH TO RIPPOLDSAU (p. 409; $2\frac{1}{4}$ hrs.), diverging from the Kniebis road at a sharp bend about 1 M. from the Kurhaus, and ascending past a waterfall and viâ the *Sophienruhe* to the *Hilda Hut* on the *Holzwälder Höhe* (3005 ft.). Thence a gradual descent brings us to the road to *Rippoldsau*. — The 'Höhenweg' (p. xvii) runs from the Holzwälder Höhe viâ the *Letterstätter Höhe* (p. 408), the *Freiersberg*, the *Littweger Höhe* (see above), the *Kreuzsattel, Hirzwasen, Ebenacker*, and *Kreuzbühl* (hence to the *Hohenlochen*, 10 min.) to ($7\frac{1}{4}$ hrs.) Hausach (p. 402).

The road now ascends in windings to the **Kniebis,** the summit of which is reached immediately beyond the Wurtemberg frontier at the ($4\frac{1}{2}$ M.) *Alexanderschanze Inn* (3170 ft.; R. $1\frac{1}{2}$, D. $1\frac{1}{2}$-$2\frac{1}{2}$ $\mathscr{M}$), where the Rossbühl road joins ours (p. 399). At the inn *Zum Lamm* (3060 ft.; R. $1\frac{1}{2}$-$1\frac{3}{4}$, pens. $4\frac{1}{2}$-5 $\mathscr{M}$), $1\frac{1}{2}$ M. to the E. of the Alexanderschanze, on the Rossbühl road, the roads to Rippoldsau and Freudenstadt diverge. The road to *Rippoldsau* ($1\frac{1}{2}$ hr.; p. 409), to the right, leads viâ the ($\frac{1}{2}$ M.) Baden village of *Kniebis* (Zum Schwarzwald; shorter footpath beyond the village, to the left) and winds down the E. side of the *Holzwälder Höhe* (see above). The road to *Freudenstadt* (7 M.; p. 410) leads straight on, viâ the Wurtemberg village of *Kniebis* (Ochs), and descends along the left bank of the *Forbach*, which it finally crosses before ascending to the town. Pedestrians take the path on the right bank of the stream.

WALKERS FROM THE ALEXANDERSCHANZE INN TO RIPPOLDSAU follow the Griesbach road for $\frac{1}{2}$ M., then take the path which leads to the left through the wood ('Höhenweg', p. xvii) to the (3 M.) Hilda Hut on the Holzwalder Höhe (see above).

1

y
st
1e
i).
n-
ht

1d
s.
3s
.0
ui

e,
1e
r-
ζs
3h
t.,
or
s.
o-

's
l;
he
to
i.)
1l-
he
od
n'
iâ
is-
in
he
ay
itt
we
ds

e,
he

up
vn
of
M.
r-
he
ro

g. Schwarzwald Railway from Offenburg to Singen.

93 M. RAILWAY in 3-4³/₄ hrs. (fares 12 ℳ 10, 7 ℳ 20, 4 ℳ 60 pf.; by express 13 ℳ 10, 8 ℳ 20, 5 ℳ 10 pf.).

The *Schwarzwald Railway, opened in 1873, is one of the most striking in Germany, both in point of scenery and construction. The most interesting part is that between Hausach and Villingen (pp. 402-406). The line attracts numerous travellers, and the inns at Hausach, Hornberg, Triberg, and other picturesque points are often full in the height of the season.

Offenburg, see p. 371. — The line traverses the populous and fertile *Kinzig-Tal*, a valley enclosed by gently-sloping mountains. 2¹/₂ M. *Ortenberg* (Krone), above which, on a vine-clad hill, rises the château of *Ortenberg* (710 ft.), built by Eisenlohr in 1834-40 on the site of an ancient stronghold destroyed by Marshal Créqui in 1668.

5¹/₂ M. **Gengenbach** (570 ft.; *Adler*, R. 1¹/₂-3 ℳ; *Sonne*, both very fair), with 3050 inhab., an independent town down to the Peace of Lunéville (1801), still exhibits traces of its former importance in its walls, gates, and towers, although most of the buildings have been erected since the destruction of the town by the French in 1689. The handsome *Benedictine Abbey*, founded in the 8th cent., to which the town owes its origin, is now a preparatory school for teachers. The Romanesque abbey-church has rococo choir-stalls. The *Rathaus* is a handsome building of 1784, lately restored. Opposite is a fountain with a statue of Charles V.

WALKS AND EXCURSIONS. In the *Nollenwald;* to the (¹/₄ hr.) *St. James's Chapel* on the Kastelberg and thence to the (¹/₂ hr. more) *Teufelskanzel;* viâ *Einach* (Rebstock, unpretending but good) up the right bank of the Kinzig, then (¹/₄ hr.) to the left up the *Hüttersbach-Tal*, and to the right to the (1¹/₂ hr.) *Hochkopf* (p. 399). — A pleasant excursion leads to the (3 hrs.) *Moosturm on the Gaisschleifkopf. The path (marked by blue parallelograms) ascends the *Haigeracher-Tal* from Gengenbach, passing the (³/₄ hr) *Waldhorn Inn*, and follows the 'Kapellen-Weg' through wood to the (1¹/₄ hr.) *Kornebene* (2130 ft.) and the (10 min.) '*Dürre Brunnen*' (2095 ft.), where the routes divide. We follow the route to the N. viâ the *Siedigkopf* (2875 ft.) to the (1 hr.) summit of the *Mooskopf* or *Gaisschleifkopf* (2870 ft.). The view from the *Moosturm*, 65 ft. in height, embraces a considerable part of the Black Forest, especially the valleys of the Rench and the Kinzig. From the Moosturm the walk may be continued to the N.E. past the *Edelmannskopf* (2828 ft.) to *Kutt* (rfmts.) and thence viâ *Börskritt* to (2 hrs.) Oppenau (p. 398). Or we may return to the Dürre Brunnen and follow the E. path, which leads to Nordrach (p. 399).

9¹/₂ M. *Schönberg.* — 11¹/₄ M. **Biberach** (635 ft.; *Sonne; Bahnhof-Hôtel*), a village of 1500 inhab., prettily situated at the mouth of the *Harmersbach.*

FROM BIBERACH TO OBER-HARMERSBACH, 7 M., railway in 37 min. up the valley of the Harmersbach. — 2 M. **Zell** *(Hirsch; Löwe)*, a small town of 1950 inhab., at the mouth of the *Nordrach-Tal*, with manufactures of stoneware and majolica, has been rebuilt since a fire in 1904. 2¹/₂ M. *Birach;* 3 M. *Unter-Harmersbach* (Adler, very fair); 5¹/₂ M. **Ober-Harmersbach** *(Sonne);* 7 M. *Ober-Harmersbach-Riersbach*. From the platform on the *Brandenkopf* (3060 ft.) a fine view is obtained. — To Löcherberg and Nordrach, see p. 399.

FROM BIBERACH TO LAHR ($8^1/_2$ M.) a road leads over the *Schönberg.*
On the top (1210 ft.), $2^3/_4$ M. from Biberach, is the good *Löwe Inn,* beyond
which a footpath diverges to the right, leading in 40 min. to a lofty
and precipitous rock, crowned with the extensive ruins of the castle of
Hohen-Geroldseck (1725 ft.), first mentioned in 1139. This castle has
been partially restored and commands a fine view. From the Schönberg
the road descends into the *Schutter-Tal,* where, at (3 M.) *Reichenbach,*
we reach the steam-tramway mentioned at p. 371. *Lahr,* see p. 371.

Before ($14^1/_2$ M.) *Steinach* is reached, the line crosses the Kinzig.
— $16^1/_4$ M. **Haslach** (710 ft.; *Kreuz,* R. $1^1/_4$-2, pens. 4-5 $\mathcal{M}$;
Europäischer Hof; Vollmer, an open-air restaurant), a prosperous
little town with 2200 inhab. and some manufactures, was destroyed,
with the exception of the church, by the French in 1704, after their
defeat at the battle of Höchstädt.

An attractive road runs to the S. from Haslach, viâ *Hofstetten,* to
(9 M.) *Elzach* (p. 415), passing halfway near the scanty ruins of the
castle of *Heidburg* (to the left).

$20^1/_2$ M. **Hausach** (790 ft.; *Bahnhof-Hôtel,* R. $1^1/_4$-$2^1/_2$, pens.
4-6 $\mathcal{M}$; *Hirsch,* R. $1^1/_4$-$1^1/_2$, pens. 4-5 $\mathcal{M}$) is a small town with
1700 inhab., commanded by the ruins of an old castle of the
Princes of Fürstenberg, destroyed by the French in 1643. — From
Hausach to *Wolfach* (Rippoldsau), *Schiltach,* and *Freudenstadt,*
see pp. 408-410.

The railway quits the Kinzig-Tal above Hausach, turns to the
right at *Am Turm,* and ascends the picturesque and fertile valley
of the *Gutach.* — 23 M. **Gutach** (920 ft.; *Löwe*). The *Farrenkopf* (2590 ft.; picturesque view) may be ascended hence in 2 hrs.,
by a good path diverging to the W. from the highroad between the
station and the Löwe inn. It may also be ascended in the same
time from Hausach viâ Breitenbach.

$26^1/_2$ M. **Hornberg.** — RAILWAY STATION (1260 ft.) on the right
bank of the Gutach, above the town. The chief hotels send omnibuses
to meet the trains.

HOTELS. **Hôtel & Kurhaus Schloss Hornberg* (see below), R. $2^1/_4$-6,
B. $1^1/_4$, D. 3, pens. $6^1/_2$-12, omn. 1 $\mathcal{M}$. — In the town: **Post,* R. from
$1^3/_4$, pens. from $5^1/_2$ $\mathcal{M}$; **Bär,* R. 2-3, pens. $5^1/_2$-7 $\mathcal{M}$; *Adler,* R. $1^1/_2$-2,
pens. $4^1/_2$-5 $\mathcal{M}$; *Rössle,* R. $1^1/_2$-$1^3/_4$, pens. $4^1/_2$-5 $\mathcal{M}$, these two well spoken
of. — *Café Bopp* (wine).

Hornberg (1180 ft.), an old town of 2800 inhab., is situated at
the mouth of the *Offenbach-Tal,* opposite the *Reichenbach-Tal,*
and is commanded by a precipitous hill crowned by a *Château*
(1500 ft.), destroyed by the French in 1703. It is one of the most
picturesque spots in the Black Forest and attracts numerous summer-
visitors. The château is reached in 20 min. by a road ascending the
Offenbach-Tal, then turning to the right, or by a shorter footpath
direct from the town. The top of the hill, on which is the hotel,
commands a fine view (adm. to tower 10 pf.).

WALKS. To the N. to the ($^3/_4$-1 hr.) *Markgrafenschanze* (1605 ft.),
with a view-pavilion; to the E. to the (1 hr.) *Windeckfels* (2020 ft.), on
the way to Althornberg (p. 403); to the *Reichenbach-Tal* (and viâ the

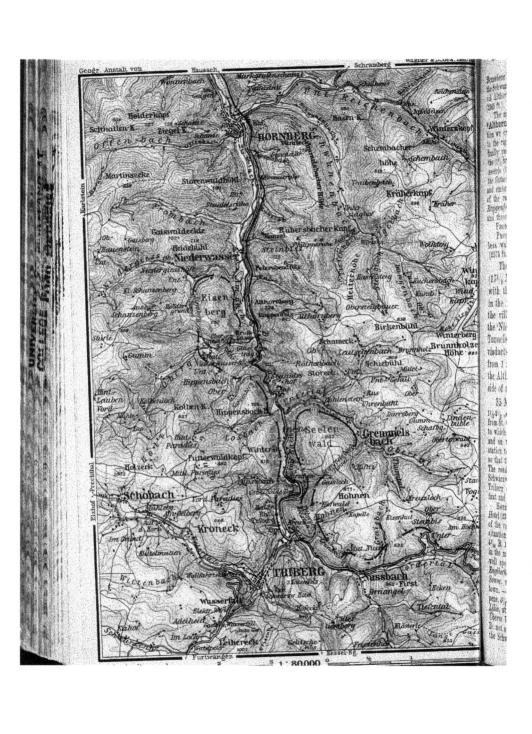

Benzebene to Thennenbronn, p. 409) or to the *Schwanenbach-Tal;* through the Schwanenbach-Tal to the (2 hrs.) top of the *Windkapf* (3030 ft.), and back viâ Althornberg; viâ the château of Hornberg to the (³/₄ hr.) *Ziegelkopf* (2365 ft.); to the (1¹/₂ hr.) top of the *Storenwaldkopf* (2515 ft.), to the S. The most attractive excursion is that to the (2 hrs.) rocky height of ***Althornberg** (2390 ft.). About 250 paces to the S. of the railway-station we cross the line, and thence ascend rapidly to the wood. We turn to the right in the wood, follow the finger-posts and way-marks, and finally pass round the upper end of the Althornberg ravine and reach the (1¹/₂ hr.) hamlet of *Althornberg.* Thence the path (marked II in red) ascends (to the right) to the summit in 20 minutes. The view hence of the Gutach-Tal is probably the finest in this part of the Black Forest, and embraces a specially interesting survey of the curves and tunnels of the railway. — The path marked III in red leads to the (8-10 min.) *Rappenfels*, commanding a similar view. — Thence viâ the Schameck and through the Röthenbach-Tal to Triberg, see p. 405.

From Hornberg to Elzach (4¹/₂ hrs.), see p. 415.

From Hornberg to Schramberg (p. 409), a charming, though shadeless walk of 10¹/₂ M. through the *Schonach-Tal*, by the *Fohrenbühl* (2575 ft.; Schwan; Adler; view) and *Lauterbach* (p. 409).

The most interesting part of the line is between Hornberg and (17¹/₂ M.) St. Georgen. For some distance the railway runs parallel with the road, which, like the line itself, is in many places hewn in the rock, and ascends the narrow, wooded Gutach-Tal. Above the village of (32 M.) *Niederwasser* (1800 ft.; Sonne; Rössle) is the 'Niederwasser Kehr-Tunnel', where the first great curve begins. Tunnels (of which there are 37 between Hornberg and St. Georgen), viaducts, and bridges follow in rapid succession. The gradient varies from 1 : 58 to 1 : 50. — The best general survey is commanded by the Althornberg (see above), which is seen from the line on the E. side of the valley.

35 M. Triberg. — The Station (2025 ft.; *Rail. Restaurant*, D. 1¹/₂-2¹/₂ ℳ) lies below the 'Kreuz-Brücke', at the junction of the roads from St. Georgen and Furtwangen, and about ¹/₂ M. from the town (2250 ft.), to which omnibuses run (¹/₂-1 ℳ). *Motor Omnibus* to the Markt-Platz and on to Schonach (p. 405) seven times daily (30-80 pf.). — From the station to the market-place 1 M.; thence to the Falls 10-15 min. more; so that the walk from the station to the Falls and back takes 1¹/₂-2 hrs. The road passes a monument to *Rob. Gerwig* (1820-85), builder of the Schwarzwald and Höllen-Tal railways. Visitors who desire to spend at Triberg only the interval between two trains should visit the waterfall first and then dine at the railway restaurant.

Hotels (often uncomfortably crowded in summer). **Schwarzwald Hotel* (2345 ft.), in a beautiful situation, ¹/₄ M. from the Falls, with view of the valley, R. 2-8, B. 1¹/₂, D. 4, pens. 9-15 ℳ. — *Bellevue*, in an open situation at the upper end of the town, on the Schönwald road, R. 2-4¹/₄, B. 1, D. 3, pens. 6-10 ℳ, closed in winter. — *Wehrle* (Zum Ochsen), in the market-place, R. from 2, B. 1¹/₄, D. 3, pens. from 6 ℳ, generally well spoken of; *Löwe & National*, R. 2-5, B. 1, D. 2-3, pens. 6-8 ℳ; *Englischer Hof*, nearly opposite the Wehrle, with beer-restaurant. — *Sonne*, with wine-room, R. 1¹/₂-3, pens. 5-7 ℳ, at the lower end of the town. — *Adler*, with brewery, opposite the Wehrle, R. 1¹/₂-2, D. 1¹/₂, pens. 4¹/₂-5 ℳ; *Post*, R. 1¹/₂-3, B. ³/₄, D. 2¹/₂, pens. 4-6 ℳ, well spoken of. — *Lilie*, at the upper end of the town, *Kreuz*, and *Bär*, unpretending. — *Überm Wasserfall* (p. 404). — Pensions. *Wetzel* (R. 2¹/₂-3¹/₂, B. 1¹/₄; D. not supplied); and many others, in the upper part of the town, near the Schwarzwald Hotel. Numerous private lodgings.

BATHS. *Municipal Swimming Bath,* above the town, near the Protestant church; *Jägerhaus,* on the Schönwald road (p. 412), 8 min. beyond
the Hôtel Bellevue. — BEER. *Café Pfaff,* in the upper part of the town,
on the left (also rooms). — *Brauerei Martin,* at the Kreuz-Brücke. —
Café-Confectioner Ketterer, Friedrich-Str. (see below; also rooms).

ENGLISH CHURCH. *Service* in summer.

VISITORS' TAX, daily 30 pf., per week 1½ *M;* band in the market-
place, etc. — On Sun. and holidays illuminations of the Waterfall.

CARRIAGE to the Retsche (see below) 6 *M,* with two horses 8 *M,* there
and back; to Schönwald (p. 412) 8 or 12 *M;* to Furtwangen (p. 413) 13 or
20 *M;* to Hornberg (p. 402) 12 or 16 *M* (up to the castle 13 or 18 *M).*

Triberg lies in the heart of the Black Forest and is one of the
principal centres of the trade in clocks, numerous specimens of
which may be seen in the *Industrial Exhibition* (adm. 30 pf.).
Pop. 3700. The lofty and yet sheltered situation of the place, and
the fine waterfall attract many summer-visitors. It contains a
Roman Catholic, a Protestant, and a small English church. The
streets and waterfall are lighted by electricity.

At the upper end of the long main street stands a finger-post,
the left arm of which indicates the road to Rohrbach and the footpath along the brook to the waterfall, while the right arm points
across the bridge to the Industrial Exhibition. In 5 min. we reach
a projecting rock, from which the best general view is obtained.
The *WATERFALL,* formed by the *Gutach,* is the finest in W. Germany. The stream, which is here of considerable volume, is precipitated from a height of 500 ft., and divided into seven distinct
leaps by huge blocks of granite. The cascade, like the fall of the
Giessbach in Switzerland, is picturesquely framed by dark pines.
A footpath ascends on the right bank, with several fine points of
view. Visitors who are pressed for time need not go beyond the
(10 min.) bridge. In 20-25 min. more, above the falls, and close
to the *Inn Überm Wasserfall* (2930 ft.), we reach the road to
Schönwald and Furtwangen (p. 413), by which we return, passing
the *Wallfahrts-Kirche* (2410 ft.).

Other walks: along the Friedrich-Str. (road to Rohrbach), passing
below the Schwarzwald Hotel and the Prot. church, then gradual ascent
to the left, past the Olga Pavilion, to the (½ hr.) *Dreikaiserfels* (2625 ft.),
on the *Retsche* (rfmts.), the height to the E. of the town; thence down
to (10 min.) the *Café zur Retsche* and by the Russenbuche, Pulverhaus,
and Schützenhaus to the lower part of Triberg. — A finger-post in the
Schwendi-Str., which begins near the Löwe Hotel, indicates the route
to the *Felsen-Pavillon,* and another in the lower town, near Siedle's
clock-factory, that to the *Bahn-Aussicht* on the *Riffhalden,* the height to
the W. of Triberg. — From the Rohrbach road, below the Schwarzwald
Hotel, the Ludwig-Str. ascends to the right to the (¾ hr.) *Geutsche*
(2980 ft.; inn) and the (¾ hr.) *Stöcklewaldkopf* (3505 ft.; belvedere with
view of the Alps); thence back to (8 min.) the road and past the Hoch-
gericht or Galgen (site of the old gallows) and the (5 min.) *Fuchsfalle
Inn* to the (10 min.) *Kesselberg* (3365 ft.) and to St. Georgen (p. 405).

FROM TRIBERG TO HORNBERG VIÂ THE ALTHORNBERG, 4 hrs. (no inns).
From the Kreuz-Brücke, at the lower end of Triberg, we follow the highroad, passing the (20 min.) *Hirsch Inn* and the (¼ hr.) *Forelle Inn,* and
20 min. farther on turn to the right to the Gremmelsbach road. We

then ascend the road to the left, turn (10 min.) to the left, and proceed
viâ *Rötenbach* to the (40 min.) crucifix at the cross-roads at the *Schameck*. Selecting the central route of the three leading to the left to the
($^1/_4$ hr.) *Rappenfels*, we descend (6-7 min.) to the rocky *Althornberg*.
Thence to *Hornberg*, see p. 403.

FROM TRIBERG TO ELZACH VIÂ SCHONACH, 4$^1/_2$ hrs. (automobile, see
p. 403). The road, from which the Furtwangen road diverges to the left
by the *Wallfahrts-Kirche* (p. 404), a few hundred paces above Triberg,
ascends the *Untertal* to the N.W. to (3 M.) **Schonach** (2910 ft.; *Rebstock; Ochs*). About 1 M. above Schonach the road forks, the right
branch leading to the 'Prechtal' (p. 415), the left crossing the 'Höhenweg' (p. xvii) on the *Vorder-Bärt* (inn) and descending to (2 M.) the *Elzhof*. From the Elzhof a cart-track (right) leads up to the (20 min.) Ochs
Inn on the *Rohrhardsberg;* then descends viâ (1$^1/_2$ hr.) *Yach* to ($^3/_4$ hr.)
Elzach (p. 415).

The train now crosses the Gutach, and in the great 'Triberg
spiral tunnel' turns direct to the N., towards the top of the hill.
Several tunnels and viaducts. For some distance we observe to the
left below us the portion of the line which we traversed before
reaching Triberg. The train turns to the S., passing through tunnels
and over viaducts. Beyond (40 M.) *Nussbach* (2460 ft.; Krone) it
again turns to the E. Among the next tunnels is one 1855 yds. in
length, which penetrates the hill (2855 ft.) of (43 M.) *Sommerau*
(2735 ft.), the watershed between the Rhine and the Danube. Many
passengers alight here (or at St. Georgen), and travel back direct,
or walk to Triberg (1$^1/_2$ hr.). Behind the station is a hotel named
the *Sommerauer Hof*.

44 M. St. Georgen (2640 ft.; *Zur Brigach ; Hirsch*). The
busy clock-manufacturing town (*Deutsches Haus*, pens. 5-8 $\mathcal{M}$;
Hirsch, pens. 4$^1/_2$-6 $\mathcal{M}$; *Adler*, these two pretty fair), with
4200 inhab., is prettily situated on a height on the left bank of the
Brigach, 200 ft. above the station. The old Benedictine abbey,
founded at the end of the 11th cent., was suppressed in 1806.

FROM ST. GEORGEN TO TRIBERG, 2$^3/_4$-3 hrs. We follow the Triberg
road for some min. to the W. from the station and cross the railway-
embankment to the left before a pond. We then proceed to the right,
along the valley road, viâ *Brigach* (with a spring) and the *Hirzwald*
(inn), with its porphyry quarries. Or, after crossing the railway, we
may keep on in a straight direction through wood, following the 'Höhenweg'
(p. xvii), to the (1$^1/_2$ hr.) *Kesselberg* (p. 404), whence we go on viâ the
Fuchsfalle Inn and the *Stöcklewaldkopf* to Triberg (see p. 404). — Ascent of the Ruppertsberg and route to the Berneck-Tal, see p. 409.

The line now traverses the plateau, not far from the Brigach.

46$^1/_2$ M. *Peterzell* (2550 ft.; Bahnhof-Hôtel), with a small church,
partly Romanesque and partly Gothic, is the station (omn. 50 pf.)
for (2$^1/_2$ M.) **Königsfeld** (*Schwarzwald-Hôtel ; Kurhaus Donis-
wald*, R. 2-3, pens. 6-7 $\mathcal{M}$; *Gasthof der Brüdergemeinde*, pens.
5-7 $\mathcal{M};$ several *Pensions*), an interesting little Moravian settlement,
much frequented by summer-visitors. — 51 M. **Kirnach** (2390 ft.;
*Wald-Hôtel, R. 2-5, B. 1$^1/_4$, D. 3$^1/_2$, pens. 8-11 $\mathcal{M}$; *Burg-Hôtel,
near the ruin of Kirneck, with mud-baths, R. 2-4, pens. 6-9 $\mathcal{M};$

Hôt. Kirneck, at the station, pens. 5-6 *M*), whence a road runs through the picturesque *Kirnach-Tal* to Vöhrenbach (8 M.; p.407), passing the ruin of *Kirneck* and the village of *Unter-Kirnach* (2¹/₂ M.; Rössle). Kirnach lies on the edge of the Villinger Stadt-wald, which is traversed by paths in all directions from this point.

53¹/₂ M. **Villingen.** — HOTELS. In the Town: **Blume* or *Post*, R. 2-2¹/₂, D. 2¹/₂, pens. 6-7 *M*; *Zähringer Hof*, R. 2-4, pens. 5¹/₂-7¹/₂ *M*; *Deutscher Kaiser*, next to the Railway Station, R. 2-3, pens. 5-7 *M*; *Falke*, R. from 1¹/₂ *M*. — Outside the Town, on the edge of the wood: *Park Hotel*, R. 1¹/₂-3¹/₂, B. 1, D. 2¹/₂, pens. 5¹/₂-7¹/₂ *M*; *Pension Quincke*, pens. 4¹/₂ *M*. Hotels at *Kirnach*, see above. — *Railway Restaurant*.

Villingen (2295 ft.), a manufacturing town (9500 inhab.), men-tioned as early as the 9th cent., and a centre of the Black Forest clock-making industry, is partly surrounded with walls and gates, which successfully resisted sieges in the Thirty Years' War (1633-34) and the War of the Spanish Succession (1703-4). Early-Gothic *Münster-Kirche* (13th cent.), with two hexagonal towers, a late-Gothic pulpit, and some good plate (now in the Rathaus). The *Rat-haus* contains well-preserved rooms in the mediæval style, and a collection of antiquities (40 pf.). The *St. Michaels-Turm*, with a portrait of the gigantic 'Landsknecht' Romeius (d. 1513), is the most interesting of the old towers. The Romanesque *Tower of the Alt-stadt-Kirche*, beside the (¹/₂ M.) cemetery, is a relic of the old town of Villingen, which was removed to its present site about 1119. The *Wanne* (2510 ft.), a neighbouring hill, commands a view of the Alps in clear weather. About 1¹/₄ M. to the S. of Villingen is the ruined *Warenburg*. — Villingen is the junction for the railway to Rottweil; see *Baedeker's Southern Germany*.

55¹/₄ M. *Marbach* (2280 ft.), the junction for the branch-line to (3¹/₂ M.) the village and baths of *Dürrheim* (2315 ft.; *Salinen-Hôtel, pens. from 5 *M*; Kreuz), whence a road leads to (5¹/₂ M.; motor-omnibus) Donaueschingen. — 56¹/₂ M. *Klengen;* 58¹/₂ M. *Grüningen.*

62 M. **Donaueschingen.** — HOTELS. In the town: **Schütze*, with saline baths, R. 1¹/₂-4, D. 2-2¹/₂, pens. from 5¹/₂ *M*, old-established; *Falke zur Post*, also very fair; *Lamm*, pens. from 4¹/₂ *M*; *Linde*, plain. — *Railway Restaurant*, D. 1¹/₄-1¹/₂ *M*; *Zur Burg*, open-air restaurant, beyond the Brigach. — Small *Saline Bath.*

Donaueschingen (2220 ft.), an ancient town with 3800 inhab. and a large brewery, the residence since 1723 of the Princes of Fürstenberg, was visited in 1908 by a destructive conflagration. From the station we follow the main street, past the *'Fürstliche Kammer'*, to a bridge, beyond which, to the left, is the Post-Platz, with the Diana Fountain (by Sauer; 1908), while to the right is the gate of the princely *Park*. The latter, with its fine trees and ponds, is always open to the public, but the *Palace* only occasionally. Farther on a descent leads down from the choir of the church to a round walled-in basin, with a spring of clear water, which is led by a subterranean channel to the Brigach, about 100 ft. distant. An inscription styles this spring the *'Source of the Danube'* (2225 ft. above the sea-level; 1763 M. from the sea), but the name Danube (Donau) is usually first applied to the stream formed by the union of the Brigach and the Brege.

On an eminence behind the church and the palace stands the *Karlsbau* (1868), dedicated 'Bonarum artium et naturæ studio'.

On the Ground Floor, to the right, *Geological Collection.* — First Floor, to the right, *Mineralogical Collection; Ethnographical Curiosities;* Prehistoric, Roman, and Frankish *Antiquities* from S.W. Germany. To the left, the *Zoological Cabinet.* — The Second Floor contains the COLLECTIONS OF ART (paintings and plaster-casts). The most important pictures, the examples of the Swabian and Frankish Schools of the 16th cent., are united in a large room lighted from the roof (also containing a bust of Prince Charles Egon, d. 1892; detailed catalogue by A. Woltmann): 1. *Unknown North German Master,* The hermits SS. Paul and Anthony (1445); 41, 42. *Barth. Zeitblom,* Wings of an altar, with the Visitation and SS. Mary Magdalen and Ursula; 43-54. *Holbein the Elder,* The Passion, 12 panels in grisaille (monogram on the painting of the Resurrection); 72. *Bernhard Strigel,* Half-length of Count John of Montfort; 76-80. *Hans Schäufelein,* Madonna with saints and donors; 97. *Lucas Cranach the Elder,* Family of fauns. — Few of the remaining paintings (end of 18th and beginning of 19th cent.), which occupy several rooms, are of importance.

The *Armoury,* which occupies a separate building, embellished by a frieze with hunting-scenes, contains a number of old implements of the chase and a few modern arms.

In the Halden-Str., to the W. of the church, are the *Library* and *Archives.* The library consists of 100,000 vols. and 1160 MSS., including the most important MS. of the Nibelungenlied after those of Munich and St. Gallen, and several others of early-German origin. The same building contains the collections of *Engravings* (Dürer, Mantegna, etc.) and *Coins.*

FROM DONAUESCHINGEN TO FURTWANGEN, 20 M., branch-railway in 1¹/₂ hr. — 1³/₄ M. *Hüfingen,* junction for the line to Neustadt (p. 420); 6 M. *Wolterdingen,* with glass-works; 12 M. *Hammereisenbach* (Hammer Inn). — 15¹/₂ M. **Vöhrenbach** (2620 ft.; *Eisernes Kreuz; Engel; Reichsadler*), with 1850 inhab., is a seat of the clock-industry. — 18 M. *Schönenbach.* — 20 M. *Furtwangen,* see p. 413.

The railway now follows the grassy valley of the *Danube.* Stations: *Pfohren, Neudingen* (with mausoleum of the Princes of Fürstenberg), *Gutmadingen, Geisingen, Hintschingen.* — 74 M. **Immendingen** (2160 ft.; *Rail. Restaurant; Falke*), with 1000 inhab., is the junction for *Waldshut* (p. 438) and for Tuttlingen and Rottweil (see *Baedeker's Southern Germany*). — The line traverses a short tunnel and beyond (77 M.) *Hattingen* intersects the watershed between the Danube and the Rhine, by a tunnel 985 yds. long. — 80¹/₂ M. *Talmühle.* — 83¹/₂ M. **Engen** (1705 ft.; *Post* or *Stern*), a quaint village with 1860 inhab., is the central point of the Höhgau, the volcanic cones of which are seen (*Neuenhöwen,* 2850 ft., 1¹/₂ hr. to the N.W.; *Hohenhöwen,* 2780 ft., 1¹/₄ hr. to the S.W.). — 85¹/₂ M. *Welschingen;* 87¹/₂ M. *Mühlhausen,* with the basaltic cone of the *Mägdeberg* (2185 ft.) to the right; 89¹/₂ M. *Hohenkrähen* (1450 ft.), with the singularly formed hill of the same name and a ruined castle (2116 ft.). The railway runs past the Hohentwiel (p. 441) to (93 M.) *Singen* (p. 441).

h. From Hausach to Freudenstadt viâ Schiltach, Rippoldsau.

24 M. RAILWAY in 1¹/₂-2 hrs. — From *Wolfach* to *Rippoldsau,* diligence daily in 2³/₄ hrs., motor-omnibus thrice daily in summer in 1¹/₄ hr. (fare 3 ℳ 20 pf.); carriage 12, with two horses 18 ℳ. From *Freudenstadt* diligence to Rippoldsau daily in summer in 2¹/₂ hrs. (also motor-omnibus).

Hausach, see p. 402. The train ascends the *Kinzig-Tal,* and at (2 M.) *Kirnbach* crosses the stream of that name.

3 M. **Wolfach.** — RAILWAY STATION on the left bank of the Kinzig, to the S. of the town. — HOTELS. *Salmen,* R. 1¹/₂-2¹/₂, pens. 5-6 ℳ; *Krone,* R. 1¹/₄-2¹/₂, pens. 4-6 ℳ, both very fair; *Ochs.* — **Kiefernadelbad,* with baths of various kinds, a little beyond the bridge.

Wolfach (860 ft.), an ancient town with 2060 inhab. and a handsome old 'Amtshaus', at the entrance to the town, is situated among abrupt mountains at the confluence of the *Wolfbach* and the *Kinzig.* Walks may be taken to the *St. Jacobs-Kapelle* (1280 ft.; to Lauterbach, see p. 409), 25 min. from the upper Kinzig bridge, and to the (³/₄ hr.) *Alte Schloss* (1135 ft.), with view.

The comparatively uninteresting ROAD TO (13¹/₂ M.) RIPPOLDSAU (diligence and motor-omnibus, see above) ascends the valley of the *Wolfbach,* which it crosses several times. About 2¹/₄ M. from the station of Wolfach it reaches the church of the scattered village of *Ober-Wolfach* (935 ft.; Linde), with the ruin of *Walkenstein* (view). Here a road (p. 400) diverges through the *Rankach-Tal* to Peterstal.

At the entrance to (6 M.) the scattered village of **Schapbach** (1375 ft.; *Ochs,* very fair, at the lower end of the village; *Adler, Sonne,* farther up), the *Wildschapbach-Tal,* through which leads another road to Peterstal (p. 399), opens to the left.

Near the (2¹/₄ M.) *Seebach Inn* the *Seebach,* formed by the discharge of the sequestered *Glaswaldsee* or *Wildsee,* a lake situated 4¹/₂ M. from the road below the *Letterstätter Höhe* (3180 ft.; view), emerges from a wild side-valley on the left. About 1 M. farther on, huge granite rocks rise to the right of the road; near them is the waterfall of the *Burbach,* only visible after rain. We next reach (³/₄ M.) the —

Klösterle (1780 ft.; Hôt. Klösterle, R. from 1¹/₂, pens. from 6 ℳ; Erbprinz, both very fair), formerly a Benedictine priory, with a church with two towers, founded in the 12th cent. by the Benedictines of St. Georgen (p. 405). It lies ³/₄ M. below Rippoldsau, visitors to the baths of which often lodge here.

FROM THE KLÖSTERLE TO FREUDENSTADT, 8½ M. The road (motor-omnibus, see p. 410) passes *Reichenbach*, ascends the *Schwabach-Tal*, and traverses the *Pfaffenwald* to *Oberzwieselberg* (2790 ft.; Hirsch; Auerhahn). Thence it proceeds in wide curves, round the valley of the *Kleine Kinzig*, to join the road from *Schömberg*, which it follows to the left to *Freudenstadt* (p. 410). — There is also a pleasant footpath (2½ hrs.) through the woods. Passing the church, we turn to the right, cross the brook, and take the broad and shady forest-path to the right (stone finger-post). At *Oberzwieselberg* the path forks, the left arm leading to *Freudenstadt* (p. 410), the right to *Schenkenzell* (p. 410).

Rippoldsau (1855 ft.; *Göringer's Hotel and Bath House*, with mineral and mud baths, R. 3-10, B. 1¼, D. 4, pens. 10-16 ℳ, closed in winter; *Rosengarten*, pens. 5-7½ ℳ), a village with 700 inhab., lies at the S.E. base of the *Kniebis* (p. 400), in a very narrow part of the Wolftal. It is the most frequented and best organized of the Kniebis Baths (1500 visitors annually). The water of the four springs, containing iron, earthy ingredients, and Glauber's salts, is considered beneficial in cases of internal complaints. It is exported in bottles (800,000 annually). The environs afford many pleasant walks (*Kastelstein* on the *Sommerberg, Badwald*, etc.).

About 1½ M. above Rippoldsau lies *Holzwald*. Thence across the Holzwälder Höhe to *Griesbach*, see p. 400; across the Kniebis to *Oppenau*, see pp. 400, 397, 399. — Through the Badwald to the *Glaswaldsee* (p. 408), 1¾ hr.; on to the Seeblick and Höhenweg (p. 400), 20 minutes.

The train continues to ascend the picturesque *Kinzig-Tal*, which again turns to the E. — Beyond (5½ M.) *Halbmeil* (Engel; Löwe) the train crosses to the right bank. Tunnel. The houses on the left bank are called the *Vordere Lehengericht* (Pflug).

8½ M. **Schiltach** (1070 ft.; *Bahnhof-Hôtel*, R. from 1, D. 2 ℳ; *Krone*, R. 1¼-2¼ ℳ; *Engel*), an old town (1860 inhab.) carrying on a brisk timber-traffic, situated at the union of the *Schiltach* and the Kinzig, with a modern Prot. church, and a ruined castle on a hill.

FROM SCHILTACH TO SCHRAMBERG, 5½ M., branch-railway. The line ascends the Schiltach-Tal, and traverses the *Hintere Lehengericht*, with the station of (2½ M.) *Lehengericht*. At the Wurtemberg frontier, above, to the right, is the ruined castle of *Schilteck*.

5½ M. **Schramberg** (1360 ft.; *Post-Krone*, pens. 6-8 ℳ; *Lamm*), an industrial town of 9800 inhab. (straw-plaiting, clock-making, and potteries), is prettily situated on the *Schiltach*, commanded by the ruined *Nippenburg* (1459). — About 2½ M. from Schramberg, on the Hornberg road (p. 403), which skirts the Lauterbach waterfalls, is the village of *Lauterbach* (*Kurhaus and Hydropathic; Schwarzwald), a health-resort. From Lauterbach to the *Moosenmättle* (2580 ft.; inn), 2 hrs., and thence by pleasant forest-paths, viâ the St. Jakobs-Kapelle, to Wolfach, 2 hrs. (comp. p. 408).

A picturesque road proceeds from Schramberg farther up the Schiltach-Tal, traversing the romantic defile of the *Berneck* and passing the ruins of *Falkenstein* (lately restored), *Berneck*, and *Ramstein*, and the *Teufels-Küche*, to (6 M.) *Thennenbronn* (2140 ft.; Krone). There we may turn to the W., cross the *Benzebene*, and reach the *Reichenbach-Tal*, in which a road descends to (6 M.) Hornberg; or, turning to the S., we may proceed over the *Ruppertsberg* (2955 ft.) to (7 M.) St. Georgen (p 405).

26*

The railway (belonging to Wurtemberg from this point) passes through a tunnel, beyond which we have another view of Schiltach. On the hill above the tunnel are the ruined *Schenkenburg* and a Kur-Hôtel. — We ascend the valley of the *Kinzig.* — 11 M. *Schenken-zell* (1170 ft.; Ochs; Sonne), another timber-trading place, with a ruined castle, is situated at the mouth of the *Kleine Kinzig*, in the pretty valley of which lies (ca. 2 M.) *Reinerzau* (Linde). The line next passes the *Krähenbad* (for nervous patients), crosses the river several times, and threads two tunnels.

14¹/₂ M. **Alpirsbach** (1425 ft.; *Löwen-Post*, pens. 4¹/₂-5 *M*, very fair; *Schwan; Bahnhof-Hôtel*), with 1400 inhab., who carry on a considerable traffic in timber and straw-hats, is the first station in Wurtemberg. The Protestant church, a Romanesque building begun in the 11th cent. with a Gothic choir, once belonged to a Benedictine abbey and was well restored in 1879. On the portal is a Romanesque relief (Christ in glory). Some of the secular buildings of the convent are also extant; the Romanesque cloisters were altered in the Gothic style in 1480-90.

20¹/₂ M. *Lossburg-Rodt*, near the source of the Kinzig.

24 M. **Freudenstadt.** — The main RAILWAY STATION (Pl. C, 2; 2180 ft.; restaurant) lies ³/₄ M. from the town; near the town is a second station (Pl. A, 1) for the branch-line from Kloster-Reichenbach (p. 394).

HOTELS. (It is advisable to engage rooms beforehand in the summer.) At the main station: *Schwarzwald Hotel*, of the first class, in an open situation, with large garden, R. 2-6, B. 1¹/₂, D. 4, pens. 8-10 *M*, also frequented by foreigners. — In the town: *Post* (Pl. b; A, B, 1), R. 2-3, B. 1, D. 2¹/₂, pens. 6-9 *M; Krone* (Pl. c; A, 1, 2), very fair, pens. 5¹/₂-7 *M; Linde* (Pl. d; A, 1), pens. 4¹/₂-5¹/₂ *M; Herzog Friedrich* (Pl. e; B, 2), pens. 5-7 *M; Rössle* (Pl. f; B, 1), R. 1¹/₂-2¹/₂, D. 1³/₄-2¹/₂, pens. 4¹/₂-6 *M; Park-Hôtel*, a dépendance of the last, on the edge of the forest, pens. 5-8 *M*. In the S.W. part of the town: *Rappen* (Pl. g; A, 2), R. from 1¹/₂, B. ³/₄, D. 2¹/₂, S. 1¹/₂, pens. from 5¹/₂ *M; Kurhaus Waldeck* (Pl. h; A, 2), with the dépendance *Christophsaue*, of the first class, on the promenade, R. from 3, B. 1¹/₄, D. 3, S. 2¹/₂, pens. 7-15 *M*. — To the S.E., above the town: *Kurhaus Waldlust* (Pl. i; B, 3), R. 3-8, pens. 12-16 *M; Kurhaus Palmenwald* (Pl. k; B, 3), R. 2¹/₂-4¹/₂, pens. 5-6¹/₂ *M*, very fair; *Hotel-Café Stokinger* (p. 411), R. 1¹/₂-5, B. ³/₄, D. 2-2¹/₂, pens. 5¹/₂-8¹/₂ *M*. Several pensions and numerous private lodgings (R. 7-10 *M* per week). — *Visitors' Tax*, for 5 days 1, for a longer stay 2-5 *M*.

CARRIAGES at all the hotels. — MOTOR OMNIBUS once daily in summer to *Baiersbronn* (p. 394) and *Ruhstein* (p. 391) in 1¹/₄ hr. (3 *M*); to the *Kniebis* (p. 400) and *Oppenau*, see p. 398; viâ Zwieselberg to *Rippoldsau* (p. 409) once or twice daily in 50 min. (2 *M* 40 pf.).

Freudenstadt (2395 ft.), a loftily-situated town of Wurtemberg (7900 inhab.), with cloth-factories and an extensive traffic in timber, was founded in 1599 by Duke Frederick I. of Wurtemberg for Salzburg Protestant refugees, and is a favourite summer-resort (ca. 7000 visitors annually), also frequented for winter-sports. The plan of the town is unusual, the centre being occupied by a large open space (now partly occupied by gardens), surrounded by houses with arcades. In or adjoining this space are the *Rathaus*, the *School*, the *Pro-*

testant Church (Pl. A, 2), the *Oberamt*, and the *Post Office* (Pl. A, 1). The curiously-constructed church, built in 1601-8, and restored in 1887-99, consists of two naves at right angles to each other, in one of which the male, and in the other the female members of the congregation used to sit, while the altar and pulpit are placed at the angle. There is a tower at the end of each nave. The parapets of the galleries are embellished with stucco-reliefs of Biblical subjects;

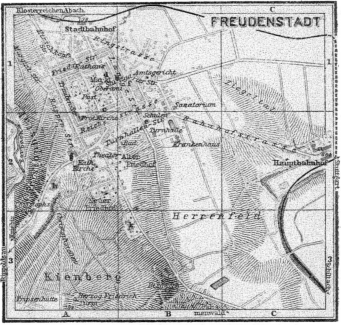

the paintings (restored) are by Jakob Zuberle. The Romanesque font, the Romanesque reading-desk, the carved choir-stalls (1488), and the beautiful crucifix (16th cent.) were all brought from the convent of Alpirsbach (sacristan, Schul-Str. 323, behind the church). — Freudenstadt is surrounded by fine pine-woods, traversed by walks and drives. On the S.W., to the left of the Kniebis road, is the *Teucheles-Weg* (Café Noll); about 1/2 M. to the S.E. is the so-called *Palmenwald* (Pl. B, 3), with its ferns and pines (Café Stokinger); between rises the *Kienberg* (2660 ft.), with the Herzog-Friedrich-Turm (Pl. A, 3; rfmts.), a fine point of view.

Branch-railway from Freudenstadt to *Kloster-Reichenbach* viâ Baiersbronn, see p. 394. — Good roads lead from Freudenstadt to the W. over the *Kniebis* (p. 400) to (12½ M.) *Griesbach* (p. 400; one-horse carr. 12, two-horse 20 ℳ); to the S.W. viâ the *Zwieselberg* to (7½ M.) *Rippoldsau* (p. 409; one-horse carr. 9, two-horse 16 ℳ).

The Wurtemberg railway goes on, passing several small stations, to *Eutlingen* (see *Baedeker's Southern Germany*).

i. From Triberg to the Simonswälder-Tal *(Waldkirch)* viâ Furtwangen.

28 M. From Triberg to (9½ M.) *Furtwangen*, diligence twice daily in 2½ hrs. (carriages, see p. 404); from Furtwangen to (18½ M.) *Waldkirch*, diligence twice daily in 3¾ hrs. (back in 4¾ hrs.). — A good route for pedestrians is as follows: from Triberg past the waterfalls to the Wasserfall Inn and viâ Schönwald to the forester's house of *Martins-Kapelle*, 2½ hrs.; thence viâ the *Brend* to *Gütenbach*, 2¼ hrs.; and past the *Zweribach Waterfall* to the top of the *Kandel*, 4¼ hrs.

Triberg (2250 ft.), see p. 403. The road to Furtwangen first ascends the 'Untertal' to the W., and at the Wallfahrts-Kirche (p. 404) turns to the left, and ascends the hill in long windings, crossing the Gutach before reaching the (2½ M.) *Inn überm Wasserfall* (p. 404; the carriage-road in the Untertal leads to Schonach, see p. 405). About ½ M. farther on are the *Linde Inn* and the *Pension Beausite*, and in 1¼ M. more, beyond a road on the right leading to Schwarzenbach and Weissenbach (see below), we reach —

4½ M. (from Triberg) **Schönwald** (3260 ft.; *Kur-Hôtel Schönwald*, R. 1½-3½, D. 3, pens. 5-8 ℳ; *Victoria*, R. 1½-4, B. 1, D. 3, S. 2, pens. 5-11 ℳ; *Adler; Sonne; Ochs;* private lodgings), a frequented summer-resort with a church, amid meadows and pine-woods.

The above-mentioned road (from the Wasserfall Inn) leads viâ *Schwarzenbach* and *Weissenbach* to the (1½ hr.) forester's house of *Martins-Kapelle* (3645 ft.; simple rfmts.), on the watershed between the Rhine and the Danube. Routes lead hence on the right viâ *Rohrhardsberg* and *Hörnleberg* to *Bleibach* (p. 415), or viâ *Griesbach* to the *Simonswald Valley* (p. 414); and on the left to *Furtwangen* (4 M.; p. 413). — Footpaths lead to the S. from the Martins-Kapelle, along the slope, to (¾ hr.) the *Brend* (3770 ft.); the tower, which is one of the finest points of view in this part of the Black Forest, stands a few paces to the W. of the Höhenweg (p. xvii). Thence we descend to the S. to (½ hr.) the farm of *Alte Eck* (3550 ft.), on the old Kilpen road, 2½ M. from Furtwangen, 4½ M. from Simonswald, and 3 M. from Gütenbach. From the *Gasthof zum Raben*, on the Kilpen road, the Höhenweg leads to the S. to the *Neue Eck* (p. 413).

Beyond Schönwald the road ascends in a wide curve. Pedestrians take the old road, diverging to the right a little before the last houses of Schönwald, and joining the new road by the (½ hr.) inn *Zum Kreuz*, at the *Escheck* (3370 ft.), or the top of the pass, which forms the watershed between the Rhine and the Danube. The new road descends circuitously. Pedestrians may shorten the distance considerably by taking the steep old road, which diverges to the right at the kilomètre-stone marked 10.5.

412

]
bron
the]
two-:
(p. 4(
r
to *E*

i. :

2
in 2[1]
kirch
route
the 1
tins-
past
/
asce]
(p. 4
cross
fall
see I
Pens
leadi
4
Sch(
B. 1
lodg]
and]
1
Schw
Mart
Rhin(
berg
wald
Foot]
to (3/
point
the V
the 1
Furt\
the G
S. to
I
trian
last
inn ,
whic
The
dista
to th

5 M. (from Schönwald) **Furtwangen** (2860 ft.; *Sonne*, R. 1³/₄-2¹/₂ ℳ; *Grieshaber zur Ochsen*, R. 1¹/₂-3, pens. 4¹/₂-7 ℳ, both very fair; *Bahnhofs-Hôtel*), on the *Brege*, a prosperous little town with 5200 inhab., where the best clocks in the Black Forest are manufactured. The 'Gewerbehalle', or industrial hall, contains an interesting collection of old Black Forest clocks, from the end of the 16th cent. onwards (adm. 50 pf.). There is a training-school for wood-carvers and clock-makers, and another for straw-plaiting. New church. — Railway to *Donaueschingen*, see p. 407.

To the (1¹/₂ hr.) *Brend* viâ the Alte Eck, see p. 412. — To WALDAU. We follow the Simonswald road for about 1 M., and then the Linach road for ¹/₂ M. Beyond the *Bregbach*, where the road bends to the left, we take the footpath ascending to the *Kaltenherberg* (3380 ft.; inn). We next follow another path as far as the *Lachhäusle* (3580 ft.; good echo). Up to this point we have followed a 'Höhenweg' route (p. xvii), from which we now diverge by a path descending to the left to (7¹/₂ M.) **Waldau** (*Traube; Sonne*), a favourite summer-resort. Thence down the Langenordnach-Tal (also reached direct from the Kaltenherberg) to (4¹/₂ M.) the railway-station of Hölzlebruck, near Neustadt; comp. p. 419.

The road to Simonswald and Waldkirch (18¹/₂ M.) ascends from Furtwangen to the S.W. About 1¹/₄ M. from the church of Furtwangen a road diverges to the left to *Linach* (see above). About 500 yds. farther on the Simonswald road turns abruptly to the E. (left). Pedestrians choose the route across the hill to the right and at the *Neue Eck* (3230 ft.; Freiburger Hof, unpretending but very fair) rejoin the road, the farther windings of which may also be cut off. In about 1¹/₂ hr. we reach (4¹/₂ M. from Furtwangen) **Gütenbach** (2850 ft.; *Zur Hochburg*, R. 1¹/₄-2, pens. 4¹/₂-5¹/₂ ℳ, very fair; *Post*, R. 1¹/₄-1¹/₂, pens. 3-4 ℳ), another busy, clock-making and straw-plaiting place, with 1900 inhab. and a pretty church. A way-post, beyond the Post Inn, indicates the route, descending to the left, to Wildgutach and St. Märgen (2¹/₂ hrs.; comp. p. 417).

The road, which is partly hewn in the solid rock, continues towards the W., then turns to the N., and descends in long windings, affording numerous beautiful views, into the valley of the *Wildgutach*. A footpath cuts off the widest curve (about 1¹/₄ M. from Gütenbach), and rejoins the road at the *Sternen Inn* (2035 ft.), about 3 M. from Gütenbach.

To THE ZWERIBACH FALL, which is seen beyond the Wildgutach-Tal, from the road, 1¹/₂ hr. We take the footpath to the left beyond the Sternen Inn; 10 min. cross the Wildgutach; ascend the grassy slope towards the high-lying cottage for ca. 10 min., cross the *Zweribach*, and ascend on the right bank; cross the brook twice, and ascend more steeply at the end to the (1 hr.) **Zweribach Fall** (2525 ft.), consisting of an upper and a lower fall, which, except at the height of summer, present a charming picture in a romantic frame. — The path (guide-posts) continues to ascend to the (³/₄ hr.) *Plattenhof* (3220 ft.; restaurant), and thence leads through wood to (³/₄ hr.) a wooden hut, where we cross the carriage-road from St. Peter (p. 416). Hence through wood to the (1 hr.) refuge on the *Kandel* (p. 414; 2¹/₂ hrs. in all).

About $1^1/_4$ M. farther down the valley, $1^3/_4$ hr.'s walk ·from Gütenbach, and beyond another path descending on the left to the Zweribach Fall, is the inn *Zum Engel* (1470 ft.; very fair), at the junction of the road with the old *Kilpen Road* (p. 412).

The road descends the picturesque valley of the Wildgutach, here called the **Simonswald Valley.** The villages of *Ober-, Alt-,* and *Unter-Simonswald* consist of scattered houses. On the right, by the church of Ober-Simonswald, 1 M. from the Engel Inn, is a finger-post, indicating the way through the Griesbach-Tal to Schönwald and Triberg (p. 412). About $2^3/_4$ M. farther on lies the inn *Zur Krone*, or *Post* (pens. $3^1/_2$-6 ℳ), near the prettily-situated church (1225 ft.) of Alt-Simonswald. A way-post near the Ochs Inn indicates a broad path leading, nearly the whole way among wood, through the *Ettersbacher-Tal* to (2 hrs.) the Kandel (see below); after about 1 hr. it ascends on the right bank of the stream. Passing *Bleibach* (p. 415), the road reaches the *Elztal*, about 11 M. from Gütenbach; thence railway to *Waldkirch* (see below).

k. Waldkirch and the Elztal.

From Denzlingen to Elzach, $12^1/_2$ M., railway in ca. 50 min. (numerous local trains to *Waldkirch* in 16 min.). — Road from Elzach to (5 M.) *Ober-Prechtal*, and thence to ($5^1/_2$ M.) *Steingrün* in the *Gutach-Tal*.

Denzlingen, see p. 372. — The line crosses the *Elz*. Near ($2^1/_2$ M.) *Buchholz* a strong variety of wine is produced. On the opposite (left) bank of the Elz are the baths of *Suggental* (815 ft.; Tritscheller-Reich's Inn, very fair, pens. from $4^1/_2$ ℳ).

5 M. **Waldkirch.** — HOTELS. *Kastelburg*, by the station, at the foot of the Schlossberg. — In the town, $1/_3$ M. from the station: *Löwe* (Post), R. $1^1/_2$-2, B. $3/_4$, D. $2^1/_4$, pens. $4^1/_2$-5 ℳ, very fair. — *Rebstock*, with brewery; *Adler; Krone; Goldener Engel*, all near the market-place. — *Garden Restaurant zur Arche*, near the station. — *Baths* in the Elz.

Waldkirch (865 ft.), a busy and prettily-situated little town of 5100 inhab. on the left bank of the Elz, with silk and cotton mills, an organ factory, and glass and stone-polishing works, is a favourite summer-resort on account of its picturesque environs. The station lies on the right bank, to the N. of the town, at the foot of the Schlossberg (1215 ft.), which is crowned with the ruin of *Kastelburg*, and may be ascended in 20 minutes. — Among the other view-points in the vicinity are the *Schänzle,* to the S. (to the highest pavilion, $1/_2$ hr.), whence the walk may be extended to *Dettenbach* (there and back in $2^3/_4$-3 hr.); and the *Thomas-Hütte* on the *Kleine Kandelfels*, reached in $1^1/_4$ hr. by woodland paths passing the ruin of *Schwarzenberg.*

The ascent of the **Kandel* (4075 ft.; $2^1/_2$-$3^1/_2$ hrs.) may be made from Waldkirch by various routes. The road leads past the Rathaus to the S.E. end of the town, and after $3/_4$ M. we take the narrow ·footpath to the right ('Altersbach, Kandel'). At the

fork, 1 M. farther on, we keep to the left. About 250 yds. farther
on is another fork, whence one route leads to the right, by the so-
called 'Damen-Pfad', to the *Thomas-Hütte* on the rugged *Kandelfels* and thence direct to the summit. An easier cart-track leads
to the left at the fork and proceeds viâ the *Vordere Holzplatz* in
the *Altersbach Tal* (1535 ft.; inn) to the ($^1/_2$ hr.) *Hintere Holzplatz* (1900 ft.), whence a footpath ascends to the ($^3/_4$ hr.) *Albin-
Hütte* (2803 ft.) and the (1 hr.) top. A third route crosses the Altersbach a little above the Vordere Holzplatz and ascends the right
bank of the stream to join the preceding path at the Albin-Hütte.
On the top are a trigonometrical pyramid with a direction-table,
indicating the chief points in the view, which includes the central
Black Forest as far as the Swabian Alb, the Vosges, and the Jura.
The Alps are visible as far as the Zugspitze. About 10 min. from
the top, to the N., is a comfortable *Rasthaus* (R. $1^1/_2$-$2^1/_2$, B. 1,
D. 2-$2^1/_2$ ℳ; telephone to Waldkirch).

The descent may be made on the N.E. to *Unter-Simonswald* (p. 414);
on the E. viâ the *Plattenhof* and the *Zweribach Fall* to the Engel Inn in
Ober-Simonswald or to *Gütenbach* (p. 413); or on the S. to *St. Peter* (p. 416).
From Waldkirch through the Simonswald Valley (p. 414) to *Güten-
bach*, $4^1/_2$ hrs.; thence to *Furtwangen*, $1^1/_2$ hr.; comp. p. 413.
From Waldkirch through the Simonswald Valley (p. 414) to *Martins-
Kapelle*, 5 hrs.; thence to *Triberg* viâ *Schönwald*, $2^1/_2$ hrs.; comp. p. 412.

The railway crosses to the left bank of the Elz, which it thenceforth follows. — $5^1/_2$ M. *Kollnau* (900 ft.), with large cotton-
factories. — 7 M. *Gutach*, with its silk-factories, lies below the
influx of the *Wilde Gutach* (to the Simonswald Valley, see p. 414).

$7^1/_2$ M. *Bleibach* (985 ft.; Sonne), with an old church. The
village extends on the right to the Simonswald road.

The *Hörnleberg* (2970 ft.; chapel on the summit), ascended hence in
$2^1/_4$ hrs., commands a fine view; the descent to the Krone Inn, at Unter-
Simonswald (p. 414), may be made in $1^1/_2$ hr.

$9^1/_2$ M. *Niederwinden;* $10^1/_2$ M. *Oberwinden.*

$12^1/_2$ M. **Elzach** (1190 ft.; *Zum Bahnhof*, clean; *Hirsch*, pens.
from 4 ℳ) with 1200 inhab., has a 16th cent. church and a silk-
factory. — From Elzach to Haslach, see p. 402.

The valley now contracts. We proceed on foot viâ *Unter-Prech-
tal* to the Sonne and Adler Inns in *Ober-Prechtal* (1510 ft.; $4^1/_2$ M.
from Elzach) whence a carriage-road leads to the right through the
Hintere Prechtal (Linde) to *Schonach* (p. 405; 15 M. from Elzach).
The main road continues to ascend to the N.E. viâ *Landwasser*,
whence détours may be made (to the right) to the Schwedenschanze
on the *Hirschlache* (2745 ft.; $^3/_4$ hr. from Ober-Prechtal; view)
and (to the left; finger-post on the top) to the *Farrenkopf* (p. 402).
Beyond Landwasser the road crosses the watershed between the
Elz-Tal and the Gutach-Tal in long curves (short-cuts for walkers),
and joins the Gutach-Tal road at the houses of ($5^1/_2$ M.) *Steingrün*
(Rössle), $1^3/_4$ M. below Hornberg (p. 402).

1. Höllen-Tal Railway (Freiburg to Donaueschingen). Feldberg.

FROM FREIBURG TO DONAUESCHINGEN, 47 M., railway in 2$^1/_4$-3 hrs. (fares 6 ℳ 60, 3 ℳ 90, 2 ℳ 60 pf.; third-class fare by slow trains 1 ℳ 70 pf.). View generally to the right, *i.e.* opposite the side by which the carriages are entered at Freiburg. — The first part (completed in 1887) of the *Höllen-Tal Railway commands for a short distance as grand and beautiful scenery as any part of the older Schwarzwald line.

A day's excursion from Freiburg may be conveniently arranged as follows: take the train to *Höllsteig* (p. 417); walk through the Ravenna-Schlucht to (1$^1/_2$ hr.) *Hinterzarten* (p. 418); take the train to the *Titisee* (p. 418) and back to *Hirschsprung* (p. 417); walk viâ the (10 min.) Hirschsprung to (3$^/_4$ hr.) *Himmelreich* (p. 417). The ascent of the Feldberg is also a day's excursion: to the *Titisee* by rail in 1$^1/_2$-1$^3/_4$ hr., thence on foot to the top of the *Feldberg* in 3$^1/_2$ hrs., descent to *Posthalde* 2$^3/_4$ hrs., rail to Freiburg 1 hr. 20 minutes. — From the Feldberg to *Schluchsee* 3$^1/_4$ hrs., thence to *St. Blasien* 2$^3/_4$ hrs.

The inns near the Feldberg, particularly at Titisee, are often overcrowded in summer, and rooms should be secured beforehand (comp. p. 385).

Starting from the principal station at *Freiburg* (p. 372), the train crosses the *Dreisam*, and halts at (2 M.) *Wiehre*, the S. suburb of Freiburg (p. 379). It continues to ascend the broad valley of the Dreisam to (3$^3/_4$ M.) *Littenweiler* (1040 ft.), with a chalybeate spring, the station for *Ebnet*, a village with an old château, on the right bank of the Dreisam. — In the *Kappeler-Tal*, to the right, the ore mined on the Schau-ins-land (p. 380) is smelted.

7 M. **Kirchzarten** (1265 ft.; *Restaurant zur Post*, at the station; *Adler, Löwe*, in the village, $^1/_4$ M. from the station), a village with 1000 inhab., $^3/_4$ M. to the N.W. of which, on the right bank of the Dreisam, is *Zarten*, with traces of the Celtic town *Tarodunum*.

FROM KIRCHZARTEN TO ST. MÄRGEN, diligence twice daily; either viâ Buchenbach (p. 417) or viâ St. Peter (12 M.; in 3$^1/_2$ hrs.); comp. Maps on pp. 416, 412. The latter route passes *Zarten* and at *Stegen* enters the valley of the *Eschbach*, which it ascends to (7$^1/_2$ M.) **St. Peter** (2370 ft.; *Hirsch*), rebuilt since a fire in 1899, with a Benedictine abbey, now a Catholic seminary, and an interesting church. Thence over the hills to (3 M.) St. Märgen (p. 417). — Pedestrians, starting from the station of Kirchzarten, walk to the N.E. viâ the *Brandenburg Inn* to *Burg*, and thence ascend the *Ibental* viâ the *Lindenberg* (2670 ft.; pilgrimage-chapel, with view) to St. Peter, in 3 hrs. — From St. Peter the **Kandel** (p. 414) may be ascended in 2 hrs. We follow the road running to the N. into the *Glotter-Tal* (p. 372) for about $^3/_4$ M.; then, at the Eckle, we turn to the right at the guide-post and proceed viâ the *Haldenhof* to the *Sägendobel* (inn). Thence we ascend to the N. (guide-posts).

FROM KIRCHZARTEN TO TODTNAU, 13 M., diligence twice daily in 4$^1/_2$ hrs. (returning in 3$^3/_4$ hrs.). The road at first ascends the broad valley between the *Brugga* and the *Osterbach*. At (2$^1/_2$ M.) **Oberried** (1500 ft.; *Stern* or *Post*, very fair), at the mouth of the *Zastler-Tal* (p. 422), a wood is entered; farther on, on a lofty rock, the ruins of the *Schneeburg*. About 3$^1/_2$ M. from Oberkirch the *St. Wilhelms-Tal* (p. 422) diverges to the left. The memorial stone known as the **Notschrei** (8$^1/_2$ M. from Kirchzarten) marks the culminating point (3695 ft.; *Kur-Hôtel Waldheim*, pens. 6$^1/_2$ ℳ, very fair) of the route; a road to the right leads to the Halde (p. 380). The main road (comp. Map, p. 417; motoromnibus from Freiburg, see p. 373) now quits the wood and descends through the upper *Wiesen-Tal* by *Muggenbrunn* (Grüner Baum; $^1/_4$ hr.

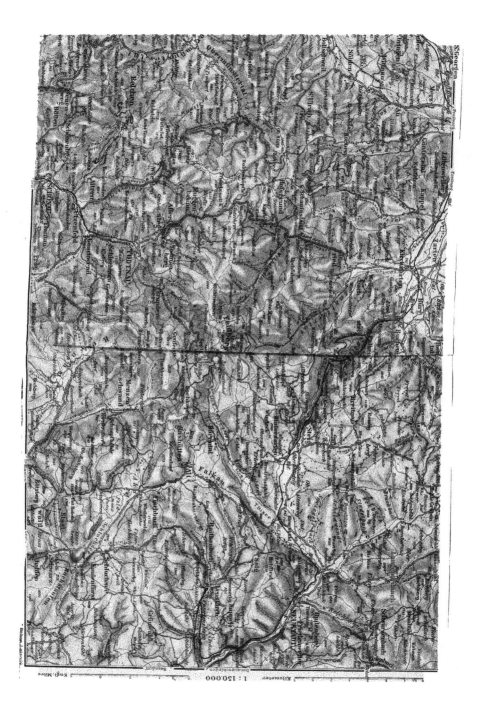

C
(:
E
t.
w
n
tl
tl
d

4
be
S
w
b
ve
fr
W
le
on
th.

farther ön, finger-post on the left indicating the way to Todtnauberg,
p. 431) and *Aftersteg* to (5¹/₄ M.) *Todtnau* (p. 431). Between Aftersteg and
Todtnau a footpath diverges to the *Todtnauberg Waterfall* (see p. 431).

The railway crosses the *Rotbach.* — 8¹/₂ M. **Himmelreich**
(1490 ft.), a farm with an inn at the entrance of the Höllen-Tal
proper. A guide-post opposite the station indicates the way to the
(³/₄ hr.) *Frauensteigfels* (2540 ft.), which commands an attractive
view of the valley of the Dreisam. Thence to the Nessellache (see
below), ³/₄ hr.

FROM HIMMELREICH TO ST. MÄRGEN, 8¹/₂ M., diligence daily in 3 hrs.
(starting from Kirchzarten; comp. Maps, pp. 416, 412). Pedestrians, following the highroad, proceed viâ (1 M.) *Buchenbach* (1470 ft.; Hirsch;
Adler), to the left of which is the ruin of *Wisneck*, and ascend the
Wagensteig-Tal (numerous short-cuts) to (6 M.) **St. Märgen** (2920 ft.;
Hirsch; Krone, pension in both 4¹/₂-6 *M*), a frequented health-resort, with
1100 inhabitants. The abbey-church was destroyed by lightning in 1907.
— A picturesque road ascends viâ (¹/₂ hr.) *Hinterstrass* (Hirsch) in 1¹/₄ hr.
to the *Thurner* (3395 ft.; inn), and then descends to (3¹/₂ M.) the *Gast-
hof zum Löwen* at *Breitnau* (p. 418). An alternative route ('Höhenweg',
p. xvii) leads from the Thurner viâ the *Weisstannhöhe* (p. 419) to (3¹/₂ hrs.)
Titisee (p. 418). Or we turn to the right, 6 min. from the top, and descend to Hinterzarten or the Ravenna-Schlucht (p. 418; guide-posts). —
Picturesque route from St. Märgen through the *Wildgutach-Tal* to (7¹/₂ M.)
Gütenbach (p. 413).

The train now passes the straggling village of *Falkensteig* (Zwei
Tauben; Löwe, pens. 4¹/₂-5 *M*), crosses the *Engebach*, passes through
a tunnel below the ruin of *Falkenstein*, and enters the *Höllen-Pass*,
the finest part of the valley, a defile with towering and overhanging
rocks, partly overgrown with firs and underwood. The line passes
through the *Lower* and *Upper Hirschsprung Tunnel*. The road
winding through the defile, side by side with the railway and the
foaming *Rotbach*, was constructed by the Austrian government in
1770, and was shortly afterwards traversed by the Archduchess
Marie Antoinette when on her way to France to marry the Dauphin,
the future Louis XVI. The pass also witnessed the celebrated retreat
of Moreau (Oct., 1796), when pursued by the Archduke Charles.

The Höllen-Tal now expands. 11 M. *Hirschsprung* (1835 ft.).

A footpath, leading to the right 4 min. above the station, ascends
through the *Laubbrunnendobel* to (1¹/₄ hr.) the fine view-point of *Nessellache* (3410 ft.; Rössle Inn, ¹/₄ hr. to the N.W.).

Beyond this station the train ascends for about 4¹/₂ M. by means
of a 'rack-and-pinion' arrangement (no change of carriages necessary). After passing through a tunnel 220 yds. long, we reach (13 M.)
Posthalde (2155 ft.; *Adler*, very fair), pleasantly situated.

From the Adler Inn to *Breitnau* (p. 418) viâ the *Neuhof*, 1³/₄ hr. About
1 hr. from the Adler and ¹/₄ hr. short of Neuhof a pretty forest-path leads
to the left to the (1¹/₂ hr.) Nessellache (see above). — A path, turning to the
right at the Neuhof, outside the wood, leads to (6 min.) the *Kaiserwacht*
(3405 ft.) and the (³/₄ hr.) *Pikettfels* (3325 ft.), whence we may descend to
(1 hr.) Höllsteig. — Ascent of the *Feldberg* from Posthalde, see p. 420.

13¹/₂ M. **Höllsteig** (2430 ft.), the station for the well-known
Sternen Inn (R. 1³/₄-3, D. 3, pens. 6¹/₂-7 *M*), with baths and several

dependencies, which lies on the road 80 ft. below. It is a good starting-point for excursions in the Höllen-Tal and for an ascent of the Feldberg (p. 421; numerous finger-posts).

A footpath constructed by the landlord of the 'Sternen', beginning opposite the inn and passing the post-office, leads under the railway-viaduct to the *Ravenna Schlucht*, a wild ravine with a fine cascade. After 12 min. the path forks: the right branch crosses the entrenchment to the road, which we follow either back to the inn (in all ³/₄-1 hr.) or on to Hinterzarten (in all 1¹/₂ hr.). The left branch leads to the upper Ravenna-Tal, reaching another fork at (20 min.) the saw-mill. There we may either keep to the left for (¹/₂ hr.) the Pikettfels (p. 417), or go on in a straight direction to the *Ravennaschlucht Hotel* in *Oedenbach*, on the road to Breitnau (see below). — A pleasant route from the 'Sternen' to Hinterzarten is as follows: we keep to the highroad for ¹/₂ M.; beyond the bridge, where it makes a sharp curve to the left, we take the road to the right, which ascends the picturesque *Löffel-Tal*, now traversed by the railway, to (1¹/₂ M.) the first houses of *Hinterzarten* (see below).

The railway crosses the *Ravenna Schlucht* (view of it to the left) by a lofty viaduct, while the road ascends the *Höllsteig* in bold windings. The last view of the Höllen-Tal is cut short by a tunnel (275 yds. long), whence we emerge in the *Löffel-Tal*. The train then passes through the seventh and last tunnel and reaches the top of the plateau and the station of —

15¹/₂ M. **Hinterzarten.** — Hotels (all well spoken of). *Adler*, near the church, pens. 5-7 *M*; *Linde* (pens. 4¹/₂-5 *M*), Bahnhof-Hôtel, at the station; *Rössle*, ¹/₂ M. to the N.W., on the edge of the forest, pens. 4¹/₂ *M*; *Lafette*, ¹/₃ M. farther to the E., unpretending. — Lodgings.

Hinterzarten (2900 ft.), a favourite summer-resort, where the rack-and-pinion section of the railway ends. — The road passing the handsome church and the footpath beyond it both lead to *Erlenbruck* (3080 ft.; Schwan), pleasantly situated among firs, whence we may go on in the one direction to the Titisee, and in the other to Bärental and the Feldberg (comp. p. 421).

About ¹/₄ M. to the W. of the Weisses Rössle a road, diverging to the N. from the Höllen-Tal road, leads viâ *Oedenbach* (see above) to the (3 M.) *Gasthof zum Löwen* (3265 ft.). Hence we may proceed to the left to (¹/₄ hr.) *Breitnau* (Kreuz) and (¹/₂ hr.) the **Hochwart** (3675 ft.), with an old entrenchment (view of the Alps). Or we may go to the right to (1 hr.) the *Weisstannhöhe* (p. 419). — From the Löwe to the *Thurner* (p. 417), 1¹/₄ hr.

Numerous erratic blocks and gravel moraines, brought to light by the construction of the railway, bear witness to the glacial conditions of this whole district in the ice age. A number of characteristic specimens of glacial striation have been collected at the railway-stations of Hinterzarten, Titisee, and Neustadt.

18 M. **Titisee** (2815 ft.; *Bär*, at the station, R. 1³/₄-3¹/₂, B. 1, D. 3, pens. from 6 *M*; *Bahnhof-Hôtel*, unpretending) is about ¹/₄ M. from the small lake of the same name, on the bank of which lie the *Schwarzwald Hotel* (R. from 2, B. 1, D. 3, pens. from 6 *M*) and the *Hôtel Titisee*, two pleasant hotels with gardens on the lake, and both often full in summer. — The *Titisee* (2780 ft.; area 265

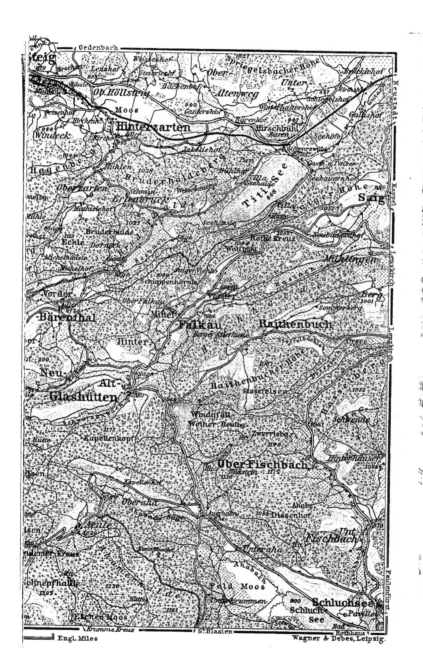

Engl. Miles

Wagner & Debes, Leipzig.

dependencies, which lies on the road 80 ft. below. It is a good starting-point for excursions in the Höllen-Tal and for an ascent of the Feldberg (p. 421; numerous finger-posts).

A footpath constructed by the landlord of the 'Sternen', beginning opposite the inn and passing the post-office, leads under the railway-viaduct to the *Ravenna Schlucht*, a wild ravine with a fine cascade. After 12 min. the path forks: the right branch crosses the entrenchment to the road, which we follow either back to the inn (in all ³/₄-1 hr.) or on to Hinterzarten (in all 1¹/₂ hr.). The left branch leads to the upper Ravenna-Tal, reaching another fork at (20 min.) the saw-mill. There we may either keep to the left for (¹/₂ hr.) the Pikettfels (p. 417), or go on in a straight direction to the *Ravennaschlucht Hotel* in *Oedenbach*, on the road to Breitnau (see below). — A pleasant route from the 'Sternen' to Hinterzarten is as follows: we keep to the highroad for ¹/₂ M.; beyond the bridge, where it makes a sharp curve to the left, we take the road to the right, which ascends the picturesque *Löffel-Tal*, now traversed by the railway, to (1¹/₂ M.) the first houses of *Hinterzarten* (see below).

The railway crosses the *Ravenna Schlucht* (view of it to the left) by a lofty viaduct, while the road ascends the *Höllsteig* in bold windings. The last view of the Höllen-Tal is cut short by a tunnel (275 yds. long), whence we emerge in the *Löffel-Tal*. The train then passes through the seventh and last tunnel and reaches the top of the plateau and the station of —

15¹/₂ M. **Hinterzarten.** — Hotels (all well spoken of). *Adler*, near the church, pens. 5-7 ℳ; *Linde* (pens. 4¹/₂-5 ℳ), *Bahnhof-Hôtel*, at the station; *Rössle*, ¹/₂ M. to the N.W., on the edge of the forest, pens. 4¹/₂ ℳ; *Lafette*, ¹/₃ M. farther to the E., unpretending. — *Lodgings*.

Hinterzarten (2900 ft.), a favourite summer-resort, where the rack-and-pinion section of the railway ends. — The road passing the handsome church and the footpath beyond it both lead to *Erlenbruck* (3080 ft.; Schwan), pleasantly situated among firs, whence we may go on in the one direction to the Titisee, and in the other to Bärental and the Feldberg (comp. p. 421).

About ¹/₄ M. to the W. of the Weisses Rössle a road, diverging to the N. from the Höllen-Tal road, leads viâ *Oedenbach* (see above) to the (3 M.) *Gasthof zum Löwen* (3265 ft.). Hence we may proceed to the left to (¹/₄ hr.) *Breitnau* (Kreuz) and (¹/₂ hr.) the **Hochwart** (3675 ft.), with an old entrenchment (view of the Alps). Or we may go to the right to (1 hr.) the *Weisstannhöhe* (p. 419). — From the Löwe to the *Thurner* (p. 417), 1¹/₄ hr.

Numerous erratic blocks and gravel moraines, brought to light by the construction of the railway, bear witness to the glacial conditions of this whole district in the ice age. A number of characteristic specimens of glacial striation have been collected at the railway-stations of Hinterzarten, Titisee, and Neustadt.

18 M. **Titisee** (2815 ft.; *Bär*, at the station, R. 1³/₄-3¹/₂, B. 1, D. 3, pens. from 6 ℳ; *Bahnhof-Hôtel*, unpretending) is about ¹/₄ M. from the small lake of the same name, on the bank of which lie the *Schwarzwald Hotel* (R. from 2, B. 1, D. 3, pens. from 6 ℳ) and the *Hôtel Titisee*, two pleasant hotels with gardens on the lake, and both often full in summer. — The *Titisee* (2780 ft.; area 265

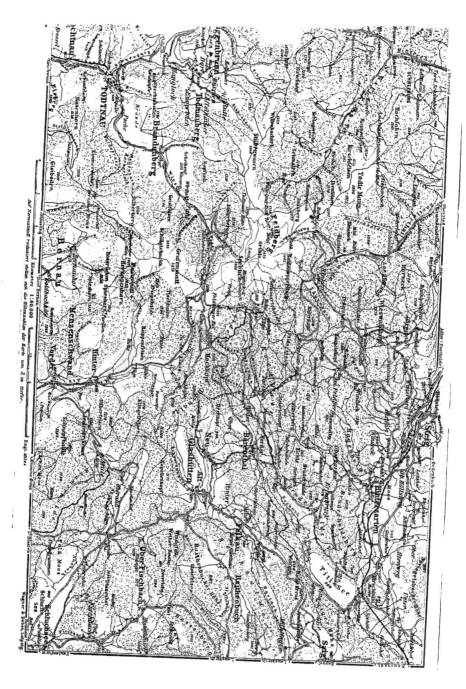

acres; 130 ft. deep), occupying, like all the Schwarzwald lakes, the bed of a former glacier, is fed by the *Seebach* (p. 421) and drained by the *Gutach*, called *Wutach* farther down. The surrounding hills are partly wooded.

At the old *Seebauernhof*, a few min. from the Hôtel Titisee, on the Lenzkirch and Schluchsee road (p. 423) which skirts the E. side of the lake, the steep old road to (40 min.) Saig diverges to the left (new road, see p. 423). **Saig** (3250 ft.; *Ochs*, with baths, pens. from 4¹/₂ ℳ, very fair) is a summer-resort. — From the first bend on the road, 7 min. from the Seebauernhof, a forest-path leads to the left to (25 min.) the lonely *Kalte Herberge*, on the Saig and Neustadt road. Crossing the latter diagonally, we ascend in ¹/₂ hr. to the wooded summit of the *****Hohfirst** (3900 ft.), on which is a view-tower with mountain-indicator (adm. 20 pf.; rfmts.). — From Saig to the Hohfirst, ³/₄ hr.; from Neustadt, see below.

At the first important bend on the Lenzkirch road (3165 ft.), 2 M. from the station and about 1³/₄ M. from the Hôtel Titisee, is a notice-board on a tree to the right, indicating the footpath to the *Feldberg* (Höhenweg, p. xvii). This path (very muddy in wet weather) leads to (1¹/₄ hr.) the 'Adler', in Bärental (p. 421).

Ascent of the *Feldberg*, see p. 421; post-gig daily (2¹/₂ ℳ, return journey 2 ℳ; carr. and pair 18 ℳ, returning viâ Menzenschwand and St. Blasien, 33 ℳ).

Another good point of view is the **Weisstannhöhe** (3890 ft.), 2 hrs. to the N.W. of Titisee. From the station we follow the Höllen-Tal road to the W., and after 20 min. take the path (Höhenweg marks; p. xvii) to the right; 50 min., *Heiliger Brunnen* (3515 ft.), with chapel and inn. Descents, see pp. 418 and 417.

Farther on we cross the Wutach or Gutach and skirt the spurs of the Hohfirst. — 20 M. *Hölzlebruck*, at the mouth of the *Langenordnacher-Tal*, in which lies (5¹/₂ M.) Waldau (p. 413). Near Hölzlebruck is the *Posthäusle*, with brewery and garden-restaurant.

22 M. **Neustadt** (2640 ft.; *Adler-Post; Krone*, both very fair; *Neustädter Hof*), an ancient town, with 3500 inhab., engaged in the timber-trade, tanning, and gold-embroidering, lies at the confluence of the *Reichenbach* and the Gutach and is the junction of a branch-line to Lenzkirch and Bonndorf (see below).

Walks may be taken to the (1 M.) *Posthäusle* (see above); to the (1 hr.) *Hohfirst* (see above), by the Saig road for ¹/₂ hr., then footpath to the left; and viâ *Rudenberg* to (1¹/₂ hr.) **Friedenweiler** (2965 ft.; *Kurhaus*, R. 1¹/₂-3, pens. 5¹/₂-9 ℳ, very fair), a favourite summer-resort. On the last excursion we follow the Löffingen road for 3 M. and then diverge to the left (omn., in ³/₄ hr., 1 ℳ; carr. with one horse 4, two horses 6 ℳ).

[From Neustadt a branch-line runs viâ *Kappel* (p. 420), *Lenzkirch* (7 M.), *Unter-Lenzkirch*, and *Gündelwangen* to (15 M.) the small town of *Bonndorf* (2780 ft.; Hirsch). — **Lenzkirch** (2660 ft.; *Adler* or *Post*, pens. from 5 ℳ, well spoken of; *Wilder Mann*, unpretending), in the valley of the Haslach, also known as *Ober-Lenzkirch*, contains 1250 inhab. and is one of the most important clock-making places in the Black Forest. Walks may be taken to the S.W. on the *Stöckleberg;* to the W. to the (¹/₂ hr.) ochschirm, on the Berger Höhe; and to the N.W. to (¹/₄ hr.) the uin of *Alturach*, on the road to Titisee.]

Beyond (24¹/₂ M.) *Kappel* (2580 ft.) the Höllen-Tal Railway
crosses the Gutach by a viaduct 210 ft. in span, and soon afterwards
it crosses the Schwändeholzdobel and threads four tunnels. Near
(28¹/₂ M.) *Rötenbach* (2725 ft.) we see a new pilgrimage-church
(Zum Schneekreuze) on the left. 32 M. *Löffingen* (2630 ft.; Löwe,
Sonne), a small town with 1100 inhab., is mentioned in a document
of 886. — 33 M. *Reiselfingen* (2570 ft.).

Löffingen and Reiselfingen are the stations for **Bad Boll** (2035 ft.;
well-equipped Kurhaus, pens. 5¹/₂-7 ℳ), which is situated in the romantic
gorge of the Wutach, 3³/₄ M. from the former and 2¹/₄ M. from the latter
(carriages to meet the train must be ordered in advance). Boll is surrounded with pine-woods (good paths). Pleasant walks may be taken
to the S., past the waterfall, to (20 min.) the ruined castle; to the E.,
through the imposing *Ravine of the Wutach,* to (1¹/₂ hr.) a point beyond
the place where the channel of the Wutach is dry for some distance
(guide-post), whence we may either descend to the left direct to (¹/₂ hr.)
Bachheim (see below) or descend along the Wutach for ³/₄ hr. more and
then ascend to the left through the wild *Gauchach-Schlucht* to (1 hr.)
Bachheim. Bonndorf (p. 419) lies about 3 M. to the S. of Bad Boll.

35 M. *Bachheim* (Hirsch); 37 M. *Unadingen.* — The train
passes over a viaduct and through a tunnel. — 40 M. *Döggingen*
(2455 ft.); 42¹/₂ M. *Hausen vor Wald.* 45 M. *Hüfingen*, with
1700 inhab. and an old castle, now converted into a hospital, is the
junction of the railway to Furtwangen (comp. p. 407). — 47 M.
Donaueschingen (p. 406).

The FELDBERG may be ascended from the Höllen-Tal by various
routes, all indicated by finger-posts and coloured marks. The easiest
routes are those from Hinterzarten and Titisee.

ASCENT OF THE FELDBERG FROM KIRCHZARTEN or from the station
of HIMMELREICH viâ *Sonneck*, *Hinterwaldkopf*, and the *Rinken* (see
below), 4¹/₂ hrs. in each case (Höhenweg, p. xvii). The descent towards
Freiburg is the most picturesque.

ASCENT OF THE FELDBERG FROM POSTHALDE (p. 417), 3¹/₄ hrs. The
footpath crosses the Höllbach beyond the Adler Inn and ascends (yellow
marks), steep at first, in view of the Ravenna viaduct, to (³/₄ hr.) *Albersbach*, where we reach the Hinterzarten road and follow it to the right.
In 10 min. more we reach the new *Gasthof zur Esche;* 5 min. farther
on we ascend to the left, finally by a broad road, to (¹/₂ hr.) the *Lochrütte* (3815 ft.) and on to (35 min.) the cottages (rfmts.) on the **Rinken**
(3920 ft.). The road forks here; by keeping to the right and following
(10 min.) the path to the left, we reach (20 min.) the *Zastler-Hütte* (inn),
whence an easy ascent of ³/₄ hr. brings us to the tower on the 'Höchste'
(p. 422); by following the left branch and soon diverging by a path to
the right, we reach the tower in 1¹/₂ hr. viâ the *Baldenweger Viehhütte.*
Or we may diverge to the left, below the Seebuck, by the so-called
'Felsen-Weg', leading to the (1¹/₄ hr.) Feldberg Hotel.

If at Albersbach (see above) we ascend the footpath instead of following the road to the right, we reach, finally by a broad track, the
(³/₄ hr.) saddle of *Fürsatz* (3675 ft.), where the road from Hinterzarten
joins ours on the left (see p. 421), while a road to the right leads to
(20 min.) the Lochrütte (see above). We follow in a straight direction
the fairly level road, indicated by a finger-post marked 'Feldsee, Feldberg', and in ³/₄ hr. reach the *Rufen-Hütte* (3545 ft.). Here we take the
footpath to the left, which passes the Rainmartehof (inn) and leads to

(25 min.) the **Feldsee** (3650 ft.), a gloomy little lake enclosed by precipitous pine-clad heights. Thence an easy zigzag path ascends to (35-45 min.) the Feldberg Hotel. — The red-marked path, diverging to the right from the Posthalde route immediately beyond the Höllbach, joins the ($1^1/_4$ hr.) path from Kirchzarten (p. 420) at a point to the W. of the Hinterwaldkopf.

Ascent of the Feldberg from Höllsteig (p. 417), 3-$3^1/_4$ hrs. We may either take the footpath, pointed out by the sign affixed to the Sternen Inn, which ascends in 40 min. to the Hinterzarten road, and then follow the continuation of the path from the Posthalde (p. 420), which joins this road 2 min. to the W. Or we may continue to follow the highroad for $^1/_2$ M. beyond the Sternen Inn and then turn to the right at the finger-post marked 'über Bisten, Fürsatz, Feldsee zum Feldberger Hof'. This ascends abruptly through wood to (ca. 40 min.) the hamlet of *Bisten* (3020 ft.), situated on the Hinterzarten road. We finally follow the upper branch of this road, avoiding the last curve by a short-cut, and so reach ($^3/_4$ hr.) the *Führsatz* (p. 420).

Ascent of the Feldberg from Hinterzarten (p. 418), 3 hrs. We may proceed to the W. from the station and follow the road diverging to the left at the railway-crossing; at (25 min.) the corner, below the hamlet of *Windeck*, we ascend to the left and traverse the beautiful Bistenwald to ($^3/_4$ hr.) the *Fürsatz* (see above). Or we may follow the road to *Erlenbruck* (p. 418), $^1/_4$ M. beyond which is a finger-post (right), indicating the forest-path to Bärental and Feldberg (see below).

The good road from the Titisee to the Feldberg (9 M.; carr. and diligence, see p. 419) diverges to the S.W. from the road coming from the station, a little on this side of the Schwarzwald Hotel. After about $1^1/_4$ M. we reach the upper end of the lake (rowing-boat from the hotel thus far, 40 pf.). Our road is joined by that from Erlenbruck and Hinterzarten (see p. 418) $^3/_4$ M. farther on, and by the forest-path from Erlenbruck (p. 418) after $^3/_4$ M. more (near the *Löffelschmiede Inn*). Beyond a saw-mill we cross the *Seebach*, continue to follow the road (from which a private road to the Feldsee diverges after $^1/_3$ M.), and ascend through wood, passing between the houses of *Bärental*, to the *Adler Inn* (3205 ft.; $4^3/_4$ M. from the station of Titisee), where the road forks, the Feldberg road ascending to the right ($3^3/_4$ M.; $1^1/_2$ hr.), while the main road leads in a straight direction viâ *Neu-Glashütten* and *Alt-Glashütten* to (9 M.) *Schluchsee* (p. 424).

About $^1/_4$ M. from the Adler Inn a path ascends on the left to the (1 hr.) 'Zweiseenblick' (view of the Titisee and Schluchsee; best in the afternoon) on the *Bärhalde* (4330 ft.); hence to the Feldberg Hotel $^3/_4$-1 hr.

The Feldberg road continues to ascend, commanding for some distance a fine survey of the Bären-Tal and the Titisee, and then enters beautiful pine-forest. About 3 M. above the Adler a new road diverges through wood to the left (Zweiseenblick, $1^1/_2$ M.; St. Blasien, 12 M.; Schluchsee, $7^3/_4$ M.), and 3 min. farther on an old road to the ($^3/_4$ M.) Feldberg Hotel leads off to the right, passing the *Menzenschwander Viehhütte*. The Todtnau road goes on viâ the (8 min.) *Jägermatte Inn* (4100 ft.; R. 1-$2^1/_2$, pens. 5-$6^1/_2$ *M*), where the new road to the Feldberg Hotel ($^1/_4$ hr.) begins.

The **Feldberg Hotel* (4195 ft.; R. $1^1/_2$-5, B. 1, D. $2^1/_2$, S. $1^3/_4$, pens. 6-10 *M*; post-office and telephone), where the road ends, is

situated on the S.E. side of the bare Feldberg ridge ($2^1/_2$ M. long,
$^1/_3$ M. broad), which culminates to the N.W. in the Feldberg proper,
to the N. in the Baldenweger Buck, and to the S.E. in the Seebuck,
while on the S. it is connected with the Herzogenhorn by a saddle.

Two paths lead from the hotel to the (1 hr.) top, diverging from
each other above the (5 min.) cattle-shed. The 'Felsenweg' to the
right, high above the Feldsee (p. 421), skirts the slope of the Seebuck, to the N. of which it rejoins the older path. The older path
(left) winds up to the (20-25 min.) top of the *Seebuck (4755 ft.),
on which is a tower bearing a large bronze relief of Bismarck (1896).
To the E. we have a picturesque view of the Bären-Tal and the
wooded basin of the Feldsee; and to the S. (in clear weather; rare
in summer) a distant survey of the Alps from the Säntis to Mont
Blanc, with the Bernese Alps rising conspicuously to the left of the
Hornberg. — In $^1/_2$ hr. more we reach the top of the Feldberg proper.

The *Feldberg (4905 ft.; 1000 ft. lower than the Rigi-Kulm)
is the highest mountain in Central Germany, with the exception of
the Schneekoppe (5260 ft.) and two other peaks (5120 and 4950 ft.)
in the Riesengebirge. On the highest point (the 'Höchste') are the
Friedrich-Luisen-Turm (adm. 20 pf.) and the *Feldberg-Turm
Inn* (R. 2-3, B. 1, D. 2, pens. 6-7 ℳ). The view from the tower
includes the Vosges and the Alps as seen from the Seebuck (mountain-indicator). The Feldberg, which is visited at all seasons, is
frequented in winter by numerous 'ski-runners'.

Ascent of the Feldberg from Oberried (p. 416) through the
St. Wilhelms-Tal (5 hrs.). We follow the Todtnau road for 3 M. to a
finger-post, indicating the way to the left to the picturesque, wooded,
and rocky *St. Wilhelms-Tal*. The broad track crosses the brook four
times; beyond the last bridge (2 hrs.) is the humble inn Zum Napf, where
carriages must stop. The footpath to the left is to be followed hence;
12 min., we ascend to the left, at first gradually, afterwards in rapid
zigzags; $^3/_4$ hr., the wood is quitted; we again ascend to the right to the
(35 min.) *St. Wilhelmer Hütte* (4520 ft.; rfmts. and nightquarters), from
which the tower is attained in $^1/_2$ hr. more.

From Oberried through the Zastler-Tal ($3^1/_2$ hrs. by road; less
by footpaths). The road is quitted at Oberried, and the *Zastler-Tal*, a
narrow and wild valley, is ascended. In $2^3/_4$ hrs. we reach *Auf dem
Rinken* and join the route described at p. 420. We may also ascend to
the top direct from the *Zastler-Hütte* (p. 420).

From Todtnau (p. 431; $3^1/_2$ hrs.). The Titisee road ascends the
Wiesen-Tal viâ the hamlets of *Brandenberg* (Hirsch) and ($1^1/_2$ hr.) *Fahl*
(2790 ft.; Adler), and then makes a wide curve to the pass of the Zeiger
(4035 ft.), where several roads meet. Walkers may avoid the last curve
by following the 'Hebelsweg durch das Fahler Loch', a footpath to the
right, $^3/_4$ M. above Fahl. From the summit of the Zeiger pass a path
diverges to the left to the Feldberg Hotel ($1^1/_4$ hr. from Fahl). — A direct footpath from Fahl to the ($1^3/_4$-2 hrs.) tower on the top leads to the
left in the village to the right bank of the Wiese, ascends past the falls
to the curve of the road, and proceeds thence to the left to the Todtnauer Hütte (4335 ft.; rfmts.; bed $1^1/_2$-2 ℳ), $^1/_2$ hr. below the tower.

From Todtnauberg (p. 431) the ascent takes 3 hrs.; the route unites
at the Todtnauer Hütte with that above described. — From the Notschrei (p. 416) to the top of the Feldberg $2^1/_2$ hrs.; numerous way-posts.

FROM MENZENSCHWAND (p. 435; 2-2¹/₂ hrs.). Just beyond Hinter-Menzenschwand the road reaches the right bank of the Alb, which it follows. The final wide bend of the road before the Zeiger is avoided by a zigzag footpath to the right at the top of the wood, which rejoins the road at the Jagermatte.

FROM ST. BLASIEN (p. 435; 3¹/₂ hrs.) we may either follow the road viâ Menzenschwand (carr. 25 ℳ), or take the following walk. About 1 M. above St. Blasien a road diverges to the right from the Menzenschwand road, mounts the *Bötzberg*, and leads to (1¹/₄ hr.) *Muchenland* (3515 ft.) and (20 min. farther) the *Krummenkreuz* (3770 ft.). Beyond it the path forks, to the right to *Aeule* (p. 424) and *Aha*, to the left, always on the same level, to the (1¹/₂-2 hrs.) *Aeulemer Kreuz*. Hence (Höhenweg, see p. xvii) we ascend the W. side of the Feldberg and the *Bärhalde* to the Bärental road in 1³/₄ hr., or, making a détour by the *Zweiseenblick* (p. 421), reach the Feldberg Hotel in 2¹/₄ hrs.

FROM SCHLUCHSEE (p. 424). The road by *Unter-Aha, Ober-Aha*, and *Altglashütten* unites at the Adler in (7 M.) Bärental with the road from the Titisee described at p. 421. From the Auerhahn Inn at Unter-Aha (p. 424; 2¹/₄ M. from Schluchsee) walkers may follow the Aeule road to the left for 8 min. and then take the path indicated by a finger-post to the right (2 hrs.; Höhenweg, see p. xvii).

From the Zeiger (p. 422; ¹/₄ hr. below the Feldberg Hotel) the Höhenweg (p. xvii) leads to the S.W., ascending at first, across the *Grafenmatt* (4445 ft.), at the (³/₄ hr.) S. end of which (the so-called *Glockenführe*, 4355 ft.) is a finger-post pointing to the left to St. Blasien (9¹/₂ M.; viâ the Spiesshorn, 2 M.). Here we turn to the right (Höhenweg) and in 20 min. reach the ***Herzogenhorn** (4650 ft.; refuge-hut; rfmts.), which affords a fine view of the Alps and the valleys to the S. — From the Herzogenhorn we may return to the Glockenführe and descend to the right (E.) through wood; then at the (1 hr.) clearing on the *Rossrücken* cross the cart-track, keeping to the left, to the *Spiesshorn* (4430 ft.) and Menzenschwand (p. 435). Or we may take the Höhenweg to the left and at 'An der Eck', instead of descending to the left to Bernauhof, we follow the ridge to the S. to (1¹/₂ hr.) the *Wacht*, on the road from St. Blasien to Geschwend (p. 435); thence by the *Blössling* (p. 435), the *Hohe Zinken* (4075 ft.), and the *Hochkopf* (4150 ft.) to Todtmoos (p. 434).

A fine MOUNTAIN WALK (Höhenweg, p. xvii) leads from the Feldberg viâ the Todtnauer Hütte (p. 422), and the *Stübenwasen* (4550 ft.) to the (2 hrs.) *Notschrei* (p. 416); thence either over the Halde to the (1³/₄-2 hrs.) *Schau-ins-Land* (p. 380), or (Höhenweg) viâ the *Trubelsmattkopf* and the *Hörnle* to the (1³/₄ hr.) *Wiedenereck* (p. 431) and on over the *Krinne* saddle to (2-2¹/₂ hrs.) the top of the *Belchen* (p. 430).

m. From Titisee to Schluchsee and St. Blasien.

18¹/₂ M. Road. Diligence twice daily in 4¹/₂ hrs., Motor Omnibus in summer 3-4 times daily in 1¹/₃ hr. (fare 4¹/₂ ℳ; to Schluchsee in ³/₄ hr., 2¹/₂ ℳ); 11 lbs. of luggage free, each 11 lbs. more 25 pf. Carriage from Titisee to Schluchsee 9, with two horses 14 ℳ, to St. Blasien 22 and 25 ℳ.

The road from Titisee (p. 418) skirts the E. end of the lake and ascends in a long curve (short-cut to the left, ³/₄ M. from the Titisee Hotel), through noble fir-woods, to (2¹/₂ M.) the *Rotenkreuz* (a cross, now of white granite; 3285 ft.). From this point the road to Lengkirch (in the middle) leads to the E. through the valley of the Haslach, while the new road to Saig (p. 419) diverges to the left and that to Schluchsee to the right. Following the last we reach *Falkau*, where walkers at the Löwe Inn may descend to the left, through the wood, to the Windgfäll-Weiher.

5¹/₂ M. *Altglashütten* (3260 ft.; Hirsch, fair), where the road
from the 'Adler' in the Bären-Tal joins ours on the right (2 M.; see
p. 421). We then descend to the E. and S.E., mostly through wood,
and passing the *Windgfäll-Weiher*, to the *Auerhahn Inn* (3055 ft.).
The road leading hence to the W. runs viâ *Aeule* (3375 ft.) to (5¹/₂ M.)
Menzenschwand (p. 435); that to the S. (recommended to walkers)
leads viâ *Muchenland* (p. 423) to (3 hrs.) St. Blasien.

The road to St. Blasien soon forks. The new road, to the right,
runs viâ *Unter-Aha* to the *Schluchsee* (2955 ft.); the old road, to
the left, which is followed by the diligence, ascends to the village
and summer-resort of —

10 M. **Schluchsee** (3120 ft.; *Stern*, R. 2-4, pens. 6¹/₂-11 ℳ;
Schiff, R. from 1¹/₂, pens. from 5¹/₂ ℳ), situated ¹/₂ M. from the
lake in the midst of pine-forest. Pop. 600. The lake, 2 M. long
and ¹/₂ M. broad, is well stocked with fish (boats for hire). On the
bank is a bath-establishment.

The (1¹/₄ hr.) *Hochstaufen* or *Wagnersberg* (3555 ft.), to the S. of
Seebrugg, is ascended by convenient paths; it affords a view of the Alps.
— The *Faulenfürst* (3405 ft.), to which a road leads from Schluchsee in
1 hr., commands a similar view. — The expedition may be extended by
descending on the E. side of the Faulenfürst to (³/₄ hr.) *Rothaus* (3190 ft.;
inn, opposite, pens. from 6 ℳ), a brewery founded by the Abbots of
St. Blasien and now government-property (Alpine view). Thence to (21 M.)
Tiengen (diligence from Schluchsee), see p. 439. The picturesque Schlücht-
Tal is the most interesting part of the route. — A road descends the
Mettma-Tal from Rothaus, ascending to the right, after about 3¹/₂ M.,
to *Brenden* (6¹/₂ M. in all). Thence to the Schlücht-Tal viâ *Berau*, 4¹/₂ M.
— From SCHLUCHSEE TO LENZKIRCH (p. 419), 5¹/₂ M., diligence daily in
1¹/₂ hr.

From Schluchsee the road descends to the new road along the
lake, which divides beyond (1¹/₂ M.) *Seebrugg* (Seebrugg; Seehof), at
the foot of the lake, the left branch leading to Rothaus and Bonndorf (p. 419), the right to St. Blasien. The latter crosses the
Schwarza, the brook by which the lake is drained, and leads
through pine-forest. About ³/₄ M. farther on a finger-post indicates
a path to the right, leading by *Blasiwald* (Sonne) and *Althütte* to
St. Blasien (6 M.; 1¹/₂ M. shorter than by the road). The highroad
now enters the *Schwarzhalde*, a deep and romantic valley, which
it follows nearly to (4¹/₂ M.) *Häusern* (p. 436). A little beyond the
village it divides (comp. p. 436), the branch to the left leading to
(1¹/₂ M.) *Höchenschwand* (p. 436), that on the right to (2¹/₄ M.) —

18¹/₂ M. *St. Blasien* (p. 435).

n. Badenweiler and Environs.

FROM MÜLLHEIM TO BADENWEILER, 4¹/₂ M., narrow-gauge railway in
¹/₂ hr. — Carriages take 1¹/₂ hr.; fare 4 ℳ 10 pf., with two horses 5¹/₂ ℳ,
fee included (luggage up to 110 lbs. 60 pf.).

Müllheim, see p. 382. The line ascends the valley of the *Klemmbach.* — 2³/₄ M. *Niederweiler* (970 ft.; Löwe), with a brewery.

3¹/₂ M. *Oberweiler* (1120 ft.; Ochsc, R. 1¹/₂-2, pens. 4¹/₂-5 *M ;*
Wilder Mann, both unpretending and with open-air restaurants), a
village with 670 inhabitants. — 4¹/₄ M. *Hasenburg* (1180 ft.), the
station for the *Hasenburg Hotel* (r.; pens. 4¹/₂-7 *M*) and for the
Kurhaus Oberweiler (pens. 50 *M* per week; with baths and large
garden), in a sheltered situation at the S.W. base of the wooded
Lausberg, much frequented in spring and autumn.

About 1 M. to the E. of Hasenburg is the *Schwärze* (1430 ft.), commanding a picturesque view of Badenweiler. Hence we may proceed to
the right to (40 min.) the ruin of *Neuenfels* (1960 ft.), returning viâ
Holden and Schweighof (p. 428).

The railway skirts the Hasenburg and reaches the station of
(4¹/₂ M.) *Badenweiler*, ¹/₄ M. below the village.

Badenweiler. — HOTELS (larger houses closed in winter). **Römerbad* (Pl. a; A, 2), ¹/₂ M. from the rail. station, a handsome building, at
the main entrance of the Kur-Park, R. 2¹/₂-6, B. 1¹/₄, D. 4, pens. from
8 *M; *Hôtel Sommer* (Pl. b; B, 2), at the E. entrance of the park, R.
2¹/₂-6, B. 1¹/₄, D. 3¹/₂, pens. 7-12 *M*, both first-class, with fine gardens and
baths; **Hôtel-Pension Saupe* (Pl. c.; C, 1), with garden, R. 2¹/₂-4, B. 1¹/₄,
D. 3, pens. 6¹/₂-10 *M; Schwarzwald Hôtel* (Pl d; A. 2), R. 2¹/₂-5, B. 1¹/₄,
D. 3, pens. from 6¹/₂ *M*, very fair; *Hôtel-Restaurant Engler* (Pl. e; B, 2),
pens. 6-9 *M; Meissburger* (Pl. f; B, 2), very fair, pens. 5-6¹/₂ *M* (Bavarian
beer on draught), with dépendance *Waldhaus*, on the edge of the wood
(pens. 6-8 *M*); *Sonne* (Pl. g; B, 2); *Bellevue* (Jewish). — PENSIONS. *Internationale* (from 6 *M*), *Pflüger* (5-7 *M*), *Windscheid* (7-10 *M*), *Händler*
(7-10 *M*), etc. — **Haus Baden* (p. 427), in an open situation on the edge
of the wood, 1 M. to the S. of Badenweiler, R. 2-5, B. 1¹/₄, D. 3¹/₂, pens.
7¹/₂-10¹/₂ *M*. — *Private Apartments* 7-25 *M* per week. List of lodgings
kept at the Kurhaus.

VISITORS' TAX at Badenweiler 50 pf. per day, 3 *M* per week, or 24 *M*
for the season; in the environs 10 or 5 *M*. — BATHS at the Marmorbad
(indoor swimming-bath with warm water) 1 *M* 20 pf., tickets per dozen
12 *M;* at the Freibad (outdoor swimming-bath with warm water) 80 pf.,
tickets per dozen 8 *M*. Gentlemen use the Marmorbad 10-1 & 2-4, and
the Freibad 7-10 & 4.30-7; ladies use the Marmorbad 7-10 & 4-6, the Freibad 10-1 & 2-4.30.

ENGLISH CHURCH SERVICE during the season.

CARRIAGES (gratuity included). For 1 hr. 2¹/₂, each additional ¹/₂ hr.
1 *M*, with two horses 3¹/₂ and 1¹/₂ *M. Ascent of the Blauen*, with one horse
11 *M* 30 pf., with two horses for 2-3 pers. 15¹/₂, for 4-5 pers. 20¹/₂ *M;* to
Bürgeln, 8 *M* 40 pf., two horses 11 *M* 40 or 14 *M* 40 pf.; to *Kandern*,
9 *M* 40 pf., two horses 17¹/₂ *M*.

Badenweiler (1450 ft. above the sea, 690 ft. above the Rhine),
a village with 650 inhab., lies among the W. spurs of the Black
Forest, on a buttress of the Blauen, and commands an unimpeded
view across the valley of the Rhine to the Vosges. The thermal springs
(77°-80°), which are almost destitute of mineral ingredients, were
known to the Romans. Badenweiler, however, owes its present prosperity to its fine air, its sheltered situation, its equable temperature,
and its beautiful walks. It is patronized by over 6-7000 visitors
annually, including many sufferers from pulmonary and nervous
ailments. The season lasts from mid-March to the end of October.

The chief resorts of visitors are the **Kurhaus** (Pl. A, 2), with

its concert, ball, and reading rooms, its terraces, and its restaurant
(D. 2-4 ℳ), and the *Wandelbahn*, or *Covered Promenade*, which
is 150 ft. in length. A band plays at the Kurhaus morning, afternoon, and evening.

The *Kur-Park (Pl. A, B, 1, 2), 15 acres in extent, is remarkable for the luxuriance of its vegetation, the native trees being
neighboured by fine coniferæ, cedars, pines, laurels, and yews. A
broad walk (fine views) encircles the conical castle-hill. The hill
is crowned with the ruins of the **Castle** (Pl. A, 2; 1500 ft.), which

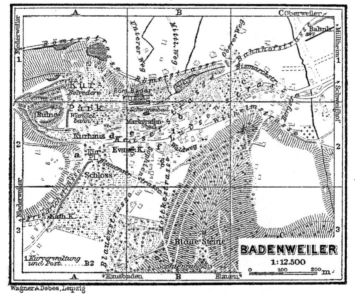

was originally built by the Dukes of Zähringen in the 11th cent.
and was destroyed by the French in 1688. Its foundations are
possibly of Roman origin. The ruin is reached by flights of steps,
and a fine prospect is enjoyed from the ivy-clad walls.

In the E. part of the park rises the handsome **Bath House**
(*Markgrafenbad*; Pl. B, 2; shown for a fee of 50 pf.); the older
part, known as the *Marmorbad*, with a colonnade, was built by
Leonhard of Carlsruhe. The arrangement of the interior somewhat
resembles that of the ancient Roman baths, all the rooms being
vaulted and lighted from above. To the right is the *Erweiterungs-
bau* or *Extension* (1908), with therapeutic baths and apparatus.
Behind the Marmorbad is the *Freibad*, also well fitted up.

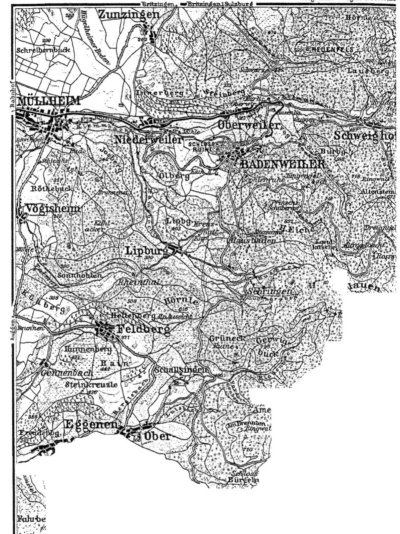

The ancient *Roman Baths (Pl. B, 1, 2), discovered in 1784, are among the finest on this side of the Alps and form an interesting monument of Roman rule on the Rhine, which was at its best in the 2nd-4th centuries. They are sheltered by a wooden roof (open 8-12.30 and 2-6.30; adm. 20 pf.).

The structure (230 ft. long and 65-80 ft. wide) is divided into two corresponding parts, the larger of which, to the W., was reserved for the men, that to the E. for the women. On each side there is a spacious forecourt, used for walking and gymnastic exercises. In the W. court is a pedestal with an inscription showing it to have supported a statue of *Diana Abnoba.* The W. vestibule is adjoined on the S. by the dressing-room *(apodyterium)* and on the N. by the vapour or hot-air bath *(sudatorium).* Farther to the E. lay two tepid swimming-baths *(piscinae),* the larger of which is 40 ft. long by 24 ft. broad. Beyond the smaller of these were other warm baths (two *tepidaria* and a *caldarium),* which were heated by means of hypocausts in the adjoining chambers. The exact use of the circular rooms here *(laconica?)* is not quite certain. — The women's department is separated by a wall from the men's baths and contains corresponding chambers arranged in inverted order from W. to E.

On the S. side of the Kur-Platz (Pl. A, 2), in front of the main entrance to the park, is the *Grand-Ducal Palace (Schloss;* Pl. A, 2), built in 1586 and remodelled in the German Renaissance style in 1887-88. — The Friedrich-Str., to the right, with numerous villas and the small *Roman Catholic Church* (Pl. A, 3), leads to Niederweiler. The Blauen-Str. (Pl. A, 2), to the left, running above the Schloss, also passes numerous villas and leads to the Blauen, Bürgeln, Kandern.

In the environs of Badenweiler are numerous picturesque and well-kept Forest Paths ('Wald-Promenaden'), leading to beautiful points of view and provided with guide-posts. The finest begin at the Blauen-Str. (Pl. A, 3) and run along the slopes of the Blauen.

From the first bend on the Kandern road (Pl. B, 2) we may ascend straight on to the 'Pfarrwald', or following the road a little farther, turn to the left beyond the last villa and then enter the wood. In the highest part of the wood, ascending to the left from the second entrance to it, we reach the (15-20 min.) *Sophienruhe* (1690 ft.; Pl. B, 3), a refuge-hut above an ancient mine, commanding a picturesque view of Badenweiler. — A no less attractive view is afforded by the *Alte Mann* (2005 ft.), a rocky height about 20 min. to the S. of the Sophienruhe, whence we may either descend to (¹/₄ hr.) Haus Baden, or ascend farther viâ the *Schuberg-Fels* (2165 ft.) and the *Prinzen-Sitz* to the (³/₄ hr.) *Vogelbach-Tal,* and return through the last, passing the *Bergmannsruhe Restaurant,* to (¹/₂ hr.) Badenweiler.

A few min. beyond the last villa on the Kandern road, the road to the Blauen diverges on the left, from which, farther on, a road, on the right, leads to the (20 min.) *Haus Baden* (1720 ft.; see p. 425), the name of which refers to an old silver-mine.

From Badenweiler to Bürgeln (5 M.). We follow the Kandern road, which diverges to the right from the road to the Blauen. — Farther on (beyond kilomètre-stone 1) a path to the right leads through oak-wood to *Lipburg* and (1¹/₂ hr.) *Vögisheim* (905 ft.; Ochs). 2 M. *Sehringen.* Beyond kilomètre-stone 4 a path diverges

to the right to the (10 min.) 'Alpenansicht', on the wooded S. flank
of the *Hörnle*, commanding in clear weather a view of the Bernese
Alps. The road to Bürgeln diverges to the left at kilomètre-stone 6
and leads through wood to the foot of the hill, where it bends
sharply to the right and ascends.

Schloss Bürgeln (2190 ft.; *Inn*, very fair, D. 2-2^1/$_2$, pens.
5-5^1/$_2$ $\mathscr{M}$) was formerly a château of the wealthy Benedictine abbey
of St. Blasien (p. 435). The stag which figures in the arms of St.
Blasien still serves as a weather-cock. The present building, adorned
with stucco-ornaments and figures of the tutelars of St. Blasien,
dates from 1762. Bürgeln commands a striking and uninterrupted
view, resembling, though less extensive than, that from the Blauen,
at the S. base of which it lies.

FROM BÜRGELN TO THE BLAUEN, 2-3 hrs. At the above-mentioned
bend on the Bürgeln road stands a finger-post, pointing to 'Vogelbach
and Hochblauen'. The route to the Blauen diverges to the left from
that to Vogelbach. The windings of the cart-track may be avoided by
pedestrians.

The ***Blauen** (3830 ft.) or *Hochblauen*, one of the highest
points of the Black Forest, and the nearest to the Rhine, is easily
ascended by the road mentioned at p. 427 in 2^1/$_2$ hrs. A pleasanter
walking route (Höhenweg, p. xvii) leads viâ the Alte Mann, Prinzen-
sitz (p. 427), Hohe Eiche, Schrennengraben (3018 ft.; refuge-hut),
Wankersfels, and Hirzenmättle. The distance, however, is only
slightly shortened towards the very end, 25 min. below the summit,
where the road is crossed. On the summit, surrounded by wood,
are a good *Hotel* (R. 1^1/$_2$-2^1/$_2$, D. 2^1/$_2$-3, pens. from 6 $\mathscr{M}$) and an iron
platform which commands an unimpeded view of the Alps from the
Glärnisch to the Matterhorn and Mont Blanc, the Jura, the plain
of the Rhine, the Vosges, and the Black Forest.

About ^{1}/$_3$ M. below the inn, beyond the second bend of the carriage-
road, is a finger-post indicating the above-mentioned route to (1^1/$_2$-1^3/$_4$ hr.)
Bürgeln.

The HÖHENWEG ROUTE TO THE BELCHEN (see p. 430) offers a fine
high-level *Walk of about 4^1/$_2$ hrs. Descending on the E. side of the
inn (way-posts) and passing to the left of the *Stockberg* (3515 ft.; early-
German ring-wall), we reach the saddle of *Egerten* (3035 ft.; 35 min.
from the inn). Here we cross the roads from Badenweiler and Schweighof to *Marzell* (2330 ft.; Sonne), to the *Friedrichsheim*, a sanatorium
for consumptives, and to the Sirnitz, and ascend from the refuge-hut to
the right. Farther on we skirt the slope of the *Brandeck* (3610 ft.) by
a fairly level path, above the road just mentioned, to (50 min.) the saddle
of *Stühle* (3435 ft.) whence a footpath to the left leads into the Klemm-
Tal and so to Schweighof. A few paces farther on two roads diverge,
that to the left to the Sirnitz, that to the right to Marzell. In ^{1}/$_4$ hr.
from the refuge-hut, where we turn to the left, we come to the *Spähne-
platz* (3450 ft.), and in a farther 10 min. we cross a logging-road and
then a stream, after which we ascend in a curve to the left, reaching in
10 min. the cross-road on the *Sirnitz-Sattel* (p. 429).

About 3^1/$_2$ M. to the S. of Bürgeln lies **Kandern** (1160 ft.;
Krone; Ochs; Blume), a busy little town with 2000 inhab., to
reach which a pleasant détour of about 2^1/$_2$ hrs. may be made viâ

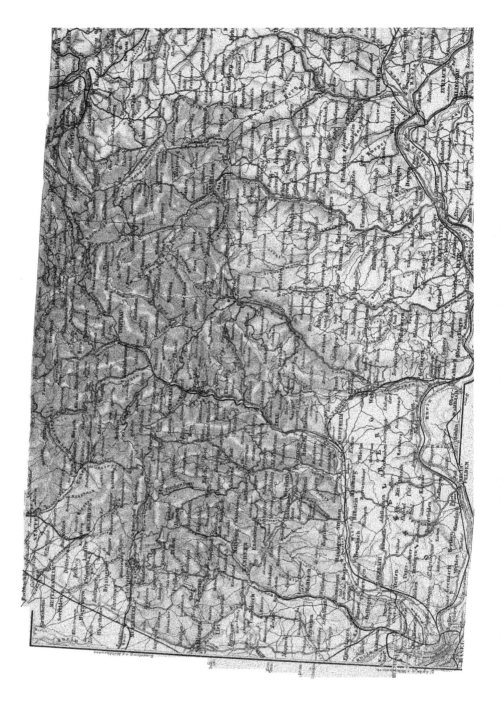

Bürgeln, Käsacker, Vogelbach, and the ruins of *Sausenburg*
(2195 ft.; key at Vogelbach), destroyed by the French in 1678.
Below Kandern is the *Wolfsschlucht,* a picturesque rocky ravine.

FROM KANDERN TO HALTINGEN (p. 382), 8 M., branch-railway in ³/₄ hr.,
descending the Kander-Tal, viâ (1³/₄ M.) *Hammerstein,* (3¹/₂ M.) *Wollbach,*
(4¹/₂ M.) *Wittlingen,* (5¹/₂ M.) *Rümmingen,* and (7 M.) *Binzen.*

o. From Badenweiler to the Belchen, and through the Münster-Tal to Staufen.

From Badenweiler to the *Belchen* in 5 hrs. (numerous finger-posts);
down to *Neumühle* 1¹/₂ hr., thence to *Staufen* 1¹/₂ hr. The ascent from
Neumühle, a favourite excursion from Freiburg, takes 2¹/₂ hrs.

A good road leads from Badenweiler to the E. to (1³/₄ M.)
Schweighof (1510 ft.; Sonne), the highest village in the valley of
the *Klemmbach* (1¹/₄ M. from Oberweiler), where roads diverge to
Marzell (r.) and Sulzburg (l.). (About ¹/₂ M. along the latter road
a footpath diverges on the right for the *Brudermatt-Fels,* 2250 ft.).

The new road (to Schönau, p. 431) ascends the valley of the
Klemmbach (short-cuts by footpaths and the old road) to the (4¹/₂ M.)
unpretending Auerhahn Inn, on the *Sirnitz* (2955 ft.), where another
road to Marzell diverges to the right, while the Schönau road ascends to the left. Walkers follow the old road, which ascends between the inn and the 'Felicitas Hut', and on the (35 min.) *Sirnitz-
Sattel* (3480 ft.) regain the highroad where it emerges from the
wood (to the right is the footpath to the Blauen, p. 428; to the
left appears the Belchen). In 20 min. more by the short-cuts we
reach the rustic *Inn zum Haldenhof* (3055 ft.) at *Hinter-Heubronn,*
where finger-posts indicate the routes to (6¹/₂ M.) Bad Sulzburg (l.;
p. 382) and (a few steps farther on) to the Münster-Tal. It takes
about 2¹/₂ hrs. to walk from the Haldenhof to Wembach (p. 431) by
the road viâ *Neuenweg, Oberböllen,* and *Niederböllen.*

To reach the top of the Belchen we take the 'Schattige Weg'
('Höhenweg', p. xvii), which, after 20 min., joins the older route
beginning 5 min. beyond the Haldenhof. We quit the latter in
2 min., but rejoin it once more ¹/₂ hr. later; from this point to the
cattle-shed 8 min.; 25 min. beyond this, along a shadeless path,
we reach the *Hohe Kelchsattel* (4090 ft.; near the rocky Hochkelch,
4135 ft.), where finger-posts point to Badenweiler and Sulzburg and
to the Unter-Münster-Tal; 6 min., finger-post pointing to the summit and (r.) the Belchenhaus (¹/₄ hr.).

ASCENT OF THE BELCHEN FROM SCHÖNAU (p. 431) in the Wiesen-Tal;
three routes. (1). Carriage-road viâ *Schönenbuchen* (passing Utzenfeld
halfway, p. 431), then to the left up the valley of the *Aiterbach,* viâ
Aitern and *Holzinshaus* (2605 ft.), to (3 M.) *Unter-Multen* (3295 ft.). Here
the new Belchen road (1904; fine views) diverges from the carriage-road
viâ *Ober-Multen* and the *Krinne* to *Neumühle* in the Unter-Münster-Tal
(p. 430) and reaches the summit in about 1 hr. (footpaths also). — (2).
A more convenient route is the footpath (2³/₄ hrs.; Höhenweg, p. xvii) indicated by a guide-post 4 min. to the N. of the Sonne Inn in Schönau;

27*

1 hr., *Holzinshaus;* at the last house, guide-post on the left; then straight
on up the right bank of the Aiterbach through wood; 1 hr., view of the
Belchen, to the summit of which (³/₄ hr.) we follow the guide-posts. —
(3). The older and shadeless route, leading to the left at the 'Sonne'
and ascending viâ (¹/₂ hr.) *Schönenberg,* and later uniting with the other
routes, is about ¹/₂ hr. shorter.

ASCENT OF THE BELCHEN FROM BAD SULZBURG (1515 ft.; p. 382), 4-4¹/₂ hrs.
(Föhenweg, p. xvii). Passing the hotel, we ascend to the right (guide-
post) along the *Sulzbach.* ¹/₂ hr., Footpath to the left ascending in zig-
za s. Several finger-posts. At (¹/₂ hr.) the finger-post pointing to the
Behaghel-Fels (2215 ft.; l.) we ascend to the right, quitting the wood
in ¹/₂ hr. more. At (¹/₄ hr.) the *Kälbelescheuer* (cattle-shed) we gain the
saddle between the *Kaibenkopf* (3075 ft.; N.) and the *Sirnitzkopf* (3910 ft.).
The Belchen is now visible. Hence we proceed to the right, through
wood; ¹/₂ hr., bench, with fine view of the Münster-Tal and the Belchen;
¹/₄ hr., *Haldenhof,* see p. 429.

The **Belchen* (4640 ft.), perhaps the finest point of view in the
Black Forest, commands a most picturesque and uninterrupted survey of the surrounding valleys, especially the attractive Münster-
Tal towards the W., the Wiesen-Tal to the S., and the Rhine Valley
stretching far into the distance to the W. In clear weather a magni-
ücent distant prospect is enjoyed. Four mountain-chains are visible:
to the E. the Black Forest with its numerous peaks, W. the Vosges,
S. the Jura and the snow-clad Alps. About 180 ft. below the summit
is **Stiefvater's Hotel* (R. 2-2¹/₂, B. 1, D. 2¹/₄-3, S. 1³/₄-2 ℳ;
post-office and telephone; closed in winter). A hut for ski-runners
has been built lower down.

FROM THE BELCHEN TO THE MÜNSTER-TAL (Höhenweg, p. xvii).
We follow the Badenweiler-Sulzburg route to (¹/₄ hr.) the saddle
mentioned above, where a guide-post indicates the way (r.) to the
lower Münster-Tal. This leads over the ridge of the *Langeck* and
descends its N. slope in windings (keeping to the right at the small
school-house) to *Neumühle* in the *Unter-Münster-Tal* (1¹/₂ hr.).
From Neumühle (motor-omnibus to Staufen, see below) we follow
the highroad (from Staufen to Neuenweg and Schopfheim) to the
right. About 220 yds. from Neumühle, below the beginning of the
route to Schönau (p. 431), stands the *Krone Inn.* At (20 min.) the
hamlet of *Wasen* (see below) the Staufen and Schopfheim road
unites with the Ober-Münster-Tal road. From this point we descend the valley of the *Neumagen-Bach* to —

3 M. **Staufen** (910 ft.; *Kreuz & Post,* very fair; *Krone*), an
ancient town with 1900 inhab., overshadowed by the ruined *Staufen-
burg,* the seat of a powerful race which became extinct in 1602.
Rathaus of the 16th century. The vineyards on the hill yield good
'Burghalder' wine.

A motor-omnibus plies from Staufen to *Wasen* (5 times daily) and
to *Neumühle* (see above; thrice daily, fare 80 pf.); also to *Spielweg*
p. 431; thrice daily, 1 ℳ).

Staufen is a station on the branch-line from *Sulzburg to Krozingen* (p. 382).

From Staufen to Utzenfeld in the Wiesen-Tal, 19½ M. To (3 M.)
Wasen, see p. 430. Ascending the *Ober-Münster-Tal* to the N.E., towards
the Schau-ins-Land (p. 380), we pass the ancient monastery of *St. Trudpert*
(1415 ft.; Linde, a few yds. farther on, pens. 3-5 *M*) and reach (4½ M.) the
inn *Zum Hirsch*, at the *Spielweg* (1795 ft.). The road ascends hence in
long windings towards the S., through wild and romantic scenery. After
2 M. the *Scharfenstein*, a precipitous rock of porphyry, crowned by the
scanty remains of a robbers' castle, rises on the left, the finest point on
the route. The road then passes *Neuhof* (inn; 3020 ft.) and reaches (5½ M.)
the culminating point of the **Wiedenereck** (3395 ft.; *Kurhaus Wiedenereck*, R. 1½-3, pens. 4½-6½ *M*), where the road from the Notschrei, mentioned at p. 423, ends. [A footpath leads hence by the *Krinne* to
(2-2½ hrs.) the Belchen.] The road descends hence in numerous windings (commanding a fine view of the Alps) by the village of *Wieden*
(2725 ft.; Tanne) to (4½ M.) *Utzenfeld* in the *Wiesen-Tal* (see below).

p. The Wiesen-Tal and the 'Strategic Line'.

The source of the *Wiese* is on the S. slope of the Seebuck, not far
from the Feldberg Hotel. The uppermost part of the valley is traversed
by the road leading from the Titisee to Todtnau (p. 422; from the Feldberg Hotel to Todtnau 3 hrs.; by the footpath, p. 422, 1½ hr.).

Todtnau (2130 ft.; *Ochs*, R. 1½-2½, B. ³/₄; pens. 5-6 *M*;
Hirsch, pens. 4-5 *M*; *Bär*, all very fair; *Sonne*), a thriving little
town in a picturesque situation, with 2370 inhab., is the highest
in the Wiesen-Tal (road to Kirchzarten, see p. 416). Pleasant excursion (turning to the right at the church) to the *Todtnauberg
Waterfall*, formed by the *Bergerbach* descending in several leaps,
altogether 300 ft. in height, and to *Todtnauberg* (3350 ft.; Stern;
Engel), whence we may return to Todtnau by *Aftersteg* (p. 417; a
circuit of 9 M.). Comp. Map, p. 418.

To *Notschrei, Schau-ins-Land,* and *Freiburg* (motor-omnibus), see
pp. 416, 417).

From Todtnau to Schopfheim, 15½ M., railway in 1¼ hr. —
The line descends the Wiesen-Tal, passing through picturesque rocky
gorges. 1 M. *Schlechtnau* (Lamm); 1½ M. *Geschwend* (Rössle),
at the mouth of the *Prägbach* (viâ Präg to Todtmoos and St. Blasien,
see pp. 433, 435). 2½ M. *Utzenfeld* (Eiche), where the Münster-Tal
road (see above) descends from the Wiedenereck.

4½ M. **Schönau.** — Hotels. *Sonne*, R. 1½-3, D. 2-3, pens.
5-8 *M*, with large garden; *Ochs*, R. 1½-2, pens. 4½-6 *M*, also very fair;
Adler; Krone; Vier Löwen.

Schönau (1780 ft.), a busy little town with 1900 inhab., prettily
situated. Pleasant walks on the *Buchenbrand* (S.) and *Galgenhalde*
(S.), and in the *Fuchswald* (1 M. to the S.E.). Ascent of the *Belchen*,
see p. 429.

The valley expands. The stream is employed in the irrigation
of the land and for the supply of numerous mills and factories. —
From (5¼ M.) *Wembach* (1700 ft.; Rabenfels Kurhaus) a carriage-
road leads to the W. through the *Böllen-Tal*, by *Neuenweg*, to
Badenweiler and Müllheim (see p. 429). — 7½ M. *Hepschingen*.

From (8¹/₂ M.) *Mambach* a route diverges to the E. through the *Angenbach-Tal* by *Rohmatt* to Todtmoos (p. 434; 8 M., 3 hrs. walking). — 10 M. *Atzenbach* (Adler).

11¹/₄ M. **Zell** (1405 ft.; *Löwe*, R. 1¹/₂-2¹/₂ *M*; *Krone*) 'im Wiesental', a prosperous manufacturing place with 3600 inhab. and important spinning and weaving works. Extensive views of the Black Forest and the Alps are commanded by the *Zeller Blauen* (3540 ft.), 1¹/₂ hr. to the N.; the *Gresgener Höhe* (2550 ft.), near the village of Gresgen, 1¹/₄ hr. to the W.; and still better from the belvedere on the *Hohe Möhr (3230 ft.), 1¹/₂ hr. to the S.E. (to the right 3 min. from the station, cross the meadow, and ascend in windings).

13 M. *Hausen* (1330 ft.; Adler), on the right bank of the stream, where Hebel (b. at Bâle 1760, d. 1826), the poet of the Black Forest, spent his early years. A *Bust of Hebel* was erected in front of the church in 1860. Opposite to it, to the right, is the house of the poet's parents (now an almshouse), indicated by an inscription. The valley here 'changes its creed', the inhabitants of the upper part of the valley being Roman Catholics, those below Hausen Protestants. — 14¹/₂ M. *Fahrnau*, has another station, on the 'strategic railway' (see below).

Among the beautiful pine-woods on the slope of the *Hohe Möhr* (see above; to the tower ³/₄ hr. more), 4¹/₂ M. to the N.E. of Fahrnau and 3 M. to the E. of Hausen, lies the health-resort of **Schweigmatt** (2560 ft.; *Kurhaus, pens. 6-8 *M*; several pensions at 3-3¹/₂ *M* per day), which commands a good view of the Wiesen-Tal, the Wehra-Tal, the Jura, and the Alps. Carriages should be ordered to meet the traveller at Schopfheim or Hausen.

15¹/₂ M. **Schopfheim** (1230 ft.; *Drei Könige*, R. 2-2¹/₂ *M*; *Pflug*, both very fair) is a small town (3800 inhab.), with two new churches and considerable manufactories of cotton, paper, and earthenware. The *Hebelshöhe*, with a temple and bronze bust of Hebel (see above), is ¹/₂ M. from the railway-station. At *Eichen*, 3 M. from Schopfheim, is the *Eichener See*, a periodic lake.

Schopfheim is the junction of the 'STRATEGIC RAILWAY' built in 1887-90, which avoids the Swiss territory near Klein-Basel, and in connection with part of the Wiesen-Tal railway and with the line from Immendingen to Waldshut (p. 439), now permits throughcommunication on German soil between S. Germany and Upper Alsace.

FROM BÂLE TO SÄCKINGEN, 26¹/₄ M., in 1¹/₂-2 hrs.; fares 2 *M* 80, 1 *M* 60, 70 pf.

Bâle (870 ft.), see p. 383. The line diverges to the left from the Schaffhausen and Constance railway and enters the Wiesen-Tal, to the N.E. On a hill to the right is the church of *St. Chrischona*, formerly a resort of pilgrims, now a Protestant missionary institution. — Beyond (3 M.) *Riehen* (Ochs), with its pleasant villas, the German frontier is crossed. From (4¹/₂ M.) *Stetten* (945 ft.: Adler) we may ascend in $^1/_2$ hr. to *Ober-Tüllingen* (restaurant near the church), situated on the *Tüllinger Höhe,* which commands a *View of Bâle, the Baden Oberland, and the mountains of Alsace and Switzerland.

$5^1/_2$ M. **Lörrach** (970 ft.; *Hirsch,* R. $1^3/_4$-$2^1/_2$ ℳ, very fair; *Krone,* R. $1^1/_2$-$2^1/_2$ ℳ; *Markgräfler Hof; Bahnhof-Hôtel*), the chief place in the valley, with 11,000 inhab. and a *Statue of Hebel* (p. 432), has shawl, cloth, chocolate, and other factories. The *Schützenhaus* (1085 ft.) on the Schädelberg commands a fine view. FROM LÖRRACH TO LEOPOLDSHÖHE, $3^3/_4$ M., railway in 16 minutes. This line forms the W. end of the 'Strategic Railway' (p. 432). Beyond (1 M.) *Stetten* (p. 432), the line passes under the *Tüllinger Höhe* (see above) by means of a tunnel 945 yds. in length. $2^1/_2$ M. *Weil,* with numerous villas, vineyards, and orchards. — $3^3/_4$ M. *Leopoldshöhe,* see p. 382.

Farther on, on a wooded eminence to the left, rises *Schloss Rötteln* (1355 ft.), one of the largest in the Duchy, commanding a fine view, once the residence of the Margraves of Hochberg, afterwards that of the Margraves of Baden. It was taken by Bernhard of Weimar in 1638, dismantled and blown up by the French in 1678, and restored in 1867. Fair inn at *Röttlerweiler,* at the foot of the hill, $1^1/_2$ M. from Lörrach; thence to the top $^1/_4$ hr.

7 M. *Haagen* (987 ft.; Krone), with cotton-mills; on the right, *Brombach,* with the ruins of a castle destroyed in the 17th century. 10 M. *Steinen;* 12 M. *Maulburg,* industrial villages. — $14^1/_2$ M. *Schopfheim,* the junction of the line to Zell and Todtnau (p. 432).

The strategic line now quits the Wiesen-Tal and, beyond (16 M.) *Fahrnau* ($^1/_2$ M. from the station of the same name mentioned at p. 432), pierces the *Dinkelberg,* the watershed between the Wiese and Wehra, by means of a tunnel 2 M. in length. — $17^1/_2$ M. *Hasel* (1320 ft.; inn). Near the village is the *Erdmanns-Höhle,* a stalactite cavern, interesting also to the zoologist on account of its white flies and blind spiders (electric light; the keeper of the inn Zur Erdmanns-Höhle has the key; 1 ℳ, members of a party 50 pf. each). The line descends the *Wehra-Tal* (see below). $19^1/_2$ M. **Wehr** (1205 ft.; **Wehrhof,* at the station, R. $1^1/_2$-3; D. $2^1/_2$, pens. from 5 ℳ; *Adler,* well spoken of; *Krone*), an industrial village with 3600 inhab., commanded by the ruined castle of *Werrach* (station for Todtmoos; carr., p. 434). — 21 M. *Oeflingen* (1085 ft.); $22^1/_2$ M. *Brennet* (Wehratal; Kreuz), about $^1/_2$ M. from the station of the same name mentioned at p. 437. — 26 M. *Säckingen* (p. 438).

q. Wehra-Tal and Albtal.

The traveller who desires to descend from the Feldberg to the Rhine by the ***Wehra-Tal** should turn to the E. at *Geschwend* (station of the Todtnau and Schopfheim railway, p. 431) and ascend the course of the *Prägbach.* For $2^1/_2$ M. we follow the road leading over the Wacht to St. Blasien (comp. p. 435), from which we diverge to the right beyond the *Hirsch Inn*, by a steep road ascending to the hamlet of *Präg* (2505 ft.). Then, leaving the road to *Herrenschwand* to the right and the *Hochkopf* ($^1/_2$ hr.; see below) to the left, we proceed to the ($1^1/_4$ hr.) *Weissbach-Sattel* (inn) and descend past *Weg* to ($3^3/_4$ hr.; 3 hrs. from Geschwend) Todtmoos.

Todtmoos. — HOTELS. *Hôtel Kurhaus*, pens. 7-11 *M*, with terraces, covered promenade, and the Luisen-Bad for nervous sufferers; *Hôtel Bellevue*, outside the village, on the Wehra road.; *Löwe*, recommended for passing visitors, R. $1^1/_2$-$2^1/_2$, pens. $4^1/_2$-$5^1/_2$ *M*; *Sonne; Zum Schwarzwald; Krone.* — *Pens. Batzenhaus, Pens. Schmidt* ($4^1/_2$-$5^1/_2$ *M*), etc. — *Visitors' Tax* from June 15th to Sept. 15th $1^1/_2$ *M* per week, before and after 1 *M*. — About $^1/_2$ M. to the W. is the **Sanatorium Wehrawald* (2825 ft.; Dr. Lips), specially adapted for sufferers from lung-diseases; R. $1^1/_2$-6, board, including medical attendance, $8^1/_2$ *M*.

The railway-station for Todtmoos is *Wehr* (p. 433); diligence thrice daily in 3 hrs., down in 2 hrs., also other vehicles (1 *M* 60 pf. per person); two-horse carr. 16 *M*.

Todtmoos (2695 ft.), a village with 1550 inhab. and a popular pilgrimage-church, is a resort both in winter and summer. It lies at the upper end of the *Wehra-Strasse*, which is here joined from the W. by a road from Mambach through the Wiesen-Tal (p. 433) and from the E. by a road from St. Blasien via Mutterslehen (p. 436). Another road to the S. goes to *Herrischried*, etc. (see p. 438). — The ascents of the *Blössling* (p. 435) and the *Hochkopf* (p. 423; $1^1/_4$ hr.), and other attractive excursions may be made from Todtmoos.

The next village in the Wehra-Tal is (3 M.) *Todtmoos-Au* (2270 ft.; Hirsch), commonly called the *Au*. The next portion of the Wehra-Tal is a magnificent rocky ravine, the most striking of all the valleys in the Black Forest. The bold pine-crowned cliffs enclosing the valley are clothed with luxuriant vegetation, broken here and there by imposing masses of barren rock. At the bottom of the valley the stream dashes impetuously over the blocks of granite which obstruct its narrow channel, frequently leaving but little space for the road. The most striking point is about halfway, at a bridge which carries the road, beyond a tunnel, to the left bank of the Wehra. On a cliff to the left at the outlet of the valley rises the ruin of *Bärenfels* (view-tower). — $10^1/_2$ M. *Wehr* (p. 433). About $1^1/_4$ M. before entering Wehr we may cross the Wehra at a saw-mill, and ascend through the wood to ($2^1/_4$ M.) Hasel.

Travellers approaching from the S. (as in the plan suggested at p. 384) quit the Wehra-Tal $7^1/_2$ M. from Wehr (see above) at Todtmoos-Au and follow the highroad diverging to the W. to the ($3/_4$ M.) 'Neusäge', where they turn to the right by the old road. This brings them in $3/_4$ hr. to *Gersbach* (2810 ft.; Krone; Pflug), where they rejoin the highroad. Beyond the village, where the road forks, they turn to the right towards 'Raitbach, Schopfheim' (p. 432). About $1/_2$ hr. later they descend to the right through wood on the E. branch of the Höhenweg (p. xvii; finger-post 'Kurhaus Schweigmatt', ca. 1 hr., p. 432) to the ($1/_4$ hr.) refuge-hut on the *Sandwürfe* (2720 ft.); then follow the finger-posts to ($1/_2$ hr.) the summit of the *Hohe Möhr* (p. 432) and descend in $1^1/_4$ hr. to *Zell* (p. 432).

ALBTAL. Another very interesting route is that from the Feldberg to St. Blasien, and through the Albtal to the railway. From the Feldberg down to (1^1/$_2$ hr.) Menzenschwand, see p. 423.

Menzenschwand consists of *Hinter-Menzenschwand* (2900 ft.; Hirsch) and *Vorder-Menzenschwand* (2805 ft.; *Kurhaus*, with good baths, R. from 2, D. 2, pens. 6-10 $\mathcal{M}$). It is well-sheltered and much frequented in summer. Ascent of the Spiesshorn 1^1/$_2$ hr., of the Feldberg 2^1/$_2$ hrs.

About 2 M. below Vorder-Menzenschwand the Albtal road joins that from the Wiesen-Tal (diligence, see below).

The latter crosses the Alb by the Bernau Bridge (2755 ft.) and ascends through the **Bernau.** 1^1/$_4$ M. *Bernau-Kaiserhaus* (3055 ft.); ^{3}/$_4$ M. *Bernau-Riggenbach* (Adler), 5^1/$_2$ M. from St. Blasien (diligence daily in 1^1/$_2$ hr.; also to Schönau viâ Geschwend, 10 M., in 3^1/$_4$ hrs.). At (1 M.) *Bernau-Dorf* (Löwe) a road diverges on the right for Bernau-Hof. The Wiesental road ascends to the W. to the mountain-saddle of the *Wacht* (3200 ft.; comp. p. 423), between the *Giesiboden* (4100 ft.; to the N.) and the *Blössling* (4300 ft.; 1^1/$_4$ hr. to the S.). It then descends the wooded valley of the *Prägbach* to *Geschwend* (p. 431; 7 M. from Bernau-Dorf).

Walkers may cross the bridge of the Bernau road and descend to the left on the right bank of the Alb. The road crosses to the right bank just short of St. Blasien (4^1/$_2$ M. from Vorder-Menzenschwand).

St. Blasien. — HOTELS. *Hôtel & Kurhaus St. Blasien,* first-class, with three dépendances and a well-fitted-up hydropathic (closed from Oct. to May 15th), R. 2-20, board 7 $\mathcal{M}$; *Hirsch*, R. 1^1/$_2$-4, D. 2^1/$_2$, pens. 6-10 $\mathcal{M}$; *Krone,* opposite the church, with garden, pens. 5-8 $\mathcal{M}$, very good. — The *St. Blasien Sanatorium* (Dr. Sander), close to the woods, well equipped with baths, shelters, and other conveniences, is frequented by consumptive patients (pens. 9-14 $\mathcal{M}$); adjoining is the *Sanatorium Luisenheim,* also with shelters, etc., but not for consumptive patients (pens. from 9 $\mathcal{M}$), these also open in winter. *Erholungsheim Friedrichshaus,* at the E. end, close to the woods, pens. 5-8^1/$_2$ $\mathcal{M}$. — *Pension Waldeck,* to the E., outside the village; *Pens. Kehrwieder* (pens. 6-8^1/$_2$ $\mathcal{M}$), at the E. end of the village; *Pens. Liebler,* at the W. end of the village, very fair. — *Municipal Hospital,* with S.E. veranda. — *Private Apartments.* — *Restaurant Felsenkeller.* — *Visitors' Tax,* 2 $\mathcal{M}$ per week. from Oct. to May 1 $\mathcal{M}$ per week.

MOTOR OMNIBUS viâ Schluchsee (35 min., 2^1/$_2$ $\mathcal{M}$) to Titisee (1 hr. 20 min., 4^1/$_2$ $\mathcal{M}$), see p. 423; viâ Höchenschwand (25 min., 1^1/$_2$ $\mathcal{M}$) to Waldshut (p. 438), 15^1/$_2$ M., 1^1/$_2$ hr. (4^1/$_2$ $\mathcal{M}$). Luggage, see p. 423. — DILIGENCE to Titisee, see p. 423; to Menzenschwand 1-2 times daily in 1^1/$_4$ hr.; to Albbruck (16 $\mathcal{M}$; p. 438) 1-2 times daily in 3-4 hrs.; to Waldshut once daily in 4-4^1/$_2$ hrs. — TWO-HORSE CARRIAGE to Albbruck 20, to Titisee or Waldshut 22 $\mathcal{M}$, to Brennet through the Wehra-Tal 25-30 $\mathcal{M}$; fee 10 per cent of the fare.

St. Blasien (2530 ft.), a village with 1800 inhab., was once celebrated for its wealthy and learned Benedictine abbey, which was founded in the middle of the 10th cent., attained the freedom of the Empire in 1611, and was secularized in 1805. It is now frequently resorted to both in summer and winter, owing to its healthy situation, which affords an agreeable mixture of mountain and forest air. The abbey-buildings are now used principally as a cotton-mill (600 hands). In the Kur-Garten is a fountain, throwing a jet 165 ft. high. The Gewerbehalle is a tasteful building.

The handsome *Church*, built by Ixnard in 1768-83, after the model of the Pantheon, was almost entirely burned down in 1874, but has been restored. The central dome is 165 ft. in diameter. The upper part of the rectangular choir, originally intended for the monks but now used for the general congregation, is decorated with Ionic columns and galleries.

The paths in the neighbourhood are distinguished by marks, for the purposes of the 'Terrain Cure'. The *Tusculum* waterfall (10 min.), the *Gross-Herzogin-Luisen-Ruhe* ($^3/_4$ hr.), the *Calvarienberg* (3465 ft.), the *Sandboden* (3270 ft.; view of Alps), on the slope of the *Bötzberg* (3970 ft.), and the *Lehenkopf* (3410 ft.; $1^1/_4$ hr.; view of Alps from tower) afford pleasant objects for walks.

To SCHLUCHSEE ($8^1/_2$ M.), see p. 423, by the Titisee road. The shorter route by Blasiwald is indicated by a finger-post 4 min. below the *Krone Inn*, to the left of the Albtal road.

To TODTMOOS (p. 434; 8 M., 3 hrs. on foot). The road leads from St. Blasien by *Mutterslehen* and past the cross on the *Hörnleberg* (3490 ft.), finally descending rather steeply.

On the plateau, $4^1/_2$ M. to the S.E. of St. Blasien, lies *Höchenschwand* (see below). This may be reached either by the highroad (motor-omnibus and diligence, see p. 435) viâ ($2^1/_2$ M.) *Häusern* (2920 ft.; Adler; Deutscher Kaiser), or by the footpath, which leads to the left into the wood (finger-post 'Windbergfälle-Häusern') at the 'Steinerne Kreuz', below St. Blasien. This path rejoins the road above Häusern, but another path ('Waldweg') soon diverges to the right ($1^1/_2$ hr. in all).

Höchenschwand (3315 ft.; *Hôtel Kurhaus*, burnt down in Nov. 1910; *Hirsch, Krone*, unpretending), one of the highest villages in Baden (300 inhab.), is now a popular health-resort. Pleasant walks in the adjacent pine-forest. From the *Belvedere* (key at the hotels), 10 min. from the village, a magnificent *View (finest at sunrise and sunset) is enjoyed in clear weather, comprising the Algäu and Vorarlberg Mts., and the entire chain of the Alps.

The road from Höchenschwand to ($10^1/_2$ M.) Waldshut (p. 438; motor-omnibus and diligence, p. 438), commanding fine views, leads viâ ($1^1/_2$ M.) *Frohnschwand*, ($2^3/_4$ M.) *Tiefenhäusern* (2935 ft.; Rössle), *Bannholz* ($4^3/_4$ M.), *Waldkirch* (6 M.; 2260 ft.; Storch), and ($8^1/_2$ M.) *Espach*. — Beyond Tiefenhäusern, at a lonely farm, a narrow road leads to the right into the Albtal, passing ($1/_2$ M.) *Brunnadern*, beyond which we turn to the right at a chapel and reach ($1/_2$ hr.) *Niedermühle* (see below).

FROM ST. BLASIEN TO ALBBRUCK, 16 M. (diligence, see p. 435). — The road descends the valley of the Alb, between wooded heights. $2^1/_4$ M. *Schmelze*, with abandoned iron-works. $2^1/_4$ M. *Kutterau* (Engel). — $1^1/_2$ M. *Immeneich* (2090 ft.; Adler), with a new chapel. About $1^1/_4$ M. farther on is the hamlet of *Niedermühle* (2005 ft.; Sonne), where the Höchenschwand road joins ours (see above).

From this point downwards the *Albtal becomes narrower and wilder. The road passes between perpendicular rocks, high above the impetuous brook, and affords occasional views of the grand and rocky ravine. The most imposing part of the route is beyond *Tiefen-stein* (Post, on the road, near the bridge), situated on the right bank, about 5 M. below Niedermühle, with a large silk-spinning mill. Beyond Tiefenstein five tunnels follow each other in rapid succession. About 2 M. farther on we pass the *Hôtel zum Hohen-fels* (1510 ft.; very fair), charmingly situated high above the river and surrounded with grounds (fine view of the Albtal and the Lower Alps). Near (2 M.) *Albbruck* (p. 438), on the Bâle-Waldshut Railway, the valley opens into that of the Rhine.

55. From Bâle to Constance. Falls of the Rhine.

89½ M. RAILWAY in 3-4½ hrs. (fares 11, 7, 4½ *M*). Views on the *right*.

Bâle, see p. 383. The line, from which the 'Strategic Railway' (p. 432) diverges to the left outside the town, traverses the fertile valley of the Rhine, here flowing in a channel of considerable depth. 3³/₄ M. *Grenzach*, where excellent 'Markgräfler' (p. xxiii) is produced. 5 M. *Wyhlen;* 7½ M. *Herthen.* The line now approaches the Rhine, which dashes impetuously over rocks and stones, forming the *Höllenhaken* and other rapids. Considerable numbers of salmon are caught here. The opposite Swiss bank is precipitous and wooded.

9½ M. **Badisch-Rheinfelden** (*Bellevue*, with salt-baths, R. 1½-3, pens. 4½-7 *M* ; *Oberrheinischer Hof; Railway Restaurant*, with garden, very fair), with important electric works and factories. — On the opposite bank lies the Swiss town of **Rheinfelden** (865 ft.; *Grand-Hôtel des Salines*, above the town, pens. 9-16 fr.; *Dietschy*, pens. 7-9 fr., with garden on the Rhine; *Schützen*, pens. 6½-9 fr.; *Schiff*, pens. 5-6¼ fr., all with salt-baths), which was in ancient times strongly fortified and repeatedly besieged.

To the right of (12 M.) *Beuggen* is a former lodge of the Teutonic Order, used since 1817 as a normal seminary and reformatory. — 15 M. *Nieder-Schwörstadt;* 17 M. *Brennet* (p. 433).

20 M. **Säckingen.** — HOTELS.. *Schützen*, R. 1½-2, D. 2 *M* ; *Gold-ener Knopf*, with a view-terrace on the Rhine. — *Schwarzer Walfisch*, Munich beer; *Löwenbräu*, at the station. — *Swimming Bath* in the Rhine.

Säckingen (960 ft.) is an important silk-manufacturing and timber-trading town with 4050 inhabitants. The old *Abbey Church*, with its two towers, rebuilt in the 18th cent., contains the remains of St. Fridolin, the apostle of this district (6th cent.). Over the portal of the .church are statues of the saint and of Count Urso of Glarus, whom he had restored to life. To the left, on the exterior of the choir, is the tombstone of Werner Kirchofer (d. 1690) and his wife Maria Ursula of Schönauw (d. 1691), which formerly stood behind the château-garden and suggested the composition of

Scheffel's 'Trompeter von Säckingen'. The abbey, subsequently a nunnery, was secularized in 1801. In the market-place is a *Monument to Scheffel*, by Menges. The château of *Schönau* on the Rhine is private property. To the right of the entrance to the covered bridge (fine view of the castle) is the house in which Scheffel lived.

Excursion to the (1½ M.) *Bergsee* or *Scheffelsee* (1250 ft.), to the N. of the station of Säckingen, on thé road to Herrischried (see below). — Line to *Schopfheim* and *Lörrach*, see p. 432.

To the left of the railway stands the church of *Ober-Säckingen*. — 23½ M. *Murg* (1025 ft.; Zum Hirsch), situated at the mouth of the Murg, in the picturesque valley of which a road ascends to (6¼ M.) *Hottingen* (Sonne); on a hill to the left rises the *Harpolinger Schloss*. Beyond Hottingen the road leads to (3 M.) *Herrischried* and (7½ M. farther) *Todtmoos* (p. 434).

Opposite (25½ M.) *Klein-Laufenburg* (Post, unpretending but very fair; Stern) is the Swiss town of **Laufenburg** (*Rheinsoolbad*, with a terrace on the river, pens. 5-7 fr.; *Adler;* beer at the *Pfau*, with view), picturesquely placed on the left bank, with its ancient castle, below which the Rhine dashes impetuously over its narrow and rocky bed. These rapids (50,000 horse-power) are now utilized for industrial purposes.

The eighth Lord Montagu, the last of his family, perished here in 1793, and by a singular coincidence his ancestral mansion of Cowdray House in Sussex was burned down almost on the same day, and has never been rebuilt. Below the cataract, salmon are caught in considerable numbers. Down to 1803 Klein-Laufenburg and Gross-Laufenburg formed a single Austrian town, but the former now belongs to Baden, the latter to Switzerland. *View of Gross-Laufenburg from the Schlossberg.

The line passes through a tunnel, and beyond (28½ M.) *Albert-Hauenstein* crosses a lofty viaduct. — 30 M. **Albbruck** (1060 ft.; *Zum Albtal*, R. 1½-2½, D. 1¾-2½ ℳ, very fair), with a large pulp-mill, at the mouth of the *Albtal* (p. 436). — 31½ M. *Dogern*.

35 M. **Waldshut.** — HOTELS. *Bahnhofs-Hôtel*, R. 2-3, D. 2, pens. 5-7 ℳ; *Blume*, at the entrance to the town; *Rebstock*, Haupt-Str. 83, with terrace on the Rhine, R. 1¼-2 ℳ; *Rheinischer Hof*. — *Löwenbrauerei* at the railway-station. — DILIGENCE to St. Blasien, see p. 435. In summer a MOTOR DILIGENCE plies once or twice daily viâ Höchenschwand (1 hr.; 3½ ℳ) to St. Blasien (1 hr. 20 min.; 4½ ℳ; luggage, see p. 423); seats should be ordered in advance at the Bahnhofs-Hôtel.

Waldshut, a quaint old town with 3800 inhab. and many industries, lies at a considerable height above the right bank of the river. The railway to Winterthur and Zürich diverges to the right. Our railway skirts the town on the side next the hill.

FROM WALDSHUT TO IMMENDINGEN, 46 M., railway (a section of the strategic line mentioned in p. 432) in 2¾-3¾ hrs. — 3 M. *Tiengen* (p. 439); 6 M. *Oberlauchringen*, see p. 439. — Diverging to the left from the Rhine valley, the line ascends. 8 M. *Horheim;* 10½ M. *Ofteringen;* 12 M. *Unteregingen;* 14½ M. *Eberfingen.* — 17 M. **Stühlingen** (1490 ft.; *Hirsch-Post*, very fair; *Adler*), an old town, commanded by the castle of *Hohenlupfen* (extensive view). A tramway runs to the E., viâ (1¼ M.) *Schleitheim* (the Roman Juliomagus, where a number of Roman and

Alemannian antiquities have been discovered), *Beringen*, and *Neuhausen* (see below), to (12 M.) *Schaffhausen* (p. 440). — 18¹/₂ M. *Weizen* (diligence to Bonndorf, p. 419). The valley contracts. The line passes under the ruin of *Blumegg* by a spiral tunnel 1300 yds. in length, and crosses the Wutach by a lofty bridge. 23 M. *Grimmelshofen*. Beyond a short tunnel, the line enters the spiral *Stockhalden Tunnel*, 1860 yds. in length, by which it ascends in corkscrew fashion. From the station of (26¹/₂ M.) *Fützen* (1930 ft.) we enjoy an interesting survey of the line just traversed. Several viaducts are passed, high above the Wutach valley. 31 M. *Epfenhofen*. After passing some more viaducts and threading a tunnel, the line reaches its culminating point at (35 M.) *Zollhaus-Blumberg* (2300 ft.) and descends past *Riedöschingen*, *Leipferdingen*, *Aulfingen*, *Kirchen-Hausen*, and *Hintschingen* to (46 M.) *Immendingen* (p. 407).

Quitting Waldshut, the train passes through a tunnel, and skirts the hills to the left. The *Schlücht* is crossed.

38 M. **Tiengen** (1140 ft.; *Ochs*, R. 1¹/₂-2, pens. 5-7 *M*; *Krone*), an industrial town with 2400 inhabitants.

A road from Tiengen up the *Schlücht-Tal* (diligence to Schluchsee viâ Birkendorf once daily in 5³/₄ hrs.) offers a very interesting walk for part of the way. At (2 M.) the *Bruckhaus Inn* (1310 ft.; pens. 4-6 *M*; baths) a covered bridge crosses the ravine; ¹/₂ M. farther on a path descends to the left to the *Haselbach Waterfall*, ¹/₄ M. beyond which is the *Guttenburg* saw-mill, at the foot of a rock (1460 ft.) crowned with a small ruined castle. About 2¹/₄ M. farther on is the **Witznauer Mühle** (1430 ft.; inn, fair), at the junction of the Schlücht-Tal and *Schwarza-Tal*. From this point the Schlücht-Tal vies in picturesqueness with the valleys of the Wehra and Alb. On each side are lofty and partly-wooded rocks. At one place the stream occupies the whole width of the valley, so that after its junction with the *Mettma* a passage for the new road had to be hewn through the rocks. — Farther on the valley again expands. 9¹/₂ M. (from Tiengen) *Uehlingen* (2120 ft.; Posthorn, fair); 12 M. *Birkendorf* (2580 ft.; Post; Hirsch); 15 M. *Grafenhausen* (2940 ft.; Hirsch); 17 M. *Rothaus* (3190 ft.; p. 424). — 18¹/₂ M. *Schluchsee,* see p. 424.

40¹/₄ M. *Oberlauchringen*, on the *Wutach* (see p. 438). We cross the Wutach. The ruined castle of *Küssenberg* stands on a wooded hill to the right. 44 M. *Griessen*. Beyond (47 M.) *Erzingen* (customs examination) the train enters Swiss territory. 49 M. *Wilchingen-Hallau;* 50¹/₂ M. *Neunkirch;* 54¹/₂ M. *Beringen.*

57 M. **Neuhausen.** Besides the *'Baden Station'*, at which we arrive, there is a *'Swiss Station'* of the same name on the Swiss railway, to the E. — ELECTRIC RAILWAY to Schaffhausen, p. 440.

HOTELS. *Schweizerhof,* R. 4-9, B. 1¹/₂, D. 5-7, pens. 10-18 fr., with large garden and beautiful views of the falls and the Alps; *Bellevue,* R. from 3, pens. from 8, D. 4 fr., with similar view. — In the village of Neuhausen: *Hôtel-Pension Germania,* R. 3-4, B. 1¹/₄, D. 2¹/₂-3, pens. 3-10 fr.; *Hôtel Oberberg; Hôt. Badischer Bahnhof; Hôtel Rheinfall,* R. 2-3 fr.; *Hôt. Schweizer Bahnhof,* 3 min. from the Swiss station, R. 2-3 fr. — *English Church* in the 'Schweizerhof' grounds (services in summer). — About 1¹/₂-2 hrs. are sufficient for a visit to the falls. In August the falls are illuminated every evening with electric light, for which a charge of ³/₄-1 fr. is made in each bill.

Neuhausen (1443 ft.) is the station for the ****Falls of the Rhine,** one of the finest cascades in Europe, locally called the Laufen', which descend in three leaps over a ledge of rock of unequal height. The breadth of the river above the falls is about

126 yds. The height of the unbroken fall is 62 ft. near the left bank and 49 ft. by the right. If the rapids above and below are taken into consideration, the whole fall is nearly 100 ft. high. The river is largest in June and July, owing to the melting of the snow.

From the Baden Station we follow the road to the left, and after a few paces descend by a path to the right to the village of *Neuhausen.* At the Hôtel Rheinfall we descend to the right by a finger-post, and after 100 paces take the shady Brücken-Weg to the left, passing the *Waggon Factory,* to the (1/4 hr.) *Rheinfall-Brücke,* which carries the Winterthur railway over the Rhine to the left bank. On the left bank a path ascends in 5 min. to the *Schloss Laufen* (inn), picturesquely situated on a wooded rock above the falls; the garden (adm. 1 fr.) affords the best points of view: *viz.* the *Pavilion,* the *Känzeli,* and in particular the *Fischez,* a gallery projecting almost into the roaring cataract. From the lower entrance to the Schloss-Garten we ferry across (50 c. each) to the *Schlösschen Wörth* (inn), on an island commanding another fine view of the falls. A boat to the central rock in the falls, which may be ascended without danger, costs 3 fr. for 1 or 2 persons. — From the Schlösschen Wörth we may either return to the station direct, or follow the path ascending on the right bank (benches at intervals), passing an *Aluminium Factory* (left), to the road, when we descend slightly to the right to a stone parapet, affording another good survey of the falls. Comp. *Baedeker's Switzerland.*

59 M. Schaffhausen. — Hotels. *Hôtel Müller* (Pl. a; A, 1), opposite the station, R. 2¹/₂-3¹/₂, B. 1¹/₄, D. 3¹/₂ fr.; **Hôtel National* (Pl. b; A, 1), R. 2-3¹/₂, B. 1¹/₄, D. 2¹/₂-3 fr., very fair; **Riese* (Pl. c; A, 1), R. 2-3, B. 1¹/₄, D. 3 fr.; *Rheinischer Hof* (Pl. d; A, 1), R. 2-3, B. 1 fr., well spoken of; *Schwan* (Pl. f; B, 2), near the station, R. 2-3, D. 2¹/₂ fr., very fair; *Bahnhof-Hôtel* (Pl. e; B, 1); *Tanne* (Pl. g; A, 2); *Löwe* (Pl. h; B, 1). — *Railway Restaurant,* D. 2¹/₂ fr. — *River Baths* above the town, open for men 6-1 and 5-8.

Electric Railway from the Bahnhof-Platz every 10 min. to Neuhausen (p. 339) in 13 min. (20 c.); continuation to Stühlingen, see pp. 439, 438. *Steamboat* to Constance (p. 442) in 4 hrs. 1-3 times daily.

Schaffhausen (1320 ft.; pop. 17,000), a free imperial town down to 1501 and now capital of the Swiss canton of Schaffhausen, retains many of its ancient characteristics. It is most picturesque when seen from the opposite village of *Feuerthalen,* on the left bank of the Rhine, or from *Villa Charlottenfels* (tramway), 25 min. to the W., on a hill on the right bank. Herr Moser (d. 1874), builder of the latter, originated the great *Water Works* in the Rhine for the supply of the factories in the town. The early-Romanesque *Münster,* a basilica supported by columns, was built in 1052-1101, and has been restored. *Schloss Munot,* which commands the town, dates from 1564-82 (view from the platform, 50 c.). The *Fäsenstaub Promenade* affords a beautiful view of the Rhine and Alps.

61¹/₂ M. *Herblingen;* 20 min. above it is the Schloss of the

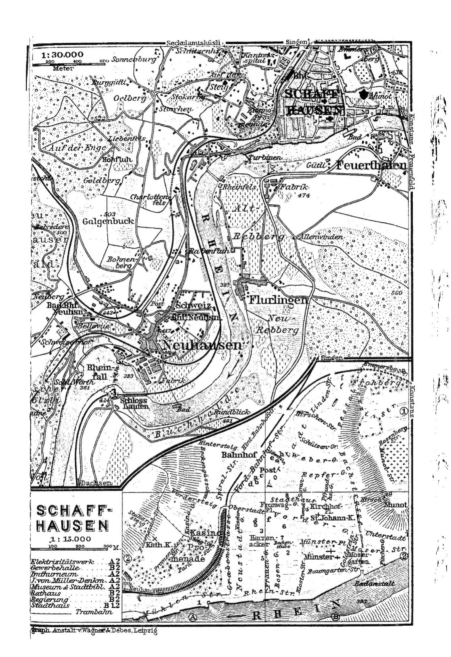

same name (1970 ft.; view). 64 M. *Thaingen.* The train now re-
enters Baden. 67 M. *Gottmadingen.*

71 M. Singen. — HOTELS. *Schweizerhof,* with lift, R. 1³/₄-3, D.
1¹/₂-3, pens. 5-8 *ℳ; Adler,* R. 1¹/₂-2¹/₂, D. 2 *ℳ,* these two at the rail.
station; *Krone,* ¹/₂ M. from the rail. station, an old-established house,
R. 1¹/₂, D. 2 *ℳ; Ekkehard,* R. 1¹/₄-1¹/₂ *ℳ.* — At the foot of the Hohentwiel is a *'Festspielhalle'* (by Bauder, 1906) for national dramatic performances. — *Luggage* is examined by the customs-officers here.

Singen (1405 ft.), a small town of 5700 inhab., on the Ache, the
junction of the Black Forest Railway (p. 408) and of the Upper
Neckar line (see *Baedeker's Southern Germany*), is the station for a
visit to the ruin of Hohentwiel, 3³/₄ M. distant. About ¹/₂ M. beyond
the Krone we turn to the right from the Gottmadingen road; 1 M.
farther on lies the Inn zum Hohentwiel, whence we reach the lower
fortification in 15-18 min. (adm. 20 pf.).

The fortress of *Hohentwiel* (2255 ft.), a small 'enclave' of
Wurtemberg, was the seat of Alemannian dukes in the 9th and
10th cent., came into the possession of the Hohenstaufens in the
11th cent., and has belonged to Wurtemberg since 1538. It was
successfully defended during the Thirty Years' War by the Wurtemberg commandant Widerhold. In 1800 it was destroyed by the
French. The ruins command a superb view of the Alps.

75 M. *Rickelshausen.* — 77 M. **Radolfzell** (1305 ft.; *Schiff,
Krone, Sonne*), an ancient town of 5200 inhab., with walls and
gates, is situated on the *Untersee.* The Gothic church, dating from
1436, contains the tomb of St. Radolf and a fine reliquary (left side-
altar), dating substantially from the 9th century. At the *Villa
Seehalde* is a monument to its former owner, the poet Victor von
Scheffel (d. 1886). Radolfzell is the junction of the line to Mengen
(Sigmaringen) and Ulm (see *Baedeker's Southern Germany*).

79 M. *Markelfingen;* 82¹/₂ M. *Allensbach;* 84 M. *Hegne.* —
85¹/₂ M. *Reichenau,* the station for the island of that name, which
is connected with the mainland by a long causeway (1 M.) and has
for some time been visible to the right.

The island of **Reichenau,** belonging to Baden, is 3 M. long and
1 M. wide. It was formerly the seat of a famous *Benedictine Abbey,*
founded in 724 and suppressed in 1799. It may be visited by the causeway (see above), by row-boat from Hegne or Allensbach (¹/₄ hr.), or by
the Constance and Schaffhausen steamers (landing-place on the S. bank).
— Approaching from the causeway, we pass the ruined tower of *Schöpfeln,*
the abbot's residence, and reach *Oberzell,* a hamlet with a Romanesque
church of the 9-10th cent., containing the oldest extant church-frescoes
in Germany (10-11th cent.). — In the middle of the island lies its largest
village (1000 inhab.), *Mittelzell* or *Münster* (Mohr; Bär), the church of
which, consecrated in 806 and dating in its present form from the 10-
12th cent. (choir, late-Gothic, 1447-1550), was the church of the above-
mentioned abbey. Charles the Fat, great-grandson of Charlemagne, who
was dethroned in 887, was interred in this church. The sacristy contains
some fine reliquaries. A fine view is obtained from the W. tower of
the *Königsegg,* a 16th cent. château, recently restored. — The church of
Unterzell, at the N.W. end of the island, is another columned basilica

of the 11-12th centuries. In the main apse are some frescoes of the 11th century. — Fine view from the belvedere on the *Friedrichshöhe* (key kept at the Mohr inn at Mittelzell).

The train passes the large arsenal of *Petershausen* and crosses the Rhine by an iron bridge adorned with statues.

89¹/₂ M. **Constance.** — HOTELS. *Insel-Hôtel* (Pl. a; C, 3), of the highest class, in the old Dominican monastery (modern frescoes in the Romanesque cloisters; church converted into the dining-room) superbly situated close to the lake, with restaurant (in the refectory) and garden, R. 3-8, B. 1¹/₂, D. 4¹/₂, S. 3¹/₂, pens. 10-16 ℳ, closed from Oct. 15th to April 15th. — *See-Hôtel* (Pl. b; D, 3), also situated on the edge of the lake, first-class, with terrace and restaurant, R. 2¹/₂-5, B. 1¹/₄, D. 3-4, pens. 8-12 ℳ, open throughout the year. — *Halm* (Pl. c; C, 5); *Schönebeck* (Pl. d; C, 5), R. 2¹/₂-5, B. 1, D. 3 ℳ, both these opposite the railway station; *Hecht* (Pl. e; C, 4), to the N. of the station, R. 2¹/₄-3¹/₂, B. 1, D. 3, pens. 7-8¹/₂ ℳ, with wine-room, good cuisine. — *Krone* (Pl. f; C, 5), R. 2-4, B. 1 ℳ; *Schnetzer* (Pl. g; C, 5), R. 2-3, B. 1 ℳ, these two in the market-place, with restaurants, very fair. — *Badischer Hof* (Pl. h; B, 5), Husen-Str. 13, R. 1³/₄-2, D. 2 ℳ; *Barbarossa* (Pl. i; B, 4), Oberer Markt, with restaurant, R. 2-3 ℳ, plain but good; *Schlüssel* (Pl. l; C, 5), Sigismund-Str. 14; *Bayrischer Hof* (Pl. m; B, 5), Rosgarten-Str. 30, R. 1³/₄-2¹/₂ ℳ; *Hohes Haus* (Pl. n; C, 4), Zollern-Str. 29, R. 1¹/₄-2 ℳ; *Hôtel-Restaurant Ehren*, Wessenberg-Str. 29; *Falke* (Pl. k; B, 6), Kreuzlinger-Str. 13, with beer-garden; *Katholisches Vereinshaus St. Johann* (Pl. o; C, 3), R. 1¹/₂-2, pens. 4-5 ℳ.

RESTAURANTS, besides those at the hotels; *Victoria*, opposite the railway-station; *Café Maximilian*, Bahnhof-Str. 4; *Café Dauner*, Husen-Str. 3 (Pl. B, 5).

MOTOR BOATS ply every 10 min., to the N., to the See-Hôtel and the Pulver-Turm (Pl. C, 3; round trip, 20 min., 20 pf.), and every ¹/₂ hr., to the S., to Bottighofen and the Waldhaus Jakob (round trip, 1 hr., 50 pf.). — SMALL BOATS (Pl. C, D, 4), per hr. for 1-2 pers. 40, each additional pers. 20 pf., with a sail 80 & 20 pf. (1 ℳ additional to the boatman). — *Bathing Establishment* (Pl. D, 5, 6), in the lake (bath with costume and towels 40 pf., ferry 10 pf.).

Constance (1335 ft.), a town of Baden with 24,800 inhab. and manufactures of iron and textiles, is situated at the N.W. extremity of the *Lake of Constance*, or *Bodensee*, at the point where the Rhine emerges from it.

Constance, which ascribes its origin to Constantius Chlorus (3rd cent.), became an episcopal see in the 6th cent. and was a free town until 1548, when it was made subject to Au⁊· ¹a. Since 1809 it has belonged to Baden. After the Reformation the bishops resided at Meersburg, and in 1827 the bishopric was merged in the archbishopric of Freiburg. The Council of Constance, held in 1414-18 at the instance of the Emp. Sigismund, suppressed the schism of the anti-popes John XXIII., Gregory XII., and Benedict XIII., and condemned the teaching of John Huss (p. 443).

The CATHEDRAL or MINSTER (Pl. C, 4), founded in 1054, was rebuilt in its present form in 1435 and 1680. Gothic tower (249 ft. high) erected in 1850-57; the spire is of light grey sandstone; on either side is a platform commanding a charming view (adm. 20 pf.).

On the *Doors* of the principal portal are *Bas-Reliefs*, in 20 compartments, representing scenes from the life of Christ, carved in oak in 1470. The organ-loft, richly ornamented in the Renaissance style, was perhaps designed by P. Flötner in 1518. In the nave, the arches of which are supported by 16 monolithic pillars (28 ft. high, 3 ft. thick), sixteen

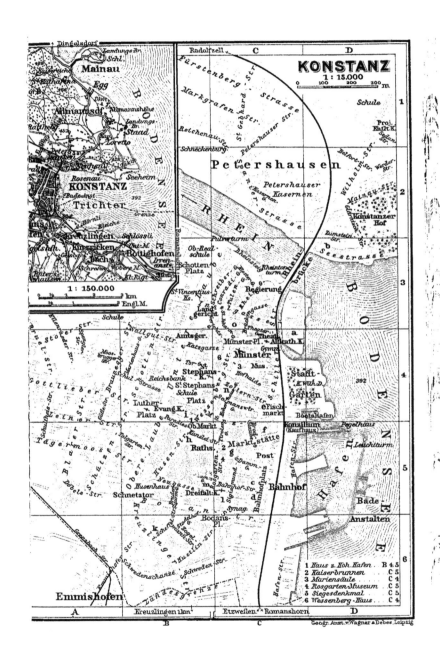

KONSTANZ

1 : 15.000

0   100   200   300 m

Petershausen

RHEIN

Konstanzer Hof

Münster

Stadt-Garten

Bahnhof

Bade-Anstalten

B O D E N S E E

Emmishofen

1 : 150.000

1   Haus z. Hoh. Hafen . B 4.5
2   Kaiserbrunnen . . . . C 5
3   Mariensäule . . . . . C 5
4   Rosgarten-Museum . . C 4
5   Siegesdenkmal . . . . C 5
6   Wessenberg-Haus . . . C 4

Geogr. Anst. v. Wagner & Debes, Leipzig.

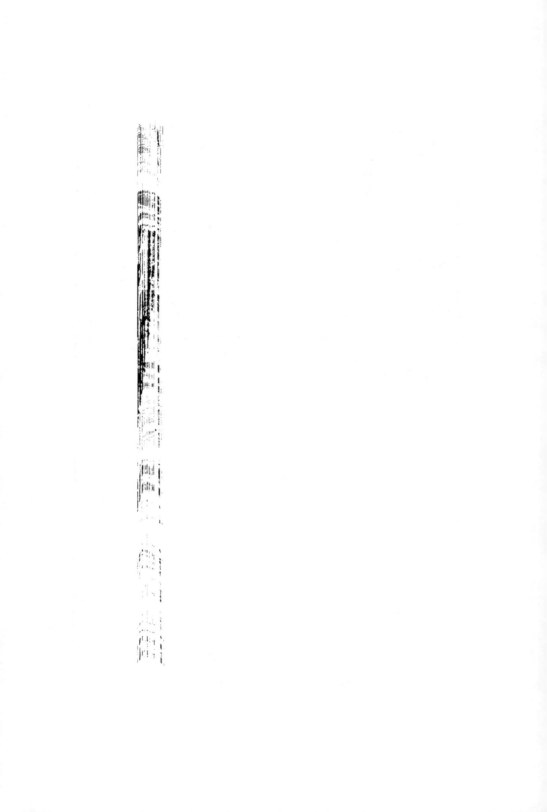

paces from the principal entrance, is a large stone slab with a white spot, on which Huss is said to have stood when the Council of 6th July, 1415, sentenced him to be burnt at the stake. The pulpit dates from the 17th century. In the choir is the tomb of Robert Hallam, Bishop of Salisbury (d. 1417). The late-Gothic choir-stalls are by the same sculptor as the reliefs on the doors. In the N. chapel, adjoining the choir, is a *Death of the Virgin*, with lifesize stone figures (1460). Adjacent is an elegant spiral staircase ('Der Schneck', 1438?). In the last chapel of the N. aisle is a large winged altar-piece of the Swabian School (1524). — The *Treasury* (custodian ½-1 ℳ) contains an illuminated missal (1496). — On the E. side is a CRYPT, containing the *Chapel of the Holy Sepulchre*, dating from the 13th century. This chapel contains a silver statuette presented by Queen Victoria, of *Bishop Conrad*, who was a member of the Guelph family. On the exterior of the N. side stand two aisles of the elaborate late-Gothic *Cloisters*. Adjacent are the late-Gothic *Chapel of St. Maurice* and the *Chapter House* (1480).

The *Wessenberg Haus* (Pl. 6; C, 4), now the property of the town, contains the public library and the collections of J. H. von Wessenberg (d. 1860), who for many years was the vicar-general of the diocese (open free on Wed. & Sat. 2-5 and on Sun. 11-1 & 2-4; on other days, 9-12, 50 pf.).

The *Church of St. Stephen* (Pl. B, C, 4), a late-Gothic building begun in 1428, with a slender tower, contains stalls, tabernacle, and reliefs by H. Morink (ca. 1594; in the choir).

The Wessenberg-Str. leads hence to the S. to the *Obere Markt* (Pl. B, 5), at the corner of which stands the house *'Zum Hohen Hafen'* (Pl. 1), where Frederick VI., Burgrave of Nuremberg, was created Elector of Brandenburg by Emp. Sigismund, 18th April, 1417. It is adorned with frescoes by Häberlin (1906). Adjacent to it is the *Hôtel Barbarossa* (Pl. i), in which Emp. Frederick I. concluded peace with the Lombard towns in 1183·

The STADT-KANZLEI, or *Town Hall* (Pl. B, 5), rebuilt in the Renaissance style in 1592, was decorated in 1864 on the exterior with frescoes by F. Wagner illustrative of the history of Constance. It contains the *Municipal Archives*, comprising 2800 documents (from the Reformation period to 1524). Fine inner court. In the lobby of the second floor are five frescoes by Häberlin (1898), also relating to the town's history.

In the ROSGARTEN (Pl. 4; C, 5), once the guild-house of the butchers, is the *Rosgarten Museum*, a good collection of local antiquities (from lake-dwellings, sculptures by H. Morink, etc.) and of objects of natural history (adm. 50 pf.; free on Wed., 2-5, & Sun., 10.30-12). — In the Markt-Stätte (Pl. C, 5) stand a *War Monument* by Baur (Pl. 5) and the *Kaiser-Brunnen* (Pl. 2; 1897).

The KAUFHAUS, or *Merchants' Hall* (Konzilium; Pl. C, 4, 5), by the lake, erected in 1388, contains the great *Council Chamber*, supported by ten massive oaken pillars, where the conclave of cardinals met at the time of the Great Council (1414-18). The hall is decorated with frescoes by *Pecht* and *Schwörer* (adm. 20 pf.).

The ancient *Dominican Monastery* (Pl. a; C, 3, 4), in which Huss was confined in 1414-15, on an island in the lake, is now the Insel-Hôtel (see p. 442). — Pleasant promenade in the *Stadt-Garten* on the lake (Pl. C, D, 4; band every evening in summer).

The house in which Huss was arrested, Husen-Str. 64, near the Schnetz-Tor (Pl. B, 5), bears a memorial tablet with his effigy, put up in 1878. Adjoining it is an old relief, dated 1415, with satirical verses. Behind it is the 'Obere Laube' (Pl. B, 5), containing a bronze tablet with an inscription which marks the spot where Jerome of Prague was imprisoned in 1415-16.

In the *Brühl*, reached viâ the Tägermoos-Str. (Pl. A, 5), is the spot where Huss and Jerome suffered martyrdom, indicated by a huge mass of rock with inscriptions ('Husenstein').

At **Kreuzlingen** (*Löwe; Schweizerhof,* very fair; *Bellevue,* for nervous patients), ¼ hr. from the S. gate, on Swiss territory, is an old Augustine abbey, now a normal school. The church contains a curious piece of wood-carving, with about 1000 small figures, executed in the 18th century.

A fine view of the lake and of the Vorarlberg and Appenzell Alps is obtained from the (1 hr.) *Allmannshöhe (1512 ft.), with belvedere, 5 min. above the village of *Allmannsdorf,* on the road to the Mainau. — Among other pleasant objects for a walk may be mentioned the *Loretto-Kapelle* (½ hr.); the *Jacob* (Hôt.-Pens. Waldhaus, pens. 5-6 ℳ; ½ hr.); *Tabor,* with a belvedere (1 hr.); and the *Kleine Rigi,* above Münsterlingen (1¼ hr.).

The excursion to the island of Mainau in the *Ueberlinger See,* or N.W. arm of the Lake of Constance, is attractive. We may reach it either by steamboat viâ *Meersburg* (on the N. bank of the lake) in ½-1 hr. or by rowing-boat in 1 hr. (5 ℳ and gratuity). Pedestrians may either follow the road (carr. 5-6, with two horses 10 ℳ), a walk of 1½ hr., or take the shorter footpaths (1 hr.). We proceed along the Wilhelm-Str. (Pl. D, 2) to (½ M.) a guide-post where we diverge to the right and pass the *Military Hospital;* about ½ M. farther on we reach another guide-post, whence we may either go straight on skirting the wood and soon joining the road, or take the preferable route to the left ('Privatweg Lützelstätten'), through the wood and past the St. Katharina tavern. — Comp. the small map on the plan of Constance.

The island of **Mainau** was from 1272 to 1809 the seat of a lodge of the Teutonic Order. Since 1853 it has been the property of the Grand-Duke of Baden, who refurnished the *Château* (1746), on the S. side of which is still visible the cross of the Teutonic Order (adm. to the interior in the absence of the family only). The island is covered with charming pleasure-grounds (open to the public) also laid out by the Grand-Duke, in which favourite spots are marked with inscriptions.

56. From Mayence to Ludwigshafen
(Mannheim).

42 M. RAILWAY in $1^1/_4$-$2^1/_4$ hrs.; fares 5 $\mathcal{M}$ 70, 3 $\mathcal{M}$ 80, 2 $\mathcal{M}$ 45 pf. *Preussisch-Hessische Staatsbahn* as far as *Worms* (in $^3/_4$-$1^1/_2$ hr.; fares 3 $\mathcal{M}$ 70, 2 $\mathcal{M}$ 30, 1 $\mathcal{M}$ 45 pf.; express fares 4 $\mathcal{M}$ 20, 2 $\mathcal{M}$ 55, 1 $\mathcal{M}$ 70 pf.) and beyond it the *Pfälzische Bahn*.

Mayence, see p. 265. — The train starts from the Central Station, traverses the tunnel under the citadel to the *South Station*, near the Neutor, and passes under the Darmstadt line (p. 313). — $4^1/_2$ M. *Laubenheim;* 6 M. *Bodenheim*, junction of a branch-line viâ Undenheim (see below) and Gau-Odernheim (p. 447) to ($19^1/_2$ M.) *Alzey* (p. 455; $1^1/_2$ hr.); $8^1/_2$ M. *Nackenheim*. These three wine-producing villages lie on the vine-clad hills to the right, not far from the Rhine.

11 M. **Nierstein** *(Rhein-Hôtel*, with restaurant, R. from $1^1/_2$ $\mathcal{M}$; *Krone)*, a town with 4450 inhab., is noted for its careful vine-culture. 'Niersteiner' is one of the best-known and most wholesome of Rhenish wines; it is marked by a mildly acid flavour with considerable aroma. Much of the wine of Rhenish Hesse has been sold under this name. The private chapel of the Von Herding family contains six large frescoes by Götzenberger. On the hill to the right rises an old watch-tower. Branch-line to (6 M.) *Undenheim* (see above).

$12^1/_2$ M. **Oppenheim** *(Ritter*, at the station, very fair), an industrial town with 3700 inhab., picturesquely situated on a hill rising above the river, is commanded by the church of St. Catharina and the ruined castle of Landskron. The town is mentioned in the Roman itineraries as *Bauconica;* it afterwards became a city of the empire and enjoyed the patronage of the Franconian emperors, particularly Henry IV.; and at a still later period it was an important member of the league of the Rhenish towns. In 1689 the town was destroyed by the French.

On leaving the station we descend the avenue in a straight

ilometer. 1:500.000. 0 1 2 3 4 5 Engl. Miles

MAINZ

direction, then turn slightly to the left, pass the lofty round clock-tower, and go through an archway below one of the streets. We then ascend, skirting the mediæval walls, to the (10-12 min.) ruins of the once famous imperial fortress of *Landskron*, which was burned down by the French in 1689. It was erected in the reign of the Emp. Lothaire, and restored by Emp. Rupert, who died here in 1410. It commands a magnificent view of Oppenheim and the valley of the Rhine. — We next descend to the —

Katharinen-Kirche, a superb Gothic edifice, erected in 1262-1317 on the site of an older church, partly destroyed in 1689, and thoroughly restored in 1878-89 from the designs of the late architect Schmidt of Vienna. The E. part of the church forms a cruciform edifice with a tower over the crossing and two W. towers. The W. choir (abbey-church), which was consecrated in 1439, is now un-used and shut off by a screen. The windows contain beautiful tra-cery; most of the stained glass is modern. There are numerous mon-uments of the Dalberg, Sickingen, and other families. The sacristan lives on an upper floor to the left of the steps at the principal S. entrance (40 pf.). To the N., in the old churchyard, is *St. Michael's Chapel* (charnel-house).

In front of the S. portal of the church is the market-place, with a *War Monument for 1870-71;* the monument incorporates a column of syenite with an inscription, dug up on the Landskron, and probably found in the Roman quarry on the Felsberg (p. 323).

$17^1/_2$ M. **Guntersblum** *(Krone),* a small town with 2000 inhab., possesses a Romanesque church with helmet-shaped towers. On the N. side of the town is the château of Count Leiningen, with its gardens.

19 M. *Alsheim;* 21 M. *Mettenheim.* — From $(23^1/_2$ M.) *Osthofen* branch-lines run to *Gau-Odernheim* (12 M., in 1 hr.) and to *West-hofen* $(3^1/_2$ M.). On the *Petersberg,* near Gau-Odernheim, are the ruins of an old abbey (ca. 1200).

$28^1/_2$ M. **Worms,** see p. 448.

From *Worms to Mannheim,* see pp. 312, 313; to *Darmstadt,* see p. 318; to *Bensheim* and *Heppenheim,* see p. 320; to *Monsheim* (Bingen), see p. 456; to *Grünstadt* (Dürkheim, etc.), see p. 457.

$31^1/_2$ M. *Bobenheim.* — $35^1/_2$ M. **Frankental** *(Hôtel Lang; Pfälzer Hof),* a town with 20,000 inhab. and considerable in-dustrial importance (sugar-refinery, machine-shops, bell-foundry), is known to have existed in the 8th cent. and after 1562 was the refuge of many Protestants who were banished from the Nether-lands by the Spaniards. It was destroyed by the French in 1689 and afterwards completely rebuilt. An important porcelain factory flourished here from 1755 to 1794. The portal of the late-Roman-esque *Abbey Church,* situated at the back of the Roman Catholic Church, founded in 1119 and consecrated in 1224, is worth in-

29*

spection. Frankental is the junction of the Ludwigshafen and Gross-Karlbach railway (p. 345) and is connected with the (3 M.) Rhine by a canal constructed in 1777.

From (Ludwigshafen) Frankental to Freinsheim (p. 457), 8 M., railway in $1/2$ hr. Stations: *Flomersheim-Eppstein, Lambsheim, Weisenheim am Sand.*

39 M. *Oggersheim* (Krone), a town with 6600 inhabitants. The Loretto Church here is a fine building. A tablet on a house in the Schiller-Str. records that Schiller resided here in 1781. He was at that time engaged in writing his 'Kabale und Liebe'. A monument has also been erected to him.

42 M. **Ludwigshafen,** see p. 345. — Passengers for Mannheim, Heidelberg, etc., change carriages here. Routes to Neustadt, Neunkirchen,-Landau, Speyer, etc., see RR. 61 & 60.

57. Worms.

Railway Stations. The Central Station (Pl. B, 2; Restaurant, very fair), for all the lines mentioned at p. 447. The Rhine Station lies about $1/2$ M. to the N. of the town, near the railway-bridge, see p. 318. Vorstadtbahnhof ('Suburban Station'), at the S. end of the town.

Hotels. *In the Town:* Alter Kaiser (Pl. c; C, 3), Andreas-Str., near the cathedral, an old-established house, R. $2^{1}/_2$-10, B. 1, D. 3 $\mathcal{M}$; Hôtel Hartmann (Pl. d; C, 3), Kämmerer-Str. 24, R. $2^{1}/_4$-$3^{1}/_2$, B. $3/_4$, D. $1^{3}/_4$-$2^{1}/_2$ $\mathcal{M}$; Wilder Mann (Pl. e; C, 3), Peters-Str. 11, near the market-place, patronized by Jews. — *Near the Station* (with restaurants): Europäischer Hof (Pl. a; B, 2); Kaiserhof (Pl. f; B, 2); Bahnhofs-Hôtel (Pl. b; B, 2), R. 2-3, B. $3/_4$. $\mathcal{M}$; Reichskrone (Pl. g; B, 2), Kaiser-Wilhelm-Str. 19, R. 2-3, B. $3/_4$ $\mathcal{M}$.

Restaurants. *Café Weiss*, Kämmerer-Str. 23, at the corner of the Hafergasse; *Festhaus Restaurant* (p. 453), with garden, D. $1^{1}/_2$ $\mathcal{M}$; *Zur Kajüte*, Woll-Str. (Munich beer); *Casino Restaurant*, Hardtgasse 4, with garden (Munich beer); *Ebertsburg*, Petersgasse; *Zwölf Apostel*, Hagen-Str. 4. — **Wine Rooms.** *Zum Toehtermann*, Hafergasse; *Clemens*, Woll-Str.; *Malepartus*, Chrimhilden-Str., with small garden. — **Cafés.** *Gregori*, Kaiser-Wilhelm-Str. 13; *Kunkel*, Wilhelm-Str. 9.

Electric Tramways (comp. the plan) from the station through the Kaiser-Wilhelm-Str. to the town and to the suburbs.

Post & Telegraph Office (Pl. C, 2), Kämmerer-Strasse. — Tourists' Enquiry Office, at Herbst's, Luther-Platz.

Steamboats to Mayence in $2^{3}/_4$-3 hrs. The Cologne & Düsseldorf boats start near the Ernst Ludwig Bridge (comp. Pl. F, 2), those of the Netherlands line $1/_2$ M. lower down (Pl. E, 1; comp. p. xvi).

Worms (325 ft.), one of the most ancient, and in the middle ages one of the most important towns in Germany, with 47,000 inhab. (nearly $2/_3$ Prot., $1/_3$ Rom. Cath., and 1400 Jews), lies in the rich plain of the *Wonnegau*, on the left bank of the Rhine. The large new harbour has an imposing warehouse in the old German style, and there are manufactories of leather, wool, yarn, and sparkling wine, etc., in the town. Of the old fortifications only four towers (two to the W. and two to the E.) and a portion of the inner wall are still extant.

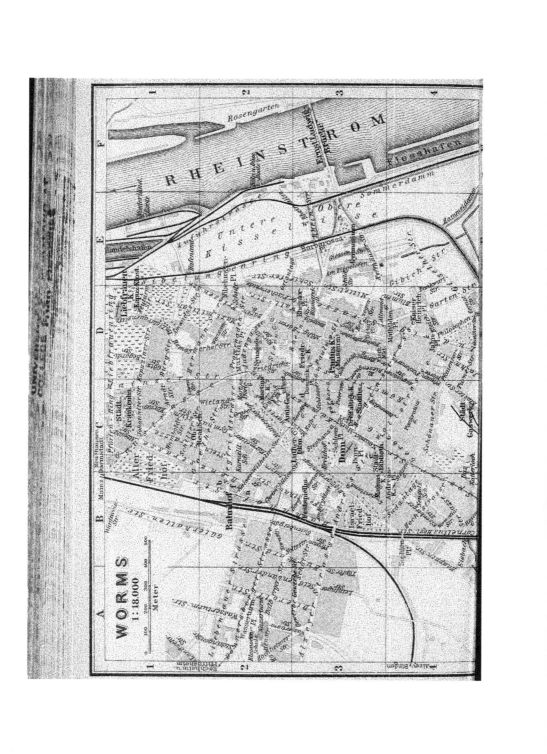

Worms is the Celtic and Roman *Borbetomagus*, the seat of the *Vangiones*. For a short time, during the period of the migrations of the barbarian hordes, it was the capital of the *Burgundians*, who had descended from the Baltic Sea, but the supremacy of that race terminated with the defeat of King Gundicar by the Huns in 437. There were bishops of Worms as early as the 5th century. The *Frankish Kings*, and afterwards *Charlemagne* and his successors, frequently resided at Worms. The war against the Saxons was planned here in 772, and here the great contest concerning the investiture of the bishops with ring and staff was adjusted by the Concordat between the Emp. Henry V. and Pope Calixtus II. (1122). As a free city of the Empire, Worms, in the disputes between the emperors and the princes, always espoused the cause of the former, and was specially faithful to the unfortunate Henry IV. Its fidelity was rewarded by the grant of various privileges, chiefly of a commercial character. The union between Worms and Mayence laid the foundation for the Confederation of Rhenish Towns (1254). At Worms, in April, 1521, was held the Imperial Diet, at which Luther defended his doctrines before the Emperor Charles V., six Electors, and a large and august assemblage, concluding with the words: '*Here I stand, I cannot act otherwise, God help me! Amen.*'

The Thirty Years' War proved very disastrous to Worms, which was repeatedly occupied and laid under contribution by Mansfeld and Tilly, the Spaniards, and the Swedes. In 1689 the town was treated with savage cruelty by Mélac and the young Duc de Créqui. After having been pillaged, it was set on fire, and, with the exception of the cathedral and synagogue, soon became one smouldering heap of ruins. The town retained its independence down to the Peace of Lunéville in 1801, and after the short-lived French supremacy was annexed to Hesse-Darmstadt in 1815, when its inhabitants numbered about 5000.

To Worms and to the Rosengarten (p. 452), on the opposite bank, attach many ancient traditions, preserved in the 'Nibelungenlied' and other heroic poems. Worms, indeed, is the centre of these romantic legends; as the city of the Burgundian King Gunther it was the scene of Siegfried's heroic achievements, of his death through the treachery of Hagen, and of the revenge of Chriemhilde.

From the *Railway Station* (Pl. B, 2) the Kaiser-Wilhelm-Strasse leads to the former Neu-Tor and to the *Luther-Platz*, situated at the entrance to the old town, the ramparts of which have been turned into promenades. The square is embellished with ***Luther's Monument** (Pl. C, 2, 3), designed by *Rietschel* (d. 1861) in 1856, and modelled by *Kietz, Donndorf*, and *Schilling* of Dresden (erected in 1868). — Best light in the morning.

A massive platform, 48 ft. square and 9½ ft. high, bears in its centre a large pedestal, surrounded by seven smaller ones. The central base or pedestal is surmounted by another pedestal in bronze, adorned with reliefs from Luther's life, and medallion-portraits of his contemporaries who contributed to the Reformation. On it stands Luther's *Statue in bronze, a commanding figure, 10½ ft. in height. In his left hand he holds a Bible, on which his right hand is placed emphatically; while his face, on which faith is admirably pourtrayed, is turned upwards. 'He is surrounded by a row of bold spirits, who before, or along with him had fought the last struggle for the freedom of the Reformation, or were privileged to promote it in various positions of life.' At the corners of the chief pedestal, in a sitting posture, are four precursors of the Reformation: in front, r. Huss (d. 1415), l. Savonarola (d. 1498); at the back, r. Wycliffe (d. 1387), l. Petrus Waldus (d. 1197). On the side-pedestals in front are Philip the Generous of Hesse on the right, and Frederick the Wise of Saxony on the left; at the back Melanchthon on the right, and Reuchlin on the left (each 9 ft. in height). Between these, on lower pedestals, are allegorical figures of the towns of (r.) Magdeburg (mourning), (l.) Augsburg (making confession), and (at the back) Speyer (protesting). Between these figures are the arms of the 24 towns of Germany which first embraced the reformed faith.

To the S. of the Luther-Platz is the *Heylshof*, built for Baron Heyl in 1884 on the site of the old *Bischofshof*, or episcopal palace. The garden is entered from the Schloss-Platz (gratuity).

The **Cathedral* (Pl. C, 3; Rom. Cath.), dedicated to SS. Peter and Paul, a very ancient building on Roman foundations, practically belongs in its present extent and ground-plan to the time of Bishop Burchard I. (1000-1025). It was, however, restored at several later epochs and partly remodelled, particularly by Bishop Conrad II. of Sternberg (1171-1192). The octagonal W. apse took the place ca. 1230 of the original round chancel-ending. The S. portal, with its elaborate plastic decoration of Biblical and allegorical import (Church and Synagogue, etc.) was renewed toward the end of the 13th cent. in the Gothic style. With its four slender round towers, two domes, and double choir, the cathedral ranks, like those of Speyer and Mayence, among the finest examples of Romanesque architecture in the Rhineland. Parts of the church have been thoroughly restored in recent years.

The INTERIOR (closed 12-2; entrance on the S. side; a boy may be sent for the sacristan; fee) is 438 ft. long, 87 ft. wide, across the transept 120 ft. wide, nave 105 ft. high. Immediately to the right, in the second S. chapel (St. Joseph's), is a whitewashed relief (12th cent.), representing Daniel in the lions' den. — The *Baptistery*, on the left side of the S. Portal, contains five large **High Reliefs* in stone, dating from 1487 and 1488, admirably executed, brought hither on the demolition of the old cloisters of 1484; they represent the Adoration of the Shepherds (l.), Annunciation, Deposition in the Tomb, Resurrection, and Genealogy of Christ. The coats-of-arms and keystones placed here are also from the cloisters. The late-Gothic *Font* is from the chapel of St. John, to the S. of the cathedral, taken down in 1807.
The *Tombstone of the Three Frankish Princesses* of the 14th cent., now in the N. aisle, is interesting. — To the left in the E. choir is a mutilated Romanesque relief of St. Juliana and the Devil, inscribed 'Otto me fecit'. The baroque choir-stalls and high-altar were designed by J. B. Neumann (p. 347).

It may interest those versed in German lore to know that the space in front of the cathedral is said to have been the scene of the quarrel between Brunhilde and Chriemhilde, recorded in the 14th Adventure of the Nibelungenlied.

In the Dechaneigasse, to the S. of the cathedral-square, are the building of the *District Office (Kreisamt;* 1738) on the right, and the *Town Library (Stadt-Bibliothek;* Pl. C, 3), containing some rare impressions, on the left. — A little to the S.W. is the late-Romanesque *Andreas-Kirche* (Pl. B, 4).

The streets to the E. lead from the cathedral to the MARKET PLACE, which contains the *Dreifaltigkeits-Kirche* (Pl. C, 3) or Church of the Trinity, built in 1709-25. To the S. between the market-place and the Hagen-Str., are the *Kornelianum* (erected by Baron von Heyl) and the new part of the Stadthaus *(Stadthausneubau)*, two modern buildings by Fischer of Munich. The old *Stadthaus* (Pl. C, 3), in the Hagen-Str., to the E. of the market-place, was rebuilt in 1883-84 after designs by Seidl. The large hall contains a fresco by *Prell,* representing Emp. Henry IV. conferring important commercial privileges on the town (1074). The extensive archives are housed in the pavilion in the court.

The KÄMMERER-STRASSE (Pl. C, 3, 2; electric tramway), leading N. from the market-place, is the chief business thoroughfare of the town. — We follow the Färbergasse to the E. to the —

Paulus-Kirche (Pl. D, 3), a Romanesque building of 1102-16, inferior in interest to the cathedral alone and, like it, founded by Burchard I. (p. 452). The choir, in the form of a half decagon, dates from the 13th, the W. porch from the 14th century. The doors of the W. portal are a reproduction of those of Hildesheim Cathedral. The interior, restored at the beginning of the 18th cent. in the baroque style, contains the **Paulus Museum,** an extensive and well-arranged collection of antiquities found in or near Worms, especially of the later Stone Age and of the Roman and Franko-Merovingian periods. Adm. on Sun., 10.30-12.30, free; on other days, on application to the custodian, 50 pf., for a party 25 pf. each.

Interior. To follow the chronological order we begin on the E. side of the CLOISTERS, which we enter direct from the vestibule. Five glass-cases and several stands contain objects of the Later Stone Age, arranged according to the four distinct periods which archæologists have been led to recognize from the antiquities found near Worms. The skulls and bones in the adjoining chapel seem to indicate the existence of various different races of men. The examples of complete tombs illustrate the various modes of burial with the bodies in different postures. In the S. wing of the cloister are Roman well-heads, roofing-tiles, and vessels, as well as a few Roman and Byzantine textiles of the 2nd-7th centuries. — We now return to the —

VESTIBULE. To the left of the entrance are objects of the Bronze Age and the First Iron Age (Hallstatt period), to the right those of the Second Iron Age (La Tène period). Here also are Roman altars, milestones, and sarcophagi, as well as piles from the Roman bridges at Mayence and Krotzenburg. In the passage-room are small Roman antiquities.

NAVE. In the front section of the nave are Roman antiquities. Three helmets; richly decorated sword; military commission of the Emperor Domitian (90 A.D.); extensive collection of Roman glass, including two Millefiori glasses, a large flask containing a smaller one inside it, two glasses in the form of human heads, a cut-glass dish with figures and inscription, and a drinking-horn; to the right, actor's mask and terracotta vessels, including many 'Gesichts-Krüge' (Worms pottery with the heads of women on the spouts) and Sigillata vessels (p. 471); to the left, tools. Here also are Frankish antiquities and objects found in graves at Worms, Wonsheim, Flonheim, and elsewhere. — The back part of the nave contains mediæval and modern objects of art (architectural fragments, tombstones of the 14-18th centuries).

CHOIR. Two painted altar-panels, with SS. Peter, Paul, and Stephen, and a bishop (ca. 1250); late-Gothic wood-carvings painted and gilded (15th cent.); objects found in the grave of Bishop Conrad II. of Sternberg (p. 450). — SACRISTY (to the right). Works in iron; collection of Worms coins, containing about 2000 'bracteates' of the 13th century. — The winding staircase to the left ascends to the —

GALLERY. In the first cabinet to the right are antiquities of the civic guilds; goblet, hat, gloves, and heralds' staves used by the delegates from Worms to the Frankfort 'Pfeifergericht', mentioned by Goethe in 'Dichtung und Wahrheit'; stoneware, porcelain, furniture; printing-press of the 16th cent.; pictures. In the side-room are ethnographical collections, views of the city, and old printed works.

A room, furnished in the Gothic style, in the N. tower beside the W. portal, contains the '*Luther Library*', with rare early editions of the works of Luther and his contemporaries and also three letters of Luther. — The S. tower contains works printed at Worms in 1516 and later.

In the LUDWIGS-PLATZ (Pl. C, 2) are an *Obelisk* to the memory of Grand-Duke Lewis IV., and reproductions of Roman milestones and memorial stones with the names of fallen warriors. Close by, in the Martinsgasse, stands the *Church of St. Martin* (Pl. C, 2), originally founded in the time of Burchard I. (p. 451), reconsecrated in 1265, destroyed in 1689, and restored in the 18th cent.; it contains some old mural paintings (restored). — In the Judengasse, to the right, is the **Synagogue** (Pl. D, 2), an outwardly insignificant building with an interesting interior (key at No. 27 Judengasse, fee 50 pf.). The part occupied by the men is Romanesque and dates from the 11th cent., that occupied by the women is Gothic of the 15th century. The building contains some fine embroideries and old brazen candelabra with curious representations on them. Behind the adjacent Raschi Chapel (which owns prayer-books of the Romanesque period) are the old *Jewish Baths* (11th cent.; restored in 1900). The Jewish community of Worms is one of the oldest in Germany.

In the modern industrial Mayence suburb stands the **Liebfrauen-Kirche** (*Church of Our Lady;* Pl. D, 1; key at Liebfrauenstift 21), a noble late-Gothic building, consecrated in 1467. The church is in the form of a cruciform basilica, with an ambulatory and two W. towers, one of which was destroyed in 1689 and was not restored until 1883. It replaces an older building erected by the town council and citizens of Worms; the keystones of the vaulted roof bear the arms of the guilds of Worms. Inside, to the right of the entrance, is a painted sculpture of the Entombment (14th cent.); on the S. side-altar is an ancient carved figure of the Virgin. — The wine called *Liebfrauenmilch* is yielded by vineyards near the church.

Worms is connected with the right bank of the Rhine by a railway-bridge (p. 318) and by the **Ernst-Ludwig-Brücke** (Pl. F, 3; toll 3 pf.), an iron bridge of three arches, erected in 1897-1900. From the centre of the latter we command a good view of the Odenwald (with the Melibocus) and of the Haardt. — The right bank of the river immediately below the bridge preserves the name of the *Rosengarten* (Pl. F, 2), of legendary fame.

In the Festhaus-Str., $^1/_4$ M. to the S.W. of the station, is the municipal *Spiel-und-Fest-Haus* (Pl. B, 3), for popular recreations, with an open-air restaurant and a good view of the cathedral. — The *Water Tower* at the end of the Dalberger-Str. (Pl. A, 2), in the new quarter of the town beyond the railway, commands a wide panorama (adm. by order from the Director of the Town Water Works, Kloster-Str.). Adjacent is the new *Eleonoren-Schule*, for girls. — Adjoining the Hochheim road is an attractive new quarter inhabited by artisans.

To the S.E. of the town is the so-called 'Wäldchen', with the *Hagen Monument* (scene from the 'Nibelungenlied') by J. Hirt (1905).

A pleasant excursion may be made by tramway to the suburb of **Hochheim**. The *Roman Catholic Church*, formerly belonging to the convent of Himmelskron, contains many monuments of the 13-15th centuries. On the heights are the *Protestant Church*, with an old Romanesque tower, and the *Worms Cemetery (Wormser Friedhof)*, affording a good view of Worms, the plain of the Rhine, and the Bergstrasse. — *Pfifligheim*, see p. 456.

On the branch-railway from *Worms* to *Gundheim* (7 M. in $^1/_2$ hr.) lies (2 M.) *Herrnsheim*, with a beautiful private park, to which visitors are admitted.

58. From Münster am Stein to Kaiserslautern and Neustadt and to Homburg.

a. To Kaiserslautern and Neustadt.

RAILWAY viâ Hochspeyer to (38 M.) *Kaiserslautern* in ca. 2 hrs. (fares 4 ℳ 60, 2 ℳ 90, 1 ℳ 85 pf.); viâ Hochspeyer to (45 M.) *Neustadt* in $1^1/_4$-$3^1/_4$ hrs. (fares 5 ℳ 90, 3 ℳ 50, 2 ℳ 30; express fares 6 ℳ 40, 4 ℳ, 2 ℳ 55 pf.).

Münster am Stein, see p. 209. — The train crosses the *Nahe*, here forming the Bavarian frontier. $^3/_4$ M. *Ebernburg* (p. 210). We then ascend the valley of the *Alsenz*, crossing the stream several times and passing through several tunnels.

2 M. *Altenbamberg;* on the hill to the left is the ruin of Altenbaumberg ($^1/_2$ hr.), mentioned at p. 211. — $3^1/_2$ M. *Hochstätten.*

7 M. **Alsenz** (Post), a town with 2200 inhab. and important sandstone quarries.

From Alsenz a diligence plies twice daily to ($4^1/_2$ M.) *Gaugrehweiler*, whence we may go on foot through the valley of the *Appel* to *Iben* (Ibener Kapelle, see p. 211) and thence viâ *Wonsheim* to *Flonheim* (p. 455). — To the W. of Alsenz, in a pleasant lateral valley, lies the little town of ($2^1/_2$ M.) *Obermoschel* (Reichshalle), reached by a branch-railway in 18 minutes. On the hill between Alsenz and Obermoschel are the extensive ruins of the fortress of *Landsberg*, destroyed by the French in 1689. From Obermoschel a diligence runs once daily to (7 M.) Meisenheim.

To the right of ($9^1/_2$ M.) *Mannweiler* is the ruin of *Randeck*. 10 M. *Bayerfeld-Cölln;* 12 M. *Dielkirchen;* $15^1/_2$ M. *Rockenhausen* (Bahnhof-Hôtel), a considerable village near the Donnersberg (see p. 456); $16^1/_2$ M. *Imsweiler.*

20 M. *Winnweiler* (Donnersberg), with iron-works and a copper-foundry, near the picturesque Falkensteiner-Tal, with the ruin of Falkenstein (route to the Donnersberg, see p. 456).

22 M. *Langmeil-Münchweiler*, the junction of the line from Alzey to Kaiserslautern (see p. 456); 24¹/₂ M. *Neuhemsbach-Sembach;* 27 M. *Enkenbach* (p. 456). Tunnel.

30¹/₂ M. *Hochspeyer*, the junction for the railway to (38 M.) *Kaiserslautern* (p. 461) and (45 M.) *Neustadt* (p. 459), described at pp. 460, 461.

b. To Homburg in the Palatinate.

54 M. RAILWAY ('Strategic Line') in 2¹/₄ hrs. (fares 4 ℳ 10, 2 ℳ 70 pf.; no first class).

The train crosses the Nahe by the bridge mentioned at p. 209 and ascends along the right bank of the river, with a view of the rocks and vine-clad slopes on the opposite side. — 5¹/₂ M. *Duchroth-Oberhausen*, whence the Lemberg (p. 211) may be ascended in ¹/₂ hr. We now thread a tunnel and enter the valley of the *Glan*. — 10 M. *Odernheim* (Bläsy-Bonnet; Krone), whence a junction-railway runs via the Disisbodenberg and across the Nahe to (2¹/₂ M.) Staudernheim (p. 209; ascent of the Disibodenberg from Odernheim 20 min.). — We ascend the valley of the Glan. 12¹/₂ M. *Rehborn;* 14¹/₂ M. *Raumbach.*

15¹/₂ M. **Meisenheim** (*Engel*, R. & B. 2, D. 1¹/₂ ℳ; *Gassen*, R. & B. 2 ℳ, both in the town; *Bahnhofs-Hôtel*, well spoken of), a small Prussian town of 1900 inhab., with some remains of its old walls. The *Schloss-Kirche*, completed in 1479 and restored in 1875-80, is a little gem of the late-Gothic style. The tower dates from 1377-1404; the vaulted burial-chapel (restored in 1896) contains the interesting tombs of Duke Charles I. of Pfalz-Zweibrücken (d. 1600), the progenitor of the present royal family of Bavaria, and of Duke Wolfgang (d. 1569) and his wife (d. 1591) and daughter, the latter by Meister Johannes of Trarbach.

At *Schweinschied*, 4¹/₂ M. to the W. of Meisenheim, is a large Roman tomb hewn out of the living rock.

We now cross the Bavarian frontier. 17¹/₂ M. *Odenbach*, at the mouth of the stream of that name; 20 M. *Medard.* — 21¹/₂ M. *Lauterecken* (Post, R. & B. 2 ℳ, in the town; Hôtel-Restaurant Bahnhof), a small town of 2300 inhab., situated at the confluence of the Lauter with the Glan, and also the station for *Grumbach*, 1¹/₂ M. to the W. For the Lauter-Tal railway to Kaiserslautern, see p. 461. — 23 M. *Wiesweiler.*

24¹/₂ M. *Offenbach* (Löwe), with the remains of an abbey-church, one of the most beautiful examples of the Transition style, built in 1170-90, but partly razed in 1810. The choir, the transept, and the two chapel-like side-apses still remain, near the modern church (visible from the railway-station). Offenbach is also the station for

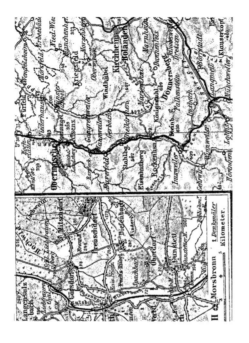

II. Morsbronn
1 *Denkmäler.*
Kilometer.

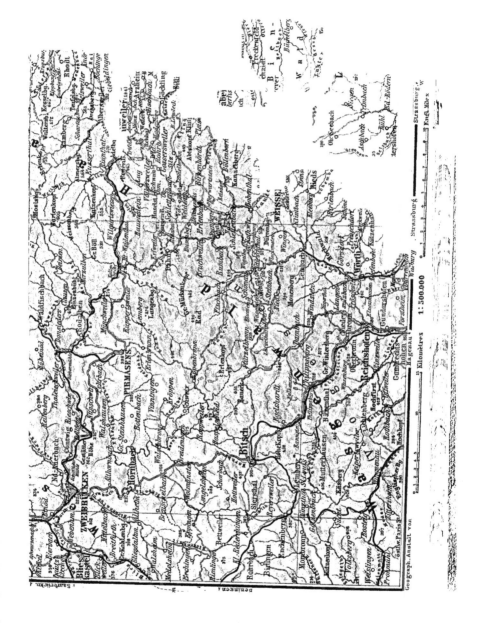

Geograph. Anstalt von 1 : 300.000

Hundheim. — 28 M. *Eschenau*; 29¹/₂ M. *Niederalben-Raths-
weiler;* 30¹/₂ M. *Ulmet.* — 32¹/₂ M. *Altenglan,* the junction of the
Kusel and Landstuhl railway (p. 462) with the Homburg line. The
stations of *Theisbergstegen, Matzenbach, Rehweiler,* and *Glan-
münchweiler* are common to the two lines. — At (45 M.) *Elsch-
bach* the train quits the valley of the Glan and enters that of the
Erbach through a tunnel. — 50 M. *Waldmohr-Jägersburg.* —
54 M. *Homburg,* see p. 301.

59. From Bingen or Mayence viâ Alzey to Kaiserslautern, Worms, or Neustadt.

RAILWAY FROM BINGEN TO ALZEY, 20¹/₂ M., in 1¹/₄ hr.; TO WORMS,
39 M., in 2¹/₄-2¹/₂ hrs. — FROM MAYENCE TO ALZEY, 25¹/₂ M., in 1¹/₂ hr. —
FROM ALZEY TO KAISERSLAUTERN, 35 M., in 2 hrs. — FROM ALZEY TO
NEUSTADT, 36 M., in 2¹/₄-3 hrs. — The route from Mayence to Neustadt
viâ Ludwigshafen is preferable (express in 2 hrs.).

FROM BINGEN (p. 243) TO ALZEY. — The train leaves the Rhine
at (2 M.) *Kempten* (Krone), and turns southwards. — 4¹/₂ M. *Büdes-
heim-Dromersheim* is also a station on the strategic line mentioned
at p. 217. Both villages produce wine. — 7 M. *Gensingen-Horr-
weiler;* 8¹/₂ M. *Welgesheim-Zotzenheim;* 10 M. *Sprendlingen*
(branch-line to *Wöllstein-Fürfeld*); 12¹/₂ M. *Gaubickelheim;*
13¹/₂ M. *Wallertheim.* At (16 M.) *Armsheim,* with a Gothic church
of 1430, a branch-line diverges for *Flonheim* and *Wendelsheim.*
19¹/₂ M. *Albig.* — 20¹/₂ M. *Alzey.*

FROM MAYENCE (p. 265) TO ALZEY. — 3¹/₂ M. *Gonsenheim,* a
favourite resort of the Mainzers (pleasant excursion through the
Mühlbach-Tal to the *Lenneberg,* ¹/₂ hr., see p. 277). To the left
is the Roman aqueduct of Zahlbach. — 6 M. *Marienborn;* 8¹/₂ M.
Klein-Winternheim; 11 M. *Nieder-Olm;* 14 M. *Nieder-Saulheim;*
16¹/₂ M. *Wörrstadt* (Krone); 20¹/₂ M. *Armsheim* (see above); 24 M.
Albig. — 25¹/₂ M. *Alzey.*

Alzey (*Darmstädter Hof,* R. & B. 2¹/₂ *ℳ,* very fair; *Hôt. Ess,*
at the railway-station), a Hessian town with 7500 inhab., on the
Selz, possesses a castle destroyed by the French in 1689, now
restored and used as dwellings for officials. It was the *Altiaia* of
the Romans, and its name occurs in the Nibelungenlied. Alzey is
the junction for several railways.

FROM ALZEY TO KAISERSLAUTERN. — 3 M. *Wahlheim;* 6 M.
Morschheim-Ilbesheim.

9¹/₂ M. **Kirchheimbolanden** (880 ft.; *Bechtelsheimer,* R.
1¹/₂-2¹/₂, B. ³/₄, D. 1¹/₂ *ℳ; Post*), a town of 3600 inhab., possesses
a pomological and viticultural school and is known for its wood-
engraving. The château of the former princes of Nassau-Weilburg,
uilt in 1753, is now private property (interesting chapel). About
1¹/₂ M. from the railway-station is the *Kurhaus Schillerhain.*

FROM KIRCHHEIMBOLANDEN TO THE DONNERSBERG. A good road ascends from the town of (4¹/₂ M.) *Dannenfels,* situated on the slope to the S. of the road, in the midst of beautiful old chestnut-trees, and visited as a summer-resort. About ³/₄ M. farther up through wood is the *Villa Donnersberg,* a hotel and pension, with a view-terrace. Pleasant paths, well-provided with finger-posts, lead from the village and from the villa to various points of view on the E. and S. slopes of the Donnersberg. In 25-30 min. more we reach the *Bismarck Tower,* on the top of the **Donnersberg** (2245 ft.), the *Mons Jovis* of the Romans, and the French *Mont Tonnerre,* which commands an extensive view. Near the tower is a firmly constructed fragment of a Celtic fort. — FROM ROCKENHAUSEN (p. 453), a railway-station on the W. side of the mountain, the ascent occupies the same time. A road leads thence to (4¹/₂ M.) the village of *Mariental,* whence the tower is reached in 1 hr. more. — The Donnersberg may also be ascended from *Winnweiler* (p. 454; through the Falkenstein valley, steep, 3 hrs.), or, most conveniently, from *Börrstadt* (see below; 1¹/₂ hr.). — From Dannenfels to *Göllheim* (see below) viâ *Jakobsweiler* and *Dreisen,* 5¹/₂ M.

13 M. *Marnheim;* branch-line to (8 M.) Monsheim (see below), viâ *Albisheim, Harxheim-Zell,* and *Wachenheim.*

15 M. *Göllheim-Dreisen.* **Göllheim** *(Ochse),* an old market-village with 1600 inhab., lies 1¹/₂ M. to the S.E. of the station. Near it is the battlefield where Emperor Adolph of Nassau was defeated and slain by Albert of Austria on 2nd July, 1298. At the S.W. end of the town, beside a venerable elm, is a modern *Chapel,* surrounded by gardens, into the walls of which is built the old 'Königskreuz', a figure of the Saviour in red sandstone, erected on the battlefield in the 14th cent. and renewed in 1611.

18 M. *Börrstadt* (ascent of the Donnersberg, see above). — 21¹/₂ M. *Langmeil-Münchweiler* (Frank). For the Alsenz line, see pp. 453, 454.

24 M. *Neuhemsbach-Sembach.* — 26¹/₂ M. *Enkenbach* (Riess) contains the late-Romanesque church of a Præmonstratensian abbey, founded in 1150 and suppressed in 1664. The church (restored since 1876) is adjoined on the S. by a cloister, one walk of which formed the S. transept of the church. Fine W. portal. — 31¹/₂ M. *Eselsfürth,* with the *Barbarossa Park,* belonging to Kaiserslautern. The (2¹/₄ M.) *Bremerhof* is a favourite pleasure-resort.

33¹/₂ M. *Kaiserslautern* (N. Station); 35 M. *Kaiserslautern* (Principal Station), see p. 461.

FROM ALZEY TO WORMS. — 2¹/₂ M. *Kettenheim;* 5 M. *Eppelsheim;* 7 M. *Gundersheim;* 9¹/₂ M. *Niederflörsheim.* — 11 M. **Monsheim,** the junction for Neustadt and for Marnheim (see above). — 15 M. *Pfeddersheim.* — 16¹/₂ M. *Pfifflingheim,* with a very ancient elm ('Luther-Baum'). About ³/₄ M. to the N. lies *Hochheim* (p. 453). — 18¹/₂ M. *Worms,* see p. 448.

FROM MONSHEIM TO NEUSTADT. — 1¹/₄ M. *Hohensülzen;* 2¹/₂ M. *Bockenheim;* 4¹/₂ M. *Albsheim* (see above).

5¹/₂ M. **Grünstadt** *(Jakobslust,* with restaurant and garden, R. 1¹/₂-1³/₄, B. ³/₄ ℳ; Station Hotel, R. 2-2¹/₂, B. ³/₄ ℳ; *Goldener*

Engel; Adler), a manufacturing town with 4600 inhabitants. Down
to the French Revolution it was the residence of the Counts of
Leiningen, whose châteaux (Unterhof and Oberhof) now serve as a
stoneware factory and a school-house. The *Stadt-Park*, on the
slope of the hill, commands a fine view. — A branch-line runs
hence to *Neu-Leiningen* and (7 M.) *Alt-Leiningen*, with châteaux
destroyed by the French in 1690. About $1^3/_4$ M. from Alt-Leiningen
is *Höringen* (Kurhaus Kochendörfer), with the ruins of an Augustine
convent, established in 1120 and suppressed in 1569. The small
Romanesque church has a beautiful portal (N. transept).

FROM GRÜNSTADT TO EISENBERG AND HETTENLEIDELHEIM, $5^1/_2$ and
6 M., in ca. $^1/_2$ hr. — The train ascends the valley of the *Eisbach*, passing numerous clay-pits and tile-works. $1^1/_4$ M. *Asselheim*. At $(2^1/_2$ M.)
Mertesheim diverges the line for *Hettenleidelheim*. — $3^1/_2$ M. *Eberts-
heim*. — $5^1/_2$ M. *Eisenberg* (Löwe), whence a diligence plies thrice daily
to *Göllheim* and *Dreisen* $(3^1/_2$ M.; p. 456). Göllheim may also be reached
in $2^1/_4$ hrs., by a pleasant détour viâ the old convent of *Rosental*, with
an interesting late-Gothic church (15th cent.). Another diligence runs
from Eisenberg twice daily to (3 M.) *Ramsen* and (9 M.) *Enkenbach*
(p. 456).

FROM GRÜNSTADT TO WORMS, $10^1/_2$ M., railway in $1^1/_4$ hr., viâ *Albsheim* (p. 456), *Offstein*, and *Weinsheim*.

8 M. *Kirchheim-an-der-Eck*. From (11 M.) *Freinsheim* a
branch-line diverges to Frankental (see p. 448). $12^1/_2$ M. *Erpolz-
heim*. Extensive vineyards in every direction.

A little farther on begin the **Haardt Mountains,** now including the entire mountain-region extending W. from Grünstadt and
Weissenburg to Kaiserslautern and Pirmasens, though originally
the name was limited to the district ending at Neustadt. The Haardt
forms a W. counterpart to the Odenwald (p. 322), from which it is
separated by a broad depression running from S.S.W. to N.N.E., now
covered with alluvial deposits from the Rhine and later tertiary
rocks. With the exception of a few spots on the E. verge where older
rocks occur, the entire Haardt consists of variegated sandstone, and
presents the appearance of a plateau gradually sloping down to the
Saar, furrowed with ravines at the edges. A considerable fault
separates it from the coal-basin of Saarbrücken.

$15^1/_2$ M. **Dürkheim.** — HOTELS. *Park-Hôtel*, near the Kur-Park,
with garden and bath-house, R. $2^1/_2$-5, B. $^3/_4$, pens. $4^1/_2$-10 $\mathcal{M}$; *Hôtel-Restaurant Terminus*, at the rail. station. — *Café-Restaurant Schüpple*
(R. & B. 2 $\mathcal{M}$), at the station; wine at *Bach-Meyer's* and *Dietz's*, Gau-Str.

Dürkheim (435 ft.), with 6300 inhab., one of the busiest towns
in the Palatinate, with its conspicuous new Gothic spire, is beautifully situated among the vineyards of the Haardt Mts. The town
was almost entirely rebuilt after the ravages of the French in 1689.
It afterwards enjoyed great prosperity as the residence of the Princes
of Leiningen-Hartenburg, whose handsome palace, which was burned
down by the French in 1794, occupied the site of the present town-
hall. There are a few antiquities in the town-hall. The neighbouring

salt-baths of *Philippshalle* attract visitors in summer and autumn.
The town is surrounded by pleasant promenades.

On an abrupt eminence at the entrance to the *Isenach-Tal*, about
2 M. to the W. of Dürkheim, lie the picturesque ruins of the Benedictine
Abbey of *Limburg*, once a château of the Salic Count Conrad the
Elder, who was elected king of Germany in 1024 (Conrad II.). On
12th July, 1030(?), he laid the foundation-stone of the church, which was
completed twelve years later and presented to the Benedictines, who soon
acquired large possessions. The abbots placed themselves under the protection of the Hartenburg Counts of Leiningen, but having quarrelled
with them, their abbey was taken and destroyed by Count Emich VIII.
in 1504. The abbey was finally suppressed by Elector Frederick III. in
1574. The ruins of the imposing BASILICA, which now belong to government, afford an admirable example of the style of the 11th cent., and are
surrounded with pleasant grounds. The S.W. tower, dating from the beginning of the 16th cent., commands a fine view (137 steps). The walls
surrounding the church, part of the original cloisters, and the burial-
chapel, which is open at the E. side, are still preserved. Charming view
in three different directions. (*Inn* at the top.)

We may now proceed towards the W., either by a hilly path along
the heights, to the **Hartenburg**, the conspicuous red ruins of which
are situated in the Isenach-Tal, 2¹/₄ M. from the Limburg. This extensive
castle was erected by the Counts of Leiningen about 1215-20, and was
afterwards enlarged; in 1510 it was restored in the Renaissance style,
and in 1794 it was blown up by the French. The ruin is surrounded
with pleasant promenades. On the E. side, on the path from the Limburg, there is a large grass-plot where tournaments were once held,
planted with fine lime-trees, and commanding a pleasing survey of the
valley. At the foot of the castle lies the village of *Hartenburg* (Hirsch),
3 M. from Dürkheim by the highroad. — A walk from Hartenburg up
the pretty *Isenach-Tal* to Frankenstein (p. 460) takes about 3 hours.

To the N.W. of Dürkheim rises the wooded *Kastanienberg*, the summit of which is enclosed by a rude stone rampart, 60-100 ft. broad, 7-13 ft.
high, and about 1¹/₄ M. in circumference, called the **Heidenmauer**,
and probably, like the similar structure on the Altkönig (p. 307), of ancient Germanic origin. On the right rises the *Teufelsstein*, a rock 13 ft.
in height. The 'heathens' wall' and the abbey of Limburg furnished
Cooper with the background for one of his novels. The paths are provided with finger-posts, which indicate the way to several good points
of view.

On the hill to the right, beyond Dürkheim, we observe the Limburg, and nearer the railway rises the 'Flaggenturm' (view). —
18 M. **Wachenheim** (*Dalberger Hof*), with 2400 inhab.; on the
hill lies the ruined *Wachtenburg* or *Geiersburg*, once the property
of the Salic dukes, and afterwards that of the Counts Palatine, destroyed in 1689. The handsome country-houses and gardens here
belong to wealthy wine-merchants. To the right lies *Forst* (Krone),
a village which yields excellent wine. — 20 M. **Deidesheim**
(*Goldene Kanne*, R. 1-1¹/₂ ℳ, B. 60 pf.; *Bayerischer Hof; Winzer-
verein Restaurant*, at the rail. station) is another wine-producing
place (2800 inhab.) and the Rome of many extensive vineyard-pro-
prietors. The late-Gothic *Parish Church* dates from the end of
the 15th, the *Château* from the beginning of the 18th century. On
the *Martenberg*, 2¹/₄ M. from Deidesheim, is a Celtic town, excavated in 1908-1910. — 21¹/₂ M. *Königsbach*, with the château

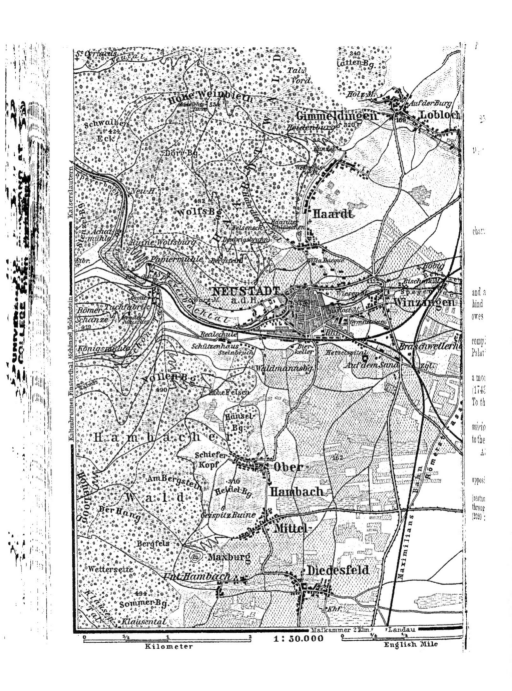

1 : 50.000
Kilometer
English Mile

of *Burckshof* and large sandstone-quarries. — 23 M. *Mussbach* (Weisses Ross), with aluminium-works and large vineyards; on the hill to the right lie the long villages of *Lobloch* and *Gimmel-dingen* (Hammel, fair, with view-terrace).

25 M. **Neustadt.** — HOTELS. *Löwe*, near the station, R. 2-3¹/₂, B. 1, D. 1¹/₂-2¹/₂ *M*, good wine, with café-restaurant; *Railway Hotel*, in the Saalbau (see below), with restaurant and garden, R. 2-5, B. ³/₄, D. 1¹/₂ *M*; *Weisses Lamm*, opposite the Löwe, R. 2-3, B. 1, D. 2-3 *M*; *Bayrischer Hof*, R. & B. 2¹/₄ *M*; *Pfälzer Hof*, R. 1¹/₂-2 *M*, these two near the station.

RESTAURANTS. *Railway Restaurant*, very fair; *Old German Wine Rooms*, Gabelsberger-Str., near the Saalbau; *Alte Pfalz*, Turm-Str. 26; *Waldmannsburg*, on the road to the Maxburg (p. 460), with view.

AMERICAN AGENT, Herr Leopold Blum.

Neustadt or *Neustadt-an-der-Haardt* (450 ft.; 18,000 inhab.), charmingly situated at the entrance to the valley of the *Speyer-bach*, the largest town in the Haardt district (p. 457), possesses several paper-mills, and carries on a considerable wine-trade. (Palatinate wines, see p. xxii.) Opposite the station is the *Saalbau*, built in 1871-2, with large halls for balls and concerts, a hotel, and a restaurant (see above). A monument in the small square behind it commemorates Herr Hetzel, a banker, to whom the town owes several benevolent institutions. The handsome Gothic *Abbey Church (Stiftskirche)*, in the market-place, founded in 1354 and completed in 1489, contains the tombstones of several of the Counts Palatine, the founders of Neustadt; the choir is used by Roman Catholics, the nave by Protestants. In the market-place are also a monumental fountain and the *Stadthaus*, formerly a Jesuit college (1743). A house to the right has carved wooden beams of 1580. To the left, beyond the Stadthaus, is the modern Gothic *Roman Catholic Church*, separated by the Speyerbach from the *Casimirianum* (1578), once a theological seminary. The *Hetzel-Anlage*, to the S.W. of the town, contains a monument to Bismarck, by Bodin.

About 1 M. to the W. of the station are the *Schützenhaus* (restaurant) and the new *Realschule*. Farther on, at about the same height above the valley, opens the *Schöntal*, with its beautiful fountains (restaurant); opposite rises the Wolfsburg (p. 460). A walk through the Schöntal brings us to the shady *Kaltenbrunner-Tal*, which begins at the *Königs-Mühle* (restaurant). — A pleasant path leads past the (3 M.) *Kalte Brunnen* and through the *Finster-Tal* (numerous finger-posts) to (2¹/₂ hrs.) the **Schänzel** (2020 ft.; view-tower; comp. p. 463), in defending which the Prussian General von Pfau fell in 1794. Refreshments may be obtained at the forester's house. Thence through the *Triefen-Tal* to *Edenkoben* (p. 460; 2 hrs.), or through the shady *Hüttenbrunner-Tal* (2¹/₂ hrs.) or viâ *Ramberg* (Löwe) and *Albersweiler* (p. 465) to (3 hrs.) *Annweiler* (p. 465).

About 1¹/₂ M. to the N. of Neustadt lies the village of **Haardt**, near which rises the château of *Winzingen*, or '*Haardter Schlösschen*', rebuilt in 1875 in the French Renaissance style. — By the third house in Haardt is a finger-post, indicating the way, leading past the vineyards, and then to the right by the *Kaiserweg*, to the **Wilhelms-Platz** (2 M. from Neustadt), which commands a superb view to the S. A zigzag path leads hence to (40 min.) the tower on the *Weinbiet* (1820 ft.; always open), which

commands a wide view. A blue-marked path indicates the way thence
to the (25 min.) **Bergstein** (1260 ft.), affording a beautiful view of Neustadt, the Speyerbach-Tal, and the Schöntal. From the Bergstein we proceed to the (40 min.) ruin of *Wolfsburg* and thence to (40 min.) Neustadt.
    FROM NEUSTADT TO THE MAXBURG, 1½ hr. From the road to the W.
of the station we cross the viaduct and follow the road to the S. to
Ober-Hambach and (2 M.) *Mittel-Hambach*. At the 'Engel' Inn we turn
to the right, at the W. end of the village-street to the left (under an
archway), and after 8 min. take the zigzag path to the left, which leads
to the (12 min.) saddle behind the Maxburg. A preferable route ('Höhenweg'; marked) ascends the 'Hambacher Treppenweg' (steps), opposite the
above-mentioned viaduct, and follows the road to the right; after ¼ hr.
we pass the Waldmannsburg and Neustadter Kurhaus restaurants and
follow the path to the left along the slope above Ober-Hambach. Or
about 20 paces beyond the path to the Waldmannsburg Restaurant, we
may ascend a path to the left, then after 10 min. (red way-marks) a path
to the right; in 5 min. more, beyond a quarry, ascend to the left, and
proceed along the slope above Ober-Hambach to the (1 hr.) Maxburg. —
The **Maxburg**, or *Hambacher Schloss*, formerly called the *Kestenburg*
('chestnut castle'), is conspicuously situated on a spur of the Haardt,
1080 ft. above the sea, and about 650 ft. above the plain (shown by the
custodian; no fee). The handsome château was re-erected in the Gothic
style by *Voit*, by order of King Max II. of Bavaria, but is in a neglected
condition. The mediæval castle is said to have been built by Emp. Henry II.
and, after various vicissitudes, was finally destroyed by the French in 1688.
    A steep path descends from the Máxburg by *Unter-Hambach* to
(½ hr.) *Diedesfeld* and (¼ hr.) the rail. station of *Maikammer* (p. 463). —
Or from the Maxburg we may go to (½ hr.) the village of *Maikammer*,
(1 hr.) *Edenkoben*, (½ hr.) *Rhodt*, and the *Villa Ludwigshöhe* (p. 463).

60. From Neustadt to Neunkirchen and Saarbrücken.

    62 M. RAILWAY (express) in 1¾ hr. (fares 8 ℳ 80, 5 ℳ 70, 3 ℳ 60 pf.) ·
to (51½ M.) Neunkirchen in 1½ hr. (fares 7 ℳ 60, 4 ℳ 90, 3 ℳ 10 pf.).

Neustadt, see p. 459. The line enters the mountain district of
the *Westrich*. For an hour the train winds up the beautiful wooded
ravine of the *Speyerbach*, and penetrates the variegated sandstone
rocks by means of 12 tunnels. Beyond Neustadt, on a hill to the
right, stand the red ruins of the *Wolfsburg* (p. 459).

3½ M. *Lambrecht* (Pfälzer Hof, very fair), a town of 3800 inhab., with extensive cloth-factories. About 1¼ M. farther on, at
Frankeneck, a paper-making village, the valley divides. The branch
to the left, through which flows the Speyerbach, is named the *Elm-
steiner-Tal;* that to the right is named the *Frankensteiner-Tal*
and is watered by the *Hochspeyerbach*. The train ascends the latter.

    A pleasant excursion may be made up the *Elmsteiner-Tal*, past
various ruined castles, to (10 M.) *Elmstein* (Becker), whence the *Eschkopf* (1975 ft.) may be ascended in 2 hrs.

Farther on, on a height to the right, are the ruins of *Neiden-
fels.* — 8½ M. *Weidental*, with two new churches. — 11 M. *Franken-
stein* (Haffen), one of the most picturesque points in the valley, with
the ruins of a castle of that name, beneath which the line passes.

On the right are the *Teufelsleiter,* and in a sequestered side-valley, also to the right, the ruin of *Diemerstein.*

From Lambrecht (3 hrs.), from Weidental (2 hrs.), or from Franken-stein (2 hrs.) we may visit the *Drachenfels* (1875 ft.), commanding a fine view; ¹/₂ hr. below the top is the *Siegfriedsbrunnen.* Thence to Dürk-heim, by the Hartenburg (4 hrs.) or viâ the Limburg (3 hrs.), see p. 458.

15¹/₂ M. *Hochspeyer* (875 ft.) is the junction for the *Alsenz-Bahn* to Münster am Stein (Kreuznach; see p. 453). The line pen-etrates the *Heiligenberg* (watershed) by a tunnel 1780 yds. long.

20¹/₂ M. **Kaiserslautern.** — HOTELS. *Schwan, Fackel-Str. 25, ¹/₂ M.. from the rail. station, R. from 2, B. 1, D. 2¹/₂ ℳ; *Karlsberg*, Theater-Str. 25, R. 2-3 ℳ; *Krafft*, Markt-Str. 19, R. & B. 2 ℳ 80 pf.; *Railway Hotel*, opposite the station, with garden, R. 2-3, D. 1¹/₂-2 ℳ; *Post*, Stein-Str. 24. — WINE RESTAURANT: *Zum Dürkheimer*, Stifts-Platz.

Kaiserslautern (775 ft.), one of the chief towns in the Pala-tinate, situated in the hilly tract of the Westrich, has 52,500 in-hab. and considerable iron-works and spinning, weaving, cigar, and sewing machine factories. From the rail. station we reach (¹/₄ hr.) the spacious Stifts-Platz viâ the Bahnhof-Str., the Eisen-bahn - Str. (with a *Monument to Bismarck* at the corner), and the Theater-Str. The *Protestant Church (Stiftskirche)* with its three towers owes its foundation to Emp. Frederick I., but in its present form belongs to the 13th and 14th centuries. It contains a marble monument in memory of the union of the Protestant churches, by Knoll, with an allegorical figure and the statues of Luther and Calvin (1883). From the choir of the Stiftskirche we next follow the Schiller-Str., leading to the *Fruchthalle* (1845-6), and then ascend the Schloss-Str., in which a memorial tablet (on the House of Correction) marks the site of the palace built here by Frederick I. in 1153. The street brings us to the terrace on which stands the *Provincial Industrial Museum (Pfälzische Ge-werbe-Museum)*, a fine building in the Italian Renaissance style, with interesting collections of furniture, metal wares, textiles, ceramics, and the like from the 14th cent. to the present day (open daily, except Frid., 10-12 and 2-4; adm. 20 pf.). We return through the Schloss-Str., Max-Str., and Pariser-Str., passing the handsome Romanesque *Apostel-Kirche* (1901; Prot.).

About 9 M. to the S. of Kaiserslautern is the *Waldkurhaus Johannis-kreuz* (1550 ft.; pens. 4¹/₂-5¹/₂ ℳ), a sanatorium situated amid beautiful woods. Excursion to the Ludwigs-Turm on the Eschkopf, see p. 460.

FROM KAISERSLAUTERN TO LAUTERECKEN, 22 M., railway in 1¹/₃ hr. The line follows the course of the *Lauter.* — 2¹/₂ M. *Kaiserslautern West Station.* — From the station of (5¹/₂ M.) *Lampertsmühle* a dili-gence plies four times daily in ¹/₂ hr. to (2¹/₂ M.) *Otterberg*, with a Cistercian abbey founded in 1134 and now suppressed. The abbey-church, an imposing structure in the Transition style, was probably completed in 1225. — 15¹/₂ M. *Wolfstein*, at the foot of the *Königsberg* (1780 ft.; ancient tombs, remains of Roman buildings). On the left are the ruins of *Neuwolfstein*, built by Rudolph I. in 1275, and of the former im-perial castle of *Altwolfstein.* — 23 M. *Lauterecken*, see p. 454.

From Kaiserslautern to *Bingen*, see pp. 455, 456; to *Münster am Stein*, see p. 453.

Beyond Kaiserslautern the line runs near the 'Kaiserstrasse', a road constructed by Napoleon, and skirts the *Landstuhler Bruch*, an extensive moor at the base of wooded hills. — 25¹/₂ M. *Einsiedlerhof;* 28 M. *Kindsbach.*

30¹/₂ M. **Landstuhl.** — Hotels. *Hôtel Finger* or *Goldener Engel*, Haupt-Str. 2, 10 min. from the station, in a pleasant site adjoining the Burg-Park, R. 1¹/₂-4, B. ³/₄, D. 1³/₄ ℳ, with a large garden and the *Sickingen Hydropathic*, in the forest; *Burgard*, at the station, R. 1¹/₂, D. 2 ℳ.

Landstuhl, a small town with 4400 inhab., was once a seat of the Sickingen family, whose castle, with its huge walls, 25 ft. thick, lies in ruins about ¹/₂ M. above the town (keys at the forester's). Franz von Sickingen (p. 210) was besieged here by the Electors of the Palatinate and Trèves in 1523, and lost his life by the splinter of a beam shattered by a cannon-ball. His tomb, erected by his sons, with a figure in full armour, is in the Roman Catholic church. A statue of Sickingen has been erected by Baron von Stumm at an old fountain-basin near the castle. Fine points in the environs are the *Bismarck Tower, Fleischhacker's Loch, Kahlenberg* (view-tower), and *Bärenloch*, all accessible by convenient paths (a round of 3-4 hrs.).

From Landstuhl to Kusel, 18 M., branch-railway in 1¹/₂-2 hrs. — The line intersects the Landstuhler Bruch (see above). Beyond (8³/₄ M.) *Glan-Münchweiler* the attractive valley of the *Glan* is entered, and followed viâ *Eisenbach-Matzenbach* and *Theisbergstegen* to (15 M.) *Altenglan* (p. 455). [From Theisbergstegen we may visit the (1¹/₂ hr.) *Potzberg* (1815 ft.; view) and the *Remigiusberg* (with a restored Romanesque church).] At Altenglan the line turns in a sharp angle towards the W. and enters the Kuseler-Tal. — 18 M. **Kusel** *(Mainzer Hof; Pfälzer Hof)*, a busy town of 3500 inhab., with cloth and other factories. In the neighbourhood are large syenite quarries.

33¹/₂ M. *Hauptstuhl;* 36 M. *Bruchmühlbach;* 40 M. *Eichelscheid-Lambshorn.*

43 M. **Homburg** (795 ft.; *Dümmler zur Pfalz*, R. from 1³/₄, B. ³/₄, D. 1³/₄-2¹/₂ ℳ, very fair; *Bach*), a small town on the Erbach, with 5500 inhab., is the junction of lines to Münster am Stein (R. 58 b), Zweibrücken (p. 466), Neunkirchen, and Saarbrücken.

Beyond (45¹/₂ M.) *Altstadt* and (47¹/₂ M.) *Bexbach* the Neunkirchen line enters a productive coal-district in Prussia. 49¹/₂ M. *Wellesweiler*. — 51¹/₂ M. *Neunkirchen* (see p. 206).

At Homburg the Saarbrücken line diverges to the left from the Neunkirchen line. 46¹/₂ M. *Limbach-Altstadt;* 48¹/₂ M. *Kirkel-Neuhäusel;* 52¹/₂ M. *Rohrbach*. — 54¹/₂ M. **St. Ingbert** *(Post,* ¹/₂ M. from the rail. station; *Bahnhof-Hôtel)*, a town with 15,500 inhab. on the Rohrbach, an affluent of the Saar, is the focus of an extensive coal-mining district. It possesses large iron and steel works, glass-works, and other factories. — 58 M. *Scheidt*. — 62 M. *Saarbrücken*, see p. 204.

61. From Ludwigshafen to Weissenburg
(Strassburg).

RAILWAY to *Weissenburg* (48 M.) in 1¹/₄-3 hrs. (fares 6 ℳ 20, 3 ℳ 70, 2 ℳ 40 pf.; express fares 7 ℳ 20, 4 ℳ 70, 2 ℳ 90 pf.). Through-express to (90 M.) *Strassburg* in 2¹/₂ hrs. (fares 11 ℳ 70, 6 ℳ 90, 4 ℳ 50 pf.). The quickest through-route to Strassburg is viâ Speyer, see R. 64.

Ludwigshafen, see p. 345. The train traverses the fertile plain of the Rhine, with its extensive vineyards and fields of corn and tobacco. — 2 M. *Mundenheim;* 3 M. *Rheingönheim;* 5 M. *Mutterstadt.*

7¹/₂ M. *Schifferstadt*, the junction for Speyer, Lauterburg, and Strassburg (see p. 472). — The train approaches the Haardt Mts. — 10¹/₂ M. *Böhl-Iggelheim;* 13 M. *Hassloch.*

18¹/₂ M. *Neustadt* (p. 459), junction for the lines to Deidesheim and Dürkheim (R. 59) and to Kaiserslautern, Neunkirchen, and Saarbrücken (R. 60). The train next skirts the extensive vineyards of the Haardt district, commanding beautiful views, especially by morning-light.

22¹/₂ M. *Maikammer-Kirrweiler* (Rail. Restaurant, very fair); to the right rises the Maxburg (p. 460; 1 hr. from here); farther distant is the *Kalmit* (2235 ft.), with a view-tower (2 hrs. from Neustadt). On a height more to the S., by the village of *St. Martin* (Goldener Wolf), are the ruins of the *Kropsburg.*

23¹/₂ M. **Edenkoben** (*Goldenes Schaf*, with garden), at the mouth of the Edenkoben Valley, a cheerful little town of 5300 inhab., with a sulphur-spring, is much frequented for the grape-cure in autumn.

Near the thriving village of *Rhodt*, 3 M. from Edenkoben station, is the royal *Villa Ludwigshöhe*, built by King Lewis I. of Bavaria, above which rises the ruined *Rietburg* or *Rippburg*. On the opposite (right) side of the *Edenkobener-Tal* (also 3 M. from the station) stands a *Monument of Victory and Peace*, unveiled in 1899, with statues and an allegorical relief. A pleasant route leads hence through the *Hüttenbrunnen-Tal* to the top of the (2¹/₂ hrs.) *Schänzel* (p. 459).

25¹/₂ M. *Edesheim;* 27¹/₂ M. *Knöringen.* The train crosses the *Queich*, which separates the Vosges and Haardt Mts.

30 M. **Landau.** — HOTELS. *Schwan*, Gerber-Str., very fair; *Körber*, Reiter-Str., unpretending, R. 2 ℳ, B. 80 pf., these two at the W. end of the town, ³/₄ M. from the station. Near the railway-station: *Terminus*, R. from 1¹/₂ ℳ, well spoken of; *Kronprinz*, R. from 1¹/₂, D. 1¹/₂ ℳ; *Bayrischer Hof*, R. from 1¹/₂, D. 1¹/₂ ℳ. — *Festhalle*, with rooms for musical and dramatic entertainments.

Landau (480 ft.), a town on the Queich with 18,000 inhab., incl. a large garrison, was a fortified place at an early period. In the Thirty Years' War it was frequently besieged, and from 1680 down to 1815 it remained in the hands of the French. In 1871 the fortifications were removed. In front of the Commandant's Residence in the Max-Joseph-Platz, at the W. end of the town, is the

Luitpoldbrunnen, with an equestrian statue of the Prince Regent of Bavaria (1892). The Trappengasse leads hence to the E. to the late-Gothic *Augustiner-Kirche* (R. C.), dating from 1407. Adjacent, to the left (König-Str. 21), in an old convent, is the *Museum* (adm. 20 pf.; catalogue 50 pf.), the first room of which contains prehistoric and Roman antiquities,.while the second has historical relics. — In the Markt-Str., a little to the S. of thé Max-Joseph-Platz, is the early-Gothic *Stiftskirche* or *Collegiate Church,* a building of 1285, with a finely sculptured W. portal. The mural paintings in the sacristy date from the 14th century.

From Landau to *Germersheim* and *Zweibrücken,* see R. 62. Branch-line to *Herxheim.*

About 5 M. to the N.W. of Landau (diligence in 1¼ hr.) is the village of **Gleisweiler** (1015 ft.), which lies at the foot of the *Teufels-berg* (1980 ft.; view), with a large *Hydropathic* (grape and diet cures). — Pleasant walk to the N.W. to the ruin of *Scharfeneck* (1½ hr.), or to the W. to the *Orensberg* (p. 465).

To the right are visible the Madenburg, the Trifels, the Münz, and the Rehberg (comp. p. 465). — 33½ M. *Insheim.* — 35 M. *Rohrbach.*

FROM ROHRBACH TO KLINGENMÜNSTER, 6 M., railway in ½ hr. — **Klingenmünster** *(Ochs)* was the seat of a Benedictine convent, founded in 650 by Dagobert II., of which only the church (rebuilt in 1735) remains. Klingenmünster also contains the extensive *District Lunatic Asylum.* Above the village rises the imposing ruin of *Landeck* (½ hr.; 12-15th cent.), with a well-preserved keep. The tower on the *Treitels-kopf* affords a fine view of the mountains of the Palatinate. — From Klingenmünster we may go on to *Mönchweiler* and *Silz* either by road (3½ M.) or by a path (1¾ hr.; red and yellow marks), passing the Land-eck and running about halfway up the Treitelskopf. Beyond Silz we may take a footpath (red and yellow marks) leading up the first side-valley to the right to (1¼ hr.) the Lindelbrunner Schloss (p. 467).

38 M. **Winden,** junction for *Maxau* and *Carlsruhe* (see p. 354).

FROM WINDEN TO BERGZABERN, 6 M., railway in ½ hr. — **Berg-zabern** (730 ft.; *Rössel,* R. 1½-2, B. ³/₄, D. 2, pens. 4½-6 ℳ; *Badischer Hof; Bahnhof-Hôtel*), a town of 2680 inhab. with old houses (*e.g.* Angel Brewery) and a castle (damaged by a fire in 1909), is of Roman origin. To the W. (³/₄ M.) is a new quarter, with the *Kurhäuser* (pens. from 3½ ℳ) and a large *Hydropathic,* on the edge of the wood. — The village of *Dörrenbach,* 1½ M. to the S., has an old Rathaus and a singular fortified church. To the W. of Dörrenbach rises the *Steffelsberg* (1580 ft.; view). — Diligence from Bergzabern to Klingenmünster (see above; 3 M., in 35 min.), twice daily to Weissenburg (see below; 6 M., in 1¾ hr.), and once daily to (17½ M.) Dahn (p. 467) in 3½ hrs.

42 M. *Schaidt-Steinfeld;* 44½ M. *Kapsweyer,* the last Bavarian station. — The train enters Alsace and crosses the *Lauter.* To the left is the Geisberg (p. 473). — The international through express-trains follow a loop-line without entering the station of Weissenburg.

48 M. *Weissenburg,* and thence to (90 M.) *Strassburg,* see R. 65.

62. From Germersheim to Saarbrücken viâ Landau and Zweibrücken.

80 M. Railway in $2^1/_4$-5 hrs. (express 10 ℳ 90, 7 ℳ 30, 4 ℳ 50 pf.).

Germersheim (junction of the line to Bruchsal), see p. 472. — The stations between Germersheim and Landau are unimportant. Near (7 M.) *Zeiskam* are large market-gardens. The railway ascends the *Queich*.

13 M. *Landau* (p. 463); the train stops at both the chief station and (15 M.) the W. station. — 16 M. *Godramstein*. From (18 M.) *Siebeldingen* (Adler) a road leads viâ *Birkweiler*, *Ransbach*, and *Leinsweiler* to ($3^1/_2$ M.) *Eschbach*, at the foot of the Madenburg (p. 466). — $19^1/_4$ M. *Albersweiler*. About $3^1/_2$ M. to the N.W. is the village of *Eussertal* (Hauck's Inn), with a Romanesque Cistercian church dating from the middle of the 13th century. The *Orensberg* (1905 ft.), $3^1/_2$ M. to the N., is a good point of view. — Short tunnel.

$22^1/_2$ M. **Annweiler** (590 ft.; *Schwan*, R. $1^3/_4$-2 ℳ, B. 60-80 pf., D. 2 ℳ, very fair; *Rehberg*, R. 1 ℳ 40 pf., both with gardens), a small and ancient town of 4000 inhab. on the right bank of the Queich (the station is on the left bank), is a good centre for excursions among the mountains of the S. Palatinate (p. 467). The *Krappenfels* and *Buchholzfels* are easily accessible points in the neighbourhood. The view-tower on the *Rehberg* (1890 ft.), to the S., is reached direct in $1^1/_2$ hr., or viâ the Trifels path (see below) in 2 hrs. (guide-posts and blue way-marks).

At the E. end of Annweiler a road ('Burg-Strasse') diverges to the S. from the Landau highroad, and from it a good footpath (blue marks) ascends to the left through wood. The ancient imperial fortress of *Trifels (1615 ft.; 1 hr.; rfmts.) was founded as early as the 10th cent., but the present scanty ruins date from about the middle of the 12th century. Trifels was not unfrequently occupied by the German emperors. Its walls protected the unhappy Henry IV., when excommunicated by Pope Gregory VII. in 1076, and deserted by his nobles. It was here that Richard Cœur-de-Lion is said to have been confined for more than a year (1193-94) by the Emp. Henry VI., until his liberation was effected by the faithful Blondel. After the Thirty Years' War the castle fell to decay. The central tower, 33 ft. in height, and the chapel have recently been restored. In cleaning the castle-well, the spring, cut in the rock, was discovered at a depth of 270 ft. The view is similar to that from the Madenburg, but less extensive towards the E.

The hill occupied by the Trifels is the northernmost eminence of a range 1 M. in length, the other two summits of which bear the ruins of *Anebos* and *Scharfenberg*, the latter, with its square tower 66 ft. in height, being usually known as the *Münz*. A blue-marked path skirts the S.W. slope of this range, passing beneath these ruins. On the ($1/_2$ hr.) saddle beyond the Münz the path forks; the right branch (blue marks) leads to (³/₄ hr.) the Rehberg (p. 465), while the Madenburg route to the left (white way-marks) runs up and down through fragrant woods of beech and pine. The *Wetterberg* and the *Schletterberg* remain to the left. In 1¹/₂ hr. (l.; yellow way-marks) we reach the **Madenburg** (locally *Eschbacher Schloss;* 1520 ft.; rfmts.), situated above the village of Esch-bach, the grandest ruin in the Rhenish Palatinate, formerly belonging to the Counts of Leiningen, afterwards to the bishopric of Speyer, and burned down by the French general Montclar in 1689. The episcopal coat-of-arms is visible on various parts of the ruin. The view from the Madenburg is one of the most extensive in the Palatinate, comprising both plain and mountain. — From the Madenburg to *Eschbach,* 25 min.; to *Klingenmünster* (p. 464), 1 hr. (the white marks lead direct to the *Landeck*).

The narrow green valley of the Queich beyond Annweiler is enclosed by wooded hills, from which the variegated sandstone protrudes in picturesque and fantastic forms. — 25 M. *Rinntal;* 27¹/₂ M. *Wilgartswiesen,* with a handsome church by Voit.

30 M. *Hauenstein.* — 34 M. *Hinterweidental-Kaltenbach* (Gerstle, very fair; Rail. Restaurant), a good centre for excursions. Diligence four times daily from Kaltenbach to Dahn (4¹/₂ M., p. 467). — The line now crosses the watershed between the Rhine and the Saar. 36¹/₂ M. *Münchweiler;* 41 M. *Rodalben.* — 43 M. *Biebermühle* (805 ft.).

Branch-line to (4¹/₂ M., in 20 min.) **Pirmasens** (1205 ft.; *Pfälzer Hof; Rail. Hotel*), an industrial town (leather and shoes) with 34,000 inhab., named after St. Pirmin, who preached here in the 8th century. From 1764 to 1790 the Landgrave Lewis IX. of Hesse-Darmstadt had his residence in the town. The Protestant church contains the landgrave's monument. — Another branch-line runs N. to (3 M.) *Waldfischbach.*

Several unimportant stations. 55 M. *Tschifflik,* once a summer-residence of Stanislaus Leszczynski, King of Poland.

57¹/₂ M. **Zweibrücken** (730 ft.; *Zweibrücker Hof,* R. 2¹/₂-3¹/₂, B. ³/₄, D. 2¹/₂, S. 1¹/₂ ℳ; *Pfälzer Hof,* both near the Herzogs-Platz, very fair; *Deutsches Haus*), formerly the residence of the Dukes of Zweibrücken, and known to the literary world as the place where the *Editiones Bipontinae* of classical authors were published. It is now a town of 14,700 inhab., and contains the chief court of the Bavarian Palatinate, which occupies the old castle. When Charles X. Gustavus of the Zweibrücken family ascended the Swedish throne in 1654, the duchy became subject to Sweden, which it continued to be till the death of Charles XII. (1719). The *Alexander-Kirche* contains the burial-vaults of the ducal house.

From Zweibrücken to Saargemünd, 23 M., railway in 1¹/₄ hr., viâ *Bierbach* (see below). — *Saargemünd,* see p. 489.

From Zweibrücken to Homburg, 7 M., railway in 20 min., viâ *Einöd* (see below) and *Schwarzenacker* (with the former convent of *Wersch-weiler*). — *Homburg,* see p. 462.

The railway goes on to (59¹/₂ M.) *Einöd* and (61¹/₂ M.) *Bierbach,* from which stations the above-mentioned two branch-lines diverge. At (72 M.) *St. Ingbert* (p. 462) our line unites with the Kaisers-lautern line (R. 60). — 80 M. *Saarbrücken,* see p. 204.

The **Mountainous District of the South Palatinate,**
with its imposing and picturesque rocks of variegated sandstone,
its romantic castles, and its beautiful forests, is best visited from
Annweiler, and may be seen in two days, with a night spent at
Dahn. We ascend by the blue-marked path indicated at p. 465 to
a point about halfway up the Rehberg, where the route from Trifels
joins ours. We then descend and turn to the right to the highroad,
which we follow to *Völkersweiler* and *Gossersweiler.* Farther on
a cart-track (blue marks) diverges on the right for the Lindelbrunner
Schloss (2¹/₂ hrs. from Annweiler). A pleasanter but somewhat
longer route diverges to the left at *Sarnstall,* 1¹/₂ M. to the W.
of Annweiler, and leads through the *Rimbach-Tal,* passing *Lug,*
Schwanheim, and (1³/₄ hr.) *Ober-Schlettenbach* (Germann, 5 min.
to the left of the path, good wine).

The **Lindelbrunner Schloss** (1445 ft.), the ruins of a castle
of the Counts of Leiningen, dating from the 11th cent., commands
a highly characteristic view of the grotesque sandstone formations
of the S. Palatinate. At the foot of the hill is the Inn zum Schlösschen.

About 2 M. from the Lindelbrunner inn lies *Vorderweidental;*
1 M. farther on a road diverges to the right for Busenberg and Dahn;
and ¹/₂ M. farther is *Erlenbach* (Hôt. Berwartstein), under the
shadow of the castle of *Berwartstein,* recently rebuilt. From Erlenbach a footpath (yellow marks) ascends in ³/₄ hr. to the massive
ruined castle of **Drachenfels,** also of ancient foundation, destroyed
by the citizens of Strassburg in 1335, but afterwards restored. The
ruins look as if they were part of the hill on which they stand, and
some of its steps and passages are hewn in the living rock. They
command a fine view of Schloss Dahn and the castellated rocks of
this district. — We descend on the E. side of the Drachenfels to
Busenberg (Zum Schlösschen), 3 M. from Erlenbach and 3³/₄ M.
from Dahn. Hence we proceed (yellow marks) to *Schindhardt* and
thence by a path (yellow and red marks; coming from Lindelbrunn)
along the slope and through the valley in which *Erfweiler* lies, to
the saddle between Hochstein and the castle-hill. Thence we ascend
to (1¹/₂ hr. from the Drachenfels) the ruins of **Schloss Dahn**
(1110 ft.), an extensive fortified area which included three separate
castles. Its passages, chambers, dungeons, and cellars have all been
hewn out of the solid rock. It commands a striking view. — About
1¹/₄ M. to the W. lies the picturesque little town of **Dahn** *(Sonne,*
R. 1¹/₂-2, B. ¹/₂, D. 1¹/₂ *M,* very fair; *Pfalz),* whence diligences
ply four times daily to Hinterweidental-Kaltenbach (p. 466), twice
daily to Schönau (p. 468), and once daily to Bergzabern and Weissenburg (pp. 464, 473). Above the lower end of the town rises the
precipitous cliff called the *Jungfernsprung.*

From Schloss Dahn we may descend direct to the highroad
which leads in the direction of Busenberg, and then descend to the

S. through the Lauter-Tal to (3 M.) *Bruchweiler* (Löwe). On the left is the cliff known as the *Fladenstein*. One mile beyond Bruchweiler the Lauter-Tal is quitted by a road leading to the right to (1 M.) *Rumbach* (Post, plain but good). Hence we follow the road to Nothweiler and take a path (red marks) to the right at a fingerpost, which leads to the (1½ hr.) Wegelnburg. Or we may proceed through the Rumbacher-Tal (passing *Birkenfels* on the right) to (3¾ M.) **Schönau** (*Löwe*, very fair), a village on the *Sauer*, with pleasant environs. From Schönau we take 1 hr. more to reach the **Wegelnburg** (1880 ft.), a hill crowned with the ruins of a castle destroyd by the French in 1679, one of the finest points in the S. Palatinate. At the top is a mountain-indicator.

The frontier of Alsace runs a few hundred paces to the S. of the Wegelnburg. Just beyond it, about ¾ M. from the Wegelnburg, is the *Hohenburg*, built of skilfully-hewn square blocks of stone, and commanding a view similar to that enjoyed from the Wegelnburg. We return to the ridge and descending to the left by a fingerpost proceed by the *Fleckensteiner Hof* to the (½ hr.) **Fleckenstein,** another rocky fastness affording a fine view of the Sauer-Tal, and perhaps the most remarkable ruin in the whole district. Hence we descend to the (20 min.) *Sauer-Tal* and to (3 M.) —

Lembach (*Weisses Rössel*, plain but good), the terminus of a branch-line from Walburg (p. 474), and a good centre for excursions.

A path (red and white marks), diverging from the route between Wegelnburg and Fleckenstein, leads viâ *Klein-Wingen*, *Klimbach* (Engel), and the *Scherhol* (p. 473) to (4½ hrs.) Weissenburg.

About 1½ hr. to the S.W. of Schönau, in the woods, on the other side of the hamlet of *Wengelsbach*, is the ancient castle of **Wasigenstein**, mentioned in the old Waltharius-Lied (10th cent.), and one of the most interesting ruins in the district; it is accessible also from Schönau in 1½ hr. by a red-marked path over the Wengelsbacher Jochhöhe. We may descend hence in ¼ hr. to *Obersteinbach* (Sensfelder; Fricker), at the foot of the ruined *Klein-Arnsberg;* a massive rock behind the village bears the ruins of *Lützelhardt*. A path leads to the S. (to the left the ruined *Wineck*), viâ the hamlet of *Windstein*, below the imposing ruins of *Alt-Windstein* and *Neu-Windstein*, to (7 M.) *Jägertal* (inn), with iron-works. From Jägertal to *Niederbronn* (p. 488), 3 M.

63. Speyer.

Railway Stations. The *Central Station* (Pl. A, 1), for Ludwigshafen and Strassburg (p. 472) and for Schwetzingen and Heidelberg (p. 342); *Rhenish Station* (Pl. E, 3), for trains of the latter line only; *Local Station* for Geinsheim and Neustadt.

Hotels. RHEINISCHER HOF (Pl. b; B, 3), Maximilian-Str. 44, very fair, R. 1½-4, B. 1, D. 3 ℳ; WITTELSBACHER HOF (Pl. a; C, 4), Ludwig-Str. 40, with garden-restaurant, R. & B. 2½-5, D. 1¾-2½, also very fair; PFÄLZER HOF (Pl. c; C, 3), Maximilian-Str. 13; ENGEL, outside the Altpörtel (Pl. B, 3; p. 471), unpretending but very fair.

Beer Houses. *Gambrinus*, at the station; *Sonne*, Maximilian-Str. 17; *Zum Storchen*, facing the Altpörtel (p. 471). — Wine at *Sick's*, Königs-Platz. — *Café Waibel*, by the Altpörtel, also beer and wine.

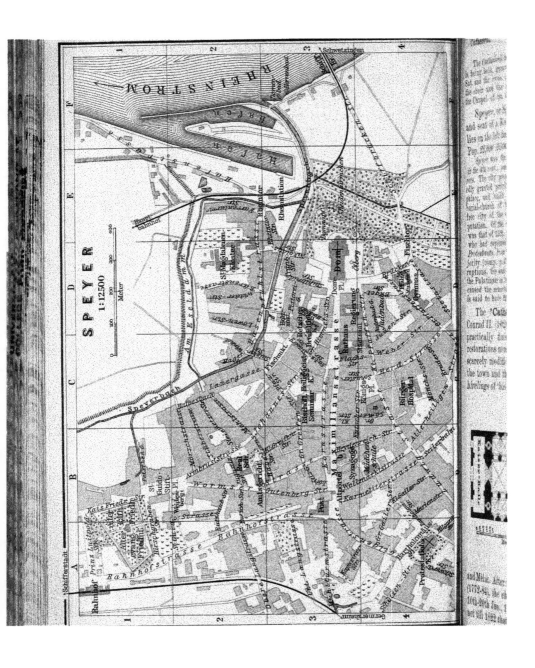

The *Cathedral* is open to visitors only during the hours when no service is being held, generally 10-11 a.m. and 2-6 p.m. (Oct.-March 2-4) except on Sat. and the eves of festivals; a fee of 35 pf. is charged for admission to the choir and the crypt (with the imperial tombs), and another fee for the Chapel of St. Catharine (with the objects found in the tombs).

Speyer, or *Spires* (325 ft.), the capital of the Bavarian Palatinate, and seat of a Roman Catholic bishop and a Protestant consistory, lies on the left bank of the Rhine, at the influx of the *Speyerbach.* Pop. 22,000 (9500 Protestants, 500 Jews).

Speyer was the Roman *Colonia Nemetum,* became an episcopal see in the 4th cent., and was frequently the residence of the German empe-rors. The city prospered greatly under the Salic emperors, who repeat-edly granted privileges to the loyal inhabitants, embellished the old palace, and built the celebrated cathedral, which was regarded as the burial-church of the German emperors for nearly five centuries. As a free city of the empire (from 1294 onwards) Speyer enjoyed a high re-putation. Of the numerous imperial diets held here the most important was that of 1529, under Charles V., after which the princes and estates who had espoused the cause of the Reformation received the name of *Protestants,* from their protest against the resolution of the hostile ma-jority (comp. p. 471). From 1527 onwards Speyer was, with few inter-ruptions, the seat of the *Reichs-Kammergericht,* until the devastation of the Palatinate in 1689 by the French, during which the city was destroyed, caused the removal of the courts to Wetzlar. — Edward VII. of England is said to have first met his future wife in Speyer Cathedral.

The **Cathedral* (*Dom;* Pl. D, 3) was founded in 1030 by Conrad II. (1024-39), continued by his son Henry III. (d. 1056), and practically finished by his grandson Henry IV. (d. 1106). The restorations necessitated by the fires of 1137, 1159, 1281, and 1450 scarcely modified the original character of the building. In 1689 the town and the cathedral were ravaged with fire and sword by the hirelings of 'his most Christian majesty' Louis XIV., under Montclar

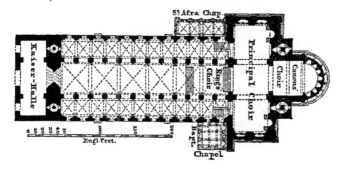

and Mélac. After the restoration by the Würzburg architect Neumann (1772-84), the church was once more subjected to devastation on 10th-20th Jan., 1794, and was converted into a magazine. It was not till 1822 that it was at length restored to its sacred purposes.

The church is a simple, but vast and imposing Romanesque basilica, with nave, aisles, transepts, two domes, and four towers. Length 440 ft., length of transept 180 ft., breadth of nave 45 ft., height of nave 105 ft. The Kaiser-Halle, or vestibule, with its three portals and large rose-window, was erected by *Hübsch* in 1854-58, while the W. towers (240 ft.) were completed on the model of the E. towers. The handsome arcade at the top runs round the whole building.

In the Kaiser-Halle are statues of the emperors buried in the church and four reliefs (foundation of the church and scenes from the life of Rudolph of Hapsburg).

The *INTERIOR (adm., see p. 469) is adorned with 32 large FRESCOES, by *Johann Schraudolph* and his pupils (1845-53), representing Old Testament events prophetic of the Redemption, scenes from the lives of Christ, the Madonna, and St. Bernard of Clairvaux, and numerous single figures of prophets and saints. — From the E. end of the nave twelve steps ascend to the KINGS' CHOIR, with statues of *Rudolph of Hapsburg*, by Schwanthaler, and *Adolph of Nassau*, by Ohnmacht. On the right and left of the approach to the principal choir are two late-Gothic *Reliefs,* formerly in the crypt, each containing likenesses of four emperors. The brasses in the floor and the gilded chandeliers are modern. — The CHAPEL OF ST. AFRA was built in 1097-1103, but was afterwards a'tered. The body of Emp. Henry IV. lay here unburied from 1106 to 1111, when the papal excommunication was revoked. — The BAPTISTERY, in the S. aisle, dates from the 12th century. Above it (entrance from the S. transept) is the CHAPEL OF ST. CATHARINE, originally dating from the 13th cent., but almost entirely rebuilt in 1857; it contains an early-German altarpiece and various articles found in the tombs of the emperors (fragments of clothes, a sapphire ring, a cross of Henry IV., etc.).

The CRYPT, beneath the choir and the transept, was consecrated in 1039 and restored in 1857. Here is the entrance to the EMPERORS' VAULT, rebuilt in 1900-1906 and containing those of the imperial tombs which escaped destruction by the French in 1689. On the E. side are the stone sarcophagi of *Emp. Conrad II.* (d. 1039) and his wife *Giseia* (d. 1043), *Henry III.* (d. 1056), *Henry IV.* (d. 1106) and his wife *Bertha* (d. 1087). The W. side was entirely destroyed. The leaden coffin of *Philip of Swabia* (d. 1208) was found on this side. The coffin of *Henry V.* (d. 1125), the last of the Salic line, which rested above that of Henr; IV., was ruthlessly desecrated. The following royal personages also were buried here: *Beatrice* (d. 1184), wife of Frederick Barbarossa, and their daughter Agnes; *Rudolph of Hapsburg* (d. 1291), whose tombstone has been preserved; and the rival monarchs, *Adolph of Nassau* (d. 1298) and *Albert I. of Austria* (d. 1308; p. 456). The bones found here have all been reinterred in their original resting-places.

Visitors with steady heads should walk round the arcaded gallery on the outside of the church (see above; fee 50-75 pf.).

The ancient CHURCHYARD (*Domkirchhof;* Pl. D, 3, 4) is now a promenade, where a military band plays on summer-evenings. Opposite the N.E. corner of the church is the *Domnapf,* or cathedral bowl, a large vessel of sandstone, once marking the boundary between the episcopal and civic jurisdiction. Every new bishop was obliged, after binding himself to respect the liberties of the town, to fill the Napf with wine, which was then drunk to his health by the townspeople. The fragments of the '*Mount of Olives*' to the S. of the cathedral, constructed in 1511, are the sole remains of the cloisters, which were built in 1437-44 and destroyed at the end of the 18th century. — Among the trees to the E. rises the *Heiden-Türmchen* (Heathens' Tower; Pl. E, 3), a relic of the town-wall built in 1080 by Bishop Rudger. — A good view of the cathedral-choir is obtained from the bank of the Rhine, below the bridge-of-boats.

The '*Judenbad*' (Pl. D, 4), in a small garden at the end of the Judenbadgasse, dates from the early 13th cent. (key at the town-hall). — Some Gothic ruins by the Protestant church preserve the name of the ancient *Retscher* (Pl. D, 3), an imperial palace where the diets were held. The fine old gate-tower, at the W. end of the Maximilian-Str., is named the *Altpörtel* (Pl. B, 3).

The **Protestations-Kirche** (Pl. A, 4), a cruciform building in the Gothic style, was erected in 1893-1903 to commemorate the Diet of 1529 (p. 469). The interior (adm. 20 pf., with ascent of tower 50 pf.; printed guide free) merits a visit. The bronze statue of Luther in the vestibule is by W. Hahn.

The ***Historical Museum of the Palatinate** (Pl. D, 4), a two-storied building in the German Renaissance style with towers and balconies, was erected from plans by Gabriel Seidl of Munich and was opened in 1910 (open daily, 10-1 & 2-5; adm. 50 pf., on Sun. and Wed. afternoons 20 pf.). The Roman section is one of the most important collections of its kind in the whole district of the Rhine.

Ground Floor. — From the vestibule we ascend the steps to the right to the NORTH WING. Through an ante-chamber, flanked by rooms containing prehistoric objects, we enter the *Roman Lapidarium*. a large hall with stone monuments, milestones, tombstones, votive stones (including 'Six God Stones' and 'Eight God Stones'), and a few complete tombs. The small cabinet to the right contains bronzes: bust of Germanicus(?); head of a Centaur, a Greek original of the school of Lysippus (ca. 300 B.C.); archaistic statuette of Apollo (2nd cent. A.D.). The W. side of the Lapidarium is adjoined by three semicircular apses divided by columns. The apse to the right contains Roman weapons, implements, and small bronzes, including a statuette of Mercury and a medallion with the rape of Ganymede. The apse to the left contains *Roman Glass;* also harness and a sword with a silver hilt. In the central apse are **Sigillata Vessels* (Roman pottery of brilliant red colouring) together with moulds, one of the most extensive collections of its kind; also bronze cooking utensils. — In the WEST WING are three other rooms containing Sigillata vessels. — SOUTH WING. The large corner-room contains the *Frankish-Alemannian Collection* of arms, vessels, and ornaments; two canoes. The next room contains the *Mediaeval Lapidarium*, with four mural paintings after miniatures from the Codex Aureus, which was formerly in Speyer but is now in the Escurial in Spain. The central room is devoted to the *Cathedral* and its history. In the next room are objects of *Mediaeval Industrial Art*, including sculptures, stoneware, glass, and vessels of various kinds. The *Gothic Room* contains an altar-piece from the Liebfrauen-Kirche at Worms, arms, vessels, objects in stone, and carvings in wood. In the *Circular Turret Chamber* and the adjoining room *(Incunabula Room)* of the EAST WING are pictures of old Speyer buildings, old furniture, three pieces of tapestry, tables with parchments and incunabula, and a Gothic cabinet (locked) with imperial documents issued at Speyer. The Corridor contains engravings, views of Speyer, furniture, glazed tiles, and so on: in a niche adjoining the vestibule is an allegorical figure of the Palatinate ('Palatia').

Upper Floor. — *Armoury*, with military trophies of 1870-71. The *Picture Gallery* chiefly contains Netherlandish works from Schleiss-heim. — *Natural History Collection.* Several rooms with *Furniture* of the Empire and 'Biedermaier' (*i.e.* middle of the 19th cent.) periods, *Costumes* of the Palatinate, *Frankental Porcelain* (p. 447), and so on.

The **Basement** (entered from the S.W. corner of the courtyard) contains collections illustrative of wine-growing: old wine-presses, carved casks, and implements of vine-culture. A glass bottle, found in Speyer and hermetically closed by a film of oil which has become resinous through age, still contains wine dating from the Roman period.

64. From Ludwigsburg to Strassburg viâ Speyer and Lauterburg.

81 M. RAILWAY (express) in 1³/₄ hr. (fares 10 ℳ 90, 7 ℳ 30, 4 ℳ 50 pf.).

From Ludwigshafen to (7¹/₂ M.) *Schifferstadt,* see p. 463. — 13 M. *Speyer* (p. 468), junction of the Heidelberg and Schwetzingen branch (p. 342).

15 M. *Berghausen;* 16¹/₂ M. *Heiligenstein;* 19¹/₂ M. *Lingenfeld.*

22 M. **Germersheim** *(Salm),* an old fortified town with 5800 inhab., lies at the confluence of the *Queich* (p. 465) and the Rhine. The latter is crossed here by a railway-bridge and a bridge-of-boats.

Railway to *Landau* and *Zweibrücken,* see R. 62; to *Bruchsal,* see p. 347.

25 M. *Sondernheim;* 28 M. *Bellheim;* 30¹/₂ M. *Rülzheim;* 33 M. *Rheinzabern,* on the *Erlenbach;* 35 M. *Jockgrim.*

38¹/₂ M. *Wörth,* the junction of the Carlsruhe and Landau line (p. 354). 41 M. *Hagenbach;* 43 M. *Neuburg;* 44¹/₂ M. *Berg.* The train then crosses the *Lauter,* which forms the boundary between the Bavarian Palatinate and Alsace.

46¹/₂ M. **Lauterburg** *(Blume),* a town of 1700 inhab., was once fortified, and is frequently mentioned in the annals of the old wars between the French and Germans. The Rathaus contains a Roman altar. Branch-line to Weissenburg, see p. 473.

48¹/₂ M. *Mothern;* 53 M. *Selz,* with a Gothic chapel, the junction of a line to Walburg (p. 474).

58 M. **Röschwoog,** junction of the strategic railway (p. 346) to Rastatt and Carlsruhe, continued towards the W. to Hagenau (p. 474) and Obermodern (p. 490).

61¹/₂ M. **Sesenheim** *(Ochs,* well spoken of; *Krone),* the scene of Goethe's intimacy with Friederike Brion (1770-71).

The parsonage has since been rebuilt. The wooded hill with the arbour in which Goethe and Friederike used to converse has been purchased by a number of the poet's admirers, and the arbour has been renewed. On the S. side of the church are the tombstones of Friederike's parents (comp. p. 370). In the church is the bench on which Goethe, by Friederike's side, 'found a somewhat dry sermon none too long'.

64 M. *Drusenheim;* 67 M. *Herlisheim*, on the *Zorn;* 70 M. *Gambsheim*, with an old chapel; 73 M. *Wanzenau*, with Fort Fransecky; 78 M. *Bischheim.* — 81 M. *Strassburg* (p. 475).

65. From Weissenburg to Strassburg.

42 M. RAILWAY in 1-2 hrs. (fares 5 ℳ 20, 3 ℳ 30, 2 ℳ 20 pf.). — Weissenburg is connected with (13 M.) *Lauterburg* (p. 472; ³/₄ hr.) by a branch-railway passing *Schleital, Salmbach*, and *Nieder-Lauterbach.*

Weissenburg (520 ft.; *Hôtel de l'Europe,* near the rail. station, R. 2-3, B. ³/₄, D. 1¹/₂-2 ℳ; *Engel,* R. 1¹/₄-2¹/₂ ℳ, B. 60 pf., D. 1¹/₂-2¹/₂ ℳ; *Schwan*, these two in the town), a very ancient town with 6900 inhab., mentioned in history as early as the Merovingian kings, was the seat of an independent abbey, founded by Dagobert II., down to 1534. Otfried, author of a poetic harmony of the Gospels, the earliest rhymed German poem of any length, was a monk here about 860. The *Abbey Church of St. Peter and St. Paul* is a noble example of the early-Gothic style (13th cent.), with a tower above the crossing of the transept, a fine portal, and a beautiful chapel opening from the S. transept. In the interior are fine stained-glass windows of the end of the 13th (Romanesque; on the S. side) and of the 14th and 15th centuries. It is adjoined on the N. side by handsome Gothic cloisters, which have been recently restored and contain a few old carvings and tombstones. The *Johannis-Kirche*, partly Romanesque in style, and many of the private houses are also interesting edifices.

On 4th Aug., 1870, part of the German army under the Crown Prince of Prussia gained a decisive victory here over the French under Abel Douay. The town, defended by a simple wall, and the **Geisberg,** 2 M. to the S., were occupied by the French, but were attacked by Prussians from the E. and Bavarians from the N., and both taken after a severe struggle. In order to form an idea of the nature of the ground, the traveller should follow the Lauterburg road, turn to the right about 1 M. from the station, cross the railway, and proceed by a footpath to the (³/₄ M.) *Gutleuthof* and the (1 M.) château of *Geisberg*, now a farmhouse (rfmts.), round which the struggle was very hotly contested. Fine view from the terrace on the E. side. Douay fell at the top of the hill, on the way to which numerous graves of the fallen are passed. The traveller may now return by the Hagenau road on the W. side, a round of 2-2¹/₂ hrs. in all. Various monuments have been erected on the battlefield.

About 3 M. from Weissenburg a footpath (red and white marks), diverging to the right from the Bitsch road, ascends in ¹/₂ hr. to the view-tower on the top of the **Scherhol** (1660 ft.). From the top we descend to the left and regain the road near the 7th kilomètre-stone. Thence we may follow the footpaths running parallel with the road viâ Klein-Wingen and Klimbach to the Fleckenstein and the Wegelnburg (p. 468).

On quitting Weissenburg the train describes a circuit round the Geisberg, and passes stations *Riedselz, Hunspach*, and *Hofen.*

10$^{1}/_{2}$ M. *Sulz unterm Wald* (Rössle), the headquarters of the Crown Prince of Prussia, commander of the Third German Army, on Aug. 5-6th, 1870. — At *Lobsann, Pechelbronn,* and *Schwab-weiler,* near Sulz, petroleum and asphalt are obtained. — The line now traverses part of the *Forest of Hagenau* (35,000 acres in extent).

15$^{1}/_{2}$ M. **Walburg,** with a fine church of the 15th cent., is the junction for several branch-lines, including one to (10$^{1}/_{2}$ M.) *Lembach,* viâ *Biblisheim, Dürrenbach, Morsbronn,* (5$^{1}/_{2}$ M.) *Wörth* (see below), *Liebfrauental,* and *Mattstall.*

Morsbronn is the best starting-point for a visit to the Battlefield of Aug. 6th, 1870 (6-8 hrs.). Comp. inset-map, p. 454. — The neighbourhood of *Morsbronn* was the scene of the attack of the 11th Prussian Army Corps and of the gallant onset (about 1 p.m.) of the French cavalry, which certainly covered the retreat of the infantry, but resulted in the destruction of the whole brigade of horse. The Germans then pressed forward and occupied the village of *Elsasshausen* (3 p.m.), which they afterwards maintained against the attempts of the French to retake it. The battlefield is now studded with monuments, the finest of which is the equestrian *Statue of Emp. Frederick,* by Max Baumbach, near *Diefenbach* (best view of the battlefield). Near Elsasshausen is the 'MacMahon Tree', where the French marshal had his stand during most of the battle.

The little town of **Wörth** (*Post,* R. 1$^{1}/_{2}$-2, D. 1$^{1}/_{2}$-2$^{1}/_{2}$ $\mathscr{M}$; *Weisses Ross;* old Roman altar in front of the Gemeindehaus), which has given its name to the battle, contains 1050 inhab., and lies on the right bank of the *Sauer.* The Germans found it unoccupied by the French, and at once took possession of it (7 a.m.), successfully resisting all attempts to dislodge them. Their efforts, however, to storm the strong position held by the French on the heights of Fröschweiler were in vain, until the success of the Prussians at Morsbronn made its influence felt on the French right wing. **Fröschweiler** (*Jäger-Zusammenkunft,* very fair), the centre of the French position, with the headquarters of MacMahon, was attacked from all sides almost simultaneously and captured between 4 and 5 p.m. Those of the French who escaped death or capture effected a disorderly retreat towards (2 M.) Reichshofen (p. 488). The church of Fröschweiler was destroyed, but a new one, the tower of which overlooks the whole of the battlefield, has been built. The largest French monument stands to the N. of the road from Wörth to Fröschweiler.

20$^{1}/_{2}$ M. **Hagenau** (*Europäischer Hof,* with garden, R. 2, D. 2-3$^{1}/_{2}$ $\mathscr{M}$; *Post; Andres,* all near the station; *Rail. Restaurant,* very fair), with 18,700 inhab., was once a free town of the German Empire and a fortress, the works of which are partly preserved. The walls were erected by Emp. Frederick I. in 1164. The palace built by the same emperor, afterwards a favourite residence of the Hohenstaufen, was burned by the French in 1678. Part of the conspicuous *Church of St. George* dates from the 12th century. The choir contains a huge wooden figure of Christ, executed in 1488. The fine candelabrum of the 13th cent., and the modern stained glass also deserve attention. The *Municipal Museum* contains a collection of antiquities. In front of it is a statue of Frederick Barbarossa. — To the E. of the town and S. of the Hagenauer Wald lie the artillery-ranges. — Railway to *Saargemünd, Metz,* and *Saarbrücken,* see R. 67; to *Röschwoog,* see p. 472; to *Zabern* (viâ Obermodern), see p. 490.

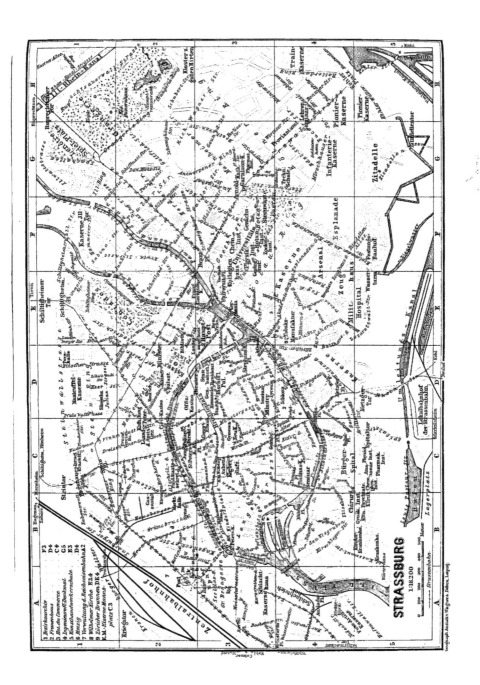

STRASSBURG

1:38,200

0 100 200 300 400 500 Meter

Geograph. Anstalt v. Wagner & Debes, Leipzig.

24¹/₂ M. *Mariental,* with a nunnery, dissolved in 1789; 25¹/₂ M. *Bischweiler,* with cloth-manufactories. The train now crosses the *Zorn.* — 26 M. *Kurzenhausen;* 30 M. *Weyersheim;* 32 M. *Hördt.*

36 M. *Vendenheim,* junction for the Saarburg-Zabern line (R. 68). Then several unimportant villages, near which are some of the outworks of Strassburg. — 42 M. *Strassburg.*

66. Strassburg.

Arrival. The *Central Railway Station* (Pl. A, 2, 3; *Restaurant, D. 2-4 ℳ), with an entrance-hall adorned with frescoes by Knackfuss, is on the W. side of the town. Omnibuses of the larger hotels (70 pf.) and cabs (see p. 476) are in waiting. — *Neudorf Station,* see p. 370.

Hotels. *At the Central Station:* Hôtel National (Pl. k; A, 2), Bahnhofs-Platz 13, R. from 2¹/₂, B. 1¹/₄, déj. 3¹/₄-3¹/₂, D. (at 6 p.m.) 4-4¹/₂ ℳ; *Hôtel Christoph (Pl. m; A, 2), Bahnhofs-Platz 15, R. from 3, B. 1¹/₄, déj. 3¹/₂, D. 7-9 p.m. 4 ℳ; Terminus Hotel (Pl. f; A, 3), with popular café-restaurant, R. 2¹/₂-5, B. 1 ℳ. — Hôtel Pfeiffer (Pl. h; A, 2), Bahnhofs-Platz 12, R. 2¹/₂-5, B. 1¹/₄, D. 3¹/₂ ℳ, very fair, with restaurant. — Elsässer Hof (Pl. n; A, 3), cor. of Bahnhofs-Platz and Küss-Str.; Victoria (Pl. i; A, 3), Küss-Str. 7, R. 2-3, B. 1, D. 2-2¹/₂ ℳ, unpretending; Schermuly (Pl. o; B, 2), Kuhngasse 13, R. 2-2¹/₂, B. 1, D. 2 ℳ; Rheinischer Hof (Pl. p; A, 3), Bahnhofs-Platz 7, both these very fair; Hôtel des Vosges, Bahnhofs-Platz 3; Royal, Küss-Str. 3, new, R. from 2 ℳ.

In the Town: *Ville de Paris (Pl. a; C, 3), Meisengasse 13a, at the cor. of the Broglie-Platz, in the busiest part of the town, R. from 3, B. 1¹/₂, D. 4 ℳ, first-class, excellent wine and cuisine; *Maison Rouge *(Palast-Hôtel Rotes Haus;* Pl. c, C 3), Kleber-Platz, R. from 3, B. 1¹/₄, déj. 3, D. 3¹/₂-4 ℳ, with café-restaurant. — Englischer Hof (Hôtel Garni; Pl. b, B 3), Pariser Staden 5; Hôtel de France (Pl. e; C, 3), Jung-St-Peters-Platz; Rebstock (Pl. g; B, 3), Gerbergraben 38, corner of the Lang-Str., R. 1¹/₂-3, B. 1, D. 2¹/₂ ℳ; Union (frequented by Roman Catholics), Kellermann-Staden 8. 2¹/₄-4, B. 1, D. 3 ℳ; Weber's Hôtel Krone (Pl. d; B, 2), Kronenburger-Str. 26, R. 2¹/₂-3, B. 1, D. 2¹/₂ ℳ: Stadt Basel (Pl. l; D, 4), Metzger-Platz; Schmutz, Züricher-Str. 7, wine and Munich beer on draught; Evangelisches Vereinshaus, Finkmatt-Str. 7 (Pl. C, 2), R. 1¹/₂-4¹/₂, D. 1¹/₂ ℳ, very fair.

Pensions. *Köbig,* Manteuffel-Str. 24; *Internationale,* Universitäts-Str. 26, first floor; *Riedmann,* Fischart-Str. 12 (Pl. F, 3).

Wine Restaurants, besides those at the hotels. *Valentin,* Alte Weinmarkt 50, first-class (no prices stated on bill of fare); *Stiftskeller,* Münster-Platz (p. 483); *Raiffeisenstube,* Alter Weinmarkt, near the Kleine Metzig; *Sorg,* Fasanengasse 4; *Kempf,* Kinderspielgasse 46; *Zum Sänger-haus,* Julian-Str. 5 (Pl. D, 1; Alsatian wine usually drunk at last five). —

Beer. *Germania* (Pl. E, 3), Universitäts-Platz 1, with seats outside in summer, D. 1¹/₂-2 ℳ; *Luxhof,* Luxhofgasse 1, to the S. of the Broglie; *Münchener Kindl* (Franciscan), Brandgasse 12; *Piton,* Alter Kornmarkt 11; *Löwenbräu,* Gewerbslauben 47 (Roman masonry in the cellar, uncovered by the new building); *Spatenbräu,* Schlossergasse 31; *Stadt München,* Küfergasse 3, with a fine old façade; *Krokodil,* Schlauchgasse. — *Strassburg Beer* (famous since 1446) is obtainable at the *Elsässer Tavern* (Gruber & Co.), Kornmarkt 18, and elsewhere. — *Automatic Restaurants* in the Alte Weinmarkt, in the Hohe Steg, etc.

Cafés. *Du Broglie,* *Wiener Café,* both in the Broglie-Platz, tables out of doors in summer. — **Beer Gardens.** *Orangerie Restaurant* (D. 2-3 ℳ), see p. 488; *Bäckehiesel* (Gruber & Co.), outside the W. entrance

of the Orangerie, with fine room; *Tivoli*, outside the Schiltigheimer-Tor,
beyond the 'Contades' (Pl. E, 1); *Rheinlust*, see p. 488.

Cab Tariff. A. ORDINARY CABS.	During the day.		In the evening (after the street-lamps are lit).	
	1-2 pers.	3-4 pers.	1-2 pers.	3-4 pers.
Per Drive:	ℳ pf.	ℳ pf.	ℳ pf.	ℳ pf.
Drive within the town and to Tivoli	—.75	—.90	1.—	1.20
To the Orangerie from the station	1.20	1.40	1.80	2.10
To the Orangerie from other parts of the town	1.—	1.20	1.60	1.90
By Time:				
Per ¹/₂ hr.	1.20	1.45	1.60	1.90
„ 1 hr.	2.—	2.40	2.60	2.90
For each ¹/₄ hr. additional	—.40	—.50	—.50	—.60

Trunk, 20 pf. — Between midnight and 6 a.m. the fares are higher.
B. TAXIMETER CABS. Within the town: 1-2 pers. per 1000 metres
50 pf., each 500 m. more 10 pf.; 3-5 pers. per 750 m. 50 pf., each 375 m.
more 10 pf. Outside the circumvallation: 1-5 pers. 50 pf. per 750 m.,
10 pf. for each 375 m. more. From 10 p.m. till 6 a.m. 50 pf. per 500 m.,
10 pf. for each 250 m. more. — Luggage, 25 pf. per 55 lbs. (25 kg.).

Tramways. — 1. From the *Central Railway Station* (Pl. A, 2, 3)
viâ the Kleber-Platz (Pl. C, 3) and Metzger-Tor (Pl. D, 3) to *Kehl* (p. 370).
— 2. From the *Central Railway Station* viâ the Stein-Platz (Pl. C, 1)
to the *Kehler-Tor* (Pl. A, 4). — 3. From the *Central Railway Station*
viâ the Broglie-Platz (Pl. C, D, 3) to the *Orangerie* (Pl. G, H, 2). — 4.
From the *Central Railway Station* viâ the Metzger-Tor (Pl. D, 3) to
Neuhof. — 5. From *Hönheim* viâ Bischheim (comp. Pl. C, 1), Stein-
Str., and the Metzger-Tor (Pl. D, 3) to *Neudorf* (Ost). — 6. From
Neudorf (West) viâ the Metzger-Tor (Pl. D, 3) and Kronenburger-Str.
(Pl. B, 2) to *Kronenburg*. — 7. From the *Kleber-Platz* (Pl. C, 3) viâ the
Broglie-Platz (Pl. C, D, 3) and Germania (Pl. E, 3) to *Ruprechtsau* (Pl.
H, 1). — 8. From *Tivoli* (comp. Pl. E, 1) viâ the Broglie-Platz to the *Schirm-
ecker-Tor* (comp. Pl. A, 4). — 9. From *Tivoli* viâ the Schirmecker-Tor (comp.
Pl. A, 4) to *Lingolsheim*. — 10. *Circular Line*. From the Central Railway
Station viâ the Stein-Platz (Pl. C, 1), Vogesen-Str., and Schwarzwald-
Str. to the Arnold-Platz (Pl. G, 3), returning viâ the Germania (Pl.
E, 3) and the Raben-Platz (Pl. C, D, 4) to the Central Railway Station. —
11. From the *Central Railway Station* (Pl. A, 2, 3) viâ Königshofen and
Eckbolsheim to *Wolfisheim* (comp. Pl. A, 4) and *Breitschwickerheim*. —
12. From the Metzger-Platz (Pl. D, 4) viâ Illkirch to *Grafenstaden* (p. 495).

Baths. *Municipal Swimming Baths*, Nikolaus-Ring 10 (Pl. E, 3).
— *River Baths* at the Kehl Bridge (tramway), on both banks.

Theatres. *Stadt-Theater* (Pl. D, 2, 3; p. 486), from 15th Sept. to
15th May; *Eden-Theater*, at the Terminus Hotel (p. 475). — **Military
Music** at midday in the Kleber-Platz or in the Broglie; in summer also
towards evening in the Broglie or in the Contades. — Art and Industrial
Exhibition in the *Elsässische Kunsthaus*, Brandgasse 6 (Pl. D, 3; adm. free).

Post & Telegraph Office (Pl. E, 3), Hohenlohe-Str. — **Strangers'
Enquiry Office** (*Fremdenverkehrsverein*), Meisengasse 1 (Pl. C, 3).

Pâtés de Foie Gras (invented by the cook of Marshal Contades,
Governor of Alsace in 1762-88). *L. Henry*, *E. Doyen*, *Feyel*, Münster-
gasse; *Gerst*, Kirchgasse; *A. Henry*, Küss-Str. 12; *J. G. Hummel*, Lange-
Str. 103; *A. Michel*, Krämergasse 11; *Ed. Artzner*, Schlossergasse 18.

Principal Attractions (collections closed on Monday): Minster
(p. 479; ascend tower); Collections in the Episcopal Palace (p. 484); Church
of St. Thomas (p. 485); Broglie (p. 486); Imperial Palace (p. 486); University (p. 487); Orangerie (p. 488). — Those who have time should take
a ride on the circular route tramway (No. 10, see above).

English Church Service once a month at the Pension Köbig
(p. 475); chaplain from Baden-Baden.

Strassburg (470 ft.), the capital of Alsace and German Lorraine, the seat of the governor and administration of that province, the headquarters of the 15th Corps of the German army, the seat of a university (see below), and the see of a Roman Catholic bishop, with 170,000 inhab. (in 1871, 78,130), including its garrison of 15,500 men, is situated on the *Ill*, 1 M. from the Rhine, with which it is connected by a canal. As a medium of communication between Germany, France, and Switzerland, Strassburg has long enjoyed extensive commercial relations. Recently it has also become a manufacturing place of some importance, with tobacco factories, breweries, engine-works, foundries, and tanneries.

Argentoratum, the oldest name of Strassburg, denotes a Celtic settlement, which probably owed its origin to the intersection here of the road from Gaul to Upper Germany with that along the Rhine valley. The Romans established a castrum at this point (in 9 A.D.?), which served, along with Mayence, as the headquarters of the legions on the Upper Rhine. The Emp. Julian gained a brilliant victory here over the Alemanni in 357. — The name *Stratisburgum* appears towards the end of the 6th cent., to which period the foundation of the bishopric is also ascribed. As an episcopal city, Strassburg attained great prosperity through its shipping and trade in wine. The inhabitants (30,000 in number) overthrew the bishop and acquired independence at the battle of Oberhausbergen in 1262. Their skill in the arts of war enabled them to maintain their position, and in 1445 they successfully defended their city against 50,000 Armagnacs who invaded Alsace under the Dauphin of France. The Reformation gained a footing at Strassburg in 1520, and for a century and a half thereafter the minster was almost uninterruptedly used for the Protestant service. On 30th Sept., 1681, Louis XIV., who had already conquered the rest of Alsace, seized the city of Strassburg, and France was confirmed in its possession by the Peace of Ryswyck in 1697. By the Peace of Frankfort, 10th May, 1871, the city was restored to the German Empire.

The **University,** founded in 1567, was closed at the time of the French Revolution, but was re-opened in 1872. Many distinguished men have been educated here, and Goethe, after a prolonged course of study in the society of Herder, Stilling, and other talented fellow-students, graduated here as a doctor of laws in 1771. In 1794 the National Convention suppressed the university as being a stronghold of the German element in Alsace, and in 1803 it was converted into a French academy, which in its turn was closed in 1870.

Strassburg has always been regarded as a place of the utmost strategical importance, and in a letter of Emp. Maximilian I. it is termed the bulwark of the Holy Roman Empire, and commended for its old-German honesty and bravery. Strassburg artillery was famous in the middle ages. The **Fortifications** were much strengthened by the French, who constituted Strassburg their third great arsenal. The siege of 1870 began on 13th Aug., the bombardment on 18th Aug.; and after a determined and gallant resistance the town capitulated on 27th September. The *Citadel*, erected by Vauban in 1682-84, was converted into a heap of ruins, while the *Steintor* on the N. and the *Weissturmtor* on the W. were almost entirely destroyed. The quarters of the town adjoining these gates suffered terribly, but no trace of the havoc now remains. The German fortifications consist of an extensive girdle of fifteen strong outworks, some of them 4-5 M. from the town (comp. pp. 475, 495), and of an inner rampart, enclosing a space nearly thrice the area of the former town.

The political vicissitudes of the city find their external counterpart in its **Architectural Character.** Its prosperity as a free imperial city is illustrated by the noble Minster and other old churches and by a few public buildings (pp. 479, 485) and private dwellings in the Renaissance style, chiefly in the side-streets near the cathedral (pp. 483, 485). A considerable layer of structures in the Louis XV. style was deposited by the 18th cent., when the noblesse of both banks of the Rhine were attracted by the brilliant court of the French Cardinal-Bishop (pp. 483, 484). The plans were furnished by *Rob. de Cotte, Blondel, Pinot,* and other Parisians, but the execution was entrusted to local architects. A third important building era set in with the recent expansion of the city under German rule. The monumental edifices, such as the University, the Emperor's Palace, and the new churches, are accompanied by a growing number of new private residences, chiefly in the Renaissance style. — The numerous storks are an unfailing source of interest to British and American visitors.

From the RAILWAY STATION (*Zentral-Bahnhof;* Pl. A, 2, 3) we follow the Kuhngasse to the canalized Ill. In the Kleber-Staden, to the left, are the *Synagogue*, a Romanesque building (1898), and the old railway-station, now a *Market* (Pl. B, 2).

Crossing the Kronenburg Bridge, we reach the ALTE WEINMARKT (Pl. B, 3), which contains a *Monumental Fountain* (1895), with reliefs of the Alsatian poets, Ehrenfried, August, and Adolf Stöber (d. 1835, 1884, & 1892). — A little to the S.W. is *Old St. Peter's Church* (Pl. B, 3), a building of the 14-15th cent., with four large reliefs in wood (right and left of the entrance) by Veit Wagener (1501). The old quarter to the S. of this church has many quaint and picturesque features.

.... The WEINMARKT-STRASSE, the HOHE STEG (Pl. B, C, 3), and the MEISENGASSE, ending at the Broglie (p. 486), form the chief artery of traffic in the old town. — At the beginning of the Hohe Steg, to the right, is the small *Eisern-Manns-Platz*, deriving its name from the 'iron man', an ancient cognizance of Strassburg to be seen on a house here. — We pass the *Kleine Metzig*, recently rebuilt in the German Renaissance style, to the KLEBER - PLATZ (Pl. C, 3), which is adorned with a bronze **Statue of Kleber,** by *Grass*, erected in 1840. The inscriptions give a brief account of the career of the general, who was a native of Strassburg (b. 1753, murdered at Cairo in 1800). — The so-called **Aubette,** on the N. side of the Platz, was totally destroyed by the bombardment of 1870, but has been tastefully restored, the former façade having been retained. It was originally used in part for military purposes, and its name is said to refer to the reveille or morning-call. The groundfloor now contains *Guard Rooms* and some shops. The upper floor is devoted to the *Conservatorium of Music.* — A little to the E. is the *Temple Neuf*, or *Neue Kirche* (Pl. C, 3), a Dominican church of the 13th cent., entirely burned down during the siege of 1870, but rebuilt in an imposing Romanesque style. It contains a fine organ, and the tombstone of the mystic Johann Tauler (1290-1361). Adjoining the church is the *Protestant Gymnasium*, an institution of which the Strassburgers have been justly proud for more than two centuries. — A little to the N. is the Protestant *Jung-St-Peter-Kirche* (Pl. C, 2), erected in 1250-1320, and restored in 1897-1901, with an interesting interior (entr. in Jung-St-Peter-gässchen).

From the Kleber-Platz the GEWERBSLAUBEN, a busy street with arcades under the houses on the E. side, leads to the S. to the Gutenberg-Platz. [At No. 12 Alte Kornmarkt (the first street parallel with the Gewerbslauben on the W.), over the middle window of the first floor, is a small relief of 1768, representing Frederick the Great playing the flute.]

The GUTENBERG-PLATZ (Pl. C, 3, 4) is so called from the *Statue of Gutenberg*, the inventor of printing, by David d'Angers (1840). The four bas-reliefs are emblematical of the blessings of the invention in the four quarters of the globe, and comprise likenesses of many celebrated men. The first Strassburg printer was *Johann Mentel* or *Mentelin*, who flourished about 1458-73, and was perhaps either a pupil or assistant of Gutenberg (comp. p. 275). — The Gutenberg-Platz is bounded on the S.W. by the **Hôtel du Commerce** (Pl. 3; C, 4), formerly the town-hall, built in the Renaissance style in 1582-85, and extended towards the S. in 1867. — The Alte Fischmarkt (see p. 485) runs to the S. from the Gutenberg-Platz.

From the Gutenberg-Platz the Krämergasse leads to the E. towards the Minster, the W. façade of which, in red sandstone from the Vosges, produces a brilliant effect in the light of a clear afternoon.

The ****Minster** (Pl. D, 3; *Monasterium Sanctae Mariae Virginis*) is the cathedral of the see of Strassburg, said to have been founded about 600 and dedicated from the very first to the Holy Virgin. The earliest building of architectural importance was begun in 1015 by *Bishop Wernher von Hapsburg* (1001-27) and continued by *Bishop William I.* (1028-47). The date of its completion is not known. Repeated fires gave occasion for the erection of a new church, which was begun in 1176 under *Bishop Conrad I.*, mainly on the existing foundations, but after a design calculated to make it one of the most considerable Romanesque edifices in Germany. While the apse and the transept were slowly progressing, Gothic architecture had become established in France, and of course exercised an influence on all buildings in course of construction. This influence is apparent in the articulation of the S. transept, in the tracery of its round and pointed windows, and in its elaborate portal. The architecture of the nave, begun about 1250 (nearly the same time as the choir of Cologne Cathedral) and finished in 1290, is almost exclusively Gothic.† The name of the

---

† In the accompanying plan the Romanesque parts of the building are shown in black, the Gothic shaded.

architect is unknown. We can gather, however, from analogies of
style that he had been a diligent student of French architecture
(such as that of the church of St. Denis, finished in 1231). He was,
however, by no means a mere servile copyist, but a thoughtful and

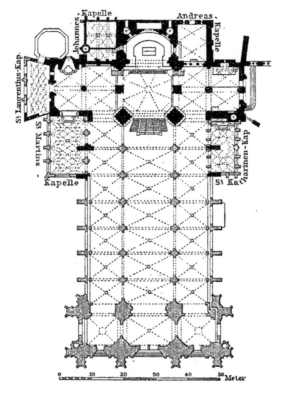

original master, who pre-eminently surpassed his contemporaries
in his keen sense of symmetry. His work may be characterized as
the first important manifestation of the Gothic style on German
soil. In 1277 the citizens, justly proud of their recently acquired
independence (p. 477), took in hand the construction of the W. façade.
It is in connection with the latter that we encounter the name of
Erwin von Steinbach for the first time. Of the origin and training of this master we know nothing, and even the accuracy of his
surname is questioned. That he was a stranger may be inferred

from the discrepancy of the style of his work from that previously exhibited in the minster. Among the extant designs ascribed (with more or less certainty) to him is one (p. 485) which accords with the execution up to the top of the gable of the side-portals. Erwin died in 1318. The office of cathedral-architect long remained in his family, the last scion of which is supposed to be *Master Gerlach*, who completed the third stage of the towers in 1365. Thereafter the idea of carrying through Erwin's designs for the façade seems to have been given up, while an important innovation, the construction of the platform between the towers, was resolved on. In 1399 *Ulrich von Ensingen* of Swabia, who showed astonishing command of the constructive possibilities, began the erection of the octagonal story of the tower, with its lofty windows and bold corner-turrets. To him is due also the heightening of the octagonal tower by another low story (1419), which completed the substruction for the spire. The identity of the '*Junker von Prag*', who also are credited with work on the tower, is uncertain. Equal technical ability is shown by the open-work spire, constructed by *Johann Hültz* of Cologne (1420-39).

The work of the following centuries was confined to renovation and small additions. Great damage was caused by a conflagration in 1759, by the fanaticism of the French Republicans in 1793, and by the German bombardment in 1870. All traces of the injury which the cathedral sustained during the siege have now been removed under the superintendence of the architect *Klotz*. The roof has been covered with copper, and a Romanesque dome was built over the crossing in 1878-79. From 1890 to 1895 the minster-architect was *Fr. Schmitz,* who completed Cologne Cathedral.

The **Façade,* by Erwin of Steinbach, is justly the most admired part of the edifice, and presents a singularly happy union of the style of N. France (horizontal members, and fine rose-window, 44 ft. in diameter) with the perpendicular tendency peculiar to German cathedrals. The walls are covered with delicate tracery, and the entire building is embellished with numerous sculptures (many of them restored in the 19th cent.).

The niches of the gallery of the first story contain equestrian figures of *Clovis* (founder of the first minster), *Dagobert* (founder of the bishopric), *Rudolph of Hapsburg* (who invested the town with many privileges; these three erected in 1291, but since renewed), and *Louis XIV.* (erected in 1823). In the niches of the second and third stories are statues of 20 other emperors and kings. — Over the rose-window are the *Virgin* and *Apostles*, with the *Saviour* above them.

The sculptures of the three portals illustrate the Christian doctrine of the Fall and Redemption. On the *Left Side Portal* are scenes from the early life of Christ and figures of the Cardinal Virtues and the Seven Works of Mercy. On the *Main Portal* are reliefs from the Passion and statues of prophets, with the Virgin and King Solomon, as the representative of the highest earthly wisdom. (The middle, beardless prophet to the left, in mediæval dress, is said by tradition to be a portrait of Erwin of Steinbach.) On the *Right Side Portal* is a relief of the Last Judgment, with figures of the Foolish Virgins and the Tempter to the left, and of the Wise Virgins and a prophet to the right.

The late-Romanesque *S. Portal* also merits examination. The
sculptures with which it is adorned date from about 1250. Of the
reliefs over the doors the Coronation of the Virgin has been restored,
while the Death of Mary remains almost in its original condition.
King Solomon between the doors is modern. The beautiful female
figures on the right and left are mediæval symbols of Christianity
and Judaism. The statues of *Erwin* and *Sabina* (the more or less
apocryphal daughter of Erwin) were erected in 1840.

On the N. side is the late-Gothic *Chapel of St. Lawrence*, with
coarsely realistic sculptures from the martyrdom of the saint (restored), built in front of the Romanesque façade of the N. transept in
1494-1505. On the pillars to the left is the Adoration of the Magi;
to the right are statues of St. Lawrence, Pope Sixtus IV., and others.

The *Interior (open 8-9, 10-12, and 2-5 or 2-6; best light in
the afternoon), consisting of a nave and aisles, with transept and
a somewhat shallow choir, is 360 ft. in length and 135 ft. in width.
It differs from that of other German cathedrals in possessing greater
width in proportion to its height, and surpasses them in harmonious
effect. The noble window-tracery and the open triforium are direct
reminiscences of St. Denis. The subdued light enters through admirable stained-glass windows of the 14-15th cent., the subjects of
which include apostles, saints, bishops, German sovereigns, and
scenes from the lives of Christ and the Virgin. The middle window
of the choir is modern. The fresco of the Last Judgment on the
triumphal arch is by Steinheil (1875). In the nave is the *Pulpit*,
richly sculptured in stone, and executed in 1485-87 for John
Geiler of Kaysersberg (d. 1510; p. 520). The *Font* in the N.
transept dates from 1453. — The *Chapel of St. Catharine*,
at the E. end of the S. aisle, was added in 1349 and revaulted in
1547. — Opposite, at the E. end of the N. aisle, is the *Chapel of
St. Martin*, of 1515-20. — The *Apse* was frescoed by E. Steinle
(p. 289) in 1877-80. — The *Chapel of St. John* (13th cent.), to
which a few steps descend to the left of the choir, contains the
Monument of Bishop Conrad of Lichtenberg (d. 1299), executed
in Erwin's workshop. The small figure of a man in a capacious
cloak and hood (below, next the window) is said to represent Erwin.
In the court behind this chapel is the *Tombstone of Erwin*, his
wife, and one of his grandchildren. — The Romanesque *Chapel
of St. Andrew*, to the right of the choir, was finished before 1190,
but its upper part was altered at a later period. — The '*Engel-
pfeiler*', a pillar in the S. transept, is adorned with late-Romanesque sculptures (ca. 1250), representing Christ, seven angels, and
the four Evangelists.

The large astronomical **Clock** in the S. transept was c nstructed in
1838-42 by *Schwilgvé*, a clock-maker of Strassburg. It replaces a similar
clock by *Dasypodius*, constructed in 1574, which was in use down to
1789, and which in its turn formed a substitute for a still older clock,

made in 1352-54. Only a few parts of the interior and some of the decorative paintings of the old clock were used in making the present one. The exterior attracts spectators at all times, especially at noon (12.29 p.m. of Central Europe time); after the closing of the cathedral at 11.30 a.m. visitors are re-admitted by the door of the S. transept, except on festivals (30 pf., free on Frid.). On the first gallery an angel strikes the quarters on a bell in his hand; while a genius at his side reverses his sand-glass every hour. Higher up, around a skeleton which strikes the hours, are grouped figures representing boyhood, youth, manhood, and old age (the four quarters of the hour). Under the first gallery the symbolic deity of each day steps out of a niche, Apollo on Sunday, Diana on Monday, and so on. In the highest niche, at noon, the Twelve Apostles move round a figure of the Saviour. On the highest pinnacle of the side-tower, which contains the weights, is perched a cock which flaps its wings, stretches its neck, and crows, awakening the echoes of the remotest nooks of the cathedral. The mechanism also sets in motion a planetarium, behind which is a perpetual calendar.

At the end of the nave is the entrance to the *Crypt* (fee), the E. part of which dates from early in the 11th century.

The *Minster Tower (p. 481) rises from the W. façade to a vast and dizzy height. The entrance is on the S. side of the unfinished tower; ticket to the platform 20 pf., up to the turrets 50 pf., to the top of the spire (steady head necessary) 2 *M*. The visitor ascends a tolerable staircase of 335 steps to the *Platform*, 216 ft. above the street, which affords a fine *View of the town and the plain of the Rhine. To the E. is seen the Black Forest from Baden to the Blauen; W. and N. the Vosges Mountains; S. the isolated Kaiserstuhl, rising from the plain; beyond it, in the extreme distance, the Jura range. A good panorama is sold by the attendants.

Innumerable names are engraved on the parapet of the platform and on the tower itself. Among them are those of *Goethe, Herder,* and *Lavater,* on a stone to the right of the small E. door of the tower leading to the gallery. *Voltaire's* is also to be found in the neighbourhood, among many others.

From the platform to the summit of the tower is a height of 249 ft.; the entire height is therefore 465 ft. (one of the highest buildings in Europe; Eiffel Tower at Paris 985 ft., Mole Antonelliana at Turin 538 ft., Ulm Cathedral 528 ft., Cologne Cathedral 512 ft., Rouen Cathedral 485 ft., the Church of St. Olaus at Reval 475 ft., the Nicolai-Kirche at Hamburg 472 ft., St. Martin's at Landshut in Germany 462 ft., St. Stephen's at Vienna 446 ft., St. Peter's at Rome 436 ft., St. Paul's at London 404 ft.). The unfinished turrets at the corners, which seem to cling precariously to the principal structure, contain winding staircases, leading to the '*Lantern*', an open space immediately below the extreme summit.

The Münster-Platz, in front of the W. façade of the cathedral, contains several ancient examples of half-timbered architecture, the finest of which is the *Kammerzell'sche Haus* (15-16th cent.), recently well restored and fitted up as a wine-saloon (Stiftskeller, see p. 475).

In the Schloss-Platz (Pl. D, 3, 4), which lies on the S. side of the Minster, are situated the *Lyceum*, or grammar-school, and the *Roman Catholic Seminary*.

The old **Episcopal Palace** (*Schloss;* Pl. D, 4), opposite the S. portal of the Minster. was built by Rob. de Cotte for Cardinal

Armand Gaston de Rohan in 1728-41, and between that date and 1789 it was the seat of the brilliant court of three other bishops of the Rohan family. It was purchased by the town during the First Revolution. The rooms on the groundfloor retain their old decoration. In 1898 the building was fitted up for the *Municipal Museum of Art.* (*Städtisches Kunst-Museum*). In the court to the right are the *Alsatian Antiquities* (open free on Sun. 10-12.30 and on Wed. 11-12.30, at other times for a fee). On the first floor is the *Picture Gallery* (open free on Tues., Frid., & Sat. 10-12.30 & 3-6, on Sun. 10-1, on Wed. & Thurs. 10-12.30 & 3-6 for a fee of 50 pf.). The earlier section of the gallery, which was founded in 1889, contains some excellent works of the Italian, German, and Netherlandish schools; the modern section is largely devoted to Alsatian works. Catalogue 80 pf.; with illustrations, 2 ℳ 50 pf. A re-arrangement of the exhibits is in prospect.

Room I. Works of the 19th century. 448. *Hornecker*, Portrait of an old woman; *499. *J. H. Zuber*, Flock of sheep at Alt-Pfirt; 418b. *A. G. Decamps*, Landscape; 462. *M. Liebermann*, Dutch orphans; *417. *Corot*, Pond at Ville d'Avray; 410. *G. Brion*, Sunday at home.

Room II. Older Schools. To the right, 85. *Van Dyck*, Portrait; 124. *Rembrandt*, Study of an old man's head. — *Rubens*, 82. Christ, 81. St. Francis (studio-pieces); 325. *Salv. Rosa*, Heroic landscape; 351. *Dom. Theotocopulo* (Spanish), Madonna; *123. *Th. de Keyser*, Officers of the Amsterdam Silversmiths' Guild. — 354, 353. *Zurbaran*, Saints (replicas of the paintings in Genoa); 352. *Ribera*, SS. Peter and Paul; 344a, 344b. *Guardi*, Venetian scenes.

Ante-Room III. Sculptures. Fine view of the Minster. — Room IV. German schools of the 15-16th cent. 13. *Hans Baldung Grien*, Martyrdom of St. Sebastian; *1. *Conrad Witz*, SS. Mary Magdalen and Catharine; 5. *B. Zeitblom*, Christ with three apostles.

Room V. Italian Masters (15-16th cent.). 271. *School of Palma Vecchio*, Head of Christ; 223. *B. Montagna*, Adoration of the Holy Child; 275. *Cariani*, Lute-player; 216a. *Piero di Cosimo*, Madonna; 219. *Cima da Conegliano*, St. Sebastian; 312a. *Tiepolo*, Madonna with saints; 265. Caritas, copy (16th cent.) of a work by *Andrea del Sarto*, now lost.

Farther on, passing through Vestibule VI (525. *L. von Kramer*, Alsatia Antiqua, a large coloured drawing) and Ante-Room IX, we enter—

Cabinet X. *51. *Hans Memling*, Six panels from a travelling-altar; 53a. *Follower of Gerard David of Bruges*, Madonna with the spoon. — Cabinet XI. 362. *Corneille de Lyon*(?), Nobleman with a falcon; 62. *Master of the Half Figures*, Triptych; 65. *Joos von Clève the Younger*, Portrait. — Cabinet XII. 91. *Dutch School* (ca. 1660-70), Astronomer and his wife; 125. *Gabriel Metsu*, Dives and Lazarus; 155. *J. de Heem*, Still-life. — Cabinet XIII. 157. *A. van de Velde*, Ferry; 128. *P. de Hooch*, The walk; 137. *J. van Ruysdael*, Mill-stream. — Cabinet XIV. 90. *Teniers the Younger*, Card-players; 138. *J. van der Meer*, Sand-dunes. — Cabinet XV. 25. *A. Altdorfer*(?), Portrait of an architect; *Hans Baldung Grien*, 14. Young man. 15. Savant; *Bernhard Strigel*, Emperor Maximilian I.; 9 b. *Hans Holbein the Elder*, The dead Christ. — Cabinet XVI. 16. *Hans Baldung Grien*, Madonna in an arbour; 11. *Bernhard Strigel*, Death of Mary.

We pass through Cab. XV. into Corridor XVII. Italian and French Works. *251-256. Heads of Apostles, old copies from Leonardo's Last Supper; 217. *Carlo Crivelli*, Adoration of the Christ Child; 270. *Correggio*, Judith (youthful work); 368. *Watteau*, Cleaning the dishes; without a number, *Rigaud*, Count de Ruel; *Botticelli*(?), Madonna (youthful work). Sculptures by *Alfred Boucher* and *F. A. Bartholdi* (p. 497). We now return to the staircase, and proceed straight on to Rooms VII & VIII, which contain modern paintings.

In the Palace are the headquarters of the *Kaiserliche Denkmal-Archiv,* a society for the preservation and study of the monuments in Alsace (open daily, except Sun., 9-12 & 3-6), and the Reading Room of the Museum of Industrial Art, with an interesting relief of the town.

The **Maison de Notre Dame,** or *Frauenhaus* (Pl. 2, D 4; adm. daily, 9-12 & 3-5, 20 pf.), Schloss-Platz 3, built in the 14-16th cent., contains an ancient plan of the cathedral, the model of the spire, several Gothic sculptures transferred from the cathedral, designs for the tower and façade (comp. p. 481), and remains of the old clock. The graceful winding staircase, in the latest Gothic style, merits attention.

Viâ the *Ferkel-Markt* (Pl. D, 4; No. 1, at the corner, a picturesque house of 1477 and 1602), we reach the ALTE FISCHMARKT (Pl. C, 4), which connects the Gutenberg-Platz (p. 479) with the Raben-Brücke. The house where Goethe lived when a student at Strassburg (1770-71; No. 36) is indicated by a bronze portrait-bust of the poet, in relief.

At the end of the Alte Fischmarkt, near the Raben-Brücke, is the **Grosse Metzig** (Pl. 6; D, 4), built in 1588, the groundfloor of which is used as a market, while the first floor harbours the *Hohenlohe Museum,* containing an interesting collection of industrial art. This includes a room in the rococo style from the Château of Linderhof, once belonging to King Lewis II. of Bavaria. The museum is open free on Sun. (10-1) and Wed. (10-12 & 2-4) and for a fee of 50 pf. on Tues., Thurs., Frid., & Sat. (10-12 & 2-4). — No. 1 in the Kaufhausgasse, which runs hence to the W., is a Renaissance structure of 1586.

Beyond the Raben-Brücke, to the left, at No. 1 Schiffleutstaden (Pl. D, 4), is the old *Raven Inn (Gasthaus zum Raben),* with an interesting court.

To the W., Nikolausstaden No. 23, is the **Alsatian Museum** (*'Elsässisches Museum'*), which was installed in 1907 in a patrician dwelling of the 17th cent. (open on Sun., Tues., Wed., Frid., & Sat., 10-12 & 2-5; adm. 50 pf.). Its contents include costumes, furniture, domestic utensils, products of cottage-art, and so on, sometimes arranged in the form of complete rooms. The court of the building, with its wooden galleries, is also noteworthy. — To the S. of the Nikolausstaden is the old *Bürgerspital* or *City Hospital,* round which are grouped the *Medical Institutes of the University* (Pl. B, C, 4, 5). An extensive district has here been opened up for building through the demolition of the old fortifications.

The Protestant **Church of St. Thomas** (Pl. C, 4) consists, like the Minster, of a Romanesque and a Gothic part. The former, to the W., dates from about 1200-1240. The latter, consisting of a short nave with double aisles, was erected in the 14th century. Open daily; tickets, 40 pf. each, obtained from the sacristan, Thomas-Platz 5 (free on Wed., 10-12).

The choir contains a magnificent **Monument* in marble, erected by Louis XV. to *Marshal Saxe* (d. 1750), son of Augustus I., Elector of Saxony (afterwards King of Poland), and the beautiful Countess Aurora von Königsmark. It was executed by *Pigalle*, who completed it in 1776 after twenty years' labour. The marshal is in the act of descending into the tomb opened for his reception by Death, while a female figure representing France strives to detain him, and Hercules at the side in mournful attitude leans upon his club; on the left, with broken flags beneath, are the Austrian eagle, the Dutch lion, and the English leopard, symbolizing the three powers defeated by the marshal in the Flemish wars. The whole is an allegory in the questionable taste of the age, but its execution is of great delicacy and vigour. — The stone sarcophagus of *Bishop Adeloch* (d. 830), in a side-chapel to the N., dates from the 12th century. The two mummies, in the same chapel, are of the 17th century.

The *Tower* of St. Thomas's commands a fine view of the Minster, rising over the pointed roofs of the old town.

In the N.E. part of o d Strassburg lies the BROGLIE (Pl. C, D, 3), a square named after the marshal of that name who laid it out in 1742, and much frequented as a promenade, especially in the evening (band, see p. 476). At the E. end stands the *Theatre*, burned down in 1870, but since restored in its former style. In front of it is the *Reinhardbrunnen*, by Hildebrand (1902). On the S. are the *Stadthaus* (1730), the *Military Headquarters (General-Kommando;* with a monument to Lewis I. of Bavaria, born here in 1786), and the *Residence of the Governor of Alsace (Statt-halterliche Residenz)*, rebuilt in 1872-74 with retention, so far as possible, of the old materials and appearance of 1730-36. At the corner is a bronze statue of the préfect *Marquis de Lézay-Marnésia* (1810-14), by Grass, erected in 1857. Behind the Stadthaus, in the Brandgasse, is the *Exhibition of the Strassburg Art Union* (open free).

The Lézay-Marnésia-Staden leads hence along the canalized Ill to the *Church of St. Stephen* (Pl. D, 3), dating from the 13th cent. but originally founded in the 8th century. The *Café zum Ritter*, Stephans-Plan No. 17, is a Renaissance building of 1598, with a painted façade. — On the opposite bank of the Ill is the *Höhere Mädchenschule* (Pl. D, E, 3), a high school for girls, by Ott. The house of the Head Master incorporates the façade of an old patrician dwelling.

In the KAISER-PLATZ (Pl. D, 2), adjoining the river, stands the **Imperial Palace** *(Kaiser-Palast)*, built in 1883-89 in the Florentine Renaissance style from *Eggert's* designs. The building (open daily 10-6, Sun. 11-6, in winter 10-4 & 11-4; adm. 25 pf.; entr. on the right side, through the garden), 240 ft. in length by 184 ft. in depth, with a portico in front and a half-round borne by columns at its back, is richly decorated with sculptures by Berlin and Frankfort artists. The dome above the audience hall is crowned

by two colossal heralds and rises to a height of 115 ft. The palace
is roofed with tiles after Olympian patterns. The imperial rooms,
on the first floor, are decorated with paintings by *Keuffel* and
Baum of Frankfort. The staircase, the audience room (under the
dome), and the three reception rooms on the W. side are all very
handsome. — To the right, opposite the palace and separated from
each other by the Kaiser-Wilhelm-Str. (see below), are the *Hall
of the Provincial Diet (Landesausschuss)* and the *University
Library,* both in the Renaissance style and built between 1888 and
1894. The latter contains the Provincial and University Library
(915,000 vols.), founded in 1871 to replace that destroyed in the
siege (open to visitors on week-days 2-3, Sun. 9-12). In the hall
is a marble statue of Emperor William I., by Zumbusch. — Behind
the Diet Hall is the *General Post Office (Hauptpost;* Pl. E, 3).

On the N. side of the Kaiser-Platz, between two *Ministerial
Offices* (Pl. D, 2), opens the Kaiser-Friedrich-Str., leading to the
Contades (Pl. E, 1, 2), a park laid out by Marshal Contades in
1764. — To the W. of the Imperial Palace is the conspicuous dome
of the *Neue-Jung-St-Peter-Kirche* or the *Church of the Sacred
Heart* (Pl. C, D, 2), erected in 1889-93.

The Kaiser-Wilhelm-Strasse leads from the Kaiser-Platz to the
S.E., crossing the Ill by the handsome *Universitäts-Brücke* (Pl.
E, 3) and passing the *Protestant Garrison Church* (1892-97), to the
UNIVERSITÄTS-PLATZ (Pl. E, 3; monument of *Goethe as a Youth,*
1904), which is bounded on the E. by the collegiate department of
the **University** (comp. p. 477) and on the S. by the building of
the *Germania Insurance Co.* (restaurant, see p. 475).

The **Collegiate Department** (*Kollegien-Gebäude;* Pl. E,
F, 3), built in the early Italian Renaissance style in 1877-84, is
adorned with 36 statues of men of learning. About 1800 students
attend the lectures. The interior contains a handsome court, lighted
from above, richly decorated vestibules, staircases, and aula, and
extensive collections of casts and objects of antiquarian and artistic
interest. — Adjoining are the *Seismological Observatory*, the
Chemical and *Physical Institutes*, the *Botanical Garden*, and
other University departments (Pl. F, 3). The collections of the
Zoological Institute are the most extensive in Germany after those
of Berlin and Hamburg (open daily, except Mon., 10-12 and 2-4
or 2-5).

The old part of the town to the S. of the University contains
several military buildings. Near the old Academy building is the
Mechanics' School of Art (Pl. 5; E, 3), the ground in front of
which, with a monument, was used as a burial-place during the
siege. At the W. end of the Wilhelmergasse is the old *Wilhelmer-
Kirche* (Pl. 8; E, 4), with a fine Gothic monument of the 14th cent.
and good stained glass (15-16th cent.). — The *Zürich Fountain*

(Pl. 9; D, 4) commemorates an old legend told in a ballad by Fischart.

At the end of the villa-lined Ruprechtsauer Allée (tramway) lies the *Orangerie (Pl. G, H, 1, 2), a beautiful park, with a fine orangery (1806), a kiosque (adm. 20 pf.), once belonging to King Lewis II. of Bavaria, a bust of the composer *Victor Nessler* (of Strassburg; 1841-90), a restaurant (p. 475) with a large concert-room, and the 'Alsatian Peasant House' (wine).

FROM STRASSBURG TO KEHL is a pleasant trip by tramway (p. 476). The cars pass through the old Metzger-Tor (Pl. D, 4) and skirt the harbours constructed to the S.E. of the town since 1891. The road leads over the *Sporen-Insel*, formed by the temporary divergence of the 'Little Rhine' from the main stream. The large new **Harbour Works** here, with magazines of coal and petroleum, indicate the growing importance of the navigation of the Upper Rhine. Beyond the bridge over the 'Little Rhine', on the Sporen-Insel, to the right of the road, is a monument erected by Napoleon I. to General Desaix, who fell at Marengo in 1800. On the E. side of the Sporen-Insel, adjoining the new iron bridge over the Rhine (1897), is the favourite open-air pleasure-resort *Rheinlust*, affording a fine view. — *Kehl*, see p. 370.

FROM STRASSBURG TO COLMAR (p. 496) VIÂ MARKOLSHEIM, 47 M., steam-tramway in ca. 5¹/₄ hrs. (fares 3 ℳ 80, 2 ℳ 50 pf.). This line skirts the E. bank of the Rhine-Rhone Canal. The intermediate stations are unimportant.

67. From Hagenau *(Strassburg)* to Saar-gemünd *(Saarbrücken and Metz)*.

52¹/₂ M. RAILWAY in 2¹/₄ hrs. (fares 6 ℳ 80, 4 ℳ 10, 2 ℳ 70 pf.). — From Strassburg to *Metz*, 4³/₄-5 hrs.; route viâ Saarburg, see R. 68.

Hagenau, see p. 474. Our line diverges to the N.W. from that to Weissenburg, passes (2¹/₂ M.) *Schweighausen* (branch-line to Obermodern and Zabern, p. 490), and traverses part of the forest of Hagenau (p. 474). 7 M. *Merzweiler*, a busy little place with iron-works (branch-line to Walburg, p. 474). 8 M. *Mietesheim;* 10 M. *Gundershofen.* — 10¹/₂ M. *Reichshofen Werk;* 12 M. *Reichshofen Stadt* (Bellevue, at the station; Dowler, well spoken of; excursion to the battlefield, see p. 474), situated on the road from Wörth to Bitsch, by which the remnants of MacMahon's army retreated on the evening of 6th Aug., 1870. — The line enters the mountains.

13¹/₂ M. **Niederbronn.** — HOTELS. *Hôtel und Villa Matthis*, Kurplatz, R. 2-3, B. 1, D. 2¹/₂, S. 2, pens. 5¹/₂-7¹/₂ ℳ, with terrace and garden; *Goldene Kette; Doersch*, R. 1¹/₂-2, B. ³/₄, D. 2, S. 1¹/₂, pens. 4-5 ℳ, very fair; *Weissler*, R. 1-2, B. ³/₄, D. 2 ℳ; *Pens. Sorg*, 4-4¹/₂ ℳ. — Visitors' tax, 10 ℳ.

Niederbronn (650 ft.), with 3120 inhab., in the pretty valley of the *Falkensteiner Bach*, is a popular summer-resort, with saline springs (65° Fahr.) which were known to the Romans and are specially beneficial for stomach and liver complaints. Pleasant walks. The hill (1415 ft.), which rises abruptly to the W. of the town, commanding a fine view, and easily ascended in ³/₄ hr., is crowned with the ruins of the *Wasenburg*, erected in the 14th century. Other excursions may be taken to the view-tower on the *Grosse Wintersberg* (1900 ft.; 1¹/₄-1¹/₂ hr.) and through the Jäger-Tal, past the ruins of *Alt-Windstein* and *Neu-Windstein*, to Philippsburg (4-4¹/₂ hrs.). — *Jägertal* and the *Wasigenstein*, see p. 468.

18 M. *Philippsburg.* About 3 M. from here, among the woods, on a lofty rock, is the ruined castle of *Falkenstein* (12th cent.), with a fine view. — 22 M. *Bannstein.*

28 M. **Bitsch** (1005 ft.; *Hôtel de Metz*), a small town with 4700 inhab., is situated on the N. slopes of the Vosges, and commanded by *Fort Bitsch*, the fortifications of which, partly hewn in the rock, still command the valley. In the Franco-German war of 1870-71 Bitsch capitulated only after the preliminary articles of the peace had been signed.

33¹/₂ M. *Lemberg,* with glass-works; 36 M. *Enchenberg;* 38¹/₂ M. *Klein-Rederchingen;* 40¹/₂ M. *Rohrbach;* 45¹/₂ M. *Wölflingen.*

52¹/₂ M. **Saargemünd,** French *Sarreguemines* (660 ft.; *Hôt. de l'Europe; Central Hotel*), a town with 15,000 inhab., at the confluence of the *Blies* and *Saar*, the latter of which here forms the boundary between German Lorraine and Rhenish Prussia, possesses large manufactories of plush, velvet, fayence, and earthenware.

From Saargemünd to *Saarburg,* see p. 492; to *Zweibrücken,* see p. 466; to *Mommenheim (Strassburg),* see below.

At Saargemünd the line divides: the branch to the N. runs by *Hanweiler* (station for the small baths of *Rilchingen*), *Klein-Blittersdorf,* and *Brebach* to (11 M.) *Saarbrücken* (p. 204); that to the W. by *Hundlingen, Farschweiler,* and *Beningen* (p. 203), to (20¹/₂ M.) *Metz* (p. 194).

68. From Strassburg to Metz viâ Saaralben or viâ Saarburg. The North Vosges Mts.

RAILWAY viâ *Saaralben,* 106 M., in 3 hrs. (express); viâ *Saarburg,* 98¹/₂ M., in 2¹/₂-3 hrs. (express; fares 13 ℳ 80, 8 ℳ 60, 5 ℳ 40 pf.).

Strassburg, see p. 475. 5 M. *Mundolsheim.* At (6 M.) *Vendenheim* the line to Weissenburg diverges to the right (R. 65). The train crosses the *Zorn* and passes the large lunatic asylum of *Stephansfeld.* 11 M. *Brumath.*

14 M. *Mommenheim,* the junction of the lines to Saaralben (Saargemünd) and Saarburg, which diverge from each other here.

RAILWAY TO BENSDORF VIÂ SAARALBEN. — 18½ M. *Alteckendorf;* 20½ M. *Ettendorf.* —· 24½ M. *Obermodern,* the junction of a line to Schweighausen and Hagenau (p. 488).

FROM OBERMODERN TO ZABERN, 14 M., railway in ¾ hr.

3½ M. **Buchsweiler** *(Sonne,* R. 1-1½, B. ½, D. with wine 2½ ℳ); a small town with 3000 inhab., in the old 'Hanauer Ländchen', which belonged to Hesse-Darmstadt down to the French Revolution. The Rathaus has a handsome portal. The Gymnasium, established in 1612, stands on the site of the old château. Many of the houses have Renaissance balconies. An admirable view is obtained from the *Bastberg* (1255 ft.), a hill of curious geological formation, abounding in coal; its fossils attracted the attention of Goethe (refuge-hut on the summit). — From Buchsweiler branch-line to INGWEILER (see below).

7 M. **Neuweiler** *(Anker, Wolff,* good red wine), a town of 1400 inhab., possesses two interesting churches: the Protestant *St. Adelphi-Kirche,* a late-Romanesque edifice of the 12th cent., and the Roman Catholic *Church of SS. Peter and Paul,* Romanesque with later additions, restored in 1852 (fine crypt). The double chapel of St. Sebastian of the latter church dates from the 11th cent. or even earlier. The N. portal of the nave deserves notice. Above the town (½ hr.) rises the ruin of *Herrenstein,* commanding a picturesque view (rfmts.).

8 M. **Dossenheim** *(Railway Hotel)* lies at the entrance of the *Zinzel-Tal,* through which a pléasant excursion may be made to (3¾ M.) *Oberhof* (Mathis, very fair), and (1½ M.) *Grauftal* (branch-line from Lützelburg; p. 492), with curious rock-dwellings. About 4½ M. to the N. of Oberhof· is *Lützelstein* (Pflug, very fair), with a picturesque old castle. Another walk from Dossenheim is the following: we ascend to the left at the beginning of the woods in the Zinzel-Tal· to the *Taubenschlagfels,* above *Ernolsheim;* then cross the hill, viâ the so-called *Heidenstadt* and *Langentaler Kreuz,* to the *Michaels-Kapelle,* above *St. Johann* (p. 493), and to *Zabern.*

9½ M. *Hattmatt;* 12 M. *Steinburg;* 13 M. *Zornhof.* — 14 M. *Zabern* (see below).

The line ascends the wide valley of the *Moder.* — 26½ M. *Menchhofen;* 28 M. *Ingweiler* (Hôtel des Vosges, very fair), connected by a branch-line with Buchsweiler (see above); 31½ M. *Wimmenau* (1 hr. from *Lichtenberg,* at the foot of a fort destroyed in 1870); 34 M. *Wingen* (branch to *Münztal,* 7½ M.). Fine woods. Long tunnel. 38 M. *Puberg;* 41 M. *Tiefenbach;* 43 M. *Adamsweiler.* Near (45½ M.) *Diemeringen* are the remains of a Roman villa. 47 M. *Domfessel,* with a fine Gothic church of the 14th cent.; 48½ M. *Völlerdingen;* 51½ M. *Oermingen.*

54 M. *Kalhausen,* junction of the line to Saargemünd and Saarbrücken; 56½ M. *Herbitzheim.* — 59 M. *Saaralben,* the junction of the Bensdorf and Saargemünd line (p. 492). — 64 M. *Ottweiler;* 70 M. *Leiningen.*

75 M. *Bensdorf,* and thence to *Metz,* see p. 492.

FROM MOMMENHEIM (p. 489) TO BENSDORF VIÂ SAARBURG. — 17½ M. *Hochfelden;* 20½ M. *Wilwisheim;* 22½ M. *Dettweiler;* 25 M. *Steinburg* (to Obermodern and Hagenau, see above).

27½ M. **Zabern.** — HOTELS. *Hôtel de la Gare (Bahnhofs-Hôtel),* at the railway-station, with popular restaurant and small garden, R. 1½-2,

B. ¹/₂, D. 1¹/₂-2 *M: Hôtel des Vosges,* on the Canal, in the Haupt-Str., with beer-garden, R. 1¹/₂-4, B. ¹/₂, D. with wine 2¹/₂ *M; Sonne,* Haupt-Str., R. from 2, B. ¹/₂ *M; Hôtel Central,* Schloss-Platz. — *Karpfen,* Haupt-Str., opposite the Schloss, good wine.

CARRIAGE to Hoh-Barr and back 6, with two horses 8 *M,* incl. stay of 3 hrs.; to Dagsburg and Wangenburg 20, to Wangenburg 18 *M;* to Pfalzburg 7, with two horses 12 *M.*

Zabern (610 ft.), also called *Elsass-Zabern* to distinguish it from Rhein-Zabern and Berg-Zabern (pp. 472, 464), the French *Saverne,* the *Tres Tabernae* of the Romans, and formerly the capital of the Wasgau, is now a dull town with 8900 inhab., lying at the entrance of the *Zaberner Senke,* a narrow defile of the Vosges, watered by the Zorn, and close to the base of the beautifully-wooded lower hills. On the latter appear the ruins of Greifenstein to the right (W.), and to the left (S.W.) Hoh-Barr (p. 493). The *Rhine-Marne Canal* also traverses the pass and intersects the town.

The former *Schloss* of the Bishops of Strassburg, with its conspicuous red sandstone walls, was erected in its present form in 1784 by Cardinal de Rohan, who held a brilliant court here; it is now used as a barrack. The principal façade is turned towards the garden. An *Obelisk* in the planted square in front of the Schloss, erected in 1666, records the distances of 100 different towns from Zabern in German miles.

. Ascending the Haupt-Str., we reach the *Haupt-Kirche,* chiefly in the late-Gothic style of the latter half of the 15th century. The pulpit dates from 1497. The decoration is modern. The court-gateway, to the N. of the church, leads to a *Museum,* in which are preserved Roman, Gallic, Celtic, and Frankish antiquities found in the neighbourhood, including several roof-shaped tombstones with Roman inscriptions from Kempel, Fallberg, and Dagsburg.

From Zabern to *Molsheim* and *Schlettstadt,* see pp. 503 & 508; to *Obermodern,* see p. 490; to the *N. Vosges,* see p. 493.

. Near Zabern the railway enters the narrow and picturesque valley of the *Zorn,* and intersects the Vosges range at its narrowest point, the *Zaberner Senke* (see above), which separates the Central from the Lower Vosges. The line runs parallel with the highroad, the brook, and the Rhine-Marne Canal. Bridges, embankments, viaducts, and tunnels follow each other in rapid succession. — From (30¹/₂ M.) *Stambach* (A. Kling; E. Kling) a marked path leads through the *Bärenbach-Tal* to (3-3¹/₂ hrs.) *Dagsburg* (p. 494). A prettier way, but about 1 hr. longer, is that by the forester's house of *Haberacker* (marked red and white to that point, and then red), comp. p. 494.

33¹/₂ M. *Lützelburg* (Gasthof zur Lützelburg), the first station in German Lorraine, is separated by the Zorn from a bold rock crowned with the ruins of the *Lützelburger Schloss,* a castle dating from the 11th cent., under which runs a tunnel.

To *Dagsburg*, see p. 494. — Branch-railway (from which a line diverges for *Pfalzburg*, p. 493; 3¹/₂ M.) viâ (7¹/₂ M.) *Grauftal* (p. 490) to *Drulingen*, 12¹/₂ M. in 1¹/₂ hr.

The line soon quits the valley of the Zorn. A handsome bridge spans the river with one of its arches, and with the other the *Rhine-Marne Canal*, which here turns to the right side of the valley. — Beyond (36¹/₂ M.) *Arzweiler* the railway penetrates the last of the obstructing hills by means of a tunnel, 2927 yds. in length, above which is another tunnel for the canal. — The hills now recede. Among the mountains to the left the two Donon peaks are prominent 42 M. *Rieding.*

44¹/₂ M. **Saarburg** (*Hôtel Abondance*, R. 1¹/₂-2, B. ³/₄, D. with wine 2¹/₂ $\mathcal{M}$; *Bayersdörfer*, at the station, R. 1³/₄-2, B. ³/₄, D. 1¹/₂ $\mathcal{M}$), on the *Saar*, a small and ancient town, with 9800 inhab. and a strong garrison, enclosed by walls and gates. It must not be confounded with Saarburg near Trèves (see p. 186).

FROM SAARBURG TO SAARGEMÜND, 34 M., railway in 1-1³/₄ hr. (fares 4 $\mathcal{M}$ 20, 2 $\mathcal{M}$ 60, 1 $\mathcal{M}$ 65 pf.). — To *Berthelmingen*, where carriages are changed, see below. 10 M. *Finstingen;* 14 M. *Wolfskirchen;* 17¹/₂ M. *Saarwerden;* 18¹/₂ M. **Saar-Union** (*Hôtel du Commerce*, very fair), a place consisting of the two small towns of *Bockenheim* and *Neu-Saarwerden* (3000 inhab.). 24¹/₂ M. *Saaralben* is the junction of the line from Mommenheim to Bensdorf (see p. 490). Then *Willerwald, Hambach, Neuscheuern.* — 34 M. *Saargemünd*, see p. 489.

FROM SAARBURG TO ALBERSCHWEILER, 10 M., railway in 1 hr. — 3¹/₂ M. *Oberhammer* (branch-line to *Vallerystal-Dreibrunn*, viâ *Hessen*, with interesting ruins of an old abbey-church). — 10 M. **Alberschweiler** (*Hôtel Cayet*, R. 1¹/₂-2, D. with wine 2¹/₂ $\mathcal{M}$, very fair) is a good starting-point for excursions into the Dagsburg district (p. 494) and the upper valley of the Saar.

FROM SAARBURG TO NANCY, 49 M., railway (express) in 2 hrs. — 12¹/₂ M. *Deutsch-Avricourt*, the German frontier-station and seat of the custom-house, connected by a branch with Bensdorf (see below); 13¹/₂ M. *Igney-Avricourt* (the French frontier-station). Thence to *Nancy*, see *Baedeker's Northern France.*

At Saarburg the line to Metz begins, and follows the course of the *Saar*. — 46¹/₂ M. *Saaraltdorf;* 51¹/₂ M. *Berthelmingen* (see above). The line now diverges to the left, intersecting a hilly and wooded country, with several large ponds. Several unimportant stations. 58¹/₂ M. *Lauterfingen;* 63¹/₂ M. *Nebing.*

66 M. *Bensdorf*, the junction for the line from Mommenheim viâ Saaralben (p. 490).

Bensdorf is connected by branch-lines with (21¹/₂ M.) *Deutsch-Avricourt* (see above) and with (21¹/₂ M.) *Moncel* (for Nancy).

68¹/₂ M. *Rodalben-Bermeringen;* 71 M. *Mörchingen*, strongly garrisoned; 73 M. *Landorf;* 76 M. *Brülingen;* 80 M. *Baudrecourt.* — At (85 M.) *Remilly* we join the line from Saarbrücken to (98¹/₂ M.) *Metz*, see p. 203.

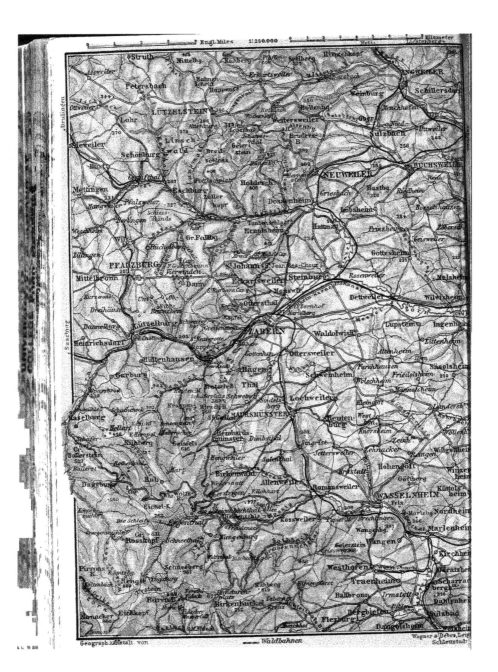

The North Vosges Mountains.

Zabern is a good starting-point for excursions among these mountains. — From Zabern to *St. Johann* and *Dossenheim*, 6 M., returning
by railway or taking the train to *Buchsweiler* (p. 490). — From Zabern
to *Pfalzburg*, 7¹/₂ M., and by a branch-line to *Lützelburg* in ¹/₂ hr. (see
p. 492). — From Zabern to the top of the *Greifenstein* and back in 2-
2¹/₂ hrs. — From Zabern viâ *Hoh-Barr, Brotschberg, Haberacker,* and
Ochsenstein to *Stambach* (p. 491), 5 hrs.; viâ *Hoh-Barr* to *Dagsburg*
and *Wangenburg*, 7-7¹/₂ hrs.

About 2¹/₄ M. to the N.E. of Zabern lies the village of **St. Johann,**
Fr. *St. Jean-des-Choux,* formerly the seat of a Benedictine Abbey,
the Romanesque church of which, re-consecrated in 1127, but partly
disfigured in the 18th cent., deserves notice. The *St. Michaels-
Kapelle* situated above it commands a fine view. Along the ridge,
past the Taubenschlag rock, to Dossenheim, see p. 490.

From Zabern to Pfalzburg, 6¹/₄ M., the road ascends the steep
slopes of the 'Pfalzburger Steig'. Pedestrians turn to the left and
pass the precipitous *Karlssprung,* above which they regain the road.
— **Pfalzburg** (1035 ft.; *Stadt Metz; Rappen,* very fair) with
3700 inhab., situated in an unattractive lofty plain, and fortified
down to 1872, possesses a monument to Marshal Mouton, Comte
Lobau, one of Napoleon's officers, who was born here in 1770
(d. 1838).

To the W. of Zabern, on the summit of a wooded hill, to the
right of the entrance of the narrower part of the valley of the Zorn,
rises the ruin of **Greifenstein** (1255 ft.). In Zabern we follow
the Greifensteiner - Str., which diverges from the main street to
the N. of the canal (or we may go along the bank of the canal), and
after about ³/₄ M. turn to the right at the finger-post. We then cross
the Zorn and the railway, and ascend through the wood to the left.
The path (indicated by finger-posts) leads hence to the summit in
about ¹/₂ hour. The ruins consist of two separate parts, chiefly dating from the 12th and 13th centuries, and command a pleasing view.
On the slope to the S.W. of the fortress, and about 1¹/₄ M. distant,
is the natural *Grotto of St. Vitus* (1280 ft.), formerly a chapel and
hermitage to which pilgrimages were made. We may return to
Zabern in ³/₄ hr., or continue along the crest to (20 min.) the *Rappenfels,* and descend thence to (25 min.) Stambach (p. 491).

On the S. side of the Zorntal rises the ruin of **Hoh-Barr**
(1505 ft.), which also occupies a wooded eminence. Starting from
the main street of Zabern, on the S. side of the canal, and ascending a few steps, we proceed along the canal and then follow the
finger-posts to the left until we reach (25 min.) the edge of the
wood, through which a footpath (red marks) leads in 20 min. to
the ruin (good inn, R. 1¹/₂-2, D. 1¹/₂-2¹/₂ ℳ). The fortress was
built in the 10-11th cent., enlarged at a later period, and restored
in 1583. The extensive ruins almost appear to grow out of the

fantastic sandstone and conglomerate rocks. The small Romanesque chapel, in the court, is perhaps of the 11th century. The highest points of the huge rocks are made accessible by ladders and bridges.

An interesting mountain-walk may be made from the Hoh-Barr. Continuing along the ridge (finger-posts and red marks), and passing between the ruins of *Gross-Geroldseck* (1580 ft.), with a huge tower, only half preserved, and *Klein-Geroldseck*, we reach (20 min.) the so-called 'Hexentisch', where notices on the trees indicate the route viâ the (20 min.) *Brotschberg* (1760 ft.; view-tower) and past the Brotsch Grotto to (25 min. more) the Schäferplatz and also the direct route to the forester's house of *Schäferplatz* (1265 ft.). Thence we follow the Hägen and Haberacker road, which, flanked by a shady footpath, descends to the S. and terminates $1^1/_2$ M. farther on in a road coming from Reinhardsmünster. We follow the latter to the right (10 min.) the two forester's houses of *Haberacker* (1575 ft.; in the first one a very fair restaurant, also rooms). The ruin of **Ochsenstein** (1915 ft.; view), which rises above ($^1/_4$ hr.), consists of three towers rendered accessible by ladders.

A footpath (red and white marks) leads viâ the *Krappenfels* (1745 ft.) to the *Druidenstein,* thence steeply down to the *Stone Hut,* and follows the Bärenbach-Tal to *Stambach* (p. 491; $1^1/_2$-$1^3/_4$ hr.). Stambach may be reached in 1 hr. by the direct way.

We continue to follow the road above the forester's, and then take the (6 min.) footpath to the left ('Hart, Hub, Dagsburg'), which soon affords a view (r.) of the Dagsburg. We proceed past the Geisfeldwasen (whence a path, marked with red and white, leads to the Obersteigen and Wangenburg road) to the (40 min.) *Hart*, whence by the wall of the farmyard, we descend to the right, following the red way-marks. $^1/_2$ hr. *Auf der Hub* (Kimmenau's Inn), the church of which has been conspicuous for some time.

Passing the E. side of the church, we reach (20 min.) the *Zollstock Inn,* on the road to *Obersteigen-Wangenburg* (ca. 6 M.; $1^1/_2$ hr. by the short-cuts indicated by notices).

A route leads towards the wood from Kimmenau's inn, descends into the valley, and then ascends again in 1 hr. to the **Dagsburg** (1675 ft.), a lofty, isolated rock, commanding an excellent view. The castle, 'hewn in a rock and inhabited by certain Counts of Leiningen-Dagsperg' (Merian, 1663), was destroyed by the French in 1675, and has left scarcely a trace behind. On its site stands a chapel (with view-tower) erected in honour of Pope Leo IX. (1048-54), who is said to have been born here. At the foot of the castle-hill lies ($^1/_4$ hr.) the village of *Dagsburg* (Schlossberg-Hôtel, on the way down, very fair, R. $1^1/_2$, D. with wine $2^1/_2$ $\mathcal{M}$; Bourg, Hôtel des Vosges, in the village).

The road from Dagsburg to ($8^1/_2$ M.) *Lützelburg* station (p. 491; motor-omnibus thrice daily) viâ *Schäferhof, Neumühl* (near the pretty valley of the Zorn), and *Sparsbrod,* is not recommended to pedestrians.

From Dagsburg to Wangenburg, a pleasant walk of $2^1/_2$ hrs.

The path, furnished with guide-posts, skirts the cliffs of the Dagsburg (without entering the village), and, after passing the forester's
house on the ridge, reaches (1 hr.) the *Schleife,* a clearing in the
woods, where paths cross each other. Continuing in the same direction by the path indicated by guide-posts, we descend into the
Engen-Tal, and then, ascending to the right, reach *Wangenburg*
(p. 503) in 1¼ hr. more.

69. From Strassburg to Bâle.

88 M. RAILWAY in 2-5 hrs. (fares 12 ℳ 70, 7 ℳ 90, 4 ℳ 90 pf.; express
fares 11 ℳ 70, 6 ℳ 90, 4 ℳ 40 pf.). For travellers in the other direction
the German custom-house examination takes place in Bâle.

Strassburg, see p. 475. The line to *Kehl* (p. 370) diverges to
the left before we cross the fortifications. To the right lies *Königshofen,* where the capitulation of Strassburg was signed in a railway-
van in Sept., 1870. The line to *Molsheim* (p. 504) diverges to the
right beyond the fortifications. On the left the tower of the cathedral
long remains visible. — 4½ M. *Grafenstaden,* with important
machine-factories. Close to the line, on the left, is Fort von der Tann.
5½ M. *Geispolsheim;* 7½ M. *Fegersheim;* 9½ M. *Limersheim.*

12½ M. *Erstein* (Löwe), a town with 5800 inhab., connected
by steam-tramways with the (1¼ M.) rail. station and with Strassburg (omnibus to Ottenheim, see p. 370). — A branch-line runs
hence to (8½ M.) *Oberehnheim* and (12 M.; 1¼-2 hrs.) *Ottrott*
(see p. 509).

The line now runs nearer the mountains. The Odilienberg
(p. 511), with its white convent, is long a conspicuous object. The
land is fertile and well-cultivated, tobacco being one of the principal
crops. The hill-slopes are covered with vineyards.

14 M. *Matzenheim;* 16½ M. *Benfeld;* 20 M. *Kogenheim;*
22½ M. *Ebersheim.* On a hill to the right of the entrance to the
Leber-Tal rise the old castles of Ortenberg and Ramstein (see p.509).

26½ M. **Schlettstadt.** — HOTELS. *Hanser,* near the station, R.
2-2½ ℳ, B. 80 pf., D. with wine 2½ ℳ, very fair; *Goldnes Lamm,* at
the entrance to the town, R. 1½-2 ℳ, B. 60 pf., D. with wine 2½ ℳ;
Adler & Bock, in the town, an old house. — *Motor Omnibus* four times
daily from the station to (7 M.) the Hoh-Königsburg in 1 hr. (fare 2½ ℳ),
returning in ¾ hr. (fare 1½ ℳ).

Schlettstadt (575 ft.), a town with 9700 inhab., once a free city
of the German Empire, attained the height of its prosperity during
the 13-15th centuries. It was fortified by Vauban after its capture
by the French, but was taken by the Germans on 24th Oct., 1870.
The church of *St. Fides,* founded in 1094 by the Hohenstaufen, but
completed at a later period, an edifice in the Romanesque and Transitional styles, with a porch, is a memorial of the town's former importance. So, likewise, is the minster of *St. George,* one of the

32*

finest specimens of Gothic architecture in Alsace, a cruciform church with an octagonal tower, founded early in the 13th cent., and lately restored. The choir was begun in 1415. At the railway-station are some new barracks. — Railway to *Markirch* and *Weiler*, see p. 513; to *Zabern*, see pp. 510-508 and 503.

Farther on, to the right, halfway up the hill, is the ruin of *Kinzheim* (p. 513). 30¹/₂ M. *St. Pilt;* the village (585 ft.; Krone) is about 1¹/₂ M. from the station (omn. 25 pf.), and is commanded by the ruins of the lofty *Hoh-Königsburg* (p. 515); farther on is the Tännchel (p. 516).

33 M. **Rappoltsweiler** (603 ft.), 2¹/₂ M. from the station (tramway), lies at the foot of the mountains. Above it rise three castles (p. 518).

35 M. *Ostheim;* 36¹/₂ M. *Bennweier*, to the right of which is the opening of the Weisstal (Kaysersberg, see p. 520). To the right is the Galz (p. 524), beside it Drei Æhren (p. 523), and behind are the Kleine and Grosse Hohnack (p. 524).

40¹/₂ M. **Colmar**. — HOTELS. *Bahnhofs-Hôtel Terminus* (Pl. a; A, 4), Bahnhofs-Str. 40, R. 2¹/₂-3¹/₂, B. 1, D. 2¹/₂ ℳ; *National,* near the station, very fair. — *Deux Clefs* (Pl. b; C, D, 3), at the corner of the Schlüssel-Str. and Langen-Str., an old-established Alsatian house, R. 2-8, B. 1, D. incl. wine 3 ℳ, with restaurant; *Park-Hôtel* (formerly *Sonne*), Rufacher-Str. 26, R. 1³/₄-3, B. ³/₄, D. 2 ℳ; *Schwarzes Lamm* (Pl. d; B, 3), in the Rapp-Platz, R. 2-3, B. ³/₄, D. with wine 2¹/₂ ℳ.

WINE at the Vintage Society in the *Kopfhaus* (Pl. 2; B, 3). — BEER at the *Café zum Marsfeld,* beside the Fountain Monument, and the *Luxhof,* near St. Martin's. — Pâtés de foie gras at *Schaerr's,* Pfaffengasse 14.

ELECTRIC TRAMWAY from the Station (Pl. A, 5) viâ the Marsfeld, Theater-Platz (Pl. B, 2), Schlüssel-Str., Vauban-Str., and Breisacher-Str., to the Canal Harbour.

TOURISTS' ENQUIRY OFFICE *(Verkehrsverein),* Schlüssel-Str. 36 (Pl. C, 3). — Baths at the *Unterlinden-Bad* (Pl. B, 2).

Railway from Colmar to *Münster,* see p. 522; to *Freiburg,* see R. 52; to *Ensisheim* and *Bollweiler,* see p. 499. — Steam-tramways to *Winzenheim* (3 M.; p. 523), to *Schnierlach* (p. 520), and to *Strassburg* (p. 475).

Colmar (640 ft.), a town with 41,600 inhab., is the capital of Upper Alsace and the seat of the court of appeal for Alsace and German Lorraine. It is situated on the *Lauch,* a tributary of the Ill, and the *Logelbach* (p. 523), which flow through the town, and is about 2 M. from the mountains and 10¹/₂ M. from the Rhine.

Colmar was declared a free town of the Empire by the Emp. Frederick II. in 1226, and became so powerful that in 1474 its inhabitants refused admittance to Charles the Bold. In the Thirty Years' War it was occupied by the Swedes, and in 1673 by the French. — In the history of Rhenish art Colmar is a place of some importance. *Caspar Isenmann* (d. 1466), who flourished here after 1436, learned oil-painting in the school of the Van Eycks and painted a large altar-piece for St. Martin's Church (1462). His pupil *Martin Schongauer,* the scion of an artist-family of Augsburg, was born at Colmar about 1450 (d. 1491), and, after also visiting the Netherlands, settled in his native town about 1470-75. He is considered the greatest German artist of the 15th cent., but, as few of his paintings have been preserved, he must be judged mainly by his engravings.

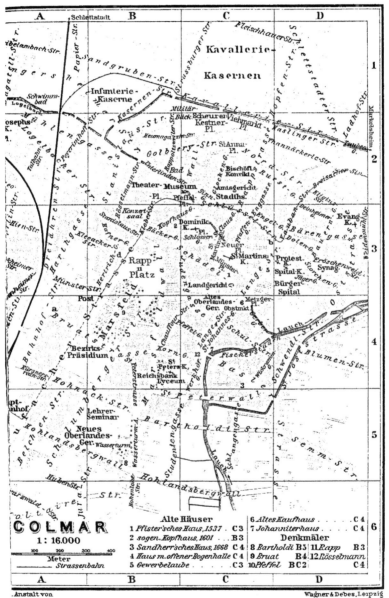

Alte Häuser

1 Pfister'sches Haus, 1537	C 3
2 sogen. Kopfhaus, 1601	B 3
3 Sandherr'sches Haus, 1668	C 4
4 Haus m. offener Bogenhalle	C 4
5 Gewerbelaube	C 3

6 Altes Kaufhaus	C 4
7 Johanniterhaus	C 4

Denkmäler

8 Bartholdi	B 3	
9 Bruat	B 4	11 Rapp B 3
10 Pfeffel	B C 2	12 Rösselmann C 4

COLMAR
1:16.000

100 200 300 400
Meter
—— Strassenbahn

Anstalt von

Wagner & Debes, Leipzig

The road from the station leads direct to the pleasant grounds
i the *Champ de Mars,* or *Marsfeld,* with a *Fountain Monument*
ɔ *Admiral Bruat* (born in Colmar in 1796, d. 1855) by Bartholdi
ɔ. 498). The large building to the S. is the *Bezirks-Präsidium*
?l. A, B, 4), or office of the President of the District. On the W.
ɪ the new *Post Office.* The *Monument of General Rapp,* another
ative of Colmar (1771-1821), in the Rapp-Platz, to the N. of the
[arsfeld, is also by Bartholdi. In the Hohlandsbergwall are the
ew *Court of Appeal (Oberlandes-Gericht;* Pl. A, B, 5) and a
Ionument to F. A. Bartholdi (1834-1904; Pl. 8, B 5), who was
native of Colmar (comp. p. 498).

In striking contrast to this quite modern part of the town is
ɪe inner town, with its narrow, picturesque streets and numerous
andsome secular buildings of the 16th and 17th centuries (the
ɪost important are marked in the plan). In the centre rises the
ɛstored *Church of St. Martin* (Pl. C, 3), a fine cruciform Gothic
uilding, with marks of French influence, begun in 1237. The choir,
·ith a narrow ambulatory and good stained glass of the 15th cent.,
ates from 1350. The fine carved reredos at the high-altar is modern.
ɪf the two W. towers, that on the S. alone is partly completed. The
. side-portal has interesting sculptures, which are, however, inferior
ɔ the contemporary work at Strassburg-Minster (13th cent.). The
ɪcristy, to the right of the choir, contains a 'Madonna in an arbour
˙ roses' by *Schongauer,* an excellent, though harsh work, the earliest
473) and best-authenticated production of the master (retouched).

The buildings of the old Dominican Nunnery of *Unterlinden,*
unded in 1232, famous in the history of the German Mysticism
the 13th and 14th cent., were restored in 1849-58, and, together
ith the early-Gothic church, have been tastefully converted into
e *Schongauer Museum* (Pl. B, 2), which is of some importance
students of German art (open 9-12 & 2-6 in summer, in winter
-12 & 2-4; 1-2 pers. 50 pf., 3-4 pers. 1 ℳ, free on Sun. and
urs.; entr. on the W. side).

To the left of the entrance is the FLEISCHHAUER ROOM, containing
tiquities from Colmar and other Alsatian towns, Roman, Celtic, Ale-
nnian, and Frankish antiquities, models of Alsatian buildings, and old
rniture.

In front are the fine early-Gothic CLOISTERS, which contain a collec-
ɔn of Roman-Gallic and mediæval stone monuments, including a num-
r of interesting Roman tomb-reliefs from Horburg, Kempel, etc., tomb-
ɔnes from Colmar and neighbourhood, and mediæval wood-carvings. In
ᵎ centre is a fine *Monument to Schongauer,* by Bartholdi (1860).

To the S. is the old ABBEY CHURCH, containing a few modern paint-
s and the *Collection of Early German Pictures.

To the left (N. side of the church). 171, 170, 167, 165. Painted wings
the *'Isenheim Altar' (from the monastery of Isenheim near Geb-
iler), to which Nos. 163, 164, 166, and 190-192 also belong. This
s the masterpiece of *Matthias Grünewald* (d. after 1529), the chief
enish painter at the beginning of the 16th cent., who worked mainly
Mayence and Aschaffenburg. 171. Madonna with the Child (monastery

of Isenheim in the background), on the back (170) Temptation of St. Anthony, St. Anthony and St. Paul the Hermit; 167. Ascension and Annunciation, on the back (165) Crucifixion. In the apse, 190-192. Three painted and carved wooden *Figures of SS. Anthony, Jerome, and Augustine. Below is another piece of painted wood-carving, representing Christ and the Apostles (according to the inscription by *Des. Beychel*, 1493), also from Isenheim. Below, 166. Entombment (easel-picture), above to the left and right, 164, 163. SS. Anthony and Sebastian, two other wings of the Isenheim altar. — To the left: 161. Pietà, by an unknown master; 157, 158. Wings of the so-called 'Stauffenberg Altar' (Annunciation and Adoration); 112. Portrait of Schongauer. — In the middle, Wooden panel of 1512 painted on both sides, with SS. Martin, Eucharius, and Sebastian, Maurice, Martin, and Ursula, from Rappoltsweiler; 132-135. *Schongauer*, Altar-wings with the Madonna and St. Anthony Abbas inside and the Annunciation outside; 179-182. Scenes of martyrdom, on the back SS.' Catharine and Laurence (painted at the Monastery of Isenheim and dated 1505). — On the N. side, 137-143. *Caspar Isenmann*, Scenes from the Passion, almost burlesqued in their crude realism; 115-130. Passion scenes by *M. Schongauer* and his assistants, among others, Entry into Jerusalem, Christ on the Mount of Olives, Christ at Gethsemane, Bearing of the Cross, Entombment, all partly repainted. — *Rembrandt*, Lady with dog (ca. 1665). — The Roman mosaic pavement is from Bergheim.

Adjoining the cloisters to the E. is a room with PLASTER CASTS and the BARTHOLDI ROOM, with models and casts of the well-known sculptor of the Statue of Liberty in New York Harbour (comp. p. 497).

On the UPPER FLOOR of the monastery are a *Natural History Collection*, an *Ethnographical Collection*, a *Cabinet of Engravings*, and the *Library*.

Beyond Colmar we observe on the right the castle of *Hohlandsburg* (see p. 523). — 43¹/₂ M. **Egisheim.** The village (1700 inhab.), which is 1 M. from the station, contains a recently restored palace ('Pfalz'), that is said to date back to the 8th cent. (the chapel, dedicated to Pope Leo IX., is modern; comp. p. 494). Above the village stands the castle of *Hohen-Egisheim* or *Dreien-Egisheim*, with its three towers, which have been for some time visible in the distance: the *Dagsburg*, of the 12th, and the *Wahlenburg* and *Wekmund*, of the 11th cent., together known as the '*Drei-Exen*'. The route from the station to the castle is by the village of *Häusern*, whence a footpath ascends through wood. — The descent may be made to the S. by the Augustine abbey of *Marbach* (now a farm and inn), founded in 1094, of which part of the church-choir and a few Romanesque columns of the cloisters are still extant.

45 M. *Herlisheim.* To the right rises the wooded *Staufen* (2950 ft.). — 49 M. **Rufach** (670 ft.; *Bär*, R. 1¹/₂-2, D. 2 ℳ, very fair), the *Rubeacum* of the Romans, a town of 2900 inhab., with an agricultural school. The *Church of St. Arbogast, a cruciform basilica, with an octagonal tower over the crossing, erected at the close of the 12th cent., partly in the Transition, and partly in the Gothic style, has lately been restored. The choir dates from the beginning of the 14th century. In the late-Gothic *Franciscan Church* is a collection of tombstones of the 14th, 17th, and 18th centuries. Close to the town is a hill, which is crowned by the castle of *Isenburg*, a modern erection on the foundations of one of

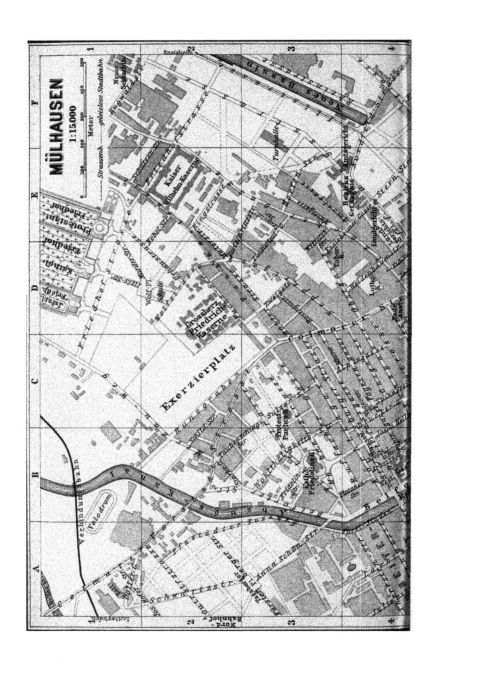

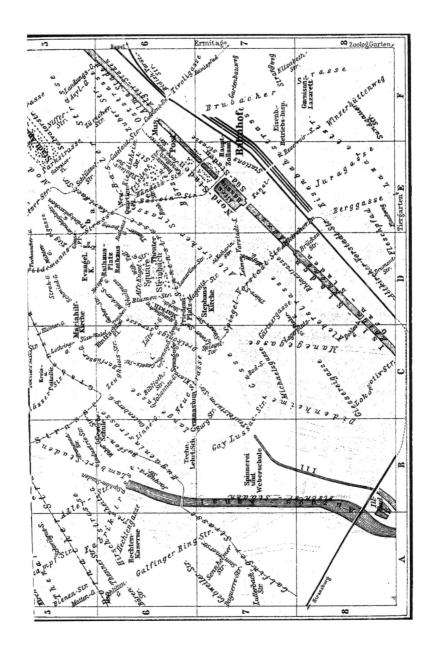

the oldest castles in Alsace, frequently occupied by the Merovingian-
Frankish kings.

52 M. *Merxheim.* To the right, in the distance, are the Kahle
Wasen (p. 524) and, beyond it the Grosse Belchen (p. 529). — 56¹/₂ M.
Bollweiler (784 ft.), the junction for Lautenbach (see p. 528). The
Baumann Arboricultural Schools here are the oldest and most
extensive in Alsace.

A narrow-gauge railway runs from Bollweiler, viâ *Feldkirch* and
Ungersheim, to (4¹/₂ M.) **Ensisheim** (*Krone*, very fair), a small town
with 2500 inhab., once the capital of the Austrian possessions in Alsace.
It is interesting for its many specimens of secular edifices of the 15th
and 16th centuries, chiefly in the Renaissance style, especially the imposing *Rathaus*, with its handsome oriel, containing a meteoric stone,
which fell here in 1492. The Jesuit college is now a penitentiary. — The
railway continues N. to (17¹/₂ M.) *Colmar* (p. 496). — Steam-tramway to
Mülhausen (10 M.; see below).

The *Thur* is now crossed. — 59 M. *Wittelsheim;* 63¹/₂ M.
Lutterbach (junction for Thann and Masmünster, p. 529). Here
the train leaves the mountains, turns to the E., and reaches (65 M.)
Dornach, an industrial suburb of Mülhausen. The photographs of
raun, Clément, & Co. of Dornach are well known in France and
Germany.

67 M. **Mülhausen.** — The *Station* (restaurant) lies on the S.E.
side of the town.

HOTELS. **Central Hotel* (Pl. A, E, 5), with good restaurant, R. 2¹/₂-6,
. 1, D. 3 *M; Wagner* (Pl. b; E, 5), *National,* these three in the Wildemann-Str.; *Hôt. de l'Europe* (Pl. e; E, 6), R. 2-3, B. ³/₄, D. 2 *M;*
Hôtel-Restaurant Berney, Ziegelgasse 9 (Pl. D, E, 5), R. 1³/₄, B. ¹/₂,
D. 2 *M.*

CAFÉ. *Moll,* Neuquartier-Platz (Pl. E, 6), Munich and Pilsen beer. —
WINE. *Landwerlin,* Rathaus-Durchgang (Pl. D, E, 6). — BEER. *Bürger-
bräu.* Modenheimer-Str. (Pl. E, 5); *Luxhof, Münchener Kindl,* both in
Wildemann-Str. (Pl. D, 5); *Spatenbräu,* Colmarer-Str. 14 (Pl. C, D, 3, 4).

POST & TELEGRAPH OFFICE (Pl. E, F, 6), near the station. — TOURISTS'
ENQUIRY OFFICE (*Verkehrsbureau*), Handels-Str. 7 (Pl. E, 6).

Cab. 1 *M* 60 pf. per hour. — *Electric Tramway* through the town. —
Steam Tramways to Ensisheim (10 M.; see above), Pfastatt (3 M.), and
Wittenheim (5 M.).

Braun's Photographs, Wildemann-Str. (Pl. E, 5, 6).

ENGLISH CHURCH SERVICE at Gesetz-Str. 3 (Pl. C, 6), on the last Frid.
of each month from Oct. to June. Chaplain from Freiburg (p. 374).

Mülhausen (785 ft.), in the *Sundgau,* once a free city of the
German Empire, and from 1515 to 1798 allied with the Swiss
Confederation, is now the most important manufacturing town in
Alsace (cotton and woollen goods, chemicals, paper, iron-ware,
machinery, etc.). It is the seat of government for the district, with
a provincial tribunal and 95,000 inhabitants.

Leaving the *Railway Station* (Pl. E, F, 7) and proceeding a
few paces towards the right, we cross the Rhine-Rhone Canal and
enter the NEW QUARTER of the town, with its large but unattractive houses, many of which have wide, arched porticoes on the
groundfloor. Here on the right is situated the large building of

the *Société Industrielle* (Pl. E, 6), an association formed in 1825 for the promotion of industrial and scientific interests of all kinds. It contains natural history collections and a library. Adjacent, in the Nordstaden, is the *Post Office* (Pl. E, F, 6). The MUSEUM (Pl. F, 6), established by the Société Industrielle in 1882, contains an interesting collection of Romano-Celtic antiquities, most of them found in Alsace, and a collection of objects illustrative of local history. On the second floor is a picture gallery, with a few good specimens of modern French masters.

Proceeding straight on we enter the Wildemann-Str., the main street of the OLD TOWN. A street, diverging to the left, leads to the Rathaus-Platz, in which is the *Rathaus* (Pl. D, 6), erected in 1552 after a fire and restored in 1846, a solitary witness of the ancient importance of Mülhausen as a free imperial city. The whole of the façade was painted by *Christian Vacksterffer* of Colmar. Opposite the Rathaus is the modern-Gothic *Protestant Church* (Pl. D, 5, 6), with a very showy façade. — The *Stephans-Kirche* (Pl. D, 7; 14-15th cent.) contains remarkable stained glass, with representations from the Old and New Testaments (restored in 1905). — The *School of Design* (*Gewerbeschule;* Pl. B, C, 5, 6) contains an interesting and extensive collection of patterns and designs for dress goods, chiefly produced by Mülhausen firms.

The ARBEITERSTADT (Pl. A, B, 3, 4), or artisans' colony, to the N.W. of the town, founded in 1853 at the suggestion of Mayor Dollfus (1800-87), was one of the earliest attempts to provide cheap and good houses for the working classes. There are also large bath and washing houses, an infant school, etc. The Arbeiterstadt, however, is now largely occupied by small shopkeepers and the like.

Near the station (to the S.E.) rises the REBBERG, with pretty villas and gardens belonging to Mülhausen manufacturers, the town-reservoir (view), and the *Zoological Garden* (best reached by the Brubacher-Str. or by the Reservoir-Str. and the Winzer-hüttenweg; Pl. E, F, 7, 8). Higher up is the *Tannenwald,* which commands a beautiful view.

FROM MÜLHAUSEN TO MÜLLHEIM (in Baden), 13½ M., railway in ca. 40 minutes. — 3 M. *Napoleons-Insel,* on the Rhine-Rhone Canal, with large paper-mills. The train then traverses the extensive *Hartwald.* 7 M. *Grünhütte.* — 8½ M. *Banzenheim,* 2½ M. to the S. of which lies *Ottmarsheim,* with an interesting octagonal chapel, consecrated in the middle of the 11th-cent., and belonging to a suppressed Benedictine abbey. It is built on the model of the Carlovingian cathedral at Aix-la-Chapelle. — The Rhine is then crossed. 12 M. *Neuenburg.* — 13½ M. *Müllheim,* see p. 382.

FROM MÜLHAUSEN TO BELFORT, 31 M., railway in 1¼-2 hrs. The railway ascends the smiling valley of the *Ill.* There were formerly about 20 castles in the district traversed by this line, which, with numerous villages, have all been destroyed by the ravages of war. At many points traces of Roman fortifications and roads are noticeable. — 4½ M. *Zillisheim;* 6 M. *Illfurt.*

10¹/₂ M. **Altkirch** (955 ft.; *Goldener Kopf*, R. from 1 ℳ 60 pf.,
D. 2 ℳ), picturesquely situated on the slope of the hill, is the capital
of the Sundgau in the narrower sense of the name. Pop. 3400. A fine
view is obtained from the vicinity of the church. The Rathaus contains
the Sundgau Museum, a small collection of antiquities. Pottery is extensively manufactured here. — Almost the whole of the *Sundgau* belonged to the Counts of Pfirt, whose castle, now in ruins, is in the Jura
Mts., above the little town (500 inhab.) of **Pfirt**, Fr. *Ferette* (1540 ft.;
Stadt New York, very fair), 15 M. to the S. of Altkirch (branch-line in
1¹/₂ hr.). Pfirt lies on the Swiss frontier, and is a good centre for excursions in the Alsatian Jura, recently opened up by the 'Vosges Club'.
Above Pfirt, to the E., is (20 min.) the ruin of *Hohenpfirt*, whence we
may go on to the *Haidenfluh* and the (¹/₂ hr.) *Erdwibelefelsen*. About
1¹/₂ M. to the N.E. of Pfirt is the old convent of *Luppach* (now a convalescent home), with interesting vaulted tombs.

16 M. *Dammerkirch*, Fr. *Dannemarie* (1040 ft.). The train then
crosses an imposing viaduct with 35 arches, and reaches (21 M.) *Alt-
Münsterol*, Fr. *Montreux-Vieux* (1135 ft.), the German frontier-station.
23 M. *Petite-Croix*, the French frontier-station. — 31 M. **Belfort** or
Béfort (Grand-Hôtel du Tonneau d'Or, first-class; *Ancienne Poste)*, a
town and fortress on the *Savoureuse*, built by Vauban under Louis XIV.,
and memorable for its long siege by the Germans from 3rd Nov., 1870,
to 16th Feb., 1871. See *Baedeker's Northern France*.

From Mülhausen to *Wesserling* and *Masmünster*, see pp. 529, 532.

70¹/₂ M. *Rixheim;* 71¹/₄ M. *Habsheim;* 77¹/₂ M. *Sierentz;*
79¹/₂ M. *Bartenheim*. Beyond (84¹/₂ M.) *St. Ludwig* (or *St. Louis*)
the line enters Switzerland and threads two tunnels.

From St. Ludwig to Leopoldshöhe (in Baden), 3³/₄ M., railway in
¹/₄ hr. — 1¹/₄ M. *Hüningen* (Gasthof zum Raben), fortified by Vauban
in 1679 and dismantled by the Austrians in 1815. — 3³/₄ M. *Leopoldshöhe*, see p. 382.

88 M. *Bâle*, see p. 383.

70. The Central and Upper Vosges Mts.

The **Vosges** (Lat. *Mons Vosegus*, Germ. *Vogesen*, or more
correctly *Wasigen* or *Wasgenwald*) form the western boundary
of the basin of the Upper Rhine, and run parallel with the Black
Forest, with which they for the most part coincide in orographical
and geological characteristics. They are generally divided into the
Upper, Central, and Lower Vosges. The Upper or High Vosges
Mts. are separated from the Jura on the S. by the depression of
Belfort (the Trouée de Belfort), and on the N. extend to the Leber-Tal
(p. 513). The highest summits are the *Grosse Belchen* (4680 ft.;
p. 529), the neighbouring *Storkenkopf* (4468 ft.), the *Hohneck*
(4465 ft.; p. 526), the *Klinzkopf* (4358 ft.; p. 524), the *Rotenbachkopf* (4305 ft.; p. 527), and the *Kahle Wasen* or *Kleine
Belchen* (4160 ft.; p. 524). The Central Vosges Mts. stretch from
the Leber-Tal to the Zaberner Senke (p. 491), the highest points
being the *Hochfeld* (3605 ft.; p. 513), the *Mutzigfels* (3310 ft.),
the *Donon* (3307 ft.; p. 507), the *Climont* (3170 ft.; p. 506), the
Schneeberg (3150 ft.; p. 503), and the *Odilienberg* (2470 ft.; p. 511),

a spur running out towards the E. The LOWER or NORTHERN VOSGES run northwards from the Zaberner Senke as far as the Queich (p. 465), where they merge with the Haardt Mts.

In contrast to the Schwarzwald (p. 383), the Vosges present their steepest side, seamed with picturesque ravines, towards the Rhine, on the E., while on the W. they gradually slope down towards the valleys of the Moselle and Saar and finally merge imperceptibly into the plateau of Lorraine. Geologically they consist of granite, slate, and older formations between the Belfort depression and the Breusch-Tal, while the crests of the High Vosges are granitic, rising in rounded summits displaying wide rocky expanses. Tarns occur in the deep depressions of the main ridge (p. 522). Throughout the entire N. region the granite is overlaid by a massive layer of variegated sandstone, which determines the long, coffin-shaped form of the heights. Seen from their narrower side the summits often exhibit a pointed triangular appearance (*e.g.* Hoh-Königsburg). Up to a height of about 3600 ft. these mountains are covered with luxuriant forests of beech and pine. The highest summits, on which only grass grows, afford excellent pasturage, and are extensively used for cattle-rearing and dairy-farming. The abrupt E. side is preceded by a narrow belt of sedimentary foot-hills, which expands into a broader zone only at the Zaberner Senke. The Vosges are poorer than the Schwarzwald in minerals and mineral springs. In the valleys, iron-working, ore-smelting, weaving, and other industries are actively prosecuted. The slopes towards Alsace are covered with vineyards (comp. p. 495).

The 'Vosges Club', instituted in 1872, has done much to facilitate a tour among these mountains by the construction of paths, the erection of finger-posts, etc. A MAIN ROUTE, traversing the entire range from N. to S. and passing all the finest points, is indicated by red rectangles. From Schönau (p. 468) this leads viâ *Niederbronn, Zabern, Wangenburg, Donon, Hohwald, Barr, Kestenholz, Rappoltsweiler, Schlucht, Metzeral,* the *Grosse Belchen, St. Amarin,* and *Masmünster* to Sewen. SIDE-ROUTES that join this main route are indicated by red rectangles with a white bar, while other colours indicate LOCAL ROUTES. — The Club is publishing a map of the district on a scale of 1 : 50,000, of which 17 sheets have appeared (2-3 ℳ each). The best detailed guidebook is *C. Mündel's* 'Handbuch für die Vogesen' (11th edit., 1907, 4½ ℳ).

Good INNS are to be found at all the most frequented points. Average charges: R. 1½-2 ℳ, B. 80 pf., D. incl. wine 2-2½, S. incl. wine 1½-2 ℳ.

I. THE CENTRAL VOSGES-MTS.

PLAN OF TOUR. The most interesting points in the Central Vosges may be conveniently visited in five days by following the above-mentioned 'Hauptroute', or 'Main Route'. — 1st Day: From Zabern viâ *Hoh-Barr, Haberacker,* and *Dagsburg* (comp. pp. 493, 494) to *Wangenburg,* 7½-8½ hrs. — 2nd Day: Viâ the *Schneeberg* and the *Nideck* to *Urmatt* (p. 505), 5-5½ hrs.; in the afternoon ascent of the *Hahnenberg.* — 3rd Day: *Türgestell, Mutzigfels, Donon,* and *Schirmeck* (pp. 507, 505), 8-9 hrs. — 4th Day: *Struthof, Münzfeld, Hochfeld,* and *Hohwald* (p. 512), 6-7 hrs. — 5th Day: *Odilienberg, Männelstein,* the ruin of *Landsberg,* and *Barr* (pp. 511, 509), 6-7 hrs.; railway to Schlettstadt.

Heiligenberg
Urmatt
Mühlbach
Lützelhausen
Wisch
Russ
Schirmeck
Barenbach
Struthof
Natzweiler
Hohbühl-kopf
Schwarzkopf
Heidenkopf
Klingenthal
Treiskopf
Münzfeld
Rothlach
Neuntenstein
Welschbruch
Rosskopf
Hohwald
Hochfeld
Breitenbach
Erlenbach
St. Martin
Weiler
Triembach
Laach
Breitenau
Neukirch
St. Moritz
St. Petersholz
Thannweiler
Diefenbach
Altenberg
Deutsch-Rumbach
Leberau (Liepvre)
St. Kreuz
Orschweiler
St. Pilt
Thannenkirch
Rodern
Dreispitz
Dorlisheim
Rosenweiler
Mollkirch
Grendelbruch
Rosheim
Bischofsheim
Börsch
St. Leonard
Oberehnheim
Ottrott
Hohenburger
Bernhardswlr.
St. Nabor
Goxweiler
Heiligenstein
Landsberg
Barr
Gertweiler
Zellweiler
Mittelbergheim
Andlau
St. Peter
Stotzheim
Itterswiller
Reichsfeld
Epfig
St. Margaretha
Nothalten
Blienschweiler
Dambach
Diefenthal
Rittersbg.
Scherweiler
Kestenholz
Hahnenbg.
Kinzheim
Schlettstadt
Ebersheim
Strassburg
Erstein

a. From Zabern to Molsheim. — Wangenburg. Schneeberg.

From Zabern to *Molsheim*, 20 M., RAILWAY in about 1 hr. (fares 1 *M* 60, 1 *M* 5 pf.). — From Romansweiler to *Wangenburg*, OMNIBUS thrice daily in summer in 1½ hr. (1 *M*).

Zabern, see p. 490. — 2½ M. *Ottersweiler.* On the right rises the Hoh-Barr (p. 493).

5 M. **Maursmünster**, Fr. *Marmoutier (Krone*, very fair; *Zwei Schlüssel)*, a small town with 1800 inhabitants. The *Church of St. Maurus*, which belonged to an ancient and once powerful Benedictine abbey, now suppressed, possesses a handsome late-Romanesque façade and a vaulted vestibule (a favourite style in Alsace; comp. the church of St. Fides at Schlettstadt, and the church at Gebweiler). — Tunnel.

8½ M. *Romansweiler.* (Route to Wangenburg, see below.) — 10 M. *Papiermühle*, with large cement-works.

11 M. **Wasselnheim**, French *Wasselonne (Railway Hotel*, well spoken of), a town with 3600 inhab., situated on the *Mossig*, with extensive stocking-factories. — 12¾ M. *Wangen;* 13¾ M. *Marlenheim*, the traditionary home of the Nibelungen hero, Hagen von Troneck.

Marlenheim is the junction of a LIGHT RAILWAY FROM STRASSBURG (13¾ M.; departure from the Markt-Halle; Pl. B, 2), which proceeds (3¾ M. in ¼ hr.) viâ *Kirchheim* to *Westhofen* (fine Gothic church of the 14th cent.).

14¼ M. *Kirchheim;* 15½ M. *Scharrachbergheim;* 17¼ M. *Sulzbad*, with a salt-spring (Kurhaus, ·pens. 4-7 *M*). — 18 M. *Avolsheim*, a village with an interesting parish church of the 15th century. About ¾ M. to the S.E. is a Romanesque church of the 11th cent. ('Dom-Peter'), the nave of which has a flat roof.

20 M. *Molsheim*, the junction of the Strassburg and Saales, and of the Strassburg, Molsheim, and Schlettstadt railways, see pp. 504, 508.

FROM ROMANSWEILER TO WANGENBURG, 7 M. (omnibus, see above). The road crosses the *Mossig*, and then ascends the wooded and confined valley watered by that stream. Pedestrians may save about 2 M. by short-cuts.

From Zabern to *Wangenburg*, 10 M., see pp. 493, 494.

Wangenburg (1485 ft.; *Hôtel Wangenburg*, R. from 1½, B. ³⁄₄, D. 2½, pens. 5-5½ *M*, very fair; *Schneeberg)*, a small, scattered village, commanded by the ruins of the castle of that name and beautifully situated among meadows surrounded by pine-forest, is an unpretending· but favourite summer-resort.

The route from Wangenburg to (1½ hr., red marks) the top of the **Schneeberg** (3150 ft.) diverges to the left near the church, passes a new red house, and, by a solitary house on the margin of the wood, ascends to the left (footpath; finger-post) to the rocky summit, just below which a shelter-hut has been built. The top (mountain-indicator) commands an extensive view over Alsace (to the E.), the plain of Lorraine (to the W.), and the Vosges. The 'Lottelfels', at the W. corner, is a 'rocking-stone' which may be set in motion by stepping on it. Between the summit and the hut is a finger-post showing the way to the Donon (red marks).

A good path (not to be mistaken) descends to the S. in $^3/_4$ hr. to the forester's house of *Nideck* (p. 506). Thence to *Nideck Castle* (see p. 506), $^1/_4$ hr.: on quitting the house, we turn to the right along the carriage-road, from which a path diverges to the left in 7 min., reaching the castle in 6 min. more. To Urmatt, see p. 506.

b. From Strassburg to Saales. — Breuschtal. Donon.

$38^1/_2$ M. RAILWAY in $2^3/_4$-3 hrs. (fares 3 $\mathcal{M}$, 1 $\mathcal{M}$ 95 pf.).

Strassburg, see p. 475. — 3 M. *Lingolsheim*, with a large tannery; 4 M. *Holzheim;* 6 M. *Enzheim;* $7^1/_2$ M. *Düppigheim; $8^1/_2$* M. *Düttlenheim; $10^1/_2$* M. *Dachstein.*

12 M. **Molsheim** (575 ft.; *Zwei Schlüssel; Rail. Restaurant*), a small town with 3200 inhab. on the *Breusch,* at the foot of the Vosges, a fortified place in the middle ages. In the church (formerly the property of the Jesuits) and the handsome meat-market (16th cent.) here the forms of the Renaissance are combined with the articulation of Gothic architecture. — Molsheim is the junction for the Zabern and the Schlettstadt lines (see pp. 503, 508).

The Saales line ascends the pleasant green valley of the Breusch, which is enclosed by wooded heights and rocks of red porphyry. The stream descends from the Climont.

13 M. **Mutzig** (615 ft.; *Felsburg*, R. $1^1/_2$-2, pens. $3^1/_2$-4 $\mathcal{M}$), a small town of 3450 inhabitants. To the right, on the Molsheimer Berg, is the large Fort Emperor William II. — $15^1/_2$ M. *Gressweiler.* — $17^1/_2$ M. *Heiligenberg* (Railway Restaurant) is the most convenient starting-point for a visit to the ruin of Girbaden ($1^1/_2$ hr.)

From the railway-station a footpath leads to the S. and enters the wood. 40 min. Finger-post pointing to the *Grauschlagfels.* In 40 min. more, latterly on the Urmatt road, we reach the forester's house of Girbaden, whence the road (better views than from the footpath) leads in 10 min. to the ruin. — **Schloss Girbaden** (1855 ft.), one of the oldest and most extensive fortresses in Alsace, is said once to have possessed 14 gates and 14 court-yards, and is still an imposing ruin. The inner castle dates from the 10th, the imposing outer castle from the early part of the 13th century. In the W. portion a hall, the handsome windows of which are bordered with clustered pillars, is still traceable. Beside the square W. tower is the *Chapel of St. Valentine.* Good view from the E. wall of the ruin.

On the S. slope of the ridge, $2^1/_4$ M. from Girbaden, lies **Grendelbruch** (1770 ft.; *Weber's Grendelbruch Hotel*, R. 2, B. $^3/_4$, D. 3, S. $1^3/_4$, pens. 4-5 $\mathcal{M}$), a favourite summer-resort. A pretty walk through the wood leads hence to ($1^1/_4$ hr.) Urmatt station; on the way another path branches off to the *Hahnenberg* (2115 ft.; view-platform).

20 M. **Urmatt** (765 ft.; *Post*, in the village, R. $1^1/_2$ $\mathscr{M}$, B. 60 pf., D. 2, pens. 4 $\mathscr{M}$, very fair) is the starting-point for a visit to *Nideck Castle*, and for the ascent of the *Donon* (see p. 507). — Above this point French is the language of the valley. The curious mixed patois of French, German, and Celtic, now rapidly disappearing, is of interest to philologists (grammar by Oberlin).

From Urmatt viâ the Hahnenberg to Grendelbruch, see p. 504.

22 M. *Lützelhausen* (830 ft.; Zwei Schlüssel), a large village, whence a pleasant excursion may be made viâ the *Grande Côte* (in German *Langenberg*), between the Mutzigfels and Narionfels, to *Alberschweiler* (p. 492; 8 hrs.). — 23 M. *Wisch* (Donon Inn); $24^1/_2$ M. *Russ-Hersbach.*

$26^1/_2$ M. **Schirmeck-Vorbruck** (1030 ft.; *Hôt. Vogt*, R. $1^1/_4$-2, D. 2 $\mathscr{M}$, in Vorbruck, opposite the station; *Hôt. Donon*, in Schirmeck, $^1/_4$ M. from the station, R. from $1^1/_2$, D. $2^1/_2$ $\mathscr{M}$, very fair), two busy little places, separated by the Breusch. *Vorbruck*, Fr. *Labroque*, with the rail. station and 3100 inhab., is on the left bank, at the mouth of the Framont (p. 507); *Schirmeck* (1700 inhab.) lies on the right bank and is commanded by the ($^1/_4$ hr.) *Schlossberg*, on which are a ruined castle of the Bishops of Strassburg and a modern statue of the Virgin (view).

From Schirmeck to Hohwald, $4^1/_2$-5 hrs. We ascend, following the red marks, to the ($1^3/_4$ hr.) *Struthof* (2330 ft.; good rustic inn). Farther on we follow a cart-road and after $^1/_2$ hr. ascend by a footpath to the right to (20 min.) the *Münzfeld* (3385 ft.). At (25 min.) the cross-roads we may either follow the red marks (straight on) to the *Rathsamhausen-Stein* and ($1^1/_2$ hr.) *Hochfeld* (p. 513), or the red and white marks (left) to the solitary inn of ($^1/_2$ hr.) *Rotlach* (p. 512), then viâ the *Neuntenstein* (p. 512) to ($1^1/_4$ hr.) Hohwald (p. 512). — From the Neuntenstein we may proceed to (20 min.) the forester's house of *Welschbruch* (p. 512), whence a new road leads to ($4^1/_2$ M.) the *Odilien Convent* (p. 511). To Barr, see p. 511.

28 M. **Rothau** (1105 ft.; *Zwei Schlüssel*, R. 1-2, pens. $3^1/_2$-5 $\mathscr{M}$, very fair), a busy village, with 1800 inhabitants. The ruined castle of *Salm*, $4^1/_2$ M. to the W., was the seat of the Princes of Salm (view). About $^1/_2$ M. from the castle is the hamlet of *Salm*. The view-tower on the *Katzenstein*, or *Chatte Pendue*, 2 M. farther on, affords a good view of the Hochfeld, the valley of the Breusch, and the valley of the Rhine.

From Rothau to Hohwald, $4^1/_2$-5 hrs. A pleasant path leads, viâ (3 M.) *Natzweiler* and past the Cascade de Servâ and the farm of *Morel* (rfmts.), to the (3 hrs.) *Hochfeld* (p. 513). Descent to *Hohwald* (p. 512), $1^1/_2$ hr.

31 M. **Urbach,** French *Fouday* (1320 ft.; *Post*), at the union of the *Chergoutte* with the Breusch.

Urbach belongs, like Rothau and five other villages, to the ancient lordship of *Steintal*, Fr. *Ban de la Roche*, which has been a desolate and sparsely-peopled district since the time of the Thirty Years' War. The places named owe their prosperity and comparative populousness to the praiseworthy philanthropic exertions of *Johann Friedrich Oberlin* (b. at Strassburg 1740, d. 1826), who is buried in the churchyard of Urbach.

The HOCHFELD (p. 513) may be reached from Urbach in about 3 hrs., viâ *Waldersbach*, where Oberlin was a Protestant pastor, and the forester's house of *Schirrgut* (rfmts.).

32$^1/_2$ M. *St. Blaise-Poutay;* 34 M. *Saulxures* (1475 ft.); 36$^1/_2$ M. *Bourg-Bruche* (1625 ft.).

38$^1/_2$ M. **Saales** (1830 ft.; *Hôt. de l'Europe; Hôt. du Com-merce*), the terminus of the railway, lies close to the frontier. — A pleasant walk may be taken hence to (6 hrs.) *Weiler* (p. 514), viâ *Voyemont,* the *Climont* (3170 ft.; view-tower), and the ruin of *Bil-stein;* or from the farms of Climont we may follow the frontier to the *St. Diedeler Höhe* and thence descend by road to *Markirch* (p. 514).

HASLACH VALLEY. Nieder-Haslach is fully 1$^1/_2$ M. by road from the station of Urmatt (p. 505). Pedestrians who have already visited the church of Nieder-Haslach should take the footpath (red marks) diverging to the right a few paces to the W. of the station at Urmatt, which leads through meadows and wood and joins the undermen-tioned road in 1$^3/_4$ hr., shortly before reaching the mouth of the valley of the Nideck.

Nieder-Haslach (730 ft.; *Delcominete*, R. 1$^1/_2$-2 ℳ, B. 60 pf., D. 1$^1/_2$-2, pens. 3-4 ℳ, very fair; *Goldener Apfel*, R. & B. 1$^1/_2$-2$^1/_2$ ℳ) was formerly the seat of a convent. The large Gothic church of *St. Florian* possesses beautiful old stained-glass windows, and fine Gothic sculptures on the W. portal. The body of the church and the tower date from the 14th cent.; the choir was begun in 1274 and rebuilt in 1290 after its destruction by fire. A side-chapel to the right contains the tombstone of a son of Meister Erwin ('Filii Erwini magistri'; d. 1330).

The road continues to ascend the Hasel, and at the end of (1$^1/_4$ M.) Ober-Haslach (beer at Fuchslock's) it divides. We follow the branch to the right, leading through a beautiful and gradually contracting dale to the (2$^1/_2$ M.) fifth saw-mill from Ober-Haslach. A few paces on this side of it a broad footpath ascends to the right into the beautiful pine-clad *Valley of the Nideck,* enclosed by rocks of porphyry, which vies with the finest scenery of the Black Forest. At the (1 M.) upper end of the valley the Nideck forms a waterfall, 80 ft. in height. High above it stands the square tower of the (25 min.) **Castle of Nideck** (13-14th cent.), to which a zigzag path ascends to the right, crossing the brook to the left above the waterfall. The tower (85 steps) commands a fine view of the valley. The relief of Chamisso over the entrance refers to his ballad ('Riesenspielzeug' or 'Plaything of the Giants') dealing with the legend of the castle. From this point to the forester's house of *Nideck* (Inn, very fair), 15-20 min., see p. 504.

From the forester's house the *Schneeberg* (p. 503) is ascended in 1$^1/_4$ hr. A few paces to the right we enter a narrow cart-road (finger-post), which presently degenerates into a footpath. In about $^3/_4$ hr. we emerge from the wood and reach the hill, 20 min. below the summit. — Another path (numerous finger-posts), avoiding the Schneeberg, leads direct to Wangenburg (p. 503) in 2 hrs. In good weather, the route over the Schneeberg is preferable (p. 503).

The **Donon,** the most frequented summit in the Central Vosges, commanding an extensive prospect, may be ascended from Nideck in $4^1/_2$, from Urmatt via the Mutzigfels in $6^1/_2$-7, or from Schirmeck in $2^1/_2$-3 hrs.

FROM NIDECK TO THE DONON ($4^1/_2$ hrs.), a fine forest-excursion (finger-posts). About 100 yds. to the W. of the forester's house we diverge from the road to the right (finger-post); 20 min., fork, where the Schneeberg route diverges to the right (see above); 20 min., another path to the Schneeberg; 10 min., saddle; 20 min., the *Urstein* (3105 ft.; fine view). In 25 min. more we join the road and follow it to the left; at the ($^1/_4$ hr.) fork we proceed to the left, on the E. slope of the *Grossmann* (3235 ft.), to (40 min.) the flat saddle of the *Altmatt.* A little farther on, past the *Noll* (see below), we descend a little to the left, where we join the path from the Mutzigfels, enjoying a view of the *Haut du Narion* (2415 ft.). $1^1/_4$ hr. Fork (left to Schirmeck, right to the Donon). In $^1/_4$ hr. more we reach the road between the Donon and Alberschweiler (p. 508). Here we follow the old road to the left to (20 min.) the saddle between the Great and the Little Donon, $^1/_2$ hr. from the summit (see p. 508).

FROM URMATT TO THE DONON. From the station we proceed through the village and along the road to the (1 M.) *Eimerbach-Tal,* which we ascend on the left bank of the stream, through wood (red marks), to *Kappelbronn* ($1^3/_4$-2 hrs. from the station). An easy path ascends hence to the ($^3/_4$ hr.) *Türgestell,* a curiously shaped rock on the saddle below the *Katzenberg* (2958 ft.), whence the commanding *Mutzigfels* (3310 ft.) is reached in 35-40 min. more. We descend to the Haut du Narion, and thence either take the shadeless path (fine views), via the *Narionfels* (3278 ft.) and the top of the *Noll* (3250 ft.), or skirt these two heights to the S. through the wood to (fully $^1/_2$ hr.) the W. side of the Noll, where we again strike the road from Nideck described above.

FROM SCHIRMECK TO THE DONON, $2^1/_2$-3 hrs. (several routes). — A finger-post near the station shows the shortest way (blue marks). We cross the Framont and (5 min.; l.) the railway, and then ascend through pasture-land and a wood to the Kohlberg road, following which we arrive at the saddle between the Grosse and Kleine Donon (p. 508).

The carriage-road from Schirmeck ascends the valley of the *Framont* (omnibus to Grandfontaine, 40 pf.). At a quarry, just beyond the first kilomètre-stone, a good path (red marks) diverges to the right, leading to the Hôt. Velleda (p. 508); and farther on

(1½ M. from Schirmeck), immediately beyond the church of *Wackenbach*, another route (red and white marks) diverges, leading straight to the saddle proper. The latter is the best route of all. — The carriage-road (no shade), with a tramway for the transport of timber, continues to ascend the left bank of stream. At a (2³/₄ M.) customhouse we cross the bridge to *Grandfontaine*, and we ascend thence, passing the church, to (³/₄ hr.) the *Platform of the Donon* (2425 ft.; Hôt. Velleda, R. 2-3, B. 1, D. 2½, pens. 5-6 ℳ, very fair; inn also at the forester's; telephone), 5½ M. from Schirmeck. The road describes a wide bend and crosses the stream higher up. Beyond the Hôtel Velleda it divides: the left branch enters France, the right branch skirts the W. slope of the Donon and follows the valley of the Rote Säar to Alberschweiler (p. 492). The top is reached in ³/₄ hr. by a footpath, diverging to the right from the Alberschweiler road, about 250 yds. beyond the Hôt. Velleda.

The *Donon (3307 ft.) affords an extensive survey of the surrounding mountains, of Alsace towards the W., and of the hills and plain of Lorraine on the E. In clear weather the Bernese Alps can be distinguished to the S. On the summit is the 'Musée', a small sandstone 'temple', built in 1869 and containing some Roman architectural fragments discovered in the neighbourhood. About 30 yds. below the summit, amid the rocks on the side next the Kleine Donon, there is a refuge-hut whence we may descend on the N.E. to the saddle (2625 ft.) between the Great and the *Little Donon* (3160 ft.; see p. 507).

c. From Molsheim to Schlettstadt. Odilienberg. Hohwald.

21 M. Railway in 1¼ hr.; through-carriages from Strassburg.

Molsheim is the junction for railways to Zabern (p. 503) and to Saales and Strassburg (p. 504). — 1¼ M. *Dorlisheim*, with a Romanesque church. In the distance, farther on, is Girbaden (p. 504).

2½ M. *Rosheim*, station for a branch-line to St. Nabor (separate station, close by) and for the small town (3200 inhab.) of **Rosheim** (*Pflug*, plain but good), which lies 1½ M. to the W. Rosheim, which was once a free city of the empire, has several times suffered destruction, but the mediæval fortifications are in good preservation, and an ancient tower-gate is still standing on its E. side. The Romanesque *Church of SS. Peter and Paul* was consecrated in 1049; the present edifice dates from the 12th cent., and has been added to in Gothic times. Several of the old houses in the main street are very picturesque.

The branch-line to (7½ M.) *St. Nabor* (Stern), the starting-point for the ascent of the Odilienberg (see p. 510), runs viâ *Börsch* (another quaint little town), *St. Leonhardt*, and *Ottrott* (p 509).

3¹/₂ M. *Bischofsheim*. In the distance are the castles of Ottrott (p. 510), farther on the Odilienberg (p. 511) and the Männelstein (p. 511).

5¹/₂ M. **Ober-Ehnheim.** — HOTELS. *Hôtel des Vosges*, R. from 1¹/₂, B. ³/₄, D. 2¹/₂, S. 1¹/₂ ℳ, very fair; *Bahnhof-Hôtel* (Wach), R. & B. 2-2¹/₂, D. 1¹/₂-2 ℳ, these two at the railway-station; *Dubs*, in the town, R. 1¹/₂-2, D. with wine 2¹/₂ ℳ. Wine Room at the *Ratskeller*. — The branch-railway from Erstein, mentioned at p. 495, stops in Ober-Ehnheim both at the main railway-station and in the market-place.

Ober-Ehnheim, French *Obernai*, a small town of 3900 inhab. and several manufactories, was made a free imperial town in the time of the Hohenstaufen and still preserves much that is quaint and interesting in its old houses and fortifications. The *Town Hall (Stadthaus)*, dating from 1523, contains a noteworthy old council-chamber; in front of it is a draw-well of 1579. The Gothic *Church*, with its two spires, is modern, but in the churchyard is a Mount of Olives of 1517. — The branch-line coming from Erstein (p. 495; viâ Schöffersheim, Meistratzheim, and Nieder-Ehnheim) goes on from Ober-Ehnheim viâ *St. Leonhardt* to (3 M.) *Ottrott* (Schwan; Grüner Baum), which is celebrated for its good red wine and is one of the starting-points for the ascent of the Odilienberg (see p. 510).

7¹/₂ M. *Goxweiler* produces a good variety of white wine ('Klevner'); the station affords a fine view of the mountains, with their numerous ruined castles. Pleasant walk through the 'Heiligensteiner Au' to Heiligenstein (p. 510). — 9¹/₄ M. *Gertweiler;* to the right the ruin of Landsberg (p. 511), opposite Schloss Andlau (p. 512).

10 M. **Barr** (660 ft.; *Rotes Haus*, R. 1¹/₂-2 ℳ; B. 60 pf., D. 2¹/₂ ℳ ; *Krone*, similar charges, both very fair; *Rail. Restaurant*), a busy little town of 5000 inhab., with extensive tanneries, is prettily situated at the mouth of the *Kirneck-Tal*. The *Town Hall* was built in 1640. In the Kirneck-Tal, 1 M. from the rail. station, is the *Bühl Hydropathic* (pens. 4 ℳ), which also receives passing visitors.

12 M. *Eichhofen*, station for Andlau (2 M.; p. 512) and *Stotzheim*, 2¹/₂ M. to the W. Then (13 M.) *Epfig*, with 2300 inhab.; at the E. end is the early-Romanesque Margareten-Kapelle. To the right, in the background, rises the *Ungersberg* (p. 513).

16 M. **Dambach** (*Krone*, very fair), a small town of 2500 inhab., with the remains of old fortifications and several late-Gothic houses. The *Chapel of St. Sebastian* to the W., with its Romanesque tower and Gothic choir, contains a richly-carved wooden altar. Passing the chapel, we reach in 40 min. the extensive ruins of the castle of *Bernstein*, whence we may proceed (red marks) by the castle of *Ortenberg*, with its bold pentagonal tower of the 13th cent., and that of *Ramstein* (the two locally known as the 'Scherweiler Schlösser'), to Weilertal station (p. 514).

18¹/₂ M. *Scherweiler*, where the insurgent peasants were defeated in the Peasants' War of 1525. In the background, to the right, the *Altenberg* (2885 ft.) and the ruined *Frankenburg* (p. 514). — 21 M. *Schlettstadt*, see p. 495.

ASCENT OF THE ODILIENBERG. — From OTTROTT (p. 504), the road leads to the N.W. round the hill (1640 ft.) crowned by the ruins of the *Lützelburg* and the *Rathsamhausen*, the so-called 'Ottrott Castles'. It then passes *Klingental* (Schwan) and ascends to the S. through the valleys of the *Ehnbach* and the *Vorbach*, finally sweeping round in a bold curve to the (9¹/₂ M.) convent. — Walkers may take the route to the right, shown by a finger-post at the exit from Ober-Ottrott, and ascending the Odilienberg in 2¹/₄ hrs. viâ the 'Ottrott Castles' and the *Elsberg* (2208 ft.; beautiful view). This charming route leads along the hill through wood. The direct route (1¹/₂ hr.; white marks) ascends through wood, passes (1 hr.) above an old Roman causeway (still in fairly good preservation), skirts the meadow below the convent, and again traverses wood.

At the station of ST. NABOR (p. 508) is a finger-post indicating the route leading to the W. through shrubbery, which farther on crosses the 'Steinbruchs-Bahn' and joins the above-mentioned direct route from Ottrott. We may also proceed to the S. from the railway-station to (10 min.) the last houses of St. Nabor and then ascend to the right through the *Dachsbach-Tal*, by the route indicated by the finger-post and the blue marks. In 1 hr. we reach the *Odilienbrunnen*, welling up in a grotto close to the road, the water of which has been used by thousands of devotees as a cure for diseases of the eyes. The distance thence to the convent along the road is ca. ³/₄ M. — Another route beginning at the end of the village follows blue and white rectangles, crosses the Dachsbach, keeps to the left at the first bend, and leads to (1 hr.) the *St. Jakob Hotel* (1805 ft.), a new and well-equipped building with a large view-terrace (R. 1-3, B. 1, D. 2¹/₂, pens. 5-7¹/₂ *M*). From the hotel we may follow the new road viâ the Odilienbrunnen, or we may take a blue-marked path passing (¹/₄ hr.) the farmhouse of *Niedermünster* and the ruined abbey-church of that name (consecrated in 1180). Thence we go on past the Odilienbrunnen to (³/₄ hr.) the convent.

FROM BARR (p. 509) 2¹/₂ hrs. The road from the railway-station leads directly to the N. (without touching the village) and then goes on viâ (1 M.) *Heiligenstein* (Stern, opposite the Rathaus; Rebstock; good 'Klevner' at both), ¹/₂ M. beyond which a finger-post indicates the way (left) to (³/₄ M.) Truttenhausen and (3³/₄ M.) Ste. Odile. The suppressed Augustine abbey of *Truttenhausen* (1230 ft.) was founded in 1181; it is now, along with the ruins of the Gothic abbey-church, dating from 1490, private property. Farther on, at

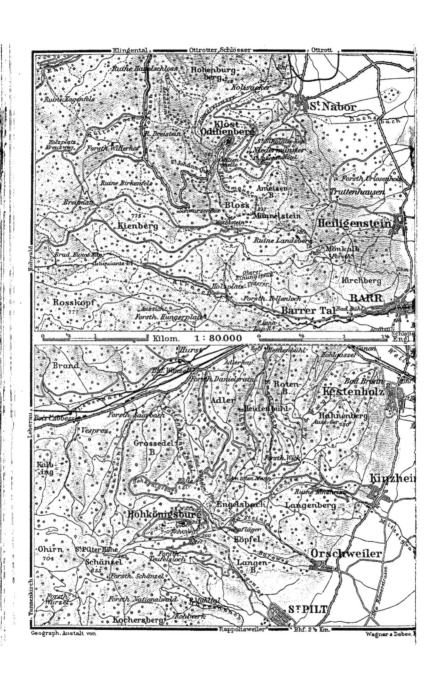

Kilom. 1:80.000 Engl.

Geograph. Anstalt von

Wagner & Debes,

the entrance to the wood, a path diverges to the left for the forester's house and ruined castle of *Landsberg* (1900 ft.), which we see on the slope of the *Bloss*, below the Männelstein (see below). From Landsberg a white-marked path leads to the Hôtel St. Jakob. The direct path from Truttenhausen to Ste. Odile also passes ($^1/_2$ hr.) the Hôtel St. Jakob (p. 510).

Another route from Barr leads past the Protestant church and through the 'Anlagen' (pleasure-grounds) on the Kirchberg to the forester's house of *Mönkalb;* thence to (1$^1/_2$ hr.) the ruin of *Landsberg* (see above), whence we may either proceed to the *Männelstein*, or go direct to the convent.

The *Odilienberg* forms a plateau-like ridge about 6 M. in circumference, surrounded by the *Heidenmauer*, a prehistoric fortified wall, parts of which are still 6-10 ft. high and 6$^1/_2$ ft. thick; it is supposed to be one of the Gaulish places of refuge (like Alesia, Bibracte, etc.) mentioned by Cæsar. The sandstone blocks of which the Heidenmauer is built are merely rough-dressed, not hewn, and were secured by oak braces in the form of a double dovetail. On the N.E. spur (2500 ft.) of the central saddle stands a *Nunnery*, founded by Ste. Odile in the 7th century. The abbey-church, which is much frequented by pilgrims, and has even been visited by emperors and popes, contains the tomb of the foundress. Tradition relates that Odile, the daughter of Eticho, Duke of Alsace (7th cent.), was born blind, but gained her sight on being baptized, and afterwards spent a long life here in all the odour of sanctity. The convent-door is closed at 9.30 p.m. Superb view from the convent-garden. In the inner court (ring) is an unpretending but very fair *Inn* (R. 1-3, B. 1, D. at 12.30 p.m. 2$^1/_2$, pension 4-7 ℳ).

The highest point of the ridge is the **Männelstein** (2680 ft.), which rises to the S.E., and may be ascended from the nunnery in 40 min. (finger-posts), the last part of the route passing extensive remains of the Heidenmauer (see above). In clear weather the Männelstein commands a view embracing almost the whole of Alsace, the Breisgau as far as the Black Forest, the Vosges (to the S. the Kirneck-Tal, the Andlauer Schloss, and the Spesburg), the Rhine, and, towards the S., the Alps. — At the N. extremity of the Odilienberg lies the ruin of *Waldsberg*, or *Hagelschloss*, which may be reached in $^3/_4$ hr. (the ruin itself is difficult of access). To the W. is the ruin of *Dreistein*, buried in wood, consisting of three castles of the 13th cent., situated on two crags.

From the Odilienberg we reach (2$^1/_2$ hrs.) HOHWALD by proceeding for 8 min. in a straight line from the nunnery-gate and then turning to the left, along a new road, passing (1$^1/_2$ hr.) the forester's house of *Welsch-bruch* (p. 512). On the way a path turns off to the right, leading to the ruin of *Birkenfels*, and subsequently rejoining the road.

FROM BARR TO HOHWALD, diligence in summer twice daily in 1$^3/_4$-2 hrs. (fare 1 ℳ 60 pf.; carr. for 1-2 pers. 6$^1/_2$, for 3 pers. 8, carr. & pair 13 ℳ).

The CARRIAGE ROAD from Barr to Hohwald (8³/₄ M.) leads by *Mittelbergheim* to **Andlau** (*Ochsen*, R. 1¹/₂-2 ℳ), a small town with 1700 inhab., prettily situated at the entrance to the Andlau-Tal, with several old timbered houses, and a Romanesque *Abbey Church* of the 12th cent., with Gothic additions, altered in 1701, and judiciously restored in 1866. The crypt (11th cent.) is borne by columns. The façade is ornamented with rude, fantastic reliefs, and the choir-stalls are very handsome. — The road then ascends the valley of the *Andlau*, through beautiful woods, passing the ruins of *Andlau* (1480 ft.) and *Spesburg* (1560 ft.) on the right, and numerous saw-mills.

PEDESTRIANS (3¹/₂ hrs.) should walk through the straggling town of Barr, about 1¹/₄ M. in length, and ascend the road on the left bank of the Kirneck as far as the (2 M.) '*Holzplatz*', and then proceed by a good footpath, frequently crossing the railway (p. 508), to (1¹/₄ hr.) the forester's house of Welschbruch. — As an alternative route we may turn to the left at the W. end of Barr (1¹/₄ M. from the station), cross the bridge, and pass to the N. of, and below, the ruins of Andlau and Spesburg. Beyond the (1¹/₄ hr.) forester's house of *Hungerplatz* (1790 ft.; rfmts.) we follow a cart-track to (³/₄ hr.) the forester's house of *Welschbruch* (2540 ft.; rfmts.), where several paths cross (comp. above). — From Welschbruch the new road to the Hohwald takes ³/₄ hr.; we may also go viâ the Neuntenstein (see below; white, then red and white marks) in 1¹/₂ hr.

Hohwald (2000 ft.; *Hôtel Kuntz*, with baths, R. from 2, B. 1, D. 3, S. 2, pens. 6¹/₂-10¹/₂ ℳ; *Stauffer*, R. 1¹/₂-2, B. ³/₄, D. 2-2¹/₂, pens. 5 ℳ, very fair; *Marchal*, R. from 1¹/₂ ℳ, B. 60 pf., D. 2, pens. 4-4¹/₂ ℳ) is a straggling village with 700 inhabitants. Its healthy and at the same time sheltered and picturesque situation has made it one of the most frequented summer-resorts in the Vosges. The *Roman Catholic Church* stands on a height to the E. of the Hôtel Kuntz, by the side of the broad Welschbruch road; the *Protestant Church* lies farther up the valley.

The wooded *ENVIRONS OF HOHWALD afford many pleasant excursions which are greatly facilitated by numerous way-posts. To the **Waterfall** (30-40 min.) and the *Grosse Tanne* (1 hr.). We ascend to the right from the road up the valley, near the old Prot. church. — From the Grosse Tanne ('Great Fir'; ca. 2790 ft.) we may proceed to the N., by the new road, to the (³/₄ hr.) *Rathsamhausen-Stein* (3440 ft.), affording a view of the Donon and the upper valley of the Breusch. Hence we may return by the forester's house of *Melkerei*, and past the *Kirchbühl-Fels* (1-1¹/₄ hr.). We may also follow the ridge to the E. from the Rathsamhausen-Stein to the (25 min.) *Rotlach Inn* (3126 ft.; comp. p. 505) and (³/₄ hr. more) the **Neuntenstein** (3185 ft.; 1 hr., back in ³/₄ hr.), a fine point of view, a good path ascends from the garden of the Hôtel Kuntz. — To the **Schöne Leite** (or 'Grosse Bellevue'; 1 hr.): we turn to the right at (5 min.) the first saw-mill below the hotel, cross the bridge, and skirt the wood for about 10 min., until we reach the beginning (on the left) of a narrow, partly grass-grown road, which afterwards widens and winds gradually round the mountain, chiefly through

wood, and keeping at nearly the same elevation. At the exit from the
wood we obtain a fine view of the valley of the Breitenbach, and 5 min.
farther on of the Weiler-Tal. Thence to the $(1^1/_4$ hr.) *Ungersberg* (2955 ft.),
with view-tower. — The *Tannenstein,* or *Pelage* (3222 ft.), another favourite point, is reached by a shady new footpath, which intersects the
Hohwald and Breitenbach road at the forester's house of *Kreuzweg* (rfmts.).

The **Hochfeld,** French *Champ-du-Feu* (3605 ft.), is ascended from
Hohwald in 2 hrs. The route (red marks) leads to the W. from the
Grosse Tanne (p. 512). At the top is the 'Hohenlohe Tower', 65 ft. high.
In returning we may follow the footpath (blue marks) towards the E.
viâ Kälberhütte, Tannenstein, and Kreuzweg (see above): 2 hrs. — Ascent
of the Hochfeld from *Schirmeck* and from *Rothau,* see p. 505.

FROM HOHWALD TO WEILER, $2^1/_4$ hrs. (carr. 10, with two horses
16 ℳ). We follow the above-described route to the *Schöne Leite,*
and then descend to $(1^1/_4$ hr.) the rail. station of Weiler (p. 514)
by the so-called Eselsweg ('donkey-road'), which traverses the ridge
dividing the valleys of *Breitenbach* on the right and *Erlenbach* on
the left (fine views, but shadeless).

II. THE UPPER OR HIGH VOSGES MTS.

PLAN OF TOUR. The 'Main Route' ('Haupt-Route') of the Vosges Club
(comp. p. 502) takes six days. — 1st Day: By railway to *Kestenholz*
(see below), ascend the *Hoh-Königsburg,* and proceed viâ *Tannkirch* to
Rappoltsweiler (p. 517), $5^1/_2$-6 hrs. — 2nd Day: Viâ *Altweier* (p. 519) to
the *Brézouard* (p. 515), descending thence viâ *Diedolshausen* to the
Weisse See (p. 522), 9-10 hrs. — 3rd Day: Along the crest of the mountain (p. 522) to the *Schlucht* (p. 526), $3^1/_2$-4 hrs.; excursion to Gérardmer. —
4th Day: Along the crest past the *Hohneck* (p. 526) and the *Rotenbachkopf* (p. 527) to the *Grosse Belchen* (p. 529), $8^1/_2$-9 hrs. — 5th Day: Descent to *St. Amarin* and by the *Belacker* dairy and the *Rossberg* to
Masmünster (p. 530), 7-8 hrs. — 6th Day: By railway to *Oberbruck*
(p. 532), walk viâ *Rimbach* to the *Stern-See* and thence to the *Welsche
Belchen* (p. 532), descending again to *Sewen* (p. 532), $7^1/_2$-$9^1/_2$ hrs.

a. From Schlettstadt to Markirch. Hoh-Königsburg. Rappoltsweiler. Altweier.

$13^1/_2$ M. RAILWAY in 1 hr. (fares 1 ℳ 20, 75 pf.; no first class).

Schlettstadt, see p. 495. — The line ascends the *Leber-Tal,* a
picturesque, industrial valley enclosed by wooded hills. On the N.
rise the *Scherweiler Schlösser* (p. 510; reached from Weilertal).

3 M. **Kestenholz,** French *Châtenois* (630 ft.; *Weisses Lamm,*
at the station; *Adler,* in the village, well spoken of; *Kur-Hôtel
Badbronn,* very comfortably fitted up, R. $1^1/_4$-4, B. $1^1/_4$, D. 3, pens.
$5^1/_2$-8 ℳ), a place with 2600 inhab., is situated at the foot of the
Hahnenberg, on which rise two tepid mineral springs (60° Fahr.).
A pleasant walk may be taken through the park, and then to the
left from the route to the Hoh-Königsburg (p. 515), to the (1 hr.)
top of the *Hahnenberg* (1740 ft.).

A road leads to the S. from Kestenholz to (1 M.) **Kinzheim,** an
ancient village, commanded by a castle of the same name, a ruin since
the Thirty Years' War. The Hoh-Königsburg may be ascended hence
in $1^1/_2$ hr.

3³/₄ M. *Weilertal* (660 ft.), French *Val-de-Villé*, a small group of houses, lies at the entrance of the valley of its own name. Above it to the right, on the hill where the two valleys unite, rises the ruin of *Frankenburg* (11-12th cent.), with its massive round tower. On the slope are remains of a prehistoric ring-wall. — A branch-railway ascends, in 35 min., through the Weiler-Tal, passing *Gereuth, Thannweiler* (with a 16th cent. château, restored in the 18th), *St. Moritz*, and *Triembach*, to (5¹/₂ M.) **Weiler** (820 ft.; *Stadt Nanzig, Post*, both very fair), the chief place in the valley, with 1000 inhab. and two churches (to Hohwald: either by the Breitenbach road or viâ the Schöne Leite, see p. 513).

The line continues to follow the Leber-Tal. — 5¹/₂ M. *Wanzel* (720 ft.; Danielsrain, R. from 1 ℳ 60, B. 80 pf., D. 2 ℳ), whence a footpath ascends to the Hoh-Königsburg (p. 515). — 8³/₄ M. *Leberau*, French *Lièpvre* (890 ft.; La Fleur), opposite the entrance to the *Rumbach-Tal*, a beautiful valley, in which the principal place is *Deutsch-Rumbach*, with a French-speaking population. — 11 M. *St. Kreuz*, French *Ste. Croix-aux-Mines*.

13¹/₂ M. **Markirch.** — HOTELS. *Grand-Hôtel*, Lange-Str. 35, ³/₄ M. from the rail. station, commercial, very fair, R. 2-3, B. ³/₄, D. 2³/₄, S. 2¹/₂ℳ; *Hôtel du Commerce*, R. 1¹/₂-2 ℳ, B. 60 pf., D. 2¹/₂ℳ; *General Kleber*; *Hôtel zum Bahnhof*, at the rail. station, R. 1¹/₂-2, B. ³/₄, D. with wine 2¹/₂ ℳ. — Beer at *Schubert's* (Munich beer), near the station, and the *Taverne Alsacienne* (Strassburg beer), by the Grand-Hôtel. — *Motor Omnibus* viâ Wisembach to (15 M.) St. Dié twice daily in 2 hrs. (3 ℳ 40 pf.).

Markirch, French *Ste. Marie-aux-Mines* (1180 ft.), the capital of the valley, with 12,400 inhab., has considerable wool and cotton factories. The once productive silver-mines are no longer worked. The boundary between the French and German languages formerly passed exactly through the middle of the town, the right bank of the *Leber* or *Lièpvrette* being German, the left French, but it is now less strongly defined. The German-speaking portion embraced the Reformation and was subject to the Counts of Rappoltstein, while the French inhabitants were Roman Catholic and under the sway of the Dukes of Lorraine.

A pleasant WALK may be taken by the St. Dié road (the bends may be avoided by short-cuts) to the forester's house of *Pflanzschule* (fair inn) and (3 M.) the frontier on the *St. Diedeler Höhe* (2500 ft.; Pfister's Inn), and then to the right, in a N. direction, along the frontier to (²/₃ M.) the *Château de Faîte* (2895 ft.), situated exactly upon the boundary-line, which commands a fine view of the valley of the Meurthe, and of St. Dié and its environs. From the St. Diedeler Höhe to Saales, see p. 506. — The limestone-quarries of (1¹/₂ M.) *St. Philip*, in the gneiss rock, are interesting.

FROM MARKIRCH TO RAPPOLTSWEILER, 11¹/₄ M., there is a good road ascending to the right about ¹/₄ M. below the rail. station. The cart-track, diverging to the left from the road, ¹/₂ M. from Markirch, effects a considerable saving, and rejoins the new road in about 1¹/₂ M. Fine retrospect of Markirch. Farther on we pass the forester's house of *Kleinhöhe* (1985 ft.) and reach (³/₄ hr.) the height of land (2430 ft.) between Markirch and Rappoltsweiler. The road then descends into the valley of the *Strengbach*, and leads through wood nearly the whole way to Rappoltsweiler. About 1¹/₂ M. from the summit, and 3³/₄ M. from Rappoltsweiler, a road ascends to the right (S.), to (3 M.) *Altweier* (p. 519). About 2¹/₂ M. farther on (1 M. from Rappoltsweiler) we reach the entrance (l.) of the Dusenbach-Tal, through which the three castles of Rappoltsweiler are easily reached in ³/₄-1 hr. (comp. p. 518).

THE ASCENT OF THE BRÉZOUARD, which may be accomplished from Markirch in 3-3¹/₂ hrs., is a very pleasant excursion. We follow the road ascending the Leber-Tal to (¹/₂ hr.) *Eckerich* or *Eschéry* (1405 ft.), where we turn to the left into the *Rauen-Tal.* Farther on we twice turn to the right at finger-posts marked 'Haïcot' and ascend through wood to (2 hrs.) the saddle and (5 min.) the farm of *Haïcot* (rfmts.). In ¹/₂ hr. more we reach the ridge connecting the two summits, whence the top is gained in ¹/₄ hr. The **Brézouard,** *Bressoir*, or *Brüschbückel* (4030 ft.), commands a most extensive view, including the Alps in clear weather. — The Brézouard may also be ascended from *Altweier* (p. 519), viâ the Dreibannstein, in 2¹/₂ hrs., or from *Schnierlach* (p. 520), viâ the *Grande Roche*, in 2³/₄ hrs. (yellow marks). — *Diedolshausen* (p. 521) is reached from the Brézouard (blue marks) either direct from the summit over the *Le Plat* saddle (1¹/₂ hr.), or by turning to the right a little below the W. summit, proceeding past the farm of Haïcot to the *Diedolshauser Höhe* (inn), and then following the short-cuts across the bends of the road (2 hrs.).

————

The HOH-KÖNIGSBURG may be reached by road (shadeless), with a short-cut through wood, from the station of *St. Pilt* (p. 496); by a carriage-road from *Weilertal* (p. 514) through the wood (5 M.); or by pleasant footpaths from *Kestenholz* (p. 513) and *Wanzel* (p. 514). Motor-omnibus from Schlettstadt, see p. 495.

From the station of KESTENHOLZ (2-2¹/₂ hrs.; red marks) we may either turn at once to the right along the main road, and then, in 5 min., to the left by the guide-post, or we may go through the Bronnbad park, skirting the N. side of the Hahnenberg (comp. p. 513) to the forester's house of *Wick*, which is about 1 hr. from the hotel. — The shortest route is that from WANZEL (red and white marks), which leads through woods the whole way, twice crossing the Weilertal road, after which we proceed either (r.; red marks) direct to the castle (1³/₄ hr.) by the 'Kaiser-Wilhelm-Pfad', or (l.) by the 'Hohenlohe-Pfad' to the hotel (1¹/₂ hr.).

About ¹/₂ hr. below the top is the *Hoh-Königsburg Hotel* (R. from 3, B. 1, D. 3, pens. from 5¹/₂ *ℳ*), commanding a view of the valley of the Rhine, the slopes of the Vosges, and (in clear weather) the Alps. An easy path leads from the hotel to the principal entrance of the castle.

The ***Hoh-Königsburg** (2475 ft.), built upon a ridge mentioned in a document of 774 as the '*Stophanberch*' (Staufenberg), was in the possession of the Hohenstaufen family about 1147 and was later held in fee by the Counts of Werd. In 1462 it was destroyed by the League of Rhenish Towns, but in 1479 it was rebuilt by the Counts of Thierstein. From 1533 to 1606 it was held in pledge by the Lords of Sickingen, from whom it passed successively into the hands of the Lords of Bollweiler and the Counts Fugger (1617). In the Thirty Year's War the castle was destroyed by the Swedes (1633). Towards the end of the 17th cent. it fell again into the hands of the Lords of Sickingen, who sold it in 1770. After various other changes of ownership it was acquired in 1865 by the town of Schlettstadt, which presented it to Emp. William II. in 1899. The Emperor caused it to be rebuilt (1901-8) at the expense of Alsace and the German Empire from the plans of Bodo Ebhardt,

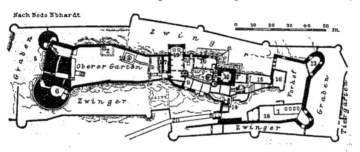

Nach Bodo Ebhardt

1. Old house above the stable (1606). — 2. Bakehouse (destroyed in 1557). — 3. Well. — 4. Drawbridge. — 5. *Great Bulwark.* — 6. *Great Tower* (1560). — 7. Main spiral stair. — 8. *Main Entrance.* — 9. Chapel (1527). — 10. *Main Building (Hauptbau;* 1558). — 11. *Löwen-Tor.* — 12. *Keep (Bergfried).* — 13. Mill and bakehouse. — 14. Porthus or Gate-keeper's Lodge. — 15. Lumber-room. — 16. Forge. — 17. Store-room (1557). — 18. Stable and inn (1530). — 19. Cisterns. — 20. *Zwinger-Tor.*

who has restored it as far as possible to its appearance in the 15th century. Its huge walls and towers of red sandstone, towering above the dark-green chestnut wood, are strikingly picturesque.

The Castle is open in summer 8-12 and 1.30-6 (in winter 9-12 and 1.30-4). The company of a guide is obligatory (1-8 pers. 2 *M*, each addit. pers. 25 pf.). Through the *Zwinger-Tor* (Pl. 20), above which is the coat-of-arms of the Counts of Thierstein, and the *Main Entrance (Haupt-Tor;* Pl. 8), above which are the arms of the Hohenzollerns, we enter the Fore-Court. On the left side of this is the *Löwen-Tor* (Pl. 11) which still bears the arms of the Hohenstaufens. Beyond the gate, to the left, is the castle-well, 200 ft. in depth. The next gate leads to the Inner Court *(Burghof).* To the right is a handsome spiral staircase (Pl. 7). The imposing *Main Building* (Pl. 16) consists of four stories, the lowest of which is the kitchen, while on the upper floor are the Ritter-Saal, the Chapel, and the dwelling-rooms. From the third floor of the structure containing the chapel we reach the Keep, which is 195 ft. in height and commands a superb view. The *Great Bulwark* (Pl. 5) and the *Great Tower* (Pl. 6), on the W. Side of the castle, were erected for purposes of defence.

From the Hoh-Königsburg a red-marked path leads to the S.W., passing the inn on the *St. Pilter Höhe* and (20 min.) the forester's house of *Schänzel* (rfmts.) to the right, which has been already visible from above, to (1-1¼ hr.) *Tannenkirch* (1730 ft.; Hôtel Tännchel, unpretending), a scattered village, lying at the foot of the *Tännchel* (2955 ft.; with curious rock-formations, and a fine view). Rappoltsweiler may be reached hence by two routes. From the fork, ³/₄ M. from Tannenkirch we may proceed either to the right, following the red marks past the castles (2 hrs.), or to the left viâ the saddle of *Renk* direct to the town (1¹/₄ hr.).

From the rail. station of Rappoltsweiler (p. 496) a steam-tram-way (35, 25 pf.) runs in ¹/₄ hr. to the town, 2¹/₂ M. to the W.

Rappoltsweiler. — HOTELS. *Stadt Nanzig*, at the foot of the main street, the nearest to the station, R. 1¹/₂-2 ℳ, B. 60 pf., D. incl. wine 2¹/₂-3, pens. 4¹/₂-5¹/₂ ℳ, good wine and cuisine; *Pfeiffer zum Lamm*, in the upper town, also good, similar charges. — *Carola Bad, ³/₄ M. to the N.E. of the station (omn. 50 pf.), on the road to Bergheim, a well-equipped bathing establishment, with excellent mineral water (swimming-bath 30 pf.; open for men 5-8 a.m. & 12-8 p.m., for women 8-12 a.m.), a beautiful garden, and a restaurant, also frequented by transient guests (closed from Oct. until the end of April); R. 2¹/₂-4, B. 1, D. 2¹/₂, S. 2¹/₂, pens. 7-9 ℳ.

Rappoltsweiler (locally called *Rapperschwier*), French *Ribeau-villé* (820 ft.), an old town, with 6000 inhab., and partly preserved walls of the 14-18th cent., lies amid productive vineyards, at the entrance of a short but beautiful valley, watered by the *Streng-bach*. On the rocks above, to the right, rise the 'Three Castles' of the Counts of Rappoltstein, a family often mentioned in the mediæval history of Alsace.

The *Count of Rappoltstein* was the 'king' of all the musicians and minstrels of the Upper Rhine, who recognized him as the head of their brotherhood and paid him a yearly tax, while he in return extended to them the benefit of his protection. Every year on 8th Sept. (which is still the date of a local feast) these wanderers assembled at Rappolts-weiler to celebrate a joyous festival, called the 'Pfeifertag'. On the death of the last Count of Rappoltstein in 1673, this singular jurisdiction, along with the title of 'king of the pipers', was conferred on the *Counts-Palatine of Birkenfeld* (afterwards *Zweibrücken-Birkenfeld*), who were in the service of France. Max Joseph, Duke of Pfalz-Zweibrücken, a colonel in the French service (1777), and afterwards King of Bavaria (d. 1825), resided in the château (now a school) down to 1782.

At the lower end of the town, near the rail. station, is the *Herren-Garten*, laid out in the 18th century. A long street, con-taining many fine old houses of the 15th and 16th centuries, inter-sects the town from E. to W. The *Metzgerturm*, in the market-place, is a remnant of the inner fortifications, which once separated the adjacent parishes, now forming the town of Rappoltsweiler. The *Rathaus* contains an interesting collection of goblets and other antiquities. Handsome fountain of 1536; farther up a modern one, with a figure representing Alsatia, by Friedrich. The Gothic *Parish Church* (R. C.) was completed in 1473.

In order to visit the three castles, we take the red marks as our guide, pass the choir of the Roman Catholic church, follow to the left (finger-post; 920 ft.) the walk in the *Lützelbach-Tal*, crossing the stream, and then ascend to the right through the coppice. In ¹/₄ hr. we cross a footpath leading from the forester's house of

Lützelbach to Giersberg, and soon after the plain of the Rhine is disclosed to view. About ¹/₂ hr. from the church we turn sharply to the left (to the right a path to the Lützelbach-Tal), and reach in ¹/₄ hr. more the ruin of **Giersberg** (13th cent.), perched boldly on a precipitous cliff (1730 ft.). A fine path leads hence, past a bench commanding a superb prospect, to (5 min.) the ***St. Ulrichs-Burg** (1710 ft.; view), the most modern of the three castles, erected in the 13th, and enlarged in the 15th cent., and abandoned since the Thirty Years' War. It is remarkable for its artistic architecture, best exhibited in the spacious 'Rittersaal', with its beautiful double windows, surrounded by niches. From the entrance to the St. Ulrichs-Burg a footpath leads to (25 min.) the saddle to the W. of the highest point (hence to Tannenkirch, 1¹/₄ hr., see p. 516) and, turning to the right, to (10 min.) **Hoh-Rappoltstein** (2105 ft.), with its lofty tower, constructed in the 14th cent. on the site of an earlier building, and affording a good view. — The best route for returning to Rappoltsweiler leads from the just-mentioned saddle (finger-post) through the *Dusenbach-Tal*, past the *Dusenbach-Kapelle* (pilgrimage-resort; rfmts.), recently rebuilt from the mediæval remains, and along the Route de Calvaire (fine retrospects), to the (¹/₄ hr.) Markirch road (p. 515), and by it to (1 M.) Rappoltsweiler.

From Rappoltsweiler to Kaysersberg (6 M.). The road leads through vineyards on the hillside to (1¹/₂ M.) *Hunaweier* (Rebstock, Traube, good wine at both), containing a church of the 15th cent., surrounded by a wall with bastions. To the E. we observe the ancient *Zellenberg*, a village and castle, also surrounded with a wall. About 1¹/₂ M. beyond Hunaweier we reach —

Reichenweier (*Hirsch, Goldene Granate*, good wine at both), a small and ancient town with 1500 inhab., surrounded by vineyards yielding excellent wine. Its walls and gates are among the finest works of the kind in Alsace, particularly the *Obertor* or *Dolder*, on the W. side of the town, with its double gateway, and the *Diebsturm*, containing a collection of antiquities. Near the Obertor is a fine *Fountain* of the 17th century. The old *Château* of the Counts of Württemberg-Mömpelgart, to whom the town was subject, is now a school. The town contains a number of handsome private dwelling-houses, built in the 16th and 17th cent. in the Gothic and Renaissance styles.

From Reichenweier to *Kaysersberg* (p. 520), 3 M.

From Rappoltsweiler to Altweier, 5¹/₂ M., diligence from April to the end of September twice daily in 2 hrs. (2 ℳ; down in 1¹/₄ hr., 1¹/₄ ℳ; carr. 6 ℳ 40, with two horses 12 ℳ 80 pf.). The road ascends the valley of the Strengbach, with the Rappoltsweiler Castles to the right and the ruin of *Bilstein* (2485 ft.) to the left. At the kilomètre-stone 6.19 (reckoned from Markirch, p. 514), the road to (2 M.) Altweier diverges to the left. — Walkers may, with advantage, diverge to the left by the new red-marked 'St. Morandsweg', pass the forester's house of *Bärenhütte* (rfmts.), below the

weg, pass the forester's house of *Bärenhütte* (rfmts.), below the

Bilstein, and go on thence by the N. slope of the *Seelburg* to Altweier in 3 hrs.

Altweier. — Hotels. *Brézouard,* R. from 2, B. 1, D. $2^{1}/_{2}$, S. 2, pens. from 5 ℳ, with baths, very fair, closed from Oct. to April; *Raffner,* R. $1^{1}/_{2}$-2, B. $^{3}/_{4}$, D. 2, pens. 4 ℳ. — Several *Pensions.*

Altweier (2625 ft.), French *Aubure,* with 300 inhab. and two churches (Prot. and Rom. Cath.), is the highest village in Alsace and is a popular summer-resort. — The road is continued towards the S. Fine view on the ($^{1}/_{2}$ M.) ridge. The road to the left leads to (6 M.) Kaysersberg (p. 520) and to (2 M.) Urbach (p. 520), that to the right to (1 M.) a *Sanatorium,* pleasantly situated in a sheltered valley.

The Brézouard (p. 515) may be ascended from Altweier, by quitting the road at the last house in the village (finger-post; $2^{1}/_{4}$-$2^{1}/_{2}$ hrs.), or by going as far as the Sanatorium and then following the red-marked winding path behind it. The latter ($2^{1}/_{2}$-3 hrs.) affords the better views. The two paths converge at the forest-clearing of the *Dreibannstein* (3675 ft.).

b. Weisstal. Weisse and Schwarze See. Reisberg.

Steam Tramway from *Colmar* viâ *Kaysersberg* to *Schnierlach,* $12^{1}/_{2}$ M., in $1^{1}/_{2}$ hr. (fares 1 ℳ 30, 90 pf.). Those who desire to visit the lakes ·leave the tramway at *Eschelmer* and walk or take the omnibus (thrice daily; 50 pf.) to (40 min.) *Urbeis,* and then proceed on foot (2 hrs. direct, or $2^{1}/_{2}$ hrs. viâ the Schwarze See) to the Weisse See; thence to the *Schlucht* ($3^{1}/_{2}$-4 hrs.).

Colmar, see p. 496. The tramway starts from the principal railway station. 2 M. *Logelbach* (p. 523). Immediately after crossing the *Fecht* we reach ($2^{1}/_{2}$ M.) *Ingersheim,* whence a good road leads viâ *Niedermorschweier* to Drei Æhren (p. 523). — $3^{3}/_{4}$ M. *Katzental;* on the left the ruined castle of *Winck* ($1^{1}/_{2}$ hr.).

5 M. **Ammerschweier** (820 ft.; *Zwei Schlüssel*), an old town with 1600 inhab., and a number of interesting buildings, among which may be named the late-Gothic parish-church, the Gothic Kaufhaus (1538), the Renaissance Rathaus (1552), and a fountain of the 16th century. There are also several handsome dwelling-houses of similar dates; and the walls and towers, of the 16th cent., particularly the Schelmen-Turm of 1535, merit attention.

From Ammerschweier to Drei Æhren (p. 523), $4^{1}/_{2}$ M. by road. Walkers should take the path viâ the *Meiweierer Köpfchen* (1395 ft.) and the *Galz* (p. 524; 2 hrs.).

The tramway next crosses the *Weiss,* a tributary of the Fecht. — $5^{1}/_{2}$ M. *Sigolsheim.* The village, which lies $^{1}/_{2}$ M. to the E., possesses a fine late-Romanesque church, with interesting sculptures on the portal; the tower over the cross is late-Gothic. Near Sigolsheim is the so-called 'Red Field', where the degenerate sons of Louis the Pious took their father prisoner in 833, after they had seduced his army from its allegiance. In consequence of this event the spot is sometimes termed the 'Lügenfeld' (*i.e.* field of lies).

6 M. *Kienzheim* is one of 'three towns in one valley' (the other
two being Kaysersberg and Ammerschweier), mentioned in a verse
quoted by Merian (1663) as characteristic of Alsace along with
'three castles on one hill, and three churches in one churchyard'.

7 M. **Kaysersberg** (*Goldener Schlüssel*, very fair; *Sonne;*
Rail. Restaurant, very fair), an old town with 2600 inhab. and
several cotton-factories, lies at the point where the picturesque
Weisstal contracts and is commanded by the ruins of the ancient
Kaiserburg, the residence of the imperial Landvogt of Alsace during
the 13-14th cent., which was destroyed in the Thirty Years' War
(view from the platform). The town was founded by Emp. Frederick II. of the Hohenstaufen family, who were Dukes of Swabia
and Alsace and were solicitous for the welfare of their land. The
famous preacher *John Geiler* (p. 482) was brought up here. The
ancient walls, the numerous quaint houses of the 15-16th cent., and
the old fountains (with inscription) combine to give the town a particularly pleasing air of antiquity. The handsome *Town Hall*, in
the Renaissance style, dates from 1604. The spacious *Church*,
dating from the 12th cent., but subsequently altered, possesses a
fine Romanesque portal, and contains a sculptured Pietà, of the
15th cent., and a winged altar-piece, of the early 16th century.
The *Sommerhaus* (¹/₄ hr.) and the *Wetterkreuz*, somewhat higher
up, are good points of view.

From Kaysersberg to *Drei Æhren* (p. 523) a blue-marked path leads
in 2¹/₂ hrs.; a shorter path, marked in yellow, is more fatiguing and less
attractive (1³/₄ hr.). — To Rappoltsweiler, see p. 518.

The steam-tramway skirts the S. side of the old town-wall of
Kaysersberg, and ascends on the right bank of the Weiss. 8¹/₂ M.
Weibel; 9¹/₄ M. *Alspach*, formerly a Clarissine nunnery, now a
factory. — 10 M. *Urbach*. The village of that name, French *Fré-
land*, lies in a side-valley, 1¹/₂ M. to the right.

12 M. **Eschelmer,** French *Hachimette* (*Grad*, R. & B. 2 ℳ,
fair), just within the bounds of the French-speaking district, which
embraces the country on the E. slope of the mountains, watered
by the Weiss and its tributary streams. Crossing the stream, we pass,
¹/₄ M. farther on, on the left, the road (finger-post) leading to Urbeis
(p. 521). The line ascends the valley of the *Béchine*.

12¹/₂ M. **Schnierlach,** French *La Poutroie* (*Post*, R. 1¹/₂-2¹/₂,
B. ³/₄, D. 2¹/₂, S. 2 ℳ; *Krone*, similar charges, both very fair), the
tramway-terminus, possessing considerable cotton-factories. — To
the S.W. of Schnierlach, beyond *Goutte*, a path ascends to the left
to (1 hr.) the top of the *Faudé* (2535 ft.). — From Schnierlach to
the Weisse See (2¹/₂ hrs.): the blue-marked and shadeless path leads
viâ Goutte to the saddle of *Bermont* (2105 ft.), and then viâ *Remo-
mont* to (1 hr.) *La Matrelle*, where it joins the route from Urbeis
(p. 521). — Ascent of the *Brézouard*, see p. 515.

The road continues to ascend along the Béchine. 3 M. **Diedols-hausen,** French *Le Bonhomme* (2200 ft.; *Cheval Blanc, Lion d'Or,* both very fair), with ca. 1000 inhab., lies $2^1/_2$ M. from the French frontier (Col du Bonhomme, 3120 ft.). It is dominated on the E. by the scanty ruins of the Gutenburg.

From Diedelshausen a red-marked path (fine views) leads to (2 hrs.) the Weisse See. It begins at the church and ascends to the W. of the *Buchenkopf* (4000 ft.) and the *Lamerlinskopf* (3985 ft.). The road ($7^1/_2$ M.) also repays the walker. We proceed in the direction of the Col du Bonhomme for $1^1/_4$ M. and then ascend to the left, through the valley of the *Bétine,* to the *Col de Luschbach* (3210 ft.; inn on the French side). The rest of the way (left) is on German soil.

From ESCHELMER we proceed towards the S.W. by the road mentioned above (omn. in connection with mail trains), up the valley of the Weiss, to (2 M.) **Urbeis** or *Orbey* (1575 ft.; *Cornelius,* R. 2-3, B. 1, D. $2^1/_2$, S. 2, pens. 5-6 ℳ, very fair; *Hôt. Vogesia; Hôt. Beck*), a scattered village, with cotton and silk mills. — At the beginning of the village diverges a road to the left, ascending the *Tannacher- Tal* (fine mountain-view) to the ($7^1/_2$ M.) Drei Æhren (footpath shorter). — The road running to the S. from Urbeis and then (1 M.) bending to the left ascends viâ *Unterhütten* to the *Wett-steinhöhe* (2885 ft.) and then descends to the Schlucht road above Sulzern (p. 525; Sulzern is $10^1/_2$ M. from Urbeis).

Most travellers pay a visit from Urbeis (or from Schnierlach) to the two lonely mountain-lakes, the Weisse See and the Schwarze See, which lie to the W. of it, nearly on the summit of the granite ridge separating Alsace from France. — The direct, but shadeless path (2 hrs.; blue marks) from Urbeis to the *Weisse See* diverges to the right in the village, passes the 'Nouveau Martinet' (forge), and follows the right bank of the brook, viâ *Basse Grange,* to the hamlet of *La Matrelle.* Hence we follow the path from Schnierlach (see p. 520), viâ *Blanc Rupt.* We may cut off the last wide bend of the road by ascending direct to the left about $1^1/_2$ hr. after leaving Urbeis. — The route viâ the *Schwarze See* ($1^1/_2$-2 hrs.; to the Weisse See $2^3/_4$-3 hrs.) is pleasanter. We follow the above-mentioned Sulzern road for 1 M. and then take the road to the right, which passes (1 M.) the hospital of **Pairis** (2130 ft.; on the site of a Cistercian abbey founded in the 12th cent.), with a new church, and two hotels (the *Hôtel Pairis,* and, a little farther on, the **Hôtel Schwarze See;* at the latter, R. $1^1/_2$-3, B. 1, D. incl. wine 3, S. 3, board 4 ℳ). In 20 min. more we reach the edge of the wood, whence a steep footpath to the left ascends to ($1/_2$ hr.) the Schwarze See. The road runs to the N., ascends in a sharp curve, and then (2 M.) forks. The branch to the right leads to the Weisse See and along its E. bank to (2 M.) the hotel. The left branch leads to ($3/_4$ M.) the refuge-hut on the Schwarze See, on the S. bank of which we may ascend (steep) to (50 min.) the Sulzerner Eck (see below).

The *Weisse See,* or Lac Blanc (3460 ft.), which derives its name from the quartz at the bottom, is the largest lake·of the German Vosges (ca. 3 M. in circumference; 200 ft. deep); it is bounded on two sides by lofty precipices, and on a third by huge masses of granite piled together. High over its N. end stands the *Hôtel zum Weissen See* (3680 ft.; R. 2¹/₂-3, B. 1, D. incl. wine 3, pens. 6¹/₂-8 ℳ; telephone to Urbeis). — The Schwarze See, or Lac Noir (3115 ft.; Gerard's Inn, R. 1¹/₂ ℳ, B. 60 pf., small but clean), about half the size of the other, lies only ³/₄ M. to the S., but the two lakes are separated by a huge wall of granite, which it takes ³/₄ hr. to circumvent. A large reservoir and dam have been constructed to supply the factories of Urbeis with water-power. The discharge of the two lakes forms the *Weiss.*

On the W. side of the lakes rises the Reisberg (4278 ft.), the northernmost eminence of the range called *Les Hautes Chaumes,* which extends to the Schlucht (about 9¹/₂ M.; fine mountain-walk of 3¹/₂-4 hrs.). The ridge, along which runs the boundary of Alsace, may be attained from the Weisse See Hotel in about 20 minutes. The view extends over the Vosges, a great part of Lorraine, the Black Forest, and the entire plain of the Rhine. The path keeps mainly on the German side of the boundary. Beyond the boundary-stone 2772, about 40 min. from the hotel, is a finger-post indicating (l.) the (¹/₄ hr.) *See-Kanzel* ('Pulpit'), commanding a view of both lakes. At the *Sulzerner Eck* (4270 ft.; stone 2779) a survey is obtained to the S. of the Münster-Tal, with the Swiss Alps in the distance. Farther on we pass the *Taubenklangfels* or *Roche du Gazon de Faing* (stone 2782) and the *Ringbühlkopf* or *Gazon de Faîte* (4270 ft.; stone 2786). Beyond stone 2789 a path leads to the left to the Sulzerner See (to Sulzern 2 hrs., comp. p. 525), while another, to the right, leads to (10 min.) Chaume du Gazon Martine (inn; thence to the Schlucht 1 hr.). We now traverse a low wood of beech and pine, and about 50 paces to the left obtain a view of the *Sulzerner See* or *Daren-See* (3425 ft.), a small, pine-girt mountain-lake, 415 acres in area. At the *Tanneckfels,* or *Roche du Tanet* (4245 ft.; stone 2800), we have our last retrospect of the lake. At stone 2816 a path leads to the left to (40 min.) the Hôt. Altenberg (p. 526). From this point we require ¹/₂ hr., passing the *Krappen-fels* (4115 ft.; stone 2826), to reach the Schlucht (see p. 526).

c. From Colmar to Münster and Metzeral. The Schlucht.

15 M. RAILWAY to (12 M.) *Münster* in ³/₄ hr. (fares 1 ℳ 60 pf., 1 ℳ, 65 pf.); to (15 M.) *Metzeral* in 1¹/₄ hr. (fares 2 ℳ, 1 ℳ 30, 85 pf.).

To the W. of Colmar (p. 496) opens the fertile *Münster-Tal,* formerly called the St. Gregorien-Tal, watered by the *Fecht.* Its inhabitants, most of whom are Protestants, carry on manufactures of various kinds and cattle-farming. The 'Münster cheese' resembles the highly-esteemed Camembert.

The line skirts the *Loqelbach*, an old canal, conducted from the Fecht at Türkheim, on which numerous cotton-manufacturies are situated. 2 M. *Logelbach* (p. 519). In the plain between Colmar and Türkheim, on 5th Jan., 1675, Turenne surprised and signally defeated the German imperial army, which had gone into winter-quarters here. This decisive engagemant drove the Germans across the Rhine and effectually expelled them from Alsace.

3³/₄ M. **Türkheim** (775 ft.; *Hôtel des Vosges*, at the rail. station, R. from 1¹/₂, B. ³/₄, D. 2¹/₂ ℳ, very fair; *Deux Clefs*, a picturesque old house, with wine-room, R. 1¹/₄-2, B. ³/₄, D. 1¹/₂-2¹/₂, S. 2 ℳ, also very good), an old town with 2500 inhab., still partly surrounded by walls and towers. One of the best wines of Alsace is yielded by the neighbouring vineyards.

On the other side of the valley, 1 M. to the S.E. of stat. Türkheim and 3 M. from Colmar (steam-tramway in ¹/₄ hr.; 40, 25 pf.), lies the village of **Winzenheim** (*Meyer*, well spoken of). A path (red and white marks), issuing from the W. end of the village, ascends to (1 hr.) the ruin of **Hohlandsburg** (2055 ft.), consisting of little more than the outer walls of an extensive castle, destroyed by the French in 1635. Fine view. — In returning we may either proceed to the N.W. by the *Plixburg* or by a direct and easy path to stat. *St. Gilgen* (p. 524), or, taking the direction indicated by the finger-post on the S. slope of the Hohlandsburg, pass mostly through wood to (3 M.) the ruins of the *Drei-Exen* (p. 498).

From Türkheim to Drei Æhren, 6 M., electric tramway in 40 min. (fare 1¹/₄ ℳ, down 50 pf., there and back 1 ℳ 55 pf.; best views to the right). The line follows the highroad for about half the distance, then traverses the Türkheim Wood, and at the top reaches the Niedermorschweier road (tramway-station). — Pedestrians (1³/₄ hr.) follow the road to the W., up the valley, for about 1¹/₄ M., and then take the shorter footpath to the right.

Drei Æhren. — Hotels. *Hôtel des Trois Rois*, with terrace; *Hôtel des Trois Épis*, two hotels belonging to the same company, closed in winter, R. 1¹/₂-3, D. 3, S. 2, pens. 6-12 ℳ; *Notre Dame*, R. 1¹/₂-3, D. 2¹/₂, S. 1³/₄, pens. 5-7 ℳ; *Bellevue*, R. 2-4 ℳ, D. 2 ℳ 60 pf., pens. 5-7 ℳ.

Drei Æhren, French *Notre Dame des Trois Épis*, German *Unsere Liebe Frau zu den drei Æhren* (1910 ft.) is a resort of pilgrims, and also a favourite summer-resort. The village consists of an unpretending Gothic church, containing a number of votive tablets, with a few houses adjacent. The view embraces the lower Münster-Tal, the slopes of the Vosges, the plain of the Rhine as far as the Black Forest, and the distant Alps to the S. To the W. of the village, near the Villa Hartmann, is the *Belvedere*.

A more extensive view, especially towards the N., is gained from the **Galz** (2395 ft.), ¹/₂ hr. to the N.E. (finger-post behind the Hôt. Trois Epis). — The *Grosse Hohnack* (3200 ft.), 2¹/₂ M. to the S.W. of Drei

Æhren (finger-post at the W. end of the village), also commands a pleasing view, with the Münster-Tal in the foreground, and opposite, on the N., the *Kleine Hohnack* (3015 ft.), crowned with the ruins of a castle restored in the 13th cent. and destroyed in 1655. — From Drei-Æhren to the lakes (p. 522), passing between the two Hohnacks, 4½ hrs.; by *Hohrodberg* to Münster (see below) 3½ hrs.; to Urbeis (p. 521) 2½ hrs.

Drei Æhren may also be reached by pleasant routes from Ingersheim (p. 519), Ammerschweier (p. 519), and Kaysersberg (p. 520).

5½ M. *St. Gilgen* (p. 523); 6¼ M. *Walbach*. — 8 M. *Weier im Tal* (1015 ft.; good inn at the station), about 1 M. to the S. of which is a small bath-establishment near the small and ancient town of *Sulzbach* (Sanssouci, with a chalybeate spring, plain; from Sulzbach to the Kahle Wasen, 4 hrs., see below). The village of Weier im Tal, with a conspicuous new church, lies 1 M. to the N. of the station, and is commanded by the pilgrimage-chapel of *Heiligkreuz*. — 10 M. *Günsbach*, with a large cotton-factory, at the foot of the Schlosswald (see below). We then cross the Fecht to —

12 M. **Münster** (1256 ft.; **Grand-Hôtel Münster*, near the station, R. 2½-4, B. 1, D. 2½, S. 2, pens. 5-7 ℳ, with garden; *Storch*, R. 1½-3, pens. 4½-5 ℳ), a manufacturing town with 6100 inhab., situated at the base of the *Mönchberg* (Hôt. Mönchberg, pens. 4-5 ℳ, well spoken of), at the union of the *Kleintal* (p. 525) with the *Grosstal* (see below). The place owes its origin to a Benedectine abbey founded here by King Childeric about 660, and in the 13th cent. it was a free town of the German Empire. Numerous modern buildings, among which the handsome Protestant church (in the Romanesque style) and the theatre are conspicuous, testify to the prosperity of the town.

The *Schlosswald*, 1¼ M. to the E., an eminence laid out in pleasure-grounds, and crowned by the ruin of *Schwarzenburg* (1705 ft.), is open to the public. *View.

From Münster to the Kahle Wasen, 3 hrs. The path (finger-post at the station; farther on red and white marks) winds upward to the *Furch*, a ditch or trench filled with water, which it skirts, to the right, as far as the *Voltaire Oak*. Here it joins the road from Luttenbach (see below), which we now follow (avoiding the wide curve by short-cuts), viâ the *Rieth* dairy (rfmts.), where a path to Sulzbach diverges on the left, to the (2¼-2½ hrs.) dairy of *Kahlenwasen*. Thence to the top, ½ hr. The **Kahle Wasen,** or *Kleine Belchen* (4160 ft.), commands a view of the Münster-Tal and the Lauchtal. In June the mountain is covered with a carpet of Vosges violets (Viola clegans). — The descent is made to (2-2¼ hrs.) *Lautenbach* (p. 529), by a path indicated by red and white marks leading viâ *Bönles Grab* (2840 ft.; inn), or we may go from the dairy-house viâ the *Steinberg* to the forester's house of *Lattern* (red rectangle with yellow disk), and by the road viâ *Landersbach* and *Sondernach* to *Metzeral* (p. 525) in 2¼-2½ hrs. — A fine walk of 6-7 hrs. may be taken by following the ridge towards the W. to the *Klinzkopf* (4355 ft.; *View) and proceeding to the S. to the Grosse Belchen (p. 529).

We now run to the S.W. up the *Grosstal*, which is watered by the Fecht. — From (12½ M.) *Luttenbach* the just-mentioned road leads to the Kahlenwasen dairy. — 13¾ M. *Breitenbach*; 14¼ M. *Mühlbach*.

15 M. **Metzeral** (1572 ft.; *Railway Hotel*, by the station; *Sonne*, both unpretending), with 1800 inhab., lies at the union of the two streams which form the Fecht.

Both valleys are ascended by roads, diverging from each other at the Sonne Inn (guide-board on the school-house opposite). That to the S. leads to *Sondernach* (p. 524) and the Kahle Wasen; that to the W. to the *Herrenberg* (see below).

ASCENT OF THE HOHNECK (p. 526) FROM METZERAL, 3¹/₂ hrs. From the Sonne Inn we follow the Herrenberg road, passing the new Protestant Church. After ³/₄ M. we diverge to the right, cross the bridge, and follow the route up the beautiful *Wolmsa-Tal*, indicated by red rectangles, to (1¹/₂ hr.) the *Fischbödle*, a small lake surrounded by wild rocks which show traces of an ancient glacier. Farther on we pass *Schiess-rotried* (rfmts.), where a pond has recently been dammed in, and ascend rapidly to (2 hrs.) the summit.

FROM METZERAL TO WILDENSTEIN (p. 531), 4¹/₂ hrs. We follow the Herrenberg road along the right bank of the Fecht to (2 M.) *Mittlach* (Fuchs), passing the Esels-Brücke, across which runs a cart-road ascending through the right lateral valley to (1 hr.) the pond of *Altenweiher*. About 3 min. beyond the Esels-Brücke we cross to the left bank of the Fecht and in ¹/₄ hr. reach the forester's house of **Herrenberg** (good inn). Hence a forest-path, indicated by a red rectangle with a yellow disc, ascends in windings to (2 hrs.) the *Herrenberg Dairy*, about ¹/₄ hr. beyond which is the *Herrenberg Saddle* (3890 ft.). Here we reach the path constructed by the Vosges Club along the ridge. On the left this leads to the Grosse Belchen (see p. 529); we, however, turn to the right, passing the dairy of *Neurod*, and then descend direct to the left by a somewhat steep path (marked by a blue H) to (1¹/₄ hr.) Wildenstein. Or we may reach Wildenstein by a détour of 1-1¹/₄ hr. viâ the Rotenbach-kopf and the dairy of Rotenbachhof (comp. p. 527).

FROM MÜNSTER TO THE SCHLUCHT, 6³/₄ M., electric railway in 1 hr. (fare 3 ℳ 40, in the reverse direction 1 ℳ 70, there and back 4 ℳ 10 pf.). The railway avoids the windings of the road (11 M.). Road and railway at first ascend side by side through the *Kleintal*, passing (1 M.) *Hohrod*, to (1¹/₂ M.) *Stossweier* (1400 ft.), where the valley forks. — The road ascends to the N. to *Sulzern* and then returns on itself in a sharp curve. At the angle of this bend, 4¹/₂ M. from Münster, a beautiful road leads in a straight direction, forking again about ²/₃ M. farther on. The left branch ascends the valley to (3 M.) the *Sulzerner-See* (p. 522), while the right branch winds up to the *Wettsteinhöhe* (2885 ft.) and then descends, also in windings, to (9¹/₂ M.) Urbeis (p. 521).

At Stossweier the electric railway turns into the W. Kleintal and runs to (2¹/₄ M.) *Ampfersbach* and (3 M.) *Schmelzwasen* (1640 ft.). From the latter an attractive footpath leads viâ *Stolz's Ablass* (waterfall) and the dairies of *Frankental* (3370 ft.) and *Schäfertal* to (3 hrs.) the Hohneck (see p. 526). — At (4 M.) *Sägmatt* (new hotel) begins the steepest part of the railway, which is run on the rack-and-pinion system.

5¹/₂ M. **Altenberg** (3610 ft.; *Hôtel Altenberg, first-class, with

modern comforts and equipment, open from June 1st to Oct. 1st,
R. 2^1/$_2$-6^1/$_2$, B. 1^1/$_2$, D. at 12.30 p.m. 5, S. at 7.30 p.m. 3 *M ;* rooms
had better be ordered in advance; in the annex is a restaurant for
tourists, D., 11-2, at 1^1/$_2$ *M*). View of the Münster-Tal. Pleasant
walks ascend through the woods behind the hotel to the Krappen-
Fels and the top of the pass (p. 522).

Beyond Altenberg the railway follows the road, which is here
cut through the granite rocks. Beyond the custom-house it passes
through a tunnel.

6^3/$_4$ M. The *Schlucht,* French *Col de la Schlucht* (3735 ft.),
a picturesque mountain-pass, surrounded by precipitous rocks and
beautiful pine-forest, lies between the *Lundenbühl* or *Montabec*
(4125 ft.) on the S. and the *Spitzenfelskopf* (4115 ft.) on the N.,
two heights of the Central Vosges Mts. The summit of the pass
forms the boundary between Germany and France (comp. p. 522).
On the German side are a house in the 'Swiss Chalet' style (belonging to Herr Hartmann) and a good inn, and on the French side is
the popular *Hôtel Français de la Schlucht* (R. 3-5, B. 1^1/$_2$, D. 4,
S. 3^1/$_2$ fr., with restaurant), the terminus of the mountain-railway
from Gérardmer (see p. 527).

From the Hartmann Chalet a good club-path (view) passing
the *Quellenfels,* ascends to the left to (1^1/$_4$ hr.) the summit of the
Hohneck (4465 ft.), which is reached in the same time also by a
path from the French hotel. The mountain-railway from Le Collet
(see below) reaches its terminus, a little below the summit, in
20 min. (2^1/$_2$ M.; 1 fr. 20 c. or 1 *M*). At the top are two restaurants (open in summer), at one of which a bed may be procured
(2^1/$_2$ fr.; D. 3 fr.). The view (mountain-indicator) extends far beyond
the Vosges Mts., embracing the plain of the Rhine as far as the
Black Forest, the Jura and the Alps towards the S., and the French
Department of the Vosges towards the W. In the foreground towards the E. is the beautiful Münster-Tal, towards the W. the valley
of Gérardmer with the Retournemer and Longemer lakes. The
Hohneck is also of great interest to the botanist.

From the Schlucht to Gerardmer (11 M., an interesting day's excursion), road and mountain-railway (there and back 4 fr. 5, ascent
2 fr. 40 c.; the trains run on Paris time, 55 min. behind German time).
The road gradually descends past the source of the Meurthe to (1^1/$_4$ M.)
Le Collet (3640 ft.), and thence in a curve to the N.W. with a fine view
of the lakes, passing through a short tunnel below the (3 M.) *Roche du
Diable,* and then running above the banks of the lake of Longemer. The
railway quits the Schlucht road beyond Le Collet (junction for the branch
to Hohneck, see above) and follows a road diverging to the left, which
runs in a curve to the S. to the pretty little lake of *Retournemer*
(2550 ft.; by footpath from the Schlucht road, 20-25 min.; small hotel
on the lake). It then skirts the *Vologne* (pretty waterfall) and the lake
of *Longemer* (2450 ft.; 1^1/$_4$ M. long), near the N. end of which it rejoins
the Schlucht road (French custom-house). Hence we descend along the
Vologne, which forms a fine fall *(Saut des Cuves)* above the bridge, by

which the road and the railway cross to the left bank (Café-Restaurant du Saut-des-Cuves). About 3¹/₂ M. farther on is —

Gérardmer (final *r* silent; 2200 ft.; *Hôt. de la Poste*, déj. 3¹/₂, D. 4 fr.; *Grand-Hôtel du Lac; Hôt. Beau Rivage; Hôt. Cholé-Terminus; Hôt. de la Providence; Hôt. des Bains; Hôt. des Vosges*, etc.), an industrial town with 10,000 inhab., at the E. end of the lake of that name (2185 ft.) and a favourite summer-resort of the French. From the station we cross an open space to the S.W. and reach the lake. Fine walk round the lake in 1¹/₂ hr. — Comp. *Baedeker's Northern France*.

From the Hohneck we may descend to the N.E. to Schmelz-wasen (p. 525), or proceed to the S.E. (finger-posts and red rectangles) viâ the Schiessrotried Pond and the Fischbödle, to (3 hrs.) Metzeral (p. 525).

The *Walk along the Ridge from the Hohneck to the Grosse Belchen* (7 hrs.) is very attractive. It is advisable to make an early start, as the midday sun shines full in our faces. From the station of the mountain-railway we follow the route along the frontier marked by red and white rectangles and in 1 hr. reach a point where the path forks. The branch to the right traverses French soil for a short distance and then descends to the dairy of *Rotenbachhof* and to (1¹/₄ hr.) Wildenstein. We however, kept to the left, follow the red rectangles, and in ¹/₂ hr. reach the *Rhein-kopf* or *Rainkopf* (4260 ft.; frontier-stone 2889; to the right, below, lies the lake of Blanchemer). The frontier here bends to the right, our route, however, descends in a straight direction and then ascends the pointed summit of the *Rotenbachkopf* (4318 ft.), which commands an extensive panorama. We may also skirt the W. side of the Rotenbachkopf, whence a path diverges to the dairy of Rotenbach. Going on from the summit and passing near the dairy of *Neurod*, we reach (³/₄ hr.) the *Herrenberg-Sattel* (3890 ft.), where the Metzeral route (p. 525) joins ours. The ridge-path main-tains its S.E. direction, keeping to the W. of the *Schweiselkopf* (4252 ft.) and the *Hundskopf* (4072 ft.). 1¹/₄ hr. *Klein-Hahne-brunnen* and *Gross-Hahnebrunnen* (3940 ft.), two dairy-farms, at the second of which refreshments may be obtained. We then follow the W. slope of the *Breitfirst* (4205 ft.) to (³/₄ hr.) the dairy of *Markstein* (rfmts.). About ¹/₂ hr. farther on we strike the so-called 'Pionier-Weg' ascending from the Lauchenweiher (p. 529) and then follow it through fine woods, passing the *Marksteinkopf* (4070 ft.) and the *Storkenkopf* (4470 ft.) to the See-Sattel on the Grosse Belchen (1¹/₄ hr.; see p. 529).

d. From Bollweiler to Lautenbach. Grosse Belchen.

8 M. RAILWAY in ³/₄-1 hr. (fares 70, 50 pf.; no first class).

Bollweiler, see p. 499. The line traverses a fertile district. — 3 M. *Obersulz*, a town of 4400 inhab., with silk-factories, contains an unpretending but tasteful parish-church, chiefly in the Gothic

34*

style, with a lofty tower above the crossing, begun in 1278, and finished in the 14th and 15th centuries.

From Obersulz there is omnibus connection, viâ *Jungholz*, with *St. Anna* (1455 ft.; 1 hr.) which has lately come into vogue as a health-resort (*Hôtel-Pension Schuller, R. 1¹/₄-3, B. ³/₄, D. 2¹/₂, S. 2, pens. 4-6 ℳ).

4¹/₂ M. **Gebweiler** (930 ft.; *Engel*, at the station, R. 1³/₄-2¹/₂, D. incl. wine 2¹/₂ ℳ; *Goldene Kanone*, in the town, R. 1¹/₂-2, B. ³/₄, D. 2¹/₂ ℳ, very fair), with 13,300 inhab., situated at the entrance to the *Lauchtal*, is an important manufacturing place, the products of which are cotton goods, cloth, sugar, and machinery. The road from the station leads straight to the *Neue Kirche*, a handsome building in the baroque style, erected in 1759 by the Prince-Abbots of Murbach, when they transferred their residence to Gebweiler. The main street leads to the right past the late-Gothic *Rathaus* to the *Parish Church (St. Leodegar)*, a fine example of the Transition style, begun in 1182 and lately restored. It possesses double aisles, a transept, three towers of unequal height, and a fine Romanesque porch occupying the whole breadth of the W. front. The choir is Gothic. The sculptures on the W. central portal merit inspection. One of the best wines of Alsace ('Kitterle') is produced near Gebweiler.

A good path, with red and white marks, beginning at the W. end of Gebweiler (1¹/₄ M. from the station), ascends viâ the saddles of *Peternit* (1845 ft.) and *Münsteräckerle* (2150 ft.) and the refuge-hut on the mountain-pasture of *Judenhutplan* to (3¹/₂-4 hrs.) the *Grosse Belchen* (p. 529).

5¹/₂ M. *Heissenstein* (1015 ft.), the upper station for Gebweiler. — The railway ascends the pretty Lauchtal, passing the ruin of *Hugstein*. — 7 M. *Buhl* (1115 ft.), another industrial village.

Near Bühl the road from Gebweiler enters the valley of the *Murbach*, passes the *Hôt. Wolff* (R. 2-2¹/₂, D. incl. wine 2¹/₂ ℳ, very fair), and leads W. to the (2 M. from Bühl station) Romanesque abbey-church of **Murbach**. This Benedictine Abbey, founded by Duke Eberhard of Swabia in 727, became one of the most powerful on the Upper Rhine and possessed extensive domains, in which three towns (including Gebweiler) and thirty villages were situated. It was presided over by an abbot of princely rank, who bore as his device a black greyhound ('haughty as the Murbach hound' was a mediæval saying). The church, of which the nave has disappeared, was consecrated in 1139, and ranks, like that of Maursmünster (p. 503), as one of the oldest and finest Romanesque buildings in Alsace. The S. transept contains a handsome Gothic tombstone of the 13th century. The house to the left, about 50 paces beyond the archway across the road, with its groundfloor borne by Romanesque columns, is an inn.

The *Belchen* is ascended from Murbach in 3 hrs. by a path crossing the brook to the left above the church and joining the 'Neuweg', which leads to the Judenhutplan (see above).

The terminus of the railway is (8 M.) *Lautenbach* (1300 ft.; Weisses Lamm), an industrial village, with cotton and thread mills. In the neighbourhood is the *Chapel of St. Gangolf*. Opposite, on the right bank of the Lauch, is the village of *Lautenbach-Zell*.

FROM LAUTENBACH TO THE GROSSE BELCHEN, 3³/₄-4 hrs. (red and white way-marks). This is the pleasantest ascent from the Lauchtal.

We follow the road up the valley to the (50 min.) forester's house of *Sägmatten,* whence we ascend the track through the woods, to the left, to ($^3/_4$ hr.) the piles of cut timber. [The road goes on to ($1^3/_4$ hr.) the *Lauchenweiher,* an artificial pond adjoined by a good inn (p. 527).] From the wood-piles we ascend to (10 min.) the picturesque falls of the *Seebach,* and continue along the left bank of the stream, crossing it above the falls, and then following the right bank until we reach the *Belchensee* (3235 ft.; 35 min.), picturesquely situated at the foot of the peak. Skirting the W. side of the lake, we gradually climb to the (50 min.) *See-Sattel,* between the Storkenkopf on the W. and the Belchen on the E.; and then, crossing the 'Pionier-Weg', we round the N. side of the peak and reach ($^1/_2$ hr.) the comfortable *Belchenhaus,* belonging to the Vosges Club (bed $2^1/_2$ ℳ; open in winter also; telephone to Gebweiler), with a meteorological station and a garden of Alpine plants. This is 5 min. below the peak of the *Grosse Belchen,* French *Ballon de Soultz* (4670 ft.), the highest point of the Vosges, commanding a wide panorama (mountain-indicator). In clear weather the Alps, from the Sentis to Mont Blanc, are plainly visible.

For travellers wishing to continue their walk farther S. the descent to *St. Amarin* is recommended (red marks; $1^3/_4$ hr.; see p. 530). — The walk along the crest to (7 hrs.) the Hohneck and (8 hrs.) the Schlucht is also worth making (see pp. 526, 527).

e. From Mülhausen to Wesserling and Krüt.

$23^1/_2$ M. RAILWAY in $1^1/_2$ hr. (fares 1 ℳ 90, 1 ℳ 25 pf.).

Mülhausen, see p. 499. This railway connects the main line with the important manufacturing places in the **St. Amarin-Tal,** the industrious valley of the *Thur,* and opens up to visitors an exceedingly picturesque tract of country. — 2 M. *Dornach;* $3^1/_2$ M. *Lutterbach* (825 ft.), see p. 499. — $9^1/_4$ M. *Sennheim* (985 ft.), Fr. *Cernay* (Bornot, R. 2-4, B. 1, D. with wine $2^3/_4$ ℳ) is the junction of a branch-line to Masmünster and Sewen (see p. 532). About $2^1/_2$ M. to the N. is *Wattweiler,* with mineral baths.

$12^1/_2$ M. **Thann** (1095 ft.; *Zum Bahnhof,* very fair; *Ortlieb,* rooms and beer), a town with 7900 inhab., a large chemical manufactory, and thriving machinery, cotton, and silk factories, is picturesquely situated at the mouth of the narrow valley of the Thur, the mountains enclosing which are covered with wood on their upper, and vineyards on their lower slopes. The *Church of St. Theobald,* the choir (1351-1421) of which is first visible in approaching from the station, is a gem of Gothic architecture. Its bold and elegant open tower, begun in 1430 and completed in 1516 by Meister Remigius Walch (inscription on the spire at the top), is one of the finest specimens of later Gothic. The handsome double portal on the W. side also deserves attention. The interior is adorned with carvéd work of the 16th cent., Gothic stained glass, and a fine painting, of the school of Martin Schongauer, of Christ amid several apostles. — The church is well seen from the *Engelburg*, a castle crowning an eminence on the left bank of the Thur (crossed by two bridges), and commanding the town and entrance to the valley. (The route to the castle diverges to the right from the main street, opposite the church.) The overthrown tower of the castle, destroyed by Turenne in 1674, somewhat resembles a huge cask. The district to the E. of the Engelburg yields the 'Rangener wine', which is mentioned by the German historian Münster as early as 1550. The *Staufen* (1685 ft.), 1¹/₂ M. from Thann, is a fine point of view.

FROM THANN TO THE GROSSE BELCHEN, 5 hrs., by an easy and attractive route. Starting from the rail. station, we proceed to the N., crossing the Thur and ascending the *Kattenbach-Tal*, viâ the *Pasteten-Platz*, to (2¹/₄ hrs.) the *Thomanns-Platz* (2980 ft.), whence a visit may be made, to the left, to the (4 min.) *Osteinfels*, commanding a splendid view of the Belchen. From the Thomanns-Platz we ascend in ¹/₂ hr. to the *Molkenrain* (3690 ft.; wide view), and thence in the same direction to the dairy of *Freundstein* (rfmts.), and, passing below the ruin of the same name, to the (1¹/₄ hr.) *Firstacker*, the saddle between the *Sudel* (3310 ft.) and the Belchen. Finally we traverse the flat pastures on the ridge to the *Belchenhütte* (rfmts.) and the (1-1¹/₄ hr.) *Belchenhaus* (p. 529).

FROM THANN TO ST. AMARIN OR MASMÜNSTER (red and white marks as far as the Rossberg). We keep to the W. over the three saddles *Napoleons-Platz, Dieboldscherer's Ebene*, and *Hundsrücken*; then proceed to the N.W. to the (2¹/₂ hrs.) *Mittlere Rossberg-Hütte* or *Kolbs-Hütte* (2950 ft.; rfmts.), situated between the *Rossberg* (3905 ft.) on the left and the *Thanner Hubel* (3875 ft.; ascent recommended in clear weather) on the right. We then ascend to the ridge of the Rossberg and proceed along the 'Hauptroute' (see below) either to the N. to (2 hrs.) *St. Amarin* (see below), or to the S. to (2¹/₂ hrs.) *Masmünster* (p. 532).

14¹/₄ M. *Bitschweiler*, 15¹/₂ M. *Weiler* (1215 ft.), two industrial villages, with modern Gothic churches. — The line now skirts the left bank of the stream. 17¹/₂ M. *Moosch.*

18¹/₂ M. **St. Amarin** (1330 ft.; *Goldener Löwe*, R. 1¹/₂-2, D. 2 ℳ 40 pf., very fair; *Kämmerlin*), one of the most ancient places in the valley, was destroyed in the Thirty Years' War.

THE GROSSE BELCHEN (p. 529) is ascended from St. Amarin by a pretty and shady path (marked red) in 2³/₄ hrs.

FROM ST. AMARIN TO MASMÜNSTER, 5-5¹/₂ hrs. by the 'Hauptroute' (red marks) of the Vosges Club. We leave the station, cross the Thur, and ascend the E. slope of the *Hirschbachkopf* to the *Drei-Markstein* (2490 ft.); then through wood, in about 2 hrs., to the meadow of the *Belacker* dairy (rfmts.; 1¹/₂ hr. to the W. is the Sternsee-Sattel, mentioned at p. 531). Proceeding viâ the *Falkensteine* or *Vogelsteine* (3870 ft.; superb view from the rocks), and continuing along the ridge, we reach the *Rossberg* (3905 ft.) in 1 hr. We next pass the *Hintere Hirzenstein* (3330 ft.; good view) and the *Vordere Hirzenstein* (3180 ft.) and descend through the *Willerbach-Tal* to (2 hrs.) *Masmünster* (p. 532). — The Mittlere Rossberg-Hütte (see above) lies about ³/₄ hr. to the E. of the Vogelsteine, in the direction of Thann.

20¹/₂ M. **Wesserling** (1433 ft.; *Hôtel de Wesserling*, R. 1¹/₂-2, B. 1, D. with wine 2³/₄, S. 2 ℳ, very fair; *Benz's Inn*, at the station), a place of modern origin, on the site of a hunting-lodge of the abbots of Murbach and built partly on what was once the moraïne of a huge glacier, is a colony of extensive cotton-factories, etc., with ca. 1000 inhabitants.

FROM WESSERLING TO BUSSANG, 9 M., by the road ascending the valley which diverges to the W. from the St. Amarin-Tal. 2¹/₂ M. *Urbis* (1475 ft.; Couronne; German custom-house), 1¹/₄ M. beyond which, to the left, opens the *Brückenbach-Tal* (see below). The road becomes steeper, with sharp bends. 6¹/₄ M. *Col de Bussang*, which is pierced by a tunnel with a boundary-stone in the middle (highest point of the road, 2360 ft.); at the entrance to the tunnel is a small inn, at the exit the French custom-house. The old road diverges to the right from the road leading to the village of *Bussang*, passes near the source of the *Moselle* (to the left, indicated by a tablet), and reaches the little mineral bath of *Bussang* (Grand-Hôtel des Sources), 1¹/₄ M. above the village (Deux Clefs, D. 3 fr.). — The *Drumont* (3935 ft.) is ascended from Wesserling in 2 hrs. We follow the Urbis road to (1¹/₄ M.) a pond, where a yellow-marked foot-path diverges to the right. At the top is a mountain-indicator, placed there by the French Vosges Club. The descent may be made on the French side to (1 hr.) Bussang. — Comp. *Baedeker's Northern France.*

FROM WESSERLING TO OBERBRUCK (6 hrs.). Viâ Urbis to the *Brückenbach-Tal,* see above. We ascend through the latter to (2³/₄ hrs.) the *Sternsee-Sattel* (3610 ft.). Thence, skirting the basin of the *Lac de Bers* (*Sternsee;* 3230 ft.), which lies far below, we proceed along a level path, past the *Upper Bers Dairy,* to the *Neuweiher,* two little lakes in an imposing setting (2700 ft.). Following the outflow of these, we reach (2 hrs.) *Oberbruck* (p. 532). — From the Obere Bers a route leads along the frontier on the crest of the hill to the Welsche Belchen (p. 532), in 2¹/₂ hrs.

21 M. *Felleringen* (Ochse, very fair). — 23 M. *Oderen* (Fischer's Hotel), between the granite cones of *Märleberg* (1790 ft.) and *Bärberg* (1815 ft.) which rise above the valley. The *Uhufels,* 1¹/₂ M. to the N., affords a fine view.

23¹/₂ M. *Krüt* (Sonne), the terminus of the railway.

The road (recommended to pedestrians) continues to ascend the valley of the Thur. About 1¹/₄ M. beyond Krüt suddenly rises the wooded *Schlossberg* (2185 ft.; 410 ft. above the valley), with the river Thur on the W., and, on the E., separated from the slope of the Griebkopf by a dale through which the road runs. On it stand the scanty ruins of *Wildenstein* (entrance from the N. side; restaurant in summer). This stronghold formerly belonged to the Abbey of Murbach and was taken by the French during the Thirty Years' War. In 1644 it was destroyed by the Weimar troops. — About 3³/₄ M. from Krüt the road reaches —

Wildenstein (1970 ft.; *Sonne*), the highest village in the valley. It then makes a sharp bend to the E., crosses the Thur, and ascends in many windings to the *Col de Bramont* (3145 ft.; 4¹/₂ M. from Wildenstein), which forms the frontier. Thence to *La Bresse,* 5 M.

A good path leads from Wildenstein to the *Rotenbachhof* and *Rotenbachkopf* (p. 527). Pleasant walk thence along the crest of the hills; either to the N. viâ the *Rheinkopf* (p. 527) and the *Hohneck* (p. 526) to the *Schlucht* (p. 526) in 4¹/₂-5 hrs., or to the S. to the Grosse Belchen (p. 529). From Wildenstein across the *Herrenberg* to *Metzeral* in 4¹/₂ hrs., see p. 525.

f. From Sennheim to Sewen. — Welsche Belchen.

17¹/₂ M. RAILWAY from Sennheim to Sewen in ca. 1¹/₂ hr.

Sennheim, see p. 529. — The line runs to the S., viâ (3 M.) *Aspach,* to the entrance of the Doller-Tal, crosses the *Doller,* and continues along its right bank to (5 M.) *Burnhaupt,* (7 M.) *Gewen-heim,* and (8¹/₂ M.) *Sentheim.* It then crosses to the left bank. 10¹/₂ M. *Aue.* — 12 M. **Masmünster,** Fr. *Massevaux* (1365 ft.; *Adler*), an old town with 4000 inhab., the principal place in the *Doller-Tal,* a picturesque valley, with imposing ramifications.

From Masmünster, viâ the Rossberg, to *Thann* or *St. Amarin,* see p. 530. — About 1¹/₂ M. to the S. of Masmünster lies the popular *Schimmel Inn* (1705 ft.; pens. 5¹/₂-6¹/₂ ℳ).

13³/₄ M. *Niederbruck;* 15 M. *Kirchberg.* — 16¹/₄ M. *Ober-bruck* (Sternsee), at the entrance to a side-valley on the N., the road through which leads to (1¹/₂ M.) *Rimbach* (Krone).

From Rimbach we may ascend to the *Sternsee* (p. 531) in 1¹/₂ hr.

17¹/₂ M. *Sewen* (Krone; Hirsch), the terminus of the line and the best starting-point for the ascent of the Welsche Belchen (3¹/₄ hrs.; guide-post beside the church, ¹/₂ M. from the station). We cross the *Seebach* and follow the road ascending on the right bank, which leads past the *Sewensee* (1645 ft.) to the (1 hr.) Alfeld-see. Halfway a finger-post indicates the path to the right over the stream to the *Hohlenbachfälle,* where some glacier-cauldrons are to be seen. The *Alfeldsee* (2035 ft.; inn at the keeper's), the largest of the reservoir-lakes in the Vosges (24 acres), occupies a lonely situation. We go on by the road on the S. side of the lake until we come to (³/₄ M.) an ascending path on the left. In 1³/₄ hr. more we reach the ridge, which forms the frontier (French custom-house), and strike, on the French side, the highroad that runs from Belfort to St. Maurice, following it past the (³/₄ M.) *Hôtel du Ballon* (very fair; D. 4 fr.) to the (1 M. more) *Hôtel Stauffer* (3880 ft.; R. 3, B. 1¹/₄, D. 4 fr.) and the *Ferme du Ballon.* Here we turn to the right across meadows and ascend in 10 min. to the top of the **Welsche Belchen** or *Ballon d'Alsace* (4085 ft.), which is crowned by an equestrian statue of Joan of Arc, erected in 1909. The view (moun-tain-indicator) is magnificent, especially in the direction of Belfort; to the N.W. it is somewhat limited by the *Ballon de Servance* (3900 ft.), which is strongly fortified.

From the Welsche Belchen a route leads along the crest of the hill to the dairy of *Obere Bers* and the *Sternsee-Sattel* (p. 531). — From the custom-house (see above) a path leads to the S. along the ridge past the frontier-stones to the *Trémont* (3570 ft.), and thence to the E. by the *Fennemattkopf* (3478 ft.) and the *Bärenkopf* (3518 ft.) to (2¹/₂ hrs.) a finger-post near the *Sudel* (3000 ft.). We may descend thence viâ *Stöcken* to (2¹/₄ hrs.) Masmünster (see above).

INDEX.

Leipzig: Printed by Breitkopf & Härtel.